D1259871

THE HISTORY OF THE JEWISH PEOPLE IN THE AGE OF JESUS CHRIST

EMIL SCHÜRER
1844 – 1910

THE HISTORY
OF THE JEWISH PEOPLE
IN THE AGE OF JESUS CHRIST
(175 B.C.–A.D. 135)

BY

EMIL SCHÜRER

A NEW ENGLISH VERSION
REVISED AND EDITED BY

GEZA VERMES & FERGUS MILLAR

Literary Editor
PAMELA VERMES

Organizing Editor
MATTHEW BLACK, F.B.A.

VOLUME I

EDINBURGH T. & T. CLARK LTD 38 GEORGE STREET

Revised English Edition

PRINTED IN GREAT BRITAIN BY
MORRISON AND GIBB LIMITED
FOR
T. & T. CLARK LTD EDINBURGH

ISBN 0 567 02242 0

FIRST EDITION AND REPRINTS 1885-1924
REVISED EDITION 1973

Preface

Emil Schürer's *Geschichte des jüdischen Volkes im Zeitalter Jesu Christi* has rendered invaluable services to scholars for nearly a century. It began its career in 1874 as *Lehrbuch der neutestamentlichen Zeitgeschichte,* acquired its definitive shape and title with its second edition (1886–1890), and was further enlarged and perfected in the so-called third/fourth edition (1901–1909).

As early as 1885–1891, Messrs. T. & T. Clark included an English version of the second German edition in their *Foreign Theological Library* under the title, *A History of the Jewish People in the Time of Jesus Christ.* The same publishing house is responsible for the present work, and the editors are most appreciative of their willingness to undertake it, and of their patience during the lengthy phase of preparation.

The idea of a new Schürer was first conceived by the late Professor H. H. Rowley of Manchester University, but credit for the actual initiation and organization of the enterprise belongs to Matthew Black, F.B.A., Principal of St. Mary's College and Professor of Biblical Criticism in the University of St. Andrews. In 1964, he commissioned a team of translators (whose names are listed on p. xii) to render into English the last German edition. Their work constituted the first phase of the present volume.

Subsequently, Professor Black invited Geza Vermes, Fellow of Wolfson College, Reader in Jewish Studies, and Fergus Millar, Fellow and Tutor in Ancient History at The Queen's College, both in the University of Oxford, to join the Schürer project, and it was decided to follow a new policy which would entail the insertion of changes at the actual points where they were needed, instead of presenting, as was initially planned, a straight translation of the original accompanied by a special volume of supplements. In the meantime, a preliminary revision of Schürer's text was requested from the translators, but the volume now published is the result of a detailed re-working of the entire manuscript, on the principles set out below, carried out jointly by Geza Vermes and Fergus Millar.

The editors are grateful to Mrs. Tessa Rajak, of Somerville College, Oxford, and Philip S. Alexander, of Pembroke College, Oxford, for their substantial contribution to the modernization of §3 C and §§2, 3 E, respectively.

Finally, to ensure a faithful, homogeneous and readable text, Pamela Vermes checked the revised copy against the German, re-translated it where necessary, and introduced throughout a quantity of stylistic improvement.

A few words of explanation must be added concerning firstly the principle of revising a classic and much used work of reference, and secondly the procedures adopted by the present editors. A modernization is justified in their view because Schürer's *History* was not intended to provide a personal synthesis, but a critical and objective presentation of all the available evidence. Failing revision, it must either be declared obsolete, which would be a tragic waste, or meet an even more undeserved fate of becoming increasingly a source of error. The aim of the present enterprise is precisely to salvage all that is still valid of Schürer's monument and to offer it in a form that will permit the work to fulfil its original purpose. In consequence, the editors have resolved not to mark additions, corrections and deletions in the text—those who wish to study Schürer and his time can always refer to the latest German edition—but to revise it directly, introducing the following main types of change.

(a) The removal of out-of-date items of bibliography, and of purely polemical material incorporated in the course of the successive German editions.

(b) The revision of the bibliographies, retaining the essential earlier items and adding the most important works published up to Spring 1972.

(c) The correction and modernization of all references to, and quotations of, literary texts, papyri, inscriptions and coin legends in Greek, Latin, Hebrew and Aramaic. This has involved (1) the use of modern methods of reference (e.g. the two numbering systems used for sections of Josephus) and the latest editions of papyri, inscriptions and coins; and (2) the correction of the texts as quoted, with the adjustment of the argument where such corrections necessitate it.

(d) The addition of relevant new archaeological, epigraphic, papyrological and numismatic material and, again, the adjustment of the notes and text of Schürer to take account of it. This has meant the introduction not only of fresh data of a type already known to Schürer, but also of wholly new areas of evidence such as the Babylonian tablets relative to Seleucid chronology, the Qumran manuscripts and the Bar Kokhba documents.

Whereas it has been the aim of the editors to make available to the reader all factual evidence affecting the fields covered by

Schürer, they have *not* attempted to record every shade of opinion voiced since Schürer wrote, and even less to refer to every book or article expressing such opinions. To do so would have been both impossible and undesirable. But, as well as the bibliographical lists, which give the major modern works, the text and notes do endeavour to take account of the more important interpretations offered during the last sixty years or so.

The numbering of the notes of the latest German edition could not be retained, but the structure of the chapters and subdivisions has been preserved, so that any reader familiar with the original ought to be able to understand without difficulty what fresh material has appeared and what its relevance is. The only wholly new section in the present volume is §3 F on the documents from the Judaean desert, which is placed so as not to interfere with the numbering of the rest.

In conclusion, two fundamental points must be stressed. Firstly, the work remains, as far as the evidence now available allows, that of Emil Schürer. That so much survives is a tribute to his immense diligence, scholarship and judgement. Secondly, the volume now presented offers material for historical research, but is not intended as an interpretative synthesis, or as a summary of contemporary interpretations. Still less is it meant to lay undue emphasis on the views of the editors themselves. It is their hope that by reminding students of the inter-Testamental era of the profound debt owed to nineteenth-century learning, and by placing within the framework of the finest product of that scholarship the vast accretion of knowledge gained in the twentieth century, the new Schürer will prove to be a secure foundation on which future historians of Judaism in the age of Jesus may build.

The substantial publication costs of this volume have been assisted by generous grants from The Queen's College, Oxford, the Oxford Centre for Post-Graduate Hebrew Studies, and another Trust which wishes to remain anonymous.

Contents

PART ONE

The First Period

From Antiochus Epiphanes to the Capture of Jerusalem by Pompey

The Maccabaean Rising and the Age of Independence
175 B.C.–63 B.C.

The Second Period

From the Capture of Jerusalem by Pompey to the Hadrianic War

The Roman-Herodian Age 63 B.C.–A.D. 135

Translators/Revisers *

T. A. BURKILL, Professor and Head of the Department of Theology, University of Rhodesia, Salisbury, Rhodesia (§16–19).

MALCOLM C. DOUBLES, Professor of New Testament, St. Andrews Presbyterian College, Laurinbourg, North Carolina, U.S.A. (Appendices IV–VIII).

H. A. KENNEDY, B.D., Newton Stewart, Wigtownshire (§4–12).

GEORGE OGG, D.D. (1890–1973), (§13–15 and Appendix III).

L. CALISTA OLDS, Professor of Religious Studies, Defiance College, Defiance, Ohio, U.S.A. (§1–3).

MAX WILCOX, Head of the Department of Religious Studies, University of Newcastle upon Tyne (§20–21 and Appendices I–II).

PAUL WINTER, D.Phil. (1904–1969) (§17, 19).

* The figures in parentheses appended to the names of Translators/Revisers indicate the sections for which they provided the first draft.

Abbreviations

AAB	Abhandlungen der Deutschen (Preussischen) Akademie der Wissenschaften zu Berlin
AAG	Abhandlungen der Akademie der Wissenschaften in Göttingen
AASOR	Annual of the American Schools of Oriental Research
ADAJ	Annual of the Department of Antiquities of Jordan
AE	Année Épigraphique
AIPhHOS	Annuaire de l'Institut de Philologie et d'Histoire Orientales et Slaves
AJA	American Journal of Archaeology
AJPh	American Journal of Philology
AJSL	American Journal of Semitic Languages and Literatures
ALUOS	Annual of Leeds University Oriental Society
ARAST	Atti della Reale Accademia delle Scienze di Torino
ASTI	Annual of the Swedish Theological Institute
BA	Biblical Archaeologist
BASOR	Bulletin of the American Schools of Oriental Research
BCH	Bulletin de Correspondance Hellénique
BE	Bulletin Épigraphique, in REG
BGU	Aegyptische Urkunden aus den Staatlichen Museen zu Berlin, Griechische Urkunden
BIES	Bulletin of the Israel Exploration Society
BJRL	Bulletin of the John Rylands Library
BMC Arabia	G. F. Hill, *Catalogue of the Greek Coins of Arabia, Mesopotamia and Persia in the British Museum* (1922)
BMC Palestine	G. F. Hill, *Catalogue of the Greek Coins of Palestine in the British Museum* (1914)
BMC Phoenicia	G. F. Hill, *Catalogue of the Greek Coins of Phoenicia in the British Museum* (1910)
BMC Roman Republic	H. A. Grueber, *Coins of the Roman Republic in the British Museum* I–III (1910)
BMC Syria	W. Wroth, *Catalogue of the Greek Coins of Galatia, Cappadocia, and Syria in the British Museum* (1899)

BZ	Biblische Zeitschrift
BZAW	Zeitschrift für die Alttestamentliche Wissenschaft, Beihefte
CAH	*Cambridge Ancient History*
CBQ	Catholic Biblical Quarterly
CCL	*Corpus Christianorum, series Latina*
CHB	*Cambridge History of the Bible*
CIG	*Corpus Inscriptionum Graecarum*
CIJ	J.-B. Frey, *Corpus Inscriptionum Iudaicarum* I–II
CIL	*Corpus Inscriptionum Latinarum*
CIS	*Corpus Inscriptionum Semiticarum*
CPh	Classical Philology
CPJ	V. Tcherikover, A. Fuks, M. Stern, *Corpus Papyrorum Judaicarum* I–III
CRAI	Comptes-rendus de l'Académie des Inscriptions
CSHB	*Corpus Scriptorum Historiae Byzantinae*
CSEL	*Corpus Scriptorum Ecclesiasticorum Latinorum*
DB Supp.	*Supplément au Dictionnaire de la Bible*
DJD	*Discoveries in the Judaean Desert*
EB	*Encyclopaedia Biblica*
EE	Ephemeris Epigraphica
EJ	*Encyclopaedia Judaica* (A–L)
Enc. Jud.	*Encyclopaedia Judaica* (1971)
ET	Expository Times
EThL	Ephemerides Theologicae Lovanienses
EvTh	Evangelische Theologie
FGrH	F. Jacoby, *Die Fragmente der griechischen Historiker*
FHG	I. Müller, *Fragmenta Historicorum Graecorum*
FIRA²	S. Riccobono, *Fontes Iuris Romani Antiqui*²
GCS	*Die Griechischen Christlichen Schriftsteller der ersten drei Jahrhunderte*
HDB	*Hastings' Dictionary of the Bible*
HERE	*Hastings' Encyclopedia of Religion and Ethics*
HSCPh	Harvard Studies in Classical Philology
HThR	Harvard Theological Review
HUCA	Hebrew Union College Annual
ICC	*International Critical Commentary*
IDB	*The Interpreter's Dictionary of the Bible*
IEJ	Israel Exploration Journal
IGLS	*Inscriptions grecques et latines de la Syrie*
IGR	R. Cagnat *et al*, *Inscriptiones Graecae ad Res Romanas Pertinentes* I, III, IV
IGUR	*Inscriptiones Graecae Urbis Romae*
JA	Journal Asiatique

JAOS	Journal of the American Oriental Society
JBL	Journal of Biblical Literature
JE	*The Jewish Encyclopedia*
JEA	Journal of Egyptian Archaeology
JHS	Journal of Hellenic Studies
JJS	Journal of Jewish Studies
JNES	Journal of Near Eastern Studies
JOAI	Jahreshefte des Österreichischen Archäologischen Instituts
JPOS	Journal of the Palestine Oriental Society
JQR	Jewish Quarterly Review
JRS	Journal of Roman Studies
JSJ	Journal for the Study of Judaism in the Persian, Hellenistic and Roman Period
JSS	Journal of Semitic Studies
JThSt	Journal of Theological Studies
JZWL	Jüdische Zeitschrift für Wissenschaft und Leben
LThK	*Lexikon für Theologie und Kirche*
MDPV	Mitteilungen und Nachrichten des Deutschen Palästina-Vereins
MGWJ	Monatschrift für Geschichte und Wissenschaft des Judentums
MRR	T. R. S. Broughton, *Magistrates of the Roman Republic* I–II
MUSJ	Mélanges de l'Université St. Joseph
NKZ	Neue Kirchliche Zeitschrift
NT	Novum Testamentum
NTS	New Testament Studies
ÖAW	Österreichische Akademie der Wissenschaften
OGIS	W. Dittenberger, *Orientis Graeci Inscriptiones Selectae* I–II
PAAJR	Proceedings of the American Academy for Jewish Research
PBSR	Papers of the British School at Rome
PEFA	Palestine Exploration Fund Annual
PEFQSt	Palestine Exploration Fund Quarterly Statement
PEQ	Palestine Exploration Quarterly
PG	J.-P. Migne, *Patrum Graecorum Cursus Completus*
PL	J.-P. Migne, *Patrum Latinorum Cursus Completus*
PIR[1]	*Prosopographia Imperii Romani*[1]
PIR[2]	*Prosopographia Imperii Romani*[2]
QDAP	Quarterly of the Department of Antiquities of Palestine
RAC	*Reallexikon für Antike und Christentum*
RB	Revue Biblique

RE	Pauly-Wissowa, *Realencyclopädie der classischen Altertumswissenschaft*
REG	Revue des Études Grecques
REJ	Revue des Études Juives
RES	Répertoire d'épigraphie sémitique I–VII
RGG	*Die Religion in Geschichte und Gegenwart*
RHR	Revue de l'Histoire des Religions
RIB	*Roman Inscriptions of Britain*
RN	Revue Numismatique
RQ	Revue de Qumrân
RSR	Recherches de Science Religieuse
SAB	Sitzungsberichte der Deutschen Akademie der Wissenschaften zu Berlin
SAH	Sitzungsberichte der Heidelberger Akademie der Wissenschaften
SAM	Sitzungsberichte der Bayerischen Akademie der Wissenschaften
SAW	Sitzungsberichte der Österreichischen Akademie der Wissenschaften
Scrip. Hier.	*Scripta Hierosolymitana*
SEG	Supplementum Epigraphicum Graecum
SIG[3]	W. Dittenberger, *Sylloge Inscriptionum Graecarum*[3]
ST	*Studi e Testi*
SThU	Schweizerische Theologische Umschau
Strack	H. L. Strack, *Introduction to Talmud and Midrash*
Str.-B.	H. L. Strack–P. Billerbeck, *Kommentar zum Neuen Testament aus Talmud und Midrasch*
TAPhA	Transactions of the American Philological Association
ThDNT	*Theological Dictionary to the New Testament*
ThLZ	Theologische Literaturzeitung
ThStKr	Theologische Studien und Kritiken
ThT	Theologisch Tijdschrift
ThWNT	*Theologisches Wörterbuch zum Neuen Testament*
ThZ	Theologische Zeitschrift
TU	*Texte und Untersuchungen*
VT	Vetus Testamentum
WKZM	Wiener Zeitschrift zur Kunde des Morgenlandes
ZA	Zeitschrift für Assyriologie
ZAW	Zeitschrift für die Alttestamentliche Wissenschaft
ZDMG	Zeitschrift der Deutschen Morgenländischen Gesellschaft
ZDPV	Zeitschrift der Deutschen Palästina-Vereins
ZNW	Zeitschrift für die Neutestamentliche Wissenschaft
Zunz	L. Zunz, *Die gottesdienstlichen Vorträge der Juden*[2]
ZWTh	Zeitschrift für Wissenschaftliche Theologie

Introduction

Introduction

§1. Scope and Purpose of the Work

Since it was from Judaism that Christianity emerged in the first century A.D., nothing in the Gospel account is understandable apart from its setting in Jewish history, no word of Jesus meaningful unless inserted into its natural context of contemporary Jewish thought. The task of the New Testament scholar, when enquiring into the phenomenon of the birth of Christianity, is to relate Jesus and the Gospel, not only to the Old Testament, but also, and above all, to the Jewish world of his time. Such an aim involves a full assimilation of the findings of students of inter-Testamental Judaism and of Hellenistic and Roman Palestine.

The chief characteristic of this period was the growing importance of Pharisaism. The legalistic orientation initiated by Ezra had slowly developed into a religio-social system in which it was no longer sufficient to fulfil the commandments of the written Torah; the generalities of biblical law were resolved into an immense number of detailed precepts, the performance of which was imposed as a most sacred duty. Though never universally followed, and never completely divorced from truly spiritual and even charismatic tendencies, this concern with the punctilious observance of the minutiae of religion became the hall-mark of mainstream Judaism.

Together with the other Palestinian religious parties, the Pharisaic movement had its origin in the conflicts of the Maccabaean period. During that time, the trend towards legal conservatism not only acted as a unitive force within Jewry by defeating the pro-Greek faction, and thus contributed to the defence of Israel's patrimony; it also helped to create a highly influential class, that of the scribes. No other power, spiritual or political, was in a position to neutralise their impact. But the battles of the Maccabaean period were also crucial for Israel's political history since they laid the ground for the emancipation of the Jews from the Seleucid kingdom, and for the establishment of an independent Judaea under native princes which endured until the

Roman conquest. Thus both the internal and external development of Judaism which took place at this time justifies the choice of the Maccabaean age for the *terminus a quo* of the present study.

Similar considerations help to fix the *terminus ad quem*. At the start of Roman rule a certain measure of political autonomy continued. The priestly line of the Maccabees was replaced by a newly created dynasty of Herodians. When they were removed by Rome, Judaea was administered by imperial prefects and procurators, but even so, a national aristocratic senate, the Sanhedrin, exercised many of the powers of government. It was only in consequence of the great insurrection under Nero and Vespasian that the independence of the Jewish people was taken from them, and only the suppression of the great rebellion under Hadrian that entailed its actual and final abolition. But if political considerations warrant the extension of the 'age of Jesus' to the reign of Hadrian, the internal evolution of Judaism does the same, for it was precisely the second century A.D. that saw the commencement of the systematic recording of laws till then transmitted mainly orally, the foundation, in other words, of the Talmudic code. It was, moreover, the period in which Pharisaism, as a result of the downfall of Jewish institutions, acquired decisive influence, both as a spiritual power and as a secular authority. For the Sadducee priesthood disappeared with the destruction of the Temple; and in the Diaspora, inconsistent Hellenistic Judaism was unable to hold its own in face of the greater consistency of the Pharisees.

It is impossible, because of the nature of the sources, to follow the doctrinal movements of this time step by step, and even more impossible to do so in regard to the development of the various institutions. First, therefore, Judaea's political destiny must be investigated in its two phases of national independence and Roman domination. The subsequent consideration of Jewish thought and institutions calls primarily for a description of the general cultural setting in Palestine with particular attention to the spread of Hellenism in territories inhabited by Gentiles and by Jews (§22). Next, community organisation will be discussed, Gentile as well as Jewish; for this belongs to internal history inasmuch as it concerns the self-administration of communes as opposed to the political history of the country as a whole. Included in the study of Jewish self-government will be an examination of the Sanhedrin and the High Priesthood (§23). But the two chief factors in interior affairs were, on the one hand, the priesthood and the Temple cult (§24), and on the other, the study and teaching of the Bible by the scribes and rabbis (§25). Whereas the leading priests in the Greek period, with the Sadducees grouped around them, were more interested in political matters than in religion, the scribes and their heirs, the Pharisees (§26), propagated and preserved the knowledge of the Torah through the institutions of school and synagogue (§27). The effects of their work upon the people at large are seen in an examination of Jewish life and religious practice (§28). But most important of all, the reward for a faithful and rigorous observance of the law was looked for in the future; zeal for the Torah during this time was inspired by a vivid Messianic and eschatological expectation (§29).

This exploration of mainstream Judaism is to be supplemented by an exposition of the community of the Essenes (§30) and of the distinctive features of Diaspora Judaism (§31). Finally, extant Palestinian Jewish literature of the period (§32), and to an even greater extent Hellenistic literature (§33), where the Jewish philosopher Philo of Alexandria merits special attention (§34), reveal that, despite the predominance of Pharisaism, the spiritual interests and aspirations of religious Jews were many and varied.

Bibliography

1. General works on inter-Testamental Jewish history and ideas.

Geiger, A., *Urschrift und Übersetzungen der Bibel in ihrer Abhängigkeit von der innern Entwickelung des Judenthums* (1857, [2]1928).

Derenbourg, J., *Essai sur l'histoire et la géographie de la Palestine d'après les Thalmuds et les autres sources rabbiniques.* I. *Histoire de la Palestine depuis Cyrus jusqu'à Adrien* (1867).

Graetz, H., *Geschichte der Juden von den ältesten Zeiten bis auf die Gegenwart* I–XI (1853–75, [4]1908).

Ewald, H., *Geschichte des Volkes Israel* I–VII ([3]1864–8).

Wellhausen, J., *Die Pharisäer und Sadduzäer* (1874, [2]1924).

Wellhausen, J., *Israelitische und jüdische Geschichte* (1894, [9]1958).

Weber, F., *Jüdische Theologie auf Grund des Talmud und verwandter Schriften gemeinfasslich dargestellt* (1897).

Schlatter, A., *Israels Geschichte von Alexander dem Grossen bis zum Hadrian* (1900).

Holtzmann, O., *Neutestamentliche Zeitgeschichte* ([2]1906).

Schechter, S., *Some Aspects of Rabbinic Theology* (1909).

Juster, J., *Les Juifs dans l'Empire romain* I–II (1914).

Radin, M., *The Jews among the Greeks and Romans* (1915).

Meyer, E., *Ursprung und Anfänge des Christentums* I–III (1921–3).

Moore, G. F., *Judaism in the First Centuries of the Christian Era* I–III (1927–30).

Bousset, W.-Gressmann, H., *Die Religion des Judentums im späthellenistischen Zeitalter* ([3]1926, [4]1966).

Herford, T. R., *Judaism in the New Testament Period* (1928).

Lagrange, M.-J., *Le judaïsme avant Jésus-Christ* (1931).

Guignebert, C., *The Jewish World in the Time of Jesus* (1939).

Lieberman, S., *Greek in Jewish Palestine* (1942, [2]1965).

Lieberman, S., *Hellenism in Jewish Palestine* (1950).

Pfeiffer, R. H., *History of New Testament Times with an Introduction to the Apocrypha* (1949).

Marmorstein, A., *Studies in Jewish Theology* (1950).

Abel, F.-M., *Histoire de la Palestine depuis la conquête d'Alexandre le Grand jusqu'à l'invasion arabe* I–II ([2]1952).
Baron, S. W., *A Social and Religious History of the Jews* I–II ([2]1952).
Goodenough, E. R., *Jewish Symbols in the Greco-Roman Period* I–XII (1953–65).
Alon, G., *Tol^edot ha-Y^ehudim b^e-'ereẓ Yisra'el bi-t^eḳufat ha-Mishnah veha-Talmud* I–II (1954).
Baer, Y. F., *Israel among the Nations* (1955) (in Hebrew).
Büchler, A., *Studies in Jewish History* (1956).
Daube, D., *The New Testament and Rabbinic Judaism* (1956).
Klausner, J., *Hisṭoryah shel ha-bayit ha-sheni* I–V ([5]1958).
Tcherikover, V., *Hellenistic Civilization and the Jews* (1959).
Vermes, G., *Scripture and Tradition in Judaism* (1961).
Bickerman, E. J., *From Ezra to the last of the Maccabees* (1962).
Zeitlin, S., *The Rise and Fall of the Judean State* I–II (1962–67).
Avi-Yonah, M., *Geschichte der Juden im Zeitalter des Talmuds: In den Tagen von Rom und Byzanz* (1962).
Noth, M., *Geschichte Israels* ([5]1963); E.T. *History of Israel* ([2]1960).
Filson, F. V., *A New Testament History* (1965).
Neusner, J., *A History of the Jews in Babylonia* I–V (1965–70).
Cohen, B., *Jewish and Roman Law, A Comparative Study* I–II (1966).
Bruce, F. F., *New Testament History* (1969).
Jeremias, J., *Jerusalem in the Time of Jesus* (1969).
Hengel, M., *Judentum und Hellenismus* (1969).
Reicke, B., *The New Testament Era. The World of the Bible from* 500 *B.C. to A.D.* 100 (1969).
Ben Sasson, H. H. (ed.), *History of the Jewish People* (Hebrew) I [The Period of the Second Temple (M. Stern); The Age of the Mishnah and the Talmud (S. Safrai)], pp. 177–367 (1969).
Urbach, E. E., *The Sages, their Concepts and Beliefs* (1969) (in Hebrew).
Guttmann, A., *Rabbinic Judaism in the Making—The Halakhah from Ezra to Judah I* (1970).
Neusner, J., *The Rabbinic Traditions about the Pharisees before 70* I–III (1971).
Maier, J., *Geschichte der jüdischen Religion* (1972).

2. The most important works of reference and periodicals dealing with inter-Testamental Jewish history.

a. Works of reference:

The Jewish Encyclopedia I–XII (1901–5).
Encyclopaedia Judaica I–X [A–L] (1928–34).
Supplément au Dictionnaire de la Bible (1928–).
The Interpreter's Dictionary of the Bible I–IV (1962).
Real-Encyclopädie der classischen Altertumswissenschaft (Pauly, A. and Wissowa, G.) (1894–).
Encyclopaedia Talmudica: *Enẓiḳlopediyah Talmudit* (1948–).
Encyclopaedia Biblica: *Enẓiḳlopediyah Miḳra'it* (1964–).
Encyclopaedia Judaica I–XVI (1971).

b. Periodicals

Monatschrift für Geschichte und Wissenschaft des Judenthums (1851–1938).
Jüdische Zeitschrift für Wissenschaft und Leben (A. Geiger) (1862–75).
Revue des Etudes Juives (1880–).
Jewish Quarterly Review (1888–).

Revue Biblique (1892–).
Biblica (1919–).
Tarbiz (1929/30–) (in Hebrew with English summaries).
Zion (1935–) (in Hebrew with English summaries).
Journal of Jewish Studies (1948–).
Israel Exploration Journal (1950–).
New Testament Studies (1954–).
Revue de Qumrân (1958–).
Journal for the Study of Judaism in the Persian, Hellenistic and Roman Period (1970–).

c. Bibliographies

Kirjath Sepher, Bibliographical Quarterly of the Jewish National and University Library, Jerusalem (1924–).

Marcus, R., 'A Selected Bibliography (1920–1945) of the Jews in the Hellenistic–Roman Period', PAAJR 16 (1946–7), pp. 97–181.

Delling, G., *Bibliographie zur jüdisch-hellenistischen und intertestamentarischen Literatur 1900–1965* (1969).

Berlin, C., *Index to Festschriften in Jewish Studies* (1971).

Rappaport, U., 'Bibliography of Works on Jewish History in the Hellenistic and Roman Periods, 1946–1970', *Studies in the History of the Jewish People and the Land of Israel*, ed. B. Obed *et al.* (1972), pp. 247–321.

§2. Auxiliary Sciences

The general literature cited in §1 requires supplementation, and the present chapter will consist of bibliographical lists relating to the main auxiliary disciplines: (A) Archaeology; (B) Geography; (C) Chronology; (D) Numismatics; and (E) Epigraphy.

A. Archaeology

a. Bibliography:

Thomsen, P., *Die Palästina Literatur* [vol. A and I–VII for 1878–1945] (1908–).
Vogel, E. K., 'Bibliography of Holy Land Sites', HUCA 42 (1971), pp. 1–96.

b. Main Periodicals:

Palestine Exploration Fund Quarterly Statement (1869–1936).
Palestine Exploration Quarterly (1937–).
Zeitschrift des Deutschen Palästina-Vereins (1878–).
Revue Biblique (1892–) containing a 'Chronique archéologique'.
Palestine Exploration Fund Annual Report (1903–).
Palästinajahrbuch des deutschen evangelischen Instituts für Altertumswissenschaft des heiligen Landes zu Jerusalem (1905–).
Annual of the American Schools of Oriental Research (1919–).
Bulletin of the American Schools of Oriental Research (1919–).
Quarterly of the Department of Antiquities of Palestine (1931–50).
The Biblical Archaeologist (1938–).
Israel Exploration Journal (1949/50–).
Eretz Yisrael (1951–).
Annual of the Department of Antiquities of Jordan (1951–).
Atiqot (1955–).
Levant (1969–).

For the archaeology of the Syrian region see

Syria (1920–).

For reports of all finds from Palestine and the surrounding areas see the relevant part of

Fasti Archaeologici I– (1946–).

c. Descriptive Works:

Krauss, S., *Talmudische Archäeologie* I–III (1910–2).
Krauss, S., *Synagogale Altertümer* (1922).
Albright, W. F., *The Archaeology of Palestine and the Bible* (1932).
Watzinger, C., *Denkmäler Palästinas* I–II (1933–5).
Barrois, A. G., *Manuel d'archéologie biblique* I–II (1939–53).
Glueck, N., *The Other Side of the Jordan* (1940; ^{2}1970).
Albright, W. F., *From the Stone Age to Christianity* (1940).

Wright, G. E., *Biblical Archaeology* (1957, rev. 1962).
Finegan, J., *Light from the Ancient Past* ([2]1959).
Glueck, N., *Rivers in the Desert* (1959).
Yeivin, S., *A Decade of Archaeology in Israel*, 1948–1958 (1960).
Kenyon, K., *Archaeology and the Holy Land* (1960).
Thomas, D. W. (ed.), *Archaeology and Old Testament Study* (1967).
Finegan, J., *Archaeology of the New Testament* (1969).

For Jerusalem see:

Vincent, L.-H., Abel, F.-M., *Jérusalem Nouvelle* (1914–26).
Dalman, G., *Jerusalem und sein Gelände* (1930).
Simons, J., *Jerusalem in the Old Testament* (1952).
Vincent, L.-H., Stève, A.-M., *Jérusalem de l'Ancien Testament* I–II and Pl. (1954–6).
Avi-Yonah, M. (ed.), *Sepher Yerushalayim* (*The Book of Jerusalem*) I (1956) (Hebrew).
Kenyon, K., *Jerusalem: Excavating 3000 Years of History* (1967).
Aviram, J. (ed.), *Jerusalem through the Ages* (1968) (mostly Hebrew).
Shiloh, Y., 'A Table of the Major Excavations in Jerusalem', Qadmoniot 1 (1968), pp. 71–8 (Hebrew).
Gray, J., *A History of Jerusalem* (1969).

For Jewish life in biblical and inter-Testamental Palestine see:

Vaux, R. de, *Ancient Israel. Its Life and Institutions* (1961).
Jeremias, J., *Jerusalem in the Time of Jesus* (1969).

B. Geography

a. Bibliography:

Bibliographiyah nivḥeret le-geographiyah hisṭorit shel Ereẓ Yisrael I–III (1961–2).
Thomsen, P., *Die Palästina Literatur*, see Archaeology a.

b. Periodicals: see Archaeology b.

c. Descriptive Works:

Robinson, E., *Biblical Researches in Palestine* I–III (1841).
Neubauer, A., *La géographie du Talmud* (1868).
Guérin, V., *Description géographique, historique et archéologique de la Palestine*: *Judée* I–III (1868–9); *Samarie* I–II (1874–5); *Galilée* I–II (1880).
Wilson, C., et al., *The Survey of Western Palestine* I–IX (1881–8).
Smith, G. A., *The Historical Geography of the Holy Land* (1894).
Abel, F.-M., *Géographie de la Palestine* I–II (1933–8).
Glueck, N., *Explorations in Eastern Palestine* I–IV (1935–49).
Baly, D., *The Geography of the Bible* (1957).
Baly, D., *A Geographical Companion to the Bible* (1963).
Avi-Yonah, M., *The Holy Land from the Persian to the Arab Conquests. A Historical Geography* (1966).
Mittmann, S., *Beiträge zur Siedlungsgeschichte des nordlichen Ostjordanlandes* (1970).

d. Atlases and Topographical Works:

Smith, G. A., *Historical Atlas of the Holy Land* (1936).
Avi-Yonah, M., *Map of Roman Palestine* (1940).

Avi-Yonah, M., *The Madaba Mosaic Map* (1954).
Avi-Yonah, M., *Carta's Atlas of the Period of the Second Temple, the Mishnah and the Talmud* (1966) (Hebrew).
Aharoni, Y., Avi-Yonah, M., *The Macmillan Bible Atlas* (1968).
Negenman, J. H., *New Atlas of the Bible* (1969).
Atlas of Israel (1970).
Miller, K., *Weltkarte des Castorius* (1887)=*Die Peutingersche Tafel* (rp. 1962).
Eusebius, *Onomasticon der biblischen Ortsnamen*, ed. E. Klostermann, GCS XI/1 (1904).
Thomsen, P., *Loca Sancta* (1907).
Miller, K., *Itineraria Romana* (1916).
Borée, W., *Die alten Ortsnamen Palästinas* (1930).
Romanoff, P., *Onomasticon of Palestine* (1937).
Fischer, H., 'Geschichte der Kartographie von Palaestina' ZDPV 62 (1939), pp. 169–89.

C. Chronology

Chronology is an auxiliary of history the purpose of which is to convert the time-reckoning of ancient sources into the chronological system used today. Since the Jewish calendar is discussed in detail in Appendix III, only basic bibliographical data will be listed here concerning ancient chronology in general as well as the chronologies of the Mesopotamian, Egyptian, Biblical and Greco-Roman worlds.

General Works:

Ideler, L., *Handbuch der Chronologie* I–II (1825–6).
Ideler, L., *Lehrbuch der Chronologie* (1831).
Ginzel, F. K., *Handbuch der mathematischen und technischen Chronologie* I–III (1906–14).
Nilsson, M. P., *Primitive Time-Reckoning* (1920).
Kubitschek, W., *Grundriss der antiken Zeitrechnung* (1928).
Neugebauer, O., *The Exact Sciences in Antiquity* (1957).
Grumel, V., *La chronologie* (1958).
Bickerman, E. J., *Chronology of the Ancient World* (1968).

Mesopotamia:

Kugler, F. X., *Sternkunde und Sterndienst in Babel* I–II (1907–24); Ergänz. Hefte I–III (1913–35).
Sidersky, D., *Etude sur la chronologie assyro-babylonienne* (1920).
Langdon, S., *Babylonian Menologies and Semitic Calendars* (1935).
Labat, R., *Hémerologies et ménologies assyriennes* (1939).
Neugebauer, O., *Astronomical Cuneiform Texts* (1955).
Parker, R. A., Dubberstein, W. H., *Babylonian Chronology 626 B.C.–A.D. 75* (1956).

Egypt:

Meyer, E., *Chronologie égyptienne* (1912).
Borchardt, L., *Aegyptische Zeitmessung* (1920).
Parker, R. A., *The Calendars of Ancient Egypt* (1950).
Neugebauer, O., Parker, R. A., *Egyptian Astronomical Texts* I–II (1962–4).

The Bible:

Mahler, E., *Handbuch der jüdischen Chronologie* (1916).
Kugler, F. X., *Von Moses bis Paulus* (1922).
Goudoever, J. van, *Biblical Calendars* ([2]1961).
Jepsen, A., Hanhardt, R., *Untersuchungen zur israelitisch-jüdischen Chronologie* (1964).
Finegan, J., *Handbook of Biblical Chronology* (1964).
See also the literature quoted in Appendix III.

Greece and Rome:

Clinton, H., *Fasti Hellenici* ([2]1841).
Clinton, H., *Fasti Romani* I–II (1845–50).
Mommsen, Th., *Römische Chronologie* ([2]1859).
Goyau, G., *Chronologie de l'Empire romain* (1891).
Nilsson, M. P., *Die Erstehung und religiöse Bedeutung des griechischen Kalendars* (1918).
Dinsmoor, W. B., *The Archons of Athens in the Hellenistic Age* (1931).
Pritchett, W. K., Neugebauer, O., *The Calendars of Athens* (1948).
Broughton, T. R. S., *The Magistrates of the Roman Republic* I–II and Suppl. (1951–60).
Degrassi, A., *I Fasti consolari dell'impero romano dal* 30 *a.C. al* 613 *d.C.* (1952).
Degrassi, A., *Fasti Capitolini* (1954).
Manni, E., *Fasti ellenistici e romani* (1957).
Merritt, B. D., *The Athenian Year* (1961).
Samuel, A. E., *Ptolemaic Chronology* (1962).
Pritchett, W. K., *Ancient Athenian Calendars on Stone* (1963).
Michels, A. K., *The Calendar of the Roman Republic* (1967).
Samuel, A. E., *Greek and Roman Chronology. Calendars and Years in Classical Antiquity* [*Handbuch der Altertumswissenschaft* I, 7] (1972).

D. Numismatics

A study of coins issued during the epoch under consideration offers valuable contributions to a better understanding of (1) Seleucid history, (2) the history of Hellenistic cities in the neighbourhood of Palestine, and (3) Jewish history.

1. Seleucid Coins

Eckhel, J., *Doctrina numorum veterum* III (1794), pp. 209–49.
Mionnet, T. E., *Description des médailles antiques* V (1811), pp. 1–109; Suppl. VIII (1837), pp. 1–81.
Saulcy, F. de, *Mémoire sur les monnaies datées des Séleucides* (1871).
Saulcy, F. de, 'Monnaies des Séleucides munies de contremarques', Mélanges de Numismatique I (1875), pp. 45–64.
Saulcy, F. de, 'Monnaies inédites de Tryphon frappées dans les villes maritimes de Phénicie', *ibid.* II (1877), pp. 76–84.
Gardner, P., *Catalogue of the Greek Coins in the British Museum. The Seleucid Kings of Syria* (1878).
Babelon, E., 'Les rois de Syrie, d'Arménie et de Commagène', *Catalogue des monnaies grecques de la Bibliothèque Nationale* (1890).

MacDonald, G., *Catalogue of the Greek Coins in the Hunterian Collection* III (1905), pp. 5–117.

Head, B. V., *Historia Numorum, a Manual of Greek Numismatics* (^{2}1911), pp. 755–73.

Newell, E. T., 'The Seleucid Mint of Antioch', Am. Journ. of Numismatics 51 (1917), pp. 1–151.

Newell, E. T., *The Seleucid Coinages of Tyre: a Supplement*. Num. Notes and Monogr. 73 (1936).

Newell, E. T., *The Coinage of the Eastern Seleucid Mints from Seleucus I to Antiochus III*, Numismatic Studies 1 (1938).

Newell, E. T., *Late Seleucid Mints in Ake-Ptolemais and Damascus*, Num. Notes and Monogr. 84 (1939).

Newell, E. T., *The Coinage of the Western Seleucid Mints from Seleucus I to Antiochus III*, Num. Studies 4 (1941).

Bellinger, A. R., 'The End of the Seleucids', Trans. Connect. Acad. 38 (1949), pp. 51–102.

Seyrig, H., 'Notes on Syrian Coins I: the Khan el-adbe Find and the Coinage of Tryphon', Num. Notes and Monogr. 119 (1950), pp. 1–23.

Brett, A. B., 'The Mint of Ascalon under the Seleucids', Am. Num. Soc., Mus. Notes 4 (1950), pp. 43–54.

Sylloge Nummorum Graecorum, Danish National Museum: Syria, Seleucid Kings (1959).

Mørkholm, O., *Studies in the Coinage of Antiochus IV of Syria* (1963).

Le Rider, G., *Suse sous les Séleucides et les Parthes* (1965).

Le Rider, G., and Seyrig, H., 'Objets de la collection Louis de Clercq: monnaies Séleucides', RN 9 (1967), pp. 11–53.

Baldus, H. R., 'Der Helm des Tryphon und die seleukidische Chronologie der Jahre 146–138 v. Chr.', Jahrbuch f. Num. u. Geldgesch. 20 (1970), pp. 217–39.

2. City Coinages of the Phoenician and Palestinian Region

For works on city mints under the Seleucids see the preceding list.

Saulcy, F. de, *Numismatique de la Terre Sainte. Description des monnaies autonomes et impériales de la Palestine et de l'Arabie Pétrée* (1874). The basic work on the coins of the Palestinian cities.

Babelon, E., *Les Perses Achéménides (les Satrapes et les Dynastes tributaires de leur empire), Cypre et Phénicie, Catalogue des monnaies grecques de la Bibliothèque nationale* (1893).

Rouvier, J., 'Numismatique des villes de la Phénicie', Journ. internat. d'arch. num. 3 (1900), pp. 125–68; 237–312.

MacDonald, G., *Catalogue of Greek Coins in the Hunterian Collection* III (1905), pp. 225–84.

Head, B. V., *Historia Numorum* (^{2}1911), pp. 783–806.

Hill, G. F., *Catalogue of the Greek Coins in the British Museum*:
Phoenicia (1910);
Palestine (1914);
Arabia, Mesopotamia, Persia (1922), pp. XXII–XLV and 15–44 on the coinage of the cities included in the Roman province of Arabia.

Sylloge Nummorum Graecorum, Danish National Museum:
Phoenicia (1961);
Palestine-Characene (1961).

Corpus Nummorum Palestinensium:

I. Kadman, L., *The Coins of Aelia Capitolina* (1956).

II. Kadman, L., *The Coins of Caesarea Maritima* (1957).

IV. Kadman, L., *The Coins of Akko-Ptolemais* (1961).

For corrections and supplements to the latter work see the review-article by H. Seyrig, RN Ser. 6 (1962), pp. 25–50.

Note also: H. Seyrig, *Antiquités Syriennes* I–VI (1934–66); in default of a modern corpus, this series of papers off-printed from 'Syria', represents the fullest treatment of the antiquities, primarily the coins, of many cities in Syria, Phoenicia, Judaea and the Decapolis.

Naster, P., 'Le développement des monayages phéniciens avant Alexandre, d'après les trésors', *The Patterns of Monetary Development in Phoenicia and Palestine in Antiquity*, ed. A. Kindler (1967), pp. 3–24.

Kadman, L., 'Temple Dues and Currency in Ancient Palestine in the Light of recently discovered Coin-Hoards', *Congresso internat. de Numismatica, Roma* II (1965), pp. 69–76.

Kindler, A., 'The Mint of Tyre—the Major Source of Silver Coins in Ancient Israel', *Eretz-Israel* VIII (1967), pp. 318–25 (Hebrew with English summary).

Ben-David, A., *Jerusalem und Tyros: ein Beitrag zur palästinensischen Münz- und Wirtschaftsgeschichte* (126 *a.C.*–57 *p.C.*) (1969).

(The latter three studies deal with the widespread circulation of Tyrian shekels in Palestine.) For the coinage of individual cities see also vol. II, §22 2, 1 and §23 1.

3. Jewish Coins

Only the most essential reference works are listed here. For a fuller bibliography, see Appendix IV.

Saulcy, F. de, *Recherches sur la numismatique judaïque* (1854).

Madden, F. W., *History of Jewish Coinage and of Money in the Old Testament* (1864).

Madden, F. W., *Coins of the Jews* (1881).

Hill, G. F., *Catalogue of the Greek Coins in the British Museum: Palestine* (1914).

Reifenberg, A., *Ancient Jewish Coins* ([2]1947).

Kadman, L., *The Coins of the Jewish War of* 66–73 *C.E.* (1960).

Mayer, L. A., *A Bibliography of Jewish Numismatics* (1966).

Kanael, B., 'Altjüdische Münzen', Jahrb. f. Num. u. Geldgesch. 17 (1967), pp. 159–298. (With discussion and full bibliography.)

Meshorer, Y., *Jewish Coins of the Second Temple Period* (1967). (Discussion, transcription, plates.)

E. Epigraphy

Inscriptions relevant to the history discussed here are of various kinds: non-Jewish and Jewish, Palestinian and extra-Palestinian, in Greek, Latin, Hebrew and Aramaic. (1) The non-Jewish Greek and Latin inscriptions from Palestine and its neighbouring areas were collected in *Corpus Inscriptionum Graecarum* III and *Corpus Inscriptionum Latinarum* III. The number of Greek and Latin epigraphic documents from this region has enormously increased since the compilation of the two monumental nineteenth-century works, but there is no modern corpus of them. The inscriptions referred to give especially valuable information on the culture of the non-Jewish areas of Palestine (see vol. II, §22). In addition to Palestinian inscriptions in classical languages, many discovered elsewhere are of importance for the present study, as are also many Semitic epigraphs from Palestine and other countries, especially the Nabataean texts (see the full bibliography in Appendix II). (2) Among the directly relevant Jewish inscriptions originating from both Palestine and the Diaspora, the majority is constituted by Greek and Latin sepulchral inscriptions. The Jewish catacombs in Rome are particularly rich in such epigraphs. The only modern collection of Jewish inscriptions in all languages, that of J.-B. Frey (see below), though very useful, is unfortunately neither complete, nor fully accurate.

1. Non-Jewish Inscriptions of the Phoenician and Palestinian Region

Only major collections and publications are listed here, together with an indication of the sources for the current bibliography of Greek and Latin inscriptions. Detailed epigraphical references in regard to individual cities will be found in vol. II, §22, 2, 1 and §23, 1. For Ituraea, Chalcis and Abilene, see Appendix I; for Nabataean inscriptions, see Appendix II.

a. Greek and Latin Inscriptions.

Corpus Inscriptionum Graecarum (CIG), III (1853), 4444–669.

Corpus Inscriptionum Latinarum (CIL), III (1873), 86–211 and 6027–49, and Suppl. to III, 6638–729.

Graham, G. C., 'Additional inscriptions from the Hauran and the eastern desert of Syria', *Transactions of the Royal Society of Literature*, ed. J. Hogg, VI, (1859), pp. 270–323.

Wetzstein, J. G., 'Ausgewählte griechische und lateinische Inschriften, gesammelt auf Reisen in den Trachonen und um das Haurangebirge', AAB (1863), pp. 255–68.

Renan, E., *Mission de Phénicie* (1864).

Le Bas, P., Waddington, H., *Inscriptions grecques et latines recueillies en Grèce et en Asie Mineure* III (1870), especially Pt. 1, pp. 449–625 and Pt. 2, pp. 435–631. A carefully prepared index was supplied by J.-B. Chabot, Revue archéol. 28–9 (1896).

Mordtmann, A. D., 'Griechische Inschriften aus dem Hauran', Archäol.-epigr. Mittheilungen aus Oesterreich 8 (1884), pp. 180–92.

Smith, G. A., 'Communication on some unpublished Inscriptions from the Hauran and Gilead', Critical Review of Theological and Philosophical Literature 2 (1892), pp. 55–64.

Ewing, W., 'Greek and other inscriptions collected in the Hauran', PEFQSt (1895), pp. 41–60, 131–60, 265–80, 346–54.

Schumacher, G., 'Dscherasch', ZDPV 18 (1895), pp. 126–40.—Buresch, K., 'Schumachers Inschriften aus Dscherasch', *ibid.*, pp. 141–8.

Fossey, C., 'Inscriptions de Syrie, II. Djolan et Hauran, III. Plaine de Damas et Antiliban', BCH 21 (1897), pp. 39–65.

Clermont-Ganneau, C., *Recueil d'archéologie orientale* I–VIII (1888–1924). *Études d'archéologie orientale* I–II (1895–7). *Archaeological Researches in Palestine* I–II (1896–9).

Conder, C. R., PEFQSt (1885), pp. 14–17, surveyed the inscriptions included in *The Survey of Western Palestine.*

Reinach, S., 'Chroniques d'Orient' I (1883–90); II (1891–5); Revue archéologique 1891, 1896.

Orientis Graeci Inscriptiones Selectae (OGIS), ed. W. Dittenberger, I (1903), 414–29, reproduces with commentary the Greek inscriptions of the Herodian dynasty, and II (1905), 586–602, other inscriptions from Syria, Phoenicia and Palestine.

Inscriptiones Graecae ad Res Romanas Pertinentes (IGR) III (1906), ed. R. Cagnat, 1015–1384, contains the Greek inscriptions of this region which are explicitly dated to the Roman period.

Publications of an American Archaeological Expedition to Syria, 1899–1900 III: *Greek and Latin Inscriptions* (1908), ed. W. K. Prentice (see pp. 287–336 for the inscriptions of the Djebel Hauran).

Thomsen, P., *Die römischen Meilsteine der Provinzen Syria, Arabia und Palaestina zusammengestellt und bearbeitet* (1917)=ZDPV 40 (1917), pp. 1–103.

Syria: Publications of the Princeton University Archaeological Expeditions to Syria in 1904–5 *and* 1909 III: *Greek and Latin Inscriptions, Section A, Southern Syria*, ed. E. Littmann, D. Magie, D. R. Stuart (1921).

Alt, A., *Die griechischen Inschriften der Palaestina Tertia westlich der Araba* (1921).

Gerasa: City of the Decapolis, ed. C. H. Kraeling (1938). The Inscriptions, by C. B. Welles, pp. 355–494.

Avi-Yonah, M., 'Greek and Latin Inscriptions from Jerusalem and Beisan', QDAP 8 (1938), pp. 54–61.

Thomsen, P., 'Die lateinischen und griechischen Inschriften der Stadt Jerusalem und ihrer nächsten Umgebung', ZDPV 64 (1941), pp. 201–56.

Avi-Yonah, M., 'Newly Discovered Latin and Greek Inscriptions', QDAP 12 (1946), pp. 84–102.

Sourdel, D., *Les cultes du Hauran à l'époque romaine* (1952), with a full bibliography of the inscriptions of this region.

Scavi di Caesarea Maritima (1965), pp. 218–28 (Inscriptions, including that of Pontius Pilatus).

Note also the selection by E. Gabba, *Iscrizione greche per lo studio della Bibbia* (1958).

For the most important periodicals publishing material, including inscriptions from the Palestinian area, see p. 6 above. Note especially IEJ and the series of studies on Palestinian epigraphy by B. Lifshitz in RB from 1960 onwards.

All publications of Greek inscriptions are surveyed in the 'Bulletin Épigraphique' in Revue des Études Grecques since 1888. The entries are arranged geographically. New and revised Greek inscriptions are also reprinted from time to time in Supplementum Epigraphicum Graecum (1923–). The arrangement is also geographical but the coverage tends to be episodic. The relevant inscriptions are included principally in vol. VII (1934), the Near-East other than Palestine;

VIII (1937), 1–353; XIV (1957), 832–47; XVI (1959), 821–53; XVII (1960), 774–88; XVIII (1962), 620–7; XIX (1963), 901–24; XX (1964), 412–95 (Palestine). A separate volume of *Indices* (1970) covers vol. XI–XX.

Newly published or revised Roman inscriptions are surveyed, and largely reprinted, in Année Épigraphique (1888–).

P. Thomsen, *Die Palästina-Literatur* I–VII (1908–70), covering the years 1895–1945, and A (1960), for the period 1878–94, devotes sections to a very full, if inevitably indiscriminate, lists of epigraphic publications from Palestine and to some extent from elsewhere. For the years subsequent to 1945 a good survey of all new material, including inscriptions, is provided by the relevant sections of Fasti Archaeologici (see above, p. 6.)

b. Semitic Inscriptions

The major collection of Semitic inscriptions is the *Corpus Inscriptionum Semiticarum* (CIS) published by the French Académie des Inscriptions et Belles-Lettres. The texts are arranged according to languages and the Corpus gives for each inscription a transcription, a Latin translation with, when necessary, a brief commentary. Separate volumes (Tabulae) contain the facsimiles. Of the planned five tomes, the following have appeared so far: Tome I, i–iii, Phoenician inscriptions begun by E. Renan (1881, 1890, 1926); Tome II, i, Aramaic inscriptions by M. de Vogué (1889); ii (1), Nabataean inscriptions from Sinai (1907); iii, Palmyrenian inscriptions by J.-B. Chabot (1926); Tome IV, i–iii, South-Arabian inscriptions started by J. Derenbourg (1889, 1911, 1926); Tome V, i, North-Arabian inscriptions edited by G. Ryckmans (1950). Tome III is reserved for Hebrew inscriptions but nothing has as yet been published.

Répertoire d'épigraphie sémitique (RES) I–VII surveys and reprints Semitic inscriptions published between 1890 and 1950.

Lidzbarski, M., *Handbuch der nordsemitischen Epigraphik nebst ausgewählten Inschriften* (1898).

'Ephemeris für semitische Epigraphik' I–III (1902–15).

Cooke, G. A., *A Text-Book of North-Semitic Inscriptions* (1903).

Donner, H., Röllig, W., *Kananäische und aramäische Inschriften* I–III (^{2}1966–9). (The most recent collection, with German translation and commentary.)

The works of Clermont-Ganneau mentioned above contain much relevant material from Semitic epigraphy.

The numerous Aramaic and Greek inscriptions from Palmyra have some relevance to the subject of this work. There are several useful collections:

Chabot, J.-B., *Choix d'inscriptions de Palmyre* (1922).
Cantineau, J., *Inventaire des inscriptions de Palmyre* I–IX (1930–6).

For the earliest Syriac inscriptions dating from the period covered here, see:

Jennin, E., 'Die altsyrischen Inschriften 1–3 Jahrhundert n. Chr.', ThZ 21 (1965), pp. 371 ff.

All publications and studies of Semitic inscriptions from 1964 onwards are surveyed in the 'Bulletin d'épigraphie sémitique' by J. Teixidor in Syria 44– (1967–).

2. Jewish Inscriptions (Hebrew, Aramaic, Greek and Latin)

Only the most essential collections are listed here. The inscriptions of the Diaspora communities will be discussed in detail in vol. III, §31.

For Jewish inscriptions and papyri from the biblical period, see:

Cooke, G. A., *A Text-book of North-Semitic Inscriptions* (1903).
Diringer, D., *Le iscrizioni antico-ebraiche palestinesi* (1934).
Moscati, S., *L'epigrafia ebraica antica* 1935–1950 (1951).
Moscati, S., *Stato e problemi dell'epigrafia ebraica antica* (1952).
Donner, H., Röllig, W., *Kananäische und aramäische Inschriften* I–III ([2]1966–9).
Gibson, J., *Syrian Semitic Inscriptions* (1969).
Sachau, E., *Aramäische Papyrus und Ostraka* (1911).
Cowley, A., *Aramaic Papyri of the Fifth Century B.C.* (1923).
Kraeling, E. G., *The Brooklyn Museum Aramaic Papyri* (1953).
Driver, G. R., *Aramaic Documents of the Fifth Century B.C.* (1954).
Koopmans, J. T., *Aramäische Chrestomathie* (1962).

For inscriptions more directly relevant to the period discussed in this work the following are to be consulted:

Frey, J.-B., *Corpus Inscriptionum Iudaicarum. Recueil des inscriptions juives qui vont du IIIe siècle avant Jésus-Christ au VIIe siècle de notre ère* I–II (1936–52). (This collection is very defective. Note the criticisms by J. Robert in REJ 101 (1937), pp. 73–86; BE 1954, no. 24, in REG 67 (1954), pp. 101–4.

Sepher Yerushalayim I, ed. M. Avi-Yonah (1956). 'Hebrew, Aramaic and Greek Inscriptions' by Y. Kutscher and M. Schwabe, pp. 349–68.

The Excavations at Dura Europos, VIII, 1. *The Synagogue*, ed. C. Kraeling (1956). Aramaic, Greek and Middle Iranian texts by C. C. Torrey, C. B. Welles and B. Geiger, pp. 261–317.

Mazar, B., *Beth She'arim. I. The Catacombs I–IV* ([2]1957). Semitic Inscriptions, pp. 132–42. (Hebrew with English summary.)

Bagatti, B., Milik, J. T., *Gli scavi del 'Dominus Flevit'* I. *La necropoli del periodo romano* (1958), pp. 70–109 ('Le iscrizioni degli ossuari', by J. T. Milik).

Leon, H. J., *The Jews of Ancient Rome* (1960). (All the Jewish inscriptions are reproduced and translated.)

Scheiber, A., *Corpus Inscriptionum Hungariae Judaicarum* (1960), pp. 13–61 (Greek and Latin inscriptions from the second to the fourth century A.D. with Hungarian translation and commentary).

Schwabe, M., Lifshitz, B., *Beth She'arim. II. The Greek Inscriptions* (1967) (Hebrew with French summary).

Lifshitz, B., *Donateurs et fondateurs dans les synagogues juives: Répertoire des dédicaces grecques relatives à la construction et à la réfection des synagogues* (1967).

Avigad, N., *Beth She'arim. III* (1971). Hebrew and Aramaic Inscriptions, pp. 169–89 (in Hebrew).

For the more than two hundred Hebrew and Aramaic inscriptions on pottery vessels and ostraca found at Masada and still awaiting publication, see the preliminary report by Y. Yadin in IEJ 15 (1965), pp. 111–4.

For current publications of Jewish inscriptions, note the collections and bulletins mentioned above under Greek, Latin and Semitic inscriptions.

For an edition with English translation and commentary of Jewish-Greek papyri see *Corpus Papyrorum Judaicarum* by V. Tcherikover, A. Fuks and M. Stern, with an epigraphic contribution by D. M. Lewis, I–III (1957–64).

§3. The Sources

The chief sources of information concerning the intellectual and spiritual life of the Jews during the period under consideration are the extant literary products of that era. They will be dealt with in §§32–4 in vol. III. The New Testament is also part of this literature insofar as it originates from Jewish writers and refers to Jewish affairs. Direct source material is further provided by the coins and inscriptions, the bibliography of which is contained in the preceding §2.

Taken singly or together, these documents would, however, not enable the scholar to write a history of the inter-Testamental age. This is possible only because the two Books of the Maccabees and the works of Josephus are available, recounting the principal events and often even the minute details of the history of that period. They form the most important, and almost exclusive, source for Jewish political history. Their contribution may be supplemented from the general and comprehensive works of Greek and Roman historians. Moreover, indirect evidence of those times concerning institutions and customs emerges from rabbinic literature (Mishnah, Tosefta, Talmud, Midrash and Targum), and from the various documents discovered during the last quarter of a century in the Judaean Desert between Qumran and Masada.

The relevant material will therefore be presented under the following six headings: A. the two Books of the Maccabees; B. the non-extant sources; C. Josephus; D. Greek and Roman historians; E. Rabbinic literature; F. the Documents from the Judaean Desert.

A. The Two Books of the Maccabees

The First Book of the Maccabees is the main source for the first forty years of the era under review (175–135/4 B.C.). The Second Book covers only the first fourteen years. Its credibility as an independent witness was erroneously thought to be restricted to the prehistory of the Maccabaean rising. It is more reasonable to adopt an eclectic principle and decide, on the basis of the evidence in each case, which of the two books offers the more reliable report. §§32 and 33 will examine in full detail the nature and origins of both compositions. Thus the only major issue to be discussed here is that of chronology, viz., how the two works apply the Seleucid era to date Jewish history and, in particular, whether the Macedonian era, beginning in the autumn of 312 B.C., or the Babylonian era counted from the spring (1 Nisan) of 311 B.C., is preferred by the Jewish writers. On the two Seleucid eras see Appendices III and V.

Since there existed in both the Hellenistic world and among the Jews two rival calendars (see Appendix III), with one New Year in the spring (1 Nisan) and one in the autumn (1 Tishri), it will surprise no-one that the chronology of the Maccabaean works is beset with complex problems requiring individual consideration. Nevertheless, analysis of the various data reveals certain common features in both the calendar and the era reckonings, and the following remarks are intended as a general guide in a highly controversial field.

1 Mac. uses the Jewish names of the months (Kislev, 1:54, 4:52; Adar, 7:43, 49; Elul, 14:27; Shebat, 16:14) and numbers them so that they represent a year commencing in the spring (i.e. Nisan). It names Kislev and Shebat the ninth and eleventh months respectively (4:52; 16:14); the feast of Tabernacles (celebrated on 15 Tishri) is placed in the seventh month (10:21), and the occupation of the citadel of Jerusalem by Simon, dated to 23 Iyyar in Megillath Taanith §5, is said to have taken place on the 23rd day of the second month. (For the list of the Jewish months see Appendix III.) It is consequently justifiable to conclude that 1 Mac. follows, in general, a calendar in which the year, like the Babylonian Seleucid year, starts in the spring. Such a calendar was in use among Jews, according to the Mishnah (mRSh 1:1, '1 Nisan is the New Year for the kings and the festivals'), and Josephus, *Ant.* i 3, 3 (80–2) asserts that Moses established Nisan as the first month. The dating of yearly seasons from autumn to autumn employed for the Jewish civil, Sabbatical and Jubilee years (see mRSh 1:1), as in the Macedonian Seleucid calendar, appears to have left no trace in 1 Mac.

Even before the fact of a separate Babylonian Seleucid era was established, a number of scholars realised that 1 Mac. reckons its dates in Seleucid years and from a vernal New Year. This view has been declared the rule in F. M. Abel's commentary, *Les livres des Maccabées* ([2]1949), pp. l–lii. Similarly, R. Hanhart in his study, 'Zur Zeitrechnung des I und II Makkabäerbücher', concludes that the starting point of the era followed in 1 Mac. is the spring of 311 B.C. See A. Jepsen, R. Hanhart, *Untersuchungen zur israelitisch-jüdischen Chronologie* (1964), p. 81. The truth of this thesis, as will be seen in the subsequent historical discussions, can be verified in a large number of cases. However, amidst the many equivocations of both Seleucid and Jewish chronological data, it seems preferable to abstain from dogmatic assertions and admit that in addition to the Babylonian era, the Macedonian calendar may also have been occasionally employed in 1 Mac., perhaps unconsciously, for certain events of Seleucid rather than Jewish history proper. See most recently O. Mørkholm, *Antiochus IV of Syria* (1966), pp. 160–1.

Apropos of the controversy concerning the determination of the sabbatical years mentioned in 1 Mac. 6:49, 53 = *Ant.* xii, 9, 5 (378) and 1 Mac. 16:14 compared with *Ant.* xii, 8, 1 (234) and *B.J.* i, 2, 4 (60), the following should be noted. Bearing in mind that the Sabbatical year begins in the autumn, the two years in question, 150 and 178 of the Seleucid era, would correspond to 163/2 and 135/4 B.C. See Abel, *ad loc.* and Marcus, *Josephus* (Loeb) VII, p. 196, note a, p. 345, note b. This is, however, irreconcilable with the view advanced below (§7, n. 33) that Simon's death at the end of the Seleucid year 177 occurred in February, 134 B.C. and not in 135 B.C. as Marcus suggests (*ibid.* p. 342, note c). The various attempts at harmonisation made by Hanhart (*op. cit.*, p. 96, n. 99) and R. North ('Maccabean Sabbath Years', Biblica 34 (1953), pp. 501–15) appear to have produced no satisfactory solution. Moreover none of the dates so far suggested can be made to correspond to the chronological scheme implied in Josephus's statement, *Ant.* xiv, 16, 2 (475), that the capture of Jerusalem by Herod, in 37 B.C., took place during a Sabbatical year. One of North's remarks aptly sums up this issue: 'The sabbath dates of Josephus are either palpably incommensurate or else insolubly obscure.' (*Op. cit.*, p. 511.)

For bibliographical information regarding Seleucid chronology, see pp. 125–6 below and Appendix III; for the Books of the Maccabees, see the literature quoted in §4 and vol. III, §32 I, 1; §33 III, 7.

B. Non-Extant Sources

The following survey includes: (1) all those works specifically on Jewish history in our period which are known only through quotations or fragments, whether used by Josephus or not; (2) general historical works now lost, the direct or indirect use of which by Josephus is discernible.

1. Jason of Cyrene

Jason of Cyrene wrote a work in five books on the history of the Maccabaean rebellion from its beginning to the victory of Judas over Nicanor (161 B.C.). This is epitomised in one book, the Second Book of Maccabees, 2 Mac. 2:23 (τὰ) *ὑπὸ Ἰάσωνος τοῦ Κυρηναίου δεδηλωμένα διὰ πέντε βιβλίων πειρασόμεθα δι' ἑνὸς συντάγματος ἐπιτεμεῖν).* He probably lived not long after the events described, somewhere in the middle of the second century B.C.; see F.-M. Abel, *Les Livres des Maccabées* (1949), pp. xlii–iii, reviewing other suggested datings. Compare O. Eissfeldt, *Old Testament*, pp. 580–1. See also a brief discussion and bibliography by S. B. Hoenig, s.v. 'Jason' (3), IDB, II (1962), pp. 804–5. For an analysis of his part in 2 Maccabees, see R. Pfeiffer, *Hist. of New Testament Times*

(1949), pp. 506–18, cf. RE, s.v. 'Jason' (10). Also S. Krauss, 'Jason of Cyrene' in JE, viii, col. 75, and Jacoby, FGrH 182. For a fuller discussion and bibliography see vol. III, §33, 3, 7. The most important treatment is still B. Niese, *Kritik der beiden Makkabäerbücher* (1900), esp. pp. 32–40; note also the recent survey in M. Hengel, *Judentum und Hellenismus* (1969), pp. 176–83.

2. The History of Hyrcanus

A history of John Hyrcanus was known to the author of the First Book of Maccabees (1 Mac. 16:24, *βιβλίον ἡμερῶν ἀρχιερωσύνης αὐτοῦ).* This apparently described his long reign in a style similar to that of the First Book of Maccabees. This book seems to have been lost at an early date, for Josephus apparently had no knowledge of it. Cf. vol. III, §32, I, 2.

3. Posidonius of Apamea

The famous Stoic philosopher and historian Posidonius stemmed from Apamea in Syria but lived mainly in Rhodes, where he founded a Stoic school (so he was called also '*ὁ Ῥόδιος*'). Since he was a student of Panaetius, who died, at the latest, in 110 B.C., he cannot have been born much later than 130 B.C. In the seventh consulship of Marius, 86 B.C., he went as an envoy to Rome and there saw Marius shortly before his death. (Plut., *Mar.* 45). Immediately after Sulla's death, 78 B.C., Cicero heard him in Rhodes (Plut., *Cic.* 4). Pompey visited him there several times. In the consulship of Marcus Marcellus, 51 B.C., he came again to Rome (the Suda, s.v. *Ποσειδώνιος* = Jacoby, FGrH 87 T1). His *floruit* was thus approximately 90–60 B.C. According to [Lucian], *Macrob.* 20, he reached the great age of eighty-four years. For the detailed evidence on his life see K. Reinhardt in RE XXII, cols. 563–7, and compare H. Strasburger, 'Posidonius on Problems of the Roman Empire', JRS 55 (1965), pp. 40–53. Of his numerous writings his major historical work is of interest to us here. It is quoted repeatedly by Athenaeus, Strabo, Plutarch and others. According to the quotations by Athenaeus it included at least forty-nine books (Ath. 168 DE = Jacoby FGrH F27). It is therefore evident that the Suda (above) had this work in view when it notes mistakenly of the Alexandrian Posidonius *ἔγραψεν Ἱστορίαν τὴν μετὰ Πολύβιον ἐν βιβλίοις νβ'*. Indeed, the remaining fragments make it clear that the work begins where Polybius concludes, in the mid-140s B.C. How far it continued is not known. According to the Suda (above), it went *ἕως τοῦ πολέμου τοῦ Κυρηναϊκοῦ καὶ Πτολεμαίου*. Müller, *Fragm. hist. graec.* (FHG) III, p. 250, believed that the above should read '*ἕως τοῦ Πτολεμαίου τοῦ*

Κυρηναϊκοῦ', namely up to the Ptolemaic King Apion of Cyrene, who died in 96 B.C. This conjecture is supported by the fact that the fragments from the 47th and 49th books cover the period from 100 to 90 B.C. But according to a large fragment in Athenaeus (Müller, F 41 = Jacoby, FGrH 87 F36) it appears that Posidonius related in detail the history of the Athenian demagogue Athenion or Aristion (87–6 B.C.). In addition, according to Strabo xi 1, 6 (492) = Müller FHG F89 = Jacoby, FGrH 87 T11, he dealt with the history of Pompey as well *(τὴν ἱστορίαν συνέγραψε τὴν περὶ αὐτόν)*. Müller concluded, therefore, that Posidonius had recounted the period after 96 in a 'second part' or continuation of the main work (*op. cit.* III, p. 251). This ingenious hypothesis is, however, not adequately supported by the words of the Suda. The fifty-two books could, indeed, have included the period from 87–6 B.C., and the work could have continued down to this period (according to Scheppig, *De Posidonio Apameo rerum gentium terrarum scriptore* (1869), pp. 27–31, until the year 86 B.C.). This end point had been assumed, apparently correctly, by Unger, Philologus 55 (1896), pp. 79–86, on the basis of the words of the Suda *ἕως τοῦ πολέμου τοῦ Κυρηναϊκοῦ*. He took this to mean the operations of Lucullus in Cyrene, referred to by Josephus, *Ant.* xiv 7, 2 (114), which fell in the year 86. Others accept Sulla's dictatorship, 82 B.C., as the end-point, (so C. F. Arnold, Jahrbb, f. class. Philol. 13 (1884), *Supp*, p. 149; F. Susemihl, *Geschichte der griechischen Literatur in der Alexandrinerzeit*, II (1892), p. 140; E. Wachsmuth, *Einleitung in das Studium der alten Geschichte* (1895), p. 651). In any case, the work cannot have continued much further if the period from 100 to 90 B.C. was included in the 47th and 49th books. The history of Pompey would, therefore, have formed a separate work—if the reference in question is at all credible, see Wachsmuth, *op. cit.*, p. 651, and compare Jacoby, *op. cit.* IIC, pp. 154–7.

The great work of Posidonius was held in high regard by later historians and seems to have been used by them in the same way as Polybius, as a major source for the period with which it deals. It is certain that Diodorus drew on it (compare xxxiv/v 2, 34 with Müller, F15 = Jacoby, F7 quoted from Athenaeus 542B; cf. in general Müller, *op. cit.* II, p. xx, III, p. 251; Susemihl, *op. cit.* II, pp 142 f.). Indeed, even Pompeius Trogus may have used him (see Heeren, 'De Trogi Pompeji fontibus et auctoritate', Commentationes Societ. scient. Götting. 15 (1804), pp. 185–245, esp. 233–41; cf. Wachsmuth, *op. cit.*, p. 115, and Schanz-Hosius, *Röm. Lit.-Gesch.* II ([4]1935), pp. 322–4. So probably did the majority who dealt with this period. It is therefore very likely that the relevant sections of Josephus depend on Posidonius, not directly, it is true, but indirectly (through the works of Strabo and Nicolaus of Damascus).

Josephus used, for this period, Strabo and Nicolaus of Damascus as his main sources (see below). That Strabo depends on Posidonius is beyond question, for he cites him in his *Geography* repeatedly and with great respect (see, for example, xvi 2, 10 (753) = Jacoby, T3). Nicolaus of Damascus also appears to have used Posidonius (Müller, F39 = Jacoby F38). Josephus mentions Posidonius only once, *Contra Apionem* ii 7/79. Definite resemblances are found, however, between his presentation and that of Diodorus and Pompeius Trogus (= Justin). Compare, for example, Josephus, *Ant.* xiii 8, 23 (236–48) with Diodorus xxxiv/v 1 (the capture of Jerusalem by Antiochus Sidetes; see Jacoby, *op. cit.* IIC, pp. 196–9); Jos. *Ant.* xiii 5, 11 (181–6) with Justin xxxvi 1, 3 (the Parthian war of Demetrius II). Cf. M. Nussbaum, *Observationes in Flavii Josephi Antiquitates XII, 3–XIII, 14* (1875), pp. 28–43, J.v. Destinon, *Die Quellen des Fl. Josephus* (1882), p. 52; J. G. Müller, ThStKr (1843), pp. 893 ff. and his commentary to Josephus' work, *Contra Apionem* (1877), pp. 214 ff.; 258 f.; Adolf Kuhn, 'Beiträge zur Gesch. der Seleukiden', *Altkirch. in E. Progr.* (1891), pp. 6 f.; this indirect dependence on Posidonius is briefly referred to by G. Hölscher, RE IX, col. 1967.

The historical and geographical fragments of Posidonius are collected in C. Müller, FHG III, pp. 245–96 and Jacoby, FGrH 87. But note J. Bake, *Posidonii Rhodii reliquiae doctrinae,* (1810) and now L. Edelstein, I. G. Kidd, *Posidonius I: the Fragments* (1972). See also V. E. P. Toepelmann, *De Posidonio Rhodio rerum scriptore* (1869); R. Scheppig, *De Posidonio Apamensi rerum gentium terrarum scriptore* (1869); F. Blass, *De Gemino et Posidonio* (1883); M. Arnold, 'Untersuchungen über Theophanes von Mytilene und Posidonius von Apamea', Jahrbb. für class. Philologie 13, Supp. (1884), pp. 75–150; F. Schühlein, *Studien zu Posidonius Rhodius* (1886) (careful establishment of the biographical details); R. Zimmermann, 'Posidonius und Strabo', Hermes 23 (1888), pp. 103–30, on the use of Posidonius by Strabo in the *Geography*; for this, see now W. Aly, *Strabon von Amaseia* (1957), *passim*; Ad. Bauer, 'Posidonius und Plutarch über die römischen Eigennamen', Philologus 47 (1889), pp. 242–73. Schühlein, *Zu Posidonius Rhodius* (1891) (examination of the tradition in the Suda); F. Susemihl, *op. cit.* II (1892), pp. 128–47, 687, 708 ff.; C. Wachsmuth, *op. cit.*, pp. 648–54 (good characterisation of Posidonius' historical work). G. F. Unger, 'Umfang und Anordnung der Geschichte des Poseidonios', Philologus 55 (1896), pp. 73–122, 245–56.

On Posidonius as a historian, the essential modern work is Jacoby's commentary, *op. cit.*, IIC (1920), pp. 154–220, to his collection of the fragments. Note also, for discussion and bibliography up to 1920, W. v. Christ-W. Schmid-O. Stählin, *Geschichte der griechischen Litteratur* II (1920), pp. 347–55, and for a recent general sketch, with bibliography, M. Laffranque, *Poseidonios d'Apamée: essai de mise au point* (1964). The most significant modern works are those of K. Reinhardt, *Poseidonios* (1921); *Kosmos und Sympathie* (1926); RE s.v. 'Poseidonios' (3) XXII 1 (1953), cols. 558–826; cols. 630–41 concern his historical work.

On Posidonius as a philosopher see E. Schmekel, *Die Philosophie der mittleren Stoa* (1892), pp. 9–14, 85–154, 238–90; E. Zeller, *Philosophie der Griechen* III 1, (^{3}1880), pp. 572–84; P. Wendland, 'Posidonius' Werk περὶ θεῶν', Archiv f. Gesch. der Philos. (1888), pp. 200–10; M. Pohlenz, *Die Stoa* (1948), pp. 208–38; Reinhardt, RE XXII, cols. 641–822 and for a perceptive survey A. D. Nock, 'Posidonius', JRS 49 (1959), pp. 1–15.

4. Timagenes of Alexandria

Timagenes was taken prisoner in Alexandria by Gabinius in his Egyptian campaign (55 B.C.) and brought to Rome, where he subsequently lived (the Suda, s.v. *Τιμαγένης* = Jacoby, FGrH 88 T1). He was notorious for his loose tongue, for which Augustus forbade him his house. In spite of that, he was commonly esteemed, and enjoyed the close companionship of Asinius Pollio in particular (Seneca, *de ira* iii 23, 5 = Jacoby, T3, *postea Timagenes in contubernio Pollionis Asinii consenuit ac tota civitate direptus* [or *dilectus*] *est: nullum illi limen praeclusa Caesaris domus abstulit*). His numerous works (Suda, *βιβλία δ' ἔγραψε πολλά)* were valued because of their learning and elegant rhetorical form (Ammianus Marcellinus, xv 9, 2 *Timagenes et diligentia Graecus et lingua*). Even Quintilian, x 1, 75, named him among the most famous historians. The meagre remaining fragments permit no certain judgment on the contents and style of his works. The citations in Josephus bear on the history of Antiochus Epiphanes, *Contra Apionem*, ii 7 (84) = Jacoby, F4; the Jewish kings Aristobulus I, *Ant.* xiii 11, 3 (319) = Jacoby, F5; and Alexander Jannaeus, *Ant.* xiii 12, 5 (344) = Jacoby, F6. Apparently, however, Josephus did not use Timagenes himself, but borrowed the quotations from other historians, see *Ant.* xiii 11, 3 (319) *μαρτυρεῖ τουτῷ καὶ Στράβων ἐκ τοῦ Τιμαγένους ὀνόματος λέγων οὕτως* = Jacoby, F5 and 91 F11 (Strabo). Similarly the quotation in *Ant.* xiii 12, 5 (344) probably stems from Strabo, from whom *Ant.* xiii 12, 6 (345–7) = Jacoby, FGrH 91 F12, following directly after, is cited.

The fragments of Timagenes are collected in Müller, FHG III, pp. 317–23, and Jacoby, FGrH 88; commentary in IIC (1926), pp. 220–8. A. von Gutschmid, 'Trogus and Timagenes', Rhein. Museum 37 (1882), pp. 548–55, *Kleine Schriften* V, pp. 218–27, tried to show that Pompeius Trogus is 'only a Latin edition of a work originally in Greek', and asserts that the latter was that of Timagenes. See C. Wachsmuth, 'Timagenes und Trogus', Rhein. Museum 46 (1891), pp. 465–79; *Einleitung in das Studium der alten Gesch.* (1895), pp. 114 f. (against Gutschmid). F. Susemihl, *op. cit.* II, pp. 377–81; O. Hirschfeld, 'Timagenes und die gallische Wandersage'. SBA (1894), pp. 331–47 = *Kleine Schiften* (1913), pp. 1–18; J. Kaerst, 'Untersuchungen über Timagenes von Alexandria' (1913), pp. 1–18; Philologus 56 (1897), pp. 621–57; see also W.v. Christ-W. Schmid-O. Stählin, *Gesch. d. gr. Lit.* II ([6]1920), p. 399; RE s.v. 'Timagenes' (2), VIA (1937), cols. 1063–71.

5. Asinius Pollio

C. Asinius Pollio, the well-known friend of Caesar and Augustus, wrote, among other works, a history of the civil wars between Caesar and Pompey in seventeen books in the Latin language (this, at least, is the apparent sense of the confused information in the Suda, s.vv. *'Ασίννος Πωλίων*, and *Πωλίων, ὁ 'Ασίνιος*). Plutarch, Appian and others used the work (Plut., *Pomp.*, 72; *Caesar* 46; Appian, B.C. ii, 82). This source, as a work of a contemporary participant, would have been of the greatest importance—and was not overlooked, for instance, by Strabo. From a reference in Josephus one learns that Strabo quoted from it, for example, on the history of the Egyptian campaign of Caesar

(Jos. *Ant.* xiv 8, 3 (138) *μαρτυρεῖ δέ μου τῷ λόγῳ Στράβων ὁ Καππάδοξ λέγων ἐξ Ἀσινίου ὀνόματος οὕτως* = Jacoby, FGrH 91 F16.

For a collection of the fragments of Asinius Pollio see H. Peter, *Historicorum Romanorum Reliquiae* II (1906), pp. 67–70; biographical references in PIR² A 1241. See also P. Groebe, s.v. 'Asinius Pollio', RE II, cols. 1589–602. E. Kornemann, 'Die historische Schriftstellerei des C. Asinius Pollio', Jahrbb. f. class. Phil. 22, Supp. (1896), pp. 555–692; Schanz-Hosius, *Geschichte der röm. Lit.* II (⁴1935), pp. 24–30; J. André, *La vie et l'oeuvre d'Asinius Pollion* (1949); A. B. Bosworth, 'Asinius Pollio and Augustus', Historia 21 (1972), pp. 441–73. On the history of the civil war in particular, G. Thouret, 'De Cicerone, Asinio Pollione, C. Oppio rerum Caesarianarum scriptoribus', Leipziger Studien zur classischen Philologie I (1878), pp. 303–60; on Asinius Pollio see pp. 324–46. In later discussions on the sources of Appian, the question of how extensively Appian used the work of Asinius Pollio has often been discussed, but no definite conclusion is possible. Compare also, E. Schwartz, s.v. 'Appianus' RE II, cols. 216–37 = *Griechische Geschichtschreiber* (1957), pp. 361–93; E. Gabba, *Appiano e la storia delle guerre civili* (1956); *idem*, *Appiani Bellorum Civilium Liber Primus* (1958), pp. xxii–v, *Appiani Bellorum Civilium Liber Quintus* (1970), pp. xxxix–xlii.

6. Hypsicrates

An author otherwise little known, Hypsicrates is quoted twice in Strabo's *Geography*. One quotation relates to the history of Asander, a king of the Bosporus in the period of Caesar and Augustus, Strabo vii 4, 6 (311) = Jacoby, FGrH 190 F2; on Asander see PIR² A 1197. The other concerns the ethnology of the Caucasian peoples, Strabo xi 5, 1 (504) = Jacoby, F3. There is perhaps also a third place, on the natural history of Libya, where Hypsicrates is to be read instead of Iphikrates, xvii 3, 5 (827) = Jacoby, F9. According to [Lucian], *Macrob.* 22, Hypsikrates came from Amisus in Pontus and reached the age of ninety-two years. According to a reference in Josephus, Strabo used this Hypsikrates in his account of the Egyptian campaign of Caesar, Jos. *Ant.* xiv 8, 3 (138–9) *ὁ δ' αὐτὸς οὗτος Στράβων καὶ ἐν ἑτέροις πάλιν ἐξ Ὑψικράτους ὀνόματος λέγει οὕτως* = Jacoby, F1.

For a discussion of Hypsicrates see Jacoby's commentary in FGrH IID (1930), pp. 618–20.

7. Q. Dellius

Dellius, a friend of Antonius, wrote a work on the latter's Parthian campaign in which he himself took part, Strabo, xi 13, 3 (523) *ὥς φησιν ὁ Δέλλιος ὁ τοῦ Ἀντωνίου φίλος, συγγράψας τὴν ἐπὶ Παρθυαίους αὐτοῦ στρατείαν, ἐν ᾗ παρῆν καὶ αὐτὸς ἡγεμονίαν ἔχων*. Cf. Plutarch, *Ant.* 59: *πολλοὺς δὲ καὶ τῶν ἄλλων φίλων οἱ Κλεοπάτρας κόλακες ἐξέβαλον . . . ὧν καὶ Μάρκος ἦν Σιλανὸς καὶ Δέλλιος ὁ ἱστορικός*. It is possible, as Bürcklein and Gutschmid conjectured, that from this work all the accounts by later historians of the Parthian campaign in the years

41–36 B.C. and, indeed, that of Josephus also, are derived directly or indirectly. Josephus mentions Dellius (not as a historian but as a general of Antonius), in *B.J.* i 15, 3 (290), *Ant.* xiv 15, 1 (394), xv 2, 6 (25).

The two fragments are given in full in H. Peter, *Historicorum Romanorum Reliquiae* II (1906), pp. 53–4, cf. Jacoby, FGrH 197; biographical references in RE IV, cols. 2447–8. Compare A. Bürcklein, *Quellen und Chronologie der römisch-parthischen Feldzüge in den Jahren 713–718* (1879) (on Josephus pp. 41–3); A. von Gutschmid, *Geschichte Irans und seiner Nachbarländer* (1888), p. 97; W. Fabricius, *Theophanes von Mytilene und Quintus Dellius als Quellen der Geographie des Strabon*, (1888). Cf. Schanz-Hosius, *Gesch. d. röm. Lit.* II ([4]1935), pp. 325–6, and the commentary by Jacoby, FGrH IID (1930), pp. 623–5.

8. Strabo

Strabo also wrote, in addition to the extant *Geography* (see on this, §3, D) a great historical work now lost except for some fragments. It was already completed before Strabo began his *Geography*, for he refers to it in the introduction, i 1, 23 (13) = Jacoby, FGrH 91 F2 *διόπερ ἡμεῖς πεποιηκότες ὑπομνήματα ἱστορικὰ χρήσιμα, ὡς ὑπολαμβάνομεν, εἰς τὴν ἠθικὴν καὶ πολιτικὴν φιλοσοφίαν.* From another reference in the *Geography* it appears that the fifth book of this work began where Polybius left off, in the 140s B.C.; see Strabo *Geog.* xi 9, 3, (515) = Jacoby, F1 *εἰρηκότες δὲ πολλὰ περὶ τῶν Παρθικῶν νομίμων ἐν τῇ ἕκτῃ τῶν ἱστορικῶν ὑπομνημάτων βίβλῳ, δευτέρᾳ δὲ τῶν μετὰ Πολύβιον.* The duplication would argue that the character of the first four books was different from that of the books *μετὰ Πολύβιον*, the former probably being more summary, the latter more detailed. The period of Alexander the Great must have been treated in the earlier books, for Strabo says, in a third place, that he recognised the unreliable nature of the detailed information on India when he dealt with the history of Alexander the Great, *Geog.* ii i, 9 (70) = Jacoby, F3, *καὶ ἡμῖν δ' ὑπῆρξεν ἐπὶ πλέον κατιδεῖν ταῦτα ὑπομνηματιζομένοις τὰς Ἀλεξάνδρου πράξεις.* According to an explanatory note in the Suda s.v. *Πολύβιος* = Jacoby, T2, the work 'after Polybius' was in forty-three books (*ἔγραψε δὲ καὶ Στράβων Ἀμασεὺς τὰ μετὰ Πολύβιον ἐν βιβλίοις μγ'*), the whole work consisting of forty-seven. From the quotations in Josephus it appears that the work continued at least until the conquest of Jerusalem by Herod (37 B.C.). It may have concluded with the establishment of the principate of Augustus. We are indebted to Josephus for the majority of the quotations, for he evidently used it as a major source for the history of the Hasmonaeans from John Hyrcanus to the defeat of Antigonus (135–37 B.C.), excerpting from this great world history those passages and items dealing with the history of Palestine—*Ant.* xiii 10, 4 (286) = F4; 11, 3 (319) = F11; 12, 6 (347) = F12; xiv 3, 1 (35–6) = F14;

4, 3 (68) = F15; 6, 4 (104) = F13; 7, 2 (111) = F6; 8, 3 (138) = F16; xv 1, 2 (9–10) = F18. Compare also the information relating to Antiochus Epiphanes in *Contra Apionem* ii 7 (83–5) = F10. Strabo's *History* is also quoted by Plutarch, *Sulla* 26 = F8; *Lucull.* 28 = F9; *Caesar* 63 = F19; and Tertullian, *De anima* 46 = F5. However greatly the loss of this work is to be regretted, it is nevertheless fortunate that Josephus used it as a major source along with Nicolaus of Damascus. For Strabo was a scholarly historian who used the best sources with caution and discrimination. Even in the few fragments included in Josephus, he quotes his authorities three times (Timagenes, Asinius Pollio, and Hypsikrates). That he also used the great work of Posidonius is not to be doubted. Josephus frequently emphasizes the agreement between Strabo and Nicolaus of Damascus (*Ant.* xiii 12, 6 (347) = F12 and 90 F93, and esp. xiv 6, 4 (104) = F13 and 90 F97: *περὶ δὲ τῆς Πομπηίου καὶ Γαβινίου στρατείας ἐπὶ Ἰουδαίους γράφει Νικόλαος ὁ Δαμασκηνὸς καὶ Στράβων ὁ Καππάδοξ οὐδὲν ἕτερος ἑτέρου καινότερον λέγων).* It is, however, not likely that one used the other, for both wrote at approximately the same time. Nicolaus of Damascus is in fact quoted by Strabo in his *Geography* xv 1, 72–3 (719). But Strabo's *History* is from an earlier period than that of Nicolaus. The agreement emphasized by Josephus probably derives from the use of identical sources.

F. Lewitz, *Quaest. Flav. specimen* (1835), pp. 1–10, was certainly mistaken in taking the view that the Strabo of the *History* and the Strabo of the *Geography*, as quoted by Josephus, were two different persons. Admittedly, Josephus continually names his authority the 'Cappadocian', whereas the geographer stemmed from Amaseia in Pontus. But the district of Pontus was called also *ἡ πρὸς τῷ Πόντῳ Καππαδοκία*, Strabo xii 1, 4, (534), and Pliny lists Amaseia among the cities of the Cappadocians, *Nat. Hist.* vi 3/8. Mithridates, the king of Pontus, is called in an inscription *Μιθραδάτης Καππαδοκί[ας βασιλεὺς]*, Le Bas and Waddington, *Inscriptions*, III, n. 136a, l.3 = Dittenberger, SIG[3] 742 = Th. Reinach, *Mithridate Eupator* (1890), p. 463, no. 13.

The fragments of Strabo's *History* are collected in Müller, FHG III, pp. 490–4 and Jacoby, FGrH 91. Many doubtful fragments are discussed by P. Otto, 'Strabonis *ἱστορικῶν ὑπομνημάτων* fragmenta collegit et enarravit adiectis quaestionibus Strabonianis,' Leipziger Studien zur class. Philologie 11, Supp. (1889); on Josephus' relation to Strabo, see pp. 225–44. Compare in general Wachsmuth, *Einleitung*, pp. 654 f. Schwartz, s.v. 'Appianus', RE II, cols. 235–7 = *Griechische Geschichtschreiber*, pp. 389–93; (against the conjecture that Strabo was a major source of Appian). For further discussion and bibliography of Strabo see Christ-Schmid-Stählin, *Gesch. d. gr. Lit.* II 1 ([6]1920), pp. 409–15; Jacoby's commentary on the historical fragments, FGrH IIC (1926), pp. 291–5; E. Honigmann s.v. 'Strabon' (3), RE IVA (1932), cols. 76–155; W. Aly, *Strabon von Amaseia: Untersuchungen über Text, Aufbau und Quellen der Geographika* (1957).

9. Herod's Memoirs

Like other princely persons of that period, such as Augustus and Agrippa, see G. Misch, *Geschichte der Autobiographie* I. 1 ([3]1949), pp.

266–98, Herod the Great also wrote his 'memoirs', which are mentioned once by Josephus, *Ant.* xv 6, 3 (174) *ταῦτα δὲ γράφομεν ἡμεῖς ὡς ἐν τοῖς ὑπομνήμασιν τοῖς τοῦ βασιλέως Ἡρώδου περιείχετο).* Whether Josephus himself saw them is very doubtful, since he follows Nicolaus of Damascus as his main source, and apart from him probably employed only a source unfavourable to Herod. Indeed, the past tense *περιείχετο* conveys the idea that the work quoted was no longer available to the writer, but was known to him only at secondhand.

On the philosophical, rhetorical and historical studies of Herod see the fragment from the autobiography of Nicolaus of Damascus in Müller, FHG III, pp. 350 f., F4 = Jacoby, FGrH 90 F135. *ὑπομνήματα* are 'memoranda'; the fullest treatment is in G. Avenarius, *Lukians Schrift zur Geschichtsschreibung* (1956), pp. 85–104. As such they are not essentially different from *ὑπομνηματισμοί* and *ἀπομνημονεύματα* (the latter expression also means essentially 'memoranda'). On *ἀπομνημονεύματα* see E. Schwartz in RE II, cols. 170–1. A direct use of the memoirs of Herod by Josephus, suggested in ThLZ (1879), pp. 570 f., and in H. Bloch, *Die Quellen des Flavius Josephus,* (1879), pp. 107 f., 140 ff., appears untenable, and was rejected, e.g., by J. von Destinon, *Die Quellen des Flavius Josephus* (1882), pp. 121 ff.

10. Ptolemaeus

In Ammonius, *De adfinium vocabulorum differentia* (ed. Nickau, Teubner, 1966) s.v. *Ἰουδαῖοι* we have: *Ἰουδαῖοι καὶ Ἰδουμαῖοι διαφέρουσιν, ὥς φησι Πτολεμαῖος ἐν πρώτῳ Περὶ Ἡρώδου τοῦ βασιλέως. Ἰουδαῖοι μὲν γάρ εἰσιν οἱ ἐξ ἀρχῆς φυσικοί. Ἰδουμαῖοι δὲ τὸ μὲν ἀρχῆθεν οὐκ Ἰουδαῖοι ἀλλὰ Φοίνικες καὶ Σύροι. κρατηθέντες δὲ ὑπ' αὐτῶν καὶ ἀναγκασθέντες περιτέμνεσθαι καὶ συντελεῖν εἰς τὸ ἔθνος* [*ἔθος*?] *καὶ τὰ αὐτὰ νόμιμα ἡγεῖσθαι ἐκλήθησαν Ἰουδαῖοι* [*Ἰδουμαῖοι*?]. The work of a Ptolemaeus on Herod mentioned here is otherwise totally unknown. The statements quoted concerning the semi-Judaism of the Idumaeans are doubtless taken from an unprejudiced discussion of Herod's true descent such as no court historian would have dared to make; compare Jos *Ant.* xiv 1, 3 (8). The author, therefore, cannot have belonged to the court officials of Herod, among whom two men of the name Ptolemaeus are recorded, one of them, a brother of Nicolaus of Damascus, taking the side of Antipas after the death of Herod, *Ant.* xvii 9, 4 (225), *B.J.* ii 2, 3 (21), the other taking that of Archelaus, as did Nicolaus of Damascus, *Ant.* xvii 8, 2 (195); 9, 3 (219), 5 (228), *B.J.* i 33, 8 (667) ii 2, 1 (14). It is much more likely to have been the grammarian, Ptolemaeus of Ascalon, the only writer of the name Ptolemaeus mentioned elsewhere by Ammonius, *De adfin. vocab. differentia* s.v. *τρίετες* and *σταφυλήν*. Indeed, Stephanus of Byzantium s.v. *Ἀσκάλων* refers to this Ptolemaeus as a contemporary of Aristarchus (*Ἀριστάρχου γνώριμος*), thus placing him in the second century B.C. But Baege, *De*

Ptolemaeo Ascalonita (1882), pp. 2–6, argued that Stephanus's estimate is incorrect and that Ptolemaeus lived at the beginning of the first century A.D. He would thus be splendidly qualified from the point of view of time, to write a biography of Herod. Jacoby, however, argues that the Suda s.v. *Πτολεμαῖος, ὁ Ἀσκαλωνίτης*, mentions only grammatical works. A. Dihle s.v. 'Ptolemaeus' (79), RE XXIII 2 (1959), col. 1863, does not discuss the possibility that he was the author of the work on Herod.

See Müller, FHG III, p. 348, IV, p. 486, and Jacoby, FGrH 199, with discussion in IID, pp. 625–6. Cf. also W. Otto, *Herodes* (1913), col. 1; and A. Schalit, *König Herodes* (1969), pp. 677–8.

The foregoing statement about the Idumaeans is also found in an abridged form in one of the works ascribed to Ptolemaeus of Ascalon, *Περὶ διαφορᾶς λέξεων*, published in part by W. Fabricius, *Biblioth. graec.* ed. Harles VI, pp. 157–63, and in full by Heylbut in Hermes 22 (1887), pp. 388–410. This reads as follows: *Ἰουδαῖοι καὶ Ἰδουμαῖοι διαφέρουσιν· οἱ μὲν γὰρ Ἰουδαῖοι ἐξ ἀρχῆς, Ἰδουμαῖοι δὲ τὸ μὲν ἀρχῆθεν οὐκ Ἰουδαῖοι ἀλλὰ Φοίνικες καὶ Σύροι.* But as does this passage, so also all the others prove that this alleged work of Ptolemaeus is rather an excerpt from Ammonius, who for his part quotes from the genuine Ptolemaeus of Ascalon. Compare Baege, *op. cit.*, pp. 15 ff.

11. Nicolaus of Damascus

No writer was used so fully by Josephus for the post-biblical period as Nicolaus of Damascus, the trusted friend and counsellor of Herod. He came from a distinguished non-Jewish family in Damascus. His father, Antipater, held the highest offices there. (The Suda, s.v. *Ἀντίπατρος*=Müller, FHG III F1=Jacoby, FGrH 90 F131, *ἀρχάς τε πάσας διεξῆλθε τὰς ἐγχωρίους*).

Since Nicolaus speaks of himself as being about sixty years old immediately after the death of Herod in 4 B.C., Jacoby, F136 (8), *καὶ γὰρ ἦν περὶ ξ′ ἔτη*, he must have been born about 64 B.C. He acquired an extensive Greek education and mainly followed Aristotle in his philosophical views (see e.g. T1 *φιλόσοφος Περιπατητικός ἢ Πλατωνικός*, and Athenaeus xiv 66 (652a)=T10a *τῶν ἀπὸ τοῦ Περιπάτου δ' ἦν*). According to Sophronius of Damascus (Patriarch of Jerusalem in the seventh century A.D.), he was tutor to the children of Antonius and Cleopatra (Sophronius, *Narratio miraculorum SS. Cyri et Johannis* 54= Migne, PG lxxxvii, col. 3621=Jacoby, T2). When Augustus was in Syria in 20 B.C. Nicolaus saw the Indian ambassadors who came to Antioch, Strabo xv 1, 73 (719)=F100. He may even by then, at the latest by 14 B.C., have been a member of the inner circle of King Herod, by whom he was also employed in important diplomatic services. In 14 B.C. he was in the retinue of Herod when the latter visited Agrippa in Asia Minor. Later he went with Herod to Rome. When Herod, as a result of his conflicts with the Nabataeans, fell into disfavour with

Augustus, Nicolaus was sent to Rome as ambassador. Similarly, in the king's conflict with his sons, Alexander, Aristobulus and Antipater, Nicolaus served prominently as counsellor. After the death of Herod he represented the interests of Archelaus before the emperor in Rome. This is attested in his *Autobiography* (F134–7) and in the relevant sections in Josephus. The closing years of his life seem to have been spent in Rome according to indications in the *Autobiography*, F138).

To cultivate his relationship with Augustus, Nicolaus is reported to have often sent the emperor the excellent dates which grew in Palestine. Augustus called these, therefore, 'Nicolaus-dates', and the name was generally adopted. Athenaeus xiv 66 (652A) = T10a *περὶ δὲ τῶν Νικολάων καλουμένων φοινίκων τοσοῦτον ὑμῖν εἰπεῖν ἔχω τῶν ἀπὸ τῆς Συρίας καταγομένων, ὅτι ταύτης τῆς προσηγορίας ἠξιώθησαν ὑπὸ τοῦ Σεβαστοῦ αὐτοκράτορος σφόδρα χαίροντος τῷ βρώματι, Νικολάου τοῦ Δαμασκηνοῦ ἑταίρου ὄντος αὐτῷ καὶ πέμποντος φοίνικας συνεχῶς*. In Plutarch, *Quaest. conviv.* viii 4, 1 (723D) = T10b, it is not Augustus but rather *ὁ βασιλεύς*, i.e. Herod, who is referred to as the inventor of the name, and he is said to have called the dates after Nicolaus because he resembled them in sweetness, slenderness and ruddiness. According to Pliny these dates were especially large, *Nat. Hist.* xiii 9/45 *sicciores ex hoc genere Nicolai, sed amplitudinis praecipuae, quaterni cubitorum longitudinem efficiunt*. In the *Descriptio totius orbis* 31, of the fourth century (see vol. II, §2, 1 and 2) they are mentioned as a major product of Palestine —*Nicolaum vero palmulam invenies abundare in Palestina regione, in loco qui dicitur Hiericho*. According to the Palestinian pilgrim Theodosius (sixth century A.D.) they grew also in the region of Livias in Transjordan, *De situ terrae sanctae* (CSEL xxxix, p. 145 = CCL clxxv, p. 121), *ibi habet dactulum Nicolaum maiorem*). There is reference to them also in the *Edictum Diocletiani* vi 81 (CIL III, 1934). See, in general, Müller, FHG III, p. 343; Lauffer, *Diokletians Preisedikt* (1971), p. 232. In addition, there exists rabbinic evidence. In the Mishnah (mAZ 1:5), R. Meir declares that נקלווס (נקליבס or נקלביס) is a kind of date forbidden to Jews because of their use in pagan cults. Hebrew parallels may be found in yAZ 39d, 40d; bAZ 14b; yShab; 14d; M. Teh. 92:11; Num. R. 3:1. For Aramaic examples see yBer. 10c, yDem. 22c; yMSh 54d. Cf. in particular, I. Löw, *Aramaeische Pflanzennamen* (1881), pp. 109–11. S. Krauss, *Griech u. lat. Lehnwörter* II (1899), pp. 366–7; S. Lieberman, 'Palestine in the Third and Fourth Centuries', JQR 37 (1946–7), pp. 51–2. See also *Aruch Completum* (ed. A. Kohut) V (1889), p. 380 s.v. נקלווס; Y. Yadin, *Bar Kokhba* (1971), p. 180. The statement in the Suda and elsewhere that Augustus named cakes, not dates, after Nicolaus is a mistake, Müller, FHG III, p. 343; B. Z. Wacholder, *Nicolaus of Damascus* (1962), p. 1, nn. 1–3.

Of the tragedies and comedies allegedly written by Nicolaus (the Suda, s.v. *Νικόλαος* = T1) no trace remains (see Jacoby, *ad loc.*; Dindorf, *Hist. gr. min.* I, p. iii; Susemihl, *op. cit.* II, p. 309). His philosophical works survive (in part) only in Syriac and Arabic translations (see below). Of his historical works, the Suda, s.v. *Νικόλαος* = T1, says, *ἔγραφεν ἱστορίαν καθολικὴν ἐν βιβλίοις † ὀγδοήκοντα, † καὶ τοῦ † βίου † Καίσαρος ἀγωγήν . . . ἔγραψε καὶ περὶ τοῦ ἰδίου βίου καὶ τῆς ἑαυτοῦ ἀγωγῆς*. In place of the traditional *βίου* in the title of the second work one should perhaps read *νέου*. In addition to these three works he wrote, according to Photius, *Bib.* 189 = T13, a *Παραδόξων ἐθῶν συναγωγή* (F103–24). More or less extensive fragments survive of all four compositions.

We are indebted for the greater number of the remaining fragments to the great undertaking of the Emperor Constantine Porphyrogenitus (A.D. 912–59) who ordered the most valuable portions of the ancient historians to be collected under fifty-three headings. Only a few of the fifty-three books have been preserved, and of those only two are relevant here: (1) the Excerpts *De Virtutibus et vitiis*, first edited by Valesius in 1634 and called also *Excerpta Peiresciana* after the earlier owner of the manuscript; and (2) the Excerpts *De insidiis*, first edited in the years 1848–55 by Feder from a codex Escurialensis—*Excerpta e Polybio, Diodoro, Dionysio Halicarnassensi atque Nicolao Damasceno etc.* ed. Feder, I–III, (1848–55). At the same time and independently of Feder, Müller included from the same manuscript the fragments of Nicolaus of Damascus in FHG III. On Constantine Porphyrogenitus' undertaking see K. Krumbacher, *Geschichte der byzantinischen Literatur* ([2]1897), pp. 258–61; C. Wachsmuth, *Einleitung in das Studium der alten Geschichte* (1895), pp. 70–5. The definitive edition of the text is U. P. Boissevain, C. De Boor, T. Büttner-Wobst, *Excerpta Historica iussu Imp. Constantini Porphyrogeniti confecta* I–IV (1903–6).

(1) The great historical work of Nicolaus comprised 144 books, Athenaeus vi 54 (249A)=T11: *ἐν τῇ πολυβίβλῳ ἱστορίᾳ· ἑκατὸν γὰρ καὶ τεσσαράκοντά εἰσι πρὸς ταῖς τέσσαρσι.* If the Suda speaks of only eighty books it is due either to a mistake in the manuscript or because the author only knew of eighty books. The extensive fragments in the Constantinian Excerpts *de virtutibus* and *de insidiis* derive entirely from the first seven books and are concerned with the ancient history of the Assyrians, Medes, Greeks, Lydians, and Persians to the time of Croesus and Cyrus. Virtually nothing remains of books 8–95. Of book 96 some fragments have been preserved, namely through Josephus and Athenaeus. Books 96, 103, 104, 107, 108, 110, 114, 116, 123, 124 are definitely cited. Books 123 and 124 describe the negotiations with Agrippa in Asia Minor in favour of the Jews of the area, in which Herod and Nicolaus of Damascus represented the interests of the Jews, Jos. *Ant.* xii 3, 2 (126–7)=F81, cf. xvi 2, 2–5 (16–57). These negotiations occurred in 14 B.C. The remaining twenty books must have been concerned with the following ten years up to the accession of Archelaus in 4 B.C. For from reading through Josephus it is at once clear that the exceptionally detailed source which he followed for the history of Herod in Books xv–xvii breaks off at the beginning of the reign of Archelaus. What he reports from then onward (book xviii) is so remarkably meagre that he cannot have had before him a source even approximately similar in scale to that which he had in books xv–xvii. This detailed source can be only Nicolaus, who is cited in *Ant.* xvi 7, 1 (183–186)= F101–2; cf. *Ant.* xii 3, 2 (126)=F81; xiv 1, 3 (9)=F96; and who in his *Autobiography* gives an account which is frequently very close to that of Josephus. Thus the author obviously included here in briefer form the events narrated in detail in his great historical work. Nicolaus's *History*

is, however, used by Josephus, not only for the history of Herod but also for that of the Hasmonaeans, in the same way as the related work of Strabo (*Ant.* xiii 8, 4 (250) = F92; 12, 6 (347) = F93; xiv 4, 3 (68) = F98; 6, 4 (104) = F97. In addition, Josephus quotes this work for the history of remote antiquity: *Ant.* i 3, 6 (94) = F72; (?) 3, 9 (108) = F141; 7, 2 (159) = F19, for the history of David, *Ant.* vii 5,2 (101) = F20, and for that of Antiochus Epiphanes, *Contra Apionem*, ii 7 (184) = F91.

(2) Of the biography of Augustus, *Βίος Καίσαρος*, two extensive parts remain, one of which, a series of fragments from the Constantinian Excerpts *de virtutibus* (= F125–9), deals with Octavian's youth and education. The other, from the Constantinian Excerpts *de insidiis* (= F130), is a very long continuous section dealing with the time immediately after the assassination of Caesar, with, in the form of an excursus, (para. 5, 19–27) an added detailed account of the plot against Caesar and the circumstances of this conspiracy. It is this second fragment, that makes possible a just evaluation of the work which, in spite of all the flattery contained in it, is not without merit, since it offers the most detailed connected historical narrative from the beginning of the conspiracy against Caesar to the raising of an army by Octavian; for a discussion of the sources see W. Schmitthenner, *Oktavian und das Testament Cäsars* (1952).

(3) The *Autobiography*, of which several fragments have been preserved in the Excerpts *de virtutibus* (= F133–9), and to which the references in the Suda s.v. *Ἀντίπατρος* (= F131) and *Νικόλαος* (= F132) may also be traced back, is interesting because of the praise that the author bestows without embarrassment upon himself. For this reason some scholars have argued that it is not by Nicolaus but by an admirer of his; see e.g., Wachsmuth, *op. cit.*, p. 104.

(4) The *Παραδόξων ἐθῶν συναγωγή* which was seen by Photius, *Bib.* 189 = T13, is known to us only through extracts in the *Florilegium* of Stobaeus (= F103–24). F. Dümmler, Rhein. Mus. 42 (1887), p. 192, n. 2, suggested that the work derives from the *νόμιμα βαρβαρικά* of Aristotle, while E. Reinmann proposed Ephorus as its source, see Philologus 8 (1895), pp. 654–709.

For collections of the historical fragments of Nicolaus see J. C. Orelli, *Nicolai Damasceni historiarum excerpta et fragmenta quae supersunt* (1804), and *idem*, *Supplementum editionis Lipsiensis Nicolai Damasceni* (1811). These, however, do not contain the fragments from the Constantinian Excerpts *de insidiis*. The latter were published by Feder, *Excerpta e Polybio, Diodoro, Dionysio Hal. atque Nicolao Dam.* I–III (1848–55). All are included in C. Müller, FHG III, (1849), pp. 343–464, with *addenda* in IV, pp. 661–8; and (without Latin translation) in Dindorf, *Hirtorici graeci minores* I (1870), pp. 1–153 (see also *Proleg.* pp. iii–xvii). The standard edition of Nicolaus, Jacoby, FGrH 90, with commentary in IIC (1926), pp. 229–91, uses the definitive edition of the Constantinian Excerpts, by U. P. Boissevain, C. De Boor and T. Büttner-Wobst (see p. 30 above).

See in general F. Susemihl, *Gesch. der griech. Lit. in der Alexandrinerzeit* II (1892), pp. 309–21; A. von Gutschmid, *Kleine Schriften* V (1894), pp. 536–42; C. Wachsmuth, *Einleitung in das Studium der alten Geschichte* (1895), pp. 104–7, 697 f. H. Peter, *Die geschichtliche Literatur über die römische Kaiserzeit* I (1897), pp. 401–4; Christ-Schmid-Stählin, *Geschichte der griech. Literatur* II, 1([6]1920), pp. 374–6; R. Laqueur, s.v. 'Nikolaos' (20), RE XVII (1937), cols. 362–424; B.Z. Wacholder, *Nicolaus of Damascus* (1962).

On his treatment of the earliest period (books 1–7) see K. Steinmetz, *Herodot und Nicolaus Damascenus* (1861); E. Jacoby, 'Zur Beurtheilung der Fragmente des Nikolaus von Damaskus', *Commentationes philologae, scripserunt seminarii phil. Lips. sodales* (1874), pp. 191–211; P. Tietz, *De Nicolai Damasceni fontibus quaestiones selectae* (1896); W. Witte, *De Nicolai Damasceni fragmentorum Romanorum fontibus* (1900); B. Z. Wacholder, *op. cit.*, pp. 52–8, 65–70; G. L. Huxley, 'Nikalaos of Damascus on Urartu', Greek, Rom. and Byz. Studies 9 (1968), pp. 319–20.

On Nicolaus as a source for Josephus: H. Bloch, *Die Quellen des Flavius Josephus* (1879), pp. 106–16; J. von Destinon, *Die Quellen des Flavius Josephus* (1882), pp. 91–120; P. Otto, Leipziger Studien zur class. Philol. 11, Supp. (1889), pp. 225–44. A. Büchler, JQR 9 (1897), pp. 325–39; G. Hölscher, *Die Quellen des Josephus für die Zeit vom Exil bis zum Juedischen Kriege* (1905); *idem*, s.v. 'Josephus', RE IX (1916), cols. 1944–9, 1970–94; R. J. M. Shutt, *Studies in Josephus* (1961), pp. 79–92.

On the *Βίος Καίσαρος* see Bürger, *De Nicolai Damasceni fragmento Escorialensi quod inscribitur Βίος Καίσαρος* (1869); A.E. Egger, 'Mémoire sur les historiens officiels et les panégyristes des princes dans l'antiquité grecque', Mémoires de l'Acad. des inscriptions 27, 2 (1873), pp. 1–42, esp. pp. 20–36; W. Witte, *De Nicolai Dam. fragmentorum Romanorum fontibus* (1900); C. M. Hall, *Nicolaus of Damascus, Life of Augustus: A Historical Commentary embodying a Translation* (1923).

The fragments of the *Παραδόξων ἐθῶν συναγωγή* were collected by A. Westermann, *Παραδοξογράφοι* (1839), pp. 166–77; see now Jacoby, F103–24. On the passage referring to the Lacedaemonians: K. Trieber, *Quaestiones Laconicae* I: *De Nicolai Damasceni Laconicis* (1867). In general: F. Dümmler, Rhein. Mus. 42 (1887), pp. 189–95. E. Reinmann, 'Quo ex fonte fluxerit Nicolai Damasceni *παραδόξων ἐθῶν συναγωγή*', Philologus 54 (1895), pp. 654–709, and Jacoby's commentary on these fragments.

Of the philosophical works of Nicolaus there remain only a number of titles and brief fragments in Greek, and some translations in Arabic and Syriac. The essential modern survey is M. J. Drossaart Lulofs, *Nicolaus Damascenus on the Philosophy of Aristotle: fragments of the first five books translated from the Syriac with an introduction and commentary* (1965); note pp. 6–19 on the evidence for his philosophical works; see also B. Hemmerdinger ,'Le De Plantis, de Nicolas de Damas à Planude', Philologus 110 (1967), pp. 56–65.

12. Vespasian's *Commentarii*

In his *Vita* 65 (342), Josephus relies for the accuracy of his account on the *Commentarii* of Vespasian (ταῦτα δὲ οὐκ ἐγὼ λέγω μόνος, ἀλλὰ καὶ ἐν τοῖς Οὐεσπασιανοῦ τοῦ αὐτοκράτορος ὑπομνήμασιν οὕτως γέγραπται), while he reproaches his opponent Justus of Tiberias with not having read these memoirs, as his account contradicts that of the emperor,

Vita 65 (358), *οὔτε γὰρ τῷ πολέμῳ παρέτυχες οὔτε τὰ Καίσαρος ἀνέγνως ὑπομνήματα μέγιστον δὲ τεκμήριον, τοῖς [γὰρ] Καίσαρος ὑπομνήμασιν ἐναντίαν πεποίησαι τὴν γραφήν).* In his *Contra Apionem,* he carries on a controversy against those who criticised his history of the Jewish wars, and denies them the right to such criticism. 'For if, as they maintain, they have read the Commentaries of the emperors, still they had no first-hand acquaintance with the actions of those of us who were in the opposite camp.' (i 10 (56) *οἳ κἂν τοῖς τῶν αὐτοκρατόρων ὑπομνήμασιν ἐντυχεῖν λέγωσιν, ἀλλ' οὔ γε καὶ τοῖς ἡμετέροις τῶν ἀντιπολεμούντων πράγμασι παρέτυχον).* These memoirs 'of the emperors' are surely to be identified with the memoirs of Vespasian referred to in the *Vita.* Nothing more is known of them. Josephus manifestly came to know them only after the composition of *B.J.*, for he does not refer to them among the sources of this work, see *Contra Apionem* i 9–10 (47–56). Cf. H. Peter, *Historicorum Romanorum Reliquiae* II (1906), pp. 108, CXXXXIII–V; note, however, the very extensive discussion by W. Weber, *Josephus und Vespasian: Untersuchungen zu dem Jüdischen Krieg des Flavius Josephus* (1921), advancing the theory that these *Commentarii* were a major source of *B.J.*

13. Antonius Julianus

Minucius Felix, *Octavius,* 33, 4, cites, as evidence for his view that the Jews were the cause of their own misfortunes, their own writings and those of the Romans: *Scripta eorum relege, vel*†, *ut transeamus veteres, Flavi Josephi,* †*vel si Romanis magis gaudes, Antoni Juliani de Judaeis require: iam scies, nequitia sua hanc eos meruisse fortunam* (following the Budé text, 1964, ed. Beaujeu; the text is corrupt and the order uncertain). The work of Antonius Julianus probably dealt with the war of Vespasian. For a *Μάρκος Ἀντώνιος Ἰουλιανός* is referred to also by Josephus as a procurator of Judaea *(ὁ τῆς Ἰουδαίας ἐπίτροπος)* during the war under Vespasian, *B.J.* vi 4, 3 (238); for the question of identity see H. Peter, *Hist. Rom. Rel.* II (1906), pp. 108–9, CXXXXV–VI; E. Norden, 'Josephus und Tacitus über Jesus Christus und eine messianische Prophetie', Neue Jahrbücher 31 (1913), pp. 637–66; E. Hertlein, 'Antonius Julianus, ein römischer Geschichtschreiber?', Philologus 77 (1921), pp. 174–93; Schanz-Hosius, *Geschichte der römischen Literatur* II ([4]1935), p. 649; cf. PIR[2] A 843–4, 846.

J. Bernays, *Über die Chronik des Sulpicius Severus* (1861), p. 56, assumed that this work by Antonius Julianus was used by Tacitus, on whom, in his turn, Sulpicius depends. This is possible, but entirely hypothetical. See the very full discussion in A. M. A. Hospers-Jansen, *Tacitus over die Joden: Hist.*5, 2–13 (1949) (Dutch with extensive English summary). It must not, however, be forgotten that there were other works dealing with the Jewish war. Josephus even distinguishes two classes of them. Some authors not having themselves been involved in the events, assembled accidental and contradictory information based on hearsay and conveyed it in a sophistic style. Others, who were present, falsified the events, either from desire to flatter the Romans or from hatred of the Jews, *B.J. Praef.*, 1 (1–2), *οἱ μὲν οὐ παρατυχόντες τοῖς πράγμασιν ἀλλ' ἀκοῇ συλλέγοντες εἰκαῖα καὶ ἀσύμφωνα διηγήματα, σοφιστικῶς ἀναγράφουσιν, οἱ παραγενόμενοι δὲ ἢ κολακείᾳ τῇ πρὸς Ῥωμαίους ἢ μίσει τῷ πρὸς Ἰουδαίους καταψεύδονται τῶν πραγμάτων).* Compare also the evidence at the end of *Ant., Praef.*, 1 (4); *Contra Apionem* I 8 (46) and the letter of Agrippa in Josephus *Vita*, 65 (365).

A. Schlatter, *Zur Topographie und Geschichte Palästinas* (1893), pp. 97–119; 344–403) advanced the opinion that the whole of *B.J.* is really a work by Antonius Julianus corrected here and there by Josephus; this view is a pure fantasy.

Antonius Julianus, a rhetorician who lived about the middle of the second century A.D., is often mentioned by Aulus Gellius, see Schanz-Hosius, *op. cit.* III (1922), pp. 137–8. F. Münter, *Der Jüdische Krieg unter den Kaisern Trajan und Hadrian,* (1821), p. 12, argued that the reference of Minucius Felix is to him, and that he wrote a history of the war of Bar–Kokhba. That is not actually impossible, but hardly probable.

14. Justus of Tiberias

On the life of Justus of Tiberias we know only what Josephus says in his *Vita* 9 (36–42), 12 (65), 17 (88), 35 (175–8), 37 (186), 54 (279), 65 (336–67), 70 (390–3), 74 (410); cf. PIR² I 872. He was a Jew of Greek education—9 (40) *οὐδ' ἄπειρος ἦν παιδείας τῆς παρ' Ἕλλησιν*—and held, together with his father Pistus, a prominent position in Tiberias during the Jewish war in A.D. 66–7. As a man of moderate views, he joined the revolution more from necessity than conviction, but left his native city before the subjugation of Galilee by Vespasian and fled to Agrippa, 70 (390). Sentenced to death by Vespasian and given over to Agrippa for execution, he was reprieved and committed to a long term of imprisonment through the intercession of Berenice, *Vita* 65 (341–3, 355), 74 (410). Subsequently, he appears to have lived once more in Tiberias but, according to Josephus, he led a far from exemplary life. Agrippa sentenced him twice to imprisonment and banished him several times from his native city, once condemning him to death and pardoning him only on the petition of Berenice. In spite of all this, Agrippa then transferred the *τάξις ἐπιστολῶν* to him. However, here also Justus proved himself useless and was finally dismissed by Agrippa, *Vita* 65 (355–6). It has been argued that he was still alive at the beginning of the second century A.D. on the grounds that his history continues until the death of Agrippa, put by Photius in Trajan's third year (A.D. 100). On the problem, which involves the dates both of the composition of Josephus' *Vita* and of the death of Agrippa II, see pp. 54 and 481–2 below. His works were probably as follows (for the Testimonia and Fragments see Jacoby, FGrH 734): (1) A *History of the Jewish war*, against which the polemic of Josephus in his *Vita* is addressed. The later writers who refer to this work, Eusebius, *H.E.*

iii 10, 8; Jerome, *De vir. ill.* 14 (and the Greek translation under the name of Sophronius) and the Suda, s.v. *Ἰοῦστος Τιβερεύς*=T1, derive solely from Josephus. Similarly, it is very doubtful whether Steph. Byz. s.v. *Τιβεριάς*=T4, had any independent knowledge of it. (2) A *Chronicle of the Jewish kings*, from Moses to Agrippa II. This seems to have been still available to Photius and is described briefly by him, *Bib.*, 33. Julius Africanus, from whom the questions in the *Chronicle* of Eusebius and in Syncellus derive, also used it. A reference in Diogenes Laertius ii, 41=F1 possibly suggests that the work was a chronicle of the world, not just one of the Jewish kings. If so, only a fragment of this was available to Photius. (3) The existence of the *Commentarioli de scripturis* mentioned by Jerome, *de vir. ill.* 14, is very questionable since no other author knows anything of it.

On the part played by Justus in the Jewish War false opinions once prevailed, based on the misleading information of Josephus. He has sometimes been reported as an extreme 'patriot' and enemy of the Romans (so, for example, A. Baerwald, *Josephus in Galiläa*, (1877); so also C. Wachsmuth, *Einleitung*, p. 438. However, a critical evaluation of all the information in Josephus yields a substantially different picture. On the one hand, Josephus admittedly portrays him as a leading agitator for the war, and maintains that he incited his own native city, Tiberias, to secession from Agrippa and the Romans, *Vita* 9 (36–42), 65 (344), 70 (391). As evidence of this, Josephus cites his campaign against the cities of Decapolis, Gadara, and Hippos, for which he was accused by their representatives before Vespasian and handed over by him to Agrippa for punishment, escaping death only by the intercession of Berenice, 9 (39–42) and 65 (341–3, 355), 74 (410). Josephus cites also Justus's association with the leaders of the revolution, John of Gischala, 17 (91) and Jesus, son of Sapphias, 54 (278). However, in spite of these efforts to lay the blame for the uprising of Galilee on Justus, Josephus is still naïve enough to assert right at the beginning that Justus had belonged neither to the Roman nor to the revolutionary party, but rather to a middle party which 'pretended to have scruples against the war', 9 (36) *ὑπεκρίνετο μὲν ἐνδοιάζειν πρὸς τὸν πόλεμον*. Moreover various facts indicate that Justus was not at all enthusiastic for the war. His nearest relatives in Gamala were murdered by the revolutionary party, 35 (177), 37 (186). He himself was one of the prominent men who opposed the destruction of Herod's palace in Tiberias, 12 (65–6). Indeed, he was among the officials whom Josephus ordered to be imprisoned precisely because they refused to join the revolution, and to whom he then declared that he too knew the power of the Romans but that for the present no other course remained but to join the 'robbers', that is, the revolutionaries, 35 (175–6), cf. *B.J.* ii 21, 8–10 (632–46), *Vita* 32–4 (155–73). Justus also left Tiberias while the revolution there was still in progress, and went over to Agrippa and the Romans, 65 (354, 357), and 70 (390–3). He was therefore entitled in his account of the war, to attribute the main blame for the revolution in Tiberias to Josephus, and to maintain that Tiberias joined the revolt unwillingly, 65 (340, 350–1). The true situation is thus very clear, Justus was a man of the very same inclination as Josephus. Both joined the revolt, but only under the pressure of circumstances. Later, they both wished they had had nothing to do with it and each tried to shift the blame onto the other.

The work against which Josephus carried on his polemic in his *Vita* cannot be identified with the *Chronicle* described by Photius. For the latter was, according to Photius, 'very scanty in detail and passed over many very necessary items', whereas the former clearly went into great detail and was characterised by Josephus as a history of the war, *Vita* 9 (40), *καὶ γὰρ οὐδ' ἄπειρος ἦν παιδείας τῆς παρ' Ἕλλησιν, ᾗ θαρρῶν ἐπεχείρησε καὶ τὴν ἱστορίαν τῶν πραγμάτων τούτων ἀναγράφειν.* Cf. 65 (336) *Ἰοῦστον καὶ αὐτὸν τὴν περὶ τούτων πραγματείαν γεγραφότα,* and 65 (338) *Ἰοῦστος γοῦν συγγράφειν τὰς περὶ τούτων ἐπιχειρήσας πράξεις τὸν πόλεμον.* In the same chapter, *Vita* 65 (357–8), Josephus speaks of his astonishment at the audacity of Justus, who insisted he was the best reporter of these events, and yet knew nothing authentic either of the proceedings in Galilee, or of the siege of Jotapata, or of the siege of Jerusalem. Plainly, therefore, the whole history of the war was treated in the work. It was not published by Justus until twenty years after its completion, when Vespasian, Titus and Agrippa II were already dead, *Vita* 65 (359–60). Since, accordingly, it was written in the lifetime of Agrippa, it cannot be identified with the *Chronicle*, which continued to the death of Agrippa. Some subsequent references are simply derived from Josephus: Eusebius, *H.E.* iii 10, 8 *Ἰοῦστον Τιβεριέα ὁμοίως αὐτῷ τὰ κατὰ τοὺς αὐτοὺς ἱστορῆσαι χρόνους πεπειραμένον,* and Jerome, *de vir. ill.* 14 (PL xxiii, col. 631) = TU XIV, 1 (1896), p. 16 (revised text) = T1: *Iustus Tiberiensis de provincia Galileae conatus est et ipse Iudaicarum rerum historiam texere et quosdam commentariolos de scripturis; sed hunc Iosephus arguit mendacii. constat autem illum eo tempore scripsisse quo et Iosephum.* The article of the Suda s.v. *Ἰοῦστος Τιβερεύς* comes verbatim from Pseudo-Sophronius (TU XIV, 2 (1896), p. 16), that is the Greek translation of Jerome. Perhaps the reference in Steph. Byz. (ed. Meineke) s.v. *Τιβεριάς* = T4, is also founded on Josephus—*ἐκ ταύτης ἦν Ἰοῦστος ὁ τὸν Ἰουδαϊκὸν πόλεμον τὸν κατὰ Οὐεσπασιανοῦ ἱστορήσας.*

On his *Chronicle*, Photius, *Bib.* 33 = T2, says *Ἀνεγνώσθη Ἰούστου Τιβεριέως χρονικόν, οὗ ἡ ἐπιγραφὴ Ἰούστου Τιβεριέως Ἰουδαίων Βασιλέων τῶν ἐν τοῖς στέμμασιν. οὗτος ἀπὸ πόλεως τῆς ἐν Γαλιλαίᾳ Τιβεριάδος ὡρμᾶτο. ἄρχεται δὲ τῆς ἱστορίας ἀπὸ Μωϋσέως, καταλήγει δὲ ἕως τελευτῆς Ἀγρίππα τοῦ ἑβδόμου μὲν τῶν ἀπὸ τῆς οἰκίας Ἡρῴδου, ὑστάτου δὲ ἐν τοῖς Ἰουδαίων βασιλεῦσιν, ὃς παρέλαβε μὲν τὴν ἀρχὴν ἐπὶ Κλαυδίου, ηὐξήθη δὲ ἐπὶ Νέρωνος καὶ ἔτι μᾶλλον ὑπὸ Οὐεσπασιανοῦ, τελευτᾷ δὲ ἔτει τρίτῳ Τραϊανοῦ, οὗ καὶ ἡ ἱστορία κατέληξεν. ἔστι δὲ τὴν φράσιν συντομώτατός τε καὶ τὰ πλεῖστα τῶν ἀναγκαιοτάτων παρατρέχων.* The quotations in the *Chronicle* of Eusebius and in Georgius Syncellus, which they probably derived from Julius Africanus, also refer to this work. In the foreword to the second book of his *Chronicle*, Eusebius says, *Chron.* ed. Schoene II, p. 4 = Syncellus, ed. Dindorf, I, p. 122 = F*2: *Μωϋσέα . . . . τοῖς χρόνοις ἀκμάσαι κατὰ Ἴναχον εἰρήκασιν ἄνδρες ἐν παιδεύσει γνώριμοι, Κλήμης, Ἀφρικανός, Τατιανός, τοῦ καθ' ἡμᾶς λόγου, τῶν τε ἐκ περιτομῆς Ἰώσηππος καὶ Ἰοῦστος ἰδίως ἕκαστος τὴν ἀπόδειξιν ἐκ παλαιᾶς ὑποσχὼν ἱστορίας.* This passage from the foreword of Eusebius is not only cited expressly by Syncellus, *loc. cit.*, but is also used by him elsewhere (ed. Dindorf, I, pp. 118, 228, 280. cf. also I, pp. 116 f.); also cited in Eustathius, *In Hexaemeron commentarius*, ed. Allatius, (1629), 1 (= PG xviii, col. 708). Eusebius also mentions Justus in his *Chronicle, ad ann. Abrah.* 2113, under the Emperor Nerva (ed. Schoene II, p. 162 (from the Armenian): *Jostus Tiberiensis Judaeorum scriptor cognoscebatur; ibid.* 163 (Jerome), *Justus a Tiberiade Judaeorum scriptor agnoscitur* = T5 = Helm, *Chronik das Hieronymus* (1956), p. 193. The same notice appears in Syncellus in the beginning of the reign of Trajan (ed. Dindorf I, p. 655), *Ἰοῦστος Τιβεριεὺς Ἰουδαῖος συγγραφεὺς ἐγνωρίζετο).* This surely reproduces the original remark in the *Chronicle* of Julius Africanus. For the statement is, without doubt, based on the fact that the *Chronicle* of Justus was supposed to have continued until the beginning of the reign of Trajan. If it is established by this evidence that Julius Africanus used the *Chronicle* of Justus, it is reasonable to suggest that certain of the references to Jewish history by chroniclers dependent on Africanus not deriving from Josephus, go back to Justus (see H. Gelzer,

Julius Africanus (1880), pp. 246–65; cf. A. von Gutschmid, *Kleine Schriften* II, p. 203).

It is possible that Philostorgius also used the *Chronicle* of Justus. One entry in the Suda s.v. *Φλέγων* (ed. Adler IV, pp. 744–5 = FGrH 257 F34) reads *τούτου τοῦ Φλέγοντος, ὥς φησι Φιλοστόργιος, † ὅσον † τὰ κατὰ τοὺς Ἰουδαίους συμπεσόντα διὰ πλείονος ἐπεξελθεῖν τοῦ πλάτους*. The word *ὅσον* is evidently a corruption for the name of a writer. It is possible that the original reading was *Ἰοῦστον*, but more likely in fact that it was *Ἰώσηπον*, for Josephus is explicitly referred to a few lines lower down.

In Diogenes Laertius ii 41 = F1 (in the biography of Socrates) we have *Κρινομένου δ' αὐτοῦ φησὶν Ἰοῦστος ὁ Τιβεριεὺς ἐν τῷ Στέμματι Πλάτωνα ἀναβῆναι ἐπὶ τὸ βῆμα καὶ εἰπεῖν· 'νεώτατος ὤν, ὦ ἄνδρες Ἀθηναῖοι, τῶν ἐπὶ τὸ βῆμα ἀναβάντων', τοὺς δὲ δικαστὰς ἐκβοῆσαι 'Κατάβα, κατάβα'*. It is very unlikely that such a specific reference to Socrates and Plato would have appeared in a short history of the Jewish kings. But the wording of Photius's title compared with that of Diogenes Laertius also leads to the conjecture that Justus wrote more than a chronicle of the Jewish kings. The title, Photius, *Bib.* 33, *Ἰουδαίων βασιλέων τῶν ἐν τοῖς στέμμασιν* cannot be read, 'History of the Crowned Kings of the Jews' even though *στέμμα* usually means crown. It is much more likely, since *στέμμα* also means genealogical table, that it should be translated 'History of the Kings of the Jews enumerated by Genealogical Tables'. But what *στέμματα* are meant? The *Chronicle* of Castor (middle of the first century B.C., see below p. 43) consisted in the main of king-lists; so also that of Julius Africanus which Eusebius followed. It may well be that the work of Justus should also be placed in the same category, and included several different *στέμματα* (genealogical tables). Then the *στέμμα* of the Jewish kings which were available to Photius formed only a portion of the work. The quotation by Diogenes Laertius would then refer to another *στέμμα*, to another part of the complete work. However, this remains a hypothesis, and we cannot confidently relate the quotation in Diogenes Laertius to the text of what we know of Justus' works. See H. Graetz, 'Das Lebensende des Königs Agrippa II, des Justus von Tiberias und des Flavius Josephus und die Agrippa-Münzen', MGWJ (1877), pp. 337 ff.; *idem*, *Gesch. der Juden* III 2 ([5]1906), pp. 555–8; A. Baerwald, *Josephus in Galiläa, sein Verhältniss zu den Parteien, insbesondere zu Justus von Tiberias und Agrippa II* (1877); A. Schlatter 'Der Chronograph aus dem zehnten Jahre Antonins', TU XII, 1 (1894), pp. 37–47; C. Wachsmuth, *Einleitung*, p. 438; B. Niese, Hist. Zeitschr. 76 (1896), pp. 227–9; M. Luther, *Josephus und Justus von Tiberias* (1910); F. Ruhl, 'Justus von Tiberias', Rh. Mus. 71 (1916), pp. 289–308; F. Jacoby s.v. 'Iustus' (9), RE X (1917), cols. 1341–6; Christ-Schmid-Stählin, *Gesch. d. gr. Lit.* II, 1 ([6]1920), pp. 601–3; R. Laqueur, *Der jüdische Historiker Flavius Josephus* (1920), pp. 6–23; M. Drexler, Klio 19 (1925), pp. 293–9; A. Schalit, 'Josephus und Justus', Klio 26 (1933), pp. 67–95; M. Gelzer, 'Die Vita des Josephos', Hermes 80 (1952), pp. 67–90; Th. Frankfort, 'La date de l'autobiographie de Flavius Josèphe et des oeuvres de Justus de Tibériade', Rev. Belge de philol. et d'hist. 39 (1961), pp. 52–8 (rightly dismissing the view that Photius, *Bib.* 33, can be used to date the works of Justus and Josephus). See p. 482 below.

15. Ariston of Pella

On Ariston of Pella and his writings we have only two independent witnesses: Eusebius and Maximus Confessor. (1) According to Eusebius, *H.E.* iv 6, 3, it was recorded in a work by Ariston of Pella that after the conquest of Beth-ther and the overthrow of Bar-Kokhba *τὸ πᾶν ἔθνος ἐξ ἐκείνου καὶ τῆς περὶ τὰ Ἱεροσόλυμα γῆς πάμπαν ἐπιβαίνειν εἴργεται νόμου δόγματι καὶ διατάξεσιν Ἀδριανοῦ, ὡς ἂν μηδ' ἐξ ἀπόπτου θεωροῖεν τὸ πατρῷον ἔδαφος ἐγκελευσαμένου. Ἀρίστων ὁ Πελλαῖος ἱστορεῖ.* It is on this passage of Eusebius that are based the remarks on Ariston of Pella given in the *Chronicon paschale* and by the Armenian historian, Moses of Chorene. (2) In the commentary of Maximus Confessor (*c.* 580–662) on Dionysius the Areopagite, *De mystica theologia*, 1 (Dionys. Areopagit., PG iv, col. 421) we have *Ἀνέγνων δὲ τοῦτο 'ἑπτὰ οὐρανοὺς' καὶ ἐν τῇ συγγεγραμμένῃ Ἀρίστωνι τῷ Πελλαίῳ διαλέξει Παπίσκου καὶ Ἰάσονος, ἣν Κλήμης ὁ Ἀλεξανδρεὺς ἐν ἕκτῳ βιβλίῳ τῶν Ὑποτυπώσεων τὸν ἅγιον Λουκᾶν φῆσιν ἀναγράψαι.* According to Maximus Confessor, therefore, Ariston was the author of the *Dialogue between Jason and Papiscus*, which is, indeed, quoted elsewhere but always as an anonymous work. It was known already to the pagan philosopher Celsus, similarly to Origen, *Contra Cels.* iv 52, and to Jerome, *Comment. ad. Gal.* 2, 14 (PL xxvi col. 361) and *Heb. Quaest. in lib. Gen.* 1, 1 (CCL lxxii, p. 3). The fullest information is provided by the extant preface to a Latin translation made by a certain Celsus, possibly in the third century; for the text see CSEL iii (1871), pp. 119–32. The principal passage is chapter 8, at the end of which the author gives his name, Celsus.

Since the *Dialogue* was known to Celsus, Origen, Jerome and the Latin translator as being anonymous (for none of them names the author), it is very questionable whether the testimony of Maximus Confessor describing Ariston as the author deserves any credit. From what source could a writer of the seventh century have obtained genuine information about the author if none of the earlier writers knew anything about it? Nevertheless, the assertion made by Maximus is not in itself unlikely. In Tertullian's *adversus Iudaeos* 13, 3–4, the imperial edict forbidding the Jews to enter the environs of Jerusalem is almost identical with the passage quoted from Ariston by Eusebius: *interdictum est, ne in confinio ipsius regionis demoretur quisquam Iudaeorum . . . post expugnationem Hierusalem prohibitis ingredi in terram vestram de longinquo eam oculis tantum videre permissum est* (cf. also Tertullian, *Apol.* 21, 5). Since Tertullian says this in an anti-Jewish treatise, it is not impossible that he derived his evidence from a similar anti-Jewish polemic. Such, however, was the *Dialogue between Jason and Papiscus* (cf. also TU I, 1–2, 127 ff.).

If then, it is to be assumed that the reference in Eusebius is to the *Dialogue of Jason and Papiscus*, no history of the war under Hadrian may be ascribed to Ariston; and it is improbable that the remaining statements by Eusebius concerning the war of Hadrian derive from Ariston, who will have referred only to that one edict in passing.

Ariston's work is to be dated to somewhere around the middle of the second century. Note, however, the view of Jacoby, FGrH 201, in his commentary, IID (1930), pp. 627–8, that the possibility of a historical work by Ariston is not to be excluded.

In *Chron. paschale*, ed. Dindorf I, p. 477, there is a reference to A.D. 134: *τούτῳ τῷ ἔτει Ἀπελλῆς καὶ Ἀρίστων, ὧν μέμνηται Εὐσέβιος ὁ Παμφίλου ἐν τῇ ἐκκλησιαστικῇ αὐτοῦ ἱστορίᾳ, ἐπιδίδωσιν ἀπολογίας σύνταξιν περὶ τῆς καθ' ἡμᾶς θεοσεβείας Ἀδριανῷ τῷ βασιλεῖ.* Since the author refers explicitly to Eusebius (confusing *H.E.* iv 3, 3 and 6, 3), his reference has no independent value. The singular *ἐπιδίδωσιν* makes it probable that he wrote *ὁ Πελλαῖος Ἀρίστων* where *Ἀπελλῆς καὶ Ἀρίστων* is found by a corruption of the text. Similarly the Armenian historian, Moses of Chorene, derived his information from Eusebius that Ariston refers to the death of King Artashes (Artaxias—the contemporary king was in fact Vologeses), but then narrates, closely following Eusebius, the history of Bar Kokhba; see V. Langlois, *Collection des historiens de l'Arménie* I = Müller, FHG v, 2, pp. 391–4; A.v. Harnack, *Texte u. Unters*, i, 1–2 (1882), p. 126; Jacoby, FGrH 201 F2.

The dialogue between Jason and Papiscus was thought to have been the source of the *Altercatio Simonis Judaei et Theophili Christiani* published by Martene, *Thesaurus novus anecdotorum* V (1717), and re-edited by Harnack. See Harnack, TU I, 3 (1883), esp. pp. 115–30; but cf. P. Corssen, 'Die "Altercatio Simonis Judaei et Theophili Christiani" auf ihre Quellen geprüft', ThLZ (1890), p. 624, and Th. Zahn, *Forschungen zur Gesch. des neutestamentl. Kanons* IV (1891), pp. 308–29. Corssen and Zahn maintained as probable that the older dialogues were used in the more recent one, yet not to the extent Harnack supposed. Harnack subsequently agreed with them himself in principle, *Gesch. der altchristl. Literatur*, I, pp. 94 f.

F. C. Conybeare, *The dialogues of Athanasius and Zachaeus and of Timothy and Aquila, edited with Prolegomena and Facsimiles* (1898) was of the opinion that both the Greek dialogues published by him go back to the Dialogue and Papiscus. This remains unproven.

See in general A. B. Hulen, 'The Dialogues with the Jews as a Source of the Early Jewish Arguments against Christianity', JBL 51 (1932), pp. 58–70; M. Simon, *Verus Israel* ([2]1964), pp. 188–213; M. Hoffmann, *Der Dialog bei den christlichen Schriftstellern der ersten drei Jahrhunderte*, TU 96 (1966), pp. 9–10.

On Ariston in general see A. von Harnack, *Die Ueberlieferung der grieschen Apologeten des zweiten Jahrhunderts in der alten Kirche und im Mittelalter*, TU I, 1–2 (1882), pp. 115–30. Harnack, *Gesch. der altchristl. Literatur* I (1893), pp. 92–95; II, 1 (1897), pp. 268 f.; Christ-Schmid-Stählin, *Gesch. d. gr. Lit.* II 2 ([6]1924), 1283, n. 3; Hulen and Hoffmann, *op. cit.* above; B. Altaner, *Patrology* (1960), pp. 120–1.

16. Papyrus Fragments

Under this heading are included, as texts of a semi-literary character which bear, or affect to bear (since it is disputed to what extent they are fictional), on the history of the Jews in Alexandria in the Roman period, a series of Greek papyri from Egypt which mainly represent diametric confrontations between leading Alexandrian Greek and

Roman office-holders, primarily various Emperors from Claudius to Commodus. They can be considered as a group, not because they were discovered as such, but because they seem to belong to a single *genre*, and to share the purpose of glorifying Alexandria and its leading citizens in the face of Roman rule.

Not all these papyri concern the Jews of Alexandria, and only those which specifically involve them will be listed here. No more than a brief tabulation of the nature of the relevant texts will be provided, since a fuller consideration of their historical setting belongs in vol. III, §31, 1, on the communities of the Diaspora. Moreover, all the texts have been collected and edited with an extensive commentary by H. A. Musurillo, *The Acts of the Pagan Martyrs: Acta Alexandrinorum* (1954); they are re-edited by Musurillo with brief notes for the Teubner *Acta Alexandrinorum* (1961), with the same numbering. Those concerning the Jews are also re-edited in V. Tcherikover and A. Fuks, *Corpus Papyrorum Judaicarum* II (1960), nos. 154–9.

(a) An Alexandrian embassy led by Isidorus and Lampon accusing Agrippa I (see p. 398 below), or Agrippa II (p. 472, n. 5) before Claudius.

A composite text from BGU 511; P. Lond. inv. 2785; P. Berl. inv. 8877; P. Cairo 10448. See Musurillo IV, CPJ 156.

(b) A confrontation of Greek and Jewish embassies before Trajan (*Acta Hermaisci*), P. Oxy. 1242. See Musurillo VIII and CPJ 157.

(c) A dispute between Jews and Greeks before a Roman Emperor, almost certainly either Trajan or Hadrian (*Acta Pauli et Antonini*).

Composite text from P. Par. 68, P. Lond. 1. 227 f., BGU 341. See Musurillo IX B and CPJ 158.

The participants seem to refer to incidents during the great revolt of A.D. 115–7.

(d) See now also P. Oxy. 3021, a first century A.D. fragment of papyrus showing ambassadors, including one called Isidorus, addressing an Emperor and referring to the Jews.

17. Teucer of Cyzicus

The Suda, s.v. *Τεῦκρος ὁ Κυζικηνός* has *ὁ γράψας Περὶ χρυσοφόρου γῆς, Περὶ τοῦ Βυζαντίου, Μιθριδατικῶν πράξεων βιβλία ϵʹ, Περὶ Τύρου ϵ́, Ἀραβικῶν ϵʹ, Ἰουδαϊκὴν ἱστορίαν ἐν βιβλίοις ζʹ, Ἐφήβων τῶν ἐν Κυζίκῳ ἄσκησιν γʹ καὶ λοιπά.* Almost nothing is known of this writer, who probably wrote in the middle of the first century B.C., and of whom nothing survives except a few fragments mainly concerned with place-names in Epirus and Euboea. See Jacoby, FGrH 274, and his discussion and commentary in FGrH IIIa (1934), pp. 314–6.

18. Various Works περὶ Ἰουδαίων.

Works specifically on the history of the Jews were produced also by Hellenistic Jewish writers, for instance, Demetrius, Eupolemus, Artapanus, Aristeas, Cleodemus (or Malchus) and Philo the epic poet. They hardly come into consideration here, however, for they dealt predominantly if not entirely with the earlier biblical period (see vol. III, §33, 3, 1–6). The book of Pseudo-Hecataeus on the Jews seems to have had more bearing than those above on the circumstances of the Jews in his own time (see vol. III, §33, 7, 4). An important source for the history of his time was provided by the five books of Philo of Alexandria on the persecution of the Jews, which must be mentioned here because they survive only in part (see vol. III, §34, 1).

From an early period mentions of the Jews appear in pagan authors. See the references collected by J. Freudenthal, *Alexander Polyhistor* (1875), pp. 177–9; cf. M. Willrich, *Juden und Griechen vor der makkabäischen Erhebung* (1895), pp. 43–63. Editions of the texts are in T. Reinach, *Textes d'auteurs grecs et romains relatifs au Judaïsme* (1895); note also that a new and expanded collection of these texts, with commentary, is being prepared by M. Stern of the Hebrew University under the title, 'Texts of Greek and Latin Authors relating to Jews and Judaism'. Many are quoted in Josephus, *Contra Apionem*, i 14–23, 73–218. But from the beginning of the first century B.C., works specifically on the Jews were written by non-Jewish authors: (1) the oldest known is the Συσκευὴ κατὰ Ἰουδαίων by Apollonius Molon (see vol. III, §33, 6, 1). (2) Not much later is the scholarly compilation of Alexander Polyhistor Περὶ Ἰουδαίων (Jacoby, FGrH 273 F19), to which we are indebted for valuable excerpts from the writings of the Hellenistic Jewish writers (see vol. III, §33, 3). (3) Herennius Philo of Byblos lived in the period of Hadrian, and was the author of, among other works, a treatise Περὶ Ἰουδαίων. In this he referred, according to Origen, to the book of Pseudo-Hecataeus on the Jews and expressed the view that either the book did not come from the historian Hecataeus, or if he were the author, he had been converted to Jewish teaching, Origen, *Contra Celsum* i 15 = Jacoby, FGrH 790 F9. The text of the passage will be given in vol. III, §33, 7, 4. Allegedly, two fragments in Eusebius derive from the same work Περὶ Ἰουδαίων (*Praep. evang.* i 10, 42 = F10—ἐν τῷ περὶ Ἰουδαίων συγγράμματι). However, the contents of these fragments relate expressly to Phoenician mythology, and the second of them is quoted again by Eusebius in another place, *Praep. evang.* iv 16, 11 = F3b, with the heading ἐκ δὲ τοῦ πρώτου συγγράμματος τῆς Φίλωνος Φοινικικῆς ἱστορίας. It was therefore once argued that the treatise Περὶ Ἰουδαίων formed only an excursus in the larger Φοινικικὴ ἱστορία of Philo (so for example, J. Freudenthal,

Alexander Polyhistor, p. 34). But it is more likely that Eusebius, in i 10, 44, wrongly ascribed the quotation from the Phoenician history to the work *Περὶ Ἰουδαίων*. Compare, on Philo in general: Müller, FHG III, pp. 560–76, Jacoby, FGrH 790; Wachsmuth, *Einleitung*, p. 406; Christ-Schmidt-Stählin, *Gesch. d. gr. Lit.* II, 2 ([6]1924), pp. 867–8; RE s.v. 'Sanchuniathon'. (4) A certain Damocritus also wrote a work *Περὶ Ἰουδαίων*. From the brief note of this in the Suda s.v. *Δαμόκριτος* = Jacoby, FGrH 730 F1, it is clear only that its viewpoint was one of hostility to the Jews. (5) The same is true of the work of a certain Nicarchus *Περὶ Ἰουδαίων*, I. Bekker, *Anecdota*, p. 381 = Jacoby FGrH 731 F1. (6) As writers on Jewish matters Alexander Polyhistor refers also to a certain Theophilus, see Eusebius, *Praep. evang.* ix 34, 19 (= Jacoby, FGrH 733 F1); and Eusebius to a Timochares *ἐν τοῖς περὶ Ἀντιόχου*, ix 35, 1 (= Jacoby, FGrH 165 F1, and 737 F15) and to an anonymous *Συρίας σχοινομέτρησις*, ix 36, 1 (= Jacoby, FGrH 849 F1). However, all three clearly dealt with Jewish matters only in passing. Theophilus discusses Solomon's relationship to the King of Tyre; both of the others give interesting details on the topography of Jerusalem. The author of the Syrian topometry is perhaps to be identified with the Xenophon cited elsewhere by Alexander Polyhistor—*Ξενοφῶν ἐν ταῖς Ἀναμετρήσεσι τῶν ὀρῶν*, Steph. Byz. s.v. *Ὠρωπός* (= F99 in Müller FHG III, p. 237 = Jacoby FGrH 273 F72) whom Müller identified with the Xenophon of Lampsacus mentioned by Pliny; see now RE s.v. 'Xenophon' (10), IXA (1967), cols. 2051–5. On these writers in general see Müller, FHG III, p. 209; pp. 515 f.; Reinach, *Textes*, pp. 51–4; for the latter two, cf. Hengel, *Judentum u. Hell.*, *pp.* 101–2.

19. The Chronographers

For the facts concerning the plundering of the Temple by Antiochus Epiphanes, Josephus, *Contra Apionem* ii 7 (84) = Jacoby, FGrH 244 F79 and 250 F13, appeals among others to the chronographers Apollodorus and Castor. He also takes from Castor the date of the battle of Gaza in 312/11 B.C., *Contra Apionem* i 22 (184–5) = Jacoby, FGrH 250 F12. Since it is possible that he also occasionally derived chronological information from them, it is necessary to say something about both these men.

(1) Apollodorus of Athens lived in the second half of the second century B.C., and wrote, in addition to other works, a *Χρονικά* in metrical form which dealt with the most important events in world history in chronological order from the Fall of Troy (placed in 1184 B.C.) to 144/3 B.C. (with a continuation, possibly by Apollodorus, to 119 B.C.). Since the metrical form allowed the contents to be memorised easily, the work became a widely-used schoolbook and handbook.

For the fragments see Müller, FHG III, pp. 435–49; Jacoby, FGrH 244, with a commentary in IID (1930), pp. 716–52, 802–12. Compare also C. Wachsmuth, *Commentatio vernaculo sermone conscripta de Erathosthene, Apollodoro, Sosibio, chronographis* (1892); *Idem, Einleitung*, pp. 131–5; E. Schwartz, RE I, cols. 2856–75 = *Griechische Geschichtschreiber* (1957), pp. 253–81; F. Jacoby, *Apollodors Chronik: eine Sammlung der Fragmente* (1902).

(2) Castor of Rhodes. This chronographer is know mainly through quotations in the Christian chroniclers, Eusebius and Syncellus. The first book of Eusebius' *Chronicle*, which is extant only in an Armenian translation, gives particularly valuable extracts. It is clear from this that the work of Castor covers the period up to the consulate of M. Valerius Messala and M. (Pupius) Piso, 61 B.C., the year in which Pompey celebrated his triumph for the subjugation of Asia (*nostrae regionis res praeclaraque gesta cessarunt*). Since the author concludes his work at this point, it cannot have been written much later than the middle of the first century before Christ. This is confirmed by the fact that it is quoted already by Varro, *de gente populi Romani* (= Jacoby, FGrH 250 F9). It comprised six books, according to Eusebius. What little is known of his origin and life is due mainly to a brief and confused entry in the Suda s.v. *Κάστωρ Ῥόδιος* (= FGrH 250 T1, with Jacoby's discussion), which at least helps to establish that he was a contemporary of Julius Caesar.

The fragments are collected by Jacoby, FGrH 250, with commentary in IID (1930), pp. 814–26. Eusebius refers to the work in a list of his sources, *Chron.* ed. Schoene I, col. 265): *E Kastoris VI libris: in quibus a Nino ac deorsum olompiades CLXXXI collegit* = T2 (in German translation). The conclusion of the work is given as follows in a passage quoted by Eusebius, *Chron.* ed. Schoene I, col. 295, *seorsum consules disponemus, incipientes a Leukio Junio Bruto, et a Leukio Tarkino Collatino et in Markum Valerium Messaliam et Marcum Pisonem desinentes: qui tempore Theophemi Atheniensium archontis consules fuerunt* = F5 (German translation); cf. *Ibid.* I, col. 183: [*archontes Atheniensium*] *desinunt sub Theophemo; cuius aetate omnino quidem nostrae regionis res praeclaraque gesta cessarunt* = F4 (German translation). See also H. Gelzer, *Sextus Julius Africanus* II (1885), pp. 63–79; E. Schwartz, *Die Königslisten des Eratosthenes und Kastor* (1895); C. Wachsmuth, *Einleitung*, pp. 139–42; W. Kubitschek, RE s.v. 'Kastor' (8), X (1919), cols. 2347–57.

C. Josephus[1]

Josephus, whose works provide the main source for the history studied here, gives in his *Life* and *Jewish War* the following facts concerning himself. He was born in Jerusalem in the first year of the reign of Caligula, A.D. 37/38[2]. His father, named Matthias, was des-

1. The name reads in Greek Ἰώσηπος (Niese, *Josephi opp.* I, p. v).
2. The first year of Caligula's reign extended from 18 March A.D. 37 to 17 March A.D. 38. As Josephus at the conclusion of the *Antiquities* notes that he was fifty-six years old in the thirteenth year of Domitian (14 September A.D. 93–13 September A.D. 94), he must have been born between 14 September A.D. 37 and 18 March A.D. 38.

cended from a distinguished priestly family whose ancestors Josephus could trace back to the time of John Hyrcanus. One of them, also called Matthias, married a daughter of the High Priest Jonathan (=Alexander Jannaeus?), *Vita* 1 (4) cf. *B.J.*, preface 1 (3), *Ant.* xvi 7, 1 (187). The young Josephus received a careful religious education and by the age of fourteen had so distinguished himself for his knowledge of the Law that the High Priests and notables of the city came to him to receive instruction. Yet he was not satisfied with this and went, when he was sixteen, through the schools of the Pharisees, Sadducees and Essenes, one after another. But even so his thirst for knowledge remained unsatisfied and he withdrew into the desert to a hermit named Bannus. After spending three years with him, he returned to Jerusalem and, in his nineteenth year, joined the Pharisees, *Vita* 2 (12). At the age of twenty-six, in A.D. 64, he travelled to Rome in order to obtain the release of certain priests, close associates of his, who had been taken there as prisoners for some trivial matter. He managed, through the good offices of a Jewish actor called Alityrus, to secure the favour of the empress Poppaea, and was thus able to achieve his purpose. Rich with gifts, he then returned to Judaea, *Vita* 3 (16). Soon afterwards, war broke out against the Romans (A.D. 66). Josephus says that at first he advised against it, *Vita* 4 (17–19); this is quite possible, as the Jewish aristocracy in general only took part in the revolt under compulsion. The fact is, however, that once the decisive blows had been struck, he joined the uprising, and even became one of its leaders, with the important post of commander-in-chief of Galilee, *B.J.* ii 20, 4 (568); *Vita* 7 (28–9). From then on, his actions and destiny were closely bound up with those of the Jewish people, and will therefore be mentioned in the history of the Jewish war (cf. *Vita* 7–74 (28–413), *B.J.* ii 20, 4–21, 10 (566–646), iii, 4, 1 (59–63), 6, 3–8, 9 (127–408), 9, 1, 5–6 (409–13, 432–42). His activities as commander-in-chief in Galilee ended, after the fall of the fortress of Jotapata in A.D. 67, with his capture by the Romans, *B.J.* iii 8, 7–8 (340–98). When he was led before Vespasian, he predicted his future elevation to the throne, *B.J.* iii 8, 9 (399–408); Suet. *Div. Vesp.* 5; Dio lxvi 1; Appian in Zonaras xi 16, with the result that he was treated from the beginning with consideration and respect, *B.J.* iii 8, 9 (399–408); *Vita* 75 (414–21). But two years later, when in A.D. 69 Vespasian was in fact proclaimed emperor by the legions in Egypt and Judaea and Josephus's prophecy was thus fulfilled, Vespasian remembered his prisoner and granted him his freedom as a mark of gratitude, *B.J.* iv 10, 7 (622–9). After his proclamation as emperor, Vespasian hastened first to Alexandria, *B.J.* iv 11, 5 (656) and Josephus accompanied him, *Vita* 75 (415). From here, Josephus returned to Palestine in the train of Titus, to whom Vespasian had delegated the continuation of the war, and remained in his entourage until it was over, *Vita* 75 (416–21); *c. Ap.* i 9 (47–9). During the siege of Jerusalem he was obliged, on Titus's orders and often to the danger of his own life, to call on the Jews to surrender, *B.J.* v 3, 3 (116–9); 6, 2 (261); 7, 4 (325); 9, 2–4 (356–419); 13, 3 (541–7); vi 2, 1–3 (93–123); 2, 5 (129); 7, 2 (365); *Vita* 75 (416). He was once struck by a stone whilst doing this and was carried away unconscious, *B.J.* v 13, 3 (541). When, after the capture of the city, Titus encouraged him to 'take what he wanted', he merely appropriated some sacred books and entreated the freedom of many prisoners who were his friends, as well as that of his own brother. Even three men who had already been crucified were taken down on his request, one of whom recovered, *Vita* 75 (418–21). As his own lands near Jerusalem were needed by the Roman garrison, Titus gave him others in the Plain, *Vita* 76 (422). After the war ended, he went with Titus to Rome, where, benefiting from the emperor's favour, he carried on with his studies and writing. The former Jewish priest became a Greek man of letters. Vespasian assigned him a dwelling in a house in which he had himself once lived, bestowed on him Roman citizenship and granted him a yearly pension, *Vita* 76 (422–3). He also gave him a splendid estate in Judaea. At the time of the suppression of the Jewish revolt in Cyrene, its captured leader, Jonathan, alleged that many respected Jews were his accomplices, among them Josephus, who had sent him weapons and gold. But Vespasian gave no credence to this information and continued to show favour to Josephus, *Vita* 76 (424–6); *B.J.* vii 11, 1–3 (437–50). He enjoyed the same patronage under Titus (A.D. 70–81) and Domitian (A.D. 81–96). The latter granted him exemption from taxation on his estate in Judaea, *Vita* 76 (429). Nothing is known of any association with later emperors, nor when Josephus died. It is not necessary to assume that he was still alive at the beginning of the second century A.D. unless Photius's statement is accepted, *Bibliotheca* 33, dating the death of Agrippa to A.D. 100. The *Life* was certainly written after this event, *Vita* 65 (359–60). According to Eusebius, *HE* iii 9, 2, Josephus was honoured in Rome by the erection of a statue.

Concerning his family, Josephus gives the following information. His ancestor Simon 'the Stutterer' *(ὁ ψελλός)* lived during the time of John Hyrcanus. He belonged to the first of the twenty-four orders of priests, i.e., the order of Jehoiarib (1 Chron. 24:7). Simon's son was Matthias ὁ *Ἡφλίου* (Niese *Ἡφαίου*), who married a daughter of the High Priest Jonathan (=Alexander Jannaeus?). From this marriage was born Matthias 'the Humpback' *(ὁ κυρτός)* in the first year of Hyrcanus (II?). Matthias the Humpback's son was Joseph, born in the ninth year of Alexandra (?). His son was Matthias the father of Josephus, born in the tenth year of Archelaus, *Vita* 1 (5).[3] The parents of Josephus were still alive at the time of the great war. While he was commander-in-chief in Galilee he received news from Jerusalem through his father, *Vita* 41 (204). His parents were in the city during the siege and were held prisoner by the rebels because they did not trust them; cf. the father, *B.J.* v 13, 1 (533); the mother, *B.J.* v 13, 3 (544); cf. also v 9, 4 (419). His brother, probably his full brother, Matthias, with whom he was brought up, *Vita* 2 (7), was released through Josephus's intervention from Roman imprisonment after the capture of Jerusalem, *Vita* 75 (419). According to *B.J.* v 9, 4 (419), his wife was also in the city during the siege. This was presumably his first wife, of whom there is otherwise no mention. As a prisoner-of-war of Vespasian, he had, at his command, married a captive Jewess from Caesarea, but she left him while he was in Alexandria with Vespasian, *Vita* 75 (414). He then married another woman in Alexandria, *Vita* 75 (415), and by her had three sons, only one of whom, Hyrcanus, born in the fourth year of Vespasian, *Vita* 1 (5) and 76 (426), was still alive at the time when he wrote the *Life*. Still during the period of Vespasian, Josephus divorced this wife and married a distinguished Jewess from Crete who bore him two sons: Justus, born in the seventh year of Vespasian, and Simonides with the surname of Agrippa, born in the ninth year of Vespasian. Both were alive at the time of the composition of the *Life*, *Vita* 1 (5) and 76 (427).

It is thanks to Josephus's literary activity in Rome that those works exist without which the present history could not have been written. The following four are extant:

(1) *The Jewish War*, *Περὶ τοῦ Ἰουδαϊκοῦ πολέμου* as Josephus himself

3. The genealogy as presented in the received text of *Vita* 1 (1–5) contains several impossibilities. If Matthias, the father of Josephus, was born in the tenth year of Archelaus (A.D. 6), Matthias's father, Joseph, could not have been born in the ninth year of Alexandra (67 B.C.). This is either an oversight on the part of Josephus, or the text is corrupt. If it is assumed that Joseph, the grandfather of Josephus, was born in about 30 B.C. (in the ninth year of Herod?), the Hyrcanus in the first year of whose reign 'Matthias the Humpback' was born, will have been Hyrcanus II, who became High Priest in 76 B.C. The Humpback's mother can then not have been a daughter of Jonathan, the first of the Maccabees (died 143/2 B.C.), but a daughter of Alexander Jannaeus (died 76 B.C.) also called Jonathan. Josephus admittedly follows *Ἰωνάθου ἀρχιερέως* with the explanatory *τοῦ πρώτου ἐκ τῶν Ἀσαμωναίου παίδων γένους ἀρχιερατεύσαντος, τοῦ ἀδελφοῦ Σίμωνος τοῦ ἀρχιερέως*. Yet the reasonable suspicion must exist that Josephus mistakenly added this explanatory note to the name of the 'High Priest Jonathan' in the list of his forefathers. If Alexander Jannaeus is meant, the statement that 'Simon the Stutterer' lived under John Hyrcanus is also correct.

entitles the work.[4] It is divided into seven books, an arrangement due, as appears from e.g., *Ant.* xiii 10, 6 (298); xviii 1, 2 (11), to Josephus himself. A very detailed introduction occupying the whole of the first book and half of the second precedes the history of the war proper. The first book begins with the period of Antiochus Epiphanes (175–164 B.C.) and extends to the death of Herod (4 B.C.). The second continues the history until the outbreak of the war (A.D. 66) and includes the first year of the war A.D. 66/67. The third discusses the war in Galilee, A.D. 67; the fourth, the further progress of the war until the complete isolation of Jerusalem; the fifth and sixth, the siege and conquest of Jerusalem; the seventh, the aftermath of the war down to the destruction of the last remaining insurgents. From the preface, 1 (3), it appears that this work was written originally in Josephus's native language, Aramaic, and was only later re-written by him in Greek. For this, he employed the help of collaborators to improve his Greek style, *c. Ap.* i 9 (50).[5] For the history of the war proper he chiefly used his own experience, since he had either participated in the events related, or was present as an eye-witness. Even during the siege of Jerusalem he made written notes for himself, for which he also used statements made by deserters concerning the situation inside the city, *c. Ap.* i 9 (49).[6] When the work was completed, he presented it to Vespasian and Titus and had the satisfaction of being assured by them, and by King Agrippa II and many Romans who had taken part in the war, that he had recounted the events correctly and faithfully *c. Ap.* i 9 (50–1); *Vita* 65 (361–6). Titus in person commanded the book to be published, *Vita* 65 (363). Agrippa wrote sixty-two letters testifying to the accuracy of the account. Josephus had submitted the individual books to him as he wrote them and had received favourable opinions from him, *Vita* 65 (365). Since the completed work was presented to Vespasian, *c. Ap.* i 9 (51), it must have been written during his reign

4. *B.J.* i 1, 1 (1); *Ant.* i 11, 4 (203); xviii 1, 2 (11); xx 11, 1 (258); *Vita* 74 (412). In cod. Parisin. 1425 the title reads *Φλαυΐου Ἰωσήπου Ἑβραίου ἱστορία Ἰουδαϊκοῦ πολέμου πρὸς Ῥωμαίους*. Niese held this to be the original one. In the majority of manuscripts the title reads *Περὶ ἁλώσεως* (see Niese, *Jos.* I, Praef. vi and VI, p. 3 on the first appearances of the two headings).

5. It is not known for sure whether these assistants played any part in the composition of the *Bellum* also, but it is assumed from the high degree of stylistic and historical expertise in the work (avoidance of hiatus, etc.). For an exaggerated view of their role in Josephus's work in general, see H. St. J. Thackeray, *Josephus the Man and the Historian* (1929), *passim*. For criticism of Thackeray, see G. C. Richards, 'The Composition of Josephus' Antiquities', CQ 33 (1939), pp. 36–40.

6. As Josephus was himself in an ideal position to observe the war, it is curious to suppose that he derived most of his material from a 'Flavian work'—so W. Weber, *Josephus und Vespasian* (1921)—or from the *Commentarii* of Vespasian—so Thackeray, *op. cit.*, pp. 37–41.

(A.D. 69–79). Nevertheless, it must have been towards the end of it, for other works on the Jewish war had preceded that of Josephus, *B.J.* Preface, 1 (1); *Ant.* Preface 1 (4). This is confirmed by *B.J.* vii 5, 7 (158), where the building of the Temple of Peace (*Εἰρήνη*) is referred to as completed; according to Dio lxvi 15, 1, it was not consecrated until A.D. 75.[7]

(2) *The Jewish Antiquities*, *Ἰουδαϊκὴ Ἀρχαιολογία* (*Antiquitates Judaicae*), covers in twenty books the history of the Jewish people from the earliest times down to the outbreak of the war with the Romans in A.D. 66. The distribution into twenty books is Josephus's own, *Ant.* xx 12, 1 (267). He may have wished to provide thereby a counterpart to the twenty books of *Ῥωμαϊκὴ Ἀρχαιολογία* by Dionysius of Halicarnassus.[8] The first ten run parallel to the narrative of the Bible and extend to the end of the Babylonian captivity. The eleventh goes from Cyrus to Alexander the Great; the twelfth, from Alexander the Great to the death of Judas Maccabaeus (161 B.C.); the thirteenth, to the death of Alexandra (67 B.C.); the fourteenth, to the accession of Herod the Great (37 B.C.); the fifteenth, sixteenth and seventeenth deal with Herod's reign (37–4 B.C.); and the last three books extend from then until A.D. 66. The work was finished after many interruptions, Preface 2 (7–9) in the thirteenth year of Domitian, when Josephus was fifty-six years old, i.e., in A.D. 93 or 94, *Ant.* xx 12, 1 (267). He was encouraged to complete it by a certain Epaphroditus in particular, a man whose lively interest in learning Josephus praised highly.[9] That the entire work was primarily intended not for Jewish but for Greek and Roman readers, and that its main purpose was to elicit from the cultivated world respect for the much calumniated Jewish people, is clear enough from its character and is declared emphatically by Josephus himself, *Ant.* xvi 6, 8 (174–8).

The sources for the earlier period (down to Nehemiah, about 440 B.C.), were almost exclusively the canonical books of the Old Testament. As a

7. A. von Gutschmid, *Kleine Schriften* IV (1893), p. 344.

8. *Ibid.*, p. 347; Thackeray, *op. cit.*, pp. 56–8.

9. Josephus also presented his *Vita*, 76 (430), and the books against Apion, *c. Ap.* i 1 (1), ii 41 (296) to this Epaphroditus. Two men named Epaphroditus are known from this period. The one was a freedman and secretary (*a libellis*) of Nero and was executed by Domitian (Tac. *Ann.* xv 55; Suet. *Nero* 49, 3; *Domit.* 14, 4, Dio lxiii 29, 12; lxvii 14. The Suda, *Lex.* s.v. Ἐπίκτητος; Epict. i, 1, 20; 19, 19–23; 26, 11–12; PIR² E 69; RE V 2, 2710). The other was a grammarian who lived in Rome from the time of Nero to that of Nerva, and formed a great library (The Suda, *Lex.* s.v. Ἐπαφρόδιτος; CIL VI 9454—probably the same Epaphroditus; RE V 2 2711–14). It cannot be established which of the two was Josephus's patron. The freedman perished in A.D. 95 (Dio lxvii 14, 4) and can only be the person to whom Josephus dedicated his latest works, if these were all written before that year. The name Epaphroditus is not rare, occurring in numerous inscriptions.

native Palestinian, Josephus shows in his use of them a wide knowledge of the Hebrew and Aramaic texts, yet he chiefly employs the Greek translation of the Septuagint, so much so that in the case of the books of Ezra and Esther he uses only those parts which appear in the Septuagint.[10] The biblical history is treated according to the following principles. (1) For apologetic purposes, modifications are not infrequently made, offensive items being omitted or altered and the history presented in the best possible light. (2) To this latter end, Josephus had already made a preliminary study of the older legends known as haggadah. Their influence is seen, in particular, in the history of the Patriarchs and of Moses. (3) Josephus did not, as it seems, derive these haggadic embellishments solely from oral tradition, but in part from earlier Hellenistic versions of the biblical history by Demetrius, Artapanus, and others.[11] (4) In expounding the law, he followed the Palestinian halakhah (see vol. II, §25 iii, 1–2). (5) The influence of Philo is also noticeable in some places.[12] (6) Non-biblical writings are sometimes interpolated in order to supplement and corroborate the biblical narrative, especially in the history of the earlier period and in later history where it touches that of neighbouring peoples.[13]

Josephus's information on the post-biblical era is uneven. The great

10. See vol. III §33, II 1–2; H. Bloch, *Die Quellen des Jos.* (1879), pp. 69–79; H. St. J. Thackeray, *Josephus, the Man and the Historian* (1929), pp. 75 ff.; A. Schalit, *Jewish Antiquities*, Introd. (1955), pp. xxxii–v (Hebrew); G. Ricciotti, 'Il testo della Bibbia in Flavio Giuseppe', *Atti del XIX Congr. Internaz. degli Orientalisti* (1935). But in ASTI 4 (1965), pp. 163–88, Schalit stresses the use of the Greek Bible more than has been done before and suggests that Josephus's reliance on the Hebrew Bible needs querying.

11. On the influence of Demetrius, see J. Freudenthal, *Alexander Polyhistor* (1874), pp. 46, 49 n. 61, n. 63; A.-M. Denis, *Introduction aux pseudépigraphes grecs d'Ancien Testament* (1970), p. 249. On that of Artapanus, Freudenthal, p. 160 n., pp. 169–71; Denis, p. 257. On both, Bloch, *Die Quellen des Flavius Josephus*, pp. 53–62; Schalit, *Introduction*, pp. xlv–xlix (Hebrew). Josephus knew them at least in part through Alexander Polyhistor, see vol. III, §33 iii. Schalit, *loc. cit.*, suggests that Josephus also knew Artapanus independently.

12. See C. Siegfried, *Philo von Alexandria* (1875), pp. 278–81; J. Freudenthal, *op. cit.*, p. 218; P. Wendland, *Jahrb. für class. Philol.* 22, Suppl. (1896), pp. 712 f.; Schalit, *Introduction*, xli (Hebrew); Thackeray, *op. cit.*, pp. 93–6. Differing, Bloch, *Die Quellen des Fl. Jos.*, pp. 117–40; S. Belkin, *Philo and the Oral Law* (1940), pp. 23–5.

13. In the first ten books the following non-biblical writers are cited: i 3, 6 (93–4): Berosus, Jerome, Mnaseas, Nicolaus of Damascus; i 3, 9 (107): Manetho, Berosus, Moschus, Hestiaeus, Jerome, Hesiod, Hecataeus, Hellanicus, Acusilaus, Ephorus, Nicolaus; i 4, 3 (118–19): Sibylla, Hestiaeus; i 7, 2 (158–9): Berosus, Hecataeus, Nicolaus; i 15 (240): Malchus after Alexander Polyhistor; vii 5, 2 (101): Nicolaus; viii 5, 3 (144–9): Menander, Dios; viii 6, 2 (157): Herodotus; viii 10, 2–3 (253, 260): Herodotus; viii 13, 2 (324): Menander; ix, 14, 2 (283): Menander; x 1, 4 (20): Herodotus, Berosus; x 2, 2 (34): Berosus; x 11, 1 (219, 227–8): Berosus, Megasthenes, Diocles, Philostratus.

gap between Nehemiah and Antiochus Epiphanes (440–175 B.C.) is filled almost solely by a few partly legendary sources, in particular by popular traditions relative to Alexander, the story of the Tobiads, and a long extract from the *Letter of Aristeas*, xii 2 (11–42).[14] For the period 175–134 B.C., the main source is 1 Maccabees, which, however, is used so summarily towards the end that it is doubtful whether Josephus had the complete book before him.[15] It is supplemented by Polybius, xii 9, 1 (358), and from the point where Polybius ends (146 B.C.), by the same sources from which the history of the Hasmonaeans from 134 B.C. onwards is, in general, derived. For this, in effect, Josephus apparently had no more written Jewish sources. He therefore obtained his material by extracting from Greek works on world history information relating to the history of Palestine. His chief informants in regard to 134–37 B.C. were the historians Strabo, xiii 10, 4 (285); 11, 3 (319); 12, 6 (347); xiv 3, 1 (35); 4, 3 (68); 6, 4 (104); 7, 2 (111); 8, 3 (138); xv 1, 2 (9), and Nicolaus of Damascus, xiii 8, 4 (249); 12, 6 (347); xiv 1, 3 (9); 4, 3 (68); 6, 4 (104).

There is no foundation for the view, formerly often expressed, that the authors repeatedly quoted here were not his main sources but were merely employed to supplement a source unnamed. Josephus uses whole excerpts from these writers, and at the same time cites individual passages of importance to him. Where the quotations are really an interpolation into the text, Josephus follows the latter and supplements it with the former. This technique explains certain inconsistencies between the text and the inserted quotation. It is a great exaggeration, however, to assert with C. Wachsmuth that the quotations are often in glaring contradiction to the text.[16] This remark is actually only valid for the history of Aristobulus I, where Josephus probably follows no written source, but Jewish traditions with which the quotation of Strabo's judgment on that prince does then stand in sharp contradiction, xiii 11, 3 (319). Strabo's method of cautiously weighing evidence, known from his *Geography*, is clearly discernible in a few

14. For the story of Alexander the Great and the Jews, see R. Marcus's discussion and bibliography in *Josephus* (Loeb) VI, App. C. For the Tobiads see A. Momigliano, 'I Tobiadi nella preistoria del moto maccabaico', ARAST 67 (1932), pp. 165–200, who assumes that Josephus drew on two different sources. This is highly conjectural. It is clear, at any rate, that the main body of the narrative is from a Hellenistic-Jewish story about the doings of the family of Tobiah. V. Tcherikover, *Hellenistic Civilization and the Jews* (1959), pp. 40–2 suggested a family chronicle. M. Stern, 'Notes on the Story of Joseph the Tobiad', Tarbiz 32 (1962), pp. 35–45 (Hebrew), rightly points out that the emphasis is on the activities of Hyrcanus, the son of Joseph.

15. On the question whether Josephus used 1 Maccabees in the traditional Greek text see vol. III §32, I 1 and R. Marcus, *Josephus* (Loeb) VIII, p. 334, note d.

16. *Einleitung in das Studium der alten Geschichte* (1895), p. 444.

passages where he is not named, as in the various numerical data of xiii 12, 5 (344). Obviously, Strabo and Nicolaus both go back to earlier sources. For the first half of the period indicated (about 134–85 B.C.) the basis is most likely to have been Posidonius (see above, pp. 20 f.). Timagenes, xiii 11, 3 (319); 12, 5 (344), Asinius Pollio and Hypsicrates, xiv 8, 3 (138–9), are all quoted in passages taken from Strabo. Livy, who is named only once, xiv 4, 3 (68), is used scarcely at all. But for internal Jewish history, Josephus supplements the material obtained in this way from Strabo and Nicolaus with stories characterised as legends by their content and standing out in clear contrast to the framework of the narratives, xiii 10, 3 (280–3); 10, 5–6 (288–96); xiv 2, 1 (22–4). These have clearly been drawn from oral tradition. For the history of Herod, Nicolaus of Damascus is acknowledged to be the chief source, xii 3, 2 (126); xiv 1, 3 (9); xvi 7, 1 (183); see pp. 28 f. above. The shorter account, the *Bellum*, appears to be taken exclusively from him. In *Antiquities*, also, the detailed study in books xvi–xvii gives an impression of definite uniformity. By contrast, joinings are noticeable in book xv which point to the use of two sources; and in effect it is evident that another source—one unfavourable to Herod—is used besides Nicolaus of Damascus. Whether Josephus himself looked into the 'Memoirs of King Herod' (ὑπομνήματα τοῦ βασιλέως Ἡρῴδου) mentioned in ix 6, 3 (174) is, to say the least, very doubtful (cf. above p. 26). But although the history of Herod is treated in great detail, that of his immediate successors is thin. It almost seems as though Josephus had no written sources to turn to here. The narrative does not fill out again until the reign of Agrippa I (A.D. 41–4). Oral tradition was in any case available to him; he could learn about Agrippa I through his son, Agrippa II. For the history of the last decades preceding the war he drew on his own reminiscences. The disproportionate thoroughness with which he recounts events in Rome at the time of the death of Caligula and the accession of Claudius in A.D. 41, which had nothing to do with Jewish history, is extremely conspicuous, xix 1–4 (1–273). There can be little doubt that this section is taken from a separate source written by a contemporary, possibly Cluvius Rufus.[17] Josephus directed particular attention to the history of the High Priests. His information makes it possible to trace the uninterrupted succession

17. Th. Mommsen, Hermes 4 (1870), pp. 322, 324, argued that the incident involving Cluvius Rufus in *Ant.* xix 1, 13 (91–2) could only have come from the historian's own pen. L. H. Feldman, *Josephus* (Loeb) IX, p. 212, note a, and Latomus 21 (1962), pp. 320 ff., does nothing to weaken the hypothesis. For the work and outlook of the historian, see also A. Momigliano, 'Osservazioni sulle fonti per la storia di Caligola, Claudio, Nerone', Rend. d. Accad. d. Lincei 8 (1932), p. 305; M. P. Charlesworth, 'The Tradition about Caligula', Cambr. Hist. Journ. 4 (1933), pp. 105–19; D. Timpe, 'Römische Geschichte bei Flavius Josephus', Historia 9 (1960), pp. 474–502.

of these religious leaders from the time of Alexander the Great to the destruction of Jerusalem. It may be assumed that priestly documents, from at least the time of Herod the Great on, were available to him for this. For great value was attached to the maintenance of the priestly records, and great care expended on them, *c. Ap.* i 7 (31); *Vita* i 1 (6).[18] Finally, the official documents which Josephus frequently incorporates into his narrative are of the greatest interest: xiii 9, 2 (259–64); xiv 8, 5 (145–55); xiv 10 (188–264); xiv 12 (306–22); xvi 6 (162–73); xix 5 (280–5); xx 1, 2 (10–14). The most numerous are those from the times of Caesar and Augustus guaranteeing to the Jews the free exercise of their religion.[19]

18. Cf. H. Bloch, *Die Quellen des Josephus* (1879), pp. 147 ff. J. von Destinon, *Die Quellen des Josephus* (1882), pp. 29 ff. G. Hölscher, *Die Hohenpriesterliste bei Josephus und die evangelische Chronologie* (1940).

19. Where Josephus took these documents from is obscure. He claims that he saw them all in the great library of the Capitol, *Ant.* xiv 10, 26 (266); cf. also xiv 10, 1 (188). This library, after its destruction by fire in the battles of A.D. 69, Tac. *Hist.* iii 71–2; Suet. *Vitell.* 15; Dio lxv 17; Jos. *B.J.* iv 11, 4 (649), was in fact restored by Vespasian, Suet. *Div. Vesp.* 8. But it can have held only a small part of the documents given by Josephus; namely, only the Roman documents, and probably only the *senatus consulta*, but certainly not the decrees (*ψηφίσματα*) of cities of Asia Minor, a great number of which are quoted (cf. in general Th. Mommsen, *Römisches Staatsrecht* III 2 (1888), pp. 1004–21; RE s.v. 'Archiv' and 'Tabularium'. The documents were doubtless assembled from various places: Rome, Asia Minor and perhaps Palestine also. Due to the lively contacts that existed between Jewish congregations, Josephus could easily have obtained from foreign communities the official documents concerning them. Jewish congregations had their archives in which such papers were kept; cf. J. B. Frey, CIJ II, 775, a Jewish tomb inscription threatening the unauthorised user of the grave with a fine, ending with *ἀντίγραφον ἀπετέθη ἐν τῷ ἀρχίῳ τῶν Ἰουδαίων*). Since in the speech which Nicolaus of Damascus delivered in favour of the Jews before M. Agrippa during his stay in Asia Minor, on the occasion of their conflict with the cities, Jos. *Ant.* xvi 2, 4 (47–8), reference was made also to earlier Roman official documents in favour of the Jews, Niese concluded, Hermes 11 (1876), pp. 477–83, that the documents communicated by Josephus had already been assembled by Nicolaus of Damascus and were taken by him from this work. But this assumption is untenable, for (1) a considerable proportion of the documents relate to release from Roman military service, xiv 10, 11–19 (223–40), which had nothing to do with the conflict in question; (2) another section concerns Judaea, xiv 10, 2–10 (190–222),the circumstances of which were equally unconnected with it; (3) one document, xvi 6, 5 (169), has to do with the Jews of Cyrene and is therefore also unconcerned with the situation in Asia Minor; (4) two documents, xvi 6, 2 (162–5) and 7 (172–3), did not exist at the time of the conflict but are of a later date. Niese himself expressed his views somewhat more cautiously in his later article, Hist. Zeitschr. 40 (1896), p. 222. H. Willrich (*Judaica* (1900), pp. 40–8) believed he improved Niese's case in that he maintained, on the basis of Philo, *Legatio* 28 (179), that the collection was assembled by King Agrippa I when he intervened with Caligula in favour of the Alexandrian Jews. But unfortunately Josephus's collection contains no documents of this period for Alexandria, but on the other hand a great many for Asia Minor,

(3) *The Life* does not give a full description of Josephus's career, but deals almost exclusively with his activities as commanding officer in Galilee in A.D. 66/67, and indeed only with the preparatory measures put into effect by him prior to actual hostilities with the Romans, 7–74 (28–413). The short biographical notes at the beginning and end of the work, 1–6, 75–6 (1–27, 404–30) act merely as an introduction and conclusion to this main body of the contents. According to his remarks at the conclusion of the *Antiquities*, Josephus intended at that time to follow on with another account of the war and 'our experiences (i.e. of Jewish history) until the present day'; *Ant.* xx 12, 1 (267), *κἂν τὸ θεῖον ἐπιτρέπῃ, κατὰ περιδρομὴν ὑπομνήσω πάλιν τοῦ τε πολέμου καὶ τῶν συμβεβηκότων ἡμῖν μέχρι τῆς νῦν ἐνεστώσης ἡμέρας.* In point of fact, the *Life* sets out to be an addendum to the *Antiquities*. It begins with the enclitic *δέ* (*ἐμοὶ δὲ γένος ἐστὶν οὐκ ἄσημον*) and concludes with the words *σοὶ δ' ἀποδεδωκώς, κράτιστε ἀνδρῶν Ἐπαφρόδιτε, τὴν πᾶσαν τῆς ἀρχαιολογίας ἀναγραφὴν ἐπὶ τοῦ παρόντος ἐνταῦθα καταπαύω τὸν λόγον.* In the manuscripts also, the *Life* always forms the conclusion of *Antiquities*. Eusebius (*HE* iii 10, 8 f.) cites a passage from the *Life* with the remark that 'the words occur at the end of the *Antiquities*', and in all the extant manuscripts the *Life* is joined to *Antiquities* (with one exception; see Niese I, Prolegom. pp. v f.). It would nevertheless be a great mistake to regard the *Life* as a realization of the purpose indicated at the end of *Antiquities*. At that time, Josephus had in mind to continue his work on Jewish history until the then present time. But the *Life* is not this at all. It was obviously occasioned by an account of the Jewish war written by Justus of Tiberias (see above pp. 34–7)[20] presenting Josephus as the real organiser of the rebellion in Galilee. For Josephus in his later position in Rome this was most inconvenient. So he wrote a refutation in which he laid all the

---

which could be of no use to the Alexandrians. They are in a very bad condition and must have been treated with great negligence. At times, it is no more than fragments that Josephus transmits. No-one today doubts the essential authenticity of the documents. See J. Juster, *Les Juifs dans l'Empire Romain* I (1914), pp. 132 ff.; E. Bikermann, 'Une question d'authenticité. Les privilèges juifs', Ann. de l'Inst. de Philol. et d'Hist. Or. 13 (1953), pp. 11–34; R. Marcus, *Josephus* (Loeb) VII, app. DJ (bibliography).

20. Other opinions have been advanced by R. Laqueur, *Der. jüd. Historiker Fl. Jos.* (1920), pp. 56 ff. who took the kernel of the work to be a report of his activities in Galilee written for the Romans by Josephus before the fall of Jotapata and thus preceding the *Bellum*, and by M. Gelzer, 'Die Vita des Josephos', Hermes 80 (1952), pp. 67–90, who suggested that this account could have been composed in Alexandria. But Thackeray, *op. cit.*, pp. 17–19, offered stylistic arguments against such a view, and Schalit, 'Josephus und Justus', Klio 26 (1933), pp. 67–95 showed that *Vita* has the internal unity of one work, written for a definite purpose, that of combating the attacks of Justus.

blame on Justus[21] and showed himself as a friend of the Romans. The attempt is miserably weak, for Josephus himself cannot help mentioning facts which prove the opposite. To the beginning and end of this heated self-vindication he adds a few biographical notes and then publishes the whole as a supplement to *Antiquities*.

In spite of the enclitic δέ, the *Life* could therefore have been written some time after the *Antiquities*. It could, as R. Laqueur suggested, *Der jüdische Historiker Flavius Josephus* (1920), pp. 1–6, have been appended to a 'second edition' of the *Antiquities*. Some evidence, hard to dismiss, recommends this view. (1) The *Life* assumes the death of Agrippa II to have already occurred, 65 (359–60); see above, p. 45, (2) There appear to be two conclusions embodied in the text of the *Antiquities* (shown by Laqueur). In *Ant.* xx 12, 1 (259) Josephus writes: 'Here will be the end of my *Antiquities*, following which begins my account of the War'. A little later, xx 12, 1 (267): 'With this I shall conclude my *Antiquities*, contained in twenty books with 60,000 lines. If God wills, I shall, in a running account, again write of the war and of what has befallen us up to the present day.' (259–66) seems to be a complete conclusion, leading directly to the *Life* with the promise in (266) to give a brief account of his own lineage and story. But (267) expresses the different intention of writing a new *Bellum*; (259–66) may then be a new conclusion, composed when the *Life* was added to *Antiquities*. But the old conclusion still remains and follows immediately after the new one.

However, there are arguments for a date for *Vita* nearer that of *Antiquities*. (1) Josephus is careful to mention in *Life* 76 (429) honours done him by Domitian and Domitia, but no subsequent emperor is named. (2) If the Epaphroditus to whom both *Antiquities* and *Life* were dedicated was the freedman of Nero, they must have been published before his fall in A.D. 95 (see above, p. 48). But he could equally well be identified with M. Mettius Epaphroditus. It remains therefore uncertain when the *Life* was issued.[22]

(4) *Against Apion* or *On the Antiquity of the Jewish People*, two books. This work is not only, or even primarily, directed against the gram-

21. Whether Justus was in fact a Zealot is disputed; see Schalit, *op. cit.*, pp. 68–9, and above, p. 35.

22. Although it does not solve all the problems, Laqueur's theory has been widely accepted as a way of maintaining the close connection between *Vita* and *Ant.* at the same time as dating *Vita* to after A.D. 100. Cf. Thackeray, *op. cit.* and A. Pelletier, *Flavius Josèphe: Autobiographie* (1959), p. xiii. But L.-H. Vincent, 'Chronologie des oeuvres de Josèphe', RB n.s. 8 (1911), pp. 376–7 and Th. Frankfort, 'La date de l'autobiographie de Flavius Josèphe et des oeuvres de Justus de Tibériade', Rev. Belge de Philol. et d'Hist. 39 (1961), pp. 52–8, adhere to an earlier date for *Vita*. For arguments supporting this view see pp. 481–2 below.

marian Apion and his defamation of the Jewish people, but in general against the many, in part absurd, prejudices and malignant attacks which Jews of that period had to endure. It is a skilfully planned, well written and clever apology for Judaism. Its particular value is that it includes excerpts from writers whose works are no longer extant. On the authors attacked by Josephus, see vol. III, §33 vi 1. The title *Against Apion* is surely not the original one. Porphyry, *De abstinentia*, iv 11, quotes the work under the title *πρὸς τοὺς Ἕλληνας*, and early patristic writers (Origen, *contra Celsum* i 16; iv 11; Eusebius, *HE* iii 9, 4; *Praep. evang.* viii 7, 21; x 6, 15), under the title *περὶ τῆς τῶν Ἰουδαίων ἀρχαιότητος*. Both titles are probably equally old and authentic, for proof of the antiquity of the Jewish people constitutes, in fact, a main point in the apology. The heading *contra Apionem* is first used by Jerome (epist. lxx *ad Magnum oratorem*, 3, ed. Hilberg, CSEL liv, p. 704; *de viris illustr.* 13; cf. *adv. Jovinian.* ii 14, where he follows the passage from Porphyry cited above, but substitutes for the title proposed by that writer the one with which he was himself familiar). See vol. II, §30.[23] Since Josephus quotes in it from the *Antiquities*, i 1 (1); 10 (54), *Against Apion* was in any case written after that work, i.e., after A.D. 93. Like *Antiquities* and the *Life*, it is dedicated to Epaphroditus, i 1 (1); ii 41 (296).

Besides these four works, several of the Church fathers ascribe to Josephus the so-called Fourth Book of the Maccabees, or treatise *περὶ αὐτοκράτορος λογισμοῦ*. Its cast of thought is certainly close to that of Josephus: Jewish-Pharisaic with a touch of Greek philosophy. But it may be taken as certain that Josephus is not the author (see vol. III, §33, V, 4.

The work mentioned by Photius, *Bibliotheca*, cod. 48—*Ἰωσήπου Περὶ τοῦ παντός* or *Περὶ τοῦ παντὸς αἰτίας* or *Περὶ τῆς τοῦ παντὸς οὐσίας*—is a philosophical refutation of Plato of Christian origin and belongs to Hippolytus, the author of *Refutatio Omnium Haeresium*, who cites such a work as his own in *Haeres.* x 32 (under the title *περὶ τῆς τοῦ παντὸς οὐσίας*). Even Photius noticed this self-quotation and the Christian character of the composition. See A. v. Harnack, *Gesch. d. altchr. Lit.* I (1893), pp. 622–3.

At the end of *Antiquities*, xx 12 (268), he expresses his intention 'to compose a work in four books on the opinions that we Jews hold concerning God and His essence, as well as concerning the laws, that is, why according to them we are permitted to do some things while we are forbidden to do others'. By this he presumably did not mean various works (as many have thought) but one alone, which would treat of God's essential nature and provide a rational interpretation of

23. Cf. also on the title Niese, *Jos. Opp.* V, p. iii.

Mosaic law in a way similar to Philo's systematic presentation of the Mosaic legislation (cf. vol. III, §34. i, iii). In the earlier books of the *Antiquities*, too, he refers frequently to this proposed work; cf. vol. III §33. vii. In it he wished, among other things, to state the reasons for circumcision, *Ant.* i 10, 5 (192), and to explain why Moses permitted some animals to be eaten and others not, *Ant.* iii 11, 2 (260). Compare also *Ant.* Preface 4 (25); i 1, 1 (29); iii 5, 6 (94); 6, 6 (143); 8, 10 (223); iv 8, 4 (198), 44 (302). The composition appears never to have been completed, however.

Several references in *Antiquities* seem to imply that Josephus also wrote a history of the Seleucids. These statements are puzzling. He often remarks, in effect, that something mentioned by him briefly is also dealt with elsewhere.[24] Where this occurs with the passive formula καθὼς καὶ ἐν ἄλλοις δεδήλωται, it can, of course, refer to the historical works of other men; so *Ant.* xi 8, 1 (305); xii 10, 1 (390); xiii 4, 8 (119), 8, 4 (253), 13, 4 (371); xiv 6, 2 (98), 7, 3 (119, 122); 11, 1 (270). But not infrequently Josephus employs the first person, καθὼς καὶ ἐν ἄλλοις δεδηλώκαμεν, see *Ant.* vii 15, 3 (393); xii 5, 2 (244); xiii 2, 1 (36), 2, 4 (61) 4, 6 (108), 5, 11 (186), 10, 1 (271), 10, 4 (285), 12, 6 (347), 13, 5 (372). Four of these citations may be understood as alluding to passages of the known works of Josephus: *Ant.* vii 15, 3 (393) = *B.J.* i 2, 5 (61); *Ant.* xiii 10, 1 (271) = xiii 7, 1 (222); *Ant.* xiii 10, 4 (285) = *B.J.* vii 10 (407–35) and *Ant.* xiii 3 (62–73); *Ant.* xiii 13, 5 (372) = iii 10, 4 (245). For the rest, however, no such correspondences are traceable. They all relate to the history of the Seleucid kingdom from Antiochus Epiphanes to the end of the second century B.C., *Ant.* xii 5, 2 (244); xiii 2 1 (36); 2, 4 (61); 4, 6 (108; 5, 11 (186); 12, 6 (347). As nothing is known of Josephus having written a history of the Seleucids, Destinon maintained, *op. cit.* pp. 21–9, that all these references existed in Josephus's source and were taken over by him unchanged. Strange as this theory may appear, it should not be rejected out of hand. It is not without parallel in ancient history-writing. A ἡμεῖς appears several times in the works of Diodorus which cannot belong to him but only to his source.[25] There is also the celebrated ἡμεῖς in the Acts of the Apostles which the compiler may have taken from the so-called 'We-Source'. In favour of Destinon's interpretation it can be said in particular that sometimes this kind of reference appears in *Antiquities* as well as in parallel passages in the *War*, although both works derive independently of one another from a common source, *Ant.* xiv 7, 3 (119) = *B.J.* i 8, 8 (179); *Ant.* xiv 7, 3

24. The most complete earlier studies of these passages are J. von Destinon, *Die Quellen des Flavius Josephus* (1882), pp. 21–3, and H. Drüner, *Untersuchungen über Josephus* (1896), pp. 82–94. See more recently, H. Petersen, 'Real and Alleged Literary Projects of Josephus', AJPh 79 (1958), pp. 259–74.

25. C. Wachsmuth, *Einleitung in das Studium der alten Geschichte* (1895), p. 96.

(122) = *B.J.* i 8, 9 (182). On the other hand, in some of the passages in question the writer speaking immediately before or afterwards in the first person is certainly Josephus himself; so xii 5, 2 (244) and xii 12, 6 (347). In addition, the suspect formulas are worded exactly the same as those which certainly originate from Josephus, xiii 10, 4 (285) and 13, 5 (372). It is therefore difficult to reach any firm conclusion.[26]

The most contradictory judgments have been expressed on the character of Josephus and his credibility as a historian. In antiquity and the Middle Ages, he was as a rule greatly overrated, Jerome going so far as to name him the 'Greek Livy'[27]; in more recent times, critics have treated him with greater harshness. It is necessary to strike the right balance. No-one would wish to defend his character. The basic features of his personality were vanity and complacency. And even if he was not the dishonourable traitor that his *Life* would seem to imply, nevertheless his going over to the Romans and his intimate alliance with the Flavian imperial house was performed with more ingenuity and indifference than was seemly in a person mourning the downfall of his nation. As a writer, too, he had his great imperfections. But to be fair, it must be said that his main weakness was not to his discredit, namely that he wrote with the intention of praising his people. It was to this end that he invested the history of the remote past with a halo, and the same interest moved him to treat more recent history similarly. The Pharisees and Sadducees were the representatives of philosophical schools concerned with the problems of freedom and immortality. Messianic expectation, which on account of the political claims attached to it constituted the more powerful incentive to rebellion, was passed over in silence in order to conceal Jewish hostility to Rome. It was not the people who wished for war against the empire; they were led astray by a few fanatics. In all these respects, Josephus certainly gives a distorted picture. Moreover, his writings are not all of equal value. The *War* is, without question, much more carefully composed than *Antiquities*. Entering into the smallest detail, he provides an account the reliability of which there is no reason to doubt. The long speeches which he places in the mouth of his heroes are, of course, free rhetorical performances, and his figures must not be taken

26. For criticism of Destinon, see Gutschmid, *Kleine Schriften* IV, pp. 372 f. (Josephus refers to a preliminary study to *Ant.*); H. Drüner, *Untersuchungen über Josephus* (1896), pp. 70–94 (the work alluded to was not published by Josephus but merely served as a preparation for *Ant.*); G. F. Unger, SAM (1897), pp. 223–44 (Josephus wrote a history of Syria, not that of the Seleucids only); H. Petersen, AJPh 79 (1958), pp. 259–74 (all the formulas refer, even if imprecisely, to surviving works of Josephus, or to extant sources for these works, 1 Mac., Polybius).

27. *Ep.* xxii *ad Eustochium* 35, 8, 'Iosephus, Graecus Livius' (ed. Hilberg, CSEL liv, p. 200).

too seriously either. But Josephus shares these frailties with many ancient historians and they do not impair the reliability of the rest. The only passage not included in this favourable judgment is his version of his capture in Jotapata *B.J.* iii 8 (340–408). The situation is considerably different in regard to *Antiquities*, the last books of which seem to have been written in weariness. Furthermore, the sources are often employed not only negligently, but also—at least, where it is possible to check them—with great freedom and arbitrariness. Yet there is occasional evidence of a critical attitude towards them, *Ant.* xiv 1, 3 (9); xvi 7, 1 (183–6); xix 1, 10 (68–9); 1, 14 (106–8). Needless to say, the value of the various sections differs according to the sources used.

Among Christians, Josephus was read diligently from the beginning. He became known in the west through a Latin translation of his works (with the exception of the *Life*) and a free paraphrase of the *War*. On the origin of these texts, the following evidence exists. (1) Jerome, *epist.* lxxi *ad Lucinium*, 5, 'Porro Iosephi libros et sanctorum Papiae et Polycarpi volumina falsus ad te rumor pertulit a me esse translata: quia nec otii mei nec virium est, tantas res eadem in alteram linguam exprimere venustate'. From this it follows not only that Jerome made no translation of Josephus, but that in his time there was still no translation of his works, or at least part of his works, available, otherwise there would have been no need of one. (2) Cassiodorus, *Institutiones* I 17, 1 (ed. Mynors, p. 55), 'Ut est Ioseppus, paene secundus Livius, in libris antiquitatum Iudaicarum late diffusus, quem pater Hieronymus scribens ad Lucinum Betticum propter magnitudinem prolixi operis a se perhibet non potuisse transferri. Hunc tamen ab amicis nostris, quoniam est subtilis nimis et multiplex, magno labore in libris viginti duobus (i.e. 20 books of *Ant.* and 2 books of *c. Ap.*) converti fecimus in Latinum. Qui etiam et alios septem libros captivitatis Iudaicae mirabili nitore conscripsit quorum translationem alii Hieronymo, alii Ambrosio, alii deputant Rufino; quae dum talibus ascribitur, omnino dictionis eximiae merita declarantur'. From this it may be taken as certain that the extant Latin translations of *Antiquities* and *contra Apionem* were prepared at the suggestion of Cassiodorus, hence in the sixth century A.D. But there is no cause whatever for ascribing this translation to a certain Epiphanius simply because Cassiodorus states two sentences later that he had made Epiphanius re-edit the *Historia tripartita*.

It is uncertain whether Cassiodorus's remarks concerning the *War* refer to the Latin translation usually ascribed to Rufinus (so Niese, *Jos. Opp.* VI, p. xx, n. 5; V. Ussani, 'Studi preparatori ad una edizione della traduzione latina in sette libri del Bellum Iudaicum', BPEC n.s. 1 (1945), p. 94; F. Blatt, *The Latin Josephus* I, introd. p. 17), or to the free Latin paraphrase which carries in the editions the name of Hegesippus (so F. Vogel, *De Hegesippo* (1881), p. 33; C. Mras, *Hegesippus* iii, CSEL lxvi, 2 (1932), Praef., p. xxv). The designation of the work as a translation permits either interpretation, for the free paraphrase has also been accepted as a translation. But Cassiodorus's comments concerning the style favour its ascription to Hegesippus. For even if Rufinus wrote in good Latin, nevertheless 'dictionis eximiae merita' can only have been in praise of Hegesippus's Sallustian style. If the latter is meant, it would follow from the words of Cassiodorus (1) that this work was anonymous, since Cassiodorus knew only of conjectures concerning the author; (2) that the literal translation did not exist at the time of Cassiodorus, otherwise he would not have been able to omit mentioning it and to refer only to the free paraphrase, since after all he wishes to say that the rendering into Latin of the *War* had already been attended to. In order to be able to settle the question with any certainty, it would be necessary to inquire whether Latin writers down to the ninth century (from which period the oldest manuscripts of the so-called Rufinus derive) used the *War* in the form of the so-called Rufinus or in that of the so-called Hegesippus. That Rufinus was responsible for the literal translation is in any case unlikely in view of the fact that no translation of Josephus is mentioned in Gennadius's catalogue of Rufinus's translations, *De viris illustr.* 17. For the arguments against Rufinus's authorship see also V. Ussani, *op. cit.*

The Latin paraphrase of the *War* carries in the editions the name Egesippus or Hegesippus. This is certainly merely a corruption of Josephus, in Greek Ἰώσηπος, Ἰώσηππος, Ἰώσιππος, in Latin *Iosepus*, *Ioseppus*, *Iosippus* (these are the oldest forms; Iosephus does not appear in manuscripts until the ninth century, see Niese's edition of Josephus, I, *proleg.* v).[28] But one ms. tradition mentions, besides the name of the Greek author Iosippus or Hegesippus, that of the work's Latin translator, Ambrose of Milan, 'Ambrosius epi. de greco transtulit in latinum'. However, although the work stems from the time of Ambrose (C. Mras dates it to *c.* A.D. 375, *Praef.*, p. xxxi), it cannot be attributed to him, as was shown by the exhaustive research of F. Vogel, *De Hegesippo* (1881). Mras, *op. cit.*, p. xxxii argues that the author was a Jew converted to Christianity.

In this free version, the original text of Josephus is frequently abridged and sometimes expanded. The longest interpolation deals with Simon Magus, iii 2; others relate to particular geographical observations. The seven books of Josephus are compressed into five.

28. The corruption to 'Hegesippus' may have been caused by a recollection of Hegesippus, the author of the five ὑπομνήματα on Church history which Eusebius used as a source (*HE* IV 22; cf. Jerome, *De viris illustr.* 22). There is no connection between the two writers. See K. Mras, 'Die Hegesippus-Frage', Anzeiger der Oesterr. Ak. d. Wiss. in Wien, Phil.-hist. Kl. 95 (1958), p. 143.

In the foreword, the writer mentions an earlier work on the history of the Jewish kings following the four biblical books of Samuel and Kings. He repeatedly introduces his Christian viewpoint, ii 12; v 2, 32, 44, and cites Josephus as though he were another author; i 1, 8; three times in ii 12, on pp. 163–5 in the ed. of Ussani. He felt that he was himself a writer, not a translator.

The work first appeared in Paris in 1510. The latest edition is by V. Ussani, *Hegesippi qui dicitur historiae libri quinque* I–II, CSEL lxvi (1932–60); cf. also *Hegessipus qui dicitur sive Egesippus de bello Iudaico ope codicis Casellani recognitus*, ed. C. F. Weber and J. Caesar (1864). On Hegesippus see F. Vogel, *De Hegesippo qui dicitur Josephi interprete* (1881); V. Ussani, 'La questione e la critica del così detto Egesippo', Studi ital. di filol. class. 14 (1906), pp. 245–361; O. Scholz, *Die Hegesippus-Ambrosius Frage* (1913); M. Schanz, *Geschichte der römischen Literatur* IV ([2]1914), pp. 109 ff.; W. F. Dwyer, *The Vocabulary of Hegesippus* (1935); K. Mras, 'Die Hegesippus-Frage', Anzeiger d. Oesterr. Ak. d. Wiss., Phil.-hist. Kl. 95 (1958), pp. 143–53; 'Drei seltsame Stellen bei Josippus', Wiener Stud. 74 (1961), pp. 138–41.

The Latin translation of the works of Josephus was first printed by Johann Schüssler in Augsburg in 1470, but the best edition of the old Latin version is that of Basel (1524); see B. Niese, *Jos. Opp.* I, p. lviii; A. v. Gutschmid, *Kleine Schriften* IV, pp. 380 f. Subsequent editions are frequently revised after the Greek text. The first volume of a new edition of the Latin Josephus, containing also a classification of the manuscripts, has been issued by F. Blatt, *The Latin Josephus. I. Introduction and Text. The Antiquities: Books I–V* (1958). *Contra Apionem* was edited by C. Boysen, CSEL xxxvii (1898). See further Gutschmid, *op. cit.* IV, pp. 378–80 and Niese's *Prolegomena* to the separate volumes of his edition. For the qualities of the translation of *Ant.* and *c. Ap.* and for evidence of Cassiodorus's influence on the work, see F. Blatt, *op. cit.*, pp. 17–24.

A Syriac translation of Book VI of the *War* is included in *Translatio Syra Pescitto Veteris Testamenti ex codice Ambrosiano saec. VI photolithographice edita* by A. M. Ceriani I–II (1876–83).

On the Hebrew Yosippon, see below pp. 117–18.

A free Slavonic version of the *War* attracted considerable attention at one time, mainly on account of a theory propounded by R. Eisler, *ΙΗΣΟΥΣ ΒΑΣΙΛΕΥΣ ΟΥ ΒΑΣΙΛΕΥΣΑΣ* (1929), translated, abridged and modified by A. H. Krappe, *The Messiah Jesus and John the Baptist according to Flavius Josephus' recently rediscovered 'Capture of Jerusalem' and other Jewish and Christian Sources* (1931). According to Eisler, the Slavonic version derives, at least indirectly, from Josephus's own Aramaic original, perhaps through an intermediate Greek version made by his assistants. The text has been edited by V. Istrin, *La prise de*

Jérusalem de Josèphe le Juif I–II (1934–8) and N. A. Meshcherskii, *Istoriga iudeskoig voiny Josifa Flaviga* (1958).

For criticism of Eisler, see H. Lewy, Deutsche Literaturzeitung 51 (1930), pp. 481–94; S. Zeitlin, *Josephus on Jesus with particular Reference to the Slavonic Josephus and the Hebrew Josippon* (1931); cf. also JQR 20 (1929–30), pp. 1–50; 21 (1930–1), pp. 377–417. Zeitlin dates the work to the seventh century; Meščerskij, on linguistic grounds, to the eleventh. The Slavonic account of the Essenes has been reconsidered since the Qumran discoveries but is unlikely to contain any original early material; see A. Rubinstein, 'Observations on the Old Russian Version of Josephus' Wars', JSS 2 (1957), pp. 329–48; cf. also E. H. del Medico, 'Les Esséniens dans l'oeuvre de Flavius Josèphe', Byzantinoslavica 13 (1952-3), pp. 193–202.

For the manuscripts of the Greek text see the Prolegomena to the individual volumes of Niese's edition.

Bibliography

No detailed list is necessary as there are two recent bibliographical surveys:

Feldman, L. H., *Studies in Judaica; Scholarship on Philo and Josephus*, 1937–62 (1963).

Schreckenburg, H., *Bibliographie zu Flavius Josephus* [1470–1968], (1968).

Editions:

Niese, B., *Flavii Josephi Opera* I–VII (1887–95).

Naber, S. A., *Flavii Josephi Opera Omnia* I–VI (1888–96).

Text and Translation:

Thackeray, H. St. J., Marcus R., Feldman, L. H., *Josephus* I–IX [Loeb Classical Library] (1926–65). The work includes also notes, appendices and specialised bibliographies.

Reinach Th., Blum, L., *Flavius Josèphe: Contre Apion* (1930).

Pelletier, A., *Flavius Josèphe: Autobiographie* (1959).

Michel, O., Bauernfeind O., *Flavius Josephus: De Bello Judaico. Der jüdische Krieg* I–III (1959–69). With notes and excursuses.

Translations:

Whiston, W., *The Genuine Works of Flavius Josephus* (1737). Rev. by Shilleto, A. R. (1900–1903).

Reinach, Th. (ed.), *Oeuvres complètes de Flavius Josèphe* I–VII (1900–32).

Ricciotti, G., *Flavio Giuseppe* I–IV (1937–63).

Schalit. A., *Ḳadmoniyot ha-Yehudim* [Jewish Antiquities] I–III (1955–63). Hebrew, with a detailed introduction.

Lexica and Concordance:

Thackeray, H. St. J., Marcus, R., *A Lexicon to Josephus* I–IV (1930–55). Incomplete.

Rengstorf, K. H. (ed.), *A Complete Concordance to Flavius Josephus* Suppl. I: *Namenwörterbuch zu Flavius Josephus*, by A. Schalit (1968).

General:
Niese, B., 'Josephus', HERE VII (1914), pp. 569–79.
Hölscher, G., 'Josephus', RE IX (1916), cols. 1934–2000.
Laqueur, R., *Der jüdische Historiker Flavius Josephus* (1920).
Thackeray, H. St. J., *Josephus, the Man and the Historian* (1929).

On Bellum and Vita:
Weber, W., *Josephus und Vespasian* (1921).
Drexler, H., 'Untersuchungen zu Josephus und zur Geschichte des jüdischen Aufstandes 66–70', Klio 19 (1925), pp. 277–312.
Schalit, A., 'Josephus und Justus. Studien zur Vita des Josephus' Klio 26 (1933), pp. 67–95.
Gelzer, M., 'Die Vita des Josephos', Hermes 80 (1952), pp. 67–90.

On philosophy and theology:
Schlatter, A., *Wie sprach Josephus von Gott?* (1910).
Guttmann, H., *Die Darstellung der jüdischen Religion bei Flavius Josephus* (1928).
Schlatter, A., *Die Theologie des Judentums nach dem Bericht des Josephus* (1932).
Delling, G., 'Josephus und das Wunderbare', NT 2 (1958), pp. 291–309.
Delling, G., 'Josephus und die heidnische Religionen', Klio 43–5 (1965), pp. 263–9.

On the text and canon of the Bible:
Mez, A., *Die Bible des Josephus untersucht für Buch V–VII des Archäologie* (1895).
Fell, W., 'Der Bibelkanon des Flavius Josephus'. BZ 7 (1909) pp. 1–16, 113–22, 235–44.
Rahlfs, A., 'Stellung des Josephus zu Lucian', *Septuagintastudien* III (1911, [2]1965), pp. 80–111.
Ricciotti, G., 'Il testo della Bibbia in Flavio Giuseppe', Atti del XIX Congr. Internaz. degli Orientalisti (1935).
Schalit, A., 'Evidence of an Aramaic Source in Josephus' Antiquities of the Jews', ASTI 4 (1965), pp. 163–88.

On haggadah and halakhah:
Bloch, H., *Die Quellen des Flavius Josephus in seiner Archäologie* (1879), pp. 23–53.
Thackeray, H. St. J., 'Josephus', HDB Extra Vol. (1904), pp. 461–73.
Rappaport, S., *Agada und Exegese bei Flavius Josephus* (1930).
Heller, B., 'Grundzüge der Aggada des Flavius Josephus', MGWJ 80 (1936), pp. 237–46, 363.
Heinemann, I., 'Josephus' Method in the Presentation of Jewish Antiquities', Zion 5 (1940), pp. 180–203 (Hebrew).
Feldman, L. H., 'Hellenizations in Josephus' Version of Esther', PAPLA 101 (1970), pp. 143–70.

On chronology and calendar:
Destinon, J. von, *Die Chronologie des Josephus* (1880).
Niese, B., 'Zur Chronologie des Josephus', Hermes 28 (1893), pp. 453–92.
Bosse, A., 'Die chronologischen Systeme im Alten Testament und bei Josephus', Mitteil. d. Vorderasiat. Gesellsch. 13 (1908), pp. 101–76.

On the non-biblical sources of Antiquities:
Bloch, H., *Die Quellen des Flavius Josephus . . .* (1879).
Destinon, J. von, *Die Quellen des Flavius Josephus in der jüdischen Archäologie Buch xii–xvii* (1882).

On documents used by Josephus:
Willrich, H., *Urkundenfälschung in der hellenistisch-jüdischen Literatur* (1924).
Bikerman, E., 'Une question d'authenticité: les privilèges juifs', AIPhHOS 13 (1953), pp. 11–34.

On geography and topography:
Klein, S., 'Hebräische Ortsnamen bei Josephus', MGWJ 59 (1915), pp. 156–69.
Kahrstedt, U., *Syrische Territorien in hellenistischer Zeit* (1926).
Hollis, F. J., *The Archaeology of Herod's Temple* (1934).
Abel, F.-M., 'Topographie du siège de Jérusalem en 70', RB 56 (1949), pp. 238–58.
Vincent, L.-H., Stève, A. M., *Jérusalem de l'Ancien Testament* I–III (1954–6), pp. 90–6, 182–95, 432–7, 517–25.
Kallai, Z., 'The Biblical Geography of Flavius Josephus', *4th World Congr. of Jew. St., Abstr. of Papers* (1965), pp. 1–2.

On c. Ap.:
Gutschmid, A. von, *Kleine Schriften* IV (1893), pp. 336–589.
Momigliano, A., 'Intorno al "Contro Apione",' Riv. di Filol. 59 (1931), pp. 485–503.

On the Testimonium Flavianum:
See below, §17.

D. Greek and Latin Authors

This section does not attempt to list all the Greek and Latin authors providing information on Jewish history, but confines itself to those who are of special significance. For the history of the Jewish people, the extant Greek and Roman historians provide relatively limited evidence. Of greater value is the insight into the general characteristics of Judaism obtainable from contemporary authors, especially the satirists such as Horace and Juvenal. The texts of some of these were collected by T. Reinach, *Textes d'auteurs grecs et romains relatifs au Judaïsme* (1895); for the new edition by M. Stern see p. 41 above. In addition, however, to texts relating directly to the Jews, particular attention must be paid to the historians on whom we depend for the history of Syria during the Seleucid and Roman periods. For the history of Palestine is intimately linked to the general history of Syria in our period. The historians, therefore, who deal with this, also belong to the sources for this era. The references to editions and commentaries are intended as no more than a selection for basic guidance. Current bibliography of all classical authors is provided by the periodical l'Année Philologique.

I. Greek Writers

1. Polybius of Megalopolis in Arcadia. One of the thousand distinguished Achaeans transported to Rome in 167 B.C., he was detained there, or at least in Italy, for sixteen years. During his long residence

in Rome and Italy he became convinced of the inevitability of the Roman domination of the world. This idea was expressed in his *History*, which described in forty books the gradual rise of Rome to world power from 220 to 146 B.C. Only the first five of these are fully extant; of the rest, only more or less extensive fragments survive, for the most part in the collection of Excerpts made under Constantine Porphyrogenitus (cf. above, p. 30). For the present purposes, only the last fifteen books, xxvi–xl, come into consideration. The standard text is the Teubner edition by Th. Büttner-Wobst (1889–1905); note also the Loeb edition by W. R. Paton (1922–7). The essential tool for the study of the remains of Books xix–xl will be vol. III of F. W. Walbank, *A Historical Commentary on Polybius*.

2. Diodorus. Born in Agyrium in Sicily (hence called 'Siculus'), he lived in the period of Caesar and Octavian. He wrote a lengthy universal history which he called *Βιβλιοθήκη*. It consisted of forty books and covered a period of eleven hundred years extending to the conquest of Gaul and Britain by Julius Caesar. Extant are Books i–v (the early history of Egypt and Ethiopia, of the Assyrians and the other peoples of the East, as well as the Greeks); Books xi–xx (from the Persian Wars, 480 B.C., to the history of the successors of Alexander the Great, ending 302 B.C.). Of the remaining books, only fragments survive, chiefly in the collection of Excerpts of Constantine Porphyrogenitus (cf. above, p. 30). Note the text with Latin translation by L. Dindorf (1860–8), and the Teubner text by F. Vogel and C. T. Fischer (1888–96). There is no modern commentary on Diodorus. The most useful instrument of study is now the Loeb text in twelve volumes (1933–67). Vol. XII (1967) contains the text and translation, with historical notes, of the fragments of Books xxxiii–xl, and a general index to the whole work.

3. Strabo of Amaseia in Pontus lived from about 64/3 B.C. to at least A.D. 21. Of his works, there remains extant only the *Geography* (in seventeen books) written towards the end of his life. Among its numerous historical passages are many which are of value for the history of Syria. In the description of Palestine, xvi 2, 28–46 (759–65), Strabo used, among others, a source which seems to present the situation in the period before Pompey, for he describes Gaza, which was destroyed by Alexander Jannaeus, as *μένουσα ἔρημος*, xvi 2, 30 (759), without mentioning its subsequent reconstruction by Gabinius, even if on a different site. Similarly the forcible conversion of Joppa and Gazara (Gadara) seems still recent to Strabo's source, xvi 2, 28–9 (759). It is possible that it is Posidonius, who is frequently cited by Strabo in this part of the *Geography*; see FGrH 87 F65–7, where Posidonius is explicitly named, and F70 = Strabo xvi 2, 34–45 (760–4), where he is not. Teubner text by A. Meinecke (1851–2); Loeb text (1917–32); F. Sbordone, *Strabonis Geographica* I–II (1963); W. Aly,

Strabonis Geographica I–II (1968); Budé text, ed. G. Aujac, F. Lasserre (1966–). See in general W. Aly, *Strabon von Amaseia: Untersuchungen über Text, Aufbau und Quellen der Geographika* (1957).

4. Plutarch. Born shortly before A.D. 50 in Chaeronea in Boeotia, Trajan honoured him with consular insignia and Hadrian named him procurator of Greece. In addition, it is known that he performed the office of Archon in Chaeronea and also acted as priest of Pythian Apollo at Delphi. He died after 120 A.D. The works of Plutarch to be considered here are the parallel biographies (*βίοι παράλληλοι*) of distinguished Greeks and Romans, of which fifty are extant. Those of Crassus, Pompey, Caesar, Brutus and Antony are of especial relevance to Jewish history. Teubner text of the *Lives* (1914–39) and revised ed. in progress (1960–); Loeb edition (1914–28); Budé text, ed. R. Flacelière, in progress (1957–). Of the *Lives* mentioned above there is a commentary on the *Caesar* by A. Garzetti (1954).

5. Appian. At the end of the preface to his *Roman History*, Appian describes himself as 'Appian of Alexandria, who attained the highest position in my native city and appeared as advocate at Rome before the Emperors, after which they considered me worthy to be made their procurator.' Scattered references in his works and in the letters of Fronto show that he lived under Trajan, Hadrian and Antoninus Pius (see PIR² A 943). His *History* was written under Antoninus Pius, about A.D. 150, and covered the history of Rome in twenty-four books, Appian chose, in place of the usual synchronistic method, the ethnographic, relating the history of each country continuously up to the moment of its conquest by Rome. In this way the history of Rome is divided into a series of separate histories of the individual lands and peoples absorbed into the Roman Empire. Of the twenty-four books the following remains: fragments of Books i–v and ix; the complete text of vi *'Ιβηρική (ἱστορία)*, vii *'Αννιβαϊκή*, viii *Λιβυκὴ καὶ Καρχηδονική*, xi *Συριακή*, xii *Μιθριδάτειος*, xiii–xvii *'Εμφύλια* (the Roman civil wars), xxiii *Δακική* or *'Ιλλυρική*. The five extant books on the civil wars (xiii–xvii) are cited usually as Appian *BC* i, ii, iii, iv, v, and the remaining books according to their contents: *Libyca* (or *Punica*), *Syriaca*, etc. Teubner text of *BC* i–v (1902), and edition and commentary by E. Gabba of i (²1967) and v (1970); revised Teubner text of the other books by P. Vierek and A. G. Roos (1962); Loeb text of *BC* (1912–13).

6. Cassius Dio. Born at Nicaea in Bithynia about A.D. 163/4, Cassius Dio followed a senatorial career in Rome and was praetor in 194 and consul about 205. In 229 he was consul for the second time and retired from public life. The writing of his *Roman History* took place approximately in the first two decades of the third century; it was subsequently continued by him up to A.D. 229. The work consists of eighty books and includes the whole of Roman history from the arrival of Aeneas in

Latium up to 229. The extant portions consist of small fragments of Books i–xxi, plus the epitome by Ioannes Zonaras; more significant passages of Books xxii–xxxv; Books xxxvi–liv complete (from the wars of Lucullus and Pompey with Mithridates to the death of Agrippa in the year 12 B.C.); significant portions of Books lv–lx; of substantial Excerpts made under Constantine Porphyrogenitus (see p. 30 above), the Epitomes made by Xiphilinus in the eleventh century and Ioannes Zonaras in the twelfth; and part of the original of Books lxxix–lxxx. The essential text is that of U. P. Boissevain, vols. I–III (1895–1901), with IV (*index historicus*, ed. Smilda). Note also the Loeb text (1914–27). There is no modern commentary. For his references to the Jews, note F. Millar, *A Study of Cassius Dio* (1964), pp. 178–9.

II. Latin Writers

1. Cicero. Born 3 January 106 B.C. at Arpinum; died 7 December 43 B.C., a victim of the proscriptions of Antonius, Octavian and Lepidus. Cicero's speeches and letters are an essential source for the history of his time, and also contain references to the history of Syria during the years 57–43 B.C. For editions of Cicero's letters in chronological order note R. Y. Tyrrell and L. C. Purser, *The Correspondence of Cicero* ([2]1885–1915), and the Budé text in progress, ed. L.-H. Constans and J. Bayet (1940–); the letters to Atticus are edited with translation and notes by D. R. Shackleton-Bailey (1965–8). There is an almost complete Budé text, with French translation and notes, of Cicero's speeches (1949–66), and a Loeb text (1923–58). Of those speeches which are particularly informative on the history of Syria, there are commentaries on *De provinciis consularibus* by H. E. Butler and M. Cary (1924), and on *In Pisonem* by R. G. M. Nisbet (1961).

2. Livy. Born in Patavium (Padua), perhaps in 64 B.C.; died in the same place, perhaps in A.D. 17 as Jerome records, but possibly earlier. His great *History* (*Ab urbe condita libri*) dealt, in 142 books, with the history of Rome from its Foundation to the death of Drusus in 9 B.C. Only 35 books are extant, namely i–x and xxi–xlv. Of these, only xli–xlv, on the years 178–167 B.C., are relevant to Jewish history. But much valuable and relevant material survives in the *Periochae*, or summaries, of xlvi to cxlii and in the Oxyrhynchus Epitome of xxxvii to xl and xlviii–lv. Books xli–v, the *Periochae* and the Oxyrhynchus fragments are available in the Teubner text of Livy, vol. IV (1959).

3. *Res Gestae Divi Augusti*. Augustus left behind him at his death an account of the most important acts of his reign, to be transcribed on brass tablets and placed before his mausoleum, Suet. *Div. Aug.* 101: *indicem rerum a se gestarum, quem vellet incidi in aeneis tabulis, quae ante Mausoleum statuerentur*. This account is available primarily from

the text inscribed in Latin and Greek on the marble walls of the Temple of Augustus at Ancyra in Galatia. Fragments of another copy of the Greek text come from a temple at Apollonia in Pisidia, and of the Latin text, from Antioch in Pisidia. This extensive work, together with Cassius Dio and Suetonius, constitutes the major source for the reign of Augustus. Note the editions by J. Gagé (1935), with a full commentary and the best account of the nature of the text; S. Riccobono (1945); H. Volkmann (1957); H. Malcovati, *Imperatoris Caesaris Augusti Operum Fragmenta* (^{5}1969), pp. lii–lxv (discussion and bibliography), 105–49 (text).

4. Tacitus. Born in A.D. 56 or 57, Tacitus was praetor in 88 and consul in 97; for the dates see R. Syme, *Tacitus* (1958), ch. vi. The date of his death is unknown, but he seems to have survived into the reign of Hadrian (A.D. 117–38). Of his two major historical works, the *Annales*, dealing in eighteen books with the reigns of Tiberius, Caligula, Claudius and Nero (i.e. A.D. 14–68) is acknowledged as the most important source for the history of that period, and also for the history of Syria. The annalistic arrangement is, however, not rigidly adhered to in relation to provincial affairs, including those of Syria and Judaea. Unfortunately, substantial parts of the text are missing. The extant sections are i–iv complete, v and vi in part, and xi–xvi with missing sections at the beginning of xi and the end of xvi. These parts cover the reign of Tiberius, except for a gap between A.D. 29 and 31, that of Claudius from A.D. 47 onwards, and that of Nero up to A.D. 66. Of his other main work, the *Historiae*, covering the reigns of Galba, Otho, Vitellius, Vespasian, Titus and Domitian (i.e. A.D. 69–96) in twelve books, only a small part remains, namely i–iv and a part of v dealing with the years A.D. 68–70. Note especially v 1–13, where Tacitus gives a brief survey of the history of the Jewish people up to the war with Titus. On this section see A. M. A. Hospers-Jansen, *Tacitus over de Joden: Hist.* 5, 2–13 (1949), in Dutch, with an extensive English summary. Teubner texts of the *Annales* (1960) and *Historiae* (1961) by E. Koestermann; commentaries on the *Annales* i–vi (^{2}1896) and xi–xvi (^{2}1907) by H. Furneaux, and on the whole *Annales* by E. Koestermann (1963–8); a commentary on the *Historiae* by H. Heubner (1963–).

5. Suetonius. In regard to his dates, it is known that Suetonius was a young man during the reign of Domitian (A.D. 81–96), that he was invested with the rank of a tribune under Trajan (98–117), and was *ab epistulis* under Hadrian (117–38), who, however, dismissed him for misconduct; for the evidence see R. Syme, *Tacitus* (1958), App. 76. Of his writings, only the *Vitae XII Imperatorum* is of concern here. The twelve Emperors are those from Caesar to Domitian. Teubner text by M. Ihm (1908); Loeb text (1914); commentaries on individual *Vitae*:

Divus Julius, H. E. Butler, M. Cary (1927); *Divus Augustus*, M. A. Levi (1951); *Divus Vespasianus*, A. W. Braithwaite (1927); *Domitianus*, J. Janssen (1919).

6. Pompeius Trogus (Justin). Trogus wrote under Augustus a universal history from Ninus to his own time, in forty-four books, with special regard to the history of Macedonia and the kingdoms of the Diadochi. It was substantial, accurate, and based on good Greek sources. The work itself is lost. There remain only the list of contents (*prologi*) of the forty-four books, an *Epitome* made by Justin (M. Iunianus Iustinus), probably in the second or third century, and a number of quotations in later writers. Even the epitome is so full of material that it constitutes an important source for the history of the Seleucids. For Justin's *Epitome Historiarum Philippicarum Pompei Trogi*, see the Teubner text by F. Ruehl and O. Seel (1935); cf. the Teubner ed. of the *Fragmenta* of Pompeius Trogus by O. Seel (1956). See O. Seel, *Eine römische Weltgeschichte: Studien zum Text der Epitome des Iustinus und zur Historik des Pompejus Trogus* (1972).

E. Rabbinic Literature

General introduction: L. Zunz, *Die gottesdienstlichen Vorträge der Juden* ([2]1892) = Zunz, hereafter; H. L. Strack, *Introduction to the Talmud and Midrash* (1945) = Strack; articles in the *Jewish Encyclopedia* I–XII (1901–6) = JE, and in *Encyclopaedia Judaica* (1971) = Enc. Jud. A useful outline may be found in M. Waxman, *A History of Jewish Literature* I (1960). These works cite selected literature. A virtually complete bibliography on any particular subject in Rabbinics may be gathered from the following sources:

S. Shunami, *Bibliography of Jewish Bibliographies* (1969).

For older works:

M. Steinschneider, *Catalogus Librorum Hebraeorum in Bibliotheca Bodleiana* (1852–60).

A. E. Cowley, *A Concise Catalogue of the Hebrew Printed Books in the Bodleian Library* (1929).

J. Zedner, *Catalogue of the Hebrew Books in the Library of the British Museum* (1867).

For more recent works:

British Museum General Catalogue of Printed Books (up to 1955); also the annual *Additions* (1963–).

Dictionary Catalog of the Jewish Collection: the New York Public Reference Library Department I–XIV (1960).

Dictionary Catalog of the Klau Library Cincinnati I–XXXII (1964).

Harvard University Library: Catalogue of Hebrew Books I–VI (1968).

Library of Congress Catalog (1950–).

For very recent literature (both books and articles):

Kirjath Sepher, Bibliographical Quarterly of the Jewish National and University Library, Jerusalem (1924–).

Some other useful sources:

Elenchus Bibliographicus Biblicus (a supplement of Biblica) (1923–).
J. R. Marcus and A. Bilgray, *An Index to Jewish Festschriften* (1937) (typescript).
J. Kohn, *Thesaurus of Hebrew Halakhic Literature* (1952).
G. Kisch and K. Roepke, *Schriften zur Geschichte der Juden* (1959).
I. Joel, *Index of Articles on Jewish Studies* I– (1966–).
C. Berlin, *Index to Festschriften in Jewish Studies* (from 1937 onwards) (1971).

Rabbinic literature is the result of the scholastic activity of the scribes and rabbis. It consists mainly, though not exclusively, of an academic exegesis of the text of the Bible. The aim pursued by them was twofold. They intended to develop Jewish law by means of an increasingly precise juridical discussion of the relevant parts of Scripture, and to enlarge on biblical history and evolve religious and moral ideas through a systematic combination of separate scriptural passages. The outcome of their legal endeavours was *halakhah*, or traditional law; that of their historico-doctrinal efforts, *haggadah*. Both concepts will be discussed more fully in vol. II, §25, iii.

Halakhah and haggadah were transmitted for several centuries mainly by oral tradition. The latter was adhered to strictly in matters of halakhah, while in the haggadic field more freedom was granted to insight and imagination. Rabbinic literature comprises the final recording of both in numerous books and tractates. Its written composition dates almost wholly from the age immediately following the period covered in the present study. Only the haggadic treatment of Genesis known as the 'Book of Jubilees', the documents discovered by the Dead Sea and elsewhere in the Judaean desert (see Section F below), and accounts of early halakhah now lost, fall within it. Although most of rabbinic literature reaches back no further than the end of the second century A.D., it is, nevertheless, an invaluable source of knowledge of the period preceding it, for the origins of the traditions it codifies may be traced back to the first century A.D., and sometimes even to the pre-Christian era.

Halakhah is partly expressed in direct connection with the text of the Bible in the form of a scriptural commentary, and partly arranged systematically according to subject-matter (e.g. prayers, tithes, sabbath, etc.). The latter type, represented by the Mishnah, the Tosefta, the Jerusalem Talmud and the Babylonian Talmud, quickly attained pre-eminence on account of its practical value. All these works may come under the collective title of Talmudic literature. In all of them, haggadah is mixed with halakhah, least in the Mishnah, most in the Babylonian Talmud.

Haggadah has been principally recorded in the form of Bible interpretation. Rabbinic commentary, whether halakhic or haggadic, is designated in general as *midrash*.

The popular and traditional (as opposed to the scholastic) exegesis of Scripture is expressed in the Aramaic Bible translations or Targums. Though no doubt pre-Christian in origin, they also have survived in compilations the earliest of which is unlikely to antedate the second century A.D.

Finally, mention must be made of historical works which transmit traditions relative to the period dealt with in the present book.

I. Talmudic Literature

1. The Mishnah

The word *Mishnah* (משנה) is rendered in patristic writings as 'repetition' (δευτέρωσις).[1] This is correct, for the root שנה signifies 'to repeat' (δευτεροῦν).[2] But in later Hebrew linguistic usage, 'to repeat' became synonymous with 'to teach or learn the oral law': the teacher recited the subject of the instruction with his students again and again.[3] In consequence, *mishnah* ('repetition') evolved into 'teaching (or study) of the law', i.e., teaching (or study) of the oral law as distinct from the written Torah.[4]

1. Cf. Jerome, *In Esaiam* 59 (CCL lxxviiiA, p. 685): 'contemnentes legem dei et sequentes traditiones hominum, quas illi δευτερώσεις vocant'. *In Mt.* 22:23 (PL, 26, 170): 'Pharisaei traditionum et observationum quas illi δευτερώσεις vocant, iustitiam praeferebant.' For passages from Epiphanius see below, n. 23. In the *Constit. apostol.* (ed. F. X. Funk, 1905): I, 6; II, 5; VI, 22, the ritual part of Mosaic law is called δευτέρωσις in distinction from the true νόμος of moral law. This δευτέρωσις was imposed on the Jews after they worshipped the golden calf. See also the Syriac *Didascalia Apostolorum*, ed. M. D. Gibson (1903), 6, 16–17. The teachers of δευτερώσεις were called δευτερωταί, Euseb., *Praep. ev.* xi 5, 3; xii 1, 4, ed. K. Mras; Jerome, *In Esaiam* 3, 14 (CCL lxxii, p. 53).

2. Cf. biblical Hebrew and mSanh. 11:2.

3. שָׁנָה=to teach. Cf. mTaan. 4:4, 'So R. Joshua used to teach' (היה שונה). Cf. Jerome, *Ep.* 121 *ad Algasiam*, 10, 21 (CSEL lvi, p. 49): 'Si quando certis diebus traditiones suas exponunt discipulis suis, solent dicere οἱ σοφοὶ δευτεροῦσιν, id est, sapientes docent traditiones'. In the sense of 'to learn', e.g., mAb. 2:4, 'Say not, I will learn (אשנה) when I have time, for perhaps you will have no time'. Cf. Strack, pp. 3, 237 and especially, W. Bacher, *Die exegetische Terminologie der jüdischen Traditionsliteratur* I (1899) pp. 193–4; II (1905), pp. 225–6.

4. Although *Mishnah* may sometimes be translated as 'repetition' or 'instruction' in general, it usually refers to the traditional doctrine of the law, especially as distinct from מקרא (the Bible): cf. mKidd. 1:10; mAb. 5:21. After a change in doctrine, the earlier teaching is called משנה ראשונה (first Mishnah), mKet. 5:3; mNaz. 6:1; mGitt. 5:6; mSanh. 3:4; mEduy. 7:2.

The work specifically designated as 'Mishnah' is the oldest extant code of traditional Jewish law.[5] Arranged according to subject matter, the material is divided into six 'Orders' (סדרים). These, in turn, are subdivided into sixty tractates (מסכתות) which have risen to sixty-three in the printed editions.[6] Each tractate is further split into chapters (פרקים) and paragraphs (משניות). The arrangement into chapters is ancient, but the rest is recent and varies according to the editions. The language of the Mishnah is post-biblical (Mishnaic) Hebrew; its contents, as may be expected, are almost purely halakhic. Apart from the predominantly haggadic Middoth and Aboth, haggadah figures only occasionally and in limited amounts at the end of tractates or in the explanation of individual halakhoth.[7]

The names and subjects of the sixty-three tractates are as follows:[8]

First Seder: *Zera'im* (Seeds)

1. *Berakhoth* (Benedictions): on blessings and prayers.
2. *Pe'ah* (Corner): on the corner of the field left unharvested for the poor, and in general on the claim of the poor to the produce of the land (cf. Lev. 19:9 f., 23:22; Dt. 24:19 ff.).
3. *Demai* (The doubtful): on the treatment of fruit when it is doubtful whether it has been tithed or not.
4. *Kila'im* (Diverse seeds): on the unlawful mixing of heterogeneous animals, plants, clothing (cf. Lev. 19:19; Dt. 22:9 ff.).
5. *Shebi'ith* (Seventh Year): on the sabbatical year (Exod. 23:11; Lev. 25:1 ff.; Dt. 15:1 ff.).
6. *Terumoth* (Heave-offerings): on priestly dues (Num. 18:8 ff.; Dt. 18:25 f.).
7. *Ma'asroth* (Tithes): on the tithe to the Levites (Num. 18:21).
8. *Ma'aser sheni* (Second Tithe): on the second tithe to be consumed in Jerusalem (Dt. 14:22 ff.).
9. *Ḥallah* (Dough): on the dough-offerings to be given to the priests (cf. Num. 15:17 ff.).

5. Earlier 'sectarian' attempts at codification have survived fragmentarily in the Dead Sea Scrolls (CDC Statutes and Temple Scroll) and Jub. 50.

6. According to the original numbering extant in cod. de Rossi 138, Baba Ḳamma, Baba Meẓi'a and Baba Bathra count as one tractate; so also Sanhedrin and Makkoth. Cf. Strack, p. 27.

7. Cf. Zunz, p. 91.

8. For a more detailed description, see Strack, pp. 29–64. The following system will be used in referring to rabbinic writings. Mishnah: chapter and paragraph (mBer. 4:3); Tosefta: chapter and paragraph according to Zuckermandel's edition (tBer. 4:3); Palestinian Talmud: tractate and folio in the Krotoschin edition (yBer. 7d); Babylonian Talmud: tractate and folio (bBer. 28b).

10. *'Orlah* (Foreskin): on the prohibition against using the fruit of newly-planted trees for the first three years (cf. Lev. 19:23–5).
11. *Bikkurim* (First Fruits): on the offering of the first fruits of the fields.

Second Seder: *Mo'ed* (Festival)

1. *Shabbath* (Sabbath): on the celebration of the Sabbath (cf. Exod. 20:10, 23:12; Dt. 5:14).
2. *'Erubin* (Blending): on the linking of separated places for freer movement on the Sabbath.
3. *Pesaḥim* (Passover Lambs): on the celebration of Passover (cf. Exod. 12, 23:15, 34:15 ff.; Lev. 23:5 ff.; Num. 28:16 ff.; Dt. 16:1 ff.).
4. *Sheḳalim* (Shekels): on the half-shekel or two drachmas tax (Exod. 30:11 ff.; Mt. 17:24).
5. *Yoma* (The Day): on the Day of Atonement (cf. Lev. 16).
6. *Sukkah* (Booth): on the Feast of Tabernacles (Lev. 23:34 ff.; Num. 29:12 ff.; Dt. 16:13 ff.).
7. *Bezah* (Egg) or *Yom Ṭob* (Festival): on whether an egg laid on a feast-day may be eaten; on the sanctification of feast-days and Sabbaths in general (cf. Exod. 12:16).
8. *Rosh ha-Shanah* (New Year): on the Feast of New Year (cf. Num. 28:11 ff.).
9. *Ta'anith* (Fast): on the days of fasting and mourning.
10. *Megillah* (The Scroll): on the reading of the 'Scroll', i.e., the Book of Esther, and on the celebration of the Feast of Purim in general (cf. Esth. 9:28).
11. *Mo'ed Ḳaṭan* (Little Feast): on the holy-days between the first and last days of a great feast.
12. *Ḥagigah* (Festival Offering): on the duty to appear and worship in Jerusalem on the three pilgrimage festivals (cf. Dt. 16:16 f.).

Third Seder: *Nashim* (Women)

1. *Yebamoth* (Sisters-in-law): on levirate marriage with a deceased husband's brother (cf. Dt. 25:5 ff.).
2. *Ketubboth* (Documents): on marriage contracts (cf. Exod. 22:16).
3. *Nedarim* (Vows): on vows, especially on the annulment of vows made by women (cf. Lev. 27 and Num. 30).
4. *Nazir* (the Nazirite): on the Nazirite vow (cf. Num. 6 and 30).
5. *Soṭah* (the Unfaithful Woman): on the procedure to be adopted against a wife suspected of adultery (cf. Num. 5:11 ff.).
6. *Giṭṭin* (Bills of Divorce): on the bill of divorce (cf. Dt. 24:1).
7. *Ḳiddushin* (Betrothals): on marriage.

Fourth Seder: *Neziḳin* (Damages)

1. *Baba Ḳamma* (the First Gate), i.e., the first of three sections relating to damages: on the legal consequences of various kinds of injury, theft and robbery (cf. Exod. 21:33, 22:5 f.).
2. *Baba Meẓi'a* (the Middle Gate): on claims in respect of property lost and found; on trusteeship, interest, borrowing and hiring.
3. *Baba Bathra* (the Last Gate): on property law and civil law.
4. *Sanhedrin* (Tribunal): on courts of justice, criminal law and capital punishment.
5. *Makkoth* (Stripes): on punishment by flogging (cf. Dt. 25:1 ff.).
6. *Shebu'oth* (Oaths): on various kinds of oaths.
7. *'Eduyoth* (Testimonies): on the validity of one hundred disputed statements made by earlier teachers 'testified to' by distinguished later authorities. Chapters 4–5 contain forty cases where the school of Shammai was more lenient than that of Hillel.
8. *'Abodah Zara* (Idolatry): on heathen worship and contact with the heathen.
9. *Aboth* (Sayings of the Fathers): a collection of sayings from the most distinguished teachers covering a period from *c.* 200 B.C. to A.D. 200.
10. *Horayoth* (Decisions): on unintentional offences caused by wrong decisions of the Sanhedrin, and on unintentional offences committed by High Priests and Princes.

Fifth Seder: *Ḳodashim* (Holy Things)

1. *Zebaḥim* (Victims): on animal sacrifice.
2. *Menaḥoth* (Meal-offerings): cf. Lev. 2; 5:11 ff., etc.
3. *Ḥullin* (Profane Things): on the correct method of slaughtering animals not intended for sacrifice, and rules concerning the eating of meat.
4. *Bekhoroth* (the First-born): rules regarding the first-born of animals and men (cf. Exod. 13:2, 12; Lev. 27:26 ff.; Num. 8:16 ff., 18:15 ff.; Dt. 15:19 ff.).
5. *'Arakhin* (Valuations): on the sum to be paid for the release of persons who have dedicated themselves, or been dedicated by others, to the service of the Sanctuary.
6. *Temurah* (Change): on the replacement of a sacrificial animal by another victim (cf. Lev. 27:10, 33).
7. *Kerithoth* (Annihilation): on what should be done in the case of the unintentional violation of a precept punishable by 'cutting off'.
8. *Me'ilah* (Trespassing): on the embezzlement of things consecrated to God (cf. Num. 5:6 ff.; Lev. 5:15 f.).

9. *Tamid* (Perpetual sacrifice): on the daily morning and evening sacrifice, and on the daily Temple service in general (cf. Exod. 29:38 ff.; Num. 28:3 ff.).
10. *Middoth* (Measures): on the dimensions and design of the Temple.
11. *Ḳinnim* (Nests): on dove sacrifice of the poor (cf. Lev. 5:1 ff., 12:8).

Sixth Seder: *Tohoroth* (Purities)

1. *Kelim* (Vessels): on household utensils and their purification (cf. Lev. 6:20 f., 11:32 ff.; Num. 19:14 ff., 31:20 ff.).
2. *Oholoth* (Tents): on the defilement of a dwelling by a corpse (cf. Num. 19:14).
3. *Nega'im* (Plagues): on leprosy (cf. Lev. 13:14).
4. *Parah* (the Red Heifer): on cleansing from defilement caused by contact with a corpse (cf. Num. 19).
5. *Tohoroth* (Purities): on minor forms of defilement lasting until sunset.
6. *Mikwa'oth* (Baths): on water suitable for bathing and washing (cf. Lev. 15:12; Num. 31:23 ff.; Lev. 12).
7. *Niddah* (Female Uncleanness): on menstruation and childbirth (cf. Lev. 15:19 ff.; Lev. 12).
8. *Makhshirin* (Predisposition to uncleanness): on liquids that render solid food impure (cf. Lev. 11:34 ff.).
9. *Zabim* (Unclean Issue): on pus and blood (cf. Lev. 15).
10. *Tebul Yom* (One who has immersed himself that day): on uncleanness lasting until sunset after the prescribed ritual bath (cf. Lev. 15:5, 22:6 f., etc.).
11. *Yadayim* (Hands): on the defilement and purification of the hands.
12. *'Uḳzin* (Handles): on the defilement of fruit through stalks, kernels and shells.

When rabbis disagree on points of law, the the Mishnah presents, not only the view of the majority, but in many cases those of dissenting scholars also. Thus, approximately one hundred and fifty authorities are cited, most of them seldom, but a few throughout almost all the tractates. The following are the teachers most frequently quoted.

First Generation (*c.* A.D. 70–100)

Rabban[9] Yoḥanan ben Zakkai (23 times).[10] R. Zadok (?).[11] R.

9. On the title Rabban see vol. II, § 25, 2.

10. The precise number of references may vary according to the different editions of the Mishnah.

11. The name of R. Zadok, or more correctly Zadduk (in Greek Σάδδωκος or Σάδδουκος), appears 16 times, but two different teachers are to be distinguished. Cf. Strack, p. 110.

Ḥananiah, captain of the priests (12 times). R. Eliezer ben Jacob (?).[12]

Second Generation (*c.* A.D. 100–130)

Earlier group

Rabban Gamaliel II (84 times). R. Joshua [ben Ḥananiah] (146 times).[13] R. Eliezer [ben Hyrcanus] (324 times). R. Eleazar ben Azariah (38 times). R. Dosa ben Arkhinas (19 times). R. Eleazar ben R. Zadduk (22 times).[14]

Later group

R. Ishmael (71 times). R. Aḳiba [ben Joseph] (278 times). R. Ṭarfon (51 times). R. Yoḥanan ben Nuri (38 times). R. Simeon ben Azzai, or simply, ben Azzai (4+21 times). R. Yoḥanan ben Beroka (11 times). R. Yose the Galilean (26 times). R. Simeon ben Nannus, or simply, Ben Nannus (5+5 times). Abba Saul (20 times). R. Judah ben Bathyra (16 times).

Third Generation (*c.* A.D. 130–160)

R. Judah [ben Ilai, or more correctly, Elai] (609 times). R. Yose [ben Ḥalafta] (335 times). R. Meir (331 times). R. Simeon [ben Yoḥai] (325 times). Rabban Simeon ben Gamaliel II (103 times). R. Neḥemiah (19 times). R. Ḥananiah ben Antigonus (13 times).

Fourth Generation (*c.* A.D. 160–200)

Rabbi, i.e., R. Judah the Prince (*ha-Nasi*) or the Saint (*ha-Ḳadosh*) (37 times). R. Yose ben Judah [ben Elai] (14 times).

The chronology presented here is not, of course, certain in every case, but only in its main outline. Each generation of rabbis can be established by the fact that its representatives appear in the Mishnah in dispute with one another. Thus, for example, Rabban Gamaliel II, R. Joshua, R. Eliezer and R. Aḳiba are frequently in conversation, and in such a way that R. Aḳiba is seen to be a younger contemporary of the three others.[15] Similarly, R. Judah ben Elai, R. Yose, R. Meir and R. Simeon ben Yoḥai are often engaged in argument. In this way, all the teachers mentioned can be assigned, with a reasonable degree of probability, to one of the four Tannaitic generations. Furthermore, the sequence of generations can also be determined on the basis of Mishnaic

12. The name of R. Eliezer ben Jacob appears 40 times. Here also, two persons are to be distinguished. Cf. Strack, pp. 110, 115.

13. Patronyms not mentioned in the Mishnah are given in brackets.

14. See n. 11 above. The same applies to this name.

15. Cf. vol. II, § 25, 4.

data. R. Joshua and R. Eliezer were pupils of Rabban Yoḥanan ben Zakkai,[16] and so was R. Aḳiba.[17] Again, men of the third generation are described as having been in personal contact with men of the second.[18] Finally, adequate clues exist for the establishment of an absolute chronology. Rabban Yoḥanan ben Zakkai issued various instructions 'after the destruction of the Temple'.[19] He was therefore alive immediately following that event. Mention of the considerably younger Aḳiba as a contemporary of Bar Kokhba and a martyr in the Hadrianic persecution, accords with this.[20]

These absolute chronological data, combined with the sequence of rabbinic generations, show that the Mishnah must have been compiled *c*. A.D. 200. If it had been redacted later, one would expect to find in it the names of rabbis active in the third century A.D. In point of fact, Jewish tradition ascribes the composition of the work to R. Judah ha-Nasi towards the end of the second, or beginning of the third century A.D.[21] From the contents of the Mishnah it may further be assumed that the thousands of statements concerning the views of individual scholars cannot have been transmitted orally. That a work was edited in about A.D. 200 containing hundreds of decisions made by a variety of teachers of earlier generations—Judah ben Elai, alone, is the author of over six hundred!—postulates the availability of written sources. It would seem probable from the statistics that the final redaction was preceded by two earlier groups of records, one from the second, and the other from the third generation of Tannaim. Certain items in the

16. mAb. 2:8. Cf. mEduy. 8:7; mYad. 4:3.

17. mSoṭ. 5:2.

18. R. Yose makes a decision in the presence of Aḳiba (mTer. 4:13). R. Yose listens to R. Ṭarfon (mNed. 6:6). R. Simeon argues with R. Aḳiba (mMakh. 6:8). R. Yose, R. Judah and R. Simeon report on the views of R. Eliezer and R. Joshua (mKer. 4:2–3).

19. mSukk. 3:12; mR.Sh. 4:1, 3, 4; mMen. 10:5.

20. In a few cases where the Mishnah gives no information, the Tosefta and Talmud may be drawn on. On personalities of the first and second generation see further vol. II, § 25, 4. For further details concerning all the Tannaim see Strack, pp. 110–8; JE (under the names of the rabbis); W. Bacher, *Die Agada der Tannaiten* I–II ([2]1903, 1890); Ch. Albeck, מבוא למשנה (1959), pp. 216–36; *Einführung in die Mischna* (1971), pp. 391–414.

21. On Judah: Strack, pp. 118, 315–6; JE VII pp. 333–7; M. Avi-Yonah, *Geschichte der Juden im Zeitalter des Talmud* (1962), pp. 38–41; W. Bacher, *Die Agada der Tannaiten* II (1890), pp. 454–86; D. Hoffmann, 'Die Antoninus-Agadot im Talmud und Midrasch', MGWJ 19 (1892), pp. 33–55, 245–55; S. Krauss, *Antoninus und Rabbi* (1910); S. Klein, 'The Estates of R. Judah ha-Nasi', JQR N.S. 2 (1911), pp. 545–56; L. Wallach, 'Colloquy of Marcus Aurelius with the Patriarch Judah I', JQR 31 (1940–1), pp. 259–86; A. Büchler, *Studies in Jewish History* (1956), pp. 179–244. The date of Rabbi's death is unknown. Scholarly opinion varies between A.D. 192/3 and 217/20. The latter is the majority view but it remains problematic.

text of the Mishnah favour this conjecture,[22] as do obscure and corrupt traditions handed down by Epiphanius.[23] The modern view, arising from a tradition contained in the Talmud,[24] assumes that the Mishnah of Judah the Prince was constructed on the groundwork of similar collections by R. Meir, and before him by R. Aḳiba.[25] Be this as it may, the Mishnah reflects the form of Jewish law elaborated in the academies of Palestine from the end of the first until the end of the second century A.D.

2. The Tosefta

The Mishnah of Judah ha-Nasi has acquired canonical rank and served as a basis for the further development of Jewish law. Another collection, the Tosefta (תוספתא) i.e. 'Supplement', has never achieved the same status. Its contents belong essentially to the period of the Tannaites, the scholars of the Mishnaic age. According to rabbinic

22. The special final benediction uttered by R. Yose ben Ḥalafta concerning the structure of the tractate Kelim would indicate that the latter was compiled in his time. See mKel. 30:4, 'R. Yose said, Happy are you, Kelim, to begin with uncleanness and end with cleanness'. Passages discussing the meaning of the sayings of earlier scholars (e.g., mOhol. 2:3; mToh. 9:3) also testify to various strata in the fixation of tradition. See also bHor. 13b concerning the redaction of 'Ukẓin.

23. Epiphanius, *Haer.* 33, 9 (ed. Holl, I, p. 459), *αἱ γὰρ παραδόσεις τῶν πρεσβυτέρων δευτερώσεις παρὰ τοῖς Ἰουδαίοις λέγονται. εἰσὶ δὲ αὗται τέσσαρες· μία μὲν ἡ εἰς ὄνομα Μωυσέως φερομένη, δευτέρα δὲ ἡ τοῦ καλουμένου Ῥαββὶ Ἀκίβα· τρίτη Ἀδδᾶ ἤτοι Ἰούδα· τετάρτη τῶν υἱῶν Ἀσαμωναίου.* Cf. *Haer.* 15, 2 (ed. Holl, I, p. 209), . . . *μία . . . εἰς ὄνομα Μωυσέως τοῦ προφήτου, δευτέρα δὲ εἰς τὸν διδάσκαλον αὐτῶν Ἀκίβαν οὕτω καλούμενον Βαρακίβαν· ἄλλη δὲ εἰς τὸν Ἀδδὰν ἢ Ἄνναν τὸν καὶ Ἰούδαν· ἑτέρα δὲ εἰς τοὺς υἱοὺς Ἀσαμωναίου.* By 'Deuteroseis of Moses', Deuteronomy is to be understood; the 'Mishnah of the Hasmonaeans' may represent the precepts of John Hyrcanus; a code of this Hasmonaean law or ספר גזרתא is mentioned in *Megillath Taanith* § 10 (ed. Lichenstein, HUCA 8–9 (1931–2), p. 331; cf. also pp. 295–7). A reference to R. Aḳiba arranging an order of halakhoth appears in tZab 1:5; the expression, 'Mishnah of R. Aḳiba', is found in mSanh. 3:4, tM.Sh. 2:1, 12, but this might signify no more than his oral teaching.

24. Cf. bSanh. 86a, 'R. Yoḥanan (bar Nappaḥa) said, Anonymous opinion in the Mishnah rests on R. Meir, in the Tosefta, on R. Neḥemiah . . . but all of them in the last resort rest on R. Aḳiba.'

25. The theory that a written compilation of the Mishnah existed before that of R. Judah ha-Nasi was advanced by Z. Frankel in *Hodegetica in Mischnam* (1859), who insisted on a Mishnah of R. Aḳiba and another of R. Meir. It is, however, thought that both were only in part recorded in script. See J. Derenbourg, *Histoire*, pp. 399–401; Strack, pp. 20–5; Ch. Albeck, *Untersuchungen über die Redaktion der Mischna* (1923), pp. 89–121; *Einführung in die Mischna* (1971), pp. 94–129; 145–70; J. N. Epstein, *Introduction to Tannaitic Literature* (1957), pp. 71 ff. (in Hebrew). On the 'First Mishnah' antedating that of Aḳiba (mSanh. 3:4) and possibly deriving from the schools of Hillel and Shammai (tM.Sh. 2:12), see D. Hoffmann, *Die erste Mischna und die Controversen der Tannaim* (1882), pp. 15–26.

tradition, the compiler of the Tosefta was R. Ḥiyya b. Abba, a pupil of Judah ha-Nasi. It is more likely, however, that the present work is a conflation of two previous halakhic collections by Ḥiyya and Hoshaiah.[26] The structure of the Tosefta resembles that of the Mishnah. Of the latter's sixty-three tractates, only Aboth, Tamid, Middoth and Ḳinnim are missing; the remainder have their exact parallels in the Tosefta. The two collections are thus closely related. The nature of their relationship has not yet received a definitive explanation, but there is agreement on two points: (1) The Tosefta follows the plan of the Mishnah in general,[27] and as the name suggests, supplements it. (2) The redactors of the Tosefta used anonymous sources older than the Mishnah. Consequently, in addition to sayings belonging to post-Mishnaic teachers, the Tosefta often cites Tannaitic dicta in their complete and original form, as against an abbreviated version preserved in the Mishnah. It contains also a greater amount of haggadah than Judah ha-Nasi's work.

3. The Jerusalem Talmud

After its codification, the Mishnah became in the third and fourth centuries A.D. the text-book for legal discussion in the schools of Palestine, especially in Tiberias. Combined with newly-collected material and with exegesis, the Mishnah grew into the so-called Jerusalem, or more correctly, Palestinian Talmud.[28] Here the text of the Mishnah is interpreted passage by passage, often casuistically. In addition to interpretation proper, the Talmud includes the views of the Amoraim (literally, 'speakers', i.e., the scholars of the post-Mishnaic period, third to fourth century A.D.), and even teachings dating from the period of the Mishnah itself, the so-called *baraytoth* (sing. בריתא), sayings unrecorded in the Mishnah and quoted in Hebrew in an Aramaic passage of the Talmud. The date of the Palestinian Talmud is disclosed by the fact that the emperors Diocletian and Julian are mentioned, but no Jewish authorities posterior to the second half of the fourth century. In fact, it acquired its present shape shortly after A.D. 400.[29] In addition to the halakhah which forms its principal

26. Cf. J. Z. Lauterbach, JE XII pp. 208–9.

27. For an independent arrangement of individual tractates, see B. de Vries, Tarbiz 26 (1957), pp. 255–61.

28. תלמוד = teaching, doctrine; e.g., mSot. 5:4–5; 6:3. תלמוד תורה, mPeah. 1:1; mKet. 5:6; mKer. 6:9. Cf. W. Bacher, *Terminologie*, I. pp. 94–6 199–202. The Talmud consists of the basic Mishnah text and the explanatory 'Gemara' (from גמר = to complete).

29. See Zunz, pp. 55–6; Strack, pp. 65–6. Cf. S. Lieberman, *The Talmud of Caesarea* (1931), pp. 70–5 (Hebr). On the problem of the *Barayta*, see B. de Vries 'Baraita', Enc. Jud. IV, cols. 189–93.

content, it includes also rich haggadic material.[30] It is disputed whether the Palestinian Talmud ever extended to include the whole Mishnah. But as it is, only the first four Sedarim have survived (with the exception of the tractates 'Eduyoth and Aboth), and the beginning of Niddah.[31] The Aramaic comments and discussions, the *Gemara*, are expressed in the Galilean dialect.

4. The Babylonian Talmud

The Mishnah is thought to have been brought to Babylon by a pupil of Judah the Prince, Abba Areka, known as Rab.[32] It served there, too, as the basis for progressive legal argument. The considerable increase of material led gradually to its codification, a work which began in the fifth, and was not completed until the sixth century A.D.[33] In the Babylonian Talmud, statements of earlier scholars are also frequently cited in Hebrew. The language of the Talmud itself is the Aramaic dialect of Babylonia. Haggadah is represented even more richly than in the Palestinian Talmud.[34] Like the latter, the Babylonian Talmud does not cover the whole Mishnah. The first Seder is entirely missing except for Berakhoth; Sheḳalim is absent from the second Seder; 'Eduyoth and Aboth from the fourth; Middoth from the fifth, together with Ḳinnim and half of Tamid; and the whole of the sixth Seder is missing except for Niddah (see Zunz, p. 58). It extends, therefore, to only thirty-six-and-a-half tractates as against thirty-nine in the Palestinian Talmud. Nevertheless, it is about four times as voluminous. From the time of the Middle Ages, the Babylonian Talmud has been studied more diligently than the Palestinian Talmud and accorded a much higher status.

Even when the Talmud was completed, halakhic discussion did not cease. It continued into the period of the Geonim (seventh to tenth century A.D.) and was practised and cultivated in the schools of

30. The haggadic portions are assembled in the work *Yephe Mar'eh* by the 16th century writer, Samuel Yaffe. See also A. Wünsche, *Der jerusalemische Talmud in seinem haggadischen Bestandtheilen zum ersten Male in's Deutsche übertragen* (1880).

31. Cf. Strack, pp. 66–9. Fragments found in the Cairo Geniza produce the same coverage. Cf. L. Ginzberg, *Yerushalmi Fragments from the Genizah* (1909). See now L. I. Rabinowitz, Enc. Jud. XV, cols. 773–4.

32. Cf. J. Neusner, *History of the Jews in Babylonia* II (1966), pp. 126–34.

33. Cf. Strack, pp. 70–1; J. Kaplan, *The Redaction of the Babylonian Talmud* (1933); *The Formation of the Babylonian Talmud*, ed. J. Neusner (1970).

34. See Zunz, p. 94. Haggadah from the Babylonian Talmud is collected in *'En Ya'aḳov* by Jacob ben Solomon ibn Habib (1516). Cf. Strack, p. 167. See A. Wünsche, *Der babylonische Talmud in seinen haggadischen Bestandtheilen* I–IV (1886–9).

Oriental and European Jews of the Middle Ages and later. Among the numerous major works dealing with Jewish law in medieval and modern times, two deserve to be singled out: the *Mishneh Torah* or *Yad ha-Ḥazaḳah* of Moses ben Maimon (Maimonides or Rambam, 1135–1204) and the *Shulḥan ʻArukh* of Joseph Karo (1488–1575). Cf. Strack, p. 166.

Additional Minor Tractates

In the editions of the Babylonian Talmud, seven extra-canonical tractates are printed at the conclusion of the fourth Seder.

(1) *Aboth de-Rabbi Nathan*: an expansion of the Mishnah tractate Aboth, with supplementary accounts from the lives of the rabbis and other haggadic material. It has survived in two recensions and first received its present form in the post-Talmudic period. But since the teachers whom it quotes all belong to the age of Mishnah, the tractate may be considered as Tannaitic in substance.

(2) *Soferim*: on the writing of the scroll of the Torah and various synagogal usages. It dates from the Gaonic period.

(3) *Ebhel rabbathi* (Mourning) or, euphemistically, *Semaḥoth* (Joys): on burial customs.

(4) *Kallah* (Bride): on marital intercourse and chastity.

(5) *Derekh Ereẓ Rabbah*: on social duties.

(6) *Derekh Ereẓ Zuṭṭa*: instructions for scholars.

(7) *Pereḳ Shalom*: on peace-making.

There are seven further small tractates:

(1) *Sefer Torah*: on the Pentateuch scrolls.

(2) *Mezuzah*: on the small parchment roll to be fixed to the door-post.

(3) *Tefillin*: on phylacteries.

(4) *Ẓiẓith*: on fringes.

(5) *ʻAbadim*: on slaves.

(6) *Kuthim*: on Samaritans.

(7) *Gerim*: on proselytes.

Bibliography

The literature on the Mishnah and the Talmuds is vast. For older works see the articles 'Talmud', 'Mishnah', etc., in JE, and Strack's Bibliography; for recent works, *Kirjath Sepher* (1924–).

1. *The Mishnah*

(a) Editions: The best is Ḥ. Albeck and Ḥ. Yalon, ששה סדרי משנה I–VI (1952–58), pointed text with brief, modern Hebrew commentary. Also useful: *Mischnayoth. Die sechs Ordnungen der Mischna. Hebräischer Text mit Punktation, deutscher Übersetzung und Erklärung* I–VI (1887), by E. Baneth and others. Cf. G. Beer and O. Holtzmann, *Die Mischna: Text, Übersetzung und Erklärung, mit Einleitungen* (1912–), still in progress, but with many tractates complete. P. Blackman, *Mishnayoth: Pointed Hebrew text, introduction, translation, notes* I–VII (1951–6).

(b) Translations: H. Danby, *The Mishnah, translated from the Hebrew with introduction and brief explanatory notes* (1933). An English translation figures also in the Soncino transl. of the Babylonian Talmud (see below). In German: P. Fiebig (ed.), *Ausgewählte Mischnatractate in deutscher Übersetzung* (1905–12).

(c) Separate tractates; a selection of editions, translations, and studies following the order of Mishnah:

W. Staerk, *Der Mischnatraktat Berakhoth im vokalisierten Text mit sprachlichen und sachlichen Bemerkungen* (1910).

H. L. Strack, *Berakot: Der Mišnatractat "Lobsagungen"* (1915).

A. Lukyn Williams, *Tractate Berakoth (Benedictions), Mishna and Tosephta translated from the Hebrew with introduction and notes* (1921).

A. Rosenthal, *Der Mišnatraktat Orlah: sein Zusammenhang und seine Quellen* (1913).

H. L. Strack, *Schabbath. Der Mischnatraktat "Sabbath" hrsg. und erklärt* (1890).

H. L. Strack, *Pesaḥim: Mišnatraktat mit Berücksichtungen des Neuen Testaments und der jetzigen Passafeier der Juden, hrsg., übers. und erläutert* (1911).

H. L. Strack, *Joma: Der Mischnatraktat "Versöhnungstag" hrsg. und erklärt* ([3]1912).

A. W. Greenup, *Tractate Sukkah, Mishnah and Tosefta on the Feast of Tabernacles* (1920).

A. W. Greenup, *The Mishna Tractate Taanith (On the Public Fasts) translated from the Hebrew with brief annotations* (1920).

J. Rabbinowitz, *Mišnah Megillah, edited with introduction, translation, commentary and critical notes* (1931).

H. E. Goldin, *Mishnah Baba Kamma (First Gate), translated and annotated* (1933).

H. E. Goldin, *Mishnah: A digest of the basic principles of early Jewish jurisprudence. Baba Mezia (Middle Gate), translated and annotated* (1913).

H. E. Goldin, *Mishnah Baba Batra (Last Gate), translated and annotated* (1933).

D. Daube, *The Civil Law of the Mishnah: the arrangement of the Three Gates* (1944).

S. Krauss, *The Mishnah Treatise Sanhedrin, edited with an introduction, notes and glossary* (1909).

H. L. Strack, *Sanhedrin-Makkoth. Die Mišnatraktate . . . nach Handschriften und alten Drucken hrsg., . . . übers. und erläutert* (1910).

H. Danby, *Tractate Sanhedrin, Mishnah and Tosefta . . . translated from the Hebrew with brief annotations* (1919).

S. Krauss, *Die Mischna Sanhedrin-Makkoṯ* (1933).

H. E. Goldin, *Hebrew Criminal law and Procedure; Mishnah, Sanhedrin-Makkoth, translated and annotated* (1952).

H. L. Strack, *'Aboda Zara. Der Mischnatraktat "Götzendienst" hrsg. und erklärt* ([2]1909).

W. A. L. Elmslie, *The Mishna on Idolatry. 'Aboda Zara, edited with translation, vocabulary and notes* (1911).

H. Blaufuss, *'Aboda Zara: Mischna und Tosefta, übersetzt und mit vornehmlicher Berücksichtigung der Altertümer erklärt* (1916).

S. T. Lachs, "A note on Genesia in 'Aboda Zara I.3", JQR 58 (1967), pp. 69–71.

P. R. Weis, *Mishnah Horayoth, its history and exposition* (1952).

Because of its popularity and importance, there is a considerable body of literature on Pirḳe Aboth. The following are only some suggestions:

In general: Z. Frankel, 'Zum Traktat Abot', MGWJ 7 (1858), pp. 419–30; A. Geiger, 'Pirke Aboth', *Nachgelassene Schriften* (1875–8), IV, pp. 281–344; R. T. Herford, 'Pirke Aboth; its purpose and significance', *Occident and Orient, being studies in honour of M. Gaster's 80th birthday* (1936), pp. 244–52; L. Finkelstein, 'Introductory Study to Pirke Aboth', JBL 57 (1938), pp. 13–50; *Introduction to the treatises Abot and Abot of Rabbi Nathan* (1950). (In Hebrew with English summary); A. Guttmann, 'Tractate Abot—its place in rabbinic literature', JQR n.s. 41 (1950–51), pp. 181–93; B. Z. Dinur, 'The Tractate Aboth (Sayings of the Fathers) as a Historical Source', Zion 35 (1970), pp. 1–34 (Hebrew with Engl. summary).

Editions, etc.: C. Taylor, *Sayings of the Jewish Fathers comprising Pirqe Aboth in Hebrew and English with notes and excursuses* (^{2}1897); *An Appendix to Sayings of the Jewish Fathers, containing a catalogue of MSS and notes on the text of Aboth* (1900); H. L. Strack, *Die Sprüche der Väter . . . hrsg. und erklärt* (^{3}1901); R. T. Herford, 'Pirke 'Aboth', translated and annotated in: *Apocrypha and Pseudepigrapha of the Old Testament*, ed. R. H. Charles (1913) II, pp. 686–714; W. O. E. Oesterley, *The Sayings of the Jewish Fathers (Pirke 'Aboth), translated from the Hebrew* (1919); R. T. Herford, *Pirke 'Aboth . . . edited with introduction, translation and commentary* (1925); K. Marti-G. Beer, *Die Mischna 'Abot* (1927).

P. Blackmann, *Tractate 'Avoth . . . text, introduction, translation, notes* (1964).

A. Brody, *Der Mišna-Traktat Tamid. Text . . . übersetzt, kommentiert und mit Einleitung versehen* (1936).

L. Ginsberg, 'Tamid, the oldest Treatise of the Mishnah', Journal of Jewish Lore and Philology 1 (1919), pp. 33–44; 197–209; 265–95.

S. Gandz, 'The Mishnat ha-Middot . . . Prolegomena to a new edition', HUCA 6 (1929), pp. 263–76.

S. Gandz, *The Mishnat ha-Middot . . . A new edition, with introduction, translation and notes* (1932).

F. J. Hollis, *The Archaeology of Herod's Temple, with a commentary on the tractate Middoth* (1934).

A. Spanier, 'Zur Analyse des Mischnatraktates Middot', *Festschrift für L. Baeck* (1938), pp. 79–90.

D. Graubert, 'Le véritable auteur de traité Kèlim', REJ 32 (1896), pp. 200–25.

A. Goldberg, *The Mishnah Treatise Ohaloth critically edited* (1955) (In Hebrew).

(d) General introduction: Cf. Strack, *Introduction* (1931); J. Z. Lauterbach, JE VIII, pp. 609–19; see also the bibliographies on the Talmuds and the Tosefta.

Z. Frankel, *Hodegetica in Mischnam* (1867).

D. Hoffmann, *Die erste Mischna und die Controversen der Tannaim. Ein Beitrag zur Einleitung in die Mischna* (1882).

J. Bassfreund, 'Zur Redaktion der Mischna', MGWJ 51 (1907), pp. 291–322; 429–44; 590–608; 678–706.

L. Ginsberg, *Zur Entstehungsgeschichte der Mischnah* (1914).

J. Z. Lauterbach, *Midrash and Mishnah: a study in the early history of the Halakah* (1916).

Ch. Albeck, *Untersuchungen über die Redaktion der Mischna* (1923).

A. Guttmann, *Das redaktionelle und sachliche Verhältnis zwischen Mišna und Tosefta* (1928).

A. Guttmann, 'Das Problem des Mišnaredaktion aus den Sätzen Rabbis in Mišna und Tosefta synoptisch beleuchtet', *Festschrift zum 75 jährigen Bestehen des jüdisch-theologischen Seminars Fraenkelscher Stiftung* II (1929), pp. 95–130.

A. Guttmann, 'The problem of the anonymous Mishna: a study in the history of the Halakah', HUCA 16 (1941), pp. 137–55.

B. de Vries, 'The older form of some Halakoth', Tarbiz 5 (1934), pp. 247–56; 22 (1951), pp. 153–6; 24 (1955), pp. 392–405; 25 (1956), pp. 369–84 (all in Hebrew).

A. Weiss, לחקר הספרותי של המשנה, HUCA 16 (1941), pp. א־לב.

J. N. Epstein, 'On the Mishnah of R. Judah', Tarbiz 15 (1943), pp. 14–26 (In Hebrew).

E. Z. Melamed, 'Tannaitic Controversies over the interpretation and text of older Mishnayoth', Tarbiz 21 (1950), 137–64 (Hebrew).

R. Margulies, יסוד המשנה ועריכתה (1956).

J. N. Epstein, *Introduction to Tannaitic Literature: Mishna, Tosephta and Halachic Midrashim* (1959) (in Hebrew).

Ch. Albeck, *Introduction to the Mishna* (1959) (in Hebrew); Reviewed by B. de Vries, JJS 10 (1959), pp. 173–81.

A. M. Goldberg, 'Purpose and Method in R. Judah haNasi's compilation of the Mishnah', Tarbiz 28 (1959), pp. 260–9 (In Hebrew).

Ch. Albeck, *Einführung in die Mischna* (1971).

2. *The Tosefta*

The only complete critical edition of the Tosefta available is still M. S. Zuckermandel, *Tosefta nach den Erfurter und Wiener Handschriften mit Parallelstellen und Varianten* (1880); *Supplement enthaltend Uebersicht, Register und Glossar zu Tosefta* (1882). This work was reissued by S. Lieberman with the addition of his own *Supplement to the Tosefta* (1937). Other editions, as yet incomplete, are: S. Lieberman, *The Tosefta according to Codex Vienna, with Variants from Codex Erfurt, Genizah MSS and Editio Princeps* I–III (1955–67). G. Kittel and K. H. Rengstorf, *Rabbinische Texte: Erste Reihe: Die Tosefta, Text, Übersetzung, Erklärung* (1953–). Also incomplete is S. Lieberman, *Tosefta Kifshuṭah, a comprehensive commentary on the Tosefta*, parts 1–7 with supplement to parts 3–5 (1955–67). Editions of individual tractates: A. Schwarz, *Die Tosifta des Traktates Nesikin Baba Kama geordnet und kommentiert mit einer Einleitung: Das Verhältnis der Tosifta zur Mischnah* (1912). O. Holtzmann, *Der Tosephtatraktat Berakot: Text, Übersetzung und Erklärung* (1912). L. C. Fiebig, *Der Tosephtatraktat Roš Haš-šanah in vokalisiertem Text mit sprachlichen, textkritischen und sachlichen Bemerkungen* (1914).

There is no complete translation of the Tosefta. The following works render individual tractates into English: H. Danby, *Tractate Sanhedrin, Mishnah and Tosefta* (1919). A. Lukyn Williams, *Tractate Berakoth, Mishnah and Tosefta* (1921). A. W. Greenup, *Sukkah, Mishna and Tosefta* (1925). An important aid to the study of the Tosefta is C. J. Kasowski, אוצר לשון התוספתא: *Thesaurus Thosephthae: Concordantiae verborum quae in sex Thosephthae ordinibus reperiuntur* I–VI (1932–61).

On the Tosefta in general see J. Z. Lauterbach, 'Tosefta', JE XII, pp. 207 ff. Strack, *Introduction* (1931), pp. 75–6, 271–3. M. D. Herr, 'Tosefta', Enc. Jud. XV, cols. 1283–5. J. N. Epstein, *Introduction to Tannaitic Literature: Mishna, Tosephta and Halakhic Midrashim* (1959), pp. 241–62 (in Hebrew). The bibliography in these works may be supplemented from M. E. Abramsky's article in *Kirjath Sepher* 29 (1953–4), 149–61.

A selection of the more important or useful works: M. S. Zuckermandel, *Tosefta Mischna und Boraitha in ihrem Verhältnis zu einander* I–II (1908–10). H. Malter, 'A Talmudic Problem and Proposed Solutions', JQR n.s. 2 (1912), pp. 75–95. L. Blau, 'Tosefta, Mischna et Baraita', REJ LXVII (1914), pp. 1–23. A. Guttmann, *Das redaktionelle und sachliche Verhältnis zwischen Mišna und Tosefta*, Breslau (1928). A. Spanier, *Die Toseftaperiode in der Tannaitischen Literatur*, Berlin (1930). B. Cohen, *Mishnah and Tosefta: A Comparative Study. Part I, Shabbat* (1935). B. de Vries, 'The Mishna and Tosefta of Baba Mezia', Tarbiz 20 (1950), pp. 79–83 (Hebr. with Eng. summary). 'The Mishna and Tosefta of Makkoth', Tarbiz 26 (1957), pp. 255–61 (Hebr. with Eng. summary). 'The Problem of the Relationship of the Two Talmuds to the Tosefta', Tarbiz 28 (1959), pp. 158–70 (Hebr. with Eng. summary). 'The Mishnah and Tosefta of Meilah', Tarbiz 29 (1960), pp. 229–49 (Hebr. with Eng. summary). Ḥ. Albeck,

מחקרים בברייתא ובתוספתא (1954). S. Zeitlin, 'The Tosefta', JQR XLVII (1957), pp. 382–99.

3. *The Palestinian Talmud*

(a) Editions: See W. Bacher, JE XII, p. 23; Strack, pp. 83–6. Most useful is Vilna (1922), I–VIII, with commentaries; cf. also Piotrikow (1898–1903); Zhitomir (1860–67); and especially Krotoschin (1866).

(b) Commentaries: see Strack, pp. 149–59; M. Richtmann, JE XII, p. 28; L. I. Rabinowitz, Enc. Jud. XV, cols. 777–9. Modern commentaries: S. Lieberman, *Ha-Yerushalmi ki-Feshuto* I (1935); Z. W. Rabinovitz, שערי תורת ארץ־ישראל (Notes and comments on the Yerushalmi) (1940); L. Ginzberg, פרושים וחדושים בירושלמי, a commentary on the Palestinian Talmud I–IV (1941–61).

(c) Translation:

M. Schwab, *Le Talmud de Jérusalem* I–IX (1871–89); I (Berakhoth) was translated from the French into English (1886); *Introduction et tables générales* (1890).

(d) Single tractates, following the order of the Talmud:

Z. Frankel, אהבת ציון (a commentary on Berakhoth—Demai) (1874–5).

C. Horowitz, *Jeruschalmi, der palästinische Talmud Sukkah, die Festhütte, übersetzt und interpretiert* (1963).

A. W. Greenup, *A translation of the treatise Ta'anith (on the Public Fasts) from the Palestinian Talmud* (1918).

C. Horowitz, *Jeruschalmi, der paläst. Talmud Nedarim (Gelübde); übersetzt und interpretiert* (1957).

S. Lieberman, תלמודה של קיסרין, *The Talmud of Caesarea. Jerushalmi tractate Nezikin*, Suppl. Tarbiz 2 (1931). *The Talmud of Caesarea* (1968).

4. *The Babylonian Talmud*

(a) Editions: On these see, W. Bacher, JE XII, pp. 7, 23; Strack, pp. 83–86; E. N. Adler, 'The Talmud MSS and Editions', *Essays in honour of J. H. Hertz* (1942), pp. 15–17; R. N. Rabinowitz, מאמר על הדפסת התלמוד, תולדות הדפסת התלמוד (1952). The most useful edition is Vilna (1880–6), I–XX, containing all the major commentaries. Cf. also L. Goldschmidt, *Der Babylonische Talmud . . . hrsg. . . . nach der Bombergschen Ausgabe . . . nebst Varianten . . . übersetzt und mit kurzen Anmerkungen versehen* I–IX (1897–1935). The Baraitot have been edited by M. Higger, אוצר הברייתות I–X (1938).

(b) Commentaries: On the traditional commentators, of whom Rashi is the most important, see Strack, pp. 149–59; M. Richtmann, JE XII, pp. 27–30. Cf. J. Leveen, 'A digest of commentaries on the Babylonian Talmud', British Museum Quarterly 7 (1933), pp. 76–7. For a sample of modern commentary see Z. W. Rabinowitz, שערי תורת בבל (Notes and comments on the Babylonian Talmud), ed. Melamed (1961).

(c) Translations:

M. L. Rodkinson and I. M. Wise, *A new Edition of the Babylonian Talmud. Original text, edited, corrected, formulated and translated into English* I–XX ([2]1918).

I. Epstein (ed.), *The Babylonian Talmud, trans. into English with notes, glossary and indices*, I–XXXIV and Index, Soncino Press (1935–52).

The Soncino Press has also begun (1960–) a Hebrew and English edition with the above translation and the Hebrew text of Vilna 1880–6 on facing pages. Cf. also M. Rawicz, *Der Traktat Megilla nebst Tosafot vollständing ins Deutsche übertragen* (1883); also Rosh ha-Shanah (1886); Sanhedrin (1892); Kethuboth (1898–1900); Ḥullin (1908).

(d) Single tractates, following the order of the Talmud:
A. Cohen, *The Babylonian Talmud: Tractate Berakot trans. into English . . . with introduction, commentary etc.* (1921).
W. H. Lowe, *The fragment of the Talmud Babli Pesaḥim . . . in the University Library, Cambridge, ed., with notes* (1897).
A. W. Streane, *A translation of the treatise Chagigah from the Babylonian Talmud, with introduction, notes, glossary and indices* (1891).
H. Malter, *The treatise Ta'anit of the Babylonian Talmud, critically edited on the basis of MSS and old editions and provided with a transl. and notes* (1928).
S. Loewinger, 'Gaonic interpretations of the tractates Gittin and Qiddushin', HUCA 23 (1950–51), pp. 475–98.
M. S. Feldblum, *Tractate Gittin. The Vilna text annotated with variant readings* (1966) (Hebrew).
L. Goldschmidt, *Der Traktat Nezikin . . . aus dem babylonischen Talmud . . . mit textkritischen Scholien versehen* (1913).
E. Z. Melamed, *Massekheth Baba Kamma, transl. with a commentary* (1952) (in Hebrew).
M. N. Zobel and H. M. Dimitrovsky, *Massekheth Baba Meẓi'a, transl. with a commentary*, ed. Melamed (1960) (in Hebrew).
S. Abramson, *Massekheth Baba Bathra, transl. with a commentary* (1952) (in Hebrew).
S. Bornstein, *Tractate Makkoth of the Babylonian Talmud* (1935) (in Hebrew).
P. Fiebig, 'Talmud Babli, Traktat Götzendienst Kap. III', ZDMG 57 (1903), pp. 581–606.
S. Abramson, *Tractate 'Aboda Zara . . . with introduction and notes* (1957) (in Hebrew).

5. *Introductory* (to both Talmuds):
(a) General: See W. Bacher, JE XII, pp. 1–27; Strack, *Introduction*, pp. 3–195; also the bibliographies of Mishnah and Tosefta.
Z. Frankel, 'Skizzen zu einer Einleitung in den Talmud', MGWJ 1 (1852), pp. 36–40; 70–80.
Z. Frankel, 'Beiträge zu einer Einleitung in den Talmud', MGWJ 10 (1861), pp. 186–94; 205–12; 258–72.
Z. Frankel, מבוא הירושלמי (1870).
W. Bacher, *Die Agada der Babylonischen Amoräer* (1878).
Die Agada der Tannaiten I (1884, [2]1903)–II (1890).
Die Agada der palästinensischen Amoräer I–III (1892–9).
Die Agada der Tannaiten und Amoräer, Bibelstellenregister (1902).
Ergänzungen und Berichtigungen zur 'Agada der Babylonischen Amoräer' (1913).
Tradition und Tradenten in den Schulen Palästinas und Babyloniens (1914).
Rabbanan, die Gelehrten der Tradition (1914).
L. Ginzberg, 'Some abbreviations, unrecognized or misunderstood in the text of the Jerusalem Talmud', *Jewish Theological Seminary Students Annual* (1914), pp. 138–51.
J. Fromer, *Der Talmud: Geschichte, Wesen, und Zukunft* (1920).
M. Mielziner, *Introduction to the Talmud* ([3]1925).
P. Fiebig, *Der Talmud: seine Entstehung, sein Wesen, sein Inhalt* (1929).
J. Kaplan, *The Redaction of the Babylonian Talmud* (1932).
J. Z. Lauterbach, 'Misunderstood chronological statements in Talmudic literature', PAAJR 5 (1934), pp. 77–84.
A. Weiss, 'Le problème de la redaction du Talmud de Babylone', REJ 102 (1937), pp. 105–14.

L. Ginzberg, *The Palestinian Talmud* (1941).

M. Higger, 'The Yerushalmi quotations in Rashi', *Rashi Anniversary Volume* (1941), pp. 191–27.

L. Finkelstein, 'The transmission of the early rabbinic traditions', HUCA 16 (1941), pp. 151–135.

Ch. Albeck, לעריכת התלמוד הבבלי, *Gulak Memorial Volume* (1942), pp. 1–12.

Ch. Albeck, 'On the editing of the Talmud Babli', Tarbiz 15 (1943), pp. 14–26 (Hebrew).

A. Weiss, *The Babylonian Talmud as a literary unit: its place of origin, development and final redaction* (1943) (Hebrew).

Z. H. Chajes, *The student's guide through the Talmud*, transl. from the Hebrew, edited and critically annotated by J. Schachter (1952).

E. Z. Melamed, מבוא לספרות התלמוד (1954).

A. Weiss, לחקר התלמוד (1954).

S. K. Mirsky, 'Types of lectures in the Babylonian Academies', *Essays presented to S. W. Baron* (1959).

T. H. Stern, *The composition of the Talmud. An analysis of the relationship between the Babylonian and the Talmud Yerushalmi* (1959).

J. N. Epstein, *Introduction to Amoraitic literature: Babylonian Talmud and Yerushalmi*, ed. E. Z. Melamed (1962) (in Hebrew).

B. de Vries, תולדות ההלכה התלמודית (1962).

A. Weiss, על היצירה הספרותית של האמראים (1962).

B. de Vries, מחקרים בספרות התלמוד (1968).

Ch. Albeck, מבוא לתלמודים (1969).

J. Newman, *Halachic Sources* (1969); cf. B. S. Jackson, JJS 23 (1972), pp. 82–9.

A. Guttmann, *Rabbinic Judaism in the Making—The Halakhah from Ezra to Judah I* (1970).

J. Neusner (ed.), *The Formation of the Babylonian Talmud* (1970).

J. Neusner, *The Rabbinic Traditions about the Pharisees before 70* I–III (1971).

(b) Textual (on both Talmuds and the Mishnah):

W. H. Lowe, *The Mishnah on which the Palestinian Talmud rests* (1883).

R. Rabbinovicz, *Variae lectiones in Mischnam et in Talmud Babylonicum* I–XVI (1867–97).

M. Jastrow, 'The history and the future of the text of the Talmud', *Gratz College Publication* (1897), pp. 75–103.

L. Ginzberg, *Yerushalmi Fragments from the Genizah* (1909).

C. B. Friedmann, 'Zur Geschichte der ältesten Mischnaüberlieferung. Bab. Mischna-Fragmente aus der Altkairoer Geniza', Jüd.-lit. Gesellschaft Jahrbuch 18 (1927), pp. 265–88.

G. Beer, *Faksimile-Ausgabe des Mishnacodex Kaufmann A 50* (1929).

S. Lieberman, על הירושלמי, On the Yerushalmi: a. Contribution to the emendation of the text of the Yerushalmi. b. Variants from the Vatican MS of Soṭah (1929).

Ch. Albeck, נוסחות במשנה של האמוראים, *Chajes Memorial Volume* (1933), pp. 1–28.

P. Kahle and J. Weinberg, 'The Mishna Text in Babylonia. Fragments from the Genizah edited and examined' I, HUCA 10 (1935), pp. 185–222; II [by Kahle alone] HUCA 12–13 (1938), pp. 275–325.

E. N. Adler, 'Talmud MSS and Editions', *Essays in Honour of J. H. Hertz* (1942), pp. 15–17.

J. N. Epstein, מבוא לנוסח המשנה I–II (1948).

M. Schachter, *The Babylonian and Jerusalem Mishnah textually compared* (1959), (in Hebrew with English preface).

(c) Reference and linguistic (to both Talmuds and Mishnah):

Concordances:

C. J. Kasovsky, *Thesaurus Talmudis: Concordantiae verborum quae in Talmude Babilonico reperiuntur* (1954–).
Thesaurus Mishnae I–IV ([2]1956–60).
Thesaurus Thosephthae I–VI (1932–61).

L. Goldschmidt, *Subject Concordance to the Babylonian Talmud* (1932–61), ed. R. Edelmann (1959).

H. Duensing, *Verzeichnis der Personen- und der geographischen Namen in der Mischna* (1960).

Encyclopaedias and works of reference:

A. Neubauer, *La géographie du Talmud* (1868).

A. Berliner, *Beiträge zur Geographie und Ethnographie im Talmud und Midrasch* (1884).

A. Hyman, **תולדות תנאים ואמוראים** I–III (1910).

S. Krauss, *Talmudische Archäologie* I–III (1910–12).

H. L. Strack and P. Billerbeck, *Kommentar zum Neuen Testament aus Talmud und Midrasch* I–IV (1922–8); V. *Rabbinischer Index*, ed. J. Jeremias (1956).

M. Margolioth (ed.), *Encyclopedia of Talmudic and Gaonic Literature* (1946).

M. Berlin and S. J. Zevin, *Encyclopedia Talmudica* (1948–) (in Hebrew); vol. I has been translated into English.

R. Margulies, **לחקר שמות וכנויים בתלמוד** (1959–60).

J. Schechter, **אוצר התלמוד** (1963).

B. Jeitteles, **אוצר תנאים ואמוראים** (1961–).

I. Löw (ed. A. Scheiber), *Fauna und Mineralien der Juden* (1969).

Dictionaries:

J. Buxtorf, *Lexicon Chaldaicum, Talmudicum et Rabbinicum* (ed. B. Fischer) I–II (1869–75).

J. Levy, *Neuhebräisches und Chaldäisches Wörterbuch über die Talmudim und Midraschim* I–IV (1876–84).

A. Kohut, **ספר ערוך השלם**, *Aruch Completum* (A Targumic, Talmudic and Midraschic Lexicon) I–VIII (1878–92).

M. Jastrow, *A Dictionary of the Targumim, the Talmud Babli and Yerushalmi, and the Midrashic Literature* I–II (1886–1903).

S. Krauss, *Griechische und lateinische Lehnwörter im Talmud, Midrasch und Targum* I–II (1898–9).

W. Bacher, *Älteste Terminologie der jüdischen Schriftauslegung* (1899).

W. Bacher, *Die Bibel- und Traditionsexegetische Terminologie der Amoräer* (1905).

J. Levy and L. Goldschmidt, *Nachträge und Berichtigungen zu J. Levys Wörterbuch* (1924).

S. Krauss, *Additamenta ad Librum Aruch Completum* (1937).

G. Dalman, *Aramäisch-neuhebräisches Handwörterbuch zu Targum, Talmud und Midrasch* ([3]1938).

Grammars:

G. Dalman, *Grammatik des jüdisch-palästinischen Aramäisch* ([2]1905).

M. L. Margolis, *A Manual of the Aramaic Language of the Babylonian Talmud* (1910).

K. Albrecht, *Neuhebräische Grammatik auf Grund der Mišna* (1913).

M. H. Segal, *A Grammar of Mishnaic Hebrew* (1927).

J. T. Marshall, *Manual of the Aramaic Language of the Palestinian Talmud* (1929).

C. Levias, *A Grammar of Babylonian Aramaic* (1930); cf. *A Grammar of the Aramaic Idiom contained in the Babylonian Talmud* (1896–1900).

J. N. Epstein, *A Grammar of Babylonian Aramaic*, ed. E. Z. Melamed (1960) (in Hebrew).

P. Fiebig, 'Das Griechisch der Mischna', ZNW 9 (1908), pp. 297–314.

M. Schlesinger, *Satzlehre der aramäischen Sprache des babylonischen Talmuds* (1928).

E. Porath, *Mishnaic Hebrew as vocalized in the early MSS of the Babylonian Jews* (1938) (Hebrew).

H. M. Orlinsky, 'Studies in Talmudic Philology', HUCA 23 (1950–1), pp. 499–514.

Ḥ. Yalon, *Introduction to the Vocalization of the Mishnah* (1964) (in Hebrew).

Methodology (cf. J. Z. Lauterbach, JE XII, pp. 30–3):

M. Mielziner, 'The Talmudic Syllogism', Hebrew Review 1 (1880), pp. 42–53.

M. Mielziner, 'The Talmudic Analogy', Hebrew Review 2 (1881–2), pp. 79–94.

A. Schwarz, *Die hermeneutische Analogie in der talmudischen Litteratur* (1897); *Syllogismus* (1901); *Induktion* (1909); *Antinomie* (1913); *Quantitätsrelation* (1916); *Kontext* (1921).

S. Schlesinger, *Beiträge zur talmudischen Methodologie* (1927).

S. Atlas, לתולדות הסוגיא, HUCA 24 (1952–3), א–כא.

L. Jacobs, *Studies in Talmudic Logic and Methodology* (1961).

E. Wiesenberg, 'Observations on Method in Talmudic Studies', JSS 11 (1966), pp. 16–36.

Rabbinic Theology:

F. Weber, *Jüdische Theologie auf Grund des Talmud und verwandter Schriften* (^{2}1897).

S. Schechter, *Aspects of Rabbinic Theology* (1909)

J. Abelson, *The Immanence of God in Rabbinical Literature* (1912).

W. Hirsch, *Rabbinic Psychology: beliefs about the soul in Rabbinic literature of the Talmudic Period* (1917).

A. Marmorstein, *The Doctrine of Merits in Old Rabbinic Literature* (1920).

G. F. Moore, *Judaism in the First Three Centuries of the Christian Era* I–III (1927–30).

A. Büchler, *Studies in Sin and Atonement in Rabbinic Literature of the first century* (1928).

A. Marmorstein, *The old Rabbinic Doctrine of God* I–II (1927–37).

R. T. Herford, *Talmud and Apocrypha* (1933).

A. Marmorstein, *Studies in Jewish Theology* (1950).

B. W. Helfgott, *The Doctrine of Election in Tannaitic Literature* (1954).

R. Mach, *Der Zaddik in Talmud und Midrasch* (1957).

S. Esh, *Der Heilige* (*Er sei gepriesen*) (1957).

G. Scholem, *Jewish Gnosticism, Merkabah Mysticism and Talmudic Tradition* (1960).

J. Heinemann, *Prayer in the Period of the Tanna'im and the Amora'im* (1964), (Hebrew with an English summary).

M. Kadushin, *The Rabbinic Mind* (^{2}1965).

A. M. Goldberg, *Untersuchungen über die Vorstellung von der Schekhinah in der frühen rabbinischen Literatur* (1969).

E. E. Urbach, *The Sages, their Concepts and Beliefs* (1969) (in Hebrew).

P. Schäfer, *Die Vorstellung vom Heiligen Geist in der rabbinischen Literatur* (1972).

6. *The Minor Tractates*

(a) *General:* The text of these tractates (fifteen in all) may be found in the

Vilna Bab. Talmud (1880–6), though it is often corrupt. For introduction see, I. H. Weiss **דר דר ודורשיו** (1904) II, pp. 216 ff; Strack, pp. 73–4; L. Ginzberg, JE VII, p. 640; *On Jewish Law and Lore* (1955); the preface and introductions in A. Cohen (ed.), *The Minor Tractates of the Talmud* I–II (Soncino Press, 1965).

(b) *Aboth deRabbi Nathan:* There are two recensions of the ARN; see S. Schechter, *Aboth deRabbi Nathan* (1887). Cf. J. Goldin, 'The two versions of Abot deRabbi Nathan', HUCA 19 (1946), pp. 97–120.

English translations: J. Goldin, *The Fathers according to Rabbi Nathan* (1955); Soncino, *Minor Tractates* I, pp. 1–210. Introduction: Zunz, p. 186; M. Mielziner, JE I, p. 81; see also the bibliography on Aboth, pp. 81–2, esp. L. Finkelstein, *Introduction to the Treatises 'Abot and 'Abot of Rabbi Nathan* (1950).

(c) *Soferim:* Editions: J. Müller, *Masechet Soferim . . . nach Handschriften hrsg. und commentiert* (1878); M. Higger, *Massekhet Soferim* (1937); cf. S. Lieberman, Kirjath Sepher 15 (1937), pp. 50–60.

English translation: Soncino, *Minor Tractates* I, pp. 211–325.

Introduction: Zunz, pp. 99–101; L. Blau, JE XI, pp. 426–8; M. Higger, 'Saadia and the treatise Soferim', *Saadia Anniversary Volume* (1943), pp. 263–70; H. Bardtke, 'Der Traktat der Schrieber (Sopherim)', Wissenschaftl. Zeitschr. der Karl Marx-Univ. Leipzig 3 (1953–4).

(d) *Ebel rabbati:* Editions: M. Higger, *Treatise Semaḥot* (1931); cf. M. Guttmann, MGWJ 80 (1931), pp. 26–38. M. Klotz, *Der talmudische Tractat, Ebel rabbathi oder S'machot nach Handschriften und Parallelstellen bearbeitet* (1891).

English translations: Soncino, *Minor Tractates* I, pp. 326–400; D. Zlotnick, *The tractate 'Mourning'* (1966), contains in an appendix the Hebrew text, edited from MSS.

Introduction: Zunz, p. 94; J. Z. Lauterbach, JE XI, pp. 180–2; Strack, p. 73.

(e) *Kallah:* Editions: M. Higger, *Massekhtot Kallah* (1936); M. Sidersky, *Meliloth: text of tractates Derekh ereṣ zuṭa and Kallah with commentary* (1967) (in Hebrew).

English translation: Soncino, *Minor Tractates* II, pp. 401–14.

Introduction: Zunz, p. 94; W. Bacher, JE VII, p. 423; V. Aptowitzer, 'Le traité de "Kalla" ', REJ 57 (1909), pp. 239–44.

The expanded version of Kallah, known as 'Kallah rabbati', is edited in Higger's *Massekhtoth Kallah* (1936); English translation in Soncino, *Minor Tractates* II, pp. 415–528. Cf. Higger, 'Yarḥi's commentary on Kallah Rabbati', JQR 24 (1934), pp. 331–48.

(f) *Derekh Erez Rabbah:* Editions: M. Goldberg, *Der talmudische Tractat Derech Erez Rabba nach Handschriften neu edirt und übersetzt* I (1888); M. Higger, *The treatises Derek erez, Pirke ben Azzai, Tosefta Derek erez, edited from MSS with an introduction, notes, variants and transl.* (1935).

English translation: Soncino, *Minor Tractates* II, pp. 529–66.

In general: Zunz, p. 93; L. Ginzberg, JE IV, pp. 526–8; S. Krauss, 'Le traité talmudique 'Derech Éreç'' ', REJ 36 (1898), pp. 27–46; 205–21; 37 (1899), pp. 45–64.

(g) *Derekh Ereẓ Zuṭṭa:* Editions: A. Tawrogi, *Der talmudische Tractat 'Derech Erez Sutta' nach Handschriften . . . kritisch bearbeitet übersetzt und erläutert* (1885); M. Higger, *Massekhtoth Ze'eroth* (1929); *Supplement* (1934); M. Sidersky, *Meliloth: text of tractates Derekh ereṣ zuṭa and Kallah with commentary* (1967) (in Hebrew).

English translation: Soncino, *Minor Tractates* II, pp. 567–96.

Introduction: Zunz, p. 93; L. Ginzberg, JE IV, pp. 528–9.

(h) *Perek Shalom:* Edition: M. Higger, *Massekhtoth Ze'eroth* (1929); Supplement (1934). This tractate is found as chap. XI of *Derekh Ereẓ Zuṭṭa* in the Vilna Talmud.

English translation: Soncino, *Minor Tractates* II, pp. 597–602.

Introduction: L. Ginsberg, JE IV, p. 529.

(i) *The other small tractates:* Edition: M. Higger, *Seven Minor Tractates: Sefer Torah; Mezuzah; Tefillin; Ẓiẓith; 'Abadim; Kutim; Gerim, and the treatise Soferim II, edited from MSS* (1930). English translations in Soncino, *Minor Tractates* II, pp. 603–64.

II. The Midrashim

In the Mishnah, Tosefta and the two Talmuds, Jewish law is systematically codified. Another type of rabbinic writings is more directly and closely bound to the Bible, in that it comments on the scriptural books passage by passage. These commentaries or Midrashim contain both halakhic and haggadic material. The earlier compositions (Mekhilta, Sifra, Sifre) are mixed, with halakhah predominating; the more recent (Midrash Rabbah, etc.) are almost exclusively haggadic. The first group is closely related to the Mishnah in regard to age and contents; the second came into being largely during the time of the Amoraim and was compiled in the subsequent period. These Midrashim are not the product of legal academic discussion, but of edifying lectures and sermons held in the synagogue.

The three older works, Mekhilta (on Exod. 12–23), Sifra (on Lev and Sifre (on Num. 5–35 and Deut.) form an independent group. (For a brief general introduction, see Strack, pp. 206–9.)

All three are used frequently in the Talmud. Sifra and Sifre are mentioned explicitly (cf. Zunz, pp. 50–1). The original title of the Tannaitic Midrashim on Exodus, Leviticus, Numbers and Deuteronomy was ספרי דבי רב (literally: 'Books of the School'). Of these, the Midrash on Leviticus became known as 'the Book' par excellence (ספרא). The designation Mekhilta ('Tractates'), referring to the Exodus part of the collection, is first attested in Gaonic times. (See J. Z. Lauterbach, *Mekilta* I, p. xxi, n. 17.) In their original form, the Tannaitic Midrashim date from the second century A.D., but they were revised later. Mekhilta is ascribed to R. Ishmael (cf. vol. II, § 25 iv) on the grounds that, as in Sifre, his sayings and those of his school are quoted very frequently there. Another recension of the same work, with R. Simeon as principal spokesman, is known as Mekhilta of R. Simeon ben Yoḥai. Lauterbach (*Mekilta* I, p. xix), adopting the theory of Geiger (*Urschrift*, pp. 184 ff., 435 ff.), considers that Mekhilta and Sifre reflect the point of view of the early halakhah, whilst the Mishnah, Tosefta and Sifra, correspond to a more recent stage of legal evolution. Haggadah is represented only weakly in Sifra, but more substantially in Mekhilta and Sifre (nearly half the contents of the latter are haggadic: cf. Zunz, pp. 88–9). The language of the Tannaitic, as well as that of the other Midrashim is almost entirely Hebrew only occasionally interspersed with Aramaic words, phrases or longer sentences.

Bibliography on the Midrashim in General

D. Hoffmann, *Zur Einleitung in die halachischen Midraschim* (1886–7).

W. Bacher, *Die Agada der Tannaiten*, I–II (1884–90); *Terminologie der Tannaiten* (1889); *Die exegetische Terminologie der jüdischen Traditionsliteratur*, I–II (1889/1905); *Die Proömien der alten jüdischen Homilie* (1913); *'Erkhe Midrash* (1923) (In Hebrew).

M. Gutmann, *Zur Einleitung in die Halacha* I–II (1909–13).

J. Z. Lauterbach, 'Midrash and Mishnah', JQR n.s. 5 (1914–15), pp. 503–27; 6 (1915–16), pp. 23–95; 303–23.

H. Albeck, *Untersuchungen über die halakischen Midraschim* (1927).

M. Kasher, *Ḥumash Torah Sheʼlemah, Talmudic-Midrashic Encyclopaedia of the Pentateuch* (1927–). *Encyclopedia of Biblical Interpretation: A Millenial Anthology* (1953–).

H. L. Strack, *Introduction to the Talmud and Midrash* (1931).

C. Tchernowitz, *Toledoth ha-Halakhah*, I–IV (1934–50).

K. H. Rengstorf (ed.), *Tannaitische Midraschim* (1933/59).

L. Finkelstein, 'The Sources of the Tannaitic Midrashim', JQR 31 (1940/41), pp. 211–43.

E. Z. Melamed, *Halachic Midrashim of the Tannaim in the Talmud Babli* (1943) (in Hebrew).

I. Heinemann, **דרכי האגדה** (The Methods of Aggada) (1949).

S. Zeitlin, 'Midrash, a historical study', JQR 44 (1953), pp. 21–36.

R. Bloch, 'Midrash', DB Supp., cols. 1263–80.

J. N. Epstein, *Introduction to Tannaitic Literature* (in Hebr.), ed. E. Z. Melamed (1957).

G. Vermes, *Scripture and Tradition in Judaism. Haggadic Studies* (1961).

G. Vermes, 'Bible and Midrash', CHB I (1970), pp. 199–231, 592.

J. Heinemann and D. Noy (eds.), *Studies in Aggadah and Folk-Literature*, Scrip. Hier. XXII (1972).

Mekhilta of R. Ishmael

J. H. Weiss, *Mechilta: der älteste halachische und hagadische Commentar zum zweiten Buche Moses kritisch bearbeitet und commentirt* (1865).

M. Friedmann, *Mechilta deRabbi Ismael, der älteste halachische und hagadische Midrasch zu Exodus* (1870).

H. S. Horovitz and I. A. Rabin, *Mechilta d'Rabbi Ismael cum variis lectionibus et adnotationibus* (1931).

J. Z. Lauterbach, *Mekilta deRabbi Ishmael: A critical edition on the basis of the MSS and early editions with an English translation, introduction and notes* I–III (1933).

J. Winter and A. Wünsche, *Mechilta: ein tannaitischer Midrasch zu Exodus, erstmalig ins Deutsche übersetzt und erläutert* (1909).

B. Kosovsky, *Otzar Leshon Hatanna'im: Concordantiae verborum quae in Mechilta d'Rabbi Ismael reperiuntur* I–IV (1965–6).

L. A. Rosenthal, 'Einiges über die Agada in der Mechilta', *Semitic Studies in Memory of A. Kohut* (1897), pp. 463–84.
J. Z. Lauterbach, 'Mekilta' in JE VIII, pp. 444–7.
J. Theodor, 'Midrash Haggadah', s.v. 'Mekilta', JE VIII, p. 554.
J. N. Epstein, *Introduction to Tannaitic Literature* (1957), pp. 545–87 (in Hebrew).
J. Z. Lauterbach, 'The Name of the Mekilta' JQR 11 (1920), pp. 169–95.
L. Finkelstein, 'The Mekilta and its Text', PAAJR 5 (1933–4), pp. 3–54.
E. Y. Kutscher, 'Geniza Fragments of the Mekhilta de-Rabbi Ishmael', Leshonenu 32 (1968), pp. 103–16 (in Hebrew).
B. Z. Wacholder, 'The Date of the Mekilta de-Rabbi Ishmael', HUCA 39 (1968), pp. 117–44.
M. D. Herr, 'Mekhilta of R. Ishmael', Enc. Jud. XI (1971), cols. 1267–9.

Mekhilta of R. Simeon b. Yoḥai:

D. Hoffmann, *Mechilta deRabbi Simeon b. Johai, ein halachischer und haggadischer Midrasch* (1905).
J. N. Epstein–E. Z. Melamed, *Mekilta deR. Simeon b. Johai* (1955).
D. Hoffmann, 'Zur Einleitung in Mechilta deR. Simeon b. Joḥai', Jahrb. f. jüd. Gesch. u. Lit. 3 (1900), pp. 191–205.
J. N. Epstein, *Introduction to Tannaitic Literature* (1957), pp. 728–40 (in Hebrew).
M. D. Herr, 'Mekhilta of R. Simeon Ben Yoḥai', Enc. Jud. XI (1971), cols. 1269–70.

Sifra

J. H. Weiss, *Barajtha zum Leviticus, mit dem Commentar des Abraham ben David* (1862).
M. Friedmann, *Sifra, der älteste Midrasch zu Leviticus. Nach Handschriften . . . und mit Anmerkungen* (1915), incomplete.
L. Finkelstein, *Sifra or Torat Kohanim according to Codex Assemani LXVI, with a Hebrew introduction* (1956).
B. Kosovsky, *Otzar Leshon Hatanna'im: Concordantiae verborum quae in Sifra . . . reperiuntur* I–IV (1967–9).
Studies on Sifra: Z. Frankel, MGWJ (1854), pp. 387–92, 453–61; A. Geiger, JZWL 11 (1875), pp. 50–60; S. Horovitz, 'Sifra', JE XI, pp. 330–2.
J. N. Epstein, *Introduction to Tannaitic Literature* (1957), pp. 645–702 (in Hebrew).
Herr, 'Sifra', Enc. Jud. XIV (1971), cols. 1517–19.

Sifre

M. Friedmann, *Sifre debe Rab, der älteste halachische und hagadische Midrasch zu Numeri und Deuteronomium* (1864).
H. S. Horovitz, *Sifre d'be Rab I: Sifre ad Numeros adjecto Siphre zutta cum variis lectionibus et adnotationibus* (1917).
S. Koleditzky, *Sifre on Numbers and Deuteronomy* (1948) (in Hebrew).
Z. H. Walk, *Sifre on Numbers and Deuteronomy* (1948) (in Hebrew).
P. P. Levertoff, *Midrash Sifre on Numbers: selections . . . translated* (1926).
L. Finkelstein, *Siphre ad Deuteronomium . . . cum variis lectionibus et ad notationibus* (1939, [2]1969) (in Hebrew).
K. G. Kuhn, *Siphre zu Numeri* (1959), German translation.
H. Ljungman, *Sifre zu Deuteronomium* (1964–), German translation in progress.
Studies on Sifre: S. Horovitz, 'Sifre', JE XI, p. 332; B. Pick, 'Text-Varianten aus Mechilta und Sifre', ZAW 6 (1886), pp. 101–21 ;L. Blau, 'Beiträge zur Erklärung der Mechilta und des Sifre', in *Festschrift M. Steinschneider* (1896), pp. 21–40.

J. N. Epstein, *Introduction to Tannaitic Literature* (1957), pp. 588–624, 703–24, 741–6 (in Hebrew).
M. D. Herr, 'Sifra', Enc. Jud. XIV (1971), cols. 1519–21.

Further Tannaitic midrash material may be collected from the *Midrash ha-Gadol*, a thirteenth-century Yemenite compilation, and from *Sifre Zuṭṭa*.

Editions: M. Margolioth, *Midrash ha-Gadol on Genesis* (1947); *Midrash ha-Gadol on Exodus* (1956). D. Hoffmann, *Midrasch ha-gadol zum Buche Exodus* (1913–21). E. N. Rabbinowitz, *Midrash ha-Gadol on Leviticus* (1932). S. Fisch, *Midrash ha-Gadol on Numbers* ([2]1957). D. Hoffmann, *Midrasch Tannaim* (Deuteronomy) (1908–9). N. Z. Hasidah, *Midrash ha-Gadol on Deut.* 1–33, Ha-Segullah 1–78 (1934–42). H. S. Horovitz, *Sifre zutta* (1917). S. Lieberman, *Siphre Zutta* (1968).

The following Midrashim consist almost entirely of haggadah.

4. *Midrash Rabbah.* A collection of Midrashim on the Pentateuch and the five Megilloth (the Song of Songs, Ruth, Lamentations, Ecclesiastes, Esther) dating from different periods but later unified into a single compilation. Midrash Rabbah on the Pentateuch has been recently edited with brief notes in modern Hebrew by E. E. Halevy, *Midrash Rabbah* I–VIII (1956–63). (Note that in this edition every Aramaic phrase is translated into Hebrew!) Another modern edition of the Pentateuch with brief Hebrew commentary is M. A. Mirkin, *Midrash Rabbah* I–XI (1956–67). A complete English translation has been issued by the Soncino Press: H. Freedman—M. Simon, *Midrash Rabbah* I–X+Index vol. ([2]1951). Still useful is A. Wünsche, *Bibliotheca Rabbinica. Eine Sammlung alter Midraschim zum ersten Male ins Deutsche übertragen* I–XII (1880–5). (Midrash Rabbah, Midrash to Proverbs and Pesikta deRav Kahana.) For a general introduction to the works in this section see J. Theodor, 'Midrash Haggadah', JE VIII, pp. 557–69.

(a) *Bereshith Rabbah* on Genesis. According to Zunz (pp. 84–7), this was compiled in the sixth century A.D. in Palestine. Cf. also Strack (pp. 217–18), who considers it roughly contemporary with the Talmud Yerushalmi (*c.* A.D. 400). The final few chapters of Gen. R. are certainly later. Editions: The best critical text is that published by J. Theodor and Ch. Albeck, *Bereschit Rabba mit kritischen Apparat und Kommentar* (1903–29), with *Einleitung und Register* by Albeck (1932). See also H. Odeberg, *The Aramaic Portions of Bereshit Rabba* (1939); Halevy, *Midrash Rabbah* I–II; Mirkin, *Midrash Rabbah* I–IV. English translation in the Soncino *Midrash Rabbah,* I–II. Studies: J. Theodor, JE III, pp. 62–5; MGWJ 37 (1892–3), pp. 169–73, 206–13, 452–8; MGWJ 38 (1893–4), pp. 9–26, 433–6; MGWJ 39 (1894–5), pp. 106–10, 241–7, 289–95, 337–43, 385–90, 433–41, 489–91. Cf. A. Marmorstein, 'The Introduction of R. Hoshaya to the First Chapter of Genesis Rabba', *L. Ginzberg Jubilee Volume* (1945), pp. 247–52; L. I. Rabinowitz, 'The Study of a Midrash', JQR 58 (1967), pp. 143–61; Herr, 'Genesis

Rabbah', Enc. Jud. VII (1971), cols. 399–401; J. Heinemann, 'The Structure and Division of Genesis Rabba', Bar Ilan 9 (1972), pp. 279–89 (Hebrew with English summary).

N.B. Bereshith Rabbah differs from the later *Bereshith rabbati*, ed. Ch. Albeck, *Midrash Bereshith Rabbati* (1940), and from *Aggadath Bereshith*, ed. A. Jellinek, *Beth ha-Midrasch* (1857), IV, 'Hagada zur Genesis', and S. Buber, *Aggadat Bereshit* (^{2}1925).

(b) *Shemoth Rabbah* on Exodus. Zunz's view that this work was compiled in the 11th–12th centuries (p. 269) has been rejected by E. E. Halevy, who places its redaction at the beginning of the seventh century. Edition: Halevy, *Midrash Rabbah* III–IV; Mirkin, *Midrash Rabbah*, V–VI, and English translation in the Soncino *Midrash Rabbah* III. Cf. Herr, 'Exodus Rabbah', Enc. Jud. VI (1971), cols. 1067–9.

(c) *Wayyikra Rabbah* on Leviticus consists of 37 homilies (cf. Strack, pp. 211–12) assembled in the middle of the seventh century A.D. according to Zunz, p. 193, but more likely in the fifth. Editions: M. Margolies, *Midrash Wayyikra Rabbah. A critical edition based on MSS. . . . and Genizah fragments with variants and notes* I–V (1953–60); Halevy's *Midrash Rabbah* V; Mirkin, *Midrash Rabbah* VII–VIII. English translation in the Soncino *Midrash Rabbah* IV. Cf. J. Z. Lauterbach, JE XII, pp. 478–9; Ch. Albeck, 'Midrash Wayyikra Rabba', *L. Ginzberg Jubilee Volume* (1946) (Hebrew Part), pp. 25–43; J. Heinemann, 'Chapters of doubtful Authenticity in Leviticus Rabba', Tarbiz 37 (1967–8), pp. 339–54 (in Hebrew with an English summary); J. Heinemann, 'Profile of a Midrash. The Art of Composition in Leviticus Rabba', Journ. Am. Acad. of Rel. 39 (1971), pp. 141–50; *idem*, 'Leviticus Rabbah', Enc. Jud. XI, cols. 147–50.

(d) *Bamidbar Rabbah* on Numbers is a composite work dating in its final form from the twelfth century (Zunz, p. 273; Strack, p. 214). Editions: E. E. Halevy, *Midrash Rabbah* VI–VII; Mirkin, *Midrash Rabbah* IX–X. English translation in the Soncino *Midrash Rabbah* V–VI. See also J. Theodor, JE II, pp. 669–71; M. D. Herr, Enc. Jud. XII, cols. 1261–3.

(e) *Debarim Rabbah* on Deuteronomy was compiled around A.D. 900 (Zunz, p. 264; Strack, p. 214). It contains 27 homilies preserved in two different manuscript traditions. Editions: S. Lieberman, *Midrash Debarim Rabbah* (^{2}1964); E. E. Halevy, *Midrash Rabbah* VIII; Mirkin, *Midrash Rabbah* XI. English translation in Soncino *Midrash Rabbah* VII. Cf. J. Theodor, JE IV, pp. 487–8; Herr, Enc. Jud. V, cols. 1584–6.

(f) *Shir ha-Shirim Rabbah* on the Song of Songs is also called *Aggadath Ḥazitha* (because of its opening words). This work belongs to the later Midrashim but is 'probably older than Pesikta Rabbati' (Zunz, p. 275: i.e. prior to the middle of the ninth century, but possibly from the seventh or eighth century; cf. S. T. Lachs JQR 55 (1965), p. 249). No critical edition is available. The most readily accessible text is that of the complete *Midrash Rabbah* published in Vilna in 1878. English translation in the Soncino *Midrash Rabbah* IX. Cf. J. Z. Lauterbach, JE XI pp. 291–2. See also S. T. Lachs, 'An Egyptian Festival in Canticles Rabba', JQR 51 (1960), pp. 47–54; 'Prolegomena to Canticles Rabba', *ibid.* 55 (1965), pp. 235–55; 'The Proems of Canticles Rabba', *ibid.* 56 (1966), pp. 225–39; Herr, Enc. Jud. XV, cols. 152–4.

Other homiletic Midrashim on the same book are:

(1) *Agadath Shir ha-Shirim*, edited by S. Schechter (1896); cf. JQR 6 (1894), pp. 672–97; *ibid.* 7 (1895), pp. 145–63, 729–54; *ibid.* 8 (1896), pp. 289–320. The same text, with the addition of similar material on Ruth, Ekhah, and Koheleth, has been edited also by S. Buber, *Midrasch Suta* (1894).

(2) *Midrash Shir ha-Shirim*, edited by L. Grünhut (1897). Cf. M. Seligsohn, JE XI, pp. 292–3.

(g) *Ruth Rabbah* was placed in about the same period as (f) by Zunz, pp. 276–7, and Strack, p. 220, but is likely to have been compiled from Amoraic material in the sixth century A.D. (cf. M. D. Herr, Enc. Jud. XIV, col. 524). Edition: S. Buber, *Midrasch Suta* (1894). English translation in Soncino *Midrash Rabbah* VIII. Cf. M. Seligsohn, JE X, pp. 577–8.

(h) *Midrash Ekhah* on Lamentations is also called *Ekhah Rabbati.* Zunz saw in this a Palestinian composition from the second half of the seventh century (pp. 189–91), but it is more likely to date to about A.D. 400 (cf. Strack, p. 219). The great number of Greek words also favours an earlier origin. Edition: S. Buber, *Midrasch Echa Rabbathi* (1899). English translation: Soncino *Midrash Rabbah* VII. Cf. also S. Buber, *Midrasch Suta* (1894). Cf. J. Theodor, JE V, pp. 85–7; Herr, Enc. Jud. X, cols. 1376–8.

(i) *Midrash Koheleth* or *Koheleth Rabbah* is from about the same period as the Midrash to the Song of Songs and Ruth (Zunz, p. 277). Edition by S. Buber, *Midrasch Suta* (1894). English translation in the Soncino *Midrash Rabbah* VIII. Cf. L. Grünhut, *Kritische Untersuchung des Midrasch Koheleth* I (1892); J. Theodor, JE VII, pp. 529–32; S. Lieberman, 'Notes on Chapter I of Midrash *Koheleth Rabbah*', *Studies in Mysticism and Religion presented to G. G. Scholem* (1967), pp. 163–79 (Hebrew Section); Herr, Enc. Jud. VI, col. 355.

(j) *Midrash Esther* or *Haggadath Megillah.* The final composition of this work includes a quotation from Yosippon (10th century): cf. Zunz, p. 276. The basic material, however, is from the age of the Amoraim (see Strack, p. 221). No critical edition of this Midrash is available. For a text see the complete edition of Midrash Rabbah, Vilna 1878. English translation in Soncino *Midrash Rabbah* IX. Cf. J. Theodor, JE V, p. 241; Herr, Enc. Jud. VI, cols. 915–6.

Other Midrashim on Esther are:

(1) *Midrash Abba Gorion*. See A. Jellinek, *Bet ha-Midrasch* I (1853), pp. 1–18; S. Buber, *Sifre d'Aggadta Megillath Esther. Sammlung agadischer Commentare zum Buche Esther* (1886).

(2) S. Buber, *Aggadath Esther* (1897), based on two Yemenite MSS. This Midrash quotes Alfasi and Maimonides, see Strack, p. 222.

(3) M. Gaster, 'The Oldest Version of Midrash Megillah', *Semitic Studies in Memory of Alex. Kohut* (1897), pp. 167–78.

(4) *Targum Sheni* on Esther. See the literature on this below, p. 114.

On the Midrash Rabbah in general: Strack, pp. 214–22; J. Theodor, 'Midrash Haggadah', JE VIII, pp. 557 ff; 'Die Midraschim zum Pentateuch und der dreijährige palästinensische Cyclus', MGWJ 34 (1885), pp. 351–66; ibid. 35 (1886), pp. 212–18; ibid. 36 (1887), pp. 35–48. Editions with Hebrew commentaries appeared in Warsaw (1874) and Vilna (1878), and have been often reprinted.

5. *Pesiḳta*

The Pesiḳta (i.e. 'sections') deals not with a whole book of the Bible, but with biblical readings for the feasts and special Sabbaths of the year, sometimes, that is, selected from the Pentateuch and sometimes from the prophets, cf. Strack, pp. 210–11. Because of its many resemblances to Bereshith Rabbah, Lev. R. and Ekhah Rabbati, Zunz (pp. 206–7) believed the text of Pesiḳta to be dependent on them and concluded that it was composed around A.D. 700. Buber, on the other hand, together with Theodor, Strack and others, maintains that Pesiḳta is older than these Midrashim. The designation of the work as 'Pesiḳta of Rab Kahana' is only an abbreviation of 'Pesiḳta of R. Abba b. Kahana'. (See W. Bacher, *Die Agada der paläst. Amoräer* III, p. 609).

Editions: S. Buber, *Pesikta. Die älteste Hagada, redigiert in Palästina von Rab Kahana* (1868). German translation by A. Wünsche, *Pesikta des Rab Kahana, nach der Buberschen Textausgabe ins Deutsche übertragen* (1885). The best edition is that by B. Mandelbaum, *Pesikta deRab Kahana*, I–II (1962), with Hebrew and English introduction. For a review of this work see A. Goldberg, Kirjath Sepher 43 (1967), pp. 68 ff. For general works see: Zunz, pp. 195–237; J. Theodor, 'Zur Composition der agadischen Homilien', MGWJ 28 (1879), 97 ff, 164 ff, 271 ff; JE VIII, pp. 559–60; Strack, pp. 210–11; W. Bacher, 'Un passage inexpliqué de la Pesikta', REJ 61 (1911), 124–6; I. Lévi, 'Le Pesikta deRab Cahana contenait-elle une section pour Simhat Tora?', *ibid.* 63 (1912), pp. 129–30; A. Perles, 'Un passage obscur dans la Pesikta', *ibid.* 62 (1911), pp. 236–9; B. Mandelbaum, 'Prolegomena to the Pesikta', PAAJR 23 (1954), pp. 41–58; Z. Zinger, 'The Bible quotations in the Pesiqta deRav Kahana', Textus 5 (1966), 114–24; A. Goldberg, 'On the authenticity of certain chapters in the Pesikta', Tarbiz 38 (1968), pp. 184 ff. (Hebr. with English summary). Mandelbaum, Enc. Jud. XIII, cols. 333–4.

In addition to the Pesiḳta deRab Kahana, or simply 'Pesiḳta', there exist three other works of the same name:

(a) *Pesiḳta Rabbati,* like the other Pesiḳta deals with biblical readings for certain feasts and Sabbaths of the Jewish year, though its homilies are differently arranged. Cf. in general Zunz, pp. 250–62. It originated in the second half of the ninth century according to Zunz (p. 255), whose opinion has been adopted by I. Lévi, W. Bacher, and V. Aptowitzer. According to the opening paragraph, 777 years had elapsed since the destruction of the Temple, the second Temple according to Zunz, hence his mid-ninth century date. But M. Friedmann understands the reference to concern the first Temple and dates the work A.D. 355. Lately, W. G. Braude has qualified the figure 777 as a gloss and has suggested the sixth or seventh centuries as the most likely date of the redaction.

Edition: M. Friedmann, *Pesikta Rabbati* (1880). Cf. A. Scheiber, 'An old MS of the Pesiqta on the Ten Commandments', Tarbiz 25 (1956), pp. 464–7 (a Geniza fragment); W. G. Braude, 'The Piska concerning the sheep which rebelled, Piska 2b edited on the basis of Parma MS 1240', PAAJR 30 (1962), pp. 1–35. English translation: W. G. Braude, *Pesikta Rabbati* I–II (1968). Cf. J. Theodor, JE VIII, pp. 561–2; W. G. Braude, 'Overlooked meanings of certain editorial terms in the Pesikta Rabbati', JQR 52 (1962), pp. 264–72; D. Sperber, Enc. Jud. XIII, cols. 335–6.

(b) *Pesiḳta Ḥadatta* (New Pesiḳta) is a more concise version of the Pesiḳta Rabbati. Edition: A. Jellinek, *Bet haMidrasch* VI (1887).

(c) *Pesiḳta zuṭarta* is a Midrash to the Pentateuch and the five Megilloth compiled by R. Tobia ben Eliezer at the beginning of the twelfth century. This work, commonly known as *Leḳaḥ Ṭob,* has been labelled Pesiḳta in error, for it bears no resemblance to the other works bearing that name.

Editions: S. Buber, *Lekach Tob* I–II (1880), Genesis–Exodus; Aaron Moses Padua, *Lekach Tob* III–V (1884), Leviticus–Deuteronomy; reprinted I–V Jerusalem (1959–60). For the Megilloth: A. Jellinek, *Commentarien zu Esther, Ruth und den Klageliedern* (1855), pp. 50–1, fragments of Tobia ben Eliezer on Lamentations. S. Bamberger, *Lekach Tob* (*Pesikta Sutarta*). *Ein agadischer Kommentar zu Megillat Ruth* (1887); G. Feinberg, *Tobia ben Elieser's Commentar zu Koheleth* (1904); J. Nacht, *Tobia ben Elieser's Commentar zu Threni* (*Lekach Tob*) (1895); A. W. Greenup, *The Commentary of R. Tobia ben Elieser on Echah* (1908); *The Commentary of R. Tobia b. Elieser on Canticles* (1909).

Further on the Pesiḳtas see I. Lévi, 'La Pesikta rabbati et le 4e Ezra', REJ 24 (1892), pp. 281–5; W. Bacher, *Die Agada der paläst. Amoräer* (1899) III, pp. 493 ff. (on the relationship of the Pesiḳta Rabbati and Tanḥuma); V. Aptowitzer, 'Untersuchungen zur gaonäischen Literatur', HUCA 8/9 (1931–2), pp. 380–410; B. J. Bamberger, 'A Messianic Document of the Seventh Century', HUCA 15 (1940), pp. 425–31. On the town mentioned in Pesiḳta Rabbati 28:2, 'Bari', to which the Israelites were deported under Nebuchadnezzar (=Titus?), see I. Lévi, REJ 32 (1896), pp. 278–82; W. Bacher, ibid. 33 (1896), pp. 40–5; Krauss, MGWJ

41 (1897), pp. 554–64 (Bari = Berytus); Bacher, ibid. 41 (1897), pp. 604–12; cf. also Bacher, ibid. 33 (1889), pp. 45 ff.; Lévi, ibid. 35 (1891), pp. 224 ff. But note Braude, *op. cit.* II, p. 557 and n. 18.

6. *Pirḳe de-Rabbi Eliezer* or *Baraitha de-Rabbi Eliezer*

A Palestinian Haggadic work in fifty-four chapters, following in the main the course of Pentateuchal history and particularly detailed in regard to the creation story and the first man, and to the patriarchal and Mosaic periods. It was written, at the earliest, in the eighth century (see Zunz, p. 289), or at the beginning of the ninth (Strack, pp. 225–6). It uses much ancient material. Edition: M. Higger, 'Pirḳe Rabbi Eliezer', Horeb 8–10 (1944–8). English translation: G. Friedländer, *Pirḳe deRabbi Eliezer* (1916). Cf. Zunz, pp. 283–90; Strack, pp. 255–6; S. Ochser, JE X, pp. 58–60; I. Lévi, 'Éléments chrétiens dans le Pirké Rabbi Eliezer', REJ 18 (1889), pp. 83–9; M. D. Herr, Enc. Jud. XIII, cols. 558–60.

7. *Tanḥuma* or *Yelammedenu*

A homiletic Midrash on the Pentateuch known also as Yelammedenu because of the frequently used formula ילמדנו רבינו, 'May our masters teach us'. Two different recensions distinguished as Yelammedenu and Tanḥuma are quoted in the Yalḳuṭ (Strack, p. 212). The text of Tanḥuma is available in three recensions: that of the common editions, that of the semi-critical version of S. Buber, and another form of the text apparent in the citations of Yalḳuṭ ha-Makhiri (see below, p. 99). No complete manuscript of Yelammedenu has survived. Tanḥuma is the oldest haggadic Midrash to the whole Pentateuch; Bacher argued convincingly that it was actually R. Tanḥuma, the last significant Palestinian haggadist (*c.* A.D. 400), who laid the foundation for this Midrashic work.

Editions: S. Buber, *Midrasch Tanchuma. Ein agadischer Commentar zum Pentateuch von Rabbi Tanchuma ben Rabbi Abba* I–III (1885). Fragments of Yelammedenu and Tanḥuma are in A. Jellinek, *Bet ha-Midrasch* VI (1877), pp. 79–105. Fragments of Yelammedenu: A. Neubauer, 'Le Midrasch Tanchuma et extraits du Yélamdénu et de petits midraschim', REJ 13 (1886), pp. 224–38; *ibid.* 14 (1887), pp. 92–113. L. Grünhut, *Sefer ha-Liḳḳuṭim*, I–V (1898–1901); L. Ginzberg, *Ginzei Schechter* I (1928), pp. 449–513. Examples of all three recensions in German translation: Winter and Wünsche, *Die jüdische Literatur seit Abschluss des Kanons* (1894) I, pp. 411–32. In general see Zunz, pp. 237–50; Strack, p. 212; J. Theodor, JE XII, pp. 45–6; 'Buber's Tanchuma', MGWJ 34 (1885), pp. 35–42, 422–31; W. Bacher, 'Zu Buber's Tanchuma-Ausgabe', MGWJ 34 (1885), pp. 551–4. J. Theodor, 'Die Midraschim zum Pentateuch und der dreijährige palästinensische Cyclus', MGWJ 34 (1885), pp. 351–66, ibid. 35 (1886), pp. 212–18, ibid. 36 (1887), pp. 35–48; ibid. 35 (1886), pp. 212–18, ibid. 36 (1887), pp. 35–48; see above p. 93. W. Bacher, *Die Agada der paläst. Amoräer* (1899), III, pp. 500–14; J. Mann, *The Bible as Read and Preached in the Old Synagogue* I–II (1940–66); Herr, Enc. Jud. XV, cols. 794–6.

8. *Yalkuṭ Shim'oni*

A large midrashic compilation covering the whole Hebrew Bible in which, as in the patristic *catenae* ('chains'), various explanations of a given passage are assembled from more than fifty works, some of them no longer extant. It was composed in the first half of the thirteenth century (Zunz, p. 312) by R. Simeon ha-Darshan, who was probably a native of Frankfurt am Main. His identification with Simeon ha-Darshan, father of Joseph Ḳara, is unlikely (cf. Strack, p. 230).

In general see Zunz, pp. 308–15; Strack, p. 230. No critical edition exists. The first edition was printed at Salonica 1521–7 and has been often reissued. The most accessible editions are New York (1944) I–III (a reprint of the Vilna edition of 1898); and B. Landau, *Yalḳuṭ Shim'oni* I–II, Jerusalem (1960). See also, J. Z. Lauterbach, JE XII, pp. 585–6; E. G. King, *The Yalkut on Zechariah, translated with notes and appendices* (1882). A. Wünsche has edited and translated Yalḳuṭ on Hosea, Micah and Jonah in Vierteljahrsschrift für Bibelkunde 1 (1903–4), pp. 66, 235, 256; ibid. 2 (1904), p. 82. See also M. Gaster, 'La source de Yalkout II', REJ 25 (1892), pp. 44–64 (Yalḳuṭ II = the second part of Yalḳuṭ on the Prophets and Writings). A. Epstein, 'Le Yalkout Schimeoni et le Yalkout ha-Makhiri', REJ 26 (1893), pp. 75–82; A. B. Hyman, *The Sources of the Yalkut Shimeoni to the Prophets and Hagiographa* (1965) (in Hebrew); Y. Elbaum, Enc. Jud. XVI, cols. 707–9.

9. Other medieval midrashic collections:

(a) *Yalḳuṭ ha-Makhiri*, compiled in the fourteenth century by Makhir ben Abba Mari, covers the Latter Prophets and part of the Writings, cf. Strack, p. 231; M. Seligsohn, JE VIII, pp. 246, 569. Editions: J. Spira, *The Yalkut on Isaiah of Machir b. Abba Mari* (1894); S. Buber, *Yalkut ha-Makiri* I–II (1899), on Psalms; L. Grünhut, *Jalkut ha-Machiri. Sammlung midraschischer Auslegungen der Sprüche Salomon von R. Machir bar Abba Mari* (1902); A. W. Greenup edited the Yalḳuṭ on the Minor Prophets from a British Museum MS I–IV (1909–13); cf. also his article, 'A fragment of the Yalkut of R. Machir bar Abba Mari on Hosea', JQR, n.s. 15 (1924), pp. 141–212; J. Z. Lauterbach, 'Unpublished parts of the Yalkut ha-Makhiri on Hosea and Micah', *Occident and Orient, being studies in honour of M. Gaster's 80th birthday* (1936), pp. 365–73; Y. Elbaum, Enc. Jud. XVI, cols. 706–7.

(b) *Leḳaḥ Ṭob:* see *Pesiḳta Zuṭarta* above, p. 97. Cf. Zunz, pp. 306–7; Strack, p. 232; M. Seligsohn, JE XII, pp. 169–71.

III. The Targums

The Targums, or Aramaic translations of the Hebrew Bible, represent the traditional interpretation of Scripture in the synagogues. This is especially true of those offering a paraphrastic rather than literal rendering. Only the Targums on the Pentateuch and on the Prophets will be discussed in any detail; those on the Writings are of lesser significance for the purpose of this work on account of their late redaction. The literature relating to them is listed in section (J) of the Bibliography below.

1. *Onkelos on the Pentateuch.* Talmudic references to a man called Onkelos represent him as a contemporary of Gamaliel II, or R. Eliezer b. Hyrcanus and R. Joshua b. Hananiah (late first and early second century A.D.). They agree that Onkelos was a proselyte.[1] The Aramaic translation attributed to him is distinguished from that of the other Targums by its greater literalness.[2] Nevertheless, it contains a substantial amount of haggadah throughout, but especially in the poetic passages (e.g. Gen. 49, Num. 24, Deut. 32–3). Compared with the haggadah of the Palestinian Targums (see below), that of Onkelos shows a tendency to present traditional exegesis in an abridged form.[3] Anthropomorphic expressions concerning the Deity are always carefully eliminated.[4] In halakhic passages, biblical law is interpreted in general in the light of its rendering in the Mishnah.

The language of Onkelos is Babylonian Aramaic according to A. Geiger.[5] Th. Nöldeke first qualified it as a later development of Palestinian Biblical Aramaic,[6] but subsequently concluded that it is a Palestinian product revised in Babylonia and greatly influenced by the Eastern Aramaic dialect.[7] G. Dalman denies such an influence, or would reduce it to a minimum.[8] In his view, Onkelos has rather preserved the purest form of the Judaean dialect. P. Kahle has renewed with emphasis Geiger's Babylonian theory.[9] Yet the affinity of the language of Onkelos to Qumran Aramaic, first shown convincingly by E. Y. Kutscher,[10] appears to favour strongly the thesis of a Palestinian origin for Onkelos. A study of its interpretative features points in the same direction.[11]

Onkelos was quick to win high esteem in Babylonia. Talmud and Midrashim frequently quote from it;[12] it is designated as 'our Targum' (תרגום דידן, bKidd. 49a) and was later provided with its own Masorah.[13]

1. Cf. tHag. 3:2; tKel. BK 2:4; tDem. 6:13; bMeg. 3a; bGit. 50a; bAZ 11a. On the relationship between Onkelos and Aquila, see below, p. 102.
2. Cf. W. Bacher, 'Targum', JE XII, p. 59.
3. G. Vermes, 'Haggadah in the Onkelos Targum', JSS 8 (1963), pp. 159–69.
4. Already noted by Zunz, p. 66.
5. 'Das nach Onkelos benannte babylonische Thargum zum Pentateuch', JZWL (1871), p. 93.
6. *Die alttestamentliche Literatur* (1868), p. 257.
7. *Mandäische Grammatik* (1877), p. xxvii.
8. *Grammatik des jüd.-pal. Aramäisch* (²1905), pp. 12–13; *Die Worte Jesu* (²1930), p. 67.
9. *Masoreten des Westens* II (1930), p. 1; *The Cairo Geniza* (²1959), p. 194.
10. 'The Language of the "Genesis Apocryphon"', Scrip. Hier. IV (1958), pp. 9–11. On Targum texts from Qumran, see below p. 105.
11. G. Vermes, *art. cit.*, p. 169.
12. Cf. Zunz, p. 67, n. bc.
13. Cf. R. Le Déaut, *Introduction à la littérature targumique* I (1966), p. 78 and n. 1.

Onkelos was printed in the rabbinical Bibles of Bomberg and Buxtorf, and the edition of Sabionetta (1577) was reissued by A. Berliner (1884). At present, the best text available is that published by A. Sperber with supra-linear vocalization and a detailed critical apparatus. The Madrid Polyglot plans to improve on it by reproducing a genuine Babylonian manuscript (MS Ebr. Vat. 448). For matters pertaining to Onkelos, see section (D) in the Bibliography below.[14]

2. *Jonathan to the Prophets*. Jonathan ben Uzziel is said to have been a pupil of Hillel and to have lived in the first decades of the first century A.D.[15] The Targum bearing his name covers the whole collection of the Prophets, i.e. both the historical books and the prophetic writings proper. It is more paraphrastic than Onkelos. 'Jonathan handles even the historical books often as an interpreter; his treatment of the prophets tends to become true haggadic commentary.'[16] Its language is similar to that of Onkelos. Jonathan also soon gained appreciation and was often cited in the Talmud and Midrashim.[17] Like Onkelos, it appears in the rabbinical Bibles of Bomberg and Buxtorf, and in the London Polyglot. P. de Lagarde published in 1872 a valuable edition based on the Codex Reuchlinianus, giving also variants belonging to a Palestinian Targum to the Prophets.[18] Again, the most up-to-date critical text is that of Sperber. See further section (I) in the Bibliography below and R. Le Déaut, *Introduction*, pp. 124–30.

Jewish tradition holds that the Targums of Onkelos and Jonathan were written around the middle of the first, or beginning of the second century A.D. This is still the view of Zunz.[19] The traditional thesis was, however, shattered by Geiger, who advanced the theory that both Targums were composed, or more precisely revised, in the fourth century in Babylonia.[20] Z. Frankel agreed with Geiger on all points save for placing Onkelos a little earlier, in the third century A.D.[21] Its Palestinian prototype dates, according to W. Bacher, from the second century A.D.[22] It should also be noted that Onkelos had already been used by Jonathan.[23] In any case, the Targum to the Prophets was in use in Babylonia in

14. For the latest full discussion of the Onkelos problem, cf. R. Le Déaut, *Introduction*, pp. 78–88.
15. Cf. bSuk. 28a; bB.B. 134a.
16. Zunz, p. 66.
17. Zunz, p. 67, n. bc.
18. *Prophetae chaldaice* (1872). The Reuchlinianus was re-edited in 1956 by A. Sperber in Copenhagen.
19. *Op. cit.*, p. 66.
20. *Urschrift*, p. 164. His view has been adopted by P. Kahle (see n. 9 above).
21. *Zu dem Thargum der Propheten* (1872), pp. 8–11.
22. *Art. cit.*, JE XII, p. 59.
23. Zunz, p. 66, n. a.

the early fourth century, since R. Joseph bar Ḥiyya, head of the academy of Pumbedita, quotes from it several times.[24]

It is uncertain whether a Targumist called Onkelos ever existed. The account in the Babylonian Talmud (bMeg 3a) crediting him with an Aramaic version of the Pentateuch, refers to Aquila and his Greek Bible translation in the parallel passage of the Jerusalem Talmud (yMeg. 71c). The latter is in any case likely to be the earlier of the two. אונקלוס and עקילס are confused elsewhere also (cf. e.g. tDem. 6:13 with yDem. 25d). It appears therefore that the ancient and correct information relative to a translation of the Pentateuch by the proselyte Aquila was erroneously transferred to an anonymous Aramaic Targum, and that the name Onkelos resulted from a corruption of Aquila.[25] It is also possible that the attribution to Jonathan of the Targum to the Prophets derives from a distorted tradition concerning a Greek Bible translation by Theodotion (the Hellenic equivalent of Jonathan).[26]

Though compiled in the third or fourth century A.D., there is no doubt that the Targums of Onkelos and Jonathan rely on older works and are the final outcome of a process covering several centuries. The Mishnah knows of an Aramaic Bible translation,[27] and the New Testament more than once echoes the Targumic exegesis of Old Testament passages. Rabbinic literature mentions, with disapproval, the existence of a Targum to Job at the beginning of the first century A.D., i.e. before the destruction of Jerusalem.[28] Qumran, moreover, has yielded various remains dating from the era of the Second Temple (see below).

In consequence, it is clear that the material used in the Targums of Onkelos and Jonathan is the product of the labour of previous generations, and that written Targums preceded the extant ones. Also, the largely literal nature of the Onkelos translation is paralleled in Palestine in the first and early second century A.D. by an identical trend manifest in Greek Bible revision and retranslation.[29]

3. *The Palestinian Targums.* In addition to Onkelos, other Targums on the Pentateuch remain, fragmentarily or *in toto*. Medieval Jewish authors (Ḥai Gaon, Nathan ben Yeḥiel) designate them as *Targum*

24. Cf. bSanh. 94b; bMK 28b; bMeg. 3a. This R. Joseph is represented as the author of the Targum to the Prophets by Ḥai Gaon in his commentary on *Seder Ṭohoroth* quoted in *'Arukh* (ed. Kohut, II, pp. 293a, 308a).

25. Cf. A. Geiger, *art. cit.*, JZWL (1871), pp. 86–7; Z. Frankel, *op. cit.*, pp. 4, 8–9; G. Dalman, *Grammatik*, p. 11; A. E. Silverstone, *Aquila and Onkelos* (1931); P. Kahle, *Cairo Geniza* ([2]1959), pp. 191–2; R. Le Déaut, *Introduction*, p. 80.

26. Cf. P. Kahle, *Cairo Gen.*[2], p. 195; D. Barthélemy, *Les devanciers d'Aquila* (1963), pp. 148–56.

27. mYad. 4:5.

28. Cf. tShab. 13:2–3; yShab. 15c; bShab. 115a. See R. Le Déaut, *Introduction*, pp. 68–70.

29. Cf. D. Barthélemy, *op. cit.*, passim.

Yerushalmi or *Targum Ereẓ Yisrael*. Their principal distinguishing features are (1) their language (a largely Galilean Aramaic dialect),[30] and (2) their tendency towards Midrash (an amalgam of translation and interpretation).[31]

Until 1930, the Palestinian Targum was extant in only two forms. The version covering the whole Pentateuch was known as the Targum of (Pseudo-) Jonathan because of its apocryphal attribution to Jonathan ben Uzziel. The probable cause of this false attribution has been identified by Zunz: the symbol ת׳ י׳, i.e. *Targum Yerushalmi*, was misinterpreted as *Targum Yonathan*.[32] The second form is known as the Fragmentary Targum, and consists of extracts corresponding to short sections, individual verses, or even single words. The continuous texts are usually haggadic.[33]

In 1930, P. Kahle published large fragments belonging to seven manuscripts of the Targum of the Pentateuch originally found in the Cairo Geniza.[34] Further documents of the same origin have since been edited by A. Díez Macho and others.[35] These fragments represent the full recension of the Aramaic Bible from which the Fragmentary Targum was derived. Finally, the first integral manuscript of the *Targum Yerushalmi* containing in its margins a rich collection of textual variants was discovered in 1956 by Díez Macho in the Vatican Library: Codex Neofiti I.[36]

The relationship of these recensions to one another and to Onkelos is still a matter for debate. Ninteenth-century scholars correctly deduced that the Fragmentary Targum was older than Pseudo-Jonathan and was extracted from a complete Targum Yerushalmi.[37] The purpose of the enterprise was to provide a haggadic supplement

30. See G. Dalman, *Grammatik*, p. 32.

31. L. Zunz, *op. cit.*, pp. 75–6. Cf. in general, G. Vermes, *Scripture and Tradition in Judaism* (1961).

32. *Op. cit.*, p. 75. On Ps.-Jonathan (=1TJ) in general, see R. Le Déaut, *Introduction*, pp. 89–101.

33. On the Fragmentary Targum (=2TJ), cf. *ibid.* pp. 102–8.

34. *Masoreten des Westens* II, pp. 1–65.

35. Cf. section (G) in the Bibliography.

36. The first three volumes of the editio princeps appeared between 1968 and 1971. *Neophyti I Targum Palestinense MS de la Biblioteca Vaticana*. They contain a lengthy introduction, a transcription of the codex accompanied by a critical apparatus and a Spanish translation of Genesis and Exodus by the editor. A translation into French by R. Le Déaut, and into English by M. McNamara and M. Maher, are also included. Vol. II comprises also a list of haggadic parallels between Ps.-Jon. and Neof. on Genesis compiled by E. B. Levine.

37. Zunz, pp. 69–75; W. Bacher, 'Kritische Untersuchungen zum Prophetentargum', ZDMG 28 (1874), p. 60; J. Bassfreund, 'Das Fragmenten-Targum zum Pentateuch', MGWJ 40 (1896), pp. 16 ff.; M. Ginsburger, 'Die Thargumim zur Thoralection,' *ibid.* 39 (1895), 97 ff.; 'Zum Fragmententhargum', *ibid.* 41 (1897), pp. 289 ff.

to Onkelos,[38] or 'a collection of individual glosses' to another version of the Yerushalmi.[39] In favour of the latter hypothesis, one might note that the marginal variants of Neofiti published separately would result in another Fragmentary Targum.

Affinity between Ps.-Jonathan and Targum Yerushalmi has long since been recognized. The former is distinguished by (1) linguistic peculiarities (it is the most literary of the Palestinian Targums); (2) a greater quantity of midrashic supplements; and (3) a special relationship to Onkelos.

The substantial amount of identical readings between these two Targums cannot be fortuitous. In explanation, it has been suggested that either Ps.-Jonathan consists of Onkelos supplemented by excerpts from the Targum Yerushalmi,[40] or that a version of Targum Yerushalmi has been revised according to Onkelos.[41] A third tentative theory has been advanced recently: namely, that it is Onkelos that depends on a proto-Ps.-Jonathan, or that both derive from a common source.[42]

Since the Palestinian Targums represent common Jewish exegesis, their dating is extremely difficult. In particular, their practical teaching purpose caused them to be subjected to a process of halakhic and historical revision for a long time after the initial recording of the substance of targumic exegesis. Yet it is undeniable that even Ps.-Jonathan, which was kept up-to-date until as late as at least the seventh century (it mentions the names of the wife and daughter of Muhammed),[43] has also preserved intact many early, sometimes pre-Christian traditions.[44] The *basic* content of the more conservative Targum Yerushalmi is likely to belong to the Tannaitic era; for when comparative material is available, Targumic haggadah is usually paralleled, not only in the Talmud and Midrash, but also in the Pseudepigrapha, Dead Sea Scrolls, New Testament, Philo, Josephus, Pseudo-Philo, etc.[45] In the light of these facts, the following rule of

38. J. Bassfreund. *art. cit.*

39. A. Geiger, *Urschrift*, p. 455.

40. Cf. G. Dalman, *Grammatik*, p. 33; P. Kahle, *Masor. d. West.* II, p. 12*; P. Grelot, 'Les Targums du Pentateuque', Semitica 9 (1959), p. 88.

41. Cf. M. Ginsburger, *Pseudo-Jonathan* (1903), pp. xii, xvii; W. Bacher, 'Targum', JE XII, p. 60; R. Bloch, 'Note pour l'utilisation des fragments de la Geniza du Caire pour l'étude du Targum palestinien', REJ n.s. 14 (1955), p. 31; A. Díez Macho, 'The recently discovered Palestinian Targum', Suppl. VT 7 (1960), pp. 239–45.

42. G. Vermes, 'The Targumic Versions of Genesis IV 3–16', ALUOS 3 (1963), p. 98. Cf. R. Le Déaut, *Introduction*, pp. 98–101.

43. See 1TJ on Gen. 21:21.

44. Cf. A. Geiger, *Urschrift*, p. 479. For a summary of modern research, see R. Le Déaut, *Introduction*, pp. 92–6.

45. Cf. G. Vermes, *Scripture and Tradition in Judaism* (1961); R. Le Déaut, *La nuit pascale* (1963); M. McNamara, *The New Testament and the Palestinian Targum to the Pentateuch* (1966).

thumb has been devised: unless there is specific proof to the contrary, the haggadah of the Palestinian Targums is likely to be Tannaitic and to antedate the outbreak of the Second Jewish Revolt in A.D. 132.[46]

There is no sure answer to the question of priority between Targum-translation of the Onkelos type and Targum-interpretation of the Palestinian variety. The issue cannot be solved by the quotation of an axiom, e.g., 'The simpler and less developed a translation, the older it is.'[47] In favour of the anteriority of the non-midrashic Targum, one may cite the fact that the Qumran Aramaic Leviticus and Job fragments are of the Onkelos type.[48] The opposite argument would emphasizethat (1) the midrashic re-telling of the Bible story has also ancient parallels;[49] (2) analysis of the haggadah in Onkelos shows signs of having been abridged from a more detailed version (cf. above, p. 100); (3) a similar tendency towards approximating the non-literal Greek translation of the LXX to the original proto-Masoretic Hebrew has been shown to have been at work in first and second century A.D. Palestine.[50]

The existence of written Aramaic Targums going back to the inter-Testamental period has been attested by Jewish tradition apropos of the book of Job.[51] Since the Qumran discoveries, fragmentary Targum specimens have become available: a Leviticus fragment (Lev. 16:12–5, 18–21) from cave IV, and, characteristically, two fragments of Job (3:4–5; 4:16–5:4) from the same cave, and a fragmentary scroll of a Targum of Job from cave XI.[52] For full details on Palestinian Targum problems, see Sections A and E–H in the Bibliography.

Bibliography

A. *Introductions with useful bibliographies*

B. J. Roberts, *The Old Testament Text and Versions* (1951), pp. 197–213.
O. Eissfeldt, *The Old Testament: An Introduction* (1965), pp. 696–8.
A. Díez Macho, 'Targum', *Enciclopedia de la Biblia* VI (1965), pp. 865–81.
R. Le Déaut, 'L'état présent de l'étude des Targums', *La Nuit Pascale* (1963), pp. 19–41.

---

46. Cf. G. Vermes, 'Bible and Midrash', CHB I (1970), p. 231.
47. A. Díez Macho, *art. cit.*, Suppl. VT (1960), p. 244.
48. Cf. R. Le Déaut, *Introduction*, pp. 64–7. Cf. also n. 52, below.
49. Cf. G. Vermes, *Scripture and Tradition*, p. 95.
50. See D. Barthélemy, *op. cit.*, passim.
51. Cf. above, n. 28.
52. Cf. J. T. Milik, *Ten Years of Discovery in the Wilderness of Judaea* (1959), p. 31; J. van der Ploeg, *Le Targum de Job de la grotte 11 de Qumran* (1962); A. S. van der Woude, 'Das Hiobtargum aus Qumran Höhle XI', Suppl. VT 9 (1963), pp. 322–31; J. P. M. van der Ploeg, A. S. van der Woude, B. Jongeling, *Le Targum de Job de la grotte XI de Qumrân* (1971). This Targum is the simple translation type. The beginning of the scroll is lost and the fragments start with Job 17:14.

R. Le Déaut, *Introduction à la littérature targumique* (1966).
M. McNamara, 'A brief sketch of Targumic Studies', *The Palestinian Targum to the Pentateuch and the New Testament* (1966), pp. 5–33.
R. Le Déaut, 'Les études targumiques', EThL 44 (1968), pp. 7–34.
J. Bowker, *The Targums and Rabbinic Literature* (1969).
A. Díez Macho, *Manuscritos hebreos y arameos de la Biblia* (1971).
A. Díez Macho, *El Targum* (1972).
M. McNamara, *Targum and Testament* (1972).

B. *A selection of books and articles* (on general and particular topics)

In general see Zunz, and W. Bacher, JE XII, pp. 57–63; B. Grossfeld, Enc. Jud. IV, cols. 841–51.
A. Geiger, *Urschrift und Uebersetzungen der Bibel* (1857; [2]1928).
A. Berliner, *Targum Onkelos* II (1884).
L. Hausdorf, 'Zur Geschichte der Targumim nach talmudischen Quellen', MGWJ 38 (1894), pp. 203–13.
M. Ginsburger, 'Verbotene Thargumim', MGWJ 44 (1900), pp. 1–2.
M. Ginsburger, 'Les introductions araméennes à la lecture du Targum', REJ 73 (1921), pp. 14–26, 186–94.
P. Kahle, 'Das palästinische Pentateuchtargum', *Masoreten des Westens* II (1930).
P. Kahle, *The Cairo Geniza* (1947; [2]1959). [*Der Kairoer Geniza* (1962).]
S. Speier, 'Beiträge zu den Targumim', SThU 20 (1950), pp. 52–61.
R. Bloch, 'Écriture et tradition dans le Judaïsme', Cahiers Sioniens 8 (1954), pp. 9–34.
R. Bloch, 'Note méthodologique pour l'étude de la littérature rabbinique', RSR 43 (1955), pp. 194–227.
R. Bloch, 'Note sur l'utilisation des fragments de la Geniza du Caire pour l'étude du Targum palestinien', REJ 114 (1955), pp. 5–35.
P. Grelot, 'Les Targums du Pentateuch, étude comparative d'après Genèse IV, 3–16', Semitica 9 (1959), pp. 59–88.
A. Díez Macho, 'The recently discovered Palestinian Targum', VT Suppl. 7 (1960), pp. 222–45.
A. Díez Macho, 'En torno a la datación del Targum palestinense', Sefarad 20 (1960), pp. 3–16.
P. Grelot, 'Sagesse X, 21 et le Targum de l'Exode', Bibl. 42 (1961), pp. 49–60.
G. Vermes, *Scripture and Tradition in Judaism* (1961).
G. Vermes, 'The Targumic Versions of Genesis IV 3–16', ALUOS 3 (1961–2), [1963], pp. 81–114.
J. Heinemann, 'Targum of Exodus 22:4 and Early Halakhah', Tarbiz 38 (1968–69), pp. 294–6.
G. Vermes, 'Bible and Midrash', CHB I (1970), pp. 199–231, 592.
J. P. Schäfer, 'Die Termini "Heiliger Geist" und "Geist der Prophetie" in den Targumim und das Verhältnis der Targumim zueinander', VT 20 (1970), pp. 304–14.
S. Isenberg, 'An Anti-Sadducee Polemic in the Palestinian Targum Tradition', HTR 63 (1970), pp. 733–44.
J. Potin, *La fête de la Pentecôte* I–II (1971) [Targ. Exod. 19–20].
M. McNamara, *Targum and Testament* (1972).
P. S. Alexander, 'The Targumim and early Exegesis of "Sons of God" in Genesis 6', JJS 23 (1972), pp. 60–71.

(a) Targumic Method in General

Ḥ. Albeck, 'Apocryphal Halakah in the Palestinian Targums and the Aggadah', *B. M. Lewin Jubilee Volume* (1940) pp. 93–104 (in Hebrew).

Y. Komloš, 'The Aggadah in the Targumim of Jacob's Blessing', Ann. of the Bar Ilan Univ. 1 (1963), pp. 195–206 (Hebr.).

R. Le Déaut, 'Un phénomène spontané de l'herméneutique juive ancienne: le "targoumisme",' Bibl. 52 (1971), pp. 505–25.

For other studies see under the separate Targumim, infra.

(b) Targum and Peshitta

A. Baumstark, 'Pĕšitta und palästinensisches Targum', BZ 19 (1931), pp. 257–70.

A. Sperber, 'Peschitta und Targum', *Jewish Studies in memory of G. A. Kohut* (1935), pp. 554–64.

C. Peters, 'Peschitta und Targumim des Pentateuchs', Muséon 48 (1935), pp. 1–54.

A. Vööbus, *Peschitta und Targumim des Pentateuchs* (1958).

P. Wernberg-Møller, 'Some observations on the relationship of the Peshitta Version of the book of Genesis to the Palestinian Targum Fragments . . . and to Targum Onkelos', ST 15 (1961), pp. 128–80.

P. Wernberg-Møller, 'Prolegomena to a re-examination of the Palestinian Targum fragments published by P. Kahle and their relationship to the Peshitta', JSS 7 (1962), pp. 253–66.

S. R. Isenberg, 'On the Jewish-Palestinian Origins of the Peshitta to the Pentateuch', JBL 90 (1971), pp. 69–81.

For other studies see under the separate Targumim, infra.

(c) Targum and Septuagint

P. Churgin, 'The Targum and the Septuagint', AJSL 50 (1933–4), pp. 41–65.

L. Delekat, 'Ein Septuagintatargum', VT 8 (1958), pp. 225–52.

See also under separate Targumim, infra.

(d) Targum and New Testament

A. T. Olmstead, 'Could an Aramaic Gospel be written?' JNES 1 (1942), pp. 41–75.

P. Winter, 'Lc. 2, 49 and Targum Yerushalmi', ZNW 45 (1954), pp. 145–79.

M. McNamara, *The Palestinian Targum to the Pentateuch and the New Testament* (1966).

P. Nickels, *Targum and New Testament: A Bibliography* (1967).

B. J. Malina, *The Palestinian Manna Tradition* (1968).

E. E. Ellis, 'Midrash, Targum and the New Testament Quotations', *Neotestamentica et Semitica* (1969), pp. 61–9.

M. McNamara, *Targum and Testament* (1972).

(e) Targum and Dead Sea Scrolls

N. Wieder, 'The Habakkuk Scroll and the Targum', JJS 4 (1953), pp. 14–18.

W. H. Brownlee, 'The Habakkuk Midrash and the Targum of Jonathan', JJS 7 (1956), pp. 169–86.

G. Vermes, 'Car le Liban, c'est le Conseil de la Communauté', *Mélanges A. Robert* (1957), pp. 316–25.

G. Vermes, 'The symbolical interpretation of Lebanon in the Targums', JThSt 9 (1958), pp. 1–12.

M. R. Lehmann, '1Q Genesis Apocryphon in the Light of the Targumim and Midrashim', RQ 1 (1958), pp. 252 ff.

J. A. Fitzmyer, 'The Genesis Apocryphon and the Targums', *The Genesis Apocryphon of Qumran Cave I* (1966), pp. 26–34.

G. J. Kuiper, 'A study of the relationship between a Genesis Apocryphon and the Pentateuchal Targumim in Gn. XIV, 1–12', *In Memoriam P. Kahle*, BZAW 103 (1968), pp. 149 ff.

(f) The Theology of the Targums

See also the works cited above on rabbinic theology, p. 88 and also passim under the separate Targumim, infra.

V. Hamp, *Der Begriff 'Wort' in den aramäischen Bibelübersetzungen* (1938).

C. *Linguistic*

See also the relevant bibliography on the Talmud; for the language of individual Targums, see below.

(a) Dictionary

J. Levy, *Chaldäisches Wörterbuch über die Targumim* I–II (1881).

M. Jastrow, *A Dictionary of the Targumim, the Talmud Babli and Yerushalmi and the Midrashic Literature* (1950).

(b) Grammars and linguistic studies

G. Dalman, *Grammatik des jüdisch-palästinischen Aramäisch* (^{2}1905).

W. B. Stevenson, *A Grammar of Palestinian Jewish Aramaic* (^{2}1962).

E. Y. Kutscher, 'The Language of the Genesis Apocryphon', Scrip. Hier. 4 (1958), pp. 1–35.

G. Vermes, 'The use of "Bar Nash" . . . in Jewish Aramaic', in M. Black, *An Aramaic Approach to the Gospels and Acts* (^{3}1967), pp. 310–28; the Targums, pp. 315–16; 322–3.

(c) The language of Jesus

M. Black, 'The recovery of the language of Jesus', NTS 3 (1956–7), pp. 305–13.

M. Black, 'Die Erforschung der Muttersprache Jesu', TLZ 82 (1957), cols. 653–68.

P. Kahle, 'Das palästinische Pentateuchtargum und das zur Zeit Jesu gesprochene Aramäisch', ZNW 49 (1958), pp. 100–16.

E. Y. Kutscher, 'Das zur Zeit Jesu gesprochene Aramäisch', ZNW 51 (1960), pp. 45–54.

M. Black, '*ΕΦΦΑθΑ* (Mk. 7:34)', *Mélanges... Béda Rigaux* (1960), pp. 57–60.

I. Rabbinowitz, ' "Be opened" = *ΕΦΦΑΘΑ*, Mk. 7:34: Did Jesus speak Hebrew?', ZNW 53 (1962), pp. 229–384.

A. Díez Macho, 'La Lengua hablada por Jesucristo', Oriens Antiquus 2 (1963), pp. 95–132.

M. Black, *An Aramaic Approach to the Gospels and Acts* (^{3}1967). 'Aramaic studies and the language of Jesus', *In Memoriam P. Kahle*, BZAW 103 (1968), pp. 17–28.

J. A. Emerton, '*Maranatha* and *Ephphatha*', JThSt 18 (1967), pp. 427–31.

J. A. Fitzmyer, 'The Language of Palestine in the First Century A.D.', CBQ 32 (1970), pp. 501–31.

J. Barr, 'Which Language did Jesus speak?', BJRL 53 (1970–71), pp. 9–29.

I. Rabinowitz, '*ΕΦΦΑΘΑ* (Mark VII. 34): Certainly Hebrew, not Aramaic', JSS 16 (1971), pp. 151–6.

S. Morag, '*'Εφφαθὰ*' (Mark VII. 34): Certainly Hebrew, not Aramaic', JSS 17 (1972), pp. 198–202.

D. *Onkelos*

(a) Editions

A. Berliner, *Targum Onkelos* I–II (1884).

A. Sperber, *The Bible in Aramaic: I The Pentateuch according to Targum Onkelos* (1959). Cf. P. Kahle, VT 10 (1960), pp. 383–4; D. W. Thomas, JSS 5 (1960), pp. 286–8.

A. Díez Macho, *Biblia Polyglotta Matritensia: Prooemium* (1957), p. 9.

A. Díez Macho, *Biblia Polyglotta Matritensia. Series IV. Targum Palestinense in Pentateuchum. Adduntur Targum Pseudo-jonatan, Targum Onqelos et Targum Palestinensis hispanica versio. Liber V. Deuteronomium Cap. I* (1965).

A. Díez Macho, 'Un importante manuscrito targumico en la Biblioteca Vaticana (MS Ebr. Vat. 448)', *Homenaje a Millás Vallicrosa* I (1954), pp. 375–463.

A. Díez Macho, 'Onqelos Manuscript with Babylonian transliterated Vocalization in the Vatican Library', VT 8 (1958), pp. 113–33.

A. Díez Macho, 'Un manuscrito babilonico de Onqelos en el que se confunden los timbres vocalicos Pataḥ y Qamez', Sefarad 19 (1959), pp. 273–82.

A. Díez Macho, 'A fundamental manuscript for an edition of the Babylonian Onqelos to Genesis', *In Memoriam P. Kahle*, BZAW 103 (1968), pp. 62–78.

(b) Translations

J. W. Etheridge, *The Targums of Onkelos and Jonathan ben Uzziel on the Pentateuch with the Fragments of the Jerusalem Targum* I–II (1862–65).

(c) Concordances

E. Brederek, *Konkordanz zum Targum Onkelos*, BZAW 9 (1906).

C. J. Kasowski, *A Concordance of the Targum of Onkelos* (1940).

(d) Massorah

A. Berliner, *Die Mâssôrâh zum Targum Onkelos* (1887).

S. Landauer, *Die Mâsôrâh zum Targum Onkelos auf Grund Quellen lexikalisch geordnet und kritisch beleuchtet* (1896).

G. E. Weil, 'La Massorah Magna du Targum du Pentateuch. Nouveaux fragments et autres. Esquisse historique', Textus 4 (1964), pp. 30–54.

G. E. Weil, 'Nouveaux fragment de la Massorah Magna du Targum de Babylone', *In Memoriam P. Kahle*, BZAW 103 (1968), pp. 241–53.

(e) Studies

S. Singer, *Onkelos und das Verhältnis seines Targums zur Halacha* (1881).

J. M. Schoenfelder, *Onkelos und Peschitto* (1896).

H. Barnstein, *The Targum Onkelos to Genesis* (1896).

M. Friedmann, *Onkelos und Akylas* (1896).

E. Brederek, 'Bemerkungen über die Art der Übersetzung in Targum Onkelos', ThSK 3 (1901), pp. 351–77.

A. E. Silverstone, *Aquila and Onkelos* (1931).

A. Sperber, 'The Targum of Onkelos in its relation to the Masoretic Hebrew Text', PAAJR 6 (1935), pp. 309–51.

M. Z. Kaddari, 'The use of *d*- clauses in the language of Targum Onkelos', Textus 3 (1963), pp. 36–59.

M. Z. Kaddari, 'Studies in the syntax of Targum Onkelos', Tarbiz 32 (1963), pp. 232–51 (Hebr. with Eng. summary).

A. M. Goldberg, 'Die spezifische Verwendung der Terminus Schekinah im Targum Onkelos als Kriterium einer relativen Datierung', Judaica 19 (1963), pp. 43–61.

G. Vermes, 'Haggadah in the Targum Onkelos', JSS 8 (1963), pp. 159–69.
J. W. Bowker, 'Haggadah in the Targum Onkelos', JSS 12 (1967), pp. 51–65.
A. Díez Macho, 'Primeros impresos del Targum de Onqelos', Sefarad 30 (1970), pp. 289–303.

E. *Pseudo-Jonathan*

(a) Editions

M. Ginsburger, *Pseudo-Jonathan: Thargum Jonathan ben Usiël zum Pentateuch nach der Londoner Handschrift* (1903).

The editio princeps, Venice 1591, is still important in that it seems to be based on a MS no longer extant. Commentary: B. Schmerler, *Sefer Ahabat Yehonatan* (1932).

(b) Translation

See J. W. Etheridge, Onkelos (b) above.

(c) Studies

S. Gronemann, *Die Jonathanische Pentateuch-Übersetzung in ihren Verhältnis zur Halacha* (1879).
J. Bassfreund, 'Die Erwähnung Jochanans des Hohenpriesters in Pseudojonathan zu Dt. 33, 11 und das angeblich hohe Alter des Targums', MGWJ 44 (1900), pp. 481–6.
M. Neumark, *Lexikalische Untersuchungen zur Sprache der jerusalemischen Pentateuch-Targume* (1905).
A. Marmorstein, *Studien zum Pseudo-Jonathan Targum. I Das Targum und die Apokryphe Literatur* (1905).
S. Speier, 'The Targum of Jonathan on Genesis 24.56', JQR 28 (1937–38), pp. 301–3.
W. Gottlieb, 'The translation of Jonathan ben Uzziel on the Pentateuch', Melilah 1 (1944), pp. 26–34 (Hebr.).
K. H. Bernhardt, 'Zu Eigenart und Alter der messianisch-eschatologischen Zusätze im Targum Jeruschalmi I', *Gott und die Götter* (*Festgabe E. Fascher*) (1958), pp. 68–83.
S. Speier, התארך של מילת אברהם וישמעל לפי התרגם המיוחס ליונתן, PAAJR 29 (1960), pp. 69 ff.
R. Meyer, 'Elia und Ahab (Targ. Ps.–Jon. zu Deut. 33, 11)', *Abraham unser Vater* (*Festschrift O. Michel*) (1963), pp. 356–68.
M. Brayer, 'The Pentateuchal Targum attributed to Jonathan ben Uziel, a source for unknown Midrashim', *Abraham Weiss Memorial Volume* (1964), pp. 201–31 (Hebr.).
D. Reider, על התרגום הלטיני של יונתן על התורה, Sinai 59 (1965), pp. 9–14.
E. B. Levine, 'Internal Contradictions in Targum Jonathan ben Uzziel to Genesis', Augustinianum 9 (1969), pp. 118–19.
G. Kuiper, 'Targum Pseudo-Jonathan: A Study of Genesis 4:7–10, 16', *ibid.* 10 (1970), pp. 533–70.
G. Kuiper, 'Targum Pseudo-Jonathan in Relation to the Remaining Targumim at Exodus 20:1–18, 25–26', *ibid.* 11 (1971), pp. 105–54.
E. Levine, 'Some Characteristics of Pseudo-Jonathan Targum to Genesis', *ibid.*, pp. 89–103.
G. Kuiper, *The Pseudo-Jonathan Targum and its Relationship to Targum Onkelos* (1972).

F. *The Fragmentary Targum*

(a) Editions

M. Ginsburger, *Das Fragmententhargum: Thargum Jeruschalmi zum Pentateuch* (1899).

M. C. Doubles, 'Toward the publication of the extant texts of the Palestinian Targum(s)', VT 15 (1965), pp. 16–26.

(b) Translation

J. W. Etheridge, see above Onkelos (b).

(c) Studies

J. Bassfreund, *Das Fragmententargum zum Pentateuch* (1896).

M. Ginsburger, 'Die Fragmente des Thargum Jeruschalmi zum Pentateuch', ZDMG 57 (1903), pp. 67–80.

M. C. Doubles, 'Indications of antiquity in the orthography and morphology of the Fragment Targum', *In Memoriam P. Kahle*, BZAW 103 (1968), pp. 79–89.

D. Reider, 'On the *Targum Yerushalmi* known as the Fragmentary Targum', Tarbiz 39 (1969), pp. 93–5.

(d) The Targumic Tosefta

See: M. Ginsburger, *Das Fragmententhargum*, p. xii; A. Sperber, *Targum Onkelos*, pp. xvii, 354–7; A. Epstein, REJ 30 (1895), pp. 44 ff.; P. Kahle, Sefarad 15 (1955), pp. 31–9; Y. Komlós, Sinai 45 (1959), pp. 223–8; A. Díez Macho, Sefarad 16 (1956), pp. 314–17; P. Grelot, REJ 16 (1957), pp. 5–26; *ibid.* 18 (1959–60), pp. 129–30; G. Vermes, *Scripture and Tradition in Judaism* (1961), pp. 11–25; 196–7: P. Grelot, RB 73 (1966), pp. 197–211; 79 (1972), pp. 511–43.

G. *The Cairo Genizah Fragments*

(a) Editions

P. Kahle, *Masoreten des Westens* II (1930).

A. Díez Macho, 'Nuevos fragmentos del Targum palestinense', Sefarad 15 (1955), pp. 1–39.

Y. Komlós, נוסח התרגום על קריעת ים סוף, Sinai 45 (1959), pp. 223–8.

W. Baars, 'A Targum on Exodus XV 7–21 from the Cairo Genizah', VT 11 (1961), pp. 340–42.

H. P. Rüger, 'Ein neues Genesis-Fragment mit komplizierter babylonischer Punktation aus Kairo-Geniza', VT 12 (1963), pp. 235–37.

A. Díez Macho, 'Un neuvo fragmento del Targum palestinense a Génesis', *Manuscritos hebreos y aramous de la Biblia* (1971), pp. 217–20.

(b) Studies

A. Marmorstein, 'Einige vorläufige Bemerkungen zu den neuentdeckten Fragmenten jerusalemischen . . . Targums', ZAW 49 (1931), pp. 231–42.

S. Wohl, *Das palästinische Pentateuch Targum* (1935).

J. L. Teicher, 'A sixth century fragment of the Palestinian Targum?', VT 1 (1951), pp. 125–9.

R. Bloch, 'Note sur l'utilisation des fragments de la Geniza du Caire pour l'étude du Targum palestinien', REJ 14 (1955), pp. 5–35.

G. Schelbert, 'Exodus XXII 4 im palästinischen Targum', VT 8 (1958), pp. 253–63.

H. *Codex Neofiti I*

(a) Editions

A. Díez Macho, *Neophyti I. Targum Palestinense MS de la Bibliotheca Vaticana*, I (Genesis) (1968); II (Éxodo) (1970); III (Levítico) (1971); includes Spanish, French and English translations.

A. Díez Macho, *Biblia Polyglotta Matritensia, Ser. IV. Targum Palestinense in Pentateuchum . . . Liber V, Deuteronomium Cap. I* (1965).

M. H. Goshen-Gottstein, *Aramaic Bible Version, comparative selections and glossary including unpublished chapters from the Palestinian Targum* (includes Gen. 3:1–24; Exod. 19:1–25; Num. 25:1–19; Deut. 28:1–69 from Cod. Neofiti I) (1963).

(b) Studies

A. Díez Macho, 'The recently discovered Palestinian Targum: its antiquity and relationship with the other Targums', VT Suppl. 7 (1960), pp. 222–45.

P. Wernberg-Møller, 'An inquiry into the validity of the text-critical argument for an early dating of the recently discovered Palestinian Targum', VT 12 (1962), pp. 312–30.

A. Díez Macho, 'El Logos y el Espíritu Santo', Atlántida 1 (1963), pp. 381–46.

M. Martin, 'The palaeographical character of Codex Neofiti I', Textus 3 (1963), pp. 1–35.

G. E. Weil, 'Le Codex Neophiti I: à propos de l'article de M. Fitzmaurice Martin', Textus 4 (1964), pp. 225–9.

M. McNamara, 'Some early citations and the Palestinian Targum to the Pentateuch', Rivista degli Studi Orientali 41 (1966), pp. 1–15.

R. Le Déaut, 'Jalons pour un histoire d'un manuscrit du Targum palestinien', Bibl. 48 (1967), pp. 509–33.

D. Reider, 'On the Targum Yerushalmi MS Neofiti I', Tarbiz 38 (1968), pp. 81–6 (in Hebrew).

S. Lund, 'The sources of the variant readings to Deut. I 1—XXIX 17 of Codex Neofiti I', *In Memoriam P. Kahle*, BZAW 103 (1968), pp. 167 ff.

G. Vermes, 'HE IS THE BREAD: Targum Neophiti Exodus 16:15', *Neotestamentica et Semitica* (1969), pp. 256–63.

M. Delcor, 'La portée chronologique de quelques interprétations du Targoum Néophyti contenues dans le cycle d'Abraham', JSJ 1 (1970), pp. 105–19.

S. Lund, 'An argument for the further study of the palaeography of Cod. Neofiti I', VT 20 (1970), pp. 56–64.

I. *The Targum to the Prophets*

(a) Editions

P. de Lagarde, *Prophetae Chaldaice* (1872).

A. Sperber, *The Bible in Aramaic:* II. *The Former Prophets according to Targum Jonathan.* III. *The Latter Prophets according to Targum Jonathan* (1959–62).

F. Praetorius, *Das Targum zu Josua in jemenischer Überlieferung* (1899).

F. Praetorius, *Das Targum zum Buch der Richter in jemenischer Überlieferung* (1900).

S. Silbermann, *Das Targum zu Ezekiel*, 1–10 (1902).

J. F. Stenning, *The Targum of Isaiah* (1949).

For the Tosefta Targumica to the prophets, see: A. Díez Macho, Sefarad 27 (1957), pp. 237–80 (Jos. 16:7–II Kings 5:24); *id.* Est. Bibl. 15 (1956), pp. 287–95 (Jos. 5:5–6:1); *id.* Bibl. 39 (1958), pp. 198–205 (Ez. 3:1–14); P. Grelot, RB 73 (1966), pp. 197–211 (Zech. 2:14–15).

(b) Studies

W. Bacher, 'Kritische Untersuchungen zum Prophetentargum', ZDMG 28 (1874), pp. 1–72.

P. Churgin, *Targum Jonathan to the Prophets* (1927).

P. Humbert, *Le Messie dans le targum des Prophètes* (1911).

A. Sperber, 'Zur Sprache des Prophetentargums', ZAW 45 (1927), pp. 267–87.

P. Seidelin, 'Der 'Ebed Yahve und die Messiasgestalt im Jesaja Targum', ZNW 35 (1936), pp. 194–231.

E. R. Rowlands, 'The Targum and the Peshitta Version of the Book of Isaiah', VT 9 (1959), pp. 178–91.

P. Grelot, 'L'exégèse messianique d'Isaïe LXIII 1–6', RB 70 (1963), pp. 371–80.

S. H. Levey, 'The Date of Targum-Jonathan to the Prophets', VT 21 (1971), pp. 186–96.

J. *Targum to the Writings*

(a) Editions

P. de Lagarde, *Hagiographa Chaldaice* (1873).

A. Sperber, *The Bible in Aramaic,* IVa (1968) (Chronicles, Ruth, Canticles, Lamentations, Ecclesiastes).

(b) Psalms

W. Bacher, 'Das Targum zu den Psalmen', MGWJ 21 (1872), pp. 408–73.

O. Komlós, 'Distinctive features in the Targum of Psalms', *Studies in the Bible, presented to Prof. M. H. Segal* (1964), pp. 265–70 (Hebrew).

(c) Job

W. Bacher, 'Das Targum zu Hiob', MGWJ 20 (1871), pp. 208–23, 283–4.

A. Weiss, *De Libri Job Paraphrasi Chaldaica* (1873).

(d) Proverbs

S. Maybaum, 'Über die Sprache des Targum zu den Sprüchen und dessen Verhältnis', Merx Archiv 2 (1871), pp. 66–93.

H. Pinkuss, 'Die syrische Übersetzung der Proverbien . . . und ihr Verhältnis zum Targum', ZAW 14 (1894), pp. 109 ff.

A. Kaminka, 'Septuagint und Targum zu Proverbia', HUCA 7–9 (1931–2), pp. 161–91.

(e) Chronicles

M. Rosenberg and K. Kohler, 'Das Targum zur Chronik', JZWL 8 (1870), pp. 72–80, 263–78.

R. Le Déaut–J. Robert, *Targum des Chroniques* I–II (1971). [Introduction, French translation, Aramaic text and glossary.]

(f) Canticles

R. H. Melamed, *The Targum to Canticles according to Six Yemen Mss. compared with the Textus Receptus* (*ed. de Lagarde*) (1921); cf. JQR 10 (1920), pp. 377–410; *ibid.* 11 (1920–1), pp. 1–20.

R. Loewe, 'Apologetic Motifs in the Targum to the Song of Songs', *Biblical Motifs*, ed. A. Altmann (1966), pp. 159–96.

E. Z. Melamed, 'Targum Canticles', Tarbiz 40 (1970–71), pp. 201–15 (in Hebrew with an English summary).

J. Heinemann, 'Targum Canticles and its Sources', Tarbiz 41 (1971), pp. 126–9 (Hebrew with an English summary).

(g) Ruth

English translation: A. Saarisalo, Studia Orientalia (1928), pp. 88–104.

A. Schlesinger, 'The Targum of Ruth, a sectarian document', *Research in the Exegesis and Language of the Bible* (1962) (Hebr.)

E. Z. Melamed, 'On the Targum of Ruth', Bar Ilan 1 (1963), pp. 190–4.

S. Speier, ' "Death by Hanging" in Targum Ruth I 17', Tarbiz 40 (1970–71), p. 259.

(h) Esther

Text: M. David, *Das Targum Scheni, nach Handschriften herausgegeben* (1898).

German translation: D. Cassel, *Das Buch Esther* (1878).

S. Gelbhaus, *Die Targum Literatur vergleichend agadisch und kritisch-philologisch beleuchtet I: Das Targum Sheni zum Buche Esther* (1893).

P. Grelot, 'Remarques sur le Second Targum du livre d'Esther', RB 77 (1970), pp. 230–9.

For the 'Additions to Esther', see Lagarde, *Hagiographa Chaldaice*, pp. 362–5; Jellinek, *Bet ha-Midrasch*, V, pp. 2–8; Merx, *Chrestomathia Targumica*, pp. 154–64.

(i) Ecclesiastes

Y. Komlós, 'PSHAT and DRASH in Targum Kohelet', Bar-Ilan 3 (1965), pp. 46–55 (Hebr. with Eng. summary).

(j) Lamentations

S. Landauer, 'Zum Targum der Klagelieder', *Orientalische Studien Th. Nöldeke gewidmet* (1906), pp. 505–12.

IV. Historical Works

In addition to the Talmud, Midrash and Targums, rabbinical circles were responsible for a few further works relating to the history of the end of the pre-Christian era and the first two centuries A.D. Apart from Megillath Taanith, their value as historical sources is limited.

1. *Megillath Taanith* (Scroll of Fasting), or more precisely, a list of days on which, in recollection of some joyful event of the recent (Maccabaean) past, fasting was forbidden. A fixed calendar of such days is already assumed in Judith 8:6. Megillath Taanith is mentioned in the Mishnah (mTaan. 2:8) and in the Talmuds (yTaan. 66a; b.RSh. 18b). It appears to have been written in the first, or at the latest at the beginning of the second century A.D. According to the Talmud, its author was Hananiah ben Hezekiah ben Garon (bShab. 13b), whilst the Hebrew scholion appended to the document ascribes it to the latter's son, Eliezer, possibly the person mentioned in Jos. *B.J.* ii 17, 2 (409) as one of the revolutionary leaders in A.D. 66. The text is Aramaic; the accompanying commentary is probably post-Talmudic.

Editions

A. Neubauer, *Mediaeval Jewish Chronicles* II (1895), pp. 3–25.

G. Dalman, *Aramäische Dialektproben* (1896), pp. 1–3, 32–4, the Aramaic text with notes.

M. Grossberg, *Tractate Megillath Taanith . . . nach alten Handschriften edirt u. mit Einleitung, Anmerkungen u. Register versehen* (1905).
H. Lichtenstein, 'Die Fastenrolle. Eine Untersuchung zur jüdisch-hellenistischen Geschichte', HUCA 8–9 (1931/2), pp. 257–351.
B. Lurie, *Megillath Ta'anith, with introduction and notes* (1964) (in Hebrew).

Translations into English:
A. Edersheim, *The Life and Times of Jesus the Messiah* II (1883), pp. 698–700;
S. Zeitlin, *Megillat Taanit*, quoted *infra*.

Translations into French:
J. Derenbourg, *Essai sur l'histoire . . . de la Palestine* (1867), pp. 439–46;
M. Schwab, *La Meghillath Taanith ou 'Anniversaires historiques'* (1898).

Studies: Zunz, p. 318; J. Z. Lauterbach, JE VIII, pp. 427–8; J. Schmilg, *Über Entstehung und historischen Werth des Siegeskalenders Megillath Ta'anith* (1874); M. Schwab, 'Quelques notes sur la Meghillath Ta'anith', REJ 41 (1900), pp. 266–8; S. Zeitlin, *Megillat Taanit as a Source for Jewish Chronology and History in the Hellenistic and Roman Periods* (1922); A. Schwarz, 'Taanith Esther' *Festkrift i Anledning af Professor D. Simonsens 70-aarige Fødelsdag* (1923), pp. 188–205; S. Zeitlin, 'Nennt Megillat Taanit antisadduzäische Gedenktage?', MGWJ 81 (1937), pp. 151–8, 205–11; H. D. Mantel, 'The Megillat Ta'anit and the Sects', *Studies in the History of the Jewish People* [Memorial Zvi Avneri] (1970), pp. 51–70 (in Hebrew); N. N. Glatzer, Enc. Jud. XI (1971), cols 1230–1.

2 (a). *Seder 'Olam*, also called *Seder 'Olam Rabbah*, an outline of biblical and Jewish history from Adam to the time of Alexander the Great, and subsequently to the end of the Herodian dynasty, with an additional reference to the age of Bar Kokhba. The Talmud ascribes the work to R. Yose b. Halafta (mid-second century A.D.). See bMeg. 11b; bYeb. 82b; bNid. 46b; bNaz. 5a; b.A.Z. 8b; bShab. 88a. R. Yose is cited nine times as an authority in the *Seder* itself. The compilation may be dated from the late second or third century A.D.

Editions
A. Neubauer, *Mediaeval Jewish Chronicles* II (1895), pp. 26–67.
B. Ratner, *Seder Olam Rabba. Die grosse Weltchronik nach Handschriften und Druckwerken* hrsg. (1897); cf. S. K. Mirsky, *Midrash Seder Olam, a photostatic reproduction of B. Ratner's edition, with a prefatory scholarly survey* (1966) (in Hebrew).
A. Marx, *Seder 'Olam (cap. 1–10), nach Handschriften und Druckwerken hrsg.* (1903).
M. J. Weinstock, סדר עולם רבה השלם (1956).

Translations into German:
Marx, *Seder 'Olam, (cap. 1–10)*, cf. above.
J. Winter and A. Wünsche, *Die jüdische Literatur seit Abschluss des Kanons* III (1896), pp. 299 ff. (selections).

Studies: Zunz, p. 89; M. Seligsohn, JE XI, pp. 147–9; M. Gaster, 'Demetrius und Seder Olam; ein Problem der hellenischen Literatur', in *Festskrift . . . Professor David Simonsen* (1923), pp. 243–52; S. Gandz, 'The Calendar of the Seder Olam', JQR 43 (1952–3), pp. 177–92, 249–70.

2 (b). *Seder Olam Zuṭṭa* is a genealogical work which first deals with the biblical period, and follows with a list of the Babylonian exilarchs. It cannot be earlier than the eighth century A.D.

Editions

A. Neubauer, *Mediaeval Jewish Chronicles* II (1895), pp. 68–73.

S. Schechter, 'Seder Olam Suta', MGWJ 39 (1895), pp. 23–8.

M. Grossberg, *Seder Olam zuta and complete Seder Tannaim v'Amoraim with introduction and notes* (1910).

M. J. Weinstock, סדר עולם זוטא השלם (1957).

Translations into German:

J. Winter and A. Wünsche, *Die jüd. Literatur seit Abschluss des Kanons* III (1896), pp. 304 ff. (selections).

Studies: M. Seligsohn, JE XI, pp. 149–50; see also the studies on *Seder 'Olam Rabbah* above.

3. *Megillath Antiochus* (Scroll of Antiochus), or *Megillath Beth Ḥashmonai* (Scroll of the House of the Hasmonaeans), or *Sepher Bene Ḥashmonai* (Book of the Hasmonaeans), is a legendary history of the persecutions ordered by Antiochus Epiphanes and the triumph of the Hasmonaeans. The original text is in Aramaic but various Hebrew versions and an Arabic translation have survived. Dating probably from the Muslim period, the work served for public reading for the Hanukkah festival in oriental, especially Yemenite, synagogues.

Editions

M. Gaster, *The Scroll of the Hasmoneans* (*Megillath Bene Ḥashmonai*) (1893).

I. Abrahams, 'An Aramaic Text of the Scroll of Antiochus' JQR 11 (1899), pp. 291–9.

L. Nemoy, *The scroll of Antiochus . . . Aramaic . . . facsimile of Codex Hebrew 51 in the Yale University Library . . . with a bibliographic note* (1952); cf. A. Jellinek, *Bet ha-Midrasch* I (1853), pp. 142–6 (Hebrew text); VI (1877), pp. 4–8 (Aramaic text).

Translation into English:

Gaster, *The Scroll* etc., see above.

Translation into German:

L. Grünhut, *Das Buch Antiochus*, see below.

Studies: L. Ginzberg, JE I, 33. 637–8; L. Grünhut, *Das Buch Antiochus, kritisch untersucht, erläutert und übersetzt* (1894); S. Krauss, 'Le livre des Asmonéens', REJ 30 (1895), pp. 214–19; I. Lévi, 'Un indice sur la date et le lieu de la composition de la Meguillat Antiochus (Rouleau d'Antiochus)', REJ 45 (1902), pp. 172–5; S. Atlas, M. Pearlmann, 'Saadia on the Scroll of the Hasmonaeans', PAAJR 14 (1935), pp. 1–23; G. Bader, מגילת אנטיוכוס in די מלחמות פון די חשמונאים (1940), pp. 347–54, in Yiddish; F.-M. Abel, *Les livres des Maccabées* ([2]1949), pp. xvii–xix; I. Lévy, 'Les deux livres des Machabées et le livre hébraïque des Asmonéens', Semitica 5 (1955), pp. 15–36; M. Z. Kaddari, 'The Aramaic Antiochus Scroll', Bar Ilan 1 (1963), pp. 81–105; 2 (1964), pp. 178–214 (Hebrew); A. Momigliano, *Prime linee di storia della tradizione maccabaica* ([2]1968), pp. 50–65; Enc. Jud. XIV (1971), cols. 1045–7.

4. *Yosippon* or *Joseph ben Gorion* is the title of an historical work written in elegant Hebrew and attributed to Flavius Josephus (Joseph son of Mattathias confused with Joseph son of Gorion). Covering the period from Adam to the destruction of Jerusalem by Titus, it incorporates a Hebrew paraphrase of the Alexander Romance and attempts to synchronize Jewish and Roman history. The author used Josephus's *Antiquities*, *War*, and *Against Apion*, as well as the Latin Hegesippus and oral traditions.

The work has survived in three recensions, the best of which, represented in older manuscripts, is still unpublished. Another figures in the *editio princeps* of Mantua (*c.* 1480), and the third and long version, in the Constantinople edition (1510). There are also Arabic, Ethiopic and Latin translations.

Linguistic, historical and geographical data suggest that Yosippon was composed in southern Italy. One manuscript states that the work was completed in A.D. 953, a date corresponding well to the internal features of the composition. A substantial part of Yosippon was included, in the early twelfth century, in the Chronicles of Yeraḥmeel, or *Sefer ha-Zikhronoth* by Yeraḥmeel ben Solomon, a Jewish author living probably in southern Italy also.

Editions

1. *The Hebrew Text:* (a) the short recension: Abraham Conat in the editio princeps (Mantua, pre-1480); cf. *Josippon qui inscribitur liber. Ad finem editionis A. Conati ante annum* 1480 *impressae, ed. denuo . . . D. Günzburg* (Berditschev 1896–1913); (b) the long recension: Constantinople 1510; cf. A. J. Wertheimer, יוסיפון ליוסף בן גוריון הכהן (1955–6) = Venice 1544 (based on Constantinople 1510), with additions and corrections from the Mantua edition. On both these editions, see Steinschneider, *Cat. Bod.*, p. 1550. Two useful texts are:

J. F. Breithaupt, *Josephus Gorionides, sive Josephus Hebraicus, Latine versus* (1707) in Hebrew and Latin.

H. Hominer, *Shearith Yisrael complete, the second volume of Josiphon, authored by Menachem Mon ben Shlomoh Halevi* (1964) (in Hebrew).

(c) Abstracts: (i) Yeraḥmeel: A. Neubauer, *Mediaeval Jewish Chronicles* I (1887), pp. xii, xx, 190–1; 'Yeraḥmeel ben Shelomoh', JQR 11 (1899), pp. 364–86; M. Gaster, *The Chronicles of Jerahmeel* (1899); (ii) Abraham Ibn Daud: G. D. Cohen, *The Book of Tradition* (1967), pp. xxxiii–xxxv, and passim.

2. The Ethiopic Text: M. Kamil, *Des Josef ben Gorion* (*Josippon*) *Geschichte der Juden; Zena Aiuhud nach den Handschriften hrsg.* (1937); reviewed by: E. Littmann, ZDMG 92 (1937), pp. 661–3; C. C. Torrey, JAOS 59 (1937), pp. 260–2; J. Simon, Orientalia 9 (1937), pp. 378–87; A. Z. Aescoly, REJ 104 (1937), pp. 133–8.

3. Arabic text: See, J. Wellhausen, AAG I, no. 4 (1897); M. Schloessinger JE XII, p. 648.

Studies: Zunz, pp. 154–62; M. Schloessinger, JE VII, pp. 259–60.

I. Lévi, 'Le Yosippon et le Roman d'Alexandre', REJ 28 (1894), pp. 147 f.

D. Gunzbourg, 'Quelques mots sur le Yosippon', REJ 31 (1895), pp. 283–8.

K. Trieber, 'Zur Kritik der Gorionides', NGG (1895), Heft. 4, pp. 381–409.

S. Fraenkel, 'Die Sprache des Josippon', ZDMG 50 (1896), pp. 418–22.
A. Neubauer, 'Pseudo-Josephus, Joseph ben Gorion', JQR 11 (1899), pp. 355–64.
L. Wolf, 'Josippon in England', Jewish Historical Society of England: Transactions 6 (1912), pp. 277–88.
J. Klausner, *Jesus of Nazareth* (1925), pp. 47–54.
S. Zeitlin, 'The Slavonic Josephus and its relation to Josippon and Hegesippus', JQR 20 (1929), pp. 1–50.
S. Zeitlin, *Josephus on Jesus, with particular reference to the Slavonic Josephus and the Hebrew Josippon* (1931).
L. Wallach, 'Quellenkritische Studien zum hebräischen Josippon', MGWJ 82 (1938), pp. 190–8.
L. Wallach, 'Alexander the Great and the Indian Gymnosophists in Hebrew tradition', PAAJR 11 (1941), pp. 47–83.
L. Wallach, 'Yosippon and the Alexander romance', JQR 37 (1947), pp. 407–22.
Y. F. Baer, ספר יוסיפון העברי, *Sefer Dinaburg* (1949), pp. 178–205.
A. A. Neuman, 'Josippon: history and pietism', *A. Marx Jubilee Volume* (1950), pp. 636–67.
A. A. Neuman, 'A note on John the Baptist and Jesus in Josippon', HUCA 23/2 (1950), pp. 137–49.
A. A. Neuman, 'Josippon and the Apocrypha', JQR 43 (1952), pp. 1–26.
S. Zeitlin, 'Josippon', JQR 53 (1953), pp. 273–97.
D. Flusser, 'The author of the book of Josippon: his personality and his age', Zion 18 (1953), pp. 109–26 (in Hebrew).
W. J. Fischel, 'Ibn Khaldun and Josippon', *Homenaje a Millas-Vallicrosa* I (1954), pp. 587–98.
J. Reiner, 'The Original Hebrew Yosippon in the Chronicle of Jeraḥmeel', JQR 60 (1969–70), pp. 128–46.
D. Flusser, 'Josippon', Enc. Jud. X (1971), cols. 296–8.

F. Manuscripts from the Judaean Desert

Since 1947, the sources of inter-Testamental Jewish history and literature have been considerably enriched by the discovery of scrolls, manuscript fragments, papyri and ostraca in various areas of the Judaean Desert. The largest find (the mostly fragmentary remains of more than 500 original documents) was made between 1947 and 1956 in the Qumran area, close to the north-western extremity of the Dead Sea. Only the non-biblical works are relevant to the present study: common scholarly opinion considers them to be prior to A.D. 70. Between 1951 and 1961, several further caves situated in Wadi Murabba'at, and other wadis west of En-Gedi (especially in Naḥal Ḥever), have yielded to Israeli archaeologists legal documents and letters dating from the first and early second century A.D., some of which represent the correspondence of the revolutionary administration of Judaea during the Bar Kosiba uprising. Finally, a smaller amount of manuscripts and ostraca was unearthed from 1963 to 1965 during the excavation of the fortress of Masada. They are necessarily older than A.D. 73/4.

As a result of these discoveries, written documents other than inscriptions belonging to the last centuries of the pre-Christian era and the first 135 years A.D. have for the first time become available in their original form and language and in their genuine archaeological context. They thus not only provide a direct insight into their respective ages, but also chronologically well-placed data for an historical reassessment of Jewish traditions surviving in later rabbinic compilations, or preserved only in Greek translation in the New Testament and Josephus.

The newly-found texts will be analysed in the chapter devoted to Palestinian Jewish literature (vol. III § 32), and the identity of the community responsible for them will be discussed in connection with the religious groups of the Essenes, Pharisees and Zealots.

The limited scope of the present paragraph is to give basic bibliographical information.

1. *The Qumran or Dead Sea Scrolls*

(a) Bibliographies and lexica:

C. Burchard, *Bibliographie zu den Handschriften vom Toten Meer* I–II (1957–65).
W. S. LaSor, *Bibliography of the Dead Sea Scrolls 1948–1957* (1958).
M. Yizhar, *Bibliography of the Hebrew Publications on the Dead Sea Scrolls 1948–1964* (1967).
J. A. Sanders, 'Palestinian Manuscripts 1947–1967', JBL 86 (1967), pp. 430–40. [A full list of edited texts; a more complete version (1947–1972) is contained in JJS 24/1 (1973), pp. 74–83.]
J. A. Fitzmyer, 'A Bibliographical Aid to the Study of the Qumran Cave IV Texts 158–186', CBQ 31 (1969), pp. 59–71.
B. Jongeling, *A Classified Bibliography of the Finds in the Desert of Judah*, 1958–1969 (1971).
See also the bibliographical section of the Revue de Qumran (1958–).
K. G. Kuhn etc., *Rückläufiges Hebräisches Wörterbuch: Retrograde Hebrew Dictionary* (1958).
K. G. Kuhn etc., *Konkordanz zu den Qumrantexte* (1960).

(b) Editions:

M. Burrows, J. C. Trever, W. H. Brownlee, *The Dead Sea Scrolls of St. Mark's Monastery*, I: *The Habbakuk Commentary* [1QpHab] (1950). II: *The Manual of Discipline* [1QS] (1951).
E. L. Sukenik, *The Dead Sea Scrolls of the Hebrew University* [War Scroll (1QM) and Thanksgiving Hymns (1QH)] (1955).
N. Avigad, Y. Yadin, *A Genesis Apocryphon* [1QGA] (1956).
D. Barthélemy, J. T. Milik, *Discoveries in the Judaean Desert I: Qumran Cave I* [Rule of the Congregation (1QSa), Benedictions (1QSb), Biblical commentaries, etc.] (1955).
M. Baillet, J. T. Milik, R. de Vaux, *Discoveries in the Judaean Desert* III*: Les 'Petites Grottes' de Qumran . . . 2Q, 3Q, 5Q, 6Q, 7Q à 10Q* [Copper Scroll, many small fragments] (1962).
J. A. Sanders, *Discoveries in the Judaean Desert of Jordan* IV*: The Psalms Scroll from Qumran Cave 11* (11QPsa) [Apocryphal Psalms] (1965).

J. M. Allegro, A. A. Anderson, *Discoveries in the Judaean Desert of Jordan* V: *Qumran Cave 4:* I (4Q 158–186) [Bible commentaries, horoscope, etc.] (1968). [Cf. J. Strugnell, 'Notes en marge du volume V des "Discoveries in the Judaean Desert of Jordan" ', RQ 7 (1970), pp. 163–276.]

J. P. M. van der Ploeg, A. S. van der Woude, B. Jongeling, *Le Targum de Job de la grotte XI de Qumrân* (1971).

Preliminary publications:

J. T. Milik, 'La prière de Nabonide', RB 63 (1956), pp. 407–11; 'Hénoch aux pays des aromates' (ch. 27 à 32), RB 65 (1958), pp. 70–7; 'Fragment d'une source du Psautier' (4Q Ps 89), RB 73 (1966), pp. 94–106.

J. M. Allegro, 'Further Messianic References in Qumran Literature', JBL (1956), pp. 174–6.

K. G. Kuhn, *Phylakterien aus Höhle 4 von Qumran* (1957).

J. Strugnell, 'The Angelic Liturgy at Qumran', Suppl. VT VII (1960), pp. 318–45.

M. Baillet, 'Les paroles des luminaires', RB 68 (1961), pp. 195–250; 'Débris de textes sur papyrus de la grotte 4 de Qumrân', RB 71 (1964), pp. 353–71.

J. Starcky, 'Un texte messianique araméen de la grotte 4 de Qumrân', *Ecole des langues orientales anciennes . . .: Mélanges du Cinquantenaire* (1964), pp. 51–66.

A. S. van der Woude, 'Melchisedek als himmlische Erlösergestalt in den neugefundenen eschatologischen Midraschim aus Qumran Höhle XI', Oudtest. Stud. 14 (1965), pp. 354–73.

M. de Jonge–A. S. van der Woude, '11Q Melchizedek and the New Testament', NTS 12 (1966), pp. 301–26.

J. Starcky, 'Psaumes apocryphes de la grotte 4 de Qumrân' (4QPs vii–x), RB 73 (1966), pp. 353–71.

Y. Yadin, *Tefillin from Qumran* (1969).

Y. Yadin, 'Pesher Nahum (4Q Nahum) Reconsidered' [Temple Scroll 64:6–13] IEJ 21 (1971), pp. 1–12 and pl. I.

J. T. Milik, 'Turfan et Qumran—Livre des Géants juif et manichéen', *Tradition und Glaube* (*Festgabe für K. G. Kuhn*) (1971), pp. 117–27 [4Q Géants[a]].

J. P. M. van der Ploeg, 'Un petit rouleau de psaumes apocryphes (11QPsAp[a])', *ibid.*, pp. 128–39.

A. S. van der Woude, 'Fragmente des Buches Jubiläen aus Höhle XI (11QJub)', *ibid.*, pp. 140–6.

J. T. Milik, '4Q Visions de ʿAmram et une citation d'Origène', RB 79 (1972), pp. 77–97.

J. T. Milik, '*Milkî-ṣedeq* et *Milkî-rešaʿ* dans les anciens écrits juifs et chrétiens' [4Q Ṭeharot D and 4Q Berakot[a]] JJS 23 (1972), pp. 95–144.

M. Baillet, 'Les manuscrits de la Règle de Guerre de la grotte 4 de Qumrân', RB 79 (1972), pp. 217–26.

Descriptions of unpublished manuscripts:

P. Benoit, *et al.*, 'Le travail d'édition des fragments manuscrits de Qumrân', RB 63 (1956), pp. 49–67.

Y. Yadin, 'The Temple Scroll', BA 30 (1967), pp. 135–9.

J. T. Milik, 'Problèmes de la littérature hénochique à la lumière des fragments araméens de Qumrân', HThR 64 (1971), pp. 333–78.

Damascus Rule from the Cairo Geniza (CDC):

S. Schechter, *Fragments of a Zadokite Work* (1910); (Repr. with a new introduction by J. A. Fitzmyer, 1970).

S. Zeitlin, *The Zadokite Fragments* [Facsimile edition] (1952).
C. Rabin, *The Zadokite Documents* (1954).

Vocalized editions:

A. M. Habermann, *Megilloth Midbar Yehuda. The Scrolls from the Judean Desert* (1959).
E. Lohse, *Die Texte aus Qumran. Hebräisch und Deutsch* (1964, [2]1971).

(c) Archaeology:

R. de Vaux, *L'archéologie et les manuscrits de la Mer Morte* (1961).

(d) General studies:

C. Rabin, *Qumran Studies* (1957).
F. M. Cross, *The Ancient Library of Qumran and Modern Biblical Study* (1958).
C. Rabin, Y. Yadin (ed.), *Aspects of the Dead Sea Scrolls*, Scrip. Hier. 4 (1958).
J. T. Milik, *Ten Years of Discovery in the Wilderness of Judaea* (1959).
G. Jeremias, *Der Lehrer der Gerechtigkeit* (1963).
G. R. Driver, *The Judaean Scrolls* (1965).
O. Eissfeldt, *The Old Testament. An Introduction* (1965), pp. 637–68; 775–8.
J. Macdonald (ed.), *Dead Sea Scroll Studies 1969*, ALUOS 6 (1969).

(e) Translations with introduction:

G. Vermes, *Les manuscrits du désert de Juda* ([2]1954); *Discovery in the Judean Desert* (1956).
T. H. Gaster, *The Scriptures of the Dead Sea Sect* (1957).
A. Dupont-Sommer, *Les écrits esséniens découverts près de la Mer Morte* (1959); *The Essene Writings from Qumran* (1961).
J. Maier, *Die Texte vom Toten Meer* I–II (1960).
J. Carmignac, P. Guilbert, E. Cothenet, H. Lignée, *Les textes de Qumrân* I–II (1961–3).
G. Vermes, *The Dead Sea Scrolls in English* (1962, revd. 1965, 1968).
L. Moraldi, *I manoscritti di Qumrân* (1971).

(f) Monograph commentaries:

P. Wernberg-Møller, *The Manual of Discipline* (1957).
J. Licht, *Megillat ha-Serakhim* (1965).
Y. Yadin, *The Scroll of the War of the Sons of Light against the Sons of Darkness* (1962).
A. Dupont-Sommer, *Le livre des Hymnes découvert près de la Mer Morte* (1957).
J. Licht, *Megillat ha-Hodayot* (1957).
M. Mansoor, *The Thanksgiving Hymns* (1961).
M. Delcor, *Les Hymnes de Qumran* (1962).
K. Elliger, *Studien zum Habakuk-Kommentar vom Toten Meer* (1954).
J. A. Fitzmyer, *The Genesis Apocryphon of Qumran Cave I* (1966, [2]1971).
R. Meyer, *Das Gebet des Nabonidus* (1962).
J. M. Allegro, *The Treasure of the Copper Scroll* (1960).
B. Lurie, *Megillat ha-Neḥoshet* (The Copper Scroll) (1963).

(g) Qumran and Jewish Bible exegesis:

F. F. Bruce, *Biblical Exegesis in the Qumran Texts* (1959).
O. Betz, *Offenbarung und Schriftforschung in der Qumransekte* (1960).

G. Vermes, *Scripture and Tradition in Judaism—Haggadic Studies* (1961).
See also 'Biblical Interpretation at Qumran' in *Dead Sea Scroll Studies 1969*, ALUOS 6 (1969), pp. 84–163 (G. Vermes and S. Lowy).

(h) Qumran and the beginnings of Christianity:

K. Stendahl (ed.), *The Scrolls and the New Testament* (1958).
G. Baumbach, *Qumran und das Johannes-Evangelium* (1958).
H. Kosmala, *Hebräer-Essener-Christen* (1959).
J. van der Ploeg (ed.), *La secte de Qumrân et les origines du Christianisme* (1959).
M. Black, *The Scrolls and Christian Origins* (1961).
L. Mowry, *The Dead Sea Scrolls and the Early Church* (1962).
J. Becker, *Das Heil Gottes: Heils- und Sündenbegriffe in den Qumrantexten und im Neuen Testament* (1964).
B. Gärtner, *The Temple and the Community in Qumran and the New Testament* (1965).
H. Braun, *Qumran und das Neue Testament* I–II (1966).
J. Murphy-O'Connor (ed.), *Paul and Qumran* (1968).
M. Black (ed.), *The Scrolls and Christianity* (1969).
G. Klinzing, *Die Umdeutung des Kultus in der Qumran Gemeinde und im Neuen Testament* (1971).
J. H. Charlesworth (ed.), *John and Qumran* (1972).

(i) Qumran and the Karaites:

N. Wieder, *The Judean Scrolls and Karaism* (1962).

2. *Judaean manuscripts found in caves outside the Qumran area:*

P. Benoit, J. T. Milik, R. de Vaux, *Discoveries in the Judaean Desert* II: *Les Grottes de Murabba'at* [Hebrew, Aramaic and Greek contracts and letters including documents relating to the second Jewish revolt] (1961).
N. Avigad, Y. Yadin, etc., 'The Expedition to the Judean Desert, 1960', IEJ 11 (1961), pp. 1–81; 'The Expedition . . . 1961', IEJ 12 (1962), pp. 167–262.
Y. Yadin, *The Finds from the Bar Kokhba Period from the Cave of Letters* (1963).
O. Eissfeldt, *The Old Testament, An Introduction* (1965), pp. 639–40, 775–6.
E. Koffmann, *Die Doppelurkunden aus der Wüste Juda* (1968).
J. A. Fitzmyer, 'The Bar Cochba Period', *Essays on the Semitic Background of the New Testament* (1971), pp. 305–54.
Y. Yadin, *Bar-Kokhba* [Letters, pp. 124–39; documents, pp. 172–83; Babata's archive, pp. 222–53] (1971) [a popular account].

3. *Documents from Masada:*

Y. Yadin, 'The Excavation of Masada—1963/64, Preliminary Report', IEJ 15 (1965), pp. 1–120.
Y. Yadin, *The Ben Sira Scroll from Masada* (1965).
Y. Yadin, *Masada: Herod's Fortress and the Zealots' Last Stand* [Inscriptions, p. 95; ostraca, pp. 190–1, 201; scrolls, p. 173] (1966) [a popular account].

Part One

The First Period

From Antiochus Epiphanes to the Capture of Jerusalem by Pompey

The Maccabaean Rising and the Age of Independence 175 B.C.–63 B.C.

Survey of the History of Syria in the Last Century of Seleucid Rule

Sources

Eusebius, *Chronicorum Libri Duo*, ed. A. Schoene I (1875), II (1866). Note the extract here from Porphyry, on which see below. A good account of Eusebius's *Chronicle* is given by C. Wachsmuth, *Einleitung in das Studium der alten Geschichte* (1895), pp. 163–76; cf. R. Helm, *Eusebius' Chronik und ihre Tabellenform*, AAB 1923, No. 4; on the revision by Jerome, A. Schoene, *Die Weltchronik des Eusebius in ihrer Bearbeitung durch Hieronymus* (1900); text in R. Helm, *Die Chronik des Hieronymus*, GCS xlvii (1956).

Appian, *Syriaca* 45/233–49/250 (ed. Viereck and Roos, Teubner, 1962), gives a brief continuous sketch.

Daniel 11, with the commentary by Jerome (CCL lxxvii, pp. 897–935), is relevant only for Antiochus Epiphanes.

Maccabees I–II ed., comm. and transl. by F.-M. Abel, *Les livres des Maccabées* (1949).

Josephus, *Ant.* xii and xiii (and, less fully, *B.J.* i) adds to the account in Maccabees valuable evidence from other sources, and is important for Seleucid history throughout the period. For Polybius, Diodorus, Strabo, Livy and Pompeius Trogus (Justin) see pp. 63–8 above.

Coins, for the bibliography of Seleucid coins see pp. 9–10 above.

General Works on Later Seleucid History:

Bevan, E. R., *The House of Seleucus* (1902).

Niese, B., *Geschichte der griechischen und makedonischen Staaten seit der Schlacht bei Chaeronea* III: *von 188 bis 120 v. Chr.* (1903).

Bouché- Leclercq, A., *Histoire des Séleucides (323–64 avant J.-C.)* I–II (1913–14).

Kolbe, W., *Beiträge zur syrischen und jüdischen Geschichte: kritische Untersuchungen zur Seleukidenliste und zu den beiden ersten Makkabäerbüchern* (1926).

Bevan, E. R., 'Syria and the Jews', CAH VIII (1930), pp. 495–533.

Bellinger, A. R., 'The End of the Seleucids', Trans. Connecticut Acad. 38 (1949), pp. 51–102.

Rostovtzeff, M., *The Social and Economic History of the Hellenistic World* (1953), pp. 695–705, 841–70.

Will, E., *Histoire politique du monde hellénistique* II (1967), pp. 253–98, 306–19, 336–85, 423–34.

Bikerman, E., *Institutions des Séleucides* (1938), is essential for the background to Seleucid-Jewish relations.

The Bases of Seleucid Chronology

The chief sources for fixing the chronological framework are (1) the *Chronicle* of Eusebius, both the section quoted from Porphyry as well as Eusebius's own statements. (2) The First Book of Maccabees. This book is dated in accordance with the Seleucid era, which in Greek sources normally begins from the autumn of 312 B.C.; 1 Mac. contains datings by both that, and the Babylonian Seleucid era (below). (3) Coins dated by the Seleucid era. (4) Greek inscriptions, similarly dated and mentioning the reigning king. (5) Cuneiform inscriptions, see R. A. Parker, W. H. Dubberstein, *Babylonian Chronology 626 B.C.–A.D. 75* (1956), esp. pp. 10–26, with references to earlier literature and a conspectus of evidence on the dating of the reigns. The Babylonian Seleucid era begins from the spring of 311 B.C.

Porphyry, the well-known neo-Platonist philosopher (3rd cent. A.D.), wrote a chronological work for which he conscientiously used the best sources. From this, Eusebius in his *Chronicle* recounts the history of the Ptolemies (ed. Schoene I, pp. 159–70 = Jacoby, FGrH 260 F2, in German translation) and of the Macedonian kings (*ibid.* 229–42 = *ibid.* F3). The corresponding section on the history of the Seleucids (*ibid.* 247–64) undoubtedly derives from the same source, although Porphyry is not mentioned by name. The complete text of this part of the *Chronicle* is only preserved in an Armenian translation, first edited by Aucher, *Eusebii Chron.* I (1818), and subsequently rendered into Latin by Petermann for Schoene's edition). The Armenian and Greek texts (the former in Aucher's translation) are given among the fragments of Porphyry's writings, with the addition of a historical commentary, in Müller, FHG III, pp. 706–17. They appear among the dubious fragments of Porphyry in Jacoby, FGrH 260 F32 (German transl.); commentary vol. II D, pp. 866–77.

In this section, Porphyry fixes the chronology of the Seleucids in accordance with the Olympic era but takes only whole years into account. As a result, the year in which a reign comes to an end is accredited to that king as a full year, and his successor's reign is not reckoned to begin until the year following. Cf. Jacoby, FGrH II D, pp. 854–6. Furthermore, when a new claimant to the throne appeared on the scene, as frequently happened, Porphyry counts the reign of the victorious pretender only from the year in which his opponent was overthrown.

In regard to Porphyry's sources, a reasonable deduction may be made from the following passage of Jerome, which admittedly refers, not to Porphyry's chronicle, but to his *Against the Christians:* 'Ad intelligendas autem extremas partes Danielis multiplex Graecorum historia necessaria est: Sutorii videlicet Callinici, Diodori, Hieronymi, Polybii, Posidonii, Claudii Theonis et Andronici cognomento Alipi, quos et Porphyrius secutum esse se dicit', *Prolog. in Dan.* (CCL lxxva, p. 775). On Porphyry's *Against the Christians*, see A. von Harnack, 'Porphyrius gegen die Christen', AAB (1916), no. 1 (note p. 12, for its relation to the *Chronicle*).

Valuable as the work of Porphyry is, it should nevertheless not be overestimated. He evidently reaches his conclusions in terms of Olympic dates 'primarily by means of a calculation from regnal years' (se A. v. Gutschmid, *Geschichte Irans und seiner Nachbarländer* (1888), p. 77) and they do not, therefore, possess the value of direct independent evidence. In addition, the figures in the Armenian text are often corrupt. Eusebius's own calculations in the second book of the *Chronicle* serve as a control. To assess the worth of both, Porphyry's statements are set beside those of Eusebius in the second book, the latter according to the version of Jerome, which is better than the Armenian translation (see Helm, *Eusebius' Chronik und ihre Tabellenform*, p. 56).

PORPHYRY		EUSEBIUS	
Euseb. *Chron.* I, pp. 247–63; Jacoby, FGrH 260 F32	Olymp.	*Chron.* II, 117–33; ed. Helm, pp. 126–49	Olymp.
Seleucus (I) Nicator	32 years, first 117,1 last 124,4	Seleucus (I) Nicator	32 years, first 117,1 last 124,4
Antiochus (I) Soter	19 years, first 125,1 last 129,3	Antiochus (I) Soter	19 years, first 125,1 last 129,3
Antiochus (II) Theos (in the index 15)	**19** years, first 129,4 last **135,3**	Antiochus (II) Theos	15 years, first 129,4 last 133,2
Seleucus (II) Callinicus	**21** years, first 133,3 last 138,2	Seleucus (II) Callinicus	20 years, first 133,3 last 138,2
Seleucus (III) Ceraunus	3 years, first last 139,1	Seleucus (III) Ceraunus	3 years, first 138,3 last 139,1
Antiochus (III) Magnus	36 years, first 139,2 last **148,2**	Antiochus (III) Magnus	36 years, first 139,2 last 148,1
Seleucus (IV) Philopator	12 years first **148,3** last 151,1	Seleucus (IV) Philopator	12 years, first 148,2 last 151,1
Antiochus (IV) Epiphanes	11 years, first **151,3** last **154,1**	Antiochus (IV) Epiphanes	11 years, first 151,2 last 153,4
Antiochus (V) Eupator	1½ years, first last	Antiochus (V) Eupator	2 years, first 154,1 last 154,2
Demetrius (I) Soter	12 years, first **154,4** last **157,4**	Demetrius (I) Soter	12 years, first 154,3 last 157,2
Alex. (Balas) (in index 15)	5 years, first 157,3 last **158,4**	Alex. (Balas)	10 years, first 157,3 last 159,4
Demetrius (II) Nicator	3 years, first 160,1 last 160,3	Demetrius (II) Nicator	3 years, first 160,1 last 160,3
Antiochus (VII) Sidetes	9 years, first 160,4 last 162,4	Antiochus (VII) Sidetes	9 years, first 160,4 last 162,4
Demetrius (III) (after captivity)	4 years, first **162,2** last **164,1**	Demetrius (III)	4 years, first 163,1 last 163,4
Antiochus (VIII) Grypus	**11** years, first **164,2** last 166,4	Antiochus (VIII) Grypus	12 years, first 164,1 last 166,4
Antiochus (IX) Cyzicenus	18 years, first 167,1 last **171,1**	Antiochus (IX) Cyzicenus	18 years, first 167,1 last 171,2
Philippus (acc. to Greek index)	2 years, first 171,3 (Greek text)	Philippus	2 years, first 171,3 last 171,4

Variants in these two tables are shown in bold figures in the text of Porphyry. In certain places, the figures of Porphyry are manifestly corrupt. A genuine variant, however, occurs from the year of the death of Antiochus III to that of Demetrius I. If the errors due to faulty textual transmissions are corrected here, Porphyry's estimates are, throughout, one year behind those of Eusebius. While most scholars have so far always followed Porphyry, Niese in his 'Kritik der beiden Makkabäerbücher', Hermes 35 (1900), pp. 491–7, argued by quoting other dates that at this point Eusebius's reckoning is to be preferred. However, one cannot explain the variants of Porphyry, as Niese does, from a later revision of the text. It is rather that Eusebius's statements are obviously independent of the texts of Porphyry contained in the first book of his *Chronicle*. A similar change has also taken place in the case of Demetrius III and Antiochus VIII (the date 162,2 instead of 163,2 for the beginning of the reign of Demetrius II is simply a textual error).

Antiochus IV Epiphanes (175–164 B.C.)

The son of Antiochus III (the Great), Antiochus IV was the brother of Seleucus IV Philopator (187–175 B.C.), during whose reign he lived in Rome as a hostage. Seleucus enabled him to return by sending in exchange his own son Demetrius as a hostage to Rome. Before Antiochus reached home, however, Seleucus was assassinated by Heliodorus. Thus Antiochus usurped the throne to which his nephew, also called Antiochus, was the rightful heir (Appian *Syr.* 45/233–4). The nephew may have been proclaimed before Antiochus's arrival and have been kept as co-regent until his death in 170 B.C. See O. Mørkholm, *Antiochus IV of Syria* (1966), pp. 38–47. Antiochus IV died after a reign of eleven years during a campaign against the Parthians in 164 B.C.

The eleven years of his reign are attested by a cuneiform tablet, see A. J. Sachs, D. J. Wiseman, 'A Babylonian king list of the Hellenistic Period', Iraq 16/17 (1954/5), pp. 202–12; cf. Parker and Dubberstein, *op. cit.*, pp. 10–11, 23; Porphyry (Euseb. *Chron.* ed. Schoene I, pp. 253, 263); Jerome *In Daniel* 21, 21 and Sulpicius Severus, *Chron.* II 22. The First Book of Maccabees (1 Mac. 1:10) dates the beginning of the reign in 137 of the Seleucid era, or 176/175 B.C. Porphyry counts Olymp. 151,3 (175/4) as the first year, Eusebius 151,2 (176/5). Since, as has been said, Eusebius is to be preferred, and since he, like Porphyry, always reckons the year following a change of reign as the first full year of a monarch, the beginning of the reign would seem to fall in Olymp. 151, 1, i.e., 176/175 B.C. This date agrees with that given by I Maccabees. But the cuneiform tablet (above) shows that Seleucus died, and Antiochus began his reign, in September 175. The death of Antiochus occurred, according to Eusebius, in Olymp. 153,4, 165/164 B.C.; according to 1 Mac (6:16) in 149 of the Seleucid era, i.e. 164/163 B.C., which would place it, if these statements are correct, during the second quarter of 164 B.C. This date is also supported by the difference between Eusebius and Porphyry, which can be explained by the fact that, according to the sources, some uncertainty might have existed as to whether Olymp. 153,4 or Olymp. 154,1 (i.e. 164/163) was to be reckoned as the time of his death. The cuneiform tablet, above, shows that his death became known in Babylon between Nov. 20 and Dec. 18, 164. The coins of Antiochus cover the years 138–147, and possibly 149, of the Seleucid era, E. Babelon, *Les rois de Syrie* (1890), pp. cix–xi; Mørkholm, *op. cit.*, pp. 126–7.

The chronology of the Egyptian campaigns of Antiochus, which is also relevant for Jewish history, is debatable. Even the Book of Daniel, which speaks of only two campaigns, is of no help, because it mentions only those that were followed by after-effects in Jerusalem. However, the view of Niese, *op. cit.*, pp. 168–76, that the campaigns were restricted to the years 169–168 B.C. appears to be incorrect. It now seems certain that the first war covered the years 170–169 B.C.; see T. C. Skeat in JEA 47 (1961), pp. 107–12. This squares also with 1 Mac. 1:20, which puts the return from the first Egyptian campaign in the year 143 of the Seleucid era. This will be autumn 169 B.C.: 1 Mac. uses both the Greek and the Babylonian starting-points for the Seleucid era, and is here using the Babylonian year 143, i.e., spring 169–spring 168 B.C. Only the Second Book of Maccabees appears to differ from this calculation in so far as it describes the same campaign as the second inroad into Egypt (2 Mac. 5:1); however, Abel, *ad. loc.*, proposes that this should be taken as a reference to the second phase, the actual penetration of Egypt, of the war of 170/169 B.C.; the first will have ended with the battle of Mt. Casius in November 170. Cf. Mørkholm, *op. cit.*, pp. 69–84. The second invasion of Egypt, ended by Roman diplomatic intervention, took place in 168 B.C.; see Mørkholm, *op. cit.*, pp. 88–101.

On Antiochus Epiphanes see (apart from the general works on the Seleucids, pp. 125–6 above, and works on the Maccabean movement, pp. 137–8 below). O. Mørkholm, *Antiochus IV of Syria:* Classica et Mediaevalia, Diss. VII (1966).

Antiochus V Eupator (164–162 B.C.)

This monarch was the son of Epiphanes. He was only nine years old when he ascended the throne (so Appian *Syr.* 46/236, 66/352; the statement by Porphyry that he was twelve must be rejected, for in that case his father would have married when he was a hostage in Rome; so Mørkholm, *op. cit.*, p. 48, n. 41). During his reign of about two years, he was merely a tool in the hands of his army commander and guardian, Lysias, together with whom he was assassinated at the command of his cousin Demetrius in 162 B.C.

Statements relating to the duration of his reign vary from a year and a half, so Porphyry in the summary of Eusebius, *Chron.* ed. Schoene I, cols. 263–4, to two years, so Jos. *Ant.* xii 10, 1 (390). The latest dating by his reign in cuneiform tablets is October 16, 162 B.C. See Parker and Dubberstein, *op. cit.*, p. 23.

Demetrius I Soter (162–150 B.C.)

Demetrius I was the son of Seleucus Philopator. Sent by his father to Rome as a hostage, he escaped, and seized power by causing his cousin Antiochus Eupator to be murdered.

In 153 B.C. he was confronted by a pretender to the throne in the person of Alexander Balas, who claimed to be a son of Antiochus Epiphanes, and therefore the legitimate heir. Demetrius fell in battle against him in 150 B.C.

The flight of Demetrius from Rome, and the events that preceded it, are very vividly described by Polybius, who, as a friend of Demetrius, was one of the persons involved. (Polyb. xxxi 12, 19–22). Polybius iii 5, 3, as well as Porphyry (in Eusebius *Chron.* ed. Schoene I, cols. 255, 263–4) and Eusebius, ascribes to Demetrius a reign of twelve years, but Josephus, *Ant.* xiii 2, 4 (61) only eleven. The First Book of Maccabees (1 Mac. 7:1) dates the beginning of the reign in 151 of the Seleucid era = 162/161 B.C. (or 161/160 by the Babylonian Seleucid era). Porphyry mentions as the first full year of his reign Olymp. 154, 4, which means that he commenced his reign in Olymp. 154, 3 = 162/161 B.C. Eusebius puts both dates back by one year, so making the reign begin in 163/162 B.C. The coins cover the years from 154 to 162 of the Seleucid era = 159/158 to 151/150 B.C., see Babelon, *op. cit.*, pp. cxix, cxxii; *Syll. Num. Gr. Danish Museum: Seleucid kings* (1959), nos. 228–48. On the date of the rise of Alexander Balas, see below. The transmitted text of Porphyry gives Olymp. 157/4 as the year of his death. Since the length of the reign would then amount to thirteen years, the proper reading of the text must be Olymp. 157, 3 = 150/149 B.C. Eusebius has Olymp. 157, 2 = 151/150 B.C. According to 1 Mac. 10:50, 57, the death of Demetrius occurred not later than 162 of the Seleucid era, 151/0 or 150/49 B.C. Cuneiform tablets mention him earliest on 14 May, 161 B.C., and latest on 1 June, 151 (or between April 6, 151 and 26 March, 150), see Parker and Dubberstein, *op. cit.*, p. 23. The fullest treatment of Demetrius is H. Volkmann, 'Demetrius I und Alexander I von Syrien', Klio 19 (1925), pp. 373–412.

Alexander Balas (150–145 B.C.)

In the same way that Alexander seized power from Demetrius, so in his turn the son of Demetrius, who was called after his father, rose against Alexander with the support of Ptolemy VI Philometor of Egypt. Alexander was defeated in battle by Ptolemy at Antioch, fled to Arabia, and was there treacherously murdered in 145 B.C. Five days after he was killed, his head was brought to Ptolemy, Jos. *Ant.* xiii 4, 8 (117).

The coins of Alexander cover the years from 162–167 of the Seleucid era = 151/150 to 146/145 B.C., Babelon, *op. cit.*, pp. cxxiii–iv. 1 Mac. 10:1 places his insurrection against Demetrius I in the year 160 of the Seleucid era = 153/152 B.C. (or spring 152–spring 151). The rising took place before the Feast of Tabernacles of the year mentioned above (1 Mac. 10:21). Porphyry and Josephus, *Ant.* xiii 4, 8 (119), give the duration of his reign proper as five years. The transmitted text of Porphyry puts the beginning of the reign at Olymp. 157, 3 and the end at 158, 4. Since this would amount to six years according to Porphyry's method of reckoning, the first figure should probably read 157, 4 (i.e. in fact 157, 3 = 150/149 B.C.). Eusebius places it a year earlier (151/150 B.C.). The earliest cuneiform dating is 21 October, 150 B.C., Parker and Dubberstein, *op. cit.*, p. 23. The First Book of Maccabees dates Alexander's death in 167 of the Seleucid era = 146/145 B.C. (or 145/4) B.C. (1 Mac. 11:19). The date given by Porphyry is Olymp. 158, 4 = 145/144 B.C. The year 145 B.C. for Alexander Balas's death is certain because of the almost simultaneous demise of Ptolemy Philometor, see RE s.v. 'Ptolemaios' (24); for the evidence of the date of his death *ibid.* xxiii 2, col. 1717. No cuneiform dating is known later than 21 November, 146 B.C., Parker and Dubberstein, *op. cit.*, p. 24. The fullest account to that of H. Volkmann, *op. cit.*, Klio 19 (1925), pp. 373–412.

Demetrius II Nicator (145–140/39 B.C.) Antiochus VI (145–142 B.C.). Tryphon (142/1–138 B.C.)

The throne of Demetrius was in its turn contested by one of Alexander's generals, Diodotus Tryphon, in the name of Alexander's son, Antiochus VI, who was still a minor.

Tryphon, however, coveted the throne for himself, had his ward

Antiochus murdered, and made himself king. Soon afterwards (or before, according to other sources), Demetrius undertook a campaign against the Parthians in the course of which he was captured in 138 B.C. But Tryphon was attacked at Dora by Antiochus VII Sidetes, the brother of Demetrius, besieged at Apamea, and compelled to take his own life, Strabo xiv 5, 2 (668); Jos. *Ant.* xiii 7, 2 (222–3); Appian *Syr.* 68/357.

The revolt of Demetrius against Alexander Balas began, according to 1 Mac. 10:67, in the Seleucid year 165 = 148/7 (or 147/6) B.C. The coins cover 167 to 173 of the Seleucid era = 146/5 to 140/139 B.C., Babelon, *op. cit.*, p. cxxxi. Coins of Antiochus VI exist from 167 to 171 of the Seleucid era = 146/5 to 142/1 B.C., Babelon, *op. cit.*, p. cxxxv; H. Seyrig, 'Notes on Syrian Coins I: the Khan el-abde Find and the Coinage of Tryphon', Num. Notes and Monog. 119 (1950), pp. 1–22; and of Tryphon with the years 2–4, Babelon *op. cit.*, p. cxxxviii; Seyrig, *op. cit.* Josephus says that the reign of Antiochus VI lasted four years and that of Tryphon three, *Ant.* xiii 7, 1–2 (218, 224). Accordingly, the first would fall in 145/1 B.C. and the second in 141/38 B.C., or, which seems more likely on account of the coins, 145/2 and 142/38 B.C. However, Porphyry and Eusebius attribute a reign of only three years to Demetrius, i.e., before his imprisonment, (Eusebius, *Chron.* ed. Schoene I, cols. 257, 263–4), namely from Olymp. 160, 1 (in fact, 159, 4 = 141/40 B.C.) to Olymp. 160, 3 = 138/7 B.C. Apparently, Porphyry and Eusebius count the years of Demetrius's reign only from the removal (by defeat or assassination) of Antiochus VI. The numismatic evidence, however, agrees with the chronology of the First Book of Maccabees, which mentions 170 of the Seleucid era = 143/2 B.C. as the approximate date of the murder of Antiochus by Tryphon (1 Mac. 13:31, cf. 13:41). Finally, there is no great difference between the First Book of Maccabees, where the Parthian campaign of Demetrius is dated in the Seleucid year 172 = 141/40 (or 140/39) B.C., and Porphyry, where the year Olymp. 160, 2 = 139/8 B.C. is given. There is, by contrast, a strong contradiction to the foregoing in the statements of some authors (Jos. *Ant.* xiii 5, 11 (184–6); 7, 1 (218); Appian *Syr.* 68/357; Justin xxxvi 1, 7), who do not place the murder of Antiochus VI by Tryphon until the time of Demetrius's Parthian expedition, and even after his capture. But this argument runs counter not only to the chronology of the First Book of Maccabees, but also to the fact that in that case Tryphon could not have reigned for three to four years, as is nevertheless to be assumed from Josephus and Tryphon's coins. (The survival of Antiochus VI to 139/8 B.C. is argued again by H. R. Baldus, 'Der Helm des Tryphon und die seleukidische Chronologie', Jahrb. f. Num. u. Geldgesch. 20 (1970), pp. 217–39.) For Tryphon's death occurs at more or less the same time as the capture of Demetrius by the Parthians (see below under Antiochus Sidetes). For a similar argument with the same conclusions, Seyrig, *op. cit.*, pp. 12–7. For a detailed discussion of Tryphon, W. Hoffmann, RE s.v. 'Tryphon' (1). For the date of Demetrius's capture see now G. Le Rider, *Suse sous les Séleucides et les Parthes* (1965), pp. 369–72.

Antiochus VII Sidetes (138–129 B.C.)

As long as Demetrius remained a prisoner of the Parthians, Antiochus VII ruled without opposition in Syria. In 130 B.C. he embarked on a campaign against the Parthians during which he met his death in

129 B.C. While the war was still in progress, the king of the Parthians released Demetrius to carry out a coup against Antiochus and thereby force him to return.

On the surname 'Sidetes', see Porphyry (Eusebius, *Chron.* ed. Schoene, I, col. 225), 'in Sida urbe educatus, quapropter Sidetes ubique vocabatur'. Side lies in Pamphylia. According to 1 Mac. 15:10, the action of Antiochus VII against Tryphon took place in the Seleucid year 174=139/8 B.C. Porphyry and Eusebius count his reign from Olymp. 160, 4 (in fact, 160, 3=138/7 B.C.). The first coins are dated 174 of the Seleucid era=139/8 B.C., and continue until 183=130/129 B.C., Babelon, *op. cit.*, pp. cxl–i. The start of the Parthian campaign, according to Livy, cannot fall later than 130 B.C. (Livy *Epit.* 59 mentions immediately before, the consul M. Perperna, *cos.* 130, and immediately after, the consul C. Sempronius, *cos.* 129). Porphyry and Eusebius place the death of Antiochus after the reign of nine years in Olymp. 162, 4=129/8 B.C. According to Justin xxxviii 10, 9–10, his death occurred in the winter; according to Diodorus xxxiv/xxxv 15–16, in the spring; therefore if we follow Livy, at the beginning of 129 B.C. A cuneiform text dates by his rule on 1 June, 130 B.C. See A. T. Olmstead, 'Cuneiform Texts and Hellenistic Chronology', CPh 32 (1937), pp. 1–14, on p. 14. Cf. N. C. Debevoise, *A Political History of Parthia* (1938), pp. 31–5; Le Rider, *op. cit.*, pp. 377–8. For the epithets *Megas* and *Kallinikos* borne by the king in 130/29, see the inscription from Ako-Ptolemais, Y. H. Landau, IEJ 11 (1961), pp. 118–26=SEG xx, 413, cf. BE 1963, 281. Note, however, T. Fischer, *Untersuchungen zum Partherkrieg Antiochos VII im Rahmen der Seleukidengeschichte* (Diss. Tübingen, 1970), pp. 102–9, who attributes the inscription to Antiochus IX Cyzicenus.

Demetrius II Nicator for the second time (129–126/5 B.C.) Alexander Zebinas (128–122 B.C.?)

After ten years of Parthian captivity (so Porphyry in Eusebius), Demetrius became once again king of Syria. Immediately, Ptolemy Physcon raised a rival to his throne in the person of Alexander Zebinas, an alleged son of Alexander Balas. Demetrius was defeated by him near Damascus. Compelled to flee, he was assassinated as he was about to land at Tyre.

The coins of Demetrius cover the years 183–7 of the Seleucid era=130/29 to 126/5 B.C., Babelon, pp. cxli, cxlv; cf. Bellinger, *op. cit.*, pp. 58–62. Porphyry and Eusebius ascribe to Demetrius another four years of reign after his captivity. The transmitted text of Porphyry gives the year Olymp. 162, 2 as the beginning of this second period. This should certainly read Olymp. 163, 2 actually, 163, 1=128/7 B.C. The year of Demetrius's death is given as 164, 1=124/3 B.C. Eusebius represents both events as occurring one year earlier. The coins confirm that this is correct, for those of Antiochus VIII Grypus and of Cleopatra begin already with the Seleucid year 187=126/5 B.C., Babelon, *op. cit.*, p. cliii. Porphyry and Eusebius do not supply direct dates for Alexander Zebinas. His coins extend from 184 to 190 of the Seleucid era=129/8 to 123/2 B.C., Babelon *op. cit.*, p. cl; cf. Bellinger, *op. cit.*, pp. 62–5.

Seleucus V (125 B.C.)

Seleucus V succeeded his father Demetrius at the instigation of his mother, but was murdered soon after his accession to the throne.

Antiochus VIII Grypus (125–113 B.C.)

Antiochus VIII was the brother of Seleucus V. He still had to contend with Alexander Zebinas, the rival to the throne, but defeated him in the third year of his reign (i.e. 123/2 B.C.) and executed him (so Justin xxxix 2, 6; cf. also Diodorus xxxiv/xxxv 28, 2–3 Porphyry records that he took his own life by poison).

After a reign of eleven to twelve years, Antiochus Grypus was superseded in 114/113 B.C. by Antiochus IX Cyzicenus, his cousin on his father's side and brother on his mother's side. Antiochus Grypus retired to Aspendus.

The relationship between the two is as follows. Cleopatra, the daughter of Ptolemy Philometor of Egypt, who had first married Alexander Balas (1 Mac. 10:58), left him and married Demetrius II Nicator (1 Mac. 11:12). From this union descended Seleucus V and Antiochus VIII Grypus. But while Demetrius was in the hands of the Parthians, Cleopatra married his brother, Antiochus VII Sidetes, Jos. *Ant.* xiii 7, 1 (222). From this union descended Antiochus IX Cyzicenus, Jos. *Ant.* xiii 10, 1 (271–2); Appian *Syr.* 68/361. Porphyry, quoted by Eusebius *Chron.* ed. Schoene I, col. 260, writes, *τῷ ὁμομητρίῳ ἀδελφῷ Ἀντιόχῳ καὶ ἀνεψιῷ τῷ ἐκ πατρός*. On the genealogy of the Seleucids in general, see the stemma on p. 612.

Porphyry calculates that Antiochus VIII reigned for eleven years until dispossessed by Antiochus IX; that is, from Olymp. 164, 2 (actually, 164, 1=124/3 B.C.) till Olymp. 166, 2=113/2 B.C. Eusebius reckons twelve years, rightly placing the beginning of the reign one year earlier (125/4 B.C.). On the coins (after a brief period in 126/5 when Cleopatra appears alone), Antiochus VIII figures as co-regent of his mother Cleopatra while she was alive, but afterwards alone. The coins of the first kind run from the Seleucid years 187 to 192=126/5 B.C. to 121/120 B.C., Babelon, *op. cit.* p. cliii. Antiochus's own coins begin with the year 192, directly following the earlier ones, Babelon, *op. cit.*, p. clv. Cf. in general A. Kuhn, *Beiträge zur Geschichte der Seleukiden*, (1891), 14 ff.; Bellinger, *op. cit.*, pp. 64–6, and Excursus I, 'The Coinage of the Wars of the Brothers' (pp. 87–91).

Antiochus IX Cyzicenus (113–95 B.C.)
Antiochus VIII Grypus (111–96 B.C.)

For two years Cyzicenus was sole ruler, but in 111 B.C., Grypus returned and seized the greater part of Syria from his cousin. Cyzicenus retained only Coele-Syria (Porphyry in Euseb. *Chron.* I, col. 260, *κρατεῖ μὲν αὐτὸς τῆς Συρίας, ὁ δὲ Κυζικηνὸς τῆς Κοίλης*). The kingdom was thus divided and the two cousins (and brothers) in conflict.

Antiochus Grypus died fifteen years after his return, in 96 B.C.; according to Jos. *Ant.* xiii 13, 4 (365) he was assassinated. His rights and claims were inherited by his son Seleucus VI, who immediately attacked Antiochus Cyzicenus and defeated him at Antioch. To avoid capture, Cyzicenus took his own life while the battle was still in progress, in 95 B.C. (Porphyry in Euseb. *Chron.* I, cols. 259–60).

Porphyry gives Antiochus IX Cyzicenus a reign of eighteen years, from Olymp. 167, 1 (actually, 166, 4=113/2 B.C.) until Olymp. 171, 1=96/5 B.C. In place of the last figure, the reading should probably be, as with Eusebius, 171, 2=95/4 B.C. The reliable dates on the coins extend from 199 to 216 of the Seleucid era=114/3 to 97/6 B.C., Babelon, *op. cit.*, p. clxiii; cf. Bellinger, *op. cit.*, pp. 68–73. (Livy, *Epit.* 62, gives a hint of disturbances in Syria at some point between 118 and 114 B.C.; cf. Bellinger, *op. cit.*, pp. 66–7). The year 113 B.C. is therefore the year of the decisive victory of Antiochus IX over Antiochus VIII. Porphyry places the return of Antiochus VIII Grypus in Olymp. 167, 2=111/110 B.C. and gives him from then on another fifteen regnal years until Olymp. 170, 4=97/6 B.C. Josephus ascribes to Antiochus VIII Grypus a reign of altogether 29 years; that is, from 125 to 96 B.C. *Ant.* xiii 13, 4 (365). An inscription (OGIS 257) found in Paphos on the island of Cyprus includes a letter of one or other Antiochus to king Ptolemy Alexander of Cyprus, dated September, 109 B.C., in which he informs him that he has just bestowed freedom on the city of Seleucia Pieria. See C. B. Welles, *Royal Correspondence in the Hellenistic Period* (1934), pp. 289–94. The coinage of Antiochus VIII Grypus in this second period covers the years 201 to 208 of the Seleucid era=112/11 to 105/4, see Babelon, *op. cit.*, p. clv; Bellinger, *op. cit.*, pp. 68–72; A. B. Brett, Museum Notes 4 (1950), pp. 51–4; H. Seyrig, RN 9 (1967), p. 40.

During the next twelve years there was almost uninterrupted fighting between the five sons of Antiochus V Grypus (Seleucus VI, Antiochus XI, Philip, Demetrius III Eucaerus and Antiochus XII) and the son of Antiochus Cyzicenus, Antiochus X Eusebes Philopator (Jos. *Ant.* xiii 13, 4 (365–71); 14, 3 (384–6); 15, 1 (387–91); Porphyry in Eusebius *Chron.* ed. Schoene, I, col. 259–62=FGrH 260 F32 (25)–(28); Appian *Syr.* 69/365–6; see Bellinger *op. cit.*, pp. 73–80).

The struggle ended when Tigranes, king of Armenia, took possession of the Syrian kingdom. His rule over Syria lasted fourteen years (83–69 B.C.)

The details (according to Josephus whose account is most exhaustive) are as follows. To avenge his father, Antiochus X Eusebes went to war against Seleucus VI, defeated him, and drove him into Cilicia, where he was killed by the citizens of Mopsuestia on account of his extortions. His brother Antiochus then took over the struggle against Antiochus Eusebes, but lost both the battle and his life. Next, the third brother, Philip, rose against Antiochus Eusebes and was able to take possession of at least part of Syria, while the fourth brother, Demetrius Eucaerus, seized another part, with the capital Damascus. Since Porphyry and Eusebius give Olymp. 171, 3=94/3 B.C. as Philip's first full regnal year and thus place his first appearance during the previous year, and since coins of Demetrius exist from 217 of the Seleucid era=96/5 B.C. (see below), both brothers will have appeared on the scene before the end of 95 B.C. For a while, Philip and Demetrius each ruled over his own part of Syria. Antiochus Eusebes, who according to Josephus had by then fallen in battle against the Parthians, seems in fact also to have maintained his hold on a part of Syria. After some time, in 88 or 87 B.C., Demetrius made war against Philip, besieged him at Beroea (east of Antioch), but was himself taken prisoner and died in captivity. Besides Antiochus Eusebes, there now still remained Philip and the youngest brother Antiochus XII, all engaged in mutual conflict. Antiochus, however, fell in battle against the Nabataean dynast Aretas, who then seized Coele-Syria. Finally, the whole of Syria fell into the hands of Tigranes. According to Appian, *Syr.* 48/248, 69/366, Antiochus X Eusebes was still alive and in power when Tigranes took possession of Syria; according to Justin xl 2 and Porphyry in Euseb. *Chron.* I, col. 262, he was even living when Pompey put an end to the Syrian empire. The latter statement results from a confusion of Antiochus X Eusebes with Antiochus XIII Asiaticus, both of whom are clearly distinguished by Appian; but the first is quite probable since Appian appears here to have made use of reliable sources. It may therefore be assumed that Antiochus Eusebes held one part, and Philip and Aretas other parts of Syria at the time when Tigranes occupied the kingdom.

The coins provide valuable evidence for the dating of events in this confused period. It is best arranged by the mints at which the coins were struck. Only those coins will be mentioned which themselves furnish dates.

(1) Antioch. See E. T. Newell, 'The Seleucid Mint of Antioch', Am. Journal of Numism. 51 (1917), pp. 1–151; G. Downey, *A History of Antioch in Syria* (1961), pp. 132–6.

Coins struck at Antioch reflect the reigns there of Seleucus VI (95–4 B.C.), Antiochus X (94–2 B.C.), Antiochus XI Epiphanes Philadelphus (93 B.C.), Demetrius III (*c.* 92–89 B.C.) and Philip Philadelphus (89–3 B.C.). However, none of these coins is dated. Dated coins of the city of Antioch itself were issued from 92/1 to 73/2 B.C.

An unsolved problem is presented by a series of tetradrachms from Antioch with the name of Philip and the numerals *Γ, Δ, H, BI, ΘI, K, KA, BK, KΔ, ΣK, IK, HK, ΘK*; see Newell, *op. cit.*, pp. 123–4. They seem to denote years, but too many for his brief reign. The Philip who appears at the time of Pompey, Euseb. *Chron.* ed. Schoene I, col. 262 = FGrH 260 F32 (28), is the son of this Philip, see Diodorus XL 1a.

(2) Damascus. See E. T. Newell, *Late Seleucid Mints in Ake-Ptolemais and Damascus*, Num. Notes and Monogr. 84 (1939), pp. 78–100. These coins are the most important for dating purposes, as indication of the Seleucid era continued, while abandoned elsewhere. So we have coins of Demetrius III from 96/5, 95/4, 94/3, 92/1, 90/89, 89/8 and 88/7 B.C., of Antiochus XII from 87/6 and 86/5 B.C., and of Tigranes from 72/1, 71/70 and 70/69 B.C.

The dates 221, 227 and 229 of the Seleucid era were once reported on the coinage of Philip, see references in Babelon, *op. cit.*, p. clxix, but have not been confirmed.

The period of Tigranes's domination can be deduced from the fact that, according to Appian. *Syr.* 48/248; 70/368 (cf. Justin xl 1, 4 and 2, 3, where the reading of the figures is dubious), he reigned for fourteen years over Syria. The end of his rule, brought about by the capture of his capital by Lucullus, occurred in 69 B.C., as we know from Roman history.

The Romans did not immediately take possession of Syria after the victory of Lucullus over Tigranes. Lucullus ceded it to Antiochus XIII Asiaticus (69–65 B.C.), a son of Antiochus Eusebes. After about a year, he was deposed in favour of Philip (Diodorus xl 1a–b), who probably ruled until *c.* 66/65 B.C. See Bellinger, *op. cit.*, pp. 83–4. Then Antiochus Asiaticus returned to power. But Pompey, during his triumphal march through Asia, brought the reign of the Seleucids finally to an end in 64 B.C. (Appian, *Syr.* 49/250, 70/367; Justin xl 2, 3–5). Syria then became a Roman province (Plut. *Pomp.* 39; cf. MRR II, pp. 163–4).

Appian, *Syr.* 70/367 asserts that Antiochus had reigned for one year only when he was deposed by Pompey (*βασιλεύσαντα ἐν ταῖς ἀσχολίαις ταῖς Πομπηίου ἐπὶ ἓν μόνον ἔτος*). A. Kuhn, in consequence, *Beiträge*, p. 44 f., assumed that the reign lasted only one year altogether, from 68–67 B.C. But Antiochus was at first king by favour of Lucullus, and Pompey did not arrive in Asia until 66 B.C. Appian's statement must therefore be understood to mean that Antiochus continued to be king for one year after Pompey's arrival. (So Bellinger, *op. cit.*, p. 84, n. 112).

Pompey first despatched his legates from Armenia to Syria in 65 B.C. He himself arrived in 64 B.C. The definite stabilisation of conditions here did not occur until 63/2 B.C.

§ 4 Religious Crisis and Revolution 175–164 B.C.

Sources

1 Maccabees 1–4; 2 Maccabees 4–11. Ed., comm. and French translation by F.-M. Abel, *Les livres des Maccabées* (1949); cf. S. Tedesche, S. Zeitlin, *The First Book of the Maccabees* (1950); *The Second Book of the Maccabees* (1954).

Josephus *B.J.* i 1, 1–4 (31–40); *Ant.* xii 5–7 (237–326); *c. Ap.* I 7–8 (79–102).

Daniel 8:23–6; 9:24–7; 11:21–45 and Jerome's commentary *ad loc.* (CCL LXXVA). pp. 865–89; 914–35.

Megillath Taanith, ed. H. Lichtenstein, 'Die Fastenrolle', HUCA 8–9 (1931–32), pp. 257–351.

For a fuller discussion and bibliography of these works and of the Scroll of Antiochus, see the general section on sources above.

Bibliography

This list contains only the essential general works relating to §§ 4–7. References to individual points are given in the relevant footnotes. For a fuller bibliography, see O. Eissfeldt, *Introduction*, pp. 576–80; A. Momigliano, *Tradizione maccabaica* (²1968), pp. 173–87.

Derenbourg, J., *Essai sur l'histoire et la geographie de la Palestine* (1867), pp. 53 ff.

Graetz, H., *Geschichte der Juden* II, 2 (⁵1902), pp. 246 ff.

Wellhausen, J., *Israelitische und jüdische Geschichte* (⁹1958), pp. 213 ff.

Willrich, H., *Juden und Griechen vor der makkabäischen Erhebung* (1895).

Büchler, A., *Die Tobiaden und die Oniaden im II. Makkabäerbuche* (1899).

Niese, B., *Kritik der beiden Makkabäerbücher* (1900).

Meyer, E., *Ursprung und Anfänge des Christentums II.* (1921), pp. 121 ff.

Kugler, F. X., *Von Moses bis Paulus* (1922), ch. VII.

Abel, F.-M., 'Topographie des campagnes machabéennes', RB 32 (1923), pp. 495–521; 33 (1924), pp. 201–17, 371–87; 34 (1925), pp. 195–216; 35 (1926), pp. 102–22, 510–33.

Kolbe, W., *Beiträge zur syrischen und jüdischen Geschichte. Kritische Untersuchungen zur Seleukidenliste und zu den beiden ersten Makkabäerbüchern* (1926).

Bousset, W., Gressmann, H., *Die Religion des Judentums im späthellenistischen Zeitalter* (³1926, ⁴1966).

Ginsburg, M. S., *Rome et la Judée* (1928), pp. 1–64.

Rankin, O. R., *The Origin of the Festival of Hanukkah* (1930).

Momigliano, A., *Prime linee di storia della tradizione maccabaica* (1930, ²1968).

Momigliano, A., 'I Tobiadi nella preistoria del moto maccabaico', ARAST 67 (1931/2), pp. 165–200.

Bickerman, E., 'La charte séleucide de Jérusalem', REJ 100 (1935), pp. 4–35.

Bickerman, E., 'Un document relatif à la persécution d'Antiochus IV Epiphane', RHR 115 (1937), pp. 188–223.

Bickermann, E. *Der Gott der Makkabäer* (1937).

Zeitlin, S., 'Hanukkah', JQR 29 (1938–39), pp. 1–36.

Abel, F.-M., 'La fête de Hanoucca', RB 53 (1946), pp. 538–46.

Abel, F.-M., *Histoire de la Palestine* I (1952), pp. 109 ff.

Schunck, K.-D., *Die Quellen des I. und II. Makkabäerbuches* (1954).

Baer, Y. F., *Israel among the Nations* (1955), pp. 26–80 (in Hebrew).
Farmer, W. R., *Maccabees, Zealots and Josephus* (1956).
Plöger, W., 'Die Feldzüge der Seleukiden gegen den Makkabäer Judas', ZDPV 74 (1958), pp. 158–88.
Tcherikover, V., *Hellenistic Civilization and the Jews* (1959).
Bickerman, E., *From Ezra to the Last of the Maccabees* (1962).
Zeitlin, S., *The Rise and Fall of the Judean State* I (1962).
Hanhart, R., 'Zur Zeitrechnung des I und II Makkabäerbücher', in A. Jepsen, R. Hanhart, *Untersuchungen zur israelitisch-jüdischen Chronologie* (1964), pp. 49–96.
Zambelli, M., 'La composizione del secondo libro dei Maccabei e la nuova cronologia di Antioco IV Epifane', *Misc. greca e romana* I (1965), pp. 195–299.
Mørkholm, O., *Antiochus IV of Syria* (1966), esp. ch. VIII.
Hengel, M., *Judentum und Hellenismus* (1969) esp. pp. 486–564.
Jeremias, J., *Jerusalem in the Time of Jesus* (1969), pp. 182–91.
Bunge, J. G., *Untersuchungen zum Zweiten Makkabäerbuch* (Diss. Bonn, 1971).

Since the conquests by the Assyrians and Babylonians, the Jewish nation had lost its political independence. The northern kingdom of the ten tribes fell to the Assyrians, and the southern kingdom of Judah to the Babylonians. From these, the power passed to the Persians, and after two hundred years, to Alexander the Great.[1] During the stormy times of the Diadochi, Palestine constituted the main bone of contention between Ptolemy Lagus and his adversaries and therefore belonged sometimes to the one, sometimes to the other. During the third century, with brief interruptions, it formed part of the kingdom of the Ptolemies. At the beginning of the second century, however, Antiochus the Great was able to secure permanent possession of Phoenicia and Palestine. In place of the Ptolemies, the Seleucids became overlords of the Jews.[2]

Already at the beginning of Persian rule, the Jews were permitted

1. According to Josephus *Ant.* xi 8, 4–5 (326–36), Alexander offered sacrifices in Jerusalem. The story is largely unhistorical. See H. Willrich, *Juden und Griechen* (1895), pp. 1–13; A Büchler, 'La relation de Josèphe concernant Alexandre le Grand', REJ 36 (1898), pp. 1–26; F.-M. Abel, 'Alexandre le Grand en Syrie et en Palestine', RB 43 (1934), pp. 528–45; 44 (1935), pp. 42–61. There are also later legends of Jewish origin concerning Alexander. See I. Levi, 'Les traductions hébraïques de l'histoire légendaire d'Alexandre', REJ 3 (1881), pp. 238–75; 'La légende d'Alexandre dans le Talmud', REJ 2 (1881), pp. 293–300; 'La légende d'Alexandre dans le Talmud et le Midrash', REJ 7 (1883), pp. 78–93; 'Le voyage d'Alexandre au Paradis', REJ 12 (1886), pp. 117 f.; 'La dispute entre les Egyptiens et les Juifs', REJ 63 (1912), pp. 211–15; G. Radet, *Alexandre le Grand* (1931), pp. 130–6; R. Marcus, *Josephus* (Loeb) VI, App. C (Alexander the Great and the Jews), pp. 512–32. For the Alexander romance and Yosippon, see above p. 117.

2. See for details the works on the history of Syria listed on pp. 125–6. From the battle of Panias in 200 B.C., Phoenicia and Palestine remained permanently in the possession of the Seleucids. Cf. Abel, *Histoire de la Palestine* I (1952), pp. 84 ff.; E. Will, *Histoire politique du monde hellénistique* II (1967), pp. 101–2; note the important series of documents of this period on an inscription from near Scythopolis, Y. H. Landau, 'A Greek Inscription found near Hefzibah', IEJ 16 (1966), pp. 54–70; cf. BE 1970, no. 627.

to organise themselves as a religious and political community. But the form in which the political system was restored after the exile was essentially different from that which existed before. The predominating authority was in the hands of the priests, at least from the time of Ezra. Indeed, a priest was the leader of the political community, too. For the so-called High Priest was by no means merely in command of religious affairs; he was at the same time head of the state, unless sovereignty was exercised by the king and his officers. The rank of High Priest was held for life and was hereditary.[3] At his side—presumably already during the Persian period but in any case from the beginning of Greek rule—stood a council of elders, the *gerousia*, whose head and executive he was. To what extent administration and jurisdiction lay in the hands of this native governing body, and how far it was carried out by the Persian or Greek overlords, cannot now be determined. Under

3. See the list of the High Priests from Joshua, the contemporary of Zerubbabel, to Jaddua in Neh. 12:10–11. Jaddua was a contemporary of Alexander the Great, Jos. *Ant.* xi 7, 2 (302); 8, 7 (347). According to Josephus, the successors of Jaddua were:

Onias I son of Jaddua, *Ant.* xi 8, 7 (347); according to 1 Mac. 12:7–8, 20, a contemporary of King Areus of Sparta 309–265 B.C.;

Simon the Just son of Onias I, *Ant.* xii 2, 4 (43); according to Aristeas, a contemporary of Ptolemy II Philadelphus, 283–46 B.C.;

Manasse uncle of Simon I, *Ant.* xii 4, 1 (147);

Onias II son of Simon the Just, *Ant.* xii 4, 1–2 (156–66), a contemporary of Ptolemy III Euergetes 246–21 B.C.; but a detailed description of this Ptolemy is lacking in some of the better manuscripts of *Ant.* xii 4, 1 (158); see also the following notes;

Simon II son of Onias II, *Ant.* xii 4, 10 (224); cf. Sir. 50:1 ff.; 3 Mac. 2:1;

Onias III son of Simon II, *Ant.* xii 4, 10 (225), at the time of Seleucus IV and Antiochus Epiphanes, 175 B.C., and therefore mentioned in the introduction to the history of the Maccabaean rising, 2 Mac. 3–4; Jos. *Ant.* xii 5, 1 (237).

The High Priest Ezekias referred to by Ps.-Hecataeus in Jos. *c. Ap.* I 22 (87), cf. FGrH 264 F21 and commentary, as a contemporary of Ptolemy Lagus, is not mentioned by Josephus in his historical narrative. On a coin possibly giving his name, see O. R. Sellers, *Citadel of Beth Zur* (1933), pp. 73 ff. Cf. also Marcus, *Josephus* (Loeb) VII, p. 6, n. 6; and Meshorer, *Jewish Coins of the Second Temple Period* (1967), p. 36. A critical examination of the whole list is made by Willrich, *op. cit.*, pp. 107 ff. Christian historians (Euseb., *Demonstr. evang.* viii 2, 62–72; *Chron.* ed. Schoene II, pp. 114–24; *Chronicon paschale* ed. Dindorf I, pp. 302–39, 356 f., 390 f.) devote particular attention to these High Priests and fix the exact dates for each of them. But it is obvious from their statements that Josephus was the only source at their disposal. Their calculations are, therefore, quite arbitrary. H. Gelzer, *Julius Africanus* (1885), II, pp. 170–6, gives a detailed critical account of the list of the High Priests compiled by the Byzantine chroniclers. See in general H. Graetz, 'Zur Geschichte der nachexilischen Hohenpriester; MGWJ 30 (1881), pp. 49–64, 97–112; E. R. Bevan, *Jerusalem under the High-Priests* (1904). On the development of the High Priesthood see R. de Vaux, *Ancient Israel* (1961), pp. 397–403. For the inter-Testamental period, see esp. J. Jeremias, *Jerusalem in the Time of Jesus* (1969), pp. 147–98, 377–8; see also M. Hengel, *Judentum und Hellenismus* (1969), pp. 44–7.

the Greeks, the political autonomy of the Jewish community will have been not less but greater than before (cf. in general § 23, iii). The most important issue was, without doubt, the payment of taxes. Until the reign of Onias II, they are said to have been paid by the High Priest personally (ἐκ τῶν ἰδίων) in a lump sum of twenty talents, but to have been leased out later to a tax-farmer.[4]

The extent of this relatively autonomous Jewish state was probably limited to Judaea proper, i.e. the province south of Samaria—corresponding approximately to the former kingdom of Judah. Excluded from it were all the coastal towns which, with their predominantly Gentile populations, constituted self-governing city-states (see vol. II, § 23, i). How far into the interior these territories reached, becomes evident from the fact that Ekron and Gazara were not part of Judaea. Ekron was not united to Jewish territory and Judaised until the time of Jonathan (1 Mac. 10:88–9), and Gazara, not until that of Simon (1 Mac. 13:43–8). On the sites of these places, see below § 6 and 7. Furthermore, none of the land east of the Jordan belonged to Jewish territory either. Some Hellenistic cities were located there (see vol. II, § 23, i), and some independent tribes under their own leaders.[5] In the

4. Jos. *Ant.* xii 4, 1–10 (154–224). The name of the tax-farmer was Joseph son of Tobias. According to the transmitted text of *Ant.* xii 4, 1 (158), his lease began during the time of Ptolemy III Euergetes, but in several reliable manuscripts the surname of the king is missing and is probably an interpolation; for (a) Josephus has previously mentioned the marriage of Ptolemy V Epiphanes with Cleopatra, the daughter of Antiochus the Great of Syria; (b) the king's spouse throughout the entire story of Joseph's tax-farming is referred to as Cleopatra, *Ant.* xii 4, 3 (167); 4, 5 (185); 4, 8 (204); 4, 9 (217). But there was no queen of Egypt by that name before the marriage of Ptolemy V in 194/3 B.C., H. L. Strack, *Die Dynastie der Ptolemäer* (1897), pp. 183, 196; cf. RE s.v. 'Kleopatra' (14). Accordingly, Joseph's whole taxation lease, which lasted for twenty-two years, *Ant.* xii 4, 6 (186) and 4, 10 (224), would fall during the period when Palestine already belonged to Syria and Cleopatra merely drew certain revenues from these as dowry (see above note 2), whereas the narrative presupposes that Palestine belonged to Egypt. The historical background of the story is therefore impossible, and its details are also obviously legendary. In so far as historical facts underlie it, they are to be situated in the period before 200 B.C. (the conquest of Palestine by Antiochus the Great). In fact, the textual variant τὸν Εὐεργέτην ὃς ἦν πατὴρ τοῦ Φιλοπάτορος may be a deliberate insertion by a scribe aware of the chronological inconsistencies of Josephus's narrative (so Marcus, Loeb text. *ad. loc.*). More recent scholars generally accept that the activity of Joseph fell in the period of Ptolemy Euergetes, 246–21 B.C. See B. Mazar, 'The Tobiads', IEJ 7 (1957), pp. 137–45, 229–38; Tcherikover, *op. cit.*, pp. 128–30; Hengel, *op. cit.*, pp. 51–3, 489–90.

5. One of these seems to have been Timotheus, the ἡγούμενος of the Ammonites against whom Judas Maccabaeus fought (1 Mac. 5:6, 11, 34, 37, 40). For in view of the independence of these tribes, clearly illustrated by the account in 1 Mac. 9:35–42, the suggestion that he was a military commander placed by the king of Syria over the Ammonites is unlikely. Aretas, the τύραννος of the Nabataeans (2 Mac. 5:8) was also one of these native dynasts. See below, pp. 576–7.

areas west of the Jordan 'Judaea' and 'Samaria' formed, towards the end of the third and the beginning of the second century, a specific administrative district alongside 'Coele-Syria' and 'Phoenicia'.[6] Galilee is not mentioned as such; it therefore belonged to one of the four districts mentioned, though scarcely to Judaea, from which it was geographically separated. Pseudo-Hecataeus maintains that Alexander the Great bestowed Samaria on the Jews as a tax-free zone.[7] But even if this statement were more reliable than it is, it would no longer apply to the era of Seleucid domination, for under the Maccabaean High Priest Jonathan it is mentioned as a special favour granted by king Demetrius II that three *νομοί* were detached from Samaria and united to Judaea, and this whole region was transferred to the Jews tax-free.[8] Traditionally, therefore, the authority of the Jewish High Priest extended only to Judaea, and indeed to Judaea in the narrower sense (without Galilee), for this is apparently the meaning of the passages cited in Maccabees.[9]

6. See Jos. *Ant.* xii 4, 1 (154) and xii 4, 4 (175), where these territories are mentioned separately in exactly the same terms. But for the full complexity of local administrative sub-divisions in early Seleucid times see M. Avi-Yonah, *The Holy Land* (1966), ch. III.

7. Ps.-Hecataeus in Jos. *c. Ap.* II 4 (43) = FGrH 264 F22, *τὴν Σαμαρεῖτιν χώραν προσέθηκεν ἔχειν αὐτοῖς ἀφορολόγητον.*

8. 1 Mac. 11:34, 'We have, therefore, settled on them the lands of Judaea and the three districts of Aphaerema, Lydda and Ramathaim' (*τοὺς τρεῖς νομοὺς Ἀφιρεμα καὶ Λυδδα καὶ Ῥαμαθαιμ*) (these were added to Judaea from the district of Samaria). Cf. 11:28. This gift was promised once before but not implemented (1 Mac. 10:30, 38); it was confirmed by Antiochus VI (1 Mac. 11:57). Cf. Avi-Yonah, *op. cit.*, pp. 55–6.

9. 'Judaea' side by side with 'Samaria' can only be Judaea in the narrower sense, i.e., the southern province. This corresponds to the linguistic usage of 1 Maccabees, where *γῆ Ἰούδα* or *Ἰουδαία* is apparently always Judaea proper (e.g. 1 Mac. 12:46–52). The prevailing usage in Josephus, the New Testament and the Mishnah, which distinguishes between 'Judaea', 'Samaria' and 'Galilee' as three separate districts (see vol. II, § 22, 1), was, in consequence, already firmly established in the Maccabaean era. If, however, it is acknowledged that Judaea in the narrower sense is meant in the passages quoted (1 Mac. 10:30, 38; 11:28, 34), then it follows that the district of Galilee lay outside the jurisdiction of the Jewish High Priest, not only before the beginning of the Maccabaean rising, but even under Jonathan and Simon. For it is always simply a question of Judaea and the three *νομοί* of Samaria added to it. Only in 1 Mac. 10:30 do we read that three *νομοί* of 'Samaria and Galilee' were to be united to Judaea. But on the one hand, this was not realised at that time and, on the other, according to other corresponding passages only three *νομοί* in Southern Samaria can be meant. In consequence, either the word *Γαλιλαίας* is just an interpolation, or 'Samaria and Galilee' is used as a comprehensive geographical term for the province of Samaria. Cf. Avi-Yonah, *op. cit.*, p. 48, who takes this passage as evidence that Galilee was included in the eparchy of Samaria. It was only by the conquests of John Hyrcanus and his successor that Galilee, as well as Samaria and Scythopolis, were joined politically to Jewish territory. (Cf. pp. 207, 217–18 below.)

The boundaries of the Jewish population did not coincide with those of Judaea in the political sense. Even the fact that in the time of the Maccabees it was considered of value that the three southern districts of Samaria—Aphaerema, Lydda and Ramathaim—should be united to Judaea, gives ground to assume that the population of these areas was predominantly Jewish; that, in other words, they did not offer sacrifice with the schismatic Samaritans on Mount Gerizim, but in Jerusalem, in religious fellowship with the Jews living there.[10] But in Galilee too, as well as in Gilead—east of Jordan therefore—there must, at the beginning of the second century B.C., have been a considerable number of Jews living in religious communion with Jerusalem; one of the first acts of the Maccabees after the restoration of the cult was to bring help to their fellow-Jews in Galilee and Gilead who were oppressed by the heathens, Simon going to Galilee and Judas to Gilead (1 Mac. 5:9–54). Yet the way in which they brought aid demonstrates that there were not yet any compact masses of Jewish population there, for neither Simon nor Judas brought these regions as such under Jewish protection. Simon, after defeating the Gentiles in Galilee, led all the Jews, with their wives, children and belongings, out of Galilee and Arbatta to Judaea, to shelter them in safety there (1 Mac. 5:23).[11] Judas proceeded in the same way with the Jews living in Gilead after he had defeated the heathens there (1 Mac. 5:45–54). It is thus clearly evident that the Jews in Galilee and Gilead still formed a Diaspora among the Gentiles; and the early Maccabees by no means set out to Judaise those regions, but on the contrary, withdrew their Jewish population.

Only a general sketch can be given of the inner development of Judaism from the time of Ezra to the Maccabaean period, or even to the beginning of the talmudic era. The point of departure is known more exactly—the promulgation of biblical laws by Ezra—and also the end—the codification of Jewish legal customs in the Mishnah (about A.D. 200). Between these two limits lies an interval of about six centuries. What stage of development had Judaism reached at the outbreak of the Maccabaean uprising? It seems that it was already on the way towards the results completed in the Mishnah; and the Maccabaean era was the time of greatest crisis which Judaism had to endure during this entire period. An attempt was made to destroy the groundwork of earlier development and to convert the Jews to

10. Note especially in 1 Mac. 5:23 that the offering of sacrifice in Jerusalem is the distinguishing characteristic of those exempted from taxes.

11. Jos. *Ant.* xii 8, 2 (334) speaks of Jews held captive by the Gentiles.But 1 Mac. 5:23 probably refers to all who wished to emigrate to Judaea. This is proved by the more explicit parallel narrative on the procedure of Judas in Gilead (1 Mac. 5:45–54). The location of Arbatta is uncertain; it may be identical with the district of 'Narbata', inland from the future Caesarea. See Abel, *ad. loc.*

heathen worship. The outcome was a consolidation of the foundations laid by Ezra, a sedulous continuation of work on the theoretical elaboration of the law and on its practical application. The reform introduced by Ezra was fundamentally ritual. It fixed the religion of Israel within firm legal forms in order to safeguard it against heathen influence. The Jew was told, in the form of a divinely given law, how he should behave as a true servant of God: which feasts he should celebrate, which sacrifices he should offer, which dues he should pay to the celebrant priests, and in general which ceremonies he should observe. The conscientiousness of his observance of all these precepts became from now on an indication of his piety. And in order to render such conscientiousness feasible, an authentic interpretation of the Torah was provided. Experts—'scribes'—devoted themselves professionally to the study and ever more subtle exposition of Scripture, and the devout saw their highest merit to consist in a zealous fulfilment of the law thus expounded. The history of the Maccabaean rebellion itself shows that the Jews had already made substantial progress along this path by the second century B.C. There were circles (the Assidaeans or Ḥasidim) in which the Sabbath commandment was interpreted so strictly that they would rather be cut down without a struggle rather than transgress the law by wielding the sword (1 Mac. 2:32–8). It was also part of the ideal of piety held up at that time by the author of the Book of Daniel that his co-religionists should not defile themselves by eating heathen food (Dan. 1).

But along with this tendency towards legal piety went, from the time of Alexander the Great, influences and aspirations of quite another kind, and the longer they existed, the more clearly they proved to be its most dangerous enemy: namely, the inclination towards Hellenism. It was the grandiose plan of Alexander the Great to found a world empire that would be held together, not only by unity of government, but also by a unity of language, customs and culture. For this reason, he saw to it that Greek colonists followed everywhere in the steps of his armies. New cities were founded inhabited only by Greeks, and old cities were provided with Greeks too. In this way a net of Greek culture was spread over half of Asia, the purpose of which was to bring all the intervening areas within its sphere of influence. Alexander's successors continued his work, and it is a brilliant testimony to the power of Greek culture that it fulfilled, in very large measure, the mission assigned to it by Alexander. The whole of the Near East—if not among the broader masses of the population then in the higher levels of society—became Hellenized. In Palestine, too, this process was in full operation at about the beginning of the second century B.C. It cannot, admittedly, be proved that every one of the cities known as Greek under the Roman empire (see vol. II, § 22, ii and 23, i) was already Hellenized at the beginning of the Maccabaean era, but most of them certainly were. Greek civilisation was advancing everywhere.[12] Gaza, as its coins testify, enjoyed lively trade relations with Greece already in pre-Hellenistic times; from the time of its conquest by Alexander it was a Macedonian garrison town, and Josephus calls it a *πόλις Ἑλληνίς*.[13] Anthedon betrays its Greek origin through its name. In Ascalon, coins of Alexander the Great were minted;[14] Joppa is the seat of the myth of Perseus and Andromeda, and in the age of the Diadochi was a Macedonian garrison town. But the Tower of Straton, in spite of its Greek name, was probably a Sidonian foundation. Dora, too, had been a dependency of Sidon, but was now a Greek city. In Acre, later Ptolemais, a Greek trading settlement existed as early as the time of Isaeus and Demosthenes; the coins of Alexander minted there are very numerous. It was an important garrison town in the period of the Diadochi; its Hellenisation proper, and refounding as Ptolemais, was the work of Ptolemy II Philadelphus. To these coastal towns must be added a number of inland cities. Samaria was colonised by Alexander the Great, or (more probably) Perdiccas.[15] Scythopolis appears under this Greek name already in the third century, and the Paneion just as early (the grotto sanctuary of Pan at the source of the Jordan). Together with Scythopolis, Polybius (V 70, 3–4) mentions, in the time of Antiochus the Great (218 B.C.), the important town, not otherwise known under this name, of Philoteria on the Lake of Gennesaret, which like the similarly named town in Upper Egypt, was probably called after a sister of Ptolemy II Philadelphus.[16] Of the cities east of the Jordan, Hippus and Gadara are distinctly described as *πόλεις Ἑλληνίδες*.[17] Pella and Dium are named after towns in Macedonia, and both were probably founded during the period of the Diadochi. The derivation of the name Gerasa from the *γέροντες* (veterans) of Alexander the Great is admittedly only an etymological absurdity. It is, however, certain that the ancient capital of the Ammonites was hellenised by Ptolemy II Philadelphus under the name of Philadelphia. Finally, 2 Maccabees speaks in general of the *πόλεις Ἑλληνίδες* in the neighbourhood of Judaea (2 Mac. 6:8).

12. See the evidence in § 22, ii and § 23, i. On the cities founded by Alexander the Great and his successors cf. A. H. M. Jones, *Cities of the Eastern Roman Provinces* (1937; [2]1971); *The Greek City* (1940), ch. I.

13. Jos. *B.J.* ii 6, 3 (97). Cf. vol. II, § 23, i.

14. For the evidence see vol. II, § 23, i.

15. For recent archaeological evidence on the question see F. M. Cross, 'Papyri of the Fourth Century B.C. from Dâliyeh', *New Directions in Biblical Archaeology*, ed. D. N. Freedman, J. C. Greenfield (Anchor, 1971), pp. 45–69.

16. On Philotera of Upper Egypt (spelled without the 'i') see Strabo, xvi 4, 5 (769). Philoteria on the Sea of Galilee is now identified with Beth Yeraḥ, near the outflow of the Jordan, see Abel, *Géog. Pal.*, p. 284; RB 1956, pp. 89–90.

17. Jos. *B.J.* ii 6, 3 (97).

Encircled by these Hellenistic towns, little Judaea could naturally not escape the influence of Greek customs and ways. They began to encroach on it more and more. Even the needs of daily life made it necessary to acquire Greek, the universal language; otherwise intercourse and trade with foreign lands would have been impossible. With the language went also the habits, and indeed the entire culture of Greece. At the beginning of the second century B.C., the progress of Hellenism in Palestine must have already been considerable. For only thus is it possible to explain the fact that part of the nation, the aristocratic and educated classes in particular, willingly consented to the Hellenising programme of Antiochus Epiphanes, and indeed promoted it.[18] If this process had been allowed to continue peacefully, presumably Judaism in Palestine would in time have become barely recognisable, and at least as syncretistic as that of Philo. For it is part of the essence of Hellenism to take over an alien religious cult and clothe it in Greek dress. This was the case in Syria as well as in Egypt. The same would most likely have happened in Judaea if things had taken their course. Needless to say, the more completely conservative Judaism and Hellenism had permitted their respective natures to develop, the more acute would the conflict between them have become. Two opposing parties came into being within the Jewish people itself: that of the Hellenists, and that of the 'Devout' (*Ἀσιδαῖοι* חסידים, 1 Mac. 2:42, 7:13) who held fast to the strict ideal of the scribes. But it appears likely from the history prior to the Maccabaean uprising that the former already had the upper hand. All was well on the way towards the acceptance and establishment of Hellenism. For the Devout there seemed no alternative but to become a sect. And then a reversal occurred which culminated in orders from Antiochus Epiphanes by which Jewish worship was to be totally abolished and purely Greek rites introduced. It was this radical attempt that saved Judaism. Now, not only the strict party of the Ḥasidim rose in defence of the ancient faith, but also the mass of the people,

18. On the dissemination of Greek culture in Palestine at the time of the Maccabees, even among loyal Jews, see, among older works, J. Freudenthal, *Alexander Polyhistor* (1875), pp. 127–9. Freudenthal drew special attention to the following facts: (1) the *Letter of Aristeas* takes for granted that the Palestinian scholars who were summoned to Alexandria for the translation of the Pentateuch had full command of the Greek language. (2) The grandson of Jesus ben Sira, who translated his sayings into Greek, was a Palestinian by birth. (3) The Greek translator of the Book of Esther was, according to the sub-title of the book in the Septuagint, also a Palestinian. But in particular, the Jewish Hellenist Eupolemus, fragments of whose works are still extant (see vol. III, § 33, 3, 2) appears to be identical with the Palestinian Eupolemus whom Judas Maccabaeus sent to Rome as head of a Jewish delegation (1 Mac. 8:17; 2 Mac. 4:11). The fullest discussion of Jewish Hellenism in the period up to the Maccabees is now M. Hengel, *op. cit.*

with the result that Hellenism, in its religious aspect at least, was wholly dislodged from Jewish soil. So far as is known, this is the only example of an eastern religion resisting by force the influence of Hellenism.[19]

Antiochus IV Epiphanes, the son of Antiochus the Great, succeeded his brother Seleucus IV after he was murdered by his minister, Heliodorus. He reigned over Syria from 175–164 B.C.[20] He was by nature a genuine despot, eccentric and unpredictable, at one moment lavishly generous, affectedly fraternising with the common people, and then again, ferocious and tyrannical, as his treatment of Judaea demonstrates. The characteristics outlined by Polybius portray the more pleasant aspect of his personality.[21]

'Sometimes he would slip away from the palace, unnoticed by his servants, appearing in the city at one time here, at another time there, sauntering along in the company of one or two others. Very frequently he could be seen in the workshops of the silversmiths and goldsmiths, where he would chat with the moulders and other workmen and seek to impress them with his love of art. Then he would condescend to engage in familiar conversation with any of the common people he happened to meet, and carouse with strangers of the lowest rank whom he stumbled upon by chance. On learning, however, that somewhere young people were holding a drinking-bout, he would march in unannounced with horn and bagpipe, so that most of them, being frightened by this strange sight, would take to flight. Quite often he would exchange his royal robes for a toga, go to the forum and apply as a candidate for an office. He would then seize some people by the hand and embrace others, asking them to give him their vote, sometimes as if for the office of aedile and sometimes as if for that of tribune. If he succeeded in obtaining the office and was seated according to Roman custom in an ivory chair, he would take note of the contracts signed in the forum and give his decisions in a serious and conscientious manner. Reasonable folk, therefore, did not know what to make of him. Some regarded him as a simple and modest man, while others said that he was mad. He acted in a similar fashion when he distributed gifts. To some he gave dice made of bone, to others dates, whilst another group received gold. When he happened to meet someone whom he had never seen before, he would bestow upon him unexpected presents. With regard to the sacrifices which he ordered to be offered in the cities and the honours to be shown to the gods, he outshone all other kings.

19. For a comparative study see S. K. Eddy, *The King is Dead: Studies in the Near Eastern Resistance to Hellenism* 334–31 *B.C.* (1961).

20. On Antiochus see now O. Mørkholm, *Antiochus IV of Syria* (1966); ch. II deals with the evidence for his accession.

21. Polyb. xxvi 1, 1–14.

As evidence we may point to the temple of Zeus at Athens and the statues around the altar at Delos. He used to frequent the public baths when they were quite full of ordinary citizens, and had vessels with precious perfumes brought to him. When somebody once said to him, "You kings are fortunate to have such ointments of exquisite fragrance", he went the next day, without saying anything to the man, to the place where he bathed, and had a large vessel of the most precious ointment, called *stacte*, poured over his head; whereupon everyone rose and rushed forward to receive a share of this aromatic perfume. But because of the slippery state of the floor, many fell over, amid shouts of laughter, the king himself joining in the mirth.' So Polybius; Diodorus and Livy give similar reports. They also emphasise his love of luxury and his munificence. Brilliant spectacles, magnificent buildings, regal presents, these were his chief delights.[22] But in everything he inclined towards senseless extremes, so that Polybius spoke of him as *ἐπιμανής* rather than *ἐπιφανής*.[23]

The policies and motives of Antiochus remain a matter of controversy. But it may be that Tacitus judged him correctly when he said that Antiochus wished to take from the Jews their superstitions and to teach them Greek customs, but that he was prevented by the Parthian war from rendering 'the detestable nation' more civilised.[24] He en-

22. Cf. in general also Polybius xxviii 22; xxix 24; xxx 25, 1–26, 9. Diodorus xxix 32; xxxi 16. Livy xli 20. Ptolemy viii Euergetes, FGrH 234 F3; Heliodorus, FGrH 373 F8.

23. Athenaeus x 439a = Polybius xxvi 1a (10) reads *Πολύβιος δ'ἐν τῇ ἕκτῃ καὶ εἰκοστῇ τῶν Ἱστοριῶν καλεῖ αὐτὸν Ἐπιμανῆ καὶ οὐκ Ἐπιφανῆ διὰ τὰς πράξεις.* The surname *Ἐπιφανής* is in fact an abbreviation of *Θεὸς Ἐπιφανής*, which Antiochus applies to himself on his coins and which means, 'the god who manifests and reveals himself'. In Egyptian texts it is rendered as 'the god who emerges, who comes out' as the morning sun, Horus, on the horizon (Wilcken in Droysen's *Kleine Schriften* (1894) II, p. 440). This epithet, therefore, identifies the king with the young Horus making his appearance as a victorious god; but cf. Mørkholm, *op. cit.*, pp. 132–3. The first monarch with this soubriquet was Ptolemy V of Egypt and after him Antiochus IV of Syria. Subsequently, the name occurred frequently among the Seleucids. It can be authenticated in the cases of Alexander Balas, Antiochus VI, VIII, IX, XII, Seleucus VI and Philip; it also is found among the kings of Commagene, Antiochus I and IV, see H. Dörrie, *Der Königskult des Antiochus von Kommagene im Lichte neuer Inschriften-Funde* (1964), pp. 29 f. Gutschmid, *op. cit.* 108 f., points out that the earliest bearers of this surname 'are merely kings who by ascending their throne brought to an end a prevailing state of distress or were able to pretend to do so'. He explains it therefore as, 'the god bringing visible help'. On the soubriquets of the Hellenistic kings see also Strack, *Die Dynastie der Ptolemäer* (1897), pp. 110–45. Cf. in general L. Cerfaux, J. Tondriau, *Le culte des souverains dans la civilisation gréco-romaine* (1957), pp. 240 ff.

24. Tacit. *Hist.* V 8, 'rex Antiochus demere superstitionem et mores Graecorum dare adnisus, quominus taeterrimam gentem in melius mutaret, Parthorum bello prohibitus est'. Tacitus may be guilty of some confusion here, see Mørkholm, *op. cit.*, pp. 175–6.

deavoured to promote the splendour of Greek culture everywhere. In doing this in Judaea, he met with the co-operation, and even the positive initiative, of a certain party of the people. Needless to say, he supported that party and entrusted the government to it. But when the Jews opposed some of these efforts, this merely roused the despot's ill-humour. The obstinate nation was first of all disciplined through the looting of the rich treasures of the Temple, which must in any case have been very tempting to the king with his need for money. Then, since resistance continued, Jewish worship was abolished and an attempt was made to introduce total Hellenisation by force.

When Antiochus Epiphanes ascended the throne, the hereditary High Priesthood was held by Onias III, a 'zealot for the laws' (2 Mac. 4:2). The leader of the pro-Greek faction was his own brother Jesus, or, as he preferred a Greek name, Jason.[25] The tendency to favour things Greek was already so strong that the pro-Greek faction could venture to seize power and attain their aims by force. Jason promised the king great sums of money (whether in the form of a single gift or as a regular tribute is not very clear) if he would transfer the High Priesthood to him, permit him to erect a gymnasium, establish a corps of ephebes, and finally, consent to 'the inscription of the inhabitants of Jerusalem as Antiochenes', *τοὺς ἐν Ἱεροσολύμοις Ἀντιοχεῖς ἀναγράψαι*, i.e. (probably) transform Jerusalem into a Greek *polis* called Antioch and draw up a list of its citizens.[26] Antiochus readily agreed to everything. Onias was deposed and Jason appointed as High Priest.[27] The process of Hellenisation was now set vigorously in motion. It is important to note, however, that there is as yet no mention of any interference with the Jewish religion. For the rest, 'lawful institutions' were abolished and 'new usages contrary to the Law' introduced (2 Mac. 4:11). A gymnasium was erected below the citadel and the young men of Jerusalem practised the athletic skills of the Greeks. Even the priests left their service at the altar and took part in the games held in the palestra. The contempt for Jewish customs went so far that many removed their circumcision

25. Jos. *Ant.* xii 5, 1 (239).

26. 2 Mac. 4:9. The meaning of this passage is not certain and various interpretations have been advanced, see Abel *ad loc.* The view followed here is that of Tcherikover, *op. cit.*, pp. 161–9; see the valuable discussion in G. Le Rider, *Suse* (1965), pp. 410–11.

27. 2 Mac. 4:7–10. Josephus tells the story differently. Whereas according to 2 Maccabees Onias was deposed, and, when Jason was deprived of the High-Priestly office in his turn, later murdered (2 Mac. 4:33–4), Josephus simply records that after the death of Onias, his brother Jesus was given the dignity of High Priest, *Ant.* xii 5, 1 (237), *ἀποθανόντος καὶ Ὀνίου τοῦ ἀρχιερέως τῷ ἀδελφῷ αὐτοῦ Ἰησοῦ τὴν ἀρχιερωσύνην Ἀντίοχος δίδωσιν*. But Josephus's narrative is obviously summary and vague, and that of 2 Maccabees is confirmed by Dan. 9:26; 11:22, inasmuch as these passages probably refer to Onias III.

artificially.[28] With true Hellenistic broadmindedness, Jason even sent a contribution to the sacrifices in honour of Heracles on the occasion of the quadrennial games at Tyre; this was so offensive to the Jews delivering it that they requested that the money should be used to build ships.[29]

Jason held office in this way for three years (probably from 174 to 171 B.C.). He then fell, as a result of the intrigues of a rival who continued his work in a manner that was even worse. A certain Menelaus (according to 2 Mac. 4:23, cf. 3:4, probably of the tribe of Benjamin and thus not of priestly descent), succeeded, by promising still larger sums of money, in having Jason expelled, and the High Priesthood transferred to himself.[30] He particularly aroused the bitter animosity of the people by profaning the Temple vessels. He also caused the

28. See in general 2 Mac. 4:11–17; 1 Mac. 1:11–15; Jos. *Ant.* xii 5, 1 (241). The purpose of disguising circumcision (1 Mac. 1:15, ἐποίησαν ἑαυτοῖς ἀκροβυστίας) was to avoid mockery in public baths and wrestling-schools. According to many reports, it seems also to have happened in later times. See esp. 1 Cor. 7:18; mAb. 3:11; tShab. 15:9; yPea 16b; yYeb. 9a; bYeb. 72 ab; Gen.R. 46:13; Epiphanius, *De mensuris et ponderibus* 16 (PG xliii, col. 264). Jerome is mistaken in denying that the operation is possible. *adv. Jovinian.* I 21 = Migne PL xxiii, col. 239; *comm. in Isa.* 52, 1 = CCL lxxiiiA, pp. 574–5. See JE IV, p. 397; J. Juster, *Les Juifs dans l'Empire romain* II (1914), p. 284; Hengel, *op. cit.*, p. 137, n. 135. See also commentaries on 1 Cor. 7:18; and Str.-B. IV, pp. 33–4. The practice of *epispasm* appears to have been so common during the Hadrianic persecution that the rabbis introduced the rule of the *peri'ah* (laying bare of the *glans penis*) in the ceremony of circumcision, thus preventing the obliteration of the 'sign of the covenant with Abraham' (see Gen.R. 46:13).

29. 2 Mac. 4:18–20. Jason's conduct calls to mind that of a certain Nicetas son of Jason Ἱεροσολυμίτης, living in Iasus on the coast of Caria between Miletus and Halicarnassus around the middle of the second century B.C., who supported the celebration of Dionysia with a contribution of money (Le Bas and Waddington, *Inscriptions* III n. 294 = Frey CIJ II 749). He may even have been a son of Jason, the brother of Onias III.

30. 2 Mac. 4:23–7. According to Jos. *Ant.* xii 5, 1 (239); cf. xv 3, 1 (41); xix 6, 2 (298); xx 10, 3 (235), the true name of Menelaus was Onias and he was a brother of Jason. But if the first statement is correct, the second is very improbable, for in that case there would have been two brothers called Onias. So 2 Maccabees must be right in regard to Menelaus's descent. See H. H. Rowley, 'Menelaus and the Abomination of Desolation', *Studia Orientalia J. Pedersen . . . dicata* (1953), pp. 303–9. It remains in dispute whether the original text of 2 Mac. 3:4 referred to the tribe of Benjamin, or to the priestly family 'Bilqa', see Abel, *ad. loc.* and Hengel, *op. cit.*, pp. 508–9. According to Jos. *Ant.* xii 5, 1 (239) the 'sons of Tobias' sided with Menelaus. Yet it does not follow from this that he was himself a 'Tobiad', as some writers suggest. On the contrary, the manner in which Josephus refers to 'the sons of Tobias' with Menelaus excludes such an assumption. According to *Ant.* xii 4, 2 (160), Tobias, the father of Joseph the tax-farmer (above), married a sister of the High Priest Onias II. They were therefore related to the old High Priestly family ousted by Menelaus. Also Onias III was kindly disposed towards a certain 'Hyrcanus son of Tobias' who had deposited money in the Temple (2 Mac. 3:11). But now 'the sons of Tobias' belong to the extreme pro-

murder, probably in 170 B.C., of the former High Priest Onias III, who was enticed from his refuge in the sanctuary at Daphne and treacherously killed.[31]

Jason in the meanwhile had not abandoned his claims to the High Priesthood. In 170/69 B.C., when Antiochus was engaged in his campaign against Egypt, he succeeded in seizing Jerusalem in a surprise attack and obliged his rival to seek refuge in the citadel. It was this success of Jason (according to 2 Maccabees) that was the reason for the king's direct intervention in Jerusalem. Antiochus saw it as a revolt against his sovereignty and decided to punish the rebellious city.[32]

Greek faction. They were, as may be seen from 2 Mac. 3:11, prominent financiers. The family fortunes were increased by Joseph son of the Tobias who married a sister of Onias II. He leased the taxes of Coele-Syria, Phoenicia, Judaea and Samaria from the Ptolemies for twenty-two years (see above, p. 140). His son Hyrcanus angered his father through his extravagance, and withdrew east of the Jordan, where he built himself a fortress, *Ant.* xii 4, 2–11 (160–236); on the surviving ruins at Araq el-Emir, where there is also an inscription (of the 6th or 5th century B.C.) with the name of a Tobias, see vol. II, §22 ii, 2; papyrological evidence shows that there was a Tobiad fortress there already in the 3rd century B.C. See Mazar, *op. cit.* [in n. 4 above], and CPJ I, no. 1 (cf. nos. 2, 4, 5). But the surviving buildings, recently excavated, appear to be of the 2nd century, see Hengel, *op. cit.*, pp. 496–503. Supposing Joseph had also a son by the name of Tobias, the family tree would then appear as follows:

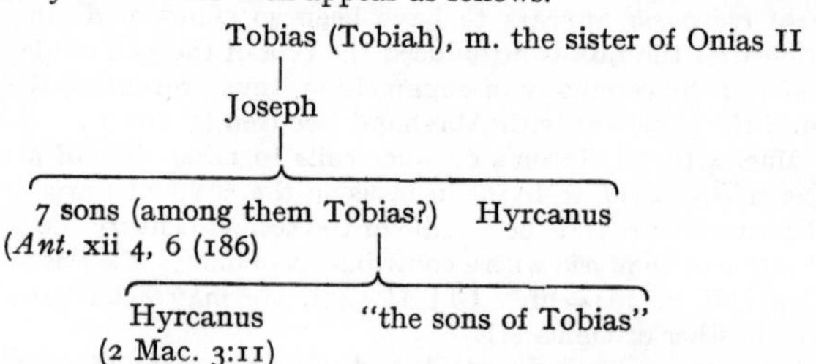

31. See in general 2 Mac. 4:27–50. On the historicity of the death of Onias cf. Niese, *op. cit.*, p. 96 = Hermes 35 (1900), pp. 509 f. (against Willrich and Wellhausen); cf. now M. Delcor, 'Le temple d'Onias en Egypte', RB 75 (1968), pp. 188–203. Dan. 9: 26; 11:22 probably refers to the murder of Onias III. Cf. also J. A. Montgomery, *The Book of Daniel* (1927), *in loc.* It is important for the chronology that the Andronicus who was executed by Antiochus for his part in this murder according to 2 Mac. 4:38 is presumably the Andronicus put to death in 170 B.C. for complicity in the murder of the young Antiochus, nephew and co-regent of Epiphanes (see Diodorus xxx 7, 2–3); so Mørkholm, *op. cit.*, pp. 45, 141, but cf. Hengel, *op. cit.*, p. 510. For an attempted identification of Onias III as the Teacher of Righteousness of the Qumran sect, see H. H. Rowley, *The Zadokite Fragments and the Dead Sea Scrolls* (1952), pp. 67–9; cf. however, G. Vermes, *Discovery in the Judean Desert* (1956), p. 89.

32. 2 Mac. 5:1–11. 2 Maccabees, from which this description of the events leading up to the Maccabaean rising is taken, presents many problems, but still provides the fullest available account of the prehistory of the Maccabaean uprising.

When he returned from Egypt towards the end of 169 B.C.,[33] he marched in person with his army against Jerusalem, executed a blood-bath there, and looted the immense treasures of the Jewish Temple, with the help, it is said, of Menelaus himself. All the valuables, amongst them the three great golden vessels from the inner Temple, the altar of incense, the seven-branched candelabrum and the table of the shew-bread, were taken back by him to Antioch.[34] According to 2 Mac. 5:22, he left a Phrygian, Philip, in charge of the city along with Menelaus.

The worst, however, was still to come. A year later, in 168 B.C., Antiochus undertook yet another expedition against Egypt. But this time the Romans confronted him. The Roman general, Popillius Laenas, presented him with a decree of the senate which required him to abandon once and for all his designs upon Egypt if he wished to avoid being regarded as an enemy of Rome. When Antiochus replied that

---

The first difficulty is chronological. It is discussed in detail in n. 37 below, but it must be noted here that Jason's attempted coup, for which 2 Mac. is the only source, is often placed in 168 B.C., between the two supposed visits of Antiochus to Jerusalem; see Tcherikover, *op. cit.*, pp. 186–7, Hengel, *op. cit.*, pp. 511–12. Note also the separate tradition as to the motivation of the struggles in Jerusalem represented by the summary of events of 169–7 B.C. in Josephus, *B.J.* i 1, 1 (31–3), where the internal strife in Judaea is attributed to a dispute among the Jewish *δυνατοί* about the supreme power (*περὶ δυναστείας*). Some had the support of the king of Syria, the others, that of the king of Egypt. The adherents of Ptolemy (*οἱ Πτολεμαίῳ προσέχοντες*) were overthrown by Antiochus IV at the instigation of the others. All this may suggest, not only that a Greek source independent of that of 2 Mac. was used here, but also that its author saw events as a Gentile observer ignorant of the internal situation in Judaea.

The identity of the sources for the two accounts of these events in Josephus, *B.J.* i 1, 1 (31–2) and *Ant.* xii 5, 1 (239–40), is a matter of speculation. It is noteworthy that they give a prominent role to the Tobiads. *B.J.* i 1, 1 (31–2) reports that the High Priest Onias (?) expelled the Tobiads, who then invited Antiochus to assault the city and plunder the Temple, killing many supporters of Ptolemy. *Ant.* xii 5, 1 (239–40) mentions the revolt of Jason, supported by the majority of the people, against Menelaus, supported by the Tobiads. He and they are represented as going now to Antiochus and asking leave to abandon their ancestral customs *καὶ τὴν Ἑλληνικὴν πολιτείαν ἔχειν*. The brevity and extreme chronological confusion of these accounts (see n. 37 below) make it wholly improper to use them, as does Hengel, *op. cit.*, pp. 514, 527, as the key to events of these years. The 'political' interpretation of the Maccabaean revolt must be no more than a hypothesis.

33. According to 1 Mac. 1:20, it was in the Seleucid year 143. This will have been in the autumn of 169 B.C. (see pp. 128–9 above); the Babylonian era beginning in spring 311 B.C. is being used. Jos. *Ant.* xii 5, 3 (246) also gives the year 143 but confuses the chronology by saying that Antiochus was retreating from Egypt *διὰ τὸ παρὰ Ῥωμαίων δέος*.

34. 1 Mac. 1:20–4; 2 Mac. 5:11–21; Jos. *Ant.* xii 5, 3 (246). On the looting of the Temple, Jos. *c. Ap.* ii 7 (84) also quotes the evidence of Polybius, Strabo, Nicolaus of Damascus, Timagenes, Castor and Apollodorus.

he would like to consider the matter, Popillius gave him the famous brief ultimatum by drawing a circle round him with his staff and ordering him formally ἐνταῦθα βουλεύου (make up your mind in here). Antiochus was obliged willy-nilly to fall in with the demands of the Romans.[35] To the author of Daniel (11:30) there seemed to be a connexion between the failure of his Egyptian plans and the fact that Antiochus undertook at that precise time a war of extermination against the Jewish religion. Since he could no longer achieve anything in Egypt, he would carry out his plans in Judaea with all the more vigour. In 167 B.C. a chief tax collector was despatched by him to Judaea (his name is not given in 1 Mac. 1:29, but in 2 Mac. 5:24 he is called Apollonius); this man began the process of massacre, pillage and destruction in Jerusalem.[36] The precise sequence of events which led to this drastic step, the identity of the person, or persons, from whom the initiative came, and their motives, remain a matter of controversy.[37] The Jewish population which refused to yield was exterminated: the men were murdered and the women and children sold into slavery. All who were

[*Text continues on page 154*

35. Polyb. xxix 27, 1–8; Diodorus xxxi 2; Livy xlv 12, 1–8; Appian *Syr.* 66/350–2; Justin xxxiv 3, 1–3. Cf. Dan. 11:29 f. See Broughton, MRR I, p. 430.

36. According to 1 Mac. 1:29 compared with 1:20 and 1:54, this Apollonius was sent on his mission in the year 145 of the Seleucid era = spring 167–spring 166 B.C. On the term *μυσάρχης* see now A. Mittwoch, 'Tribute and Land-tax in Seleucid Judaea', Bibl. 36 (1955), pp. 352–61.

37. Only the essentials of the acutely controversial question of the chronology of these events can be given here, and no attempt is made to provide a complete bibliographical account. The reconstruction offered takes the view that Antiochus visited Jerusalem only once in the 160s, viz. in the autumn of 169 B.C., and that it was on this occasion that the despoliation of the Temple took place; hence the looting described in 1 Mac. 1:20–3 is identical with that in 2 Mac. 5:11–21, and referred to in Jos. *B.J.* i 1, 1 (32); the account in *Ant.* xii 5, 2–4 (242–50) is inextricably confused (see below).

There are three reasons for supposing that Antiochus visited Jerusalem twice. The first, it is claimed (Tcherikover, *op. cit.*, p. 186), is that 'the Book of Daniel speaks explicitly of two visits'. But this does not appear to be so. Dan. 11:28–31 runs as follows: 'He (Antiochus) will return (from Egypt, 169 B.C.) greatly enriched to his own country, his heart set against the holy covenant; he will take action (ועשה; in Greek just *καὶ ποιήσει*), and next go home. In due time he will make his way southwards again, but this time the outcome will not be as before. The ships of Kittim (Rome, 168 B.C.) will oppose him and he will be worsted. He will retire and take furious action against the holy covenant and, as before, will favour those who forsake it. Forces of his will come and profane the sanctuary citadel; they will abolish the perpetual sacrifice (167 B.C.), and install the disastrous abomination there.' Thus Daniel clearly refers to two phases of action, one after the campaign of 169 B.C., and one subsequent to that of 168; but he does not explicitly and concretely refer to the presence of Antiochus in Jerusalem on either occasion.

Secondly, 1 Mac. and 2 Mac. each mention one visit by the king after an Egyptian campaign, but have been thought to speak of different visits, in 169 and 168 B.C. 1 Mac. 1:20 dates the journey in the Seleucid year 143 (spring 169–spring 168 B.C.). Its chronology is consistent. 1 Mac. 1:29 has the arrival of the *μυσάρχης* '*μετὰ δύο ἔτη*'. Then there follows the Abomination of Desolation on 25 Kislev of the Seleucid year 145, spring 167–spring 166 (1 Mac. 1:54), and the restoration of the cult on 25 Kislev of 148, i.e. December 164 B.C. (1 Mac. 4:52).

2 Mac. gives no datings by Seleucid years for these events. But 4:38 mentions the execution of Andronicus, which will date to 170 B.C. (see above), followed by a couple of paragraphs on events in Jerusalem. Then 5:1 reads *περὶ δὲ τὸν καιρὸν τοῦτον τὴν δευτέραν ἄφοδον ὁ 'Αντίοχος εἰς Αἴγυπτον ἐστείλατο.*. Since it is known that Antiochus invaded Egypt in both 169 and 168 B.C., it is natural to take this as a reference to that of 168, even though 2 Mac. contains no mention of the 'first' campaign. But the account of the despoliation of the Temple, 5:11–21, is markedly similar to that of 1 Mac. 1:20–3; and, as has been seen (pp. 128–9) it is possible to take *τὴν δευτέραν ἄφοδον* as a reference to the second phase (169 B.C.) of the campaign of 170/69 B.C.

The only source that speaks explicitly of two visits by Antiochus to Jerusalem is Jos. *Ant.* xii 5, 2–4 (242–50). But his narrative is filled with confusions, apparently resulting from an over-hasty conflation of earlier documents. (1) Like 1 Mac., he places the arrival of Antiochus in Jerusalem, on his return from Egypt, in the Seleucid year 143 (169 B.C.), but attributes this return, 5, 3 (246) to the fear of the Romans (168 B.C.). (2) He then borrows from 1 Mac. the interval *μετὰ δύο ἔτη* and the date 25 Kislev of the Seleucid year 145, 5, 4 (248), but applies these to a second visit of Antiochus, which he makes the occasion of the looting of the Temple treasures. Josephus's evidence has therefore no independent value.

In consequence, it must be concluded that Antiochus visited Jerusalem in 169 B.C., and that the attempted coup by Jason took place previously in that year. There is no reason to doubt that the 'Mysarch', Apollonius (the name is given in 2 Mac. 5:24), arrived in 167 B.C.

If this reconstruction is correct, there is a further ground (cf. Hengel, *op. cit.*, pp. 508 f.) for rejecting the hypothesis of Tcherikover, *op. cit.*, pp. 188–9, that Jason's intervention (in 168 B.C.) was followed by a temporary military victory of the orthodox party, then suppressed by Antiochus. This is the starting-point of his theory (pp. 188–98) that continuous armed resistance by the conservatives is the explanation of the decrees of 167 B.C. abolishing both the Temple cult and the observation of the Torah.

Similarly, as pointed out in n. 32 above, Hengel's own interpretation relies essentially on the references to the Tobiads in the brief and confused accounts of Josephus, and is therefore unacceptable.

In fact, there is no reliable account of the actual series of events leading to the persecution proper, and the student is reduced to hypotheses based on his knowledge of the general situation. At this level there is of course abundant evidence that the imposition of Gentile cults was welcomed or accepted by a substantial section of the Jewish population, cf. Hengel, *op. cit.*, pp. 532 f. The possibility of an actual initiative on their part is suggested by the parallel case of the Samaritan request (made, however, after the inception of the persecution) to have their temple dedicated to Zeus Hellenios, Jos. *Ant.* xii 5, 5 (257–64); cf. 2 Mac. 6:2, which has Zeus Xenios. For the significance of this evidence, see Bickerman, *op. cit.*, pp. 90 f. and his article, 'Un document relatif à la persécution d'Antiochus IV Epiphane', RHR 115 (1937), pp. 188–223. See also Y. Baer, 'The Persecution of Monotheistic Religion by Antiochus Epiphanes', Zion 33 (1968), pp. 101–24 (in Hebrew with an English summary).

able to do so, left the city.[38] To ensure that these measures would be permanently implemented, the walls of the city were torn down. The old Davidic city, however, was re-fortified and converted into a powerful stronghold (the 'Akra', on which see below) occupied from then on by a pagan garrison. 'He will use the people of an alien god to defend the fortress', as the author of Daniel 11:39 wrote; or in the words of 1 Mac. 1:34, *ἔθηκαν ἐκεῖ ἔθνος ἁμαρτωλόν, ἄνδρας παρονόμους, καὶ ἐνίσχυσαν ἐν αὐτῇ* (cf. 1 Mac. 3:45, *υἱοὶ ἀλλογενῶν ἐν τῇ Ἄκρᾳ*). This was, as Tcherikover states, *op. cit.*, p. 189, a military *cleruchy* or *κατοικία*. The word is in fact used of them in 1 Mac. 1:38, *καὶ ἐγένετο κατοικία ἀλλοτρίων*. This force remained in control of the citadel during all the subsequent successes of the Maccabees and maintained the supremacy of the Syrian kings through every vicissitude. It was not until twenty-six years later that Simon, in 142/1 B.C., was able to gain possession of the citadel and thereby seal the independence of the Jews.[39]

38. 1 Mac. 1:29–30; 2 Mac. 23–26; Jos. *Ant.* xii 4, 4 (251). It seems from 1 Mac. 1:38 compared with 1 Mac. 1:30–2 and 2 Mac. 5:24, that one aim was the annihilation of the Jewish population and the settlement of the city by Greek or Hellenized inhabitants. It was therefore exactly the same process as that adopted by the Jews themselves at a later period in Joppa and Gazara (1 Mac. 13:11 and 43–8). On the consequences of these measures, see 1 Mac. 2:18; 3:35, 45.

39. An *ἀκρόπολις* of Jerusalem is often mentioned in preceding years (2 Mac. 4:12, 27; 5:5). But this cannot be identical with the fortress built by Antiochus Epiphanes. The 'Acropolis' of 2 Maccabees is more likely to be the castle close to the north side of the Temple known already from Neh. 2:8; 7:2. It is also probably that referred to in the *Letter of Aristeas*, 100–4, and in the history of Antiochus the Great, Jos. *Ant.* xii 3, 3 (133, 138). It was later rebuilt by the Hasmonaeans, and then again by Herod, who called it Antonia, *Ant.* xv 11, 4 (403), xviii 4, 3 (91). So this citadel near the Temple is distinct from the fortress built by Antiochus (1 Mac. 1:33–6; Jos. *Ant.* xii 5, 4 (252)) when the walls of the city were demolished (1 Mac. 1:31). On the capture of the Acra by Simon, see 1 Mac. 13:49–52. It is often mentioned in 1 Mac. (2:31; 3:45; 4:2, 41; 6:18–21, 26, 32; 7:32; 9:52–3; 10:32; 11:20–1, 41; 12:36; 13:21). The site of this Acra is one of the most controversial questions in the topography of Jerusalem. It is probable that it lay on the southern spur of the eastern hill; south, that is to say, of the Temple mount. There can be little doubt that it was built on the site of the ancient Davidic city (1 Mac. 1:33; 2:31; 7:32; 14:36). But the city of David, according to Neh. 3:15, obviously stood in the vicinity of Shiloh, south of the Temple, and thus not on the great western hill on which the main part of the city lies even today, but on a separate elevation of the eastern chain of hills, i.e., of the Temple mount. For the archaeological evidence confirming that the Jerusalem of the Old Testament was situated on the southern spur of the eastern ridge see K. M. Kenyon, *Jerusalem* (1967), ch. 2–6. The Zion on which David's city lay (2 Sam. 5:7; 1 Kg. 8:1) is not, as later Christian tradition claims, the western hill, but the same chain on which the Temple stood; the eastern hill therefore. This is confirmed by the literary usage of 1 Maccabees in which 'Zion' and 'Temple mount' are identical concepts (see 1 Mac. 4:37–60; 5:54; 6:48–62; 7:33). This view remains the most probable, though definitive archaeological evidence is still lacking. For a full

Both 1 Maccabees (1:41–51) and 2 Maccabees (6:1–2) mark as a new phase the arrival of instructions from Antiochus for the abolition of the Temple cult and of the observance of the Law, and the substitution of pagan cults. The observance of all Jewish ordinances, in particular those relating to the Sabbath and circumcision, was prohibited on pain of death. In every town in Judaea sacrifice was to be offered to the heathen gods. Overseers were sent everywhere to see that the royal command was carried out. Where the people did not comply willingly, they were obliged to do so by force. Once a month a check was made, and whoever was found with a scroll of the Torah or had had a child circumcised, was put to death. On 15 Kislev of the Seleucid year 145 = December 167 B.C., a heathen altar was built in Jerusalem on the great altar of burnt-offering, and on 25 Kislev the first heathen sacrifice was offered on it (1 Mac. 1:54, 59); this is 'the abomination of desolation', the שקוץ משמם or שקוץ שמם LXX: *βδέλυγμα τῆς ἐρημώσεως* to which the Book of Daniel refers (Dan. 11:31, 12:11). The sacrifice, according to 2 Maccabees, was offered to Olympian Zeus, to whom the Temple in Jerusalem had been dedicated.[40] On the feast of Dionysus, the Jews were compelled to walk in bacchanalian procession with their heads crowned with ivy.[41]

2 Maccabees has wonderful stories of the glad courage with which some of the people defended their ancient faith at that time. It describes at length how a ninety-year-old man called Eleazar was put to death, and how seven brothers suffered martyrdom one after another before the eyes of their mother, she too finally dying for her

---

discussion of the archaeological and literary evidence, see J. Simons, *Jerusalem in the Old Testament: Researches and Theories* (1952), pp. 144–57. He concludes that the term designated the entire fortified city on the south-east hill, rather than a fortress within it. L.-H. Vincent and M.-A. Stève, *Jerusalem de l'Ancien Testament* (1954), pp. 175–92, argue that the Akra was situated on a spur of the south-west hill, opposite the Temple. This view is adequately disproved by W. A. Shotwell, 'The Problem of the Syrian Akra', BASOR 176 (Dec. 1964), pp. 10–19; but his own contention that the identification of a Maccabaean tower (i.e. a tower of the Maccabaean period) on the eastern side of the south-east hill shows that this area must have lain outside the Akra, is a logical confusion. Kenyon, *op. cit.*, p. 113, suggests that the Akra may have stood on the upper western ridge.

40. E. R. Bevan, 'A Note on Antiochus Epiphanes', JHS 20 (1900), pp. 26–30, suggested that the cult was actually intended for Antiochus himself, on the grounds that coins showed portraits of Antiochus impersonating Zeus Olympios. But this view is in fact mistaken. See O. Mørkholm, *op. cit.*, pp. 130–1.

41. See in general 1 Mac. 1:41–64; 2 Mac. 6:1–11. Jos. *Ant.* xii 5, 4 (253); Dan. 7: 25; 8:11 f.; 11:31 ff.; 12:11. According to 2 Mac. 6:17, the Jews were also forced to participate in the sacrificial meal at the monthly celebration of the royal birthday. On the monthly birthday festivities, see ZNW (1901), pp. 48–52.

faith.[42] The details must remain uncertain. But the fact is that, despite all the violence, a wide circle of the people stayed loyal to the faith and customs of their forefathers. To strengthen their resolve, an unknown writer published at that time under the pseudonym of Daniel an exhortation in which he set before his co-religionists, stories of earlier days to admonish and encourage them, and foretold with bold confidence the impending downfall of heathen rule and the transfer of world-government to the people of God (see vol. III, § 32, 5, 1). The effect of this work can be easily imagined.

Passive resistance was soon accompanied by open insurrection—a most foolhardy undertaking, seen from the practical point of view. For how could the small Jewish nation permanently defy the power of the king? But religious enthusiasm does not inquire whether success is possible. Incitement to rebellion was instigated by a priest of the order of Joarib called Mattathias, together with his five sons—John, Simon, Eleazar, Judas and Jonathan—in the town of Modein.[43] When the king's officer arrived there to demand the offering of heathen sacrifice, Mattathias refused to obey the command. 'Though all the nations in the king's realm lapse from the religion of their fathers, yet will I, with my sons and brothers, walk in the covenant of our fathers.

42. 2 Mac. 6:18–7:42. The story also forms the theme of 4 Maccabees (cf. vol. III, §33, 5, 4), and is introduced into subsequent Jewish literature. Cf. G. D. Cohen, 'The Story of Hannah and her seven Sons in Hebrew Literature', *M. M. Kaplan Jubilee Volume*, Hebrew Section (1953), pp. 109–22.

43. 1 Mac. 2:1, 15. Jos. *Ant.* xii 6, 1 (265). The family did not move to Modein just then, as might appear from 2:1, but had lived there already for some considerable time, 13:25. The name of the place is given in 1 Maccabees, according to the great majority of the Mss., as *Μωδεείν* or *Μωδεῖν*. Other forms also occur, e.g., *Μωδεεῖμ* in Jos. *Ant.* xii 6, 1 (265) (Niese gives *ἐν Μωδαΐ*); 6, 2 (268) *τὴν Μωδαΐν*; 6, 4 (285), *ἐν Μωδαΐ*; 11, 2 (432) *τὴν Μωδεεῖν*; xiii, 6, 5 (210) *ἐν Μωδεεῖ*; *B.J.* i, 1, 3 (36) *ἀπὸ κώμης Μωδεεὶν ὄνομα*. In Eusebius's *Onomasticon* we find *Μηδεείμ*: Jerome has Modeim. The plural is sometimes found in the Hebrew, sometimes in the Aramaic, and sometimes elided. In mPes. 9:2 and mḤag. 3:15 the reading varies between מודיעים and מודיעית in such a way that the latter form predominates in both. A surprising confirmation of it is to be found in the nomenclature of the mosaic map of Madaba: *Μωδεειμ ἡ νῦν Μωδιθα*, see M. Avi-Yonah, *The Madaba Mosaic Map* (1954), p. 58; cf. Abel, *Géog. Pal.* II, p. 391. A man from Modein is called in mAb. 3:11 המודעי. For the establishment of the exact location it is important to take into account: (a) the fact that the splendid monument built there by Simon for his parents and brothers was visible from the sea, 1 Mac. 13:27–30, *εἰς τὸ θεωρεῖσθαι ὑπὸ παντῶν τῶν πλεόντων τὴν θάλασσαν*; and (b) its mention by Eusebius, who still knew the place, *Onomast.* ed. Klostermann, p. 132, *Μηδεείμ κώμη πλησίον Διοσπόλεως, ὅθεν ἦσαν οἱ Μακκαβαῖοι, ὧν καὶ τὰ μνήματα εἰς ἔτι νῦν δείκνυται.* Jerome, *Onomast.* ad. loc. gives the same: 'Modeim vicus juxta Diospolim unde fuerunt Maccabaei, quorum hodieque ibidem sepulchra monstrantur'. It lay, therefore, in the vicinity of Lydda (Diospolis), on higher ground, i.e., in the direction of the hills. It can now be taken as settled that the modern Arab village of el-Medieh east of Lydda, at the entrance to the hills, marks the position of ancient Modein. Cf. Abel, *Géog. Pal.* II, p. 391.

May God preserve us from abandoning the law and the commandments!' Seeing a Jew about to offer sacrifice, he struck him down at the altar. He also killed the king's officer—and destroyed the altar.[44]

He then fled with his sons into the mountains. Numerous like-minded people had also withdrawn to hiding-places in the desert. There they were hunted out by a detachment of the Syrian garrison of Jerusalem, attacked on the Sabbath, and because they offered no resistance, were massacred together with their wives and children.[45] A martyrdom of this order seemed to the energetic Mattathias to be a poor way of serving God's cause. He and his people resolved to take action, and not to shirk fighting even on the Sabbath if it were necessary. They were joined now by the 'Devout' (Ἀσιδαῖοι = חסידים), i.e. those faithful to the Torah who had hitherto shown their steadfastness only in patient endurance.[46] Mattathias now gathered together all those who

44. 1 Mac. 2:15–26. Jos. *Ant.* xii 6, 2 (268–71). On Josephus's account of Mattathias see A. Büchler, REJ 34 (1897), pp. 69–76; Niese, *op. cit.*, p. 100. Mattathias is not mentioned in 2 Maccabees. Niese was therefore inclined to doubt his existence, *op. cit.*, pp. 44–7; in general, he gave greater weight to 2 Maccabees compared with 1 Maccabees (see *op. cit.*, p. 94). He saw in 1 Maccabees, in so far as it coincides with 2 Maccabees (chapters 1–7), merely a tendentious adaptation, formulated in the interest of the dynasty, of the same source as that which forms the basis of 2 Maccabees, namely that of Jason of Cyrene (*op. cit.*, p. 94). It does not seem possible to explain the pronounced differences between 1 and 2 Maccabees in this way. They are comprehensible only on the premise that they are largely independent of one another. For the fullest modern discussion of their sources see Momigliano, *Prime Linee* . . . (1931), with Schunck, *op. cit.* (1954) and Bunge, *op. cit.* (1971).

45. 1 Mac., 2:27–38; Jos. *Ant.* xii 6, 2 (272–5).

46. That the Asidaeans were not identical with the circle of Mattathias was stressed in particular by J. Wellhausen in *Pharisäer und Sadducäer*, pp. 78–86. They certainly made common cause with the Maccabees, but later (1 Mac. 7:13) parted company with them. Cf. R. Meyer, *Tradition und Neuschöpfung im antiken Judentum*, SAW, Phil.-hist. Kl. 110/2 (1965), pp. 16–17. The word חסידים occurs frequently in the OT (e.g. Ps. 30:5; 31:24; 37:28), and means simply 'the devout'; but it signifies in particular those who took their piety, that is their faithful observance of the Torah, seriously. For a recent treatment of the Hasidim see J. Morgenstern, 'The HᴬSÎDÎM—Who were They?', HUCA 38 (1967), pp. 59–73.

For a comprehensive, though not always historically perspicacious, survey of the later stages of ancient Hasidism, see A. Büchler, *Types of Jewish-Palestinian Piety from 70 B.C.E. to 70 C.E. The Ancient Pious Men* (1922). According to this author, the rabbinic concept of the *ḥasid* includes both strict legal observance and a deeply charitable attitude towards people. Büchler rejects all basic distinction between the Ḥasidim and the Pharisees/rabbis. A more accurate picture is offered by S. Safrai, namely that in some respects (e.g. Sabbath observances) Hasidic halakhah was more rigid than the common Pharisaic kind but, at the same time, it was less concerned with questions of ritual cleanness and uncleanness; see 'The Teaching of Pietists in Mishnaic Literature', JJS 16 (1965), pp. 15–33. See also G. B. Sarfatti, 'Pious Men, Men of Deeds and the Early Prophets' Tarbiz 26 (1956–57), pp. 126–53 (in Hebrew), and G. Vermes, 'Ḥanina ben Dosa', JJS 23 (1972), pp. 37–9.

were fit and willing to fight for their faith and travelled with them up and down the country destroying altars, killing lapsed Jews, circumcising the children, and encouraging everyone to offer open resistance to their heathen persecutors.[47]

He was not able to pursue this work for long. Soon after the beginning of the uprising, in the Seleucid year 146, i.e. spring 166–spring 165 B.C. (1 Mac. 2:70), Mattathias died, after exhorting his sons to continue, and recommending Simon as their adviser and Judas as their battle commander. Amid deep mourning, he was buried at Modein.[48]

Judas thus took over the leadership of the movement. His surname *ὁ Μακκαβαῖος*, from which the whole party has received the name of Maccabees, is often interpreted as meaning a warrior quick to strike (מקבה=hammer).[49] 'In his deeds he was like a lion, and like a lion's whelp roaring after prey.' In 1 Maccabees 3:4 he is depicted as a chivalrous hero, bold and eager, not weighing the possibilities of success but staking his all for the sake of the great cause.[50] With his forces so outnumbered, his successes could, of course, only be temporary ones. The cause he represented must certainly have been lost if it had depended only on the sword.

At first all went very well with the uprising. With blow after blow Judas won decisive victories and even succeeded in restoring Jewish worship on Mount Zion. He defeated a Syrian force under the command of Apollonius (probably identical with the person mentioned earlier on

47. 1 Mac. 2:39–48; Jos. *Ant.* xii 6, 2 (276–8).

48. 1 Mac. 2:49–70; Jos. *Ant.* xii 6, 3–4 (279–86).

49. The etymology of the name is still disputed. *Μακκαβαῖος* (on the vocalisation see G. Dalman, *Grammatik*, p. 178, n. 3) is usually derived from מקבה. S. I. Curtiss objected to this interpretation, *The Name Machabee* (1876), on the grounds that in the O.T. (e.g. 1 Kg. 6:7; Isa. 44:12; Jer. 10:4) it does not refer to the large club or battle mace, but to the ordinary hammer. It has also been remarked that the nickname 'Maccabee' is unconnected with military feats but appears to have distinguished Judas from his childhood from other persons bearing the same common name. Hence the interpretation suggested by Dalman (*Grammatik*, p. 178, n.3) that 'Maccabee' like מקבן (mBekh. 7:1; bBekh. 43b) indicates a peculiarity of the body, viz., a hammer-shaped head, or, if one is to rely on the Syriac with F. Perles (JQR 17 (1926/7), pp. 403–6), a man with unusual nostrils. Another derivation advanced by A. A. Bevan (JThSt 30 (1929), pp. 191–2) and adopted by Abel (*op. cit.*, p. III) is from נקב (to name, designate). *Makkabaï* would then be a contraction from Makkabiah, i.e. 'designation by the Lord.' The latest theory put forward by R. Marcus, viz. that the basis of Maccabee is the Hebrew מקוה '(source of) hope' ('The Name *Makkabaios*', *Joshua Starr Memorial Vol.* (1953), pp. 59–66), is unconvincing. Apropos of the interpretation 'hammer-shaped', it should be noted that a nickname originally indicating a bodily peculiarity could easily have acquired, in changed circumstances, the meaning 'hammer (of God)'.

50. Cf. in general the description in 1 Mac. 3:3–9.

p. 152) in a battle in which Apollonius himself was slain, and from then on used Apollonius's sword in all his fighting.[51] A second Syrian army, led by Seron, the 'commander-in-chief of the Syrian forces', was also repulsed by Judas at Beth-horon, north-west of Jerusalem.[52]

The king realized that he would have to adopt stringent measures to put down the revolt in Judaea. While he himself undertook in 165 B.C. (1 Mac. 3:37, Seleucid year 147) a campaign against the Parthians,[53] he left Lysias in Syria as imperial vice-regent and tutor to the minor Antiochus V, and charged him with the task of sending a large army to Judaea for the purpose of exterminating the rebellious Jews.[54] Lysias despatched three generals, Ptolemy, Nicanor and Gorgias, with a large contingent of troops, to Judaea. The defeat of the Jews seemed so certain that foreign merchants were already in the Syrian camp ready to buy the expected Jewish slaves.[55]

In the meantime, Judas and his followers were not inactive either. Since Jerusalem was occupied by the Gentiles, he assembled his fighting forces in Mizpah.[56] It was now no longer a small band of enthusiastic warriors, but a regular, organised Jewish army; he appointed as leaders of the people 'commanders of every Thousand, Hundred, Fifty and Ten'. They prepared for the unequal struggle with prayer and fasting. In the region of Emmaus, west of Jerusalem, the two armies confronted one another.[57]

While the main body of the Syrian army remained encamped near Emmaus, Gorgias, with a strong detachment of troops, went in search

51. 1 Mac. 3:10–12; Jos. *Ant.* xii 7, 1 (287).

52. 1 Mac. 3:13–26. Jos. *Ant.* xii 7, 1 (289), *Βαιθωρων* is the OT בית חורון, according to Eusebius, *Onomast.* ed. Klostermann, p. 46, twelve miles north-west of Jerusalem, and consequently identical with modern Beit-ur. Cf. Abel. *Géog. Pal.* II, pp. 274–5.

53. 1 Mac. 3:31; Tac. *Hist.* V 8.

54. 1 Mac. 3:27–37; Jos. *Ant.* xii 7, 2 (293–7). 2 Mac. 10:9–11, 12, places the appointment of Lysias and the subsequent campaigns in the reign of Antiochus V Eupator. See below. The problems presented by the evidence are not appreciated in the sketch by O. Plöger, 'Die Feldzüge der Seleukiden gegen den Makkabäer Judas', ZDPV 74 (1958), pp. 158–88.

55. 1 Mac. 3:38–41; Jos. *Ant.* xii 7, 3 (298–9). 2 Mac. 8:8–11. According to 2 Maccabees, Ptolemy was the governor of Coele-Syria and Phoenicia who delegated the military operations to Nicanor and Gorgias. During the following years, Jewish slaves were in fact sold as far away as Greece; see vol. III, § 31, 1.

56. The *Μασσηφά* of 1 Mac. 3:46 is ancient Mizpah. Mizpah was the religious and political centre of Israel during the period of the Judges (Jg. 20–1; 1 Sam. 7:5 ff.; 10:17 ff.); see R. de Vaux, *Ancient Israel* (1961), pp. 304–5. According to 1 Mac. 3:46, it was situated *κατέναντι Ἰερουσαλήμ*, not far, therefore, from Jerusalem. Its location is not certain, but may well be Tell en Nasbeh, 13 km. north of Jerusalem, see Abel, *Géog. Pal.* II, pp. 388–90.

57. 1 Mac. 3:42–60. Jos. *Ant.* xii 7, 3 (298). *Ἐμμαούμ*, 1 Mac. 3:40, 57, in Roman times capital of a toparchy, exists today under the name of 'Amwas (the Emmaus of the NT is probably another place nearer to Jerusalem). See vol. II, § 23, ii.

of the Jewish army. When Judas heard of this, he evaded him and attacked the main force at Emmaus. His address to the Jews stimulated them to such bravery that the Syrian army was completely routed. When the detachment under Gorgias returned, the camp was already in flames and the Jews ready to resume battle with them, but they fled instead to Philistia. The Jews had won a total victory (166/5 B.C.).[58]

In the following year (165/4 B.C.), according to the account in 1 Maccabees 4:28–35, condensed in *Ant.* xii 7, 5 (313–15), Lysias himself led a fresh attack against Judaea with a still more powerful army. But there is some doubt as to whether this campaign actually occurred.[59] According to the narrative, he did not launch the assault directly from the north, but approached from Idumaea in the south (1 Mac. 4:29). He must therefore have made a detour round Judaea either to the east round the Dead Sea, or as seems more likely, to the west, by marching along the Philistine coast and round the hills. The

58. 1 Mac. 4:1–25; 2 Mac. 8:12–36; Jos. *Ant.* xii 7, 4 (305–12). The evidence for the chronology of these events is as follows. 1 Mac. 3:37 dates the departure of Antiochus on his Parthian campaign to 147 of the Seleucid era. The author will here be using the Greek Seleucid era, from autumn 312 B.C., see Mørkholm, *op. cit.*, p. 161, so 166/5 B.C. Antiochus will presumably have left in fact in the spring of 165 B.C., *ibid.*, p. 166. Then 1 Mac. 4:28 reads, after the account of the victory at Emmaus, *καὶ ἐν τῷ ἐρχομένῳ* (or *ἐχομένῳ*) *ἐνιαυτῷ* introducing Lysias's campaign. This will be 165/4 B.C., as is shown by the dating of the consequent restoration of the Temple cult to 25 Kislev of the Seleucid year 148, 1 Mac. 4:52, i.e. December 164 B.C., using the era starting in the spring of 311 B.C. But the historicity of Lysias's campaign is disputed (see below). 1 Mac. mentions only Gorgias as enemy commander, and 2 Mac. only Nicanor, both possibly being correct in so far as Gorgias commanded the raiding force and Nicanor the main army. On other differences between 1 and 2 Mac. regarding this expedition, see Niese, *op. cit.*, pp. 53–5.

59. The arguments against the historicity of this campaign are given by Kolbe, *op. cit.*, pp. 79–81, and extended by Mørkholm, *op. cit.*, pp. 152–4. (1) The brief account of the campaign in 1 Mac. 4:28–35 could well be a doublet of the longer account in 1 Mac. 6:20–49 of the campaign by Lysias and Antiochus Eupator in 163 B.C., which however ended with the capitulation of Beth-Zur; similarly 2 Mac. 11:5–12 (placed under Antiochus Eupator and after the rededication of the Temple, see below) could be a doublet of the second campaign, 2 Mac. 13:1–22. Josephus also gives two campaigns, *Ant.* xii 2, 5 (313–15) and 9, 4–7 (375–83). (2) The battle at Beth-Zur is more intelligible after the fortification of the place by Judas, 1 Mac. 4:61, and raids into Idumaea by him, 1 Mac. 5:3–8, 65–8. But 1 Mac. 4 says only that Judas advanced to meet Lysias at Beth-Zur. (3) It is unlikely that the campaign will have been started in the autumn of 165 B.C. (but this may equally account for the fact that a relatively slight defeat brought it to an end). If it began in the spring of 164 B.C. it is difficult to relate it chronologically to the amnesty-letter issued by Antiochus Epiphanes on 15 Xanthicus in the year 148 of the Seleucid era = about March 164 B.C., 2 Mac. 11:22–33 (see below).

None of the objections to the historicity of the first campaign seems conclusive.

armies met near Beth-Zur, south of Jerusalem, on the road to Hebron.[60] Although the Syrian army was far superior, Judas once again gained a total victory and Lysias was obliged to return to Antioch to collect reinforcements.[61]

This victory may have occurred as early as the autumn of 165 B.C.

60. *Βαιθσούρα* (ἡ and τά) 1 Mac. 4: 29, 61; 6:7, 26, 31, 49, 50; 9:52; 10:14; 11:65; 14:7, 33, is also frequently mentioned in the OT as בית צור. Euseb. *Onomast.* ed. Klostermann, p. 52, places it twenty Roman miles south of Jerusalem in the direction of Hebron (*καὶ ἔστι νῦν κώμη Βηθσωρὼ ἀπιόντων ἀπὸ Αἰλίας εἰς Χεβρὼν ἐν κʹ σημείῳ*); approximately confirmed by the position of the modern Beit-Sur. The distance of four plus two plus fourteen Roman miles is also given by the pilgrim of Bordeaux, *Itinera Hierosol.* ed. Geyer (1898), p. 25 = CCL clxxv, p. 20. He names the place *Bethasora*; on the mosaic map of Madaba it is [*ΒΕΘ*]*ΩΡΑ*, see M. Avi-Yonah, *The Madaba Mosaic Map* (1954), p. 61. For excavations there, with extensive finds of the Maccabaean period, see O. R. Sellers, *The Citadel of Beth-Zur* (1933); cf. Abel, *Géog. Pal.* II, p. 283, and now O. R. Sellers *et al.*, *The 1957 Excavation at Beth-Zur*, AASOR XXXVIII (1968).

61. 1 Mac. 4:26–35; 2 Mac. 11:1–15; Jos. *Ant.* xii 7, 5 (313–15). The identity of 2 Mac. 11:1–15 with 1 Mac. 4:26–35 cannot really be in doubt. Cf. Abel, *in loc.* None the less, the reports diverge noticeably in two main points: (a) 1 Maccabees knows nothing of the peace treaty which followed this campaign according to 2 Maccabees, which provides as documentary evidence four letters (from Lysias, the king and the Roman ambassadors), 2 Mac. 11:16–38. Their authenticity, and with it the historicity of this account, is defended by Niese (*op. cit.*, pp. 63 ff. = Hermes 35 (1908), pp. 476 ff., 489). (b) 2 Maccabees places this expedition of Lysias considerably later, i.e., after the re-dedication of the Temple, and also presents the events which followed in another order. The divagations of the two narratives are illustrated by Niese, *op. cit.*, 56 = Hermes 35 (1900), p. 469, in the following paradigm:

1 Mac. 4 ff.	2 Mac. 8 ff.
Victory over Gorgias and Nicanor.	Victory over Gorgias and Nicanor.
1. Campaign of Lysias.	Occupation of Jerusalem.
Occupation of Jerusalem.	Death of Epiphanes (9).
Purification of the Temple.	Purification of the Temple (10).
Border warfare (5).	Accession of Eupator.
Death of Epiphanes.	Border warfare.
Accession of Eupator (6).	1. Campaign of Lysias and peace (11).
2. Campaign of Lysias with Eupator.	New border warfare (12).
Peace with the Jews.	2. Campaign of Lysias with Eupator.
	Peace with the Jews.

The divergence in the sequence of events can be traced, according to Niese, *op. cit.*, p. 60, in the main to (a) the smaller military expeditions against neighbouring tribes, which in 2 Maccabees are spread over various points of time but in 1 Maccabees, chapter 5, are collected together; (b) the death of Antiochus Epiphanes in 1 Maccabees occurs a year later than in the second book; (c) the first attack of Lysias is antedated by approximately the same time, so these two events, the death of Antiochus and the campaign of Lysias more or less change places in 1 and 2 Maccabees. On all three points, Niese prefers 2 Maccabees. His attempt to explain the divergencies of 1 Maccabees as having been deliberately brought about by the author's inflexible views, p. 55–63 = Hermes 35, 468–76, may be correct, but only in the sense that chronological conflation came about for literary reasons.

(see n. 59). This possibility depends, however, on the apparent identity of the present campaign with that of Lysias in 2 Mac. 11:1–12, placed after the death of Antiochus Epiphanes, and on the genuineness of the four documents given there (11:16–38); it is important to note that three of them carry a dating to the Seleucid year 148 = 165/4 B.C. On the hypothesis that these documents are genuine, or at least go back to genuine originals, there is evidence here for two important stages of the Maccabaean victory not reflected in 1 Mac., which passes straight from the victory over Lysias to the restoration of the Temple cult. The first is represented by the letter of Lysias to the Jews (11:16–21) dated *Διοσκόρου/Διοσκορινθίου εἰκοστῇ τετάρτῇ* of the Seleucid year 148. The most probable of several amendments (see Abel, *ad loc.*) is the Macedonian month Dios (November). The letter, in which Lysias says that he has granted various requests made by Jewish envoys and passed others on to the king, could then date after his brief and unsuccessful campaign in autumn 165 B.C. Subsequent to this is the letter of the king himself (11:27–33), in which he offers amnesty to all Jews who return to their homes before the end of the month Xanthicus (April) and allows them *χρῆσθαι . . . τοῖς ἑαυτῶν δαπανήμασι καὶ νόμοις καθὰ καὶ τὸ πρότερον*. The letter is dated, exactly like that of two Roman *legati* which follows (11:34–8)[62], in the year 148—*Ξανθικοῦ πέμπτῃ καὶ δεκάτῃ*. This seems to indicate an impossibly short time for the fulfilment of the terms of the amnesty, and is perhaps a doublet from the letter of the *legati*. But the letter itself may well be a genuine document of the early part of 164 B.C. If so, it marks a significant stage in the abandonment of active persecution in the face of Jewish resistance.

After these successes, Judas again took Jerusalem and directed his attention to restoring the Temple cult. The Akra was still occupied by Syrian troops, but Judas kept them continually in check so that work in the Temple could proceed without interruption. Everything impure was removed. The altar of burnt-offering, defiled by heathen sacrifice, was demolished, and a new one erected in its place.[63] The

62. There is good evidence that two Roman *legati* were in the East in 164 B.C., and heard complaints against Antiochus IV. See Broughton, MRR I, pp. 439–40, and J. Briscoe, 'Eastern Policy and Senatorial Politics 168–146 B.C.', Historia 18 (1969), pp. 49–70, on p. 53. However, the authenticity of the document has often been questioned. For the latest discussion and bibliography see Th. Liebmann-Frankfort, 'Rome et le conflit judéo-syrien (164–161 avant notre ère)', Antiquité Classique 38 (1969), pp. 101–20, who dates it to 163 B.C.

63. The stones of the pagan sacrificial altar (or perhaps of several such altars) were carried to 'an unclean place', i.e. removed from the Temple precincts (1 Mac. 4:43), and the stones of the former Jewish altar of burnt-offering were laid in a suitable place on the Temple mount, 'until a prophet should arise to show what would be done with them' (1 Mac. 4:46). According to mMid. 1:6, the stones of the Jewish altar were deposited in a chamber within the bounds of the inner court, but

sacred vessels were replaced by new ones and when everything was completed, the Temple was re-dedicated amidst splendid celebrations. This occurred (according to 1 Maccabees 4:52) on 25 Kislev, in the Seleucid year 148 = December 164 B.C., on the same day on which, three years previously, the altar had first been profaned by heathen sacrifice.[64] The festivities lasted for eight days, and it was resolved that they should be renewed yearly as a reminder of these events.[65]

The re-dedication of the Temple constituted the first phase in the history of the Maccabaean revolt. Until this point, the struggles of the Jews were crowned with success. Judas had led his followers from victory to victory. The future was now to show whether their strength was sufficient and their enthusiasm enduring enough for them to keep permanent hold of what they had so rapidly won.

---

no longer on 'holy' ground. Derenbourg, *op. cit.*, pp. 60–1, combining 1 Mac. 4:43 and 46 with two obscure passages in Megillath Taanith (§ 17 and 20; cf. ed. Lichtenstein, pp. 337, 339), advanced the highly questionable theory that the stones of the Jewish altar (סוריגה) were removed on 23 Marḥeshwan (November) and those of the heathen altar (סימואתא) some time later, on 3 Kislev (December). But since סימא means 'sign', 'standard' (σημεῖον = signum), the latter event is perhaps more likely to refer to the removal of the Roman emblems under Pontius Pilate, *B.J.* ii 9, 2–3 (169–74); *Ant.* xviii 3, 1 (55–9). Cf. Abel, *op. cit.*, p. 80; Lichtenstein, *op. cit.*, pp. 299–300.

64. The date of 25 Kislev as the day of the dedication of the Temple is confirmed by the Megillath Taanith § 23. See Derenbourg, *op. cit.*, p. 62; Lichtenstein, *op. cit.*, pp. 275–6; Abel, *op. cit.*, p. 85.

65. Cf. in general 1 Mac. 4:36–59; 2 Mac. 10:1–8; Jos. *Ant.* xii 7, 6–7 (316–26). This is the origin of the 'Feast of the Dedication of the Temple', τὰ ἐγκαίνια, Jn. 10:22. Cf. Jos. *Ant.* xii 7, 7 (325) καὶ ἐξ ἐκείνου μέχρι τοῦ δεῦρο τὴν ἑορτὴν ἄγομεν, καλοῦντες αὐτὴν φῶτα (because during the festival it was the custom to light lamps, see mB.K. 6:6). According to 2 Maccabees 10:6 it was celebrated in the manner of the Feast of Tabernacles, and is therefore actually called in 2 Mac. 1:9 'The Feast of Tabernacles in the month Kislev'. This expression comes from one of two letters preserved at the beginning of 2 Maccabees, in which the Jews of Egypt are invited to celebrate this Feast, cf. vol. III, § 31, 1. In Hebrew it is called Hanukkah (חנוכה), and is celebrated for eight days. Cf. mBik. 1:6; mR.Sh. 1:3; mTaan. 2:10; mMg. 3:4, 6; mM.K. 3:9; mB.K. 6:6; Meg. Taan. § 23. A complete description of the festival in post-talmudic times is given by Maimonides, *Hilkhoth Megillah wa-Ḥanukkah* 3–4 in *Mishneh Torah, Sefer Zemanim* (ed. M. D. Rabinowitz) V (1916), pp. 545–65; E.T. in Yale Judaica Series XIV, *Code of Maimonides, Book* 3, *The Book of Seasons* (1961), pp. 453–71. At the service in the synagogue Num. 7 was read (mMeg. 3:6) and the festal psalm was Ps. 30 (Soferim 18:2). Hence Ps. 30 bears the title שיר חנוכת הבית. Cf. in general S. Krauss, 'La fête de Hanoucca', REJ 30 (1895), pp. 24–43, 204–19; I. Levi, *ibid.*, pp. 220–31; 31 (1895), pp. 119 f. Krauss, *ibid.* 32 (1896), pp. 39–50; S. Zeitlin, JQR 29 (1938/9), pp. 1–36; F.-M. Abel, 'La fête de Hanoucca', RB 53 (1946), pp. 538–46; S. Stein, 'The Liturgy of Hanukkah and the First Two Books of the Maccabees', JJS 5 (1954), pp. 100–6, 148–55. See O. S. Rankin, *The Origins of the Festival of Hanukkah* (1930); R. de Vaux, *Ancient Israel* (1961), pp. 510–14, 552; M. D. Herr, 'Hanukkah', Enc. Jud. 7 (1971), cols. 1080–88.

§ 5 Judas Maccabaeus 164–161 B.C.

Sources

1 Maccabees 5–9:22; 2 Maccabees 12–15.
Josephus *Ant.* xii 8–11 (327–434).
Megillath Taanith § 30; cf. H. Lichtenstein, HUCA 8–9 (1931–2), p. 346; cf. pp. 279–80.

Bibliography

Cf. § 4 on pp. 137–8 above.

During the period after the rededication of the Temple to the summer of 162 B.C., Judas remained master of Judaea. The central government of Syria took no interest in its affairs because of its pre-occupations elsewhere. Moreover, 2 Mac. 11:22–6 contains what appears to be a letter of Antiochus V Eupator to Lysias, written soon after his accession, guaranteeing the right of the Jews to their Temple and the observance of the Law.[1] Judas could therefore concentrate on the strengthening of his position. The Temple mount was equipped with strong fortifications. Beth-Zur, on the southern frontier and the key to Judaea, was similarly fortified and garrisoned with Jewish troops.[2] But in particular, military raids were made on neighbouring territories, partly to protect the Jews living there, and partly to consolidate Judas's own power. One after another, the Edomites, the sons of Baean and the Ammonites, all of whom had shown their hostility, were punished.[3]

Soon, complaints came from Gilead (east of Jordan) and Galilee of the persecutions to which the Jews living there were being subjected by the Gentiles. It was decided to send assistance to both places. Simon marched to Galilee with three thousand men, and Judas to Gilead with eight thousand.[4] In neither case was there any intention

1. The letter contains no date and is given along with three letters from the reign of Antiochus Epiphanes, on which see p. 162 above. But the phrase τοῦ πατρὸς ἡμῶν εἰς θεοὺς μεταστάντος clearly indicates that the death of Antiochus was recent.

2. 1 Mac. 4:60–1; Jos. *Ant.* xii 7, 7 (326). Beth-Zur is frequently mentioned in subsequent history as an important place. See the references quoted above on p. 161.

3. 1 Mac. 5:1–8. Jos. *Ant.* xii 8, 1 (327–31). The Edomite province of Akrabattene (1 Mac. 5:3) probably owes its name to the mountain range Akrabbim, Num. 34:4; Jos, 15:3; Jg. 1:36, and is not to be confused with the better-known toparchy of Akrabatene. See vol. II, § 23 ii.

4. 1 Mac. 5:9–20; Jos. *Ant.* xii 8, 1–2 (330–4).

of conquering these provinces permanently. After 'many battles' against the Gentiles in Galilee, Simon took the Jews, with their wives and children and all their belongings, and led them amid great jubilation to Judaea, where they were sheltered in safety.[5] Judeas acted similarly in Gilead. In a series of successful engagements, especially in the north of the area east of Jordan, he subdued the native tribes, whose leader seems to have been a certain Timotheus. He then assembled all the Israelites in Gilead, great and small, women and children, with all their possessions, and after having to force his way near Ephron (a town east of Jordan), led them safe and sound through Bethshean (Scythopolis) to Judaea.[6]

While Judas and Simon were absent from Judaea, the leadership there was entrusted to Joseph son of Zechariah, and Azariah. Against the express instructions of Judas, these two launched a campaign against Jamnia, but were repulsed with considerable losses by Gorgias (who had therefore remained in Philistia since his defeat at Emmaus). 1 Maccabees does not neglect this opportunity to point out that it was the family of the Maccabees 'by whose hand deliverance was to be wrought for Israel'.[7]

Judas, however, continued his military exploits. He marched once more against the Edomites, and besieged and destroyed Hebron. He then advanced through Marisa (this, not 'Samaria', is the correct reading in 1 Mac. 5:66) into the land of the Philistines, overran Ashdod, destroyed the altars there and the idols, and returned to Judaea with rich booty.[8] It was quite clearly no longer a matter of protecting the Jewish faith but of consolidating and extending Jewish power.

Meanwhile circumstances had also altered in Syria. Antiochus Epiphanes had met with as little good fortune in the east of his empire as his generals had in Judaea. He had advanced as far as the province of Elymais, but after trying in vain to appropriate the rich treasures of the temple of Artemis, he was compelled to withdraw to Babylon and died on the way in the Persian town of Tabae in the autumn of

5. 1 Mac. 5:21–3; Jos. *Ant.* xii 8, 2 (334). 1 Mac. 5:23, cf. above p. 142.

6. 1 Mac. 5:24–54; 2 Mac. 12:10–31; Jos. *Ant.* xii 8, 3–5 (335–49). On the geography, see Abel, *in loc.* Ephron is probably identical with the *Γεφροῦς* or *Γεφροῦν* (Polyb. V 70, 12) conquered by Alexander the Great, situated at eṭ-Ṭaiyibeh. See Abel, *op. cit.*, p. 102; *Géog. Pal.* II, pp. 318–19.

7. 1 Mac. 5:18–19, 55–62. Jos. *Ant.* xii 8, 6 (350–2). On Jamnia, see vol. II, § 23, 1.

8. 1 Mac. 5:63–8. Instead of *Σαμάρειαν* 1 Mac. 5:66, Jos. *Ant.* xii 8, 6 (353) reads *Μάρισαν*, as do also the best Latin manuscripts; see Abel, *in loc.* Cf. also 2 Mac. 12:35. Marisa, in the OT Mareshah, is a well-known town in southern Judaea, at that time under Edomite rule, *Ant.* xiii 9, 1 (257) and lying, according to Eusebius, *Onomast.* ed. Klostermann, p. 130, in the vicinity of Eleutheropolis, i.e. between Hebron and Ashdod. Cf. Abel, *Géog. Pal.* I, p. 379.

164 B.C. (1 Mac. 6:16: in the Seleucid year 149=164/3 B.C.).[9] Before he died, he appointed one of his generals, Philip, to be imperial vice-regent and tutor to his son Antiochus V Eupator. But Lysias seized the person of the young king instead, and assumed supreme power.[10]

It might have been some time before steps were taken against the disloyal Jews had not urgent requests for such measures reached Antioch direct from Judaea. Judas now besieged the Syrian garrison in the citadel of Jerusalem, the date being the Seleucid year 150 (1 Mac. 6:20), that is, either autumn 163–autumn 162 B.C., or spring 162–spring 161 B.C. Some of the garrison escaped despite the siege, and in company with representatives of the Jewish pro-Greek faction, went to the king to persuade him of the need for his intervention. The Jewish represesentatives in particular complained of how much they had to suffer from their hostile fellow countrymen, mentioning that many of them had been killed and robbed.[11]

Only then did the government in Antioch decide to intervene. Lysias, accompanied by the young king, set off against Judaea at the head of a powerful army. He attacked once again from the south and first besieged Beth-Zur. Judas was obliged to raise the siege of the citadel of Jerusalem and to advance against the king. The two armies met at Beth-Zachariah, between Jerusalem and Beth-Zur.[12] It soon became evident that, faced with a serious onslaught by the Syrians, the Jews, in spite of all their bravery, were in the long run unable to secure a decisive victory. Courageously they threw themselves into the battle. Judas's own brother, Eleazar, distinguished himself more than any. Thinking that he had discovered the elephant carrying the young king, he pressed forward, stabbed it from below, and was crushed to death by the beast as it fell. His self-sacrifice and all the exertions of the Jews were however in vain. The Jewish army was beaten, and indeed so decisively that the king's army soon appeared before the walls of Jerusalem and laid siege to Zion, the Temple mount.[13]

9. 1 Mac. 6:1–16; Jos. *Ant.* xii 9, 1 (354–9); Polyb. xxxi 9 (11); Porphyry in Jerome on Daniel 11:44–5 (CCL lxxvA, pp. 931–2). In place of Artemis referred to by Polybius, Appian, *Syriaca* 66/352 names Aphrodite. On the chronology, cf. p. 128 above. The narratives of 2 Maccabees (1:13–16 and chapter 9) represent popular stories; see Abel, *in loc.*

10. 1 Mac. 6:14–17; Jos. *Ant.* xii 9, 2 (360–1).

11. 1 Mac. 6:18–24; Jos. *Ant.* xii 9, 3 (364–6).

12. *Βαιθζαχαρία* (1 Mac. 6:32), according to Jos. *Ant.* xii 9, 4 (369) seventy stadia north of Beth-Zur, is the modern Beit-Zakaria. See Abel, *Géog. Pal.* II, p. 284.

13. 1 Mac. 6:28–48; 2 Mac. 13:1–17; Jos. *Ant.* xii 9, 3–5 (369–75); *B.J.* i 1, 5 (41–6). The defeat is very vaguely referred to in 1 Mac. 6:47, while in 2 Mac. 13:15–17 it is actually transformed into a victory!

Beth-Zur was also forced to surrender, and occupied by the Syrians. But those besieged on Mount Zion soon began to suffer from hunger; because it was a sabbatical year, no supplies were available.[14] The complete submission of the Jews seemed imminent when suddenly Lysias found himself compelled, because of events in Syria, to make peace with them on lenient terms. The same Philip, in effect, whom Antiochus Epiphanes had appointed as imperial vice-regent and tutor to his son Antiochus V during his minority, had marched against Antioch in order to seize power for himself. To leave himself a free hand, Lysias conceded to the Jews the right for which they had been fighting: namely, the free exercise of their religion. From then on, they were to be permitted to 'walk in accordance with their ordinances as formerly'. On this condition, those besieged on Zion withdrew; its fortifications were demolished (contrary to the king's sworn promise). The Jews were once more subjugated, but they had attained the goal for which they had risen against Syrian rule five years earlier.[15]

The concession which Lysias and Antiochus V, in their own interests, made to the Jews, was not revoked by later kings. None of them reverted to the foolish idea of Antiochus Epiphanes of enforcing a Gentile culture on the Jews. The Israelite cult, which had been restored by Judas Maccabaeus, remained on the whole intact throughout all the vicissitudes of the ensuing years. This should be borne in mind if a correct estimate is to be made of the conflicts which followed. The aim of the struggle now became a different one from hitherto. It was no longer a question of preserving the Jewish religion, but—as once before in the pre-history of the Maccabaean uprising—of the domination within Jewry itself of the pro-Greek faction or the nationalists. It was essentially an internal struggle in which the Seleucid régime took part only in so far as they sometimes supported the one party and placed it in power, and sometimes the other. To a certain extent, of course, religious interests also came into consideration. For in their promotion of Greek culture, the pro-Greeks went further than seemed to their

14. 1 Mac. 6:49–54; 2 Mac. 13:18–22; Jos. *Ant.* xii 9, 5 (378). Mention of the Sabbatical year (1 Mac. 6:49: ὅτι σάββατον ἦν τῇ γῇ and 6:53: διὰ τὸ ἕβδομον ἔτος εἶναι) suggests that these events occurred in 162 B.C. For the Seleucid year 150 (in which they are placed, according to 1 Mac. 6:20, cf. 7:1) runs, according to the reckoning adopted in 1 Maccabees, either from autumn 163 to autumn 162 B.C., or from spring 162 to spring 161 B.C. The sabbatical year, however, always begins in the autumn (mR.Sh. 1:1), and this one seems to have fallen in 163/2 B.C. Since there was already a shortage of food, it must have been the second half of the sabbatical year, after the fields had been left uncultivated during the winter and spring: the summer, therefore, of 162 B.C. See also R. North, 'Maccabean Sabbath Years', Bibl. 34 (1953), pp. 501–15.

15. 1 Mac. 6:55–62; 2 Mac. 13:23–6; Jos. *Ant.* xii 9, 6–7 (379–83).

nationalist opponents to be compatible with the religion of Israel. Its basis, however, was no longer threatened.[16]

As a result of the events of the last few years, the pro-Greeks in Judaea had been removed from the leadership of affairs and even to a large extent oppressed. It was Judas who stood at the head of the Jewish people.[17] As may well be imagined, the opposition party did not submit quietly to this arrangement but made strenuous efforts to regain power. This, however, did not come about until after another change of sovereign in Syria. Antiochus V and Lysias had defeated, after a short struggle, that same Philip who had contended with them for the supremacy.[18] But they were themselves soon removed by a new pretender to the throne. Demetrius I—afterwards surnamed Soter—the son of Seleucus IV Philopator and therefore nephew of Antiochus Epiphanes and cousin of Antiochus Eupator, who had until then lived as a hostage in Rome and had tried in vain to obtain permission from the Roman senate to return home, managed to escape in secret and landed at Tripolis on the Phoenician coast.[19] He was soon able to gain adherents;[20] indeed, King Antiochus's own forces surrendered him, and his guardian Lysias, to Demetrius. On the latter's command, both were murdered, and he became king, in 162 B.C.[21] The Roman senate was at first greatly alarmed at Demetrius's flight; he was nevertheless soon able to procure their recognition of him as king.[22]

Soon after his accession, the leaders of the pro-Greek party with at their head a certain Alcimus (or Yakim, his Hebrew name)[23], made

16. Cf. Wellhausen, *Pharisäer und Sadducäer*, p. 84.

17. The identity of the person who acted as High Priest after the restoration of the cult does not emerge from 1 Maccabees. Nominally, Menelaus was still High Priest, the man said to have been executed by Antiochus V Eupator for having been the cause of the rebellion 'by persuading the king's father to compel the Jews to abandon their ancestral religion', Jos. *Ant.* xii 9, 7 (383–5); cf. 2 Mac. 13:3–8. But Menelaus could not exercise the functions of High Priest while Judas was in power. Was the person in office at that time Onias IV son of Onias III? According to one of Josephus's versions, Onias IV was still a minor when his father died, *Ant.* xii 5, 1 (237) and went to Egypt straight afterwards because the High Priesthood was not transferred to him after Menelaus's execution, but to Alcimus, *Ant.* xii 9, 7 (385–7); but compare *B.J.* vii 10, 2 (423).

18. 1 Mac. 6:63; Jos. *Ant.* xii 9, 7 (386).

19. 2 Mac. 14:1; Euseb. *Chron.* ed. Schoene I, p. 254=Syncell. ed. Dindorf I, pp. 550–1; Jerome, *Chron.* ed. Helm, p. 141.

20. Justin xxxiv 3, 9, 'delatus in Syrian secundo favore omnium excipitur'.

21. 1 Mac. 7:1–4; 2 Mac. 14:1–2; Jos. *Ant.* xii 10, 1 (389–90); Livy *Epit.* xlvi; Appian *Syr.* 47/242. On the chronology, see above pp. 129 f.

22. Polyb. xxxi 15 (23); 33 (xxxii 4).

23. Jos. *Ant.* xii 9, 7 (385) Ἄλκιμος ὁ καὶ Ἰάκειμος κληθείς. In the synopsis given in *Ant.* xx 10, 3 (235), Josephus refers to him as Ἰάκιμος. In the text of 1 Maccabees, 7:5, 12, 20–1, 23, 25 and 9:54–7, as well as 2 Mac. 14:3 various manuscripts have the addition, ὁ καὶ Ἰάκιμος.

representations to the king on account of their ill-treatment by the party of Judas. Judas and his brothers had just at that time killed the king's supporters or expelled them from the country. This factor naturally made an impact on Demetrius. Alcimus was appointed High Priest, and a Syrian army, under the command of Bacchides, was sent to Judaea to install Alcimus in office, if necessary by force.[24]

The way in which matters developed from then on is characteristic of the Maccabaean struggles. Resistance to Alcimus on the part of the strictly religious Jews was by no means general. As a result of his soothing promises, he was acknowledged as lawful High Priest descended from Aaron by the very representatives of the strictest branch of Jewry themselves—the scribes and the 'Devout' (*'Ασιδαῖοι*, 1 Mac. 7:13). Only Judas and his followers persisted in their opposition. They did not take Alcimus at his word, and believed that their religious interests would be secure only if they were in control.[25]

In the event, they were shown to be right. One of the first acts of Alcimus was to order the execution of sixty men of the Asidaean party. This, needless to say, created fear and alarm; but it also sharpened antagonism. Nevertheless, Bacchides judged his presence in Judaea to be no longer necessary. Leaving a military force for the protection of Alcimus, he himself returned to Syria. Thus Alcimus and Judas were in the main left to contend against each other by means of their own resources. But the open warfare which now began between the two parties seemed more and more to incline in favour of the Maccabees, and Alcimus found it necessary to go to the king and plead for further support.[26]

Demetrius sent another general, Nicanor, with a large army against Judaea. Nicanor first tried to seize Judas by cunning, but the Jewish leader was informed of the plot and it misfired. An engagement then took place at Capharsalama[27] in which Nicanor suffered some losses. He then went to Jerusalem and vented his fury on the innocent priests, returning their respectful greetings with mockery and ridicule, and

24. 1 Mac. 7:5–9; 2 Mac. 14:3–10; Jos. *Ant.* xii 10:1–2 (391–3). According to *Ant.* xii 9, 7 (385), Alcimus had already been nominated High Priest by Antiochus V Eupator. According to 2 Mac. 14:3 ff. he had been High Priest once before. Cf. RE s.v. 'Alkimos' (15).

25. 1 Mac. 7:10–15; Jos. *Ant.* xii 10, 2 (395–6). 2 Mac. 14:6 wrongly identifies the Asidaeans with the party of Judas. Cf. Wellhausen, *Pharisäer und Sadducäer*, pp. 79 ff.; Abel, *Histoire de la Palestine* I, p. 158.

26. 1 Mac. 7:16–25; Jos. *Ant.* xii 10, 2–3 (396–49). On the place Beth-zaith mentioned in 1 Mac. 7:19, see Abel, *Géog. Pal.* II, p. 284.

27. 1 Mac. 7:31. The site of this place is uncertain. Abel, *ad loc.* suggests the village of Salem (Euseb. *Onomast.* ed. Klostermann, p. 153) west of Jerusalem and a kilometre north-west of el-Gib, now known as Khirbet Selma. This is to be preferred to Kafar Sallam in the Plain of Sharon mentioned by Arab geographers; see *Géog. Pal.* II, p. 293.

threatening them that if Judas and his army were not surrendered to him, he would on his triumphant return set fire to the Temple.[28]

He marched off to the region of Beth-horon, north-west of Jerusalem, where he collected reinforcements from Syria. Judas was encamped opposite him near Adasa.[29] On 13 Adar 161 B.C., the decisive battle was fought which ended with the total defeat of the Syrians. Nicanor himself fell in the tumult. When his people saw this, they threw away their arms and fled. Pursuing them, the Jews surrounded and cut them down to the last man (so, at least, 1 Maccabees asserts). The victory must in any case have been striking and decisive. For from then on, 13 Adar (March) was celebrated annually as 'Nicanor's Day'.[30]

Judas was thus once more master of the situation. Josephus dates to this time the death of Alcimus and the subsequent assumption of the High Priesthood by Judas. But according to 1 Maccabees, Alcimus died considerably later, and it is very improbable that Judas ever exercised the functions of High Priest.[31]

He was, nevertheless, as Josephus's statement correctly conveys,

28. 1 Mac. 7:26–38; 2 Mac. 14:11–36; Jos. *Ant.* xii 10, 4–5 (405–6).

29. Ἀδασά (1 Mac. 7:40, 45), according to Jos. *Ant.* xii 10, 5 (408) thirty stadia from Beth-horon, is presumably identical with the Ἀδασά in the vicinity of Gophna which was known to Eusebius (*Onomast.* ed. Klostermann, p. 26, καὶ ἔστι νῦν κώμη ἐγγὺς Γουφνῶν). It therefore lay to the north-east of Beth-horon. It is to be distinguished from the similarly named Hadashah in the tribe of Judah (Jos. 15:37, mErub. 5:6) which, precisely because it belonged to the tribe of Judah, cannot have lain in the neighbourhood of Gophna, as was mistakenly assumed by Eusebius. Some scholars identify this Adasa with Khirbet 'Adaseh, 8 km. north of Jerusalem on the Beth-horon road, see Guérin, *Judée* III, pp. 5–6; Conder and Kitchener, *The Survey of Western Palestine*, III, pp. 30, 105 f. and Abel on 1 Mac. 7:40. The identification involves rejecting the evidence of Josephus, *loc. cit.* (above), since Khirbet 'Adaseh is situated sixty stadia from Beth-horon, and not in the direction of Gophna, but towards the south-east.

30. 1 Mac. 7:39–50; 2 Mac. 15:1–36; Jos. *Ant.* xii 10, 5 (408–12); Megillath Taanith § 30: יום נקנור. The year in which Nicanor's defeat occurred is not directly stated in 1 Maccabees. But by comparing 1 Mac. 7:1 (151 of the Seleucid era) with 9:3 (152), it seems clear that the month of the victory, Adar, roughly March, fell in 161 B.C. The year is certain if 1 Mac. 9:3, relating that the *next* expedition sent by Demetrius (see below) was encamped at Jerusalem in the first month of the year 152, is using the Macedonian era, as this date will then be autumn 161 B.C. It is also all but certain if the Babylonian era beginning the following spring is being used.

31. On the death of Alcimus, see 1 Mac. 9:54–6. On the High Priesthood of Judas, Jos. *Ant.* xii 10, 6 (414); 11, 2 (434). It is not in itself inconceivable that Judas also usurped the functions of the High Priest. But 1 Maccabees says nothing about it; in addition, a legitimate claimant was present in the person of Onias IV (see above, p. 168), who would probably be respected as such by Judas. Josephus himself in another place expressly states that after the death of Alcimus the High-Priestly office remained unoccupied for seven years, *Ant.* xx 10, 3 (237) διεδέξατο δ' αὐτὸν οὐδείς, ἀλλὰ διετελέσεν ἡ πόλις ἐνιαυτοὺς ἑπτὰ χωρὶς ἀρχιερέως οὖσα.

the effective leader of the Jewish community, and it was his intention that he, or at least his party, should be permanently in this commanding position. Events had taught him, however, that this was only possible in complete separation from the Syrian empire. The Syrian king had meant to ensure by force of arms that power in Judaea should pass into the hands of the opposing party. It was imperative, therefore, to shake off the Syrian yoke. To achieve this, Judas turned for assistance to the Romans. These had taken the liveliest interest in events in Syria and kept a suspicious watch on them ever since the battles with Antiochus the Great (192–189 B.C.). They had repeatedly intervened in Syrian affairs.[32] Any centrifugal pressures could count on their certain support. It was consequently very reasonable of Judas to try to ensure permanence for the briefly won freedom with the help of the Romans. 1 Maccabees gives a vivid description of how Judas heard of the deeds and might of the Romans and how this led him to seek their aid. The very inaccuracies of the narrative make clear the extent of what was known in Judaea about the Romans in those days. So Judas sent two men of his party, Eupolemus son of John, and Jason son of Eleazar, as emissaries to Rome (the former perhaps identical with the Eupolemus known as a Hellenistic writer, see vol. III, § 33, 3, 2). His object in doing so was the overthrow of Syrian domination (1 Mac. 8:18, *τοῦ ἆραι τὸν ζυγὸν ἀπ᾽ αὐτῶν*). The Roman senate willingly granted an audience to the Jewish delegation, and a treaty of friendship was signed, the essential provisions of which were that Jews and Romans were to render each other mutual aid in the event of war, though not on identical terms, and in every instance 'as the circumstances demanded' (1 Mac. 8:25, 27: *ὡς ἂν ὁ καιρὸς ὑπογράφῃ αὐτοῖς*). It rather depended, therefore, on the discretion of the Romans how far they wished to consider themselves bound by it.[33]

Simultaneously with the conclusion of this treaty, the Romans sent a letter to Demetrius prohibiting all hostilities against the Jews as allies

[*Text continues on page 173*

32. Thus Antiochus Epiphanes was compelled by Popillius Laenas to give up Egypt (see above pp. 151–2). After the death of Antiochus Epiphanes, the Roman senate demanded from Antiochus Eupator and his guardian Lysias a considerable reduction of the Syrian armed forces, Polyb. xxxi 2, 9–11; Appian *Syr.* 46/239.

33. 1 Mac. 8; Jos. *Ant.* xii 10, 6 (414–19). For similar documents known from epigraphic texts see R. K. Sherk, *Roman Documents from the Greek East: Senatus Consulta and Epistulae to the Age of Augustus* (1969), esp. no. 10 (*senatus consultum* and treaty with Astypalaea, 105 B.C.). For comment and criticism of 1 Mac. 8 cf. apart from the commentaries (e.g. Abel), especially Grimm, ZWTh (1874), 231–8 (with notes by Mommsen) and I. Mendelssohn, 'Senatus consulta Romanorum quae sunt in Josephi Antiquitatibus', *Acta societatis philologae Lipsiensis* 5 (1875), pp. 91–100; H. Willrich, *Judaica* (1900), pp. 62–85; cf. *Urkundenfälschung in der hellenistisch-jüdischen Literatur* (1924), pp. 44–50, repeating the same views; B. Niese, 'Eine Urkunde aus der Makkabäerzeit', *Orient. Studien, Th. Nöldeke*

(1906), pp. 817–29; E. Täubler, *Imperium Romanum* I (1913), pp. 239–54; O. Roth, *Rom und die Hasmonäer*, Beitr. z. Wiss. vom AT 17 (1914), pp. 3–18; W. Kolbe, *op. cit.*, pp. 36–8; R. Laqueur, 'Griechische Urkunden in der jüdisch-hellenistischen Literatur', Hist. Zeitschr. 136 (1927), pp. 229–52, esp. pp. 243 ff.; E. Meyer, *op. cit.*, pp. 246–7; M. S. Ginsburg, *Rome et la Judée* (1928), pp. 34–49; A. Momigliano, *Tradizione maccabaica*, pp. 159–62; M. Sordi, 'Il valore politico del trattato fra i Romani e i Giudei nel 161 a. C.' Acme 5 (1952), pp. 502–19; K.-D. Schunck, *op. cit.*, pp. 32–6; Th. Liebmann-Frankfort, *op. cit.*, p. 162; A. Giovannini, H. Müller, 'Die Beziehungen zw. Rom. u. den Juden im 2 Jh. v. Chr.', Mus. Helv. 28 (1971), pp. 156–71. The authenticity of the treaty (1 Mac. 8:23–30), questioned by Mommsen and Mendelssohn, was later flatly denied. Willrich went furthest in his radical criticism in that he struck out from history all diplomatic relations between the Jews and the Romans at the time of the three Maccabee brothers, Judas, Jonathan and Simon, and argued that they did not begin until the time of John Hyrcanus I, see *Judaica*, pp. 62–85. He deduced this from a remark in Caesar's decree, *Ant.* xiv 10, 6 (205), that the Jews possessed Joppa from the time that they stood in friendly relation with the Romans (*'Ιόππην τε πόλιν, ἣν ἀπ' ἀρχῆς ἔσχον οἱ 'Ιουδαῖοι ποιούμενοι τὴν πρὸς 'Ρωμαίους φιλίαν αὐτῶν εἶναι καθὼς καὶ τὸ πρῶτον*). It is true that Joppa did not come into Jewish possession until under Jonathan. But for this very reason, the argument is not applicable to the time of Simon. It is not applicable at all, in fact, for this passage merely proves that the Jews informed Caesar of their ancient and legitimate claim to Joppa. Caesar, the friend of the Jews, would have hardly carried out subtle historical investigations regarding the substance of their claim. On the other hand, the narrative of 1 Maccabees on the relations of Judas to the Romans corresponds so closely to the historical situation that there need be no doubt on this point. The historicity of the Jewish appeal to Rome may also be confirmed by Justin xxxvi 3, 9, and possibly by Diodorus xl 2. See AJP 77 (1956), pp. 413–4. Somewhat different is the question of the authenticity of the treaty itself (1 Mac. 8:23–30). It was, for instance, denied by Niese, who otherwise considered the relations between Judas and the Romans as historical (*op. cit.* p. 88 f. = Hermes 35 (1900), pp. 501 f.). Yet bearing in mind that a connecting link of a Hebrew translation is interposed between the original and the text now extant, it is not clear which reasons should decide against its authenticity. It ought, in particular, to be an argument in its favour that the treaty clauses are unequal to the disadvantage of the Jews (Grimm, ZWTh (1874), 234); but cf. Täubler, *op. cit.*, pp. 245 ff. Willrich considered the document authentic but placed it, because Josephus, *Ant.* xii 10, 6 (419) dates it by the 'High Priest Judas', in the time of Aristobulus I, also called Judas, *Judaica*, pp. 71 ff. This seems to lay too much weight on Josephus, who used here only 1 Maccabees.

The basic discussion of the text of the treaty, from which the general modern acceptance of its authenticity (see Schunck, *op. cit.*, pp. 32–4) derives, is that of Täubler *loc. cit.*, who shows (a) that making allowances for the successive re-translations mentioned above, the form of the document can be regarded as going back to a *senatus consultum* expressing the terms of a treaty, and (b) that there are no decisive historical objections to the possibility of such a treaty.

Niese, *op. cit.*, followed by Täubler, *op. cit.*, p. 249 and Kolbe, *op. cit.*, finds is further confirmation of the authenticity of this document in the letter given by Josephus *Ant.* xiv 10, 15 (233), addressed to Cos by *Γαίος Φάννιος Γαίου υἱὸς στρατηγὸς ὕπατος* and giving instructions for the same conduct of Jewish envoys returning home with *senatus consulta*. Niese suggested that the writer was to be identified with the consul of 161 B.C., C. Fannius Strabo, see Broughton, MRR I, p. 443.

of the Romans.[34] Their message came too late. Demetrius acted so swiftly and vigorously that Judas's catastrophe was complete before there could be any question of intervention by the Romans.[35] Immediately after receiving news of the death and defeat of Nicanor, he had sent a strong force under Bacchides to Judaea, which arrived in the vicinity of Jerusalem in the first month of the Seleucid year 152 (1 Mac. 9:3)—probably Autumn 161 B.C., some months after the fall of Nicanor.[36] Bacchides pitched camp near Berea (Beerzath or Berzetho), and Judas near Elasa (also written as Eleasa and Alasa).[37] The superiority of the Syrians was so conspicuous that in the ranks of Judas himself there was no longer any confidence in victory. His followers deserted in crowds. With the few who remained faithful he nevertheless threw himself fearlessly into the desperate struggle. The result was a foregone conclusion: Judas's band was wiped out and he himself fell in the battle. The only satisfaction remaining to his brothers Jonathan and Simon was that they were able to bury him in the grave of his forefathers at Modein.[38]

The downfall of Judas offered final proof of the futility of any opposition by the nationalists to Syrian power. However brilliant the earlier achievements of Judas had been, he owed them primarily to the rashness and conceit of his opponents. Lasting military success was unthinkable so long as Syrian power remained to some degree united. In the following years there was not even a passing victory of the kind won by Judas. What the Maccabees finally achieved, they won through the voluntary concessions of the rival pretenders to the Syrian throne, and as a result of the internal disorganisation of the Syrian empire.

34. 1 Mac. 8:31–2.

35. From the narrative of 1 Maccabees it appears that Judas sent the embassy only after the victory over Nicanor. Assuming this was so, it is unlikely that he was alive when his ambassador returned, for his death occurred only a few months after Nicanor's defeat.

36. Nicanor fell in battle on 13 Adar, March (1 Mac. 7:43–9), and Bacchides appeared at the gates of Jerusalem 'in the first month' of the Seleucid year 152 (1 Mac. 9:3), i.e. probably in the autumn. See p. 170 above.

37. Neither place can be identified with certainty. Instead of *Βερέαν* some MSS. of 1 Mac. 9:4 have *Βερεθ* or *Βεηρζαθ*, and Jos. *Ant.* xii 11, 1 (422) *Βηρζηθοῖ*, *Βαρζηθὼ*, *Βιρζηθὼ* etc. It is therefore possible to consider an identification with Bir ez-Zeit near Gophna (north-west); see Guérin, *Judée* III, pp. 33–4; Conder and Kitchener, *The Survey of Western Palestine* III, p. 329. Alternatively, see Abel *ad loc.* and *Géog. Pal.* II, p. 262, it may be el-Bireh, 16 km. north of Jerusalem. In that case, Elasa could be the modern el-'Aššy, which lies less than a mile south-west of el-Bireh. Otherwise, it could be present-day Ilasa, in the north-west, near Beth-horon; the note in 1 Mac. 9:15 *ἕως Ἀζώτου ὄρους* offers no clue since it certainly does not refer to the well-known Azotus, but is probably a corruption of the text. Abel emends to *ἕως ἀσηδωθ τοῦ ὄρους* 'jusqu' aux dernières rampes de la montagne'. Jos. *Ant.* xii 11, 2 (429) gives *μέχρι Ἀζᾶ* (or *Ἐζᾶ*) *ὄρους*. For a discussion see Abel, RB 55 (1948), pp. 187–8.

38. 1 Mac. 9:6–21; Jos. *Ant.* xii 11, 1–2 (422–34).

§ 6 JONATHAN 161–143/2 B.C.

Sources

1 Maccabees 9:23–13:30.
Josephus *Ant.* xiii 1–6 (1–212).
Megillath Taanith § 33; cf. H. Lichtenstein, HUCA 8–9 (1931–2), pp. 322, 347–8.

Bibliography

Cf. § 4 on pp. 137–8 above.

The defeat and death of Judas completely destroyed the effectiveness of the Jewish nationalists. The pro-Greek faction, with the High Priest Alcimus at their head, was able to exercise unopposed the authority conferred on it by the king. Whatever resistance still remained was suppressed by force. The friends of Judas were searched out and brought before Bacchides who 'took vengeance on them'. The 'unrighteous' and 'ungodly' (as they are described in 1 Maccabees) were now in command in Judaea.[1]

The friends of Judas were nevertheless not yet disposed to renounce their resistance altogether and elected Jonathan, the brother of Judas, as their new leader.[2] There was at first no question of any serious undertaking. They had instead to regain their strength and then await a favourable opportunity. The earliest incidents reported represent Jonathan's companions more as bandits than as members of a religious party. Since their possessions were not safe in Judaea, they sent them with John, a brother of Jonathan, to the friendly Nabataeans. On the way there, John and his baggage train were attacked near Medeba (east of Jordan) by a tribe of brigands known as the 'sons of Jambri', carried off and killed.[3] To avenge his death, Jonathan and Simon crossed the Jordan and attacked the sons of Jambri whilst they were walking with great pageantry in a wedding procession. Many died, and the rest fled to the mountains. On their return, Jonathan and his men were met

1. 1 Mac. 9:23–7; Jos. *Ant.* xiii 1, 1 (1–4).
2. 1 Mac. 9:28–31; Jos. *Ant.* xiii 1, 1 (5–6).
3. Instead of *υἱοὶ 'Αμβρί*, which Fritzsche read in 1 Mac. 9:36–7 and Josephus (*οἱ 'Αμαραίου παῖδες*), the form *υἱοὶ 'Ιαμβρί* is probably to be retained on the basis of A (*'Ιαμβρείν, 'Ιαμβρείν*), Ven. (*'Ιαμβρεί, 'Ιαμβρί*) and Sin. (*'Αμβρεί, 'Ιαμβρί*). C. Clermont-Ganneau compared with it the name of the Nabataean *strategos* Ya'amru found in an inscription in the neighbourhood of Medeba, *Recueil d'archéologie orientale* II, pp. 207–15: cf. Abel, *Géog. Pal.* II, pp. 381–2.

by Bacchides and a Syrian force and found themselves heavily pressed, but they escaped by swimming across the Jordan.[4]

Bacchides meantime made arrangements to ensure the confirmation of Judaea's subjection to Syrian supremacy. He fortified the towns of Jericho, Emmaus, Beth-Horon, Bethel, Thammatha, Pharaton and Tephon, and furnished them with Syrian garrisons. He also strengthened the fortifications of Beth-Zur, Gazara and the fortress in Jerusalem. Finally, he took the sons of distinguished Jews as hostages and kept them in custody in the fortress in Jerusalem.[5]

About this time, in the second month of the Seleucid year 153 = May 160 B.C. (1 Mac. 9:54), the High Priest Alcimus gave offence to observant Jews. He demolished the walls of the inner court and thus 'destroyed the works of the prophets'. His death, which occurred shortly afterwards, was seen as God's righteous punishment for such an outrage.[6]

4. 1 Mac. 9:32–49; Jos. *Ant.* xiii 1, 3 (12–14). The battle against Bacchides took place on the eastern bank of the Jordan. For after the interpolated narrative of 1 Mac. 9:35–42, the report goes back again to the point reached 1 Mac. 9:34 (*Βακχίδης . . . ἦλθεν . . . πέραν τοῦ Ἰορδάνου*). So when Jonathan and his companions escaped by swimming across the Jordan, they reached the western bank and probably remained in the desert of Judaea (cf. 9:33).

5. 1 Mac. 9:50–3; Jos. *Ant.* xiii 1, 3 (15–17). Most of the towns mentioned are known from other evidence. On Emmaus see vol. II, § 23, ii; on Beth-horon cf. above p. 159. Bethel is the well-known ancient Israelite cult centre, twelve Roman miles north of Jerusalem according to Euseb. *Onomast.* ed. Klostermann, p. 40. Tamnatha is the Hebrew Timnatah or Timnah, the name of three localities in southern Palestine, see vol. II, § 23, 2. The best-known among them is Timnath Seraḥ, where Joshua's grave was situated. See Abel, *Géog. Pal.* II, pp. 481–2. According to the traditional texts of 1 Mac. 9:50, Tamnatha-Pharaton is one place-name. But Jos., Syr. and Vet.Lat. are probably correct in that they read *καί* between the two names. Pharaton is the Hebrew Pir'aton, a town of the tribe of Benjamin, Jg. 12:13, 15, and perhaps the modern Far'atha to the south-west of Nablus, Guérin, *Samarie* II, pp. 179 f.; Abel, *Géog. Pal.* II, p. 409. But this Pirathon as well as Timnath-Seraḥ belonged to Samaria (1 Mac. 11:34). On Beth-Zur, see above p. 161; on Gazara below, p. 191.

6. 1 Mac. 9:54–6; Jos. *Ant.* xii 10, 6 (413); Josephus places the death of Alcimus prior to the death of Judas, see above p. 170). The demolition of the walls was, according to 1 Mac. 9:54, only partially carried out. The meaning of *τεῖχος τῆς αὐλῆς τῶν ἁγίων τῆς ἐσωτέρας* in 1 Mac. 9:54 is debatable. In the Temple of the Herodian period, the inner court (i.e. the 'forecourt' in the real and narrower sense) was first surrounded by a strong wall. Outside it ran a narrow terrace (the so-called *Ḥel*, cf. mMidd. 1:5), from which steps led down to the outer court. Below the steps ran another low parapet (the so-called *Soreg*) marking the boundary beyond which no Gentile was allowed. Since 1 Maccabees speaks of a *τεῖχος*, there seems to be no doubt that the real wall of the forecourt is meant. On the other hand, the Mishnah presents the tradition that the *Soreg* was demolished by the Greek kings (מלכי יון) at thirteen places, and that these thirteen 'breaches' (פרצות) were later closed, and that the thirteen bows towards it were ordered as a reminder of this (mMidd. 2:3). It seems reasonable to combine this tradition with the event under discussion, in which case *τεῖχος* should be con-

The High-Priestly office seems not to have been reoccupied for some time.[7]

Soon after the death of Alcimus, Bacchides, believing that he had ensured the subjugation of Judaea, returned to Syria.[8] There followed a period of seven years (160–53 B.C.) about which 1 Maccabees says almost nothing. Yet these seven years must have been of great significance for the reinvigoration of the Maccabaean party. For at the end of this time it emerged as the one party really capable of governing, with Judaea in fact under its control. Its adherence was therefore eagerly sought by the rival Syrian kings in their struggles against each other. The obscurity of this interval is lightened by only one episode in the narrative of 1 Maccabees. Two years after the departure of Bacchides, in 158 B.C., the dominant pro-Greek faction among the Jews made pressing representations at the royal court concerning the restoration of the Maccabaean party. As a result, Bacchides came back with an even larger military force to exterminate Jonathan and his followers. This force was, however, already so powerful that Bacchides found himself faced with no easy task. Some of them, under the leadership of Simon, entrenched themselves in Beth Bassi in the desert, where Bacchides besieged them unsuccessfully. Others, under Jonathan, raided the land. When Bacchides realised what difficulties confronted him, he was indignant at the pro-Greeks for having involved him in such embarrassment, and having made peace with Jonathan, returned again to Syria.[9]

The Jewish parties were now willing to tolerate each other. This

---

sidered as an inexact translation of סורג. But it is very questionable whether, in the simpler construction of the pre-Herodian temple, the wall and *Soreg* existed next to one another at all. At all events, Alcimus's offence consisted in removing the boundary between the 'holy' area of the forecourt and the 'unholy' outer area, thus making it possible for Gentiles to gain access to forbidden places. It is certainly a mistake to suggest that the 'inner court' was the so-called court of the priests, and that the *τεῖχος* was the barrier dividing, in the inner court itself, the area allotted to the priests from that of the Israelites; so e.g. Büchler, JQR 10 (1898), pp. 708 f. This barrier was no *τεῖχος*, but a *δρύφακτος*, *Ant.* xiii 13, 5 (373), or *γείσιον*, *B.J.* v 5, 6 (226); cf. *Ant.* viii 3, 9 (95), and probably did not even exist before the time of Alexander Jannaeus (*Ant.* xiii 13, 5 (373) is anyway far from clear). The *αὐλῇ ἐσωτέρα* is undoubtedly Josephus's *ἡ ἔνδον αὐλῇ* *B.J.* v 5, 6 (227); *ὁ ἐνδότερος περίβολος* *B.J.* v 1, 2 (7); *ὁ ἐντὸς περίβολος* *Ant.* xv 11, 5 (418); *τὸ ἐνδοτέρω ἱερόν* *B.J.* iv 5, 1 (305); v 3, 1 (104); vi 1, 8 (82); *τὸ ἔνδον ἱερόν* *B.J.* vi 4, 4 (248); *τὸ εἴσω ἱερόν* *B.J.* vi 2, 7 (150); *τὸ ἔσωθεν ἱερόν* *B.J.* vi 4, 1 (220), i.e., the forecourt in the real and strict sense, to which Israelites, but not gentiles, had access. Cf. also vol. II, § 24 iii, iv.

7. Cf. also Jos. *Ant.* xx 10, 3 (237) and p. 170 above.

8. 1 Mac. 9:57; Jos. *Ant.* xiii 1, 5 (22).

9. 1 Mac. 9:57–72; Jos. *Ant.* xiii 1, 5–6 (22–23). On Beth Bassi, see Abel, *Géog. Pal.* II, p. 269.

seems to have resulted in an increasing assumption of power by Jonathan. As 1 Maccabees remarks laconically of the next five years, 'The sword no longer hung over Israel, and Jonathan settled in Michmash, where he began to judge the people and to rid Israel of the godless'.[10] This can only mean that whereas the official Sanhedrin of Jerusalem still consisted of pro-Greeks, Jonathan established in Michmash a rival government which grew to be the chief influence in the country, to the extent that it could even venture to exterminate (*ἀφανίζειν*), the 'godless', i.e., the Hellenizing party. Pro-Hellenism had in fact no roots among the people. They were well aware that even though it allowed the religion of Israel to continue, it was incompatible with the ideal of the religious teachers. As soon, therefore, as the pressure from above was removed, the mass of the people turned to the aspirations of national Judaism defended by the Maccabees. And this is the reason why, in the struggles for the Syrian throne which began at this time, the rival claimants endeavoured to obtain Maccabee goodwill. The Syrian kings were no longer strong enough to impose a Hellenistic government on the people, but had to conciliate them and keep them in a favourable mood. This was only possible under Maccabaean leadership. Needless to say, these favourable concessions simultaneously furthered the endeavours which in fact ended in separation from the Syrian empire.

In the Seleucid year 160=153–152 B.C. by the Macedonian era, 152–1 by the Babylonian (note that 1 Mac. 10:21 puts the Feast of Tabernacles in the seventh month of the same year), Alexander Balas, a young man of humble descent and merely an agent of the kings allied against Demetrius, opposed him as pretender to his throne.[11]

10. 1 Mac. 9:73; Jos. *Ant.* xiii 1, 6 (34). *Μαχμάς*=Mikhmash is situated nine Roman miles north of Jerusalem in the neighbourhood of Rama according to Euseb. *Onomast.* ed. Klostermann, p. 132. Its modern Arabic name is still Mukhmas. See Guérin, *Judée* III, pp. 63–5; Abel, *Géog. Pal.* II, p. 386.

11. The details are as follows. In Smyrna lived a youth by the name of Balas (Justin) who strongly resembled Antiochus Eupator and claimed to be son of Antiochus Epiphanes, but who was in reality of lowly origin ('sortis extremae iuvenis'). Attalus II, king of Pergamum, ordered Balas to appear before him, placed on his head the royal diadem, named him Alexander, and set him up against Demetrius as pretender to the throne (Diodorus xxxi 32a; Justin xxxv 1, 6–7). Led by Heraclides, the former finance minister of Antiochus Epiphanes whom Demetrius had exiled, Appian *Syr.* 42/235, 47/242, Alexander went to Rome and sought recognition by the Roman Senate. Although the deception was obvious, the Senate complied and promised its support, Polybius xxxiii 15 (14), 1–2; 18 (16). In addition, Alexander was backed not only by Attalus II of Pergamum, but also by Ptolemy VI Philometor of Egypt, and Ariarathes V of Cappadocia, Justin xxxv 1, 6; Strabo xiii 4, 2 (624); Appian *Syr.* 67/354–5; Euseb. *Chron.* ed. Schoene I, p. 255). The people in Syria itself also favoured the new pretender on account of Demetrius's arrogant and surly nature, Diodorus and Justin, *loc. cit.*;

The despotic Demetrius was unloved in the country itself, so the danger threatened by the power of the confederate kings was all the greater. There was also the fear that the Jews might go over to his opponent if he allowed them to establish a national government. Demetrius tried to forestall this danger by granting concessions to Jonathan himself. He gave him full authority to assemble an army with which to support the king, and for this purpose agreed to surrender the Jewish hostages still detained in the fortress in Jerusalem. Invested with this authority, Jonathan went to Jerusalem. The hostages were surrendered and handed over to their parents. But Jonathan then formally occupied Jerusalem and fortified the city and the Temple mount. In addition, the Syrian garrisons of most of the strongholds erected by Bacchides were withdrawn. They remained only in Beth-Zur and the fortress in Jerusalem.[12]

Yet Demetrius had still not gone far enough in his concessions to Jonathan. Alexander Balas outbid him immediately by naming Jonathan High Priest of the Jews, and sending him, as a token of princely rank, the purple and the diadem. Jonathan was not slow to grasp these new favours. On the feast of Tabernacles in the Seleucid year 160 = the autumn of 153 or 152 B.C., he donned the sacred vestments.[13] He was now also formally head of the Jewish people. The pro-Greek faction was driven from government in Judaea and never returned. For Jonathan maintained his position even in the vicissitudes of the following years. In his case, circumstances favoured the objectives which Judas, with all his bravery, had been unable to attain.

When Demetrius heard that Jonathan had gone over to the party of Alexander Balas, he attempted by means of even bigger promises to win him back. The privileges assured him were incredible: taxes would be remitted, the fortress in Jerusalem would be transferred to the Jews, Jewish territory would be enlarged by the addition of three regions of Samaria, the Temple would be endowed with rich gifts and prerogatives, the building of the walls of Jerusalem would be paid for from the royal treasury.[14]

---

cf. Jos. *Ant.* xiii 2, 1 (35). Alexander thus started the war against Demetrius 'totius ferme orientis viribus succinctus' (Justin). It follows from this (cf. esp. Justin) that it is incorrect to consider 'Balas' as the surname of Alexander after Josephus, *Ant.* xiii 4, 8 (119), *'Αλέξανδρος ὁ Βάλας ἐπιλεγόμενος*. Balas was his real name, *τὸν Βάλαν 'Αλέξανδρον*, as Strabo xvi 2, 8 (751) correctly calls him.

12. 1 Mac. 10: 1–14; Jos. *Ant.* xiii 2, 1 (37–42).

13. 1 Mac. 10:15–21; Jos. *Ant.* xiii 2, 2–3 (43–6).

14. 1 Mac. 10:22–45; Jos. *Ant.* xiii 2, 3 (47–57). Although it is in itself quite credible that Demetrius at that time made more promises than he contemplated keeping, nevertheless the concessions contained in the letter of 1 Mac. 10:25–45 exceed the bounds of probability: the release throughout Demetrius's entire

Jonathan was shrewd enough not to comply with Demetrius's proposals. It was likely that the king would succumb to his enemy's superior strength, but even if he emerged victorious from the struggle, it was not to be expected that he would keep such extensive promises. Jonathan, therefore, remained with Alexander Balas and was not to

---

kingdom of all the Jewish slaves captured in war (10:33), the gift of the town of Ptolemais to the Temple (10:39), a rich endowment of the Temple from royal funds (10:40), the renewal of the Temple edifice and the city walls at the royal expense (10:44–5). Noteworthy, also, is the parallel between 10:36–7 and the *Letter of Aristeas* 3 (13). Where the latter describes Ptolemy Lagus as employing 30,000 Jews to garrison his fortresses, Demetrius, *loc. cit.* promises to take 30,000 Jews (the same number!) into his army as troops of occupation. It is therefore possible that this statement originated from the pen of a Jewish author familiar with the *Letter of Aristeas*. It would follow that the character of the letter is similar to that of the speeches which ancient authors incorporated in historical works. The Jewish author makes Demetrius write what was appropriate to the situation at that time and of which he probably had some general knowledge. In this respect, Willrich's criticism, *Judaica* (1900), pp. 52–8 (Cf. *Urkundenfälschung*, pp. 39 ff.), has some justification. By contrast, there seems to be no reason for considering the letters as a later interpolation into 1 Maccabees, or for regarding it as a forgery from Roman times, even placing it as late as the reign of Caligula; cf. Willrich, *op. cit.*, p. 56. According to Willrich, mention of the poll-tax (10:29) is decisive in marking it as a forgery from the Roman period, for it was not introduced until the time of Augustus; so Wilcken, *Grieschiche Ostraka* I, pp. 245 f., is reported to have proved. The latter will apply to the Egyptian 'poll-tax', though Wilcken makes this assumption with great diffidence. But even if it is probable that there was no poll-tax in Ptolemaic Egypt, see V. Tcherikover, '*Syntaxis* and *Laographia*', Journal of Juristic Papyrology 4 (1950), pp. 179–207, this does not positively prove anything in relation to the conditions prevailing in Syria. 1 Mac. 10:29 has ἀφίημι πάντας τοὺς Ἰουδαίους ἀπὸ τῶν φόρων, and there is ample evidence of the φόρος on subject communities in the Seleucid empire, see E. Bikerman, *Institutions des Séleucides* (1938), pp. 106–11. Here, incidentally, the expression 'poll-tax' is not used at all; it appears only in the parallel account of Josephus, which Willrich erroneously considers to be the original, *Ant.* xiii 2, 3 (50) ὑπὲρ κεφαλῆς ἑκάστης ὅ ἔδει μοι δίδοσθαι. Nevertheless it seems probable on account of the parallel in a related passage in the letter of Antiochus the Great, Jos. *Ant.* xii 3, 5 (142), ὧν ὑπὲρ τῆς κεφαλῆς τελοῦσι, that by φόροι one should understand a head tax or poll-tax in that general sense. Some further evidence for a poll-tax in the Seleucid empire *may* be provided by [Aristotle], *Oeconomica* 1346a 4 ἡ ἀπὸ τῶν ἀνθρώπων, ἐπικεφάλαιόν τε καὶ χειρωνάξιον προσαγορευομένη. This work probably dates to the last quarter of the fourth century B.C. See B. A. van Groningen, A. Wartelle, *Aristotle, Économique* (1968), p. xiii. Arguments from the possible mention of a poll-tax thus provide no evidence for the date of the letter. The mention of military service by the Jews also points more to the Hellenistic period (see the parallels by Abel, *ad loc.*), and does not support the notion of composition in the Roman period. If the references to military service by 30,000 Jews show any connection between 1 Mac. and the *Letter of Aristeas*, it is more likely that the latter derives from the former; so Momigliano, *Tradizione maccabaica*, pp. 163–5. Cf. O. Murray, 'Aristeas and Ptolemaic Kingship', JThSt 18 (1967), pp. 337–71, on pp. 338–40.

regret this decision. In 150 B.C., Demetrius was defeated by Alexander and lost his life in the battle. Alexander was crowned king.[15]

Very shortly afterwards, in the Seleucid year 162 (1 Mac. 10:57) = 151/50 or 150/49 B.C., an occasion presented itself in which Jonathan was remembered by Alexander with the highest honours and distinctions. Alexander had asked King Ptolemy Philometor of Egypt for the hand of his daughter Cleopatra. Ptolemy had given his consent, and the two kings met in Ptolemais, where Ptolemy himself brought his daughter to Alexander, and the marriage was celebrated with great splendour. Alexander invited Jonathan there also, and received him with marked respect. Emissaries of the pro-Greek party in Judaea were present as well, with complaints against Jonathan, but the king granted them no audience, heaping Jonathan instead with even more distinctions. He made him sit at his side clothed in purple, and appointed him *στρατηγός* and *μεριδάρχης*, presumably for the province of Judaea, thus formally confirming the political powers which he in fact already exercised.[16]

During the next few years, Jonathan's position was in no danger from either side. The Hellenising party had been silenced. Alexander Balas was an incompetent ruler addicted only to sensual pleasures, and it never occurred to him to restrict the concessions made to the Jewish High Priest.[17] Syrian sovereignty, indeed, continued, but as Jonathan and his party ruled in Judaea, the aims of the Maccabees were in fact achieved. Nevertheless, the struggles for the Syrian throne soon brought fresh dangers, but at the same time a new opportunity to extend political power. Jonathan now appears as supporting sometimes one pretender and sometimes the other, shrewdly exploiting the weakness of the Syrian empire for the purpose of strengthening the Jewish

15. 1 Mac. 10:46–50; Jos. *Ant.* xiii 2, 4 (58–61); Polyb. iii 5, 3; Justin xxxv 1, 8–11; Appian *Syr.* 67/354–5. The death of Demetrius is narrated in greatest detail by Josephus, *loc. cit.* His account is corroborated by Justin, 'invicto animo inter confertissimos fortissime dimicans cecidit'.

16. 1 Mac. 10:51–66; Jos. *Ant.* xiii 4, 1–2 (80–5), *στρατηγός* and *μεριδάρχης* are more or less equivalent in meaning to a military and civil governor. For further details useful parallels are not available, see Bikerman, *op. cit.*, 198–9, except for the newly-discovered inscription of the correspondence of Ptolemaeus, *strategos* and *archiereus* of Coele Syria and Phoenicia under Antiochus III, cf. *Ant.* xii 3, 3 (138–44), see Y. Landau, 'A Greek Inscription Found near Hefzibah', IEJ 16 (1966), pp. 54–70. Incidentally it is worth noting that in spite of Jonathan's appointment as *στρατηγός*, a Syrian garrison still remained stationed in the fortress in Jerusalem.

17. On Alexander's character, see Diodorus xxxii 27, 9c; Livy *Epit.* 50, 'In Syria, quae eo tempore stirpe generis parem Macedonum regis, inertia socordiaque similem Prusiae regem habebat, iacente eo in ganea et lustris, Hammonius regnabat'; Justin xxxv 2, 2 '(Alexandrum) insperatae opes et alienae felicitatis ornamenta velut captum inter scortorum greges desidem in regia tenebant'.

position. Maccabaean aspirations are once more set higher. It is no longer enough that Jonathan's party rules unopposed in internal affairs. The predicaments of the Syrian empire are used to extend Jewish territory partly through gifts, partly by force, and finally to work with tenacity and persistence for the total severance of the Jewish state from the Syrian empire.

In the Seleucid year 165 (1 Mac. 10:67) = 148/7 or 147/6 B.C., Demetrius II, a son of Demetrius I, set himself up as a rival against the unworthy weakling, Alexander Balas. He was immediately joined by Apollonius, the governor of Coele-Syria, whilst Jonathan continued to support Alexander. Fighting broke out on this account between Apollonius and Jonathan, from which Jonathan emerged victor. He dislodged a garrison of Apollonius from Joppa, defeated an army under the command of Apollonius in the vicinity of Ashdod, destroyed the town itself and its temple of Dagon, and returned to Jerusalem with rich booty.[18] In gratitude for this assistance, Alexander Balas made him a gift of the city of Ekron and its surrounding territory.[19]

Jonathan, however, was alone in supporting Alexander against Demetrius. The inhabitants of Antioch, and Alexander's own soldiers, declared themselves in favour of Demetrius.[20] Even Ptolemy, his own father-in-law, sided with Demetrius. He took back Cleopatra from Alexander and gave her to the new pretender to the throne as his wife.[21] Ptolemy also led a strong force against Alexander and defeated him by the river Oenoparas on the plain of Antioch. Alexander fled to Arabia and met his end there at the hand of an assassin. Immediately afterwards, Ptolemy also died of wounds received in the battle.[22] Thus Demetrius became king in 145 B.C. (cf. p. 130 above).

As the ally of Alexander Balas, Jonathan had confronted Demetrius as an enemy. He now seems to have felt strong enough to attempt to break away by force from the Syrian empire. He laid siege to the fortress in Jerusalem, still occupied by Syrian troops. Once again, as so

18. 1 Mac. 10:67–87; Jos. *Ant.* xiii 4, 3–4 (86–102). Josephus misrepresents the affair so far as to indicate that Apollonius sided with Alexander Balas. On Joppa and Ashdod see vol. II § 23, 1.

19. 1 Mac. 10:88–9; Jos. *Ant.* xiii 4, 4 (102). Josephus sees the motive for this gift as being Alexander Balas's desire to make it appear as if his general, Apollonius, had launched the attack upon Jonathan against the king's will. Ἀκκαρών is the ancient Philistine city of Ekron. Eusebius, *Onomast.* ed. Klostermann, p. 22, places it between Ashdod and Jamnia and to the East. It is therefore probably identical with modern 'Aḳir, east of Yavneh. See Guérin, *Judée* II, pp. 36–44; cf. Abel, *Géog. Pal.* II, p. 319.

20. Justin xxxv 2, 3.

21. 1 Mac. 11:1–13; Jos. *Ant.* xiii 4, 5–7 (103–10); Diodorus xxxii 27, 9c; Livy *Epit.* 52.

22. 1 Mac. 11:14–19; Jos. *Ant.* xiii 4, 8 (116–19); Diodorus xxxii 27, 9d and 10, 1; Livy *Epit.* 52. The site of the battle is given by Strabo xvi 2, 8 (751).

frequently happened in similar cases, it was the opposition party among his own people (the *ἄνδρες παράνομοι* and *ἄνομοι* as they are called in 1 Mac. 11:21, 25) that drew the Syrian king's attention to his revolutionary moves. As a result, Demetrius summoned Jonathan to Ptolemais to account for his conduct. But Jonathan was audacious enough to extort concessions from Demetrius. He ordered that the siege should continue, travelled to Ptolemais with magnificent gifts, and demanded of Demetrius the cession to Judaea of three provinces of Samaria and exemption from taxation for the entire region. These were some of the essential points among the offers which Demetrius I had already made to Jonathan. Demetrius dared not refuse these demands. He authorised the union of the three Samaritan districts of Aphaerema, Lydda and Ramathaim with Judaea, ceded the whole to Jonathan free of tax, and confirmed him in all the titles which he had until then. Of the fortress in Jerusalem no mention was made. These concessions were obviously the price for which Jonathan agreed to raise the siege.[23]

Ten years earlier, such a retreat before Jewish demands on the part of the Syrian king would have been quite inconceivable. But now the power of the Seleucids was broken. From this time on, no king of Syria was sure of his throne, and Jonathan was able to exploit this weakness with good luck as well as skill. The next few years offered him ample opportunity to continue his policy of annexation. Demetrius had no sooner granted these concessions when he found himself forced into new

23. 1 Mac. 11:20–37; Jos. *Ant.* xiii 4, 9 (120–8). Confirmation of former dignities: 1 Mac. 11:27. The three districts: 11:34 (cf. 10:30, 38; 11:28, 57); freedom from tribute: 11:34–35. *'Αφαίρεμα*, probably the Ephraim where Jesus is said to have withdrawn shortly before the Passover (Jn. 11:54), was situated, according to Jos. *B.J.* iv 9, 9 (551), in the neighbourhood of Bethel; according to Euseb. *Onomast.* ed. Klostermann, p. 86, twenty Roman miles north of Jerusalem (*καὶ ἔστι νῦν κώμη 'Εφραεὶμ μεγίστη περὶ τὰ βόρεια Αἰλίας ὡς ἀπὸ σημείων κ'*), and five Roman miles east of Bethel, Jerome in Euseb. *Onomast.* ed. Klostermann, p. 29, 'est et hodie vicus Efraim in quinto miliario Bethelis ad orientem respiciens'; the parallel Greek text of Eusebius, *loc. cit.*, is defective. Ephraim in 2 Sam. 13:23 and Ephron in 2 Chr. 13:19 are also undoubtedly the same place. For suggestions concerning its situation see Guérin, *Judée* III, pp. 45–51; F. Buhl, *Geogr. des alten Palästinas*, p. 177; Abel, *Géog. Pal.* II, p. 402. On Lydda, the modern Lod, see vol. II, § 23, 2. *'Ραμαθάιμ* is certainly the town of Samuel, רמתים צופים, 1 Sam. 1:1, elsewhere named הרמה. It is probably to be identified with Rentis north-east of Lod; see Abel, *Géog. Pal.* II, pp. 428–9. According to 1 Sam. 1:1, it lay in the mountains of Ephraim. Eusebius locates it in the vicinity of Diospolis-Lydda *Onomast.* ed. Klostermann, p. 32. *'Αρμαθὲμ Σειφά· πόλις 'Ελκανὰ καὶ Σαμουήλ· κεῖται δὲ αὕτη πλησίον Διοσπόλεως, ὅθεν ἦν 'Ιωσήφ <ὁ> ἐν εὐαγγελίοις ἀπὸ 'Αριμαθίας.* In Jerome *Onomast.* ed. Klostermann, p. 33, the passage runs, 'Armathem Sofim civitas Elcanae et Samuelis in regione Thamnitica iuxta Diospolim, unde fuit Joseph, qui in evangeliis de Arimathia scribitur'. The accuracy of this statement is supported by 1 Mac. 11:34, according to which the town belonged to Samaria until the time of Jonathan.

promises to Jonathan to obtain his assistance when he was in serious danger. A certain Diodotus of Apamea, called Tryphon,[24] a former general of Alexander Balas, succeeded in seizing Alexander's young son, Antiochus, who had been brought up by an Arab, Imalcue, and set him up as a rival to Demetrius.[25] The latter's situation became very critical, for his own troops deserted and the inhabitants of Antioch were hostile to him. In face of these perils, he promised to hand over the fortress in Jerusalem and the other strongholds of Judaea to Jonathan if he would provide him with auxiliary troops. Jonathan immediately sent three thousand men, who arrived just in time to give powerful support to the king in the insurrection in Antioch which was then breaking out. It was substantially due to their aid that the revolt was crushed. The Jewish troops retreated to Jerusalem with the king's thanks and rich spoils.[26]

Demetrius, however, did not keep his word. Also, it soon looked as though he were going to yield to the new pretender. Tryphon and Antiochus seized the capital, Antioch, with the help of his deserters, and thereby won control of the heart of the empire. They straightaway tried to win Jonathan over to their side, Antiochus confirming him in the possession of everything given him by Demetrius. His brother Simon was simultaneously appointed royal *strategos* from the Ladder of Tyre to the Egyptian border.[27]

Faced with Demetrius's treachery and weakness, Jonathan considered it justified as well as useful to go over to Antiochus, and in association with his brother, Simon, undertook the subjugation to the new pretender of the territories lying closest to Judaea. They first turned their attention to the regions over which Simon had been nominated *strategos*. Jonathan thus marched at the head of Jewish and Syrian troops against the towns of Ascalon and Gaza. The first sub-

24. Jos. *Ant.* xiii 5, 1 (131), Ἀπαμεὺς τὸ γένος. Cf. Strabo xvi 2, 10 (752).

25. 1 Mac. 11:39–40, 54; Jos. *Ant.* xiii 5, 1 and 3 (131–2, 144); Diodorus xxxiii 4a; Livy *Epit.* 52. Appian *Syr.* 68/357, mistakenly names the young king Alexander. The name of the Arab Εἰμαλκουαί or Ἰμαλκουέ (1 Mac. 11:39) corresponds to ימלכו occurring in Palmyrene inscriptions; see Abel, *in loc.* Jos. *Ant.* xiii 5, 1 (131) reads here Malchus. Diodorus gives Iamblichus (for the equivalence of ימלכו and the Greek Ἰάμλιχος, see Waddington, *Inscr.* n.2614). Cf. also the Latin 'Iamlicus', CIL XIII 7040.

26. 1 Mac. 11:38, 41–52; Jos. *Ant.* xiii 5, 2–3 (133–44).

27. 1 Mac. 11:53–9; Jos. *Ant.* xiii 5, 3–4 (144–7). The κλίμαξ Τύρου or Τυρίων is, according to Jos. *B.J.* ii 10, 2 (188) a high hill one hundred stades north of Ptolemais. For the topography of the area see M. Dunand, R. Duru, *Oumm El-'Amed, une ville de l'époque hellénistique aux Echelles de Tyre* (1962), pp. 9–17, By his appointment as στρατηγός over the district named, Simon became a royal official of the highest rank, and at that, outside Judaea. The position must first, of course, have been obtained by him in opposition to the *Strategoi* of Demetrius.

mitted willingly to Antiochus; the second, only after Jonathan had used force. He compelled the city to hand over hostages and took them with him to Jerusalem.[28] After this, he advanced into northern Galilee and fought against Demetrius's *strategos* on the plain of Hazor. At first, the fight went against him, but it ended with his victory.[29] At the same time, Simon besieged the fortress of Beth-Zur in southern Judaea where the garrison was still loyal to Demetrius. After a long struggle, he forced the town to surrender and installed a Jewish garrison.[30]

Whilst consolidating his power in this way, Jonathan may have created for himself further support by means of diplomatic relations with foreign countries. 1 Maccabees and Josephus record that he sent two envoys, Numenius and Antipater, to Rome to renew the treaty of friendship with the Romans concluded during the time of Judas.[31] The same ambassadors also brought letters from the High Priest and the Jewish people to Sparta and other places, in order to establish and cultivate friendly relations with them.[32] These documents, if genuine, reveal that such relations between the Jews and foreign nations were not without example in earlier times. In his letter to the Spartans, Jonathan refers to the fact that King Areus of Sparta had directed a friendly message to the High Priest Onias.[33]

28. 1 Mac. 11:60–2; Jos. *Ant.* xiii 5, 5 (148–53). On Ascalon and Gaza, see vol. II, § 23, 1. Note that Jonathan is regarded as a partisan of Antiochus and Tryphon. It was therefore not intended to unite these towns to Jewish territory, but only to compel them to join the party championed by Jonathan.

29. 1 Mac. 11:63–74; Jos. *Ant.* xiii 5, 6–7 (154, 158–62). Ἀσώρ (1 Mac. 11:67) is חצור, cf. Jos. 11:1, 10–13; 12:19; 19:36; Jg. 4:2, 17; 1 Sam. 12:9; 1 Kg. 9:15; 2 Kg. 15:29. According to Jos. *Ant.* v 5, 1 (199) (cf. Jos. 11:5), it was situated not far from Lake Semachonitis or Merom (ὑπέρκειται τῆς Σεμαχωνίτιδος λίμνης), i.e., in the extreme north of Palestine. It has now been securely identified with Tell el-Qedah or Tell Waqqas, 5 km south-west of L. Huleh, see Y. Yadin *et al.*, *Hazor* I (1958), p. 3. The site has been extensively excavated.

30. 1 Mac. 11:65–6; Jos. *Ant.* xiii 5, 6 (155–7). On the site see p. 161 above.

31. 1 Mac. 12:1–4; on the names of the ambassadors see 12:16. Jos. *Ant.* xiii 5, 8 (163–70). Cf. Mendelssohn in Acta Societatis philologae Lipsiensis 5 (1875), pp. 101–4. Ginsburg, *op. cit.*, pp. 53 f., and Momigliano, *Tradizione maccabaica*, pp. 148 f., argue that this embassy is unhistorical, being a doublet of that which was shortly afterwards sent to Rome by Simon (see below, p. 194). T. Fischer, *Untersuchungen zum Partherkrieg Antiochos' VII* (1970), pp. 96 ff., claims that the embassy set off under Jonathan and returned under Simon.

32. 1 Mac. 12:2, πρὸς Σπαρτιάτας καὶ τόπους ἑτέρους. The letter to the Spartans 1 Mac. 12:5–23; Jos. *Ant.* xiii 5, 8 (166–70). The Spartan reply, 1 Mac. 14:16–23. The authenticity of the documents is subject to serious doubts, see e.g., Willrich, *Urkundenfälschung*, pp. 23–7; Momigliano, *Tradizione Maccabaica*, pp. 141–70. Cf., however, Abel, *op. cit.*, pp. 231–3.

33. 1 Mac. 12:7–8 (a reference in Jonathan's letter); 19–22 (text) = Jos. *Ant.* xii 4, 10 (226–7); cf. *Ant.* xiii 5, 8 (167), a reference in Josephus's version of Jonathan's letter. The name of the Spartan king is oddly mutilated in the manuscripts of 1 Maccabees. In 1 Mac. 12:7 it is given as Δαρεῖος and in 1 Mac. 12:20 as Ὀνιάρης

In the meanwhile, Jonathan's battles against Demetrius continued, and were conducted by him in such a way that he kept in view, not only the interests of Tryphon and Antiochus, but his own as well. Soon after Demetrius's troops were defeated on the plain of Hazor, he sent a new army against Jonathan. This time, the Jewish leader advanced much farther north to meet him, as far as the district of Hamath north of Lebanon. But no decisive battle was fought, for the Syrian army avoided contact.[34] Jonathan next turned his forces against the Arab tribe of the Zabadaeans, then towards Damascus, and from there southwards again. After his return to Jerusalem, he saw to the

---

(for which the Codex Sinaiticus has the better *ΟΝΙΑΑΡΗΣ*, i.e. *'Ονίᾳ "Αρης*, for the rare name Oniares is formed only by contraction of the preceding name of Onias). Both texts, as may be confirmed by Jos. and Vet. Lat., originally read *"Αρειος*. The more correct form is *'Αρεύς* (so on an inscription, SIG[3] 433). There were two Spartan kings by this name, Areus I, who according to Diodorus xx 29, reigned for forty-four years from 309–265 B.C., and Areus II, who reigned *c.* 255 B.C., but died as a child at the age of eight, see Pausanias iii 6, 6. On the Spartan kings see E. Manni, *Fasti ellenistici e romani* (1961), pp. 73–4; Niese in RE s.v. 'Areus' (1) and (2). As Onias II can hardly have been a contemporary of Areus II, Areus I and Onias I must be meant here (Josephus's combination, which places the letter in the period of Onias III, *Ant.* xii 4, 10 (225–7), is certainly mistaken). Relations between the two would therefore fall in the era of the Diadochi, when the Spartans, in conflict with Antigonus and his son Demetrius Poliorcetes, could perhaps have thought of creating difficulties for their enemies by stirring up trouble in the east. For a bibliography of the relations between Jews and Spartans see R. Marcus, *Josephus* (Loeb) VII, App. F, pp. 769 f. Hitzig's idea of looking for the Spartans in Asia Minor was an original one, ZDMG 9 (1855), pp. 731–7, as was that of A. Büchler that they were Greeks from Cyrenaica, see *Die Tobiaden und Oniaden*, p. 126 ff. The fiction of a relationship between Jews and Spartans, which constituted the Spartans' motive for writing their letter (1 Mac. 12:6–7, 21; cf. 2 Mac. 5:9) is not unprecedented in the Hellenistic period. Cf. Freudenthal, *Alexander Polyhistor*, p. 29, referring to Stephanus of Byzantium s.v. *'Ιουδαία ... ὡς Κλαύδιος 'Ιούλιος* (or *'Ιόλαος*), *ἀπὸ Οὐδαίου Σπάρτων ἑνὸς ἐκ Θήβης μετὰ Διονύσου ἐστρατευκότος*. Cf. Jacoby, FGrH 788 F4. In a decree of the Pergamenes, Jos. *Ant.* xiv 10, 22 (255) there is also mention of friendly relations between the Jews and the Pergamenes in the time of Abraham. For more recent views, see Momigliano, *loc. cit.*; M. S. Ginsburg, 'Sparta and Judaea', Class. Philol. 29 (1934), pp. 117–22; S. Schüller, 'Some Problems connected with the supposed Common Ancestry of Jews and Spartans', JSS 1 (1956), pp. 257–68; B. Cardauns, 'Juden und Spartaner: zur hellenistisch-jüdischen Literatur', Hermes 95 (1967), pp. 317–24.

34. 1 Mac. 12:24–30; Jos. *Ant.* xiii 5, 10 (174–8). Derenbourg, *op. cit.*, pp. 99–100 attempted to connect this and what follows with Megillath Taanith § 33: 'On 17 Adar, as the Gentiles rose against the remnant of the scribes in the districts of Chalcis and Zabadaea, deliverance came to the house of Israel'. This hypothetical combination has since been adopted by Wellhausen, *Pharisäer und Sadducäer*, p. 58, and Abel, *in loc.* Note, however, that Josephus refers to Jonathan's war against the Nabataeans in Arabia, *Ant.* xiii 5, 10 (179). See also the comment in H. Lichtenstein, 'Die Fastenrolle', HUCA 8–9 (1931–2), p. 293.

strengthening of the city's fortifications, and by erecting a high wall cut the communication between the Syrian garrison in the fortress and the town.[35] Simon had already installed a Jewish garrison at Joppa before Jonathan's return; he now also fortified Adida in the 'Shephelah', i.e. in the lowlands of western Judaea.[36]

All these operations were undertaken by Jonathan and Simon ostensibly in the interests of the young king Antiochus and his guardian Tryphon. But by now, Tryphon seems to have found the increase in Jewish power somewhat disquieting. And not without justification. For as it developed, the greater grew the danger of a total Jewish severance from the Syrian empire. It is therefore very understandable that as soon as Demetrius allowed him a free hand, Tryphon turned against Jonathan. According to 1 Maccabees, the reason for this was that Tryphon wished to wear the crown himself and Jonathan would not tolerate this. It may well have been so, but Jonathan's motives will have been not so much moral as political.[37]

Tryphon therefore marched with an army into Palestine in order to contain the disturbing increase of Jewish power. He found Jonathan near Beth-Shean (Scythopolis). The encounter was at first friendly, although Jonathan, like Tryphon, had a large army with him. Tryphon tried to remove Jonathan's suspicions by showering him with honours.

35. 1 Mac. 12:31–7; Jos. *Ant.* xiii 5, 10–11 (179–83).

36. 1 Mac. 12:33–4, 38; cf. Jos. *Ant.* xiii 5, 10 (180). *Σεφήλα* (thus also LXX Jer. 32:44; 33:13; Ob. 19; 2 Chr. 26:10) is the Hebrew *Shephelah*, the low-lying country west of the mountainous region of Judaea. In mSheb 9:2 a distinction is made between שפלת לוד (lowlands near Lydda) and שפלת הדרום (lowlands of the south). So, too, Jerome *Com. in Abd.* 19 (CCL lxxvi, p. 370), 'qui autem habitabant in Sephela, id est in campestribus, Liddam et Emmaus, Diospolim scilicet, Nicopolimque significans. . . . Alii vero putant eam Sephelam, id est campestrem regionem, quae circa Eleutheropolim est, repromitti' etc. Less definite, Eusebius, *Onomast.* ed. Klostermann, p. 162, *Σεφηλά . . . καὶ εἰς ἔτι νῦν Σεφηλὰ καλεῖται. αὕτη ἐστὶν πᾶσα ἡ περὶ τὴν Ἐλευθερόπολιν πεδινὴ χώρα πρὸς βορρᾶν καὶ δυσμάς.* In the present passage, the district of Lydda is meant. *Ἀδιδά*, 1 Mac. 12:38 and 13:13, is *Ḥadid*, Ezra 2:33; Neh. 7:37; 11:34. In mArak. 9:6 חדיד is mentioned as one of the ancient towns which were surrounded with walls as early as the time of Joshua. A R. Yakim of Ḥadid appears in mEdu. 7:5. The Greek forms *Ἄδδιδα* or *Ἄδιδα* are also found in Jos. *Ant.* xiii 6, 5 (203); 15, 2 (392); *B.J.* iv 9, 1 (486). According to the last, it commanded the main road leading (from the west and therefore from Joppa) to Jerusalem. This is in agreement with Ezr. 2:24 and Neh. 7:37, where it is mentioned together with Lydda and Ono. Probably, therefore, it is identical with 'Aditha circa Diospolim quasi ad orientalem plagam respiciens' referred to by Jerome, *Onomast.* ed. Klostermann, p. 25, i.e. the modern Ḥaditheh, or Ḥadid, east of Lod. It appears as *Ἀδιαθημ ἡ νῦν Ἀδιθα·* on the mosaic map of Madaba, M. Avi-Yonah, *The Madaba Mosaic Map* (1954), p. 61. See Abel, *Géog. Pal.* II, pp. 340–1.

37. 1 Mac. 12:30–40; Jos. *Ant.* xiii 6, 1 (187).

He pointed out to him that a great army was superfluous since they were not at war with each other. If Jonathan would follow him with a small, select company to Ptolemais, he would hand over the town to him and 'the remaining fortresses and troops', probably meaning those between the Ladder of Tyre and the Egyptian border, over which Simon had been appointed *strategos*.[38] Jonathan actually allowed himself to be hoodwinked by these bland promises; he dismissed his army and followed Tryphon with only one thousand men to Ptolemais. But hardly had he arrived, when he was taken into custody and his force treacherously massacred.[39]

The news of this treachery on the part of Tryphon caused great consternation throughout Judaea. Simon, the only other survivor of the five Maccabee brothers, naturally took over the leadership. By the decree of an assembly of the people he was formally elected head. His first acts were to speed up work on the fortification of Jerusalem and to take definite possession of Joppa, which had never yet belonged to Jewish territory. He had already in his capacity as *strategos* of the coastal districts, placed a Jewish garrison there (see above p. 186). Now, the Gentile inhabitants were expelled from Joppa, and the town was Judaized and joined to Jewish territory.[40]

Tryphon, with Jonathan as his prisoner, came with an army to Judaea. Near Adida, Simon barred him with his troops from marching into the interior. Tryphon consequently sent envoys to Simon and let him know that he was keeping Jonathan prisoner only because he owed money for the official appointments conferred on him. If the money were paid, and as a guarantee of future loyalty the sons of Jonathan were handed over as hostages, he would free him. Although Simon sent everything that was demanded, Jonathan was nevertheless not released. On the contrary, Tryphon endeavoured, by making a detour round the mountains, to push towards Jerusalem from the south via Adora in Idumaea. When he was again prevented, this time by a heavy fall of snow, he marched his troops to Gilead (east of Jordan), ordered Jonathan to be murdered at Bascama, and returned to Syria.[41]

38. On Beth-shean or Scythopolis, and Ptolemais, see vol. II, § 23, 1.

39. 1 Mac. 12:41–53; Jos. *Ant.* xiii 6, 1–2 (188–92).

40. 1 Mac. 13:1–11; Jos. *Ant.* xiii 6, 3–4 (196–202). On Joppa see vol. II, § 23, 1.

41. 1 Mac. 13:12–24; Jos. *Ant.* xiii 6, 5–6 (203–12). Adora is an Idumaean town later conquered by John Hyrcanus I, *Ant.* xiii 9, 1 (257). See § 8 below. Bascama, which Josephus gives as Basca, appears to have been situated east of the Jordan. See, however, Abel, *Géog. Pal.* II, p. 261, suggesting hypothetically a place north-west of Lake Tiberias, el-Gummezeh ('the sycamore') from the interpretation of Bascama as ב׳ שקמה, House of the Sycamore.

With this, Simon took the place of his brother as High Priest of the Jews. He brought Jonathan's bones from Bascama and buried him beside his parents and his three brothers in their native town of Modein. Over their common grave he later erected a magnificent memorial stone.[42]

42. 1 Mac. 13:25–30; Jos. *Ant.* xiii 6, 5 (210–12). The sepulchral monument at Modiim still existed at the time of Eusebius; see above p. 156. On the Hellenistic features of the monument see C. Watzinger, *Denkmäler Palästinas* II (1935), pp. 22–3.

The identification of the 'Wicked Priest' in the Qumran texts with Jonathan and/or Simon Maccabee, has been advanced by G. Vermes, *Les manuscrits du désert de Juda* (1953), pp. 92–100; *Discovery in the Judean Desert* (1956), pp. 89–97; J. T. Milik, *Ten years of Discovery in the Wilderness of Judaea* (1959), pp. 84–7; F. M. Cross, *The Ancient Library of Qumran and Modern Biblical Studies* (1958), pp. 107–16; P. Winter, 'Two non-allegorical Expressions in the Dead Sea Scrolls', PEQ 91 (1959), pp. 38–46; R. de Vaux, *L'archéologie et les manuscrits de la Mer Morte* (1961), pp. 90–1; G. Vermes, *The Dead Sea Scrolls in English* (1968), pp. 61–5; F. M. Cross, 'The Early History of the Qumran Community', *New Directions in Biblical Archaeology*, ed. D. N. Freedman, J. C. Greenfield (Anchor, 1971), pp. 70–89.

§ 7. SIMON 143/2–135/4 B.C.[1]

Sources

1 Maccabees 13:31–16:22.
Josephus *Ant.* xiii 6–7 (213–29).
Megillath Taanith § 5–6, 15; cf. H. Lichtenstein, HUCA 8–9 (1931–2), pp. 319–20, 327, 336.

Bibliography

Cf. § 4 on pp. 137–8 above.

The original aims of the Maccabaean party, the restoration of Temple worship and the free exercise of the Jewish religion, had been far surpassed through Jonathan's deeds. Judas, who achieved them, was already dissatisfied, and sought in addition control of the country's internal affairs. Under Jonathan, this target too was reached. With his appointment as High Priest, the powers of government were placed in the hands of the Maccabaean party and the pro-Greek faction was ousted. Yet even this was no longer sufficient. The favourable circumstances and the weakness of the Syrian empire aroused the temptation to shake off its supremacy altogether. The last acts of Jonathan were already important moves in this direction. The significance of the reign of Simon is that he completed Jonathan's work and made the Jews totally independent of the Syrian empire.

In Syria, the confrontation continued between Demetrius II and Tryphon, the guardian of the youthful Antiochus VI. Tryphon, who until now had appeared only as the representative of his young protégé, dropped his mask at about this time, ordered the assassination of Antiochus VI, and set the crown on his own head.[2]

Following Tryphon's hostile behaviour, Simon naturally attached himself once more to Demetrius. But the price he demanded was Demetrius's recognition of Jewish freedom. Whilst proceeding assidu-

1. The year of Jonathan's death is not mentioned in 1 Maccabees (which gives no dates between 11:19 and 13:41). According to 13:41 and 14:27, the years of Simon's rule were reckoned from the Seleucid year 170=143/2 or 142/1 B.C. 1 Mac. 13:22 asserts that Jonathan died in the winter. This will be 143/2 or 142/1 B.C., probably the former in view of Josephus's statement that Simon reigned for eight years, *Ant.* xiii 7, 4 (228), so from 142 to 135 or 134 B.C. (the Seleucid year 177, 1 Mac. 16:14). The statement in *Ant.* xiii 6, 5 (212) that Jonathan was High Priest for four years is erroneous. Equally mistaken is the reference to seven years in *Ant.* xx 10, 3 (238).

2. 1 Mac. 13:31–2; Jos. *Ant.* xiii 7, 1 (218–22); Diodorus xxxiii 28; Livy *Epit.* 55; Appian *Syr.* 68/357; Justin xxxvi 1, 7. The murder was committed by surgeons. Cf. Livy, 'Alexandri filius, rex Syriae, decem annos admodum habens, a Diodoto, qui Tryphon cognominabatur, tutore suo, per fraudem occisus est

ously to build Judaea's fortresses, he sent an embassy to Demetrius 'to secure for his country exemption from tribute'. As Demetrius in fact no longer possessed control over the south of the empire, it was in his interest to play a magnanimous role and grant the Jews all their requests. He therefore consented not only to a remission of their tax arrears, but also to a complete exemption from future tribute.[3] With this, the political independence of Judaea was acknowledged. 'The yoke of the Gentile', as 1 Maccabees expresses it, 'was taken from Israel'. In recognition of the fact, the Jews began in the Seleucid year 170 = 143/2 B.C. to employ their own chronology. Documents and treaties were dated according to the years of Simon, High Priest and Prince of the Jews.[4]

It was once usual to combine this statement from 1 Maccabees with numismatic data, and to ascribe Jewish shekels and half-shekels dated from Year 1 to Year 5 to the time of Simon. But today it is clear that the shekels, half-shekels and quarter-shekels in question were struck during the First War against Rome (A.D. 66–70).[5] The recent excavations at Masada produced three groups of such silver coins of the Years 1 to 5, in an archaeological context which is indubitably that of the First Revolt.[6] On the other hand, the exploration of Simon's fortress at Beth-Zur revealed none of these.[7] It is to be recognised, therefore, that Simon did not issue coins at all: the grant made by Antiochus

---

corruptis medicis, qui illum calculi dolore consumi ad populum mentiti, dum secant, occiderunt'. Josephus reads, *τὸν μὲν ὡς χειριζόμενος ἀποθάνοι διήγγειλεν*. Josephus and the non-Jewish sources place the murder of Antiochus a little later, after the capture of Demetrius II by the Parthians. 1 Mac. mentions it in the above context, still prior to Demetrius's campaign against the Parthians. The coins, in particular, support this version. Cf. on this difference, p. 131 above.

3. Graetz, *Geschichte der Juden* III ([5]1905–6), p. 52; Derenbourg, *op. cit.*, p. 69 and Abel, *in loc.* refer to Megillath Taanith § 6. According to this document, 27 Iyyar (= May) was the day when the crown-tax (כליליא) was abolished in Judaea and Jerusalem. Cf. Lichtenstein, HUCA 8–9 (1931–2), p. 286.

4. 1 Mac. 13:33–42; cf. 14:27; Jos. *Ant.* xiii 6, 6 (214). Justin, in his extract from Pompeius Trogus, dates the freedom of the Jews from the time of Demetrius I. He says of Antiochus VII Sidetes, xxxvi 1, 10, 'Iudaeos quoque, qui a Macedonico imperio sub Demetrio patre armis se in libertatem vindicaverant, subigit'. Cf. xxxvi 3, 9, 'A Demetrio cum descivissent, amicitia Romanorum petita primi omnium ex Orientalibus libertatem acceperunt, facile tunc Romanis de alieno largientibus'. The relevant statement in 1 Mac. 13:42 reads, *καὶ ἤρξατο ὁ λαὸς γράφειν ἐν ταῖς συγγραφαῖς καὶ συναλλάγμασιν· Ἔτους πρώτου ἐπὶ Σίμωνος ἀρχιερέως μεγάλου καὶ στρατηγοῦ καὶ ἡγουμένου Ἰουδαίων.*

5. For the latest discussions of the issue, cf. B. Kanael, 'Altjüdische Münzen', Jahrb. f. Numism. u. Geldgesch. 17 (1967), pp. 165–7; Y. Meshorer, *Jewish Coins of the Second Temple Period* (1967), pp. 41–2; A. Ben-David, PEQ 104 (1972), pp. 93–103.

6. See Y. Yadin, IEJ 15 (1965), pp. 80–1; *Masada* (1966), pp. 108–9.

7. For Beth-Zur see O. R. Sellers, *The Citadel of Beth-Zur* (1933); cf. p. 161 above.

(1 Mac. 15:6) was, if historical, evidently withdrawn as soon as he was in a strong enough position to do so. The date of the origin of Hasmonaean coinage remains controversial (see below and App. IV), but it can be taken as certain that it was later than the period of Simon.

The charter of Demetrius conferred privileges which, in reality, he was in no position to grant. In the face of Tryphon's more dangerous power, Simon made it his business to give them substance. To consolidate his position, he sought above all to seize two important fortified places, the town of Gazara and the fortress in Jerusalem, in both cases with success. Gazara, the ancient Gezer, not far from Emmaus-Nicopolis in a westerly direction, at the foot of the mountains, had been until then a Gentile city. Its possession was of importance to the Jews because it was one of the places which dominated the mountain passes and, in consequence, communications between Jerusalem and the port of Joppa annexed by the Jews. Simon besieged the city skilfully, conquered it, expelled its Gentile inhabitants, and replaced them by 'men who observed the law'.[8] His son John was appointed governor.[9]

8. 1 Mac. 13:43–8; cf. 14:34; Jos. *Ant.* xiii 6, 7 (215); Strabo xvi 2, 29 (759) ἐν δὲ τῷ μεταξὺ καὶ ἡ Γαδαρὶς ἔστιν, ἣν καὶ αὐτὴν ἐξιδιάσαντο οἱ Ἰουδαῖοι (Strabo's Gadaris is identical with Gazara). The manuscripts of 1 Mac. 13:73 all have *Γάζαν*. That *Γάζαρα* should be read instead, is proved not only by the parallel text of Josephus, but also by the text of 1 Mac. in the parallel passages (1 Mac. 13:53; 14:7, 34; 15:28, 35; 16:1; 19:21). It is the Gezer of the Old Testament, an important Canaanite town, concerning which Eusebius remarks, *Onomast.* ed. Klostermann, p. 66, καὶ νῦν καλεῖται Γαζάρα κώμη Νικοπόλεως ἀπέχουσα σημείοις δ' ἐν βορείοις. This information has been corroborated by later research. For Tel Jazer, discovered by Clermont-Ganneau in 1873, lies four Roman miles from Emmaus-Nicopolis, though more in a westerly than a northern direction. The data given in the Old Testament and 1 Maccabees accord with this site, in particular 1 Mac. 4:15, but also 1 Mac. 7:45 (a day's journey from Adasa) and 1 Mac. 14:34 (τὴν Γαζάραν τὴν ἐπὶ τῶν ὁρίων Ἀζώτου), that the territory of Gazara bordered on that of Ashdod is very possible, considering the great spread of these city territories). Finally, several inscriptions bearing the name of גזר were discovered in the neighbourhood, probably indicating the town's Sabbath boundaries. (1) Clermont-Ganneau discovered in 1874 two Hebrew-Greek inscriptions תחם גזר/Ἀλκίου, and one in Hebrew alone, all three close together, approximately 800 metres east of Tel-Jazer (the reading of the Hebrew inscription is uncertain). (2) In 1881 Clermont-Ganneau found a third Hebrew-Greek inscription not far from the others. (3) In 1898 Lagrange came across a fourth Hebrew-Greek inscription, with the same wording as the others, but at approximately the same distance south of Tel-Jazer as the others were east of it. A fifth was published by Macalister, *The Excavation of Gezer* I (1912), pp. 33–41, and a sixth by W. R. Taylor, BASOR 41 (1931), pp. 28 f.; see Frey, CIJ II no. 1183. תחם גזר can only mean, 'boundary of Gezer'; Ἄλκιος (possibly a Hellenistic form of Helkias) is perhaps the name of the official who ordered the inscription. Cf. Clermont-Ganneau, CRAI, 1874, pp. 201, 213 f.; PEFQSt (1873), pp. 78 f.; (1874), pp. 56, 276 ff.; (1875), pp. 5 ,74 ff. *Archaeological Researches in Palestine* II (1896), pp. 224–75. Cf. Abel, *Géog. Pal.* II, pp. 332–3.

9. 1 Mac. 13:53; 16:1; 19:21.

Soon after the conquest of Gazara, Simon also forced the Syrian garrison of the fortress in Jerusalem to capitulate through famine. The nationalist aspirations of the Maccabees had long been directed towards this aim, for whilst the fortress was in the hands of the Syrian kings, the Jews remained subject to them. Simon now succeeded in conquering this bulwark also. On the 23rd day of the second month of the Seleucid year 171 = early June 141 B.C., he entered the fortress with great pomp and ceremony.[10]

As the Syrian kings were unable to pay much attention to events in Judaea, the next few years were ones of undisturbed prosperity and peace for the Jews. The period of Simon's rule is on the whole characterized as such a time in 1 Maccabees. His chief merits are represented there as having been the acquisition of Joppa as a port, and the conquest of Gazara, Beth-Zur and the fortress in Jerusalem.[11] There is also particular praise for his care for the spiritual and material well-being of the country, for his strict administration of justice, and for his implementation of Jewish law. 'They farmed their land in peace, the land gave its produce, the trees of the plain their fruit. The elders sat at ease in the streets, all their talk was of their prosperity; the young men wore finery and armour. He kept the towns supplied with provisions and furnished them with fortifications, so that his fame resounded to the ends of the earth. He established peace in the land, and Israel knew

10. 1 Mac. 13:14–52; cf. 14:7, 36–7; Jos. *Ant.* xiii 6, 7 (215–17). The date of 23 Iyyar (the second month) is given not only in 1 Mac. 13:51, but also in Megillath Taanith § 5. Cf. Graetz, *Gesch. der Juden* III ([5]1905–6), p. 54; Derenbourg, *op. cit.*, p. 67; Abel, *in loc.*; Lichtenstein, HUCA 8–9 (1931–2), pp. 286–7. 'On 23 Iyyar the occupants of Akra left Jerusalem', נפקו בני חקרא מירושלם. If the conjecture is correct that 1 Mac. follows here the Babylonian Seleucid era, i.e. that the year begins in the spring (Nisan), then Iyyar 171 = May–June 141 B.C. To the story of the conquest of the fortress, Josephus, *Ant.* xiii 6, 7 (217), cf. *B.J.* V 4, 1 (139), is joined the remarkable statement that not only the fortress was destroyed; the entire hill on which it stood was levelled by the people during three years of uninterrupted labour, so that the site of the Temple should be higher than that where the earlier fortress once was. As 1 Mac. says nothing of this, but on the contrary asserts that Simon fortified the place and installed a Jewish garrison, 1 Mac. 14:36–7, cf. also 15:28, the levelling cannot have taken place in this time. In the parallel account of *B.J.* v 4, 1 (139), it is also only generally referred to as the work of the Hasmonaeans. In this form, the statement has more chance of being correct, for the south-easterly hill is now in fact almost level, whereas *if* it was the site of the Akra, one would expect a different configuration. Certainly unhistorical, therefore, is only the assertion by Josephus in *Ant.* xiii 6, 7 (217) that the levelling occurred under Simon. This, according to 1 Mac. 14:36–7 and 15:28 is not possible. But cf. on this whole question the literature cited above pp. 154–5.

11. 1 Mac. 14:33–7. Cf. also the theme of the ode in 1 Mac. 14:4–15. Both passages summarise events recounted previously in the narrative of 1 Mac. Cf. on Beth-Zur, 1 Mac. 11:65 f.; on Joppa, 1 Mac. 12:33 f., 13:11; on Gazara and the citadel, 13:43–52.

great joy. Each man sat under his own vine and his own fig tree, and there was no one to make them afraid. No enemy was left in the land to fight them, and the kings in those days were crushed. He gave strength to all the humble among his people and did away with every lawless and wicked man. He observed the Law, and gave new splendour to the Temple, replenishing it with sacred vessels.'[12]

These words from 1 Maccabees express the feeling of satisfaction experienced by the majority of the people under Simon's rule. The final object of Maccabaean aspiration was attained. Government was in the hands of the national party, and the country was independent of Syrian hegemony. So now Simon also reaped the last fruit of their common labours: the formal legitimization of his family by the people as the ruling High-Priestly family. The sons of Mattathias had obtained power by an act of usurpation. Until the outbreak of the Maccabaean revolt, the office of High Priest had been hereditary in another family. In the course of events, that family had been displaced. The Maccabee brothers had taken over the leadership of the nationalist party and the Syrian kings had conferred upon them High-Priestly rank. It was of the greatest importance to the continuance of Simon's rule that the legitimacy of his government for himself and his descendants should be expressly recognised by a popular decree. Such an act was passed in the third year of Simon's rule. On 18 Elul of the Seleucid year 172 = September 140 B.C., it was resolved in a great assembly of 'the priests and the people and the princes of the people and the elders of the land', that Simon should be High Priest, military commander and ethnarch of the Jews (*ἀρχιερεύς, στρατηγός* and *ἐθνάρχης*), and that he should be 'their leader and High Priest for ever until a trustworthy prophet should arise' (1 Mac. 14:41).[13] The implication of this formula was that the people's decree was to remain valid until God decreed otherwise. Until then, Simon's dignities were to be 'for ever', i.e., hereditary.

12. 1 Mac. 14:8–15. On the severe measures taken by Simon against apostates, see Derenbourg, *op. cit.*, pp. 68 f., who refers to Megillath Taanith § 15. 'On 22 Elul we came back to kill the wicked', תבנא לקטלא רשיעיא. Cf. Lichtenstein, HUCA 8–9 (1931–2), pp. 305–6.

13. See in general 1 Mac. 14:25–49. The content of the decree (14:41–6) is made dependent on a *ὅτι* in 14:41 from the preceding *ἠκούσθη* in 14:40. Commentators have normally taken the view that the *ὅτι* should be eliminated; but see Abel, *ad loc*. Simon's full title is a triple one, as may be seen from the following essentially similar passages: 1 Mac. 13:42 *ἐπὶ Σίμωνος ἀρχιερέως μεγάλου καὶ στρατηγοῦ καὶ ἡγουμένου Ἰουδαίων*. 1 Mac. 14:41–2; *τοῦ εἶναι αὐτῶν Σίμωνα ἡγούμενον καὶ ἀρχιερέα . . . καὶ τοῦ εἶναι ἐπ' αὐτῶν στρατηγόν*. 1 Mac. 14:47; *ἀρχιερατεύειν καὶ εἶναι στρατηγὸς καὶ ἐθνάρχης τῶν Ἰουδαίων καὶ ἱερέων*. A little less complete is 1 Mac. 15:1; *ἱερεῖ καὶ ἐθνάρχῃ τῶν Ἰουδαίων*; 15:2, *ἱερεῖ μεγάλῳ καὶ ἐθνάρχῃ*. Also in 1 Mac. 14:27 *ἐπὶ Σίμωνος ἀρχιερέως ἐνσαραμελ*. The mysterious words *ἐνσαραμελ* or *ἐνασαραμελ* have been interpreted as part of the titulature; see

Thus was founded a new High-Priestly and princely dynasty, that of the Hasmonaeans.[14] The terms of the decree were engraved on bronze tablets which were displayed in the Temple.[15]

Legitimization by the people was soon followed by recognition by the Romans. At about the time of the popular decree, Simon sent a delegation to Rome under the leadership of Numenius. These men handed over the gift of a gold shield weighing one thousand *minae* and requested the renewal of the alliance. The embassy was courteously received by the Senate, and obtained a *senatus consultum* guaranteeing to the Jews undisputed possession of their territory. According to 1 Mac. 15:16–24, the kings of Egypt, Syria, Pergamum, Cappadocia and Parthia, and of several independent smaller states and communes in Greece and Asia Minor, were informed of this, and at the same time instructed to surrender to the Jewish High Priest any evil-doers who had fled to them from Palestine. But the authenticity of the last clause, and of the letter of 'Lucius, consul of the Romans', to Ptolemy

---

Derenbourg, *op. cit.*, pp. 450–1. σαραμελ, presumably חצר עם אל = ἐθνάρχης. But the εν preceding it remains a puzzle. Possibly σεγεν = סגן stood here originally, corresponding to the Greek στρατηγός (cf. vol. II, § 24, 3). See R. H. Charles, *Apocr.* I, p. 119. Abel, *in loc.*, sees in the phrase a geographical expression חצר עם אל 'Courtyard of the People of God'. For a full discussion, see now Schalit, *op. cit.*, Anhang XIV, although his own theory, εν ασαραμελ = ἐν ασαρᾷ (= עזרה) μεγάλῃ, 'in the great Temple courtyard', seems far fetched.

14. The family name of the dynasty is οἱ Ἀσαμωναίου παῖδες, Jos. *Vita* 1 (2, 4); *Ant.* xx 8, 11 (190), xx 10, 3 (247) τὸ Ἀσαμωναίων γένος, *Ant.* xv 11, 4 (403), οἱ Ἀσαμωναῖοι, *B.J.* ii 16, 3 (344); v 4, 1 (139), after the ancestor Ἀσαμωναῖος, mentioned in 1 Mac., *Ant.* xii 6, 1 (265); xiv 16, 4 (490–1); xvi 7, 1 (187). In mMid. 1:6 they are בני חשמונאי or בני חשמוני (the latter form in the Cambridge manuscript, edited by Lowe); in the Targum to 1 Sam. 2:4, בית חשמונאי; for other rabbinic passages see Levy, *Chald. Wörterb.* and *Neuhebr. Wörterb.*, and Jastrow, *Dictionary*, s.v. חשמונאי—Wellhausen, *Pharisäer und Sadducäer*, p. 94 (n.) suggested that Hasmon was the grandfather of Mattathias, and that in 1 Mac. 2:1 Ben Ḥashmon stood in place of τοῦ Συμεών.

15. 1 Mac. 14:27, 48–9. The text of the document given in 1 Maccabees 14:27–45 is represented as an ἀντίγραφον of the authentic text (14:27). Nevertheless, the remark in 14:38–40 is to be noted, namely that Demetrius confirmed Simon in the office of High Priest because he heard that the Romans had received his delegation honourably. Demetrius's charter for the Jews, 1 Mac. 13:36–40, cf. above p. 190, is probably to be dated some years before Simon's embassy to the Romans, which may not (see below) have set off until around the time of the decree, and returned still later. Therefore, if the facts in the rest of the narrative of 1 Mac. are correct, the circumstance stated cannot be right, and in consequence the wording of the people's decree cannot be authentic in all its details. It would then be a free rendering, rather than a diplomatically exact duplicate. However, the assumption that it was merely inserted by a later interpolator, see e.g. Willrich, *Juden und Griechen*, p. 69 f., cf. *Urkundenfälschung*, p. 42, appears to be without foundation.

(VIII Euergetes) quoted in 15:16–21, is very dubious.[16] The terms of the senate's resolution are probably reproduced in the *senatus consultum* given by Josephus, *Ant.* xiv 8, 5 (145–8), and assigned by him to the time of Hyrcanus II. The circumstances described in this document are precisely the same as those of 1 Mac. 14:24 and 15:15–24: Jewish ambassadors, one of them named Numenius, took with them a gift of a gold shield and requested a renewal of the alliance, and the senate, as a result of this, resolved to instruct the autonomous cities and kings to respect the integrity of Jewish territory. According to Josephus, the relevant session of Senate took place *εἰδοῖς Δεκεμβρίαις* = 13 December, under the presidency of *Λεύκιος Οὐαλέριος Λευκίου υἱὸς στρατηγός* (i.e. praetor). He is possibly identical with the *Λεύκιος ὕπατος Ῥωμαίων* (i.e. consul) who according to 1 Mac. 15:16 despatched the circular letter to the kings and cities. It was previously thought that Calpurnius Piso, consul of 139 B.C., had the *praenomen* 'Lucius' (see Val. Max. I 3, 2)[17]; but the Oxyrhynchus papyrus text of Livy, *Per.* liv, and the

[*Text continues on page* 197

16. Cf. in general, 1 Mac. 14:24, 15:15–24. 1 Mac. 14:16–18 seems to imply that the Romans had already, of their own accord, addressed a letter to the Jews concerning the renewal of the alliance (though only the letter from Sparta is actually given, 14:20–3). This is scarcely historical. From 1 Mac. 14:24, cf. 14:40, it should be assumed that the embassy left before the decree of 18 Elul of the Seleucid year 172 = September 140 B.C. It did not return, however, before the Seleucid year 174 = 139–8 or 138–7 B.C. (1 Mac. 15:10, 15). Perhaps the author inserted the report of the departure of the embassy before that of the people's decree because he was misled by an error in the transmitted text of the decree (1 Mac. 14:40) into thinking that it occurred previously. It should furthermore be noted that the list of states to which the Roman circular letter was addressed (1 Mac. 15:16, 22–3) corresponds exactly to the circumstances prevailing at that time. For almost all the minor states and cities mentioned with the kings of Egypt, Syria, Pergamum, Cappadocia and Parthia were at that time in fact not subject, either to the Romans, or to any of these kings. Cf. Marquardt, *Römische Staatsverwaltung* I ([2]1881), pp. 333 ff.; Mommsen, *Römisches Staatsrecht* III, 1 ([3]1887), pp. 670 ff. Willrich, *Judaica*, p. 76, cf. *Urkundenfälschung*, p. 58 f., raised two objections against this list: (a) Demetrius of Syria, to whom the letter was also addressed, according to 1 Mac. 15:22, was by then a prisoner of the Parthians; (b) Cyprus and Cyrene, mentioned with the king of Egypt, belonged to Egypt at that time. The first point cannot be substantiated however (cf. pp. 130–1 above), and there is nothing remarkable about the second, since the Romans could certainly write separately to the Egyptian governors of Cyprus and Cyrene. Cf. G. F. Unger, *loc. cit.*, and now de Sanctis, *Storia dei Romani* IV, 3 (1964), p. 195, n. 77.

17. Thus F. Ritschl, 'Römische Senatusconsulte bei Josephus', Rhein. Mus. 29 (1874), pp. 337 ff.; 30 (1875), pp. 428 ff. Cf. also Abel, *in loc.* The identity of the *senatus consultum* in *Ant.* xiv 8, 5 (144–8) with that in response to Simon's embassy was assumed by H. Ewald, *Gesch. des Volkes Israel* [3]IV, p. 438, and W. Grimm, *Exeget. Handb. zu 1 Makk.*, p. 226 f. Independently of them, Mendelssohn came to the same conclusion and substantiated it in more detail. Through his enquiries into this question and others connected with it, a whole body of literature emerged in the late nineteenth century. L. Mendelssohn, 'Senati consulta Romanorum

quae sunt in Josephi Antiquitatibus', Act. Soc. Philol. Lips. 5 (1875), pp. 87–288; D. Ritschl, 'Eine Berichtigung der republikanischen Consularfasten', Rhein. Mus. 28 (1873), pp. 586–614; Grimm, 'Ueber I Makk. 8 und 15:16–21 nach Mommsen's und Ritschl's Forschungen', ZWTh (1874), pp. 231–8; Mommsen, 'Der Senatsbeschluss Josephus Ant. XIV, 8, 5', Hermes 9 (1875), pp. 281–91; K. Wieseler, ThStKr (1875), pp. 524 ff.; W. Judeich, *Cäsar im Orient* (1885), pp. 129–36; P. Viereck, *Sermo Graecus, quo senatus populusque Romanus* etc. *usi sunt* (1888), pp. 103–6; Unger, SAM, 1895, pp. 553–75; Willrich, *Juden und Griechen* (1895), pp. 71 f., cf. *Urkundenfälschung*, p. 60 f. After giving the text of the *senatus consultum*, Josephus remarks in *Ant.* xiv 8, 5 (148) *ταῦτα ἐγένετο ἐπὶ Ὑρκανοῦ ἀρχιερέως καὶ ἐθνάρχου ἔτους ἐνάτου μηνὸς Πανέμου.* By this he means Hyrcanus II. It was on the strength of this that Mommsen, and after him Judeich, dated the *senatus consultum* to 47 B.C., when Caesar was settling affairs in Syria; and Willrich wrote that he was sure that Mommsen had proved irrefutably that the document belonged to the period of Hyrcanus II. In fact, Mommsen's view is untenable because 47 B.C. was not the ninth year of Hyrcanus II, either as *ἀρχιερεύς* or as *ἐθνάρχης*. He had been High Priest since 63 B.C., and only became ethnarch through Caesar. (Mommsen's dating from the decrees of Gabinius onward is impossible, for nothing was given to Hyrcanus through Gabinius, but all his political power was taken away, see Mendelssohn, Rhein. Mus. 30 (1875), pp. 424 f.; 32 (1877), p. 256. Furthermore, the security of their 'harbours' could not be guaranteed to the Jews in 47 B.C., as happens in the *S.C.*, because since Pompey they no longer possessed any (it was only after 47 B.C. that they reacquired Joppa through Caesar's favour). Far more weight, therefore, is to be given to the opinion of Scaliger and earlier scholars, which was supported by Viereck and Unger, that the ninth year of Hyrcanus I is meant. Cf. Marcus, *ad loc.* (Loeb text), supporting attribution to Hyrcanus I but suggesting that the date applies to the following document, from Athens. The similarity of circumstances in 1 Mac. 15:16–21 and Jos. *Ant.* xiv 8, 5 (145–8) is so noticeable that the probability of identity cannot be denied. The question should therefore be whether, in respect to the dating, 1 Mac. is to be preferred, which mentions Simon's name in the document itself (15:17), or Josephus. But if this is so, the authority of the latter seems too weak to supplant that of the former. It is also an argument in favour of the era of Simon that the *senatus consultum* which belongs to the early period of Hyrcanus, *Ant.* xiii 9, 2 (260–4), probably refers back to this *S.C.* Against its dating to 139 B.C., Mommsen raised the point as a decisive objection that the relevant session of the senate took place, according to Josephus, in the temple of Concordia (*ἐν τῷ τῆς Ὁμονοίας ναῷ*), whereas this temple, in which sessions of the senate were later held, was not constructed until 121 B.C. But Mommsen himself mentioned another temple of Concordia, built in 366 B.C. by M. Furius Camillus (Plutarch, *Cam.* 42) and restored in 121 B.C. and under Augustus (Ovid. *Fasti* I, 639–48; see Frazer's commentary *ad loc.* and Platner and Ashby, *Topographical Dictionary of Ancient Rome*, pp. 138–40) and Ritschl argued that it was very suitable for a session of the senate, Rhein. Mus. 30 (1875), pp. 428–32. Cf. also Excursus III in Abel, *op. cit.*, pp. 275–6. For doubts about the fourth-century temple of Concordia see K. Latte, *Römische Religionsgeschichte* (1960), p. 237, n. 8. But Livy xxvi 23, 4, mentions it under 211 B.C.

For further discussion of the authenticity and dating of both documents see e.g. Ginsburg, *op. cit.*, pp. 59–64; Momigliano, *Prime Linee*, pp. 151–7; T. Fischer, *Untersuchungen zum Partherkrieg Antiochos VII* (1970), pp. 97–101; A. Giovannini, H. Müller, 'Die Beziehungen zw. Rom und den Juden im 2 Jh. v. Chr.', Museum Helveticum 28 (1971), pp. 156–71.

Fasti Antiates (*Ins. Italiae* XIII, 1, p. 161) show that his *praenomen* was Gnaeus. It is not easy to find another Lucius holding an appropriate office in this period, unless it is L. Caecilius Metellus Calvus, the consul of 142 B.C.[18] But the envoys seem to have returned to Palestine in the Seleucid year 174 = 139–8 or 138–7 B.C. (1 Mac. 15:10 and 15). However, L. Valerius Flaccus, consul in 131 B.C., may have been praetor about this time. The presence of the envoys has often been hypothetically linked with the beginnings of Jewish propaganda in Rome in 139 B.C., known from a report by Valerius Maximus.[19]

Meanwhile, the government of Simon was not destined to progress as peacefully as it had done hitherto. He, too, became involved once more in Syrian affairs. At about this time, Demetrius II disappeared temporarily from the scene. He had allowed himself to become embroiled in a protracted war with Mithridates I, king of the Parthians, which ended with his capture by the Parthians in 140/39 B.C.[20] In place of Demetrius, his brother Antiochus VII Sidetes now took over the struggle against Tryphon. Like all the Syrian pretenders, who had first to conquer their thrones, Antiochus hastened also to heap favours on the Jews. He had heard in Rhodes of the capture of Demetrius. Before landing on the Syro-Phoenician coast ('from the islands of the sea'),[21] he sent a letter to Simon confirming all the privileges conferred on him by former kings, and granting him, in particular, the right to mint his own coinage.[22] Soon afterwards, still in the Seleucid year 174 = 139–8 (or 138–7) B.C. (1 Mac. 15:10), Antiochus landed in Syria and

18. See Broughton MRR I, pp. 474 and 476, n. 1. In this case, it would have to be accepted that there is a basic chronological confusion in the narrative. This would, however, remove one difficulty: the reference to Roman favour to Simon in 1 Mac. 14:38–40, see n. 15 above.

19. Valerius Maximus I, 3, 2, 'Idem'—the praetor, Cn. Cornelius Scipio Hispanus (for the correct form of the name see Broughton, MRR I, p. 482)—'Iudaeos, qui Sabazi Iovis cultu Romanos inficere mores conati erant, repetere domos suas coegit'. Cf. vol. III, § 31, 1. The Jewish proselytizers expelled by the praetor cannot, of course, have been the envoys themselves, but probably members of their retinue.

20. 1 Mac. 14:1–3; Jos. *Ant.* xiii 5, 11 (184–6); Appian, *Syr.* 67/356; Justin xxxvi 1, 1–6; xxxviii 9, 2; Euseb. *Chron.*, ed. Schoene I, pp. 255 f.; Syncellus, ed. Dindorf I, p. 554. On the chronology, see above p. 130. Almost all sources refer to the king of the Parthians as Arsaces, the name, according to Strabo xv 1, 36 (702) and Justin xli 5, 6, common to all the Parthian kings. According to Justin xxxviii 9, 2–10, however, Demetrius was taken prisoner by the predecessor of the Phraates who later set him at liberty. But the predecessor of Phraates was Mithidrates. Cf., in general, J. Neusner, *A History of the Jews in Babylonia* I (1965), pp. 20–5.

21. 1 Mac. 15:1–9: ἀπὸ τῶν νήσων τῆς θαλάσσης is explained by Appian, *Syr.* 68/358: πυθόμενος ἐν Ῥόδῳ περὶ τῆς αἰχμαλωσίας.

22. 1 Mac. 15:10–14; Jos. *Ant.* xiii 7, 1–2. On the coins erroneously attributed to Simon, see above, pp. 190–1. On Dora see vol. ii, § 21, 1.

quickly gained the upper hand over Tryphon, who was forced to withdraw to Dora, the powerful fortress on the Phoenician coast. There Antiochus besieged him. Tryphon managed to escape and fled to Apamea by way of Ptolemais[23] and Orthosias.[24] But here he was besieged once more and in the fighting lost his life.[25]

As soon as Antiochus had obtained a few successes over Tryphon, he adopted a different attitude towards the Jews. During the siege of Dora, Simon sent him two thousand auxiliary troops together with silver, gold and weapons. Antiochus, however, rejected the offerings, revoked all his earlier concessions, and sent one of his friends, Athenobius, to Jerusalem to demand from Simon the surrender of the conquered towns of Joppa, Gazara and the fortress in Jerusalem, as well as all the places outside Judaea possessed by the Jews. If he were unwilling to return them, he was to pay the sum of one thousand talents for them (as a single sum of indemnity). The demands were definitely justified, for the Jews could make no valid claim to their conquest. But Simon refused to comply; he declared that he was ready to pay only one hundred talents. With this answer Athenobius returned to the king.[26]

Antiochus was resolved to enforce his demands. While he himself was still dealing with Tryphon, he handed over the campaign against Simon to his general Cendebaeus. Cendebaeus set up his headquarters at Jamnia, fortified Cedron (probably modern Katra near Jamnia), and launched assaults on Judaea.[27] Simon was prevented by age from personally taking to the field once more. He therefore sent his sons Judas and John with an army against Cendebaeus. Both of them justified the confidence placed in them by their father. In a decisive engagement Cendebaeus was completely routed. As Judas was wounded,

23. Charax in Steph. Byz., s.v. *Δῶρος* = Jacoby, FGrH 103 F 29.

24. 1 Mac. 15:37. Orthosias lies north of Tripoli on the Phoenician coast. See RE s.v. 'Orthosia' (3).

25. Jos. *Ant.* xiii 7, 2 (224). Cf. also Appian, *Syr.* 68/358, and Strabo xiv 5, 2 (668).

26. 1 Mac. 15:25–36; Jos. *Ant.* xiii 7, 2–3 (223–5). The sum of one thousand talents asked for can only have been intended as a single payment of indemnity. Withdrawal from individual towns in exchange for large sums of money happened also elsewhere (cf. the inscription of Eshmunazar on the transfer of Joppa and Dora to the Sidonians, vol. II, § 23 i, 7, 10). A permanent tribute of thousand talents for a few towns would have been beyond all proportion, considering that later, for instance, the entire territory of Archelaus, which was far more extensive than that of Simon, yielded only six hundred talents a year, *Ant.* xvii 11, 4 (320).

27. 1 Mac. 15:38–41; Jos. *Ant.* xiii 7, 3 (225). On Cedron, see Abel, *Géog. Pal.* II, p. 296. *Κενδεβαῖος* is, perhaps equivalent to *Κανδυβεύς*, a name taken from the town of *Κάνδυβα* in Lycia, Steph. Byz. s.v.; Pliny *NH* v 28/101. Cf. RE s.v. 'Kandyba'.

John took over the pursuit of the enemy as far as Cedron and the territory of Ashdod. He returned to Jerusalem as conqueror.[28]

While Simon lived, the attack by Antiochus was not repeated.

It seemed therefore that Simon was destined to spend his last days in peace. But this was not to be so. Like all his brothers he, too, died a violent death. His own son-in-law, Ptolemy, who was *strategos* over the plain of Jericho, had ambitious plans. He wished to seize power for himself and plotted to rid himself of Simon and his sons by cunning. He therefore gave a great banquet when Simon, who was on a tour of inspection through the cities of the land in the month of Shebat of the Seleucid year 177 = February 135 or 134 B.C. (1 Mac. 16:14), visited him in the fortress of Dok near Jericho.[29] And in the course of it, he caused Simon and his two sons Mattathias and Judas, who were all drunk, to be assassinated.[30]

28. 1 Mac. 16:1–10; Jos. *loc. cit.*

29. 1 Mac. 16:11–17; Jos. *Ant.* xiii 7, 4 (228). The Δώκ of 1 Mac. 16:15 is identical with the Δαγών of Jos. *Ant.* xiii 8, 1 (230); *B.J.* i 2, 3 (56). The name is still preserved in that of the spring Ain Duk, north of Jericho, on the fringe of the mountains, at a place eminently suitable for the site of a fortress. See Abel, *Géog. Pal.* II, p. 307. As elsewhere, the dating by the Seleucid year 177 in 1 Mac. 16:14 is ambiguous as between 135 and 134 B.C. The latter would be supported by the reference to Simon's eight-year rule in *Ant.* xiii 7, 4 (228).

30. For the identification of Simon as the 'Wicked Priest' in the Qumran scrolls, or one of the two 'Wicked Priests'—the other being Jonathan—see the works by Vermes, Cross and de Vaux quoted on p. 188, n. 42 above.

§ 8 John Hyrcanus I 135/4–104 B.C.[1]

Sources

I Maccabees 16:23–4 (but the annals mentioned there have not been preserved).
Josephus *Ant.* xiii 8–10 (230–300); *B.J.* i 2, 3–8 (55–69).
Mishnah Ma'aser Sheni 5:15; Soṭah 9:10. Cf. also Derenbourg, *op. cit.*, pp. 70–82; S. Lieberman, *Hellenism in Jewish Palestine* (1950), pp. 139–43.

On the disputed question of whether any coinage is to be attributed to the reign of Hyrcanus I see below pp. 210-11.

Bibliography

Graetz, H., *Geschichte der Juden* III (⁵1905–6), pp. 79–116.
Derenbourg, J., *Essai sur l'histoire et la géographie de la Palestine* (1867), pp. 70–82.
Otto, W., 'Hyrkanos' RE IX, cols. 527–34.
Bickermann, E., 'Ein jüdischer Festbrief vom Jahre 124 v. Chr. (II Macc. i 1–9)', ZNW 32 (1933), pp. 233–54.
Abel, F.-M., *Histoire de la Palestine* I (1952), pp. 206–23.
Stern, M., 'The Relations between Judaea and Rome during the Rule of John Hyrcanus', Zion 26 (1961), pp. 1–22 (in Hebrew with Engl. summary).

As Simon's titles of High Priest and Prince had been declared hereditary, his third surviving son, John Hyrcanus, governor of

1. On the chronology of the Hasmonaeans, cf. Niese, Hermes 28 (1893), pp. 216–28; Unger, SMA (1896), pp. 357–82. Josephus gives the regnal periods of the rulers from John Hyrcanus I to Alexandra inclusive as follows:

John Hyrcanus	31 years, *Ant.* xiii 10, 7 (299).
Aristobulus I	1 year, *Ant.* xiii 11, 3 (318).
Alexander Jannaeus . .	27 years, *Ant.* xiii 15, 5 (404).
Alexandra	9 years, *Ant.* xiii 16, 6 (430).

The same figures are given by Josephus in two other passages: *Ant.* xx 10, 3–4 (240–2) and *B.J.* i 2, 8 (68), 3, 6 (84), 4, 8 (106), 5, 4 (119). The only difference is to be found in *B.J.* i 2, 8 (68), where the MSS give the length of Hyrcanus's reign as 33 years. But this too may be only a slip of the pen, for the Latin version of Hegesippus has *trigesimo et primo anno* (ed. Ussani I, 1, 10). See Niese, *op. cit.*, p. 217, and compare his edition of *B.J.*, Proleg., p. lxii. In any case, 31 is the correct number, for Josephus, if he wrote 33 at all, corrected it in *Antiquities* on the basis of better information.

The following points are well established: (1) the death of Simon in the month Shebat of the Seleucid year 177=February 135 or 134 B.C. (1 Mac. 16:14); (2) the start of the fratricidal war between Aristobulus II and Hyrcanus II immediately after the death of Alexandra, in the third year of the 177th Olympiad according to Josephus *Ant.* xiv 1, 2 (4), under the consuls Q. Hortensius (Hortalus) and Q. (Caecilius) Metellus Creticus, i.e., in 69 B.C. Accordingly, this war started, and Alexandra died, in the first half of 69 B.C. But there are only 66 or 65 years from

Gazara, was his lawful successor.[2] It was therefore against him that

---

135 or 134 B.C. to 69 B.C., whereas addition of the above regnal years results in 68. One possible solution might be that Josephus, in reckoning from the time of accession without regard to the calendar year, always counted the last fraction of the year as a whole one, so in fact a certain fraction of the year should be deducted from every reign. Nevertheless, this does not correspond to the method of reckoning employed by the ancient historians and chronographers, who count full years in such a way that the calendar year during which a change of government has taken place is assigned in its entirety either to the departing ruler, or to the new one (cf. pp. 126–7, the lists of Porphyry and Eusebius). For this reason, Niese *loc. cit.* thought that the regnal years given by Josephus should simply be added, and that accordingly, Alexandra's death took place in 67 B.C. He found confirmation for this in the fact that Alexandra must have survived the departure of Tigranes from Syria (69 B.C.) for some time, and also in that Josephus reckons only 3 years and 9 months altogether for Alexandra's successors, Hyrcanus II and Aristobulus II—Hyrcanus II, 3 months, *Ant.* xv 6, 4 (180); Aristobulus, 3 years 6 months, *Ant.* xiv 6, 1 (97)—this then corresponding to the interval between Alexandra's death and Aristobulus's dismissal by Pompey (67–3 B.C.). These estimates are, of course, contradicted by the information concerning the Olympic and consular year in *Ant.* xiv 1, 2 (4). But this objection must not be regarded as decisive. Josephus is not always accurate in his synchronisations, which he perhaps derives from a chronographic handbook, possibly that of Castor (see above p. 43); he is definitely wrong, for instance, in placing the first year of John Hyrcanus during the 162nd Olympiad = 132–128 B.C. Thus the synchronisation to 69 B.C. also seems to rest on an mistaken combination, perhaps that of identifying Alexandra's death with the defeat of Tigranes by Lucullus in 69 B.C. The chronology of the Hasmonaeans is therefore as follows:

John Hyrcanus	135/4–104 B.C.
Aristobulus.	104–103 B.C.
Alexander Jannaeus . . .	103–76 B.C.
Alexandra	76–67 B.C.

Instead of the calculation of regnal years suggested here, another is admittedly possible. Taking the calendar year as a basis, they could be counted in such a way that the fraction of a calendar year at the beginning and end of a reign is always counted as a full year. Josephus seems to reckon, for example the regnal years of Herod according to this method (see the remarks at the end of § 15). But then, in order to arrive by addition at the correct final figure, one year would have to be subtracted from each reign; and in order to reach the date of 69 B.C. indicated by Josephus it would be necessary to attach the figure of thirty-three years to John Hyrcanus, as in *B.J.* i 2, 8 (28). This was Unger's choice. But the very preference given to *B.J.* is risky. What is more, Unger had to change the 3½ years given for Aristobulus to 6½ years by emending the text in order to rescue all Josephus's statements. This amounts to an admission that the problem cannot be resolved without rejecting one or other of them. Niese's solution therefore seems preferable.

2. Eusebius and others explain the sobriquet 'Hyrcanus' by saying that John conquered the Hyrcanians, Euseb. *Chron.* ed. Schoene II, pp. 130–1; in Greek, in Syncellus, I, p. 548 Ὑρκανοὺς νικήσας Ὑρκανὸς ὠνομάσθη; in Latin in Jerome, *ad. loc.* 'adversum Hyrcanos bellum gerens Hyrcani nomen accepit'; cf. Sulpicius Severus ii, 26, 'qui cum adversum Hyrcanos, gentem validissimam, egregie pugnasset,

the pretender Ptolemy, who had murdered his father and two brothers, directed his next ventures. Immediately after that deed, he sent assassins to Gazara to do away with John, but warned by friendly messengers, John had the murderers killed as soon as they entered the town. Then he hurried to Jerusalem and was fortunate enough to anticipate Ptolemy here too. When the latter arrived, he found the city already in Hyrcanus's power.[3]

Ptolemy then marched to the fortress of Dagon (identical with Dok) in the neighbourhood of Jericho. There Hyrcanus besieged him, and would undoubtedly soon have conquered the town and handed over the murderer to the fate he deserved had he not been impeded by consideration for his mother. She was in Ptolemy's power and whenever Hyrcanus threatened to storm the fortress, Ptolemy ordered her to be brought out onto the walls and threatened to throw her down if Hyrcanus did not desist. This crippled his advance. The siege was prolonged until it finally had to be abandoned on account of the Sabbatical year. Ptolemy was thereby freed, but he nevertheless killed the mother of Hyrcanus, and then fled.[4]

Through Ptolemy, Hyrcanus had thus lost parents and brothers without having succeeded in avenging them.

Worse awaited him, however. For reasons unknown, but presumably because affairs in Syria claimed his attention, Antiochus VII Sidetes had made no further move against Judaea. But it was not his intention to forego the demands made earlier on Simon. He invaded Judaea in the first year of Hyrcanus's reign (135/4 B.C.), devastated the whole country, and finally besieged Hyrcanus in his capital, Jerusalem.[5] He

---

Hyrcani cognomen accepit'. In support of this explanation it can be said that John actually did participate in the campaign of Antiochus VII Sidetes against the Parthians (see below). But it founders on the fact that the name 'Hyrcanus' appears in Jewish circles long before John Hyrcanus, Jos. *Ant.* xii 4, 6–11 (186–236); 2 Mac. 3:11. It is therefore presumably to be explained according to the analogy of Yaddua הבבלי (mB.M. 7:9); Nahum המדי (mShab. 2:1; mNaz. 5:4; mB.B. 5:2). Hyrcania was the place to which Jews were deported, particularly by Artaxerxes Ochus (see vol. III, § 31, 1). A Jew from there who settled in Palestine would at first be called '*ὁ 'Υρκανός*' And in this way, the name became generally adopted. cf. 1Q Gen. Ap. 20:8, 21, 24 where חרקנוש is the name of one of Pharaoh's princes. Cf. J. A. Fitzmyer, *The Genesis Apocryphon of Qumran Cave I* (1966), pp. 111–12.

3. 1 Mac. 16:19–22. Jos. *Ant.* xiii 7, 4 (228–9).

4. Jos. *Ant.* xiii 8, 1 (230–5); *B.J.* i 2, 3–4 (59–60). On the Sabbatical year cf. above p. 19.

5. The sources do not agree in regard to the date. According to Jos. *Ant.* xiii 8, 2 (236), the invasion by Antiochus took place *τετάρτῳ μὲν ἔτει τῆς βασιλείας αὐτοῦ, πρώτῳ δὲ τῆς 'Υρκανοῦ ἀρχῆς, ὀλυμπιάδι ἑκατοστῇ καὶ ἑξηκοστῇ καὶ δευτέρᾳ.* The fourth year of Antiochus and the first of Hyrcanus are both 135/4 B.C.; the 162nd Olympiad, by contrast, is 132–128 B.C. Porphyry gives the

encircled the entire city with a rampart and a ditch, and cut off its supplies. Hyrcanus, for his part, tried to harass the besiegers, and, to make the provisions last longer, sent all those who were incapable of fighting out of the town. But Antiochus would not let them pass through and drove them back again, so they were obliged to wander between the city and its besiegers and many of them died of hunger. It was not till the Feast of Tabernacles that Hyrcanus allowed them in again. He also requested a truce of seven days for this feast, and Antiochus not only complied, but even sent sacrificial gifts to be offered in the Temple. This indulgent behaviour encouraged Hyrcanus and he now hoped that his eventual capitulation would meet with favourable terms. He therefore sent a deputation to Antiochus to enquire about them. After much deliberation a settlement was reached. According to this, the Jews were to surrender their arms, pay tribute for Joppa and the other towns outside Judaea which they had conquered, give hostages, and in addition pay a further five hundred talents. The terms were certainly oppressive. But in the circumstances, Hyrcanus must nevertheless have been happy, even at this price, to

---

date for the capture of Jerusalem by Antiochus by this last reckoning, i.e., Ol.162, 3=130–129 B.C., Euseb. *Chron.* ed. Schoene I, p. 255: 'Judaeosque hic subegit, per obsidionem muros urbis evertebat, atque electissimos ipsorum trucidabat anno tertio CLXII olympiadis'. It is only possible to combine these statements by assuming that the war dragged on for four years, which seems improbable. But it must be accepted as having lasted for more than one year, for the siege of Jerusalem alone appears to have continued for longer than that. For at the beginning of it Josephus mentions the setting of the Pleiades, *Ant.* xiii 8, 2 (237), δυομένης πλειάδος, which occurs in November (Pliny *N.H.* ii 47/125 'post id aequinoctium diebus fere quattuor et quadraginta Vergiliarum occasus hiemen inchoat, quod tempus in III. idus Novembres incidere consuevit'. And the siege was still not lifted by the following Feast of Tabernacles, i.e. in October, *Ant.* xiii 8, 2 (241). Sieges of a year are not rare in the history of those times, see Samaria, *Ant.* xiii 10, 3 (281); Gaza, *Ant.* xiii 13, 3 (364); Gadara, ten months, *Ant.* xiii 13, 3 (356). The agreement between Josephus and Porphyry in regard to 162nd Olympiad may suggest that this date has some foundation. On the other hand, its intrinsic probability argues in favour of the first year of Hyrcanus (it is difficult to believe that Antiochus did not proceed against the Jews until 130 B.C., i.e. eight years after his accession to the throne), as well as the fact that the correct identification of Hyrcanus's first year with Antiochus's fourth year must stem from a reliable source. In addition, Porphyry's 130–129 B.C. would place the siege of Jerusalem in the same year in which Antiochus's campaign against the Parthians most likely took place (see above p. 132). It is therefore probable that the Olympic year 162, 3 transmitted only through the unreliable Armenian text of Eusebius, should be rejected. On the other hand it is possible that the war lasted from 134 to 132 B.C., i.e., until the beginning of the 162nd Olympiad. All in all, it is more likely that either Josephus made a mistake in referring to the Olympic year, or that there is an early corruption in the MSS which influenced Porphyry.

have secured the raising of the siege and the departure of the Syrian army. The city walls were also demolished.[6]

It is possible that the decree of the Roman senate reported by Josephus in *Ant.* xiii 9, 2 (260–6) should be attributed to the time of this war. It suggests that a king Antiochus had, contrary to the will of the senate, seized from the Jews the towns of Joppa, Gazara and other places (πολεμῶν ἔλαβεν Ἀντίοχος παρὰ τὸ τῆς συγκλήτου δόγμα), and that because of this a Jewish embassy (ὑπὸ δήμου τοῦ Ἰουδαίων) had been sent to Rome with the request that the senate might effect a return of the cities taken from them by Antiochus. The senate decreed a renewal of φιλία and συμμαχία with the Jews, but postponed making a decision on their request until time could be spared from attending to its own affairs (ὅταν ἀπὸ τῶν ἰδίων ἡ σύγκλητος εὐσχολήσῃ). As the Jews had not possessed Joppa and Gazara under an earlier Antiochus, and as the surrender of both towns constituted the chief demand made by Antiochus VII to the Jews during the time of Simon (1 Mac. 15:28), there can be little doubt that it is he who is meant in the decree of senate referred to. He must therefore, as is inherently likely, have begun the war with the seizure of these towns; and the Jews sought the support of the Romans while the war was still in progress by appealing to the decree of the senate issued in the time of Simon. Considering that the Romans, in spite of the promised φιλία and συμμαχία, left the Jews at first to their own devices, it is rather remarkable that when peace was concluded Antiochus handed back the towns he had captured against payment of tribute. Perhaps this relative disclaimer may be explained by the fact that the Romans had intervened beforehand. It seems in fact that another decree of the senate, reported by Josephus in *Ant.* xiv 10, 22 (248–50) and inserted (probably by mistake) in a decree of the people of Pergamum, should be attributed to this time. This *senatus consultum* was occasioned by a deputation sent by 'the nation of the Jews and the High Priest Hyrcanus', and states that

6. Jos. *Ant.* xiii 8, 2–3 (236–48). Diodorus xxxiv/v 1–5; Porphyry in Euseb. *Chron.* ed. Schoene I, p. 255; Justin xxxvi, 1 'Iudaeos quoque, qui in Macedonia imperio sub Demetrio patre armis se in libertatem vindicaverant, subigit'. Several scholars (e.g. Graetz, *Gesch.* III ([5]1905–6), pp. 67 f.) have taken the words of Josephus καθεῖλε δὲ καὶ τὴν στεφάνην τῆς πόλεως as referring not to the destruction of the entire wall but only of the top of the wall, in which case his account would diverge from those of Diodorus and Porphyry. But such an interpretation is not necessary. In any case, according to Diodorus and Porphyry the wall itself was demolished. Among the praiseworthy actions of John Hyrcanus, 1 Mac. 16:23 especially emphasizes its reconstruction. Hyrcanus is said to have obtained the sum demanded by Antiochus by extracting three thousand talents from the tomb of David, so Jos. *Ant.* vii 15, 3 (393), whereas *Ant.* xiii 8, 4 (249) merely recounts that Hyrcanus employed stolen money to pay his mercenaries). On David's tomb, cf. Neh. 3:16; Jos. *Ant.* xvi 7, 1 (179); Acts 2:29. According to Neh. 3:15–16, it lay to the south of the city, not far from the Pool of Shelah.

King Antiochus, the son of Antiochus, must return to the Jews the fortresses, ports and land which he had taken from them, and that no-one must export anything tax-free from Jewish territory except King Ptolemy, the ally and friend of the Romans, and that the garrison must be removed from Joppa (τήν ἐν Ἰόππῃ φρουρὰν ἐκβαλεῖν). Since the seizure of Jewish towns and ports by an Antiochus is mentioned here too, and Joppa is a principal bone of contention, it is reasonable to suppose that this decree of the senate relates to the same circumstances as the previous one. It would explain why Antiochus returned to the Jews, against payment of tribute, towns that he had already conquered. It would admittedly be necessary to accept that a textual corruption exists in regard to the name, for Antiochus VII Sidetes was a son not of Antiochus but of Demetrius. This intrinsically precarious assumption is not inadmissible because none of the later Seleucids (it could only be a question of Antiochus IX Cyzicenus) confronted the Jews with such a display of force as is ascribed to the Antiochus mentioned here. The statements, in so far as they emanate from Josephus, fit only Antiochus VII. All the same, the text as transmitted permits no definite decision. If both decrees of the senate are to be attributed to the period of the war between Antiochus VII and Hyrcanus I, it must have lasted for some time.[7]

7. The above hypothesis, according to which both these *senatus consulta* are to be attributed to the period of this war, was advanced by Mendelssohn in Acta societatis philologae Lipsiensis 5 (1875), pp. 123–58; cf. also Mendelssohn, Rhein. Museum 30 (1875), pp. 118 f. Compare M. S. Ginsburg, *Rome et la Judée* (1928), pp. 65–77. On the emendations of the names in *Ant.* xiii 9, 2 (260–4), see Th. Mommsen's observations on the decree of the council of Adramyttium, *Ephemeris Epigr.* IV, p. 217. Mendelssohn's conclusions have not invariably been accepted by those who have since occupied themselves with these two *senatus consulta*. See Gutschmid, *Kleine Schriften* II, pp. 303–15; Viereck, *Sermo graecus, quo senatus populusque Romanus etc. usi sunt* (1888), pp. 93–6; A. Kuhn, *Beiträge zur Gesch. der Seleukiden* (1891), pp. 3–14; J. Wellhausen, *Israelitische und jüdische Geschichte* ([9]1958), pp. 259, 261; Unger, SMA (1895), pp. 575–604; Th. Reinach, 'Antiochus Cyzicène et les Juifs', REJ 38 (1899), pp. 161–71; H. Willrich, *Judaica* (1900), pp. 69–71; *idem*, *Urkundenfälschung in der hellenistisch-jüdischen Literatur* (1924), pp. 63–4. On the geographical references in *Ant.* xiii 9, 2 (261) see also J. Levy, '*Λιμένες et Πηγαί*', REJ 41 (1900), pp. 176–80. Many scholars relate only *Ant.* xiii 9, 2 (260–6) to Antiochus VII Sidetes, and *Ant.* xiv 10, 22 (248–50) to Antiochus IX Cyzicenus; Reinach and Willrich associate both *senatus consulta* with the last-named. In regard to *Ant.* xiii 9, 2 (260–2), the majority do not link it to the actual period of the war, but to that following it. Said to be decisive in this respect is the fact that the Jewish envoys wished to have τὰ κατὰ τὸν πόλεμον ἐκεῖνον ψηφισθέντα ὑπὸ Ἀντιόχου revoked. But instead of ψηφισθέντα a number of manuscripts have the difficult ψηλαφηθέντα ('handled' or 'touched'='attempted'; cf. Nah. 3:1 LXX), which may perhaps be accepted (the old Latin text has *gesta*). The choice of a period subsequent to the conclusion of peace is contradicted by the fact that by the signing of the treaty the Jews were given back Joppa and the other towns on payment of tribute, whereas they were in the hands of Antiochus at the time

The conflicts of these early years under Hyrcanus showed once more that the small Jewish state could only remain free from Syrian domination as long as the Syrian empire was itself weak. With the first forceful moves by Antiochus, the freedom won by Simon was lost once again. Hyrcanus's dependence on Antiochus VII also obliged him to participate in the Syrian monarch's campaign against the Parthians in 130/29 B.C. But he escaped the disaster that overtook Antiochus.[8]

---

when the Jewish delegation complained to the Senate. Gutschmid, *op. cit.*, and Schlatter, *Topographie*, pp. 3–14, therefore assumed that Antiochus did not surrender them at all, which is dubious in view of his famous εὐσέβεια. The *senatus consultum* seems to fit into the war period provided that it is accepted that the war had already lasted for some time before Jerusalem was besieged. If, on the other hand, the Φάννιος named as praetor in xiii 9, 2 (260) is C. Fannius, the consul of 122 B.C., his praetorship would be expected to have been later than this, say about 126 B.C., so Broughton, MRR II, pp. 508–9. But the evidence on the Fannii known from this period is confused. It remains possible that one was praetor in 132 B.C., so RE VI, cols. 1988–9.

It is much more difficult to reach a decision in regard to *Ant.* xiv 10, 22 (248–50). The designation of the king as 'Antiochus son of Antiochus' is a forceful argument against Mendelssohn's conclusion. If the description is correct, it can in fact only mean Antiochus IX Cyzicenus (for Antiochus VII Sidetes was a son of Demetrius I, and Antiochus VII Grypus a son of Demetrius II). But it is said of this Antiochus that he 'wrested fortresses, ports and territory' from the Jews, *Ant.* xiv 10, 22 (249–50), *φρούρια καὶ λιμένας καὶ χώραν καὶ εἴ τι ἄλλο ἀφείλετο αὐτῶν*, and in particular that he was in possession of Joppa. If one wished to dissociate, with Gutschmid, this last-mentioned fact also from the time of Antiochus VII, Antiochus IX must himself have made considerable conquests in Palestine and have appeared so powerful that the Jews felt obliged to enlist Roman support. Yet this contradicts all that is known of Antiochus IX. Josephus emphasises most strongly that he was unable to do anything against John Hyrcanus. When Antiochus wished to undertake some aggressive move, 'Hyrcanus disclosed his own will' and despised Antiochus IX as he did his brother Antiochus VIII, *Ant.* xiii 10, 1 (274). It is true that with Egyptian support Antiochus devastated Hyrcanus's territory with acts of brigandage, but he did not dare to fight him openly because he was too weak, *Ant.* xiii 10, 2 (278). Presumably, this was not Josephus's own account but one found in his sources. But can what appears in the *senatus consultum* be accepted of such a ruler? It is also improbable that Hyrcanus sought the legal protection of the Romans for the preservation of the *status quo* against the conquests of Antiochus IX, whilst he himself was engaged in making conquests. The dating of this document remains controversial. M. Stern, 'The Relations between Judaea and Rome during the Rule of John Hyrcanus', Zion 26 (1961), pp. 1–22 (in Hebrew with an Engl. summary), explains *Ant.* xiii 9, 2 (260–6) against the background of political events of the years 128–5 B.C., and places *Ant.* xiv 10, 22 (248–50) in 113–12 B.C.

See also T. Fischer, *Untersuchungen zum Partherkrieg Antiochos' VII* (Diss. Tübingen, 1970), who dates the first document to 126/5 B.C. (pp. 64–73), and the second to 114–104 B.C. (pp. 73–82), and A. Giovannini, H. Müller, 'Die Beziehungen zwischen Rom und den Juden im 2 Jh. v. Chr.', Museum Helveticum 28 (1971), pp. 156–71, dating both to the reign of Antiochus IX.

8. *Ant.* xiii 8, 4 (250–1) quoting Nicolaus of Damascus (= Jacoby FGrH 90 F 92). Cf. J. Neusner, *A History of the Jews in Babylonia* I (1965), pp. 24–5.

For Hyrcanus, Antiochus's death in the Parthian campaign in 129 B.C. was providential.[9] His place on the Syrian throne was taken for the second time by the weak Demetrius II, previously released from captivity by the Parthians.[10] He was immediately involved in internal struggles which prevented him from attending to the Jews.

Hyrcanus at once set out to benefit from the altered circumstances. Disregarding Demetrius, he began to appropriate considerable territories in the vicinity of Judaea, to the east, north and south. First he marched into Transjordan and conquered Medeba after siege of six months.[11] Then he turned towards the north and captured Shechem and Mount Gerizim, subdued the Samaritans, and destroyed their temple. Finally, he marched southward, took the Idumaean towns of Adora and Marissa and forced the Idumaeans to submit to circumcision and to accept the Jewish law.[12] The policy of conquest begun by Jonathan and Simon was thus vigorously continued by Hyrcanus. But the purely secular nature of his policy is revealed by the fact that he no longer fought these wars with a Jewish army, but was the first of the Jewish princes to hire mercenaries.[13]

This independent behaviour on the part of Hyrcanus was made possible by Syria's internal weakness. Soon after his re-accession to the throne, Demetrius II committed the folly of going to war against

9. On the campaign and death of Antiochus, compare Justin xxxviii 10, xxxix, 1, 1; Diodorus xxxiv/v, 15–17; Livy *Epit*, lix; Appian, *Syr.* 68/359; Jos. *Ant.* xiii 8, 4 (250–3); Porphyry in Eusebius *Chron.* ed. Schoene I, p. 255. On the chronology, cf. above p. 132.

10. On Demetrius II see Justin xxxvi 1, 1, 'Demetrius, et ipse rerum successu corruptus, vitiis adulescentiae in segnitiam labitur tantumque contemptum apud omnes inertiae, quantum odium ex superbia pater habuerat, contraxit'. On the other hand, Justin xxxix 1, 3, also speaks of a 'superbia regis, quae conversatione Parthicae crudelitatis intolerabilis facta erat'. On the actions and fortunes of Demetrius during his captivity, and his ultimate release, see Justin xxxvi 1; xxxviii 9–10; Appian, *Syr.* 67/355–6, 68/360; Jos. *Ant.* xiii 8, 4 (253); Porphyry in Euseb. *Chron.* ed. Schoene I, p. 255.

11. Medeba, already mentioned in the Mesha inscription, is a well-known town in Transjordan, south of Heshbon, the name and ruins of which have survived. Cf. Num. 21:30; Jos. 13:9, 16; Isa. 15:2; 1 Chr. 19:7. Cf. 1 Mac. 9:36; Jos. *Ant.* xiii 1, 2 (11); 15, 4 (397); xiv 1, 4 (18); Ptolemy v 17, 6; viii 20, 20. mMikw. 7:1; Euseb. *Onomast.* ed. Klostermann, p. 128; *The Survey of Eastern Palestine* I (1889), pp. 178–83; Abel, *Géog.* Pal. II, pp. 381–2. On the mosaic map found at Medeba, see M. Avi-Yonah, *The Madaba Mosaic Map* (1954).

12. Jos. *Ant.* xiii 9, 1 (255–8); *B.J.* i 2, 6 (63). Cf. *Ant.* xv 7, 9 (254). Adora is modern Dura, west-south-west of Hebron; see Abel, *Géog. Pal.* II, p. 239. On Marissa see above p. 165 (1 Mac. 5:66). As a result of the Judaization by John Hyrcanus, the Idumaeans later regarded themselves as wholly Jewish, *B.J.* iv 4, 4 (270–84). To the Jewish aristocracy, they counted only as ἡμιιουδαῖοι and for this reason the Idumaean Herod was regarded as an inferior, *Ant.* xiv 15, 2 (403) Ἡρῴδῃ . . . ἰδιώτῃ τε ὄντι καὶ Ἰδουμαίῳ, τουτέστιν ἡμιιουδαίῳ.

13. Jos. *Ant.* xiii 8, 4 (249).

Ptolemy VII Physcon of Egypt. In return, the Egyptian monarch nominated a rival pretender to Demetrius's throne in the person of a young Egyptian whom he presented, according to some, as an adopted son of Antiochus Sidetes, and according to others, as a son of Alexander Balas,[14] naming him Alexander (the Syrians gave him the nickname Zebinas, i.e., 'the bought one').[15] Defeated by Alexander near Damascus, Demetrius was obliged to flee to Ptolemais and from there by ship to Tyre, and was murdered there just as he was about to land, in 125 B.C.[16]

Alexander Zebinas, for his part, had to struggle once more for the throne against Demetrius's son, Antiochus VIII Grypus. He was therefore obliged to live in peace and friendship with Hyrcanus.[17]

After several years, in about 123/2 B.C., Alexander Zebinas was defeated by his adversary, Antiochus VIII Grypus, and executed; according to others, he poisoned himself (see above, p. 133). A period of quiet then ensued, during which Antiochus VIII Grypus wielded undisputed authority in Syria.[18] None the less he, too, took no action against John Hyrcanus. He no longer entertained any ambition to restore the old Syrian frontiers. He was deposed in 113 B.C. by his cousin and step-brother. Antiochus IX Cyzicenus, who governed the whole of Syria for two years, and then, when Antiochus Grypus re-

14. The first according to Justin, xxxix 1–4; the second according to Porphyry in Eusebius *Chron.* ed. Schoene I, pp. 257 f.

15. Porphyry in Euseb. *Chron.* ed. Schoene I, p. 258 correctly interprets the nickname Zebinas (Ezr. 10:43 also has זבינא) by ἀγοραστός. The orthography varies between *Ζεβινᾶς*, Jos. *Ant.* xiii 9, 3 (268), and *Ζαβινᾶς*, Diodorus xxxiv/v 22; Porphyry in Euseb. *loc. cit.*; inscription in Letronne, *Recueil des inscriptions grecques et latines de l'Égypte* II, p. 61 = Bernand, *Inscriptions grecques de Philae* I (1969), no. 31. 'Zabbinaeus' in Justin *Prolog.* xxxix. See in general Letronne *op. cit.* II, pp. 62 f., and Bernand, *op. cit.*, p. 235.

16. Jos. *Ant.* xiii 9, 3 (268); Justin xxxix 1, 7–8; Porphyry in Euseb. *Chron.* ed. Schoene I, pp. 257 f. On his death see especially Justin, *loc. cit.* 'Cum Tyrum religione se templi defensurus petisset, navi egrediens praefecti iussu interficitur.' According to Appian, *Syr.* 68/360, his wife Cleopatra was the instigator of the murder. Cf. Livy *Epit.* lx 'motus quoque Syriae referentur, in quibus Cleopatra Demetrium virum suum . . . interemit'.

17. Jos. *Ant.* xiii 9, 3 (269) *φιλίαν ποιεῖται πρὸς τὸν ἀρχιερέα.*

18. Justin xxxix 2, 9, 'Parta igitur regni securitate Grypos octo annis quietem et ipse habuit et regno suo praestitit'. Immediately before this Justin mentions the forced death of Cleopatra, the mother and hitherto co-regent of Antiochus VIII (121–120 B.C., see above p. 133). By eight years he means, therefore, the period from then until the displacement of Antiochus VIII by Antiochus IX (i.e., 113 B.C.). This, however, was not entirely an era of peace, for Antiochus IX was in opposition to his brother already some time prior to 113 B.C. (see above p. 134 A. Kuhn, *Beiträge zur Gesch. der Seleukiden*, p. 19; Wilcken RE I, 2481). But Josephus is not correct in saying of Antiochus VIII that he had to fight against his brother Antiochus IX during the whole period, *Ant.* xiii 10, 1 (270–2).

possessed the greater portion of the country, stood his ground in just that part that adjoins Palestine, namely Coele-Syria.[19]

Diodorus gives the following description of Antiochus IX Cyzicenus, ruler of Coele-Syria from 113–95 B.C. 'No sooner had Antiochus obtained the throne than he lapsed into drunkenness and unworthy debauchery, and into pursuits quite unfitting in a king. He had a liking, that is to say, for mimes and comedians, and for conjurers in general, and endeavoured to learn their skills. He also practised puppetry assiduously and took pains to make the silver and gold animals, five cubits high, that moved automatically, and other clever gadgets. He failed, on the other hand, to make the battering-rams and engines of war which would have brought him renown and considerable advantage. But unfortunately, he was also passionately fond of adventurous hunting expeditions, and without telling his friends, frequently went off by night with two or three servants into the country to hunt lion, panthers and boars. In doing so, he often exposed himself to extreme danger by engaging in foolhardy encounters with wild animals.'[20]

The portrait given here is a debased version of that of an earlier Antiochus, Epiphanes. Hyrcanus had nothing to fear from a ruler interested in such things as these. So in fact, after the death of Antiochus Sidetes in 129 B.C., Judaea was completely independent of Syria once more. The tributes imposed by Antiochus Sidetes were paid to none of the following kings. Hyrcanus 'no longer furnished them with anything, neither as a subject, nor as a friend'.[21]

During the last years of his reign, Hyrcanus once more launched invasions into neighbouring territories. Having subdued the district around Shechem and Mount Gerizim, he now directed his attacks against the town of Samaria, whose inhabitants had given him cause for complaint. He surrounded it with a rampart and a ditch and entrusted the conduct of the siege to his sons Antigonus and Aristobulus. The hard-pressed Samaritans called for help to Antiochus Cyzicenus, who came willingly but was driven back by the Jews. Appealed to for support a second time, Antiochus brought up Egyptian military forces supplied by Ptolemy Lathyrus, and with their assistance ravaged Jewish territory, but without achieving any decisive result. After heavy

19. Porphyry, *loc. cit.*, I, p. 260; Jos. *Ant.* xiii 10, 1 (273–4); Justin xxxix 2, 10-3. 12; Appian, *Syr.* 69/314. See above p. 134.

20. Diodorus xxxiv/v 34.

21. Jos. *Ant.* xiii 10, 1 (273) *οὔτε ὡς ὑπήκοος οὔτε ὡς φίλος αὐτοῖς οὐδὲν ἔτι παρεῖχεν*. Another picture would emerge if the confiscation of Jewish fortresses and ports associated with an Antiochus in the *senatus consultum* in *Ant.* xiv 10, 22 (249), was due to Antiochus IX. He must then have used similar force towards the Jews as did his father, Antiochus VII. Cf. on this point p. 206 above.

losses, Antiochus withdrew from the scene of battle and left the continuation of the campaign to his generals, Callimandrus and Epicrates. Of these, one was defeated by the Jews and lost his life, and the other, Epicrates, accomplished nothing either; indeed he treacherously surrendered Scythopolis to the Jews. Samaria thus fell into the hands of the Jews after a year-long siege, and was completely razed to the ground.[22] Jewish legends relate that on the day of the decisive victory of Antigonus and Aristobulus over Antiochus Cyzicenus, the event was made known to Hyrcanus by a voice from heaven as he was presenting a burnt-offering in the Temple.[23]

Nothing more is known of the external events in what seems to have been the brilliant rule of Hyrcanus. It is little enough. But reliable information relating to internal circumstances is still more meagre. A certain amount may probably be gathered from numismatic sources.[24]

22. Jos. *Ant.* xiii 10, 2–3 (275–81). *B.J.* i 2, 7 (65). *B.J.* names, not Antiochus Cyzicenus, but Antiochus Aspendius, i.e. Grypus, as the one to whom the Samaritans called for aid. These events must then have taken place earlier, during the time when Antiochus Grypus still ruled unopposed throughout the whole of Syria. But the statements concerning Ptolemy Lathyrus do not fit into this picture (see below). According to *B.J.*, Scythopolis was not surrendered to the Jews by treachery, but was conquered by them (cf. on this important city vol. II, § 23, 1). Megillath Taanith § 8 also seems to refer to the seizure of Scythopolis by the Jews on 15 and 16 Siwan. Cf. Derenbourg, *op. cit.*, pp. 72 ff.; Lichtenstein, HUCA 8–9 (1931–2), pp. 288–9. The date of the conquest of Samaria was, according to Megillath Taanith, 25 Marḥeshwan (=November). See Derenbourg, *op. cit.*, pp. 72–3; Lichtenstein, *ibid.*, p. 289. The year may be approximately fixed from the fact that, on the one hand, Antiochus Cyzicenus was already in undisputed possession of Coele-Syria (since 111 B.C.), and on the other, Ptolemy Lathyrus was still co-regent with his mother Cleopatra (till 107 B.C.); see H. L. Strack, *Die Dynastie der Ptolemäer* (1897), pp. 185, 202 f.; cf. T. C. Skeat, *The Reigns of the Ptolemies* (1954), pp. 15–16. The conquest of Samaria therefore occurred, in any case between 111–107 B.C., and probably not long before 107 B.C., for Cleopatra was so enraged at Ptolemy for assisting Antiochus that she 'very nearly' dispossessed him of power, see Jos. *Ant.* xiii 10, 2 (278) ὅσον οὔπω τῆς ἀρχῆς αὐτὸν ἐκβεβληκυίας. There is some archaeological evidence of the destruction of Samaria at this moment, see J. W. Crowfoot, K. M. Kenyon, E. L. Sukenik, *The Buildings at Samaria* (1942), p. 121, and G. A. Reisner, C. S. Fisher, D. G. Lyon, *Harvard Excavations at Samaria* I (1924), pp. 50–8. For the historical and religious significance of the destruction in the light of recent evidence see F. M. Cross, 'Aspects of Samaritan and Jewish History in Late Persian and Hellenistic Times', HThR 59 (1966), pp. 201–11; 'Papyri of the Fourth Century B.C. from Dâliyeh', *New Directions in Bibl. Arch.*, ed. D. N. Freedman, J. C. Greenfield (Anchor, 1971), pp. 45–69.

23. Jos. *Ant.* xiii 10, 3 (282–3). For the rabbinic passages (tSoṭ. 13:5; ySoṭ 24b; bSoṭ 33a) see Derenbourg, *op. cit.*, p. 74; E. E. Urbach, 'When did Prophecy end?', Tarbiz 17 (1946/7), pp. 1–11 (in Hebrew with an Engl. summary).

24. Contrary to the opinion of earlier numismatists, the majority, or even the totality, of the Yehoḥanan coins are ascribed today to Hyrcanus II (see below, Appendix IV, p. 604). Y. Meshorer, *Jewish Coins of the Second Temple Period* (1967), pp. 41–5, argues that Hyrcanus I issued no coins at all. It seems, however,

The coins attributed to Hyrcanus bear the following inscription:

יהוחנן הכהן הגדל וחבר היהודים

The meaning of the penultimate word, much disputed by earlier scholars, is now generally accepted to be 'congregation', i.e. the *γερουσία* of the Jewish nation known from later documents as the Sanhedrin. The inscription would therefore run: 'John the High Priest and the Congregation of the Jews'.[25] This official title shows that John Hyrcanus still regarded himself first and foremost as a priest. As in pre-Maccabaean Jewry, the Hasmonaean state was administered by priests. The ruling chief priest was, however, not an autocrat, but governed his people and issued coins in conjunction with the 'congregation of the Jews', i.e. the national assembly. Nevertheless, the very fact that he stamped his name on his coins seems to reveal that John was increasingly aware of himself as a prince. In addition to the numismatic evidence reflecting, possibly, the constitution of the Jewish state under Hyrcanus I, the letter prefacing 2 Maccabees testifies to a religious custom in his time. This was addressed in 124 B.C. to the Jewish community in Egypt and urged them to observe the festival of Hanukkah.[26]

With regard to the internal policy adopted by Hyrcanus during his thirty years' reign, one very important fact is well established at least: his breach with the Pharisees and dependence on the Sadducees. The two parties now appear on the stage of history for the first time under

---

safer to assign to him, with B. Kanael, IEJ 2 (1952), pp. 170–5, and A. Kindler, *ibid.*, 4 (1954), Pl. 14, a limited number of the standard coinage, probably minted during the last years of his reign (*c.* 110 B.C.). Cf. Appendix IV, p. 603. See now also A. Ben-David, 'When did the Maccabees begin to strike their first Coins?', PEQ 124 (1972), pp. 93–103.

25. For nineteenth-century views concerning the sense of חבר, see F. W. Madden, *Coins of the Jews*, p. 77 f. Since then substantial agreement has been achieved on explaining the term as 'congregation', designating either the whole Jewish community (so Schürer), or the senate of the Jews (e.g. Geiger, *Urschrift*, pp. 121–2; Derenbourg, *op. cit.*, p. 83; Wellhausen, *Isr. u. jüd. Gesch.* ([9]1958), p. 269; J. Klausner, *Historiyah shel ha-Bayit ha-sheni* III ([3]1952), p. 97; B. Kanael, 'Altjüd. Münzen', Jahrb. f. Numism. u. Geldgesch. 17 (1967), p. 167; Meshorer, *op. cit.*, p. 49. A linguistic parallel appears in CDC 12:8, where חבור/חבר describes an authoritative body within Jewry. Cf. C. Rabin, *The Zadokite Documents* (1954), pp. 60–1. The Phoenician phrase attested in CIS I 165, 'the two suffets and חברנם = their colleagues' has been understood by most scholars since Renan as alluding either to a senate, or its executive committee. See G. A. Cooke, *A Text-Book of North-Semitic Inscriptions* (1903), p. 116; H. Donner-W. Röllig, *Kananäische u. aramäische Inschriften* II ([2]1968), p. 84. It has also been argued that the expression חבר העיר can mean 'council of the city community', e.g. in bMeg. 27b; see R. Meyer, *Tradition und Neuschöpfung* (1965), pp. 25–6.

26. 2 Mac. 1:19. It encapsulates (7–8) a quotation from a previous letter written in the Seleucid year 169 (143/2 B.C.) with the same object. See Abel, *ad loc.* and Excursus IV (pp. 299–302); E. Bickermann, 'Ein jüdischer Festbrief vom Jahre 124 v. Chr.', ZNW 32 (1933), pp. 233–54.

these names. Their beginnings reach far back into the past, but their consolidation seems to have been a consequence of the Maccabaean movement.[27] The Pharisees were simply the party of the strict observers of the Law; they belonged in essence to the same circles as those encountered at the start of the Maccabaean movement under the name of the 'Devout', or Hasidim. At that time, their extreme opposites were the pro-Greeks who co-operated so thoroughly with the aspirations of Antiochus Epiphanes that they not only opened the gates to Hellenism within the field of civil life, but also within that of religious worship. These phil-Hellenes, who were drawn in particular from the upper ranks of the priesthood, were swept away in the turmoil of the Maccabaean movement. Voices of this kind were no longer allowed to make themselves heard in the Jewish community. Nevertheless, the base from which the tendency had sprung still remained, namely, the essentially worldly spirit, antipathetic to any religious enthusiasm, of the high-ranking priesthood. They doubtless intended to abide by the Law of Moses, but whatever went beyond its letter they rejected with cool superiority. Their real interests were concerned more with this life and the present than with the life to come and the future. This tendency, which was mainly represented by the higher priests, the 'Sons of Zadok', was now called that of the Zadokites or Sadducees.[28]

Originally, the Maccabees belonged neither to the Pharisees nor the Sadducees. The zeal for the Law which had pressed their swords into their hands bound them to the Hasidim, who in the beginning had also participated in the struggle for independence. But soon they both went their divided ways, more beside one another than with one another.

27. Josephus mentions them first, together with the Essenes, during the period of Jonathan, *Ant.* xiii 5, 9 (171–3).

28. For further details concerning the nature and origin of the Pharisees and Sadducees, see § 26. On the Essenes, see § 30.

The origin of the Qumran community and its relation to the Essenes will also be discussed fully in § 30. But in order to provide a more complete picture of the religious parties under John Hyrcanus, it seems appropriate to outline here a few basic data on which there is substantial agreement among experts.

The beginnings of the Qumran sect are connected generally with the emergence and subsequent disintegration of the Hasidic movement. Unlike those Hasidim (the Pharisees) who until John Hyrcanus collaborated with the Maccabees, another group with priestly members and Zadokite loyalties broke away from the new rulers, probably at the time of Jonathan's acceptance from Alexander Balas of the High Priesthood. Whether the Hasmonaean enemy of the sect is to be identified with Jonathan, or Simon, or both (4Q Testimonia, DJD V, no. 175, p. 58 speaks of 'two instruments of violence'), it can be accepted as certain on archaelogical grounds that the sectarian establishment at Qumran existed during the time of Hyrcanus I, or even perhaps that of Simon. According to R. de Vaux, Period I of the site's occupation falls into two parts, the second of which (Ib) corresponds, on numismatic evidence, to the reign of Alexander Jannaeus (103–

The Hasidim were not concerned with political supremacy or political freedom. For the Maccabees, these were points of vital importance. They did not of course abandon their original aim, the preservation of the religion of their fathers. But as time wore on, it became increasingly bound up with quite other political aims. And it was precisely these that brought them into closer relation with the Sadducees. As political parvenus, the Maccabees dared not ignore the influential Sadducean nobility. It may be taken for granted that in the *γερουσία* of the Maccabaean period the 'Sadducees' were also represented. Despite all this, however, in religious matters the Maccabees were originally closer to the Pharisees than to the Sadducees. They were the guardians of the ancestral faith and the ancestral law. In the case of Hyrcanus, it is definitely assumed that in the early years of his reign he followed the observances of the Pharisees. For it was his abrogation of Pharisaic precepts that constituted the chief accusation levelled against him by the more strictly observant Jews.[29]

This dual position of the Maccabees explains the swing which occurred during Hyrcanus's reign. The more his political interests came to the fore, the more those concerned with religion receded into the background. But he was correspondingly obliged to move away from the Pharisees and closer to the Sadducees. For in view of the distinctly worldly character of his policies, no sincere association with the Pharisees was in the long run possible. It is therefore not surprising that he broke openly with the Pharisees and adopted unreservedly the Sadducean outlook.

The ostensible occasion of the breach between Hyrcanus and the Pharisees is described by Josephus and the Talmud as follows. Once, when a number of Pharisees were in his home as guests, Hyrcanus asked them, if they observed him doing anything unlawful, to call his attention to it and point out the right way to him. All those present were full of his praises. But one of them, Eleazar, stood up and said: 'As you wish to hear the truth, then know that if you seek to be

---

76 B.C.). In consequence, Period Ia, beginning with the foundation of the communal settlement, must have preceded Jannaeus by several decades, and may go back to the middle of the second century B.C. See R. de Vaux, *L'archéologie et les manuscrits de la Mer Morte* (1961), pp. 3–4, 15. Cf. also G. Vermes, *Discovery*, pp. 12–18; *The Dead Sea Scrolls in English*, pp. 53–4; F. M. Cross. *The Ancient Library of Qumran*, pp. 42–4; J. T. Milik, *Ten Years of Discovery*, p. 51; F. M. Cross, 'The Early History of the Qumran Community', *New Directions in Biblical Archaeology*, ed. D. N. Freedman, J. C. Greenfield (Anchor, 1971), pp. 71–2 [the Qumran site was founded between 150–100 B.C., more probably between 140–120 B.C.].

29. Josephus even says in *Ant.* xiii 10, 5 (289): *μαθητὴς δ' αὐτῶν καὶ Ὑρκανὸς ἐγεγόνει καὶ σφόδρα ὑπ' αὐτῶν ἠγαπᾶτο.*

righteous, lay down the office of High Priest and content yourself with ruling the nation'. When Hyrcanus asked for the reason, the other replied: 'Because we hear from our elders that your mother was taken captive under King Antiochus Epiphanes'. This allegation being incorrect, Hyrcanus flew into a rage. When he then enquired of the Pharisees what punishment Eleazar deserved, they said, 'stripes and chains'. Hyrcanus, who believed that death was the fitting consequence of such abuse, became even more furious and thought Eleazar had spoken with the approval of his party. From then on, he dissociated himself entirely from the Pharisees, forbad on pain of punishment all observance of the laws drawn up by them, and joined the ranks of the Sadducees.[30]

In its anecdotal form, the story certainly bears the stamp of a legend and it was probably derived by Josephus solely from an oral tradition. Nevertheless, it may be considered as a fact that Hyrcanus unquestionably turned away from the Pharisees and abolished their ordinances. For Alexandra's reintroduction of Pharisaic laws was a conscious reaction against the policy pursued from the time of Hyrcanus.[31] A few ordinances set aside by Hyrcanus are mentioned in the Mishnah. But in view of Hyrcanus's total opposition to everything Pharisaic, the cases cited in the Mishnah are to be regarded merely as details selected at random.[32]

Reviewing Hyrcanus's period of rule, Josephus judges him fortunate to have been 'thought worthy by God of three of the greatest things: government of his people, the priestly honour, and the gift of

30. Jos. *Ant.* xiii 10, 5–6 (288–98). For the rabbinic tradition, see Graetz, *Gesch.* III ([5]1905–6), pp. 687–9; Derenbourg, *op. cit.*, pp. 79–80. Note that bKidd. 66a confuses John Hyrcanus with his son Alexander Jannaeus (ינאי המלך). But the Babylonian teacher who told the story (Abayye) asserted elsewhere (bBer. 29a) the identity of ינאי and יוחנן. See below p. 223, n. 16. Cf. in general Wellhausen, *Die Pharisäer und Sadducäer*, pp. 89–95. R. Marcus, 'The Pharisees in the Light of Modern Scholarship', Journ. of Rel. 23 (1952), pp. 153–64; L. Finkelstein, *The Pharisees* ([3]1962), pp. 762–3; A. Michel, J. Le Moyne, 'Pharisiens', DB Suppl. (1964), cols. 1022–1115.

31. Jos. *Ant.* xiii 16, 2 (408).

32. See mM.Sh. 5:15=mSoṭ. 9:10,'Yoḥanan, the High Priest, abolished confession concerning the Second Tithe. He also abolished the singing of the verse "Awake" (Ps. 44:24) and the stunning of the sacrificial victim. Until his time, the hammer was in use in Jerusalem (on intermediary days between the first and the last day of a festival season). In his time, no man needed to enquire concerning Demai (i.e. whether tithes had been paid on the corn bought).' See W. Bunte, *Maaserot/Maaser Scheni* (1962), pp. 243–5; H. Bietenhard, *Soṭa* (1956), pp. 157–60. Cf. Derenbourg, *op. cit.*, p. 71. On confession relative to tithing, see Dt. 26:12–15; Jos. *Ant.* iv 8, 22 (242–3); mM.Sh. 5:6–15. See also mPar. 3:5 mentioning Yoḥanan among the High Priests under whom, according to the law in Num. 19, a red heifer was burnt. See also S. Zeitlin, 'Johanan the High Priest's Abrogations and Decrees', *Studies and Essays in Honor of A. A. Neuman* (1962), pp. 569–79.

prophecy'.[33] His reign appears to the Jewish historian to have been a pre-eminently happy one.[34] He is right if political power is regarded as the measure of prosperity. Following his ancestors' advancement of Jewish territory as far as the sea by means of the acquisition of Joppa and Gazara and other conquests in the west, Hyrcanus had, by new conquests in the east, south and north, and by ensuring his independence of Syria, created a Jewish state such as had not existed since the dispersal of the ten tribes, and perhaps not since the partition of the kingdom after the death of Solomon.

Among the great sepulchral monuments in the vicinity of Jerusalem, Josephus frequently mentions in the *Jewish War* that of the 'High Priest John'.[35]

33. Jos. *Ant.* xiii 10, 7 (299–300). An Aramaic echo of the belief in the prophetic character of Hyrcanus I may be detected in a pro-Hasmonaean relic surviving in Tg. Ps.Jon. on Dt. 33:11 (the blessing of Levi): 'Bless o Lord the sacrifices of the House of Levi, those who give the tenth from the tithe, and receive with pleasure the oblation from the hand of Elijah the priest which he offered on Mount Carmel. Break the loins of Ahab, his enemy, and the neck of the false prophets who rose against him. As for the enemies of John the High Priest, may they have no foot to stand on.' The exegesis underlying this Targum passage associates Elijah, the model of the true prophet opposed by false teachers, with John Hyrcanus, hated by his enemies (the Pharisees). See A. Geiger, *Urschrift*, p. 479; P. Kahle, *The Cairo Geniza* ([2]1959), pp. 202–3; R. Meyer, 'Elijah und Ahab', *Abraham unser Vater, Festschr. O. Michel* (1963), pp. 356–68; R. Le Déaut, *Introduction*, pp. 92–3. See also J. Bassfreund, MGWJ 44 (1900), pp. 481–6; G. Dalman, *Grammatik*, p. 30; *Die Worte Jesu* ([2]1930), pp. 68–9.

34. Jos. *Ant.* xiii 10, 7 (299).

35. Jos. *B.J.* v 6, 2 (259); 7, 3 (304); 9, 2 (356); 11, 4 (468); vi 2, 10 (169).

For an identification of John Hyrcanus as one of 'the last Priests of Jerusalem' in IQpHab., see G. Vermes, *Discovery in the Judean Desert* (1956), p. 79; *The Dead Sea Scrolls in English* (1968), p. 65.

§ 9 ARISTOBULUS I 104–103 B.C.

Sources

Josephus *Ant.* xiii 11 (301–19); *B.J.* i 3 (70–84).

On the disputed question of his coins see n. 7 below and Appendix IV.

Bibliography

Graetz, H., *Geschichte der Juden* III ([5]1905–6), pp. 117–20.
Wellhausen, J., *Israelitische und jüdische Geschichte* ([9]1958), pp. 262–3.
Abel, F.-M., *Histoire de la Palestine* I (1952), pp. 224–5.
Schalit, A., *König Herodes* (1969), pp. 708–9, 743–4.

John Hyrcanus left five sons.[1] He nevertheless stipulated in his will that the secular authority should devolve upon his wife,[2] whereas his eldest son Aristobulus should receive only the office of High Priest. The young man was not satisfied with this. He committed his mother to prison, and to death there by starvation, and assumed power himself.[3] With the exception of Antigonus, he also incarcerated all his brothers. Only in Antigonus had he enough trust to allow him a share in the government. But it was this privileged position that proved fatal to Antigonus. It aroused the jealousy of many, and their intrigues in the end succeeded in causing Aristobulus to murder the brother whom he loved. Told that Antigonus himself aspired after supreme power, Aristobulus became suspicious, and gave the order to his bodyguard that if Antigonus should come to him armed he should be struck down. At the same time, he asked his brother to come to him unarmed. The enemies of Antigonus bribed the messenger, however, and made him say instead that Aristobulus had heard that he had acquired new weapons and armour, and invited him to visit him fully armed so that he could see them. Antigonus did so, and entering the citadel unsuspectingly, was killed by the guard. Aristobulus is said to have suffered bitter regret after the deed was done, so much so that it hastened his death.[4]

This whole domestic tragedy—if it may be taken as historical—reveals Aristobulus's character in a very poor light. His only interest was the exercise of power. All regard for piety was sacrificed to this. In other ways, too, Aristobulus departed further than his father from the ancient traditions of the Maccabees. Monarchical pride drove him

1. Jos. *Ant.* xiii 10, 7 (299).
2. *Ant.* xiii 11, 1 (302); *B.J.* i 3, 1 (71).
3. *Ant.* xiii 11, 1 (302); *B.J.* i 3, 1 (71). On the chronology, see above pp. 200–1.
4. *Ant.* xiii 11, 1–3 (303–17); *B.J.* i 3, 2–6 (72–84).

(according to Josephus) to assume the royal title borne by his descendants from this period onward until the time of Pompey.[5] Greek culture, the spread of which was once opposed by the Maccabees, was directly favoured by him; that he also bore the title *Φιλέλλην* appears probable from the words of Josephus.[6] As his father, Hyrcanus, had given purely Greek names to his sons (Aristobulus, Antigonus, Alexander), it may be assumed that is was he who paved the way for the views eventually adopted by Aristobulus.

It is not certain whether Aristobulus minted coins, but if he did, he made no use on them, either of his royal title, or his Greek name. The coins in question have the legend:

יהודה הכהן הגדל וחבר היהודים

Judas the High Priest and the Congregation of the Jews.[7]

Notwithstanding his phil-Hellenism, Aristobulus remained fundamentally Jewish, as is shown by the most important event of his short reign; namely, the conquest and Judaizing of the northern districts of Palestine. He undertook a campaign against the Ituraeans, conquered a large part of their land, united it with Judaea, and forced its inhabitants to be circumcised and to live according to the Jewish Law.[8] The Ituraeans resided in the Lebanon.[9] Since Josephus does not say that Aristobulus subdued 'the Ituraeans', but only that he conquered and Judaized part of their country; since, furthermore, Galilee had not hitherto belonged to the territory of the Jewish High Priest (see above p. 141; the conquests of John Hyrcanus I in the north had only extended as far as Samaria and Scythopolis; and since also, the population of Galilee was until this time more Gentile than Jewish (see above p. 142),

5. *Ant.* xiii 11, 1 (301); *B.J.* i 3, 1 (70). Strabo, xvi 2, 40 (762), relates this of Alexander Jannaeus, possibly because he overlooked the short reign of Aristobulus. But E. Meyer, *Ursprung und Anfänge* II, pp. 275–6, argues that Strabo is correct. Priestly kings ruled, for instance, in Sidon. Cf. vol. II, § 23, 4.

6. *Ant.* xiii 11, 3 (318): *χρηματίσας μὲν φιλέλλην*. From the context, this probably means, 'he called himself *Φιλέλλην*', rather than, 'he acted as someone friendly towards the Greeks'; see Meyer, *op. cit.*, II, p. 277. For various Parthian kings with the title *Φιλέλλην*, see *BMC Parthia*, pp. 275–80; J. Neusner, *A History of the Jews in Babylonia* I (1965), p. 8. Cf. also the Nabataean king, Aretas (see Appendix II, pp. 578–9).

7. On Aristobulus's Hebrew name, cf. Jos. *Ant.* xx 10, 3 (240) *'Ιούδᾳ τῷ καὶ 'Αριστοβούλῳ κληθέντι*. On the coins see, for their attribution to Aristobulus I, most recently B. Kanael, 'Altjüdische Münzen', Jahrb. f. Numism. u. Geldgesch. 17 (1967), p. 167; and for their attribution to Aristobulus II (see below, p. 233), Y. Meshorer, *Jewish Coins*, pp. 41–55. Cf. Appendix IV, p. 605.

8. Jos. *Ant.* xiii 11, 3 (318) *πολεμήσας 'Ιτουραίους καὶ πολλὴν αὐτῶν τῆς χώρας τῇ 'Ιουδαίᾳ προσκτησάμενος*. Strabo, following Timagenes and quoted by Josephus *ibid.* (319), has *χώραν τε γὰρ αὐτοῖς προσεκτήσατο καὶ τὸ μέρος τοῦ τῶν Ιτουραίων ἔθνους ᾠκειώσατο*. This passage is Jacoby FGrH 88 F 5 (Timagenes) = 91 F 11 (Strabo).

9. See Appendix I, p. 562.

it is justifiable to presume that the region conquered by Aristobulus was mainly Galilee, and that it was through him that Galilee was first Judaized.[10] In any case, he extended Judaism further to the north, as Hyrcanus had done toward the south.

Aristobulus died of a painful disease after a reign of only one year.[11] Since Gentile historians judge him favourably,[12] it is possible that the charge of cruelty towards his relatives laid against this Hellenophile Sadducee was an invention of his political opponents, the Pharisees.

10. This interpretation is supported by the fact that the territories north and east of Galilee were still predominantly Gentile in the Herodian period. They cannot therefore have already been Judaized by Aristobulus. Consequently, the area annexed by Aristobulus must have been Galilee. That Josephus does not call it Galilee, may be explained by his use of a non-Jewish source. Another objection may be raised against the thesis that Galilee first came under Hasmonaean rule under Aristobulus, viz. that John Hyrcanus caused his son, Alexander Jannaeus, to be brought up there, *Ant.* xiii 12, 1 (322). But the implication of this may be precisely that Hyrcanus, not wishing his son to succeed to the throne, had him educated outside the country. It is also possible that Hyrcanus was already in possession of the southern parts of Galilee. The above remarks would then only refer to the northern parts. The statement concerning Alexander's upbringing in Galilee is, moreover, open to considerable suspicion because of the context in which it appears.

11. *Ant.* xiii 11, 3 (318); *B.J.* i 3, 6 (84).

12. Strabo, following Timagenes, quoted by Jos. *Ant.* xiii 11, 3 (319) ἐπιεικής τε ἐγένετο οὗτος ὁ ἀνὴρ καὶ πολλὰ τοῖς Ἰουδαίοις χρήσιμος. See n. 8 above.

§ 10 ALEXANDER JANNAEUS 103–76 B.C.

Sources

Josephus *Ant.* xiii 12, 1–16, 1 (320–406); *B.J.* i 4 (85–106).
Syncellus, ed. Dindorf I, pp. 558–9.
Rabbinic literature: Genesis Rabbah 91:3
yBerakhoth 11b; bBerakhoth 48a
bYoma 26b
bSukkah 48b
bKiddushin 66a.
Cf. Derenbourg, *op. cit.*, pp. 96–102.

For the Qumran evidence see n. 22 below.

For the coins see n. 28 below and Appendix IV.

Bibliography

Derenbourg, J., *Essai sur l'histoire et la géographie de la Palestine* (1867), pp. 95–102.

Graetz, H., *Geschichte der Juden* III ([5]1905–6), pp. 123–35.

Abel, F.-M., *Histoire de la Palestine* I (1952), pp. 225–39.

Aptowitzer, V., *Parteipolitik der Hasmonäerzeit in rabbinischen und pseudo-epigraphischen Schrifttum* (1927).

Schalit, A., 'The Conquests of Alexander Jannaeus in Moab', Ereẓ Yisrael I (1951), pp. 104–21 (Hebrew) = 'Die Eroberungen des Alexander Jannäus in Moab', *Theokratia* 1 (1967/9), pp. 3–50 (revised and expanded).

Kanael, B., 'Notes on Alexander Jannaeus' Campaigns in the Coastal Region', Tarbiz 24 (1954–5), pp. 9–15 (Hebrew with Engl. summary).

Rabin, C., 'Alexander Jannaeus and the Pharisees', JJS 7 (1956), pp. 3–11.

Galling, K., 'Die τερπωλή des Alexander Jannäus', *Von Ugarit nach Qumran* [O. Eissfeldt Festschrift], BZAW 77 (1958), pp. 49–62.

Stern, M., 'The Political Background of the Wars of Alexander Yannai', Tarbiz 33 (1963–4), pp. 325–36 (Hebrew with Engl. summary).

Rappaport, U., 'La Judée et Rome pendant le règne d'Alexandre Jannée', REJ 127 (1968), pp. 129–45.

Efron, Y., 'Simeon ben Shetaḥ and King Yannai', *In Memory of Gedaliahu Alon—Essays in Jewish History and Philology* (1970), pp. 69–132 (Hebrew).

When Aristobulus died, his widow Salome Alexandra released his three brothers whom he had imprisoned, and raised the eldest, Alexander Yannai or Jannaeus, to the throne and the High-Priesthood,[1] offering him at the same time her hand in marriage.[2]

1. *Ant.* xiii 12, 1 (320–3); *B.J.* i 4, 1 (85).

2. There is no direct evidence for this last statement. But since Josephus calls Aristobulus's wife Salome (or Salina?) Alexandra, *Ant.* xiii 12, 1 (320), both of which names were also borne by the wife of Alexander Jannaeus, there can be little doubt about the identity. On the Hebrew name of Alexandra, see below § 11.

Alexander Jannaeus (103–76 B.C.)[3] was, during his reign of twenty-seven years, almost continuously involved in foreign and internal wars for the most part deliberately provoked by him, and which by no means always turned out well.

He began by launching hostilities against the citizens of Ptolemais,[4] whom he defeated and whose city he surrounded. They turned for help to the Egyptian king, Ptolemy Lathyrus, who having been thrust from the throne by his mother Cleopatra, was at that time ruling in Cyprus. Ptolemy arrived with an army, and Alexander through fear of him raised the siege.[5] He then tried to rid himself of Ptolemy by overtly concluding treaties of peace and of friendship with him whilst secretly appealing for assistance to his mother. At first, Ptolemy consented willingly to the alliance, but when he heard that Alexander had secretly asked for help against him from his mother, he broke the truce and advanced with an army against Alexander. He conquered and plundered the town of Asochis in Galilee,[6] and then confronted Alexander near Asophon (or Asaphon) on the Jordan.[7] Alexander had an impressive army, excellently equipped. That of Ptolemy was not nearly so well armed, but his soldiers were more agile and had confidence in the tactical skill of their general, Philostephanus. As the river separated the two armies, the Egyptian troops crossed over, and Alexander allowed this to happen, hoping to crush them all the more surely. Both sides fought bravely and Alexander's army even won the initial advantages. But then the Egyptian general, by skilful manoeuvres, succeeded in forcing a section of the Jewish army to fall back; and once one part fled, the rest were unable to hold their ground. The whole Jewish army took to flight and the Egyptians hunted them down, killing them 'until their swords were blunt from murder and their hands were weary'.[8]

The whole country now lay exposed to Ptolemy. However, to counter her son's increasing power, Cleopatra sent an army to Palestine. While

3. On the chronology, see above p. 200.

4. On Ptolemais, ancient Akko, one of the most important coastal towns of Phoenicia in the immediate neighbourhood of Galilee, see vol. II, § 23, 1.

5. *Ant.* xiii 12, 2–4 (324–34).

6. Asochis is also frequently mentioned by Josephus in the *Vita*, 41 (207); 45 (233); 68 (384)). It lay close to Sepphoris, *Ant.* xiii 12, 5 (338) *μικρὸν ἄπωθεν*, *Vita* 45 (233) *παρὰ δὲ Σεπφωριτῶν εἰς 'Ασωχὶν καταβάντες*, in the plain, *Vita* 41 (207), and thus in the present plain of Beth Netophah. On its probable situation, see Guérin, *Galilée*, I, pp. 494–7; references in Avi-Yonah, *Map of Roman Palestine* ([2]1940), p. 32.

7. *'Ασωφών* or *'Ασαφῶν* (as given by some MSS.) is otherwise unknown. It is probably identical with צפון (Jos. 13:27). See Abel, *Géog. Pal.* II, p. 448.

8. *Ant.* xiii 12, 5 (343) *ἕως οὗ καὶ ὁ σίδηρος αὐτοῖς ἠμβλύνθη κτείνουσι καὶ αἱ χεῖρες παρείθησαν*. For the full account, Jos. *Ant.* xiii 12, 4–5 (326–44).

it was operating there, Ptolemy succeeded in advancing as far as Egypt. He was nevertheless driven back and compelled to retreat to Gaza, and Cleopatra took possession of the whole of Palestine. Once the power was in her hands, some of her friends advised her to unite the land of the Jews with Egypt. But her Jewish general Ananias was able to divert her from this plan and to persuade her instead to conclude an alliance with Alexander. Ptolemy was now no longer able to hold out in Jewish territory, and returned to Cyprus. Cleopatra also withdrew her army, and Alexander was once again master of the land.[9]

Now he could think about further conquests. He began east of Jordan by capturing Gadara[10] and the strongly fortified bastion of Amathus on the Jordan,[11] taking the former after a siege lasting ten months. Then he turned against Philistia, conquering Raphia, Anthedon, and finally the illustrious ancient city of Gaza.[12] He was outside that town for a full year, and in the end only seized it through treachery, whereupon he gave it up to be sacked and burnt.[13]

The conquest of Gaza must have taken place in 96 B.C., for it was about the same time that Antiochus VIII Grypus died.[14]

No sooner was there peace outside the frontiers of Palestine, than strife began within them. The damaging party-antagonism that had already cast its shadow over the reign of Hyrcanus, turned that of Alexander into a period of internal agitation and dissension. A rabbinic tradition of little historical value relates that there was friction between the king and the head of the school of the Pharisees, Simeon ben Shetaḥ, reputed to be a brother of Alexander's wife, Salome. According to this story, 'three hundred Nazirites came to Jerusalem to offer the prescribed sacrifices. Simeon found ways and means of dispensing half of them from doing so, but was unable to include the other half, and therefore petitioned the king to defray the costs, pretending that he, Simeon, was paying them. The king complied. But when he discovered that Simeon had lied to him, he was very vexed, and Simon had to go into hiding to escape his wrath. Some time later, Parthian envoys arrived

9. *Ant.* xiii 13, 1–3 (348–56).

10. Gadara is the place well known from the Gospels, south-east of Lake Gennesaret, and at that time an important Hellenistic town. For further details see vol. II, § 23, 1.

11. *Ant.* xiii 13, 3 (356): *μέγιστον ἔρυμα τῶν ὑπὲρ τὸν Ἰορδάνην κατῳκημένων*, later the seat of one of the five councils instituted by Gabinius, Jos. *Ant.* xiv 5, 4 (91); *B.J.* i 8, 5 (170). According to Eusebius, it lay twenty-one Roman miles south of Pella, *Onomast.* ed. Klostermann, p. 22, *λέγεται δὲ καὶ νῦν Ἀμμαθοῦς κώμη ἐν τῇ Περαίᾳ τῇ κατωτέρᾳ Πέλλων διεστῶσα σημείοις κά εἰς νότον*. This statement agrees with the position of the modern site of Amatha near the Jordan, north of the Jabbok. See Abel. *Géog. Pal.* II, pp. 242–3.

12. On Raphia, Anthedon and Gaza see vol. II, § 23, 1.

13. *Ant.* xiii 13, 3 (356–64); *B.J.* i 4, 2 (87).

14. *Ant.* xiii 13, 4 (365). See above p. 134.

at the royal court wishing to see the celebrated rabbis. The king turned to his wife, who knew where Simeon was, and asked her to persuade her brother to come out into the open. The queen made Alexander promise that no harm would come to him and induced him to appear. Seated between the king and the queen, Simeon then had the following conversation with Yannai:

King: 'Why did you flee?'

Simeon: 'Because I heard that my Lord, the King, was angry with me.'

King: 'And why did you deceive me?'

Simeon: 'I did not deceive you. You have given your gold, and I my wisdom.'

King: 'But why did you not tell me this?'

Simeon: 'If I had told you, then you would not have given it to me.'

King: 'Why have you seated yourself between the king and the queen?'

Simeon: 'Because it is written in the Book of Ben Sira, "Exalt wisdom and it will raise you up; it will seat you between the princes" ' (Sir. 11:1). At this, the king ordered wine to be set before him and asked him to say the grace. Simeon began, 'Praised be God for the food which Yannai and his companions have received.'

King: 'So you are just as obstinate as ever. I have never before heard the name of Yannai mentioned in the grace.'

Simeon: 'Could I say that we praise Thee for that which we have eaten, when I as yet have received nothing?' The king ordered that Simeon should be brought food to eat, and when he had finished, he said, 'Praised be God for that which we have eaten.'[15]

Alexander's real conflicts with the Pharisees, and the people led by them, were of an entirely different and more serious nature. Their deeper cause was to be found in the general development of internal conditions since the establishment of the Hasmonaean dynasty. The Pharisees had acquired more and more power and influence among the people. Hasmonaean policy had increasingly deviated from their aspirations and now stood in glaring opposition to them. It could only be with suppressed rage that they saw that a fierce warrior like Alexander Jannaeus discharged the office of High Priest in the sanctuary, certainly not with a scrupulous observance of ordinances regarded by the Pharisees as of divine origin. It was in fact while he was exercising his priestly office that open rebellion broke out for the first time. On the Feast of Tabernacles, when it was customary for every participant

15. See Gen.R. 91:3; yBer 11b; bBer. 48a. Cf. Derenbourg, *op. cit.*, pp. 96–8, I. Levi, REJ 35 (1897), pp. 213–17. Cf. also Graetz, *op. cit.*, III ([5]1905–6), pp. 125 f., 705 f. (n. 13).

to carry a palm-branch (*lulab*, φοίνιξ) and a lemon (*ethrog*, κίτρον), he was once pelted with lemons by the assembled people whilst standing before the altar about to offer sacrifice. He was taunted with shouts that as the son of a prisoner of war he was unworthy to offer sacrifice. Alexander was not a man to accept this quietly. He ordered his mercenaries to intervene and six thousand Jews were massacred.[16] From then on, the people's animosity was so great that they waited only for a favourable opportunity to shake off the hated yoke.

Through his love of war, Alexander was soon involved in fresh embroilments. He marched against the Arab tribes east of the Jordan and placed the Moabites and Gileadites under an obligation to pay tribute. Amathus, conquered previously but not held, was now levelled to the ground. He then commenced hostilities against the Nabataean king Obedas, but whilst fighting him in the region of Gaulanitis,[17] he once fell into an ambush in which he found himself in such difficulties that he barely escaped with his life. He went as a fugitive to Jerusalem, but a poor reception awaited him. The Pharisees took advantage of the hour of Alexander's political weakness to break down his power internally as well. An open rebellion was launched against him, and with the help of foreign mercenaries, Alexander had to fight for six long years against his own people. No less than fifty thousand Jews are said to have lost their lives during this period of civil conflict. When at last his strength was exhausted he offered to make peace. But the Pharisees wished to exploit the situation so as to secure complete victory for their party. In consequence, when Alexander inquired what they wanted from him, and under what conditions they would agree to peace and obedience, they asked only for his death. At the same time, they called to their aid Demetrius III Eucaerus, a son of

16. Jos. *Ant.* xiii 13, 5 (372–3); *B.J.* i 4, 3 (88). In the Talmud (bSukk. 48b; cf. bYom. 26b), the story is told of a Sadducee who, on the Feast of Tabernacles, once poured the customary libation of water, not on the altar, but on his feet, whereupon the people pelted him with lemons. Alexander's name is not mentioned, but he may well be meant. See Wellhausen, *Pharisäer und Sadducäer*, p. 96; Graetz, III (^{5}1905–6), pp. 127 f., 706–7; Derenbourg, *op. cit.*, pp. 98 f. On the Hasmonaean unfitness to hold the office of High Priest, see *Ant.* xiii 10, 5 (292), apropos of John Hyrcanus. Cf. bKidd. 66a, where Yannai is named as the person whose mother was captured by the enemy in Modiim, which disqualified him from acting as a priest. The story is probably unhistorical but even so it fits Hyrcanus better than Alexander. See p. 214 above.

17. The name of the place is given in *B.J.* i 4, 4 (90) as κατὰ τὴν Γαυλάνην. This is ancient Golan, the capital of the region of Gaulanitis, east of Lake Tiberias. In *Ant.* xiii 13, 5 (375), the best manuscript gives κατὰ Γάδαρα κώμην τῆς Ἰουδάνιδος. Instead of Γάδαρα, other manuscripts have Γαραδα or Χαραδρα; in place of Ἰουδάνιδος most read Γαλααδίτιδος. The term κώμη shows that the well-known town of Gadara cannot be meant. The correct form of the name of the district is probably, from *B.J.* i 4, 4 (90), Γαυλανίτιδος. See Abel, *Géog. Pal.* II, p. 149.

Antiochus Grypus and at that time ruler of part of Syria[18]—this being about 88 B.C.[19]

Demetrius came with an army. The Jewish people's party joined him at Shechem and Alexander was totally defeated; he lost all his mercenaries and was forced to flee to the mountains.[20] But now a feeling of national solidarity seems to have made itself felt among the Jews allied to Demetrius. They preferred to be subject to a Hasmonaean prince in a free Jewish state than to be annexed to the empire of a descendant of the Seleucids. Six thousand Jews went over to Alexander, and Demetrius subsequently returned to his own land. The remaining Jews, who persisted in their rebellion, tried to deal with Alexander on their own. But they were defeated in several battles and many of them were slain. The leaders of the revolt finally fled to Bethome (or Bethoma) or Bemeselis,[21] where they were besieged by Alexander. After capturing the town, Alexander took them as prisoners to Jerusalem, and whilst carousing with his mistresses—according to the account of Josephus—had about eight hundred of them crucified before his eyes in the centre of the city. Furthermore, he obliged them while they were still alive to watch the slaughter of their wives and children. His opponents in Jerusalem were so terrified at this that eight thousand of them fled by night and avoided Judaea for as long as he lived.[22]

For the rest of his reign, Alexander enjoyed peace at home. But not so abroad.

18. *Ant.* xiii 13, 5 (375–6); *B.J.* i 4, 4 (90–2).

19. I.e., more than six years after the conquest of Gaza (96 B.C.). therefore after 90 B.C., but still prior to 86 B.C., as the coinage of Demetrius III Eucaerus in Damascus continues down to 88/7 B.C., but is then replaced in 87/6 B.C. by that of Antiochus XII. See pp. 134–5 above.

20. *Ant.* xiii 14, 1–2 (377–9). *B.J.* i 4, 4–5 (92–5).

21. The former according to *Ant.* xiii 14, 2 (380), the latter according to *B.J.* i 4, 6 (96). Neither can be proved. Bemeselis may be properly Bemelchis = Beth ha-Melekh, see S. Klein, Tarbiz 1 (1930), p. 157, and is commonly identified with Misilye, some 10 miles north-east of Samaria. See Abel, *Géog. Pal.* II, p. 178.

22. *Ant.* xiii 15, 2 (389–91); *B.J.* i 4, 6 (96–8). Jannaeus's conflict with Demetrius III and his cruelty towards his political opponents appear to be echoed in the Qumran literature. Whilst the theory advanced by some scholars (e.g. M. Delcor, *Essai sur le Midrash d'Habacuc* (1951), pp. 56–61; M. H. Segal, 'The Habakkuk "Commentary" and the Damascus Fragments', JBL 71 (1952), pp. 131–47; F. F. Bruce, *Second Thoughts on the Dead Sea Scrolls* (1956), pp. 91–8; J. van der Ploeg, *Excavations at Qumran* (1958), pp. 60–1) concerning the identity of the Wicked Priest and Alexander Jannaeus is seriously weakened by the findings of archaeology (viz. the Qumran establishment was founded 30 to 40 years before the time of Jannaeus), most historians agree in recognising in him the villain of the Nahum Commentary (see J. M. Allegro, DJD V, *Qumran Cave* 4, I (1968), pp. 37–42; preliminary publications in JBL 75 (1956), pp. 89–95; JSS 7 (1962), pp. 304–8; see PEQ 91 (1959), pp. 47–51; cf. A. Dupont-Sommer, *The Essene Writings from Qumran* (1961), pp. 268–70; G. Vermes, *The Dead Sea Scrolls in English* (1968), pp. 65, 231–5; J. Carmignac, *Les textes de Qumran* II (1963), pp.

The Seleucid empire was at that time in its death throes. But its last convulsions brought unrest to Judaea also. Antiochus XII, the youngest of the five sons of Antiochus Grypus, was at war simultaneously with his brother Philip, and the king of the Nabataeans. Once when he intended to pass through Judaea on his way to Arabia, Alexander Jannaeus wished to prevent him from doing so by throwing up a great wall and a trench from Joppa to Capharsaba, fortifying the

---

53–4, 85–7; A. Dupont-Sommer, 'Observations sur le Commentaire de Nahum', Journ. des Savants (1963), pp. 201–27, etc.).

The two most important passages are: (1) 1 QpNah I 2 on Nah. 2:12 (Whither the lion goes, there is the lion's cub with none to disturb it):

'[Interpreted this concerns Deme]trius king of Greece (ד[מי]טרוס מלך יון) who sought on the counsel of those who seek smooth things to enter Jerusalem . . .'

(2) 1QpNah I 6–8 on Nah. 2:13 (And [the lion] chokes [מחנק] prey for its lionesses and it fills its caves with prey and its dens with victims):

'Interpreted it concerns the furious young lion (כפיר החרון) [who executes re-]venge on those who seek smooth things and hangs men alive (יתלה אנשים חיים), [a thing never done] formerly in Israel. Because of a man hanged alive on the tree (לתלוי חי על העץ) He proclaims, 'Behold I am against you, says the Lord of Hosts . . . (Nah. 2:14)'.

It is clear that the 'Furious Young Lion' is a Jewish ruler accused of having 'hanged men alive', a shocking novelty in Israel. The phrase 'to hang a man alive' means 'to crucify'; see Sifre on Dt. 21:22 § 221, תולין אותו חי כדרך שהמלכות עושין, cf. N. Wieder, 'Notes on the New Documents from the Fourth Cave of Qumran', JJS 7 (1956), pp. 71–2. Note also that the story interprets the term חנק 'to choke, to strangle' in the Nahum text. For an assimilation of the fourth Mishnaic death penalty, strangulation (*ḥenek*) with crucifixion, see Tg Ruth 1:17 (צליבת קיסא); cf. also J. Heinemann, 'The *Targum* of Ex. xxii, 4 and the Ancient *Halakha*', Tarbiz 38 (1968–9), pp. 294–6 (in Hebrew with an Engl. summary). This 'hanging men alive' is an act of vengeance on 'those who seek smooth things' (דורשי החלקות) an expression referring to a group, most likely the Pharisees, whose doctrines and customs were condemned by the Qumran writers (cf. pNah I 2; II 2, 4; III 3, 6–7; 1QHod. 2:12, 32; CDC 1:18).

Bearing all this in mind, one can have little doubt concerning the identification of the 'Furious Young Lion' as Alexander Jannaeus. Moreover, if a distinction between the 'Wicked Priest' and 'the last Priests of Jerusalem' mentioned in 1QpHab. IX 4–7 is recognised, Yannai is bound to be counted among the latter; cf. G. Vermes, *Discovery*, pp. 78–9; *The Dead Sea Scrolls in English*, pp. 64–5. For the 143 coins of Alexander Jannaeus found at Qumran see R. de Vaux, *L'archéologie et les manuscrits de la Mer Morte* (1961), p. 15.

For a fresh approach to this text in the light of the Temple Scroll (col. LXIV, lines 6–13), see Y. Yadin, 'Pesher Nahum (4Q pNahum) reconsidered', IEJ 21 (1971), pp. 1–12. Yadin argues that execution by 'hanging' was not an innovation by Jannaeus but a traditional penalty inflicted on persons guilty of a crime against the state. Cf. however J. M. Baumgarten, JBL 91 (1972), pp. 472–81.

On Alexander's proverbial cruelty, see Jos. *Ant.* xiii 14, 2 (383). The nickname *Thrakidas* (*ibid.*) is associated by J. M. Allegro, PEQ 91 (1959), pp. 47–51, with the 'Lion of Wrath' of 4Q pNahum, but without valid reasons, as is shown by M. Stern, 'Thrachides—Surname of Alexander Yannai in Josephus and Syncellus', Tarbiz 29 (1959–60), pp. 207–9. R. Marcus, *Josephus* (Loeb) VII (1957), p. 419 renders *Thrakidas* (the Thracian) as 'the "Cossack" '.

wall with wooden towers. But Antiochus set the whole structure alight and marched over it.[23]

As Antiochus met his death in battle against the king of the Nabataeans (Aretas), whose authority stretched as far as Damascus, the latter became from then on the Jews' most powerful and dangerous neighbour. In the south and east, Palestine bordered on regions within the Nabataean sphere of influence. Alexander Jannaeus felt its effect directly. He was obliged to retreat before an attack by Aretas on Adida (in the heart of Judaea), where he suffered a considerable defeat, and was able to persuade the Nabataean king to withdraw only by making concessions.[24]

He had more success in the campaigns which he undertook during the next three years (about 83–80 B.C.) east of the Jordan, with the object of extending his power in that direction. He conquered Pella, Dium and Gerasa, then advanced further north and took Gaulana and Seleucia, and finally the strong fortress of Gamala. On his return to Jerusalem after these exploits, he was received by the people, this time with rejoicing.[25] Not long afterwards, he contracted, as a result of over-drinking, an illness which lasted for the three remaining years of his life (79–6 B.C.). He nevertheless carried on with his military enterprises until, in the midst of the turmoil of the siege of the fortress of Ragaba,

23. *Ant.* xiii 15, 1 (389–91); *B.J.* i 4, 7 (99–102). Capharsaba (K^e^phar Saba), north-east of Tel-Aviv, lay near the later Antipatris. See vol. II, § 23, 1.

24. *Ant.* xiii 15, 2 (392); *B.J.* i 4, 8 (103). On Adida (Ḥadid), see above p. 186 on 1 Mac. 12:38. It lay east of Lydda and commanded the road leading from Joppa to Jerusalem. On Aretas and the Nabataean kings in general, see Appendix II below.

25. *Ant.* xiii 15, 3 (393–4); *B.J.* i 4, 8 (104–5). These all lie east of the Jordan. On Pella, Dium and Gerasa see vol. II, § 23, 1. In *B.J.*, Josephus mentions only Pella and Gerasa, and in *Ant.* only Dium and Essa, the latter certainly a textual corruption for Gerasa since the more detailed statements in regard to both places are identical. Instead of Dium, the manuscripts in our passage give the form *Δίαν* which is also found elsewhere (see vol. II, § 23, 1). Gaulana is ancient Golan east of Lake Tiberias, from which the province of Gaulanitis derives its name (Dt. 4:43; Jos. 20:8; 21:27; 1 Chr. 6:56). Eusebius knew it still as a large village, *Onomast.* ed. Klostermann, p. 64: *καὶ νῦν Γαυλὼν καλεῖται κώμη μεγίστη ἐν τῇ Βαταναίᾳ*. But its position has not been determined, see Abel. *Géog. Pal.*, pp. 338–9. Seleucia is also frequently mentioned by Josephus in the history of the Jewish war, *B.J.* ii 20, 6 (574); iv 1, 1 (2); *Vita* 37 (187). According to *B.J.* iv 1, 1 (2), it lay on Lake Semechonitis. It can be identified as the modern Seluqiye, south-east of Lake Huleh, Abel, *Géog. Pal.* II, pp. 453–4. On Gamala, the conquest of which by Vespasian is related in detail by Josephus in *B.J.* iv 1, 3–10 (11–83), see § 20. From the list of Nabataean towns, *Ant.* xiv 1, 4 (18), inherited by Hyrcanus II from his father Yannai, M. Stern concludes that the defeat by Aretas at Ḥadid must have been followed by a Jewish victory over the Nabataeans some time between 83 and 76 B.C. Josephus's silence is explained by his use of a Hellenistic source, probably Nicolaus of Damascus, hostile to Alexander and ignoring his victory. See 'The Political Background of the Wars of Alexander Yannai', Tarbiz 33 (1963–4), pp. 335–6.

he at last succumbed to his illness and his exertions, in 76 B.C.[26] His body was brought to Jerusalem, where he was buried with great pomp.[27]

Of the coins minted by Alexander Jannaeus,[28] the most interesting are those with the bi-lingual inscription:

יהונתן המלך *ΒΑΣΙΛΕΩΣ ΑΛΕΞΑΝΔΡΟΥ*

Yehonathan the King—King Alexander

F. de Saulcy was the first to realise that the Hebrew inscription gives the Hebrew name of Alexander. Yannai is thus an abbreviation of Jonathan, and not, as was formerly assumed, of Yehoḥanan. Other coins issued by him bear the inscription:

יהונתן [ינתן] הכהן הגדל וחבר היהודים

Yehonathan (or Yonathan) the High Priest and the Congregation of the Jews.[29]

As a result of Alexander's conquests, the frontiers of the Jewish state now extended far beyond those established by John Hyrcanus. In the south, the Idumaeans were subjugated and Judaized. In the north, Alexander's rule reached as far as Seleucia on Lake Merom. The sea-coast, where once Joppa had been the first conquest of the Maccabees, was now almost entirely under Jewish control. With the sole exception of Ascalon, which had managed to preserve its independence, all the coastal towns from the Egyptian frontier to Mount Carmel

26. *Ant.* xiii 15, 5 (398); *B.J.* i 4, 8 (106). According to Josephus, Ragaba was situated in the region of Gerasa (*ἐν τοῖς Γερασηνῶν ὅροις*), i.e., east of Jordan. It may be identical with Regeb in Perea, mentioned in the Mishnah, mMen. 8:3, as yielding the second best oil in Palestine, but it was certainly not *Ἐργά*, fifteen Roman miles west of Gerasa, Eusebius, *Onomast.* ed. Klostermann, p. 16, for the latter must have long since been in Jannaeus's possession. For the same reason it cannot be identified with the modern Ragib near Amathus. Cf. Abel, *Géog. Pal.* II, p. 427.

27. *Ant.* xiii 16 1 (405–6). The monument of Alexander is mentioned by Josephus in *B.J.* v 7, 3 (304).

28. On the coins of Alexander Jannaeus, see A. Kindler, 'The Jaffa Hoard of Alexander Jannaeus', IEJ 4 (1954), pp. 170–85; Y. Meshorer, *Jewish Coins of the Second Temple Period* (1967), pp. 56–9, 118–21; cf. B. Kanael, 'Altjüdische Münzen', Jahrb. f. Num. u. Geldgesch. 17 (1967), pp. 167–71. For the view that some of his Aramaic and Greek coins are dated to his 20th and 25th years, see J. Naveh, 'Dated Coins of Alexander Janneus', IEJ 18 (1968), pp. 20–5, and A. Kindler, 'Addendum to the Dated Coins of Alexander Janneus', *ibid.*, pp. 188–91. Cf. Appendix IV below.

29. According to Kanael, *op. cit.*, pp. 169–71, High Priest, King, High Priest, is the probable sequence of the titles used by Yannai. His relinquishment of the royal style may have resulted from his conflict with the Pharisees. However the Aramaic-Greek coins (מלכא אלסנדרוס/*ΒΑΣΙΛΕΩΣ ΑΛΕΞΑΝΔΡΟΥ*) dating to the 25th year of his rule would indicate that two years before his death he still used, or reverted again to the title 'King'. Cf. Appendix IV, below.

had been conquered by Alexander.[30] But in addition, all the country east of the Jordan, from Lake Merom to the Dead Sea, came under his jurisdiction, including a number of important towns which had until then been centres of Greek culture, such as Hippos, Gadara, Pella, Dium and others.[31]

This work of conquest proved, however, to be at the same time a work of destruction. It was not a question of the advancement of Greek civilisation, as in the conquests of Alexander the Great, but of its annihilation. For in this, Alexander Jannaeus was still Jew enough to subject conquered territories as far as possible to Jewish customs. If the captured towns refused to comply, they were razed to the ground.[32] In particular, this was the fate of the large and hitherto prosperous coastal towns and of the Hellenistic cities east of Jordan. It was not until the time of the Romans, Pompey and Gabinius, that these ruined places were rebuilt and helped to a new prosperity.

30. Josephus in *Ant.* xiii 15, 4 (395–7), expressly names the following places as having been at that time in Jewish possession: Rhinocorura on the Egyptian border, Raphia, Gaza, Anthedon, Azotus, Jamnia, Joppa, Apollonia, Straton's Tower (see vol. II, § 23, 1). But Dora must also have been part of Alexander's domain, for Straton's Tower and Dora had previously belonged to a tyrant called Zoilus, who was subdued by Alexander, *Ant.* xiii 12, 2 (324–9) and 4 (334–5). On the other hand, it is no accident that Ascalon is not mentioned. It had been an independent city since 104/3 B.C., as is attested by the era it used, and by Roman recognition of its freedom (see vol. II, § 23, 1). Cf. M. Avi-Yonah, *The Holy Land* (1966), pp. 67–8.

31. A sketch of the extent of Jewish territory at the death of Alexander is given in Josephus *Ant.* xiii 15, 4 (395–7). See also the list of places taken from the Nabataeans in *Ant.* xiv 1, 4 (18). A similar survey, derived from a source independent of Josephus, is given by the Byzantine chronicler, Georgius Syncellus, ed. Dindorf I, pp. 558–9. On the reliability of this evidence, see H. Gelzer, *Julius Africanus* I (1880), pp. 256–8. Syncellus relies on Africanus, and he in turn on older Jewish sources, possibly Justus of Tiberias (see above p 36.). He mentions several towns absent from Josephus, e.g. Abila, Hippus and Philoteria. The reference to Philoteria is especially significant, since this place is quite unknown at a later period. According to Polybius v 70,3–4, it was one of the most important towns on Lake Tiberias at the time of Antiochus the Great. See p. 144 above. Although Josephus does not say so expressly, it may safely be assumed that Alexander Yannai built the fortresses of Alexandrium and Machaerus, both used by his widow Alexandra; see *Ant.* xiii 16, 3 (417); cf. Abel, *Histoire de la Palestine* I, pp. 238–9. On the two strongholds, see further pp. 307–8 and 511 below.

32. This is expressly said of Pella at least, *Ant.* xiii 15, 4 (397) *ταύτην δὲ κατέσκαψαν οὐχ ὑποσχομένων τῶν ἐνοικούντων ἐς τὰ πάτρια τῶν Ἰουδάιων ἔθη μεταβαλεῖσθαι.* (The *οὐχ* before *ὑποσχομένων*, omitted by Niese, but found in almost all the manuscripts, is certainly to be retained, since the text otherwise becomes meaningless.) The fact that such destruction took place is also mentioned in connexion with several other towns, or may be deduced from what is known of Pompey and Gabinius with regard to their reconstruction, *Ant.* xiv 4, 4 (75–6); 5, 3 (88); *B.J.* i 7, 7 (155–6); 8, 4 (166). See esp. *Ant.* xiv 5, 3 (88) *τὰς πόλεις πολὺν χρόνον ἐρήμους γενομένας.*

§ 11 Alexandra 76–67 B.C.

Sources

Josephus *Ant.* xiii 16 (405–32); *B.J.* i 5 (107–19).
Rabbinic traditions: bSoṭah 22b
bTaanith 23a
bShabbath 16b
Sifra *B[e]-Ḥuḳḳothay* 1 (ed. I. H. Weiss, p. 110b)
Leviticus Rabbah 35:10.

Cf. Derenbourg, *op. cit.*, pp. 102–12.

Coins: see n. 1 below.

Bibliography

Derenbourg, J., *Essai sur l'histoire et la géographie de la Palestine* (1867), pp. 102–12.

Graetz, H., *Geschichte der Juden* III ([5]1905–6), pp. 135–49.

Abel, F.-M., *Histoire de la Palestine* I (1952), pp. 239–44.

Schalit, A., *König Herodes, der Mann und sein Werk* (1969), pp. 679–80.

According to Alexander's will, the throne went to his widow, Alexandra, who in turn nominated her eldest son, Hyrcanus, High Priest.[1] Alexandra, whose transliterated Hebrew name appears in Greek texts as Salome or Salina (76–67 B.C.), was in all respects the antithesis of her husband.[2] Whereas he hated, and was hated by, the Pharisees, Alexandra was well disposed towards them and entrusted

1. *Ant.* xiii 16, 1–2 (405–8); *B.J.* i 5, 1 (107–9). It is now generally accepted that there are no coins certainly attributable to Alexandra. F. de Saulcy, *Recherches sur la numismatique judaïque* (1854), pl. IV, 13, listed two with the alleged reading *ΒΑΣΙΛΙΣ. ΑΛΕΞΑΝΔ*. But both the decipherment and the attribution are highly uncertain, see U. Kahrstedt, Klio 10 (1910), pp. 284–5, and *BMC Palestine*, p. xcv. It is, however, sometimes suggested that the coins of John Hyrcanus II with the Greek letter A on the obverse refer to Alexandra, and were minted during her lifetime (see Y. Meshorer, *Jewish Coins*, p. 121, n. 14; cf. also R. de Vaux, *L'archéologie et les manuscrits de la Mer Morte*, p. 15).

2. On the chronology, see above p. 200. The Hebrew name of Alexandra has been handed down in various forms. In rabbinic sources she is referred to as שלמצה, שלמצו, שלמתו or שלציון (see Jastrow, *Dictionary*, p. 1587). All these forms as well as שלמינון (Meg. Taan. § 24, gloss) no doubt derive from an original שלמציון attested epigraphically as a Jewish woman's name. See C. Clermont-Ganneau, *Archaeological Researches in Palestine* I (1899), pp. 386–92 = J.-B. Frey, CIJ II, 1317; cf. 1223, 1253, 1265, 1297, 1353, 1363. A daughter of Herod is called *Σαλαμψιώ*, Jos. *Ant.* xviii 5, 4 (130) and Babata's step-daughter bore the same name: see Y. Yadin, *Bar-Kokhba* (1971), pp. 246–8. If J. T. Milik's statement (*Ten Years of Discovery*, p. 73) concerning a reference to Alexandra as שלמציון in an unpublished calendar from 4Q is confirmed, the issue will be definitely settled. Eusebius, *Chron., ad. ann. Abr.* 1941, mentions 'Alexandra quae et Salina' (= the Armenian translation and Jerome in Euseb. *Chron.*, ed. Schoene II, pp. 134–5). Cf. also

them with the reins of government. Whereas he was a despot after the oriental pattern, she was a God-fearing ruler after their own hearts. By their standards, her administration of power was blameless.

Alexander is said to have advised his wife on his deathbed to make peace with the Pharisees.[3] Whether this is true or not, the fact is that from the start of her reign Alexandra placed herself firmly on their side; she listened to their claims and wishes, and in particular restored legality to all the Pharisaic ordinances abrogated since the time of John Hyrcanus. The Pharisees were, during her reign the *de facto* rulers of the land. 'She had the name of royalty, but the Pharisees had the power. They recalled fugitives and released the imprisoned, and were in a word in no respect different from absolute rulers.'[4] They could only have wielded such authority if they were a determining factor in the supreme administrative body, the Gerusia. This must therefore have undergone an important transformation. Whereas it had hitherto consisted of the nobility and the priesthood, it must now have admitted Pharisaic teachers also.[5] A series of Pharisee triumphs reported by rabbinic tradition (Megillath Taanith) may also belong to this period of Pharisaic reaction. But the references are very brief and enigmatic, and the relatively late Hebrew glosses appended to the Aramaic text, expounding it as an account of a Pharisee victory over the Sadducees, provide no reliable historical evidence.[6] Neither

---

Chron. pasch., ed. Dindorf, I, p. 351; Syncellus, ed. Dindorf, I, p. 559; Jerome, *In Danielem* 9:24 (CCL lxxvA, p. 874), 'Alexandra quae et Salina vocabatur'. In consequence, *Σααλίνα* in Euseb. *Chron.*, ed. Schoene I, p. 130 should be read as *Σαλίνα*. Eusebius undoubtedly derived this name from Jos. *Ant.* xiii 12, 1 (320), where the wife of Aristobulus I, who is almost certainly to be identified with the spouse of Alexander Jannaeus, is called *Σαλίνα* in two manuscripts, whereas the rest give, with Epitome and Vet.Lat., *Σαλώμη ἡ γυνὴ αὐτοῦ, λεγομένη δὲ ὑπὸ Ἑλλήνων Ἀλεξάνδρα*.

3. *Ant.* xiii 15, 5 (401–4). According to the Talmud, bSoṭ. 22b, he said to her: 'Fear neither the Pharisees, nor those who are not Pharisees (Sadducees), but beware the hypocrites who behave like Zimri but seek Pinḥas's reward' Cf. Derenbourg, *op. cit.*, p. 101; Finkelstein, *The Pharisees* I ([3]1962), pp. xxiii, 837, n. 52.

4. *Ant.* xiii 16, 2 (408–9) *πάντα τοῖς Φαρισαίοις ἐπιτρέπει ποιεῖν, οἷς καὶ τὸ πλῆθος ἐκέλευσε πειθαρχεῖν, καὶ εἴ τι δὲ καὶ τῶν νομίμων Ὑρκανὸς ὁ πενθερὸς αὐτῆς κατέλυσεν ὧν εἰσήνεγκαν οἱ Φαρισαῖοι κατὰ τὴν πατρῴαν παράδοσιν, τοῦτο πάλιν ἀποκατέστησεν. τὸ μὲν οὖν ὄνομα τῆς βασιλείας εἶχεν αὐτή, τὴν δὲ δύναμιν οἱ Φαρισαῖοι· καὶ γὰρ φυγάδας οὗτοι κατῆγον καὶ δεσμώτας ἔλυον, καὶ καθάπαξ οὐδὲν δεσποτῶν διέφερον.* Cf. also *B.J.* I 5, 2 (110–12).

5. The importance of Alexandra's reign for the transformation of the Sanhedrin was aptly emphasised by Wellhausen in *Isr. und jüd. Gesch.* ([9]1958), pp. 267–71. Cf. H. Mantel, *Studies in the History of the Sanhedrin* (1961), pp. 56–7, 99–100; R. Meyer, *Tradition u. Neuschöpfung im antiken Judentum* (1965), pp. 47–50.

6. On Megillath Taanith, see above p. 114 f. The references in question are analysed by Lichtenstein, HUCA 8–9 (1931–2), pp. 290–8. See also Graetz, *Gesch.* III ([5]1905–6), pp. 567–72 (note 1). Derenbourg, *op. cit.*, pp. 102 f.; Wellhausen, *Pharisäer und Sadducäer*, pp. 56–63.

does the statement in the Mishnah, to the effect that Simeon ben Shetaḥ was once responsible for hanging eighty women in Ascalon, offer any solid basis for an historical conclusion. This famous Pharisee does not seem to have possessed judicial authority in that city.[7] Historical information can thus be obtained solely from Josephus. And the clarity of his account is commendable. The Pharisees, in consciousness of their power, went so far as to order the execution of the former counsellors of King Alexander (who had advised him to massacre eight hundred rebels). Such despotic behaviour did not please the Jerusalem nobility, and they sent a deputation, which included Alexandra's own son, Aristobulus, to the queen to ask her to put an end to the Pharisees' activities; whether she liked it or not, she was obliged to comply.[8]

In her foreign policy, Alexandra showed prudence and energy.[9] Nevertheless, no political events of any importance occurred during her reign. The most significant was a military expedition undertaken by her son Aristobulus against Damascus, which, however, was without result.[10] The Syrian empire was at that time in the hands of the Armenian king, Tigranes, but although he assumed a threatening attitude towards the end of her reign, the dreaded invasion of Judaea did not take place, partly because Alexandra purchased peace with substantial gifts, and partly for the more cogent reason that the Romans under Lucullus invaded Tigranes's empire, thereby compelling him to abandon his plans in regard to Judaea.[11]

On the whole, Alexandra's reign was felt by the people to be a time of prosperity. Peace with other nations was matched by peace at home. The Pharisees were satisfied, and the people, too, were favourably disposed to the God-fearing queen. In Pharisaic tradition, the days of Alexandra are of course praised as a golden age in which—as though to reward the queen's piety—even the soil was astonishingly fruitful. 'In the days of Simeon ben Shetaḥ [and queen Salome], rain fell in the night of every Wednesday and Sabbath, so that the grains of wheat were like kidneys, the grains of barley like olives, and the lentils like

7. mSanh. 6:5; cf. ySanh. 23c; yḤag. 77d; Sifre Dt. § 221. Derenbourg, *op cit.*, p. 69, conjectured that the Simon in question was Simon Maccabee; cf. however, p. 106. Against historicity speaks the fact that Ascalon did not belong to Jewish territory; see above, p. 228. On the other hand, as rabbinic sources show, the story proved to be a considerable embarrassment to rabbis of later generations, who are therefore unlikely to have invented it, and could justify it only as a measure of expediency rather than one corresponding to Jewish law. Cf. Mantel, *op. cit.*, p. 9, n. 51.

8. *Ant.* xiii 16, 2–3 (410–17); *B.J.* i 5, 3 (113–14).

9. *Ant.* xiii 16, 2 (409), 3–4 (418–19); cf. *B.J.* i 5, 2 (112), 3 (115–16).

10. *Ant.* xiii 16, 3 (418); *B.J.* i 5, 3 (115–16).

11. *Ant.* xiii 16, 4 (419–21); *B.J.* i 5, 3 (116).

golden denarii; the scribes gathered such grains and preserved samples of them in order to show future generations the effect of sin.'[12]

On the other hand, the Pharisees did not hold power so exclusively that the queen could, without danger, rely on them alone. The strength of the Sadducees was not yet broken. And the discontent among these circles was all the more dangerous since Alexandra's own son, Aristobulus, was at their head. The queen was herself to discover the instability of her position towards the end of her life. When she fell gravely ill at the age of seventy-three, and it was expected that her elder son, Hyrcanus, would succeed to the throne, Judas Aristobulus judged that the time had come to raise the banner of insurrection. As the number of his followers rapidly increased, the elders of the people[13] and Hyrcanus became seriously alarmed, and remonstrated with the queen that it was necessary to take steps against him. The queen granted the authority for this, but died before the outbreak of war, in 67 B.C.[14]

12. bTaan 23a. The text only mentions Simeon ben Shetaḥ, but when quoted in Tosaphoth to Shabb. 16b, both Simeon and the queen are named. See Derenbourg, *op. cit.*, p. 102; cf. also Sifra B^{e}ḥuḳḳ. 1; Lev. R. 35:10. Be this as it may, it is clear that the period of Alexandra is meant.

13. *Ant.* xiii 16, 5 (428) *τῶν δὲ Ἰουδαίων οἱ πρεσβύτεροι.*

14. *Ant.* xiii 16, 5–6 (422–32); *B.J.* i 5, 4 (117–19). For the date see above pp. 200–1.

§ 12 ARISTOBULUS II 67–63 B.C.

Sources

Josephus *Ant.* xiv 1–4 (1–79); *B.J.* i 6–7 (120–58).
Rabbinic traditions: mTaanith 3:8
yTaanith 66d–67a
bTaanith 23a
bSoṭah 49b
bBaba Ḳamma 82b
bMenaḥoth 64b
See Derenbourg, *op. cit.*, pp. 112–18.
Psalms of Solomon and Qumran documents: see n. 30 below.
Coins: for the controversial view that Aristobulus II issued his own coinage, see Appendix IV, 2.

Bibliography

Derenbourg, J., *Essai sur l'histoire et la géographie de la Palestine* (1867), pp. 112–18.
Graetz, H., *Geschichte der Juden* III ([5]1905–6), pp. 151–65.
Abel, F.-M., *Histoire de la Palestine* I (1952), pp. 247–61.
Ginsburg, M. S., *Rome et la Judée* (1928), pp. 78–84
Jones, A. H. M., *The Cities of the Eastern Roman Provinces* (1937; [2]1971), pp. 238 ff., 447 ff.
Abel, F.-M., 'Le Siège de Jérusalem par Pompée', RB 54 (1947), pp. 243–55.
Bammel, E., 'Die Neuordnung des Pompejus und das römisch-jüdische Bündnis', ZDPV 75 (1959), pp. 76–82.
Schalit, A., *König Herodes, der Mann und sein Werk* (1969), pp. 1–19.

The Hasmonaean star was now in its decline. War broke out immediately after Alexandra's death between her sons Aristobulus II and Hyrcanus II, and after a few years ended with the loss to the Romans of the freedom won in battle against the Syrians. Alexandra had died just at the critical moment at which her son Aristobulus was on the point of seizing power by force. Her legitimate successor was her eldest son,[1] John Hyrcanus, who had already been appointed High Priest during his mother's reign. He now assumed the duties of ruler also. But his brother Judas Aristobulus had no intention of abandoning his plans. He marched against Hyrcanus with an army. Their forces clashed near Jericho, and many of Hyrcanus's men went over to Aristobulus, thereby securing the latter's victory. Hyrcanus fled to the fortress in Jerusalem but was forced to surrender there to Aristobulus. A truce was then arranged between the brothers, according to which Hyrcanus, who was in any case a weak and idle man, renounced his

1. *Ant.* xiii 16, 2 (408); xiv 1, 3 (11); 3, 2 (42).

royal and High Priestly titles in favour of his brother. In return, he was left to enjoy his revenues undisturbed.[2]

The issue was nevertheless by no means settled. For now the Idumaean Antipater, the father of the future King Herod, began to interfere.[3] His father, also named Antipater, had been appointed *strategos* of Idumaea by Alexander Jannaeus, and his sons seem to have followed him in this position. But he saw very clearly that he would be far better off under the weak and unmanly Hyrcanus than under the bellicose and energetic Aristobulus. He therefore did his utmost to bring Aristobulus down and help Hyrcanus back to power. First he managed to win adherents among the most distinguished of the Jews by

2. *Ant.* xiv 1, 2 (4–7); *B.J.* i 6, 1 (120–2). According to *Ant.* xv 6, 4 (180), Hyrcanus's rule lasted for three months. Graetz, *op. cit.*, III, p. 154, and Derenbourg, *op. cit.*, p. 113, assumed that Hyrcanus retained the office of High Priest. That this was not the case can be deduced from *Ant.* xiv 1, 2 (6) αὐτὸν δὲ ζῆν ἀπραγμόνως, and is expressly stated in *Ant.* xv 3, 1 (41); xx 10, 4 (243).

3. On the origin of the family there exist the most contradictory reports. According to Nicolaus of Damascus, quoted in Jos. *Ant.* xiv 1, 3 (9) = Jacoby FGrH 90 A F96, Antipater was a descendant of the first Jews to return from Babylon. As this assertion contradicts all the other sources, Josephus is doubtless correct in regarding it simply as flattery of Herod on the part of Nicolaus (ταῦτα δὲ λέγει χαριζόμενος Ἡρῴδῃ); see B. Z. Wacholder, *Nicolaus of Damascus* (1962), pp. 78–9. According to Josephus, Antipater was an Idumaean of noble descent, *B.J.* i 6, 2 (123) γένος δ' ἦν Ἰδουμαῖος, προγόνων τε ἕνεκα καὶ πλούτου καὶ τῆς ἄλλης ἰσχύος πρωτεύων τοῦ ἔθνους. Justin Martyr, on the other hand, mentions the Jewish statement that he was a native of Ascalon, *Dial. c. Trypho.* 52 Ἡρώδην Ἀσκαλωνίτην γεγονέναι. This view appears in the writings of Julius Africanus in the more definite form that Antipater's father, Herod, was a temple attendant of Apollo in Ascalon, and that Antipater was carried off as a boy by the Idumaeans in a sack of the temple and grew up among them as one of themselves, Julius Africanus, *Epist. ad. Aristidem*, in Euseb. *HE* i 7, 11, cf. 6, 2–3; also in the chronicle of Julius Africanus cited by Syncellus ed. Dindorf I, p. 561. Julius Africanus is followed by Euseb. *Chron.* ed. Schoene I, p. 130; II, pp. 134, 138; *Chron. paschale* ed. Dindorf I, pp. 351, 358; Sulpicius Severus ii 26; Epiphanius *Haer.* 20, 1, 3–4, and other Christian writers. Josephus and Julius Africanus are basically in agreement in regard to the Idumaean descent, the only difference being that according to Josephus, Antipater's background was distinguished, and according to Africanus, lowly (he particularly emphasizes the poverty). In addition, Josephus gives the father of Antipater as Antipater, whereas for Africanus it is Herod. Certain connexions of King Herod with this town speak in favour of an Ascalonite descent (see vol. II, § 23, 1). But for the rest, the story of Julius Africanus reveals so much spite and malice that it is impossible to avoid the suspicion that it is a Jewish or Christian fabrication. Julius Africanus appeals to the συγγενεῖς of Jesus Christ, Euseb. *HE* i 7, 11, τοῦ γοῦν σωτῆρος οἱ κατὰ σάρκα συγγενεῖς . . . . παρέδοσαν καὶ ταῦτα. Cf. i 7, 14, οἱ προειρημένοι δεσπόσυνοι καλούμενοι διὰ τὴν πρὸς τὸ σωτήριον γένος συνάφειαν, and therefore seems to have derived it from Christian sources. Its credibility was argued by H. Gelzer, *Julius Africanus* I, pp. 258–61. See RE I, col. 2509 s.v. 'Antipatros' (16). See also W. Otto, *Herodes* (1913), cols. 1–2 (correctly rejecting the Ascalon tradition), and A. Schalit, *König Herodes* (1969), pp. 45, 677–8.

arguing that Aristobulus's occupation of the throne was unlawful and that Hyrcanus was the legitimate ruler. Then he attached himself to Hyrcanus and tried to make him believe that his life was in danger so long as Aristobulus was in power, and that he must overthrow him. To begin with, the dull and indifferent Hyrcanus paid no attention. But in the end, Antipatur's intrigues were successful. He had, in effect, also persuaded the Nabataean prince, Aretas, into an alliance with him and made him promise that if Hyrcanus fled to him for refuge, he would receive him as a friend. Hyrcanus finally decided to yield to Antipater's representations, and in his company fled by night from Jerusalem to Petra, the capital of Aretas.[4] He promised the Nabataean that when he regained power, he would return the twelve towns taken from him by Alexander Jannaeus, whereupon Aretas assured him of his support in recovering his throne.[5]

Aretas accordingly set out with an army against Aristobulus and defeated him in battle. As a result of the victory, a great part of Aristobulus's troops went over to Hyrcanus; indeed, the whole people joined him. Only a few remained loyal to Aristobulus and he was obliged to retreat to the Temple Mount, where he was besieged by Aretas and Hyrcanus. Josephus relates episodes from the time of this siege which are highly characteristic of Jewish piety at that time. On Hyrcanus's side was a certain Onias who had acquired great fame from having once prayed to God for rain during a drought, with immediate happy results. It was hoped that this man, or rather, the irresistible power of his prayer, might bring about the destruction of the besieged. He was therefore led into the camp and invited solemnly to invoke the curse of God on Aristobulus and his followers. But instead, Onias stepped into the centre and said: 'O God, Thou King of all things, since they who now stand around me are Thy people, and they who are besieged are Thy priests, I beseech thee not to hearken to either, nor to do anything that either invokes against the other'. But the people approved so little of Onias's brotherly attitude that they immediately stoned him to death.[6] Josephus also tells the story of another incident

4. On Petra as capital of the Nabataean kingdom, see App. II below.

5. *Ant.* xiv 1, 3–4 (10–18); *B.J.* i 6, 2 (123–6). Cf. above, p. 226.

6. *Ant.* xiv 2, 1 (22–4). For an (unsatisfactory) attempt to identify this man with the Qumran Teacher of Righteousness see R. Goossens, 'Les éléments messianiques des traditions sur Onias le Juste chez Josèphe et dans le Talmud', Bull. Ac. Roy. Belg. Cl. de Lett. 5 sér., 3b (1950), pp. 440–69; 'Onias le Juste, Messie de la Nouvelle Alliance', Nouv. Clio 2 (1950), pp. 336–53. The story of the hearing of Onias's prayer when he once prayed for rain appears, with much embellishment, in the Mishnah, in Taan. 3:8. He is called there Ḥoni 'the circle-drawer' (מעגל) from the circle which he drew on the ground round his feet. Cf. yTaan. 66d–67a; bTaan. 23a. See also Derenbourg, *op. cit.*, pp. 112 f. A. Büchler, *Types of Jewish-Palestinian Piety* (1922), pp. 196–264. The rabbinic report tinged with criticism contrasts interestingly with Josephus's wholehearted praise of Onias.

which, again, does not reflect well on the besiegers. The Feast of Passover was approaching, and the priests in Aristobulus's entourage wished at all costs to offer the prescribed sacrifices.[7] There was, however, a shortage of sacrificial animals, and they knew of no other way of obtaining a supply except by buying from Hyrcanus's people. The latter demanded one thousand drachmas a head. The price was unprecedently high. Nevertheless, the besieged agreed, and let down the money through a hole in the wall. The besiegers, however, took it and kept the animals for themselves. In Josephus's opinion, it was because of this wickedness that the merited punishment soon overtook them: a violent storm broke out which destroyed all the crops, with the result that a *modius* of wheat cost the exorbitant price of eleven drachmas.[8]

While this was taking place in Judaea, Pompey had already begun his victorious campaign in Asia.[9] He had defeated Mithridates in 66 B.C., and had accepted in the same year the voluntary submission of Tigranes. While he himself now penetrated deeper into Asia, he sent Scaurus to Syria in 65 B.C.[10] When the latter reached Damascus, he heard of the war between the brothers in Judaea and set off without delay in order to derive some advantage from the conflict for himself. He had hardly entered Judaea when emissaries appeared, sent by Aristobulus as well as by Hyrcanus. Both pleaded for Scaurus's favour and support. Aristobulus offered him in return four hundred talents, and as Hyrcanus could not then do less, he promised him the same sum. Scaurus, however, believed that Aristobulus was more likely to make good his offer, and he took his side. He commanded Aretas to withdraw, otherwise he would declare him an enemy of Rome. Aretas dared not resist and raised the siege, whereupon Scaurus returned to Damascus. But Aristobulus pursued Aretas as he retreated and inflicted on him a crushing defeat.[11]

Roman favour, for which Aristobulus had struggled so hard, and under whose protection he now thought himself safe, was to prove fatal to him and his land. He himself did all in his power to win the approval of Pompey, as well as that of Scaurus. He sent Pompey a precious gift, a grape-vine of gold worth five hundred talents which

7. This will probably have been Passover 65 B.C., for immediately afterwards Scaurus arrived in Judaea; cf. Broughton, MRR II, pp. 159, 163, 165, n. 7.

8. *Ant.* xiv 2, 2 (25–8). For rabbinic traditions in bSoṭ. 49b, bMen. 64b; bB.K. 82b, see Derenbourg, *op. cit.*, pp. 113–14.

9. On Pompey's wars in the east (66–62 B.C.) see Broughton, MRR II, pp. 155, 159–60, 163–4, 169–70, 176; M. Gelzer, *Pompeius* (1949), pp. 87–120; J. Van Ooteghem, *Pompée le Grand* (1954), pp. 204–77; E. Will, *Histoire politique du monde hellénistique* II (1967), pp. 419–34.

10. See n. 7 above.

11. *Ant.* xiv 2, 3 (29–33); *B.J.* i 6, 2–3 (127–30).

Strabo saw exhibited in the temple of Jupiter Capitolinus in Rome.[12] Yet none of this was able to save Aristobulus once Pompey found it convenient to withdraw his favour from him and to turn it towards Hyrcanus. In the spring of 63 B.C., Pompey left his winter quarters in Syria,[13] subjugated the greater and lesser dynasts in the Lebanon,[14] and advanced through Heliopolis and Chalcis to Damascus.[15] Here three Jewish parties appeared before him; not only Aristobulus and Hyrcanus, but, in addition, envoys of the Jewish people. Hyrcanus complained that Aristobulus had seized power unlawfully, and Aristobulus defended himself by pointing to Hyrcanus's incompetence. The people, however, wished to have nothing to do with either of them, and desired the constitution created by the Hasmonaean priests to be abolished and the ancient sacerdotal theocracy restored.[16] Pompey listened to them, but temporarily postponed his decision, declaring that

12. *Ant.* xiv 3, 1 (34–6). The words *τοῦτο μέντοι τὸ δῶρον ἱστορήκαμεν καὶ ἡμεῖς ἀνακείμενον ἐν Ῥώμῃ* are not those of Josephus, but form part of the quotation of Strabo (=Jacoby, FGrH 91 F 14), as the narrative goes on to demonstrate (the value of the golden vine is given once more, although Josephus has already mentioned it). It is true that Josephus could have seen it on his first visit to Rome in A.D. 64–5. But he would then not have omitted to remark that this had taken place before the great fire. For the Capitol was burned down in A.D. 69, Tac. *Hist.* iii 71–2; Suet. *Vit.* 15; Dio lxiv/v 17, 3.

13. According to Dio xxxvii 7, 5, Pompey spent the winter of 65–4 B.C. in the town of Aspis, the exact location of which is not known. R. Dussaud, *Topographie historique de la Syrie antique et medièvale* (1927), p. 237, suggests that Aspis was near Hama. But during this winter Pompey was still in Asia Minor. The winter of 64–3 was probably spent in Antioch, see Gelzer, *Pompeius* (1949), p. 108, and Schalit, *König Herodes* (1969), p. 7, notes 6–7.

14. Among the subjugated dynasts Josephus mentions in *Ant.* xiv 3, 2 (40) a Jew named Silas, tyrant of Lysias, a strongpoint near Apamea, see RE s.v. 'Lysias' (5). A similar lesser dynast is presumably also 'Bacchius Judaeus', whose submission is recorded by a coin of Aulus Plautius, aedile 54 B.C. See *BMC Roman Republic* I (1910), pp. 490–1. This 'Bacchius the Jew' might be identical with Dionysius of Tripolis, mentioned in Jos. *Ant.* xiv 3, 3 (39).

15. *Ant.* xiv 3, 2 (40). The text of most manuscripts reads here *διελθὼν δὲ τὰς πόλεις τήν τε Ἡλιούπολιν καὶ τὴν Χαλκίδα καὶ τὸ διεῖργον ὄρος ὑπερβαλὼν τὴν κοίλην προσαγορευομένην Συρίαν ἀπὸ τῆς Πέλλης εἰς Δαμασκὸν ἧκεν*. This would result in the impossible march route Heliopolis–Chalcis–Pella–Damascus. Niese rightly chose *ἄλλης* found in the best manuscripts (cod. Palat.), rather than *Πέλλης* ('crossing the mountains dividing Coele-Syria from the rest of Syria'). *Ἡ ἄλλη Συρία* in contrast to *κοίλη* is supported by *Ant.* xiv 4, 5 (79) and Philo. *Leg. ad Gaium* 36 (281). It should also be noted that the golden vine of Aristobulus was presented to Pompey in Damascus, *Ant.* xiv 3, 1 (34). Josephus, it is true, mentions this before his report of Pompey's advance out of Syria through Heliopolis and Chalcis to Damascus, which makes it appear as if Pompey went to Damascus twice, in 64 and 63 B.C. But it is clear that Josephus derived the account of the golden vine from another source and did not insert it into the right place in the context of the main narrative. Cf. Niese, Hermes 11 (1876), p. 471.

16. *Ant.* xiv 3, 2 (41–5); Diodorus xl 2.

it was his intention to regulate matters as soon as he had completed the campaign planned against the Nabataeans. Till then, they were all to maintain the peace.[17]

Aristobulus was not satisfied with this, and betrayed his discontent by suddenly parting from Pompey at Dium, where he had accompanied him in his campaign against the Nabataeans.[18] Pompey became suspicious, put off his expedition against the Nabataeans, and marched at once against Aristobulus. He skirted Pella, crossed the Jordan at Scythopolis, and entered Judaea proper at Corea (*Κορέα*).[19] From there, he sent messengers to Alexandrium, where Aristobulus had fled, and ordered him to surrender the fortress. After long hesitation and much negotiation, Aristobulus did so, but travelled immediately to Jerusalem to mobilize resistance there.[20] Pompey followed him through Jericho and soon appeared in the vicinity of Jerusalem. But then Aristobulus lost courage. He went to Pompey's camp, brought him new gifts, and promised to surrender the city to him if Pompey would suspend hostilities. Pompey was satisfied, and despatched his general Gabinius to take possession of the city while he detained Aristobulus in the camp. Gabinius, however, returned with nothing done because the people of the city had barred their gates to him. Pompey became so enraged at this that he took Aristobulus prisoner and advanced immediately against the city.[21] In Jerusalem, opinions were now divided. Aristobulus's followers wished to hear nothing of peace and were prepared to defend themselves to the utmost. Those of Hyrcanus, on the other hand, saw Pompey as their ally and wanted to open the gates to him. The latter were in the majority and had their way. The city was surrendered to Pompey, who sent in his legate, Piso, and took possession of it without striking a blow. But the war party had assembled on the Temple mount and mobilized resistance there.[22]

The Temple mount was then, as later, the strongpoint of Jerusalem.

17. *Ant.* xiv 3, 3 (46).

18. *Ant.* xiv 3, 3 (47); *B.J.* i 6, 4 (132). On the location of Dium and the reading in this passage, see vol. II, § 23, 1. Compare also Schalit, *König Herodes*, p. 11, n. 38.

19. On the location of Corea, see Abel, *Géog. Pal.* II, pp. 300–1. It is to be identified with Tel Mazar near modern Qarawa at the mouth of Wadi el-Far'a. The neighbouring fortress of Alexandrium must therefore have been Sartabeh. Cf. Abel, *Géog. Pal.* II, pp. 241–2. On the mosaic of Medeba also, *Κορεους* is marked as being south of Scythopolis; see Avi-Yonah, *The Madaba Mosaic Map* (1954). Pompey thus marched from Scythopolis in the Jordan valley directly south to Jericho.

20. *Ant.* xiv 3, 4 (48–53); *B.J.* i 6, 5 (133–7).

21. *Ant.* xiv 4, 1 (54–7); *B.J.* i 6, 6–7, 1 (138–41). Pompey's camp is also mentioned in *B.J.* v 12, 2 (506).

22. *Ant.* xiv 4, 2 (58–60); *B.J.* i 7, 2 (142–4).

It fell steeply away to the east and the south. To the west, also, it was divided from the city by a deep ravine. The terrain was level only to the north, but even here access was almost impossible on account of strong fortifications. It was in this mighty bulwark that the followers of Aristobulus entrenched themselves, and Pompey was obliged, whether he liked it or not, to decide on a regular siege. Naturally, he selected the northern side for his point of attack. A rampart was thrown up, and the great siege engines brought from Tyre were mounted on it. For a long time the powerful walls withstood the impact of the missiles. But at last, after a siege lasting three months, a breach was made at one place. A son of the dictator Sulla was the first to go through with his men. Others followed. A fearful blood-bath then ensued. The priests, who were at that moment offering sacrifice, would not allow themselves to be diverted from the exercise of their duties and were cut down at the altar. No less than twelve thousand Jews are said to have perished in the general massacre. It was in the late autumn of 63 B.C., in the consulship of Cicero, on the Day of Atonement, according to Josephus, on a Sabbath according to Dio, that the holy city capitulated to the Roman commander.[23]

23. *Ant.* xiv 4, 2–4 (61–71); *B.J.* i 7, 3–5 (145–51). Dio xxxvii 16, 1–4. In general see also Strabo xvi 2, 40 (762–3); Livy, *Epit.* 102; Tac. *Hist.* v 9; Appian, *Syr.* 50/252; *Mithridat.* 106/498. The Day of Atonement: *τῇ τῆς νηστεία sῆμέρᾳ*, *Ant.* xiv 4, 3 (66). The Sabbath: *ἐν τῇ τοῦ Κρόνου ἡμέρᾳ*, Dio xxxvii 16, 4. Cf. Strabo, *loc. cit.* The Day of Atonement falls on 10 Tishri (=September/October). There can be no doubt, from the established Jewish usage of the term, that this is what Josephus means by 'Day of Fasting', *Ant.* xvii 6, 4 (165); xviii 4, 3 (94); Philo, *Vita Mos.* II 4 (23); *Spec. leg.* I 168–93; II 193–203; *Leg. ad Gaium* 39 (306–7); Acts 27:9; mMen. 11:9 יום צום; cf. the Aramaic צומא רבא, yMK. 83a, yTaan. 67c, etc.; see also Dalman, *Grammatik*, p. 248. The most important parallel comes from 1QpHab. XI 6–8, where the sect's 'Day of Atonement' (יום הכפורים) is paraphrased as 'the Day of Fasting, their Sabbath of repose' (יום צום). See below, n. 30. The third month, *περὶ τρίτον μῆνα*, *Ant.* xiv 4, 3 (66) is not the third month of the year, Jewish or Greek, but the third month of the siege, as Josephus explicitly states in *B.J.* i 7, 4 (149) *τρίτῳ γὰρ μηνὶ τῆς πολιορκίας*. Cf. *B.J.* v 9, 4 (397), *τρισὶ γοῦν μησὶ πολιορκηθέντες*. Herzfeld, MGWJ 4 (1855), pp. 109–15, suggested that the date of the Day of Atonement rests on a mistake by Josephus, who discovered in his pagan sources that the conquest took place on a fast-day, but which meant, not the Day of Atonement, but (in accordance with the misapprehension widespread in the Graeco-Roman world that Jews fast on that day) the Sabbath, see Suet. *Div. Aug.* 76; Justin xxxvi 2, 14; Petronius F. 37, ed. Bücheler=Reinach, *Textes d'auteurs grecs et romains sur les juifs et le Judaïsme* (1895), p. 266. This is rendered almost a certainty by the fact that Josephus in *Ant.* xiv 4, 3 (68) quotes among his authorities Strabo (i.e. his *History*, see Jacoby, FGrH 91 F 15), who in his *Geography* xvi 2, 40 (763) writes concerning the conquest of Jerusalem *κατελάβετο* (scil. *Πομπήιος*) *δ' ὥς φασι, τηρήσας τὴν τῆς νηστείας ἡμέραν, ἡνίκα ἀπείχοντο οἱ Ἰουδαῖοι παντὸς ἔργου.* This do es indeed read 'a Sabbath fast-day'. But even if it is not proved that the

Pompey himself broke into the Holy of Holies, where only the High Priest was allowed to enter. But he left untouched the treasures and precious things of the Temple, and took care to ensure that divine worship should continue undisturbed. His judgment on the vanquished was severe. Those responsible for the war were beheaded, and the city and land were made subject to tribute, *τῇ τε χώρᾳ καὶ τοῖς Ἱεροσολύμοις ἐπιτάσσει φόρον*.[24] The extent of Jewish territory was greatly reduced. All the coastal towns, from Raphia to Dora, were taken from it; similarly, all the non-Jewish towns east of Jordan such as Hippos, Gadara, Pella, Dium and others, and also Scythopolis and Samaria with considerable territories. All these towns were placed under the immediate jurisdiction of the governor of the newly-established Roman province of Syria.[25] The diminished Jewish territory was awarded to Hyrcanus II as High Priest without royal title.[26]

After Pompey had thus regulated affairs in Palestine, he sent Scaurus back to Syria as governor, while he himself hastened back to Asia Minor. He took Aristobulus with him as a prisoner of war, as well as the latter's two daughters and his sons Alexander and Antigonus, the first of whom managed to escape on the way.[27] When Pompey celebrated his triumph in Rome in 61 B.C. with great pomp and splendour, the Jewish Priest-King, the descendant of the Maccabees, was made to

---

event took place on the Day of Atonement, it must nevertheless be maintained that it occurred in the late autumn. For the long sequence of events between Pompey's start in the spring of 63 B.C., *Ant.* xiv 3, 2 (38), and the conquest of the city, cannot have happened within the space of a few months. It is therefore very unlikely that the conquest could have taken place as early as June, as might be suggested if the phrase 'third month' were understood as the third month of the Jewish year.

24. *Ant.* xiv 4, 4 (71–3); *B.J.* i 7, 6 (152–5). Cf. Cicero *pro Flacco* 28/67, 'Cn. Pompeius captis Hierosolymis victor ex illo fano nihil attigit.' Cf. however, Dio xxxvii 16, 4.

25. On all these towns and their location in the Roman period compare vol. II, § 23, 1. Josephus's list in *Ant.* xiv 4, 4 (75–6); *B.J.* i 7, 7 (155–6) is not complete. He names only the most important. Without doubt, not only all the coastal towns received their freedom, but also all those east of Jordan which afterwards formed the so-called Decapolis. For in most of the cities of the Decapolis the coinage shows that the Pompeian era was used. See e.g. *BMC Syria*, pp. lxxxiii f. It should however be noted that an actual minting of coins did not begin in these places until later, see A. R. Bellinger, 'The Early Coinage of Roman Syria', *Studies in Roman Economic and Social History presented to A. C. Johnson* (1951), pp. 58–67. For a survey see H. Bietenhard, 'Die Dekapolis von Pompeius bis Traian', ZDPV 79 (1963), pp. 24–58.

26. *Ant.* xiv 4, 4 (73); *B.J.* i 7, 6–7 (153). Cf. *Ant.* xx 10, 4 (244) *τῷ δ' Ὑρκανῷ πάλιν τὴν ἀρχιερωσύνην ἀποδοὺς τὴν μὲν τοῦ ἔθνους προστασίαν ἐπετρέψεν, διάδημα δὲ φορεῖν ἐκώλυσεν.*

27. *Ant.* xiv 4, 5 (77–9); *B.J.* i 7, 7 (137–8).

walk in front of the conqueror's chariot.[28] In addition to Aristobulus and his family, Pompey was also accompanied by a great number of Jewish captives. When these were later set free, they formed the basis of an extensive Jewish community in Rome.[29]

With Pompey's decrees the freedom of the Jewish nation was carried to its grave after barely eighty years of existence (reckoning from 142 B.C.) He was admittedly shrewd enough not to make any essential changes in the internal conditions of the country. He left the hierarchical constitution unaltered, and gave the people Hyrcanus II, the man favoured by the Pharisees, as their High Priest. But their independence was at an end, and the Jewish High Priest was merely a Roman vassal. This result was, of course, inevitable once the Romans had set foot in Syria. For their power was of a different order from that of the Seleucid rulers. And even the mightiest and most popular dynast would not have been able to resist permanently in face of Rome's superiority. However, Rome's work of conquest was facilitated by the fact that the country was disunited and that the contending parties were foolish enough to call for protection and help from strangers. There was little trace left of that spirit which a hundred years earlier had led the nation into battle.[30]

28. Compare the description of the triumph in Plut. *Pomp.* 45; Appian *Mithridat.* 117/571–8; Pliny, *NH* VII 26/98; full references in Broughton, MRR II, p. 181. Appian *loc. cit.* erroneously states that Aristobulus's death took place after the triumph, whereas he did not die until 49 B.C. (see below).

29. See Philo, *Leg. ad Gaium* 23 (155), and Smallwood, *ad loc.* The origins of the Jewish community in Rome go back to before 61 B.C., for Jewish money was exported from Italy to Jerusalem already when Flaccus was pro-praetor of Asia (62 B.C.), Cicero, *pro Flacco* 28/67. See H. J. Leon, *The Jews of Ancient Rome* (1960), ch. i, and vol. III, § 31, 1.

30. Contemporary Jewish Bible interpretation (Qumran commentaries on Habakkuk and Nahum) and religious poetry (Sibylline Oracles and Psalms of Solomon) shed indirect but valuable light on Palestinian society and its attitude towards Rome at the time of the conquest of Jerusalem by Pompey.

Today there is quasi-unanimity in identifying the victorious Kittim of Qumran literature with the Romans; see A. Dupont-Sommer, *The Essene Writings from Qumran* (1961), pp. 341–51; cf. G. Vermes, *Discovery*, pp. 79–84; *Dead Sea Scrolls*, p. 65). The one major divergence concerns the dating of the events described in the Habakkuk commentary to the period immediately following Pompey (Dupont-Sommer) or preceding it (Vermes). The main arguments in favour of the latter alternative are as follows. (1) In 1QpHab II–VI the Kittim are depicted as world conquerors about to invade Judaea. They are not associated with past history; in fact, none of the verbs used in relation to them appears in the perfect tense. The 'last Priests of Jerusalem' still commanding the Palestinian scene at the time of the composition of the Commentary are portrayed as their contemporaries whose riches the Kittim are to appropriate, see 1QpHab. IX 4–7. (2) In 4QpNah I 2–4, Demetrius, king of Greece is said to have failed to enter Jerusalem (see above, p. 224, n. 22) and the city was not to be subjugated by the Gentiles (the sense is assured despite gaps in the text) from the time of Antiochus (IV Epiphanes) until the arrival of the rulers of the Kittim: מאנטיוכוס עד עמוד מושלי כתיים. If therefore the occupation of Jerusalem was to mark a new era, the period dealt with in 1QpHab, during which the Kittim were not yet masters of Judaea, necessarily falls prior to 63 B.C.

Dupont-Sommer's argument (see RHR 137 (1950), pp. 149–50, 168–9; *Essene Writings*, pp. 166–7) that pHab. XI 6–8 hints at the actual fall of Jerusalem on the Day of Atonement (see above, p. 239, n. 23) is far from cogent; it entails in particular an unnecessary and unjustified change of subject. In the first of two sentences this was the Wicked Priest. It is normal, therefore, to understand the key verb 'he appeared to them' (הופיע עליהם) as indicating the Wicked Priest's sudden and unexpected visit to the Teacher of Righteousness and his followers. Dupont-Sommer, by contrast, applies it to a supernatural manifestation of the dead Teacher himself. See G. Vermes, Cahiers Sioniens 5 (1951), pp. 63-5; M. B. Dagut, Biblica 32 (1951), pp. 542–8; S. Talmon, *ibid.*, pp. 549–51.

If it is accepted that the Kittim of 1QpHab are the Romans of the mid-sixties B.C., the picture contained there points to a shift in Jewish attitudes towards the Romans compared with the praises showered on them in 1 Mac. (see above, pp. 171, 194). They are no longer depicted as benevolence incarnate, but as hard, cunning and cruel conquerors (1QpHab. II 12–VI 12), the 'remnant of the peoples' chosen by God to punish the 'last Priests of Jerusalem' (IX 4–7). However, since the writer hoped that his Hasmonaean opponents would be humiliated by them, he refrained from passing judgment on the Kittim.

A similar politically unbiased view of the conquering Romans is included in a perhaps somewhat earlier passage of the Jewish Sibylline Oracles (III, 75–80) mentioning that 'an empire . . . from the Western sea . . . shall frighten many kings . . . and rob much silver and gold from many cities'. On the Sibylline Oracles see vol. III, § 33.

The author of the Psalms of Solomon, possibly a Pharisee (see Eissfeldt, *Introduction*, pp. 612–13; cf. vol. III, § 32) writing around the middle of the first century B.C., is the first Jewish author to express unmitigated hostility to Rome. He and the party of 'the Pious' which he represents, were opposed to 'the sinners' guilty of profanation of the sanctuary (2:3; 8:12–14) and of the creation of a non-Davidic monarchy (17:7–8), i.e. the Sadducaean supporters of the Hasmonaeans. The Psalmist of Ps of Sol. 2 manifests bitter hatred towards Pompey, and reproaches this 'proud sinner' with the destruction of the walls of Jerusalem and the desecration of the altar in the Temple (2:1–2). He is 'the lawless one' who 'ravaged our land' killing all indiscriminately. (Note the reference to a 'massacre by אמליוס, no doubt Aemilius Scaurus, Pompey's general, in the unpublished calendar from 4Q; see Milik, *Ten Years of Discovery*, p. 73.) Characterized as a 'dragon' (2:25), the Roman general's inglorious end is foretold in a pseudo-prophetic vision: 'I had not long to wait before God showed me the insolent one slain on the mountains of Egypt, esteemed of less account than the least on land and sea' (2:26). 'He reflected not that he was but a man . . . He said, I will be lord of land and sea, and recognized not that God alone is great' (2:28–9; probably a pun on Pompey's epithet, Magnus). See G. B. Gray in Charles, *Apocr. and Pseudep.* II, pp. 628–30 and *ad loc.*

For an identification of the opponent of the Qumran Community as Hyrcanus II and Aristobulus II, see A. Dupont-Sommer, *The Essene Writings from Qumran* (1961), pp. 351–7; 'Observations sur le Commentaire de Nahum découvert près de la Mer Morte', Journal des Savants (1963), pp. 201–26.

The Second Period

From the Capture of Jerusalem by Pompey to the Hadrianic War

The Roman-Herodian Age 63 B.C.–A.D. 135

From 65 B.C. to A.D. 70, Palestine, although not directly annexed to the province of Syria, was nevertheless subject to the supervision of the Roman governor of Syria. During this period, therefore, it was even more involved in the destiny of Syria than in the preceding one, and we accordingly begin once more with a survey of the history of that region.

Survey of the History of the Roman Province of Syria from 65 B.C. to A.D. 70

Sources

For the period of the Republic and the Civil Wars (65–30 B.C.), the main sources are Josephus, Cassius Dio, Appian, Cicero and Plutarch. For the period of the Empire (30 B.C.–A.D. 70): Josephus, Cassius Dio, Tacitus and Suetonius. See pp. 63–8 above.

Bibliography

1. *Provincial Government:*

Abbott, F. F. and Johnson, A. C., *Municipal Administration in the Roman Empire* (1926).
Badian, E., *Roman Imperialism in the Late Republic* ([2]1968).
Bowersock, G. W., *Augustus and the Greek World* (1965).
Ganter, L., *Die Provinzialverwaltung der Triumvirn* (1892).
Hirschfeld, O., *Die kaiserlichen Verwaltungsbeamten bis auf Diocletian* ([2]1905).
Jones, A. H. M., *The Greek City* (1940).
Pflaum, H.-G., *Les procurateurs équestres* (1950).
Stevenson, G. H., *Roman Provincial Administration* (1939).

2. *The Province of Syria:*

Bouchier, E. S., *Syria as a Roman Province* (1911).
Downey, G., *A History of Antioch in Syria from Seleucus to the Arab Conquest* (1961).
Harrer, G. A., *Studies in the History of the Roman Province of Syria* (1915).
Hitti, P. K., *History of Syria including Lebanon and Palestine* ([2]1957), pp. 280–98.
Honigmann, E., 'Syria' RE IVA (1932), cols 1549 f., esp. 1622 f.
Jones, A. H. M., *Cities of the Eastern Roman Provinces* (1937; [2]1971), ch. X.

3. *Reference works relating to Roman office-bearers:*

(a) General:

Drumann, W., Groebe, P., *Geschichte Roms in seinem Übergange von der republikanischen zur monarchischen Verfassung oder Pompeius, Caesar, Cicero und ihre Zeitgenossen nach Geschlechtern und mit genealogischen Tabellen* I (1899), II (1902), III (1906), IV (1908), V (1912–19), VI (1929).
Pauly-Wissowa, *Real-encyclopädie der classischen Altertumswissenschaft* (RE).

(b) Republican period:

Broughton, T. R. S., *Magistrates of the Roman Republic* I-II (1952) (MRR).

(c) Imperial period:

Prosopographia Imperii Romani[1] (1898–8), ed. Klebs, Dessau, de Rohden (PIR[1]).
Prosopographia Imperii Romani[2] (1933–), ed. Groag, Stein, Petersen (PIR[2]).

I. The Downfall of the Republic 65–30 B.C.

1. Syria under the settlement by Pompey 65–48 B.C.

M. Aemilius Scaurus 65–62 B.C.

While serving as pro-quaestor of Pompey in Armenia, Scaurus was sent by him in 65 B.C. to Damascus, occupied shortly beforehand by Lollius and Metellus, Jos. *Ant.* xiv 2, 3 (29); *B.J.* i 6, 2 (127). In 64 to 63 B.C. Pompey himself was in Syria (MRR II, pp. 163–4, 169–70). In 63 B.C. he captured Jerusalem, and on his return to Pontus left Scaurus in Syria as governor *proquaestore propraetore* (Appian, *Syr.* 51/255; Jos. *Ant.* xiv 4, 5 (79); IGR III 1102 (Tyre) *Μᾶρκον Αἰμύλιον Μάρκου υἱὸν Σκαῦρον ἀντιταμίαν ἀντιστράτηγον*). The latter carried out the campaign, planned by Pompey against the Nabataean king Aretas; Aretas secured peace on payment of 300 talents, Jos. *Ant.* xiv 5, 1–2 (80); *B.J.* i 8, 1 (159). Reference is made to this on coins minted by Scaurus as aedile of 58 B.C. with the inscription *M. Scaur. Aed. cur., ex S.C. Rex Aretas* (Babelon, *Monnaies de la république romaine* I (1885), pp. 120 f.; E. A. Sydenham, *The Coinage of the Roman Republic* (1952), pp. 151–2, Pl. 913). Scaurus took with him from Joppa the skeleton of the sea-monster to which Andromeda had been exposed (Pliny, *N.H.* ix 4/11). See Drumann-Groebe, *op. cit.*, I, pp. 20–3; RE s.v. 'Aemilius' (141).

L. Marcius Philippus 61–60 B.C.

According to Appian, *Syr.* 51/255–6, Marcius Philippus and Lentulus Marcellinus were governors of Syria (*τῶνδε μὲν ἑκατέρῳ διετὴς ἐτρίφθη χρόνος*) between Scaurus and Gabinius, each for two years, and both with praetorian rank. Since Gabinius arrived in Syria in the beginning of 57 B.C., the years 61–60 B.C. must be assigned to L. Marcius Philippus, and the years 59–58 B.C. to Cn. Cornelius Lentulus Marcellinus. Cf. RE s.v. 'Marcius' (76).

Cn. Cornelius Lentulus Marcellinus 59–58 B.C.

See the preceding paragraph. Like his predecessor, he had to fight against the Nabataeans. Cf. RE s.v. 'Cornelius' (228).

Aulus Gabinius 57–55 B.C.

In 58 B.C., Syria was made a consular province (App. *Syr.* 51/256). In legislation passed by the tribune P. Clodius (MRR II, pp. 195–6), one of the consuls of 58 B.C., Aulus Gabinius, was assigned first Cilicia and then Syria. He arrived in the province in 57 B.C.[1] In this year he crushed a Jewish revolt under Alexander and Aristobulus, Jos. *B.J.* i 8, 2–6 (160–74); *Ant.* xiv 5, 2–6, 1 (82–97). Cicero, in speeches delivered in the spring and summer of 56 B.C., makes frequent attacks on his government of Syria for corruption, extortion and measures against the *publicani*, see e.g. *Pro Sestio* 71, 93; *De prov. cons.* 9–16. He was refused the vote of a *supplicatio*. See MRR II, p. 203.

In 56 B.C., he made preparations for an invasion of Parthia, and his command was continued for 55 B.C. (MRR II, p. 211). But in the spring of 55 B.C. he was commissioned by Pompey to reinstate King Ptolemy Auletes, who had been expelled from Alexandria in a popular rising. Ptolemy himself gave the needed stimulus to this commission by a gift of 10,000 talents. With Gabinius these two reasons outweighed both the opposition of the senate, and the prevailing law strictly prohibiting a proconsul from overstepping the limits of his province. He discontinued the expedition against the Parthians, made for Egypt, brought the Egyptian army to defeat—in the course of which young M. Antonius, the future triumvir, especially distinguished himself—and

1. In this period consuls and praetors proceeded to their provinces immediately after their tems of office expired. This was altered in 52 B.C., when it was enacted that there must always be an interval of five years. Cf. Marquardt, *Römische Staatsverwaltung* I (²1881), p. 522; G. H. Stevenson, *Roman Provincial Administration* (1939), p. 64.

reinstated Ptolemy as king in the beginning of 55 B.C. (Dio xxxix 56–8; Cic. *In Pison.* 48–50; Jos. *Ant.* xiv 6, 2 (98); Plut. *Ant.* 3, Appian, *Syr.* 51/257–9). He was for this reason accused *de maiestate* in Rome in the same year 55 B.C., at the instigation of Cicero in particular. The trial was already in progress when—after Crassus had meanwhile acquired the province—he arrived in September 54 B.C. in Rome (Cic. *ad Q.f.* iii 1, 5–7). His wealth and Pompey's influence succeeded in procuring for him a verdict of acquittal. But he was condemned on a charge of extortion, despite the fact that Cicero himself, persuaded by Pompey, undertook his defence (Dio xxxix 59–63, cf. 55; App. *B.C.* ii 24/90–2; Cic. *ad Q.f.* iii 1–4; *pro Rab. Post.* 8, 12; MRR II, p. 218). See Drumann-Groebe, *op. cit.* III, pp. 31–58; RE s.v. 'Gabinius' (11); T. Rice Holmes, *The Roman Republic* II, pp. 149–50, 155–8; E. Badian, Philologus 103 (1959), pp. 87–99.

M. Licinius Crassus 54–53 B.C.

In 60 B.C. Caesar, Pompey and Crassus had concluded the so-called first triumvirate. In 56 B.C. their agreement was renewed. It was in consequence of this that in 55 B.C., two of them, Pompey and Crassus, attained to the consulship. Whilst they held the consulship, Pompey undertook the administration of Spain, and Crassus that of Syria, each for five years (Dio xxxix 33–6; Liv. *Epit.* 105; Plut. *Pomp.* 52; Crass. 15; App. *B.C.* ii 18/65). Crassus left Rome and went to Syria even before the expiry of his consulship, in November of 55 B.C. (MRR II, pp. 214–15). In 54 B.C., he organised a campaign against the Parthians and advanced beyond the Euphrates, but returned to spend the winter in Syria. In the spring of 53 B.C., he renewed the campaign, crossed the Euphrates at Zeugma, but suffered a considerable defeat and had to withdraw to Carrhae. As he was unable to hold his ground here either, he continued his retreat, and had already reached the mountains of Armenia when the Parthian general Surenas offered him terms of peace on condition that the Romans should give up their claim to the territory on the further side of the Euphrates. Crassus was inclined to negotiate, but whilst on his way with a small escort to meet Surenas in 53 B.C., he was treacherously attacked and murdered by Parthian troops (according to Ovid, *Fast.* vi 465, *v Idus Junias*=9 June. MRR II, p. 230). Many of his men were taken prisoner by the Parthians, but some of them succeeded in escaping, and others had already got away to Syria under the leadership of the quaestor Cassius Longinus (Dio xl 12–27; Plut. *Crass.* 17–31; Liv. *Epit.* 106; Justin. xlii 4). See Drumann-Groebe, *op. cit.* IV, pp. 84–127; RE s.v. 'Crassus' (68); F. E. Adcock, *Marcus Crassus, Millionaire* (1966). On the Parthian campaign see T. Rice Holmes, *The Roman Republic* II, pp. 312–15; N. C. Debevoise, *A Political History of Parthia* (1938), pp. 78–93.

C. Cassius Longinus 53–51 B.C.

After the death of Crassus, the supreme command in Syria was assumed by Cassius Longinus, the quaestor of the province. The Parthians now made incursions into Roman territory, and in 51 B.C. advanced as far as Antioch, but were repelled by Cassius in the autumn of 51 B.C. (Dio xl 28–9; Jos. *Ant.* xiv 7, 3 (119); Liv. *Epit.* 108; Justin xlii 4; Cic. *ad Att.* V 20, 1–7; *ad Fam.* ii 10; *Phil.* xi 14/35; Drumann-Groebe, *op. cit.* II 2, pp. 98–128; RE s.v. 'Cassius' (59). See MRR II, pp. 229, 237, 242–5.

M. Calpurnius Bibulus 51–50 B.C.

Cassius Longinus was succeeded by a certain Bibulus (according to Cic. *ad fam.* ii 10; *ad Att.* v 20; Dio xl 30–1). Appian in *Syr.* 51/259 calls him *Λευκίου Βύβλου*. But from the testimony of Cicero, *ad fam*, xii 19, xv 1 and 3, Liv. *Epit.* 108 and Caesar, *B.C.* iii 31, it is certain that this was M. Bibulus, Caesar's colleague in the consulship in 59 B.C. He arrived in Syria in the autumn of 51 B.C. (Cic. *ad Att.* v 18 and 20). He too had dealings with the Parthians (cf. Cic. *ad fam.* xii 19), but was able to get rid of them by inciting them to strife among themselves (according to Dio xl 30–1), as early as 51 B.C. Cf. Cic. *ad Att.* vii 2 'Parthi . . . repente Bibulum semivivum reliquerunt'. See MRR II, pp. 242, 250, and in general Drumann-Groebe, *op. cit.* II, pp. 80–6; RE s.v. 'Calpurnius' (28).

Veiento 50/49 B.C.

'Bibulus de provincia decessit, Veientonem praefecit', writes Cicero, in the beginning of December 50 B.C. (*ad Att.* vii 3, 5). Veiento was probably his *legatus*. MRR II, p. 253; RE s.v. 'Veiento' (2).

Q. Caecilius Metellus Pius Scipio Nasica 49–48 B.C.

When, in the first days of 49 B.C., civil war broke out between Caesar and Pompey, the provinces had just been distributed by Pompey's party and the province of Syria assigned to his father-in-law, Q. Metellus Scipio, who had held the consulship in 52 B.C. (Caesar, *B.C.* i 6; cf. Cic. *ad Att.* ix 1). Towards the end of 49 B.C. he brought two legions from Syria to assist Pompey, and spent the winter with them in the region of Pergamum (Caesar, *B.C.* iii 4 and 31). In the following year, he crossed over to Macedonia and joined Pompey shortly before the battle of Pharsalus (Caesar, *B.C.* iii 33, 78–82). In the battle of Pharsalus he commanded the centre of the Pompeian army (Caesar, *B.C.* iii 88). See MRR II, pp. 260–1, 275. See Drumann-Groebe, *op. cit.* II, pp. 36–50; RE s.v. 'Caecilius' (99).

2. The age of Caesar 47–44 B.C.

Sex. Iulius Caesar 47–46 B.C.

After the battle of Pharsalus (9 August 48 B.C.), Caesar followed Pompey by sea to Egypt, arriving there in the beginning of October, shortly after the assassination of Pompey on 28 September. Contrary to expectation, he became embroiled there in a war with King Ptolemy which detained him for nine months (App. *B.C.* ii 90/378). It was not until the beginning of June 47 B.C. that he was able to depart. He then went quickly (Dio xlii 47, 1) through Syria to Asia Minor to campaign against Pharnaces, the king of Pontus (*Bell. Alex.* 33, 65 ff.; Plut. *Caesar* 49, 50; Suet. *Div. Jul.* 35; App. *B.C.* ii 91/381).[2] Syria seems to have been left more or less to itself until then, but during his short stay there (according to Cic. *ad Att.* xi 20, 1, Caesar was in Antioch in the middle of July 47 B.C. by the Roman calendar), Caesar set the affairs of Syria in order by appointing one of his own relatives, Sex. Iulius Caesar, as governor, probably as *proquaestore pro praetore*, *Bell. Alex.* 66; Dio xlvii 26, 3. Cf. Jos. *Ant.* xiv 9, 2 (160). See MRR II, pp. 289, 297. Many Syrian cities obtained valuable privileges from Caesar (see *Bell. Alex.* 65) and for this reason instituted a new chronology (*aera Caesariana*): thus Antioch, Gabala, Laodicea. See Jones, *Cities*, p. 261; G. Downey, *A History of Antioch*, pp. 152 ff.; *BMC Syria* (1899), pp. 154 f.; A. R. Bellinger, 'The Early Coinage of Roman Syria', *Stud. in Rom. Soc. and Econ. Hist. pres. A. C. Johnson* (1951), pp. 58–67. See W. Judeich, *Caesar im Orient, kritische Uebersicht der Ereignisse vom.* 9 *Aug.* 48 *bis October* 47 (1885). On Sex. Iulius Caesar see RE s.v. 'Iulius' (153).

(*Q. Caecilius Bassus* 46–44 B.C.)

While Caesar was engaged in Africa in 46 B.C. against the Pompeian party, one of their number, Q. Caecilius Bassus, endeavoured to seize the governorship of Syria. He was defeated by Sextus, but managed to rid himself of him by assassination, to win over the soldiers to his side, and thus make himself master of Syria, Dio xlvii 26–27; Liv. *Epit.* 114; Jos. *Ant.* xiv 11, 1 (268); App. *B.C.* iii 77/312–15; compare iv 58/249–52; Drumann-Groebe, *op. cit.* II, pp. 106–8, 125; RE s.v. 'Caecilius' (36); Rice Holmes, *Roman Republic* III, p. 326 and n. 5.

2. Caesar journeyed by sea from Egypt to Syria and from Syria to Cilicia; cf. Jos. *Ant.* xiv 8, 3 (137); 9, 1 (156); *Bell. Alex.* 66, 'eadem classe, qua venerat, proficiscitur in Ciliciam'. In the earlier passage, *Bell. Alex.* 33, 'sic rebus omnibus confectis et collocatis ipse itinere terrestri profectus est in Syriam' the words 'itinere terrestri' ought to be deleted. Cf. J. Andrieu, *César, Guerre d'Alexandrie* (Budé ed., 1954), p. 83.

C. Antistius Vetus 45 B.C.

Antistius Vetus was probably appointed by Caesar to govern Syria as *quaestor pro praetore*.[3] In the autumn of 45 B.C. he besieged Bassus in Apamea, but was unable to defeat him decisively because the Parthians brought assistance to Bassus, Dio xlvii 27, 2–5. Cf. Jos. *Ant.* xiv 11, 1 (268). The chronology is given by Cicero, *ad Att.* xiv 9, 3 and Dio *l.c.*: διὰ τὸν χειμῶνα.) Cf. RE s.v. 'Antistius' (47); PIR² A 770.

L. Staius Murcus 44 B.C.

For the fight against Caecilius Bassus, Caesar sent L. Staius Murcus to Syria with three legions (probably at the beginning of 44 B.C.). He left after the Ides of March, suffered a reverse against Bassus, and was reinforced by the governor of Bithynia, Q. Marcius Crispus, who also had three legions at his disposal. Both then besieged Bassus again in Apamea (App. *B.C.* iii 77/316–7; iv 58/253–5; Dio xlvii 27, 5; Jos. *Ant.* xiv 11, 1 (270). Cf. Strabo xvi 2, 10 (752). See MRR II, p. 330.

3. Syria under the administration of Cassius (44–42 B.C.)

C. Cassius Longinus 44–42 B.C.

The assassination of Caesar on 15 March 44 B.C. gave a new turn to affairs. Among the conspirators responsible for the deed, the most prominent, apart from M. Brutus, was C. Cassius Longinus, the same man who had successfully defended Syria against the attacks of the Parthians in 53–51 B.C. He had been designated by Caesar as governor of Syria for 43 B.C. (App. *B.C.* iii 2/5; iv 57). But after Caesar's death, M. Antonius assigned Syria to Dolabella, and another province (Cyrene?) to Cassius (App. *B.C.* iii 7–8/22–9; iv 57/245). Cassius, however, did not submit to these arrangements, but proceeded to Syria, the province allotted to him by Caesar, arriving there before Dolabella (App. *B.C.* iii 24/91–2; iv 58/248–9; Dio xlvii 21, 26).[4] At the time of his arrival early in 43 B.C., Caecilius Bassus was still besieged in Apamea by Staius Murcus and Marcius Crispus. He succeeded in winning over both

3. From Cicero, *ad fam.* xii 19, 1, it appears that at one time Caesar designated Q. Cornificius governor of Syria (Cicero writes to Cornificius: 'Bellum, quod est in Syria, Syriamque provinciam tibi tributam esse a Caesare ex tuis litteris cognovi'). The letter is undated, but it is plausibly argued by Ganter, Philologus 53 (1894), pp. 132–46, followed in RE s.v. 'Cornificius' (8), R. Syme, *Anatolian Studies pres. Buckler* (1939), pp. 320, 324, and MRR II, p. 297), that Cornificius was *quaestor pro praetore* in Cilicia in 46 B.C., and was briefly responsible also for operations in Syria.

4. On the transactions in reference to the provinces in the year 44 B.C. see further Drumann-Groebe, *op. cit.*, I, pp. 101–5; II, pp. 103 f.; T. Rice Holmes, *The Architect of the Roman Empire* (1928), pp. 188–90; Syme, *Roman Revolution*, pp. 97 f.

of these men, whereupon the legion of Bassus joined him also, as Cassius himself reports to Cicero in March and May 43 B.C., Cic. *ad fam.* xii 11 and 12. Cf. *ad Brut.* ii 5; *Phil.* xi 12/30; App. *B.C.* iii 78/317; iv 59/225; Dio xlvii 28; Jos. *Ant.* xiv 11, 2 (272). Cassius had thus considerable forces at his disposal when Dolabella, who in the meantime had made himself master of Asia Minor in the interests of Antonius, also invaded Syria and advanced as far as Laodicea, on the seashore south of Antioch (App. *B.C.* iii 78/320; iv 60/258–60; Dio xlvii 29–30). Cassius besieged him there (Cic. *ad fam.* xii 13–15) and obliged him to surrender, whereupon Dolabella ordered one of the soldiers of his bodyguard to kill him (App. *B.C.* iv 60–2/258–68; Dio xlvii 30). After the defeat of Dolabella, Cassius intended to make for Egypt, but was called urgently to Asia Minor by Brutus in 42 B.C. (See MRR II, pp. 343–4.) Accordingly, he left his nephew with one legion in Syria (App. *B.C.* iv 63/272), met Brutus in Smyrna, undertook an expedition against Rhodes, rejoined Brutus in Sardis, and then went with him to Macedonia. Here, at Philippi in the late autumn of 42 B.C., the armies of the conspirators were defeated by M. Antonius and Octavian, and Cassius, like his comrade Brutus, ended his life by his own hand, App. *B.C.* iv 63/270–138/581; Dio xlvii 31–49; Plut. *Brut.* 28–53. See RE s.v. 'Cassius' (59).

4. Syria under the domination of M. Antonius 41–30 B.C.

L. Decidius Saxa 41–40 B.C.

After the battle of Philippi, Octavian went to Italy, while Antonius made first for Greece and then for Asia (Plut. *Ant.* 23–4). On his way through Asia in 41 B.C., he met Cleopatra for the first time in Tarsus. She so captivated him by her charm that he followed her to Egypt, where he spent the winter 41/40 B.C. in idleness and revelry (according to Plut. *Ant.* 25–8). Before leaving for Egypt, he set in order the affairs of Syria, exacted on all sides an enormous tribute (App. *B.C.* v 7/29–31), and appointed L. Decidius Saxa *legatus*, probably with *imperium*; Dio xlviii 24, 3; Liv. *Epit.* 127; see MRR II, p. 376.

In the spring of 40 B.C., Antonius left Egypt and came in the summer of that year to Italy with the intention of fighting against Octavian; but after some insignificant skirmishing he concluded an agreement with him at Brundisium according to which the provinces were divided between Octavian and Antonius in such a way that the West fell to the former and the East to the latter (App. *B.C.* v 52/216–65/275; Dio xlviii 27–8. Scodra (now Scutari) in Illyria formed the boundary, App. *B.C.* v 65/274). Antonius remained for a year or so in Italy, during which time he nominated several vassal kings, among them Herod,[5] and then went to Athens in the autumn of 39 B.C. (App. *B.C.* v 75/318–76/324; Dio xlviii 39, 1–2). There he stayed, though not continuously, until the spring of 36 B.C.

At the time when Antonius secured from Octavian the rule over the East, a large part of the eastern territory, in particular the whole province of Syria, had already been lost to the Parthians. In 42 B.C., about the time when Cassius left Syria (App. *B.C.* iv 63/271), they had been invited by Cassius to form an alliance against Antonius and Octavian. Nothing came of it, however, the decisive battle of Philippi having taken place before the long-protracted negotiations had ended. But Labienus, the chief of the embassy, remained at the Parthian court, and at length managed by his unremitting representations to persuade King Orodes to invade Roman territory. As early perhaps as the autumn of 41 B.C., but at the latest in the spring of 40 B.C., a large Parthian army under the command of Labienus and Pacorus, the son of King Orodes, invaded Syria, defeated Decidius Saxa—he himself was killed—conquered all Syria, Phoenicia (with the exception only of Tyre) and Palestine, and finally forced its way into Asia Minor as far as the Ionian coast (Dio xlviii, 24–6; App. *Syr.* 51/259; *B.C.* v 65/276; Plut. *Ant.* 30; Liv. *Epit.* 127). See Debevoise, *Political History of Parthia* (1938), pp. 108–14; CAH X, pp. 47–50.

P. Ventidius Bassus 39–38 B.C.

Probably in the winter of 40–39 B.C., Antonius sent P. Ventidius Bassus with an army to Asia; at this time he had the status of *legatus* (Liv. *Epit.* 127), but had *imperium pro consule* at his triumph in 38 B.C. He drove Labienus back to the Taurus (in 39 B.C.) and defeated him there in a decisive battle (Labienus himself was afterwards taken prisoner and put to death). Ventidius then conquered Cilicia, and at the Amanus, the mountain boundary between Cilicia and Syria, defeated Pharnapates, Pacorus's second in command. He then without difficulty took possession of Syria and Palestine (Dio xlviii 39–41; Liv. *Epit.* 127; Plut. *Ant.* 33). In 38 B.C. the Parthians made another invasion, but sustained a complete defeat at the hands of Ventidius in the district of Cyrrhestica. Pacorus met his death in this battle, on the same day on which Crassus had fallen fifteen years earlier, 9 June (Dio xlix 19–20, cf. 21, 2; Liv. *Epit.* 128; Plut. *Ant.* 34). Ventidius next turned against Antiochus of Commagene. While he was besieging

5. Appian, *B.C.* v 75/319 *ἵστη δέ πῃ καὶ βασιλέας, οὓς δοκιμάσειεν, ἐπὶ φόροις ἄρα τεταγμένοις, , Πόντου μὲν Δαρεῖον τὸν Φαράκους τοῦ Μιθριδάτου, Ἰδουμαίων δὲ καὶ Σαμαρέων Ἡρῴδην, Ἀμύνταν δὲ Πισιδῶν καὶ Πολέμωνα μέρους Κιλικίας καὶ ἑτέρους ἐς ἕτερα ἔθνη.* See H. Buchheim, *Die Orientpolitik des Triumvirn M. Antonius* (1960), pp. 50 f., 66 f., etc. There are also nominations from a later time (36/35 B.C.) in Dio xlix 32, 3–5. Cf. Plut. *Ant.* 36.

him in Samosata, Antonius himself arrived, dismissed Ventidius, and continued the siege. But he accomplished little, contented himself with the formal submission of Antiochus, and returned to Athens, leaving C. Sosius behind as governor of Syria and Cilicia (Dio xlix 20–2; Plut. *Ant.* 34). In Rome on 27 Nov. 38 B.C. Ventidius celebrated a triumph *ex Tauro monte et Partheis* (CIL I², pp. 50, 76–7, 180). See MRR II, pp. 388, 392; RE s.v. 'Ventidius' (5).

C. Sosius 38–37 B.C.

Sosius completed the conquest of Syria by defeating the Jewish king Antigonus, the protégé of the Parthians, and conquering Jerusalem, where he installed Herod, whom Antonius had nominated king (Dio xlix 23, 1, transfers this to 38, the consulship of Ap. Claudius Pulcher and C. Norbanus Flaccus. But cf. § 14 below). For this, Sosius received the title *imperator* and was granted a triumph (*ex Judaea*), which he did not celebrate until 3 September 34 B.C. Cf. PIR¹ S 556; RE s.v. 'Sosius' (2).

In 36 B.C. Antonius himself went again to the East. Resolved to strike a decisive blow at the Parthians, he proceeded against them with a large force, but accomplished nothing, and when winter set in, was obliged to turn back with huge losses (Debevoise, *op. cit.*, pp. 123–31; MRR II, p. 400). He had rejoined Cleopatra in Syria in the spring of 36 B.C., before setting out against the Parthians. And after his return from that unfortunate expedition, he went to Leuce Come, between Sidon and Berytus, and in her company indulged in his usual amusements (Dio xlix 23–31; Plut. *Ant.* 36–51). He then (before the end of 36 B.C.) followed her to Egypt, and remained there till 33 B.C., devoting himself to a life of pleasure and extravagance interrupted by only two short campaigns against Armenia in 34 and 33 B.C. (Dio xlix 33, 29–41, 44; Plut. *Ant.* 52–3; Drumann-Groebe, *op. cit.* I pp. 336–42; R. Syme, *The Roman Revolution* (1939), pp. 264 f.; Buchheim, *Die Orientpolitik des Triumvirn M. Antonius* (1960), pp. 84 f.

From this period to the time of the battle at Actium, only two governors of Syria are known.

L. Munatius Plancus 35 B.C.

In 35 B.C., Sextus Pompeius, who had fled to Asia Minor after his defeat by Octavian, was put to death there. App. *B.C.* v 144/598 notes that it is uncertain whether his execution was ordered by Antonius himself or by Plancus, the governor of Syria (*εἰσὶ δ'οἳ Πλάγκον, οὐκ Ἀντώνιον λέγουσιν ἐπιστεῖλαι, ἄρχοντα Συρίας*). From this incidental note it seems possible that L. Munatius Plancus was then governor of Syria. He was one of Antonius's most intimate friends, but went over to the side of Octavian even before the outbreak of the war between Octavian and Antonius in 32 B.C. See Drumann-Groebe, *op. cit.* IV, pp. 223–29; RE s.v. 'Munatius' (30); PIR[1] M 534; MRR II, pp. 408–9.

L. Calpurnius Bibulus, c. 34/3–33/2 B.C.

App. *B.C.* iv 38/162 also mentions L. Bibulus among the proscribed who later made their peace with Antonius and Octavian: 'But Bibulus made his peace with Antonius and Octavian at the same time as Messala, and rendered service to Antonius as the commander of a ship, frequently effected settlements between Antonius and Octavian, was appointed by Antonius as governor of Syria and died whilst he was still governor'.[6] Since, according to this statement, Bibulus died when he was governor, but according to the evidence of his coins was alive at least in 33 B.C., it is probable that this governorship falls in the period of the war between Antonius and Octavian. RE s.v. 'Calpurnius' (27); PIR[2] C 253.

Meanwhile, Antonius had become increasingly the slave of Cleopatra's whims. He had even allowed himself to be persuaded to make a gift of Roman territory to her and her children. Cleopatra thus acquired Coele Syria, or as Dio says, a great portion of the land of the Ituraeans, whose king Lysanias was put to death (cf. App. I); Phoenicia, as far as the Eleutherus, with the exception of Tyre and Sidon; and parts of Judaea and Arabia, which were taken from their kings, Herod and Malchus (Jos. *Ant.* xv 3, 8 (74–9); 4, 1–2 (88–103); *B.J.* i 18, 5 (361–3); Dio xlix 32, 4–5; Plut. *Ant.* 36; on the date of these gifts see § 15 below). Somewhat later, Ptolemy, Cleopatra's son by Antonius, acquired Syria as far as the Euphrates and Phoenicia, whilst Coele Syria continued to belong to his mother (so Plut. *Ant.* 54; cf. Dio xlix 41). See Buchheim, *Orientpolitik*, pp. 81 f. These gifts were certainly not confirmed by the senate (Dio xlix 41, 4). After the last Armenian campaign in 33 B.C., Antonius went to Greece. While he was there, war broke out between him and Octavian in 32 B.C., and in the following year, in the battle of Actium (2 September 31 B.C.), his power was finally and permanently broken.

II. The Period of the Empire 30 B.C.–A.D. 70

1. Octavian/Augustus 30 B.C. to 19 August A.D. 14

Q. Didius 30 B.C.

After the battle of Actium, Antonius fled to Egypt. Octavian followed

6. *Βύβλος δὲ ἐσπείσατο ἅμα τῷ Μεσσάλᾳ, καὶ ναυάρχησεν Ἀντωνίῳ, διαλλαγάς τε πολλάκις Ἀντωνίῳ καὶ Καίσαρι ἐς ἀλλήλους ἐπόρθμευσε, καὶ στρατηγὸς ἀπεδείχθη Συρίας ὑπ Ἀντωνίου καὶ στρατηγῶν ἔτι αὐτῆς ἀπέθανεν.*

him, but because the year was well advanced, was obliged to spend the winter in Samos (Suet. *Div. Aug.* 17). It was not until 30 B.C. that he travelled by land through Asia and Syria ('Asiae Syriaeque circuitu Aegyptum petit', Suet. *Div. Aug.* 17) to Egypt. There, on 1 August 30 B.C., before the gates of Alexandria, an engagement took place in which Antonius was defeated, while at the same time his fleet went over to Octavian. As a result, Antonius and Cleopatra committed suicide, leaving Octavian absolute master of the Roman empire (Dio li 1–14; Plut. *Ant.* 69–86).

In this period, between the battle of Actium and the death of Antonius (Sept. 31–Aug. 30 B.C.), Q. Didius is mentioned as a governor of Syria who provoked the Arabian tribes to burn ships built for Antonius in the Arabian Gulf, and prevented gladiators anxious to hasten from Cyzicus to the help of Antonius from marching through to Egypt, in which connexion King Herod also lent him aid, Dio li 7; Jos. *Ant.* xv 6, 7 (195). It is possible that Didius had been appointed by Antonius, but that he sided with Octavian after the battle of Actium, when he saw that Antonius's cause was lost.[7] See PIR² D 69.

Towards the end of 30 B.C., Octavian returned to Syria on his way back from Egypt, and probably only then set affairs in order there. He spent the winter 30/29 B.C. in Asia. (Dio li 18, 1).

M. Valerius Messalla Corvinus 29 B.C.

The gladiators prevented by Didius from marching to Egypt were dispersed to various places and put to death as occasion arose by Messalla (i.e. M. Valerius Messalla Corvinus, consul of 31 B.C., Dio li 7, 7; see Tibullus I 7, 13 f.). Messalla must therefore have been governor of Syria after Didius. From App. *B.C.* iv 38/162, Ganter (*Provinzialerwaltung der Triumvirn*, p. 44) argued that Messalla's administration of Syria cannot have occurred until after his governorship of Gaul (28–27 B.C.), since Appian mentions his mission to Gaul immediately after his participation in the battle of Actium. But this does not exclude the possibility that his administration of Syria fell in the interval between the two. See PIR¹ V 90; RE s.v. 'Valerius' (261).

M. Tullius Cicero 29–27? (27–25?)

From App. *B.C.* iv 51/221 it emerges that after holding the consulship in 30 B.C., Cicero was also governor of Syria. But nothing certain is known concerning the date of his administration. Appian's words (*αὐτὸν ὁ Καῖσαρ . . . ἱερέα τε εὐθὺς ἀπέφηνε καὶ ὕπατον οὐ πολὺ ὕστερον καὶ*

7. This conjecture was rejected by Ganter, *Provinzialverwaltung der Triumvirn*, p. 44. But its probability emerges from the fact that already very soon after the battle of Actium Didius appears in control of Syria; see Syme, *Roman Revolution*, p. 266, n. 3.

Συρίας στρατηγόν) point to a period soon after 30 B.C. The inscription on which Cicero is mentioned as governor of Syria is now held to be spurious (CIL x, *falsae* no. 704). See PIR[1] T 272; Drumann-Groebe, *op. cit.* VI, pp. 711–19; Syme, *Roman Revolution*, pp. 302–3; RE s.v. 'Tullius' (30).

In 27 B.C., the provinces were divided between Augustus and the senate. Hitherto, Augustus had appointed the governors of all the provinces under the powers conferred on the Triumvirate in 43 B.C. But now he returned part of them to the rule of proconsuls appointed by lot, retaining for himself the right to appoint the governors (*legati Augusti pro praetore*) of others, mainly those in which there were substantial military forces. Among the latter was Syria, in itself one of the most important provinces; because its eastern frontier was constantly threatened, it could not be left without a strong military defence.[8]

8. On this division of the provinces, cf. in particular Dio liii 12; also Strabo xvii 3, 25 (840) and Suet. *Div. Aug.* 47. The more specific regulations concerning the administration of the provinces made by Augustus partly now, and partly at a later time, are in substance the following (see especially Dio liii 13–15; Marquardt, *Römische Staatsverwaltung* i ([2]1881), pp. 543–57; Mommsen, *Römisches Staatsrecht* II ([3]1887), pp. 243–66; G. H. Stevenson, *Roman Provincial Administration* (1939), pp. 94 ff.; F. Millar, JRS 56 (1966), pp. 156–66):

a. The senatorial provinces. They were divided into two classes, those administered by former consuls, and those administered by former praetors. Only Africa and Asia were consular provinces; all the rest were praetorian. All governors were chosen by lot, each for one year; but, as had been laid down in the *lex Pompeia* of 52 B.C., at least five years had to elapse between the holding of office in Rome and departure to a province. The interval was frequently longer. The two consuls first entitled cast lots for the two consular provinces of Africa and Asia (the first entitled were not always the oldest, see Zippel, *Die Losung der konsularischen Prokonsuln in der früheren Kaiserzeit*, Königsberg, Progr. 1883); similarly, entitled praetors cast lots for the praetorian provinces (nothing certain is known of this however). The governors of all the senatorial provinces were called *proconsules*, whether they were former consuls or only former praetors; but the proconsuls of Africa and Asia had twelve lictors, the rest of them six. None of the governors of the senatorial provinces had legions at his disposal, but only a small force sufficient for the maintenance of order. Exceptions were Macedonia and Africa, where a legion was stationed, but in the latter case it was later handed over to a separate *legatus* appointed by the Emperor.

b. The imperial provinces. They too were divided into those administered by former consuls and those administered by former praetors; in addition, some were administered by mere knights. All governors were of course nominated by the emperor, and the length of their term of office depended entirely on him. The governors of both consular and praetorian provinces (Syria belonged to the former) were known as *legati Augusti pro praetore* (Dio liii 13, 5 τοὺς δὲ ἑτέρους ὑπό τε ἑαυτοῦ αἱρεῖσθαι καὶ πρεσβευτὰς αὐτοῦ ἀντιστρατήγους τε ὀνομάζεσθαι, κἂν ἐκ τῶν ὑπατευκότων ὦσι, διέταξε. Unlike the governors of the senatorial provinces, they had the *paludamentum* and went out *cum gladio*.

(M. Terentius?) Varro 24–23 B.C.?

Immediately before Agrippa's mission to the East (23 B.C.), a certain Varro is mentioned as governor of Syria, Jos. *Ant.* xv 10, 1 (345); *B.J.* i 20, 4 (398). He may be identical with the Terentius Varro mentioned by Dio liii 25, 3–5 and Strabo iv 6, 7 (205), who in 25 B.C. as legate of Augustus subdued the Salassi; or with the [*Μᾶρκος Τερέντ*]*ιος Μάρκου υἱὸς Παπειρίᾳ Οὐάρρων* in the *SC de Mytileneis* of 25 B.C. (IGR IV 33, B 42 = R. K. Sherk, *Roman Documents from the Greek East* (1969), no. 26). From Josephus it emerges definitely that our Varro was still in Syria when Augustus bestowed the district of Trachonitis upon Herod,[9] i.e., at the end of 24 B.C. or the beginning of 23 B.C. The opinion of Mommsen (*Res Gest.*, pp. 165 f.) that Varro was a legate of Agrippa is improbable, for Josephus places Varro before the time when Agrippa was sent to the East. Cf. M. Reinhold, *Marcus Agrippa: A Biography* (1933), p. 175. See PIR[1] T 195; RE s.v. 'Terentius' (86); Syme, *Roman Revolution*, pp. 330, 338.

M. Vipsanius Agrippa 23–13 B.C.

In 23 B.C. Augustus sent to Syria M. Agrippa, his intimate friend and counsellor, and in 21 B.C. his son-in-law (Dio liv 6, 5). Josephus describes him as the 'deputy of Caesar in the countries beyond the Ionian Sea' (*Ant.* xv 10, 2 (350) *τῶν πέραν Ἰονίου διάδοχος Καίσαρι*). He possessed in any case very extensive powers, more than an ordinary *legatus Augusti pro praetore.* According to Jos. *Ant.* xvi 3, 3 (86) he held this position (*τὴν διοίκησιν τῶν ἐπὶ τῆς Ἀσίας*) for ten years, until 13 B.C. Agrippa did not in fact go to Syria in 23 B.C. at all, but stayed in Mytilene on the island of Lesbos from 23–21 B.C., and then returned to Rome, Dio liii 32, 1; liv 6, 5; Suet. *Div. Aug.* 66. Cf. Jos. *Ant.* xv 10, 2 (350). During the four following years, he was busy in the West, and it was not until 16 B.C. that he went again to the East, where he remained until 13 B.C., Dio liv 19, 6; 24, 5–8; 28, 1; Jos. *Ant.* xvi 2, 1–5 (12–62); 3, 3 (86). He was thus by no means always in the East during the ten years, let alone in Syria. He could, however, exercise his official powers *in absentia* through legates, as he in fact did in 23 B.C. (*τοὺς ὑποστρατήγους*, Dio liii 32, 1), when he sent his legate from Lesbos to Syria. He is therefore to be regarded as the governor of Syria during this period, at least during 23–21 B.C., and perhaps 17–13 B.C. It is not possible to give a precise account of the constitutional powers of Agrippa during this period, or of the status of his *legati*. See, however, the discussion and conclusions of M. Reinhold, *Marcus Agrippa*, pp. 167–75. Cf. PIR[1] V 457; RE s.v. 'Vipsanius' (2) IXA. 1, cols. 1226 f.);

9. Augustus commanded Varro to extirpate the gangs of robbers in Trachonitis, and at the same time bestowed the territory on Herod, *Ant.* xv 10, 1 (345).

and now E. W. Gray, 'The Imperium of M. Agrippa: a note on P. Colon. inv. nr. 4701', Zeitschr. f. Pap. u. Epig. 6 (1970), pp. 227–38.

During the two years 21–19 B.C. Augustus was in the East, Dio liv 7–10; cf. Jos. *Ant.* xv 10, 3 (354); *B.J.* i 20, 4 (399).

M. Titius c. 10 B.C.

At the time of Herod's quarrel with his sons, probably *c.* 10 B.C., M. Titius, suffect consul in 31 B.C., is mentioned as governor of Syria, Jos. *Ant.* xvi 8, 6 (270). Cf. Strabo xvi 1, 28 (748); RE s.v. 'Titius' (18); PIR[1] T 196. T. Corbishley, JRS 24 (1934), pp. 43–9; L. R. Taylor, JRS 26 (1936), pp. 161–73; R. Syme, *Roman Revolution*, p. 398; G. W. Bowersock, *Augustus and the Greek World* (1965), pp. 21–2.

C. Sentius Saturninus ?10/9–?7/6 B.C.

The immediate successor of M. Titius was possibly C. Sentius Saturninus, Jos. *Ant.* xvi 9, 1 (280), consul in 19 B.C. Josephus names Volumnius with him also, as τῶν Συρίας ἐπισταтούντων. But in *B.J.* i 27, 1 (535) he calls Volumnius τὸν στρατοπεδάρχην, and in i 27, 2 (538) ἐπίτροπος. So he was an equestrian subordinate of Saturninus, and probably procurator of the province. Sentius Saturninus is also mentioned in Jos. *Ant.* xvi 10, 8 (344); 11, 3 (368); xvii 1, 1 (6); 2, 1 (24); 3, 2 (57). Tertullian places the census during which Christ was born in the period of his administration: 'sed et census constat actos sub Augusto nunc in Iudaea per Sentium Saturninum, apud quos genus eius inquirere potuissent' (*adv. Marcion.* iv 19, 10). This statement is at variance with the account given by Josephus and is certainly erroneous. See PIR[1] S 293; RE s.v. 'Sentius' (9).

P. Quinctilius Varus 7/6–4 B.C.

The immediate successor of Saturninus was Quinctilius Varus, Jos. *Ant.* xvii 5, 2 (89), consul in 13 B.C., who later undertook the disastrous campaign in Germany. On the evidence of coins (*BMC Syria*, pp. 158 f., nos. 357–9; G. Macdonald, Num. Chron. 4 (1904), pp. 106–9; D. B. Waage, *Antioch on the Orontes* IV 2 (1952), p. 29, nos. 300–3) it is established that Varus was governor of Syria in the years 25, 26 and 27 of the *aera Actiaca*. Since the Actian era begins on 2 September 31 B.C. (E. J. Bickerman, *Chronology of the Ancient World* (1968), pp. 73), its 25th year runs from autumn 7 B.C. to autumn 6 B.C. Varus must therefore have arrived in Syria before autumn 6 B.C. He remained there until after the death of Herod, Jos. *Ant.* xvii 9, 3 (221); 10, 1 (250); 10, 9 (286); 11, 1 (299), i.e. probably into the summer of 4 B.C. or longer (on the date of Herod's death, see p. 326 below), Velleius ii 117, 2 says of his administration of Syria, 'Varus . . . pecuniae vero quam non contemptor, Syria cui praefuerat declaravit, quam pauper divitem ingressus dives pauperem reliquit'. See PIR[1] Q 27; B. E. Thomasson, *Die Statthalter der röm. Provinzen Nordafrikas* II (1964), p. 13; RE s.v. 'Quinctilius' (20).

? *L. Calpurnius Piso* ? *c.* 4–1 B.C.

The much discussed acephalous inscription from Tibur (ILS 918) does not show an earlier governorship of Syria by P. Sulpicius Quirinius (see below), and may well, as has been argued in recent years (Syme, *Roman Revolution*, p. 398; B. M. Levick, *Roman Colonies in Southern Asia Minor* (1967), pp. 208–9), relate to L. Calpurnius Piso, the *pontifex*, consul in 15 B.C. (PIR[2] C 289); cf. however, P. Herrmann, Ath. Mitt. 75 (1960), pp. 130–4, and C. Habicht, *Alt. v. Pergamon VIII* 3 (1969), p. 40. In that case, the inscription refers to Piso's campaign against the Thracian Bessi, culminating in 11 B.C. (cf. Dio liv 34, 5–7; Tac. *Ann.* vi 10 f.), his proconsulate of Asia, perhaps in 3/2 B.C. or earlier (Levick, *op. cit.*, p. 209), and then his legateship of Syria, for which Syme, Klio 27 (1934), pp. 127–35, suggested the period 4–1 B.C. It may well be that the *Λεύκιον Κ[α]λπόρνιον Πείσωνα, πρεσβυτὴν καὶ ἀντιστράτηγον* honoured at Hierapolis-Castabala in Cilicia, JOAI 18 (1915), Beiheft, p. 51, is this Piso as *legatus* of Syria.

(? *P. Sulpicius Quirinius* ? 4–2 B.C.)

It has often been argued that P. Sulpicius Quirinius was twice *legatus* of Syria, once from about A.D. 6 (see below), and once earlier. The case for the latter rests on (a) Luke 2: 1, *ἐξῆλθε δόγμα παρὰ Καίσαρος Αὐγούστου, ἀπογράφεσθαι πᾶσαν τὴν οἰκουμένην. αὕτη ἡ ἀπογραφὴ πρώτη ἐγένετο ἡγεμονεύοντος τῆς Συριάς Κυρηνίου*, which thus seems (cf. Luke 1: 5) to date a Roman census conducted by Quirinius to the lifetime of Herod the Great; hence, such a census, and a governorship of Quirinius, would have to be an earlier one than that of A.D. 6, in which year he also conducted a census both of Syria and of the newly-absorbed province of Judaea. This thesis has seemed to be supported by the inscription from Tibur (ILS 918) which records *int. al.* that the unnamed senator whose career is described '[legatus pr. pr] divi Augusti iterum Syriam et Ph[oenicem optinuit]'. In spite of the recent doubts of A. N. Sherwin-White, *Roman Society and Roman Law in the New Testament* (1963), pp. 163–4, this will, however, mean not that the man was twice *legatus* of Syria, but that his second legateship was that of Syria. The inscription more probably relates to L. Calpurnius Piso (see above). The problem of the census, which cannot have taken place while Judaea was a client kingdom, is discussed on pp. 399–427. There is no good reason to think that Quirinius was governor of Syria at any time before A.D. 6. During the war which he fought against the Homonadenses (Strabo xii 6, 5 (567); Tac. *Ann.* iii 48), probably in the period *c.* 4–3 B.C., he was probably *legatus* of Galatia-Pamphylia, not of Syria (see Levick, *Roman Colonies*, pp. 203–14).

(? *C. Iulius Caesar* 1 B.C.–A.D. 4)

Gaius, the grandson of Augustus, was sent to the East with proconsular *imperium* in 1 B.C., and remained there until his death in A.D. 4. The expressions used by literary sources to describe his position are very varied (see PIR² I 1216), and only Orosius vii 3, 4 'ad ordinandas Aegypti Syriaeque provincias missus', implies clearly that he was specifically in charge of Syria. The contemporary evidence of Ovid, *Ars Amat.* 1 177 f. and an inscription from Messene (AE 1967, 458 ὑπὲρ τᾶς ἀνθρώπων πάντων σωτηρίας τοῖς βαρβάροις μαχόμενον) clearly envisages him as primarily engaged against the Parthians. There is therefore no definite reason to think that he replaced the normal governor of Syria during this period.

L. Volusius Saturninus A.D. 4–5

Consul suffectus in 12 B.C. It is known from coins that he was governor of Syria in the year 35 of the Actian era = autumn A.D. 4 to A.D. 5 (Mionnet V, p. 156; *BMC Syria*, p. 159; Macdonald, Num. Chron. 4 (1904), p. 109. See PIR¹ V 660; RE s.v. 'Volusius' (16) (Supp. IV, cols. 1857 f.).

P. Sulpicius Quirinius A.D. 6

After the banishment of Archelaus, the ethnarch of Judaea, in A.D. 6, P. Sulpicius Quirinius travelled to Syria and immediately after his arrival undertook a census in Judaea (Jos. *Ant.* xvii 13, 5 (355); xviii 1, 1 (1); 2, 1 (26); referred to in Luke 2:1; see above and pp. 399–427). How long he remained governor of Syria cannot be determined. Reference is also made to his activity in Syria in an inscription which was once supposed to be spurious. Since the discovery of the second half in the original, its authenticity is, however, assured (see especially Mommsen, *Ephemeris Epigraphica* IV (1881), pp. 537–42 = CIL III 6687 = ILS 2683; a facsimile of the surviving portion in De Rossi, Bull. di arch. crist (1880), tav. ix, cf. p. 174). On the inscription Q. Aemilius Q. f. Pal. Secundus says of himself among other things: 'iussu Quirini censum egi Apamenae civitatis millium homin(um) civium CXVII. Idem missu Quirini adversus Ituraeos in Libano monte castellum eorum cepi'. See PIR¹ S 732; RE s.v. 'Sulpicius' (90); Levick, *Roman Colonies*, pp. 206–13.

Q. Caecilius Metellus Creticus Silanus A.D. 12–17

Consul in A.D. 7. His coins show that he arrived in Syria as governor in A.D. 12 at the latest. On them occur the year numbers 43, 44, 45, 47 of the Actian era (Mionnet V, pp. 156–9, 276; Leake, *Numismata Hellenica, Asiatic Greece*, p. 15; *BMC Syria*, pp. 159, 169, 273; but see Macdonald, Num. Chron. 4 (1904), pp. 113–17; D. B. Waage, *Antioch on-the-Orontes* IV. 2, nos. 311, 312, 324, 325. Those of the years 43–46 were minted in Antioch; those of 47, in Seleucia; those of 45 have the head of Tiberius and the date A = the first year of Tiberius; those of the year 47 have the head of Tiberius and the date *Γ* = the third year of Tiberius. The year 43 of the Actian era is autumn A.D. 12–13. The latest coin of Silanus (47 *aer. Act.*) belongs to A.D. 16–17. In agreement with this, Tac. *Ann.* ii 43 records the recall of Silanus by Tiberius in A.D. 17. Cf. also Tac. *Ann.* ii 4; Jos. *Ant.* xviii 2, 4 (52). See PIR² C 64; add IGLS V 2550.

2. Tiberius, 19 Aug. 14 to 16 March 37

Cn. Calpurnius Piso A.D. 17–19

In A.D. 17, perhaps toward the end of the year, Tiberius sent his nephew and adopted son Germanicus to the East. Germanicus was invested with an authority higher than that of the governors of the provinces into which he went 'decreto patrum permissae Germanico provinciae quae mari dividuntur, maiusque imperium, quoquo adisset, quam iis qui sorte aut missu principis obtinerent', Tac. *Ann.* ii 43). At the same time, Silanus was recalled, and in his place, Cn. Calpurnius Piso, consul in 7 B.C. and a man of a domineering and obstinate character 'ingenio violentum et obsequii ignarum', Tac. *Ann.* ii 43), was appointed governor of Syria.

Germanicus went in the first place to Greece, where he entered on his second consulship at the beginning of A.D. 18, then by way of Byzantium to Troy, down the Ionian coast to Rhodes, and thence to Armenia. Having attended to affairs there, he travelled to Syria, where Piso had already hurried ahead of him (Tac. *Ann.* ii 53–7), Because of Piso's domineering nature, hostilities between the two were inevitable. Nevertheless these were at first without consequence (Tac. *Ann.* ii 57–8). In A.D. 19 Germanicus undertook a journey to Egypt, mainly to see the antiquities there (Tac. *Ann.* ii 59–61). Soon after his return to Syria he fell ill and died on 10 October A.D. 19. Common report laid the blame for his death on Piso (Tac. *Ann.* ii 69–73), who had already left Syria on Germanicus's order (Tac. *Ann.* ii 70). See PIR² C 287.

Cn. Sentius Saturninus A.D. 19–21

After the death of Germanicus, his staff conferred supreme command in Syria on Cn. Sentius Saturninus, consul in A.D. 4 (Tac. *Ann.* ii 74). But Piso received news of the death of Germanicus on his return journey, and decided to take possession of Syria by force. He landed in Cilicia and occupied the fortress of Celenderis, Κελένδερις, Strabo, 670, 760; cf. Jos. *Ant.* xvii 5, 1 (86); *B.J.* i 31, 3 (610), but was obliged to surrender to Sentius and agree to return to Rome (Tac. *Ann.* ii 75–81). Arrived there at the beginning of A.D. 20, he was accused by the friends of Germanicus, but evaded condemnation by committing suicide (Tac. *Ann.* ii 8–15).

It is not known how much longer Sentius Saturninus remained in Syria. He is mentioned as *legatus Caesaris* in an inscription found at Nicopolis on the borders of Syria and Cilicia on the Gulf of Issus, and dating from A.D. 21 at the earliest (CIL III 6703=IGLS I 164). According to this, he appears to have been also formally appointed governor of Syria, for the title *leg. Caes.* is probably to be understood in this sense. PIR[1] S 295; RE s.v. 'Sentius' (11).

L. Aelius Lamia, until A.D. 32

From Tac. *Ann.* i 80 and Suet. *Tib.* 41, 63, it is clear that Tiberius repeatedly appointed legates without actually permitting them to proceed to their provinces (Tac.: 'qua haesitatione postremo eo provectus est, ut mandaverit quibusdam provincias, quos egredi urbe non erat passurus'). L. Aelius Lamia, among others, was affected by this measure. Tacitus in *Ann.* vi 27, when recording his death, gives the following account: 'Extremo anni (33) mors Aelii Lamiae funere censorio celebrata, qui administrandae Suriae imagine tandem exsolutus urbi praefuerat. genus illi decorum, vivida senectus; et non permissa provincia dignationem addiderat'. From this it appears that Aelius Lamia was appointed *praefectus urbi* immediately after being relieved of the *imago administrandi Suriae*, i.e., of the apparent, but not real, administration of Syria. But he did not receive the office of *praefectus urbi* until after the death of L. Piso, see Dio lviii 19, 5: τόν τε Πίσωνα τὸν πολίαρχον τελευτήσαντα δημοσίᾳ ταφῇ ἐτίμησεν . . . καὶ Λούκιον ἀντ' αὐτοῦ Λαμίαν ἀνθείλετο, ὃν πρόπαλαι τῇ Συρίᾳ προστάξας κατεῖχεν ἐν τῇ 'Ρώμῃ. Since according to Tac. *Ann.* vi 10 and Dio *loc. cit.*, Piso died in A.D. 32, it follows that Aelius Lamia was appointed *praefectus urbi* in that year, and was therefore governor of Syria, in name at least, until then. (The Piso mentioned by Jos. *Ant.* xviii 6, 5 (169) as *praefectus urbi* in A. D. 36, is a different man, consul in A.D. 27, PIR[2] C 293; see Syme 'Some Pisones in Tacitus', JRS 46 (1956), pp. 17–21=*Ten Studies in Tacitus* (1970), pp. 50–7. It cannot be determined when the governorship of Syria was conferred on him. At all events, he held it for a long time, as is evident from the 'tandem' of Tacitus and the 'προπάλαι' of Dio.[10] See PIR[2] A 200.

10. It is perhaps because no governor was present in Syria at the time (A.D. 29) that none is named in Luke 3: 1.

L. Pomponius Flaccus A.D. 32–35 (?)

Since Lamia was relieved of his post as governor in A.D. 32, Flaccus, consul in A.D. 17, will have succeeded him in the same year. In *Ann.* vi 27, in a passage immediately following the account of Aelius Lamia, Tacitus records the death of Flaccus in the following terms: 'exin (i.e. after the death of Lamia) Flacco Pomponio Syriae pro praetore defuncto recitantur Caesaris litterae, quis incusabat egregium quemque et regendis exercitibus idoneum abnuere id munus, seque ea necessitudine ad preces cogi, per quas consularium aliqui capessere provincias adigerentur, oblitus Arruntium, ne in Hispaniam pergret, decimum iam annum attineri'. As Tacitus records this among the events of A.D. 33, the obvious assumption is that the death of Flaccus took place in that year. It is nevertheless not impossible that Tacitus associated the report concerning Lamia with that of Flaccus on practical grounds, and that the death of Flaccus did not take place until later, perhaps in A.D. 35. In favour of this is (1) the observation by Tacitus that at the time of the death of Flaccus, Arruntius had already been prevented for ten years from setting out for Spain, his province, i.e. Tarraconensis, governed by a consular legate. An earlier governor of this province appears to be mentioned in A.D. 25 (Tac. *Ann.* iv 45. But Syme, JRS 56 (1956), pp. 20–1, has shown that this should refer to a praetorian legate serving there). (2) Agrippa I arrived in Rome in the spring of A.D. 36, ἐνιαυτῷ πρότερον ἢ τελευτῆσαι Τιβέριον ἐπὶ Ῥώμης ἄνεισι, Jos. *Ant.* xviii 5, 3 (126), having visited Flaccus in Syria not long before Jos. *Ant.* xviii 6, 2–3 (147–60). If a whole year is allowed for Agrippa's journey—which was certainly attended by difficulties—from the time of his visit to Flaccus to that of his arrival in Rome, then Flaccus must still have been in Syria in A.D. 35. Finally, in favour of 35 as the year of the death of Flaccus is the fact that his successor Vitellius, who arrived in Syria in A.D. 35, followed him immediately, whereas otherwise there would be an interval.

There are coins of Flaccus of the year 82 of the Caesarian era[11] = A.D. 33–4; see Mionnet V, p. 167; *BMC Syria*, p. 170, no. 161; Dieudonné, RN, Ser. 4, 30 (1927), p. 36, no. 4. See PIR[1] P 538

L. Vitellius A.D. 35–39?

In A.D. 35 Tiberius sent L. Vitellius, consul in A.D. 34 and father of the subsequent emperor of that name, as legate to Syria (Tac. *Ann.* vi

11. The Caesarian era at Antioch ran from 1.10.49 B.C.; see G. Downey, *History of Antioch*, pp. 157–8; cf. Ginzel, *Chronologie* III, pp. 43–5.

32).[12] Tacitus testifies of him that, by contrast with his later life, his administration of the province was blameless 'eo de homine haud sum ignarus sinistram in urbe famam, pleraque foeda memorari; ceterum in regendis provinciis prisca virtute egit'. Recalled by Caligula, probably in A.D. 39, he was succeeded by Petronius (Jos. *Ant.* xviii 8, 2 (261)).[13] Cf. also generally, Suet. *Vit.* 2; Dio lix 27; Pliny, *N.H.* xv 21/83; PIR¹ V 500; RE s.v. 'Vitellius' (7c) (Supp. IX, cols. 1733 f.).

3. Caligula, 16 March A.D. 37 to 24 Jan. A.D. 41

P. Petronius A.D. 39?–41/2

Petronius was sent to Syria by Caligula in A.D. 39 (see the foregoing paragraph). From a coin (Mionnet V, pp. 167, 173; Dieudonné, RN, Ser. 4, 30 (1927), p. 38) it is evident that he was still governor in the year 90 of the Caesarian era = A.D. 41–42, for about a year, therefore, during the reign of Claudius. See Jos. *Ant.* xviii 8, 2–9 (261–309); xix 6, 3 (299–311); Philo, *Leg.* 31–34/576–84; PIR¹ P 198; RE s.v. 'Petronius' (24).

4. Claudius, 24 Jan. A.D. 41 to 13 Oct. A.D. 54

C. Vibius Marsus A.D. 41/2–44/5

As successor of Petronius, Claudius sent C. Vibius Marsus, *consul suffectus* in A.D. 17, to Syria, Jos. *Ant.* xix 6, 4 (316). He had occasion several times to safeguard Roman interests against king Agrippa, *Ant.* xix 7, 2 (326–7); 8, 1 (338–42). His recall took place soon after Agrippa's death in A.D. 44, i.e., at the end of A.D. 44, or the beginning of A.D. 45,

12. From the words of Tacitus, 'cunctis quae apud orientem parabantur L. Vitellium praefecit', it should perhaps be assumed that Vitellius obtained a wider sphere of activity than the province of Syria. But Tacitus himself, in *Ann.* vi 41, calls him *praeses Syriae*; so does Jos. *Ant.* xviii 4, 2 (88) ὑπατικὸν . . ἄνδρα Συρίας τὴν ἡγεμονίαν ἔχοντα; cf. also Suet. *Vit.* 2; Dio lix 27, 2; and Pliny, *N.H.* xv 21/83. So he was in any case governor of Syria, but may have possessed additional powers. But see D. Magie, *Roman Rule in Asia Minor* ii (1950), p. 1364, n. 39.

13. From Josephus it seems as if the recall of Vitellius and the arrival of Petronius did not take place until autumn A.D. 40. After his arrival, Petronius took up winter quarters in Ptolemais, *Ant.* xviii 8, 2 (262). The negotiations immediately started with the Jews took place during the sowing season, *Ant.* xviii 8, 3 (272); 8, 6 (284), i.e. in November or December, see IDB I, p. 58. Petronius reported on them to Caligula, who received and answered the letter shortly before his death on 24 January A.D. 41, *Ant.* xviii 8, 8–9 (298–309). Josephus therefore seems to place the arrival of Petronius in the autmn of A.D. 40. On the other hand, according to the contemporary testimony of Philo, *Legatio ad Gaium* (see Smallwood, Latomus 16 (1957), pp. 3–17, and her *Philonis Alexandrini legatio ad Gaium* (1961; ²1970), esp. pp. 31 f., 260 f., and cf. p. 210), Petronius was already in Palestine in the spring of A.D. 40.

Ant. xx I, I (I). Cf. Tac. *Ann.* xi 10. See PIR[1] V 388; RE s.v. 'Vibius' (39).

C. Cassius Longinus A.D. 44/5–*c.* 50

Marsus was succeeded by C. Cassius Longinus, Jos. *Ant.* xx I, I (I), *consul suffectus* in A.D. 30, a famous jurist ('ceteros praeminebat peritia legum', Tac. *Ann.* xii 12), and founder of a school of jurists ('Cassianae scholae princeps et parens', Pliny, *Ep.* vii 24, 8). Coins of his from the years 94 and 96 of the Caesarian era = A.D. 45/46 and 47/48 are given in Eckhel, *Doctr. Num.* III p. 280; Mionnet V, pp. 167, 175; (only that of 96 is above suspicion). Tacitus mentions him as still in office as governor of Syria in A.D. 49 (*Ann.* xii 11–12). He seems to have been recalled by Claudius not long after that. Cf. Tac. *Ann.* xvi 7 and 9; Suet. *Nero* 37. *Digest.* I 2, 2, 51. See PIR[2] C 501. Legal fragments in O. Lenel, *Palingenesia juris civilis* I, pp. 109–26 and F. P. Bremer, *Jurisprudentiae Antehadrianae quae supersunt* II 2 (1901), pp. 9–79.

C. Ummidius Durmius Quadratus A.D. 50–60

Ummidius Quadratus is mentioned by Tacitus (*Ann.* xii 45) as governor of Syria in A.D. 51. He may well have gone there in A.D. 50. Coins of his from the years 104–108 of the Caesarian era = 55/56–59/60 are given in Eckhel, *Doctr. Num.* III, p. 280; Mionnet V, p. 159. Only those of the years 104, 105 and 105 are reliable. W. M. Leake, *Numismata Hellenica, Asiatic Greece*, p. 16; *BMC Syria*, pp. 160, 173; A. Dieudonné, RN, Ser. 4, 30 (1927), p. 40. He died as governor of Syria in A.D. 60 (Tac. *Ann.* xiv 26). His career (he had been quaestor as early as A.D. 14) is given in CIL X 5182 = ILS 972. Cf. Tac. *Ann.* xii 54; xiii 8–9; Jos. *Ant.* xx 6, 2 (125–33). See PIR[1] U 800; RE s.v. 'Ummidius' (4) (Supp. IX, cols. 1827 f.); R. Syme, Historia 17 (1968), pp. 72–5.

5. Nero 13 Oct. A.D. 54 to 9 June A.D. 68

Cn. Domitius Corbulo A.D. 60–63

After the death of Ummidius Quadratus in A.D. 60, Domitius Corbulo went to Syria as governor (Tac. *Ann.* xiv 26). On his activities there see Tac. *Ann.* xv 1–17; Dio lxii 10 ff. One of his decrees is mentioned in the customs tariff of Palmyra (IGR III 1056 = OGIS 629, l.168). He held the governorship of the province until A.D. 63, in which year a higher *imperium* was given him, while another governor was sent to Syria, Tac. *Ann.* xv 25, 'Suriae executio ‹C.› Ce‹s›tio, copiae militares Corbuloni permissae; et quinta decuma legio ducente Mario Celso e Pannonia adiecta est. scribitur tetrarchis ac regibus praefectisque et procuratoribus et qui praetorum finitimas provincias regebant, iussis

Corbulonis obsequi, in tantum ferme modum aucta potestate, quem populus Romanus Cn. Pompeio bellum piraticum gesturo dederat'. The name of the person to whom the province of Syria was awarded cannot be established with certainty. It is most likely to have been Cestius, since he appears as governor of Syria in A.D. 65. On the death of Corbulo (in A.D. 67) see Dio lxiii 17, 2–5. On an inscription of A.D. 64 (CIL III 6741–2 = ILS 232) found in Armenia, he is named *leg. Aug. pr. pr.* His daughter Domitia was Domitian's wife (Dio lxvi 3, 4; CIL XIV 2795 = ILS 272). See PIR² D 142; M. Hammond, Harv. Stud. Class. Phil. 45 (1934), pp. 81–104; R. Syme, *Tacitus* (1958), esp. pp. 391–2, 395–6, 493–5 and JRS 60 (1970), pp. 27–39.

C. Cestius Gallus A.D. ?63–66

If the above surmise is correct, Cestius Gallus arrived in Syria as early as A.D. 63. He was in any case there in A.D. 65, for he went to Jerusalem at the Passover of A.D. 66 (in the twelfth year of Nero = Oct. A.D. 65–66; Jos. *Ant.* xx 11, 1 (257); *B.J.* ii 14, 4 (284) after a prolonged stay in Syria, *B.J.* ii 14, 3 (280). For coins of his from the years 114 and 115 of the Caesarian era = A.D. 65/66 and A.D. 66/67, see Eckhel, *Doctr. Num.* III 281 f.; Mionnet V, p. 169; suppl. VIII, p. 131; Leake, *Numismata Hellenica, Asiatic Greece*, p. 16; *BMC Syria*, p. 175. Dieudonné, RN, Ser. 4, 30 (1927), p. 45. The Jewish war broke out in May A.D. 66, in the month Artemisios, *B.J.* ii 14, 4 (284), when he was governor of Syria, but he lived to see only its beginning, as he died in the winter of A.D. 66/67 'by accident or of ennui' ('fato aut taedio occidit', Tacitus, *Hist.* v 10).[14] See PIR² C 691.

C. Licinius Mucianus A.D. 67–69

When Vespasian was appointed as *legatus* to take command in the Jewish war—probably also being considered as the governor of Judaea[15]—Syria was assigned to C. Licinius Mucianus. Josephus mentions him in A.D. 67 during the siege of Gamala, *B.J.* iv 1, 5 (32), and in A.D. 69 on Vespasian's election as emperor, *B.J.* iv 10, 5–6 (605–21). Cf. also Tac. *Hist.* i 10; Jos. *Ant.* xii 3, 1 (120). For coins of his from the reign of Galba (9 June 68 to 15 Jan. 69) and of Otho (15 Jan. to 16 Apr. 69)[16] see Eckhel III, p. 282, Mionnet V, p. 169,

14. Cestius Gallus was still in Syria in the winter of A.D. 66/67, Jos. *Vita* 8/30–31, 43/214, 65/347, 67/373, 71/394. But before the start of spring, the conduct of the war was transferred to Vespasian, *B.J.* iii 4, 2 (64–9).

15. The sources describe Vespasian's appointment in varying terms: Suet. *Div. Vesp.* 4, 'ad hunc motum comprimendum cum exercitu ampliore et non instrenuo duce . . . opus esset . . . ipse potissium delectus est'; Jos. *B.J.* iii 1, 3 (7) πέμπει τὸν ἄνδρα ληψόμενον τὴν ἡγεμονίαν τῶν ἐπὶ Συρίας στρατευμάτων. Cf. PIR² F 398.

16. Both coins bear the year 117 of the Caesarian era, and for that very reason afford a reliable clue to the reckoning of the era.

suppl. VIII, 131, *BMC Syria*, p. 176. In the autumn of A.D. 69 he led an army from Syria to Rome to assist in the fighting against Vitellius, Jos. *B.J.* iv 11, 1 (632); Tac. Hist. ii 82 f.; Suet. *Div. Vesp.* 6; Dio lxv 9. He did not, however, arrive there until after the death of Vitellius, which occurred on 20 December A.D. 69, but then wielded supreme power for some time (Jos. *B.J.* iv 11, 4 (654); Tac. *Hist.* iv 11, 39, 49, 80; Dio lxv 22; lxvi 2). See PIR² L 216; RE s.v. 'Licinius' (116a).

Later governors of Syria do not concern us since Palestine now became a full province governed by a senatorial *legatus pro praetore*. For the governors of Palestine from the time of Vespasian to that of Hadrian see § 21.

§ 13 HYRCANUS II 63–40 B.C.; THE RISE OF ANTIPATER AND HIS SONS PHASAEL AND HEROD

Sources

Jos. *Ant.* xiv 5–13 (80–369); *B.J.* i 8–13 (159–273).

Literature

Graetz, H., *Geschichte der Juden* III ([5]1905–6), pp. 162–88.
Wellhausen, J., *Israelitische und jüdische Geschichte* ([9]1958), pp. 294–304.
Ginsburg, M. S., *Rome et la Judée* (1929), pp. 78–106.
Momigliano, A. D., *Ricerche sull' organizzazione della Giudea sotto il dominio romano. Ann. della r. Scuola Normale Superiore di Pisa*, ser. i, vol. III (1934–XII), pp. 183–221, repr. Amsterdam (1967).
Abel, F.-M., *Histoire de la Palestine* I (1952), pp. 287–334.
Jones, A. H. M., *The Herods of Judaea* (1938, [2]1967), pp. 22–39.
Schalit, A., *König Herodes: der Mann und sein Werk* (1969), pp. 1–74.

Because of the scantiness of the sources it is difficult to give an accurate account of the position of Palestine at this time in relation to Rome. This much is certain, however: it was tributary, Jos. *Ant.* xiv 4, 4 (74); *B.J.* i 7, 6 (154), and under the control of the Roman governor of Syria. The question is whether or not it was directly incorporated in the province of Syria. A later observation made by Josephus constitutes an argument for the latter alternative, namely that by the enactment of Gabinius, who divided Palestine into five districts, the land was free from 'monarchical government', *B.J.* i 8, 5 (170). Hyrcanus will consequently have stood at the head of the government of the country, and been subject only to the control of the Roman governor.[1]

After Pompey's departure, Palestine at first enjoyed a few years of peace. Scaurus, like his two successors Marcius Philippus and Lentulus Marcellinus, admittedly still had trouble with the Nabataeans,[2] but this had no influence on the fortunes of Palestine. In 57 B.C., however, Aristobulus's son, Alexander, who had escaped from captivity when on

1. So also E. Kuhn, *Die städtische und bürgerl. Verfassung des röm. Reichs* (1865) II, p. 163; cf. Schalit, *op. cit.*, pp. 14–15. For some hypotheses on the constitutional position, cf. E. Bammel, 'Die Neuordnung des Pompeius und das römisch-jüdische Bündnis', ZDPV 75 (1959), pp. 76–82.

2. Jos. *Ant.* xiv 5, 1 (80 f.); *B.J.* i 8, 1 (159); Appian, *Syr.* 51/255–6.

the way to Rome (see p. 240 above), tried to seize power in Palestine. He succeeded in collecting an army of 10,000 heavy infantry and 1,500 horsemen, and held in his power the fortresses of Alexandrium, Hyrcania and Machaerus.[3] Gabinius, who had just arrived in Syria as proconsul, first sent against him his second in command, M. Antonius, the future triumvir, and followed soon after with the main army. Alexander was defeated in an encounter near Jerusalem and withdrew to the fortress of Alexandrium. There he was besieged by Gabinius and was obliged to surrender, but seems to have obtained his freedom in exchange for the fortresses in his possession.[4] At the same time, Gabinius effected an important change in Palestine's political circumstances: he left to Hyrcanus only the care and custody of the Temple, but took his political status from him by dividing the country into five districts (σύνοδοι, συνέδρια) with Jerusalem, Amathus, Jericho, Sepphoris, and probably Adora in Idumaea (or possibly Gazara) as their capitals.[5] The language in which Josephus describes these five σύνοδοι or συνέδρια

3. On Alexandrium see p. 238. Hyrcania is probably Kh. Mird in the Judaean desert, see Avi-Yonah, *Holy Land*, p. 101; Abel, *Géog. Pal.* II, p. 350; Schalit, *op. cit.*, p. 341; cf. G. R. H. Wright, 'The Archaeological Remains at El Mird in the Wilderness of Judaea', Biblica 42 (1961), pp. 1–21. Machaerus, still called el Mukawer in Arabic, lay east of the Dead Sea; for details see p. 511, n. 135.

4. Jos. *Ant.* xiv 5, 2–4 (82–9); *B.J.* i 8, 2–5 (160–8).

5. Jos. *Ant.* xiv 5, 4 (90–1); *B.J.* i 8, 5 (169–70). On Amathus in the country east of the Jordan see p. 221 above; on Sepphoris in Galilee see vol. II, §23 i. The remaining three fortresses were in Judaea proper. On Gazara see p. 191 above. In *Ant.* xiv 5, 4 (91) Josephus has Γαδάροις or Γαδώροις, in *B.J.* i 8, 5 (170) Γαδάροις. But by this he cannot mean the Greek city of Gadara (or Gadora) in Peraea, the population of which was mainly Gentile and which had been separated from Jewish territory by Pompey, nor a Jewish Gadara in the south of Peraea as once argued by A. Schlatter, *Zur Topographie und Geschichte Palästinas* (1893), pp. 44–51, the existence of which is not proved by Jos. *B.J.* iv 7, 3 (413). He may however mean the Gazara Judaized by Simon Maccabaeus, for which the form Gadara also occurs elsewhere; thus Jos. *Ant.* xii 7, 4 (308) in some manuscripts (=1 Mac. 4:15). Also Strabo xvi 2, 29 (759) Γαδαρὶς, ἣν καὶ αὐτὴν ἐξιδιάσαντο οἱ Ἰουδαῖοι, probably indicates the territory of Gazara, which he admittedly mistakes for Gadara in Perea; (it was from here that the famous men came whom he mentions). In a *Notitia episcopatuum* a Ῥεγεὼν Γαδάρων appears in the neighbourhood of Azotus distinct from Γάδειρα between Pella and Capitolias (*Hieroclis Synecdemus et notitiae graecae episcopat.* ed. Parthey (1866), p. 144). At a synod in Jerusalem in A.D. 536, a bishop Ἀράξιος Γαδάρων and a bishop Θεόδωρος Γαδάρων were both present. There were therefore two places called Gadara in Palestine. A better solution has been proposed, however, by B. Kanael, 'The Partition of Judea by Gabinius', IEJ 7 (1957), pp. 98–106, and accepted by Avi-Yonah, *Holy Land*, p. 84, and Schalit, *op. cit.*, p. 32. He proposes to read Ἀδώροις, which will then refer to Adora in Idumaea, which will itself have been the fifth district. Cf. some speculations by E. Bammel, 'The Organisation of Palestine by Gabinius', JJS 12 (1961), pp. 159–62; and see also E. M. Smallwood, 'Gabinius' Organisation of Palestine', JJS 18 (1967), pp. 89–92.

is not entirely consistent,[6] but the general sense, namely that these districts were placed under separate aristocratic councils, is quite clear.[7] At all events, Gabinius's enactment signified the removal of that remnant of political power which Hyrcanus had still possessed. Pompey had already deprived him of the title of king; now he was stripped of all political authority and restricted to his priestly functions. The country was divided into five districts and 'liberated' from his rule. This arrangement did not in fact last for long. It was cancelled by the decrees of Caesar.

Soon after this, in 56 B.C., the country was again set in commotion by Aristobulus and his son Antigonus, both of whom had likewise escaped from Roman imprisonment. Aristobulus had learnt so little from the abortive undertaking of his son Alexander that he now attempted the very same venture in which his son had failed. Moreover, he was just as unfortunate. A Roman division easily drove him and his small army back over the Jordan. He tried to defend himself in Machaerus, but after a siege of only two days was obliged to surrender and was sent again as a prisoner to Rome; his children, however, were set free by the senate.[8] It was at that time that Gabinius, contrary to the will of the senate, undertook an expedition to Egypt with the intention of reinstating Ptolemy Auletes as king (see pp. 245–6 above). On his return in 55 B.C. he again had to deal with an insurrection in Judaea. Alexander had made a fresh attempt to seize power and had won over to his side at least a part of the nation. But on this occasion also his activities were soon brought to an end.[9]

In 54 B.C. M. Licinius Crassus came to Syria as proconsul in place of Gabinius. Whereas Gabinius had harshly oppressed the country with his extortions, Crassus now indulged in open robbery. Pompey, on capturing the Temple, had left its rich treasures untouched. Crassus now took possession of them all—2000 talents in gold alone, besides 8000 talents worth of precious objects.[10] But Palestine was soon delivered from his greed, for in 53 B.C. he met his death in the expedition against the Parthians.

6. In *Ant.* xiv 5, 4 (91) Josephus writes *πέντε δὲ συνέδρια καταστήσας εἰς ἴσας μοίρας διένειμε τὸ ἔθνος, καὶ ἐπολιτεύοντο οἱ μὲν ἐν Ἱεροσολύμοις οἱ δὲ ἐν Γαδάροις οἱ δὲ ἐν Ἀμαθοῦντι, τέταρτοι δ' ἦσαν ἐν Ἱεριχοῦντι, καὶ τὸ πέμπτον ἐν Σαπφώροις τῆς Γαλιλαίας. καὶ οἱ μὲν ἀπηλλαγμένοι δυναστείας ἐν ἀριστοκρατίᾳ διῆγον.* In *B.J.* i 8, 5 (169–70) he writes: *καθίστατο τὴν ἄλλην πολιτείαν* [i.e. apart from the provision for the Temple] *ἐπὶ προστασίᾳ τῶν ἀρίστων. διεῖλεν δὲ πᾶν τὸ ἔθνος εἰς πέντε συνόδους, τὸ μὲν Ἱεροσολύμοις προστάξας, τὸ δὲ Γαδάροις, οἱ δὲ ἵνα συντελῶσιν εἰς Ἀμαθοῦντα, τὸ δὲ τέταρτον εἰς Ἱεριχοῦντα κεκλήρωτο, καὶ τῷ πέμπτῳ Σέπφωρις ἀπεδείχθη πόλις τῆς Γαλιλαίας. ἀσμένως δὲ τῆς ἐξ ἑνὸς ἐπικρατείας ἐλευθερωθέντες τὸ λοιπὸν ἀριστοκρατίᾳ διῳκοῦντο.*

7. So Rice Holmes, *The Roman Republic* II (1923), pp. 311–12.

8. Jos. *Ant.* xiv 6, 1 (97); *B.J.* i 8, 6 (174); Dio xxxix 56, 6. Plut. *Ant.* 3.

9. Jos. *Ant.* xiv 6, 2–3 (98–102); *B.J.* i 8, 7 (175–8).

10. Jos. *Ant.* xiv 7, 1 (105–9); *B.J.* i 8, 8 (179).

During the years 53–51 B.C., C. Cassius Longinus, the quaestor of Crassus, held supreme power in Syria. He had not only to repulse the Parthians, but also to suppress the insurrectionary elements still present in Palestine. Aristobulus, it is true, was a prisoner in Rome, and his sons had for the time being no inclination to try their luck again. But a certain Pitholaus now assumed their role and rallied the disgruntled elements. He had as little success in attaining his end, for the final result of his enterprise was that he himself was executed and 30,000 of his supporters were sold into slavery.[11]

In 49 B.C. the fateful period of the civil wars began, disastrous for Italy and the provinces alike, but particularly disastrous for the provinces in that they had to provide the enormous sums required by the belligerent parties. During these twenty years, from Caesar's crossing of the Rubicon to the death of Antonius (49–30 B.C.), the whole course of Roman history was reflected in the history of Syria, and thus in that of Palestine also. Every change in the one represented a change in the other, and during this short period Syria and Palestine acquired new masters no less than four times.

When at the beginning of 49 B.C. Pompey and the party of the senate fled from Italy, and Caesar seized Rome, the latter wished among other things to make use of the imprisoned Aristobulus. He released him, and gave him two legions with which to fight against the party of Pompey in Syria. But the supporters of Pompey who remained in Rome frustrated the scheme by poisoning Aristobulus. At the same time, one of Aristobulus's sons, Alexander, also fell victim to the Roman civil war. He, too, wished to appear as a supporter of Caesar, and was beheaded at Antioch, on the express command of Pompey, by Q. Metellus Scipio, Pompey's father-in-law, who was then proconsul of Syria (see p. 247 above).[12]

After the battle of Pharsalus (9 Aug. 48 B.C.) and the death of Pompey (28 Sept. 48 B.C.), Hyrcanus and Antipater at once joined Caesar's party.[13] They understood that their salvation now depended on his

11. Jos. *Ant.* xiv 7, 3 (119–22); *B.J.* i 8, 9 (180).

12. Jos. *Ant.* xiv 7, 4 (123–5); *B.J.* i 9, 1–2 (183–6). Cf. Dio xli 18, 1.

13. Antipater is described as *ἐπιμελητής* of Judaea even before Caesar's intervention in the affairs of Palestine, not only by Josephus, *Ant.* xiv 8, 1 (127) *ὁ τῶν Ἰουδαίων ἐπιμελητής*, but also by Strabo, who in his turn is using Hypsicrates, *Jos. Ant.* xiv 8, 3 (139) *τὸν τῆς Ἰουδαίας ἐπιμελητήν*; cf. FGrH 190 F 1. It is possible that he obtained this position through Gabinius, who on account of Antipater's numerous services to the Roman cause 'settled affairs at Jerusalem in accordance with the wishes of Antipater' (*Ant.* xiv 6, 4 (103) *καταστησάμενος δὲ Γαβίνιος τὰ κατὰ τὴν Ἱεροσολυμιτῶν πόλιν ὡς ἦν Ἀντιπάτρῳ θέλοντι*, and *B. J.* i 8, 7 (178) *Γαβίνιος ἐλθὼν εἰς Ἱεροσόλυμα πρὸς τὸ Ἀντιπάτρου βούλημα κατεστήσατο τὴν πολιτείαν*). Since this arrangement must have been in accordance with the rest of Gabinius's dispositions, it is possible that the word, which is used in a variety of senses by Josephus, refers to Antipater's role in the collection of taxes. In any case, Anti-

favour and hastened to prove their eagerness to serve him. After his landing in Egypt (Oct. 48 B.C.), Caesar became involved in a war with King Ptolemy. To reinforce him, Mithridates of Pergamum took an auxiliary force to Egypt in the spring of 47 B.C.[14] When he met with difficulties near Pelusium, Antipater came to his aid with 3000 Jewish troops (probably assembled for the purpose) on the order of Hyrcanus, and also induced the neighbouring dynasts to furnish auxiliaries. With these troops, Antipater rendered Mithridates great services, not only in the capture of Pelusium but also during the whole Egyptian campaign. Hyrcanus acquired no little credit by inducing the Egyptian Jews to fight on Caesar's side.[15]

Thus, when Caesar came to Syria in the summer of 47 B.C. after the conclusion of the Alexandrian war, and rewarded with proofs of his favour those dynasts who paid him homage,[16] Hyrcanus and Antipater were also most generously remembered. Antigonus, the only remaining son of Aristobulus, also appeared before Caesar to complain of the violent self-assertiveness of Antipater and Hyrcanus and urge his own previous and superior claims.[17] But Caesar prized the reliability and usefulness of Hyrcanus and Antipater more highly than he valued Antigonus, took no notice of the latter's claims, and bestowed his favour exclusively on the other two. Hyrcanus seems to have been confirmed as High Priest even prior to the intervention of Antigonus, and Roman citizenship and exemption from taxation were conferred on Antipater.[18] Hyrcanus, it appears, was now nominated *ἐθνάρχης* of the Jews, i.e. restored to the political status from which Gabinius had removed him. But Antipater was nominated procurator (*ἐπίτροπος*) of

---

pater cannot have been a political officer in the service of Hyrcanus because the latter no longer had any political standing after the time of Gabinius's enactment. So if he acts *ἐξ ἐντολῆς Ὑρκανοῦ*, *Ant.* xiv 8, 1 (127), this is perhaps to be explained by the spiritual authority which Hyrcanus had as High Priest (*Ant.* xiv 5, 1 (80) *κατ' ἐντολὴν Ὑρκανοῦ*, belongs to the time when Hyrcanus still had political status); cf. however Schalit, *op. cit.*, Anhang V. On Antipater's services to the Roman cause in the period 63–48 B.C. see *Ant.* xiv 5, 1–2 (80–5); 6, 2–3 (98–102); 7, 3 (119–22); *B.J.* i 8, 1 (159), 3 (162 f.), 7 (175–8), 9 (180–2). On Antipater see Wilcken in RE I, cols. 2509 ff.; Schalit, *op. cit.*, p. 33 f.

14. *Bell. Alex.* 26.

15. *Ant.* xiv 8, 1–3 (127–39); *B.J.* i 9, 3–5 (187–94). In the decree of Caesar *Ant.* xiv 10, 2 (193) the number of the Jewish auxiliary troops is given as only 1500.

16. *Bell. Alex.* 65 'reges, tyrannos, dynastas provinciae finitimos[que], qui omnes ad eum concurrerant, receptos in fidem condicionibus inpositis provinciae tuendae ac defendendae, dimittit et sibi et populo Romano amicissimos'. Cf. M. Gelzer, *Caesar, Politician and Statesman* (1968), pp. 258–9.

17. *Ant.* xiv 8, 4 (140–2); *B.J.* i 10, 1–2 (195–8).

18. *Ant.* xiv 8, 3 (137) *Ὑρκανῷ μὲν τὴν ἀρχιερωσύνην βεβαιώσας, Ἀντιπάτρῳ δὲ πολιτείαν ἐν Ῥώμῃ δοὺς καὶ ἀτέλειαν πανταχοῦ.* So also *B.J.* i 9, 5 (194).

Judaea and thus confirmed in the position he had held hitherto. At the same time permission was granted to rebuild the walls of Jerusalem.[19]

More detailed information concerning Caesar's decrees appears in the documents given by Josephus in *Ant.* xiv 10, 2–10 (190–222), but they have unfortunately been transmitted in so poor and fragmentary a condition that on many questions no sure conclusions can be reached.[20] It is certain that Caesar's letter to the Sidonians, *Ant.* xiv 10, 2 (190–5), dates from 47 B.C. and contains the actual decree of Caesar nominating Hyrcanus.[21] In this Hyrcanus is established as hereditary ἐθνάρχης and ἀρχιερεύς of the Jews and confirmed in all the rights pertaining to him as High Priest according to Jewish law; and jurisdiction in Jewish affairs is conceded to the Jews. In addition, Hyrcanus was appointed, for himself and his children, συμμάχος of the Romans, and it was decreed that Roman troops should not winter in his country or raise

19. *Ant.* xiv 8, 5 (143–4) Ὑρκανὸν μὲν ἀποδείκνυσιν ἀρχιερέα . . . [Ἀντίπατρον] ἐπίτροπον ἀποδείκνυσιν τῆς Ἰουδαίας. ἐπιτρέπει δὲ καὶ Ὑρκανῷ τὰ τῆς πατρίδος ἀναστῆσαι τείχη. Similarly *B.J.* i 10, 3 (199). These decrees seem to be distinct from those mentioned in the foregoing note, the first having been issued before the intervention of Antigonus, and the present decrees after it (thus Mendelssohn, Acta soc. philol. Lips. 5 (1875), pp. 190 ff.; Judeich, *Cäsar im Orient* (1885), pp. 123 f.; see especially *B.J.* i 10, 1 (195) Ἀντίγονος . . . γίνεται παραδόξως Ἀντιπάτρῳ μείζονος προκοπῆς αἴτιος). As is evident from the decrees of Caesar, which are discussed below, Hyrcanus was in any case nominated by Caesar as High Priest with political powers, that is ἀρχιερεύς and ἐθνάρχης. The *senatus consultum* given by Josephus in *Ant.* xiv 8, 5 (145–8) belongs to a much earlier period. See pp. 195–7 above.

20. Cf. on these especially: Mendelssohn *op. cit.*, pp. 191–246 (reviewed in ThLZ 1876 no. 15, cols. 394 f.) and Niese, Hermes 11 (1876), pp. 483–8 (against this Mendelssohn in Rhein. Museum, n.s. 32 (1877), pp. 249–58); Mommsen, *Römische Geschichte* V, pp. 501 f.; Judeich, *Cäsar im Orient* (1885), pp. 119–41, only on the events and documents of 47 B.C., in which year Judeich places *Ant.* xiv 8, 5 (145–8); Graetz, *Gesch. der Juden* III ([5]1905–6), pp. 662–73, Viereck, *Sermo graecus quo senatus populusque Romanus . . . usi sunt* (1888), pp. 96–103; Büchler, 'Die priesterlichen Zehnten und die römischen Steuern in den Erlassen Caesars', *Festschr, zum* 80. *Geburtstage M. Steinschneiders* (1896), pp. 91–109; E. Täubler, *Imperium Romanum* (1913), pp. 157 ff., 239 ff.; J. Juster, *Les Juifs dans l'Empire romain* I (1914), pp. 129–58; T. Rice Holmes, *The Roman Republic* III (1923), pp. 507–9; E. Meyer, *Ursprung und Anfänge des Christentums* II (1925), pp. 246–78; Momigliano, *Ricerche*, pp. 193–201. See also R. Marcus, *Josephus* (Loeb) VIII, App. J (for bibliography).

21. In this same letter Caesar designates himself αὐτοκράτωρ καὶ ἀρχιερεὺς, δικτάτωρ τὸ δεύτερον (*imperator et pontifex maximus, dictator* II). Caesar's second dictatorship ran, according to Mommsen (in CIL i 2, pp. 40–2), from Oct. 48 B.C. to the end of 46 B.C., according to Ganter (in Zeitschr. für Numismatik 19 (1895), pp. 190–5), from Oct. 48 B.C. to April 46 B.C.; but more probably from Oct. 48 B.C. for one year (Broughton, MRR II, pp. 272, 285). Since consul is not among his titles, whereas Caesar was consul in 48, 46, 45 and 44 B.C., the letter must belong to 47 B.C.

levies.[22] Whether any other documents belong to the same year is unsure. It is by contrast certain that not long before Caesar's death, perhaps towards the end of 45 B.C., Hyrcanus sent an embassy to Rome which procured a *senatus consultum* with new privileges for the Jews. The beginning of this *senatus consultum*, under Caesar's fourth dictatorship and fifth consulship, and so of 44 B.C., is given in *Ant.* xiv 10, 7 (211–12). Its date is probably preserved in *Ant.* xiv 10, 10 (222): πρὸ πέντε εἰδῶν Φεβρουαρίων = 9 February. As it was not registered forthwith in the aerarium, a new *senatus consultum* was passed after Caesar's death, under the consulship of Antonius and Dolabella, πρὸ τρίων εἰδῶν Ἀπριλλίων, therefore on 11 April 44 B.C., directing the deposition of the earlier order in the aerarium, *Ant.* xiv 10, 9–10 (217–22). As the new decree is purely formal in character, nothing is to be learnt from it regarding the gist of the rights granted to the Jews. Also, the portion of the earlier decree given in *Ant.* xiv 10, 7 (211–12) comprises only the formal introduction. It is, however, extremely probable that other portions of it are preserved among the fragments in Jos. *Ant.* xiv 10, 3–6 (196–210). Yet it is precisely here that the difficulties of the investigation begin. The question is, which of these fragments belong to the *senatus consultum* of 44 B.C., and which derive from earlier years (47 B.C. or so)? Due to the corruption of the text, no sure result can ever be secured.[23] It is possible that the bulk of

22. *Ant.* xiv 10, 2 (194–5) διὰ ταύτας τὰς αἰτίας Ὑρκανὸν Ἀλεξάνδρου καὶ τὰ τέκνα αὐτοῦ ἐθνάρχας Ἰουδαίων εἶναι, ἀρχιερωσύνην τε Ἰουδαίων διὰ παντὸς ἔχειν κατὰ τὰ πάτρια ἔθη, εἶναί τε αὐτὸν καὶ τοὺς παῖδας αὐτοῦ συμμάχους ἡμῖν, ἔτι τε καὶ ἐν τοῖς κατ' ἄνδρα φίλοις ἀριθμεῖσθαι· ὅσα τε κατὰ τοὺς ἰδίους αὐτῶν νόμους ἐστὶν ἀρχιερατικὰ ἢ φιλάνθρωπα, ταῦτα κελεύω κατέχειν αὐτὸν καὶ τὰ τέκνα αὐτοῦ· ἂν δὲ μεταξὺ γένηταί τις ζήτησις περὶ τῆς Ἰουδαίων ἀγωγῆς, ἀρέσκει μοι κρίσιν γίνεσθαι [παρ' αὐτοῖς]. παραχειμασίαν δὲ ἢ χρήματα πράσσεσθαι οὐ δοκιμάζω. On the interpretation cf. Mendelssohn, *op. cit.*, pp. 195–7; Mommsen, *Römische Geschichte* V pp. 501 f. Cf. Schalit, *op. cit.*, pp. 148 f.

23. The document in *Ant.* xiv 10, 3–4 (196–8) contains scarcely anything different in content from Caesar's decree of 47 B.C., *Ant.* xiv 10, 2 (190–5). Since, on the face of it, it dates from a year in which Caesar was consul (the number of the consulship is lacking), and so from either 46, 45 or 44 B.C., Mendelssohn (*op. cit.*, pp. 205–11) considers it—and the decree in (199) for which see below—as a fragment of a *senatus consultum* of 46 B.C. which simply confirmed the ordinances of Caesar of 47 B.C. (on the confirmation by the senate of agreements made by generals see especially Mommsen, *Röm. Staatsrecht* III 2 (1888), pp. 1166–8); Momigliano, *op. cit.*, p. 197 regards the heading in (196) as confused and not documentary, and (197–8) as part of an S.C. of 47 B.C. The fragments given in xiv 10, 5–6 (200–10) contain detailed decisions regarding taxation, and seem to belong together. According to the opening words of xiv 10, 5 (200) they date from 44 B.C. (Caesar's fifth consulship). But against this is the fact that in them permission is granted to build the walls of Jerusalem, xiv 10, 5 (200), a permission already given in 47 B.C., *Ant.* xiv 8, 5 (144); *B.J.* i 10, 3 (199); and in fact the building of the walls had already been completed by that time, *Ant.* xiv 9, 1 (156); *B.J.* i 10, 4 (201); but (200–1) may contain a document of 44 B.C. which merely confirms or refers back to the earlier permission. Further, it is to 47 B.C. that we are perhaps led by the heading of the second document, *Ant.* xiv

the substantial fragment preserved in *Ant.* xiv 10, 6 (202–10) belongs to 44 B.C. Among the concessions granted in it to the Jews, the most important are that Joppa, 'which the Jews had possessed from ancient times since they made a treaty of friendship with the Romans', was ceded to them; that the villages in the Great Plain which they had previously possessed, were transferred to them; and finally, that still other places which 'had belonged to the kings of Syria and Phoenicia', were made over to them.[24] Presumably, these were simply territories

---

10, 6 (202–10): *Γαίος Καῖσαρ, αὐτοκράτωρ τὸ δεύτερον* (it should perhaps be *αὐτοκράτωρ, δικτάτωρ τὸ δεύτερον*). Finally, *Ant.* xiv 10, 6 (202–10) contains various decisions with regard to Joppa which seem to belong to different periods. On this basis, Mendelssohn, *op. cit.*, pp. 197 f., assumed that the fragments in xiv 10, 5–6 (200–10) belonged indeed to the *senatus consultum* of 44 B.C., but that a decree of Caesar from 47 B.C. is cited at the beginning, xiv 10, 5 and 6a (200–4). Mendelssohn distinguished this decree from the one given in *Ant.* xiv 10, 2 (190–5), arguing that the latter was issued before the intervention of Antigonus, and the former, after it. (This combination is scarcely admissible, since after the decree of nomination, *Ant.* xiv 10, 2 (190–5), Antigonus no longer dared remonstrate. In other respects, however, Mendelssohn's hypothesis that the fragments in *Ant.* xiv 10, 5 and 6a (200–4) belong to 47 B.C., is very attractive.) Mendelssohn found the new order of the *senatus consultum* of 44 B.C. only in the second half of *Ant.* xiv 10, 6 (204–10) (perhaps from the words *ὅσα τε μετὰ ταῦτα ἔσχον* onwards). Niese, Hermes 11 (1876), pp. 484 ff., ascribed all the fragments in *Ant.* xiv 10, 3–6 (196–210) to the *senatus consultum* of 44 B.C., assuming that the permission to build the walls given by Caesar earlier, and possiblv by word of mouth, was not granted formally by the senate until then, and reading in *Ant.* xiv 10, 6 (202) *τὸ δ'* (for the fourth time) instead of *τὸ δεύτερον*. Viereck (*Sermo graecus*, p. 101) agreed with Mendelssohn. He placed xiv 10, 3–4 (196–9) and 6a (202–4) in 47 B.C. (xiv 10, 3 (196–8) = the *senatus consultum*; xiv 10, 4 (199) and 6a (202–4) = Caesar's edict) and xiv 10, 5 (200–1) in 44 B.C. (Caesar's edict). Like Mendelssohn, he regarded xiv 10, 6b–7 (205–12) as fragments of the *senatus consultum* of February 44 B.C., to which reference is made in the *senatus consultum* of April 44 B.C., (xiv 10, 10 (219–22). Momigliano, *op. cit.*, p. 194, argues, correctly, that the earliest in the series is the pronouncement xiv 10, 4 (199) in which Hyrcanus is mentioned as High Priest but not ethnarch; this document, in which Caesar has the titles *αὐτοκράτωρ δικτάτωρ ὕπατος* will date to October–December 48 B.C.

24. *Ant.* xiv 10, 6 (209). If it is correct that the commencement of xiv 10, 6 (202–4) belongs to a decree of 47 B.C., part of the taxes of Joppa must already have been ceded to the Jews (i.e. we have to restore from the old Latin text, *ἔτους*). Niese and R. Marcus, *Josephus* (Loeb) VII, keep *ὅπως . . . Ἰόππης ὑπεξαιρουμένης, χωρὶς τοῦ ἑβδόμου ἔτους*. For a full discussion of the taxation regulations in (202–6) see Schalit, *op. cit.*, Anhang XIII. In any case they were awarded Joppa in 44 B.C. entirely as their own property: *Ἰόππην τε πόλιν, ἣν ἀπ' ἀρχῆς ἔσχον Ἰουδαῖοι ποιούμενοι τὴν πρὸς Ῥωμαίους φιλίαν, αὐτῶν εἶναι, καθὼς καὶ τὸ πρῶτον, ἡμῖν ἀρέσκει* (205). We are completely in the dark concerning who is meant in (209) by 'the kings of Syria and Phoenicia, allies of the Romans', who had earlier possessed some of the territories now ceded to the Jews. It is possible that they were dynasts to whom Pompey had granted Jewish territory. But it may also be that the text is corrupt. Schalit, *op. cit.*, Anhang VI, suggests rearranging the text to read *τούς τε τόπους καὶ χώραν καὶ ἐποίκια, ὅσα βασιλεῦσι Συρίας καὶ Φοινίκης ὑπῆρχε καρποῦσθαι, ταῦτα δοκιμάζει ἡ σύγκλητος Ὑρκανὸν τὸν ἐθνάρχην καὶ Ἰουδαίους συμμάχους ὄντας Ῥωμαίων κατὰ δωρεὰν ἔχειν,*

which Pompey had once taken from the Jews. Among the places restored, Joppa as a seaport was especially valuable.

Through Caesar's favour, Jews living outside Palestine were also granted important privileges. The Jews in Alexandria were secured in the possession of their rights;[25] the Jews of Asia Minor were guaranteed the exercise without let or hindrance of their religion.[26] It was above all Caesar's aspiration to satisfy the provincials in order to safeguard the empire. But none of them mourned his death so sorely as the Jews.[27]

The weak Hyrcanus, who had been installed in Palestine as 'ethnarch' of the Jews, governed only in name. In reality, it was the shrewd and active Antipater who did so. Moreover, he now nominated his two sons Phasael and Herod as governors (*στρατηγοί*), one in Jerusalem, the other in Galilee.[28] Herod, now encountered for the first time, was then a young man twenty-five years old.[29] But he was already giving signs of the drive which subsequently brought him to the throne. In Galilee, a robber named Ezekias and his band were making the country unsafe. Herod seized him and put him to death with many of his companions.[30] In Jerusalem, the people were not prepared to acquiesce in such summary procedures. The aristocracy there saw them as an infringement of the rights of the court empowered to pass the death sentence, and Hyrcanus was asked to call the young Herod to account. Hyrcanus agreed to do so, and summoned Herod before the Sanhedrin in Jerusalem. Herod appeared but instead of wearing mourning as befitted an accused person, he came clothed in purple and surrounded by a bodyguard. When he stood thus before the Sanhedrin, the prosecution was struck dumb, and he would doubtless have been acquitted had not the celebrated Pharisee, Sameas (Shemaiah?), risen and pricked the conscience of his colleagues. They were then inclined to allow the law to

25. See vol. III, § 31.

26. *Ant.* xiv 10, 8 (213–16) and 20–4 (241–61). The decrees assembled here were not actually issued directly by Caesar, but very probably on his suggestion. See also vol. III, § 31.

27. Suet. *Div. Iul.* 84: 'In summo publico luctu exterarum gentium multitudo circulatim suo quaeque more lamentata est, praecipueque Iudaei, qui etiam noctibus continuis bustum frequentarunt'.

28. *Ant.* xiv 9, 2 (158); *B.J.* i 10, 4 (203).

29. The traditional text of Jos. *Ant.* xiv 9, 2 (158) has 15. The number 25 which Dindorf and Bekker restored is merely a conjecture. But it is necessary, (1) because a boy of 15 years of age could not possibly have played the role that Herod was already playing; (2) because Herod is described as about seventy years old at the time of his death, *Ant.* xvii 6, 1 (148); *B.J.* i 33, 1 (647). Some (e.g. Lewin, *Fasti Sacri*, p. xii) have suggested that in the original text Herod's age was given as 25 (*κε*′) years and that a scribe altered *κε*′ to *ιε*′ (15). But others (e.g. Otto, *Herodes*, p. 18) call attention to the emphasis which Josephus lays upon Herod's youth at the time Galilee was put under his command, and maintain that he has represented him as being then younger than in fact he was.

30. *Ant.* xiv 9, 2 (159); *B.J.* i 10, 5 (204).

run its course and to pass sentence on Herod. But Hyrcanus had been ordered by Sextus Iulius Caesar, the governor of Syria, to acquit him. Accordingly, when he saw that matters were taking a dangerous turn, he suspended the sitting and advised Herod to leave the city. Herod did so; but soon afterwards marched with an army against Jerusalem to take revenge for the insult. Only the most urgent expostulations of his father Antipater succeeded in soothing his resentment and restraining him from open violence. He returned to Galilee, consoling himself that he had at least displayed his power and engendered wholesome terror in his opponents.[31] During this conflict with the Sanhedrin, he was nominated by Sextus Caesar as *strategos* of Coele-Syria and probably Samaria also.[32]

All this took place in 47 B.C., or the beginning of 46 B.C. In 46 B.C., while Caesar was fighting the party of Pompey in Africa, Caecilius Bassus, one of their number, managed to make himself master of Syria by assassinating Sextus Caesar. He was in turn besieged in Apamea in the autumn of 45 B.C. by Caesar's party under the leadership of C. Antistius Vetus (see pp. 248–9 above), whose army also included some of Antipater's troops, sent by him as a new proof of his loyalty to Caesar.[33] The conflict nevertheless had no decisive result; and the new governor, L. Staius Murcus, who arrived in Syria in the beginning of 44 B.C. and was reinforced by Marcius Crispus, the governor of Bithynia, failed to secure any decisive advantage over Caecilius Bassus either.

In the meantime, on 15 March 44 B.C., Caesar was murdered. M. Antonius was resolved to avenge his death and continue his work. But his initially cautious attitude also prevented the conspirators from taking decisive steps. It was not until he came forward in open hostility to them that their leaders proceeded to the East to assemble forces there, M. Brutus going to Macedonia and C. Cassius to Syria. When the latter arrived in Syria towards the end of 44 B.C., Caecilius Bassus was still being besieged in Apamea by Staius Murcus and Marcius Crispus. Although these two had until then belonged to Caesar's party, they nevertheless placed their army at the disposal of Cassius, Staius Murcus even offering his own person. The legion of Caecilius Bassus also went over to Cassius.[34] Thus Cassius was now

31. Jos. *Ant.* xiv 9, 3–5 (163–84); *B.J.* i 10, 6–9 (208–15). Rabbinic tradition is also acquainted with the scene before the Sanhedrin, but the names given there are quite different: Jannaeus instead of Hyrcanus; a slave of Jannaeus instead of Herod; Simeon ben Shetaḥ instead of Shemaiah. See Derenbourg, *Hist. de la Palestine*, pp. 146-8, and Schalit, *op. cit.*, pp. 45–6 and Anhang X.

32. *B.J.* i 10, 8 (213) *στρατηγὸς ἀνεδείχθη κοίλης Συρίας καὶ Σαμαρείας*. *Ant.* xiv 9, 5 (180) *στρατηγὸν τῆς κοίλης Συρίας (χρημάτων γὰρ αὐτῷ τοῦτο ἀπέδοτο)*. Cf. Schalit, *op. cit.*, p. 46, n. 154.

33. *Ant.* xiv 11, 1 (268–70); *B.J.* i 10, 10 (216–17).

34. Cf. pp. 249–50 above.

master of Syria and the possessor of a considerable force. But for the maintenance of this large and still growing army immense funds were needed, to which the small land of Judaea was also obliged to contribute its portion. A tax of 700 talents was imposed. Antipater and his son Herod showed themselves particularly zealous in this respect. For they now set out to earn Cassius's favour with the same eagerness as they once applied to winning Caesar's. The usefulness of this display of zeal was demonstrated by some shocking events in Judaea itself. Because the inhabitants of the towns of Gophna, Emmaus, Lydda and Thamna did not raise their share, they were sold by Cassius as slaves.[35] But as a reward for his services, the young Herod was appointed by Cassius, as earlier by Sextus Caesar, *strategos* of Coele-Syria.[36]

At about this time (43 B.C.), Antipater fell victim to personal enmity. A certain Malichus[37] aspired, like Antipater, to obtain a position of influence in Judaea. Antipater was the chief obstacle in his way. To attain his end he therefore had to get rid of him. He bribed Hyrcanus's cupbearer, who put Antipater to death by poison when he was dining with Hyrcanus.[38]

Herod undertook to avenge his father's death. As Malichus was thinking of implementating his plans and setting himself up as the master of Judaea, he was murdered one day in the neighbourhood of Tyre by assassins sent by Herod in connivance with Cassius.[39]

After Cassius had left Syria (42 B.C.), the province suffered still harder times. Cassius had extorted exorbitant sums, but now that the province was left to itself a state of complete anarchy arose, in which only the right of the stronger prevailed. In this period, Antigonus, with the aid of Ptolemy son of Mennaeus, the dynast of Chalcis, also tried to seize the sovereignty in Palestine. Herod repulsed this attempt with luck and skill, but was unable to prevent Marion, the tyrant of Tyre, from seizing portions of Galilean territory.[40]

35. *Ant.* xiv 11, 2 (271–6); *B.J.* i 11, 1–2 (218–22).

36. *Ant.* xiv 11, 4 (280) *στρατηγὸν . . . κοίλης Συρίας*. *B.J.* i 11, 4 (225) *Συριάς ἁπάσης ἐπιμελητήν*.

37. His name is consistently spelt by Josephus *Μάλιχος* (almost without variants in the manuscripts), whilst in other cases, e.g. for the Nabataean kings of the same name, the spelling *Μάλχος* is the prevailing one. Both forms are found in contemporary inscriptions, see indexes to IGLS; cf. Schalit, *op. cit.*, Anhang IV.

38. *Ant.* xiv 11, 4 (281); *B.J.* i 11, 4 (226).

39. *Ant.* xiv 11, 6 (288–92); *B.J.* i 11, 8 (233–5). The murder of Antipater took place before the capture of Laodicea (summer 43 B.C., see p. 250 above), that of Malichus immediately after it; consequently both occurred in 43 B.C., *Ant.* xiv 11, 6 (289); *B.J.* i 11, 7 (231).

40. *Ant.* xiv 12, 1 (297–9); *B.J.* i 12, 2–3 (238–40). The account given by Josephus, which goes back to Nicolaus of Damascus, omits the fact that Herod was unable to prevent the conquests by the Tyrians. This is evident from the subsequent letter of Antonius ordering the Tyrians to return the conquered places (see n. 42 below).

A new crisis developed for Palestine, and in particular for the two Idumaeans, Phasael and Herod, when in the late autumn of 42 B.C. Brutus and Cassius were defeated at Philippi by Antonius and Octavian. With this victory the whole of Asia fell into the hands of Antonius. For Phasael and Herod the situation was made more critical by the fact that an embassy of the Jewish nobility presented itself before Antonius in Bithynia (about the beginning of 41 B.C.) to complain about the two of them. But Herod, by appearing in person, was able to nullify these complaints for the time being.[41] Soon afterwards, an embassy from Hyrcanus approached Antonius when he was staying in Ephesus, asking him to order the emancipation of the Jews sold by Cassius as slaves, and the restoration of the places conquered by the Tyrians. Antonius willingly undertook the role of defender of their rights, and with violent invectives against Cassius's unjust conduct, issued the appropriate orders.[42] Later (in the autumn of 41 B.C.), when Antonius had come to Antioch, the Jewish aristocracy renewed their complaints against Phasael and Herod, but once again without success. Some years earlier, when he was serving under Gabinius in Syria (57–55 B.C.), Antonius had been Antipater's guest. He now recalled that friendship. And since Hyrcanus, who had also come to Antioch, gave the two brothers a favourable character, Antonius nominated Phasael and Herod as tetrarchs of the Jewish territory.[43] It does not follow that Hyrcanus was thereby deprived of his formal status as ethnarch. Besides, he had already for a long time possessed political power only in name.[44]

The period of Antonius's residence in Syria was one of great oppression for the province. His extravagance led to the consumption of astounding sums, and these had to be provided by the provinces. Thus wherever Antonius went, heavy tribute was exacted; and Palestine had to bear its share.[45]

In 40 B.C., when Antonius was partly detained in Egypt by Cleopatra and partly engaged in the concerns of Italy, occurred the great invasion of the Parthians, who overran the whole of the Near East. And on this

41. *Ant.* xiv 12, 2 (301–3); *B.J.* i 12, 4 (242).

42. *Ant.* xiv 12, 2 (304–5). The official documents (a letter of Antonius to Hyrcanus and two letters to the Tyrians) are in *Ant.* xiv 12, 3–5 (306–22). One of the letters to the Tyrians, *Ant.* xiv 12, 4 (314–18), relates especially to the restoration of the conquered places, the other, *Ant.* xiv 12, 5 (319–22), to the emancipation of the Jewish slaves. Similar letters were also issued to the cities of Sidon, Antioch and Aradus, *Ant.* xiv 12, 6 (323). Cf. on these documents Mendelssohn, *op. cit.*, pp. 254–63.

43. *Ant.* xiv 13, 1 (324–326); *B.J.* i 12, 5 (243–4).

44. See Schalit, *op. cit.*, pp. 69, 70.

45. App., *B.C.* v 7/31 *ἐπιπαριὼν δὲ Φρυγίαν τε καὶ Μυσίαν καὶ Γαλάτας τοὺς ἐν Ἀσίᾳ, Καππαδοκίαν τε καὶ Κιλικίαν καὶ Συρίαν τὴν κοίλην καί Παλαιστίνην καὶ τὴν Ἰτουραίαν καὶ ὅσα ἄλλα γένη Σύρων, ἅπασιν ἐσφορὰς ἐπέβαλλε βαρείας.*

occasion Antigonus, too, succeeded at least for a time in attaining his objective.

When the Parthians under Pacorus and Barzaphranes (the former a son of King Orodes, the latter a Parthian satrap)[46] had already occupied northern Syria, Antigonus, by making huge promises, managed to persuade them to help him to acquire the Jewish throne. Pacorus marched along the Phoenician coast, while Barzaphranes travelled inland towards the south. Pacorus sent a detachment to Jerusalem under the command of a royal cupbearer, also called Pacorus. Before this detachment arrived there, Antigonus had already succeeded in collecting adherents from among the Jews, and in entering with them into Jerusalem, where there were now daily encounters between him and Phasael and Herod.[47] Meanwhile, the Parthian army under Pacorus arrived. He pretended that he desired to make peace, and called on Phasael to go to Barzaphranes to settle the strife. Although Herod earnestly warned his brother, Phasael nevertheless walked into the trap, and together with Hyrcanus and Pacorus (the cupbearer), went to the camp of Barzaphranes. A small detachment of Parthian horsemen remained behind in Jerusalem.[48] In the Parthian camp the mask was soon thrown off and both Phasael and Hyrcanus were put in irons.[49] When Herod heard of this, he decided, since he was too weak to offer open resistance, to escape from Jerusalem. Unnoticed by the Parthians, he led the women and children of his family out of the city and brought them to the fortress of Masada, the defence of which he committed to his brother Joseph.[50] On the way there, in the place where he later built the fortress of Herodium, he fought a battle with hostile Jews. But he successfully resisted their attack. After he had thus brought his relations into safety, he continued his flight further to the south, first of all to Petra in Arabia.[51]

The Parthians did not allow their friendship with Antigonus to restrain them from plundering the land and the capital. But Phasael and Hyrcanus were put at Antigonus's disposal. The ears of Hyrcanus

46. The spelling *Βαρζαφράνης* (*Ant.* xiv 13, 3 (330)) seems to be required by the admittedly variable evidence of the manuscripts. This is apparently a transliteration of the Iranian 'Barzafarna'. See *Josephus* (Loeb) VII, *ad. loc.* The spelling *Βαζαφράνης* preferred by Niese is not justified by the manuscript tradition.

47. *Ant.* xiv 13, 3 (330–6); *B.J.* i 13, 1–2 (248–52).

48. *Ant.* xiv 13, 4–5 (337–42); *B.J.* i 13, 3 (253–5).

49. *Ant.* xiv 13, 5–6 (343–51); *B.J.* i 13, 4–5 (256–60).

50. Masada was situated on a precipitous rock on the west shore of the Dead Sea. In the war of Vespasian it was the rebels' last place of refuge and was reduced to submission only after difficult siege-operations by the Romans (*c.* A.D. 74). On its situation and history see § 20 below (where the extensive recent literature is also listed).

51. *Ant.* xiv 13, 6–9 (348–62); *B.J.* i 13, 6–8 (261–7).

were cut off to disqualify him permanently from being High Priest. Phasael escaped his enemies by dashing his head against a rock, after receiving the good news of his brother's successful escape.

The Parthians then took Hyrcanus with them as a prisoner, and installed Antigonus as king.[52]

52. *Ant.* xiv 13, 9–10 (363–9); *B.J.* i 13, 9–11 (268–73). Dio xlviii 26, 2 erroneously gives the name Aristobulus instead of Antigonus. Of the years 43–40 B.C., Julius Africanus in Georgius Syncellus (ed. Dindorf I, pp. 581 f.) and Syncellus himself (ed. Dindorf I, pp. 576 f. and 579), each give a brief account containing details at variance from those given by Josephus, and probably deriving from another source (Justus of Tiberias?). Note especially that according to this account Phasael does not take his own life when a prisoner, but falls in battle (Julius Africanus in Syncellus I, p. 581: *Φασάηλος δὲ ἐν τῇ μάχῃ ἀναιρεῖται*). Also, the sum which Cassius exacted in Palestine is given, not as 700, but as 800 talents (Syncellus I, p. 576). Cf. H. Gelzer, *Sextus Julius Africanus* I (1880), pp. 261–5. There is no reason however, to prefer these brief references to the very exhaustive account of Josephus.

On the theory identifying the 'Wicked Priest' of the Qumran documents with Hyrcanus II, see § 12, n. 30.

§ 14 Antigonus (40–37 B.C.)

Sources

Jos. *Ant.* xiv 14–16 (370–491); *B.J.* i 14–18 (274–375).

Bibliography

Graetz, H., *Geschichte der Juden* III ([5]1905–6), pp. 189–95.
Otto, W., *Herodes* (1913), cols. 25–37.
Debevoise, N. C., *A Political History of Parthia* (1938), pp. 111–20.
Jones, A. H. M., *The Herods of Judaea* (1938, [2]1967), pp. 39–48.
Abel, F.-M., *Histoire de la Palestine* I (1952), pp. 334–46.
Schalit, A., *König Herodes* (1969), pp. 79–97.

Antigonus, or according to coin evidence, Mattathias, his Hebrew name, achieved through the favour of the Parthians the position for which his father and brother had struggled in vain. Like his ancestors from the time of Aristobulus I, he now also styled himself on his coins 'King' and 'High Priest'—*ΒΑΣΙΛΕΩΣ ΑΝΤΙΓΟΝΟΥ* (rev.)/ מתתיה הכהן הגדל (obv.).[1]

Herod's hopes rested simply and solely on Roman help. Without going to Petra—for the Nabataean prince Malchus had begged him not to visit him—he proceeded to Alexandria and took ship for Rome, although the autumn storms had already begun. After perils of many sorts, he reached Rome by way of Rhodes and Brundisium and immediately brought his complaint before Antonius.[2] Whatever was lacking in favour, Herod was able to obtain by bribes. And so it came about that, after Octavian had also given his consent, he was declared king of Judaea at a formal session of the Senate. The appointment was celebrated with a sacrifice on the Capitol and a banquet given by Antonius.[3]

1. Cf. on the coins of Antigonus Eckhel III, pp. 480–1; Mionnet V, pp. 563 f.; de Saulcy, *Recherches*, pp. 109–13; Madden, *History of the Jewish Coinage*, pp. 76–9; *id.*, *Coins of the Jews*, pp. 99–103; A. Reifenberg, *Ancient Jewish Coins* ([2]1947), pp. 17–18; Y. Meshorer, *Jewish Coins of the Second Temple Period* (1967), pp. 60–3. One coin, Meshorer, *op. cit.*, no. 30, has a longer title—

מתתיה [ה]כהן הגדל וחבר היהודים

2. *Ant.* xiv 14, 1–3 (370–80); *B.J.* i 14, 1–3 (271–81).

3. *Ant.* xiv 14, 4–5 (381–93); *B.J.* i 14, 4 (282–5). Cf. Appian, *B.C.* v 75/319 (see p. 251 above). The nomination took place in 40 B.C., in the consulship of Cn. Domitius Calvinus and C. Asinius Pollio, *Ant.* xiv 14, 5 (389), but in any case fairly near the end of the year, for it was already late autumn when Herod took ship at Alexandria, *Ant.* xiv 14, 2 (376); *B.J.* i 14, 2 (279). The statement of Josephus that the nomination occurred in the 184th Olympiad, *Ant.* xiv 14, 5 (389), is strictly incorrect, for it had ended in the summer of 40 B.C. Other evidence

From nomination to actual possession was another and more difficult step. For the time being, the Parthians and their protégé Antigonus were still in occupation of the land. The former were admittedly expelled from Syria in 39 B.C. by Ventidius, the legate of Antonius (see pp. 251–2 above), but Ventidius merely exacted a heavy tribute from Antigonus, and for the rest left him unmolested. A similar policy was pursued, after the departure of Ventidius, by Silo, his second in command.[4]

Such was the situation when Herod landed at Ptolemais in 39 B.C. He quickly assembled an army, and since, on the orders of Antonius, Ventidius and Silo now supported him, he soon made progress. First, Joppa fell into his hands, and then Masada, where his family had been besieged. With his success the number of his followers also increased, and he could set about besieging Jerusalem. But he did nothing about it for the time being because Silo's Roman troops, which should have supported him, adopted a troublesome attitude and had to be dismissed to winter quarters.[5]

In the spring of 38 B.C. the Parthians renewed their invasion of Syria. While Ventidius and Silo engaged them, Herod attempted to subjugate the land completely to himself and purge it of its numerous desperadoes. Galilee, in particular, sheltered vast hordes of brigands in inaccessible caves. But he managed to capture even these by letting his soldiers down in huge boxes (λάρνακες) from the tops of the cliffs and thus enabling them to enter the caves.[6]

---

on the movement of the Triumvirs shows that it will have been towards the end of 40 B.C. (the last time, as Josephus's narrative requires, that Antonius and Octavian were in Rome together towards the end of a year); see MRR II, pp. 379–40 and cf. 386–7. The argument of W. E. Filmer, 'The Chronology of the Reign of Herod the Great', JThSt 17 (1966), pp. 283–98, on p. 285 that the formal appointment dates to 39 B.C., has no weight whatever, relying as it does solely on a resumptive reference to client kings appointed by Antonius, in App. *B.C.* v 75/319.

4. *Ant.* xiv 14, 6 (392–3); *B.J.* i 15, 2 (288–9); Dio xlviii 41, 1–6.

5. *Ant.* xiv 15, 1–3 (394–412); *B.J.* i 15, 3–6 (290–302).

6. *Ant.* xiv 15, 5 (420–30); *B.J.* i 16, 4 (309–13). According to *Ant.* xiv 15, 4 (415) and *B.J.* i 16, 2 (305), these caves were in the neighbourhood of Arbela. Josephus frequently mentions them elsewhere; *Ant.* xii 11, 1 (421); *Vita* 37 (188). The description he gives in *Ant.* xiv 15, 5 (420–30)=*B.J.* i 16, 4 (309–13) agrees accurately with the caves still situated in the neighbourhood of Khirbet Irbîd (Arbed) not far from the Lake of Gennesaret and north-west of Tiberias. Accordingly, there can be no doubt that Irbîd is identical with Arbela, and that the caves there are those described by Josephus. The form Arbela occurs five times in Josephus (cf. A. Schalit, *Namenwörterbuch* s.v. Ἄρβηλα), add to this 1 Mac. 9:2 and the Rabbinic ארבל. The place with the ancient synagogue (Carmoly, *Itinéraires* (1847), pp. 131, 259) is certainly our Arbel=Irbîd (cf. vol. II, § 27); in other cases, also, this is probably what is meant (Neubauer, *Géographie du Talmud*, p. 219). The transition from *l* to *d* is certainly surprising, but not without

Meanwhile, the Parthians were once more defeated by Ventidius (9 June 38 B.C.), who then turned against Antiochus of Commagene and besieged him in Samosata, his capital. During the siege, Antonius himself arrived before Samosata. Herod could not lose this opportunity of speaking to his patron, for he had good reason to complain of the support given him till then. He therefore went to Samosata to pay his respects to Antonius, who received him very graciously, and, as the surrender of Samosata took place soon afterwards, instructed Sosius, the successor of Ventidius, to lend Herod powerful assistance.[7]

In Palestine things had gone badly during Herod's absence. His brother, Joseph, to whom he had transferred supreme command, had been attacked by an army of Antigonus and fallen in the battle, whereupon Antigonus had ordered his head to be struck off. As a result, the Galileans too had risen against Herod, and had drowned his followers in the Lake of Gennesaret.[8]

Herod heard about all this when he was in Antioch, and hastened to avenge his brother's death. Galilee was subdued without difficulty. Near Jericho he encountered the army of Antigonus, but seems to have not risked any decisive engagement. It was only when Antigonus divided his army and sent part of it under Pappus to Samaria that Herod sought him out. They met at Isana. Pappus attacked first, but was completely defeated by Herod and thrown into the city, where all those unable to escape were cut to pieces. Pappus himself met his death at this time. The whole of Palestine, with the exception of the capital, thus fell into Herod's hands. And only the advent of winter prevented him from starting an immediate siege of Jerusalem.[9]

In the spring of 37 B.C., as soon as the season permitted, Herod camped before the capital and commenced siege operations. When these were in progress, he left the army for a short time and went to Samaria to celebrate his marriage with Mariamme, a granddaughter

---

parallel; cf. Aram. אזד and אזל (Kautzsch, *Grammatik des Biblisch-Aramäischen*, p. 63; Kampffmeyer, ZDPV 15 (1892), pp. 32 f.; Y. Aharoni, *The Land of the Bible* (1967), p. 111). On Arbela generally, see Robinson, *Biblical Researches in Palestine* II, p. 398; Guérin, *Galilée* I, pp. 198–203; *The Survey of Western Palestine, Memoirs of Conder and Kitchener* I, pp. 409–11. Cf. Abel, *Géog. Pal.* II, p. 249.

7. *Ant.* xiv 15, 7–9 (434–47); *B.J.* i 16, 6–7 (317–22).

8. *Ant.* xiv 15, 10 (448–50); *B.J.* i 17, 1–2 (323–7).

9. *Ant.* xiv 15, 11–13 (451–64); *B.J.* i 17, 3–8 (328–44). Instead of *ΙΣΑΝΑ*, *Ant.* xiv 15, 12 (458), *B.J.* i 17, 5 (334) has *ΚΑΝΑ*, which is probably only a corruption of the text. The context indicates that the place lay either in the south of Samaria, or in the north of Judaea; for Pappus was sent to Samaria, but Herod fell in with him as he was coming from Jericho. Accordingly our Isana is undoubtedly identical with ישנה, which is mentioned with Bethel in 2 Chr. 13:19 (in Jos. *Ant.* viii 11, 3 (284) *'Ισανά*). W. F. Albright in BASOR 9 (1923), p. 7 identifies Isana with Burj el-Isâneh, about twenty miles north of Jerusalem on the Nablus road; cf. Abel, *Géog. Pal.* II, p. 364.

of Hyrcanus, to whom he had already been engaged for five years from 42 B.C., see *Ant.* xiv 12, 1 (300); *B.J.* i 12, 3 (241).[10]

The wedding over, he returned to the camp. Sosius too now appeared before Jerusalem with a large army, and together he and Herod led the attack on the city from the north as Pompey had done. Here mighty ramparts were raised and the catapults began their work. Forty days after the start of the bombardment the first wall was taken, and a further fifteen days later, the second one also. But the inner court of the Temple and the upper city still remained in the hands of the besieged. Finally, these too were stormed, and the besiegers murdered whoever in the city fell into their hands. Antigonus himself dropped at the feet of Sosius and entreated him for mercy. Sosius made fun of him, called him 'Antigone' and had him clapped in irons. Herod's greatest preoccupation now was to be rid of his Roman allies as soon as possible, for murder and plundering in what was now his capital were against his interests. By means of lavish gifts he managed at last to induce Sosius and his troops to withdraw.[11] [*Text continues on p.* 286

10. *Ant.* xiv 15, 14 (467); *B.J.* i 17, 8 (344). Mariamme (Μαριάμμη, it should not be spelt Μαριάμνη) was a daughter of Alexander, the son of Aristobulus II, and Alexandra, a daughter of Hyrcanus II, *Ant.* xv 2, 5 (23). She was Herod's second wife. His first wife was Doris, from whom he had a son named Antipater, *Ant.* xiv 12, 1 (300).

11. *Ant.* xiv 16, 1–3 (468–86); *B.J.* i 17, 9 (345–6); 18, 1–3 (347–57); Dio xlix 22, 3–6; Seneca, *Suas.* ii 21, 'Sosio illi qui Iudaeos subegerat'; Tac. *Hist.* v 9 'Iudaeos C. Sosius subegit'. On Sosius's title 'Imperator' and his triumph *ex Judaea*, see p. 252 above. The date of the conquest of Jerusalem is given differently in the two sources at our disposal. Dio xlix 22, 3–23, 1 puts it in the consulship of Claudius and Norbanus, 38 B.C., along with Antonius's actions up to the siege of Samosata. Josephus, on the other hand, says that it took place under the consuls M. Agrippa and Caninius Gallus, e.g. in 37 B.C., *Ant.* xiv 16, 4 (487). Almost all more recent scholars follow him, and there can in fact be no question that the brief and summary account given by Dio is not to be compared with Josephus's narrative, which is full and detailed, and manifestly rests on very good sources. From this narrative it emerges without doubt that the conquest did not take place until 37 B.C. It is known that Pacorus was defeated by Ventidius on 9 June 38 B.C. After this, Ventidius turned against Antiochus of Commagene and besieged him in Samosata. It was not until the siege was in progress (cf. esp. Plut. *Ant.* 34), i.e. at the earliest in July 38 B.C., that Antonius arrived before Samosata. There he was visited by Herod, and when Samosata capitulated after a long siege (Plut., *Ant.* 34 τῆς δὲ πολιορκίας μῆκος λαμβανούσης), and he himself returned to Athens, he left Sosius behind with orders to reinforce Herod, *Ant.* xiv 15, 8–9 (439–47). It must then already have been the autumn of 38 B.C. before Herod received this reinforcement, and Josephus's account leaves us in no doubt that a winter still intervened before the conquest of Jerusalem (*Ant.* xiv 15, 11 (453) πολλοῦ χειμῶνος καταρραγέντος, 15, 12 (461), χειμὼν ἐπέσχε βαθύς: after that 15, 14 (465) λήξαντος δὲ τοῦ χειμῶνος: and finally 16, 2 (473) θέρος τε γὰρ ἦν). Note also *Ant.* xiv 15, 14 (465), on the beginning of the siege—τρίτον δὲ αὐτῷ τοῦτο ἔτος ἦν ἐξ οὗ βασιλεὺς ἐν Ῥωμῇ ἀποδέδεικτο (40 B.C.). Therefore the capture of Jerusalem cannot have taken place earlier than the Summer of 37 B.C.

So Otto, *op. cit.*, pp. 31 f.; A. D. Momigliano, CAH X p. 321; PIR² H 153; MRR II, pp. 397–8; Schalit, *op. cit.*, pp. 96–7, and Anhang IX. But there is one further problem. Josephus in *Ant.* xiv 16, 4 (487) says that the conquest took place τῇ ἑορτῇ τῆς νηστείας, by which he appears to mean the Day of Atonement (10 Tishri = September/October). V. Lewin, T. H. Gardthausen, G. F. Unger and others accepted this. On the other hand, L. Herzfeld, 'Wann war die Eroberung Jerusalem's durch Pompejus, und wann die durch Herodes?', MGWJ 1855, pp. 109–15, attempted to show that the conquest must have taken place earlier, in the summer, on the following arguments. Herod began the siege as soon as the weather allowed (λήξαντος τοῦ χειμῶνος), probably in February therefore, at the latest in March. Consequently, although according to *B.J.* i 18, 2 (351) it lasted for five months, it can hardly have dragged on into October. The surrender must have rather have taken place some time in July 37 B.C. The ἑορτὴ τῆς νηστείας which Josephus found in his pagan sources must, as in the account of the conquest of the city by Pompey, once more have been not the Day of Atonement, but an ordinary Sabbath, for Dio again says that the city was taken ἐν τῇ τοῦ Κρόνου ἡμέρᾳ (xlix 22, 5). Mention has still to be made of Josephus's statement that the capture took place τῷ τρίτῳ μηνί, *Ant.* xiv 16, 4 (487). By this he does not in any case mean the third month of the Olympic year, for the Greek months were never numbered; he means either the third month of the Jewish calendar, or the third month of the siege. The first of these views is accepted by Graetz, *op. cit.* III, p. 195, who accordingly places the conquest in June 37 B.C. But this cannot be Josephus's meaning since at the same time he postpones the conquest to the Day of Atonement. It is therefore preferable to understand by 'the third month' the third month of the siege. The three months are then presumably to be reckoned from the beginning of the bombardment, *Ant.* xiv 16, 2 (473), and the five months of *B.J.* from the start of the erection of the earthworks, *Ant.* xiv 15, 14 (466). Cf. Herzfeld, *op. cit.*, pp. 113 f.

The opinion of C. E. Caspari, *Chronologisch-geographische Einleitung in das Leben Jesu Christi*, pp. 18 ff., that the conquest did not take place until 36 B.C., is revived by W. E. Filmer, 'The Chronology of the Reign of Herod the Great', JThSt n.s. 17 (1966), pp. 283–98, on pp. 285–91. The chronological correlations indicated above make it unacceptable, but the argument does serve to point to unsolved difficulties arising from Josephus's reference to a sabbatical year and from his statement that the conquest took place 27 years after that by Pompey (on both points see below). For further discussion of the date of Herod's capture of Jerusalem see W. Otto, *Herodes* (1913), p. 33, n. 2; R. Laqueur, *Der jüdische Historiker Flavius Josephus* (1920), pp. 211 f.; F. X. Kugler, *Von Moses bis Paul* (1922), pp. 418–22; S. Zeitlin, *Megillat Taanit as a Source for Jewish Chronology* (1922), pp. 20–7; Schalit, *op. cit.*, Anhang IX; W. Aly, *Strabon von Amaseia* (1957), pp. 166–8. Otto suggests that if the date τῇ ἑορτῇ τῆς νηστείας means the Day of Atonement, it may rest on a popular tradition, the aim of which was to discredit Herod by representing him as having invaded the city on a day of very great solemnity. Josephus also dates Herod's capture of Jerusalem in 'the hundred and eighty-fifth Olympiad'. This Olympiad ended on 30 June 37 B.C.; but it does not necessarily follow that the capture took place in the first half, and cannot have taken place in the second half of that year; see p. 281, n. 3 above. Schalit, *loc. cit.*, dismisses the expression τριτῷ μηνί in *Ant.* xiv 16, 4 (487) as a repetition of xiv 4, 3 (66), and accepts the five months of *B.J.* i 18, 2 (351), but argues that τῇ ἑορτῇ τῆς νηστείας may refer to *a* day of public fasting during the siege.

Earlier, in *Ant.* xiv 16, 2 (475) Josephus relates that the Jews within the besieged city were distressed by famine and a lack of necessities, for a sabbatical year happened to fall at that time (τὸν γὰρ ἑβδοματικὸν ἐνιαυτὸν συνέβη κατὰ ταῦτ' εἶναι). This presents a considerable difficulty since, see R. Marcus, *Josephus*

Thus, almost three years after his nomination, Herod came into actual possession of his sovereignty. Antigonus was taken by Sosius to Antioch, and there beheaded in conformity with Herod's wish and by order of Antonius. It was the first time that the Romans had executed such a sentence on a king.[12]

With this the rule of the Hasmoneans was ended for ever.

(Loeb) VI, p. 694, note a, there is good reason to conclude that the year 37 B.C. (Oct.)–36 B.C. and not the year 38 B.C. (Oct.)–37 B.C. was sabbatical. The statement in *Ant.* xiv 16, 4 (488) that Herod took Jerusalem on the same day on which it was captured by Pompey twenty-seven years before, points according to some, e.g. von Gumpach, *Über den altjüdischen Kalender*, pp. 269–71 and Caspari, *Chron.-geographische Einleitung in das Leben Jesu Christi*, pp. 18 f., to 36 B.C., according to others, e.g. Lewin, *Fasti Sacri*, no. 524, to 37 B.C., while yet others think that Josephus made a mistake in calculation and so has given here twenty-seven instead of twenty-six.

12. *Ant.* xiv 16, 4 (487–91); xv 1, 2 (5–10). In (9–10) Josephus also quotes a passage from the lost *History* of Strabo (=FGrH 91 F 18), *B.J.* i 18, 3 (354–7); Dio xlix 22–6; Plut. *Ant.* 36.

§ 15. Herod the Great 37–4 B.C.

Sources

Jos. *Ant.* xv, xvi, xvii 1–8 (1–205); *B.J.* i 18–33 (347–673).
On the lost works of Herod, Ptolemy, Nicolaus of Damascus and Justus of Tiberias, see pp. 26–37 above.
Rabbinic traditions: bBaba Bathra 3b–4a
bTaanith 23a
Leviticus Rabbah 35:8
Numbers Rabbah 14:20
Cf. Derenbourg, *op. cit.*, pp. 149–65.
The coins are given in *BMC Palestine*, pp. 220–7; A. Reifenberg, *Ancient Jewish Coins* ([2]1947), pp. 42–3; Y. Meshorer, *Jewish Coins of the Second Temple Period* (1967), pp. 127–30. See n. 85 below

Bibliography

Graetz, H., *Geschichte der Juden* III ([5]1905–6), pp. 196–244.
Renan, E., *Histoire du peuple d'Israël* V (1893), pp. 248–304.
Wellhausen, J., *Israelitische und jüdische Geschichte*, ([9]1958), pp. 304–26.
Otto, H., 'Herodes' RE VIII, Suppl. 2 (1913), cols. 1–158 (the basic modern study).
Momigliano, A. D., 'Herod of Judaea', CAH X (1934), pp. 316–39.
Jones, A. H. M., *The Herods of Judaea* (1938, [2]1967), pp. 39–155.
Abel, F.-M., *Histoire de la Palestine I* (1952), pp. 347–406.
Buchheim, H., *Die Orientpolitik des Triumvirn M. Antonius* (1960), pp. 68–74.
Bowersock, G. W., *Augustus and the Greek World* (1965), esp. pp. 54–7.
Schalit, A., *König Herodes: der Mann und sein Werk* (1969).
Applebaum, Sh., 'Herod I', Enc. Jud. VIII (1971), cols. 375–85, 387.

Chronological Summary[1]

B.C.

37 Conquest of Jerusalem (some time in July?).
Executions, *Ant.* xv 1, 2 (5–10), cf. xiv 9, 4 (175); *B.J.* i 18, 4 (358–60).

37/6? Antonius grants to Cleopatra Chalcis, Coele-Syria, the coastal strip from the Eleutherus to Egypt (except Tyre and Sidon), Cilicia and Cyprus. For the date, Plut. *Ant.* 36; Porphyry, FGrH 260 F 2 (17); cf. *Ant.* xv 3, 8 (79), 4, 1 (95); Dio xlix 32 4–5 (under 36 B.C.).[2]

36 Hyrcanus II returns from his Parthian imprisonment, *Ant.* xv 2, 1–4 (11–22).

35 Beginning of the year: Aristobulus III, Mariamme's brother, is nominated

1. We start with this summary because the following sections do not keep entirely to a chronological sequence.

2. For the evidence for the chronology of Antonius's territorial grants to Cleopatra see n. 5 below.

B.C.

High Priest by Herod at the instigation of his mother Alexandra, *Ant.* xv 2, 5–7 (23–38); 3, 1 (39–41).[3]

End of the year: on the instructions of Herod, Aristobulus III is drowned in the bath at Jericho (soon after the Feast of Tabernacles), τὴν δ' ἀρχιερωσύνην κατασχὼν ἐνιαυτόν, *Ant.* xv 3, 3 (50–6); *B.J.* i 22, 2 (437).

35/4 Herod is summoned by Antonius to Laodicea to answer for the death of Aristobulus but is graciously released by Antonius, *Ant.* xv 3, 5 (62–7) and 8–9 (74–87).[4]

34 Joseph, the husband of Herod's sister Salome, is executed, *Ant.* xv 3, 9 (80–7).

Antonius grants to Cleopatra the balsam plantations near Jericho and some parts of the territory of Malchus of Nabataea, *B.J.* i 18, 5 (361–2), *Ant.* xv 4, 2 (96).[5]

---

3. The nomination was made some time after Alexandra had sent the portraits of Aristobulus and Mariamme to Antonius in Egypt, *Ant.* xv 2, 6 (27); *B.J.* i 22, 3 (439). Since Antonius did not arrive in Egypt until the end of 36 B.C. (see p. 252 above), the nomination cannot have taken place earlier than the beginning of 35 B.C.

4. Since, as stated above, Aristobulus died at the end of 35 B.C., this summons to Laodicea fell in the winter of 35/34 B.C., before Antonius undertook the campaign against Armenia (Dio xlix 39); when Josephus states that Antonius advanced at that time against the Parthians, *Ant.* xv 3, 9 (80), he is inaccurate but not positively wrong, for Antonius did in fact assert that he was advancing against the Parthians (see Dio xlix 39, 3). Moreover, in *B.J.* i 18, 5 (362) Josephus also writes erroneously 'Parthians' instead of 'Armenians'. The campaign (ἐπὶ Πάρθους) mentioned in *Ant.* xv 3, 9 (80) is accordingly identical with the one ἐπ' Ἀρμενίαν mentioned in *Ant.* xv 4, 2 (96).

5. These donations are also mentioned by Plut. *Ant.* 36 (Φοινίκην, κοίλην Συρίαν, Κύπρον, Κιλικίας πολλήν, ἔτι δὲ τῆς τε Ἰουδαίων τὴν τὸ βάλσαμον φέρουσαν καὶ τῆς Ναβαταίων Ἀραβίας ὅση πρὸς τὴν ἐκτὸς ἀποκλίνει θάλασσαν) and by Dio xlix 32, 5 (πολλὰ μὲν τῆς Ἀραβίας τῆς τε Μάλχου καὶ τῆς τῶν Ἰτυραίων, τὸν γὰρ Λυσανίαν . . . ἀπέκτεινεν . . ., πολλὰ δὲ καὶ τῆς Φοινίκης τῆς τε Παλαιστίνης, Κρήτης τέ τινα καὶ Κυρήνην τήν τε Κύπρον). Both place them in 36 B.C., before the beginning of the Parthian campaign, in the case of Plutarch, and after the return from it, in that of Dio. On the other hand, according to Josephus the gift of parts of Arabia, Judaea and Phoenicia took place in 34 B.C., when Antonius was about to advance against Armenia. For comparison with Dio xlix 39–40 shows without doubt that this is the campaign alluded to in *Ant.* xv 4, 1–5 (88–105), *B.J.* i 18, 5 (361–3). The date given by Plutarch and Dio is seemingly confirmed by Porphyry's observation that Cleopatra counted the sixteenth year of her reign also as its first, because that was the year in which Antonius, after the death of Lysimachus (Lysanias is intended) had bestowed upon her the kingdom of Chalcis (Porphyry in Euseb. *Chron.*, ed. Schoene I, p. 170 (=FGrH 260 F2 (17), τὸ δ' ἑκκαιδέκατον ὠνομάσθη τὸ καὶ πρῶτον, ἐπειδὴ τελευτήσαντος Λυσιμάχου [l. Λυσανίου] τῆς ἐν Συρίᾳ Χαλκίδος βασιλέως, Μάρκος Ἀντώνιος ὁ αὐτοκράτωρ τήν τε Χαλκίδα καὶ τοὺς περὶ αὐτὴν τόπους παρέδωκε τῇ Κλεοπάτρᾳ). This dual reckoning of the years of Cleopatra's reign is attested by various papyri and inscriptions, see T. C. Skeat, *The Reigns of the Ptolemies* (1954), p. 42, and by coins of Cleopatra, struck in Berytus, J. N. Svoronos, *Die Münzen der Ptolemaeer* IV (1908), pp. 377 and 385–7, but not those of Egypt itself, *op. cit.* p. 377. For the view that the first year of the Syrian era of Cleopatra was 37/6 see the valuable studies of the coinage by H. Seyrig, 'Sur les ères de quelques

B.C.

Cleopatra with Herod in Jerusalem, *Ant.* xv 4, 2 (96–103); *B.J.* i 18, 5 (362).

32/1 War of Herod with the Nabataeans after the outbreak of hostilities between Antonius and Octavian, *Ant.* xv 5, 1 (108–20); *B.J.* i 19, 1–3 (334–72).

31 Earthquake in Palestine, *Ant.* xv 5, 2 (121–2); *B.J.* i 19, 3 (370) κατ' ἔτος μὲν τῆς βασιλείας ἕβδομον, ἀκμάζοντος δὲ τοῦ περὶ Ἄκτιον πολέμου, ἀρχομένου ἔαρος.[6]

Herod defeats the Nabataeans, *Ant.* xv 5, 2–5 (123–60); *B.J.* i 19, 3–6 (371–85).

After the battle of Actium (2 Sept.) Herod sides with Octavian, supporting Didius in the fighting against the gladiators of Antonius, *Ant.* xv 6, 7 (194–201); *B.J.* i 20, 2 (391–2). Cf. p. 254 above.

30 Spring: Hyrcanus II is executed, *Ant.* xv 6, 1–4 (161–82); *B.J.* i 22, 1 (431–4); πλείω μὲν ἢ ὀγδοήκοντα γεγονὼς ἐτύγχανεν ἔτη, *Ant.* xv 6, 3 (178).[7]

Herod visits Octavian at Rhodes and is confirmed by him as king, *Ant.* xv 6, 5–7 (183–97); *B.J.* i 20, 1–3 (386–93).

At Ptolemais he welcomes Octavian on his march to Egypt, *Ant.* xv 6, 7 (198–201); *B.J.* i 20, 3 (394–5).

Autumn: Herod visits Octavian in Egypt and receives back from him Jericho and also Gadara, Hippos, Samaria, Gaza, Anthedon, Joppa and Straton's Tower, *Ant.* xv 7, 3 (215–17); *B.J.* i 20, 3 (396–7).

End of the year: He accompanies Augustus on his return from Egypt as far as Antioch, *Ant.* xv 7, 4 (218).

29 End of the year: Mariamme is executed, *Ant.* xv 7, 4–6 (218–39); *B.J.* i 22, 3–5 (438–44), *Ant.* xv 7, 4 (221) ἥ τε ὑποψία τρεφομένη παρέτεινεν ἐνιαυτοῦ μῆκος ἐξ οὗ παρὰ Καίσαρος Ἡρῴδης ὑπεστρόφει.

28? Alexandra is executed, *Ant.* xv 7, 8 (247–52).

27? Costobar, the second husband of Salome, and the sons of Babas, are executed, *Ant.* xv 7, 10 (259–66). A later date is indicated by the statement of Salome: ὅτι διασῴζοιντο παρ' αὐτῷ χρόνον ἐνιαυτῶν ἤδη δώδεκα

---

villes de Syrie', Syria 27 (1950), pp. 5–50, on pp. 110–13; and 'Le monnayage de Ptolemais de Phénicie', RN 4 (1962), pp. 25–50. Since the 16th year of Cleopatra runs from 1 Thoth = 1 Sept. 37 to 5 Epag. = 31 Aug. 36 (Skeat, *op. cit.*, p. 18), her new era commences precisely with this year. Cf. however A. E. Samuel, *Ptolemaic Chronology* (1962), p. 159, who explains the new era as marking the joint rule of Cleopatra and Caesarion. The appearance of the double era on the coins of Berytus but not those of Egypt is, however, a strong argument for accepting Porphyry's statement. Without further documentary evidence, the statements of Josephus, Plutarch and Dio about the various territorial grants by Antonius to Cleopatra cannot be reconciled in any universally acceptable way. For a full discussion see J. Dobiaš, 'La donation d' Antoine à Cléopatre en l'an 34 av. J.-C.', *Mélanges Bidez* (1934), pp. 287–314. The chronology suggested here is that of H. Buchheim, *op. cit.*, pp. 68–74, and Schalit, *op. cit.*, Anhang XII.

6. The 7th year of Herod = 31/30 B.C. reckoned from 1st Nisan to 1st Nisan. See n. 165 below. The earthquake therefore took place in Nisan 31 B.C. Elsewhere also Nisan is considered the beginning of spring. See *B.J.* iv 8, 1 (443) (ὑπὸ τὴν ἀρχὴν τοῦ ἔαρος); cf. iv 7, 3 (413) (τετράδι Δύστρου). According to the Mishnah, Taan. 1:2, Ned. 8:5, B.M. 8:6, the rainy season was reckoned from the Feast of Tabernacles to Passover, i.e., to the middle or even the end of Nisan.

7. Zonaras, V 14 *fin.* ἦν ἐτῶν ὀγδοήκοντα πρὸς ἑνί. Some of the manuscripts of Josephus also have 81. Hyrcanus, however, cannot have been so old in 27 B.C. for his mother Alexandra Salome did not marry his father Alexander Jannaeus until after the death of her first husband Aristobulus I in 104 B.C.

B.C.

[al. δεκαδύο], i.e. after the conquest of Jerusalem in 37 B.C.; but see Otto, *op. cit.*, cols. 53–4, 56.

? Start of the quadrennial athletic contests. Theatre and amphitheatre built in Jerusalem, *Ant.* xv 8, 1 (267–76).

Conspiracy against Herod, *Ant.* xv 8, 3–4 (280–91).

27/25? Herod sends 500 soldiers to the campaign of Aelius Gallus against Arabia, *Ant.* xv 9, 3 (317), cf. Strabo xvi 4, 23 (780) τῶν συμμάχων, ὧν ἦσαν Ἰουδαῖοι μὲν πεντακόσιοι. The campaign probably ended in 25 B.C., having caused heavy losses and brought no tangible results.[8]

25? Samaria rebuilt and named Sebaste in honour of Augustus, *Ant.* xv 8, 5 (292–8); *B.J.* i 21, 2 (403).[9]

---

8. The most detailed description of the campaign is given by Strabo, xvi 4, 22–4 (780–2), shorter accounts by Dio liii 29, Pliny, *NH* vi 32/160–1, and in *Res Gestae* 26. Cf. generally, Mommsen, *Röm. Geschichte* V, pp. 608 ff. T. Rice Holmes, *The Architect of the Roman Empire* II, pp. 18–20; J. G. C. Anderson in CAH X, pp. 248–52. For the geography see D. H. Müller, 'Arabia', RE II, 344–59; Abel, *Géog. Pal.* I (1933), pp. 288–98; map in Rice Holmes, *op. cit.*, facing p. 15. The chronological problem has been newly discussed by S. Jameson 'Chronology of the Campaigns of Aelius Gallus and C. Petronius' JRS 58 (1968), pp. 71–84. Dio places the whole campaign in the tenth consulship of Augustus, 24 B.C. But according to Strabo the campaign proper did not take place until after Aelius Gallus had gone with great losses, the year before, to Leuce Come, and had been obliged to spend the winter there because of much sickness in his army (Strabo xvi 4, 24 (781) ἠναγκάσθη γοῦν τό τε θέρος καὶ τὸν χειμῶνα διατελέσαι αὐτόθι τοὺς ἀσθενοῦντας ἀνακτώμενος). But since Petronius's prefecture began in 25 B.C. (below) Aelius's campaign must be earlier, probably 26–5 B.C. On the other hand it has sometimes been doubted whether Aelius Gallus conducted the campaign as governor of Egypt and was followed in this office by Petronius, or whether Petronius was governor of Egypt at the time of the Arabian campaign and was succeeded by Gallus. It is known for certain that both held the office of *praefectus Aegypti* (see on Aelius Gallus: Strabo ii 5, 12 (118) and xvii 1, 29 (806); Dio liii 29, 3; on Petronius: Strabo xvii 1, 3 (788) and 1, 53 (819); Dio liv 5, 4; Pliny *NH* vi 35/181). It is also known that Petronius undertook several campaigns against the Ethiopians at about the same time as the expedition of Aelius Gallus to Arabia, *RG* 26 'Meo iussu at auspicio ducti sunt duo exercitus eodem fere tempore in Aethiopiam et in Arabiam quae appellatur Eudaemon'; Strabo xvii i, 54 (820–1); Dio liv 5, 4–6; Pliny *NH* vi 35/181; according to Strabo the Ethiopians invaded the Thebaid when the Egyptian garrison was weakened by the departure of Aelius Gallus; it was this that necessitated the expedition of Petronius. Dio puts this expedition under 22 B.C. On the other hand, it is clear that Aelius Gallus conducted the Arabian campaign as prefect of Egypt (Dio liii 29, 3 ὁ τῆς Αἰγύπτου ἄρχων) and that Petronius was his successor in Egypt (Strabo 820). Since according to Strabo, Petronius conducted two Ethiopian campaigns, they should date to 25–4 B.C.—at the conclusion of which he sent captives to Augustus νεωστὶ ἐκ Καντάβρων ἥκοντι (Strabo 821), i.e., 24 B.C.—and the second in perhaps 23–2 B.C. Petronius will have succeeded Gallus in the second half of 25 B.C., the 13th year of Herod, cf. *Ant.* xv 9, 1–2 (299–307).

9. According to Josephus it certainly appears as if the rebuilding took place in 25 B.C. For after reporting it in *Ant.* xv 8, 5 (292–8), he continues in xv 9, 1 (299) κατὰ τοῦτον μὲν οὖν τὸν ἐνιαυτὸν τρισκαιδέκατον ὄντα τῆς Ἡρώδου βασιλείας. But the 13th year of Herod began on 1st Nisan 25 B.C. The coins of Samaria (see *BMC Palestine*. pp. xxxvii–xli, do not provide any reliable evidence for putting

B.C.

Famine and pestilence, *κατὰ τοῦτον μὲν οὖν τὸν ἐνιαυτὸν, τρισκαιδέκατον ὄντα τῆς Ἡρώδου βασιλείας* = 25/24 B.C., from Nisan to Nisan, *Ant.* xv 9, 1 (299). The famine persisted through a further failure of the harvest, *Ant.* xv 9, 1 (302), and Herod appealed for aid to Petronius, Prefect of Egypt, *Ant.* xv 9, 2 (307).

? Herod builds himself a royal palace and marries the priest's daughter, Mariamme, *Ant.* xv 9, 3 (317–22). For the name see *B.J.* i 28, 4 (562); 29, 2 (573); 30, 7 (599).

23/2 The sons of the first Mariamme, Alexander and Aristobulus, are sent to Rome for their education, *Ant.* xv 10, 1 (342); cf. Otto, *op. cit.*, col. 70 and note.

Augustus gives Herod the districts of Trachonitis, Batanaea and Auranitis, *Ant.* xv 10, 1 (343–8); *B.J.* i 20, 4 (398–400) *μετὰ δὲ τὴν πρώτην Ἀκτιάδα*).[10]

Herod visits Agrippa in Mytilene in Lesbos, *Ant.* xv 10, 2 (350).[11]

The building of Caesarea is started, *Ant.* xv 9, 6 (331–41). As it was completed in 10 B.C. after twelve years of work (see below), operations must have begun in 22 B.C.

20 Augustus comes to Syria and presents Herod with the territory of Zenodorus, *Ant.* xv 10, 3 (354) *ἤδη δ' αὐτοῦ τῆς βασιλείας ἑπτακαιδεκάτου*

---

the date any further back; the name of the city at any rate cannot precede 27 B.C., the year in which (in January) the Emperor received the name "Augustus". There are, however, clear chronological uncertainties here. The execution of Costobar, recorded in *Ant.* xv 7, 10 (259–66), took place apparently in the 13th year of Herod. After this, in xv 8, 1–5 (267–98), follows a whole series of happenings which cannot possibly all have occurred within one year. And then, in xv 9, 1 (299), we find ourselves still in the 13th year of Herod. In addition, the whole section xv 8, 1–5 (267–98) has obviously been composed for a particular purpose, in that Josephus is assembling accounts of how Herod caused offence and annoyance through illegal actions; of how the people's irritation expressed itself in words and deeds; and of the precautions Herod took to control the masses inclined to rebellion. Considering all this, and bearing in mind that Josephus worked from several sources (see p. 51 above), it is highly probable that in Josephus's main source xv 9, 1 (299 ff.) followed immediately xv 7, 10 (259–66); that xv 8, 1–5 (267–98) has been interpolated from another source; and that the words *κατὰ τοῦτον μὲν οὖν τὸν ἐνιαυτόν* etc. of Josephus have been taken over without alteration from his main source where it referred, not to the time of the rebuilding of Samaria, but to that of Costobar's execution. In this way, all the difficulties are solved. Otto, *Herodes*, col. 80 also dissociates xv 9, 1 (299 ff.) from xv 8, 1–5 (267–98), but he does not regard it as the immediate continuation of xv 7, 10 (259–66). Moreover, Otto, col. 56, note, suggests a textual emendation by which the execution of Costobar would date to 28/7 B.C.

10. The games at Actium were celebrated on 2 Sept., for the first time in 28 B.C., then in the years, 24, 20, 16 etc. The extension of territory made 'on the completion of the first Actiad' thus took place at the end of 24 or the beginning of 23 B.C.

11. Josephus says merely that Herod visited Agrippa *περὶ Μυτιλήνην χειμάζοντι*. Since Agrippa was in Mytilene from the spring of 23 to the spring of 21 B.C., this can have been the winter of either 23/22 or 22/21 B.C. Otto, *Herodes* (1913), p. 70, prefers the latter date. But if, as is generally agreed, the chief aim of Herod's visit was to prove his loyalty, he is likely to have made it as soon as possible, i.e. in the winter of 23/22 rather than that of 22/21 B.C.; thus M. Reinhold, *Marcus Agrippa* (1933), p. 84, n. 47.

B.C.

παρελθόντος ἔτους (the 17th year of Herod ended on 1 Nisan 20 B.C.), *B.J.* i 20, 4 (399) *ἔτει δεκάτῳ πάλιν ἐλθὼν εἰς τὴν ἐπαρχίαν* (i.e. reckoned from the end of 30 B.C.). Dio liv 7, 4–6, places the journey of Augustus to Syria in the consulship of M. Appuleius and P. Silius Nerva (20 B.C.). Dio liv 9, 3 also mentions the gift.

Pheroras is named tetrarch of Peraea, *Ant.* xv 10, 3 (362); *B.J.* i 24, 5 (483), cf. 30, 3 (586).

20/19 Herod remits one third of the taxes, *Ant.* xv 10, 4 (365).

The building of the Temple starts, *Ant.* xv 11, 1 (380) *ὀκτωκαιδεκάτου τῆς Ἡρῴδου βασιλείας γεγονότος ἐνιαυτοῦ* (=20/19).[12]

18/17 Herod brings home his sons Alexander and Aristobulus from Rome (Herod's first Roman journey),[13] *Ant.* xvi 1, 2 (6). Since Herod met Augustus in Italy but Augustus did not return there till the summer of 19 B.C., Herod's journey must have occurred after the middle of 19 B.C., but before the summer of 16 B.C., since Augustus was in Gaul from the summer of 16 to the spring of 13 B.C.[14]

15 Agrippa visits Herod in Jerusalem, *Ant.* xvi 2, 1 (13); Philo, *Legatio* 37 (294–7). He leaves Judaea again before the end of the year: *ἐπιβαίνοντος τοῦ χειμῶνος*.[15]

14 Herod with Agrippa in Asia Minor, *Ant.* xvi 2, 2–5 (16–62) *ἔαρος ἠπείγετο συντυχεῖν αὐτῷ*. Cf. also *Ant.* xii 3, 2 (125–6); Nic. Dam., FGrH 90 F 134.

On his return he remits a quarter of the taxes, *Ant.* xvi 2, 5 (64).

---

12. According to *B.J.* i 21, 1 (401) in the 15th year, which is either incorrect or refers to the start of building preparations. That the construction of the Temple began in 20/19 B.C. is certain because it coincided with the arrival of the emperor in Syria, which according to Dio liv 7, 6, took place in the spring or summer of 20 B.C. Construction of the outer courts lasted eight years, and that of the Temple itself a year and a half (*Ant.* xv 11, 5–6 (410–23); it is not clear whether these $8 + 1\frac{1}{2}$ years should be added together, or whether the year and a half represents the first part of the building period as a whole). After the completion of the Temple a great festival was arranged. As this occurred on the day of Herod's accession to the throne, *Ant.* xv 11, 6 (423), the building of the Temple began—provided we are right in assuming that the accession took place in July—in the winter, i.e. at the end of 20, or the beginning of 19 B.C. Accordingly, the statement in Jn. 2:20, at the time of a Passover, that the Temple was built in forty-six years (*τεσσαράκοντα καὶ ἓξ ἔτεσιν ᾠκοδομήθη ὁ ναὸς οὗτος*), points—depending on whether the 46th year is regarded as current or ended—to the Passover of A.D. 27 or A.D. 28. See C. Wieseler, *Chronolog. Synopse*, pp. 165 f. (E.T. pp. 151 ff.); *Beiträge*, pp. 156 ff.; J. van Bebber, *Zur Chronologie des Lebens Jesu* (1898), pp. 123 ff.; T. Corbishley, 'The Chronology of the Reign of Herod the Great', JThSt 36 (1935), pp. 22–32; G. Ogg, *The Chronology of the Public Ministry of Jesus* (1940), pp. 153–67; C. K. Barrett, *The Gospel according to St. John* (1955), p. 167; J. Jeremias, *Jerusalem in the Time of Jesus* (1969), pp. 21–2.

13. I.e. since his accession to the throne, therefore without counting the journey made in 40/39 B.C.

14. For the evidence on Augustus's movements see RE X, cols. 355–8.

15. For the chronology of Agrippa's movements in the East, to which he went in late 17 or early 16 B.C., see M. Reinhold, *Marcus Agrippa* (1933), pp. 106–23. That Agrippa did not arrive in Palestine till 15 B.C., and that Herod did not go to Agrippa in Asia Minor till 14 B.C., follows from the fact that Herod met Agrippa in Sinope on his expedition to the Crimea, and that expedition, according to Dio liv 24 (cf. Euseb. *Chron. ad ann. Abr.* 2003) took place in 14 B.C.

B.C.

Beginning of the dissensions with Alexander and Aristobulus, the sons of Mariamme. Antipater is brought to the court, *Ant.* xvi 3, 1–3 (66–85); *B.J.* i 23, 1 (445–48).

13 Antipater is sent to Rome with Agrippa to present himself to the emperor, *Ant.* xvi 3, 3 (86); *B.J.* i 23, 2 (451). On the date cf. Dio liv 28, 1.

12 Herod goes to Rome with his sons Alexander and Aristobulus to accuse them before the emperor (Herod's second Roman journey). He meets the emperor in Aquileia. Augustus settles the quarrel. Antipater accompanies them back to Judaea, *Ant.* xvi 4, 1–6 (87–135); *B.J.* i 23, 3–5 (452–66).[16]

10 The dedication of Caesarea takes place εἰς ὄγδοον καὶ εἰκοστὸν ἔτος τῆς ἀρχῆς (=10/9 B.C.), *Ant.* xvi 5, 1 (136), after 12 years of building, *Ant.* xv 9, 6 (341) ἐξετελέσθη δωδεκαετεῖ χρόνῳ. xvi 5, 1 (136) is probably wrong in giving ten years). On the building cf. also *B.J.* i 21, 5–8 (408–16).

? The discord in Herod's family grows increasingly serious and complex, *Ant.* xvi 7, 2–6 (188–228); *B.J.* i 24, 1–6 (467–87).

? Herod tries to establish Alexander's guilt by torturing his supporters; Alexander is imprisoned, *Ant.* xvi 8, 1–5 (229–60); *B.J.* i 24, 7–8 (488–97).

10? Archelaus, king of Cappadocia and Alexander's father-in-law, effects another reconciliation between Herod and his sons, *Ant.* xvi 8, 6 (261–70). *B.J.* i 25, 1–6 (498–512).

? Herod's third journey to Rome, *Ant.* xvi 8, 6–9, 1 (270–1).[17]

9? Campaign against the Nabataeans, *Ant.* xvi 9, 2 (282–5).

8? Herod in disfavour with Augustus, *Ant.* xvi 9, 3 (286–92).

Herod extorts by torture new incriminatory statements against Alexander and Aristobulus, has them both imprisoned, and brings an accusation against them of high treason to Augustus, *Ant.* xvi 10, 3–7 (313–34); *B.J.* i 26, 3 (526–9), 27, 1 (534–7).

---

16. Decisive for this date is the fact that during Herod's stay on that occasion in Rome, Augustus promoted games and 'distributed presents among the Roman people' (Jos. *Ant.* xvi 4, 5 (128): Ἡρῴδης μὲν ἐδωρεῖτο Καίσαρα τριακοσίοις ταλάντοις θέας τε καὶ διανομὰς ποιούμενον τῷ Ῥωμαίων δήμῳ). This must be the fourth *liberalitas* of Augustus dating to 12 B.C.; there was no other between 24 B.C. and 5 B.C. (they are listed in *Res Gestae*, 15); see *Dizionario Epigrafico* s.v. 'liberalitas', p. 840. There is admittedly no direct evidence that Augustus went to Aquileia in this year. But he may well have done so on the occasion of Tiberius's Pannonian campaign, which took place then (Dio liv 31; cf. Suet. *Div. Aug.* 20: 'Reliqua bella per legatos administravit, ut tamen quibusdam Pannonicis atque Germanicis aut interveniret aut non longe abesset, Ravennam vel Mediolanium vel Aquileiam usque ab urbe progrediens').

17. It is not universally accepted that Herod made a third journey to Rome. Concluding his account of the reconciliation affected by Archelaus, Josephus in *B.J.* i 25, 5 (510) has δεῖν μέντοι πάντως ἔφη πέμπειν αὐτὸν (Alexander) εἰς Ῥώμην Καίσαρι διαλεξόμενον, but in *Ant.* xvi 8, 6–9, 1 (270–1) he has (Herod) ἐποιήσατο δὲ καὶ συνθήκας εἰς Ῥώμην ἐλθεῖν . . . γενομένῳ δὲ ἐν τῇ Ῥώμῃ κἀκεῖθεν ἐπανήκοντι συνέστη πόλεμος πρὸς τοὺς Ἄραβας ἐξ αἰτίας τοιαύτης. The subsequent narrative (273) refers to Herod πλεύσαντος δ' εἰς τὴν Ῥώμην ὅτε καὶ τοῦ παιδὸς Ἀλεξάνδρου κατηγόρει (clearly the second journey of 12 B.C.) and then a second time to Herod's return from Rome (276). Otto, *op. cit.*, cols. 125–6 therefore argues, probably correctly, that this evidence does not support the view that there was a third journey. Schalit, *op. cit.*, p. 613, accepts the third journey but without detailed discussion.

B.C.

7? Augustus, with whom, through the good offices of Nicolaus of Damascus, Herod is once more in favour, *Ant.* xvi 10, 8–9 (335–55), authorizes him to deal with his sons according to his own discretion, *Ant.* xvi 11, 1 (356); *B.J.* i 27, 1 (537).

Alexander and Aristobulus are condemned to death at Berytus and strangled at Sebaste (Samaria), *Ant.* xvi 11, 2–7 (361–94); *B.J.* i 27, 2–6 (538–51).[18]

Antipater is all-powerful at Herod's court, *Ant.* xvii 1, 1 (1–11), 2, 4 (32–40); *B.J.* i 28, 1 (552–5), 29, 1 (567–70).

Execution of suspected Pharisees, *Ant.* xvii 2, 4 (41–5).

6? Antipater goes to Rome, *Ant.* xvii 3, 2 (52 f.); *B.J.* i 29, 2 (573).

Herod's first will, nominating Antipater as his successor, or if the latter should predecease him, the son of the second Mariamme, *Ant.* xvii 3, 2 (53); *B.J.* i 29, 2 (573).

5 Beginning of the year: death of Pheroras, Herod's brother, *Ant.* xvii 3, 3 (59); *B.J.* i 29, 4 (580).

Herod learns of Antipater's conspiracy, *Ant.* xvii 4, 1–2 (61–78); *B.J.* i 30, 1–7 (582–600).

Antipater returns to Judaea, *Ant.* xvii 5, 1–2 (83–92); *B.J.* i 31, 3–5 (608–19), seven months after Herod made his discovery, *Ant.* xvii 4, 3 (82); *B.J.* i 1, 32 (606).

Antipater on trial; he defends himself without success and is put in irons, *Ant.* xvii 5, 3–7 (93–132); *B.J.* i 32, 1–5 (620–40).

Herod sends a report to the emperor, *Ant.* xvii 5, 7–8 (133–45); *B.J.* i 32, 5 (640).

Herod falls ill and makes a second will naming his youngest son, Antipas, as his successor, *Ant.* xvii 6, 1 (146); *B.J.* i 32, 7 (645–6).

4 Popular uprising under the leadership of the rabbis Judas and Matthias sternly avenged by Herod, *Ant.* xvii 6, 2–4 (149–67); *B.J.* i 33, 1–4 (647–55).

Herod's health deteriorates, *Ant.* xvii 6, 5 (168–79); *B.J.* i 33, 5 (656–8).

On the authority of the emperor, Antipater is executed, *Ant.* xvii 7 (182–7); *B.J.* i 33, 7 (661–4).

Herod alters his will once more, naming Archelaus king, and Antipas and Philip tetrarchs, *Ant.* xvii 8, 1 (189–90); *B.J.* i 33 ,7 (664).

Herod dies five days after Antipater's execution βασιλεύσας μεθ' ὃ μὲν ἀνεῖλεν 'Αντίγονον, ἔτη τέσσαρα καὶ τριάκοντα, μεθ' ὃ δὲ ὑπὸ 'Ρωμαίων ἀπεδέδεικτο, ἑπτὰ καὶ τριάκοντα, *Ant.* xvii 8, 1 (191); *B.J.* i 33 ,8 (665).[19]

Herod[20], it seemed, was born to rule. Endowed with strength and stamina, he accustomed himself from an early age to hardships of

18. Since Saturninus was governor of Syria at the time of the condemnation, *Ant,* xvi 11, 3 (368), and indeed for some time afterwards, *Ant.* xvii 1, 1 (6); 2, 1 (24); 3, 2 (37), it must have taken place in 7 B.C., for he left Syria not later than the first half of 6 B.C. (see p. 257).

19. On the year of Herod's death, see note 165 below.

20. The name Ἡρῴδης (from ἥρως) also occurs elsewhere, see CIG, index p. 92, Pape-Benseler, *Wörterb. der griech. Eigennamen*, *s.v.* For Athenians of this name in the pre-Christian period, see Kirchner, *Prosopographia* (1901–3), nos. 6537–45.

all sorts. He was an excellent horseman and a good hunter. In contests he was feared. His lance went home unfailingly, and his arrow seldom missed its mark.[21] He was trained in war from his youth. By the time he was twenty-five years old, he had already won a reputation by his campaign against the brigands in Galilee. And again in the last years of his life, as a man over sixty, he personally led a campaign against the Nabataeans.[22] Success seldom eluded him when he himself directed a military enterprise.

By nature he was wild, passionate, hard and unyielding. Finer feelings and tenderness were foreign to him. Wherever his own interests seemed to demand it, he wielded an iron hand even at the cost of rivers of blood. If necessary, he spared neither his nearest relations nor his passionately loved wife.

He was furthermore shrewd, clever and resourceful, with a clear understanding of what measures to apply to an existing situation. Hard and relentless towards all who were in his power, he was nevertheless meek and pliable towards his superiors. His eye was sufficiently wide in its range, and his judgment sufficiently acute, to perceive that in the international position of that time nothing could be achieved except through the favour, and with the help, of the Romans. It was, therefore, an inviolable principle of his policy to maintain his friendship with Rome under all circumstances and at any price. And he managed with luck and skill to implement this principle. Thus in him cunning and enterprise went hand in hand. These conspicuous talents were set in motion by an insatiable ambition. All his thoughts, desires, plans and actions were at all times directed to the one end, the extension of his power, dominion and glory.[23] This stimulus kept all his resources ceaselessly active. Difficulties and hindrances were for him just so many incentives to increased effort. And this flexibility, this spirit of untiring endeavour, remained with him until extreme old age.

It was only through the combination of all these qualities that he

---

Compare the famous second century A.D. rhetor Herodes Atticus, i.e. L. Vibullius Hipparchus T. Claudius Atticus Herodes, PIR² C 802, cf. 801. Since the name is doubtless contracted from *Ἡρωΐδης*, the spelling with iota subscript (*Ἡρῴδης*) is certainly preferable. In inscriptions we find *Ἡρώιδης*, *IG*² II 4992, OGIS III, I. 14; 130, II. 3, 18, also *Ἡρωΐδας* (e.g. OGIS 8 I. 37, also *Ἡρώιδεια*, e.g. IG XIV 645, II. 15, 42, 55, 87, 89, 114. One of the manuscripts of Josephus, the very correct *cod. Ambrosianus* has *Ἡρώιδης* throughout (Niese III, p. vii). *The Etymologicum magnum* ed. Gaisford, col. 397, states *s.v.* *Ἡρώιδης*: *Ἔχει τὸ ι προσγεγραμμένον etc.*

21. Cf. the description given in *B.J.* i 21, 13 (429–30).

22. *Ant.* xvi 9, 2 (282–5).

23. Cf. the apposite characterization in Jos. *Ant.* xvi 5, 4 (150–9).

was able, in such testing conditions, to achieve as much as he undoubtedly did.[24]

His reign may be divided into three periods.[25] The first, extending from about 37 to 25 B.C., sees the consolidation of his authority. He has still to contend with many hostile powers, but emerges victorious from all his battles. The second period, 25–13 B.C., is the era of his prosperity. His friendship of Rome is at its zenith. Agrippa visits Herod in Jerusalem. Herod is repeatedly received by the emperor. It is also the period of his great buildings, of works of peace in general. The third period, 13–4 B.C., sees his domestic miseries, which now take precedence over everything else.

I

In the first period of his reign Herod had to contend with four hostile forces: the people, the nobility, the Hasmonaean family and Cleopatra.

The people, who were largely influenced by the Pharisees, bore with profound reluctance the rule of the Idumaean, a half-Jew and friend of the Romans.[26] Herod's first preoccupation must have been to ensure their obedience. By using the utmost severity he managed to suppress the opposition, and won over the more tractable with favours and honours. Two of the Pharisees themselves, Pollio (Abtalion), and his pupil Sameas (Shemaiah or Shammai?), rendered Herod good service in this connexion. They saw subjection to a foreigner as a divine punishment which should be borne willingly.[27] Among the Jerusalem nobility there were still numerous adherents of Antigonus. Herod disposed of these by executing forty-five of the most eminent and wealthy among them. By confiscating their property, he came at the same time into possession of great wealth, which he badly needed if he were to keep his patron Antonius in good humour.[28]

Of the members of the Hasmonaean family, Herod's mother-in-law

24. Unfortunately, no portrait exists of Herod the Great. A statue of him must have stood in the temple at Si'a near Kanawat, but only its base has been preserved, OGIS 415 (see note 61 below); see D. Sourdel, *Les cultes du Hauran à l'époque romaine* (1952), p. 21. Herod's coins never show his effigy. Cf. A. Reifenberg, 'Portrait Coins of the Herodian Kings', Numismatic Circular 43 (1935), pp. 172–6.

25. Compare the slightly different periodisation in Otto *op. cit.*

26. Herod is called *Ἡμιιουδαῖος* in *Ant.* xiv 15, 2 (403). The Idumaeans were first converted by John Hyrcanus. See p. 207 above. On Herod's ancestry see p. 234.

27. *Ant.* xv 1, 1 (3 f.); cf. xiv 9, 4 (172–6). On Pollio and Sameas see vol. II, § 25, iv; cf. Schalit, *op. cit.*, Anhang X.

28. *Ant.* xv 1, 2 (5–7); cf. xiv 9, 4 (175); *B.J.* i 18, 4 (358).

in particular, Alexandra, the mother of Mariamme, treated him with undisguised enmity. The aged Hyrcanus had of course returned from his Parthian captivity,[29] but he had always been on good terms with Herod. And this harmony continued undisturbed. As Hyrcanus was unable to resume the office of High Priest because of his physical mutilation, Herod chose as High Priest a completely unknown and insignificant Babylonian Jew of sacerdotal lineage named Hananel.[30] But Alexandra regarded even this as an infringement of Hasmonaean privileges. In her opinion, her young son Aristobulus, Mariamme's brother, was the only person entitled to be High Priest. She accordingly set out to enforce her claim. In particular, she turned to Cleopatra with the idea that, through her influence with Antonius, Herod might be compelled to install Aristobulus. Mariamme also importuned her husband with petitions in favour of her brother. In the end, Herod found himself obliged to remove Hananel (which was unlawful since the High Priest held office for life), and to install the seventeen-year-old Aristobulus as High Priest (beginning of 35 B.C.).[31]

Peace, however, did not last for long. Not without reason, Herod saw all the members of the Hasmonaean family as his natural enemies. He could not rid himself of suspicion and distrust, especially in regard to Alexandra, and had her carefully watched. Alexandra for her part found this intolerable and planned to escape his supervision. Coffins were prepared in which she and her son Aristobulus were to be carried out of the city by night so that they could then travel by sea to Egypt and Cleopatra. But the scheme was betrayed and thwarted, and served merely to intensify Herod's mistrust.[32] When, in addition to all this, the people at the next Feast of Tabernacles (35 B.C.) openly acclaimed the young Aristobulus while he officiated as High Priest, Herod firmly determined to rid himself of him without delay as his most dangerous rival. The opportunity to do so soon came. Herod was invited by Alexandra to a banquet in Jericho. As the young Aristobulus was amusing himself after the meal with the others in the bath, he was ducked as though in fun by some companions bribed by Herod and held under until he drowned. Afterwards, Herod stimulated the deepest grief and shed tears, which no one regarded as genuine.[33]

Alexandra, who realized the true facts of the case, again agitated

29. *Ant.* xv 2, 1–4 (11–22).

30. *Ant.* xv 2, 4 (22). Herod could not himself assume the dignity because he was not even of pure Jewish descent, let alone of sacerdotal lineage. On Hananel see Schalit, *op. cit.*, pp. 693–5; J. Neusner, *A History of the Jews in Babylonia* I ([2]1969), pp. 37–8.

31. *Ant.* xv 2, 5–7 (23–38); 3, 1 (39–41). For the chronology, the reader is referred once and for all to the summary given above.

32. *Ant.* xv 3, 2 (42–9).

33. *Ant.* xv 3, 3–4 (50–61); *B.J.* i 22, 2 (435–7).

with Cleopatra that Herod should be held to account before Antonius. Antonius, who had again been in the east since the spring of 36 B.C. under the spell of Cleopatra, was just then (spring of 34 B.C.) undertaking a new expedition eastwards, ostensibly against the Parthians, but actually against the Armenian king Artavasdes. When he arrived in Laodicea (no doubt the Laodicea on the coast south of Antioch) Herod was summoned to meet him there—for Alexandra with the help of Cleopatra had obtained her wish—to account for the misdeed. Herod dared not refuse, and although with a heavy heart, presented himself before Antonius. Needless to say he did not arrive empty-handed, and this circumstance, together with his adroit performance, soon dispelled the clouds. He was acquitted, and returned to Jerusalem.[34]

His absence was the cause of fresh difficulties. On his departure, he had appointed as regent his uncle Joseph (who was also his brother-in-law, for he had married his sister Salome), and had entrusted Mariamme to his care. Regarding his journey to Antonius as dangerous, he had commanded Joseph, if he failed to return, to put Mariamme to death also, for in his passionate love of her he could not bear the thought that anyone else should have his beloved. But when he came back, Salome slandered her own husband, alleging that he had been guilty of adultery with Mariamme. At first, Herod turned a deaf ear to the slander, since Mariamme protested her innocence. But on learning that she was aware of his secret command, which the garrulous old man had imparted to her as proof of Herod's special love, Herod saw this as confirming the charges and ordered Joseph to be executed without a hearing.[35]

The fourth hostile force in this first period of Herod's reign was Cleopatra. She had already brought him trouble through her association with Alexandra. Worse than this, however, she now wished to employ her influence over Antonius to acquire new territories. Antonius first offered some resistance to her demands. But probably in 37/6 B.C. he was persuaded to grant her the whole Phoenician and Philistine coast south of the Eleutherus, with the exception of Tyre and Sidon, and in addition, in 34 B.C., a part of Nabataean territory and the most beautiful and fertile region of Herod's kingdom, the celebrated district of Jericho with its palm and balsam plantations.[36] Opposition on the

[*Text continues on p.* 300

34. *Ant.* xv 3, 5 (62–7), 8–9 (74–87).

35. *Ant.* xv 3, 5–6 (62–70), 9 (80–7). On the parallel passages *B.J.* i 22, 4–5 (441–4) see n. 51 below.

36. The region of Jericho was at that time the most fertile and productive part of Palestine. This is stated in clear terms by Strabo xvi 2, 41 (763) and Josephus *B.J.* iv 8, 3 (459–75). Near *Ἱερικοῦς* there was, according to Strabo, the palm grove (*ὁ φοινικών*) extending to a hundred stadia, and the balsam garden (*ὁ τοῦ*

βαλσάμου παράδεισος) which yielded the expensive balsam resin used as a medicament. Josephus, also, emphasises that the date palm and the balsam bush were the two main crops of the district. The area, which owing to its abundant water and hot climate was peculiarly productive, is estimated by Josephus as extending to twenty stadia in breadth and seventy in length. Because of the high value of both these products, cf. Strabo xvii 15 (800), Josephus rightly designates the district a θεῖον χωρίον, ἐν ᾧ δαψιλῆ τὰ σπανιώτατα καὶ κάλλιστα γεννᾶται, *B.J.* iv 8, 3 (469). Elsewhere, also, he takes every opportunity to emphasize the fertility of the district of Jericho with its palm and balsam plantations, *Ant.* iv 6, 1 (100); xiv 4, 1 (54) = *B.J.* i 6, 6 (138); *Ant.* xv 4, 2 (96) = *B.J.* i 18, 5 (361). In one passage he expressly declares it the most fruitful district of Judaea, *B.J.* i 6, 6 (138) τὸ τῆς Ἰουδαίας πιότατον. Herod later extended the palm plantations as far as Phasaelis (see vol. II, § 23, 1). Archelaus built near Jericho a new aqueduct to irrigate the palm grove there, *Ant.* xvii 13, 1 (340). In Pompeius Trogus also Jericho is mentioned as the centre of the palm and balsam plantations of the Jordan valley, Justin, *Epit.* xxxvi 3, 1–3, 'Opes genti ex vectigalibus opobalsami crevere, quod in his tantum regionibus gignitur. Est namque vallis, quae continuis montibus velut muro quodam ad instar hortorum clauditur (spatium loci ducenta iugera; nomine Ericus dicitur). In ea silva est et ubertate et amoenitate insignis, siquidem palmeto et opobalsameto distinguitur'. (There follows a description of the balsam bush, which is cultivated in the same way as the vine and exudes balsam yearly at a certain season.) Diodorus places the palm and balsam plantations in general in the neighbourhood of the Dead Sea, for after describing the latter he proceeds (ii 48, 9, almost word-for-word as in xix 98, 4): ἀγαθὴ δ᾽ἐστὶ φοινικόφυτος . . . γίνεται δὲ περὶ τοὺς τόπους τούτους ἐν αὐλῶνί τινι καὶ τὸ καλούμενον βάλσαμον, ἐξ οὗ πρόσοδον λαμπρὰν, [xix 98, 4: ἁδρὰν] λαμβάνουσιν, οὐδαμοῦ μὲν τῆς ἄλλης οἰκουμένης εὑρισκομένου τοῦ φυτοῦ τούτου, τῆς δ᾽ ἐξ αὐτοῦ χρείας εἰς φάρμακα τοῖς ἰατροῖς καθ᾽ ὑπερβολὴν εὐθετούσης. According to Pliny the dates of Jericho were the choicest in the world, *NH* xiii 9/44 'sed ut copia ibi [in Aethiopiae fine] atque fertilitas, ita nobilitas in Iudaea, nec in tota, sed Hiericunte maxime, quamquam laudata et Archelaide et Phaselide atque Liviade, gentis eiusdem convallibus'. Cf. xiii 6/26 'Iudaea vero incluta est vel magis palmis'; xiii 9/49 'Servantur hi demum qui nascuntur in salsis atque sabulosis, ut in Iudaea atque Cyrenaica Africa'. Pliny's detailed discussion of the balsam (*NH* xii 54/111–23) opens with the following words: 'Sed omnibus odoribus praefertur balsamum, uni terrarum Iudaeae concessum, quondam in duobus tantum hortis, utroque regio, altero iugerum XX non amplius, altero pauciorum'. The extraction of the balsam was effected in this way: the bark was slit with a stone, not iron, instrument; the thick sap then gushed out and was collected in small vessels. Tacitus also in *Hist.* v 6 mentions 'balsamum et palmae' as peculiar products of Palestine. He describes the extraction of the balsam as does Pliny, cf. also Strabo xvi, 2 41 (763) and Josephus, *Ant.* xiv 4, 1 (54); *B.J.* i 6, 6 (138); Pausanias stresses as a special excellence of Palestine the fact that in it the palm trees 'always' (i.e. every year) yield an enjoyable fruit (in ix 19, 8 he says of the shrine at Mycalessus in Boeotia Φοίνικες δὲ πρὸ τοῦ ἱεροῦ πεφύκασιν οὐκ ἐς ἅπαν ἐδώδιμον παρεχόμενοι καρπὸν ὥσπερ ἐν τῇ Παλαιστίνῃ). To Horace the material worth of these plantations was well known. He speaks of 'Herodis palmetis pinguibus' (*Epist.* ii 2, 184) as an example of a particularly rich and productive estate. According to Dioscorides i 19, 1, the balsam used as a medicament grew only in Judaea and Egypt, βάλσαμον . . . γεννώμενον ἐν μόνῃ Ἰουδαίᾳ κατά τινα αὐλῶνα [καὶ ἐν Αἰγύπτῳ]. The existence of the palm groves of Jericho can be traced throughout a period of some two thousand years. In the Old Testament Jericho is already called 'the city of palm trees' (עיר התמרים, Dt. 34:3; Jg. 1:16; 3:13; 2 Chr. 28:15). Among Greek writers, Theophrastus, the pupil of Aristotle, already mentions the palm and balsam plantations of the Jordan valley. He says of the

part of Herod was unthinkable, and he was now obliged to lease his own land from Cleopatra.[37] Moreover, he had to put a good face on it, and receive Cleopatra with all honours and entertain her royally when she visited Judaea on her way back from the Euphrates, where she had accompanied Antonius. But when she tried to seduce him too, and thus trap him, he was astute enough not have closer dealings with her.[38]

The first four or five years of Herod's reign were thus spent in various struggles for his own existence. The outbreak of the war between Antonius and Octavian in 32 B.C. brought fresh anxieties. Herod wished to hasten to Antonius's aid with a considerable military force, but at Cleopatra's instigation, was commanded by Antonius to make war on the Nabataean king. Latterly, this king had not been paying his regular tribute to Cleopatra and was to be punished for it. And Cleopatra desired the war to be transferred to Herod so that the two vassal princes might weaken and exhaust one another. So, instead of advancing against Octavian, Herod marched against the Nabataeans. At first he was successful. But when Athenion, Cleopatra's general,

---

palms that it is only in three places in Coele-Syria with a saline soil that fruit can be grown suitable for preservation (*Hist. Plant.* ii 6, 2 *καὶ τῆς Συρίας δὲ τῆς Κοίλης, ἐν ᾗ γ' οἱ πλεῖστοι τυγχάνουσιν, ἐν τρισὶ μόνοις τόποις ἁλμώδεσιν εἶναι τοὺς δυναμένους θησαυρίζεσθαι.* Cf. ii 6, 8 *θησαυρίζεσθαι δὲ μόνους δύνασθαί φασι τῶν ἐν Συρίᾳ τοὺς ἐν τῷ αὐλῶνι.* According to ii 6, 5 this *αὐλών* of Syria, where the palms grow, extends to the Red Sea). With regard to the balsam he says in *Hist. Plant.* ix 6, 1 *τὸ δὲ βάλσαμον γίνεται μὲν ἐν τῷ αὐλῶνι τῷ περὶ Συρίαν. παραδείσους δ' εἶναί φασι δύο μόνους, τὸν μὲν ὅσον εἴκοσι πλέθρων τὸν δ' ἕτερον πολλῷ ἐλάττονα* (Pliny follows this in the passage given above). In the Mishnah it is related that the inhabitants of Jericho are in the habit of grafting the palm (mPes. 4:8). Cf. *Expositio totius mundi* (ed. Rougé, 1966), 31. The existence of the palm groves there continues to be attested by the Christian pilgrims Arculf in the seventh century (see Tobler and Molinier, *Itinera Hierosolymitana* I (1879), p. 176=Geyer, *Itinera Hierosol.* (1898), pp. 263 f.; *Early Travels in Palestine*, ed. T. Wright (1848), p. 7), and Saewulf in the beginning of the twelfth century (see Guérin, *Samarie* I, p. 49; *Early Travels in Palestine*, p. 45). In 1838, Robinson saw there one palm tree (Robinson, *Biblical Researches in Palestine* (^{2}1856) I, p. 559), which in 1888 was only a stump (ZDPV 11 (1888), p. 98). Cf. the articles 'Balsambaum' RE II, 2836 ff.; 'Balsam' and 'Palm Tree' in *Ency. Bibl.* I, cols. 466–8; III, cols. 3551–3 and in JE, I, pp. 466–7; IX, pp. 505–6; H.N. and A. L. Moldenke, *Plants of the Bible* (1952), pp. 169–72 (on the palm tree), pp. 183 f. (on balsam); W. Walker, *All the Plants of the Bible* (1958). On Jericho and its neighbourhood, see *The Survey of Western Palestine, Memoirs by Conder and Kitchener* III, p. 222 (with plan of the aqueducts near Jericho in Roman times); E. Sellin and C. Watzinger, *Jericho. Die Ergebnisse der Ausgrabungen* (1913); J. and J. B. E. Garstang, *The Story of Jericho* (1948); J. L. Kelso and D. C. Baramki, *Excavations at N.T. Jericho and Kherbet en-Nitla* (1955); K. M. Kenyon: *Digging up Jericho* (1957); J. B. Pritchard, *The Excavations at Herodian Jericho, 1951* (1958).

37. *Ant.* xv 4, 1–2 (88–103); *B.J.* i 18, 5 (361–2). Plut., *Ant.* 36.

38. *Ant.* xv 4, 2 (97–103); *B.J.* i 18, 5 (361–2).

went to their help, Herod was severely defeated and found himself obliged to discontinue the major war and apply himself merely to expeditions of robbery and plunder.[39]

Meanwhile, in the spring of 31 B.C., he was overcome by a new calamity: a terrible earthquake struck the country, costing the lives of 30,000 people. Herod now wished to negotiate for peace with the Nabataeans, but they assassinated his envoys and renewed their attack. Herod needed to use all his eloquence to induce his dejected troops to renew the struggle. But this time his fortune in war once more held good. He completely routed the Nabataean army, and compelled the remnant, which had taken refuge in a fortress, into an early surrender. Proud of this brilliant success, he returned home.[40]

Soon afterwards, on 2 Sept. 31 B.C., the decisive battle of Actium was fought in which Antonius lost his power for good. It was at the same time a severe blow for Herod. But with the adroitness characteristic of him, he went over at the right time to the victor's camp, and soon found an opportunity to give concrete proof of his change of heart. In Cyzicus, a troop of Antonius's gladiators had been training for the games with which Antonius had intended to celebrate his victory over Octavian. When these men heard of their master's defeat, they wished to hurry to Egypt to his help. But Didius, the governor of Syria, prevented them from marching through, and in this Herod lent him enthusiastic and effective assistance.[41]

Having thus proved himself, he could go before Augustus. But to be quite sure, he first had the aged Hyrcanus removed, the only person who could be dangerous to him as having a more valid claim to the throne. Taking into consideration Hyrcanus's character and great age, it is very improbable that, as Herod's own annals assert, he brought death on himself by conspiring with the Nabataean king. Other sources, *Ant.* xv 6, 3 (174), expressly declare his innocence. For Herod in his critical situation, the mere existence of Hyrcanus was sufficient motive for the murder. Thus fell the last of the Hasmonaeans, an old man and a memorial of bygone times, as a sacrifice to Herod's suspicion and ambition.[42]

Herod now set out to meet Augustus in Rhodes in the spring of 30 B.C. In the encounter, Herod played his part daringly. He boasted of his friendship with Antonius, and of the services he had rendered him, with the intention of showing how useful he could be to those with whom he sided. Augustus set little store by these speeches but found it advantageous to win the adherence of this Idumaean, who

39. *Ant.* xv 5, 1 (108–20); *B.J.* i 19, 1–3 (364–72).
40. *Ant.* xv 5, 2–5 (121–60); *B.J.* i 19, 3–6 (369–85).
41. *Ant.* xv 6, 7 (195); *B.J.* i 20, 2 (392); Dio li 7.
42. *Ant.* xv 6, 1–4 (161–82); *B.J.* i 22, 1 (431–4).

was as clever and energetic as he was friendly to the Romans. He was very gracious to him, and confirmed him in his royal status. On receiving this happy response, Herod returned to his homeland.[43]

Soon afterwards, in the summer, Augustus marched from Asia Minor along the Phoenician coast towards Egypt, and Herod did not fail to receive him with all pomp at Ptolemais and to arrange that the army should want for nothing in its travels during the hot season of the year.[44]

After Augustus had finished with Antonius in Egypt, and the latter, like Cleopatra, had committed suicide (August 30 B.C.), Herod once more visited him, doubtless to wish him success, and if possible to be rewarded for doing so. And this he achieved. For Augustus returned to him not only the region of Jericho, but also Gadara, Hippos, Samaria, Gaza, Anthedon, Joppa and Straton's Tower.[45] As proof of his gratitude, Herod escorted his patron as far as Antioch on his return from Egypt at the end of 30 B.C.[46]

While danger from without turned to good fortune, in his own house Herod experienced nothing but misery. Before travelling to Rhodes, he committed Mariamme to the protection of a certain Soaemus, and gave him the same order as he had once given to Joseph.[47] Again Mariamme came to know of it, and on Herod's return showed unconcealed signs of her dislike.[48] Herod's mother, Cyprus, and his sister Salome, both of whom had long been ill-disposed towards the proud Mariamme, welcomed this misunderstanding and managed to intensify it by spreading scandalous rumours. Finally, Salome bribed the king's cupbearer to declare that Mariamme had given him a poisoned drink to hand to Herod. When Herod heard of this, he had Mariamme's eunuch interrogated under torture. The latter knew nothing of the poisoned drink, but admitted that Mariamme hated her husband because of his order to Soaemus. Discovering that, like Joseph, Soaemus had also divulged his order, he again saw in this proof of unlawful relation and, frantic with rage, claimed that now he had proof of his wife's infidelity. Soaemus was executed immediately; Mariamme was tried, condemned, and at the end of 29 B.C. executed also.[49]

43. *Ant.* xv 6, 5–7 (183–98); *B.J.* i 20, 1–3 (386–93).
44. *Ant.* xv 6, 7 (198–201); *B.J.* i 20, 3 (394–7).
45. *Ant.* xv 7, 3 (217); *B.J.* i 20, 3 (396). On all these cities see vol. II, § 23, I.
46. *Ant.* xv 7, 4 (218).
47. *Ant.* xv 6, 5 (185–6).
48. *Ant.* xv 7, 1–2 (202–12).
49. *Ant.* xv 7, 3–6 (213–39). For a legendary Talmudic account of Mariamme's death see bB. B. 3b; bKid. 70b. In criticism of the story told by Josephus and repeated here, J. von Destinon *Die Quellen des Flavius Josephus* (1882), p. 113, observes: 'It is striking with what uniformity the events connected with the two journeys of the king, the one to Antonius and the other to Augustus, run their

All Herod's savagery and sensuality revealed themselves in his relationship with Mariamme. His hatred was as ungovernable and passionate as his love the moment he thought his wife had deceived him. But just as ungovernable and passionate was his longing for the loved one whom he himself had murdered. To deaden his grief, he sought distraction in wild entertainments, drinking bouts and hunting. But even his strong body could not endure such immoderation. He fell ill while hunting in Samaria and had to take to his bed. As it was doubtful whether he would recover, Alexandra turned her mind to how she could secure the throne for herself in the event of his death. She approached the commanders of the two fortresses in Jerusalem and attempted to win them over. But they denounced her to Herod, and Alexandra, who had long deserved it far more than the others, was likewise executed (in about 28 B.C.).[50]

Herod gradually recovered and soon found occasion for further executions. An eminent Idumaean, Costobar, was appointed governor of Idumaea by Herod soon after his accession to the throne, and later married Salome, whose first husband, Joseph, was executed in 34 B.C. Even in this first period he had conspired secretly with Cleopatra against Herod, but at Salome's request, had been pardoned.[51] But now Salome herself was tired of her husband, and to get rid of him grasped at an opportunity to denounce him. She knew that the sons

---

course, *Ant.* xv 3, 5–6 (62–70) and 9 (80–7); xv 6, 5 (183–6); 7, 1–6 (202–39). On both occasions he leaves his wife in the care of a friend with the command to put her to death if something should happen to him; on both occasions the guardians, meaning no harm, impart the secret to her; the king returns, discovers this, suspects a greater familiarity, and has the culprits executed. . . . Moreover, in *Jewish War* the whole of the second account is missing, *B.J.* i 22, 4–5 (441–4). In this work, Herod kills Joseph as well as Mariamme immediately after his return from Antonius. It may be thought that the two accounts in *Antiquities* refer to one and the same event; perhaps Josephus found the second report in a secondary source, regarded it because of the different name, Soaemus, as distinct from that contained in his main source, and in order not to miss anything out, linked it to Herod's journey to Augustus.' One would accept this interpretation without further argument were it not for the fact that *Bellum Judaicum* frequently reproduces in a greatly abridged form the same source as is used in *Antiquities*, and that in the second story in the *Antiquities* the first is expressly presupposed, xv 7, 1 (204) τὰς Ἰωσήπῳ δοθείσας ἐντολὰς ἀνεμνημόνευεν. That the same story is repeated in an almost identical form is of course improbable. But it seems that both stories were given in Josephus's main source, in particular because in both passages the domestic narrative is closely bound up with the political story (the latter being inserted between the beginning and end of the domestic narrative). According to R. Marcus in *Josephus* (Loeb) VIII, pp. 42 f., note a, 'the accounts in *Ant.* appear preferable to that in *B.J.* with its evident anachronisms'.

50. *Ant.* xv 7, 7–8 (240–52).

1. *Ant.* xv 7, 9 (253–8).

of Babas,[52] who were apparently distantly related to the Hasmonaean house, and whom since his conquest of Jerusalem Herod had tried in vain to trace, were concealed by her husband in his home. She informed her brother Herod of this. When he heard he quickly made up his mind. Costobar and his protégées, whose hiding-place Salome had disclosed, were seized and executed (in about 27 B.C.). And Herod was then able to tell himself with an easy mind that of all the relatives of the aged Hyrcanus, none was left to dispute his claim to the throne.[53] With this, the first period ends, the period of conflict.

II

The period 25–13 B.C. is the one of splendour and enjoyment, though not of uninterrupted and unclouded enjoyment.

To the splendour of the time belong, above all, magnificent building enterprises. All the provinces at that time competed with one another in emperor worship, and in celebrating the quadrennial games in Caesar's honour; temples to the emperor (*Καισάρεια*) were raised, and theatres, amphitheatres, stadia and hippodromes. New cities, too, were founded in Caesar's honour and named after him. 'Provinciarum pleraeque super templa et aras ludos quoque quinquennales paene oppidatim constituerunt. Reges amici atque socii et singuli in suo quisque regno Caesareas urbes condiderunt.'[54] All these ventures were tackled by Herod with the energy characteristic of him. But he was also tireless in erecting other buildings for purposes of utility and luxury, and in founding whole cities.[55]

In Jerusalem a theatre was constructed, and in the plain near Jerusalem, an amphitheatre.[56] Some time later, about 24 B.C., Herod built himself a royal palace adorned with marble and gold. It was

52. Instead of *Βαβας* Niese reads *Σαββας* with *cod. Pal.*, but says *utrum verius difficile dictu*. The name *Βαβας* occurs in an inscription given by J. Euting, SAB (1885), p. 685, table xi, n. 80. בבא בן בוטא appears in mKer. 6:3; יהודה בן בבא in mErub. 2:4–5; mYeb. 16:3, 5, 7; mEduy. 6:1; 8:2 (the Cambridge manuscript has בן בבא four times, בן אבא three times: cf. W. H. Lowe, *The Mishnah on which the Palestinian Talmud rests* (1883) *in loc.*).

53. *Ant.* xv 7, 10 (259–66). At the close of the narrative Josephus says expressly: *ὥστ' εἶναι μηδὲν ὑπόλοιπον ἐκ τῆς Ὑρκανοῦ συγγενείας*. By this he probably means only the male relatives. For according to *Ant.* xvii 5, 2 (92) the daughter of Antigonus, the last Hasmonaean king, who married Herod's oldest son Antipater, was still alive about twenty years later.

54. Suet. *Div. Aug.* 59–60. On the imperial cult cf. vol. II, § 22, ii, 1.

55. On Herod's buildings cf. C. Watzinger, *Denkmäler Palästinas* II (1935), pp. 31–78; F.-M. Abel, *Hist. Pal.* I (1952), pp. 363–79; G. E. Wright, *Biblical Archaeology* (1957), pp. 218–26; Schalit, *op. cit.*, pp. 328–403.

56. *Ant.* xv 8, 1 (268) *καὶ θέατρον ἐν Ἱεροσολύμοις ᾠκοδόμησεν, αὖθις τ' ἐν τῷ πεδίῳ μέγιστον ἀμφιθέατρον*. The hippodrome in Jerusalem which is mentioned occasionally, *Ant.* xvii 10, 3 (255); *B.J.* ii 3, 1 (44), was also doubtless built by Herod; so too, the theatre, amphitheatre and hippodrome in Jericho (on which

provided with stout fortifications, and so also served as a castle for the upper city.[57] Already in Antonius's time he had had the fortress north of the Temple reconstructed and named Antonia in honour of his patron.[58] In the non-Jewish cities of his realm, and farther afield in the province of Syria, he built numerous temples, especially temples in honour of Caesar (*Καισάρεια*), and adorned them with most beautiful sculpture.[59]

---

see vol. II, § 22, ii, 2). An interesting report concerning a theatre near Jerusalem which he discovered is given by C. Schick in PEFQS (1887), pp. 161–6 (with plans). It lies south of the city (south-south-west of Bir Eiyub, north of Wadi Yasul). The semicircular auditorium can still be clearly recognized; it is cut from the natural rock on the north side of a hill so that spectators had a glimpse of the city. The diameter below the seats amounts to 132 feet and the seats rise at a regular angle of 37 degrees. But it is curious that Schick should describe his discovery as an amphitheatre, for his sketch and description leave no doubt that it is, on the contrary, a theatre (the amphitheatre was always an ellipse, in the middle of which was the arena for gladiatorial contests and animal baiting, whereas the theatre was in the form of a semicircle, on the open side of which was the stage for dramatic performances). Schick was led to this mistake by Josephus's statement that Herod's theatre was *ἐν Ἱεροσολύμοις*, whereas the site discovered by Schick lies outside the city. But he himself has to admit that his discovery is by no means *ἐν τῷ πεδίῳ*, which according to Josephus was true of the amphitheatre built by Herod. If then *ἐν Ἱεροσολύμοις* meant 'within the city walls', the site found by Schick could not be either Herod's theatre or amphitheatre. But such an interpretation is in no way inevitable; the identification of Schick's theatre with that of Herod is therefore quite possible and even probable. Even in Hadrian's restoration of the city, the site once prepared by Herod will not have been abandoned. On the theatre and amphitheatre built by Herod see G. A. Smith, *Jerusalem. The Topography, Economics and History from the Earliest Times to A.D.* 70 II (1908), pp. 492–4; Schalit, *op. cit.*, pp. 370–1. On the hippodrome probably built by Herod see L. H. Vincent and F.-M. Abel, *Jérusalem* II, p. 34, pl. I; cf. L. H. Vincent and A. M. Stève, *Jérusalem de l'Ancien Testament* II–III (1956), pp. 708–9.

57. *Ant.* xv 9, 3 (318); *B.J.* i 21, 1 (402). Cf. the description given in *B.J.* v 4, 3–4 (156–85). One tower of Herod's palace is today still in a partial state of preservation, the so-called Tower of David. See the description of it given by Schick in ZDPV 1 (1878), pp. 226–37; see also G. A. Smith, *op. cit.*, II, pp. 486–90; Abel, *Histoire de la Palestine* I, pp. 365–7; C. N. Johns, 'The Citadel, Jerusalem—A Summary of Work since 1934', *QDAP* 14 (1950), pp. 121–90. Schalit, *op. cit.*, pp. 371–2. R. Amiran, A. Eitan, 'Excavations in the Courtyard of the Citadel, Jerusalem'. IEJ 20 (1970), pp. 9–17.

58. *Ant.* xv 8, 5 (292); 11, 4 (409); xviii 4, 3 (91); *B.J.* i 21, 1 (401). Cf. the description in *B.J.* v 5, 8 (238–47); Tac. *Hist.* v 11. On the earlier history of the fortress see note on p. 154 above; cf. J. Simons, *Jerusalem in the O.T.* (1952); Vincent, *Jérusalem de l'A.T.* I (1954), pp. 193–221; S. M. Aline de Sion, *La Forteresse Antonia à Jérusalem et la question du Prétoire* (1955); see now P. Benoit, 'L'Antonia d'Hérode le Grand et le Forum Oriental d'Aelia Capitolina,' HThR 64 (1971), pp. 135–67.

59. *Ant.* xv 9, 5 (328 f.); *B.J.* i 21, 4 (407). Cf. *Ant.* xv 10, 3 (363); *B.J.* i 21, 3 (404) (the temple at Paneion); cf. RE XXXVI 3, 594–600. It was of white marble and apparently stood on the hill above Caesarea Philippi, the ancient Panias,

A whole group of new cities took shape at his command. He was responsible for a most impressive reconstruction of the former city of Samaria, which had already been rebuilt by Gabinius after its destruction by John Hyrcanus. Herod re-named it Sebaste.[60] Not content with this, in around 22 B.C. he embarked on the even grander undertaking of establishing a new city of enormous size on the coast, on the site of Straton's Tower, giving it the name of Caesarea. Josephus mentions the town's great harbour as particularly noteworthy. To protect ships from storms, a powerful breakwater was thrown up far out into the sea, the material for which must have been brought from a considerable distance. On this breakwater, dwellings were built for the seamen, and in front of them a promenade. In the middle of the city there was a hill, and on this a temple of Caesar was built which could be seen well out to sea. The building of the city lasted twelve full years. And when it was finished, it was dedicated with great pomp in the 28th year of Herod (=10/9 B.C.).[61]

Herod's enthusiasm for building was, however, still not satisfied. On the site of ancient Capharsaba he laid out a city which he called Antipatris, in honour of his father. At Jericho he built a fortress to which he gave the name of his mother, Cyprus. In the Jordan valley, north of Jericho, he founded a new city in a fertile but undeveloped area and called it after his brother Phasaelis.[62] He rebuilt ancient Anthedon and named it Agrippium in honour of Agrippa.[63] In his own honour the name Herodium was given to two new fortresses, one of them in the mountains towards Arabia, the other three hours' journey south of Jerusalem, on the site of his victory over the Jews who

---

but its exact site is not known; it is possibly the temple represented on coins of the tetrarch Herod Philip; cf. Hill, *BMC Syria*, pl. xxiv no. 21; Reifenberg, *Ancient Jewish Coins*,[2] pl. iv, nos. 42, 44). There was also a temple of Augustus in each of the reconstructed cities of Sebaste and Caesarea. De Vogüé and Waddington found at Si'a ($\frac{1}{2}$ hour from El-Kanawat, at the western foot of the Hauran) the ruins of a temple of the Herodian period (illustrated in de Vogüé, *Syrie Centrale, Architecture Civile et Religieuse*, pl. 2 and 3). Among them was also found the following inscription on the lower part of what had once been a statue of Herod; [βα]σιλεῖ Ἡρῴδει κυρίῳ Ὀβαίσατος Σαύδου ἔθηκα τὸν ἀνδριάντα ταῖς ἐμαῖς δαπάναι[ς], OGIS 415. Cf. n. 24 above.

60. *Ant.* xv 8, 5 (292 f.); *B.J.* i 21, 2 (403); Strabo xvi 2, 34 (760). For further particulars see vol. II, § 23, i; on the time of its construction see p. 293 above.

61. *Ant.* xv 9, 6 (331–41); xvi 5, 1 (136–41); *B.J.* i 21, 5–8 (408–16). Cf. also *Ant.* xv 8, 5 (292–8); Pliny, *NH* v 14/69. For the rest of the history of Caesarea see vol. II, § 23 i.

62. *Ant.* xvi 5, 2 (142–5); *B.J.* i 21, 9 (417 f.). On Antipatris and Phasaelis see vol. II, § 23, 1. Note G. Harder, 'Herodes-Burgen und Herodes-Städte im Jordangraben', ZDPV 78 (1962), pp. 49–63.

63. *B.J.* i 21, 8 (416); cf. *Ant.* xiii 13, 3 (357); *B.J.* i 4, 2 (87). In the two latter passages the name given is Agrippias. On the history of the city see vol. II, § 23, i.

pursued him when he fled from the city. This second fortress was also furnished with magnificent quarters for the king.[64] He re-fortified the strongholds of Alexandrium and Hyrcania, built by the Hasmonaeans but destroyed by Gabinius,[65] and dealt similarly with the fortresses of Machaerus and Masada, both of which he embellished with royal

64. *B.J.* i 21, 10 (419). On the second named and more important of these fortresses see also *Ant.* xv 9, 4 (323–5); cf. *Ant.* xiv 13, 9 (360); *B.J.* i 13, 8 (265). In the Roman period it was the centre of a toparchy (*B.J.* iii 3, 5 (55); Pliny, *NH* v 14/70: 'Herodium cum oppido inlustri eiusdem nominis'; in the war of Vespasian it was one of the last of the rebels' sanctuaries, *B.J.* vii 6, 1 (163). According to *B.J.* iv 9, 5 (518), Herodium lay in the neighbourhood of Tekoa (στρατοπεδευσάμενος δὲ κατά τινα κώμην, Θεκουὲ καλεῖται, πρὸς τοὺς ἐν Ἡρωδείῳ φρουρούς, ὅπερ ἦν πλησίον); according to *Ant.* xiv 13, 9 (359), xv 9, 4 (324), *B.J.* i 13, 8 (265), i 21, 10 (419), its position was sixty stadia south of Jerusalem. As modern Tekoa is more than sixty stadia from Jerusalem, Herodium must have been situated somewhat to the north of it. Cf. also Petrus Diaconus (in Geyer, *Itinera Hierosolymitana* (1898), p. 110) 'in quo itinere (from Jerusalem to Tekoa) contra mons est, quem excavavit Erodes et fecit sibi palatium super heremum contra mare mortuum'. From this there can be no doubt that the steep conical mass known as Jebel el-Fureidis (paradise, orchard) is to be identified as Herodium. Its distance from Jerusalem is exactly 8 Roman miles, i.e. 64 stadia, as the crow flies. On the hill are still to be found the remains of the round towers, which according to Josephus in *Ant.* xv 9, 4 (324), *B.J.* i 21, 10 (420), Herod built there. Traces are also still discernible of the stone steps described by Josephus as leading up the citadel. Cf. Schick, ZDPV 3 (1880), pp. 88–99 (with plans); *The Survey of Western Palestine, Memoirs of Conder and Kitchener* III, pp. 315 f. 330–2; A. Schlatter, *Zur Topographie und Geschichte Palästina's* (1893), pp. 120 ff.; Schick's map of the more distant environs of Jerusalem, ZDPV 19 (1896); Abel, *Géog. Pal.* II, p. 348; Schalit, *op. cit.*, pp. 357–8; for recent excavations see V. Corbo, 'L'Herodion di Gebal Fureidis', Liber Annuus Studii Biblici Franciscani 13 (1962–3), pp. 219–77; 17 (1967), pp. 65–121; cf. RB 71 (1964), pp. 158–63, and 75 (1968), pp. 424–8. On the other Herodium see A. Mallon, 'Deux forteresses au pied des monts de Moab', Biblica 14 (1933), pp. 401–7.

65. Both fortresses are first mentioned in the time of Alexandra, *Ant.* xiii 16, 3 (417). In Alexandrium Aristobulus awaited the arrival of Pompey but was obliged to surrender the fortress to him, *Ant.* xiv 3, 4 (48–53); *B.J.* i 6, 5 (133–7). Both fortresses were razed by Gabinius because they had served Alexander as bastions at the time of his revolt, *Ant.* xiv 5, 2–4 (82–91); *B.J.* i 8, 2–5 (160–70). Alexandrium was re-fortified by Pheroras, *Ant.* xiv 15, 4 (419); *B.J.* i 16, 3 (308). Hyrcania served for a long time as a refuge to the sister of Antigonus; it was not until shortly before the battle of Actium that Herod acquired control of it, *B.J.* i 19, 1 (364). The new fortresses which Herod established in both these places were so remarkable that he showed them to Agrippa on the occasion of the latter's visit, *Ant.* xvi 2, 1 (13). The site of Hyrcania has been identified with Khirbet Mird in the wilderness of Judaea, about 8 miles south-east of Jerusalem; so Abel, *Géog. Pal.* II, p. 350. See also A. E. Mader, *Oriens Christianus* 34 (1937) pp. 27–58, 192–212; G. R. H. Wright, 'The Archaeological Remains at El Mird in the Wilderness of Judaea', Biblica 43 (1961), pp. 1–27. Alexandrium is probably identical with the present-day Qarn Sartaba on the edge of the Jordan plain north of Jericho (see p. 238 above). Cf. Abel in RB 10 (1913), pp. 227–34; *Géog. Pal.* II, pp. 241 f.; W. J. Moulton, 'A Visit to Qarn Sartabeh', BASOR 62 (1936), pp. 14–18.

palaces.[66] Military purposes were also served by the rebuilding of Gaba in Galilee and Heshbon in Peraea, where he established military colonies.[67]

Architecture far beyond the borders of Palestine also testified to Herod's liberality. For the Rhodians he built at his own expense a Pythian temple. He assisted the city of Nicopolis, founded near Actium by Augustus, to erect most of its public buildings. In Antioch he built colonnades on both sides of the main street.[68] When he was once in Chios, he contributed an enormous sum towards the rebuilding of the pillared hall destroyed in the Mithridatic war.[69] In Ashkelon he built baths and fountains; and Tyre, Sidon, Byblus and Berytus, Tripolis, Ptolemais and Damascus were also indebted to him. In fact, proofs of his generosity reached as far as Athens.[70]

The most magnificent of all his building operations was, however, the reconstruction of the Temple of Jerusalem. The old Temple built by Zerubbabel no longer corresponded to the splendour of the new age. The palaces nearby surpassed it in magnificence. Now, as was fitting, it was to be made to conform to these splendid environs. The undertaking began in the 18th year of Herod's reign (20/19 B.C.). When the Temple proper was completed, it was provisionally consecrated, but work on it continued long afterwards until the time of Albinus (A.D. 62–4), a few years before its destruction. Its grandeur was proverbial. 'Whoever has not seen Herod's building, has never seen anything beautiful', was a proverb of that time.[71]

66. Machaerus was first fortified by Alexander Jannaeus, *B.J.* vii 6, 2 (171). Herod's new buildings are described by Josephus in detail in *B.J.* vii 6, 2 (172–7). Masada is said to have been fortified by the High Priest Jonathan, *B.J.* vii 8, 3 (285), which is hardly possible since in Jonathan's time Jewish territory did not reach as far as Masada. On Herod's new buildings see *B.J.* vii 8, 3 (285–94). On the archaeological remains of Herodian Masada, see Y. Yadin, *Masada, Herod's Fortress and the Zealots' Last Stand* (1966), esp. pp. 40–156. Both fortresses played an important part in the war of Vespasian. For fuller details of their sites and history, see pp. 511–12.

67. *Ant.* xv 8, 5 (294). Cf. *B.J.* iii 3, 1 (36). For further evidence on these two places, see vol. II, § 23, i.

68. *Ant.* xvi 5, 3 (146–9).

69. *Ant.* xvi 2, 2 (18–19).

70. *B.J.* i 21, 11 (422–5). Berenice (PIR^2 I 651), the daughter of Agrippa I, is called on an inscription in Athens (IG^2 II 3449=OGIS 428) *μεγάλων βασιλέων εὐεργετῶν τῆς πόλεως ἔκγονος*. Cf. IG^2 II 3440=OGIS 414 *Ὁ δῆμος βασιλέα Ἡρῴδην φιλορωμαῖον εὐεργεσίας ἕνεκεν καὶ εὐνοίας τῆς εἰς ἑαυτόν* (the people of Athens). Cf. IG^2 II 3441.

71. On the history of its construction see *Ant.* xv 11 (380–425); *B.J.* i 21, 1 (401–2). In the first text, Josephus also gives a detailed description of the whole Temple area with its splendid porticoes. (On a fragment of a pillar probably deriving from Herod's building, see Clermont-Ganneau, *Archaeological Researches in Palestine* I (1899), pp. 254–8). The inner courts and the Temple proper are described most minutely in *B.J.* v 15 (184–247). The statements of Josephus are

In addition to architecture, spectacular games ranked among the splendours of the Augustan age. In this connexion Herod again did not fall short of the requirements of the time. He instituted four-yearly athletic contests, not only in Caesarea, which was predominantly Gentile, but even in Jerusalem.[72] In the eyes of orthodox Jews, these pagan spectacles with their disregard for the life of men and animals were a grievous offence only tolerated under the pressure of external

---

well assembled by F. Spiess in *Das Jerusalem des Josephus* (1881), pp. 46–94; also in ZDPV 15 (1892), pp. 234–56. The account appearing in the Mišhnah tractate Middoth agrees in essentials with that of Josephus; see I. Hildesheimer, *Die Beschreibung des herodianischen Tempels im Tractate Middoth und bei Flavius Josephus* (*Jahresbericht des Rabbiner-Seminars für das orthodoxe Judenth.* (1876/77); F. J. Hollis, *The Archaeology of Herod's Temple: with a Commentary on the Tractate Middoth* (1934); L. H. Vincent, 'Le Temple hérodien d'après la Mišnah', RB 61 (1954), pp. 5–35, 398–418; cf. Schalit, *op. cit.*, pp. 372–97 and J. Jeremias, *Jerusalem in the Time of Jesus* (1969), pp. 21–7. A brief description is given in Philo, *Spec. leg.* I 13 (71–5). On the Jewish proverb and other rabbinical traditions see bB.B. 4a; bTaan. 23a. With all its magnificence the Temple was nevertheless inferior to Herod's palace, *B.J.* i 21, 1 (402). On the duration of the construction work, see p. 292 above. On its completion in the time of Albinus, see *Ant.* xx 9, 7 (219). On the measures taken to avoid disturbance of worship see mEduy. 8:6: 'R. Eliezer said: I have heard that when the Temple (היכל) was being built, curtains (קלעים) were drawn round the Temple and curtains round the courtyards; and the walls of the Temple were built outside the curtains, whereas those of the courtyards were built inside the curtains'. It is said that while the Temple was being built it rained only by night (Jos. *Ant.* xv 11, 7 (425); bTaan. 23a). On the basis of the description given by Josephus and in the tractate Middoth, Herod's Temple has been dealt with countless times in more recent literature. Comprehensive accounts are given in articles on the Temple; IDB IV, pp. 534–60 and esp. JE XIII, pp. 85–9 (Temple of Herod), pp. 92–7 (rabbinical literature). See also H. Schmidt, *Der heilige Fels in Jerusalem: eine archäologische und religionsgeschichtliche Studie* (1933); J. Simons, *Jerusalem in the Old Testament* (1952), pp. 391–429; Vincent, *Jérusalem* I, pp. 193–221; II–III, pp. 373–610; A. Parrot, *The Temple of Jerusalem* (1957). For the determination of questions of topography, particularly in regard to the outer Temple area and its gates, an accurate description is given by M. De Vogüé, *Le temple de Jérusalem* (1864). On the Temple gates see J. Jeremias and A. M. Schneider, 'Das westliche Südtor des herodianischen Tempels', ZDPV 65 (1942), pp. 112–21; S. Corbett, 'Some Observations on the Gateways to the Herodian Temple in Jerusalem', PEQ 84 (1952), pp. 7–14, pls. I–V; M. Avi-Yonah, 'The Façade of Herod's Temple—An attempted Reconstruction', *Religions in Antiquity—Essays in Memory of E. R. Goodenough* (1968), pp. 327–35. See now Enc. Jud. XV, cols. 960–9.

Note the recently-published Aramaic ossuary inscription, from Giv'at ha-Mivtar, סמון בנה הכלה, 'Simon, builder of the Sanctuary'. J. Naveh, IEJ 20 (1970), pp. 33–4.

72. In Caesarea: *Ant.* xvi 5, 1 (137); *B.J.* i 21, 8 (415). In Jerusalem: *Ant.* xv 8, 1 (268). The expressions κατὰ πενταετηρίδα, *Ant.* xvi 5, 1 (138), πενταετηρικοὶ ἀγῶνες, *B.J.* i 21, 8 (415) and πανήγυρις τῆς πενταετηρίδος, *Ant.* xv 8, 1 (269) do not mean that the games were celebrated every fifth year, but every fourth year. See vol. II, § 22, ii, 2.

authority.[73] But the king's enthusiasm was such that he even gave generous financial support to the ancient Olympic Games.[74]

How tirelessly and unsparingly Herod promoted culture and luxury in other ways also may be deduced from Josephus. He colonized the districts east of the Lake of Gennesaret, through which until then only thieving nomads had roamed.[75] He adorned the parks about his palace in Jerusalem at great expense. Walks and water channels traversed the gardens; everywhere there were pools, with bronze statuary through which the water streamed. Nearby stood many towers with tamed wild doves.[76] The king seems to have had a special fondness for the breeding of doves; it is in fact only due to this that his name is mentioned in the Mishnah. 'Herodian doves' is a phrase used here to describe birds kept in captivity.[77] So it looks as though Herod was the first person in Judaea to keep and breed wild doves in enclosures.

To prove himself a man of culture in the eyes of the Graeco-Roman world, Herod—who in his inmost heart remained a barbarian—surrounded himself with men of Greek education. The highest offices of state were entrusted to Greek rhetoricians, and in all matters of importance he availed himself of their counsel and collaboration. The most eminent among them was Nicolaus of Damascus, a man of wide erudition, well acquainted with natural science, conversant with Aristotle and renowned as a historian.[78] He enjoyed Herod's absolute confidence, and all the more difficult diplomatic missions were delegated to him. With him was his brother Ptolemy, likewise a trusted friend of

73. On the attitude to the games of orthodox Judaism see vol. II, § 22, ii, 2, and the literature mentioned there.

74. *Ant.* xvi 5, 3 (149); *B.J.* i 21, 12 (427).

75. *Ant.* xvi 9, 2 (285) (a colony of three thousand Idumaeans); *Ant.* xvii 2, 1–3 (23–31) (a colony of Babylonian Jews). Cf. also § 17a and Vol. II, § 22, 1.

76. *B.J.* v 4, 4 (181): *πολλοὶ . . . πύργοι πελειάδων ἡμέρων* (in the same place there is a general description of the park).

77. In the Mishnah Herod's name occurs only in the following two passages: mShab. 24:3: 'Water may not be set before bees and doves on the Sabbath, but before geese and hens and Herodian doves (יוני הרדסיות)'. mHul. 12:1: The law of Deut. 22:6–7 (that only fledglings may be taken from the nest, but the mother must be allowed to fly) holds good only for birds that nest in the open, e.g. geese and barnyard fowls, but not for those that nest in the house, e.g. Herodian doves (יוני הרדסיות). In both passages 'Herodian doves', refers to birds kept in captivity as distinct from those that fly free. The Josephus passage *B.J.* v 4, 4 (181) shows that wild doves (*πελειάδες*) are meant, not domestic doves (*περιστεραί*). The reading (הדרסיות) appears already in bHul. 139b alongside the other, but it is certainly false. The *Arukh*, the rabbinical lexicon of Nathan ben Yeḥiel (ed. Kohut, IV, pp. 116–17) gives *s.v.* יון the following explanation: 'King Herod brought doves from the wilderness and bred them in inhabited places'. Cf. Buxtorf, *Lex. Chald.* (s.v. הרדסי); HDB I, pp. 619 f. (s.v. 'Dove'); JE IV, pp. 644–5. See, however, E. D. Oren, 'The "Herodian Doves' in the light of recent archaeological discoveries', PEQ 100/101 (1968–9), pp. 56–61.

78. Cf. pp. 28–32 above.

the king. Another Ptolemy was head of the financial administration and had the king's signet-ring.[79] Two further Greeks formed part of the king's immediate entourage, Andromachus and Gemellus, the latter of whom was tutor to Herod's son Alexander.[80] Finally a Greek rhetorician, Irenaeus, is encountered in the proceedings following Herod's death.[81] Distinguished Greeks also spent short periods as guests at the king's court, among them Euaratus of Cos,[82] and the ill-reputed Lacedaemonian, Eurycles, who contributed not a little to the dissension between Herod and his sons.[83]

Herod's Judaism was, by all accounts, very superficial. His ambition was directed towards promoting education and culture. But the world of that time scarcely recognised any culture other than that of

79. That there were two men called Ptolemy at Herod's court is quite clear from events immediately following his death. At that time, Ptolemy the brother of Nicolaus of Damascus stood on the side of Antipas, *Ant.* xvii 9, 4 (225); *B.J.* ii 2, 3 (21), whilst another Ptolemy attended to the interests of Archelaus (*Ant.* xvii 8, 2 (195) = *B.J.* i 33, 8 (667); *Ant.* xvii 9, 3 and 5 (219 and 228) = *B.J.* ii 2, 1 and 4 (14 and 24). It was through the latter that Archelaus handed over Herod's accounts and signet-ring to the emperor in Rome, *Ant.* xvii 9, 5 (228) Καῖσαρ δὲ Ἀρχελάου εἰσπέμψαντος . . . τοὺς λογισμοὺς τῶν Ἡρῴδου χρημάτων σὺν τῷ σημαντῆρι κομίζοντα Πτολεμαῖον, *B.J.* ii 2, 4 (24): Ἀρχέλαος . . . τὸν δακτύλιον τοῦ πατρὸς καὶ τοὺς λόγους εἰσπέμπει διὰ Πτολεμαίου. In Herod's lifetime this same Ptolemy had charge of his signet-ring, and on his death read out his will, *Ant.* xvii 8, 2 (195) = *B.J.* i 23, 8 (667). The διοικητὴς τῶν τῆς βασιλείας πραγμάτων of *Ant.* xvi 7, 2–3 (191, 197) is doubtless identical with him, as also the person mentioned in the parallel passage *B.J.* i 24, 2 (473). Cf. also *Ant.* xvi 8, 5 (257); cf. Schalit, *Namenwörterbuch* s.v. 'Ptolemaios' 7 and 8.

80. *Ant.* xvi 8, 3 (241–3).

81. *Ant.* xvii 9, 4 (226); *B.J.* ii, 2, 3 (21).

82. Euaratus, the correct reading in *Ant.* xvi 10, 2 (312); *B.J.* i 26, 5 (532), is conceivably identical with the Γάιος Ἰούλιος Εὐαράτου υἱὸς Εὐάρατος whose name appears in a list of priests of Apollo at Halasarna on the island of Cos about 12 B.C. (IGR IV 1101). In any case, the name Εὐάρατος recurs fairly often in this list and also appears elsewhere in Cos (Paton and Hicks, *Inscriptions of Cos*, index p. 371).

83. *Ant.* xvi 10, 1 (300–10); *B.J.* i 26, 1–4 (513–31). Eurycles is described by Josephus as a distinguished person (*Ant.*, *loc. cit.*, οὐκ ἄσημος τῶν ἐκεῖ). Of his later destiny, Josephus writes in *Ant.* xvi, 10, 1 (310) that he continued his intrigues in Lacadaemon and because of his misdeeds was in the end banished from his land. In *B.J.* i 26, 4 (531) it is reported in more detail that on two occasions he was accused before the emperor of plunging the whole of Achaia into uproar and plundering the cities (ἐπὶ τῷ στάσεως ἐμπλῆσαι τὴν Ἀχαίαν καὶ περιδύειν τὰς πόλεις), and that he was therefore banished. He is in consequence certainly the Eurycles who according to Strabo, 'introduced unrest among the Lacedaemonians, inasmuch as he thought he could misuse the emperor's friendship to obtain domination over them; but the tumult soon ended when he died and his son rejected all such ambition': Strabo viii 5, 5 (366) νεωστὶ δ' Εὐρυκλῆς αὐτοὺς ἐτάραξε δόξας ἀποχρήσασθαι τῇ Καίσαρος φιλίᾳ πέρα τοῦ μετρίου πρὸς τὴν ἐπιστασίαν αὐτῶν, ἐπαύσατο δ' ἡ ἀρχὴ [palimpsest ταραχή] ταχέως, ἐκείνου μὲν παραχωρήσαντος εἰς τὸ χρέων, τοῦ δ' υἱοῦ τὴν φιλίαν [pal. φιλοτιμίαν] ἀπεστραμμένου τὴν τοιαύτην πᾶσαν. The correct explanation of this frequently misunderstood

Hellenism. So, under the guidance of Nicolaus of Damascus, he submitted to instruction in Greek philosophy, rhetoric and history, and prided himself on being closer to the Hellenes than to the Jews.[84] But the culture which he endeavoured to spread throughout his land was essentially Gentile. He even erected pagan temples in the non-Jewish cities of his kingdom. Under these circumstances, it is interesting to note his attitude towards the Law and the national outlook of his people. Since the reaction under Alexandra, the Pharisaic movement had grown so powerful, and had become so firmly rooted, that forcible Hellenization under Herod similar to that carried out by Antiochus Epiphanes was unthinkable. He was clever enough to respect the views of the Pharisees on many points. Thus it is particularly noteworthy that his coins bear no human likeness, but only innocuous symbols such as those on Maccabaean coins; one coin at the most, perhaps from Herod's latest period, has the image of an eagle.[85] When he was

---

passage is given by Bowersock *op. cit.* (below), pp. 113–14. In another passage Strabo viii 5, 1 (363), calls him *ὁ τῶν Λακεδαιμονίων ἡγεμών*. On coins also he appears as a dynast. His full name, C. Iulius Eurycles, is given in the inscription *Syll.*[3] 787, cf. 788. In Corinth he built baths, and in Sparta a gymnasium (Pausan. ii 3, 5; iii 14, 6). Games founded by him, or in his honour, were still being celebrated at a later time. Cf. G. W. Bowersock, 'Eurycles of Sparta', JRS 51 (1961), pp. 112–18; PIR² I 301.

84. *Ant.* xix 7, 3 (329): *Ἕλλησι πλέον ἢ Ἰουδαίοις οἰκείως ἔχειν*. On the literary studies in which Herod engaged under the direction of Nicolaus of Damascus, see Nic. Dam. FGrH 90 F 135 *Ἡρῴδης πάλιν διαμεθεὶς τὸν φιλοσοφίας ἔρωτα . . . ἐπεθύμησε πάλιν ῥητορικῆς, καὶ Νικόλαον ἠνάγκαζε συρρητορεύειν αὐτῷ, καὶ κοινῇ ἐρρητόρευον. αὖθις δ' ἱστορίας αὐτὸν [ἔρως] ἔλαβεν, ἐπαινέσαντος Νικολάου τὸ πρᾶγμα καὶ πολιτικώτατον εἶναι λέγοντος, χρήσιμον δὲ καὶ βασιλεῖ, ὡς τὰ τῶν προτέρων ἔργα καὶ πράξεις ἱστοροίη . . . ἐκ τούτου πλέων εἰς Ῥώμην ὡς Καίσαρα Ἡρῴδης ἐπήγε[το] τὸν Νικόλαον ὁμοῦ ἐπὶ τῆς αὐτῆς νηός, καὶ κοινῇ ἐφιλοσόφουν.*

85. On the coins of Herod see Eckhel III, pp. 483–6; Mionnet V, pp. 565; de Saulcy, *Recherches sur la Numismatique judaïque*, pp. 127–33; Madden, *History of the Jewish Coinage*, pp. 81–91; *Coins of the Jews*, pp. 105–14. *BMC Palestine*, pp. xcvi f.; Reifenberg, *Ancient Jewish Coins*², pp. 18–19; Y. Meshorer, *Jewish Coins of the Second Temple Period* (1967), pp. 64–8. The coins have the simple inscription *ΗΡΩΔΟΥ ΒΑΣΙΛΕΩΣ* or *ΗΡΩΔΗΣ ΒΑΣΙΛΕΥΣ* and various emblems; some have the number of the year 3 (*LΓ*); cf. B. Kanael, JQR 42 (1951/2), pp. 261–4, and U. Rappaport, RN 10 (1968), pp. 64–75. No effigy is found on any coin; on the other hand, it is probable that a small copper coin bearing an eagle (Reifenberg, *op. cit.*, no 34), of which various exemplars have been found in Jerusalem, belongs to Herod the Great and not to Herod of Chalcis, who never reigned in Jerusalem; see de Saulcy, *Recherches*, p. 131; C. Wieseler, *Beiträge zur rightigen Würdigung der Evangelien*, pp. 86–8; Madden, *Coins*, p. 114; for Herod of Chalcis: Madden, *History*, pp. 111–13. Reinach dated it to the last period of Herod's reign, when he treated Jewish feelings with less consideration than previously, Reinach, *Les monnaies juives* (1887), p. 32; cf. Meshorer, *op. cit.*, p. 66, and J. Meyshan, 'The Symbols on the Coinage of Herod the Great and their Meanings', PEQ 91 (1959), pp. 109–21.

Note the stone weight dated by the 32nd year of Herod published by Y. Meshorer, IEJ 20 (1970), pp. 97–8.

building the Temple he was at great pains to avoid giving offence. He permitted only priests to build the Temple itself, and did not himself dare to set foot in the inner precincts where only priests were allowed.[86] No images were placed on any of the many splendid buildings in Jerusalem. And when on one occasion the people greeted with suspicion the imperial victory trophies which had been set up in the theatre at Jerusalem, thinking they were statues dressed with armour, Herod had the trophies taken down in the presence of the most distinguished, and showed them, to everyone's amusement, the bare wooden framework.[87] When the Nabataean Syllaeus sought the hand of Herod's sister Salome, he was required to adopt Jewish customs (*ἐγγραφῆναι τοῖς τῶν Ἰουδαίων ἔθεσι*), whereupon the marriage plans broke down.[88] Herod even held in high esteem some of the most reputable Pharisees, among whom Pollio and Sameas are mentioned in particular, and allowed them to go unpunished when they refused to take the oath of allegiance.[89]

However, in view of his cultural aspirations, strict observance of Pharisaic principles was not possible, or even intended. What he gave with the one hand, he occasionally withdrew with the other. Having scrupulously satisfied Pharisaic demands in the building of the Temple, he mounted, as though in mockery, an eagle over the Temple gate.[90] Theatres and amphitheatres were in themselves pagan abominations. The king's Greek entourage, the administration of state affairs by men of Greek education, the display of heathen pomp in the Holy Land, the furtherance of Hellenistic worship on the borders of Judaea, in the king's own land, all heavily outweighed the concessions made to Pharisaism, and in spite of them imparted to Herod's reign a character that was more Gentile than Jewish. The Sanhedrin, which in the people's view constituted the only rightful tribunal, lost all significance under Herod, so that it has even been doubted whether it existed.[91] The High Priests, whom he removed and installed as he pleased, were his creatures, and furthermore in part Alexandrians: men, that is to say, with a smattering of Hellenistic culture, and in consequence offensive to the Pharisees.[92] His treatment of the High Priesthood is quite typical of the king's domestic politics. Whereas on the one hand he thrust aside with reckless brutality the old Sadducean aristocracy because of their Hasmonaean sentiments (see p. 296 above), on the

86. *Ant.* xv 11, 5–6 (410–23).
87. *Ant.* xv 8, 1–2 (267–79).
88. *Ant.* xvi 7, 6 (220–8).
89. *Ant.* xv 1, 1 (3); 10, 4 (370).
90. *Ant.* xvii 6, 2 (149–54); *B.J.* i 33, 2 (648–50).
91. Cf., however, H. Mantel, *Studies in the History of the Sanhedrin* (1961), pp. 54–101; P. Winter, *On the Trial of Jesus* (1961), pp. 75–6.
92. On the High Priests see vol. II, § 23. iv.

other, he did anything but satisfy the Pharisees. Their ideals extended far beyond the king's concessions, and his Pharisaic friendships were merely exceptions.[93]

Bearing in mind that this disregard of the opinions and actual or supposed rights of the people was accompanied by the pressure of heavy taxes, it is understandable that Herod's rule aroused resentment. All the outward brilliance could not but be offensive to the people so long as it was secured by oppressing the citizens and slighting the statutes of their fathers. Most Pharisees refused to recognize the government of the Roman vassal king as legally valid, and twice refused to take the oath of loyalty, which Herod demanded first for himself, and then for the emperor.[94] On one occasion during the earlier period of his reign (*c.* 25 B.C.), the general dissatisfaction found vent in conspiracy.

93. J. Wellhausen, *Die Pharisäer und die Sadducäer*, pp. 105–9, has rightly pointed out that the Pharisees could accept Herod more readily than the Sadducees. But while this reflection is correct, he emphasised it too strongly; cf. J. Jeremias, *Jerusalem in the Time of Jesus*, pp. 228–32, 246–67; G. Allon, 'The Attitude of the Pharisees to the Roman Government and the House of Herod', Scrip. Hier. 7 (1961), pp. 53–78.

94. The two cases of refusal to take the oath reported in *Ant.* xv 10, 4 (368–72) and xvii 2, 4 (42) seem to be quite distinct. In the first passage it is said that Herod persecuted his enemies in all kinds of ways; as for the rest of the populace he demanded that they submit to taking an oath of loyalty, and he compelled them to make a sworn declaration that they would maintain a friendly attitude to his rule (*Ant.* xv 10, 4 (368) *τὸ δ' ἄλλο πλῆθος ὅρκοις ἠξίου πρὸς τὴν πίστιν ὑπάγεσθαι, καὶ συνηνάγκαζεν ἐνώμοτον αὐτῷ τὴν εὔνοιαν ἦ μὴν διαφυλάξειν ἐπὶ τῆς ἀρχῆς ὁμολογεῖν*). It was a question, therefore, of an oath of loyalty to the king. The Pharisees who refused went unmolested out of regard for Pollio and Sameas; similarly the Essenes; but others were punished. The other passage recounts that when the whole Jewish people vowed on oath to submit to the emperor and the king, more than 6,000 Pharisees refused to swear (*Ant.* xvii 2, 4 (42) *παντὸς γοῦν τοῦ Ἰουδαϊκοῦ βεβαιώσαντος δι' ὅρκων ἦ μὴν εὐνοῆσαι Καίσαρι καὶ τοῖς βασιλέως πράγμασι, οἵδε οἱ ἄνδρες οὐκ ὤμοσαν, ὄντες ὑπὲρ ἑξακισχίλιοι*). Here the oath to the emperor seems to have been the main issue. The objectors were sentenced to pay a fine, which was settled by the wife of Pheroras. Cf. G. Allon, *art. cit.*, pp. 53–78. The latter passage is possibly the earliest evidence we have that in the period of the empire not only soldiers and officials, but also the people in Italy and the provinces, had to take an oath of loyalty to the emperor. Note, however, the inscription from Samos published by P. Herrmann, Ath. Mitt. 75 (1960), pp. 70 ff., mentioning a *ὅρκος* to Augustus and probably dating to 5 B.C. Subsequent examples, see in general S. Weinstock, 'Treueid und Kaiserkult', Ath. Mitt. 77 (1962), pp. 306–27, are (1) the oath of Gangra in Paphlagonia, 3 B.C.: OGIS 532 = ILS 878; 2) the Cypriot oath of A.D. 14: T. B. Mitford, JRS 50 (1960), pp. 75–9 = AE 1962, 248; cf. Tac. *Ann.* I 34 (Germanicus administering the oath in Gaul); (3) two oaths of A.D. 37, (a) from Aritium in Lusitania, ILS 190, (b) from Assos in the Troad, *Syll.*[3] 797 = IGR IV 251; cf. Jos. *Ant.* xviii 5, 3 (124)—Vitellius, *legatus* of Syria, administering the oath in Jerusalem—and IG VII 2711 (Acraephia, Boeotia), referring to the oath taken in 37 by the League of Achaeans, Boeotians, Locrians and Euboeans. Compare Pliny, *Ep.* X, 52 and 102. See now P. Herrmann, *Der römische Kaisereid* (1968), esp. pp. 122–6 (texts of surviving oaths).

Ten citizens conspired to murder the king in the theatre. Their plan failed because it was betrayed beforehand. They were seized as they were about to set off, and were brought before Herod and immediately condemned to death.[95]

To keep the refractory populace in check, Herod used force; thus the longer his reign lasted, the more despotic it became. The fortresses, some of which were his own new foundations, and some refortified by him, served as a protection, not only against external enemies, but also as a means of suppressing his own people. The most important of them were Herodium, Alexandrium, Hyrcania, Machaerus and Masada, as well as the military colonies at Gaba in Galilee and Heshbon in Peraea (cf. pp. 307–8 above). Hyrcania, in particular, was a centre to which many political offenders were transported, to vanish there for ever.[96] To support his government against internal as well as external enemies, Herod possessed a dependable army of mercenaries composed of numerous Thracians, Germans and Gauls.[97] But in the last resort, he set out to smother in embryo every attempt at insurrection by means of rigorous police measures. Loitering in the streets, gatherings, indeed even walking together, was forbidden. And where anything contrary was done, the king heard of it immediately through his spies. He is even said sometimes to have acted the spy himself.[98]

To be just, it must nevertheless be acknowledged that his government had also its good points. Among his buildings, many were of great benefit. One has only to think of the harbour at Caesarea. His strong hand created orderly conditions conducive to the security of trade and traffic. Also, he made at least some attempts to win over his subjects with proofs of his magnanimity. Thus, in 20 B.C., he cut taxes by a third,[99] and in 14 B.C. by a quarter.[100] He also showed admirable energy in trying to check the great famine which afflicted his land in 25 B.C. He is said at that time to have sent even his own table-ware to the mint.[101]

But in face of the evil for which he was responsible, the people's memory of his benefits was short. So although, by and large, his reign was brilliant, it was not happy.

The glory of his reign was his foreign policy, in which field his accomplishments were undeniably great. He succeeded in gaining the

95. *Ant.* xv 8, 3–4 (280–91).
96. *Ant.* xv 10, 4 (365–7).
97. *Ant.* xvii 8, 3 (198); *B.J.* i 33, 9 (672). The army also included substantial levies from both the Jewish and the non-Jewish inhabitants of his kingdom; cf. Schalit, *op. cit.*, pp. 167–83.
98. *Ant.* xv 10, 4 (366–7).
99. *Ant.* xv 10, 4 (365).
100. *Ant.* xvi 2, 5 (64).
101. *Ant.* xv 9, 1–2 (299–316).

confidence of Augustus to such a degree that through imperial favour the extent of his territory was about doubled.

A description is called for at this juncture of the essential features of the constitutional position of a *rex socius* in the Roman empire of that time.[102] The dependence on Roman power of all the kings this side of the Euphrates was primarily manifest in the inability of any of them to exercise royal authority, or bear the title of king, without the emperor's explicit sanction (with or without the senate's confirmation).[103] The title was, as a rule, only conferred on princes reigning over larger territories; lesser princes had to be satisfied with the title of tetrarch or something similar. The title held good only for the person on whom it was bestowed and became extinct on his death. There were, strictly speaking, no hereditary monarchies within the domain of Roman power. Even a son appointed by his father as his successor could not assume office until his appointment had been ratified by the emperor. This ratification was refused if there were reasons for doing so, and the paternal territory was either bestowed on the son with its boundaries reduced and his title diminished, or it was given to another, or it was even brought under direct Roman administration, i.e. turned into a province. All this is evident from the history of the Herodian dynasty; but it is also confirmed by all other evidence. The title *socius et amicus populi Romani* (φίλος καὶ σύμμαχος Ῥωμαίων) seems to have been bestowed as a special distinction on particular individuals; not all of those who actually assumed this position were permitted to adopt the title formally.[104] Possession of Roman citizenship, although explicitly attested only in relation to a few, was probably a characteristic of them all. Herod's family obtained such citizenships through his father,

102. Cf. Th. Mommsen, *Röm. Staatsrecht* III, 1 (^{3}1887), pp. 645–715; W. T. Arnold, *Roman Provincial Administration* (^{3}1914); J. Gagé, 'L'Empereur romain et les rois', Revue Historique 221 (1959), pp. 221–60; M. Lemosse, *Le régime des relations internationales dans le Haut-Empire romain* (1967), pp. 20–126 *passim*.

103. Herod had his kingdom δόσει Καίσαρος καὶ δόγματι Ῥωμαίων, *Ant.* xv 6, 7 (196).

104. Even in the case of Herod whom *Ant.* xvii 9, 6 (246) calls φίλος καὶ σύμμαχος, there have been doubts whether the title was officially due to him. But the συμμαχία of King Agrippa I (Herod's grandson) with the Roman senate and people in the time of the emperor Claudius is testified by a coin (Madden, *Coins of the Jews*, pp. 136 f.; Reifenberg, *Ancient Jewish Coins*^{2}, no. 63 cf. § 18 below). Since his authority was certainly not greater than that of his grandfather, the latter will also have been recognised officially as σύμμαχος of the Romans. Even in regard to Hyrcanus II, who was nominated by Caesar merely as ἐθνάρχης, it is said in the decree of his appointment, *Ant.* xiv 10, 2 (194) εἶναί τε αὐτὸν καὶ τοὺς παῖδας αὐτοῦ συμμάχους ἡμῖν. On the title *amicus populi Romani* see RE I, cols. 1832–3; F. C. Sands, *The Client Princes of the Roman Empire under the Republic* (1908), pp. 10–48; cf. H. Heuss, *Die völkerrechtliche Grundlagen der römischen Aussenpolitik in republikanischer Zeit*, Klio Beiheft 31 (1933), pp. 1–59; A. J. Marshall, 'Friends of the Roman People', AJPh 89 (1968), pp. 39–55.

Antipater.[105] From the time of Caligula, senatorial rights (praetorian and consular rank) were also occasionally bestowed upon confederate kings.[106] Their power was restricted in the following respects. (1) They were not supposed to conclude alliances with other states or to engage in war independently, and could thus only exercise their sovereignty within the boundaries of their own land. (2) They had only a limited right of coinage. Almost all of them seem to have been prohibited from minting gold coins, and many, among them Herod and his successors, were also forbidden to mint silver coins; at any rate, only copper coins survive from the time of Herodian princes. This fact is particularly instructive as it shows that Herod was by no means one of the most privileged of these kings, whatever may be implied by Josephus.[107] (3) One of their essential obligations was to supply auxiliary troops in the event of war and to protect the empire's boundaries against foreign enemies. In special instances contributions in the form of money were also demanded. But during the earlier period of the empire, no regular tribute seems to have been levied on the kings. It is testified only of Antonius that he appointed kings ἐπὶ φόροις τεταγμένοις. There was a similar occurrence in the second century also. But there seems to have been no fixed rule. It is improbable, from all the information available, that Herod paid tribute under Augustus.[108] The rights of sovereignty allowed to dependent kings comprised, under the restrictions already described, the administration of internal affairs and the judicature. They had unlimited power over the life and death of their subjects. No part of their territory was regarded as belonging to the province. They could levy taxes at will within the boundaries of their land, and could regulate the administration of their revenue independently. Their army, also, was under their own command and organized by themselves.

105. *Ant.* xiv 8, 3 (137); *B.J.* i 9, 5 (194).

106. Agrippa I was given firstly praetorian rank, Philo, *Flacc.* 6 (40), and later consular rank (Dio lx 8, 2), cf. PIR² I 131; Herod of Chalcis, praetorian rank (Dio lx 8, 3), cf. PIR² H 156; Agrippa II, likewise praetorian rank (Dio lxvi 15, 4), cf. PIR² I 132. The bestowal of senatorial rights (*ornamenta*, τιμαί) on non-senators is first encountered in the time of Tiberius (Mommsen, *Röm. Staatsrecht*³ I, p. 463). It was a matter simply of the right to sit among the senators on public occasions and to appear in the *insignia* of their respective ranks (Mommsen, *op. cit.*, pp. 455–67).

107. Cf. on the rights of coinage of *reges socii*: Mommsen, *Geschichte des römischen Münzwesens* (1860), pp. 661–736; *Röm. Staatsrecht*³ III, 1, pp. 709–14, Bohn, *Qua condicione iuris reges socii populi Romani fuerint* (1877), pp.42–9.

108. On Antonius's procedure see Appian, *BC* v 75/319. Later, in the time of Lucian, king Eupator of the Bosporus paid a yearly tribute to the governor of Bithynia (Lucian, *Alexander* 57 *ἔνθα ἐγὼ παραπλέοντας εὑρὼν Βοσποριανούς τινας πρέσβεις παρ' Εὐπάτορος τοῦ βασιλέως ἐς τὴν Βιθυνίαν ἀπιόντας ἐπὶ κομιδῇ τῆς ἐπετείου συντάξεως*). On Herod and his successors see further details below

Of the position thus assigned to them, one that afforded ample scope for individual devotion, Herod took full advantage. He availed himself, like the others, of every opportunity of presenting himself before the emperor with proofs of his loyalty.[109] By late 30 B.C. he had already visited Augustus several times.[110] Ten years later, in 20 B.C., Augustus returned to Syria, and Herod did not fail to pay his respects once again.[111] In 18 or 17 B.C. Herod fetched his two sons, Alexander and Aristobulus, from Rome, where they had been receiving their education, and on this occasion, too, he was graciously received by the emperor.[112] Later he was with Augustus once or twice more (in 12 B.C. and about 10 B.C.),[113] Herod was also on friendly relations with Agrippa, the intimate friend and son-in-law of Augustus. Agrippa was visited by Herod when he was staying in Mytilene (23–21 B.C.).[114] In 15 B.C. Agrippa himself went to Judaea and offered a hecatomb in the Temple in Jerusalem. The people were so charmed by this Roman friendly to the Jews that they accompanied him with blessings to his ship, strewing his path with flowers and admiring his piety.[115] In the following spring (14 B.C.), Herod returned Agrippa's visit and, knowing that Agrippa intended to lead an expedition to the Crimea, even took a fleet with him to render him assistance. He met his noble friend in Sinope and after the business of the war had been attended to, traversed a large part of Asia Minor with him, everywhere distributing gifts and dealing with petitions.[116] His relations with Augustus and Agrippa were so intimate that flatterers asserted that Augustus liked him best after Agrippa, and Agrippa liked him best after Augustus.[117]

---

in the Excursus on the census of Quirinius (§ 17, Appendix I). The view that *reges socii* paid a regular tribute was advocated by Marquardt, *Römische Staatsverwaltung* I (1881), pp. 405–8 (in reference to Judaea). Against this: Bohn, *Qua condicione juris* etc., pp. 55–64. Cf. Mommsen, *Staatsrecht*[3] III, p. 683, and Momigliano, *Ricerche*, pp. 41–4.

109. Cf. Suet. *Div. Aug.* 60 'Reges amici atque socii . . . saepe regnis relictis, non Romae modo sed et provincias peragranti cotidiana officia togati ac sine regio insigni, more clientium praestiterunt'.

110. See p. 289 above.

111. *Ant.* xv 10, 3 (354–64). Augustus does not seem to have visited Judaea.

112. *Ant.* xvi 1, 2 (6).

113. *Ant.* xvi 4, 1–5 (87–129) and 9, 1 (271). Cf. p. 293 above.

114. *Ant.* xv 10, 2 (350).

115. *Ant.* xvi 2, 1 (12–15); Philo, *Legatio* 37 (294–7) εὐφημηθεὶς μυρία παρεπέμφθη μέχρι λιμένων, οὐχ ὑπὸ μιᾶς πόλεως, ἀλλ' ὑπὸ τῆς χώρας ἁπάσης, φυλλοβολούμενός τε καὶ θαυμαζόμενος ἐπ' εὐσεβείᾳ. In regard to the hecatomb cf. vol. II, § 24, iv. (On sacrifices by pagans in Jerusalem see § 24, iv, Appendix.) On Agrippa and Herod see V. Gardthausen, *Augustus und seine Zeit* I 2, pp. 838 ff., II 2, pp. 486 ff.; M. Reinhold, *Marcus Agrippa* (1933), pp. 84–5, 106, 112–13, 114–18, 133–4.

116. *Ant.* xvi 2, 2–5 (16–65). Cf. Nic. Dam., FGrH 90 F 134.

117. *Ant.* xv 10, 3 (361); *B.J.* i 20, 4 (400).

These Roman friendships also bore fruit. As early as 30 B.C., when Herod was with Augustus in Egypt, he received from him an important territorial increase (see p. 289 above). New gifts were added later. In 27/25 B.C., Herod supplied the campaign of Aelius Gallus against the Arabians with five hundred selected auxiliaries.[118] There is possibly a connection between this and the fact that soon afterwards, in 23 B.C., at about the time when he sent his sons Alexander and Aristobulus to Rome for their education, he was awarded the districts of Trachonitis, Batanaea and Auranitis; previously this country had been inhabited by thieving nomads with whom the neighbouring tetrarch Zenodorus had made common cause.[119] When Augustus went to Syria some years later, in 20 B.C., he presented Herod with Zenodorus's own tetrarchy, the districts of Ulatha and Panias, and the surrounding territory north and north-east of the lake of Gennesaret.[120] At the same time, Herod obtained permission to appoint his brother Pheroras tetrarch of Peraea.[121] But the absolute confidence placed in him by Augustus is evident, especially from the fact that (perhaps only while Agrippa was absent from the East, see p. 256 above) he commanded the procurators of Syria (Coele-Syria?) to seek Herod's advice in all matters.[122]

It should also be mentioned that Herod applied his influence with his Roman masters to securing Jews in the Diaspora against oppression and impairment of their rights on the part of the non-Jewish world.[123] The powerful position of the Jewish king thus proved beneficial even for Jews not directly under his rule.

The period 20 to 14 B.C. was the most splendid in his reign. In spite of dependence on Rome, in so far as external grandeur was concerned it could bear comparison with the best times the nation had known.

118. *Ant.* xv 9, 3 (317); Strabo xvi 4, 23 (780). For further details see p. 290 above.

119. *Ant.* xv 10, 1 (342–8); *B.J.* i 20, 4 (398–400). The districts named all lie east of the Lake of Gennesaret (cf. § 17a). On Zenodorus, see Appendix I.

120. *Ant.* xv 10, 3 (354–64); *B.J.* i 20, 4 (398–400); Dio liv 9, 3.

121. *Ant.* xv 10, 3 (362); *B.J.* i 24, 5 (483).

122. *Ant.* xv 10, 3 (360); *B.J.* i 20, 4 (399). The somewhat obscure reference to the procurators in *Ant.* xv 10, 3 (360) reads *ἐγκαταμίγνυσι δ' αὐτὸν* [Niese *αὐτὴν*] *τοῖς ἐπιτροπεύουσι τῆς Συρίας ἐντειλάμενος μετὰ τῆς ἐκείνου γνώμης τὰ πάντα ποιεῖν*, but in *B.J.* i 20, 4 (399) *κατέστησε δὲ αὐτὸν καὶ Συρίας ὅλης ἐπίτροπον, . . . ὡς μηδὲν ἐξεῖναι δίχα τῆς ἐκείνου συμβουλίας τοῖς ἐπιτρόποις διοικεῖν*. There cannot in the nature of things be any question of a formal subordination to Herod of the procurators of Syria, but, as is clear from the expression *συμβουλίας* in the second passage, only of instructions to the procurators (the finance officials of the province) to make use of Herod's counsel. It is also possible that instead of *Συρίας ὅλης* (or *Συριάς*) we should read *Συρίας κοίλης*. Cf. Marquardt, *Römische Staatsverwaltung*[2] I (1881), p. 408; Otto, *Herodes*, col. 74 note. This evidence should perhaps not be taken too seriously, since it probably comes from the flattering pen of Nicolaus of Damascus.

123. *Ant.* xvi 2, 3–5 (27–65). Cf. also xvi 6, 1–8 (160–78) and xii 3, 2 (125–8).

Internally there was of course much that was bad. It was only with distaste that the people suffered the Idumaean's semi-pagan rule and only his iron, despotic fist that prevented the outbreak of rebellion.

III

Herod's last nine years (13–4 B.C.) was a time of domestic misery during which, in particular, his irreparable quarrel with the sons of Mariamme cast a profound shadow.[124]

Herod's family was a large one. He altogether had ten wives, which as Josephus points out, was permitted by the Law but nevertheless proof of his sensuality.[125] His first wife was Doris, by whom he had one son, Antipater.[126] He repudiated them both, and Antipater was only allowed in Jerusalem at the great feasts.[127] In 37 B.C. Herod married Mariamme, the grand-daughter of Hyrcanus (see p. 283 above), who bore him five children, three sons and two daughters. The youngest of these sons died in Rome,[128] the two older ones, Alexander and Aristobulus, are the heroes of the following events.[129] The third wife, whom Herod married about 24 B.C., was likewise called Mariamme. She was the daughter of a distinguished priest from Alexandria who was appointed High Priest by Herod when he married his daughter.[130] By

124. During this time occurs much of what has already been dealt with in the preceding section. But there can be no firm demarcation of periods. It is at all events generally correct that domestic conflict was the predominating factor in the years 13 B.C. to 4 B.C.

125. *B.J.* i 24, 2 (477); *Ant.* xvii 1, 2 (14): πάτριον γὰρ πλείοσιν ἐν ταὐτῷ ἡμῖν συνοικεῖν. According to the Mishnah (mSanh. 2:4) eighteen wives were allowed to the king. How many a private man could have, is not stated expressly; it is assumed, however, that he could have four or five (four: mYeb 4:11; mKet. 10:1–6; five: mKer. 3:7; cf. in general also mKid. 2:7; mBekh. 8:4). In noteworthy agreement with this is Justin, *Dial.* 134 βελτιόν ἐστιν, ὑμας τῷ θεῷ ἕπεσθαι ἢ τοῖς ἀσυνέτοις καὶ τυφλοῖς διδασκάλοις ὑμῶν, οἵτινες καὶ μέχρι νῦν καὶ τέσσαρας καὶ πέντε ἔχειν ὑμᾶς γυναῖκας ἕκαστον συγχωροῦσι. Cf. J. Jeremias, *Jerusalem in the Time of Jesus*, pp. 90, 93 f., 369. According to the Qumran sect, both the king and the commoners were to be monogamous (cf. CDC iv 20–v 2; G. Vermes, ALUOS 6 (1969), pp. 88–9).

126. *Ant.* xiv 12, 1 (300). According to *Ant.* xvii 5, 2 (92) Antipater married a daughter of the last Hasmonaean, Antigonus.

127. *Ant.* xvi 3, 3 (78, 85); *B.J.* i 22, 1 (433).

128. *B.J.* i 22, 2 (435).

129. The two daughters were called Salampsio and Cyprus. Their descendants are listed in *Ant.* xviii 5, 4 (130–42). The name Salampsio, Σαλαμψιώ is the same as the Hebrew שלמציון which occurs in inscriptions as a Hebrew woman's name, C. Clermont-Ganneau, *Archaeological Researches* I (1899), pp. 386–92; cf. J. B. Frey, CIJ nos. 1223, 1265, 1297. For examples found in the Judaean Desert, cf. above p. 229, n. 2.

130. *Ant.* xv 9, 3 (319–22). The name Mariamme is given in *B.J.* i 28, 4 (562) and elsewhere. Josephus in *Ant.* xv 9, 3 (320) gives her father's name as Simon and her grandfather's as Boethus. According to other passages Boethus was her father. See vol. II, § 23, iv.

her he had a son called Herod.[131] Of the remaining seven wives, whom Josephus carefully lists in *Ant.* xvii 1, 3 (19–32) and *B.J.* i 28, 4 (562–3), only the Samaritan, Malthace, the mother of Archelaus and Antipas, and Cleopatra of Jerusalem, the mother of Philip, are of interest.

About 23 B.C., Herod sent the sons of the first Mariamme, Alexander and Aristobulus, for their education to Rome, where they were hospitably received in the house of Pollio.[132] Some five years later, in 18 or 17 B.C., he himself fetched them home, and kept them from then on at the court in Jerusalem.[133] They would then have been about 17 or 18 years old and, in accordance with the custom of time and country, were soon married. Alexander was given Glaphyra, a daughter of the Cappadocian king Archelaus, and Aristobulus Berenice, daughter of Herod's sister Salome.[134] But although the Hasmonaean and Idumaean lines of the Herodian house were thus most closely related by marriage, hostility between them was acute. The sons of Mariamme, conscious of their royal blood, looked down on their Idumaean relations, and these, particularly the worthy Salome, retaliated with common slander. Thus hardly had the sons re-entered their father's house when the plot began to thicken, to become eventually more and more insoluble. Nevertheless for the time being Herod did not allow these slanders to affect his love for his sons.[135]

The king's guilty conscience was, however, too fertile a soil for such seed not to take root and bear fruit. He had to admit that it was the natural heritage of sons to avenge their mother's death, and with Salome constantly depicting the danger with which they both threatened him, he began at last to believe in it, and to view the sons with suspicion.[136]

To counter their ambition and show them that there was someone else who might possibly inherit the throne, he recalled Antipater, whom he had repudiated, and soon afterwards sent him to Rome in the company of Agrippa, who just then, in 13 B.C., was leaving the East to present himself to the emperor.[137] But in doing so, he put power into

131. *Ant.* xvii 1, 2 (14).

132. *Ant.* xv 10, 1 (342). This is almost universally assumed to be Asinius Pollio; cf. L. H. Feldman, 'Asinius Pollio and his Jewish Interests', TAPhA 84 (1953), pp. 73–80; but possibly Vedius Pollio, the notorious friend of Augustus, see R. Syme, 'Who was Vedius Pollio?', JRS 51 (1961), pp. 23–30.

133. *Ant.* xvi 1, 2 (6).

134. *Ant.* xvi 1, 2 (11). Berenice was a daughter of Salome and Costobar, *Ant.* xviii 5, 4 (133). She is also mentioned by Strabo xvi 2, 46 (765). King Archelaus of Cappadocia reigned from probably 36 B.C. to A.D. 17; cf. PIR² A 1023.

135. *Ant.* xvi 1, 2 (6–11).

136. *Ant.* xvi 3, 1–2 (66–77).

137. *Ant.* xvi 3, 3 (78–86); *B.J.* i 23, 1–2 (445–51).

the hands of the worst enemy of his domestic peace. For from then on, Antipater worked unceasingly, by slandering his half-brothers, to prepare his own way to the throne. The change in their father's mood was naturally not without effect on Alexander and Aristobulus. They responded to his suspicion with undisguised dislike, and complained publicly of their mother's death and their own mortifying treatment.[138] The rift between father and sons thus deepened, until finally, in 12 B.C., Herod decided to denounce his sons before the emperor. He made the journey with them, and appeared before the emperor at Aquileia as accuser of his sons. By his mild earnestness Augustus succeeded on this occasion in settling the quarrel and re-establishing domestic peace. Having thanked the emperor, father and sons returned home; and Antipater joined them and pretended to be glad at the reconciliation.[139]

Hardly were they back when trouble began once more. Antipater, who was again in the king's entourage, continued tirelessly with his scandalmongering, loyally supported by Herod's brother and sister, Pheroras and Salome. On the other side, Alexander and Aristobulus adopted an increasingly hostile attitude.[140] Peace between father and sons was therefore soon over. The king's suspicion, daily provided with fresh nourishment, became more and more unhealthy until it bordered on mania.[141] He had Alexander's supporters interrogated under torture, at first unsuccessfully, until finally one of them made incriminating statements. Thereupon Alexander was committed to prison.[142] When the Cappadocian king Archelaus, Alexander's father-in-law, heard of the ugly situation at the Jewish court, he began to fear for his daughter and son-in-law, and travelled to Jerusalem to attempt a reconciliation. He presented himself to Herod as being very angry with his ill-advised son-in-law, threatened to take his daughter home, and generally behaved with such fury that Herod himself sided with his son and took him under his protection against Archelaus. By this ruse, the crafty Cappadocian brought about the desired reconciliation and was able to return home well satisfied.[143] The storm was thus once more interrupted by a brief lull.

During this troubled period Herod had also to contend with external enemies, and even with imperial disfavour. The lawless inhabitants of Trachonitis were no longer willing to submit to his severe rule, and some forty of the worst disturbers of the peace found admission to neighbouring Nabataea, where a certain Syllaeus had taken over power

138. *Ant.* xvi 3, 3 (84).
139. *Ant.* xvi 4, 1–6 (87–135); *B.J.* i 23, 3–5 (452–66).
140. *Ant.* xvi 7, 2 ff. (188 ff.); *B.J.* i 24, 1 ff. (467 ff.).
141. Cf. especially *Ant.* xvi 8, 2 (235–40), 5 (254–60); *B.J.* i 24, 8 (492–7).
142. *Ant.* xvi 8, 4 (244–53); *B.J.* i 24, 8 (492–7).
143. *Ant.* xvi 8, 6 (261–70); *B.J.* i 25 ,1–6 (498–512).

in place of the weak king, Obodas. When Syllaeus refused to surrender them, Herod, with the consent of Saturninus, the governor of Syria, launched a campaign against the Nabataeans and enforced his rights.[144] But Syllaeus then agitated in Rome. He represented the matter as an unlawful breach of the peace, and was able to go so far as to cause Herod a serious fall from the emperor's favour.[145] To justify his conduct, Herod sent an embassy to Rome, and when this was not received, he sent a second delegation led by Nicolaus of Damascus.[146]

Meanwhile, the family discord was rapidly approaching its tragic end. The reconciliation, needless to say, did not last long. To complete the unhappiness, the scheming Lacedaemonian dynast, Eurycles, now came to the court and incited father against sons, and sons against father.[147] The rest of the scandalmongers also continued their work. In the end, matters came to such a pass that Herod committed Alexander and Aristobulus to prison and accused them of high treason before the emperor.[148]

Nicolaus of Damascus had in the meantime accomplished his task and won over the emperor to Herod.[149] When the messengers arrived with their accusation, they therefore found Augustus in a favourable mood, and at once handed over their documents. Augustus gave Herod full power to proceed in the matter himself, but advised him to assemble a judicial council at Berytus consisting of Roman officials and his own friends, and to have it examine his sons' guilt.[150]

Herod followed the emperor's counsel. The judicial council pronounced the death sentence almost unanimously. Only the governor Saturninus and his three sons opposed it. Yet it was still doubtful

144. *Ant.* xvi 9, 1–2 (271–85).

145. *Ant.* xvi 9, 3 (286–92). Cf. Nic. Dam. FGrH 90 F 136.

146. *Ant.* xvi 9, 4 (293–9).

147. *Ant.* xvi 10, 1 (300–10); *B.J.* i 26, 1–4 (513–33). On Eurycles see pp. 311–12 above.

148. *Ant.* xvi 10, 5–7 (320–34); *B.J.* i 27, 1 (534–7).

149. *Ant.* xvi 10, 8–9 (335–55). Nic. Dam., *loc. cit.* (n. 145).

150. *Ant.* xvi 11, 1 (356–60); *B.J.* i 27, 1 (534–7). Berytus was recommended by Augustus because it was a Roman colony, i.e. a centre of Roman life in the neighbourhood of Palestine. According to Strabo xvi 2, 19 (755–6) Agrippa settled two legions (i.e. the veterans of two legions) at Berytus. This he will have done in 15 B.C., on the occasion of his visit to that region (see p. 292 above). Eusebius dates the founding of the colony of Berytus (from the text of Jerome, which is to be preferred to the Armenian) in the year 2003 from Abraham or the 30th of Augustus (Euseb. *Chron.* ed. Schoene II, p. 143), i.e. 14 B.C. (for Eusebius reckons 43 B.C., as the first year of Augustus). Augustus states in the *Res Gestae* 16 that in 14 B.C., *consulibus M. Crasso et Cn. Lentulo,* he paid large sums to cities for estates which he assigned to veterans. The two legions were leg. V Mac. and VIII Aug. The full name of Berytus as a colony was *Colonia Iulia Augusta Felix Berytus* (CIL III, nos. 161, 165, 166, 6041). Cf. also Pliny, *NH* v 20/78; Jos. *B.J.* vii 3, 1 (39); *Digest.* 15, 1, 1; 7, 8, 3. The coins are in Eckhel,

whether Herod would carry out the sentence; an old soldier, Teron, even ventured to plead publicly in favour of the condemned. But he and 300 others denounced as adherents of Alexander and Aristobulus, paid for it with their lives. The sentence was then executed without delay. In Sebaste (Samaria), where Mariamme's marriage had been celebrated thirty years earlier, her sons were executed by strangulation (probably in 7 B.C.).[151]

Peace, however, did not return to Herod's house. Antipater was now all-powerful at court and enjoyed his father's absolute confidence. But he was not satisfied. He wanted total power, and could hardly wait for his father to die. In the meantime, he set out to secure a following by giving lavish presents. He also had secret conferences with Herod's brother, Pheroras, the tetrarch of Peraea, which aroused suspicion. Salome soon heard of them and secretly informed the king.[152] As a result, relations between Herod and Antipater gradually became strained, and to avoid conflict Antipater found it convenient to have himself sent to Rome. That Herod still did not suspect him is evident from his will at that time naming Antipater as heir to the throne; Herod, the son of the High Priest's daughter Mariamme, was named successor, only in the event that Antipater died before his father.[153]

When Antipater was in Rome, Pheroras died.[154] With this, the fate of Antipater was also sealed. A number of Pheroras's freedmen went to Herod and advanced the opinion that Pheroras had been poisoned; Herod should investigate the matter more closely. The investigation proved that poison was present, but that although it had come from Antipater, was not intended for Pheroras. It had been handed to him by Antipater so that he would administer it to Herod. Herod now also heard through the female slaves of Pheroras's house about the statements which Antipater had made during his secret conferences, about his complaints over the king's longevity, about the uncertainty of his

---

Doctr. Num. III, 354–9; Mionnet, *Descr. de médailles ant.* V, 334–51, Suppl. VIII, 238–50; Babelon, *Catalogues des monnaies grecques de la Bibliothèque nationale, Les Perses Achéménides etc.* (1893), pp. 166–91; *BMC Phoenicia*, pp. xlvi–lx. See in general R. Mouterde, J. Lauffray, *Beyrouth ville romaine: histoire et monuments* (1952); R. Mouterde, 'Regards sur Beyrouth phénicienne, hellénistique et romaine', Mél. Univ. St. Joseph 40 (1964), pp. 145–90. In the later period of the empire there was in Berytus a celebrated school of Roman law, *Cod. Just.* I, 17, 2, 9; X 49, 1; P. Collinet, *Histoire de l'École de droit de Beyrouth* (1925).

151. *Ant.* xvi 11, 2–7 (361–94); *B.J.* i 27, 2–6 (538–51). Nic. Dam. FGrH 90 F 136 (4). On punishment by strangulation among the Jews: mSanh. 7:1, 3; also mTer. 7:2; mKet. 4:3; mSanh. 6:5; 9:3, 6; 11:1; cf. P. Winter, *Trial*, pp. 70–4; among the Romans: RE s.v. 'Laqueus'. See also § 10, n. 22 above.

152. *Ant.* xvii 1, 1 (1–11); 2, 4 (32–45); *B.J.* i 28, 1 (552–5); 29, 1 (567–70).

153. *Ant.* xvii 3, 2 (52–3); *B.J.* i 29, 2 (573).

154. *Ant.* xvii 3, 3 (59–60); *B.J.* i 29, 4 (580).

prospects, and much else.[155] Herod could no longer be in any doubt concerning the hostile designs of his favourite son. Making all sorts of pretences he recalled him from Rome to put him on trial at home. Antipater, suspecting nothing, came and to his great surprise—for although his plots had been discovered seven months ago, he had heard nothing about it—was taken prisoner as he entered the royal palace.[156] The next day he was brought for trial before Varus, the governor of Syria. Since in the face of the factual evidence he was unable to produce anything in his defence, Herod put him in chains and sent a report to the emperor.[157]

Herod was now almost seventy years old. His days, too, were numbered. He suffered from a malady from which he would not recover. In the new will which he now made, he named as his successor his youngest son Antipas, the son of the Samaritan Malthace.[158]

During his sickness he was also to find out how anxiously the people longed to be free of him, and yearned for the moment when they would be able to cast off his semi-pagan rule. When news spread that his illness was incurable, two rabbis, Judas the son of Sapphoraeus and Matthias the son of Margaloth, incited the people to tear down the offensive eagle from the Temple gate.[159] They were listened to only too readily, and amidst a great hubbub the work pleasing to God was done. But Herod, in spite of his malady, was still strong enough to pronounce the death sentence, and he commanded the ringleaders to be burned alive.[160]

The old king became increasingly sick; even the baths of Callirrhoe across the Jordan failed to bring him relief.[161] On his return to Jericho,

155. *Ant.* xvii 4, 1–2 (61–78); *B.J.* i 30, 1–7 (582–600).

156. *Ant.* xvii 4, 3 (79–82); 5, 1–2 (83–92); *B.J.* i 31, 2–5 (604–19).

157. *Ant.* xvii 5, 3–7 (93–141); *B.J.* i 32, 1–5 (620–40). Cf. also Nic. Dam., FGrH 90 F 136 (5)–(7).

158. *Ant.* xvii 6, 1 (146–8); *B.J.* i 32, 7 (644–6).

159. The names of the rabbis are given in *Ant.* xvii 6, 2 (149) as: *'Ιούδας ὁ Σαριφαίου καὶ Ματθίας ὁ Μαργαλώθου* [Niese *Μεργαλώθου*], but in *B.J.* i 33, 2 (648): *'Ιούδας τε υἱὸς Σεπφωραίου* [Niese *Σεπφεραίου*] *καὶ Ματθίας ἕτερος Μαργάλου.* See Schalit, *op. cit.*, p. 638.

160. *Ant.* xvii 6, 2–4 (149–67); *B.J.* i 33, 1–4 (647–55).

161. *Ant.* xvii 6, 5 (168–79); *B.J.* i 33, 5 (656–8). Callirrhoe is also mentioned by Pliny, *NH* v 16/72; Ptolem. v 16, 9; Jerome, *Quaest. in Gen.* 10:19; on the mosaic map at Madaba (*θερμα Καλλιροης*), M. Avi-Yonah, *The Madaba Mosaic Map* (1954), p. 40, and in rabbinical literature (S. Krauss, *Griech. und lat. Lehnwörter im Talmud etc.* II, p. 550; קלרה). Jewish tradition identifies Callirrhoe and the Biblical לשע: Tg. Ps.-Jon. and Neof. on Gen. 10:19 (קלרהי); Ber. R., 37:6; following this, Jerome, *Quaest. Hebr. in Genes.* 10:19 (*opp.* ed. Vallarsi III, p. 321; PL xxiii, col. 955) 'hoc tantum adnotandum videtur, quod Lise ipsa sit quae nunc Callirhoë dicitur, ubi aquae calidae prorumpentes in mare mortuum fluunt'. For a closer definition of its site, two warm springs (or groups of springs) have to be considered: (1) those in Wadi Zerka Ma'in (Conder, *The Survey of Eastern Palestine* I (1889), p. 102; Buhl, *Geogr.*, pp. 50 f.; Legendre, 'Callirrhoé'

he is said to have given orders that the distinguished men whom he had locked in the hippodrome should be shot down when he died so that at his funeral the mourning should be worthy of him.[162] In all the suffering which his sickness caused him, he nevertheless experienced the satisfaction of promoting the death of his son Antipater, the principal instigator of his domestic misery. Permission arrived from the emperor for Antipater's execution in the very last days of Herod's life, and was soon afterwards carried out.[163]

A few days before his death, Herod once again altered his will. This time he named Archelaus, the elder son of Malthace, as king, his brother Antipas as tetrarch of Galilee and Peraea, and Philip, the son of Cleopatra of Jerusalem, as tetrarch of Gaulanitis, Trachonitis, Batanaea and Panias.[164]

Finally, five days after the execution of Antipater, he died in Jericho, unmourned by his family and hated by the whole nation (4 B.C.).[165]

[*Text continues on p.* 328

in DB II, pp. 69–72); (2) the springs of Es-Sara, on the Dead Sea, south of the mouth of Wadi Zerka Ma'in (Dechent in ZDPV 7 (1884), pp. 196–201; Buhl, p. 41). Earlier authorities associated Callirrhoe with the former. Dechent, *loc. cit.* (pp. 196–201), however, identified Callirrhoe with the springs of Es-Sara, and rightly so. For (1) they alone flow into the Dead Sea, as Josephus and Jerome assert of the springs of Callirrhoe. (2) The springs in Wadi Zerka, at some distance from its mouth, are obviously to be identified with the place *Βαάρας* described by Josephus in *B.J.* vii 6, 2 (178–89) (in the gorge north of Machaerus, with various hot springs). These springs of Baaru are also mentioned by Jerome (Euseb., *Onomast.*, ed. Klostermann, pp. 45–7 'iuxta Baaru in Arabia, ubi aquas calidas sponte humus effert', in the account of the life of Peter the Iberian (Raabe, *Petrus der Iberer* (1895), pp. 82 and 87), and on the Madaba mosaic map (for the mutilated . . . *αρου*, characterized in the accompanying vignette as a place of warm springs, ought certainly to be restored as *Βααρου*, see Avi-Yonah, *op. cit.*, pp. 39–40). But according to the mosaic map, Baaru and Callirrhoe are different places, which is in any case likely because Josephus does not mention the name Callirrhoe in his description of Baaras. Callirrhoe is therefore to be identified with the springs south of the mouth of the Zerka. See also Abel, *Géog. Pal.* I, pp. 87, 156, 461; H. Donner, 'Kallirhoë', ZDPV 79 (1963), pp. 59–89.

162. *Ant.* xvii 6, 5 (173–5); *B.J.* i 33, 6 (659–60). The orders were not carried out, *Ant.* xvii 8, 2 (193); *B.J.* i 33, 8 (666). Cf. a similar rabbinic tradition in Meg. Taan. § 25 in connection with the death of Alexander Jannaeus. See Lichtenstein, *op. cit.*, pp. 271, 343; Derenbourg, *op. cit.*, pp. 164–5.

163. *Ant.* xvii 7 (182–7); *B.J.* i 33, 7 (661–4); Nic. Dam. *loc. cit.*

164. *Ant.* xvii 8, 1 (188–90); *B.J.* i 33, 7–8 (664–9).

165. *Ant.* xvii 8, 1 (191); *B.J.* i 33, 8 (665). On the actual date of his death we have the following evidence. Herod died shortly before a Passover, *Ant.* xvii 9, 3 (213); *B.J.* ii 1, 3 (10), therefore probably in March or April. Since Josephus states that he reigned 37 years from the date of his appointment (40 B.C.), 34 years from his conquest of Jerusalem, 37 B.C. Cf. *Ant.* xvii 8, 1 (191); *B.J.* i 33, 8 (665), it might appear as though he died in 3 B.C. But we know that Josephus reckons one year too many—according to our method of counting: e.g. 27 years from the conquest of Jerusalem by Pompey to its conquest by Herod, *Ant.* xiv 16, 4 (488), whereas it is only 26 (63–37 B.C.); 107 years from the conquest by Herod to that

by Titus, *Ant.* xx 10, 5 (250), whereas it is only 106 (37 B.C.–A.D. 70). He counts the spring of 31 B.C. as Herod's seventh year, *Ant.* xv 5, 2 (121); *B.J.* i 19, 3 (370), whereas it was only the sixth from July 37 B.C. From this it is evident that he reckoned the portions of a year as full years, and probably counted regnal years (as the Mishnah suggests, from Nisan to Nisan (cf. mR.Sh. 1:1: באחד בניסן ראש השנה למלכים). If this be the case, Herod's 34th year began on 1 Nisan of 4 B.C., and since he died before Passover, his death must have taken place between 1 and 14 Nisan 4 B.C. This reckoning is confirmed by an astronomical datum and the chronology of Herod's successors.

1. Shortly before Herod's death there was an eclipse of the moon, *Ant.* xvii 6, 4 (167). This probably indicates 4 B.C., in which year an eclipse of the moon was visible in Jerusalem during the night of 12/13 March, whereas in the years 3 and 2 B.C. there was no such phenomenon at all in Palestine; F. K. Ginzel, *Specieller Kanon der Sonnen-und Mondfinsternisse für das Ländergebiet der klassischen Altertumswissenschaften und den Zeitraum von 900 vor Chr. bis 600 nach Chr.* (1899), pp. 195–6; see also Ginzel, *Handbuch de math. und techn. Chronologie* II (1911), pp. 535–43. Only in 5 B.C., on 15 Sept., and in 1 B.C., on 9 Jan. were there also eclipses of the moon visible in Jerusalem (Ginzel, *op. cit.*). But from other evidence the later of these dates is excluded (see below), though the earlier remains at least possible. In 4 B.C. Passover (15 Nisan) fell on 11 April (Ginzel, *op. cit.*).

2. The chronology of Herod's two successors, Archelaus and Antipas, requires 4 B.C. as the year of Herod's death.

(a) Archelaus. According to Dio lv 27, 6, Archelaus was deposed by Augustus in A.D. 6 (the consulship of Aemilius Lepidus and L. Arruntius), in the tenth year of his reign (so *Ant.* xvii 13, 2 (342), cf. *Vita* 1 (5), correcting the earlier statement of *B.J.* ii 7, 3 (111) 'in the ninth'). Accordingly, he began his reign in 4 B.C.

(b) Antipas. Antipas was deposed by Caligula in the summer of A.D. 39 (see § 17b below). Since we have coins dating from the 43rd year of his reign, it began at the latest in 4 B.C.

From all the data, it thus emerges that Herod died in 4 B.C. shortly before Passover.

In reference to matters of detail the following points may be noted:

(1) The custom of reckoning a part, however small, of the calendar year at the beginning and end of a reign, as a full regnal year, undoubtedly holds good for Egypt. Not only the years of the Ptolemies, but also those of the Roman emperors were reckoned in this way in Egypt (cf. E. J. Bickerman, *Chronology of the Ancient World* (1968), p. 66). Later this reckoning of the years of an emperor became usual outside Egypt (Mommsen, I, pp. 501 f., II 2, pp. 756 ff.). Unger believed that Josephus also reckoned the regnal years of the Hasmonaeans in this way (see pp. 200–1 above). (2) Of the coins of Antipas of the year 43 (*MΓ*) three exemplars are now known (Madden, *Coins of the Jews* (1881), pp. 121 f., two according to Lenormant, *Trésor de Numismatique*, p. 125, pl. LIX, nos. 19 and 20, one according to de Saulcy, *Mélanges de Numismatique* II (1877), p. 92). Their existence is thus beyond doubt. Difficulties, however, are created by coins alleged to bear the dates 44 (*MΔ*) and 45 (*ME*). The coin of the year 44 (*MΔ*) is not only described by the rather unreliable Vaillant, but also, in a manuscript travel narrative by Galand, who found it near Jericho in 1674 (communicated by Fréret in *Mémoires de l'Académie des inscr. et belles-lettres* 21 (1754), pp. 292 f.). In particular, Sanclemente, pp. 315–19 and Eckhel, *Doctr. Num.* III, 487 f. have dealt with it thoroughly. Both conjecture that the date has been incorrectly read (it may well have been *ΛΔ* = 34). Cf. also *pro* and *contra*: Madden, *History*, p. 99

A solemn funeral procession accompanied the royal corpse for eight stadia from Jericho in the direction of Herodium, where he was buried.[166]

---

and *Coins*, p. 122; Riess (1880), pp. 55–7; Kellner, p. 176. Eckhel's reasons are very plausible; he points out in particular that, as regards its condition in other respects, the coin described by Galand agrees with those of the year 34, but not with those of 43. Difficulty arises only from the fact that in Fréret, p. 293 we read in reference to Galand's description: 'les lettres de l'époque *MΔ* sont très nettement figurées dans son manuscrit et absolument séparées l'une de l'autre'. But the drawing in Galand's manuscript is not decisive, and the coin itself can no longer be traced. During the last century a coin appeared with the year number 45 (*ME*) (see Wandel in Neue kirchl. Zeitschrift (1894), pp. 302 f.). According to an illustration of it produced by Wandel, it is related to the coin of the year 43, having on the reverse the inscription *Γαιω Καισαρι Γερ Σε*. If as is asserted the date *ME* can really be read clearly, this must be a forgery. In no case can the death of Herod be placed earlier than 4 B.C. It would be preferable to extend the period of Antipas's reign to A.D. 40, although it would still not cope with the coin of the year 45. Later discussions (*BMC Palestine*, p. xcvii; Reifenberg, *op. cit.*, p. 19; Meshorer, *op. cit.*, pp. 72–5) implicitly accept these conclusions, but add nothing. (3) Attempts to determine the day of Herod's death more closely with the help of Jewish tradition are untenable. In Megillath Taanith 7 Kislev and 2 Shebat are described as days of rejoicing (see Derenbourg, *Histoire*, pp. 442–6, §§ 21 and 25; H. Lichtenstein, 'Die Fastenrolle', HUCA (1931–32), pp. 271–2, 293–5, 339, 343; S. Zeitlin, 'Megillat Taanit' JQR 10 (1919–20), pp. 272–6, 279–80; B. Z. Lurie, *Megillath Taanith* (1964), pp. 161–3. But only the Hebrew scholion, which is late and unsupported by any real tradition, observes that 7 Kislev was the day of Herod's death, and 2 Shebat that of the death of Jannaeus. Therefore 4 B.C. is the generally accepted date for Herod's death, e.g. Otto, *op. cit.*, cols. 147–9, PIR² H 153; Schalit, *op. cit.*, p. 643. The argument for putting his death as late as 1 B.C. recently advanced by W. E. Filmer, 'The Chronology of the Reign of Herod the Great', JThSt. 17 (1966), pp. 283–98, has been conclusively refuted by T. D. Barnes, 'The Date of Herod's Death', JThSt 19 (1968), pp. 204–9, who further revives the suggestion that the eclipse of the moon mentioned as occurring shortly before Herod's death, *Ant.* xvii 6, 4 (167), normally taken to be that of 13 March 4 B.C., could have been that of 15/16 Sept. 5 B.C. Herod's death may then have happened on 7 Kislev (December) 5 B.C. the date of the festival mentioned in Megillath Taanith and explained (see above) by a late commentator as the anniversary of his death. But 4 B.C. remains the most satisfactory solution.

166. *Ant.* xvii 8, 3 (199) *ᾔεσαν δὲ ἐπὶ Ἡρῳδείου στάδια ὀκτώ*. *B.J.* i 33, 9 (673) *σταδίους δὲ ἐκομίσθη τὸ σῶμα διακοσίους εἰς Ἡρῴδειον*. The former passage states how far the solemn procession accompanied the corpse, the latter gives the distance from Jericho to Herodium. By the reading *ἑβδομήκοντα* which is given in two manuscripts in *B.J.* i 33, 9 (673) must be meant the distance from Jerusalem, and for that very reason it cannot be original. Undoubtedly, the more important of the two fortresses of the same name is intended (see p. 307 above), nearly two hundred stadia from Jericho. Since Herod was buried there, the *μνημεῖον* of Herod near Jerusalem, *B.J.* v 3, 2 (109); 12, 2 (507), is only a memorial and does not mark the actual grave. On the hypogaeum in the Wadi Rababy commonly identified as the *μνημεῖον* of Herod, see L. H. Vincent and M. H. Stève, *Jérusalem de l'Ancient Testament* (1954), pp. 342–6 and 710; it was quite possibly a family tomb for the house of Herod.

The end of his reign was as bloody as its beginning. Its better times lay between the two. But even then, Herod was a despot, and despite all the brilliance of his reign, not a man of personal distinction. The epithet 'Great' by which it is customary to differentiate him from lesser descendants of the same name is justified only in this relative sense.[167]

167. It is in this sense that ὁ μέγας is meant by Josephus in the sole passage where it appears, *Ant.* xviii 5, 4 (130).

§ 16. Disturbances after Herod's Death 4 b.c.

Sources

Josephus, *Ant.* xvii 9–11 (206–323); *B.J.* ii 1–6 (1–100).
Nicolaus of Damascus, FGrH 90 F 136 (8)–(11).

Bibliography

Graetz, H., *Geschichte der Juden* III ([5]1905–6), pp. 245–53.
Brann, M., *De Herodis qui dicitur Magni filiis patrem in imperio secutis* I (1873) (deals only with the events of 4 b.c.).
Jones, A. H. M., *The Herods of Judaea* (1938, [2]1967), pp. 156–66.
Kennard, J. S., 'Judas of Galilee and his Clan', JQR 36 (1945–46), pp. 281–6.
Abel, F.-M., *Histoire de la Palestine* I (1952), pp. 407–14.
Hengel, M., *Die Zeloten: Untersuchungen zur jüdischen Freiheitsbewegung in der Zeit von Herodes I bis 70 n. Chr.* (1961), esp. pp. 331–6.

In Herod's last will and testament Archelaus had been named as successor to the throne. His first business therefore was to secure the emperor's confirmation of his father's instruction and, with this end in view, he resolved to journey to Rome. But before starting, he had to quell another rebellion in Jerusalem. The people could not easily forget the execution of the two rabbis, Judas and Matthias, and clamoured for the punishment of Herod's counsellors. Archelaus tried at first to conciliate the people. But when this had no effect other than to cause an increased uproar, and since the matter was disquieting on account of the approaching Passover festival when great crowds gathered in Jerusalem, he sent a detachment of soldiers against those assembled in the Temple to put down the riot by force. But the detachment was too weak to do anything against the infuriated masses. Some of the soldiers were stoned; the rest fled, together with their leader. It was not until Archelaus called out his whole force that he was able, amid great bloodshed, to suppress the rebellion.[1]

After he had thus restored peace by force, Archelaus hastened to Rome, leaving his brother Philip as administrator of the kingdom. Scarcely had he gone, when Antipas also started for Rome to press his own claims there. By Herod's third and last will he had received only Galilee and Peraea, whereas in the earlier second will he had been appointed successor to the throne. He therefore wished to point out to the emperor that the kingdom properly belonged to him and not to

1. *Ant.* xvii 9, 1–3 (206–18); *B.J.* ii 1, 1–3 (1–13).

Archelaus. Many other members of the Herodian family were also present in Rome at the same time as Archelaus and Antipas, and they too opposed Archelaus and expressed a strong desire that Palestine should be put under direct Roman government; if not, they would rather have Antipas than Archelaus.[2]

The sons of Herod thus plotted and schemed against one another in Rome. Augustus, in whose hands the decision lay, meanwhile convoked at his palace a council at which the brothers were called on to argue their conflicting claims. A certain Antipater spoke on behalf of Antipas, while Nicolaus of Damascus, Herod's former minister, appeared on behalf of Archelaus. Each sought to win over the emperor, partly by reasoning, partly by casting suspicion on his opponent. When Augustus had heard both parties, he inclined more to Archelaus and declared him to be the most worthy of the two to mount the throne. Yet he did not wish to decide the matter immediately, and dismissed the council without pronouncing final judgment.[3]

But before the question of the succession to the throne was settled in Rome, new troubles broke out in Judaea. The Jews had again risen in revolt soon after Archelaus's departure, but had been restored to order by Varus, the governor of Syria. Varus had then returned to Antioch, leaving behind in Jerusalem a legion to maintain the peace. But no sooner had he gone than the storm broke out afresh. After Herod's death, pending the settlement of the question of his successor, the emperor had sent into Judaea a procurator, Sabinus. This person oppressed the people in every sort of way, and generally behaved most recklessly. As a result, immediately Varus left, there was another rebellion. It was the season of the Feast of Weeks (Pentecost) and crowds of people were present in Jerusalem. They divided into three bands and attacked the Romans at three different points: north of the Temple, south beside the hippodrome, and west of the city near the royal palace. The keenest struggle took place first of all near the Temple. The Romans pressed forward successfully into the Temple court, but the Jews offered stiff resistance, climbing on to the roofs of the buildings surrounding the Temple court and hurling down stones upon the soldiers. These were obliged to resort to fire; they set the buildings alight and in this way finally gained the Temple mount. The Temple treasure fell to them as loot, of which Sabinus took 400 talents for himself.[4]

This first defeat was merely the signal for a further spread of the rebellion. In Jerusalem some of Herod's soldiers joined the rebels, and

2. *Ant.* xvii 9, 3–4 (218–27); *B.J.* ii 2, 1–3 (14–22). Nic. Dam., FGrH 90 F 136 (9).
3. *Ant.* xviii 9, 5–7 (228–49); *B.J.* ii 2, 4–7 (25–38).
4. *Ant.* xvii 10, 1–2 (250–64); *B.J.* ii 3, 1–3 (39–50).

they were in consequence able to subject Sabinus and his detachment to a formal siege in Herod's palace.[5] In the neighbourhood of Sepphoris in Galilee, Judas, son of the Hezekiah/Ezekias with whom Herod had once, to the great indignation of the Sanhedrin, made such short shrift (see above, p. 275), collected around him a group, gained possession of the weapons stored in the royal arsenal, distributed these among his followers and made the whole of Galilee unsafe. He is even said to have coveted the royal crown.[6] In Peraea, a former slave of Herod called Simon assembled a band and had himself proclaimed king by his followers; but he was defeated by a Roman detachment soon afterwards, and put to death.[7] Finally, it is reported that a former shepherd named Athronges put on the royal crown and, with his four brothers, for a long time made the country insecure.[8] It was a period of general upheaval from which each tried to obtain the maximum benefit for himself.

When Varus was informed of these events, he hastened from Antioch, with the two legions which he still had to restore order in Judaea. On the way, he was joined by Nabataean auxiliary troops sent by King Aretas, as well as by other auxiliaries. With this force he first of all cleared Galilee. Sepphoris, where Judas had been causing mischief, was set on fire and its inhabitants sold as slaves. From there, Varus proceeded to Samaria, which he spared because it had not taken part in the revolt, and then marched towards Jerusalem, where the legion stationed there was still being besieged by the Jews in the royal palace. Here, Varus had an easy task, for when the besiegers saw the powerful Roman forces approach, they lost courage and fled. With this, he became master of the city and the country. But Sabinus, whose conscience was uneasy because of the Temple robberies and other misdeeds, made off as quickly as possible. Varus then sent his troops up and down through the country to capture those rebels who were still wandering about in small groups. He had two thousand of them crucified, but he granted pardon to the mass of the people. After stamping out the rebellion in this way, he returned to Antioch.[9]

5. *Ant.* xvii 10, 3 (265–8); *B.J.* ii 3, 4 (51–4).

6. *Ant.* xvii 10, 5 (271–2); *B.J.* ii 4, 1 (56). Concerning the identity of this Judas and Judas the Galilean, see below p. 381. Cf. also J. S. Kennard, 'Judas of Galilee and his Clan', JQR 36 (1945–6), pp. 281–6.

7. *Ant.* xvii 10, 6 (273–7); *B.J.* ii 4, 2 (57–9).

8. *Ant.* xvii 10, 7 (278–84); *B.J.* ii 4, 3 (60–5).

9. *Ant.* xvii 10, 9–10 (286–98); *B.J.* ii 5, 1–3 (66–79). This war of Varus is also referred to in *c. Ap.* i, 7 (34) as one of the most important between the conquest of Pompey and that of Vespasian. The name Varus is therefore probably to be restored in a corrupt passage in *Seder Olam*, in which it is said that 'from the war of Asveros to the war of Vespasian there were eighty years'. Although the number eighty is somewhat too high, and although the best texts give **אסוירוס**, it is

While this was going on in Judaea, Archelaus and Antipas were still in Rome awaiting the emperor's decision. Before it was given, yet another embassy from the people of Judaea appeared before Augustus, asking that none of the Herodians should be appointed king, but that they should be permitted to live in accordance with their own laws. About the same time, Philip, the last of the three brothers to whom territories had been bequeathed by Herod, made his appearance in Rome to press his own claims, and so support those of his brother Archelaus.[10] Augustus was finally obliged to make a decision. In a council which he called for this purpose in the temple of Apollo he heard first the delegation of the Jewish people. These presented him with a long list of Herod's scandalous misdeeds and sought thereby to buttress their demand that no Herodian should again rule in Palestine, but that they should be permitted to live according to their own laws under Roman suzerainty. When they had finished, Nicolaus of Damascus rose and spoke on behalf of his master Archelaus.[11] A few days after Augustus had thus heard both sides, he issued his decision. The will of Herod was confirmed in all its essential points. Archelaus was awarded the territory assigned to him: Judaea, Samaria, Idumaea. But the cities of Gaza, Gadara, and Hippus were detached from it and joined to the province of Syria. And instead of the title of king, he was given that of ethnarch. Antipas obtained Galilee and Peraea, with the title of tetrarch; Philip, also as tetrarch, received the regions of Batanaea, Trachonitis, and Auranitis. Archelaus was to derive from his territories an income of 600 talents, Antipas 200 talents, and Philip 100 talents. Salome, the sister of Herod the Great, also obtained the portion bequeathed to her, the cities of Jamnia, Azotus, Phasaelis, and 500,000 pieces of silver, in addition to the palace of Ascalon.[12] Salome

[*Text continues on p.* 335

nevertheless highly probable that ורוס should be read, that is, Varus (so Graetz, *op. cit.*, pp. 249, 714 ff. (note 18); Derenbourg, *Histoire*, p. 194. On the textual tradition, see A. Neubauer, *Mediaeval Jewish Chronicles* II (*Anecdota Oxoniensia*, Semitic Series, vol. I, Part vi), 1895, p. 66, and B. Ratner, *Seder Olam, die grosse Weltchronik* (1897), p. 145. The whole passage will be quoted below, p. 534, n. 92.

10. *Ant.* xvii 11, 1 (299–303); *B.J.* ii 6, 1 (83). The facts here related may have provided the framework for the Parable of the Pounds (Lk. 19:12–27). Cf. especially v. 12: 'A nobleman [Archelaus] went into a far country [Rome] to receive a kingdom [Judaea] and then returned;' v. 14: 'But his citizens hated him, and sent an embassy after him, saying, "We do not want this man to reign over us".'

11. *Ant.* xvii, 11, 2–3 (304–16); *B.J.* ii 6, 2 (92).

12. *Ant.* xvii 11, 4–5 (317–23); *B.J.* ii 6, 3 (93–100); cf. also Nic. Dam. FGrH 90 F 136 (11); Strabo, xvi 2, 46 (765). On the cities mentioned above (Gaza, Gadara, Hippus, Jamnia, Azotus, Phasaelis), see vol. II, § 23, 1. The title of *ἐθνάρχης* evidently signifies a rank somewhat higher than that of *τετράρχης*. The Hasmonaean princes, for example, bore the former before assuming the royal

title (1 Mac. 14:47; 15:1–2). It was also conferred upon Hyrcanus II by Caesar, *Ant.* xiv 10, 2 (191). The title τετράρχης is much more common. Herod the Great and his brother Phasael had already received it from Antonius, *Ant.* xiv 13, 1 (326); *B.J.* i 12, 5 (244). In 20 B.C. Pheroras was made tetrach of Peraea, *Ant.* xv, 10, 3 (362); *B.J.* i 24, 5 (483). The expression τετραρχία is first attested in the fifth century B.C. with regard to Thessaly, which from ancient times was divided into four districts (Euripides, *Alcestis* 1154; Syll.³ 274; see Harpocration, *Lex.*, ed. Dindorf, *s.v.* 'Τετραρχία' . . . καὶ 'Αριστοτέλης δὲ ἐν τῇ κοινῇ Θετταλῶν πολιτείᾳ ἐπὶ 'Αλεύα τοῦ Πύρρου διῃρῆσθαί φησιν εἰς δ' μοίρας τὴν Θετταλίαν. When Philip of Macedon brought all Thessaly under his rule, he appointed an ἄρχων over each τετράς (Harpocration, *loc. cit.*=FGrH 115 F 208: ὅτι δὲ Φίλιππος καθ' ἑκάστην τούτων τῶν μοιρῶν ἄρχοντα κατέστησε δεδηλώκασιν ἄλλοι τε καὶ Θεόπομπος ἐν τῇ μδ'). In this connection Demosthenes states that Philip had established tetrarchies in Thessaly (Demosth. *Philipp.* iii, 26: ἀλλὰ Θετταλία πῶς ἔχει; οὐχὶ τὰς πολιτείας καὶ τὰς πόλεις αὐτῶν παρῄρηται καὶ τετραρχίας κατέστησεν). Thus in Demosthenes τετραρχία means 'domination of a quarter' (government over a τετράς, whence is derived also τετραδαρχία). Similarly, the expression occurs in Galatia in this original sense. According to Strabo it was ruled by twelve tetrarchs, *viz.* four over each of three tribes of Trocmi, Tolistobogi and Tectosagi, Strabo, xii 5, 1 (566 ff.); less accurately, Pliny, *NH* v 42/146. As most of these were murdered by Mithridates (App. *Mith.* 46/178), Pompey so arranged things that he appointed one tetrach over each of the three races. Later, their number was reduced to two, and finally to one, Deiotarus (Strabo, xii 5, 1 (567); see the detailed account of these conditions in Niese, RhMus, 38 (1883), pp. 583–600, and B. A. Zwintscher, *De Galatarum tetrarchis et Amynta rege quaestiones* (1892), pp. 1–26.) However, although the title of tetrach had in this way completely lost its original meaning, it was still retained; for the title of king, which some assumed at the same time, did not apply to Galatia, but to other possessions, Strabo xii 3, 13 (547); xiii 4, 3 (625); Niese, *loc. cit.* Moreover, the title τετράρχης completely denuded of its original meaning is encountered quite frequently in Roman times. It then denoted simply a minor dependent prince whose rank and political power were less than that of a king. There seem to have been many such tetrachs, especially in Syria. See Pliny, *NH* v 16/74 f. 'intercurrent cinguntque has urbes (Decapoleos) tetrachiae, regnorum instar singulae', *ibid.* 17/77: 'Decapolitana regio praedictaeque cum ea tetrarchiae'; *ibid.* 19/81: 'Nazerinorum tetrarchia'; *ibid.*: 'tetrarchias duas quae Granucomatitae vocantur'; *ibid.* 19/82: 'tetrarchiam quae Mammisea appellatur'; *ibid.*: 'tetrarchias in regna descriptas barbaris nominibus XVII'; Jos. *Vita* 11 (52) ἔγγονος Σοέμου τοῦ περὶ τὸν Λίβανον τετραρχοῦντος. Antonius gave away 'tetrarchies and kingdoms' (Plut. *Ant.* 36: πολλοῖς ἐχαρίζετο τετραρχίας καὶ βασιλείας ἐθνῶν μεγάλων). Varus's army in 4 B.C. included auxiliaries, whom ἢ βασιλεῖς ἤ τινες τετράρχαι τότε παρεῖχον (*Ant.* xvii 10, 9 (286). In Nero's time, 'tetrarchs and kings' in Asia were instructed to obey the commands of Corbulo (Tac. *Ann.* xv, 25: 'scribitur tetrarchis ac regibus praefectisque et procuratoribus . . . iussis Corbulonis obsequi'. And so generally in Roman times *tetrarchae* often appear as minor princes of subordinate rank beside the *reges*; (*e.g.*, Cicero, *in Vatinium*, 12/29; *pro Balbo*, 5/13; *pro Milone*, 28/76; *Philipp.* xi 12/31; Caesar, *Bell. Civ.* iii 3; *Bell. Alex.* 78; Horace, *Sat.* i 3, 12; further examples may be found in the literature cited below). Better known than the Galatian tetrarchs and Herodian princes are the names of tetrarchs of Chalcis or Ituraea: Ptolemy, Lysanias, Zenodorus (for these see Appendix I). From the limited importance of these minor princes, it is not surprising that the title τετράρχης figures comparatively seldom on inscriptions and coins. On inscriptions, see IGR III 200=SEG VI 56; OGIS 349; 549 (on Galatian tetrarchs); OGIS 416, 417 (both refer to Herod Antipas); OGIS 606, IGLS 2851 (Chalcis dynasty);

lived to enjoy these possessions for some twelve or fourteen years. She died about A.D. 10, in the time of the procurator M. Ambivius, and bequeathed her property to the Empress Livia.[13]

The former kingdom of Herod was thereby divided into three territories, each of which had for a while its own history.

OGIS 543, 544. Of coins, besides those of Philip and Herod Antipas, only those of Ptolemy, Lysanias and Zenodorus need to be considered (see Appendix I). Cf. Stephanus, *Thesaurus*, *s.v.* *τετράρχης* and *τετραρχία*; RE s.v. 'Tetrarch'; Bohn, *Qua condicione juris reges socii populi Romani fuerint* (1877), p. 9–11; Niese, 'Galatien und seine Tetrarchen', Rh.Mus. 38 (1883), pp. 583–600; Zwintscher, *op. cit.*; D. Magie, *Roman Rule in Asia Minor* (1950), ch. xix, n. 8.

13. *Ant.* xviii 2, 2 (31).

§ 17. From the Death of Herod the Great to Agrippa I
4 B.C.–A.D. 41

The Sons of Herod

1. *Philip* 4 B.C.–A.D. 33/4

Sources

Josephus, *Ant.* xviii 2, 1 (27–8); 4, 6 (106–8); 6, 10 (237); *B.J.* ii 9, 1 (167–8); 6 (181).
On the coins, see n. 9 below.

Bibliography

Brann, M., *Die Söhne des Herodes* (1873), pp. 77–87.
Schalit, A., 'Herodes und seine Nachfolger', *Kontexte*, III *Die Zeit Jesu* (1966), pp. 34–42.
Jones, A. H. M., *The Herods of Judaea* ([2]1967), pp. 156–66.

The extent of the territory which Philip received is variously stated by Josephus in different passages.[1] Altogether, it comprised the regions of Batanaea, Trachonitis, Auranitis, Gaulanitis, Panias, and, according to Lk. 3:1, Ituraea also.[2] The areas named were not ancient tribal [*Text continues on p.* 338

1. *Ant.* xvii 8, 1 (189); 11, 4 (319); xviii 4, 6 (106); *B.J.* ii 6, 3 (95). In the latter passage there follows after Batanaea, Trachonitis and Auranitis, *καὶ μέρη τινὰ τοῦ Ζήνωνος οἴκου τὰ περὶ Ἰάμνειαν*. So the printed common text supported by two manuscripts; in place of *Ἰάμνειαν* three manuscripts have *Ἰνναvω*, two *Ἰναν*. It should certainly read *Πανειάδα* in accordance with *Ant.* xvii 8, 1 (189).

2. Batanaea corresponds to the Old Testament Bashan, Euseb. *Onomast.*, ed. Klostermann, p. 44, *Βασάν . . . αὕτη ἐστὶ Βασανῖτις, ἡ νῦν καλουμένη Βαταναία.* Yet ancient Bashan was of larger extent than the later Batanaea, comprising as it did the whole region beyond the Jordan, between Hermon in the north and the district of Gilead in the south, and extending eastward as far as Salcah (on the southern slope of the Hauran); see Dt. 3:10, 13; Jos. 12:4; 13:11 f.; 13:30 f.; 17:1, 5; 1 Chr. 5:23. But within this region lay the later provinces of Trachonitis, Auranitis and Gaulanitis; Batanaea was therefore only a part of ancient Bashan. However, the expression is sometimes used even by later writers in the wider sense, *e.g.* Jos. *Vita* 11 (54) *μετὰ τῶν ἐν Βαταναίᾳ Τραχωνιτῶν.* Since the cities of Ashtaroth and Edrei are named as the chief cities of Bashan (Jos. 12:4; 13:11 f.; 13:30 f.) it may be assumed that these marked the centre of the later Batanaea also. Edrei, later Adraa, the modern Der'a, lies almost exactly halfway between the southern point of Lake Gennesaret and the southern end of the mountains of Hauran. That Ashtaroth and Adraa lay in Batanaea is stated by Eusebius, *Onomast.*, ed. Kloster-

mann, p. 12, s.v. *'Ασταρώθ* (cf. p. 112 s.v. *Καρνείμ*). The Greek *Βαταναία* appears also in Polybius, xvi 39 = Jos. *Ant.* xii 3, 3 (135–6) and Ptolemy, V 15, 26. For the most detailed available maps of this area see H. C. Butler, F. A. Norris, E. R. Stoever, *Syria: Publications of the Princeton University Archaeological Expeditions to Syria in 1904–5 and 1909 I: Geography and Itinerary* (1930).

Trachonitis or *ὁ Τράχων* (so Josephus, *Ant.* xiii 16, 5 (427); xv 10, 1 (343); *B.J.* ii 6, 3 (95), and the inscription from Phaena) is the rugged plateau south of Damascus extending towards Boẓra now called the Lejah. It therefore lies north-east of Batanaea proper. Proof of this is afforded by the following data. On an inscription at Phaena, in the north of the Lejah, this place is characterized as *μητροκωμία τοῦ Τράχωνος* (OGIS 609 = IGR III 1119. Strabo mentions the *Τράχωνες* as two hills in the neighbourhood of Damascus, Strabo, xvi 2, 20 (756) *ὑπέρκεινται δ' αὐτῆς δύο λεγόμενοι λόφοι Τραχῶνες*. Cf. xvi 2, 16 (755). Eusebius consistently assigns Trachonitis to the immediate neighbourhood of Boẓra (*Onomast.*, s.v. *'Ιτουραία*, ed. Klostermann, p. 110 *Τραχωνῖτις δὲ καλεῖται ἡ παρακειμένη χώρα τῇ ἐρήμῳ τῇ κατὰ Βόστραν τῆς 'Αραβίας· ibid.*, s.v. *Κανάθ*, p. 112 *κεῖται δὲ εἰς ἔτι καὶ νῦν ἐν Τραχῶνι πλησίον Βόστρων· ibid.*, s.v. *Τραχωνῖτις*, p. 166 *ἔστιν δὲ καὶ ἐπέκεινα Βόστρων κατὰ τὴν ἔρημον πρὸς νότον ὡς ἐπὶ Δαμασκόν*. Also, a rabbinical passage concerning the boundaries of Palestine reads: 'Trakhon, in the neighbourhood of Boẓra' (ySheb. 36c.; tSheb. 4:11, ed. Zuckermandel, p. 66; Siphre-Dt. (51); the Jerusalem Talmud has טרכון דמתחם לבצרה ('Trakhon, which borders on Boẓra'); likewise a Tosephta MS.; another reads: ט' דבתחום ב' ('Trakhon, on the border of Boẓra'); cf. A. Neubauer, *Géographie du Talmud*, pp. 10–21, and especially I. Hildesheimer, *Beiträge zur Geographie Palästinas* (1886) (on Trakhon, pp. 55–7); on the rabbinical passages, see S. Krauss, *Griechische u. lateinische Lehnwörter im Talmud* . . . II, p. 275. The Targums identify טרכונא with the Biblical Argob (cf. Onk. Dt. 3:4, 13 f.; Ps.-Jon. reads טרגונא). Pliny refers to Trachonitis as being in the neighbourhood of Panias (Plin. *NH* V 16/74). Ptolemy mentions the *Τραχωνῖται Ἄραβες* as east of Batanaea (Ptolem. V 15, 26). Regarding Lk. 3:1, it is of interest to note that Philo, or rather Agrippa in the letter quoted by Philo, uses the abbreviated designation *τὴν Τραχωνῖτιν λεγομένην* for Philip's territory as a whole (just as he employs for the territories of Herod Antipas the designation *τὴν Γαλιλαίαν* both *a parte potiori*, as in Luke; see Philo, *Leg.* 41 (326). Similarly, Josephus also, *Ant.* xviii 5, 4 (137) *Φιλίππῳ . . . τῷ τετραρχῇ τῆς Τραχωνίτιδος*, immediately after, of Antipas, *τὴν δὲ Γαλιλαίων τετραρχίαν οὗτος εἶχεν*.

Auranitis is the חורן of Ezek. 47:16, 18, which is also mentioned in the Mishnah (mR. Sh. 2:4) as one of the stations for the fire signals from Judaea to Babylon. Since from the context of the Mishnah, Hauran must be a mountain, Auranitis is undoubtedly the country around the mountain peak called Jebel Hauran. For a map see Butler, Norris, Stoever, *Syria* (see above), p. 17. See also R. E. Brünnow, A. von Domaszewski, *Die Provincia Arabia* III (1909); M. Dunand, 'Rapport sur une mission archéologique au Djebel Druze', Syria 7 (1926), pp. 326–35; D. Sourdel, *Les cultes du Hauran à l'époque romaine* (1952); note pp. v–xiv for a full bibliography of the region.

Gaulanitis has its name from the place Golan, considered in the Bible to be in Bashan (Dt. 4:43; Jos. 20:8; 21:27; 1 Chr. 6:56; Euseb. *Onomast.*, ed. Klostermann, p. 64). Josephus distinguishes Upper and Lower Gaulanitis, and remarks that Gamala lay in the latter, *B.J.* iv 1, 1 (2); the same passage locates Gamala east of Lake Gennesaret. According to *B.J.* iii 3, 1 (37), Gaulanitis provided the eastern boundary of Galilee. Gaulanitis is therefore the same area as the lowlands east of the Jordan, from its source to the southern tip of Lake Gennesaret. For a map see ZDPV 22 (1899), pp. 178–88.

The district of Panias, at the sources of the Jordan (see vol. II, § 23, i, on the town of Panias) belonged in earlier times to Zenodorus, and before that, to the possessions of the Jewish people, but were for the most part added to Jewish territory in later times. The population was mixed, and the non-Jewish (Syrian or Greek) element prevailed.[3] Philip himself was

---

kingdom of the Ituraeans (see Appendix I). In this respect, Luke's statement that Philip also ruled over Ituraea is not altogether incorrect. But that region constituted only a small portion of what had formerly been the kingdom of the Ituraeans. The Ituraeans proper inhabited the Lebanon (see Appendix I) and during the period A.D. 38–49 were under the sovereignty of a certain Soaemus (Dio lix 12, 2; Tac. *Ann.* xii 23) while at the same time Agrippa I possessed the entire tetrarchy of Philip, Jos. *Ant.* xviii 6, 10 (237); xix 8, 2 (351). The bulk of the Ituraean territory cannot therefore have belonged to the domain of Philip.

Cf. on the areas mentioned above: H. Reland, *Palaestina* (1714), pp. 106–10, 193–203; Waddington, CRAI (1865), pp. 82–9, 102–9; G. Schumacher, *Across the Jordan, being an Exploration and Survey of Part of Hauran and Jaulan* (1886), and his *Northern Ajlûn* (1890); Schumacher, 'Der Dscholan, zum ersten Male aufgenommen u. beschrieben, mit Karte', ZDPV 9 (1886), pp. 165–363; and ZDPV 22 (1899), pp. 178–88; *idem*, 'Das südliche Basan, zum ersten Male aufgenommen u. beschrieben, mit Karte', ZDPV 20 (1897), pp. 65–227; Guthe, ZDPV 12 (1889), pp. 230 ff.; H. Fischer, *ibid.*, 248 ff. (good survey of exploration work in the Hauran region); F. Buhl, *Studien zur Topographie des nördlichen Ostjordanlandes* (1894); G. A. Smith, *Historical Geography of the Holy Land* (1894), pp. 538–47, 554, 665 ff. (with bibliography); W. Ewing, PEFQSt (1895), pp. 73–82 (the borders between Auranitis and Arabia); R. Dussaud, *Topographie historique de la Syrie antique et médiévale* (1927), pp. 523–412; A. H. M. Jones, *Cities of the Eastern Roman Provinces* (1937; ²1971), esp. pp. 284–91; M. Avi-Yonah, *The Holy Land* (1966), pp. 164–8.

With regard to the southern borders of the tetrarchy of Philip, the region around present-day Boẓra and Salcah (south of the Hauran) did not belong to his domain, as is proved by inscriptions with the names of the Nabataean kings Malchus and Aretas, discovered in these cities. See M. de Vogüé, *Syrie centrale, Inscriptions sémitiques* (1868), p. 103 p, 107=CIS II *Aram.*, n. 174, 182. On the other hand, Hebrân on the southern slope of the Hauran still belonged to his territory for an Aramaic inscription found there is dated, not according to the regnal years of a Nabataean king but of Claudius: ('in the month Tishri in the 7th year of the Emperor Claudius'=A.D. 47; see de Vogüé, *loc. cit.*, p. 100=CIS II *Aram.*, n. 170). From this one may conclude that Hebrân belonged to the domain of Philip, which in A.D. 37 was given to Agrippa I and after his death placed under Roman administration; cf. remarks in P. Le Bas, H. Waddington, *Inscriptions* III, n. 2286.

3. During the last years of his reign Herod the Great settled Jewish colonists from Babylon in Batanaea under the leadership of a certain Zamaris, and conferred on them the privilege of complete freedom from taxation, which was in all essential points also respected by Philip; see *Ant.* xvii 2, 1–3 (23–30). For the history of this colony, cf. also Josephus, *Vita* 11 (56–7); F. de Saulcy, 'Monnaies des Zamarides'; Num. Chron., 11 (1871), pp. 157–61; these 'coins of the Zamaridae' are in the highest degree problematical. In Trachonitis, Herod the Great had likewise settled 3,000 Idumaeans, to whom he assigned the task of maintaining the peace of the district against the robber bands that inhabited it; see *Ant.* xvi 9, 2 (285). The majority of the inhabitants were Gentiles, as is proved by the great number of Greek inscriptions still preserved in that region. Cf. also in general, *B.J.* iii 3, 5 (56–8) οἰκοῦσι δὲ αὐτὴν μιγάδες Ἰουδαῖοί τε καὶ Σύροι, and vol. II, § 22, i.

certainly an exception among the sons and grandsons of Herod. Whereas all the others, in imitation of their father and grandfather, were ambitious, domineering, harsh and tyrannical toward their subjects, of Philip only praiseworthy reports are given. His reign was mild, just and peaceful. He was faithful to the traditions of his father only in so far as he sought fame in the construction of great edifices. He is reported in particular to have raised two cities. He rebuilt and enlarged ancient Panias, at the sources of the Jordan north of Lake Gennesaret, and named it Caesarea in honour of the emperor. To distinguish it from the better known Caesarea on the coast, it was called Caesarea Philippi, under which name it appears in the Gospels (Mt. 16:13; Mk. 8:27). The other city he rebuilt was Bethsaida,[4] situated at the point where the Jordan enters Lake Gennesaret; he named it Julias, in honour of the daughter of Augustus.[5] Josephus writes that it was he who first discovered and proved that the supposed source of the Jordan at Panias obtained its water by an underground stream from the so-called Phiale. Philip demonstrated this by throwing chaff into Phiale which reappeared at Panias.[6]

Otherwise nothing more is known about his reign beyond Josephus's observation on the occasion of his death: 'He showed himself in his government to be of a modest and peace-loving disposition. He spent his whole life in his own land. When he went on circuit, he was accompanied only by a few chosen companions and he always had with him the throne on which he pronounced judgment. Whenever he encountered anyone needing his help, he had the throne set up immediately, wherever it might be. He took his seat and heard the case, sentenced the guilty and released those unjustly accused.'[7] All that is known of his private life is that he married Salome, daughter of Herodias, and that there were no children by the marriage.[8] Politically, he was a consistent friend of the Romans and attached great value to imperial favour. This may be gathered not only from the names he gave to the cities of Caesarea and Julias, but also from the images of Augustus and Tiberius impressed on his coins. This was for the first time that human effigies

4. See vol. II, § 23, i.

5. *Ant.* xviii 2, 1 (28); *B.J.* ii 9, 1 (168). On both cities, the date of their reconstruction and earlier history, see vol. II, § 23, i.

6. *B.J.* iii 10, 7 (509–15). From Josephus's description Phiale should be Birket er-Ram. But his story is impossible owing to the relative water levels. See Guérin, *Galilée* II, pp. 329–31; Schumacher, ZDPV 9 (1886), pp. 256 f. (with map).

7. *Ant.* xviii 4, 6 (106–7). The seating of a judge upon the *sella* was a necessary formality without which his words had no validity. For examples, see Mt. 27:19; Jn. 19:13; Acts 25:6; Jos. *B.J.* ii 9, 3 (172)—Pilate; ii 14, 8 (301)—Florus; iii 10, 10 (532)—Vespasian. On the *sella curulis* of the magistrates in Rome cf. Mommsen, *Röm. Staatsrecht* III[3], p. 399; RE s.v. 'sella curulis'.

8. *Ant.* xviii 5, 4 (139).

including, it now seems, his own, were engraved on the coins of a Jewish prince.[9]

Philip died, after a reign of 37 years, in the 20th year of Tiberius (=A.D. 33/34) and was buried in a tomb built by himself.[10] His territory was added to the province of Syria but retained the right of administering its own revenues[11], and after a few years was again made over to a prince of the Herodian family. The emperor Caligula, immediately after his accession to the throne (March, A.D. 37), bestowed the tetrarchy of Philip on Agrippa, a son of the Aristobulus executed by his father Herod, and therefore a grandson of Herod and Mariamme.[12]

2. *Herod Antipas* 4 B.C.–A.D. 39

Sources

Josephus, *Ant.* xviii 2, 1 (27); 3 (36–8); 4, 5 (101–5); 5, 1–3 (109–29); 7, 1–2 (240–56); *B.J.* ii 9, 1 (167–8); 6 (181–3).

New Testament: Mt. 14:1–12; Mk. 6:14–29; Lk. 3:19–20; 9:7–9; 13:31–2; 23:6–12.

On the coins, see n. 16 below.

---

9. It should of course be borne in mind that Philip's domain was predominantly pagan. Cf. on the coins, Madden, *History*, pp. 100–2; Madden, *Coins of the Jews* (1881), pp. 123–7; *BMC Palestine*, pp. xcvii, 228; A. Reifenberg, *Ancient Jewish Coins* (²1947), pp. 19, 43–5; Y. Meshorer, *Jewish Coins of the Second Temple Period* (1967), pp. 76–7. The coins have on the one side the name of Philip *ΦΙΛΙΠΠΟΥ ΤΕΤΡΑΡΧΟΥ* together with the image of a temple and the year numbers 5, 9, 12, 16, 19, 30, 33, 34, 37. The year numbers 26 and 29 given by Mionnet are regarded by de Saulcy as erroneous readings. The coin of the year 37 (first communicated by Madden, *History*, p. 102) is from the last year of Philip=A.D. 33/34. The coins of the years 12 and 16 (=A.D. 8/9 and 12/13) have on the obverse the head of Augustus and on the reverse the inscription *ΚΑΙΣΑΡΙ ΣΕΒΑΣΤΩ* (fragmentary); those of the years 19, 30, 34 and 37 the head of Tiberius and the full name *ΤΙΒΕΡΙΟΣ ΣΕΒΑΣΤΟΣ ΚΑΙΣΑΡ*. The temple engraved on all the coins is doubtless the temple of Augustus at Panias which Herod the Great had built, *Ant.* xv 10, 3 (363); *B.J.* i 21, 3 (404). The type is therefore wholly pagan. The image and name of the emperor are also found on the coins of many other dependent kings from the time of Augustus onward; but there are also instances in which all allusion to the supreme imperial authority is lacking; see Bohn, *Qua condicione juris reges socii populi Romani fuerint* (1877), pp. 45–9.

See now A. Kindler, 'A Coin of Herod Philip—the Earliest Portrait of a Herodian Ruler', IEJ 21 (1971), pp. 161–3.

10. *Ant.* xviii 4, 6 (106, 108). The 20th year of Tiberius was probably calculated subsequently from the day of Augustus's death, 19th August A.D. 33; but see D. M. Pippidi, *Autour de Tibère* (1944), pp. 125–32. The 37th year of Philip ends (reckoning from Nisan to Nisan; cf. p. 327) in the spring of A.D. 34. Philip therefore died in the winter of A.D. 33/34.

11. *Ant.* xviii 4, 6 (108).

12. *Ant.* xviii 6, 10 (237); *B.J.* ii 9, 6 (183).

Bibliography

Brann, M., *Die Söhne des Herodes* (1873), pp. 17–76.
Otto, W., RE s.v. 'Herodes' (4).
PIR[2] A 746 (Antipas Herodes).
Abel, F.-M., *Histoire de la Palestine* I (1952), pp. 440–4.
Bruce, F. F., 'Herod Antipas, Tetrarch of Galilee and Peraea', ALUOS 5 (1963–65), pp. 6–23.
Jones, A. H. M., *The Herods of Judaea* ([2]1967), pp. 176–83.
Hoehner, H. W., *Herod Antipas* (1972).

In the partition of their father's possessions, a larger share was allotted to Antipas, or Herod—as he is frequently called by Josephus and always on coins and in the New Testament—than was given to his half-brother Philip. But like him, he received the title of tetrarch.[1] His territory (Galilee and Peraea) was divided into two parts by the so-called Decapolis, which formed a wedge between Galilee and Peraea.[2] But for this he was amply compensated by the fact that half of it consisted of the beautiful, fertile and densely populated Galilee, with its vigorous, stalwart and freedom-loving inhabitants.[3] In character, Antipas was a true son of his father, astute, ambitious and a lover of luxury; but he was less able than Herod the Great.[4] Jesus is said to

1. He is thus correctly described in Mt. 14:1; Lk. 3:19, but incorrectly in Mk. 6:14, *βασιλεύς*. Since Herod Antipas is the only Herod to have borne the title of tetrarch, the two following inscriptions undoubtedly refer to him and testify at the same time of his foreign travels.

(a) On the island of Cos (Paton and Hicks, *Inscriptions of Cos*, no. 75= OGIS 416):

Ἡρῴδην
Ἡρῴδου τοῦ βασιλέως υἱόν,
τετράρχην,
Φίλων Ἀγλαοῦ, φύσει δὲ Νίκωνος,
τὸν αὑτοῦ ξένον καὶ φίλον.

(b) On the island of Delos (OGIS 417=*Ins. de Délos* no. 1586):

Ὁ δῆμος ὁ Ἀθ[η]ν[αίων καὶ οἱ]
κατοικοῦ[ντ]ε[ς] τὴ[ν νῆσον]
Ἡρῴδην βασιλέω[ς Ἡ]ρ[ῴδου υἱὸν]
τετράρχην ἀρετῆς [ἕνεκεν καὶ εὐνοί-]
ας τῆς εἰς ἑαυτοὺ[ς . . . ἀνέθηκαν?].

2. See e.g. *The Macmillan Bible Atlas* (1968), p. 145. On the Decapolis (Mt. 4:25; Mk. 5:20; 7:31), see vol. II, § 22.

3. Cf. the description of Galilee in *B.J.* iii 3, 2–3 (41–7); 10, 8 (516–21); see in general S. Klein, *Galiläa von der Römerzeit bis 67 n. Chr.* (1928); cf. *Galilee: Geography and History of Galilee from the Return from Babylonia to the Conclusion of the Talmud* (1967) (in Hebrew), and G. Vermes, *Jesus the Jew* (1973), ch II. On the borders of Galilee and Peraea, see vol. II, § 22, i.

4. Josephus, *Ant.* xviii 7, 2 (245), characterizes him as ἀγαπῶν τὴν ἡσυχίαν.

have testified to his cunning when he called him 'that fox'.[5] Astuteness was in any case necessary if the Galileans were to be kept in order and the frontiers of Peraea guarded against Nabataean raiders. To make Galilee safe, he rebuilt Sepphoris which had been destroyed by fire at the hands of the soldiers of Varus (see above, p. 332), and surrounded it with strong walls. And for the defence of Peraea he fortified Betharamphtha and named it Livias after the emperor's wife, and later Julias.[6] It was undoubtedly for political motives also that he married the daughter of the Nabataean king Aretas.[7] He believed that in doing so he would provide a better protection for his land against the inroads of the Nabataeans than any amount of fortifications; and perhaps it was Augustus himself who persuaded him to enter into this marriage.[8]

Like all the Herods, Herod Antipas delighted in magnificent architecture. Particularly excellent in this respect was the splendid capital which he built during the time of Tiberius.[9] He selected for it 'the best locality in Galilee' (Josephus: *τοῖς κρατίστοις . . . τῆς Γαλιλαίας*), the western bank of the lake of Gennesaret, near the warm springs of Emmaus. The choice of site was in one sense unfortunate, for, as became apparent from the sepulchral monuments exposed by the building operations, it was an ancient burial ground and as such forbidden to observant Jews as a place of habitation: any contact with graves rendered them ritually impure for seven days.[10] To people the city, Herod was therefore obliged to colonize it by force with many foreigners, adventurers and beggars; the population was consequently of a very mixed character. But the magnificence of the buildings left nothing to be desired. It had, among other public edifices, a *στάδιον*[11] and a royal palace, which gave offence because of its animal images

5. Lk. 13:32. A. R. C. Leaney, *Commentary on . . . Luke* (1958), p. 209, considers 'that fox' not as a symbol of craftiness but of destruction. See, on the other hand, W. Manson, *The Gospel of Luke* (1937), p. 169. In the Talmud the fox is expressly described as 'that which is called the most cunning of beasts'—**שאומרים עליו פקח שבחיות** (bBer. 61b). (Cf. Str.-B. II, pp. 200–1, showing that the term may indicate slyness, but more often insignificance (the fox is proverbially contrasted with the lion). Cf. also H. W. Hoehner, *Herod Antipas* (1972), pp. 343–7.

6. *Ant.* xviii 2, 1 (27); *B.J.* ii 9, 1 (168). On both cities and on the change of name from Livias to Julias, see Hoehner, *op. cit.*, pp. 84–91, and vol. II, § 23, i.

7. *Ant.* xviii 5, 1 (109). On Aretas and the Nabataean kings generally, see Appendix II.

8. Cf. Suet. *Div. Aug.*, 48 'Reges socios etiam inter semet ipsos necessitudinibus mutuis iunxit, promptissimus affinitatis, cuiusque atque amicitiae conciliator et fautor'.

9. On the date of the building of Tiberias, see Hoehner, *op. cit.*, pp. 93–5, and vol. II, § 23, i.

10. Num. 19:16; Jos. *Ant.* xviii 2, 3 (38). For more details concerning impurity caused by graves, see mOhol. 17–18.

11. *B.J.* ii 21, 6 (618); iii 10, 10 (539); *Vita* 17 (92); 64 (331).

and fell victim to Jewish zeal at the time of the war with the Romans.[12] There was also a Jewish *προσευχή*, a *μέγιστον οἴκημα*.[13] The city's constitution was modelled entirely on the Hellenistic pattern. It had a council (*βουλή*) of 600 members, with an *ἄρχων* and a council of the *δέκα πρῶτοι*, as well as hyparchs and an agoranomos. In honour of the emperor the new capital was named Tiberias.[14]

During the time of Pilate (A.D. 26–36), Antipas, together with his brothers, brought a successful complaint against him over the erection of an offensive votive shield in the palace at Jerusalem.[15] And just as he represented Jewish demands on this occasion, so—despite his heathen buildings at Tiberias—he dared not evade the claims of Judaism entirely in other respects also. Here, too, he was a true son of his father. According to the Gospel tradition, he went up to Jerusalem for the feasts (Lk. 23:7) and his coins, like those of the elder Herod, bear no image.[16]

The complaint against Pilate was possibly not made before A.D. 31.[17] All that is otherwise known of Herod Antipas also belongs to the same

12. *Vita* 12 (65–7).

13. *Vita* 54 (277).

14. On the building of Tiberias in general, see *Ant.* xviii 2, 3 (36 ff.); *B.J.* ii 9, 1 (168); *Vita* 9 (37–9); cf. M. Avi-Yonah, 'The Foundation of Tiberias', IEJ (1951), pp. 160–9. For further details concerning the city and its institutions, see Hoehner, *op. cit.*, pp. 91–100, and vol. II, § 23, i.

15. Philo, *Leg.* 38 (299–305). Philo does not mention the name of Antipas, but states that *τούς τε βασιλέως* [*Ἡρῴδου*] *υἱεῖς τέτταρας οὐκ ἀποδέοντας τό τε ἀξίωμα καὶ τὰς τύχας βασιλέων* made themselves especially prominent in the business. Philip and Antipas were primarily intended by this statement (Archelaus was no longer in Palestine after A.D. 6). But the identity of the other two is uncertain. We know of course from *Ant.* xvii 1, 3 (19–22); *B.J.* i 28, 4 (562–3) of three other sons of Herod who might be named in this connexion: (1) Herod, son of Mariamme; (2) Herod, son of Cleopatra; (3) Phasael, son of Pallas; on the identity of the sons see E. M. Smallwood, *Leg. ad Gaium* (1961, ²1969), *ad loc.*

16. On the coins of Herod Antipas, Madden, *History*, pp. 95–9; *BMC Palestine*, pp. xcvii, 229; Reifenberg, *Ancient Jewish Coins* (²1947), p. 19; *Coins of the Jews* (1881), pp. 118–22; Y. Meshorer, *Jewish Coins of the Second Temple Period* (1967), pp. 72–5, 133–5. The coins fall into two categories: (1) One class has the inscription *ΗΡΩΔΟΥ ΤΕΤΡΑΡΧΟΥ* with the year numbers 24, 31?, 33, 34, 36, 37, 38; on the other side the name of the city *ΤΙΒΕΡΙΑΣ*; (2) The second class has the inscription *ΗΡΩΔΗΣ ΤΕΤΡΑΡΧΗΣ*; on the other side, *ΓΑΙΩ ΚΑΙΣΑ*[*ΡΙ*] *ΓΕΡΜΑΝΙΚΩ*. Of this (second) class, only three examples can be identified with certainty, all with the year *ΜΓ*=43 (*i.e.* A.D. 39/40). The coins of Antipas bearing the name of the emperor (without his image) occupy a middle position between those of Herod the Great, which carry neither the emperor's name nor his image, and those of Philip, which have both.

17. As may be suggested by Philo, *Leg.* 24 (159–61), according to which Tiberius was unfavourably disposed towards the Jews during the lifetime of Sejanus (died A.D. 31) but after his death behaved with great indulgence towards their religious peculiarities. Cf. E. M. Smallwood, 'Some Notes on the Jews under Tiberius', Latomus 15 (1956), pp. 314–29.

period, the last ten years or so of his reign. During that time he was almost entirely under the influence of a woman who caused him a whole series of misfortunes. Once, shortly before he made a journey to Rome—we do not know why, nor exactly when—he visited his half-brother Herod, the son of Mariamme the High Priest's daughter, who had been designated eventual successor to the throne in Herod's first will (see above, p. 324). This Herod was married to Herodias, a daughter of the Aristobulus who had been executed in 7 B.C.[18] From the marriage of these two was born Salome, the wife of the tetrarch Philip, who was therefore not, as the Gospels report, the first husband of Herodias, but her son-in-law.[19] When Antipas visited the house of his brother, he was attracted to Herodias and proposed marriage to her, which the ambitious woman readily accepted. It was arranged that on his return from Rome, Antipas should divorce his wife, the daughter of Aretas, and marry Herodias. With this promise, he set off on his journey to Rome. On his return, his wife, who had meanwhile heard of these arrangements, begged him to have her sent to Machaerus, the fortress east of the Dead Sea. Since Antipas did not suspect that his wife knew about his secret plans, he granted her wish. But scarcely had the daughter of Aretas reached Machaerus than she escaped from there to her father and told him of her husband's unfriendly intentions towards her. From then on, the Nabataean king was on bad terms with Herod Antipas.[20] He nevertheless seems to have proceeded immediately with his marriage to Herodias.

18. On Herodias, see RE s.v. 'Herodias' Supp. II, cols. 202–5; PIR² H 161.

19. *Ant.* xviii 5, 4 (136–42). Philip is named as the first husband of Herodias in Mk. 6:17. In the parallel passage, Mt. 14:3, the name is absent from cod. D., and is placed in brackets by Tischendorf. In Lk. 3:19, on the other hand, where the name similarly appears in the *textus receptus*, it is deleted by Nestle and Aland. Since according to Josephus it was not the tetrarch Philip, but the Herod mentioned above, who was the first husband of Herodias, Mark's statement must be an error. Many, it is true have tried to explain the mistake by assuming that the person referred to in Mark as Herod Philip was distinct from the tetrarch. But it would be very remarkable that one designation should have been chosen by Josephus and another by the New Testament writers, and still more peculiar that the elder Herod should have had two sons called Philip. If by way of analogy it is pointed out that several of his sons bore the name of Herod, the argument is not conclusive for this was the family name. And the analogy of the two brothers Antipater and Antipas is just as inconclusive for these are in fact quite different names.

20. *Ant.* xviii 5, 1 (113). On Machaerus, see above, p. 308 and § 20. According to the traditional Josephus text, Machaerus must at that time have belonged to the Nabataean king for it states that the princess, intending to flee, had previously sent (messengers) εἰς τὸν Μαχαιροῦντα τότε πατρὶ αὐτῆς ὑποτελῆ (thus all editions from *ed. princ.* to Hudson, Havercamp and Dindorf inclusive; only Bekker conjectured τὸν τῷ instead of τότε). This seems very strange, for Machaerus both earlier and later belonged continuously to Jewish territory (Alexander Jannaeus

It was at this time, or soon afterwards, that John the Baptist and Jesus made their appearance, both of them carrying on their work in territories belonging to Antipas, the Baptist in Peraea[21] and Jesus in Galilee. Of John the Baptist, Josephus gives the following account:[22] 'He was a good man, and exhorted the Jews to lead righteous lives, practise justice towards one another and piety towards God, and so to join in baptism. In his view this was a necessary preliminary if baptism was to be acceptable to God. They must not use it to gain pardon for whatever sins they committed, but as a consecration of the body, implying that the soul was thoroughly purified beforehand by right behaviour. When many others joined the crowds about him, for they were greatly moved on hearing his words, Herod feared that John's great influence over the people would lead to a rebellion (for they seemed ready to do anything he might advise). Herod decided therefore that it would be much better to strike first and be rid of him before his work led to an uprising, than to wait for an upheaval, become involved in a difficult situation and see his mistake. Accordingly John was sent as a prisoner to Machaerus, the fortress mentioned before, because of Herod's suspicious temper, and was there put to death.'

---

fortified it, and so did Herod the Great, *B.J.* vii 6, 2 (171–7); Herod Antipas imprisoned John the Baptist there; in the war under Vespasian it was one of the last places of refuge for the rebels, *B.J.* ii 18, 6 (486); vii 6 (163–209)). Also, it is unlikely that Antipas would so unsuspectingly have allowed his wife to go to a fortress he did not possess. Actually, there is nothing in the text of Josephus to indicate that Machaerus belonged to the Nabataean king at that time for all the manuscripts (according to Niese) have *εἰς τὸν Μαχαιροῦντα τῷ τε πατρὶ αὐτῆς ὑποτελεῖ* (not *ὑποτελῆ*). This can only mean 'to Machaerus and to the subjects of her father' (that is, to the tribes subject to her father). For surveys of the site of Machaerus, and the archaeological indications that it lay near, but not beyond, the Nabataean border, see N. Glueck in BASOR 68 (Dec. 1937), pp. 15–16, and AASOR 18/19 (1937/9), pp. 131–5. On the journey through Nabataean territory, the daughter of Aretas was supported by her father's military officers (*στρατηγοί*). The title **אסרתגא** occurs frequently on Nabataean inscriptions; see vol. II, § 22, ii.

21. The scene of the Baptist's activity may have been mostly on the West bank of the Jordan, and therefore in Judaea. He did, however, also operate on the East bank, in Peraea, as is shown not only by the Fourth Gospel (1:28; 3:26; 10:40) but especially by the fact of his arrest by Antipas.

22. *Ant.* xviii 5, 2 (117–19) *κτείνει γὰρ δὴ τοῦτον Ἡρῴδης ἀγαθὸν ἄνδρα, καὶ τοῖς Ἰουδαίοις κελεύοντα ἀρετὴν ἐπασκοῦσιν καὶ τὰ πρὸς ἀλλήλους δικαιοσύνῃ καὶ πρὸς τὸν θεὸν εὐσεβείᾳ χρωμένοις βαπτισμῷ συνιέναι· οὕτω γὰρ δὴ καὶ τὴν βάπτισιν ἀποδεκτὴν αὐτῷ φανεῖσθαι, μὴ ἐπί τινων ἁμαρτάδων παραιτήσει χρωμένων, ἀλλ' ἐφ' ἁγνείᾳ τοῦ σώματος, ἅτε δὴ καὶ τῆς ψυχῆς δικαιοσύνῃ προεκκεκαθαρμένης. καὶ τῶν ἄλλων συστρεφομένων, καὶ γὰρ ἤρθησαν ἐπὶ πλεῖστον τῇ ἀκροάσει τῶν λόγων, δείσας Ἡρῴδης τὸ ἐπὶ τοσόνδε πιθανὸν αὐτοῦ τοῖς ἀνθρώποις μὴ ἐπὶ ἀποστάσει τινὶ φέροι, πάντα γὰρ ἐῴκεσαν συμβουλῇ τῇ ἐκείνου πράξοντες, πολὺ κρεῖττον ἡγεῖται, πρίν τι νεώτερον ἐξ αὐτοῦ γενέσθαι, προλαβὼν ἀνελεῖν τοῦ μεταβολῆς γενομένης εἰς πράγματα ἐμπεσὼν μετανοεῖν. καὶ ὁ μὲν ὑποψίᾳ τῇ Ἡρῴδου δέσμιος εἰς τὸν Μαχαιροῦντα πεμπφθεὶς, τὸ προειρημένον φρούριον, ταύτῃ κτίννυται.* Cf. L. H. Feldman's translation and comments in *Josephus* (Loeb) IX, pp. 82–5.

This report by Josephus and the New Testament accounts of the Baptist and his relation with the tetrarch Herod complement each other. Josephus's version of John's preaching seems to be adapted to Graeco-Roman taste. From this point of view, the short statements of the synoptic Gospels may strike a more genuine note.[23] On the other hand, it is highly probable that the real motive for the imprisonment of the Baptist by Antipas was, as Josephus states, fear of political unrest. The powerful preacher undoubtedly caused a great stir which was indeed primarily religious but was certainly not without a political impact. For at that time the mass of the people were unable to differentiate between their religious and political hopes. It is therefore quite credible that Antipas feared political troubles from the Baptist's preaching and that he ordered his arrest when he extended his activity to Peraea. Nevertheless, the evangelists may be right (Mt. 14:3 f.; Mk. 6:17 f.; Lk. 3:19 f.), when they state that he did this because John condemned his marriage with Herodias. The two statements are not inconsistent.[24] The place of John's imprisonment is not named by the evangelists. According to Josephus, it was at Machaerus, the fortress east of the Dead Sea. From his account, the Baptist's imprisonment seems to have been followed immediately by his execution. But from the evangelists' it appears that Herod kept the Baptist in prison for a protracted period, uncertain what to do with him.[25] In the end, a decision was precipitated by Herodias, the principal enemy of the austere preacher of repentance. At a great banquet in celebration of Antipas's birthday[26] in the palace of Machaerus—for it was there that

[*Text continues on p.* 348

23. For literature on the Josephus passage cf. L. H. Feldman, *op. cit.*, Appendix M, p. 577. For modern discussions see C. H. Kraeling, *John the Baptist* (1951) and IDB s.v. 'John the Baptist'.

24. The passage of Josephus was known to Origen (*c. Cels.* I, 47). Eusebius quotes it in full (*HE* i 11, 4–6; *DE* ix 5, 15). Its genuineness is rarely disputed. In its favour is the fact that the motives for the imprisonment and execution of the Baptist are entirely different from the Gospel version. But since the text of Josephus has certainly been retouched by Christian scribes in other passages, the theory of an interpolation cannot be absolutely excluded. Suspicion is aroused by the favourable verdict on John, but against this it should be borne in mind that as an ascetic and moral preacher, he might have been viewed sympathetically by Josephus.

25. Mt. 14:5; Mk. 6:20; Mt. 11:2–6.

26. The meaning of *γενέσια* (Mt. 14:6; Mk. 6:21) is a matter of controversy. Instead of the ordinary meaning 'birthday', many commentators understand it to mean 'the anniversary day of his accession to the throne'. But this sense is not positively demonstrable in the field of Greek literature. Thus if occasionally the anniversary of the day of accession to the throne is called *γενέθλιος διαδήματος* (OGIS 383=IGLS 1 ll. 83–4 (see below); cf. however, H. Dörrie, *Der Königskult des Antiochus von Kommagene im Lichte neuer Inschriften-Funde* (1964), p. 65–274) or *natalis imperii* (SHA *Vita Hadr.* 4; SHA *Vita Pert.* 15), this does not prove that *γενέθλιος* or *γενέσιος* without addition can also have this meaning (for *natalis* or

natalicia this usage is traceable only in the fourth-century calendar of Philocalus; see Mommsen, *Staatsrecht* II[3], 2, pp. 812 f.). Rabbinical support is also very weak. The principal passage is mA.Z. 1:3, 'The following are the festivals of the heathen: the *Calendae* and the *Saturnalia* and the κρατήσεις (קרטסים) and the day of the γενέσια (גיניסיא) of the kings and the day of birth and the day of death. Thus R. Meir.' (Cf. W. A. L. Emslie, *The Mishna on Idolatry 'Aboda Zara* (1911), pp. 4–6.) No explanation of the expressions used is given in the Mishnah. In the Palestinian Talmud (yA.Z. 39c) יום גיניסיא is interpreted by יום הלידה 'birthday'. The Babylonian Talmud (bA.Z. 10a) presents a detailed discussion on the meaning and reasons are advanced in favour of the interpretation 'birthday', but preference is finally given to the interpretation שמעמידין בו מלך—'the day on which the king ascended the throne' (see J. Levy, *Neuhebr. Wörterb.* I,349a; M. Jastrow, *Dictionary*, p. 240 and the English translation of the text of the whole discussion in the Soncino Talmud, ed. I. Epstein, *Nezikin* VII (1935), pp. 39–50). It is substantially on the basis of this that the interpretation 'anniversary of accession to the throne' is adopted by many modern scholars. But since the Palestinians were doubtless better informed about such matters than the Babylonians, who mostly guessed without knowing, the interpretation of the latter should not be accepted when it is opposed to all other instances (so also G. Dalman, ThLZ, 1889, p. 172). Also, the context in the Mishnah favours the interpretation 'birthday', for קרטיסים is the anniversary of attainment to power (cf. S. Lieberman, *Greek in Jewish Palestine* ([2]1965), pp. 9–10; for κράτησις in the sense of 'prohibition', see *ibid.*, pp. 10–12). גיניסיא must thus be distinguished from it. But the 'day of birth' mentioned nearby, is not, as further investigation of the Mishnah shows, the anniversary of a birth but simply the day on which a child is born. In the Palestinian Targum (Ps.–Jon. and Neof.) also, in Gen. 40, 20, יום גניסיא appears with the meaning 'birthday'. On rabbinic linguistic usage generally, cf. S. Krauss, *Griechische und lat. Lehnwörter im Talmud* . . . II (1899), p. 180; L. Blau, REJ, 27 (1893), pp. 298 f.; E. E. Urbach, 'The Rabbinical Laws of Idolatry in the Second and Third Centuries', IEJ 9 (1959), pp. 240–1; see also pp. 149–65; 229–45.

The custom of celebrating the birthday of princes and private persons is very old. Already in Genesis, there is reference to the Pharaoh's birthday (Gen. 40:20). King Amasis of Egypt, when still a private individual, is said to have presented a splendid wreath of flowers to his predecessor, King Patarmis, on his birthday (γενέθλια ἐπιτελοῦντι Πατάρμιδι; thus Hellanicus, in FGrH 4 F 55. Plato remarks that all Asia celebrated the birthday of the Persian king (Plato, *Alcib.* i, 121C: βασιλέως γενέθλια ἅπασα θύει καὶ ἑορτάζει ἡ 'Ασία). Cf. K. F. Hermann *Lehrbuch der griech. Privatalterthümer* ([3]1882), ed. Blümner, pp. 285 f., 501; RE s.v. 'γενέθλιος ἡμέρα'; Marquardt, *Das Privatleben der Römer* I (1879), pp. 244 f.; Ernst Curtius, *Geburtstagsfeier im Alterthum, Festrede* (*Monatsberichte der Berliner Akademie*, 1876, pp. 31–7=*Alterthum u. Gegenwart, Gesammelte Reden u. Vorträge* II, pp. 15–21). As birthday celebrations with great banquets are mentioned in the Bible only in connexion with Pharaoh and Herod Antipas, Origen and Jerome were of the opinion that only wicked persons did this. Origen on Matthew 10:22 (*Origenes Werke* X, ed. Klostermann, GCS (1935), p. 30; Jerome, *Opp.*, ed. Vallarsi, VII, 101 (PL xxvi, col. 97)—both in their notes on Mt. 14:6). The Herodian princes celebrated not only their birthdays—besides Herod Antipas see also Agrippa I, Jos. *Ant.* xix 7, 1 (321)—but also the anniversary of their accession to the throne, *Ant.* xv 11, 6 (423). These two customs were very widespread. The decree of Canopus (under Ptolemy III, 239/238 B.C.) relates to priests, who assembled εἰς τὴν πέμπτην τοῦ Δίου, ἐν ᾗ ἄγεται τὰ γενέθλια τοῦ βασιλέως, καὶ εἰς τὴν πέμπτην καὶ εἰκάδα τοῦ αὐτοῦ μηνός, ἐν ᾗ παρέλαβεν τὴν βασιλείαν παρὰ τοῦ πατρός. (Strack, *Die Dynastie der Ptolemäer*, 1897, pp. 227 ff.=OGIS 56 ll. 5–6.) The

the whole business took place[27]—Salome the daughter of Herodias (she was still a *κοράσιον*, Mt. 14:11; Mk. 6:22, 28 and therefore not yet married to Philip) so delighted the tetrarch by her dancing that he promised to fulfil any wish she might express. At the instigation of her mother, she demanded the head of the Baptist. And Herod was weak enough to gratify her desire immediately and had him beheaded then and there.[28]

Rosetta Stone (under Ptolemy V, 196 B.C.) mentions *τὴν τρια[κ]άδα τοῦ Μεσορῆ, ἐν ᾗ τὰ γενέθλια τοῦ βασιλέως ἄγεται, ὁμοίως δὲ καὶ [τὴν ἑπτακαιδεκάτην τοῦ Φαωφὶ], ἐν ᾗ παρέλαβεν τὴν βασιλείαν παρὰ τοῦ πατρός* (Letronne, *Receuil des inscr. grecques et lat. de l'Egypte* I, 241 ff. = Strack, pp. 240 ff. = OGIS 90, ll. 46–7; cf. on both decrees also Niese, *Gesch. der griech. u. makedon. Staaten* II, pp. 171, 673). According to both decrees, the days were celebrated not only yearly but also monthly (Canopus, ll. 33–4, Rosetta, line 48). King Antiochus I of Commagene (1st cent. B.C.) tells us in the inscription he composed for his own tomb: *σώματος μὲγα γὰρ ἐμοῦ γενέθλιον Αὐδναίου ἑκκαιδεκάτην, διαδήματος δὲ Λῴου δεκάτην ἀφιέρωσα μεγάλων δαιμόνων ἐπιφανείαις*. (IGLS 1, ll. 83–6). The celebration of these days was also both yearly and monthly (ll. 99–105; cf. also on monthly birthdays, 2 Mac 6:7; E. Rohde, *Psyche* ([2]1894), p. 235 and ZNW 2 (1901), pp. 48–52, on the arguments of H. Willrich, *Judaica*, p. 164. In Rome the emperor's birthday and the anniversary of his accession were celebrated as public festivals (CIL I[2], pp. 301–3; Mommsen, *Röm. Staatsrecht* II, 2 ([3]1887), pp. 812 f.); G. Wissowa, *Religion und Kultus der Römer* ([2]1911), pp. 344 f.; W. F. Snyder, 'Public Anniversaries in the Roman Empire', YCS 7 (1940), pp. 223–317.

The birthdays of the dead were also celebrated; on the frequency of this custom, see the literature cited, and Rohde, *Psyche* I, pp. 235 f. On the inscription of Antiochus I of Commagene already mentioned, the king stipulates precisely how his birthday is to be celebrated yearly and monthly after his death for all time.

Attic linguistic usage distinguished between *γενέθλια* and *γενέσια* in such a way that the former was employed in connexion with the living and the latter in connexion with the dead (Ammonius, *de adf. vocab. differentia*, 116: *γενέθλια τάσσεται ἐπὶ τῶν ζώντων . . . γενέσια δὲ ἐπὶ τῶν τεθνηκότων, ἐν ᾗ ἕκαστος ἡμέρᾳ τετελεύτηκε* cf. Stephanus, *Thes.*, *s.v. γενέσιος*.) In later Greek, however, *γενέσια* is also used of the living (Alciphron, *Epp.* II, 15; III, 19 (Schepers); Josephus, *Ant.* xii 4, 7 (196); xii 4, 9 (215); in the last-mentioned passage some codices have *γενεθλίῳ*). In Philo, *de opif. mundi* 30 (89), one manuscript and the editions before Mangey have *τοῦ κόσμου γενέσιον* but the correct reading here is *γενέθλιον*. Cassius Dio uses *γενέσια* only in connexion with the dead, but *γενέθλια* in connexion with the living. Cf. W. Nawijn, *Cassii Dionis Cocceiani Historiarum Romanarum Index Graecitatis* (1931), p. 158.

27. The Gospels (Matthew and Mark) evidently assume that the banquet was given at the place where the Baptist lay imprisoned, i.e., Machaerus. And in fact the banquet may have taken place there, in the beautiful palace which Herod the Great had built, *B.J.* vii 6, 2 (175). The Gospels are silent in regard to the place; for from Mk. 6:21 it is not necessary to conclude that Mark assumes Galilee (i.e. Tiberias) to be the scene of action (cf. e.g. E. Klostermann, *Das Markusevangelium* ([4]1950), p. 60).

28. Mt. 14:6–11; Mk. 6:21–8; Lk. 9:9. In Mk. 6:22 some very important MSS. (the Hesychian text and D) read *τῆς θυγατρὸς αὐτοῦ Ἡρῳδιάδος*. According to this, the young woman herself was called Herodias and was a daughter of Herod

Even before John disappeared from the scene, Jesus had already made his appearance and begun to preach the gospel in Galilee. He, too, could not remain unnoticed by the tetrarch. But Antipas did not hear of his activities until after the Baptist had been put to death, and conscience-stricken, imagined that the Baptist had risen again and was continuing his great work.[29] To make sure, he wished to see the miracle-worker who was preaching in Capernaum and converting the multitudes.[30] He meant apparently to get rid of him also.[31] Subsequently, Jesus left Galilee to make his last journey to Jerusalem. And there, according to Luke's Gospel alone, Antipas, who was staying in the city for the Feast of Passover, had the satisfaction of meeting his enigmatic subject. Pilate sent the prisoner to him so that as ruler of Galilee he might pronounce sentence on him. But Antipas refused to

---

Antipas, and not just of Herodias. But a child of the marriage of Antipas with Herodias could at that time have been only a year or two old; on the other hand, it is known from *Ant.* xviii 5, 4 (136), that Herodias had a daughter called Salome by her first marriage. Moreover, in the Gospel narrative itself the young woman figures simply as a daughter of Herodias. Hence, such a reading of Mark (however ancient) can in no case be historically correct. On the imprisonment and execution of the Baptist in general, see the literature cited in n. 23 above. The Gospel narrative contains much that arouses suspicion, for instance that Salome is still designated as *κοράσιον* whereas one would think from Josephus that in A.D. 28–30 she had been for a long time married to the tetrarch Philip, who began his reign in 4 B.C. and died in A.D. 33/4 (see above, p. 340). But careful investigation shows that even on this weak point the narrative is not unlikely. The facts emerging from Josephus are summarised by Gutschmid (*Kleine Schriften* II, p. 318): 'Aristobulus, Salome's second husband, was a son of Herod of Chalcis by Mariam, the daughter of Joseph and Olympias, a sister of Archelaus, who married after 7 B.C. but before 4 B.C. Therefore Mariam can have been born not earlier than 5 B.C., and her son Aristobulus, scarcely before A.D. 14. This gives an approximate clue to determining the age of Salome, who should not necessarily be regarded as much older than Aristobulus since her second marriage, by which she had three sons, evidently took place while she was still young. Philip, her first husband, was of an age to rule in 4 or 3 B.C., and must therefore have been born in 21 B.C. at the latest. However great the disparity between them, there is nevertheless little likelihood of it having exceeded 30 years. This would give A.D. 10 as the latest date for the birth of Salome.' Gutschmid therefore assumes that Salome was born in about A.D. 10 and regards it as quite possible that she was still a *κοράσιον* in A.D. 28 and married the forty-nine-year-old Philip when she was nineteen. On a coin of Aristobulus there is also an image of his wife Salome (cf. PIR² A 1052). See Appendix I below.

29. Mt. 14:1 f.; Mk. 6:14–16; Lk. 9:7–9.

30. Lk. 9:9. Among the women followers of Jesus was the wife of one of Antipas's officials (Lk. 8:3 *Ἰωάννα γυνὴ Χουζᾶ ἐπιτρόπου Ἡρῴδου*). The name כוזא occurs on a Nabataean epitaph (F. C. Burkitt, Expositor 9 (1899) pp. 118–22; CIS II 1, p. 227). Cf. Hoehner, *op. cit.*, pp. 303–4.

31. Lk. 13:31–2.

co-operate and was content to ridicule Jesus and return him to Pilate.[32]

His union with Herodias brought Antipas little good. The Nabataean king Aretas could not forget that Antipas had repudiated his daughter because of her. The enmity thus generated was aggravated by boundary disputes about Gabalitis—this, rather than 'Galaaditis', is the most probable correction of the manuscript readings 'Gamalitis' or 'Gamalia'.[33] At last, in A.D. 36, it came to a war between the two neighbours, which ended in the total defeat of Antipas.[34] The only resort now left to the conquered tetrarch was to bring a charge against his victorious opponent before the emperor Tiberius.[35]

When Tiberius heard of the Nabataean prince's bold enterprise, he gave Vitellius, governor of Syria, express orders to capture him, dead or alive. Vitellius decided on the venture somewhat unwillingly for he was not greatly drawn to Antipas. But since he could not disobey the imperial command, he prepared for war against Aretas. Ordering his army to march against Petra with a detour round Judaea, he himself went on a visit to Jerusalem, where a feast was being celebrated, probably Passover. He stayed there for three days. On the fourth day, he received news of the death of Tiberius (16 March A.D. 37). He considered himself thereby relieved of his task and turned back with his army to Antioch.[36] The defeat of Antipas remained therefore unavenged.

At about this time, the tetrarch was once present on the Euphrates during important negotiations between Vitellius and the king of the Parthians. But it seems that Josephus's account of this is not free from error. It is known for instance that in A.D. 35 and 36 the Parthian king Artabanus had repeated dealings with the Romans. His affairs seemed to be taking a favourable turn when the threats of Vitellius and the defection of his own subjects obliged him to flee to the remoter provinces. Vitellius then went to the Euphrates in the summer of A.D. 36

32. Lk. 23:7–12. On the chronology of the ministry of John the Baptist and the corresponding question of the date of Jesus' death, see now the detailed discussion in H. W. Hoehner, *Herod Antipas* (1972), pp. 307–12.

33. The district of Gamala belonged to the former tetrarchy of Philip and cannot therefore have been a subject of dispute between Aretas and Antipas. The province of Galaaditis (Gilead) lay on the borders of their territories; *ΓΑΛΑΑΔΙΤΙΣ* could have become *ΓΑΜΑΛΙΤΙΣ*. But *ΓΑΒΑΛΙΤΙΣ* is palaeographically even more likely, and the area in question east of the southern half of the Dead Sea is also more probable as the subject of a dispute. Undoubtedly the text of the passage *Ant.* xviii 5, 1 (113) is defective. Cf. L. H. Feldman in *Josephus* (Loeb) IX, *ad loc.*

34. The date is derived from the fact that the defeat of Antipas occurred, as is shown by what follows, about six months before the death of Tiberius (March A.D. 37).

35. *Ant.* xviii 5, 1 (115).

36. *Ant.* xviii 5, 1 (115); 3 (120–6).

together with the pretender appointed by the Romans, Tiridates, and established the latter as ruler over the Parthian kingdom. However, before the end of that same year Artabanus returned, drove out Tiridates and regained power.[37] Subsequently Vitellius arranged a meeting on the Euphrates with Artabanus at which Artabanus concluded a peace with the Romans, leaving as a pledge his son Darius as hostage.[38] According to Josephus, Herod Antipas was also present at this encounter. He entertained Vitellius and Artabanus in a sumptuous tent erected on the Euphrates bridge, and as soon as the negotiations were concluded hastened to communicate in person the favourable result to the emperor—an officiousness that annoyed Vitellius exceedingly because Antipas thereby anticipated his official report.[39] Josephus places this meeting in the reign of Tiberius and considers the tension it engendered between Vitellius and Herod Antipas as the reason why Vitellius abandoned the campaign against Aretas immediately after the death of Tiberius. But Suetonius and Cassius Dio say expressly, and the silence of Tacitus in the 6th Book of his *Annals* attests it indirectly, that the meeting between Vitellius and Artabanus took place under Caligula. Josephus is therefore wrong in one particular. But which one? If it is correct that Herod Antipas took part in Parthian negotiations on the Euphrates in the reign of Tiberius, these must have been the negotiations between Vitellius and Tiridates in the summer of A.D. 36 (Tac. *Ann.* vi 37). But if it is correct that he took part in the negotiations between Vitellius and Artabanus, it cannot have been before the time of Caligula. The second supposition is the most likely. For in the summer of A.D. 36 Herod was engaged in the war against Aretas.[40]

If Antipas had his passion for Herodias to thank for the losses he sustained at the hands of Aretas, in the end it was his wife's ambition that cost him his position and his freedom. One of the first acts of the new emperor Caligula on taking office was to assign Agrippa, the brother of Herodias, Philip's former tetrarchy and the royal title. Agrippa at first remained in Rome. But in the second year of Caligula (March A.D. 38–March 39) he went to Palestine and made his appearance there as king. The success of the once penurious adventurer, who had even sought aid from Antipas, excited the envy of Herodias and

37. Tac. *Ann.* vi 31–7; 41–4 (with respect to the date, cf. also vi 38, beginning); Dio lviii 26; *Ant.* xviii 4, 4 (100). The establishment of the date is based on the statements of Tacitus.

38. Suet. *Cal.* 14; *Vit.* 2; Dio lix 27; Jos. *Ant.* xviii 4, 5 (101–3). Besides Josephus, Dio lix 17, 5, and Suet. *Cal.* 19, also mention Darius as being in Rome in A.D. 39.

39. *Ant.* xviii 4, 5 (104–5).

40. On Parthian history generally, cf. N. C. Debevoise, *A Political History of Parthia* (1938); M. A. R. Colledge, *The Parthians* (1967); for modern discussions of the date of the meeting on the Euphrates see K.-H. Ziegler, *Die Beziehungen zwischen Rom und dem Partherreich* (1964), p. 62.

she urged her husband to petition the emperor for a royal title for himself. Herod Antipas was disinclined but finally succumbed to his wife's insistence and set off with her for Rome to plead his cause. They were followed, however, by Agrippa's freedman, Fortunatus, with a list of charges against Herod Antipas accusing him of old and new offences, of collusion with Sejanus (who died in A.D. 31) and with the Parthian king Artabanus. As evidence of this, Antipas's store of weapons was referred to. Both parties arrived simultaneously in Baiae before Caligula. After the emperor had heard the petition and the indictment, he asked Antipas about the stockpile of weapons. And when Antipas could not deny it, Caligula credited him with the remaining charges, deposed him from his tetrarchy and banished him to Lugdunum in Gaul.[41] He wished to allow Herodias, as a sister of Agrippa, to live on her private estate. But the proud woman scorned the imperial favour and followed her husband into exile. As further proof of imperial benevolence, the accuser Agrippa was awarded the tetrarchy.[42]

41. So Josephus, *Ant.* xviii 7, 2 (252); on the other hand, *B.J.* ii 9, 6 (183): εἰς Σπανίαν or Ἰσπανίαν (which Niese corrects against all manuscript evidence to Γαλλίαν). Since besides the well-known Lugdunum (Lyons), there was another Lugdunum in Gaul, on the northern slopes of the Pyrenees in the territory of the Convenae (whence Lugdunum Convenarum), it could be this that is meant. The erroneous statement in *B.J.* (corrected in *Ant.*) would then be most easily explained, for it lay on the Spanish border. So *e.g.*, H. Schiller, *Gesch. der röm. Kaiserzeit* I, 383; O. Hirschfeld, *Kleine Schriften*, p. 173, n. 2; so also Otto, 'Herodes Antipas', cols. 195–6.

42. *Ant.* xviii 7, 1–2 (252); *B.J.* ii 9, 6 (183). According to the latter passage, Agrippa himself followed Herod Antipas; according to *Ant.*, he sent Fortunatus. On the discrepancy regarding the place of banishment, see the previous note. The date of the deposition of Antipas is determined partly from *Ant.* xviii 71–2 (240–56); cf. 6, 11 (238), partly from xix 8, 2 (351). In the latter passage it is said of Agrippa: *τέτταρας μὲν οὖν ἐπὶ Γαΐου Καίσαρος ἐβασίλευσεν ἐνιαυτούς, τῆς Φιλίππου μὲν τετραρχίας εἰς τριετίαν ἄρξας, τῷ τετάρτῳ δὲ καὶ τὴν Ἡρῴδου προσειληφώς*. As Caligula reigned from March A.D. 37 to January 41, Agrippa will thus have obtained the tetrarchy of Antipas at the beginning of A.D. 40. But according to *Ant.* xviii 6, 11 (238), Agrippa returned to Palestine in the second year of Caligula (March A.D. 38–39) with the benefit of the trade winds, ἐτησίαι—Philo, *In Flaccum* 5 (26), which blow from the 20th July for 30 days (Pliny, *NH* II 47/124). Consequently, since he visited Alexandria on the way (Philo, *loc. cit.*), he may have arrived in Palestine about the end of September in A.D. 38. As Antipas's deposition was closely connected with this, it would seem to have occurred, if not in A.D. 38, at least in 39. In fact, it can be proved that it occurred not earlier and not later than the summer of A.D. 39. Not earlier, for the 43rd year of Antipas, from which we have coins, did not begin till 1st Nisan A.D. 39. But not later either for Caligula was out of Rome from the autumn of 39 to the 31st August A.D. 40 on an expedition to Gaul, Germany and Britain (Dio lix 21–25; Suet. *Cal.* 17, 43–9; for his entry into Rome, 'natali suo' *i.e.*, 31st August, see Suet. *Cal.* 8). Bearing in mind, therefore, that Antipas was deposed while Caligula was at Baiae, and further that according to Josephus, *Ant.* xix 8, 2 (351) (which states that Agrippa had already reigned for one year under Caligula), it could not have taken place *after* the

Herod Antipas died in exile. A confused statement in Dio seems to imply that he was put to death by Caligula.[43]

3. (i) *Archelaus* 4 B.C.–A.D. 6

Sources

Josephus, *Ant.* xvii 13 (339–55); xviii, 1–4 (1–108); *B.J.* ii 7, 3–9, 4 (111–17).
Philo, *Legatio ad Gaium* (ed. Smallwood, 1961, ²1969).
On the coins, see n. 4 below.

Bibliography (i): Archelaus

Graetz, H., *Geschichte der Juden* III (⁵1905–6), pp. 252–3, 315–17, 341–4.
Brann, M., 'Die Söhne des Herodes' (1873), pp. 1–16.
Otto, W., RE s.v. 'Herodes Archelaos'.
Abel, F.-M., *Histoire de la Palestine* I (1952), pp. 417–20.
Jones, A. H. M., *The Herods of Judaea* (²1967), pp. 166–8.

German campaign (which is also impossible for the reason that Agrippa was again with the emperor from autumn A.D. 40 until Caligula's death—Philo, *Legatio* 35 (261 ff.); Josephus, *Ant.* xviii 8, 7 (289–93); Dio lix 24—whereas he was in Palestine at the time of Antipas's deposition; as well as for the reason that according to Philo, *Legatio* 41 (326), he was in possession of Galilee in the autumn of A.D. 40—from which it may be concluded that Tiberias no longer belonged to Herod Antipas at that time)—the deposition must have occurred *before* the German expedition, that is, before the autumn of A.D. 39. In that year, Caligula was twice in Campania (Baiae and Puteoli), the one visit being referred to in Dio lix 13, 7, and the other in Dio lix 17; Suet. *Cal.* 19. But after his second absence, he was probably again in Rome for his birthday, the 31st August (Dio lix 20; Suet. *Cal.* 26), after which he went on the German expedition. In consequence, the deposition of Antipas in Baiae probably occurred before the 31st August A.D. 39. But since Agrippa probably only obtained the tetrarchy of Antipas at the beginning of A.D. 40, Josephus, *Ant.* xix 8, 2 (351), it may be assumed that an interval of several months separated the deposition of Antipas and the conferment of his tetrarchy on Agrippa, and that this latter event did not take place until the time of Caligula's Gallo-German campaign.

43. Dio lix 8, 2 (Caligula) Ἀγρίππαν τὸν τοῦ Ἡρῴδου ἔγγονον λύσας τε . . . καὶ τῇ τοῦ πάππου ἀρχῇ προστάξας, τὸν ἀδελφὸν ἢ καὶ τὸν υἱὸν οὐχ ὅτι τῶν πατρῴων ἀπεστέρησεν, ἀλλὰ καὶ κατέσφαξε. Although the relationship is incorrectly expressed, the reference can only be to Herod Antipas. The execution of those whom he banished was a habit of Caligula; see Suet. *Cal.* 28; Dio lix 18, 3; Philo, *In Flaccum* 21 (180–3). According to Josephus, *B.J.* ii 9, 6 (183), Antipas died in exile. On the contradiction regarding the location in *B.J.* ii 9, 6 (183) and *Ant.* xviii 7, 2 (252), see above, p. 352. Since according to *B.J.*, Antipas was banished to Spain from the first and died there, we have no right to combine Josephus's contradictory statements by suggesting that he was later transferred from Lyons to Spain.

Bibliography (2): The Events of A.D. 6–41

Derenbourg, J., *Essai sur l'histoire et la géographie de la Palestine* (1867), pp. 195–204.
Graetz, H., *Geschichte der Juden* III ([5]1905–6), pp. 259–316.
Jackson, Foakes and Lake, Kirsopp, *The Beginnings of Christianity* I: *The Acts of the Apostles* I–V (1920–33).
Abel, F.-M., *Histoire de la Palestine* I (1952), pp. 421–43.
Lohse, E., 'Die römischen Statthalter in Jerusalem', ZDPV 74 (1958), pp. 69–78.
Winter, P., *On the Trial of Jesus* (1961).
Sherwin-White, A. N., *Roman Society and Roman Law in the New Testament* (1963).
For works on the background of the Roman administration of Judaea, see note 16.

(1) *Archelaus* 4 B.C.–A.D. 6

Judaea proper, with Samaria and Idumaea (including the large cities of Caesarea, Samaria, Joppa and Jerusalem, but excluding Gaza, Gadara and Hippus), was awarded as his share of Herod's kingdom to Archelaus, the elder brother[1] of Antipas, though not with the title of king, as Herod had intended, but only that of ethnarch.[2] Yet Augustus promised him royal status too if he should prove himself worthy of it.[3] Like Antipas, Archelaus adopted the family name of Herod on coins and elsewhere.[4]

Of all the sons of Herod, his reputation was the worst. His rule was brutal and tyrannical.[5] He appointed and dismissed the High Priests at will.[6] His marriage with Glaphyra, daughter of the Cappadocian king Archelaus, caused particular scandal. She had been married first to Alexander, the half-brother of Archelaus executed in 7 B.C. (see above, p. 324). After his death she married Juba, king of Mauretania.[7] When

1. *B.J.* i 32, 7 (646); 33, 7 (664).
2. He is inaccurately styled βασιλεύς in Mt. 2:22 and *Ant.* xviii 4, 3 (93). On the title ἐθνάρχης, see above, p. 333.
3. *Ant.* xvii 11, 4 (317); *B.J.* ii 6, 3 (93).
4. Josephus never calls him Herod, but Dio does in lv, 27, 6. And there is no doubt that the coins inscribed *ΗΡΩΔΟΥ ΕΘΝΑΡΧΟΥ* are his, for no other Herodian bore the title ἐθνάρχης (cf. Eckhel, *op. cit.* III, p. 484). Noteworthy is the fact that the coins of Archelaus, also, do not bear an image. On the coins, cf. de Saulcy, *Recherches*, pp. 133 f.; Madden, *History*, pp. 91–5; *Coins of the Jews*, pp. 114–18; Reifenberg, *Ancient Jewish Coins* ([2]1947), p. 20, 45–6; Meshorer, *Jewish Coins of the Second Temple Period* (1967), pp. 69–70, 130–2.
5. Ὠμότης καὶ τυραννίς are attributed to him in *Ant.* xvii 13, 2 (342). Cf. also *B.J.* ii 7, 3 (111).
6. *Ant.* xvii 13, 1 (339–41).
7. This king Juba was also a well-known scholar. Testimonia and fragments in Jacoby, FGrH 275. Cf. also RE s.v. 'Iuba' (2); F. Susemihl, *Gesch. der griech. Literatur in der Alexandrinerzeit* II (1892), pp. 402–14 (with extensive literary references); PIR[2] I 65. As a child (βρέφος, Appian; κομιδῇ νήπιος, Plutarch) Juba was led in triumph by Caesar in 46 B.C. (App. *BC* II 101/418; Plut. *Caesar*, 55). In 29 B.C. he received from Augustus his father's kingdom of Numidia (Dio li 15, 6). Four years later, in 25 B.C., Augustus gave him instead the lands of Bocchus and

this marriage was dissolved[8] Glaphyra went to live in her father's house. There Archelaus became acquainted with her, fell in love, and eventually married her, after divorcing his first wife Mariamme. As Glaphyra had children by Alexander, the marriage was unlawful and therefore gave great offence.[9] But it did not last long, for Glaphyra died soon after her arrival in Judaea[10] after a remarkable dream in which her first husband Alexander appeared to her and announced her approaching death.[11]

It goes without saying that Archelaus, as a son of Herod, also embarked on great building projects. The palace in Jericho was magnificently restored. An aqueduct was constructed to bring water from the village of Na'ara to the newly-planted palm-groves in the plain north of Jericho. He founded in his own honour a place to which he gave the name of Archelais.[12]

Boguas (*Mauretania Tingitana* and *Caesariensis*) and part of Gaetulia (Dio liii 26, 2). The numismatic evidence shows that he did not die until A.D. 23 (PIR² I 65). The marriage with Glaphyra probably occurred some time in the years 1 B.C. to A.D. 4 if Müller's conjecture is correct (*Fragm. Hist. Graec.* III, 465–84), namely that Juba became acquainted with Glaphyra whilst accompanying C. Caesar on his eastern expedition. An inscription in Athens refers to Glaphyra, OGIS 363 = IG II/III² 3437/8:

Ἡ βουλὴ καὶ [ὁ δ]ῆμος
[β]ασίλισσαν [Γλαφύραν] βασιλέω[ς]
Ἀρχελάου θυγ[ατέρα,] βασιλέως Ἰοβ[α]
γυναῖκ[α ἀρε]τῆς ἕνε[κ]α.

8. Josephus says 'after the death of Juba', which is incorrect. See the previous note.

9. Cf. in general *Ant.* xvii 13, 1 (341) and 4 (349–53); *B.J.* ii 7, 4 (114–16).

10. *Μετ' ὀλίγον τῆς ἀφίξεως χρόνον*, *B.J.* ii 7, 4 (116).

11. *Ant.* xvii 13, 4 (351–3); *B.J.* ii 7, 4 (116).

12. *Ant.* xvii 13, 1 (340). On the palm groves near Jericho, see above, p. 298; on the village of Archelais, vol. II, § 23, i. It was situated, according to the *Tabula Peutingeriana* (ed. Miller, 1888), on the road from Jericho to Scythopolis, 12 *m.p.* north from Jericho, 12+12 *m.p.* south of Scythopolis. As the actual distance between Jericho and Scythopolis is about 50 *m.p.*, there is a mistake in the figures somewhere. If the distance of 12 *m.p.* between Jericho and Archelais is accepted as correct, Archelais must have lain a little to the south of Phasaelis (not to the north of it, as was once supposed). For its location at Ḫirbet 'Auga et-Taḥtani, seven miles N. of Jericho, see A.Alt, Pal. Jahrb. 27 (1931), p. 46; M. Avi-Yonah, *Map of Roman Palestine* (²1940), p. 27; but Abel, *Géog. Pal.* II, p. 249 leaves the identification undecided. The mosaic map of Madaba shows Archelais lying between Phasaelis and Jericho. See M. Avi-Yonah, *The Madaba Mosaic Map* (1954), p. 36 and pl. 1. Archelais, like Phasaelis, was renowned for its palm-groves (Josephus, *Ant.* xviii 2, 2 (31); Pliny, *NH* xiii 9/44). The palm-groves newly laid out by Archelaus, for which he had water brought from Na'ara, should therefore be located in the immediate neighbourhood of the Archelais founded by him. Na'ara is most probably identical with the Naaratha mentioned by Eusebius (*Onomast.*, ed. Klostermann, p. 136), which is only 5 *m.p.* from Jericho; in which case it will not have been too far from Archelais either.

But these splendid and beneficial undertakings could not reconcile his subjects to his misgovernment. After tolerating his regime for more than nine years, a deputation of the Jewish and Samaritan aristocracy set out for Rome to lay their complaints against him before Augustus. Their accusations must have been very serious, for the emperor felt obliged to summon Archelaus to Rome. Having interrogated him, he dismissed him from office and banished him to Vienne in Gaul in A.D. 6. Like his wife, Archelaus also learnt of his fate in a remarkable dream.[13]

The territory of Archelaus was placed under direct Roman rule; as an annexe of the province of Syria it was provided with a governor of its own from the equestrian order.[14] With this, Judaea's position underwent a radical change. Despite their friendship with the Romans, Herod the Great and his sons had such an understanding of their own people that, with the occasional exception, they did not wantonly injure their most sacred feelings. Common prudence demanded care and caution in this regard. The Romans, on the other hand, had practically no comprehension of the Jewish character. As they knew nothing of the religious views of the Jews or of the many laws governing daily life, so they had no idea either that for the sake of superficial and apparently unimportant things an entire people would be capable of offering the most extreme resistance, even to the point of death and self-annihilation. The Jews saw in the simplest administrative rulings, such as the initial census, an encroachment on their most sacred rights and came increasingly to believe that direct Roman rule, which they had desired at Herod's death,[15] was incompatible with the principles of theocracy. Even with the best of intentions on both sides, tension and hostility were therefore inevitable. But such goodwill as existed was only partial. Except during the reign of Caligula, those at the head of government were ready to make concessions and exercise forbearance, sometimes in very large measure. But their good intentions were always foiled by the ineptitude of the governors, and not infrequently also by

13. *Ant.* xvii 13, 2–3 (342–3); *B.J.* ii 7, 3 (111–13); Dio, lv 27, 6. Without mentioning the name of Archelaus, Strabo, xvi 2, 46 (765), writes that a son of Herod *ἐν φυγῇ διετέλει παρὰ τοῖς Ἀλλόβριξι Γαλάταις λαβὼν οἴκησιν*. Vienne, south of Lyons, was the capital of the Allobroges. As regards the chronology, Dio, lv 27, 6, dates the banishment of Archelaus during the consulship of Aemilius Lepidus and Lucius Arruntius (A.D. 6). The statements of Josephus agree with this, *Ant.* xvii 13, 2 (342), in the 10th year of Archelaus; *B.J.* ii 7, 3 (111), in the 9th. According to Jerome, the grave of Archelaus was shown near Bethlehem (*Onomast.*, ed. Klostermann, p. 45: 'sed et propter eandem Bethleem regis quondam Iudaeae Archelai tumulus ostenditur'); if this is correct he must have died in Palestine.

14. *Ant.* xvii 13, 5 (355); xviii 1, 1 (2); *B.J.* ii 8, 1 (117).

15. *Ant.* xvii, 11, 2 (314); *B.J.* ii 6, 2 (91).

gross miscarriages of justice on their part. These officials of lower rank were, like all petty rulers, above all conscious of their own arbitrary power, and through their infringements they in the end so aggravated the people that in wild despair they plunged into a war of self-annihilation.

(2) *Judaea under Roman Governors* A.D. 6–41

As the political situation in Judaea during the period A.D. 6–41 was essentially the same as that of Palestine as a whole during A.D. 44–66, the following discussion combines the two periods and makes use of evidence relating to both.[16]

Judaea (and subsequently all Palestine) was not in the strict sense of the term incorporated into the province of Syria. It had a governor of its own, of equestrian rank, who was only to some extent subordinate to the imperial legate, *legatus Augusti pro praetore*, in Syria.[17] According to Strabo's classification,[18] Judaea belonged to the third class of imperial provinces. And this third class must be considered an exception to the rule. For most of the imperial provinces were, like the senatorial provinces, administered by men of senatorial rank, the larger ones (like Syria) by former consuls, the smaller by former praetors.[19] Only a few provinces were by way of exception placed under governors of equestrian rank, namely those in which, owing to a tenacious and individual culture, or a lack of it, the strict implementation of ordinary regulations

16. For the background see Th. Mommsen, *Römische Geschichte* V ([5]1904); O. Hirschfeld, *Die kaiserlichen Verwaltungsbeamten* ([2]1905); J. Juster, *Les Juifs dans l'Empire romain. Leur condition juridique, économique et sociale* I–II (1914); M. I. Rostovtseff, *Social and Economic History of the Roman Empire* (ed. P. M. Fraser, [2]1957); A. Momigliano, *Ricerche sull' organizzazione della Giudea sotto il dominio romano, Annali della Reale Scuola normale Superiore di Pisa,* 2nd ser., 3 (1934); G. H. Stevenson, *Roman Provincial Administration* (1939); H. G. Pflaum, *Les procurateurs équestres sous le Haut-Empire romain* (1950); *idem*, *Les carrières procuratoriennes équestres sous le Haut-Empire romain,* I–III (1960); A. H. M. Jones, *Studies in Roman Government and Law* (1960).

17. Josephus, *B.J.* ii 8, 1 (117): 'The territory of Archelaus was now reduced to a province, and Coponius, a Roman of the equestrian order, was sent out as procurator (ἐπίτροπος). *Ant.* xviii 1, 1 (2): 'Coponius . . . a man of equestrian rank, was appointed governor (ἡγησόμενος) over the Jews with full authority'.

18. Strabo, xvii 3, 25 (840) 'to some, the Emperor sent to take charge (ἐπιμελησόμενοι) men of consular rank, to others men of praetorian rank, and to some of equestrian rank'.

19. To describe the imperial governor of Syria as a 'proconsul', a mistake which New Testament scholars have sometimes made, is not in accord with conditions under the Principate.

seemed impossible. The best-known example is Egypt. Otherwise it was in particular territories inhabited by semi-barbarous peoples that were administered in this manner.[20]

Under Augustus and Tiberius, the usual title for a governor of equestrian rank, in Judaea as in Egypt and elsewhere, was *praefectus* (ἔπαρχος).[21] An inscription discovered in Caesarea in 1961 shows that this was the official title by which Pontius Pilate was known.[22] Very soon, however, at least from Claudius onwards, the title *procurator* (ἐπίτροπος) came to be used for the governors of provinces of this type, Egypt excepted. The designation *praefectus* stresses the military character of the post, whereas *procurator* was used in the earliest period of the Principate only of financial officials, in imperial as well as in senatorial provinces. Originally, in its ordinary and non-technical sense, the word denoted the administrator of an estate; occasionally it occurs in the New Testament with this meaning.[23] The procurator was someone who administered the revenue of imperial domains, the emperor's *res familiares*, and in senatorial provinces his function was (and remained) to act as the emperor's personal agent. With the gradual ascendancy of the *princeps* over the *senatus*, a title which originally applied to the emperor's agent came to replace that of a public official. The procurators in imperial provinces were in every sense the representatives of the

20. Egypt was governed by a prefect. Other provinces of this type are mentioned by Tac. *Hist.* I 11 'duae Mauretaniae, Raetia, Noricum, Thracia et quae aliae procuratoribus cohibentur'. A complete list is given by O. Hirschfeld, SAB (1889), pp. 419–23. See Pflaum, *Carrières*, pp. 1044–1103.

21. O. Hirschfeld, *op. cit.*, pp. 425–7, and *Die kaiserlichen Verwaltungsbeamten*², pp. 384 ff., and A. H. M. Jones, 'Procurators and Prefects', *Studies in Roman Government and Law*, pp. 115–25, maintained this even before the inscription mentioned in the next note was discovered.

22. The inscription reads:

TIBERIEVM
PON]TIVS PILATVS
PRAEF]ECTVS IVDA[EA]E

and was discovered in the Roman theatre of Caesarea by an Italian archaeological expedition under Professor Antonio Frova. See A. Frova, 'L'iscrizione di Ponzio Pilato a Cesarea', Rendiconti dell'Istituto Lombardo, Academia di Scienze e Lettere, Classe di Lettre 95 (1961), pp. 419–34; *idem*, 'Quattro campagne di scavo della Missione Archeologica Milanese a Caesarea Maritima (Israele) 1959–1962', *Atti del Convegno La Lombardia e l'Oriente* (1963), p. 175; B. Lifshitz, 'Inscriptions latines de Césarée (Caesarea Palestinae) 1. Le Tibereum', Latomus 22 (1963), p. 783; C. B. Gerra in *Scavi di Caesarea Maritima* (1966), pp. 217–20; H. Volkmann, Gymnasium 75 (1968), pp. 124–35; E. Weber, Bonner Jahrbücher 171 (1971), pp. 194–200.

23. Mt. 20:8, Lk. 8:3, Gal. 4:2. See W. F. Arndt and F. W. Gingrich, *A Greek-English Lexicon of the New Testament* (1957), p. 303, *s.v.* ἐπίτροπος (1). The loan word אפיטרופוס is used in both meanings in Jewish Aramaic (cf. e.g. Tg. Neof. Gen. 39:4 and 41:34).

state. Besides taking care of financial affairs,[24] they also exercised military and juridical authority. Thus the difference between *praefectus* and *procurator* in imperial provinces was one in name only; by whatever title the bearer was known, his office combined military, financial and judicial powers. It is not surprising that our sources rarely distinguish properly between these two designations. Philo uses ἐπίτροπος,[25] even of the Prefect of Egypt. Josephus as a rule designates the governor of Judaea by the title ἐπίτροπος, occasionally ἔπαρχος or ἡγεμών, and also uses other names.[26] In the New Testament the term most often used is ἡγεμών,[27] i.e. *praeses*.[28] Tacitus uses the title *procurator* indiscriminately of Pontius Pilate[29] as well as of Cumanus and Felix.[30] Later writers, *e.g.* Justin Martyr, continue in the use of this expression (ἐπίτροπος), applying it also, as Tacitus had done, to officials who should have been called *praefecti*.[31] Whereas the financial administrators in provinces governed by senators, and known by the title *procuratores*, were not in-

24. Cf. A. N. Sherwin-White, 'Procurator Augusti', PBSR 15 n.s. 2 (1939), pp. 11–26; H. G. Pflaum, *Les carrières procuratoriennes*, ch. 3, 'Le pouvoir des procurateurs-gouverneurs', pp. 110–60, and esp. 'Le pouvoir des procurateurs-gouverneurs en leur qualité d'agents financiers de l'Empereur', pp. 151–7. Further see F. Millar, Historia 13 (1964), pp. 180–7, and 14 (1965), pp. 362–7; cf. P. A. Brunt, 'Procuratorial Jurisdiction', Latomus 25 (1966), pp. 461–89.

25. *Legatio* 20 (132) (the word actually occurs in a letter written by Agrippa I), *In Flaccum* 19 (163) (here of the Prefect of Egypt).

26. ἐπίτροπος in the following passages: *B.J.* ii 8, 1 (117); 9, 2 (169), 11, 6 (220) (in the parallel passage *Ant.* xix 9, 2 (363) ἔπαρχος); 12, 8 (247); *Ant.* xx 1, 2 (14) (in a letter by Claudius to Cuspius Fadus); 6, 2 (132). ἔπαρχος in *B.J.* vi 5, 3 (303, 305); *Ant.* xviii 2, 2 (33); xix 9, 2 (363) (see above); xx 9, 1 (197). ἡγησόμενος in *Ant.* xviii 1, 1 (2). ἡγεμών in *Ant.* xviii 3, 1 (55). προστησόμενος in *Ant.* xx 7, 1 (137). ἐπιμελητής in *Ant.* xviii 4, 2 (89); Josephus gives the same title to Antipater, the father of Herod the Great, in his capacity of chief officer of Hyrcanus II; see *Ant.* xiv 8, 3 (139). ἱππάρχης in *Ant.* xviii 6, 10 (237).

In *B.J.* ii 8, 1 (117) Josephus calls Judaea an ἐπαρχία (in Augustus's reign, with Coponius as prefect; cf. n. 17 above). After the death of Agrippa I, when Palestine reverted to direct Roman administration, the region around Chalcis was bestowed on Agrippa II, and of the rest of the former kingdom Josephus says: τῆς δ' ἄλλης ἐπαρχίας διαδέχεται τὴν ἐπιτροπὴν ἀπὸ 'Αλεξάνδρου Κουμανός, *B.J.* ii 12, 1 (223), cf. *Ant.* xx 5, 1 (99).

27. Mt. 27:2, 11, 14, 15, 21, 27; 28:14; Lk. 3:1; 20:20; Acts 23:24, 26, 33; 24:1, 10; 26:30.

28. A more or less general title, strictly applied to governors of senatorial rank: 'praesidis nomen generale est eoque et proconsules et legati Caesaris et omnes provincias regentes licet senatores sint praesides appellantur' (*Dig.* I 18, 1). However, a distinction is made between *praeses* and *procurator Caesaris* (e.g. *Dig.* IV 4, 9).

29. *Ann.* xv 44, 4.

30. *Ann.* xii 54, 4.

31. 1 *Apol.* 13, 2 etc.

frequently chosen from among the emperor's freedmen,[32] the governors of procuratorial provinces were normally chosen from among citizens of equestrian rank on account of the military command connected with such an appointment. It was an unprecedented innovation when in A.D. 52 a freedman, Felix, was appointed to the office of governor of Judaea (see below, § 19).

The governors of Judaea seem to have been subordinate to the legates of Syria only to the extent that it was the right and duty of the latter to exercise their superior authority whenever the need arose.[33] Ancient writers sometimes express themselves as if Judaea had been incorporated into the province of Syria, but they are not constant in this. Josephus, for instance, says that after the deposition of Archelaus (A.D. 6) Judaea became a *προσθήκη τῆς Συρίας*.[34] This must be taken with a grain of salt. Judaea remained until A.D. 70 an administrative unit with its own provincial government. Investing the prefect—or procurator, as the case may be—with a military command and independent jurisdiction, conferred on him a position which equalled in normal times that of the governors of other provinces. Only when there were grounds for fearing unrest, or when other serious difficulties arose, was it within the discretion of the legate of Syria to interfere. He would then take command in Judaea as the superior of the procurator.[35] Whether this superior authority went so far as to empower him to call the procurator to account seems questionable. In the two cases in which this happened,

32. Augustus's freedman, Licinus, appears to have been procurator in Gaul (Dio liv 21); cf. Millar in Historia 13 (1964), pp. 180–7.

33. Cf. Mommsen, *Röm. Gesch.* V, p. 509, note. Hirschfeld, SAB (1889), pp. 440–2.

34. *Ant.* xviii 1, 1 (2).

35. Josephus, *Ant.* xvii 13, 5 (355), writes: 'The territory subject to Archelaus was added to [the province of the] Syrians'. Immediately following on this passage in *Ant.* xviii 1, 1 (2), he calls Judaea a *προσθήκη* ('annex') of Syria and thus evidently does not intend to describe it as an integral part of that province, but only as being somehow attached to Syria. According to *B.J.* ii 8, 1 (117), the territory of Archelaus became a province, *ἐπαρχία*, hence directly subordinated to the emperor. Reporting on the state of affairs after the death of Agrippa, Josephus definitely affirms that the Syrian legate was not set over Agrippa's kingdom, *Ant.* xix 9, 2 (363). Subsequently, of course, he does mention that it became necessary for the legate to interfere in Judaean affairs, *Ant.* xx 1, 1 (7). Tacitus mentions Syria and Judaea as being two provinces in A.D. 17 alongside one another, *Ann.* ii 42: 'provinciae Syria atque Iudaea', and says of the arrangements after the death of King Agrippa, *Hist.* v 9: 'Claudius . . . Iudaeam provinciam equitibus Romanis aut libertis permisit'. Hence when he reports the same fact in another place, *Ann.* xii 23, in the words 'Ituraeique et Iudaei defunctis regibus, Sohaemo atque Agrippa, provinciae Syriae additi', the expression *additi* might be understood in the same way as when Josephus, *Ant.* xviii 1, 1 (2) speaks of a *προσθήκη*. Suetonius also calls Judaea simply a province (*Div. Claud.* 28: 'Felicem, quem cohortibus et alis provinciaeque Iudaeae praeposuit').

the particular legates had probably been entrusted with a special commission.[36]

The residence of the prefect or procurator of Judaea was not Jerusalem but Caesarea.[37] Since the dwelling of the commander-in-chief or governor was called *praetorium*, the *πραιτώριον τοῦ Ἡρῴδου* in Caesarea (Acts 23:35) was presumably a palace built by Herod, which now served as the residence of the imperial representative. On particular occasions, especially during the main Jewish festivals, when more than ordinary precautions had to be taken on account of the crowds that poured into Jerusalem, the Roman governor went up to the city and resided in Herod's former palace. The *praetorium* in Jerusalem in which Pilate was staying at the time when Jesus was condemned (Mk. 15:16; Mt. 26:27; Jn. 18:28, 33; 19:9) was therefore almost certainly the palace of Herod in the west of the city.[38] It was not only a princely dwelling, but also a citadel, in which more than once (e.g. during the rebellions of 4 B.C. and A.D. 66) large detachments of troops were able to hold out against the attacks of the masses.[39] When the governor was in residence,

36. For instance Vitellius, who deposed Pilate, *Ant.* xviii 4, 2 (89). Tac. *Ann.* vi 32, explicitly says of him: 'cunctis quae apud orientem parabantur L. Vitellium praefecit', thus indicating the special emergency in this instance. Similarly, of Ummidius Quadratus who ordered Cumanus to report to Rome, Josephus *B.J.* ii 12, 6 (244); *Ant.* 6, 12 (132), Tacitus says in *Ann.* xii 54: 'Claudius . . . ius statuendi etiam de procuratoribus dederat'. The legates had in these cases a special commission. Only when serious disorder threatened to break out, or actually did break out in Judaea, and the procurator was unable to cope with the situation, did the governor of the neighbouring Syrian province come to his assistance—as to a client-king—and in such circumstances assumed command. Examples are: Petronius, *B.J.* ii 10, 1–5 (185–203); *Ant.* xviii 8, 2–9 (261–309); Cassius Longinus, *Ant.* xx 1, 1 (7); Cestius Gallus, *B.J.* ii 14, 3 (280–2) 16, 1 (333–5), 18, 9 (499–512), 19, 1–9 (513–55).

37. Jos. *B.J.* ii 9, 2 (171); *Ant.* xviii 3, 1 (55, 57) (Pilate). *B.J.* ii 12, 2 (230); *Ant.* xx 5, 4 (116) (Cumanus). Acts 23:23–33 (Felix), *ibid.* 25: 1–13 (Festus). Jos. *B.J.* II 14, 4 (288), 14, 6 (296), 17, 1 (407) (Florus). Tacitus, *Hist.* ii 78: 'Caesarea . . . Iudaeae caput'.

38. Josephus *B.J.* ii 14 8 (301) 15, 5 (328). Philo, *Legatio* 38 (299) calls the procuratorial residence in Jerusalem *τοτι καῖα τὴν ἱερόπολιν Ἡρῴδου βασιλείοις*. F.-M. Abel, in H. Vincent et F.-M. Abel, *Jérusalem. Recherches de topographie, d'archéologie et d'histoire* I–III (1912–1926), vol. II, fasc. 3, pp. 562–71, remains undecided between Herod's palace and the Antonia. S. Marie-Aline de Sion, *La forteresse Antonia à Jérusalem et la question du prétoire* (1956), on archeological evidence, comes out in favour of the Antonia. P. Benoit, 'Prétoire, Lithostroton et Gabbatha', RB 59 (1952), pp. 531–50, re-states the reasons for identifying the *πραιτώριον* with Herod's palace. See now *idem*, 'L'Antonia d'Hérode le Grand et le forum oriental d'Aelia Capitolina', HThR 64 (1971), pp. 135–67. The literary evidence points overwhelmingly in this direction. Cf. in general R. Egger, *Das Praetorium als Amtssitz und Quartier römischer Spitzenfunktiäre*, SAW 250 (1966) Abh. 4.

39. Jos. *B.J.* ii 31, 1 (44), 3, 4 (51–4), 17, 7 (430–2), 17, 8 (434–9), *Ant.* xvii 10, 2 (255), 10, 3 (265). Compare the description in *B.J.* v 4, 3–4 (156–83).

his accompanying detachment of troops would therefore also have been quartered there (cf. Mk. 15:16; Mt. 27:27).

As regards the military arrangements in the province, it should be borne in mind that under the Empire Roman troops fell into two distinct categories: the legions and the auxiliaries. The legions formed the real nucleus of the army and only Roman citizens served in them: provincials recruited to serve in the legions immediately obtained full citizenship rights. Each legion consisted of ten cohorts or 60 centuries comprising altogether 5,000–6,000 men. Auxiliary troops were made up of provincials who, at all events in the early days of the Empire, did not as a rule have rights of citizenship. Their weapons were lighter and less uniform than those of the legionaries; often they were allowed to keep their own national armoury. Their infantry was grouped into cohorts, the strength of which varied (500 or 1,000 men); the cavalry was formed into *alae* of similarly varying strength. Cohorts and *alae* were named after the ethnic groups from which they had been recruited.[40]

Normally, only auxiliary troops were stationed in provinces administered by a prefect or procurator, and they served under his command.[41] This was the case also in Judaea. Legions were stationed in Syria, three in 4 B.C. and four from Tiberius onward.[42] But until Vespasian, only auxiliary troops were stationed in Judaea, and most of these were recruited in the country itself.[43] The honour and burden of this levy fell exclusively on the non-Jewish inhabitants of Palestine. The Jews were exempt. This is proved to have been so at least in the time of Caesar,[44] and, from all that is known of the Roman military organisation

40. To give only a few examples from Palestine and Syria: *cohors Ascalonitarum, Canathenorum, Damascenorum, Ituraeorum, Sebastenorum, Tyriorum*. See G. L. Cheesman, *The Auxilia of the Roman Imperial Army* (1914); K. Kraft, *Zur Rekrutierung der Alen und Kohorten am Rhein und Donau* (1951).

41. O. Hirschfeld, SAB (1889), pp. 431–7.

42. Three legions in 4 B.C.: Jos. *B.J.* ii 3, 1 (40), 5, 1 (66); *Ant.* xvii 10, 9 (286); four under Tiberius (and probably in the latter part of Augustus's reign): Tac. *Ann.* iv 5. Of the four Syrian legions, only two are known with certainty: the *legio VI Ferrata* (Tac. *Ann.* ii 79, 81; xiii 38, 40; xv 6, 26) and the *legio X Fretensis* (*Ann.* ii 57; xiii 40; xv 6). The other two were probably the *legio III Gallica* (*Ann.* xiii 40; xv 6, 26) which according to Tacitus, *Hist.* iii 24 had already fought under M. Antonius against the Parthians, and the *legio XII Fulminata* (*Ann.* xv 6, 7, 10, 26). See Ritterling in RE s.v. 'Legio'; R. Syme, 'Some Notes on the Legions under Augustus', JRS 23 (1933), pp. 13–33; A. Betz, 'Zur Dislokation der Legionen in der Zeit von dem Tode des Augustus bis zum Ende der Prinzipatsepoche', *Carnuntina*, ed. E. Swoboda (1956), pp. 17–24.

43. On the garrisoning of Judaea up to the time of Vespasian, see Th. Mommsen, in Hermes 19 (1884), p. 217, note; O. Hirschfeld, SAB (1889), pp. 433 f.; T. R. S. Broughton in Jackson and Lake, *Beginnings* . . ., Additional Note xxxiii.

44. *Ant.* xiv 10, 6 (204): 'No one, whether magistrate (ἄρχων) [or pro-magistrate (ἀντάρχων)] or praetor (στρατηγός) or legate (πρεσβευτής) shall raise auxiliary troops in the country (ὅροι) of the Jews'. Apart from the *cod. Pal.* all manuscripts give this text, as also the Old Latin (*ut nullus vel preses vel dux vel legatus in finibus*

in Palestine until the time of Vespasian, may be safely taken to apply to the early Principate. Jews were exempted from serving in the Roman armies to avoid conflict with their observation of Jewish festivals and the sabbath regulations.[45]

For the years A.D. 6–41 there is no specific information concerning the troops stationed in Judaea. It appears, however, that the Sebastenes (i.e. soldiers recruited in and around Sebaste or Samaria), who will be encountered later, constituted even then a considerable part of the garrison. In the upheaval following the death of Herod in 4 B.C., the most proficient sector of Herod's troops, the *Σεβαστηνοὶ τρισχίλιοι*, fought alongside the Romans under the command of Rufus and Gratus, the former commanding the cavalry, the latter the infantry.[46] Archelaus undoubtedly retained the troops thus proved, and it is highly probable that after his deposition in A.D. 6 they were taken over by the Romans, then from A.D. 41–44 by Agrippa, and after his death by the Romans once more. This supposition is borne out by the following. When Agrippa died in A.D. 44, the king's troops stationed in Caesarea—the *Καισαρεῖς καὶ Σεβαστηνοί*—expressed their joy in a very unseemly manner at the death of a ruler who had shown his sympathy for the Jews. To honour Agrippa's memory, the emperor wished these troops, namely the *ἴλη τῶν Καισαρέων καὶ τῶν Σεβαστηνῶν καὶ αἱ πέντε σπεῖραι* (therefore an *ala* of cavalry and five cohorts), to be transferred as a punishment to Pontus. By means of a petition, however, they managed to stay in Judaea until eventually removed by Vespasian.[47] This shows that Agrippa's troops were simply taken over by the Romans.[48] It may consequently be assumed that the same happened when Archelaus was deposed. It is remarkable that the one cavalry *ala* and five cohorts of infantry (if these are assessed at 500 men each) together amount to 3,000 men, i.e., the same number of Sebastene troops as is attested for 4 B.C. These troops are frequently mentioned in the period from

Iudeorum auxilia colligat). Niese accepts, however, the reading in the *cod. Pal.* The Jews of Asia Minor were exempt from conscription for military service when Pompey's party took to arms in 49 B.C., Jos. *Ant.* xiv 10, 13 (228); 10, 14 (232); 10, 16 (234); 10, 18 (237); 10, 14 (240) on account of their religious objections. Six years later, this exemption was confirmed by Dolabella at Ephesus, *Ant.* xiv 10, 12 (226): 'Those Jews who are Roman citizens and observe Jewish rites and practise them in Ephesus, I release from military service . . . in consideration of their religious scruples'. For Jewish soldiers in both Hellenistic armies and the Roman army after A.D. 70, see J. Juster, *Les Juifs dans l'empire romain* II (1914), pp. 265–76.

45. Cf. *Ant.* xiii 8, 4 (251–2).

46. *B.J.* ii 3, 4 (52); 4, 2 (58); 4, 3 (63). Cf. *Ant.* xvii 10, 3 (266).

47. *Ant.* xix 9, 1–2 (356–66).

48. Analogous cases are also known elsewhere. See Mommsen, 'Die Conscriptionsordnung der römischen Kaiserzeit', Hermes 19 (1884), pp. 1–79, 210–34, esp. pp. 51, 217 f.

A.D. 44 to 66. The procurator Cumanus led the *ala Sebastenorum* and four cohorts of infantry from Caesarea against the Jews.[49] In the conflicts between the Jewish and Gentile inhabitants of Caesarea, the latter relied on the fact that Roman troops in Caesarea consisted mostly of Caesareans and Sebastenes.[50] Finally, in A.D. 67 Vespasian was able to enlist in his army five cohorts and one *ala* of cavalry from Caesarea,[51] the same units as had been stationed there in A.D. 44. They are probably identical with the *Sebasteni* so often referred to on inscriptions. The σπεῖρα Σεβαστή, mentioned in Acts 27:1 as having been stationed in Caesarea at the time of the imprisonment of the apostle Paul, about A.D. 60, may have been one of the five cohorts mentioned by Josephus. But many New Testament scholars have incorrectly supposed that the expression σπεῖρα Σεβαστή is synonymous with σπεῖρα Σεβαστηνῶν. This is unlikely (unless Σεβαστή is an inaccurate equivalent to 'Sebastena'). Σεβαστή seems rather to be the equivalent of *Augusta*, a title of honour very frequently bestowed upon auxiliary troops. The cohort in question may therefore have been named *cohors Augusta Sebastenorum*. In Caesarea it would simply be called σπεῖρα Σεβαστή since this was sufficient to distinguish it from the others.[52] An inscription from

49. *B.J.* ii 12, 5 (236); *Ant.* xx 6, 1 (122).
50. *Ant.* xx 8, 7 (176).
51. *B.J.* iii 4, 2 (66).
52. Evidence exists of *ala I Flavia Sabastenorum* (EE V, p. 699), *ala gemina Sebastenorum* (CIL VIII 9358=ILS 2738, 9359), *ala Sebastenorum* (EE V 1000), *cohors I Sebastenorum* (CIL III 2916); whether the figure I is the correct reading is doubtful; see EE IV 370=CIL III 9984. A *cohors I Sebastena* was in Syria in A.D. 88 (CIL XVI 35); a *cohors I Seb(astenorum) miliaria* was stationed in Palestine in A.D. 139 (CIL XVI 87). Although there were other cities with the name of Sebaste, from the material supplied by Josephus it is nevertheless probable that these troops were drawn from Palestinian Sebaste. Cf. also Mommsen, 'Die Conscriptionsordnung der römischen Kaiserzeit', Hermes 19 (1884), p. 217. In support of this view, Cichorius (RE I, col. 1260) asserts that two of the inscriptions mentioned testify to the presence of the *ala Sebastenorum* in Mauretania, while an *ala I Thracum Mauretana* went to Palestine in A.D. 86 (see below, note 67). The regiments therefore appear to have been exchanged. Mommsen's conjecture, that among the five cohorts in Caesarea were a *cohors Ascalonitarum* and a *cohors Canathenorum*, Hermes, *l.c.* and SAB (1895), pp. 501 f., cannot be reconciled with the definite statements of Josephus, for the latter says of the Caesarean garrison as a whole that it mainly consisted of Caesareans and Sebastenes, *Ant.* xx 8, 7 (176); *Ant.* xix 9, 1 (356); 9, 2 (361, 364–5). There cannot, therefore, have been one cohort of Ascalonites and one of Canathenians among the five cohorts. The honorific, *Augusta*, which was bestowed on three legions, is rendered by Ptolemy Σεβαστή (*Geog.* ii 3, 30, ii 9, 18, iv 3, 30). It is not surprising therefore that the same title should be similarly reproduced when attached to an auxiliary cohort. Since the *ala* referred to by Josephus, although consisting of Caesareans and Sebastenes, *Ant.* xix 9, 2 (365), was nevertheless named only *ala Sebastenorum*, *B.J.* ii 12, 5 (236), it may be assumed that other conditions being equal, the other σπεῖραι were also called *cohortes Sebastenorum*. This view is supported by surviving inscriptions.

Sebaste reads A R R [? . . .]/tesse[rarius] coh. V [Augustae?]/c(ivium R(omanorum) [Sebastenae?].[53] Considering that only auxiliary troops were stationed in peace time in Judaea, it is surprising to read (Acts 10:1) that a *σπεῖρα Ἰταλική* was garrisoned in Caesarea around A.D. 40, for this expression probably means a cohort consisting of Roman citizens from Italy. Such a unit cannot have served in Caesarea under the Jewish king Agrippa from A.D. 41 to 44. But in the light of the above considerations it appears unlikely even before this. The story of the centurion Cornelius (Acts 10) is also open to suspicion in this respect, and it may be that circumstances prevailing at a later period were assumed to have existed at an earlier one. That a *cohors Italica* was stationed in Syria for some considerable time, from at least A.D. 69 to 157, is attested by three surviving inscriptions.[54]

Besides that of Caesarea, small garrisons were stationed in other cities and towns of Palestine. At the outbreak of the Jewish war in A.D. 66 there were Roman garrisons in fortified places such as Jericho and Machaerus.[55] Various detachments were distributed throughout Samaria;[56] in the Great Plain a minor detachment was posted with a decurion in charge[57]; in Ascalon (which was at least in the early period part of an imperial estate) there were a cohort and an *ala*.[58] In the

53. AE 1948, 150, cf. 151.

54. On inscriptions (Mommsen, EE V, p. 249), appear *cohors I Italica civium Romanorum voluntariorum* (CIL XIV 171), *cohors II Italica civium Romanorum . . . exercitus Syriaci* (CIL III 13483 a), *cohors II Italica civium Romanorum*, mentioned under the cohorts *quae sunt in Suria sub Arridio Corneliano legato*, A.D. 157 (CIL XVI 106), *cohors miliaria Italica voluntariorum quae est in Syria* (CIL XI 6117), *cohors II Italica* (CIL VI 3528). The last four are very probably identical. In a passage of Arrian (*Acies contra Alanos* in *Arriani Scripta minora*, ed. Roos, Wirth, 1968), the expression ἡ σπεῖρα ἡ Ἰταλική alternates with οἱ Ἰταλοί (3, 9, 13). For this reason, and with regard to the three inscriptions first mentioned, it is probable that a *cohors Italica* consisted mainly of Roman citizens from Italy. Of particular interest among the above inscriptions is the epitaph from Carnuntum in Pannonia, AE 1896 27=CIL III, 13483a=ILS 9168. It reads: *Proculus Rabili f(ilius) Col(lina) Philadel(phia) mil(es) optio coh(ortis) II Italic(ae) c(ivium) R(omanorum) (centuria) Fa[us]tini, ex vexil(lariis?) sagit(tariis?) exer(citus) Syriaci stip(endiorum) VII. vixit an(nos) XXVI. Apuleius frater f(aciundum) c(uravit).* Since Proculus had served in the Syrian army, and since 'Rabilus' is a Syrian name ('Rabbula', Rab'ulla', 'Rabel') there is no doubt of the latter's having come from Philadelphia in Palestine (Amman). It is very probable that the epitaph was placed before A.D. 73. Hence the *vexillatio* belonged to the troops which Mucianus had led from Syria to the West towards the end of A.D. 69. However the existence of a *cohors Italica* in Syria around A.D. 69 does not prove that there was one stationed in Judaea in or around A.D. 40. Cf. RE IV, cols. 304–5, and E. Gabba, *Iscrizioni greche e latine per lo studio della Bibbia* (1958), nos. 25–6.

55. *B.J.* ii 18, 6 (484–5).

56. *B.J.* iii 7, 32 (309).

57. *Vita* 24 (115).

58. *B.J.* iii 2, 1 (12).

winter of A.D. 67/68, Vespasian placed garrisons in every conquered village and town, those in the villages under the command of decurions and those in the towns under centurions.[59] This was of course an exceptional measure, not to be assumed as applying to times of peace.

In Jerusalem only one cohort was stationed. The *χιλίαρχος* referred to in the New Testament (Jn. 18:12 *ἡ σπεῖρα καὶ ὁ χιλίαρχος*; Acts 21:31 *ὁ χιλίαρχος τῆς σπείρης*='tribune of the cohort') appears throughout as the commander-in-chief in Jerusalem.[60] This is in accord with Josephus's statement that a *τάγμα* of Romans was permanently stationed in the Antonia,[61] for *τάγμα* implies here not a legion, as it often does, but, as in the passage quoted above in n. 49, a cohort. The Antonia citadel described by Josephus as the permanent quarters of this unit, lay north of the Temple. At two points, steps (*καταβάσεις*) led down from the fortress to the Temple-court.[62] This is precisely the situation that emerges from the Acts. For when Paul was taken into custody by the soldiers during the uproar in the courtyard of the Temple, and was led away to the barracks (*παρεμβολή*), he was carried up the steps (*ἀναβαθμοί*) by the soldiers to protect him from the crowd, and from there, with the permission of the 'chiliarch', addressed the people once more (Acts 21:31–40). The officer in command of the Antonia, who is certainly identical with the chiliarch, is also called *φρούραρχος* by Josephus.[63] The direct connexion between citadel and Temple court was of importance, for the latter had to be under constant surveillance. At the high festivals, guards were posted in the arcades surrounding the Temple-courts.[64] Acts 23:23 also indicates that a cavalry detachment accompanied the cohort in Jerusalem, a not uncommon arrangement.[65] But it is a puzzle to know who are meant by the *δεξιολάβοι* (from *λαβή*='grip'; therefore 'those who grasped their weapons by the right hand') mentioned in the same passage with the ordinary foot-soldiers and the cavalry. As this expression occurs only twice elsewhere, and even then without explanation, it is not possible to explain it. But it certainly seems to describe a particular kind of

59. *B.J.* iv 8, 1 (442).

60. Acts 21:31, 37; 22:24, 29; 23:10, 15, 22; 24:7, 22. The normal title of the commander of an auxiliary cohort was *praefectus* (*ἔπαρχος*). Therefore either the writer of Acts has made a slip, or this was in fact a *cohors Italica* (see above) or a *cohors milliaria* (a cohort of double the normal size), both of which were commanded by *tribuni*. See RE s.v. 'tribunus cohortis' (XII, cols. 304–5). Cf. A. N. Sherwin-White, *Roman Society*, p. 155.

61. *B.J.* v 5, 8 (244).

62. *B.J.* v 5, 8 (243).

63. *Ant.* xv 11, 1 (408); xviii 4, 3 (93).

64. *B.J.* v 5, 8 (244); *B.J.* ii 12, 1 (223)=*Ant.* xx 5, 3 (106); *Ant.* xx 8, 11 (192).

65. There was a distinction between *cohortes peditatae* and *equitatae*. See RE IV, col. 235.

light-armed soldiery (javelin-throwers or foot-soldiers using other missiles).

After the great war of A.D. 66–73/4, a radical change took place in the garrisoning of Palestine. The governor was no longer a procurator of the equestrian order but a legate of senatorial rank (in the first period, a former praetor, and later a former consul). A legion (*Legio X Fretensis*) was quartered on the site of the destroyed city of Jerusalem (see below, § 20). The native troops who for decades had formed the garrison of Caesarea were transferred by Vespasian to other provinces.[66] Their place was taken by auxiliary troops of foreign origin, some of them from the farthest West.[67] Under Hadrian, the garrison in Palestine was substantially reinforced. Instead of one legion, it was given two,[68] and the number of auxiliary troops was likewise considerably increased.[69]

In addition to the standing army, the provincial governors occasionally organized a militia when the need for reinforcements arose. Those of the population, that is to say, who were capable of bearing arms were temporarily drafted into military service without becoming permanently part of the army. A case in point was the arming of the Samaritans by Cumanus to assist in fighting the Jews.[70]

Like the governors of senatorial rank, the prefects or procurators exercised supreme judicial authority as well as the military command within their province.[71] The procurators of Judaea did so only in

66. *Ant.* xix 9, 2 (366).

67. On a *diploma* from A.D. 86 (CIL XVI 33) veterans are mentioned who served in Judaea, namely, *in alis duabus quae appellantur veterana Gaetulorum et I Thracum Mauretana et cohortibus quattuor I Augusta Lusitanorum et I et II Thracum et II Cantabrorum.*

68. See below, p. 514.

69. On a *diploma* from A.D. 139, CIL XVI 87 (ad lacum Tiberiadem), there is mention of *alae III et cohortes XII quae . . . sunt in Syria Palaestina,* namely (1) the *alae Gallorum et Thracum et Antoniniana Gallorum et VII Phrygum,* and (2) the *cohortes I Thracum milliaria et I Sebastenorum milliaria et I Damascenorum et I Montanorum et I Flavia civium Romanorum et I et II Galatarum et III et IV Bracarum et IV et VI Petraeorum et V Gemina civium Romanorum.*

70. *Ant.* xx 6, 1 (122): 'Cumanus . . . took over the squadron of the Sebastenes and four infantry units, and armed the Samaritans.' With regard to the provincial militia, see Th. Mommsen, 'Die Conscriptionsordnung der römischen Kaiserzeit', Hermes 19 (1884), pp. 219 ff.; 22 (1887), pp. 547 ff.

On the prefect's, or procurator's, authority as commander-in-chief of troops, see H. G. Pflaum, 'Les attributions militaires des procurateurs-gouverneurs' in *Les procurateurs équestres* (1950), pp. 124–34, and F.-M. Abel, *Histoire de la Palestine* I (1952), pp. 426–8.

71. On prefectorial (and procuratorial) jurisdiction, see O. Hirschfeld, in SAB (1899), pp. 437–9, and H. G. Pflaum, 'L'indépendence des procurateurs-gouverneurs' in *Les procurateurs équestres* (1950), pp. 146–8; on the governor's right of punishment in general, Th. Mommsen, *Röm. Strafrecht* (1899), pp. 229–50; particularly, H. G. Pflaum, 'Le pouvoir judiciaire des procurateurs-gouverneurs',

exceptional cases, for the ordinary administration of the law, both in criminal and civil matters, was left to the native and local courts (see vol. II, § 23). [72] The governor's judicial competence included the *ius gladii* or *potestas gladii*, the right of decision over life and death.[73] Several inscriptions testify that governors of procuratorial rank were vested with the same authority as governors of higher status.[74] With reference to Judaea, Josephus states explicitly that the emperor delegated to Coponius, Judaea's first Roman prefect, the power to rule on his behalf, and exercise his authority, including the right to inflict capital punishment.[75] He does not, however, imply that there existed in the country no other judiciary authority besides that of the

---

op. cit., pp. 110–17; F.-M. Abel, *op. cit.*, pp. 428–9; A. H. M. Jones, 'I Appeal unto Caesar' in *Studies in Roman Government and Law*, pp. 51–65; F. Millar, Historia 13 (1964), pp. 180–7; 14 (1965), pp. 362–7; P. A. Brunt, 'Procuratorial Jurisdiction', Latomus, 25 (1966), pp. 461–89.

72. This applies generally also to the administration of law in the provinces; see Th. Mommsen, *Röm. Staatsrecht* II, p. 244: 'The ordinary jurisdiction in criminal cases was left in the provinces to their inhabitants, whilst the courts of the governor, like consular courts in Italy, are to be regarded, at least in the formal sense, as being an exception'. See especially: J. Juster, *Les Juifs dans l'Empire romain* II (1914), 'Juridiction en Palestine', pp. 93–109, 127–49.

73. *Dig.* I 18, 6, 8 (from Ulpian, beginning of 3rd century A.D.): 'Qui universas provincias regunt, ius gladii habent et in metallum dandi potestas eis permissa est'. The *ius gladii* is also called *potestas gladii, Dig.* I 16, 6 *pr.*=L 17, 70, II 1, 3 (all from Ulpian). There is no proof that either expression was in use as a *terminus technicus* before the beginning of the 3rd century A.D. (the Acts of Perpetua and Felicitas belong to A.D. 203. The inscriptions scarcely go back beyond this time). On the *ius gladii*, see H. G. Pflaum, 'L'évolution du *jus gladii* sous le Haut-Empire', in *Les procurateurs équestres* (1950), pp. 117–25; further A. Berger, *Encyclopedic Dictionary of Roman Law* (1953), p. 529, and the literature quoted there.

74. See the treatments by Th. Mommsen, *Röm. Staatsrecht*, II 1, p. 246; *Röm. Strafrecht*, p. 244; O. Hirschfeld, *op. cit.*, p. 438. Only two inscriptions belong here: CIL IX 5439 *proc. Alpium Atractianar*[*um*] *et Poeninar*[*um*] *iur*[*e*] *glad*[*ii*], and CIL VIII 9367, cf. EE V, no. 968: *praeses* (*scil. Mauretaniae Caesariensis*) *iure gla*[*dii*]. The following two cases belong to different categories: (1) CIL II 484 =ILS 1372 *proc. prov. M*[*oe*]*siae inferioris, eiusdem provinciae ius gladii*; this is the temporary replacement of a senatorial legate as governor by the procurator of the province, Pflaum, *Carrières*, no. 330. (2) CIL III 1919 (with add.)=ILS 2770: *proc. centenarius provinciae Li*[*burniae iure*?] *gladii*. This is an exceptional *ad hoc* procuratorial governorship of an area normally part of a province governed by a senatorial legate, Pflaum, *Carrières*, no. 196.

A third situation is represented by the *Acta Perpetuae et Felicitatis* 6, 2 (Knopf-Krüger-Ruhbach, *Ausgewählte Martyrerakten* (^{3}1965), p. 38) 'Hilarianus procurator tunc loco proconsulis Minuci Timiniani defuncti ius gladii acceperat'. This is the temporary replacement of a deceased proconsul by the (in principle) private financial procurator of the province.

75. *B.J.* ii 8, 1 (117).

prefect empowered to administer the death penalty. The exact extent of the *ius gladii* delegated to provincial governors in the early Principate is not known for certain; at least from the third century A.D. onwards it embraced even the right over life and death of Roman citizens (with the reservation that these could appeal to the emperor against the governor's sentence), but in the early days of the Principate, provincial governors were perhaps not entitled to impose the death penalty upon persons possessing Roman citizen-rights, or, at all events, not if they appealed. Such persons, when accused of an offence constituting a capital charge, might at the beginning of the proceedings, or at any subsequent stage of their trial, request that the investigation be carried out in Rome and judgment passed by the emperor himself.[76] The governor's absolute penal jurisdiction probably extended therefore only to non-citizens. But Florus, in Jerusalem in A.D. 66, ordered the crucifixion of Jews who were of Roman equestrian rank.[77] Even non-citizens might be sent by the governor to Rome for trial, if on

76. Acts 25:10 f., 21; 26:32. Cf. Pliny, *Epp.* x, 96: 'fuerunt alii similis amentiae, quos quia cives Romani erant adnotavi in urbem remittendos'. There is very little clear evidence on the limits which existed in the early Empire on the powers of governors to execute citizens. For relevant cases see Suet. *Galba* 9; Dio lxiii 2, 3; Pliny, *Epp.* ii, 11, 8. Consequently, there is no general agreement on either the legal background or the current practice in this period. See Th. Mommsen, *Röm. Strafrecht* (1899), pp. 235–6; A. H. M. Jones, 'I appeal unto Caesar', *Studies in Roman Government and Law* (1960), pp. 51–65; A. N. Sherwin-White, *Roman Society* (1963), pp. 58–70; *The Letters of Pliny* (1966), pp. 164–5; P. Garnsey, 'The *Lex Iulia* and Appeal under the Empire', JRS 56 (1966), pp. 167–89; *idem*, *Social Status and Legal Privilege in the Roman Empire* (1970), pp. 260–71.

The most important case known is that of Paul. It would be possible to deduce from it that the governor was not in all circumstances obliged to send accused citizens to Rome for judgment, for the procurator on his own authority takes up the case of Paul, although Felix at least was aware of Paul's Roman citizenship (Acts 22:25 f., 23:27), and in the beginning Paul allowed matters to proceed without protest. Only after two years does he speak the word that determines the trial's future course: 'I appeal to Caesar' (Acts 25:11). It might therefore be supposed that the procurator could judge even a Roman citizen unless the latter lodged a protest. But if the accused made the claim to be judged in Rome, the governor was obliged to give effect to his request. Cf. *Sententiae Pauli* V 26, 1: 'Lege Iulia de vi publica damnatur qui aliqua potestate praeditus civem Romanum, antea ad populum, nunc ad imperatorem appellantem, necaverit, necarive iusserit, torserit, verbaverit, condemnaverit'. In the half century between Porcius Festus's procuratorship in Palestine and Pliny's term of office in Bithynia, a change in Roman procedural law may have taken place: Pliny did not wait for the accused Roman citizens to lodge objections to his judicial competence, but sent them to Rome on his own initiative.

77. *B.J.* ii 14, 9 (308): 'Florus ventured to do what none had done ever before, namely, to scourge before his tribunal and nail to the cross men of equestrian rank who, though Jews by birth, were none the less invested with that Roman dignity'.

account of the difficulty of the case, he wished to refer the decision to the emperor.[78] The procurator of Judaea's customary right, mentioned in the Gospels, to release a prisoner at the feast of Passover, is not known from any source of Roman law. Provincial governors had no right to grant a pardon.[79]

Although the governor as sole judge had to make his own decision, he normally took counsel with his *comites*. These were in part higher officials from his entourage, and in part younger people who accompanied the governor for the sake of their own training. They not only supported him in the exercise of his office, but also assisted him in the discharge of legal duties as a *consilium, συμβούλιον*. In certain instances, dignitaries from the native population of the province had a voice in the deliberations of the *consilium*.[80]

The death sentence was as a rule executed by soldiers.[81] For the

78. E.g. *B.J.* ii 12, 6 (243); *Ant.* xx 6, 2 (131–2): Ummidius Quadratus sent prominent Samaritans and Jews to Rome; *B.J.* ii 13, 2 (253); *Ant.* xx 8, 5 (161): Felix sent Eleazar and other Zealots to Rome; Jos. *Vita* 3 (13); Felix sent some Jewish priests; Acts 27:1: Festus despatched Paul and other captives; cf. JRS 56 (1966), p. 156.

79. See O. Hirschfeld, SAB (1889), p. 439. Also P. Winter, *On the Trial of Jesus* (1961), p. 97. *Dig.* XLVIII 19, 31: 'Ad bestias damnatos favore populi praeses dimittere non debet, sed principem consultare debet' (Modestinus, 3rd cent.).

80. Such consultants or assessors are found attached to various officials; see e.g. Jos. *Ant.* xiv 10, 2 (192); Philo, *Legatio* 33 (244); ILS 5947. Of interest is the composition and authority of the *συμβούλιον* (Acts 25:12) which advised Festus. If it was identical with the group of persons who in addition to Festus and Agrippa II interrogated Paul once more after he had lodged his appeal (Acts 25:53), it would have consisted partly of high-ranking Roman military officers and partly of civilians from the local population ('the principal men of the city').

Philo, *Legatio* 33 (244), uses the word *σύνεδρος* to designate an individual member of the governor's council; Josephus, *c. Ap.* ii 18 (177), uses the term *ἐπιστάτης*. Philo, *l.c.*, mentions that Petronius, the Syrian legate, when faced with the difficult decision how to evade complying with Caligula's order to erect the emperor's statue in the sanctuary in Jerusalem—see below, pp. 394–6—'took advice with his assessors (*μετὰ τῶν συνέδρων ἐβουλεύετο*)' on the course of action he should take. Josephus, *B.J.* ii 10, 5 (199), merely mentions Petronius's private conferences with the Jewish leaders (*οἱ δυνατοί*) and public meetings with the ordinary petitioners (*τὸ πλῆθος*).

In *c. Ap.* ii 18 (177), Josephus speaks generally of 'the holders of the highest governatorial offices' employing assessors (*ἐπιστάται*).

On *comites*, in general, see RE s.v. 'adsessor' and 'consilium'; cf. G. Cicogna, *I consigli dei magistrati romani e il consilium principis* (1910); Adolf Berger, *Encyclopedic Dictionary of Roman Law*, p. 408; W. Kunkel, Zeitschr. d. Sav. Stiftung, Röm. Abt. 84 (1967), pp. 218–44.

81. See, e.g. Suet. *Caligula* 32: 'Saepe in conspectu prandentis vel comissantis . . . miles decollandi artifex quibuscumque e custodia capita amputabat'. Tertullian, wishing to prove the incompatibility of the Christian faith with military

imperial governors were military officers and their individual power derived from their military office.[82] The numerous executions of noble Romans carried out in the reigns of Claudius and Nero were without exception effected by military personnel, often by high-ranking officers.[83] Not infrequently *speculatores* are mentioned as carrying out executions.[84] These were military men; occasionally they are explicitly described as holding military rank, in other cases they are definitely characterized as soldiers.[85] Those mentioned elsewhere by the same title and as discharging the same functions must also have been soldiers. The New Testament names the agents entrusted with the

---

pursuits, asks in *De corona militis* 11, 2: 'et vincula et carcerem et tormenta et supplicia administrabit, nec suarum ultor iniuriarum?' The passage indicates that the execution of death sentences was one of the duties of soldiers. See O. Hirschfeld, 'Die Sicherheitspolizei im römischen Kaiserzeit', *Kleine Schriften* (1913), pp. 576–612. Cf. G. Lopuszanski, 'La police romaine et les Chrétiens', Ant. Class. 20 (1951), pp. 5–46.

82. Dio liii 13; cf. Th. Mommsen, *Röm. Staatsrecht* II 1, p. 245. Compare however P. Garnsey, 'The Criminal Jurisdiction of Governors', JRS 58 (1968), pp. 51–9.

83. Tac. *Ann.* i 53; xi 37, 38; xii 22; xiv 8, 59; xv 59–61, 64, 65, 67, 69.

84. Mk. 6:27: 'The king sent forth a *σπεκουλάτωρ* and ordered him to bring [John the Baptist's] head'. Seneca, *De ira* I 18, 4: 'Tunc centurio supplicio praepositus condere gladium speculatorem iubet'; the same, *De ben.* III 25: 'speculatoribus occurrit nihilque se deprecari, quominus imperata peragerent, dixit et deinde cervicem porrexit'; Firmicus Maternus, *Mathes.* VIII 26, 6: 'faciet spiculatores, sed his ipsis gladio cervices amputabuntur'; *Dig.* XLVIII 20, 6 (from Ulpian): 'neque speculatores ultro sibi vindicent neque optiones ea desiderent, quibus spoliatur, quo momento quis punitus est' (hence soldiers who carried out executions in later times were no longer allowed to divide among themselves the garments of the executed person as they had been in the time of Jesus. Cf. RE s.v. 'speculatores'). In rabbinical literature ספקלטור or אספקלטור is encountered in the sense of 'executioner'. See especially the passage quoted in Levy, *Neuhebr. Wörterbuch* III, p. 573; *Chald. Wörterbuch* II, p. 182, add Tg. Neof. Gen. 37:36; 40:3 f.; 41:10 ff.; cf. also S. Krauss, *Griechische und lateinische Lehnwörter im Talmud* II (1899), p. 409. The form *spiculator* is a corruption from *speculator*, as is proved by many inscriptions, see for example ILS 2375, 2380–2.

85. See Seneca, *De ira* I 18, 4 (mentioning the execution of a soldier). The *optiones* and *commentarienses* referred to with the *speculatores* as carrying out executions, were also frequently, though not exclusively, military appointments (for *optiones*, see *Dig.* XLVIII 20, 6; for *commentarienses*, *Acta Claudii, Asterii et aliorum*, 4, 5).

The terms *speculator* and *lictor* are used by some writers as though synonymous; cf. Jerome, *Ep. I ad Innocentium*, 7, 8. The *lictor* however was not a soldier but belonged to the class of *apparitores*. But already in republican times he carried out death sentences on Roman citizens only, and under the Empire his duties in this direction probably extended no further (Mommsen, *Röm. Staatsrecht* I, pp. 301 f.).

arrest,[86] scourging,[87] and crucifixion[88] of Jesus as military personnel. Likewise, those charged with the imprisonment of Paul[89] are plainly described as soldiers.

The third main duty of procuratorial governors, besides the command of troops and the exercise of judiciary functions, was the administration of financial affairs.[90] It is in fact from this office that the title *procurator*, given generally to imperial finance officers, derives. Since everything of consequence concerning the different sorts of revenue and methods of taxation will be considered in the section dealing with the Census of Quirinius (Excursus I to this chapter), it is only necessary to mention here that revenues from Judaea, though an imperial province, will still have gone to the public treasury (*aerarium*) rather than to the imperial treasury (*fiscus*).[91] None the less, people in Judaea spoke of paying taxes 'to Caesar' (Mk. 12:14 ff.; Mt. 22:17 ff.; Lk. 20:22 ff.). It was probably for the purposes of tax collection that Judaea was divided into eleven toparchies (see vol. II, § 23). In collecting the revenue, the Romans seem to have made use of the Jewish authorities, as was in any case usual (see vol. II, § 23). Taxation was oppressive, as may be seen from

86. Jn. 18:3, 12. The word *σπεῖρα* has here precisely the same meaning as in Mk. 15:16; Mt. 27:27; Acts 10:1; 21:31; 27:1. It always denotes a detachment or unit of soldiers in the Roman service. When J. Blinzler, *Der Prozess Jesu* (1960), pp. 67–73, argues that the Evangelist uses the word *στρατιῶται* for soldiers in the Roman service and that therefore *σπεῖρα* in Jn. 18:3, 12 must refer to Jewish troops, his explanation is far-fetched. The *σπεῖρα* indicates the detachment as a whole; it consists of individual *στρατιῶται* (cf. Mk. 15:16, Mt. 27:27). While the Fourth Gospel undoubtedly states that Jesus was arrested by military personnel in the Roman service, the designation of the unit which carried out the arrest as a *σπεῖρα* is clearly an exaggeration. Not 500 or 600 men were despatched to apprehend Jesus, but a small detachment commanded perhaps by a *decurio* rather than a *tribunus* or *χιλίαρχος* (see P. Winter, *On the Trial of Jesus*, p. 29). On the possible identification of the *σπεῖρα* in Jn. 18:3, 12 with the *ὄχλος μετὰ μαχαιρῶν* in Mk. 14:43, see *idem*, 'Zum Prozess Jesu', in *Antijudaismus im Neuen Testament? Exegetische und systematische Beiträge*, ed. W. P. Eckert (1967), pp. 95–104, esp. on pp. 97 f.

87. Mk. 15:15, 16, 19; Mt. 27:26, 27; Lk. 23:36.

88. Mk. 15:20; Mt. 27:31.

89. Acts 21:35; 22:25, 26; 23: 23; 27:31, 32, 42; 28:16. On Paul's arrest and detention, see e.g. Jackson and Lake, *op. cit.*, *ad loc.*, and Additional Note xxvi; P. Winter, *On the Trial of Jesus*, pp. 76–87; Sherwin-White, *op cit.*, pp. 48–70.

90. On this, see H. G. Pflaum, 'Le pouvoir des procurateurs en leur qualité d'agents financiers de l'empereur', *op.cit.*, pp. 151–7; further F.-M. Abel, *op. cit.*, pp. 429 f.

91. On these distinctions, which are the subject of debate, see O. Hirschfeld, *Die kaiserlichen Verwaltungsbeamten* ([2]1905), pp. 1 ff. Cf. especially A. H. M. Jones, 'The Aerarium and the Fiscus', *Studies in Roman Government and Law*, pp. 99–114; F. Millar, 'The Fiscus in the First Two Centuries', JRS 53 (1963), pp. 29–42; P. A. Brunt, 'The "Fiscus" and its Development', JRS 66 (1966), pp. 75–91.

the fact that the provinces of Syria and Judaea complained of it in A.D. 17.[92]

From taxes in the proper sense of the word, must be distinguished customs, i.e., irregular and indirect duties, particularly those imposed on goods in transit.[93] Such customs were levied in all the provinces of the Roman Empire. The classic case in this respect was Egypt, where a system was devised of exceptional complexity. No object, and no sector of the country's economic life, remained untaxed; even its position as an entrepot for the lucrative trade between India and Europe was exploited. But in Palestine also, tolls and other levies were not unknown from as early as the Persian era (Ezra 4:13, 20; 7:24). The territorial units in which the same tariffs applied varied according to circumstances; it may not even be supposed that each province of the Roman Empire constituted a self-contained customs district.

Cities and client-kingdoms recognised as autonomous by the Romans, and their number was considerable, were also entitled to levy tolls on their borders.[94] Evidence of these matters was greatly amplified by the discovery of a lengthy inscription in Greek and Aramaic containing the customs tariff of the city of Palmyra in the time of Hadrian.[95] From this it appears that Palmyra, although at that time a Roman city in the same sense as many other self-governing cities within the Empire, nevertheless administered its own customs independently and profited from their revenues. It therefore goes without saying that the kings and tetrarchs who were 'allied' to Rome could levy customs on their

92. Tac. *Ann.* ii 42: 'provinciae Syria atque Iudaea, fessae oneribus, deminutionem tributi orabant'.

93. See RE s.v. 'portorium', 'publicanus', 'vectigal', and S. J. de Laet, *Portorium* (1949). L. Herzfeld, *Handelsgeschichte der Juden des Altherthums* (1879), pp. 159-62; J. Levy, *Neuhebr. Wörterbuch* III (1883), pp. 113–15 (art. מכס, מכסא etc.); L. Goldschmid, 'Les impots et droit de douane en Judée sous les Romains', REJ 34 (1897), pp. 192–217 (especially on the various kinds of taxes: גולגולת מכס, δημόσια, *annona*, ἀγγαρεία, קנס = census); M. Avi-Yonah, *Geschichte der Juden im Zeitalter des Talmud* (1962), pp. 92–102.

94. Mommsen, *Röm. Staatsrecht* III 1, p. 691. See especially Livy xxxviii 44: 'senatus consultum factum est, ut Ambraciensibus suae res omnes redderentur; in libertate essent ac legibus suis uterentur; portoria quae vellent terra marique caperent, dum eorum immunes Romani ac socii nominis Latini essent'. For the plebiscite for Termessus in Pisidia of 71 B.C., cf. CIL I 204 = ILS 38 = FIRA[2] I no. 11, col. II, lines 31 ff.: *Quam legem portorieis terrestribus maritumeisque Termenses maiores Phisidae capiundeis intra suos fineis deixserint, ea lex ieis portorieis capiundeis esto, dum nei quid portori ab ieis capiatur, quei publica populi Romani vectigalia redempta habebunt.*

95. The inscription was discovered in 1881. For an edition of the Aramaic text see CIS II, 3, 1, no. 3913. For the Greek text see IGR III 1056 = OGIS 629. Both texts, with an English translation and an explanation of the Aramaic text, appear in G. A. Cooke, *A Text-book of North Semitic Inscriptions* (1903), pp. 313–40.

borders to their own advantage[96]: it is uncertain whether Roman citizens were exempt.[97] The customs levied at Capernaum, close to the frontier of Galilee, in the time of Jesus (Mk. 2:14; Mt. 9:9; Lk. 5:27) undoubtedly went into the treasury of Herod Antipas, and not into the imperial treasury. In Judaea, on the other hand, customs were levied at that time in the interests of the emperor. It is known from the Gospels that an ἀρχιτελώνης (Lk. 19:1, 2) was established in Jericho, on Judaea's eastern border. In the seaport of Caesarea there is mention, among the influential men of the local Jewish community in A.D. 66 of a τελώνης by the name of John.[98] From Pliny it is known that merchants who exported incense from Central Arabia through Gaza had to pay high duties, not only to the Arabs on passing through their territory, but also to the Roman customs officers stationed, presumably in Gaza.[99] In addition to import and export duties, in Judaea as elsewhere indirect duties of another sort had to be paid: for instance, a market toll in Jerusalem, introduced by Herod but abolished by Vitellius in A.D. 36.[100]

The customs were not collected by civil servants, but by lessees, the so-called *publicani*, who leased the customs of a particular district for a fixed annual sum. Whatever the revenue yielded in excess of that sum was their gain, but if the revenue fell short of the rental, they had to bear the loss.[101] This system was prevalent in ancient times and

96. Suet. *Caligula* 16: 'whenever he [i.e. Caligula] restored kings to their thrones adiecit et omnem fructum vectigaliorum et reditum medii temporis'. Only the last point was unusual.

97. See Mommsen, *Röm. Staatsrecht* III 1, p. 691, and the passages quoted above in note 94. The Romans made arbitrary exceptions in favour of their nationals or others at certain times. Thus according to the *senatus consultum* given in Jos. *Ant.* xiv 10, 22 (248–51) (applying probably to Hyrcanus I, see above, p. 206), the Jews were allowed to levy customs within their own borders on condition that the king of Egypt was exempt.

98. Jos. *B.J.* ii 14, 4 (287).

99. Pliny, *NH* xii 32/63–5: 'Evehi non potest nisi per Gebbanitas, itaque et horum regi penditur vectigal . . . Iam quacumque iter est aliubi pro aqua aliubi pro pabulo aut pro mansionibus variisque portoriis pendunt, ut sumptus in singulos camelos * DCLXXXVIII ad nostrum litus [i.e. as far as Gaza] colligat, iterumque imperi nostri publicanis penditur', cf. de Laet, *Portorium*, pp. 333–4. There is also mention elsewhere of duties levied by uncivilized tribes. Thus, merchants trading between Syria and Babylon were forced to pay customs to the tribes through whose country they passed; and the σκηνῖται i.e. tent-dwellers of the desert, were actually more reasonable in their demands than the φύλαρχοι on both sides of the Euphrates (Strabo, p. 748).

100. Jos. *Ant.* xvii 8, 4 (205); xviii 4, 3 (90): 'Vitellius remitted to the inhabitants of the city all taxes'.

101. Cf. RE s.v. 'Publicani'; Prax, *Essai sur les sociétés vectigaliennes précédé d'un exposé sommaire du système fiscal des Romains* (1884); Rémondière, *De la levée des impôts en droit romain* (1886); Deloume, *Les manieurs d'argent à Rome jusqu'à l'empire. Les grandes compagnies de Publicains* . . . ([2]1892); F. Ziebarth, *Das*

was frequently applied, not only to customs, but even to taxes proper. Thus, for instance, during the Ptolemaic rule in Palestine, each city's tax collection was annually leased out to the highest bidder.[102] In Roman imperial times the system of leasing out was no longer used for direct taxes (the land tax and poll-tax). These were collected by state officials: in senatorial provinces by the quaestor; in imperial provinces by an imperial procurator[103] attached to the governor. In provinces, like Judaea, administered by an equestrian, the governor himself was procurator as well. Customs, on the other hand, were still commonly leased out to *publicani*, even under the Principate. This was undoubtedly the case in Judaea. The passage cited from Pliny (n. 99) states explicitly that duty had to be paid to the Roman *publicani*, among others, on incense exported from Arabia via Gaza. The general application of this system suggests that minor potentates such as Herod Antipas would also have adopted it. Even in city communes such as Palmyra, customs were not collected by municipal officials but were rented out to lessees.[104] These in turn naturally had their underlings,

---

griechische Vereinswesen (1896), pp. 19–26; U. Wilcken, *Griechische Ostraka*, I, pp. 513–630. See further M. Rostovtzeff, *Geschichte der Staatspacht in der römischer Kaiserzeit bis Diokletian* (1902); S. J. de Laet, *Portorium* (1949); E. Badian, *Publicans and Sinners* (1972).

102. Jos. *Ant.* xii 4, 3 (169): 'It so happened that at that time all the chief men and magistrates of the cities of Syria and Phoenicia were coming to bid for the tax-farming rights which the king used to sell every year to the wealthy men in each city'; *ibid.*, xii 4, 4 (175); cf. also xii 4, 5 (184). From the latter passage it is plain that taxes (φόροι) are alluded to, and not customs. The most important of these was the poll-tax, *Ant.* xii 4, 1 (155): 'prominent men purchased the right to farm taxes in their own respective provinces, and collecting the fixed poll-tax (τὸ προστεταγμένον κεφάλαιον) paid it to the kings'. But there were other taxes too; the Jerusalem priesthood had been freed by Antiochus the Great from the duty to pay 'the poll-tax' the crown tax and other (ἄλλων, perhaps to be emended to read ἁλῶν = salt) taxes'. Cf. C. Préaux, *L'économie royale des Lagides* (1939), pp. 420, 450 f.

103. This is confirmed for Egypt also. In Ptolemaic times all taxes were farmed out; in the days of the Empire a mixed system prevailed, partly farming out and partly direct collection; U. Wilcken, *Griechische Ostraka* I, pp. 515–55, 572–601; S. L. Wallace, *Taxation in Egypt from Augustus to Diocletian* (1938).

104. In the decree of the Council of Palmyra concerning the city's customs tariff in Hadrian's time (see n. 95 above) we read that the older customs tariffs had omitted a number of items; it was therefore always stipulated in an agreement of tenancy or lease that the amount of taxes to be levied by the tax-collector (τελώνης) would be determined in accordance with tariff and traditional usage. This, however, had led to disputes between merchants and collectors. The Council therefore decided that the municipal authorities would make a list of the items previously omitted and have them inserted in future lease-contracts in addition to the 'customary' taxes. If this tariff was then accepted by the lessee, it should be made publicly known, as was formerly done, by engraving it on stone tablets. But the authorities should see to it that the lessee exacted nothing illegally.

usually chosen from the native population. But even the principal lessees were by no means necessarily Romans. The above-mentioned tax-collectors of Jericho and Caesarea, Zacchaeus and John by name, were apparently Jews. Since they are described as well-to-do and respectable people, they certainly did not belong to the lowest class of publicans.[105] The amount of customs to be levied was indeed laid down by the authorities, but as is clear from the case of Palmyra, as these tariffs were in earlier times often very indefinite, there was plenty of scope for the arbitrariness and rapacity of the tax-collectors. The exploitation of such opportunities and the not infrequent overcharges made by these officials caused them, as a class, to be loathed by the people. As the poet Herodas had stated it: 'every door shudders before the tax-collectors'.[106] In the New Testament, 'publicans and sinners' appear almost as synonyms, and similar opinions are expressed in non-Jewish literature.[107] Rabbinical writings, too, display a marked aversion for customs officials.[108]

Within the limits set by the institutions themselves, the Jewish people none the less enjoyed a considerable measure of freedom in home affairs and self-government. The oath of allegiance to the emperor which the people were obliged to take, presumably on every change of reign, was, to judge from analogous cases, couched in fairly general terms, as was mandatory already in the days of Herod.[109] The internal constitution during the time of the procurators, in contrast to the monarchical rule of Herod and Archelaus, is characterized by

105. Tertullian's statement that all tax-gatherers were pagans, *De pudicitia*, 9, was contested already by Jerome, *Ep.* 21 *ad Damasum* 3.

106. *Herodas* (1892) vi 64: τοὺς γὰρ τελώνας πᾶσα νῦν θύρη φρίσσει. Cf. Wilcken, *Griechische Ostraka* I, p. 568.

107. E.g. Lucian, *Necyomantes* 11.

108. According to mB.K. 10:1, money may not be cashed from the cashbox of tax-gatherers, or alms accepted from them (because their money counts as stolen goods). But if a tax-gatherer has taken a person's ass and given another in exchange, or if a robber has deprived a person of his robe and given another in exchange, they may be kept, since the lawful owner has given up hope of recovering them (mB.K. 10:2). According to mNed. 3:4, it is permitted to swear to a robber or tax-gatherer that a certain thing belongs to the priests or the king, even if this is not so. (It was hoped that such an oath might induce the tax-gatherer or robber to desist from his unlawful demand for the property concerned). Tax-gatherers (מוכסין) are throughout equated with robbers. See J. Levy, *Neuhebr. Wörterbuch* III, p. 114; I. Abrahams, 'Publicans and Sinners', *Studies in Pharisaism and the Gospels*, 1st Ser. (1917), pp. 54–61. The meaning of the term is confirmed by the appearance of cognate expressions (מוכסיא, מוכסא) on the Palmyrene tax-law.

109. The taking of the oath of allegiance on the accession of Caligula is attested by Jos. *Ant.* xviii 5, 3 (124). For the inscriptional evidence compare S. Weinstock, 'Treueid und Kaiserkult', Ath. Mitt. 77 (1962), pp. 306–27; P. Herrmann, *Der römische Kaisereid* (1968).

Josephus as follows: 'the constitution became an aristocracy, and the High Priests were entrusted with the leadership of the nation'.[110] Josephus sees in the change which took place after the deposition of Archelaus a transition from monarchic to aristocratic rule, and considers, not incorrectly, the Roman governor only as an overseer, while the aristocratic Sanhedrin acted as the real governing body. The holder of the office of High Priest at any given time, who also held the presidency of the Sanhedrin, is called by Josephus *προστάτης τοῦ ἔθνους*. True, these High Priests were installed and deposed at the arbitrary pleasure of the Roman governor. But even in this respect the Romans observed certain bounds. In the years A.D. 6 to 41, appointments to the High Priestly office were made by the Roman governors (either by the legate of Syria or the prefect of Judaea), but during the period A.D. 44–66 the right of nomination was transferred to Jewish client-kings (Herod of Chalcis and Agrippa II), even though they did not reign in Judaea. In neither period were appointments to the office of High Priest purely arbitrary but were respectful of the precedence of certain old-established houses (Phiabi, Boethus, Ananus, Camith).[111]

More importantly, the Sanhedrin exercised a very wide range of legislative and executive powers, certainly much wider than in non-autonomous communities within the Roman Empire.[112] The legal position in general was that communities recognized by Rome as 'free' or 'autonomous' had the right to their own legislative and judicial organs, in principle exercising these rights even over resident Roman citizens. In Judaea the situation was practically the same,[113] with two reservations: (1) the state of public affairs existing *de facto* was not guaranteed; and (2) resident Roman citizens had their own law and their own jurisdiction. The existence, side by side, of a dual organization in the country, Jewish and Roman, each with its own legal system and its own judiciary institutions, occasionally had irregular results. The juridical competence of the local authorities was recognized by the

110. *Ant.* xx 10, 5 (251).

111. For the evidence, see vol. II, § 23. Cf. E. M. Smallwood, 'High Priests and Politics in Roman Palestine', JThSt 13 (1962), pp. 14–34; J. Jeremias, *Jerusalem in the Time of Jesus* (1969), pp. 147–81. On the High Priest as president of the Sanhedrin see vol. II, § 23.

112. On the status of non-autonomous communities, see Mommsen, *Röm. Staatsrecht* III 1, pp. 716–64, especially pp. 744 ff. L. Mitteis, *Reichsrecht und Volksrecht in den östlichen Provinzen des römischen Kaiserreichs* (1891), pp. 90 ff. (showing that even the *civitates non liberae* exercised their own jurisdiction). Cf. D. Nörr, *Imperium und Polis in der hohen Prinzipatszeit* (1966).

113. Mommsen, *Röm. Staatsrecht* III 1, p. 748: 'In regard to the extent of their jurisdiction, native magistrates in communities subject to Rome's rule were more or less in the same position as the magistrates of associate communes. As in administration and civil jurisdiction, the same principles were applied in the procedure governing criminal law cases.'

suzerain power, yet the governor could, if he wished, bring certain cases before his own tribunal whenever he thought that imperial interests were involved. On the whole this seems to have happened rarely. A decision of this type was taken, on the procurator's behalf, by the commander of the Roman garrison in Jerusalem, Claudius Lysias, who on learning that Paul claimed Roman citizenship, prevented the Sanhedrin from carrying the case to its conclusion and despatched the prisoner on his own initiative from Jerusalem to Caesarea (Acts 23:23-24). Felix, procrastinating, kept the apostle in a Roman prison and neither handed him back to the Jewish authorities nor took a decision of his own.

Crimes of a political nature came within the jurisdiction of the governor. Otherwise the Romans refrained from interfering in the customary functioning of the native law courts. Jurisdiction in cases of civil law was wholly in the hands of the Sanhedrin and subordinate tribunals: Jewish courts decided in accordance with Jewish law. Even in cases of criminal law the same situation almost always prevailed, with the exception, however, of political offences. It is still debated whether Jewish law courts were entitled to pass and administer sentence of death without endorsement by the Roman governor. This problem will be dealt with in connexion with the trial and condemnation of Jesus.[114] Even Roman citizens were not totally exempt from complying with the requirements of the Jewish law. A Jewish ordinance prevented Gentiles (ἀλλογενεῖς) from entering the inner courtyards of the Temple. Anyone acting contrary to this prohibition was punished with death, even if he was a Roman citizen. The Romans confirmed Jewish capital jurisdiction in such cases even over non-Jews.[115] When the procurator Festus proposed dealing with Paul in accordance with Jewish law, only Paul's appeal to the emperor (*provocatio*) prevented this from happening (Acts 25:9–12—see above p. 369).

Jewish cult and worship were not merely tolerated, but enjoyed the

114. For more details, see vol. II, § 23.

115. Josephus, *B.J.* vi 2, 4 (125–6), confirmed by two inscriptions, the more complete of which was found by C. Clermont-Ganneau in 1871; on its discovery and the text see Clermont-Ganneau, 'Une stèle du Temple de Jérusalem' in Rev. arch. 23 (1872), pp. 214–34, 290–6 = OGIS 598 = Frey, CIJ 1400; the second copy, SEG VIII 109. See E. Gabba, *Iscrizioni greche e latine per lo studio della Bibbia* (1958), no. 4 (cf. P. Winter, *On the Trial of Jesus*, p. 155 f., n. 37). This point is of considerable importance in assessing the charges in the trial of Paul. The main charge brought against him by the Jewish authorities was that he had facilitated entry into the inner Temple Courts by a 'Greek', Trophimus (Acts 21:28–9). The accusers wished to impress the procurator that Paul was punishable even under Roman law, namely the ordinance referred to in Titus's speech, *B.J.* vi 2, 4 (125–6). Cf. Acts 24:6. It is not certain whether Paul actually took Trophimus with him into the inner Temple Court. Acts 21:29 leaves this in doubt: ἐνόμιζον ὅτι εἰς τὸ ἱερὸν εἰσήγαγεν ὁ Παῦλος [τὸν Τρόφιμον].

protection of the Roman State, as is shown by the ordinance concerning trespass on the Temple Mount.[116] The cosmopolitan trend characteristic of pagan piety of that time even made it easy for noble Romans to present votive gifts to the Jewish Temple and have sacrifices offered there on their behalf.[117] State supervision of the Temple, especially of the administration of its vast finances, seems from A.D. 6–41 to have been conducted by the Roman authorities. In the years A.D. 44–66 it was transferred to the same Jewish rulers to whom the prerogative of appointing High Priests had been entrusted, namely, Herod of Chalcis first, and then Agrippa II.[118] A restriction on freedom of worship, small in itself but regarded as oppressive by the Jews, was removed in A.D. 36. From A.D. 6 the High Priest's costly stole had been in the keeping of the Roman military commander of the Antonia and was brought out for use only four times a year (on the three main festivals and the Day of Atonement). At the request of the Jews, Vitellius ordered in A.D. 36 that the High Priest's vestments should be handed over to them. And when in A.D. 44 the procurator Cuspius Fadus wished to bring the vestments back into Roman keeping, a Jewish delegation went to Rome and secured a letter from the Emperor Claudius confirming the order of Vitellius.[119]

Great deference was shown to Jewish religious sensitivity. Whereas in some provinces (Gaul and Britain, for instance) emperor-worship was instituted, and in others at least encouraged, no demands of this sort were ever made of the Jews except in Caligula's time. Out of respect for Jewish religious customs, the Roman authorities exempted the Jews from appearing before a magistrate on a sabbath or Jewish holiday, not in Judaea alone but throughout the Empire. The Romans were satisfied with a sacrifice offered by the Jews twice daily in the Temple 'for Caesar and the Roman nation'. The sacrifice consisted of

116. This protection extended in practice to synagogue services and the Torah. When the pagan inhabitants of Dora erected a statue of the emperor in the Jewish synagogue of that town, the legate Petronius ordered the town council to surrender the culprits and ensure that such outrages did not recur, cf. Jos. *Ant.* xix 6 3 (308). A soldier who capriciously tore up a Torah scroll was put to death for this by the procurator Cumanus, *B.J.* ii 12, 2 (231); *Ant.* xx 5, 4 (115–17).

117. Augustus and his wife sent wine vessels as their gift to the Temple in Jerusalem, *B.J.* v 13, 6 (562), and other costly presents, Philo, *Legatio* 23 (157), 40 (319). Marcus Agrippa gave presents on the occasion of his visit to Jerusalem, *Legatio* 37 (297), and offered 100 oxen in sacrifice, *Ant.* xvi 2, 1 (14). Vitellius also sacrificed there, *Ant.* xviii 5, 3 (122).

118. On the exercise of this prerogative by Herod of Chalcis, see *Ant.* xx 1, 3 (15); by Agrippa *Ant.* xx 9, 7 (222). On the administration of the finances of the Temple, see vol. II, § 24.

119. *Ant.* xviii 4, 3 (95); xx 1, 1 (6); cf. xv 11, 4 (403–8). Cf. P. Winter, *On the Trial of Jesus*, pp. 16–19. When Titus took Jerusalem, the High Priest's robes fell into the hands of the Romans, *B.J.* vi 8, 3 (389).

two lambs and an ox per day—provided either by Augustus himself out of his own revenue, or by the Jews, according to the conflicting testimony of Philo and Josephus.[120] On special occasions the Jews showed their loyal sentiments by a great offering in honour of the emperor.[121] In the Diaspora, donations in his honour were exhibited in the *aula* of synagogues.[122] Next to the worship of the emperor, the Jews took particular offence at portraits of him on coins and military standards. Here, too, their scruples were respected. The circulation in Judaea of Roman *denarii* bearing the emperor's image could not be avoided (Mk. 12:16; Mt. 22:20; Lk. 20:24), for gold and silver coins were not minted in the province. But the copper coins manufactured in the country carried no human portrait in the time of Roman rule (as under the Herodians) but only the emperor's name and inoffensive emblems.[123] Roman troops dispensed with their standards, which bore the emperor's image, when entering Jerusalem. Pilate's wilful attempt to contravene

120. Philo, *Legatio* 23 (157); 40 (317). Jos. *B.J.* ii 10, 4 (197); 17, 2 (409–10); 17, 3 (412–17). *C. Ap.* ii 6 (77). For further details see vol. II, § 24.

121. Three times in Caligula's time; see Philo, *Legatio* 45 (356), cf. 32 (232): an offering presented on the occasion of Caligula's accession.

122. Philo, *Legatio* 2 (133): Along with the synagogues, the Alexandrians also destroyed 'the tributes to the emperors, the shields and gilded wreaths, the slabs with dedicatory inscriptions'. *In Flaccum* 7 (48): 'The Jews . . . by losing their synagogues (*προσευχαί*), were also losing . . . their means of showing reverence to their benefactors, since they no longer had the sacred buildings where they could offer their thanksgiving'; *ibid.* 49: by depriving the Jews of their synagogues no honour was rendered to the *κυρίοι* (i.e. the Roman emperors), but honour was taken away from them. For the synagogues are to the Jews *ὁρμητήρια τῆς εἰς τὸν Σεβαστὸν οἶκον ὁσιότητος . . . ὧν ἡμῖν ἀναιρεθεισῶν τίς ἕτερος ἀπολείπεται τόπος ἢ τρόπος τιμῆς*; on the placing of honorific dedications in the forecourts of synagogues, see vol. III, § 31.

123. On the coins minted in Judaea in the time of the procurators, see Th. Mommsen, *Geschichte des römischen Münzwesens* (1860), p. 719; J. Levy, *Geschichte der jüdischen Münzen*, pp. 74–9; F. W. Madden, *History of Jewish Coinage* (1864), pp. 134–53; *Jewish Numismatics* (1874–6), *Coins of the Jews* (1874), pp. 170–87. F. de Saulcy, *Numismatique de la Terre Sainte* (1874), pp. 69–78, plates III–IV. See now A. Reifenberg, *Ancient Jewish Coins* ([2]1947), pp. 54–7, Y. Meshorer, *Jewish Coins of the Second Temple Period* (1967), pp. 102–6. On the coins of Augustus with the superscription *Καίσαρος* the years 36, 39, 40, 41 are engraved. The coins of Tiberius (with the name *Τιβερίου Καίσαρος* in most cases given in abbreviated form) are dated by the years of Tiberius's reign; we have examples of the numbers 2–5, 11. On many coins the name of Julia is mentioned with that of Tiberius, until the 16th year of Tiberius, i.e. A.D. 29, when Julia Livia died. Some coins have Julia's name alone. Coins of Claudius exist from the 13th and 14th year of his reign, and coins of Nero from his 5th year. The latter bear only the emperor's name; those of Claudius, the name of his wife also, Julia Agrippina.

On the coinage minted in the interval between the last prefect and the first procurator in Judaea, see J. Meyshan, 'The Coinage of Agrippa I', IEJ 4 (1954), pp. 186–200 = *Recent Studies and Discoveries on Ancient Jewish and Syrian Coins* (1954), pp. 50–64.

this custom was frustrated by the people's fierce opposition and he found himself compelled to withdraw the standards from Jerusalem.[124] When Vitellius, the legate of Syria, embarked on a campaign against Aretas, king of Nabataea, he yielded to Jewish entreaties and ordered the troops carrying images of the emperor on their standards not to march through Judaean territory.[125]

As regards the general institutions and principles of government, the Jews had therefore no cause to complain of any lack of consideration. But in practice they worked out rather differently. Roman officials on the spot were constantly inclined to treat these niceties with indifference. Unfortunately, also, Judaea, especially in the last decades before their rebellion against Rome, had to endure more than one governor lacking all sense of right and wrong. Moreover, despite the careful attention of Roman officials to the feelings of the Jews, their condition may itself have been viewed by many as an insult to the rights of God's chosen people, who instead of paying tribute to the emperor in Rome should themselves have been called to rule over the pagan world.[126]

The difficulty of the task which the Romans had set for themselves when they incorporated Judaea into the Empire became apparent with their first administrative act in that country. Contemporaneously with the appointment of Coponius as first prefect of Judaea, the emperor despatched a new legate to Syria in the person of Quirinius. It became his task to take a census of the population of the newly acquired territory so that taxes could be levied in accordance with Roman usage. But no sooner had Quirinius, in A.D. 6 or 7, begun to carry out this measure than he met with opposition from every quarter. It was only due to the mild persuasion of the High Priest Joazar, who evidently realised that open rebellion would lead nowhere, that the initial opposition was gradually abandoned. The people submitted in silent resignation to the inevitable, and the census was allowed to proceed.[127] No permanent peace was gained, however, but only a truce of uncertain duration. Judas of Gamala in the Golan, called the Galilean (he is no doubt identical with Judas son of Hezekiah mentioned on p. 332), made it his mission in company with a Pharisee named Ẓadduk to

124. *B.J.* ii 9, 3 (174); *Ant.* xviii 3, 1 (59). See below, p. 384.

125. *Ant.* xviii 5, 3 (121–2).

126. Such, at least, was the popular sentiment. From the same religious premises the contrary conclusion could have been drawn, namely, that the pagan government had also been sent by God and should be obeyed for as long as God willed. (In the third century, Simeon b. Lakish interpreted Gen 1:31 'Behold, it was very good' as applying to the Roman empire; cf. Gen. R. 9:15.) But from A.D. 6–41 and A.D. 44–66 this view was held by an ever-diminishing minority.

127. According to Jos. *Ant.* xviii 2, 1 26, in the 37th year of the *aera Actiaca*, i.e. in the autumn of A.D. 6/7. The Actian era begins on 2nd September 31 B.C. On its use in Syria, see above p. 257. Josephus's statement is confirmed by Dio lv 27, 6: Archelaus was deposed in A.D. 6 (see above, p. 327).

rouse the people to resistance and preach revolt and insurrection in the name of religion. They met with no significant success at first, but were nevertheless responsible for the emergence, as an offshoot from the Pharisees, of a stricter and more fanatical party of resolute patriots, or as they called themselves, activists or Zealots, unwilling to wait in quiet submission for the fulfilment, with God's help, of Israel's messianic hope, but desirous rather of bringing it to reality by means of the sword in battle against the godless enemy.[128] It was due to their activities that the spark of rebellion continued to smoulder for sixty years, when it finally burst into flame.[129]

Of Coponius and some of his successors little more is known than their names. Altogether there were seven—possibly only six—prefects who held office as governors of Judaea from A.D. 6 to 41. (1) Coponius, about A.D. 6 to 9, *B.J.* ii 8, 1 (117); *Ant.* xviii 2, 2 (29–31); (2) Marcus Ambibulus, named in our manuscripts Ambibuchus, about A.D. 9 to 12, *Ant.* xviii 2, 2 (31); (3) Annius Rufus about A.D. 12 to 15, *Ant.* xviii 2, 2 (32–3);[130] (4) Valerius Gratus A.D. 15 to 26, *Ant.* xviii 2, 2 (33);

128. *Ζηλωταί*, see Lk. 6:15; Acts 1:13; Jos. *B.J.* iv 3, 9 (160); 4, 6 (291); 5, 1 (305); 6, 3 (377); vii 8, 1 (268). Instead of the קנא of Biblical Hebrew, later Hebrew and Aramaic use also קנאי and קנאן (see Levy, *Neuhebr. Wörterbuch*, and Jastrow, *Dictionary*, s.v.). From the plural of the latter form (קנאניא) is derived the Greek *Καναναῖος* which should be read in Mt. 10:4 and Mk. 3:18 rather than *Κανανίτης*. For recent treatments of the subject see W. R. Farmer, *Maccabees, Zealots and Josephus* (1957); M. Hengel, *Die Zeloten* (1961)—the major modern study; S. G. F. Brandon, *Jesus and the Zealots* (1967); M. Smith, 'Zealots and Sicarii: their Origins and Relations', HThR 64 (1971), pp. 1–19; S. Applebaum, 'The Zealots: the Case for Revaluation', JRS 61 (1971), pp. 156–70; M. Borg, 'The Currency of the Term "Zealot",' JThSt 22 (1971), pp. 504–12.

129. Cf. in general *B.J.* ii 8, 1 (118), *Ant.* xviii 1, 1 (4–10), Acts 5:37. The descendants of Judas also distinguished themselves as Zealots. His sons Jacob and Simon were executed by Tiberius Julius Alexander, *Ant.* xx 5, 2 (102); his son (or grandson?) Menahem (Manaim) was one of the principal leaders at the beginning of the rebellion in A.D. 66, *B.J.* ii 17, 8–9 (433–48). A descendant of Judas and relative of Menahem by the name of Eleazar directed the defence of Masada in A.D. 74, *B.J.* ii 17, 9 (447); vii 8, 1 (253); 8, 2 (275); 8, 6–7 (320–88); 9, 1 (399). See Yigael Yadin, *Masada: Herod's Fortress and the Zealots' Last Stand* (1966), and below pp. 511–12. See also Vermes, *Jesus the Jew* (1973), pp. 46–7.

130. The term of office of the first three Roman prefects cannot be precisely dated. That of the following two is fixed by the fact that Valerius Gratus held office for 11 years, *Ant.* xviii 2, 2 (35) and Pontius Pilate for 10 years, *Ant.* xviii 4, 2 (89). Pilate was deposed before Vitellius made his first visit to Jerusalem, i.e. shortly before Easter A.D. 36, as a comparison of *Ant.* xviii 4, 3 (90) with 5, 3 (122–3) shows. The period during which the last two were in office can be deduced from the fact that Marullus was installed immediately after Caligula's accession in March A.D. 37, *Ant.* xviii 6, 10 (237). Eusebius *HE* i 9, 2 states that Josephus sets the date of Pilate's assumption of office in the 12th year of Tiberius (A.D. 25/26), which is correct only in that such a dating may be inferred from Josephus. In his *Chronicle* (ed. Schoene II, p. 147), Eusebius dates Pilate's instalment in office in the 13th year of Tiberius.

(5) Pontius Pilate A.D. 26 to 36, *B.J.* ii 9, 2 (169); *Ant.* xviii 2, 2 (35); Tacitus, *Ann.* xv 44; (6) Marcellus in A.D. 36 or 37, *Ant.* xviii 4, 2 (89); and (7) Marullus A.D. 37 to 41, *Ant.* xviii 6, 10 (237). It is debatable whether the two last-named were really two different persons. The reading Μαρκέλλος in *Ant.* xviii 4, 2 (89) may be corrupt for Μαρούλλος which appears in *Ant.* xviii 6, 10 (237). Marullus may have been appointed acting High Commissioner for Judaea by Vitellius, the appointment being later confirmed by Caligula in Rome. It is true that Josephus writes that the emperor 'sent' Marullus, and that this seems to indicate that he was someone else than Marcellus, who apparently was already in Judaea at the time. But the word ἐκπέμπειν need not be taken literally; Josephus could have used it as a stereotype phrase simply to denote official appointment.[131] The long term of office held by Valerius Gratus and Pontius Pilate corresponded to the general rules adopted by Tiberius when appointing provincial governors. For the good of the provinces concerned, he left then as long as possible in their posts because he thought governors behaved like flies on a wounded body: once sated, they then temper their extortions, whereas new men would start with a keen appetite.[132]

Among those named, Pontius Pilate is of special interest, not only as the judge of Jesus, but also because he is the only one discussed in

131. The reading in *Ant.* xviii 4, 2 (89) is: 'Vitellius, having despatched (ἐκπέμψας) one of his friends, Μαρκέλλος, whom he had made governor (ἐπιμελητής) over the Jews, ordered Pilate to return to Rome'. From this it appears that Marcellus, one of Vitellius's subalterns, was staying in Syria before he was appointed in Pilate's place to become the governor of Judaea. Subsequently, in *Ant.* xviii 6, 10 (237), the appointment of Marullus is reported as follows: '[The emperor] despatched (ἐκπέμπει) Marullus as cavalry commander (ἱππάρχης)', which *prima facie* indicates that Marullus was sent to Judaea from Rome. Hence Marcellus and Marullus would be two different persons. As Marcellus is otherwise unknown, it has been suggested by S. L. de Laet, 'Le Successeur de Ponce-Pilate', Ant. class. 8 (1939), pp. 418 f., that we have in *Ant.* xviii 4, 2 (89) a scribal error, and that instead of Μαρκέλλος Josephus actually wrote Μαρούλλος in both places. De Laet is followed by E. M. Smallwood in 'The Date of the Dismissal of Pontius Pilate from Judaea', JJS 5 (1954), pp. 12–21. In view of the fact that Josephus uses the term ἐκπέμπειν when reporting Marullus's appointment, de Laet's explanation can be accepted only if it is assumed that Josephus used figurative language, meaning by ἐκπέμπειν no more than that Marullus was appointed, or rather that the earlier provisional appointment made by Vitellius was confirmed by the emperor. It is not possible to arrive at a definite conclusion, but de Laet's suggestion sounds attractive, as it was not the Syrian legate's prerogative to make definite appointments in Judaea; on the other hand, it can be assumed that the emperor would in such a situation heed the legate's recommendation to appoint an experienced officer for the post.

132. *Ant.* xviii 6, 5 (172–6). Tac. *Ann.* i 80; iv 6 also mentions the long periods which the emperor allowed his governors. That Tiberius had the well-being of the provinces in mind is attested by Suet. *Tib.* 32 'praesidibus onerandas tributo provincias suadentibus rescripsit: boni pastoris esse tondere pecus, non deglubere'.

any detail in the writings of Philo and Josephus.[133] Philo (or rather Agrippa I, in his letter which Philo reproduces) describes him as unbending and callously hard by nature, 'a man of inflexible disposition, harsh and obdurate', and has a low opinion of the manner in which Pilate discharged his official duties. He charges Pilate with greed, vindictiveness and cruelty. As Agrippa's testimony on Pontius Pilate's conduct of affairs in Judaea is the only one extant from any of the prefect's own contemporaries, it cannot be dismissed.[134]

The very first action with which Pilate began his term of office as governor of Judaea was characteristic of a man who treated Jewish customs and privileges with contempt. In order not to offend Jewish religious feelings, care had always been taken by previous prefects to provide that troops entering Jerusalem should not carry ensigns bearing the image of the emperor (see above, p. 381). Pilate, however, to whom such tolerance may have appeared as an unworthy weakness, ordered the Jerusalem garrison to enter the city by night with their standards. When the people learned what had happened, they flocked in crowds to Caesarea and besieged the governor for five days and nights with entreaties to remove the abomination. At last, on the sixth day, Pilate admitted the people into the stadium, into which he had at the same time ordered a detachment of his soldiers. When the Jews continued their complaints here too, he gave a signal and the soldiers surrounded the people on all sides with drawn swords. But the Jews stood firm, bared their necks, and protested that they would rather die than submit to a breach of the law. Pilate may have thought it dangerous to insist further, for he ordered the offensive images to be removed from Jerusalem.[135]

133. On Pontius Pilate see RE XX, cols. 1322–3; S. Sandmel in IDB s.v. 'Pilate, Pontius'.

134. Philo, *Legatio* 38 (302).

135. *B.J.* ii 9, 2–3 (169–74). *Ant.* xviii 3, 1 (55–9). In *HE* ii 6, 4, Eusebius quotes Josephus; according to his *Dem. Ev.* viii 2, 123 (403), the episode of the standards was also related by Philo in the latter's work on the persecutions of the Jews under Tiberius and Caligula. Of this work, only the treatises *Legatio* and *In Flaccum* are extant, whilst other sections no longer exist. Cf. vol. III, § 34.

That the standards bearing images were erected within the Temple area (ἐν τῷ ἱερῷ) is known only from Eusebius's report in *Dem. Ev.*, *loc. cit.*, referring to Philo's lost work as Eusebius's source. Josephus, less definite on this point, speaks of Jerusalem as the place where it occurred.

It is due to an inexact recollection of his reading that Origen says of Pilate that, like Caligula later, he wished to force the Jews ἀνδριάντα Καίσαρος ἀναθεῖναι ἐν τῷ ναῷ, *Commentary on Matthew* xvii, 25, on Mt. 22:15 ff. (GCS, *Origenes Werke* X, pp. 653–4). So also Jerome on Mt. 24:15: 'potest autem simpliciter aut de Antichristo accipi aut de imagine Caesaris quam Pilatus posuit in templo' (PL xxvi, col. 177). See C. H. Kraeling, 'The Episode of the Roman Standards at Jerusalem', HThR 35 (1942), pp. 263–89.

A new storm erupted when he applied the rich treasures of the Temple to the very useful purpose of building an aqueduct to Jerusalem. Such an appropriation of the sacred treasures seemed no less offensive than setting up images of the emperor. Consequently, when he once visited Jerusalem while building was in progress, he was again surrounded by a complaining, shrieking mob. But he had been told of the expected outburst, and had given orders to his soldiers to mingle with the demonstrators in civilian dress and armed with clubs. Then when the crowd's complaints and entreaties turned to abuse, he gave the agreed signal and the soldiers pulled the clubs from under their garments and lashed into the people without mercy. Many lost their lives in the ensuing panic, and although resistance was crushed, hatred for Pilate was stirred up anew.[136]

The New Testament contains hints of other outrages in the time of Pilate. 'There were present at that time', runs the narrative in Luke 13:1, 'some who had told Jesus of the Galileans whose blood Pilate had mingled with their sacrifices'. This statement is to be understood as indicating that Pilate put to the sword a number of Galileans who were preparing to present their offerings at Jerusalem. Nothing more definite is known of this incident. There is no record of it outside the third Gospel.[137]

Just as little is known of 'the rebels who had committed murder in the insurrection' (Mk. 15:7) with whom Barabbas[138] was thrown into prison, to be released at the time of Jesus' trial.

136. *B.J.* ii 9, 4 (175–7); *Ant.* xviii 3, 2 (60–2); Eusebius, *HE* ii 6, 6–7. The length of the aqueduct is given by Josephus in *Ant.* xviii 3, 2 (60) as 200 stadia; in *B.J.* ii 9, 4 (175) as 400 stadia; the Latin Josephus, and Eusebius, *HE* ii 6, 6 make it 300 stadia. It is noteworthy that the Slavonic Josephus, which is essentially based on *Bellum*, gives the same figure of 200 stadia as do the *Antiquities*.

From these measurements there can be no doubt that the construction referred to is an aqueduct from the so-called Pool of Solomon southwest of Bethlehem. In the Jerusalem Talmud it is stated that an aqueduct led from Etam to the Temple (yYoma 41a). In fact 'Eṭam was according to 2 Chron. 11:6 situated between Bethlehem and Tekoa, without any doubt near the spring now called 'Ayin Atan, in close vicinity to Solomon's Pool.

137. For discussion of the possible setting of this episode see J. Blinzler, 'Die Niedermetzelung von Galiläern durch Pilatus', NT 2 (1957), pp. 24–49 and Winter, *Trial*, pp. 54, 176 f., nn. 8–10.

138. **בר אבא**: cf. Str.-B. I, p. 1031; Bauer, Arndt, Gingrich, *Lexicon*, p. 132. CIJ no. 1285 reproduces an inscription in which the words **בר רבן**, apparently a patronym, can be made out. This spelling agrees with that given in Mt. 27:17 in Codex Koridethi: *ΙΗΣΟΥΣ ΒΑΡ ΡΑΒΒΑΝ*. The name may not have been uncommon at the time. See Winter, *Trial*, p. 95. The reading Rabban is supported by the Gospel according to the Hebrews quoted by Jerome (*in Mt.* 27:16–8): 'filius magistri eorum'. For the Beth Shearim inscription of *ΒΑΡΑΒΑΙ*, see CIJ no. 1110; M. Schwabe, B. Lifshitz, *Beth She'arim* II (1967), no. 89.

An event mentioned in the letter, reproduced by Philo, from Agrippa I to Caligula, probably took place in the latter days of Pilate's governorship.[139] Pilate had realised from the outburst at Caesarea that the erection of images of the emperor in Jerusalem was impossible because of Jewish obduracy but he thought he might try to introduce votive shields without images but carrying the emperor's name. He raised such shields, richly gilt, in Herod's former palace, now his own residence, 'less to honour Tiberius than to annoy the people'. But even this the people would not tolerate. First, they approached Pilate in company with the aristocracy of Jerusalem and Herod's four sons (who happened to be in the city, probably to attend a feast) to induce him to remove the shields. As this met with no success, the notables amongst them, including, certainly, the four sons of Herod, addressed a petition to the emperor asking him to order the removal of the offending shields. Tiberius, who probably perceived that it was simply a piece of arbitrary bravado on the part of Pilate, ordered him with tokens of extreme displeasure to remove the shields from Jerusalem at once and to set them up in the temple of Augustus at Caesarea. This was done. 'And thus were preserved both the honour of the emperor, and the ancient customs of the city.'[140]

In the end, Pilate's recklessness caused his downfall. It was an ancient belief among the Samaritans that the sacred Temple vessels had been buried since the time of Moses on Mount Gerizim.[141] A Samaritan pseudo-prophet promised (in A.D. 35) to produce these vessels if the people would assemble on that mountain. The credulous listened to him and great crowds of armed Samaritans flocked to the village of Tirathana at the foot of Mount Gerizim ready to climb the mountain and see the holy spectacle.[142] But before they could carry out their intention, they were attacked by a strong force in the village, as a result of which some were killed, some put to flight, and still others

139. The argument that the incident connected with the introduction of votive shields into Jerusalem occurred later than the incident of the standards rests on rather shaky ground. The prefect, it is argued, having failed in his effort to persuade the citizens of Jerusalem to allow imperial standards among them, tried to get his own back by taking image-less votive shields into their city. This interpretation may well be right, but it remains speculative. As Philo (or Agrippa) reports only the incident of the shields and Josephus only that of the standards, there is no certainty in regard to the chronological sequence of these two happenings.

140. Philo, *Legatio* 38 (299–306). See Smallwood *ad loc.* and P. L. Maier, 'The Episode of the Golden Roman Shields at Jerusalem', HThR 62 (1969), pp. 109–21.

141. *Ant.* xviii 4, 1–2 (85–9). On this tradition see M. Gaster, *The Samaritans* (1925), p. 9.

142. Tirathana is possibly present-day Tire, see J. A. Montgomery, *The Samaritans* (1907), p. 146, n. 15. Cf. Abel, *Géog. Pal.* II, p. 484.

were captured. Of these, Pilate executed the most respected and distinguished.[143] The Samaritans, who knew that there was no revolutionary motive in the pilgrimage to Mount Gerizim, accused Pilate before Vitellius, the legate in Syria at that time, with the result that Vitellius sent Pilate to Rome to answer for his conduct, and handed over the administration of Judaea to Marcellus.[144]

143. *Ant.* xviii 4, 1 (87).

144. *Ant.* xviii 4, 2 (89). See E. M. Smallwood, *op. cit.* n. 131 above. It may have taken Pilate about a year to travel from Judaea to Rome, for he did not arrive in the capital until after Tiberius's death. Josephus says nothing of his subsequent fate. With the spread of Christianity in the Roman Empire, Pilate's personality caught the imagination of historiographers. A spurious letter dating from the second century makes Pilate the author of a report to the emperor Claudius (whose Principate fell in the years A.D. 41–54, after Pilate had been recalled from office). The report describes in some detail Pilate's unsuccessful attempt to save the life of Jesus. On epistles supposed to have been written by Pilate, cf. M. R. James, *The Apocryphal New Testament* (1924), p. 146. Tertullian speaks of Pilate as being at the time of Jesus' trial a secret Christian, *Apologeticum* 21, 24, and he mentions an official despatch in which the prefect suggested to the emperor Tiberius that Jesus should be included in the Pantheon, *ibid.*, 5, 2; see T. D. Barnes in JRS 58 (1968), pp. 32–3. The fourth-century *Gospel of Nicodemus*, sometimes called *The Acts of Pilate*, purports to contain official records of the governor's dealings with Jesus, M. R. James, *op. cit.*, pp. 94–145; P. Vannutelli, *Actorum Pilati textus synoptici* (1938); E. Hennecke, *New Testament Apocrypha* I (1963), pp. 444–84; S. Brock, 'A Fragment of the *Acta Pilati* in Christian Palestinian Aramaic', JThSt 22 (1971), pp. 157–8; Pilate's fame, however, reached its zenith when the Prefect of Judaea became a saint in the monophysite Coptic Church. He is still venerated as such.

From Eusebius, *Chron.* II, ed. Schoene, pp. 150–1, and *EH* ii 7, onward, a different but equally legendary tradition begins to gain circulation. The story now goes that Pilate ended his own life by suicide, or suffered death at the hands of the emperor as a punishment for his iniquitous proceedings against Jesus. According to Jerome, 'Romanorum historici scribunt [quod] in multas incidens calamitates; Pontius Pilatus propria se manu interficit' (Schoene, *op. cit.*, p. 151; R. Helm, *Die Chronik des Hieronymus*, p. 178). From what sources Jerome derived this piece of intelligence is not known. The legend of Pilate's suicide is further expanded in the *Mors Pilati* (*Evangelia apocrypha*, ed. C. Tischendorf (1876), pp. 456–8). Demons crowding around Pilate's corpse utter dreadful shrieks and his body is transported from Rome to Vienne on the Rhone, but the waters of the Rhone refuse to receive it, the river starts to boil and spits out the corpse. It is then transported to Lausanne on Lake Geneva, or to Lucerne on Lake Lucerne, but the inhabitants of whatever the city may be cannot stand the proximity of Pilate's dead body and 'a se removerunt eum et in quodam puteo montibus circumsepto immerserunt, ubi adhuc . . . diabolicae machinationes ebullire dicuntur'. The place can still be visited by tourists and other interested persons on Mount Pilate (*Pilatusberg*) in the lovely surroundings of Lake Lucerne. According to another form of Christian legend, Pilate was executed by Nero (this is reported by John Malalas, ed. Dindorf, pp. 250–7) or by Tiberius (thus in a text edited by Tischendorf in *Evangelica apocrypha*, pp. 449–55), having at last repented of his misdeeds and dying a convinced Christian.

Soon after, on the Feast of Passover A.D. 36,[145] Vitellius himself came to Jerusalem and won the goodwill of the inhabitants of the capital by remitting the taxes on fruit sold in the city, and by handing over for free use the High Priest's vestments kept in Roman custody since A.D. 6.[146]

After he had meanwhile been occupied with the Parthian expedition, the campaign against the Nabataean Aretas which he had been ordered by Tiberius to undertake in the spring of A.D. 37 brought Vitellius to Jerusalem once more (see above, pp. 349–50). On this occasion, too, he proved his understanding of Jewish sentiments. The route from Antioch to Petra would have led him and his army through Judaea proper. But Roman standards were a notorious cause of offence to the Jews. The Jewish authorities therefore sent an embassy to Vitellius at Ptolemais, beseeching him not to lead his army through their land. Vitellius was reasonable enough to see their point of view; he ordered his army to march across the Great Plain and went to Jerusalem alone. On the fourth day of his stay there he received news of Tiberius's death, whereupon he returned with his whole army to Antioch.[147]

After the reign of Tiberius, that of Caligula (A.D. 37–41) was at first

145. Josephus, *Ant.* xviii 4, 3 (90); cf. xv 11, 4 (403–8), writes that it was at the time of Passover. That it was the Passover of A.D. 36 may be deduced, partly from the fact that Vitellius only arrived in Syria in the summer or autumn of A.D. 35 (Tac. *Ann.* vi 32), partly from the fact that on his second visit to Jerusalem he received the news of the death of Tiberius (died 16 March A.D. 37), Josephus *Ant.* xviii 5, 3 (122–3). We must suppose that some time elapsed between the first and second of Vitellius's visits to Jerusalem.

146. *Ant.* xviii 4, 3 (90); cf. xv 11, 4 (405).

147. *Ant.* xviii 5, 3 (120–5). The expression 'the Great Plain' was used for two different plains in Palestine; see Abel, *Géog. Pal.* I (1933), pp. 411–13 and 425–9. (1) It is most commonly applied to the plain beginning at Acco-Ptolemais and stretching south-eastwards along the north side of Mount Carmel. At its south-east end lies the battlefield of Jezreel (יזרעאל or Esdrelon) which has also given its name to the plain as a whole. Cf. Judith 1:5, 8; τὸ μέγα πεδίον Ἐσδρήλομ. 1 Mac. 12:49; Jos. *B.J.* ii 10, 2 (188): Ptolemais κατὰ τὸ μέγα πεδίον ἐκτισμένη. *Ant.* v 1, 22 (83); viii 2, 3 (36; xv 8, 5 (294); xx 6, 1 (118); *B.J.* iii 3, 1 (39); 4, 1 (59); *Vita* 24 (115); 26 (126); 62 (318). (2) The same expression is however also used for the Jordan Valley between the Sea of Galilee and the Dead Sea. Jos. *B.J.* iv 8, 2 (455) τὸ μέγα πεδίον καλεῖται, ἀπὸ κώμης Γινναβρὶν διῆκον μέχρι τῆς Ἀσφαλτίτιδος λίμνης (Ginnabris is beyond doubt identical with the place named Sennabris (or Ennabris) in *B.J.* iii 9, 7 (447) which lay near Tiberias. (See A. Schalit, *Namenwörterbuch*, p. 110). *Ant.* iv 6, 1 (100) ἐπὶ τῷ Ἰορδάνῳ κατὰ τὸ μέγα πεδίον Ἱεριχοῦντος ἀντικρύ. It is also the Jordan Valley which is referred to in 1 Mac. 5:32 = *Ant.* xii 8, 5 (348).

A third plain, that of Asochis north of Sepphoris, also seems to be designated as 'the Great Plain' in *Vita* 41 (207). But this joined the plain of Jezreel and was probably reckoned as part of it. This supposition would explain *B.J.* iv 1, 8 (54) where Mt. Tabor is described as lying between Scythopolis and the Great Plain.

In the passage under discussion the plain referred to is that beginning at Ptolemais. Vitellius made his army march through it south-eastwards, and then presumably across the Jordan and further southward.

greeted joyfully by all the nations of the empire, the Jews among them. As Vitellius happened to be in Jerusalem when news of the change of government arrived, the Jews were the first of the peoples of Syria to swear allegiance to the new emperor and offer sacrifice for him.[148] The first eighteen months of his government passed peacefully for them.[149] But in the autumn of A.D. 38 a bloody pogrom broke out in Alexandria, apparently staged by the Alexandrian mob, but actually instigated by the emperor himself.[150] In his conceit and mental derangement, he took the idea of his divine office as Caesar very seriously. To him, worship of the emperor was not just a form of homage inherited from the Greek kings; he actually believed in his divinity, and regarded the refusal to worship him as a proof of hostility towards his person.[151] During the second year of his reign this fixed belief seems to have taken complete hold of him and to have become known in the provinces. Their inhabitants showed appropriate zeal. The Jews, unable to follow suit, fell under suspicion of hostility towards Caesar. To the anti-Jewish Alexandrians this was a welcome opportunity to give free rein to their hatred; for they could assume that by persecuting the Jews they would earn the emperor's favour. The then governor of Egypt, A. Avillius Flaccus, was weak enough to fall in with the plans of the Jew-haters to suit his own advantage. He had been governor of Egypt under Tiberius for five years (A.D. 32–37) and according to Philo had carried out his duties blamelessly during that time.[152] Under Caligula, he lost his grip more and more. As an intimate friend of Tiberius he was a priori in disfavour with Caligula. With the death of the young Tiberius Gemellus (grandson of the emperor Tiberius) and of the prefect of the praetorian guard, Sutorius Macro, both driven to suicide

148. Philo, *Legatio* 32 (231–2): 'When Gaius succeeded to the sovereignty, we were the first of the inhabitants of Syria to show our joy. Vitellius . . . during his stay in [our] city [received the news], and it was from our city that the glad tidings spread. Our Temple was the first to accept sacrifices on behalf of Gaius's reign.' On the sacrifices *ibid.* 45 (356); on the oath of loyalty, see Jos. *Ant.* xviii 5, 3 (124). Further on this point, above p. 376.

149. *Ant.* xviii 7, 2 (256).

150. On the persecution of the Jews under Caligula, see Graetz, *Gesch. der Juden* III ([5]1905–6), pp. 322–40; Mommsen, *Röm. Geschichte* V, pp. 515–19; J. P. V. D. Balsdon, *The Emperor Gaius* (1934), pp. 111–41. For further bibliography see L. H. Feldman, *Josephus* (Loeb) IX, pp. 580–1.

151. Philo, *Legatio* 11 (75–7); 13–16 (93–118); 43 (346); Jos. *Ant.* xviii 7, 2 (256); xix 1, 1 (4–5); 1, 2 (11); Dio lix 26, 28; Suet. *Caligula* 22. On emperor worship generally see vol. II, § 22.

152. Philo, *In Flaccum* 3 (8). The name is given as *Φλάκκος 'Aουίλλιος* in *In Flaccum* 1 (1) and Eusebius, *Chron.*, ed. Schoene II, p. 150. For the full name see OGIS 661. Cf. PIR[2] A 1414; A. Stein, *Die Präfekten von Agypten* (1950), pp. 26 f., and H. A. Murusillo, *The Acts of the Pagan Martyrs* (1954), text II (P. Oxy. 1089) =CPJ no. 154.

by Caligula, he lost all support at court. From then on, he had no other aim but to secure by any means he could the favour of the young Caesar. It was this that determined his attitude towards the Jews.[153]

The visit of the Jewish king Agrippa to Alexandria was the signal for the outbreak of the pogrom. He arrived there in August, A.D. 38, on his way home to Palestine from Rome. Although, according to Philo's assurance, he avoided any provocative action; nevertheless the very sight of a Jewish king was a vexation to the Alexandrians. First Agrippa was exposed to taunts and insults in the gymnasium and then made to look ridiculous in a pantomime performance. A lunatic called Carabas was decked out in imitation royal state and paid mock homage as king, the people addressing him in Aramaic as *μάριν*, Lord.[154] Not content with this, the enraged crowds next demanded that statues of the emperor should be placed in Jewish synagogues (always called *προσευχαί* by Philo). Flaccus dared not oppose them but on the contrary agreed to all their increasingly impudent requests. Having permitted the images to be set up in the synagogues, he went on to promulgate an edict depriving the Jews of their rights of citizenship and finally sanctioned a general persecution.[155] Dreadful sufferings now afflicted the Jewish population of Alexandria. Their houses and shops were looted and the people themselves ill-treated, murdered, and their bodies mutilated; others were publicly burned and yet others dragged alive through the streets. Some of the synagogues were destroyed, others profaned by the erection of a statue of Caligula as a god; in the largest synagogue, Caligula's image was placed on an old dilapidated quadriga dragged there from the gymnasium.[156] The governor Flaccus not only allowed all this to go on without interference, but himself

153. Philo, *In Flaccum* 3 (8–11, 14–18); 4 (20–4). For commentaries on the *In Flaccum* see H. Box, *Philonis Alexandrini In Flaccum* (1939) and A. Pelletier, *Les Oeuvres de Philon d' Alexandrie* 31, *In Flaccum* (1967).

154. Philo, *In Flaccum* 61 (36–9). On Carabas, see A. Loisy, *L'évangile selon Marc* (1912), p. 454; P. Winter, *Trial*, pp 94 f. For a detailed account of the position of the Jews in Alexandria, the 'Jewish question' there in the first century, and the events under Caligula see V. Tcherikover and A. Fuks, *Corpus Papyrorum Judaicarum* (CPJ) I–II (1957, 1960); see the general survey in vol. I, pp. 48–78; II, pp. 1–24 (Jews in Alexandria in the Early Roman period) and pp. 25–81 'The Jewish Question' in Alexandria). For *μάριν* = מרי, cf. Dalman, *Grammatik* ([2]1905), p. 152, n. 3. See also Vermes, *Jesus the Jew*, p. 248, n. 55.

155. Philo, *In Flaccum*, 6–7 (40–7, 52–7). Philo distinguishes three stages in Flaccus's anti-Jewish measures: (a) he permitted the installation of emperor images in the synagogues (43); (b) a few days afterwards, he issued a proclamation depriving the Alexandrian Jews of their rights of citizenship (54); (c) he allowed the plunder of Jewish property, treating Jews as if they were the inhabitants of a conuqered city (54).

156. Plundering of houses: *In Flaccum* 8 (56) = *Legatio* 18 (121–2). Killing of the Jews: *In Flaccum* 9 (65–72) = *Legatio* 10 (127–31). Destruction and profanation of synagogues (*προσευχαί*): *Legatio* 20 (132–4, 137).

adopted oppressive measures against the Jews in the city, for which, according to Philo, no other reason was given than that they refused to take part in emperor-worship. He had thirty-eight members of the Jewish gerousia bound and dragged into the theatre, there to be flogged before the eyes of their enemies so that some died under the lash and others after prolonged illness.[157] A centurion with a picked band was commanded to search the houses of the Jews for arms.[158] Jewish women were compelled to eat pork before spectators in the theatre.[159] Flaccus had already shown his hostility to the Jews by failing to fulfil his promise to despatch a letter from the Jewish community to Caligula in which the emperor was assured of the honour in which the Jews of the city held him. This letter was now sent off by Agrippa, with an explanation of the reason for its delay.[160]

It is not known how the Alexandrian community fared after the severe persecution in autumn A.D. 38 until the emperor's death in January A.D. 41. In autumn 38, Flaccus was suddenly sent as a prisoner to Rome at the emperor's command, and banished to the island of Andros in the Aegean Sea, where he was later put to death together with other distinguished exiles on the order of Caligula.[161] His successor was C. Vitrasius Pollio.[162] It is very probable that the Jews did not

157. *In Flaccum* 10 (73–85).

158. The long-standing prohibition in Egypt on carrying arms had been re-emphasized by Flaccus in A.D. 34/5; see the edict partially preserved on a papyrus. L. Mitteis, U. Wilcken, *Grundzüge und Chrestomathie der Papyruskunde* I, 2 (1912), no. 13.

159. *In Flaccum* 11 (86–96).

160. *In Flaccum* 12 (97–107).

161. *In Flaccum* 12–21 (97–191). The chronological data for the incidents recorded above all point to autumn A.D. 38. (1) Agrippa sailed to Alexandria with the aid of the Etesian winds, *In Flaccum* 5 (26), which blew for 30 days from July 20, Pliny *NH* ii 47/124, xviii 28/270. (2) The flogging of the 38 members of the Jewish *gerousia* took place on Caligula's birthday, *In Flaccum* 10 (81), see Box *ad loc.*, which was August 31 (Suet. *Calig.* 8). (3) The arrest of Flaccus soon after took place during the Feast of Tabernacles, *In Flaccum* 14 (116), i.e. September or October. The year is arrived at as follows: (1) Agrippa returned from Rome to Palestine in the second year of Caligula, Jos. *Ant.* xviii 6, 11 (238). (2) The Jewish shops were plundered while they were closed on account of mourning for Drusilla, the sister of Caligula, *In Flaccum* 8 (56). Drusilla died on 10 June A.D. 38 (Dio lix 10–11; see PIR² I 668).

162. According to Dio lix 10, Caligula had appointed Macro prefect of Egypt (his full name, as is shown by AE 1957, 250, was (Q. Naevius Cordus) Sutorius, not Sertorius, Macro). But he never took up his governorship, having fallen into disgrace with Caligula, and was replaced by Flaccus, Philo, *In Flaccum* 3 (14); 4 (16). The successor to Flaccus was C. Vitrasius Pollio, attested from 28 April A.D. 39 (ILS 8899) to A.D. 41, P. Lond. 1912 43 f. (=CPJ 153); Pliny *NH* xxxvi 11/57. See A. Stein, *Die Präfekten von Aegypten in der römischer Kaiserzeit* (1950), pp. 28 f.; O. W. Reinmuth in Bull. Am. Soc. Pap. 4 (1967), p. 80; cf. RE s.v. 'Vitrasius' (7).

receive back their synagogues in Caligula's lifetime and that emperor-worship continued to be a burning, and for the Jews a perilous, problem. However, from the fact that Vitrasius Pollio, the governor appointed by Caligula, remained in office under Claudius, it may be deduced that no further severe persecution occurred while he was governor, for otherwise Claudius, who ultimately settled the conflict in favour of the Jews, would not have left him in office. In A.D. 40, probably in the spring, the persisting disputes between the pagan and Jewish populations of Alexandria resulted in the sending of an embassy from each party to the emperor. The leader of the Jewish delegation was Philo and his opposite number the pamphleteer Apion. The outcome was unfavourable to the Jews. They were received ungraciously by the emperor and had to return without having achieved their object. Such is Josephus's brief report.[163] A few incidents connected with this embassy are also told by Philo in his work on Caligula. But it is difficult to determine much from these fragmentary notes. Without mentioning the despatch of either of the two delegations, Philo emphasises that the Alexandrian envoys won over completely the slave Helicon, a favourite of Caligula's. When the Jews noticed this, they made similar efforts, but in vain.[164] They then decided to hand the emperor a written statement (which was essentially the same as the petition sent 'shortly before' by Agrippa). Caligula first received the Jewish envoys in the Field of Mars, not far from Rome, and promised to hear them when he found it convenient.[165] The delegation then followed the emperor to Puteoli but was not received by him.[166] It was not until later—how much later is not known—that the promised audience took place in Rome, in the Gardens of Maecenas and Lamia on the Esquiline. The emperor kept the Jews trailing behind him while he inspected his building projects and gave orders concerning them, throwing out an occasional contemptuous remark amid the applause of the opposing delegates who were also there. Finally he dismissed them, declaring them more foolish than wicked since they would not believe in his divinity.[167]

163. *Ant.* xviii 8, 1 (257). According to Josephus, the two embassies each consisted of three men; according to Philo, *Legatio* 46 (370), the Jewish embassy included five men.

164. Philo, *Legatio* 26 (166); 27 (172) (the Alexandrian ambassadors); *ibid.* 27 (174); 28 (178) (the Jewish ambassadors vainly entreated Helicon to secure them an audience); cf. Dio lix 5, 2. Caligula's courtiers, Helicon and Apelles, *Legatio* 30 (203–5) promoted the cause of the anti-Jewish party.

165. *Legatio* 28 (181) (the narrator speaks on occasion in the first person, evidently of himself).

166. *Legatio* 29 (185–94).

167. *Legatio* 44–6 (349–73). It is remarkable that Philo speaks of the ambassadors' exertions in Rome without having mentioned their departure from Alexandria. There may be some lacuna in the text. But this assumption is not

It appears that affairs in Alexandria remained unsettled until Caligula's death. One of the first acts of the new emperor, Claudius, was to issue an edict confirming the former privileges of the Alexandrian Jews and restoring to them unrestricted liberty in the practice of their

---

imperative, for Philo did not set out to tell the history of the embassy (as might be supposed from the misleading title, which is Philo's own). His theme is rather the same as that of Lactantius in the latter's treatise *De Mortibus Persecutorum*. He wishes to show that the persecutors of the pious do not escape God's punishment. As with Flaccus, so with Caligula: their evil deeds are enumerated, and the divine retribution then recorded (unfortunately, the second half of the treatise on Caligula is no longer extant). In *Legatio*, the principal figure is Caligula, not the Jews; the Jewish embassy from Alexandria is a totally secondary matter. This may also explain other difficulties. Caligula was absent from Rome on an expedition to Gaul and Germany from the autumn of A.D. 39 until 31st August A.D. 40 (see above, p. 352). Did the two receptions of the embassy take place before or after this expedition? According to Philo, *Legatio* 29 (190), the ambassadors made the sea journey in the middle of winter. Since the business on which they were engaged had already become urgent on account of the great persecution in autumn A.D. 38, it would seem at first that the date was winter 38/39. This view seems to be supported by the fact that the written apology handed over by ambassadors is said to have been similar in content to that sent to the emperor by Agrippa on the occasion of his Alexandrian visit, *Legatio* 28 (179). Some writers therefore place the departure of the embassy at the end of A.D. 38, its first reception in the Campus Martius and journey to Puteoli in the beginning of A.D. 39, before Caligula's campaign in Gaul and Germany, and the second audience in the gardens of Maecenas and Lamia after that campaign, in autumn A.D. 40. This time-sequence has its difficulties. It was at Puteoli that the ambassadors first received the news of Caligula's order to erect his statue in the Temple in Jerusalem (Philo, *Legatio* 29 (186–8). This cannot have happened before the spring of A.D. 40. The first reception of the Jewish embassy by Caligula and their journey to Puteoli must therefore have occurred in the autumn of A.D. 40, after the Gallic-Germanic campaign. In any case, the second audience in the gardens of Maecemas and Lamia took place after the campaign, for the ambassadors there refer to the fact that the Jews had offered sacrifices for the emperor, *Legatio* 45 (356). If the audiences of the Jews with Caligula took place not earlier than in the autumn of A.D. 40, their winter journey would have been made that autumn. But such a date would be too late, for then how did the ambassadors hear for the first time in Puteoli of events in Palestine that had taken place after the beginning of the summer of A.D. 40? It is therefore preferable to date the ambassadors' journey to the end of the winter of A.D. 39/40, and assume that they waited in Rome for Caligula's return from his campaign and were received by him in the autumn of A.D. 40. But whichever combination is accepted, Philo's exposition not only fails to report the despatch of the Jewish-Alexandrian embassy, but also give no full, comprehensive account of what went on in Rome. It is even more surprising that Philo says nothing of the position in Alexandria itself from autumn A.D. 38 to Caligula's death. There is no explanation, either, of why the embassy did not set out until one and a half years after the great persecution. The justifiable suspicion remains that Philo's *Legatio* has not been transmitted intact. On the chronolological problem see E. M. Smallwood, *Philonis Alexandrini legatio ad Gaium* (1961; [2]1969), esp. pp. 47–50 (arguing for 39/40; *contra*, P. J. Sijpestein, 'The Legationes ad Gaium', JJS 15 (1964), pp. 87–96 (not convincing).

religion.[168] The chief instigators of the Alexandrian Jew-baiting were brought to account: Philo names as such Isidorus and Lampo. From certain papyrus discoveries it emerges that the former was a gymnasiarch and that both were sentenced to death and executed under Claudius (see above, p. 40).

While the Alexandrian embassy to Rome waited for the imperial decision, storms blew up over the mother country, Palestine. They broke out at Jamnia, a town in the coastal plain at that time mainly inhabited by Jews. When the Gentile inhabitants of the place set up a crude altar to the emperor to show their zeal for Caesar and to annoy the Jews, the latter immediately destroyed it. The imperial procurator of the city, Herennius Capito,[169] reported this to the emperor, who avenged himself on the refractory Jews by giving orders that a statue with his effigy be set up in the Temple in Jerusalem.[170] As it was anticipated that such a demand would arouse fierce Jewish opposition, the governor of Syria, Publius Petronius, received the command that half of the army stationed 'on the Euphrates', i.e. in Syria,[171] was to proceed to Palestine to enforce compliance with the emperor's will. It was with a heavy heart that Petronius, who was a reasonable man, obeyed this childish demand (winter, A.D. 39/40). While the statue was being prepared in Sidon, he sent for the Jewish leaders and tried to persuade them to yield with good grace, but without success.[172]

The news of what was in store soon spread all over Palestine and the people gathered in great masses at Ptolemais, where Petronius had his headquarters. 'The multitude of the Jews covered all Phoenicia like a cloud.' Divided into six orderly groups (old men, men, boys, old women, women and girls), the large deputation appeared before Petronius. Their impassioned complaints made such an impression on

168. Jos. *Ant.* xix 5, 2–3 (279–8)7.

169. He was probably not, as Philo, *Legatio* 30 (199), calls him, 'the tax-collector for Judaea', but merely the financial procurator of Jamnia, a town belonging to the emperor's private domains; see Josephus, *Ant.* xviii 6, 3 (158). Should not 'Ιαμνείας be read also in the text of Philo instead of 'Ιουδαίας? (so Smallwood, *ad loc.*). Cf. PIR² H 103, Pflaum, *Carrières*, no. 9, and Millar in JRS 53 (1963), p. 33.

170. Philo, *Legatio* 30 (203).

171. According to *Ant.* xviii 8, 2 (262), two legions; according to *B.J.* ii 10, 1 (186), three. The first figure is the correct one for there were four legions in Syria (see above, p. 362).

172. Philo, *Legatio* 31 (207–23). The date is determined by the fact that the negotiations at Ptolemais took place at harvest time, therefore between Passover and Pentecost, in A.D. 40. But since according to *Ant.* xviii 8, 2 (262) Petronius had moved into winter quarters at Ptolemais, he must have gone there in the winter of A.D. 39/40. Josephus's words are certainly calculated to give the impression that this did not occur till the winter of A.D. 40/41. See above, p. 263.

Petronius that he resolved to try his utmost to postpone the decision, temporarily at least.[173] He dared not write the truth to Caligula, namely that he really wished to put a stop to the whole undertaking. Instead, he asked for respite, partly because time was needed for the preparation of the statue, and partly because the harvest was approaching and it was advisable to wait till it was gathered in case the exasperated Jews in the end destroyed it. If that happened, a famine might ensue which would endanger the emperor's proposed visit to Egypt via Palestine. When Caligula received this report, he was very annoyed at the slowness of his legate. But he dared not give expression to his anger. Instead, he wrote Petronius a letter of acknowledgment congratulating him on his prudence and merely urging him to proceed as quickly as possible with the erection of the statue, since the harvest would soon be completed.[174]

Petronius still did not treat the matter urgently, but started fresh negotiations with the Jews. By the late autumn, at the sowing season (November), he was in Tiberias for forty days, besieged by people in their thousands imploring him more than ever to save the country from the threatened horror of profanation of the Temple. When Aristobulus, King Agrippa's brother, and other of his relatives joined their entreaties to those of the people, Petronius resolved on the decisive step of requesting the emperor to revoke his order. He led his army from Ptolemais back to Antioch, and pointed out in a letter to Caligula the advisability on grounds of equity and prudence of revoking the edict.[175]

Meanwhile, affairs in Rome had taken a more favourable turn. King Agrippa I, who had left Palestine in the spring of A.D. 40, met Caligula in Rome or Puteoli in the autumn when the emperor had just returned from his German campaign.[176] He had as yet heard nothing

173. Philo, *Legatio* 32 (225–43); Josephus, *B.J.* ii 10, 3–5 (192–201); *Ant.* xviii 8, 2–3 (263–72).

174. Philo, *Legatio* 33 (248–9); 34–5 (255–69).

175. *B.J.* ii 10, 3–5 (193–202); *Ant.* xviii 8, 5–6 (279–88). The recall of the army is only mentioned in *Bellum*.

176. That Agrippa had already left Palestine in the spring may be deduced from the fact that on his arrival in Rome he knew nothing of what had been going on in Palestine. But he cannot have been with Caligula in Gaul (as Dio lix 24, 1 conjectures), but must have gone to Rome or Puteoli some time after Caligula's return from his campaign (31 August A.D. 40). For if Agrippa's successful intervention had already taken place in Gaul, the Alexandrian ambassadors would not, as was the case, have first heard the bad news of affairs in Palestine after Caligula's return and after following the emperor to Puteoli, Philo, *Legatio* 29 (188). The intervention of Agrippa must therefore have taken place after that time. It follows that Petronius asked for the edict to be revoked in the late autumn (the sowing season and not long before Caligula's death, i.e. in about November). So he had not yet received Caligula's decision, which cannot have

of what was going on in Palestine but could see from the emperor's expression that he was furious. While he looked in vain for the cause, Caligula observed his uneasiness and informed him in a very ungracious tone of the cause of his displeasure. The king was so alarmed by what he heard that he fell into a faint, from which he did not recover until the evening of the following day.[177] He then made it his first business to address a supplication to the emperor in which he endeavoured to persuade him to revoke his order, pointing out that none of his predecessors had ever demanded anything of that sort.[178] Contrary to every expectation, Agrippa's letter had the desired effect. Caligula caused a letter to be sent to Petronius, telling him that nothing was to be changed in the Temple at Jerusalem. The favour was admittedly not unmixed. For joined to it was an injunction that no one erecting an altar or temple to the emperor outside Jerusalem should be hindered from doing so. A good part of the concession granted was thus taken back, and it was only because no advantage was taken of this right that no new disturbances arose from it. In fact, the emperor soon regretted having made the concession at all, and as he had no further use for the statue at Sidon, he ordered a new one to be made in Rome which he planned to put ashore on the coast of Palestine while on his projected journey to Alexandria, and send secretly to Jerusalem.[179] Only Caligula's death, which occurred soon after, prevented this enterprise from being carried out.

The emperor's death was a stroke of good fortune for the inhabitants of Judaea as well as for Petronius. When Caligula received Petronius's letter begging him to revoke his edict after he had already decreed that this should be done, he fell into a furious rage over the disobedience of his officer and commanded him to commit suicide immediately in retribution. Soon afterwards, however, Caligula himself was murdered (on 24 January, A.D. 41). Petronius received the news twenty-seven days before the messengers arrived with the order for his own suicide; they had been three months on the way because of bad weather. There

---

been made in Rome earlier than about September or October. That the intervention of Agrippa took place in A.D. 40 is also plain on general grounds from the contents of his petition, in which he describes himself as already in possession of Galilee, Philo, *Legatio* 41 (326).

177. *Legatio* 35 (261–9).

178. *Legatio* 36–41 (276–329).

179. *Legatio* 42 (331–7) (the intended journey to Alexandria is mentioned also by Suet. *Calig*. 40). A somewhat different account of Agrippa's intervention is given by Josephus, *Ant*. xviii 8, 7–8 (289–301). According to him, once when Agrippa had humoured Caligula with a luxurious banquet, the emperor told Agrippa to ask for any favour he desired; whereupon Agrippa petitioned for the revocation of the order to set up the emperor's statue in the Temple. The result, according to Josephus, was the same: the request was granted.

was now as little point in obeying the order to commit suicide as there was in setting up the statue in the Temple.[180]

The Emperor Claudius, who was raised by the soldiers to the throne, immediately after his succession bestowed Judaea and Samaria on Agrippa, besides the domain which he already received from Caligula.

180. *B.J.* ii 10, 5 (203). *Ant.* xviii 8, 8–9 (302–5, 307–8). On Jewish traditions (Meg. Taan. § 26, ed. Lichtenstein, pp. 344–5, cf. pp. 300–1; ySot. 24b; bSot. 33a), see Derenbourg, *op. cit.*, pp. 207 ff., also P. Winter, 'Simeon der Gerechte und Caius Caligula', Judaica 12 (1956), pp. 129–32.

The time-sequence of the events reported may be considered as follows (the transmission of news from Rome or Gaul to Jerusalem, and vice versa, is supposed to have normally required about two months):

Winter A.D. 39/40	Petronius receives Caligula's order to erect his statue in the Temple at Jerusalem and goes with two legions to Palestine.
April/May 40	(Not long before harvest-time), negotiations take place at Ptolemais. Petronius's first report to Caligula, *Legatio* 33 (248); Josephus, *B.J.* ii 10, 2–3 (188–92); *Ant.* xviii 8, 2 (262).
June	Caligula receives Petronius's first report and answers him, urging him to expedite matters, *Legatio* 34 (254–60).
August	Petronius receives Caligula's reply but still hesitates to make a decision.
End of September	Agrippa visits Caligula in Rome (or Puteoli), learns what has happened and intervenes. Caligula sends instructions to Petronius to stop the undertaking, *Legatio* 42 (333), Josephus, *Ant.* xviii 8, 8 (300–1).
Beginning of November	Negotiations take place at Tiberias at the season of sowing; Petronius begs the emperor not to erect the statue, *B.J.* ii 10, 3–5 (193–202); *Ant.* xviii 8, 4 (277), 8, 5 (283), 8, 6 (287).
End of November	Petronius receives instructions to abandon the undertaking.
Beginning of January A.D. 41	Caligula receives Petronius's petition not to have the statue erected and sends him the order to commit suicide, *Ant.* xviii 8, 9 (303–4).
24th January 41	Caligula murdered, *Ant.* xviii 8, 9 (307).
Beginning of March	Petronius receives the news of Caligula's death, *Ant.* xviii 8, 9 (308).
Beginning of April	Petronius receives the letter with the order to kill himself, *B.J.* ii 10, 5 (203), *Ant.* xviii 8, 9 (308).

This table may be regarded as essentially correct, even if the time taken for a letter to travel from Italy or Gaul to Palestine, and vice versa, may on occasion have been shorter than has been assumed. On average, it took between one and two months. It should be borne in mind, however, that in the summer of A.D. 40 Caligula was still in Gaul and that during winter news travelled slowly and irregularly. The main difficulty in plotting an exact chronology of events is that Agrippa, as well as the Alexandrian Jewish embassy, did not hear of Caligula's order in respect to the Jerusalem Temple until sometime in September A.D. 40, whereas according to Philo the affair was already a matter of common talk in

Consequently, all Palestine was now re-united in the hands of a Herodian just as it had been under Herod the Great.[181]

Meanwhile the divisions between Jews and Greeks in Alexandria were not yet ended. On the development of this issue in the reign of Claudius (A.D. 41–54) we have three papyrus documents, only one of which is of undisputed authenticity. This is the now famous letter of Claudius to the Alexandrians, first published in 1924.[182] It is addressed to the city of Alexandria in response to an embassy, and was written in about October A.D. 41. The first part (ll. 1–72) concerns offers of honours to the emperor and requests for benefits to themselves made by the embassy. In lines 73–104 Claudius turns to the Jewish question and mentions that the Jews had sent two embassies (possibly that of Philo and another despatched after his accession). In the context of a strongly-worded general warning to both sides to keep the peace, he orders the Alexandrians not to interfere with the customs of the Jews, and the Jews 'not to intrude themselves into the games presided over by the *gymnasiarchoi* and the *kosmetai*, since they enjoy what is their own, and in a city which is not their own they possess an abundance of all good things'. This letter probably shows that the edict preserved by Josephus, *Ant.* xix 5, 2 (279–85) cannot be genuine as it stands, for it emphasises precisely the equal rights of the Jews in Alexandria—τοὺς ἐν Ἀλεξανδρείᾳ Ἰουδαίους Ἀλεξανδρεῖς λεγομένους συγκατοικισθέντας τοῖς πρώτοις εὐθὺ καιροῖς Ἀλεξανδρεῦσι καὶ ἴσης πολιτείας παρὰ τῶν βασιλέων τετευχότας.[183] Finally, a number of papyri report parts of the hearing before Claudius in which the leading Alexandrian anti-Semite, Isidorus, accuses the Jewish king Agrippa—either Agrippa I in A.D. 41 or Agrippa II in about A.D. 53. The question whether this text, like the other 'Acts of the Alexandrian Martyrs' is documentary or fictional is not yet decided.[184]

Palestine from the harvest season in April/May. Philo's statements in *Legatio* 34–5 (255–69) are too definite and detailed to be dismissed as unhistorical.

Another chronology has been suggested by E. M. Smallwood, 'The Chronology of Gaius' Attempt to Desecrate the Temple', Latomus 16 (1957), pp. 3–17. She places the events a few months earlier. See also J. P. V. D. Balsdon, 'Notes Concerning the Principate of Gaius', JRS 24 (1934), pp. 19–24, and *idem, The Emperor Gaius* (*Caligula*) (1934), pp. 135–40.

181. *B.J.* ii 11, 4 (215); *Ant.* xix 5, 1 (274).

182. P. Lond. 19, 2. H. I. Bell, *Jews and Christians in Egypt* (1924), pp. 23–4. For a full treatment listing the immense subsequent bibliography, see CPJ no. 153. The translation of lines 92–5 above is taken from CPJ.

183. Note, however, L. H. Feldman, *Josephus* (Loeb) IX, *ad loc.*, who argues that the two documents are not irreconcilable.

184. See H. A. Musurillo, *Acts of the Pagan Martyrs: Acta Alexandrinorum* (1954), Text IV (arguing for A.D. 53); CPJ no. 156 (arguing for A.D. 41).

Excursus I—The Census of Quirinius, Luke 2:1–5

Bibliography[1]

Huschke, P. E., *Ueber den zur Zeit der Geburt Jesu Christi gehaltenen Census* (1840).
Wieseler, K., *Chronologische Synopse der vier Evangelien* (1843), pp. 73–122.
Huschke, P. E., *Über den Census und die Steuerverfassung der früheren römischen Kaiserzeit* (1847).
Gumpach, J. von, 'Die Schatzung', ThStKr 1852, pp. 663–84.
Bleek, F., *Synoptische Erklärung der drei ersten Evangelien* I (1862), pp. 66–75.
Strauss, D. F., *Leben Jesu* (1864), pp. 336–40; *idem. Die Halben und die Ganzen* (1865), pp. 70–9.
Hilgenfeld, A., 'Quirinius als Statthalter Syriens', ZWTh, 1865, pp. 408–21; *ibid.*, 1870, pp. 151–67).
Gerlach, H., *Die römischen Statthalter in Syrien und Judäa* (1865), pp. 22–42.
Lutteroth, H., *Le recensement de Quirinius en Judée* (1865).
Desjardins, A., 'Le recensement de Quirinius', Revue des quest. hist. 2 (1867), pp. 1–65.
Rodbertus, J. K., 'Zur Geschichte der römischen Tributsteuern seit Augustus', Jahrbb. für Nationalökonomie und Statistik 4 (1865), pp. 341–427; 5 (1865), pp. 135–71, 241–315; 8 (1867), pp. 81–126, 385–475.
Ewald, H., *Geschichte des Volkes Israel* V (^{3}1867), pp. 204–7.
Keim, K. T., *Geschichte Jesu* I (1867), pp. 398–405.
Ebrard, J. M. A., *Wissenschaftliche Kritik der evangelischen Geschichte* (^{3}1868), pp. 198–234.
Wieseler, K., *Beiträge zur richtigen Würdigung der Evangelien* (1869), pp. 16–107; *idem.*, ThStKr (1875), pp. 535–49.
Caspari, C. P., *Chronologische-geographische Einleitung in das Leben Jesu Christi* (1869), pp. 30–3.
Zumpt, A. W., *Das Geburtsjahr Christi* (1869), pp. 20–224.
Steinmeyer, F. L., 'Die Geschichte der Geburt des Herrn und seiner ersten Schritte in Leben', *Apologetische Beiträge* IV (1873), pp. 29–41.
Sevin, H., *Chronologie des Lebens Jesu* (^{2}1874), pp. 20–39.
Marquardt, J., *Römische Staatsverwaltung* II (^{2}1884), pp. 204–23.
Riess, F., *Das Geburtsjahr Christi* (1880), pp. 66–78; *Nochmals das Geburtsjahr Jesu Christi* (1883), pp. 59–68.
Hofmann, J. Chr. K. v., *Die heilige Schrift des Neuen Testaments zusammenhängend untersucht* VIII, 1 (1878), pp. 46 ff.; X (1883), pp. 64 ff.
Lecoultre, H., *De censu Quiriniano et anno nativitatis Christi secundum Lucam evangelistam* (1883).
Mommsen, Th., *Res gestae divi Augusti* (^{2}1883), pp. 175–7; *idem.*, *Römisches Staatsrecht*, II (^{3}1887), pp. 1091–5.
Unger, G. F., 'De censibus provinciarum Romanarum', Leipziger Studien zur class. Philologie 10 (1887), pp. 1–76 (mainly a collection of inscriptions, in which tax-collectors are mentioned).
Wandel, G., 'Der römische Statthalter C. Sentius Saturninus', ThStKr (1892), pp. 105–43; NKZ, 1892, pp. 732–44.

1. The structure of this classic treatment of the census, as a critical review of current works, has deliberately been preserved substantially intact. For the bibliography of this question see D. Lazzarato, *Chronologia Christi seu discordantium fontium concordantia ad iuris normam* (1952), p. 44, n. 7; F. X. Steinmetzer, s.v. 'Census', RAC II (1954), cols. 969–72; L. H. Feldman, *Josephus* (Loeb) IX (1965), pp. 556–7.

Nebe, A., *Die Kindheitsgeschichte unseres Herrn Jesu Christi nach Matthäus und Lukas ausgelegt* (1893), pp. 256–72.
Zahn, Th., 'Die syrische Statthalterschaft und die Schatzung des Quirinius', NKZ 1893, pp. 633–54; *Einleitung in das Neue Testament* II, pp. 395–6, 415–16.
Gardthausen, V., *Augustus und seine Zeit* I, 2 (1896), pp. 913–24; II, 2 (1896), pp. 531–40.
Marucchi, O., *L'iscrizione di Quirinio nel Museo Lateranense ed il censo di S. Luca* (1897); DB II (1899).
Ramsay, W. M., 'The census of Quirinius', Expositor I (1897), pp. 274–86, 425–35.
Kubitschek, W., s.v. 'Census', RE III, cols. 1914–24.
Weber, W., 'Der Census des Quirinius nach Josephus', ZNW 10 (1909), pp. 307–19.
Lagrange, M.-J., 'Où en est la question du recensement de Quirinius?', RB 8 (1911), pp. 60–84.
Ramsay, W. M., *The Bearing of Recent Discovery on the Trustworthiness of the New Testament* (1915), pp. 238–300.
Lodder, W., *Die Schätzung des Quirinius bei Flavius Josephus* (1930).
Taylor, L. R., 'Quirinius and the Census of Judaea', AJPh 54 (1933), pp. 120–33.
Corbishley, T., 'Quirinius and the Census: a Restudy of the Evidence', Klio 19 (1936), pp. 81–93.
Accame, S., 'Il primo censimento di Giudea', Riv. di filol. 72/3 N.S. 22/3 (1944–5), pp. 138–70.
Steinmetzer, F. X. RAC s.v. 'Census', II (1954), cols. 967–72.
Stauffer, E., *Jesus, Gestalt und Geschichte* (1957), pp. 26–34. [E.T. *Jesus and his Story* (1960), pp. 27–36.]
Instinsky, H., *Das Jahr der Geburt Christi* (1957).
Braunert, H., 'Der römische Provinzialzensus und der Schätzungsbericht des Lukas-Evangeliums', Historia 6 (1957), pp. 192–214.
Sherwin-White, A. N., *Roman Society and Roman Law in the New Testament* (1963), pp. 162–71.
Schalit, A., *König Herodes—Der Mann und sein Werk* (1969), pp. 274–81 (during the reign of Herod several censuses took place).
Moehring, H. R., 'The Census in Luke as an Apologetic Device', *Studies in New Testament and Early Christian Literature—Essays in Honor of A. P. Wikgren* (1972), pp. 144–60.

As has been already mentioned (p. 381), after the banishment of Archelaus, the imperial legate Quirinius went to Judaea and in A.D. 6 or 7 conducted a census, *i.e.* registration, of the inhabitants and their property for taxation purposes. The evangelist Luke (2:1–5) writes of a valuation census such as that made by Quirinius, but he appears to date it near the end of the reign of Herod the Great, some ten or twelve years earlier (the preceding story of the birth of John begins, 1:5: ἐγένετο ἐν ταῖς ἡμέραις Ἡρώδου βασιλέως τῆς Ἰουδαίας). The question is, how is this report related to the similar one presented by Josephus? Were two different censuses conducted in Judaea by Quirinius, or has Luke mistakenly placed the census of A.D. 6/7 in the last two years of Herod the Great? To arrive at a sound conclusion on this much-debated matter, it is necessary to have some general idea of the Roman system of taxation during the imperial period.

The original Roman census as it developed during the time of the Republic[2] concerned only Roman citizens. It was an inventory of Roman citizens and their possessions taken for two purposes: (1) the regulation of military service, and (2) the collection of direct taxes. The person to be assessed had to report to the censor and declare his possessions; but it was the custom for the head of the family to make the declaration for himself and the whole family. No regular census was taken in Republican times of the nations subject to Rome. They were conducted here and there, but were not closely connected either with each other, or with the census of Roman citizens.[3]

Under the Empire, and even in the later years of the Republic, the census of Roman citizens had completely lost its original significance since they (*i.e.* the whole of Italy and colonies with *Ius Italicum*) no longer paid direct taxes or were liable to regular and universal conscription.[4] If therefore Augustus, Claudius and Vespasian still took censuses of Roman citizens, it was only for the purpose of statistics or because of the religious ceremonies connected with them, but not for the levying of taxes. The provincial census was fundamentally different, the control of taxation being its main function.[5] There was great diversity, too, even in this respect in the early years of the Empire. In general, however, the same principles were applied which in later juristic documents (*Digest.* L, 15: *De censibus*) are presumed to prevail everywhere. From these it is evident that there were two kinds of direct taxes for the provinces: (1) a tax on agricultural produce, *tributum soli*; and (2) a poll-tax, *tributum capitis*.[6] The first

2. On the census of citizens in the Republic see Mommsen, *Röm. Staatsrecht* II 1 ([5]1887), pp. 332–415; E. Herzog, *Geschichte u. System der römischen Staatsverfassung* I (1884), pp. 754–97; Kubitschek, s.v. 'Census', RE III, cols. 1914–18; G. Pieri, *L'histoire du cens jusqu'à la fin de la République romaine* (1968); T. P. Wiseman, 'The Census in the First Century B.C.', JRS 59 (1969), pp. 59–75.

3. On the provincial census in republican times see Marquardt, *Römische Staatsverwaltung* II ([2]1884), pp. 180–204.

4. On the census of citizens in imperial times see Mommsen, *Röm. Staatsrecht* II, 1 ([3]1887), pp. 336–9, 415–17. The last citizen census to be fully carried out was Vespasian's in A.D. 73/4.

5. On the provincial census under the Empire see J. Marquardt, *Römische Staatsverwaltung* II ([2]1884), pp. 204–23; Mommsen, *op. cit.*, pp. 1091–5; Kubitschek, s.v., 'Census', RE III, cols. 1918–22. For Egypt, the papyrus finds have yielded abundant material; see the literature quoted below, n. 16.

6. That there were only these two kinds of direct taxes is clear from *Digest.* L 15, 8, 7 (from Paulus, early 3rd century A.D.) 'Divus Vespasianus Caesarienses colonos fecit, non adiecto, ut et iuris Italici essent, sed tributum his remisit capitis; sed Divus Titus etiam solum immune factum interpretatus est'. Cf. Appian, *Libyca*, 135/641: τοῖς δὲ λοιποῖς φόρον ὥρισαν ἐπὶ τῇ γῇ καὶ ἐπὶ τοῖς σώμασιν. Dio lxii, 3, 2–3; Tertullian, *Apologet.* 13, 'agri tributo onusti viliores, hominum capita stipendio censa ignobiliora'. See RE s.v. 'tributum', VII A, cols. 1–78.

was paid partly in kind, partly in money.[7] The second (*tributum capitis*) included various kinds of personal taxes, namely, a property tax which varied according to a person's capital valuation, as well as a poll-tax proper at a flat rate for all *capita*.[8] In Syria, in for example Appian's time, a personal tax was levied amounting to 1% of the property valuation.[9] In Egypt, on the other hand, a poll-tax was levied that was not identical for all the inhabitants (as was formerly supposed from Josephus), but varied for each category of the population.[10] During the earlier years of the Empire, the taxes were of many

7. According to Josephus, *B.J.* ii 16, 4 (382–6): 'the third part of the world', i.e. North Africa excluding Egypt, yielded yearly enough grain to meet the needs of the city of Rome for eight months, the deliveries from Alexandria providing for four months. The land taxes in Egypt, concerning which very precise information exists, were also paid partly in kind and partly in money; see U. Wilcken, *Griechische Ostraka aus Aegypten u. Nubien* I (1899), pp. 194–215; S. L. Wallace, *Taxation in Egypt from Augustus to Diocletian* (1938), pp. 11–16.

8. RE VII A, cols. 11, 68–70.

9. Appian, *Syr.* 50/253 καὶ διὰ ταῦτ' ἐστὶν 'Ιουδαίοις ἅπασιν ὁ φόρος τῶν σωμάτων βαρύτερος τῆς ἄλλης περιουσίας (or better, περοικίας). ἔστι δὲ καὶ Σύροις καὶ Κίλιξιν ἐτήσιος, ἑκατοστὴ τοῦ τιμήματος ἑκάστῳ. The meaning of Appian's allusion to the Jews is obscure. Instead of the received περιουσίας, many would read περιοικίας, the sense being: the Jews have to pay a higher poll-tax than the neighbouring peoples because after the war of Vespasian the additional δίδραχμον was imposed on them, Jos. *B.J.* vii 6, 6 (218); Dio lxvi 7, 2. But even so, the terminology remains surprising. Wilamowitz tried to help by resorting to more vigorous textual emendation, Hermes, 35 (1900), pp. 546 f. If περιουσίας of the received text is retained, the φόρος τῶν σωμάτων must be a tax on property, namely, the tax on moveable possessions as distinguished from the tax on ἄλλη περιουσία, i.e. landed property. In any case it is reported in the following passage that the Syrians and Cilicians have to pay a personal tax of 1% of the amount of the valuation. For as subject it is here necessary to read φόρος τῶν σωμάτων, not merely φόρος, as U. Wilcken proposes, *Griechische Ostraka* I, p. 247. Cf. also A. D. Momigliano, *Ann. Scuola Normale Sup. Pisa* ser. II, 3 (1934), pp. 204–13 approving the restoration 'περοικίας', and the Teubner text of Appian, vol. I, ed. P. Viereck and E. Roos (1962), pp. 543–4.

10. On the poll-tax in Egypt, cf. especially Wilcken, *Griechische Ostraka* I, pp. 230–49, and the supplements: Archiv für Papyrus-Forschung I, pp. 135–9 (following F. G. Kenyon, *Greek Papyri in the British Museum* II (1898), pp. 17–65); see now S. L. Wallace, *op. cit.*, pp. 116–34, and V. Tcherikover 'Syntaxis and Laographia', Journ. Juristic Pap. 4 (1950), pp. 179–217. Wilcken showed from the ostraka that the basic rate of poll-tax was not the same all over Egypt but was specifically determined for each community (*Ostraka* I, p. 234). Moreover, within each area the privileged class of 'metropolites' paid at a lower rate. Accordingly, what had been assumed formerly on the strength of Josephus must be rectified. He writes, *B.J.* ii 16, 4 (385) πεντήκοντα πρὸς ταῖς ἑπτακοσίαις ἔχουσα μυριάδας ἀνθρώπων δίχα τῶν 'Αλεξάνδρειαν κατοικούντων, ὡς ἔνεστιν ἐκ τῆς καθ' ἑκάστην κεφαλὴν εἰσφορᾶς τεκμήρασθαι. Formerly, this was generally understood to mean that Josephus simply divided the total yield of the poll-tax, which was known to him, by the number of the population, *viz.* 7½ millions (so also Wilcken, *Ostraka* I, p. 239, who sharply criticises Josephus on this score). This would be misleading, not only because of the inequality of the poll-tax, but also because

kinds.[11] Women and slaves were also liable to the poll-tax. Only children and old people were exempt. In Syria, for example, men had to pay poll-tax from the age of fourteen to sixty-five, and women from twelve to sixty-five.[12] In Egypt, the obligation lasted from the age of fourteen years to sixty or sixty-one.[13] As far as the provincial census is concerned, *i.e.* the preparation of lists for the purpose of taxation, this was conducted in the same manner as the census of Roman citizens.[14] In both cases the expressions *edere, deferre censum, profiteri* were used, from which it is evident that the taxpayer himself had to submit the necessary data, which were then checked by the officials. The declarations had to be made in the chief town of each taxation district; indeed, landed estates were required to be registered for taxation in the communes in which they were situated.[15] It is not known for sure how often the census was renewed. A clear idea of this can only be gained in the case of Egypt, because of the abundant material which the papyrus finds in that country have brought to light. In Roman times there were two kinds of periodic registration (*ἀπογραφαί*), for which the inhabitants themselves were obliged to supply the information. (1) Every fourteen years each house-owner was required to deliver to the authorities a list of those residing in his house during the past year.[16] These registers, called *κατ' οἰκίαν ἀπογραφαί*, served

---

children and old people were exempt from it. On the other hand, it does seem clear that Josephus used an extremely reliable statistical source in the report, *B.J.* ii 16, 4 (385); see Domaszewski, Rhein. Museum 47 (1892), pp. 207–18. The papyrus finds have shown that the Roman authorities at that time knew the exact number of inhabitants of Egypt through the periodical population count (see the literature mentioned in n. 16 and 21 below). It seems very likely, therefore, that Josephus obtained the figure of 7½ millions directly from an official source, and that it is only his mode of expression that is careless. Instead of saying, 'as shown by the poll-tax', he ought to have said, 'as shown by the population lists made for taxation purposes'. So also Wilamowitz in Hermes 35 (1900), pp. 545 f.

11. Of North Africa, Josephus says, *B.J.* ii 16, 4 (383) *χωρὶς τῶν ἐτησίων καρπῶν, οἳ μησὶν ὀκτὼ τὸ κατὰ τὴν Ῥώμην πλῆθος τρέφουσι, καὶ ἔξωθεν παντοίως φορολογοῦνται, καὶ ταῖς χρείαις τῆς ἡγεμονίας παρέχουσιν ἑτοίμως τὰς εἰσφοράς.*

12. *Digest*, L 15, 3 *pr.* (Ulpian, early 3rd century A.D.): 'Aetatem in censendo significare necesse est, quia quibusdam aetas tribuit, ne tributo onerentur; veluti in Syriis a quattuordecim annis masculi, a duodecim feminae usque ad sexagesimum quintum annum tributo capitis obligantur; aetas autem spectatur censendi tempore'.

13. S. L. Wallace, *op. cit.*, pp. 107–9.

14. For what follows see RE III, cols. 1918–22, s.v. 'Census'.

15. *Digest* L 15, 4, 2 (Ulpian, early 3rd century A.D.): 'Is vero, qui agrum in alia civitate habet, in ea civitate profiteri debet, in qua ager est; agri enim tributum in eam civitatem debet levare, in cuius territorio possidetur'.

16. For a survey of the *κατ' οἰκίαν ἀπογραφαί* see Wallace, *op. cit.*, pp. 96–115, and especially M. Hombert, C. Préaux, *Recherches sur le recensement dans l'Égypte romaine* (1952), which is now the standard work.

mainly in the assessment of poll-tax.[17] Presumably, the reason for the fourteen-year period was that liability to pay poll-tax began at the age of fourteen. It was therefore not necessary to supplement the lists with birth notices within the period. On the other hand, deaths appear to have been regularly registered with the authorities.[18] The lists supplied evidence for the *ἐπικρίσις*, or examination to determine status, and the consequent liability for poll-tax.[19] (2) Each year every property-owner had to give a written record, applying to the current year, of his moveable possessions such as cattle, ships and slaves. These declarations for tax purposes were also called *ἀπογραφαί*.[20] The tax was then determined on the basis of the details supplied, these latter having been checked by the authorities. The fifteen-year indiction cycle, first attested in Egypt in A.D. 312, conceivably arose from the fourteen-year cycle of the population counts combined with a five-year indiction period first attested in A.D. 287.[21]

17. It is possible but not certain that these regular population counts were introduced under Augustus. The earliest actually attested is that of A.D. 33/4, (or possibly A.D. 19/20, see P. Mich. 478), and there is evidence for every census of the fourteen-year cycle from then till A.D. 258. It has been argued, however, that the cycle actually began in 10/9 B.C.—see esp. B. P. Grenfell and A. S. Hunt on P. Oxy. 254—and even as early as 24/23 B.C., see Wallace, *op. cit.*, pp. 97–8, and Tcherikover in Journ. Juristic Pap. 4 (1950), p. 187; for a sceptical view of the theory that the cycle began under Augustus see Hombert, Préaux, *op. cit.*, pp. 47–55.

18. On death notices, cf. Wilcken, *Griechische Ostraka* I, p. 454 f.; Wallace, *op. cit.*, p. 106. Notices of births occurring after the last *ἀπογραφή* do not appear to have been demanded and were in practice sent in regularly only by members of the privileged classes in order to secure the same privileges for their children, see Wallace, *op. cit.*, p. 105.

19. C. F. J. Wessely, 'Epikrisis, eine Untersuchung zur hellenistischen Amtssprache', SAW 142 (1900), no. IX. He showed that *ἐπίκρισις* is used in various connections, particularly as test of liability or non-liability to poll-tax. Cf. Wallace, *op. cit.*, pp. 104–12.

20. Wilcken supposed, in his *Ostraka* I, pp. 456–69, that the annual property declarations included landed property as well, and not only moveable possessions. However, Grenfell and Hunt, *Oxyrhynchus Papyri* II, pp. 177 ff., showed, on the basis of an edict of Marcus Mettius Rufus of the year A.D. 90 (P. Oxy, 237) that these declarations concerned only moveable possessions. The general inclusion of landed property only took place when there was a need for it, and was specially ordered in each case. Moreover, the official registers of landed property were kept up to date because of the notices served on each change of ownership. Cf. L. Mitteis, U. Wilcken, *Grundzüge und Chrestomathie der Papyruskunde* I (1912), pp. 202–5.

21. For this view see O. Seeck, 'Die Entstehung des Indictionencyclus', Deutsche Zeitschrift für Geschichtswissenschaft 12 (1896), pp. 279–96; likewise, Mitteis, 'Aus den griechischen Papyrusurkunden', *Vortrag* (1900), pp. 12–15. On traces of a five-yearly census period and the origin of the indiction cycle, see also Marquardt, *Staatsverwaltung* II, pp. 243–5; cf. A. H. M. Jones, *Later Roman Empire* (1964), p. 61. However, one cannot conclude from the expression *πενταετία*

The task of Quirinius in A.D. 6/7 concerned not only Judaea but the whole of Syria. But in Judaea, a Roman 'valuation' (*ἀποτίμησις*) was necessary at precisely that time because it was then, following the deposition of Archelaus, that the territory was transferred for the first time to direct Roman administration.[22] That the census covered the whole of Syria is further attested by the inscription (mentioned above, p. 259) of Aemilius Secundus, who took the census in Apamea on Quirinius's order (*iussu Quirini censum egi Apamenae civitatis millium homin(um) civium CXVII*). The year A.D. 6/7 in which the census was undertaken in Judaea (see above, p. 381) coincides approximately with the fourteen-year population-count cycle in Egypt. If this cycle dates back to the time of Augustus, Egypt must also have had a population count in the same year.[23] If it is traced back one more unit, and if one assumes that the cycle applied to Syria also, there would also have been a population count in that territory towards the end of Herod's reign in 9/8 B.C. Ramsay (in the essay mentioned on p. 400 above) followed up all these combinations and saw in them a vindication of Luke. It is, however, only possible to repeat in this context the remarks concerning the *cohors Italica* (p. 365 and n. 54). For even if all these combinations were correct, the objections to the Lucan narrative would still remain in full force, for a population count in the Roman

---

in the edict of Tiberius Iulius Alexander, CIG 4957=OGIS 669=G. Chalon, *L'Édit de Tiberius Julius Alexander* (1964), that there already existed in Egypt at that time a general five-yearly census period; against this, see RE III col. 1921, and Wilcken, *Ostraka* I, p. 451.

22. The following are Josephus's statements on the census of Quirinius. *Ant.* xvii 13, 5 (355) *τῆς δ' Ἀρχελάου χώρας ὑποτελοῦς προσνεμηθείσης τῇ Σύρων πέμπεται Κυρίνιος ὑπὸ Καίσαρος ἀνὴρ ὑπατικὸς, ἀποτιμησόμενός τε τὰ ἐν Συρίᾳ καὶ τὸν Ἀρχελάου ἀποδωσόμενος οἶκον* (the private property of Archelaus was sold or leased for the benefit of the imperial fiscus). Immediately after this observation at the end of the 17th book, there follows *Ant.* xviii 1, 1 (1–2) *Κυρίνιος δὲ . . . ἐπὶ Συρίας παρῆν, ὑπὸ Καίσαρος δικαιοδότης τοῦ ἔθνους ἀπεσταλμένος καὶ τιμητὴς τῶν οὐσιῶν γενησόμενος, Κωπώνιός τε αὐτῷ συγκαταπέμπεται . . . ἡγησόμενος Ἰουδαίων . . . παρῆν δὲ καὶ Κυρίνιος εἰς τὴν Ἰουδαίαν προσθήκην τῆς Συρίας γενομένην ἀποτιμησόμενός τε αὐτῶν τὰς οὐσίας καὶ ἀποδωσόμενος τὰ Ἀρχελάου χρήματα.* The passage is given *in extenso* since (read as a whole) it implies that Quirinius undertook the census in the whole of Syria. On its execution in Judaea the same passage continues: *ἐν δεινῷ φέροντες τὴν ἐπὶ ταῖς ἀπογραφαῖς ἀκρόασιν* (therefore 'interrogations' took place when the declarations were made). *Ant.* xviii 2, 1 (26) *Κυρίνιος δὲ . . . τῶν ἀποτιμήσεων πέρας ἐχουσῶν. Ant.* xx 5, 2 (102) *Κυρινίου τῆς Ἰουδαίας τιμητεύοντος (al.τιμητοῦ ὄντος). B.J.* vii 8, 1 (253) Eleazar, a son of Judas *τοῦ πείσαντος Ἰουδαίους . . . μὴ ποιεῖσθαι τὰς ἀπογραφάς, ὅτε Κυρίνιος τιμητὴς εἰς τὴν Ἰουδαίαν ἐπέμφθη.*

23. The years mentioned in n. 17 above are the years for which the declarations were to be made. The *ἀπογραφαί* themselves, however, always took place in the following year. Hence, if it is permissible to go so far back, an *ἀπογραφή* for the year A.D. 5/6 must have taken place in the year A.D. 6/7.

province of Syria would not prove that a similar count took place in King Herod's territory, and in any case, a population count in the year 9/8 B.C. would in no circumstances have occurred in the time of Quirinius, but in that of Sentius Saturninus. Moreover, these combinations are extremely questionable. It is difficult to accept that the fourteen-year Egyptian cycle applied also to Syria, since the census of Quirinius was not based on a fixed cycle, but was a special mission, as Josephus's statements clearly show. The mission to Judaea in A.D. 6/7 was brought about directly by the deposition of Archelaus, the temporal coincidence with the Egyptian cycle being quite fortuitous. Besides, the direct evidence available for the Egyptian cycle does not begin until A.D. 33/4.[24]

In the passage referred to (2:1–5), Luke states that around the time of the birth of Jesus, apparently still during the reign of Herod the Great (Lk. 1:5; cf. Mt. 2:1–22), a decree (*δόγμα*) went out from the emperor Augustus requiring that 'the whole world should be registered', *ἀπογράφεσθαι πᾶσαν τὴν οἰκουμένην*. From the known usage of the phrase among the Romans, 'the whole world' can only mean the whole Roman empire, the *orbis Romanus*. Strictly speaking, this concept includes both Italy and the provinces. But it would be a pardonable inaccuracy if it in fact concerned only the provinces.[25] The verb *ἀπογράφειν* primarily means 'to register', and is therefore more general than the definite *ἀποτιμᾶν*, 'to value'.[26] But no other purpose of the 'register' is conceivable other than that of taxation (for the Jews were exempt from military service); and Luke understood the word in that sense anyway, for in v. 2 he associates this 'register' with the well-known census of Quirinius, whether identifying the two or not. In v. 2 he continues: *αὕτη [ἡ] ἀπογραφὴ πρώτη ἐγένετο ἡγεμονεύοντος τῆς Συρίας Κυρηνίου*. Whether the article is to be inserted before *ἀπογραφή* or not, is difficult to say; important manuscripts may be cited in favour of both readings.[27] At any rate, the order *πρώτη ἐγένετο* is to be maintained against the isolated readings *ἐγένετο πρώτη* (א) and *ἐγένετο ἀπογραφή πρώτη* (D). As far as the sense is concerned, it is almost immaterial whether the article is retained or not, for in the first case a translation would run, 'This census took place as the first', and in the second, 'This took place as the first census[28] while Quirinius was governor of Syria'. But in what sense does Luke use 'first'? Does he

24. See Hombert, Préaux, *op. cit.*, pp. 47–53. Cf. n. 17 above.
25. So Wieseler, *Beiträge*, pp. 20–2.
26. Cf. Wieseler, *Beitr.*, pp. 19 f.; Zumpt, *op. cit.*, pp. 94–6. On *ἀπογραφή*, see RE I, col. 2822; on the Egyptian *ἀπογραφαί* see above pp. 403–4.
27. Most manuscripts have the article; it is missing in BD, also in א, which reads *αυτην απογραφην*.
28. P. Buttmann, *Grammatik des neutestamentl. Sprachgebrauchs*, p. 105.

mean that it was the first general imperial census,[29] or the first Roman census in Judaea,[30] or that it was the first among several taken by Quirinius?[31] The first of these alternatives would show that Luke believed in several general imperial censuses. But if, as will become apparent, even the one imperial census under Augustus is doubtful, several repetitions of it is still more dubious. It would be well, therefore, not to ascribe unnecessarily such a serious error to the evangelist. As for the second alternative, this should stand if it emerges that Quirinius organized only one census in Judaea and that Luke had this in mind. Provisionally, therefore, the words may be taken to mean that the general imperial census ordered by Augustus for Judaea was the first taken there by the Romans, and that it occurred while Quirinius was governor of Syria. In verses 3–5, Luke reports further that, in compliance with the decree, all (in Jewish territory) went to be taxed, each εἰς τὴν ἑαυτοῦ πόλιν;[32] everyone, that is to say, who was not in his ancestral place (his οἶκος) had to go there to be registered. So Joseph travelled from Galilee to Bethlehem because he was of the house of David, to be registered together with Mary to whom he was betrothed (σὺν Μαριάμ should be read with ἀπογράψασθαι, not with ἀνέβη which is much further removed).

This account raises five issues.

I. *History does not otherwise record a general imperial census in the time of Augustus.*

Apologetical: Huschke, *Census z. Zeit d. Geb. J. Chr.*, pp. 2–59; Wieseler, *Synopse*, pp. 75–93, *idem*, *Beiträge*, pp. 50–64; Rodbertus, Jahrbb. für Nationalökonomie und Statistik, 5, pp. 145 ff., 241 ff.; Zumpt, *Geburtsjahr Christi*, pp. 147–60; Marquardt, *Römische Staatsverwaltung*, II (=1884), pp. 211 f.

Huschke endeavoured to establish that such an imperial census actually took place by means of data the inconclusiveness of which is now recognized, to some extent at least, by even the firmest defenders of Luke's narrative. Thus Huschke (p. 11 ff.) and even Wieseler[33] appealed to the *rationarium* or *breviarium totius imperii*, a register of the resources of the whole empire which Augustus as a good financier drew up with

29. So Huschke, *Ueber den zur Zeit der Geburt Jesu Christi gehaltenen Census*, p. 89.

30. So, for example, Wieseler, *Beiträge*, pp. 24, 27; Hilgenfeld, ZWT (1870), p. 157; A. Höck, *Röm. Gesch.* I, 2, p. 417.

31. So Zumpt, *Geburtsjahr Christi*, pp. 188–90.

32. To be read thus, according to ℵ′ BDL Ξ, with Tischendorf (ed. 8), Weiss, Westcott and Hort, and Nestle, instead of the εἰς τὴν ἰδίαν πόλιν of the *textus receptus*.

33. *Synopse*, pp. 82 f.; *Beiträge*, pp. 52, 93.

the idea of introducing some order into the badly disorganized imperial economy (Suet. *Div. Aug.* 28, 101; Dio liii 30, 2; lvi 33, 2; Tac. *Ann.* i 11).[34] But Zumpt rightly remarked[35] that while this speaks for the soundness of the political administration, it provides no argument for an imperial census.[36] More unfortunate still was Huschke's appeal (pp. 37–45) to Dio liv 35, 1, and lv 13, 4; for the former passage seems to be a reference to a registration of senatorial property (including that of Augustus himself), and the other alludes only to a census of Roman citizens in Italy with property of over 200,000 *sesterces*; it probably concerned the establishment of a jury panel of *ducenarii.*[37] Finally, Huschke's attempt to use the *Res Gestae* (on which, cf. p. 66 above) as evidence for a general imperial census breaks down completely, in proof of which it is enough to refer to Marquardt.[38]

Accordingly, of the numerous items of evidence which Huschke assembled as pointing to a general imperial census there remain only Cassiodorus, Isidorus Hispalensis and the Suda.[39] These undoubtedly speak of such a census in the time of Augustus.[40] But their testimony

34. Tacitus, *loc. cit.*, describes its contents as follows: 'Opes publicae continebantur, quantum civium sociorumque in armis, quot classes, regna, provinciae, tributa aut vectigalia, et necessitates ac largitiones. Quae cuncta sua manu perscripserat Augustus addideratque consilium coercendi intra terminos imperii, incertum metu an per invidiam'.

35. *Geburtsjahr Christi*, p. 154.

36. It has been deduced from Tacitus's statement that Augustus held censuses even in the territories of *reges socii*. But, as may be seen, there is no suggestion here that the *regna* paid tribute, let alone that censuses were taken in their territories.

37. See A. H. M. Jones, 'The Censorial Powers of Augustus', *Studies in Roman Government and Law* (1960), pp. 21–6.

38. *Röm. Staatsverwaltung* II ([2]1884), pp. 211–12.

39. Cf. Huschke, *op. cit.*, pp. 3 ff.; Wieseler, *Synopse*, pp. 77 f.; *Beiträge*, pp. 53–6; Rodbertus, *op. cit.*, V, pp. 241 ff.; Zumpt, *op. cit.*, pp. 149–55; Marquardt, *op. cit.*, p. 212, n. 2.

40. Cassiodorus, *Variae* iii 52, 6–7 'Augusti siquidem temporibus orbis Romanus agris divisus censuque descriptus est, ut possessio sua nulli haberetur incerta, quam pro tributorum susceperat quantitate solvenda. Hoc auctor Heron metricus redegit ad dogma conscriptum, quatenus studiosus legendo possit agnoscere, quod deberet oculis absolute monstrare'.

Isidorus, *Etymologiae* v 36 4, 'Aera singulorum annorum constituta est a Caesare Augusto, quando primum censu exagitato romanum orbem descripsit. Dicta autem aera ex eo, quod omnis orbis aes reddere professus est reipublicae'. On the Spanish era of 38 B.C., the origin of which Isidorus here seeks to explain, see RE I, cols. 639–40.

The Suda, *Lex.*, *s.v.* ἀπογραφή (ed. Adler, I, p. 293) *ὁ δὲ Καῖσαρ Αὔγουστος ὁ μοναρχήσας εἴκοσιν ἄνδρας τοὺς ἀρίστους τὸν βίον καὶ τὸν τρόπον ἐπιλεξάμενος ἐπὶ πᾶσαν τὴν γῆν τῶν ὑπηκόων ἐξέπεμψε, δι' ὧν ἀπογραφὰς ἐποιήσατο τῶν τε ἀνθρώπων καὶ οὐσιῶν, αὐτάρκη τινὰ προστάξας τῷ δημοσίῳ μοῖραν ἐκ τούτων εἰσφέρεσθαι. αὕτη ἡ ἀπογραφὴ πρώτη ἐγένετο, τῶν πρὸ αὐτοῦ τοῖς κεκτημένοις τι μὴ ἀφαιρουμένων, ὡς εἶναι τοῖς εὐπόροις δημόσιον ἔγκλημα τὸν πλοῦτον.*

loses much of its value in that all three were Christians and lived in a much later period (in the 6th, 7th, and 10th centuries A.D.); there is thus a very strong suspicion that they simply drew their information from Luke. The confused report of the Spaniard Isidorus was not considered even by Wieseler[41] and Zumpt[42] as independent evidence. As for the Suda, his dependence upon Luke is evident. Finally, Cassiodorus certainly used older sources, namely, the writings of the land surveyors, but who can guarantee that he did not take over from Luke his statement about the census? At any rate it is hazardous, in view of the silence of all the older sources (the *Res Gestae*, Cassius Dio, Suetonius), to accept his isolated notice as historical.[43] The 'testimony' of Orosius, on which Riess again laid great stress, undoubtedly also rests only on Luke.[44]

Many have found indirect support for the hypothesis of an imperial census during the time of Augustus in his alleged imperial land-survey. But even this is very doubtful.[45] It is known that Agrippa, the friend of Augustus, collected material for a map of the world, and that after his death this map was executed in marble and exhibited in the *Porticus Vipsania*. These *commentarii* of Agrippa were especially valuable for

41. *Synopse*, p. 78.

42. *Geburtsjahr Christi*, p. 151.

43. Mommsen also thought that Cassiodorus derived his statement about the census from Luke. See 'Die *libri coloniarum*' in *Die Schriften der römischen Feldmesser*, ed. Blume, Lachmann and Rudorff, II (1852), p. 177.

44. Orosius, vi 22, 6 'Eodem quoque anno (2 B.C.) tunc primum idem Caesar . . . censum agi singularum ubique provinciarum et censeri omnes homines iussit, quando et Deus homo videri et esse dignatus est. tunc igitur natus est Christus. Romano censui adscriptus ut natus est'. Cf. Riess, *Das Geburtsjahr Christi* (1880), pp. 69 ff.

45. The material relating to this question is well summed up in Marquardt, *Römische Staatsverwaltung* (²1884), pp. 207–11. In this work, p. 207, the special literature is also given, to which may be added: F. Philippi, *Zur Reconstruction der Weltkarte des Agrippa* (1880); E. Schweder, *Beiträge zur Kritik der Chorographie des Augustus* I–III (1876–83); D. Detlefsen, *Untersuchungen zu den geographischen Büchern des Plinius*, 1. *Die Weltkarte des M. Agrippa* (1884); O. Cuntz, 'Agrippa und Augustus als Quellenschriftseller des Plinius in den geogr. Büchern der *naturalis historia*', Jahrbb. für class. Philol. 17 Supplbd. (1890), pp. 473–526; L. Traube, 'Zur Chorographie des Augustus', SAM, 1891, pp. 406–9; Schweder, 'Ueber die Weltkarte und Chorographie des Kaisers Augustus', Jahrbb. für class. Philol. (1892), pp. 113–32, and 'Ueber die Weltkarte und Chorographie des Kaisers Augustus', Philologus 54 (1895), pp. 528–59; 56 (1897), pp. 130–62. Cf. also E. Hübner, *Grundriss zu Vorlesungen über die röm Literaturgesch.* (⁴1878), p. 180 (bibliographical list); M. Schanz–C. Hosius, *Gesch. der röm. Literatur* II (⁴1935), pp. 329–35; A. Klotz, 'Die geographischen Commentarii des Agrippa und ihre Überreste', Klio 24 (1931), pp. 38–58, 386–466; M. Reinhold, *Marcus Agrippa* (1933), pp. 142–8; J. O. Thomson, *History of Ancient Geography* (1948), pp. 332–4.

their numerous and exact measurements.[46] But it is very doubtful whether they were based on a general survey of the empire undertaken by Augustus. It is asserted by a few late cosmographers (Iulius Honorius and Aethicus Ister) that such a survey was begun under Caesar and completed under Augustus. But it is questionable whether this statement derives from ancient sources.[47] And even if Augustus did undertake a general imperial survey, this probably had nothing to do with a census. As geographical sources of the following period show, it could have been concerned only with geographical facts, and above all with road surveys and distances from one place to another.

In consequence, even though it is established that apart from Luke no historical evidence exists of a general imperial census under Augustus, the possibility still remains that Luke alone has preserved a record of it. But this possibility needs to be qualified. There can, above all, be no question of an imperial census but, at the most, only of one involving the provinces, since Italy is to be excluded (cf. pp. 401–2). But even with respect to the provinces, the great difference between them was that some were governed by imperial *legati*, others by *proconsules*. It is not very likely that the cautious Augustus, always careful to respect the rights of the Senate, would have ordered, by means of one and the same edict, a census for his provinces and for those of the Senate.[48] In addition, it is definitely known that during

46. The extant observations regarding them (especially those made by Pliny) were collected by A. Riese, *Geographi Latini minores* (1878), pp. 1–8; cf. his *Proleg.*, pp. vii–xvii; see now Klotz, *op. cit.*, pp. 386–466. The principal evidence is Pliny, *NH* iii 2/17, 'Agrippam quidem in tanta viri diligentia praeterque in hoc opere cura, cum orbem terrarum urbi spectandum propositurus esset, errasse quis credat? et cum eo divum Augustum? Is namque complexam eum porticum ex destinatione et commentariis M. Agrippae a sorore eius inchoatam peregit'.

47. The texts of Iulius Honorius and Aethicus Ister are given in Riese, *op. cit.*, pp. 21–55 and 71–103. The statement concerning the imperial survey is made by both at the very beginning. Iulius Honorius is earlier than Cassiodorus. But it is worthy of note that in the *Cod. Parisin.* 4808, saec. VI, which contains the oldest recension of his work (in Riese designated as A), the statement about the imperial survey is missing. On Aethicus Ister, see A. v. Gutschmid, *Kleine Schriften* V, pp. 418–25; H. Berger, RE I, cols. 697–9.

48. In general, it may be assumed that the emperors claimed from the outset the right to order censuses, even in senatorial provinces. Dio liii 17, 7, reckons it as a matter of course among the privileges of the emperors that they *ἀπογραφὰς ποιοῦνται*. But in spite of the dearth of material, Mommsen and Hirschfeld found it worthy of remark that there is as yet no evidence of imperial valuation officers in the senatorial provinces during the first century of the Empire. Among the instances assembled by Marquardt (*op. cit.*, p. 216) and G. F. Unger, Leipziger Studien zur class. Philol. 10 (1887), pp. 1 ff., are two *legati ad census accipiendos* in the senatorial provinces, one in Gallia Narbonensis (Unger, *op. cit.*, n. 1 = CIL XIV 3602 = ILS 950) and the other in Macedonia (Unger, *op. cit.*, n. 6 = CIL III 1463 = ILS 1046). But the former was the regular proconsul of the province and as such had been appointed to organise the census; in the case of the latter,

the reign of Augustus no Roman census had yet been organized in certain provinces.[49] All that can be conceded therefore is that in the time of Augustus censuses were taken in many provinces.[50] And this is in any case probable, for there must have been a need for them after the confusions of the civil war and Augustus doubtless regarded it as his duty to restore order. Juristic sources from the beginning of the 3rd century A.D. (*Digest.* L 15) already presuppose a fair amount of uniformity in regard to the valuation procedure, but there is no justification for supposing that this unifying process was due to Augustus.

II. *Under a Roman census, Joseph would not have been obliged to travel to Bethlehem, and Mary would not have been required to accompany him there.*

Apologetical: Huschke, *Census z. Zeit d. Geb. J.Chr.*, pp. 116–25; Wieseler, *Synopse*, pp. 105–8; *Beiträge*, pp. 65–9, 46–9; Zumpt, *Geburtsjahr Christi*, pp. 193–6, 203 f.

In a Roman census, landed property had to be registered for taxation in the locality within which it was situated (see above, p. 403). Moreover, the person to be taxed had to register in the place where he lived or in the chief town of his taxation district. By contrast, Luke's report that Joseph travelled to Bethlehem because he was of the house of David implies that the preparation of the taxation lists was made according to tribes, genealogies and families, which was by no means

whose abbreviated title was only *cens(itor) provinciae Macedoniae*, his position was perhaps the same (so Unger). Moreover, the inscription belongs to the second century A.D. An imperial *procurator ad census accipiendos Macedoniae* (therefore in a senatorial province alongside the proconsul) appears on an inscription at Thysdrus in Africa (Unger, *op. cit.*, n. 31=CIL VIII 10500=ILS 1409). But this is also from the second, or third, century (Pflaum, *Carrières*, no. 217). Great weight should, admittedly, not be laid on these facts, for it is possible that the same principles apply even to the imperial provinces, namely, that in the earlier days of the Empire the governors were entrusted with censuses, and that it was not until later that special census officers were appointed to work with the governors. Cf. generally on the imperial right of a census in the senatorial provinces (and against the hypothesis of an imperial census under Augustus): Mommsen, *Staatsrecht* II 2 ([3]1887), pp. 1091–3; O. Hirschfeld, *Die kaiserlichen Verwaltungsbeamten* ([2]1905), pp. 55–68. Cf. P. A. Brunt, *Italian Manpower 223 B.C.–A.D. 14* (1971), pp. 113 f.

49. Zumpt, *op. cit.*, pp. 176 f.

50. Zumpt is in basic agreement here; cf. *op. cit.*, p. 147 f., 163 ff., 211 f. (only he traces back to one edict the various provincial censuses held at different times). So, too, Marquardt, *op. cit.*, pp. 211 f.; Sherwin-White, *Roman Society and Roman Law in the New Testament* (1963), pp. 168–9.

the Roman custom. It is therefore usually assumed that in this census a concession was made to Jewish practice. But whereas it is true that the Romans frequently adapted their measures to institutions already in existence, in this particular case an 'indulgence' of such a nature would have been very odd, for it would have resulted in much more trouble and inconvenience than the Roman method. In addition, it is very doubtful whether a registration according to tribes and genealogies was possible; many were no longer able to establish that they belonged to this or that family.[51] It is strange, also, that Luke gives the impression that Mary was obliged to travel with Joseph for the census (verse 5: *ἀπογράψασθαι σὺν Μαριάμ*). There would have been no such necessity in a Roman census. For although women were liable to poll-tax, in Syria at least (see above, p. 403), there is no evidence that they were required to appear personally.[52] The particulars needed, as may be concluded from the analogy of the earlier Roman censuses, could be supplied by the father of the family.

There is in fact no detailed evidence as to the nature of the procedures imposed on individuals by the carrying out of a provincial census, except in Egypt. But even where the evidence of Egyptian papyri is clear in itself, it remains an open question whether it can be applied to other provinces.

None the less, it has been widely held that Egyptian evidence shows that there every person was invariably required to return to his *ἰδία* for the census, and hence offers confirmation for Luke's narrative. But the precise significance of the term *ἰδία*, whether 'place of birth', 'place of legal enrolment', or actual 'place of residence', remains obscure;[53] moreover, the order by the Prefect for each person to return to his *ἰδία* was made separately from the order for the census itself and cannot be shown to have followed it invariably.[54] It is precisely the Prefectoral edict most quoted in this context, that of C. Vibius Maximus in A.D. 103/4, that indicates how dubious is the

51. See vol. II, § 23. The 15th Ab, on which, according to mTaan. 4:5, 'those of unknown descent' brought wood for the altar of burnt-offerings, is described elsewhere as the day when everyone brought wood. Only particular families delivered it on special days. With these families are also connected the traces of a register of genealogies still extant in the time of Jesus (see vol. II, § 24). On the establishment of genealogies in this period, see J. Jeremias, *Jerusalem in the Time of Jesus* (1969), pp. 275–302.

52. As was assumed by Wieseler, *Beitr.*, pp. 46–9, and Zumpt, *op. cit.*, pp. 203–4.

53. See Hombert, Préaux, *op. cit.*, pp. 67–70; H. Braunert, '*ΙΔΙΑ*', Journ. of Jur. Papyrology 9–10 (1955–6), pp. 211–328.

54. V. Martin, 'Recensement périodique et réintégration du domicile légal', *Atti IV Cong. int. di papirologia* (1936), pp. 225–50. Cf. O. W. Reinmuth, *The Prefect of Egypt from Augustus to Diocletian* (1955), pp. 67–8; Wallace, *op. cit.*, p. 398, n. 29.

support given by this evidence. For the relevant part runs: 'The house-to-house census having started, it is essential that all persons who for any reason whatever are absent from their nomes be summoned to return to their own hearths, in order that they may perform the customary business of registration and apply themselves to the cultivation which concerns them.'[55] The intention was for people to return to their normal places of residence and work. Luke's own narrative represents this as having been Nazareth (2:4, 39). Furthermore, the Egyptian evidence suggests that normally the person responsible for making the return on each house had to present it personally, but gives no indication that others had to appear in person.[56] In short, the papyri do not disprove, but do nothing to prove, the historicity of the narrative of Luke.

III. *A Roman census could not have been carried out in Palestine during the time of King Herod.*

Apologetical: Huschke, *Census z. Zeit d. Geb. J.Chr.*, pp. 99–116; Wieseler, *Synopse*, pp. 93–8; *Beiträge*, pp. 79–94; Zumpt, *Geburtsjahr Christi*, pp. 178–86, 212 f.

It was quite in order for Quirinius to organize a Judaean census in A.D. 6/7, for by that time the territory had become a province. Luke, on the other hand, suggests that a Roman census took place in Palestine during the reign of Herod the Great, when the country was still an independent kingdom though under the ultimate suzerainty of Rome. From everything known of the position of the *reges socii* in relation to the Romans, and particularly of Herod's position, this seems impossible. Pompey admittedly imposed a tribute on Jewish territory[57] and Caesar reorganized the system of taxation by means of a series of edicts.[58] Also, Antonius imposed a tribute on Herod when he appointed him king.[59] But even granting that Herod continued to pay this tribute under Augustus, it is still unthinkable that a Roman census should have been organized within the bounds of his kingdom. Augustus

55. P. Lond. 904 II. 18–38; Mitteis, Wilcken, *Grundzüge und Chrestomathie* I_2, no. 202; A. S. Hunt and C. C. Edgar, *Select Papyri* II (1934), no. 220, from which this translation is quoted.

56. See Hombert, Préaux, *op. cit.*, pp. 75–6.

57. *Ant.* xiv 4, 4 (74); *B.J.* i 7, 6 (154).

58. *Ant.* xiv 10, 5 (201). Cf. above, pp. 271f.

59. Appian, *B.C.* v 75/319: *ἵστη δέ πῃ καὶ βασιλέας, οὓς δοκιμάσειεν, ἐπὶ φόροις ἄρα τεταγμένοις, Πόντου μὲν Δαρεῖον τὸν Φαρνάκους τοῦ Μιθριδάτου, Ἰδουμαίων δὲ καὶ Σαμαρέων Ἡρῴδην, κ. τ. λ.* See A. Momigliano, *Ricerche sull' organizzazione della Giudea, Ann. d. r. scuola norm. sup. Pisa*, ser. 2, III (1934), pp. 41–4; cf. A. Schalit, *König Herodes* (1969), pp. 161–2.

might have ordered such an internal administrative measure after Palestine had become a province, but not while it was the territory of a *rex socius*.

Similar instances have been pointed to in which an allegedly Roman census took place in the domain of a *rex socius*. Thus Tacitus remarks on a census undertaken among the Cietae,[60] Tac. *Ann.* vi 41: 'Per idem tempus Cietarum natio Cappadoci Archelao subiecta, quia nostrum in modum deferre census, pati tributa adigebatur, in iuga Tauri montis abscessit locorumque ingenio sese contra imbelles regis copias tutabatur'. But there is no mention here of a Roman census being held in the realm of King Archelaus; it is said only that Archelaus wished to make a census according to the Roman pattern (*nostrum in modum*) among the Cietae subject to him.[61] Zumpt argued that the revolt of Judas the Galilean on the occasion of the census of Quirinius in A.D. 6/7 proves that this census extended not only over the territory of Archelaus (Judaea and Samaria) then made into a province, but also over Galilee, since Judas must have received his nickname from the scene of his activities.[62] But Josephus writes expressly only of the territory of Archelaus as that affected by the census;[63] and the nickname is to be explained by the fact that Judas, who came from Gaulanitis,[64] which in the wider sense could be attributed to Galilee, organized the revolt not in Galilee but in Judaea, and was then named 'the Galilean' after his homeland by the inhabitants of Judaea.[65]

To prove Herod's subjection and the possibility of a Roman census in his domain, it is recalled that he was not allowed to wage war independently,[66] that he asked the emperor's permission to execute his sons,[67] that his subjects had to take the oath of allegiance to the

60. Huschke, *op. cit.*, pp. 102–4; Wieseler, *Synopse*, p. 94, and *Beiträge*, p. 94.
61. On Archelaus, cf. p. 321 above.
62. *Geburtsjahr Christi*, p. 191, note. On the description of Judas as a Galilean, see *Ant.* xviii 1, 6 (23) *ὁ Γαλιλαῖος Ἰούδας*. *Ibid.* xx 5, 2 (102) *Ἰούδα τοῦ Γαλιλαίου*. *B.J.* ii 8, 1 (118) *τις ἀνὴρ Γαλιλαῖος Ἰούδας*. *Ibid.* ii 17, 8 (433) *Ἰούδα τοῦ καλουμένου Γαλιλαίου*. Acts 5:37 *Ἰούδας ὁ Γαλιλαῖος*.
63. *Ant.* xviii 1, 1 (2) *παρῆν δὲ καὶ Κυρίνιος εἰς τὴν Ἰουδαίαν, προσθήκην τῆς Συρίας γενομένην, ἀποτιμησόμενός τε αὐτῶν τὰς οὐσίας καὶ ἀποδωσόμενος τὰ Ἀρχελάου χρήματα*. Cf. in general the passages cited on p. 405 above. Notice that it is Pharisees of Judaea who (in Jerusalem) put the question to Jesus about the tribute money (Mt. 22:17; Mk. 12:14; Lk.20:22). Galilee at that time paid no imperial *κῆνσος* or *φόρος*.
64. *Ant.* xviii 1, 1 (4).
65. That this is correct becomes quite evident especially from *B.J.* ii 8, 1 (118), where Judas is called *τις ἀνὴρ Γαλιλαῖος*, which can only mean a native of Galilee. On the issue of the census and tribute in Zealot thought see M. Hengel, *Die Zeloten* (1961), pp. 132–45.
66. *Ant.* xvi 9, 3 (289–91).
67. *Ant.* xvi 10–11 (300–404); xvii 5, 7 (131–41); xvii 7 (182–7).

emperor as well,[68] that his will required the emperor's confirmation[69]; even the athletic contests in honour of Augustus and the temples dedicated to him are made to prove the possibility of a census.[70] As though this were evidence of anything but the undoubted dependence of the Jewish vassal king on the Roman emperor! Wieseler believed also that he could turn Jewish coins to good account in defence of Luke.[71] The only noteworthy point in this is that Palestinian coins of Augustus exist from the years 36, 39, 40 and 41, which, reckoning by the Actian era (31 B.C.), would partly belong to the age of Archelaus, and therefore to the time when Judaea still possessed a native prince. But these numbers are based on the Augustan era from the 1st January 27 B.C. So the year 36 would correspond to A.D. 5/6.[72] It is quite wrong to invoke the fact that Augustus 'included him [Herod] among the procurators of Syria, and ordered that everything was to be done in accordance with his judgement'.[73] For this is evidence, not of Herod's subjection,[74] but on the contrary, of the great trust he enjoyed with his patron and friend. The same applies to the threat once uttered by Augustus under extreme provocation, when he said *ὅτι πάλαι χρώμενος αὐτῷ φίλῳ, νῦν ὑπηκόῳ χρήσεται*, *Ant.* xvi 9, 3 (290), a passage which, oddly enough, Wieseler used in support of his thesis.[75]

An exact definition of Herod's constitutional position is assuredly not easy to give since Josephus fails to provide one in the very passage where it might have been expected.[76] In 30 B.C. Herod was again apparently confirmed in the possession of his kingdom by a *senatus consultum*.[77] But Josephus gives no details regarding the contents of this decree. Even Cassius Dio's observation that Augustus, when he was regulating conditions in Syria in 20 B.C., 'organized the subject territory according to the Roman method, while allowing the confederate princes to rule in accordance with customs of their forefathers',[78] is too general to permit any very definite inference. But in

68. *Ant.* xvii 2, 4 (42). On this oath, cf. above, p. 376. From other known forms of oath, its wording may be presumed to have been fairly general.

69. *Ant.* xvii 8, 4 (202); 11, 4–5 (317–23).

70. Wieseler, *Beiträge*, pp. 90–2.

71. *Beiträge*, pp. 83–9.

72. On these coins, cf. above, p. 380, and the bibliography given there.

73. *Ant.* xv 10, 3 (360) *ἐγκαταμίγνυσι δ' αὐτὸν* [*αὐτὴν*, Niese] *τοῖς ἐπιτροπεύουσι τῆς Συρίας ἐντειλάμενος μετὰ τῆς ἐκείνου γνώμης τὰ πάντα ποιεῖν*. Somewhat different is *B.J.* i 20, 4 (399) *κατέστησε δὲ αὐτὸν καὶ Συρίας ὅλης ἐπίτροπον . . . ὡς μηδὲν ἐξεῖναι δίχα τῆς ἐκείνου συμβουλίας τοῖς ἐπιτρόποις διοικεῖν*. Cf. above, p. 319.

74. As suggested by Wieseler, *Beitr.*, pp. 89 f.

75. *Synopse*, p. 96; *Beiträge*, p. 83.

76. On the constitutional position of *reges socii* see above, pp. 316–17.

77. *Ant.* xv 6, 7 (196); cf. *B.J.* i 20, 2–3 (391–7).

78. Dio liv 9, 1 *ὁ δὲ Αὔγουστος τὸ μὲν ὑπήκοον κατὰ τὰ τῶν Ῥωμαίων ἔθη διῴκει, τὸ δὲ ἔνσπονδον τῷ πατρίῳ σφίσι τρόπῳ εἴα ἄρχεσθαι.*

any case it does not encourage the view that a Roman census took place in Herod's territory. And the same may be said of the expressions used by Josephus to describe the conversion of Judaea into a province. They prove fully that in his opinion Judaea only then became Roman territory subject to the Romans.[79]

A study of the Herodian taxation system as revealed by Josephus leads further than these general observations. It appears throughout that Herod acted independently with regard to taxes and there is no sign whatever of his paying any dues to the Romans. He remits now a third,[80] now a quarter[81] of the taxes; he even exempts the Jewish colony in Batanaea from taxes altogether.[82] After his death the Jews demanded from Archelaus (who was therefore also independent in this respect) a reduction of the oppressive taxation,[83] and the Jewish deputation in Rome complained of the burdensome taxes under Herod to support their request that no Herodian should again rule over Palestine. But there is no mention of Roman taxes.[84] Herod in other words dealt without restriction with taxation in Palestine. It is therefore legitimate to sustain the view that even if he did pay tribute to Rome, a Roman census and a Roman system of taxation could not have been introduced in his kingdom.[85]

IV. *Josephus knows nothing of a Roman census in Palestine during the reign of Herod; he refers rather to the census of* A.D. *6/7 as something new and unprecedented.*

Apologetical: Wieseler, *Synopse*, pp. 98–105; *Beiträge*, pp. 94–104.

To weaken the force of the *argumentum e silentio* drawn from Josephus, there have been attempts, either to discover in his writings

79. *Ant.* xvii 13, 5 (355) *τῆς Ἀρχελάου χώρας ὑποτελοῦς προσνεμηθείσης τῇ Σύρων.* *B.J.* ii 8, 1 (117) *τῆς Ἀρχελάου χώρας εἰς ἐπαρχίαν περιγραφείσης.* *B.J.* ii 9, 1 (167) *τῆς Ἀρχελάου δ' ἐθναρχίας μεταπεσούσης εἰς ἐπαρχίαν.* *Ant.* xviii 4, 3 (93) *οὗ* (Archelaus) *Ῥωμαῖοι παραδεξάμενοι τὴν ἀρχήν.*

80. *Ant.* xv 10, 4 (365). On Herod's finances compare in general Schalit, *König Herodes*, pp. 262–98.

81. *Ant.* xvi 2, 5 (64).

82. *Ant.* xvii 2, 1 (25) *ἀτελῆ τε τὴν χῶραν ἐπηγγέλλετο, καὶ αὐτοὺς εἰσφορῶν ἀπηλλαγμένους ἁπασῶν.*

83. *Ant.* xvii 8, 4 (205). Wieseler attempted to argue that the tax about which the Jews complained was a Roman one (*Synopses*, pp. 102 f.; *Beiträge*, pp. 98 f.).

84. *Ant.* xvii 11, 2 (304–14).

85. The question of whether Herod paid a tribute to the Romans has no bearing on the subject under consideration (the possibility of a Roman census) for the payment of a lump sum as tribute is quite different from an exaction by the Romans of direct taxes from the individual citizens of the country. But even the tribute is not at all certain; at least there is no proof of it. That Antonius imposed a tribute on Herod (Appian, *B.C.* v 75/319; see above, p. 413), proves nothing

traces of a Roman census in the time of Herod, or to deny that his silence proves anything.

Wieseler claimed to find such a trace in the revolt of Judas and Matthias shortly before Herod's death,[86] the cause of which is said to have been the census, whereas Josephus indicates as clearly as possible quite another reason.[87] Another trace is seen in the detailed information concerning the level of the revenues of Judaea, Galilee and Trachonitis given by Josephus in his reference to the partition of Palestine among Herod's three sons,[88] as though a census, and a Roman one at that, would have been necessary for him to have known these figures! It is of much greater significance that when that partition took place, Augustus stipulated that the Samaritan taxation rate should be reduced by a quarter because they had not taken part in the war against Varus.[89] It is important because it is the only reported instance of imperial interference in the matter of Judaean taxation before the territory became a Roman province. But of course it does not follow, as Wieseler argued,[90] that a Roman tax was concerned. On the contrary, it is throughout a question of the revenues of the native princes, Archelaus, Antipas and Philip, and the very absence of any reference at this juncture to a Roman tax speaks for its non-existence. Finally, the argument by means of which Zumpt discovered the required census (prior to the one in A.D. 6/7) is particularly ingenious.[91] For him,

---

in regard to the time of Augustus. It is said of Caligula that when he restored kings to their patrimonies he granted them 'full enjoyment of the revenues and also the produce of the interval' (during which the kingdom had been confiscated), Suet. *Calig.* 16, 'si quibus regna restituit adiecit et fructum omnem vectigaliorum et reditum medii temporis', it should not be concluded that normally the contrary of both was the rule. For Suetonius is not reporting here on a particular foolishness of Caligula, but on his generosity. Probably, it was only the reimbursement of the *reditus medii temporis* that was extraordinary. But in any case, the passage shows that there was no binding rule in such matters. In the time of Lucian, King Eupator of the Bosporus paid an annual tribute to the Romans (Lucian, *Alexander*, 57; for the text, see above, p. 317). On the other hand, there were *πόλεις αὐτόνομοί τε καὶ φόρων ἀτελεῖς* (Appian, *B.C.* i 102/475); and it is unlikely that the kings were placed in a worse position. In general, payment of tribute is more likely for the later period of the Empire, when the political power of the *reges socii* was subjected to greater limitation than for the earlier. Cf. above, pp. 316–17.

86. *Ant.* xvii 6, 2 (149–54). Cf. Wieseler, *Synopse*, pp. 100–5; *Beiträge*, pp. 98–104.

87. See above, p. 325.

88. *Ant.* xvii 11, 4 (318–20); *B.J.* ii 6, 3 (95–100). Cf. Wieseler, *Beiträge*, p. 99.

89. *Ant.* xvii 11, 4 (319) *τετάρτου μέρους* [Niese: *τετάρτην μοῖραν*] *οὗτοι τῶν φόρων παραλέλυντο, Καίσαρος αὐτοῖς κούφισιν ψηφισαμένου διὰ τὸ μὴ συναποστῆναι τῇ λοιπῇ πληθύι.* Cf. *B.J.* ii 6, 3 (96).

90. *Beiträge*, p. 99.

91. *Geburtsjahr Christi*, pp. 201 f.

it follows from Josephus's report concerning the census of A.D. 6/7 'that Quirinius only made a valuation of Jewish assets at that time and therefore took no consideration of those who were poor and without assets'. But since the poll-tax existing in the time of Jesus presupposes a register of those without property, it must have been drawn up earlier under Herod. In this connexion only three points require to be proved: (1) that Quirinius valued 'only the assets' of the Jews; (2) that in Palestine in the time of Jesus a poll-tax was also levied on those without property;[92] and (3) that this poll-tax was already introduced under Herod.

So, in fact, Josephus knows nothing of a Roman census during the time of Herod. One is, admittedly, disinclined to place too much reliance on *argumenta e silentio*. But in this case it has meaning. On no other period is Josephus so well informed, on none is he so thorough, as on that of Herod's last years. It is almost inconceivable that he would have ignored a measure such as a Roman census of that time, which would have offended the people to the quick, whilst faithfully describing the census of A.D. 6/7, which occurred in a period of which he reports very much less.[93] It should be borne in mind that a Roman census left behind it an effect; like that of A.D. 6/7, it would have provoked a revolt. Zumpt tried to weaken this argument by maintaining that the alleged Herodian census was a blameless registration (ἀπογραφή) of the people for the purpose of the poll-tax, whereas the census of A.D. 6/7 was a property valuation (ἀποτίμησις), and for that reason extremely offensive.[94] The poll-tax had to yield the tribute to be paid to the Romans, whereas the property tax had to defray the internal administrative expenses of the country.[95] But it is most improbable that the tribute to be paid to the Romans should have consisted simply of an equal amount of poll-tax for each *caput*. Appian says expressly that the Syrians paid a poll-tax of 1% of their property valuation. So if a Roman tax had been imposed in Palestine at all, it would certainly not have been a plain poll-tax. And in any case it would still have been a Roman tax. A population count, with the introduction of this tax as its aim, would therefore have provoked a rebellion just as much as a population census. But finally, the distinction between the ἀπογραφή mentioned in Luke 2:2 and the ἀποτίμησις of A.D. 6/7 breaks down before the fact that the latter, which sparked off the revolt of Judas

92. Compare the Syrian poll-tax referred to by Appian, *Syr.* 50/253. See above, p. 402.

93. Cf. above, p. 51.

94. So also Rodbertus, Jahrbücher für Nationalökonomie und Statistik 5 (1865), pp. 155 ff.

95. Zumpt, *Geburtsjahr Christi*, p. 196–202. Wieseler previously expressed a similar opinion (*Synopse*, p. 107; cf. 95 f., 102 f.), whereas he subsequently reverted to the idea of a poll- and land-tax (*Beiträge*, pp. 98 f.).

the Galilean, is referred to by Luke in Acts 5:37 with the same word as that used of the alleged census in the time of Herod and is called *ἀπογραφή*, which is clear proof that in both passages he has in mind the same event.

The most decisive argument, however, against a census in the reign of Herod is that Josephus characterizes the census of A.D. 6/7 as something entirely new and unprecedented among the Jews. Zumpt attempted to represent the novelty as consisting only in the property census (*ἀποτίμησις*), and Wieseler thought that only the form of the census was new and offensive, namely, the judicial examination (*ἡ ἀκρόασις*) and the obligation to confirm the evidence before a Gentile tribunal by means of a prescribed oath.[96] But these fine distinctions which can perhaps be spun from the report in *Ant.* immediately collapse when faced with the parallel account in *B.J.* ii 8, 1 (118), where Josephus expresses himself as follows: *ἐπὶ τούτου* (under Coponius) *τις ἀνὴρ Γαλιλαῖος Ἰούδας ὄνομα εἰς ἀπόστασιν ἐνῆγε τοὺς ἐπιχωρίους, κακίζων εἰ φόρον τε Ῥωμαίοις τελεῖν ὑπομενοῦσι καὶ μετὰ τὸν θεὸν οἴσουσι θνητοὺς δεσπότας*. It was therefore not the property census nor its form that was offensive, but the Roman tax itself. Such is also the assumption underlying the accounts of the rebellion given elsewhere: *B.J.* vii 8, 1 (253) *Ἰούδα τοῦ πείσαντος Ἰουδαίων οὐκ ὀλίγους . . . μὴ ποιεῖσθαι τὰς ἀπογραφάς*. *B.J.* ii 17, 8 (433) *Ἰουδαίους ὀνειδίσας ὅτι Ῥωμαίοις ὑπετάσσοντο μετὰ τὸν θεόν*. That the Romans should wish to raise a tax at all in Palestine was *novum et inauditum*. Also, from the words quoted above with which Josephus reports the establishment of Judaea as a province, *Ant.* xvii 13, 5 (355) *τῆς δ' Ἀρχελάου χώρας ὑποτελοῦς προσνεμηθείσης τῇ Σύρων*, it should necessarily be concluded, if they are taken strictly, that during the reigns of Herod and Archelaus no taxes were paid to the Romans. For if it was only after the banishment of Archelaus that Judaea was obliged to pay tribute, it follows that it had not been liable previously. The same conclusion may be drawn from two other passages. After his death the tetrarchy of Philip was added by Tiberius to the province of Syria, *τοὺς μέντοι φόρους ἐκέλευσε συλλεγομένους ἐν τῇ τετραρχίᾳ τῇ ἐκείνου γενομένῃ κατατίθεσθαι*, *Ant.* xviii 4, 6 (108). If no taxes flowed from his tetrarchy into the Roman treasury even after Philip's death, much less would this have been the case during his lifetime. But of the Jewish colony at Batanaea on which Herod conferred the privilege of absolute freedom from taxation, Josephus reports as follows, *Ant.* xvii 2, 2 (27–8) *ἐγένετο ἡ χώρα σφόδρα πολυάνθρωπος ἀδείᾳ τοῦ ἐπὶ πᾶσιν ἀτελοῦς, ἃ παρέμεινεν αὐτοῖς Ἡρῴδου ζῶντος. Φίλιππος δὲ υἱὸς ἐκείνου παραλαβὼν τὴν ἀρχὴν*

96. *Beiträge*, pp. 95–7; ThStKr (1875), p. 546. Cf. *Ant.* xviii 1, 1 (3) *ἐν δεινῷ φέροντες τὴν ἐπὶ ταῖς ἀπογραφαῖς ἀκρόασιν* ('the judicial examination in connexion with the registrations').

ὀλίγα τε καὶ ἐπ' ὀλίγοις αὐτοὺς ἐπράξετο. Ἀγρίππας μέντοι γε ὁ μέγας καὶ ὁ παῖς αὐτοῦ καὶ ὁμώνυμος καὶ πάνυ ἐξετρύχωσαν αὐτούς, οὐ μέντοι τὰ τῆς ἐλευθερίας κινεῖν ἠθέλησαν. παρ' ὧν Ῥωμαῖοι δεξάμενοι τὴν ἀρχὴν τοῦ μὲν ἐλευθέρου καὶ αὐτοὶ τηροῦσι τὴν ἀξίωσιν, ἐπιβολαῖς δὲ τῶν φόρων εἰς τὸ πάμπαν ἐπίεσαν αὐτούς. Hence it is quite evident that the imposition of a Roman tax in that region began only when it was no longer ruled by its own princes, whereas formerly, these (Herod the Great, Philip, Agrippa I, Agrippa II) levied or did not levy taxes as each of them thought best.

From all this it must be concluded that Roman taxes could not possibly have been levied in Palestine during the reign of Herod, and in consequence no Roman census was taken either.

V. *A census held under Quirinius could not have taken place in the time of Herod, for Quirinius was never governor of Syria during Herod's lifetime.*

Like Matthew (2:1 ff.), Luke (1:5) supposes that Jesus was born during the lifetime of Herod; he therefore places the census mentioned by him during Herod's reign. But he also says expressly that it was held ἡγεμονεύοντος τῆς Συρίας Κυρηνίου, which can only mean 'while Quirinius had supreme command over Syria', i.e. when he was governor of Syria.[97] Now it is known that Quirinius arrived in Syria as governor in A.D. 6; it has also been argued, incorrectly, that he may have held the same office even earlier, in 3–2 B.C.[98] But in any case, he cannot have been governor in Herod's time. For from about 10/9 B.C. to about 7/6 B.C. the office was held by Sentius Saturninus, and from 7/6–4 B.C. by Quinctilius Varus. The latter had to suppress the revolt which broke out in Palestine after Herod's death and was therefore in Syria for at least the following six months. But the probable predecessor of Saturninus was Titius.[99] Thus during the last five or six years of Herod's reign—it can be a matter of only this period—there is definitely no room for Quirinius.

This point has caused the greatest difficulties even to the defenders of Luke. Some of the arguments advanced may be considered here.

1. Lutteroth devised the following explanation to dispose of the above exegetical points.[100] When it is said of John the Baptist in Lk. 1:80 that he remained in the desert ἕως ἡμέρας ἀναδείξεως αὐτοῦ πρὸς τὸν Ἰσραήλ, by ἀνάδειξις is to be understood, not his public appearance

97. The official title is *legatus Augusti pro praetore*. See above, p. 255.
98. See above, pp. 257–8.
99. For the evidence, see above, p. 257.
100. *Le recensement de Quirinius en Judée* (1865), pp. 29–44.

as a preacher of repentance, but his 'presentation before the people' as a 12-year-old boy according to the requirements of the law. To this occasion belongs the following notice, that ἐν ταῖς ἡμέραις ἐκείναις was issued the emperor's census edict carried out by Quirinius, which also led to Joseph's journey to Bethlehem. As a subject of Herod Antipas, he was of course under no obligation to do this, for the census applied only to Judaea, but he wished to emphasize that he was a native of Bethlehem by making a voluntary appearance there. So Luke quite correctly dates the census of Quirinius to the time when John the Baptist was twelve years old. The end of Lk. 2:5 should be translated, 'to be registered with Mary, whom he had married when she was already pregnant' (hence twelve years before the census). Verse 6 then refers back again to this earlier time: it was also in Bethlehem that Mary (twelve years before the census) bore her first son. It is one of those explanations which arouse admiration for their ingenuity but need no refutation.

Huschke,[101] Wieseler,[102] Ewald,[103] Caspari,[104] Lagrange[105] and Heichelheim[106] understand the superlative πρῶτος comparatively, and translate: this census occurred as the first, before (or earlier than) Quirinius was governor of Syria. Luke therefore expressly distinguishes between the earlier census taken under Herod and the later one under Quirinius. This translation can if necessary be justified grammatically (cf. Jn. 1:15, 30).[107] But this does not mean that it is also the right one. Why should Luke have made the futile observation that this census took place earlier than when Quirinius was governor of Syria? Why does he not name the governor under whom it did take place? It is said that he distinguishes between the earlier census under Herod, and the later one under Quirinius. But according to this translation, this is precisely what he does not do. He does not say, 'this census took place earlier than that taken under Quirinius' (which would have

101. *Census z. Zeit d. Geb. J. Chr.*, pp. 78 ff.

102. *Synopse*, pp. 116–21; *Beiträge*, pp. 26–32; *Stud. und Krit.* (1875), pp. 546 ff.

103. *Gesch. d. Volkes Israel* V ([3]1868), p. 205.

104. *Chronolog.-geogr. Einl. in d. Leben J. Chr.*, p. 31.

105. M.-J. Lagrange, 'Où en est la question du recensement de Quirinius?' RB 8 (1911), pp. 60–84.

106. *Economic Survey of Ancient Rome*, ed. Tenney Frank, IV (1938) *Roman Syria*, pp. 160–2.

107. But only if need be, for of the many instances which Huschke (*op. cit.*, pp. 83–5) assembled to show that πρῶτος can have a comparative sense, if the totally irrelevant are set aside, there remain only those in which two parallel or analogous ideas are compared with each other, but not, as here, two wholly disparate ideas (the census under Herod and the governorship of Quirinius). For uses of πρῶτος see W. Bauer, *Wörterbuch zum Neuen Testament* ([5]1958), s.v.; Bauer-Arndt-Gingrich, *Lexicon*, s.v.

required something like this: *αὕτη ἡ ἀπογραφὴ πρώτη ἐγένετο τῆς Κυρηνίου Συρίας ἡγεμονεύοντος γενομένης*), but, 'this census took place earlier than when Quirinius was governor of Syria'. Wieseler translated similarly, and the analogy of all the instances adduced by him (*Synopse*, pp. 118 f.; *Beiträge*, pp. 30–2) admits of no other rendering. But an unprejudiced person would have difficulty in making sense of these words. Moreover, it is strange that Luke should express himself so clumsily and misleadingly, when elsewhere he shows such lucidity and polish. No one, except by using fragile hypotheses, can take *πρώτη* otherwise than as a superlative, and *ἡγεμονεύοντος τῆς Συρίας Κυρηνίου* otherwise than as a genitive absolute. This is the view of Winer,[108] Buttman,[109] Zumpt,[110] Bleek,[111] to name only a few.

3. Others, for instance Gumpach,[112] Steinmeyer,[113] and J. C. K. v. Hofmann,[114] emphasize *ἐγένετο* and translate: this census 'came into effect' (Gumpach) or 'was carried out' (Steinmeyer, Hofmann) while Quirinius was governor of Syria. Luke distinguishes between the promulgation of the order for the census under Herod, and its implementation ten to twelve years later under Quirinius. This hypothesis, which is apparently the simplest but in fact the weakest, founders, as one sees immediately, on the story of the journey of Joseph and Mary to Bethlehem, according to which not only the order for the census, but its implementation also, fell in the time of Herod. Such an interpretation would only make sense if another meaning were given to the simple *ἐγένετο*, i.e., 'came to a close'; but even the above-named commentators have not dared to do this.[115]

Ebrard [116] effected a supposed improvement by accentuating *αὐτὴ ἡ ἀπογραφή* and translating, 'the tax levy itself, however, took place only when Quirinius was governor of Syria'. Luke therefore does not distinguish, as the others believe, between the order for the property census and its implementation, but between the property census (its order as well as its implementation) and the tax levy based on it. The noun *ἀπογραφή* thus acquires a completely different meaning from that given to the verb *ἀπογράφεσθαι*, which in view of the close coherence of the passage is quite impossible. Noun and verb alike mean, 'to

108. *Grammatik*, sect. 35, 4, note 1.
109. *Grammatik des neutestamentl. Sprachgebr.*, p. 74.
110. *Geburtsjahr Christi*, p. 22.
111. *Synopt. Erkl. der drei ersten Evangelien* I, p. 71.
112. ThStKr (1852), pp. 666–9.
113. *Die Geschichte der Geburt des Herrn*, pp. 36 ff.
114. *Die heilige Schrift des Neuen Testaments zusammenhängend untersucht* VIII, 1, p. 49; X, pp. 64 ff.
115. Against this view, cf. especially Wieseler, *Synopse*, pp. 114–16; *Beiträge*, pp. 25 f.
116. *Wissenschaftl. Kritik d. ev. Gesch.*[3], pp. 227–31.

register' and 'registration', and in the narrower sense are both used specifically of the valuation and registration of property. The contention that the census of Quirinius was ordinarily designated by the term ἀπογραφή, and that in consequence the word (in this one particular instance) means the levying of a tax (pp. 224 f., 229 f.), is wholly without basis. For an appeal to Acts 5:37 and *Ant.* xviii 1, 1 (1–3) is inappropriate here. Instead of αὐτὴ ἡ ἀπογραφή it should read something like ἡ δὲ τῶν φόρων ἐκλογή or εἴσπραξις. Finally, history also contradicts this view. For Quirinius did not simply levy taxes in A.D. 6/7 on the basis of an earlier census, but first and foremost undertook an ἀποτίμησις himself.

4. Since nothing is to be gained by exegesis, attempts have been made to justify Luke's report without it by resorting to historical speculation. Indeed, since the discovery of the inscription supposedly showing two governorships of Quirinius in Syria, some have thought that everything has been cleared up. But as we have seen (p. 420), the inscription in fact settles nothing. Even a dual governorship (which is in any case not proved by the inscription) would not justify Luke's report. For the first governorship of Quirinius cannot have begun, at the earliest, until six months after Herod's death (see above, p. 258), whereas according to Luke, Quirinius must already have been governor in Herod's lifetime. Zumpt[117] and later Pölzl[118] and Corbishley[119] assumed—relying on a passage in Tertullian[120]—that the census was started by Sentius Saturninus (9–6 B.C.), continued by Quinctilius Varus (6–4 B.C.) and finished by Quirinius during his first governorship. It was from Quirinius, as the person who completed the work, that the census received its name; it is also why Luke states that it took place under him. As far as Tertullian is concerned, however, Zumpt himself asserts in another passage[121] that the church fathers 'generally lack all historical sense in their interpretation of the Gospel narrative'. Nothing may safely be built on their statements, therefore. For the rest, Zumpt's theory only harks back to that of Gumpach and others, referred to above. If the situation was as Zumpt envisaged it, either a verb such as ἐτελέσθη should be in place of ἐγένετο, or instead of Quirinius, that governor should be named in whose term of office the fact recorded by Luke (the journey of Joseph and Mary

117. *Geburtsjahr Christi*, pp. 207–24.

118. Wetzer-Welte, *Kirchenlex.*, ed. 2, III, cols. 5–7.

119. Th. Corbishley, 'Quirinius and the Census: a Re-study of the Evidence', Klio 29, N.F. 11 (1936), pp. 81–93.

120. Tertullian, *adv. Marcion.* IV 19 'Sed et census constat actos sub Augusto nunc in Iudaea per Sentium Saturninum, apud quos genus eius inquirere potuissent'.

121. *Geburtsjahr Christi*, p. 189, note. Cf. also Wieseler, *Synopse*, p. 113, note.

to Bethlehem) took place;[122] for the mention of the name is intended to define the time of which the evangelist is speaking. Thus, as the words read, there is necessarily the underlying idea that the birth of Jesus occurred in the time of Quirinius, which is impossible. Moreover, it is inconceivable that the *ἀπογραφή* as represented by Zumpt, viz. as a mere registration of the people without a property census, should have lasted from three to four years, while the much more difficult *ἀποτίμησις* of A.D. 6/7, which had in addition to cope with popular opposition, was completed within one year.[123]

Wandel agreed with Zumpt to the extent that he too placed the census under Sentius Saturninus. He thereby openly acknowledged Luke's error:[124] 'He was aware of the second census under Quirinius, he knew that Quirinius had been in Syria once before at about the time of Herod's death; he knew further that Christ was born in the period of a census, and mistakenly conjectured that the census under which the Saviour was born was also held under Quirinius and in the time of his first praetorship.'

The difficulties of Zumpt's interpretation disappear, of course, if it is accepted with Gerlach,[125] Quandt,[126] and Hahn,[127] that Quirinius was sent to Syria with Quinctilius Varus (6–4 B.C.) as extraordinary legate and undertook the census as such. Sanclemente presented this theory most precisely by assuming that Quirinius was despatched to Syria as *legatus ad census accipiendos*, equipped with a higher authority than the regular Syrian legate of that time, Sentius Saturninus.[128] But the evangelist's words do not admit of this expedient, since *ἡγεμονεύοντος τῆς Συρίας Κυρηνίου* can only mean 'when Quirinius had supreme command (or the office of governor, which is the same thing) over Syria'. Luke without doubt, that is to say, considers Quirinius to be the regular legate of Syria. But it is historically established that this office was occupied in the last years of Herod, not by Quirinius, but by Sentius Saturninus (?10/9–?7/6 B.C.), and then Quinctilius Varus (7/6–4 B.C.).[129] It was a step back from Sanclemente's argument when Ramsay suggested that authority was divided in such a way that

122. Therefore, according to Zumpt, Sentius Saturninus.

123. It was started after the banishment of Archelaus, at the earliest in the summer of A.D. 6, and, according to *Ant.* xviii 2, 1 (26), completed in the year 37 of the Actian era = autumn A.D. 6–7, hence at the latest in the autumn of A.D. 7.

124. NKZ 1892, p. 743.

125. *Die römischen Statthalter in Syrien und Judäa*, pp. 33–5.

126. *Zeitordnung und Zeitbestimmungen in den Evangelien* (1872), pp. 18–25.

127. *Das Evangelium des Lucas* I, p. 177.

128. Sanclemente, *De vulgaris aerae emendatione* IV, 6 (pp. 443–8). For the evidence on *legati* and *procuratores ad census accipiendas* see above, n. 48.

129. Cf. Huschke, *Ueber den zur Zeit der Geburt Jesu Christi gehaltenen Census*, pp. 75 f., who also argued against the theory in question.

Saturninus or Varus controlled the internal administration of Syria, while the military command was transferred to Quirinius in view of the war against the Homonadenses.[130] It would have been very odd if Luke had dated the census by the governor who had nothing whatever to do with the internal administration and therefore with the census! Thus the Lucan report can be justified historically only if it can be proved that Quirinius was already in the time of Herod the regular and sole governor of Syria. But such a proof can never be produced, since the contrary is an established fact. A further variant of this view was provided by Accame,[131] who argued that in 9–8 B.C., while Sentius Saturninus was the regular *legatus* of Syria, Quirinius had a *maius imperium* which included Syria in order to fight the Homanadenses.

Zahn, Weber and Lodder were more radical in their attempt to salvage Luke; they simply rejected the precise statements of Josephus.[132] Quirinius was only once governor of Syria, not as Josephus states in A.D. 6/7, but after the death of Herod in 4/3 B.C. (the governorship began a few months after Herod's death in the autumn of 4 B.C.; see NKZ (1893), pp. 647, 650). Zahn justified his criticism of Josephus's account on the following grounds. Josephus reports two depositions from office of the High Priest Joazar, (1) by Archelaus after the death of Herod, *Ant.* xvii 13, 1 (339), and (2) by Quirinius at the time of the census of A.D. 6/7, *Ant.* xviii 2, 1 (26). He also reports two rebellions by Judas, (1) during the troubles after the death of Herod, *Ant.* xvii 10, 5 (271–2); *B.J.* ii 4, 1 (56); cf. above, p. 332, and (2) on the occasion of the census under Quirinius in A.D. 6/7, *Ant.* xviii 1, 1 (4–10). In both cases, Josephus duplicates a single fact, but both are connected with the census. This took place either in 4/3 B.C. or A.D. 6/7, and Luke shows that the first date is the correct one. The ingenuity of this criticism is attractive and stimulating. Nevertheless, it must certainly be rejected. Josephus is so well informed on the history of the High Priests, and the stories of the two rebellions of Judas are so different, that in both cases the theory of a mistaken duplication is unjustifiable. Equally unwarranted is the rejection of the exact date of the census, *Ant.* xviii 2, 1 (26): in the 37th year after the battle of Actium, which implies that the census was necessarily connected with the deposition

130. The Expositor (1897), p. 431; *Was Christ born at Bethlehem?* (1898), p. 238. *The Bearing of Recent Discovery on the Trustworthiness of the New Testament* (1915), pp. 293–4 (cf. the full discussion of the census question here, pp. 238–300); JRS 7 (1917), pp. 271–5.

131. S. Accame, 'Il primo censimento della Giudea', Riv. di filol. 72/3 n.s. 22/3 (1944/5), pp. 138–70.

132. Th. Zahn, 'Die syrische Statthalterschaft und die Schatzung des Quirinius', NKZ 4 (1893), pp. 633–4, and *Einl. in das Neue Testament* II, pp. 395 f., 415 f. Cf. W. Weber, 'Der Census der Quirinius nach Josephus', ZNW 10 (1909), pp. 307–19; W. Lodder, *Die Schätzung des Quirinius bei Flavius Josephus* (1930).

of Archelaus; and, according to Dio (lv 27, 6), this took place in A.D. 6. But even if all Zahn's arguments were sound, nothing would be gained for New Testament apologetics. For again according to Zahn, Quirinius did not become governor until some months after the death of Herod, and only then undertook the census. Luke's error is thus exposed.

Finally, the suggestion made by H. Braunert[133] and A. N. Sherwin-White[134] may be noted, that Luke did in fact explicitly intend to date the birth of Jesus by the well-known census of Quirinius in A.D. 6/7. Braunert further infers that Luke derived the synchronism from a tradition in the Palestinian church which linked the birth with the origin of the Zealot movement. This view may gain further support from P. Winter's argument[135] that Luke 1:5–80 is in origin a birth narrative of John, subsequently adapted for insertion into the Gospel. Consequently there is no need to be troubled by the discrepancy between 2:1 and 1:5, ἐγένετο ἐν ταῖς ἡμέραις Ἡρώδου βασιλέως τῆς Ἰουδαίας.

This interpretation does less violence to the text of Luke than any other. But it does so only at the cost of the conclusion that Luke both followed a different chronology from Matthew (2:1) and asserted an historical absurdity, namely that Joseph and Mary travelled from Nazareth in the tetrarchy of Herod Antipas (which was their normal residence, see above p. 413) to the new Roman province of Judaea in order to be enrolled in the census, and then returned.

There is in fact no alternative but to recognize that the evangelist based his statement on uncertain historical information. The discrepancy is a dual one: (1) Luke ascribes to Augustus the order that a census should be taken throughout the whole empire. There is no historical record of such an imperial census. It is possible that Augustus undertook censuses in many, perhaps in most, of the provinces, and that Luke had some vague information about them. But these varied provincial censuses, differing in time and form, cannot be traced back to one particular edict. Luke therefore generalizes here, as he does in connection with the famine under Claudius. In the same way that, of the numerous famines that afflicted various parts of the empire in quite an unusual manner in the time of Claudius, he makes one extending ἐφ' ὅλην τὴν οἰκουμένην (Acts 11:28; see below, § 19), so the various provincial censuses of which he knew have been combined to form a single imperial census. (2) The evangelist also knows that at about the time of the birth of Jesus a census took place in Judaea under

133. H. Braunert, 'Der römische Provinzialzensus . . .', Historia 6 (1957), pp. 192–214.

134. A. N. Sherwin-White, *Roman Society and Roman Law* . . . (1963), pp. 162–71.

135. P. Winter, 'The Proto-Source of Luke I', NT 1 (1956), pp. 184–99.

Quirinius. He uses it to account for the journey from Nazareth to Bethlehem made by the parents of Jesus and therefore seems to place it exactly at the time of his birth, under Herod, i.e. about ten to twelve years too early. For that Luke had in mind the census of Quirinius, and was aware only of that one, is confirmed by Acts 5:37, where he refers to it simply as 'the census'.

Whoever believes that Luke could not have made such 'mistakes' needs only to be reminded that Justin Martyr, who was also an educated man, regarded King Ptolemy, at whose instance the Hebrew Bible was translated into Greek, as a contemporary of King Herod (*Apol.* I, 31). Moreover, this would not be the only historical error in Luke. For Theudas, who in the speech of Gamaliel is placed chronologically before Judas the Galilean (Acts 5:36 ff.) must, in fact, be the Theudas known to have lived about forty years later (see § 19).[136]

136. H. R. Moehring's final paragraph is worth quoting (*op. cit.*, p. 160): 'Once we recognize [the] apologetic function of the census in Luke we need no longer worry about the details of chronology. Luke was a forthright and open apologist for Christianity. He has no need of the forced apologetic devices of modern scholars more interested in pseudo-orthodoxy than history.'

Excursus II—Josephus on Jesus and James
Ant. xviii 3, 3 (63–4) and xx 9, 1 (200–3)*

The literature on this subject is so vast that only a selection of references can be given here. A few of the more important older works are mentioned with several recent ones. The division into three groups, in accordance with the authors' views, is only approximately accurate. Some writers maintain that our text of the two passages is authentic in all essentials, whilst not disputing that minor alterations may have been made in Josephus's own text. Others consider the possibility—or even claim—that Josephus wrote about Jesus, but think that what he wrote has been changed by a later hand out of all recognition, and that the extant text is spurious.

1. *Defending authenticity:*

C. G. Bretschneider: *Capita theologiae Iudaeorum dogmaticae e Flauii Iosephi scriptis collecta* (1812), pp. 59–66.

F. C. Burkitt, 'Josephus and Christ', ThT 47 (1913), pp. 135–44.

A. von Harnack 'Der jüdische Geschichtsschreiber Josephus und Jesus Christus', Internationale Monatsschrift für Wissenschaft, Kunst und Technik 7 (1913), cols. 1037–68; cf.: *Geschichte der altchristlichen Literatur bis Eusebius* I (1893), pp. 858–9, 2 (1897), p. 581.

B. Brüne, 'Zeugnis des Josephus über Christus', ThStKr 92 (1919), pp. 139–47 ('genuine, but a Christian censor deleted something Josephus had written').

W. E. Barnes, *The Testimony of Josephus to Jesus Christ* (1920).

R. Laqueur, *Der jüdische Historiker Josephus* (1920), pp. 274–8 ('Josephus himself added the passage, when he published a second edition of the Antiquities').

L. van Liempt, 'De testimonio Flaviano', Mnemosyne n.s. 55 (1927), pp. 109–16.

F. Dornseiff, 'Lukas der Schriftsteller, mit einem Anhang: Josephus und Tacitus', ZNW 35 (1936), pp. 129–55, esp. 145–8; 'Zum Testimonium Flavianum', *ibid.*, 46 (1955), pp. 245–50.

R. H. J. Shutt, *Studies in Josephus* (1961), p. 121 ('the *Testimonium*, as Josephus probably wrote it, was long enough to arouse suspicion, and not long enough or bitter enough to win commendation from Jews').

2. *Against authenticity:*

H. C. A. Eichstädt, *Flaviani de Iesu Christo testimonii αὐθεντία quo iure nuper rursus defenda sit* (1813–1841); *Questionibus sex super Flaviano de Iesu Christo testimonio auctarium* (1841).

H. Ewald, *Geschichte des Volkes Israel bis Christus* V, *Geschichte Christus' und seiner Zeit* ([3]1867), pp. 181–6 ('Josephus could not fail to write about the Christians, but the passage about Jesus has unmistakably been refashioned by a Christian').

E. Gerlach, *Die Weissagungen des Alten Testaments in den Schriften des Flavius Josephus und das angebliche Zeugniss von Christo* (1863), pp. 90–109.

---

* This excursus originally published by Paul Winter under the title 'Josephus on Jesus', Journ. of Hist. Studies 1 (1968), pp. 289–302, was revised by him shortly before his death in 1969.

B. Niese, *De Testimonio Christiano quod est apud Iosephum ant. Iud. XVIII, 63 sq. disputatio* (1893/4).

E. Schürer, 'Josephus', *Realenzyklopädie für die protestantische Theologie und Kirche* IX (1901), pp. 377–86.

G. Hölscher, *Die Quellen des Josephus für die Zeit vom Exil bis zum Jüdischen Krieg* (1904), p. 62; 'Josephus', RE IX, cols. 1934–2000, col. 1993–4.

W. Bauer, *Das Leben Jesu im Zeitalter der neutestamentlichen Apokryphen* (1909), p. 344; E. Hennecke's *Neutestamentliche Apokryphen* (ed. W. Schneemelcher) I (1959), pp. 324–5. [E. T. *New Testament Apocrypha* I (1963), pp. 436–7].

P. Battifol, *Orpheus et l'Évangile* (1911).

E. Norden, 'Josephus und Tacitus über Jesus Christus und eine messianische Prophetie', Neue Jahrbücher für das klassische Altertum, Geschichte und deutsche Literatur 16 (1913), pp. 637–66.

J. Juster, *Les Juifs dans l'Empire romain. Leur condition juridique, économique et sociale* II (1914), pp. 127–49, esp. pp. 139–40, n. 2.

P. Corssen, 'Die Zeugnisse des Tacitus und des Pseudo-Josephus über Christus', ZNW 15 (1914), pp. 114–40 ('Wir können der Frage nicht ausweichen, ob nicht etwa an Stelle dessen, was wir jetzt lesen, vorher etwas anderes gestanden hat', p. 128; 'man versteht . . . dass ein Christ auf den Gedanken kam, den Josephus mit einem Zeugnis für Jesus zu belasten, wenn er bereits einen Satz bei ihm vorfand, der ihn zum Widerspruch reizte', p. 132).

E. Meyer, 'Das angebliche Zeugnis des Josephus über Jesus', *Ursprung und Anfänge des Christentums* I (1921), pp. 206–11.

L. Wohleb, 'Das Testimonium Flavianum', Römische Quartalschrift 35 (1927), pp. 151–69 (he does not reject the view that something that Josephus wrote about Jesus may have been distorted by a copyist).

S. Zeitlin, 'The Christ Passage in Josephus', JQR n.s. 18 (1928), pp. 231–55.

G. Mathieu et L. Herrmann, *Oeuvres complètes de Flavius Josephus* IV (1929), p. 145.

H. Conzelmann, 'Jesus Christus', RGG III (^{3}1959) cols. 619–53, on col. 622 ('the passage reflects the Lucan kerygma, and was added as a whole to the text of Josephus').

F. Hahn, 'Die Frage nach dem historischen Jesus und die Eigenart der uns zur Verfügung stehenden Quellen' in F. Hahn, W. Lohff u. G. Bornkamm, *Die Frage nach dem historischen Jesus* (1966), pp. 7–40, on pp. 18 f.

3. *Maintaining the theory of interpolation:*

J. C. L. Gieseler, *Lehrbuch der Kirchengeschichte* I (^{2}1844, pp. 81 f.).

F. A. Heinichen, *Eusebii Pamphili Scripta Historica—Meletemata Eusebiana* III (1870), pp. 623–54.

K. Wieseler, 'Des Josephus Zeugnisse über Christus und Jakobus den Bruder des Herrn', JDTh 23 (1878), pp. 86–109.

G. Müller, *Christus bei Josephus Flavius* (^{2}1895).

A. v. Gutschmid, 'Vorlesungen über Josephos' Bücher gegen Apion', *Kleine Schriften* IV (1893), pp. 352–3.

Th. Reinach, 'Josèphe sur Jésus', REJ 35 (1897), pp. 1–18.

K. Linck, *De antiquissimis veterum quae ad Iesum Nazarenum spectant testimoniis, Religionsgeschichtliche Versuche und Vorarbeiten,* XIV 1 (1913).

R. Götz, 'Die ursprüngliche Fassung der Stelle Josephus Antiquit. XVIII 3, 3 und ihr Verhältnis zu Tacitus Annal. XV, 44', ZNW 14 (1913), pp. 286–97 ('zu kleinerem Teile echt, in der längeren jetzigen Fassung dagegen stark von einem christlichen Fälscher ergänzt und zurechtgestutzt nach christlichem Gutdünken', p. 291).

J. Klausner, *Jesus of Nazareth. His Life, Times and Teaching* (1925), pp. 55–8.
R. Eisler, *ΙΗΣΟΥΣ ΒΑΣΙΛΕΥΣ ΟΥ ΒΑΣΙΛΕΥΣΑΣ* (1928–30).
H. St. J. Thackeray, *Josephus, The Man and the Historian* (1929) ('The paragraph in the main comes from Josephus or his secretary, but the Christian censor or copyist has, by slight omissions and alterations, so distorted it as to give it a wholly different complexion', p. 148).
M. Goguel, *The Life of Jesus* (1933), pp. 75–82 (91).
W. Bienert, *Der älteste nichtchristliche Jesusbericht. Josephus über Jesus* (1936).
Ch. Martin, 'Le Testimonium Flavianum. Vers une solution définitive?' Revue belge de philologie et d'histoire 20 (1941), pp. 409–65.
F. Scheidweiler, 'Sind die Interpolationen im altrussischen Josephus wertlos?', ZNW 43 (1950/51), pp. 155–78; 'Das Testimonium Flavianum', *ibid.* 45 1954), pp. 230–43.
C. K. Barrett, *The New Testament Background. Selected Documents* (1956), p. 198.
P. Winter, *On the Trial of Jesus* (Berlin, 1961), pp. 27, 165, n. 25; 'The Trial of Jesus', Commentary 38 (1964), p. 35.
T. W. Manson, *Studies in the Gospels and Epistles* (1962), pp. 18–19.
A. Pelletier, 'L'originalité du témoignage de Flavius Josèphe sur Jésus', RSR 52 (1964), pp. 177–203.
L. H. Feldman, *Josephus* (Loeb) IX (1965), p. 49.
S. G. F. Brandon, *Jesus and the Zealots* (1967), pp. 121, 359–68; *The Trial of Jesus of Nazareth* (1968), pp. 52–55, 151–2.

In our texts of the *Antiquities* of Josephus are two passages that refer to Jesus of Nazareth, *viz. Ant.* xviii 3, 3 (63–4) and xx 9, 1 (200). Neither of them is universally accepted as authentic, but scholars who consider the second passage genuine are more numerous[1] than those who accept the first. Since the explanation of *Ant.* xx 9, 1 (200) does not involve as many difficulties as the interpretation of the other text, we may deal with the easier passage first.

Writing about James, the leader of the Jerusalem community of Jewish Christians (Acts 15:1 ff., 21:18 ff.), Josephus refers to him with the words ὁ ἀδελφὸς Ἰησοῦ τοῦ λεγομένου Χριστοῦ. We need to rid our

1. Most authors who reject *Ant.* xviii 3, 3 (63–4) as spurious have no doubts about the genuineness of *Ant.* xx 9, 1 (200). Exceptions are B. Niese, *De testimonio Christiano quod est apud Iosephum ant. Iud. XVIII, 63 sq. disputatio* (1893/4); E. Schürer, *Geschichte* I (1901), pp. 548, 581 f., n. 45; J. Juster, *Les Juifs dans l'Empire romain* II (1914), pp. 139–41; and G. Hölscher, in RE IX cols. 1934–2000, on col. 1993.

Schürer's objection was based on Origen's statement in *Contra Celsum* I 47, where Origen mentioned that Josephus thought of the fall of Jerusalem and the destruction of the Temple as God's punishment for the stoning of James. A similar statement, in *Contra Celsum* II 13, says: 'Titus destroyed Jerusalem, as Josephus reports, [in retribution] for the execution of James the Just, the brother of Jesus called Christ'. Yet no manuscript of Josephus extant today connects the destruction of Jerusalem with James's stoning. Schürer thought that Origen's statement proved the existence of several Christian interpolations in the Antiquities, of which that quoted by Origen failed to survive. It is, however, possible that Origen's memory was at fault, and that he assumed to have read in Josephus what he may have found in Hegesippus (in Eusebius, *HE* ii 23, 11–18).

minds of the notion that λεγόμενος implies doubt, as though it meant 'so-called' or 'alleged'. The word is rather similar to ἐπικαλούμενος which Josephus applies to John the Baptist, Ἰωάννης ὁ ἐπικαλούμενος βαπτιστής.[2] While ἐπικαλούμενος is best translated, 'with the byname', and therefore requires always that the actual name should be mentioned—Ἰωάννης in the case of the Baptist—λεγόμενος introduces an alternative name which might stand by itself.[3] It should be translated, according to its context, as 'said to be', or 'who is spoken of as', or simply 'called'. The usage in *Ant.* xx 9, 1 (200) also occurs in Mt. 1:16, where certainly no doubt is involved about the appropriateness of the title.[4] In *Ant.* xx 9, 1 (200) we have a statement which any writer of the first century could have used to describe the family relationship between James and Jesus, without intending to express doubts as to whether the latter was rightly or wrongly called Χριστός. A considerable number of persons with the name Jesus are mentioned by Josephus,[5] who therefore found it necessary to distinguish between them. For instance, he called the Jesus who succeeded Ananus in the high-priesthood τὸν τοῦ Δαμναίου[6] so as to avoid confusion with Jesus the son of Gamaliel, or any other bearer of the same name. 'λεγόμενος Χριστός' would be enough to specify Jesus of Nazareth.

However, the matter takes on a different aspect if it is assumed that the words, 'the brother of Jesus called Christ', were interpolated at a later time into Josephus's text. If a Christian forger had inserted a reference to Jesus, he would scarcely have been content to mention Jesus in such non-committal fashion. In all likelihood, he would have used a more direct expression to make clear the reality of the messiahship of Jesus. Furthermore, the word Χριστός soon came to be used among Christians of Gentile descent as a proper name. The phrase λεγόμενος Χριστός betrays awareness that 'messiah' was not a proper name, and therefore reflects Jewish rather than later Christian usage.

2. *Ant.* xviii 5, 2 (116–19).

3. Χριστός without Ἰησοῦς, is fairly often used as a proper name in the NT.

4. A scholion to Codex Vaticanus Graecus 354 (S) gives Pilate's question in Mt. xxvii 17 in the following form: τίνα θέλετε τῶν δύο ἀπολύσω ὑμῖν· Ἰησοῦν τὸν Βαραββᾶν ἢ Ἰησοῦν τόν λεγόμενον χριστόν.

5. Jesus son of Phabi, *Ant.* xv 9, 3 (322); Jesus son of See, *Ant.* xvii 13, 1 (341); Jesus son of Damnai, *Ant.* xx 9, 1 (203), 9, 4 (213); Jesus son of Gamaliel, *Ant.* xx 9, 4 (213), 9, 7 (223); Jesus son of Gamala, *B.J.* iv 3, 9 (160), 4, 3 (238), 4, 4 (283), 5, 2 (316), 322, 325), *Vita* 38/193, 41/204; Jesus son of Sapphas, *B.J.* ii 20, 4 (566); Jesus son of Sapphias, *B.J.* ii 21, 3 (599), iii 9, 7 (450–2), 9, 8 (457), 10, 1 (498) etc.; Jesus son of Thebuti, *B.J.* vi 8, 3 (387–9); Jesus son of Ananias, *B.J.* vi 5, 3 (300–9); Jesus, the rival of Josephus, *Vita* 22/105–11; Jesus, the Galilean, who attempted to depose Josephus from his command of Jewish troops, possibly identical with the last-named, *Vita* 40/200; Jesus, the brother-in-law of Justus of Tiberias, *Vita* 35/178, 37/186; and an undefined Jesus, *Vita* 48/246.

6. *Ant.* xx 9, 1 (203).

Origen, who was familiar with Josephus's writings,[7] expressed astonishment that Josephus, *disbelieving in the messiahship of Jesus* (ἀπιστῶν τῷ Ἰησοῦ ὡς Χριστῷ), should write in a deferential manner about James, his brother.[8] Hence the reading in *Ant.* xx 9, 1 (200) is attested as existing before the time of Origen, and there is no good reason for thinking that the words ὁ ἀδελφὸς Ἰησοῦ τοῦ λεγομένου Χριστοῦ in the passage about James were written by somebody other than Josephus.

If, then, in *Ant.* xx 9, 1 (200) Josephus referred to James as being 'the brother of Jesus who is called Christ', without more ado, we have to assume that in an earlier passage he had already told his readers about Jesus himself. Thus we are led to consider the passage in *Ant.* xviii 3, 3 (63–4). It reads:

> (63) At about this time lived Jesus, a wise man, if indeed one might call him a man. For he was one who accomplished surprising feats and was a teacher of such people as accept the truth with pleasure. He won over many Jews and many of the Greeks. (64) He was the Messiah. When Pilate, upon an indictment brought by the principal men among us, condemned him to the cross, those who had loved him from the very first did not cease to be attached to him. On the third day he appeared to them restored to life, for the holy prophets had foretold this and myriads of other marvels concerning him. And the tribe of the Christians, so called after him, has to this day still not disappeared.

Throughout the Middle Ages the authenticity of this passage was undisputed. Indeed, it considerably helped to exalt the reputation of Josephus in the Christian world; it was eagerly seized upon as impartial proof of the gospel story. But from the sixteenth century onward critical voices were raised and the dispute has continued since then.

The bibliography at the heading of this Excursus indicates the variety of views held by different scholars on the origin of our text. When examining it, we should not proceed in the same manner as did our predecessors in the main. Since all extant manuscripts of the eighteenth book of the Antiquities contain the passage—there are only three such manuscripts in existence, and none of them is earlier than the eleventh century—they started from the premise that the onus of proving lack of authenticity rests on those who refuse to accept it. This situation

7. He mentioned Josephus in *Contra Celsum* I 47, II 13 and *Com. in Matthaeum* X 17. Christian writers prior to Origen who also mention Josephus include Theophilus of Antioch (*Ad Autolycum* III 23; GCS VI, 1156); Tertullian (*Apologeticum adversus gentes pro christianis* 19, 6; PL i, 445, CSEL lxix 51; Clement of Alexandria, *Stromata* I 21, 147, 2 (GCS lii 91). None of these authors shows any acquaintance with the passage in *Ant.* xviii 3, 3 (63–4).

8. Origen's testimony is important, and may be quoted. *Com. in Matthaeum* 10:17 (ad Mt. 13:55): θαυμαστόν ἐστιν ὅτι τὸν Ἰησοῦν ἡμῶν οὐ καταδεξάμενος εἶναι Χριστόν, οὐδὲν ἧττον Ἰακώβῳ δικαιοσύνην ἐμαρτύρησε τοσαύτην. *Contra Celsum* I 47: καίτοι γε ἀπιστῶν τῷ Ἰησοῦ ὡς Χριστῷ . . . . . This proves beyond dispute that Origen found Jesus mentioned in his copy of Josephus, but that this mention did not give him the impression that Josephus considered Jesus to be the Christ.

no longer obtains. Doubt has won the day, and scholars of established reputation—Niese, Norden, Eduard Meyer, Conzelmann—consider our passage a complete fabrication. It is largely recognized by other authorities that Josephus could not have been the author of the passage as it stands. Today, the onus of proof lies on those who either maintain the genuineness of the entire passage, or maintain at least that Josephus did write something about Jesus, and that parts of *Ant.* xviii 3, 3 (63–4) —even single sentences or perhaps isolated words—preserve a trace, however incomplete, of what he wrote. Unlike our predecessors, therefore, we shall attempt to show first that certain parts of the testimonium Flavianum are not compatible with a Christian interpolator's outlook. *Σοφὸς ἀνήρ* is not an expression which a Christian would normally have used when speaking of Jesus for it contradicts the notion of Jesus' uniqueness. Certainly, an interpolator, aware that he was supposed to express a Jewish view, might have checked his habitual, more reverential, mode of speaking about Jesus, and might have employed a phrase he thought fit for a Jew to use. Nevertheless, the expression sounds doubtful in the mouth of a Christian. The phrase agrees with Josephus's own manner of writing,[9] and the case for its authenticity is strengthened when it is compared with the words immediately following, *εἴγε ἄνδρα αὐτὸν λέγειν χρή*, with which we shall deal later on.

In the sentence containing the words, 'upon an indictment (or accusation) brought by the principal men from our midst, Pilate condemned him to be crucified,' a distinction is made between the part played by Pilate and the part played by Jewish notables in Jesus' trial. While implying that charges were laid against Jesus by some Jewish nobles, these words state that it was the Roman prefect who pronounced a death sentence on him. None of the evangelists states the fact quite unambiguously.[10] The distinction between the functions of Jewish priests and Roman governor betrays some awareness of what legal proceedings in Judaea were like in the time of Jesus. Further, this distinction between the Roman and the Jewish role in Jesus' trial conflicts with all notions held by Christians of the second and the third century. From the time of the writers of the Acts of the Apostles and of the Fourth Gospel[11] onward, it was being claimed by Christian preachers, apologists and historians, that the Jews acted, not only as accusers of Jesus, but also as his judges and executioners. The array of charges against them on this count is impressive.[12] It is hard to believe that a Christian forger, bent as he would have been on extolling

9. *Ant.* viii 2, 7 (53) (of King Solomon); x 11, 2 (237) (of Daniel).
10. Mk. 15:5, Mt. 27:26, Lk. 23:24, Jn. 19:16; cf. Winter, *Trial*, p. 56.
11. Acts 2:22, 36, 3:15, 4:10, 5:30, 7:52, 10:39; Jn. 19:16b–18.
12. See Winter, *op. cit.*, pp. 58–61, 179–83.

the status of Jesus and lowering that of the Jews, might have been the author of the words in question.

To some critics of the passage in *Ant.* xviii 3, 3 (64) the words οἱ πρῶτοι ἄνδρες παρ' ἡμῖν appear suspicious for two reasons. They argue that it would accord with Josephus's habit to have inserted παρ' ἡμῖν between the words πρῶτοι and ἄνδρες. They argue further that Josephus, wishing to appear an objective historian who wrote 'from a neutral point of view', would have been careful to avoid using 'we', ἡμεῖς, and would rather have written οἱ πρῶτοι τῶν Ἰουδαίων ἄνδρες. The first objection is not really weighty. As to the second, it has to be admitted that Josephus, in *Bellum*, avoided speaking of himself or the Jewish people in the first person, singular or plural, but he abandoned this attitude when he wrote the Antiquities, a work undertaken with the explicit purpose of presenting the case for the Jews. He identified himself and his nation, on several occasions.

In the final sentence of our passage we read of τῶν Χριστιανῶν . . . τὸ φῦλον, the *tribe of Christians*. There are scholars who see in this phrase proof of Josephus's own hand and explain it as a derisive reference to Christianity. No Christian, it is argued, would have called Christians a 'tribe'. Yet though the word may have a pejorative connotation to modern ears, this was not so for first-century Jews. Steeped in the OT, Josephus would have found it natural to refer to divisions within the body politic of the Jewish people by the word 'tribe'. He even called the Jewish nation as a whole 'the tribe of the Jews'[13] or mentioned a speech, by the Jewish king of Chalcis, who addressed the inhabitants of Jerusalem with the words 'your tribe'.[14] While indeed it would be strange for a Christian to speak of the ἐξ ἐθνῶν λαός (Acts 15:14) as being a 'tribe', the phrase sounds plausible coming from Josephus.

Having made out, as we think, a *prima facie* case for the ascription to Josephus of certain turns of speech, however fragmentary, we shall in the next stage of this examination call attention to those parts of the testimonium that could not have been written by Josephus, but are clearly either Christian interpolations, or present an adulterated text.

Ὁ Χριστὸς οὗτος ἦν. This is a declaration of faith, of the Christian faith. Josephus was not a Christian. In fact, these words seem to have been lifted from Lk. 23:35, or Jn. 7:26, or perhaps from Acts 9:22, where the Apostle Paul confounded the Jews at Damascus, proving ὅτι οὗτός ἐστιν ὁ Χριστός. There is little reason to assume that Josephus had read the NT, even if it were definitely settled that the three of its

13. *B.J.* iii 8, 3 (354) τὸ Ἰουδαίων φῦλον (Josephus's own utterance), vii 8, 6 (327) τὸ φίλον [τῷ θεῷ] φῦλον Ἰουδαίων (in the speech of Eleazar, the defender of Masada).

14. *B.J.* ii 16, 4 (397) πᾶν ὑμῶν τὸ φῦλον (in Agrippa II's speech).

books quoted had been in existence at the time when he was completing his Antiquities (towards A.D. 93/4). Josephus could quite well refer to Jesus with the words ὁ λεγόμενος Χριστός to distinguish him from other persons named Jesus, in which case λεγόμενος prefacing the appellation 'Christ' makes it clear that he was following current custom and not expressing his own personal view. The definite assertion, 'He was the Christ', is, however, inconceivable in the mouth of anyone but a Christian. There are writers who think that a copyist found in his manuscript of Josephus a derogatory or malevolent reference to Jesus, crossed it out, and wrote on the margin the indignant exclamation: 'This was the Christ!' Later copyists, it is thought, inserted the marginal annotation in the text, where we now find it in all the manuscripts. It is not necessary to go to such lengths to explain the unexpected appearance of these four words. Rather, it seems that Josephus did use the word Χριστός, qualifying it in some way or other, perhaps as in *Ant.* xx 9, 1 (200), for otherwise the reference to the tribe of Χριστιανοί, 'so called after him', would be incomprehensible. What the qualification was which Josephus used, we cannot say. It may have been strong enough to irritate a copyist, who therefore left it out and replaced it by the definite assertion which we now read in our texts.[15]

Josephus nowhere informs his pagan readers what is meant by the expression, 'Christ', or 'Messiah'. It would have been necessary to elucidate the term to them. Already Bretschneider, who defended the authenticity of the testimonium, had to admit: *Bene enim tenendum est, Iosephum scripsisse non Iudaeis sed Graecis, ignorantibus sensum vocis χριστὸς dogmaticum apud Iudaeos notissimum.*[16] Without explanation, the four words now in the text would have been incomprehensible to Josephus's readers. A Christian interpolator quite sure of what he himself meant by the word χριστός would not have felt an explanation necessary. His readers would be Christians, as he was.

The words, 'if indeed one might call him a man', following on the description of Jesus as a wise man, seem to presuppose belief in the divinity of Jesus. That would not accord with what Josephus believed. If, however, these words have been added by a Christian interpolator, they considerably strengthen the case for the authenticity of Josephus's

15. In regard to the original text, T. W. Manson, *Studies in the Gospels and Epistles* (1962), p. 19, argued that the statements of Origen (cf. above n. 8) together with Jerome's variant reading 'credebatur', *de vir. inlustr.* (Teubner, 1879), p. 19, suggest that Josephus wrote ἐνομίζετο and that some pious Christian made what appeared to him the obvious and necessary correction. His conjecture, however, is tenable only if 'credebatur esse Christus' is not taken as a straight assertion, 'he was believed to be the Christ', but as a remark with ironic overtones: 'he was reputedly the Messiah'.

16. Bretschneider, *Capita theologiae Iudaeorum dogmaticae e Flauii Iosephi scriptis collecta* (1812), p. 63.

characterization of Jesus as a σοφὸς ἀνήρ. The interpolator may have thought it an inadequate description of Jesus' person to call him merely a wise man, and though in this instance he took no offence at the expression, he would have thought it necessary to note down his reservations.

'A teacher of people who accept the truth with pleasure (ἡδονῇ)' is a puzzling reading. Ἡδονή normally denotes sensual pleasure. On the one hand it is doubtful that Josephus would have said of people who embraced Christianity that they had accepted the truth; on the other, it would be most unusual for a Christian to refer to the acceptance of the Eternal Word by the turn of speech, ἡδονῇ δέχεσθαι. In juxtaposition to the παράδοξα ἔργα mentioned in the same sentence a few words earlier, the phrase has a slightly ironical undertone. Both expressions, παράδοξα ἔργα,[17] as well as ἡδονῇ δέχεσθαι,[18] occur in Josephus elsewhere, but ἡδονῇ δέχεσθαι τὴν ἀλήθειαν or τὰ ἀληθῆ sounds extraordinary. To write, or speak, πρὸς ἡδονήν, carries for Josephus the connotation of 'vain flattery'.[19]

As long ago as in 1749 the suggestion was made, and has since been repeated, that Josephus actually wrote *ΤΑΑΗΘΗ*, and not *ΤΑΛΗΘΗ*.[20] With no interval between the words, and majuscule writing, the letter *Α* could have easily been mistaken for a *Λ*. If we accept τὰ ἀηθῆ, the unusual, slightly freakish, ἡδονῇ fits the sense perfectly and agrees with the description of Jesus as a worker of παράδοξα ἔργα. The emendation has much in its favour, but it remains conjectural.

17. *Ant.* ix 8, 6 (182), xii 2, 8 (63).

18. *Ant.* xvii 12, 1 (329); xviii 1, 1 (6), 3, 1 (59), 3, 4 (70), 6, 10 (236), 9, 4 (333); xix 1, 16 (127), 2, 2 (185).

19. *Ant.* ii 5, 5 (80); cf. viii 15, 6 (418).

20. Nathaniel Forster seems to have been the first to suggest this emendation in an anonymously published treatise, *A Dissertation upon the Account suppos'd to have been given of Jesus Christ by Josephus, being an attempt to shew that this celebrated Passage, some slight corruptions only excepted, may reasonably be esteem'd genuine* (1749), p. 27. Apparently the same suggestion was also advanced by Jacob Serenius in a book published in Stockholm in 1752, and by Franz Anton Knittel in *Neue Kritiken über das weltberühmte Zeugnis des alten Juden Flavius Josephus von Iesus Christus* (1779).

Acknowledging that this emendation was not his own, Friedrich Adolf Heinichen repeated it in *Eusebii Scripta Historica* III, *Meletemata Eusebiana* (1870), pp. 623–54, on p. 647. Heinichen observed: παραδόξων ἔργων ποιητής *quamvis Iesus a Iosepho dici potuerit, idem tamen* διδάσκαλος ἀνθρώπων τῶν ἡδονῇ τἀληθῆ δεχομένων *dici minime potuit* (p. 642).

The conjecture has been accepted by Théodore Reinach, 'Josèphe sur Jésus', REJ 35 (1897), pp. 1–18, Robert Eisler, *ΙΗΣΟΥΣ ΒΑΣΙΛΕΥΣ ΟΥ ΒΑΣΙΛΕΥΣΑΣ. Die messianische Unabhängigkeitsbewegung vom Aufreten Johannes des Täufers bis zum Untergang Jakob des Gerechten* (1928–30), English version [abridged]: *The Messiah Jesus and John the Baptist* (1931), and by Walther Bienert, *Der älteste nichtchristliche Jesusbericht. Josephus über Jesus* (1936).

The words, 'He appeared to them on the third day . . . as the holy prophets had foretold this and myriads of other marvels', do not come from Josephus.[21]

So far, we have dealt with one set of sentences, or phrases, with the appearance of being non-Christian, and another set of sentences or phrases expressing Christian sentiments. We are left with a third set of expressions that are neutral. They may have been written by the Jew Josephus, or may have come from a Christian interpolator of his *Antiquities*. Josephus could have described Jesus as a performer of astonishing feats, and he is more likely to have done so than a Christian copyist. The sentence, 'He won over many Jews and many of the Greeks', could also have been written by Josephus, not as a testimony of Jesus' achievements in the course of his life, but as a description of affairs known to Josephus from his own experience. Living in Rome, he was aware that many of the local Christians were of 'Greek', i.e. Gentile, descent. The same applies to the remaining sentence, 'those who had come to love him from the very first (viz. in his life) did not cease to be attached to him (after his death)'; it may well have come from Josephus's hand.

The few sentences, or phrases, described above as being compatible with Josephus's outlook, are disconnected fragments. Even including parts considered 'neutral', the passage is disconcertingly colourless. The non-Christian and the neutral sentences together would give the following text:

(63) At about this time lived Jesus, a wise man . . . He performed astonishing feats (and was a teacher of such people as are eager for novelties?). He attracted many Jews and many of the Greeks . . . (64) . . . Upon an indictment brought by leading members of our society, Pilate sentenced him to the cross, but those who had loved him from the very first did not cease to be attached to him. . . . The brotherhood of the Christians, named after him, is still in existence.

This statement is amazingly brief in what it says about Jesus.

Once it is recognized that an interpolator altered what Josephus had written, and that he added something of his own, we should not suppose that the interpolator merely *expanded* the original wording, but consider the possibility that he also *omitted* part of what he found in his copy of Josephus. On reading the above excerpt one is led to the conclusion

21. Adolf Harnack, 'Der jüdische Geschichtsschreiber Josephus und Jesus Christus', Internationale Monatsschrift für Wissenschaft, Kunst und Technik 7 (1913), cols. 1037–68, found difficulty in reconciling these words with his assumption of the authenticity of the testimonium. André Pelletier, 'L'originalité du témoignage de Flavius Josephe sur Jésus', RSR 52 (1964), pp. 177–203, in spite of admitting that there are interpolations in the text of Josephus, strangely thinks this sentence to have come from Josephus himself.

that Josephus wrote more than what has survived. Something is now missing from the context, and has been replaced by a few not very illuminating sentences inserted by an interpolator. 'It is possible that Christian omissions as well as Christian interpolations should be allowed for; Christian writers, adding material in praise of Jesus, may quite well have omitted what they thought derogatory to his person.'[22] We cannot reliably guess what Josephus may have written and what our censorious copyist thought best to displace in favour of his own contribution.[23] It is possible, even probable, that Josephus wrote something about Jesus' deeds, as he did about the activity of John the Baptist. The mention of miracles, or astonishing feats, would scarcely fill this lacuna. It is also probable that Josephus recorded the reason why leading members of the Jewish community accused Jesus before Pilate, and that he revealed the grounds for the governor's decision to award him with the cross. As (65) in Book xviii 3, 4 of the *Antiquities*, immediately following on our passage, begins with the words, 'Some other dreadful event (*ἕτερόν τι δεινόν*) provoked agitation (*ἐθορύβει*) among the Jews', it may be that Josephus's own report, set between (62) and (65), mentioned a *θόρυβος*, an uproar or disturbance. If so, that report is now missing.

The entire section in the *Antiquities* dealing with Pilate's term of office is uneven. Apparently, Josephus used some sort of a chronicle, or annals, as a source for his report on Palestinian events,[24] and inserted in it two episodes for which he utilized a Roman source. *Ant.* xviii 3, 1 (55–9) contains a concise report on the tumult caused by the episode of the standards,[25] and is followed in xviii 3, 2 (60–2) by the account of the tumult in Jerusalem ensuing from Pilate's appropriation of money from the Temple treasury to finance the construction of an aqueduct.[26] Then comes our testimonium. The story about the affair between Decius Mundus and the noble but gullible Paulina, told by Josephus at length and with relish, *Ant.* xviii 3, 4 (65–80), interrupts the chronicler's report of Pilate's governorship in Judaea. The next section, *Ant.* xviii 3, 5 (81–4), also has its setting in Rome, but has at

22. C. K. Barrett, *The New Testament Background. Selected Documents*, p. 198.

23. 'Even though it may be possible to discover what Josephus did not say, it is . . . impossible to discover what the Christian editor omitted, or even to say with any certainty at what point the omission took place', M. Goguel, *The Life of Jesus* (1933), p. 81.

24. Cf. G. Hölscher, *Die Quellen des Josephus für die Zeit vom Exil bis zum Jüdischen Krieg* (1904) and *Die Hohenpriesterliste bei Josephus und die evangelische Chronologie* (SAH, Phil.-hist. Klasse, 1939/40, Abh. 3).

25. See above, p. 384.

26. See above, p. 385.

least some Jewish point of interest.[27] In *Ant.* xviii 4, 1 (85–7) we are back in Palestine; Josephus writes again of what happened under Pilate's rule in that country and mentions the governor's recall. The general unevenness of chapter 3 in the eighteenth book of the *Antiquities* is due to two different reasons; first, the fact that Josephus interspersed his Palestinian source with materials derived from a Roman source (65–84), and second, the disjunction caused in our text by a Christian insertion into, and omission from, what Josephus actually wrote between (62) and (65).

When the sections based on a source of information of Roman provenance are eliminated—as they should be, because Josephus was mistaken in assigning them to the time of Pilate's term of office—we are left with an account of three riots in Palestine, with the testimonium set between them: the riot resulting from the introduction of military standards (55–9); the riot caused by the profane use of Qorban money (60–2); the Testimonium (63–4); and the final upheaval which occurred in Samaria during Pilate's governorship (85–7). This strange context of the passage about Jesus also lends support to the surmise that a reference now missing (63–4)—missing after this passage had been dealt with by a Christian copyist—was concerned with a riot in Jerusalem.[28] Strong as these indications are, the argument is still based

27. Josephus must have found a report of the events he mentioned in *Ant.* xviii 3, 4 (65–80), 3, 5 (81–4) in some Roman source which dealt with the reign of Tiberius. Knowing that Pilate had been appointed prefect of Judaea by Tiberius, he inserted the report of the proscription of Egyptian and Jewish rites in Rome and Italy in this place. He was mistaken in his chronology as the events he reports occurred already in the year A.D. 19, well before Pilate became governor of Judaea. Compare Tacitus, *Annales* ii 85, and Suetonius, *Tiberius* 36.

28. That some rioting, or even an abortive rebellion, occurred in Jerusalem shortly before the arrest of Jesus, is suggested by the cryptic reference to ἡ στάσις in Mk. 15:7. The text of Mark has not escaped remoulding; the parallel passage in Mt. 27:16, brief as it is, was apparently based on an older Marcan text, as it does not connect Barabbas with any στασιασταί (see Winter, *op. cit.*, pp. 95 ff.). However, we ought not to jump to the conclusion that Jesus took any part in the στάσις. We lack the evidence for such a hypothesis.

The point is often missed, but it should be noticed that in the speech which the author of Acts attributes to Gamaliel—this speech is a Christian composition: the author of the Acts makes Gamaliel proclaim the supernatural origin of the Christian faith—the movement inaugurated by Jesus of Nazareth is paralleled by the movements connected with Judah, the Galilean or Gaulanite founder of Zealotism, and with the pseudo-prophet Theudas who had promised to liberate the Jews from the Romans (Acts 5:36, 37); see below, § 19, p. 456. When the Apostle Paul was arrested, he was mistaken for another leader of a seditous gathering (Acts 21:38); see below, § 19, pp. 463–4.

We cannot say from what sources Celsus, in his *True Treatise*, drew his information about Jesus, but we do know that he referred to him as a 'rebel leader', a λῄσταρχος or τῆς στάσεως ἀρχηγέτης (Origen, *Contra Celsum* II 12 and VIII 14, respectively). The expression λῃσταί occurs in the Gospel account of Jesus'

only on surmise. We have no means of restoring what Josephus wrote and what has been excised from his text by some copyist.

Various authors have tried to 'reconstruct' Josephus's own text by complementing the genuine Josephus passages in the Testimonium with the Old Russian (often called 'Slavonic') text of *Bellum Judaicum.* Such a procedure does not commend itself. In the Greek text of *Bellum* we have two consecutive accounts of disturbances: *B.J.* ii 9, 2–3 (169–74) concerns the riot caused by the introduction of Roman standards into Jerusalem; ii 9, 4 (175–7) deals with the riot provoked by the use of money from the Temple to build a new aqueduct; there is no mention of Jesus. The *Antiquities,* xviii 3, 1 (55–9) and 3, 2 (60–2), record the same events in the same sequence. The Testimonium Flavianum follows in 3, 3 (63–4). The Old Russian text of Bellum inserts *between* the two reports of *θόρυβοι* its own report on Jesus' appearance. But the riot occasioned in Jerusalem because of Pilate's use of money from the Temple (*B.J.* ii 9, 4 (175–7) or *Ant.* xviii 3, 3 (60–2), is called in the Old Russian text 'the second riot'—and this numeration corresponds exactly to the sequence given in the Greek text of *War* and *Antiquities,* but not in the Slavonic work itself. There it would be the third riot. The discrepancy between the numbering and the actual contents in the Old Russian version of the Jewish War would suggest that what we read about Jesus in that version was not based on a more original text of Josephus, but is an addition composed even later than the time at which the testimonium in its present form came into existence.[29]

To conclude our examination: Josephus mentioned Jesus. The present text of *Ant.* xviii (63–4) is only to some extent his own. Josephus wrote more about Jesus than we are able to extract from this text.

Although Josephus certainly did not call Jesus the Messiah, and did not assert that his resurrection on the third day had been announced by divine prophets, the impression gained from an intimate study of his report is that he was not on the whole unsympathetic towards Jesus. The words *ἕτερόν τι δεινὸν ἐθορύβει τοὺς Ἰουδαίους*, which introduce the paragraph following immediately on the Jesus passage, indicate that Josephus viewed the execution of Jesus as a 'dreadful

---

crucifixion as a description of the men who were crucified with him (Mk. 15:27 and par.). The charge that Jesus himself was a rebel was constantly repeated by ancient Greek and Roman authors up to the time of Constantine. The statements made by these authors are not sufficient to attribute to Jesus' rebellious intentions, but they are enough to prove that his activity was viewed in this light by the authorities of his day and by pagan writers of later days.

29. Nevertheless there are theories according to which the Old Russian translator used as his *Vorlage* a genuine Josephus text which is supposed to have come from *Bellum* (so R. Eisler in the work mentioned in n. 20 above) or from the *Antiquities* (so W. Bienert in his book, *ibidem*).

event' and that the Jews were disturbed by the outcome of the case.

Nothing that Josephus wrote lends any support to the theory that Jesus was caught up in revolutionary, Zealotic or quasi-Zealotic activities. The NT provides ample evidence that Jesus was tried and executed on political grounds. Josephus does not round off what remains unsaid in the NT of Jesus' own thoughts and aims. The relatively friendly attitude of Josephus towards Jesus contrasts with his severe stricture of the Zealots and kindred activist groups among the Jews responsible for encouraging the people to defy Roman rule. Of such groups Josephus spoke with undisguised scorn and summarily labelled them, *γόητες καὶ ληστρικοί*.[30] Whereas Josephus called Judah, the founder of Zealotism, and his grandson Menahem, the actual leader of the Zealot faction during the great revolt, *σοφισταί*,[31] he referred to Jesus as a *σοφὸς ἀνήρ*. And this indicates that Jews belonging to the circle to which Josephus belonged—a Pharisaic group, no doubt—had not at that time given Jesus a bad name as a heretic, or denounced him as a rebel. That various Pharisaic circles entertained friendly relations with Jewish Christians for a long time after the crucifixion is attested, not only by the report on the resentment caused by the stoning of Jesus' brother at the order of a Sadducaean High Priest, but also by the significant fact that certain communal Christian traditions of Palestinian provenance (part of the so-called 'Special Source' of Luke) depict various Pharisees or other Jews not members of Jesus' own companionship as harbouring feelings and intentions of friendship for Jesus and maintaining social contact with him (e.g. Lk. 7:16 f., 23:17, 31, 14:1, 17:20 f., 19:38, 48, 26:38, 23:27, 48).[32]

30. *B.J.* ii 8, 1 (118) and 13, 6 (264), respectively.

31. *B.J.* ii 17, 8 (433).

32. S. Pines, *An Arabic Version of the Testimonium Flavianum and its Implications* (1971) draws attention to a citation of the Testimonium by a 10th century Arabic Christian writer, Agapius: 'At this time there was a wise man who was called Jesus. And his conduct was good, and (he) was known to be virtuous. And many people from among the Jews and the other nations became his disciples. Pilate condemned him to be crucified and to die. And those who had become his disciples did not abandon his discipleship. They reported that he had appeared to them three days after his crucifixion and that he was alive; accordingly, he was perhaps the Messiah, concerning whom the prophets have recounted wonders'. No historical value may safely be attributed to this text, though it is correct to point out that it contains 'none of the suspicious phraseology of the "vulgate recension" that has led many modern scholars to reject the entire passage as a Christian interpolation.' Cf. S. P. Brock, JThSt 23 (1972), p. 491.

§ 18. Agrippa I a.d. 37, 40, 41–44

Sources

Josephus, *Ant.* xviii 6 (143–239); xix 5–9 (274–359); *B.J.* ii 9, 5–6 (178–82), 11, 2–6 (206–22).
New Testament: Acts 12.
Rabbinical traditions: mBik. 3:4; mSot. 7:8; ySot. 22a; bSot. 41b; Sifre-Dt. (157); bKet. 17a; cf. J. Derenbourg, *op. cit.*, pp. 205–19.
Coins: See n. 40 below.

Bibliography

Graetz, H., *Geschichte der Juden* III ([5]1905–6), pp. 317–59.
Saulcy, F. de, 'Étude chronologique de la vie et des monnaies des rois juifs Agrippa I et Agrippa II', Mém. Soc. Franç. de Num. et d'Arch. 3 (1869), pp. 26–56.
Sukenik, E., and Mayer, A. L., *The Third Wall of Jerusalem* (1930).
Krauss, S., 'Die jüdische Siedlung in Samaria (Sebaste)', MGWJ 75 (1931), pp. 191–9.
Swain, J. W., 'Gamaliel's Speech and Caligula's Statue', HThR 37 (1944), pp. 341–9.
Abel, F.-M., *Histoire de la Palestine* I (1952), pp. 448–55.
Meyshan, J., 'The Coinage of Agrippa the First', IEJ 4 (1954), pp. 186–200 = *Essays in Jewish Numismatics* (1968), pp. 105–19.
Kenyon, K. M., *Jerusalem* (1967), pp. 155–86.

See also the bibliographies above, in §§ 16 and 17.

On the Acts of the Apostles:

Loisy, A., *Les actes des apôtres* (1920).
Meyer, E., *Ursprung und Anfänge des Christentums* III (1923).
Jackson, Foakes, and Lake, Kirsopp, *The Beginnings of Christianity* I: *the Acts of the Apostles* I–V (1920–33).
Trocmé, E., *Le 'Livre des Actes' et l'histoire* (1957).
Menoud, P. H., *Les actes des apôtres* (1963).
Conzelmann, H., *Die Apostelgeschichte* (1965).
Haenchen, E., *Die Apostelgeschichte* (1965) = *The Acts of the Apostles* (1971).

I

When Agrippa I[1] ascended the throne of Herod the Great, he had already an eventful and adventurous career behind him. He was born

1. The New Testament (Acts 12) names him simply Herod. In Josephus and on the coins, however, he is always called Agrippa. An inscription from Athens (see below n. 41) reveals that his name was Iulius Agrippa, and from the *praenomen* of his son it is virtually certain that his father too had as his full Roman name, M. Iulius Agrippa. See PIR[2] I 131.

in 10 B.C.,[2] the son of Aristobulus, who was executed in 7 B.C., and Berenice a daughter of Salome and Costobar.[3] Shortly before the death of his grandfather, he was sent, as a boy scarcely six years old, to Rome to be educated. His mother Berenice was befriended there by Antonia, the widow of the elder Drusus, while he himself became attached to the younger Drusus, the son of the emperor Tiberius. The influence of Roman society seems not to have been entirely favourable. He became accustomed to unlimited luxury and extravagance, especially after the death of his mother. His means were soon exhausted and debts piled up. And when with the death of Drusus (A.D. 23) he also lost his support at court, he found himself obliged to leave Rome and return to Palestine.[4] He went to Malatha, a fortress in Idumaea,[5] and contemplated suicide. When his wife Cyprus heard of this, she wrote to Agrippa's sister, Herodias, who was by this time married to Antipas, and entreated her assistance. Herod Antipas was in this way induced to give his distressed brother-in-law at least sufficient to live on, and in addition he appointed him *agoranomos* (overseer of markets) in the capital city of Tiberias. But this new position in life did not last for long. At a banquet in Tyre the two brothers-in-law engaged in a quarrel, as a result of which Agrippa resigned his post at Tiberias and made his way to the Roman governor Flaccus in Antioch.[6] But there too his stay was of short duration. In a dispute that developed between the inhabitants of Sidon and Damascus, Agrippa took the side of the latter, apparently disinterestedly, but really in consequence of bribes he had accepted from them. When this came to the ears of Flaccus, he withdrew his friendship and Agrippa found himself once again deprived of all means of subsistence. He then resolved to try his fortune again in Rome. After raising a loan in Ptolemais with the assistance of a freedman of his mother Berenice, called Peter, and then in Anthedon barely evading capture by Capito, the procurator of Jamnia, who wished to apprehend him as a debtor of the emperor, he

2. As is evident from *Ant.* xix 8, 2 (350), according to which he was fifty-four years old when he died (A.D. 44).

3. *Ant.* xviii 5, 4 (130–42).

4. *Ant.* xviii 6, 1 (143–6). Wieseler, *Beweis des Glaubens* (1870), pp. 168 f., places the journey of Agrippa from Rome to Palestine in A.D. 29 or 30, which is more or less correct. At any rate, as will be shown, it did not take place until after the marriage of Herodias and Antipas.

5. *Μαλαθά* or *Μαλααθά* is also referred to several times in the *Onomasticon* of Eusebius (ed. Klostermann (1904), pp. 14, 88, 108). It lay 20+4 Roman miles south of Hebron, probably on the site of the modern Tell-el-Milh. See Robinson, *Palästina* III, pp. 184 f.; Guérin, *Judée* II, pp. 184–8; *The Survey of Western Palestine, Memoirs by Conder and Kitchener* III, pp. 404, 415 f. M. Avi-Yonah, *The Holy Land* (1966), p. 120.

6. *Ant.* xviii 6, 2 (147–50).

finally succeeded in obtaining large sums in Alexandria on the credit of his wife. He arrived in Italy in the spring of A.D. 36[7] and on the island of Capri[8] presented himself before Tiberius.[9] The emperor entrusted him with his grandson Tiberius Gemellus. In addition, he became closely associated with Gaius Caligula, the grandson of his patroness Antonia and later emperor. But even so he could not keep out of debt. In fact, to appease his old creditors he was obliged continually to borrow new and larger sums.[10] It was therefore understandable that he eagerly desired an improvement in his circumstances, but there seemed no prospect of this unless the friendly Caligula were to come to the throne in place of the aged Tiberius. Unwisely, he once openly expressed this wish to Caligula in the presence of his coachman Eutychus. When he later brought a charge of theft against Eutychus and had him brought before the city prefect, Piso,[11] Eutychus announced that he had an important secret to communicate to the emperor. At first Tiberius took no notice.[12] But when after some time a hearing was granted[13] and Tiberius learned what Agrippa had said, he had him immediately put in fetters and cast into prison, where he remained for six months until the emperor died (16 March A.D. 37).[14]

With the death of Tiberius and the accession of Caligula a period of good fortune began for Agrippa. Caligula scarcely waited for Tiberius's obsequies to be over before releasing his friend from prison and conferring on him the former tetrarchy of Philip and that of Lysanias, together with the title of king; to this gift the senate added the honorary rank of a praetor.[15] In place of his iron chains, Caligula gave him a gold chain of equal weight.[16] But Agrippa stayed on in Rome for a year and a half. It was not till the autumn of A.D. 38 that

7. *Ant.* xviii 5, 3 (126) ἐνιαυτῷ πρότερον ἢ τελευτῆσαι Τιβέριον.

8. Where Tiberius lived almost without interruption from A.D. 27 (Tacitus, *Ann.* iv, 67) until the time of his death.

9. *Ant.* xviii 6, 3 (151–60).

10. *Ant.* xviii 6, 4 (161–7).

11. The Piso referred to here, *Ant.* xviii 6, 5 (169), cannot have been the one who (according to Tacitus, *Ann.* vi, 10) died in A.D. 32 for he is still mentioned after Tiberius's death, *Ant.* xviii 6, 10 (235); cf. above, p. 261. In both passages Josephus calls him φύλαξ τῆς πόλεως. On other Greek designations of the *praefectus urbi*, see Mommsen, *Röm. Staatsrecht* II, 2, p. 981.

12. *Ant.* xviii 6, 5 (168–78).

13. *Ant.* xviii 6, 6 (179) χρόνου ἐγγενομένου.

14. *Ant.* xviii 6, 6–7 (179–204); *B.J.* ii 9, 5 (180).

15. Philo, *in Flaccum* 6 (40). Cf. above, p. 317. The title was conferred not by the emperor but by the senate, see Philo, *loc. cit.* βασιλέα καὶ φίλον Καίσαρος καὶ ὑπὸ τῆς Ῥωμαίων βουλῆς τετιμημένον στρατηγικαῖς τιμαῖς.

16. *Ant.* xviii 6, 10 (224–37); *B.J.* ii 9, 6 (181); Philo, *in Flaccum* 5 (25); Dio lix 8. From the inscription at El-Mushennef (OGIS 418) it appears that Agrippa's territory extended beyond the Hauran.

he returned to Palestine by way of Alexandria to set in order the affairs of his kingdom.[17]

Soon afterwards he obtained by imperial favour still further important increases of territory. An account has already been given (p. 352) of how Herod Antipas had lost his tetrarchy in A.D. 39 through his own indiscretion; Caligula bestowed this also on Agrippa, probably not before A.D. 40.

In the autumn of that year Agrippa was once more in Rome (or Puteoli), where he contrived by personal intercession to prevent Caligula, temporarily at least, from persisting in his project to have his statue set up in the Temple in Jerusalem (see above, p. 396). He then remained in Caligula's vicinity. He was also in Rome when his patron was murdered by Chaerea on 24 January A.D. 41, and contributed not a little to secure the succession of the weak Claudius to the imperial throne.[18] Needless to say, he was not a man to perform such services unrewarded. The new emperor not only confirmed him in his royal possessions but supplemented them with Judaea and Samaria, so that he now united under his rule the whole of his grandfather's kingdom. Besides this, he received consular rank. To ratify this grant, a solemn treaty was concluded at the Forum according to ancient custom, and the deed of gift was engraved on bronze tablets and placed in the Capitol.[19]

II

Agrippa's first act on his return to Palestine was characteristic of the spirit in which he governed his kingdom from then on. It was an act

17. *Ant.* xviii 6, 11 (238–9); Philo, *in Flaccum* 5 (25 f.). Cf. above, pp. 352 and 390.

18. *Ant.* xix 1–4 (1–273); *B.J.* ii 11 (204–22). On the events preceding Claudius's accession to the throne, see RE III, 2786 f.

19. *Ant.* xix 5, 1 (274–7); *B.J.* ii 11, 5 (215–16); Dio lx 8, 2–3. Josephus expresses himself so as to imply that the tetarchy of Lysanias was now re-conferred on Agrippa. But as he had already received it from Caligula, it can only be a question of confirming the gift. It is highly probable that Josephus found in his sources that, besides the whole of his grandather's kingdom, Agrippa, by the favour of Claudius, possessed in addition the tetrarchy of Lysanias. The conclusion of the treaty is represented on a coin the superscription of which is no longer completely legible but which mentions a συμμαχία of King Agrippa with the Roman Senate and people (σύνκλητος καὶ δῆμος Ῥωμαίων). See Madden, *Coins of the Jews* (1881), p. 139 f.; so also Meyshan, *op. cit.*, p. 191 (see Pl. 17, no. 14). That Claudius liked such ancient treaties is indicated by Suet. *Div. Claudius*, 25 'Cum regibus foedus in foro icit porca caesa ac vetere fetialium praefatione adhibita'. A home-coming of Agrippa I or II (possibly the present return of Agrippa I) is referred to in the inscription of El Mushennef (OGIS 418):

Ὑπὲρ σωτηρίας κυρίου βασιλέως Ἀγρίππα καὶ ἐπανόδου κα-
τ' εὐχὴν Διὸς καὶ πατρί(κ)οῦ(?) . . . .
. . . . . ὁμονοίας τὸν οἶκον ᾠκοδόμ[ησεν].

of piety. He hung the gold chain presented to him by Caligula on his liberation from prison 'within the limits of the Temple, over the treasury, that it might be a memorial of his earlier misfortune and a witness to the turn of events in his favour; and that it might serve to demonstrate how the greatest are liable to fall, and how God can raise up the fallen'.[20] At the same time he brought a thank-offering, 'inasmuch as he disregarded no precept of the law', and defrayed the costs of a large number of Nazirites entailed by the fulfilment of their vow.[21]

It was with acts such as these that the one-time adventurer began his new reign, and he maintained the same tone throughout his remaining three years of life and rule. They were golden days again for Pharisaism, a revival of the age of Alexandra, which is why Josephus and the Talmud are unanimous in his praise. 'It was his pleasure to reside continually in Jerusalem, and he meticulously observed the precepts of his fathers. He neglected no rite of purification and not a day passed without its appointed sacrifice.' Thus eulogizes Josephus;[22] and the Mishnah relates that he brought the first fruits to the Temple with his own hands like any other Israelite.[23] He represented the claims of Judaism abroad also. When on one occasion a gang of young Greeks in the Phoenician city of Dora set up a statue of the emperor in the Jewish synagogue, he used his influence with the governor of Syria, P. Petronius, so that not only were such outrages strictly forbidden but the culprits also called to account.[24] And when he betrothed his daughter Drusilla to Epiphanes, the son of King Antiochus

20. *Ant.* xix 6, 1 (294). It is unlikely that there is any connexion between these, and the gold chains which, according to mMid. 3:8 hung on the roof-beam of the temple Porch (against Derenbourg, *op. cit.*, p. 209).

21. *Ant.* xix 6, 1 (294).

22. *Ant.* xix 7, 3 (331) *ἡδεῖα γοῦν αὐτῷ δίαιτα καὶ συνεχὴς ἐν τοῖς Ἱεροσολύμοις ἦν, καὶ τὰ πάτρια καθαρῶς ἐτήρει. διὰ πάσης γοῦν αὐτὸν ἦγεν ἁγνείας, οὐδὲ ἡμέρα τις παρώδευεν αὐτῷ τῆς νομίμης χηρεύουσα θυσίας.* In place of *τῆς νομίμης* (so the *Epitome*, supported by *Vet. Lat.: hostiis viduata sollemnibus*) our three manuscripts have *τὰ νόμιμα*, likewise the older editions. Hudson, Havercamp, Oberthür read *τῆς νομίμης*; Dindorf and Bekker delete it (a possibility already suggested by Hudson, since *τὰ νόμιμα* occurs immediately afterwards); Niese reads *τὰ νόμιμα*, and Naber *τῆς νομίμης*.

23. mBik. 3:4: 'When they (i.e. the procession with the first-fruits of the fields) reached the Temple mount, even King Agrippa himself took his basket on his shoulder and entered as far as the Temple Court'. Here, as in other rabbinic passages, it is not quite certain whether Agrippa I or II is meant. On ceremonial ritual at the presentation of the first-fruits, see, in addition to mBik. 3:1–9, Philo's tract *de spec. leg.* ii 29 (162–75), and generally the literature referred to in vol. II, § 24.

24. *Ant.* xix 6, 3 (300–11).

of Commagene, he made him promise to submit to circumcision.[25] Because of his piety, the people led by the Pharisees were completely satisfied with him. This was strikingly demonstrated when, at the Feast of Tabernacles in A.D. 41, he read the Book of Deuteronomy according to ancient custom.[26] When he came to the passage, 'You may not put a foreigner over you, who is not your brother' (Dt. 17:15), he burst into tears because he felt that the reference was to himself. But the people cried out, 'Grieve not, Agrippa. You are our brother! You are our brother!'[27]

His meticulous observance of the Mosaic law does not, however, seem to have been the sole reason for his popularity. He evidently possessed a certain natural amiability. Josephus in any case ascribes to him an agreeable disposition and unbounded generosity.[28] That he was grateful for services rendered to him is indicated by his appointment of Silas, a faithful companion of his earlier adventures, to the supreme command of his troops.[29] He was to have unpleasant experiences with this Silas, who frequently reminded him in a tactless manner of his earlier misery and the services he had given. To be rid of the troublesome chatterbox, Agrippa had to send him to prison. However, it was fresh proof of his goodheartedness that on the next celebration of his birthday, he had the prisoner called so that he could share in the joys of the banquet; but in vain, for Silas wanted no favours and therefore was obliged to remain in jail.[30] On another occasion Agrippa showed his clemency towards Simon the Pharisee,[31] who in the king's

25. *Ant.* xx 7, 1 (139). Epiphanes afterwards refused to fulfil his promise and the marriage did not take place.

26. At the close of each sabbatical year, i.e. at the beginning of the 8th year, Deuteronomy was to be read at the Feast of Tabernacles (Dt. 31: 10 ff.; mSot. 7:8). Since A.D. 68/69 was a sabbatical year (cf. above, p. 19), A.D. 40/41 must also have been such; indeed it would be the only one occurring during Agrippa's reign. Accordingly, this incident took place in A.D. 41.

27. mSot. 7:8. The people's declaration can be justified even on the basis of strictly Pharisaic principles, for when Edomites (Idumaeans) went over to Judaism, their descendants of the third generation became full citizens of the Israelite commonwealth (Dt. 23, 7–8). M. Brann, MGWJ (1870), pp. 541–8, argued that this refers to Agrippa II. But the majority of scholars (see the list given by Brann, *ibid.*, p. 541) prefer Agrippa I, on the ground that a definite inclination to favour the Pharisees is more clearly evident in the case of Agrippa I than in that of his son. Cf. Abel, *Histoire* I, p. 449. For Agrippa II, cf. A. Büchler, *Die Priester und der Cultus im letzten Jahrzehnt des jerusalemischen Tempels* (1895), pp. 14 f.

28. *Ant.* xix 7, 3 (330) πραΰς δὸ τρόπος Ἀγρίππᾳ, καὶ πρὸς πάντας τὸ εὐεργετικὸν ὅμοιον.

29. *Ant.* xix 6, 3 (299).

30. *Ant.* xix 7, 1 (317–25).

31. Z. Frankel, *Darkhe ha-Mishnah* (1859), pp. 58–9, regarded him as identical with Simon, the son of Hillel and father of Gamaliel I. But the existence of this Simon is questionable (see vol. II, § 25). Besides, the chronology hardly fits if Gamaliel I was already head of the party before the time of Agrippa (Acts 5:34).

absence had called a public meeting in Jerusalem and charged him with transgressing the law. Agrippa heard of this while he was at Caesarea, sent for Simon, and making him sit beside him in the theatre, asked him quietly and mildly: 'Tell me, what is happening here that is unlawful?' Overcome with shame, the learned teacher could give no answer and was dismissed by the king with presents.[32]

With a Jewish national policy went a loosening of dependence on Rome, and here, also, Agrippa made at least two somewhat timid attempts. To strengthen the fortifications of Jerusalem, he began to build to the north of the city a strong new wall which, in Josephus's opinion, would have made the city impregnable if the project had been completed. But unfortunately this was not possible because the emperor, at the instigation of Marsus, the governor of Syria, objected to it.[33] Of even greater significance for Rome was the conference of kings convened by Agrippa at Tiberias. No fewer than five Roman client kings responded to the invitation: Antiochus of Commagene, Sampsigeramus of Emesa, Cotys of Lesser Armenia, Polemon of Pontus and Herod of Chalcis. But this enterprise was also broken up by Marsus. The governor of Syria himself appeared at Tiberias and advised the other guests to return home immediately.[34]

Finally, it was a necessary consequence of his internal policy that the otherwise good-natured king became an opponent of the young Christian community. It is reported that the apostle James, the son of Zebedee, was put to death by him, and that Peter escaped his

[*Text continues on page* 451

32. *Ant.* xix 7, 4 (332–4).

33. *Ant.* xix 7, 2 (326–7); *B.J.* ii 11, 6 (218–22); v 4, 2 (147–55); cf. tSanh. 3:4; bSheb. 16a; see Derenbourg, *op. cit.*, pp. 218 f.; A. Neubauer, *La géographie du Talmud* (1868), p. 138. Agrippa seems to have obtained the emperor's original indulgence over the building of the wall by bribing his counsellors; cf. Tacitus, *Hist.* v 12 'per avaritiam Claudianorum temporum empto iure muniendi struxere muros in pace tamquam ad bellum'. On the much-debated problem of the 'third wall'. Jos. *B.J.* v 4, 2 (147), see Vincent and Stève, *Jérusalem de l'Ancien Testament* (1954), pp. 114–45; for a recent survey, including the results of excavations showing also the considerable southern extension of the city, and construction of a wall there, see K. M. Kenyon, *Jerusalem* (1967), pp. 155–86. She argues that Herod Agrippa's third wall lies under the present North Wall of the Old City. But, for a contrary view, see M. Avi-Yonah, 'The Third and Second Walls of Jerusalem', IEJ 18 (1968), pp. 98–125.

34. *Ant.* xix 8, 1 (338–42). The five kings named are all known from other evidence.

(1) On the dynasty of Commagene, see Magie, *Roman Rule*, pp. 1239–40. In A.D. 17 Commagene was incorporated into the Roman province of Syria (Tacitus, *Ann.* ii 42, 56); in A.D. 38 Caligula bestowed it on Antiochus IV (Dio lix 8, 2), who was later deposed by Caligula but reinstated by Claudius in A.D. 41, Dio lx 8, 1; Jos. *Ant.* xix 5, 1 (276), and then reigned until A.D. 72. He is mentioned in Tacitus, *Ann.* xii 55; xiii 7, 37; xiv 26. According to Tacitus, *Hist.* ii 81, he was

'vetustis opibus ingens et inservientium regum ditissimus'. For the Jewish war under Nero, Vespasian and Titus, he repeatedly furnished auxiliary troops, Jos. *B.J.* ii 18, 9 (500); iii 4, 2 (68); v 11, 3 (460). The story of his deposition is related in detail by Josephus, *B.J.* vii 7, 1–3 (219–43). Through the betrothal of his son Antiochus Epiphanes to Drusilla, the daughter of King Agrippa, ties of kinship would have been formed between both kings, *Ant.* xix 9, 1 (355); but the marriage did not take place because the Commagenian prince refused to submit to circumcision, *Ant.* xx 7, 1 (139). For full details on Antiochus IV (C. Iulius Antiochus Epiphanes) see PIR² I 149.

(2) On the dynasty of Emesa, see Marquardt, *Römische Staatsverwaltung* I (1881), pp. 403 f. The earliest attested Sampsigeramus comes from the time of Pompey and Caesar, RE s.v. 'Sampsigeramus' (1). Under Augustus the dynasty continued, with varying fortunes (G. W. Bowersock, *Augustus and the Greek World* (1965), p. 47), and the Iamblichus restored by Augustus in 20 B.C. was eventually succeeded by the Sampsigeramus mentioned in the present passage, *Ant.* xix 8, 1 (338), whose daughter Iotape married Aristobulus, the brother of King Agrippa, *Ant.* xviii 5, 4 (135). The earliest mention of him is a Palmyrene inscription relating to Germanicus, so A.D. 17–19; Syria 12 (1931), p. 319; 13 (1932), pp. 266 ff. He is also referred to in the Roman inscription of a freedman, CIL VI 35556a=AE 1900 134 *C. Iulio regis Samsicerami l(iberto) Glaco*; cf. RE s.v. 'Sampsigeramus' (2). His successor was Azizus, who married Drusilla, the daughter of Agrippa, *Ant.* xx 7, 1 (139). This man (Azizus) was succeeded in A.D. 54 by his brother (C. Iulius) Soaemus, *Ant.* xx 8, 4 (158), who repeatedly supplied the Romans with auxiliary troops in the years A.D. 66–72, Jos. *B.J.* ii 18, 9 (501); iii 4, 2 (68); Tacitus, *Hist.* ii, 81; Jos. *B.J.* vii 7, 1 (226). See ILS 8958=IGLS 2760 (Baalbek) and PIR² I 582. The name Sampsigeramus (*Σαμσιγέραμος*) still occurs on an inscription from A.D. 78/79 found at the place itself (OGIS 604=IGR III 1023=IGLS 2212) and also on other inscriptions from the area into the second century, see IGLS 2216–7, 2362, 2385, 2707. The (C. Iulius) Sampsigeramus of A.D. 78/9 seems already to indicate the end of the regal status of the dynasty (cf. com. to IGLS 2217). The name Sampsigeramus=Aramaic שמשגרם; see M. de Vogüé, *Syrie Centrale, Inscriptions*, p. 54 (n. 75).

(3) On Cotys of Lesser Armenia, see Marquardt, *op. cit.* I, p. 369; PIR² C 1555. He was a brother of King Polemon II of Pontus (below) and received his kingdom at the same time through the favour of Caligula in A.D. 38; cf. the inscription from Cyzicus, Syll.³ 798 and IGR IV 147 (see below) and Dio lix 12, 2. Tacitus mentions him in connexion with A.D. 47 (*Ann.* xi 9). In A.D. 54 Lesser Armenia was bestowed by Nero on Aristobulus, the son of Herod of Chalcis (see below, Appendix I).

(4) The dynasty of the kings of Pontus in Roman times goes back to the rhetor Zeno of Laodicea, who assisted the Roman cause at the time of the invasion of the Parthians and of Labienus (Strabo, 660). Apparently, it was out of gratitude for this service that his son Polemon was made king by Antonius (Strabo, 578). He received first of all part of Cilicia (App., *BC* v 75/319); a few years later the kingdom of Pontus (Dio xlix 25, 4); in 33 B.C. Lesser Armenia also (Dio xlix 33, 1–2; 44, 3). Under Augustus he was confirmed as king of Pontus (Dio liii 25, 1), and in 14 B.C. received the Bosporus too (Dio liv 24, 5–6; see PIR¹ P 405; RE s.v. 'Polemon' (2); Bowersock, *op. cit.*, pp. 51, 53). When he died about 8 B.C., his wife Pythodoris (see RE s.v. 'Pythodoris' (1)) succeeded him in the government. From Strabo 555–6 and 649 and OGIS 377, it is now clear that she came from a distinguished family in Tralles, see Bowersock, *op. cit.*, p. 8. The further genealogy of the family is revealed by two inscriptions from Cyzicus, Syll.³ 798 and IGR IV 147.

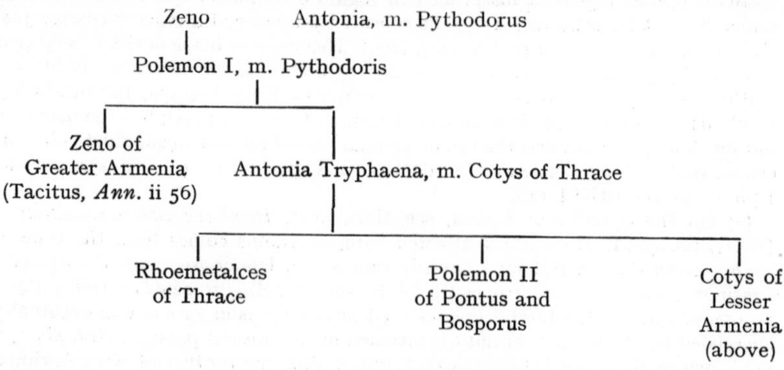

Accordingly, Polemon II was not, as Dio lix 12, asserts, the son, but the grandson of Polemon I, and Tryphaena was not, as was earlier supposed on the basis of the coins, his wife, but his mother (see PIR² A 900); she is mentioned—not by name—in Strabo 556; in the *Acta Pauli et Theclae* 36 a Queen Tryphaena, a relative of the emperor, is referred to. On Polemon II, see RE s.v. 'Polemon' (3); D. Magie, *Roman Rule in Asia Minor* (1950), ch. 21, n. 53, and ch. 23, n. 26; on the coins, *BMC Pontus*, p. 46; Head, *HN*², p. 503. According to the second inscription on the monument at Cyzicus, it was Caligula who installed the three sons of Antonia Tryphaena in their father's kingdoms. Since according to the coins A.D. 54 is the 17th year of Polemon II, he became king in A.D. 38; so Dio lix 12, 2. In place of the Bosporus (while retaining Pontus) he received in A.D. 41 part of Cilicia (Dio lx 8, 2; cf. Jos. *Ant.* xx 7, 3 (145), *Κιλικίας βασιλεύς*). In A.D. 60 Nero gave him also a part of Lesser Armenia (Tacitus, *Ann.* xiv 26). Soon afterwards, in A.D. 64, the kingdom of Pontus *concedente Polemone* became a Roman province (Suet. *Nero*, 18; cf. Tac. *Hist.* iii 47; on the date see D. Magie, *op. cit.*, pp. 1417–18). However, the designation *Πόντος Πολεμωνιακός* persisted into the middle Byzantine period: cf. Ptolemy, v 6, 4 and 10; CIL III 291 = 6818 = ILS 1017 (here *Pontus Ptolemonianus*); Hierocles, *Synecdemus*, ed. Burckhardt (1893), p. 34; the *Notitiae episcopatuum* in Gelzer, *AAM* XXI. 3 (1900), pp. 539, 554, 569, 585. The conclusion often drawn from Tacitus, *Hist.* iii 47, that Polemon was already dead in A.D. 69 is not proved. At all events, he was still alive in the time of Galba, and ruled in a part of Cilicia: see *BMC Cilicia*, pp. xxix–xxx; Head, *HN*², p. 227. His marriage with Berenice, the daughter of Agrippa I, lasted only a short time. She herself persuaded him to marry her when she had been a widow for a long time, her second husband, Herod of Chalcis, having died in A.D. 48. Polemon agreed to the marriage mainly for the sake of her wealth, and he even submitted to circumcision. But when after a short time Berenice left him, he relinquished Jewish practices, *Ant.* xx 7, 3 (146). Since Josephus designates him on the occasion of this marriage merely as *Κιλικίας βασιλεύς*, it must have taken place after A.D. 63, when Polemon no longer possessed the kingdom of Pontus. A coin shows that he re-married, to a woman named Iulia Mamaea, H. Seyrig, RN 11 (1969), pp. 45–7. A descendant of his is possibly the M. Antonius Polemon, known from coins as dynast of Olbe in Cilicia (*δυνάστης Ὀλβέων*; see PIR² A 864), whom many place in the time of the triumvir M. Antonius; see Marquardt, *op. cit.* I, pp. 385 f.; V. Gardthausen, *Augustus und seine Zeit* II 1, pp. 124 f.; J. Raillard, Wiener Numismat. Zeitschr. 27 (1895), pp. 23–26; (a few of the above identify him with King Polemon I of Pontus); against the theory,

hands only by a miracle.[35] Moreover, his pro-Jewish leanings excited enmity in certain Gentile quarters, as is shown by the unconcealed pleasure with which the Sebastenes and Caesareans received the news of his death.[36]

In view of his earlier life, the sincerity of Agrippa's devotion to Judaism has been questioned, and in this connexion it is pointed out that his Jewish piety was maintained only within the borders of Palestine. When abroad he was, like his grandfather, a generous patron of Greek culture. At Berytus, for example, he built at his own expense a splendid theatre, an amphitheatre, baths and porticoes. When they were opened, games of all sorts were performed, among them a gladiatorial combat in the amphitheatre at which 1400 criminals were compelled to slaughter one another.[37] He also sponsored games in Caesarea.[38] Statues of his daughters were even erected there.[39] Of the coins minted during his reign only those stamped in Jerusalem bear no effigy, whereas among those produced in other cities, some bear the image of Agrippa and others that of the emperor.[40] His official title is the same as that of other Roman vassal kings of the time. An

---

see Mommsen, *Ephemeris Epigr.*, 1, p. 275. Earlier, this M. Antonius Polemon was identified with the son of Polemon I mentioned (without a name) by Strabo, p. 556 (so G. F. Hill, Num. Chron. 19 (1899), pp. 181–207, and in *BMC Cilicia*, pp. lii ff., 119 ff.). See Magie, *Roman Rule*, ch. 23, n. 26.

(5) On Herod of Chalcis, brother of Agrippa I, see below, Appendix I.

35. Acts 12:1–19.

36. *Ant.* xix 9, 1 (356).

37. *Ant.* xix 7, 5 (335–7). The favour shown to Berytus is due to the fact that it was a Roman colony. Cf. above, p. 323.

38. *Ant.* xix 8, 2 (343).

39. *Ant.* xix 9, 1 (357).

40. On the coins of Agrippa in general, cf. F. W. Madden, *History of Jewish Coinage*, pp. 103–111; F. de Saulcy, 'Étude chronologique de la vie et des monnaies des rois juifs Agrippa I et Agrippa II', 1869 (cf. above, p. 442); Madden, Numismatic Chronicle (1875), pp. 58–80; Madden, *Coins of the Jews* (1881), pp. 129–39; *BMC Palestine*, pp. xcvii–111; A. Reifenberg, *Ancient Jewish Coins* ([2]1947), pp. 20–3; 46–7; J. Meyshan, 'The Coinage of Agrippa I', IEJ 4 (1954), pp. 186–200; Y. Meshorer, *Jewish Coins of the Second Temple Period* (1967), pp. 78–80, 138–41. Those of most frequent occurrence among the coins of Agrippa are imageless, being decorated with the emblem of a canopy—see Meyshan, BIES 22 (1958), pp. 157–60; most have the year number VI and the simple inscription *ΒΑΣΙΛΕΩΣ ΑΓΡΙΠΠΑ*. Besides these coins properly attributed to Agrippa, there were also minted during his reign: (1) In Caesarea Maritima (*Καισαρία ἡ πρὸς τῷ Σεβαστῷ λίμενι*) coins with the image of Agrippa and the superscription *Βασιλεὺς μέγας Ἀγρίππας φιλόκαισαρ*. (2) In Caesarea Panias, coins with the image of Caligula and the (more or less defective) name of the emperor, or without his name; (3) In Tiberias, coins with the image of Claudius, and on the reverse side: *επι βασιλε. Αγριπ. Τιβεριεων* (omitted by Meshorer, *loc. cit.*). And besides these we have (4) the coins referred to above (note 19) commemorating the treaty between Agrippa and the Roman people.

inscription shows that his family had taken the Roman *nomen* 'Iulius';[41] and another designates him as βασιλεὺς μέγας φιλόκαισαρ εὐσεβὴς καὶ φιλορώμαιος.[42] So perhaps Agrippa's concessions to Pharisaism were purely matters of policy, in which case he was truly a descendant of Herod the Great. On the other hand, it is arguable that he was seriously concerned to promote peace and saw that the explosive situation within his bicultural kingdom called for tact, as well as for a measure of compromise.

The country did not enjoy his rule for long. After a reign of scarcely more than three years (reckoned from A.D. 41) he died suddenly at Caesarea in A.D. 44.[43] The two extant accounts of his death, Acts 12: 19–

41. On the inscription at Athens, OGIS 428=IG II/III² 3449, his daughter Berenice is called Ἰουλία Βερενείκη βασίλισσα μεγάλη, Ἰουλίου Ἀγρίππα βασιλέως θυγατήρ. There is also evidence that other members of the Herodian family bore the gentilician name of the Iulii: Agrippa II is so named in OGIS 421=IGR III 1136. A son-in-law of Agrippa I is called Ἰούλιος Ἀρχέλαος, Jos. *Ant.* xix 9, 1 (355); *c.Ap.* i 9 (51). Possibly the Γάϊος Ἰούλιος βασιλέως Ἀλεξάνδρου υἱὸς Ἀγρίππας ταμίας καὶ ἀντιστράτηγος τῆς Ἀσίας mentioned in an inscription at Ephesus (OGIS 429=ILS 8823; see PIR² I 130) descended from the Herodian family; presumably the same βασιλεὺς Ἀλέξανδρος (PIR² A 500) is also referred to as consular, ὑπατικός, and as a relative of a prominent Ancyran, Iulius Severus, on an inscription of Ancyra from the time of Trajan (OGIS 544=IGR III 173; cf. PIR² I 573). On the frequent occurrence of the gentilician name of the Iulii among the vassal kings of the empire, cf. E. Renan, *Mission de Phénicie*, p. 310; O. Bohn, *Qua condicione juris reges socii populi Romani fuerint* (1877), pp. 25 f.

42. The most complete form of the titles of Agrippa I and II is given in the interesting inscription found by Waddington at Si'a (close to Kanawat, at the western foot of Hauran). See Le Bas et Waddington, *Inscriptions Grecques et Latines* III, n. 2365=OGIS 419. When W. Ewing saw the inscription later, it was already mutilated; cf. PEFQSt 1895, p. 272. According to Waddington it runs: Ἐπὶ βασιλέως μεγάλου Ἀγρίππα φιλοκαίσαρος εὐσεβοῦς καὶ φιλορωμα[ί]ου, τοῦ ἐκ βασιλέως μεγάλου Ἀγρίππα φιλοκαίσαρος εὐσεβοῦς καὶ [φι]λορωμαίου, Ἀφαρεὺς ἀπελεύθερος καὶ Ἀγρίππας υἱὸς ἀνέθηκαν. The titles φιλόκαισαρ and φιλορώμαιος occur very frequently during that period; cf. OGIS index s.v. Most precisely and completely in accordance with the titles of the two Agrippas are those of the kings of the Bosporus, from the beginning of the 2nd to the end of the 3rd century A.D. See the collection in Latyschev, *Inscriptiones antiquae orae septentrionalis Ponti Euxini graecae et latinae* II (1890), pp. xlvi–lii; cf. V. V. Struve, *Korpus Bosporshich Nadpic'e* (1965), p. 845. On the meaning of the titles, see A. v. Gutschmid, *Kleine Schriften* IV, pp. 116–19. Βασιλεὺς μέγας indicates that its bearer held more than one kingdom; φιλόκαισαρ and φιλορώμαιος are primarily passive: one to whom Caesar and the Roman people are friendly (cf. Jos. *Ant.* xix 5, 3 (288): Ἀγρίππα καὶ Ἡρῴδου τῶν φιλτάτων μοι, cf. J. Reinach, RETh. 31 (1895), p. 174; but naturally the friendship is reciprocal.

43. The date of Agrippa's death is dealt with in detail by K. Wieseler, *Chronologie des apostol. Zeitalters*, pp. 129–36. Agrippa died after reigning three full years over all Palestine, *Ant.* xix 8, 2 (343) τρίτον δὲ ἔτος αὐτῷ βασιλεύοντι τῆς ὅλης Ἰουδαίας πεπλήρωτο, consequently in A.D. 44, soon after the feast of the Passover (Acts 12:3–5), while the games in honour of the emperor were taking place at Caesarea (εἰς τὴν Καίσαρος τιμὴν ὑπὲρ τῆς ἐκείνου σωτηρίας—Jos. *loc. cit.*). By these

23 and Jos. *Ant.* xix, 8, 2 (343–52), though they vary in detail, agree on the principal points.[44] The Acts of the Apostles relates that in Caesarea, seated on the throne (βῆμα) and dressed in his royal robes, he delivered an oration to the ambassadors representing the citizens of Tyre and Sidon, with whom (it is not known why) he was displeased. While he was speaking, the people shouted, 'That is the voice of a god, and not of a man!' Immediately an angel of the Lord struck him down because he did not give the honour to God; and he was eaten by worms and gave up the ghost. According to Josephus, he was in Caesarea when the festive games in honour of the emperor were being celebrated. On the second day he appeared in the amphitheatre wearing a robe made entirely of silver. When it sparkled in the sunshine, flatterers cried out to him, and called him God (θεὸν προσαγορεύοντες) and begged him for mercy. The king was pleased by the flattery. Soon afterwards he saw an owl perched on a rope, and recalled that a German prisoner had predicted that it would be an omen of death.[45] He realised that his hour had come and at that moment felt the severest abdominal pains. He had to be carried to his house and within five days was a corpse. Thus the main points—Caesarea as the scene of the incident, the splendid robe, the flattering shout, the sudden death—are common to both narratives, although the details have become somewhat diversified in the course of transmission.

Agrippa was survived by three daughters (Berenice, Mariamme and Drusilla) and a seventeen-year-old son, also named Agrippa. The emperor Claudius was disposed to give him his father's kingdom, but

---

games Wieseler understood the regular athletic contests at Caesarea established by Herod the Great and celebrated every four years; on the hypothesis that they began on 1st August, he places the death of Agrippa on the 6th of that month. But the supposition that the games began on 1st August is quite arbitrary; furthermore, Josephus shows plainly (ὑπὲρ τῆς ἐκείνου σωτηρίας) that it was not a question of regular games but of special ones, namely those celebrated in honour of Claudius's return from Britain in the spring of A.D. 44 (Dio lx 23, 4–5; RE III, 2797), and no doubt subsequently in the provinces. The regular games of Caesarea, celebrated every four years (not every five years, see above, p. 309), would not fall in A.D. 44, but in A.D. 43, since, according to Jos. *Ant.* xvi 5, 1 (136–41), they were instituted in the 28th year of Herod (10 B.C.). Cf., however, Jackson and Lake, *op. cit.*, pp. 446–52.

44. There is agreement in all essential points in Eusebius, *HE* II, 10, although he changes the owl of Josephus into an angel; cf. H. Gerlach, *Zeitschr. f. luth. Theol.* (1869), pp. 57–62; M. Krenkel, *Josephus and Lucas* (1894), pp. 203 ff. (endeavours in spite of the divergences to prove the dependence of Luke on Josephus). On the transformation of the owl into an angel, see F. A. Heinichen, *Eusebii Scripta Historica* III, pp. 654–56.

45. *Ant.* xviii 6, 7 (200). On the owl as a bird of evil omen, see Pliny, *NH* x 12/34–35.

his advisers reminded him of the risk involved in such a move. And thus the whole of Palestine, as earlier Judaea and Samaria, was taken over as Roman territory, to be administered by a procurator under the supervision of the governor of Syria.[46] Meanwhile, the young Agrippa continued to live in retirement.

46. *Ant.* xix 9, 1–2 (354–66); *B.J.* ii 11, 6 (220). According to Bormann, *De Syriae provinciae Romanae partibus capita nonnulla* (1865), pp. 3–5, Palestine was administered from A.D. 44 to 49 by a procurator independent of the legate of Syria; and in A.D. 49 the country was attached to the province of Syria, as is shown by Tacitus, *Ann.* xii 23, where his narrative of the events of A.D. 49 begins with the words: 'Ituraei et Iudaei defunctis regibus, Sohaemo atque Agrippa, provinciae Suriae additi'. But it is evident that the narrative in question is very schematic and brings together matters chronologically widely separated; hence Bormann's conclusion has no sound basis. In A.D. 44 or 45, directly after the death of Agrippa I, the legate of Syria, Cassius Longinus, did intervene in the affairs of Judaea. The independence of the procurator of Judaea was thus no greater then than it was later, and subsequently no less than it was earlier. Cf. above, p. 360, and Marquardt, *Römische Staatsverwaltung* I ([2]1881), p. 411, n. 11.

§ 19. THE ROMAN PROCURATORS A.D. 44–66

Sources

Josephus, *Ant.* xx 1 (1–16); 5–11 (97–258); *B.J.* ii 11–14 (204–308).
Tacitus, *Ann.* xv 44; *Hist.* v 9–10.

Bibliography

Derenbourg, J., *Essai sur l'histoire et la géographie de la Palestine* (1867), pp. 220–59.
Graetz, H., *Geschichte der Juden* III (⁵1905–6), pp. 359–63, 414–53.
Jackson, Foakes and Lake, Kirsopp, *The Beginnings of Christianity* I: *The Acts of the Apostles* I–V (1920–33).
Meyer, E., *Ursprung und Anfänge des Christentums* III (1923), pp. 42–54.
Abel, F.-M., *Histoire de la Palestine* I (1952), pp. 455–79.
Stern, M. 'The Description of Palestine by Pliny the Elder and the Administrative Division of Judea, at the End of the Period of the Second Temple', Tarbiz 37 (1967–8), pp. 215–29 (in Hebrew with an English summary).

It might be thought, from the record of the Roman procurators to whom, from now on, public affairs in Palestine were entrusted, that they all, as if by secret arrangement, systematically and deliberately set out to drive the people to revolt. Even the best of them—to say nothing of the others who totally disregarded every law—had no idea that a nation like the Jews required above all consideration for their religious customs. Instead of showing moderation and indulgence, they severely clamped down on any manifestation of the people's national character. The least guilty in this respect were the first two procurators, who by refraining from any interference with ancestral customs, kept the nation at peace'.[1]

1. The first procurator whom Claudius sent to Palestine was Cuspius Fadus (A.D. 44–?46).[2] He had the opportunity as soon as he assumed office to show his determination to maintain order. When he arrived in Palestine, the inhabitants of Peraea were in a state of open war with the citizens of Philadelphia.[3] The conflict had arisen over disputes about the boundaries of their respective territories. As the Peraeans were at fault, Fadus had one of the three ringleaders executed and the other two banished from the country. But for all his love of justice, Fadus had no understanding of the peculiar characteristics of the Jewish

1. *B.J.* ii 11, 6 (220).
2. *B.J.* ii 11, 6 (220); *Ant.* xix 9, 2 (363).
3. *Ant.* xx 1, 1 (2).

people, as was proved by his demand that the vestments of the High Priest, which in earlier times (A.D. 6–36) had been kept in Roman custody but had then been released by Vitellius (see above, p. 388), should again be committed to the Romans for safe keeping.[4] Thus the feelings of the people, so sensitive in matters of this sort, were unnecessarily outraged by petty vexations. Fortunately, Fadus and the governor of Syria, Cassius Longinus, who had gone to Jerusalem in connexion with this important affair, were at least considerate enough to allow a Jewish delegation to proceed to Rome. There through the mediation of the younger Agrippa, a directive was obtained from Claudius that in the affair of the vestments matters should remain as they were.[5]

A later conflict was more serious and led to open war and bloodshed. A self-styled prophet called Theudas gathered a large crowd of followers around him and marched down to the Jordan, asserting that at his command the waters would part and let them pass across to the other bank. This was probably only to serve as proof of his divine mission; the main issue, namely the contest with Rome, would follow. Fadus in any case became suspicious. He sent a detachment of cavalry against Theudas, which attacked him by surprise, killed or captured some of his followers, and captured and subsequently beheaded Theudas himself. His head was carried to Jerusalem as a military trophy.[6]

2. Fadus's successor was Tiberius Iulius Alexander (A.D. ? 46–48), a scion of one of the most illustrious Jewish families of Alexandria, the

4. *Ant.* xx 1, 1 (6).

5. *Ant.* xx 1, 1–2 (7–14); cf. xv 11, 4 (403–8). The letter of Claudius to the city authorities of Jerusalem, in which the emperor communicated his decision to them, is dated 28 June, A.D. 45, *Claud. tribunic. potest. V*, during the consulship of Rufus and Pompeius Silvanus (on these *consules suffecti*, see A. Degrassi, *I Fasti Consolari* (1952), pp. 12–13).

6. *Ant.* xx 5, 1 (97–9) = Eusebius, *HE* II 11. The name *Θευδᾶς* also occurs elsewhere (CIG 2684, 3563, 3920, 5698; BCH 11 (1887), pp. 213, 214, 215; W. Bauer, *Griechisch-Deutsches Wörterbuch zu den Schriften des N.T.*, *s.v.*). In rabbinical writings we find the form תודוס; however, the best MSS., such as the Cambridge MS. and Codex de Rossi 138, spell the name of the physician mentioned in mBekh, 4:4 תודרוס i.e. *Θεόδωρος*. Cf. H. L. Strack, P. Billerbeck, *Kommentar zum Neuen Testament aus Talmud und Midrasch* II (1924), p. 639. Some writers think that *Θευδᾶς* represents the short form of a name compounded with *θεός* and is of Greek origin; others suggest a Semitic etymology deriving the word from the root עד (nominal form תעודה). See JE XII, p. 140; Foakes Jackson, Kirsopp Lake, *The Beginnings of Christianity* I: *Acts* IV, *ad loc.*; J. W. Swain, HThR 37 (1944), pp. 341–9; P. Winter, EvTh 17 (1957), pp. 398 f.; S. B. Hoenig, IDB IV, p. 629. A similar-sounding name, *Θευδιών*, occurs in Josephus, *Ant.* xvii 4, 2 (70, 73), xx 1, 2 (14); *B.J.* i 30, 5 (592)

Our rebel chief Theudas is also mentioned in Acts 5:36, in a speech attributed to Gamaliel I and apparently delivered long before the actual appearance of Theudas; indeed, in the speech itself, his appearance is mentioned as preceding that of Judas of Galilee (A.D. 6). A few authors have assumed the existence of

son of the alabarch Alexander and a nephew of Philo the philosopher.[7] He had abandoned the religion of his fathers and taken service under the Romans. During the period of his government Palestine was afflicted by a severe famine.[8] The one fact of importance recorded of him is that he ordered James and Simon, the sons of Judas the Galilean, to be crucified—presumably because they followed in their father's footsteps.[9]

---

two different rebels named Theudas, but such an assumption is not justified in view of the slight authority of the Acts in such matters. See M. Krenkel, *Josephus und Lucas* (Leipzig, 1894), pp. 162 ff.; Jackson-Lake, *op. cit.* I: *Acts* IV, *ad loc.*, the commentaries by A. Wikenhauser, E. Haenchen, H. Conzelmann and others; P. Winter, 'Miszellen zur Apostelgeschichte', EvTh 17 (1957), pp. 398 f.

Curious is the fact that the followers of Jesus in Acts 5:36–7 (the speech ascribed to Gamaliel is a Christian composition) are aligned with the followers of Judas the Galilean, and of Theudas, both of whom had clashed with Rome's political interests in Palestine.

7. *Ant.* xx 5, 2 (100); xviii 8, 1 (259). On the office of *alabarch*, see vol. III, § 31.

8. Compare on this, besides *Ant.* xx 5, 2 (101), also *Ant.* iii 15, 3 (320); xx 2, 5 (51); Acts 11:28–30. Josephus mentions the famine in the time of Tiberius Iulius Alexander, but states that it began in the days of his predecessor: *ἐπὶ τούτοις δὲ καὶ τὸν μέγαν λιμὸν κατὰ τὴν Ἰουδαίαν συνέβη γενέσθαι.* Instead of *ἐπὶ τούτοις*, Niese reads in accordance with the *Epitome*, *ἐπὶ τούτου.* But the reading *ἐπὶ τούτοις*, found in all the manuscripts, is confirmed by Eusebius, *EH* ii 12, 1. It is certainly not to be rendered *propter haec*, nor even *ad haec* or *post haec*, but by *horum temporibus*, as in the Old Latin. The account in Acts is in agreement with this when it describes the famine as having occurred at about the time of Agrippa's death (A.D. 44). In all three passages Josephus speaks only of Judaea being affected by the famine (xx 5, 2 (101), *Judaea*; iii 15, 3 (320), *our country*; xx 2, 5 (51), *the city*). The author of the Acts of the Apostles speaks of a world-wide famine (11:28). This is a generalization, and as unhistorical as the similar expression used of the census under Quirinius. The writer of Acts, perhaps using a source in this instance, may have seen in the 'famine in diverse places' a sign of 'the things which are coming upon the world' (cf. Lk. 21:11, 26). The reign of Claudius was certainly afflicted by *assiduae sterilitates* (Suet. *Div. Claud.* 18), including, besides the famine in Palestine, the following: (1) a famine in Rome at the beginning of Claudius's reign (Dio lx 11, 1; Aurelius Victor, *De Caes.* 4, 3); (2) a famine in Greece in the 8th or 9th year of his rule (Euseb. *Chron.*, ed. Schoene II, pp. 152–3, in the Armenian, and according to Jerome); (3) a famine in Rome in the 11th year of his rule (so Tac. *Ann.* xii 43, 1; or, according to Euseb. *Chron.*, *loc. cit.*, in the 10th or 9th year; Orosius vii 6, 17, also gives the 10th year as the date). But a famine extending over the whole world is as improbable in itself as it is unattested by any of our historical sources. K. S. Gapp, 'The Universal Famine under Claudius', HThR 28 (1935), pp. 258–65, considers the words *ἐφ' ὅλην τὴν οἰκουμένην* in Acts 11:28 justified because of the spread of famine over various parts of the Roman Empire, even if this did not occur all at once.

9. *Ant.* xx 5, 2 (102). Tiberius Iulius Alexander served later under Corbulo against the Parthians (Tac. *Ann.* xv 28, 4), and was then made Prefect of Egypt (Jos. *B.J.* ii 15, 1 (309), 18, 7 (492); iv 10, 6 (616); Tac. *Hist.* i 11, 2; ii 74, 2; 79, 1; Suet. *Div. Vesp.* 6). He was Titus's most distinguished adviser during the siege of Jerusalem, *B.J.* v 1, 6 (45); vi 4, 3 (237). He was possibly later Praetorian

If the years of these first two procurators did not pass without disturbances, they were totally insignificant in comparison with what followed. Already under the next governor, Cumanus, and not without faults on both sides, popular uprisings broke out on a more formidable scale.

3. The first rebellion with which Ventidius Cumanus (A.D. 48–*c*.52)[10] had to contend was triggered off by the insolence of a Roman soldier. At the feast of Passover, when a detachment of Roman soldiers was regularly stationed on the outskirts of the Temple[11] to maintain order, one of them had the temerity to insult the festive gathering by committing an indecency.[12] The angry crowd demanded satisfaction from the procurator, but when he tried to pacify them he was so overwhelmed with abuse that in the end he called in his forces, who routed the excited crowds so completely that (according to Josephus's estimate) 20,000 people lost their lives in the ensuing stampede.[13]

The fault in this case lay with the Romans; but in the next upheaval the provocation came from the people. An imperial slave named Stephanus was attacked on the public highway not far from Jerusalem and robbed of his possessions. As a punishment, the villages in the

---

Prefect. His full name is given in an edict which he issued as Prefect of Egypt, CIG 4957 = OGIS 669 = IGR I 1263 = G. Chalon, *L'édit de Tiberius Iulius Alexander* (1964). On Tiberius Iulius Alexander and his family see E. G. Turner, 'Tiberius Iulius Alexander', JRS 44 (1954), pp. 54–64; CPJ nos. 418–20; V. Burr, *Tiberius Julius Alexander* (1955); PIR² I 139.

The family of Tiberius Alexander, completely alienated from Judaism, continued in later times to serve the Roman administration. A certain Iulius Alexander, probably a son or grandson of the one mentioned, served as legate under Trajan in the Parthian war (Dio lxviii 30, 12); an Alexander, probably identical, was consul in A.D. 117, and in 118, one Tiberius Iulius Alexander appears among the *Fratres Arvales*; see PIR² I 142; but cf. RE s.v. 'Julius' (61). One *Τιβέριος Ἰούλιος Ἀλέξανδρος*, commander of the *Cohors Prima Flavia* and former *eutheniarch* of the second district of Alexandria, erected a monument to the goddess Isis in the 21st year of Antoninus Pius, OGIS 705 = IGR I 1044.

10. *B.J.* ii 12, 1–7 (223-46), *Ant.* xx 5, 2 (103); 5, 3–6, 5 (105–36). His name was Ventidius Cumanus according to Tac. *Ann.* xii 54, 3; Josephus calls him simply Cumanus. The date of Cumanus's introduction into office may be assessed, though only approximately, from Josephus's reference to the death of Herod of Chalcis, which occurred in the 8th year of Claudius's reign, i.e. in A.D. 48, *Ant.* xx 5, 2 (103). See F. D. Gerlach, *Die römischen Statthalter*, p. 71; P. v. Rohden, *De Palaestina et Arabia* (1885), p. 35; RE s.v. 'Ventidius' (7); M. Aberbach, 'The conflicting Accounts of Josephus and Tacitus concerning Cumanus' and Felix' Terms of Office', JQR 40 (1949–50), pp. 1–14.

11. *B.J.* v 5, 8 (244); *Ant.* xx 8, 11 (192).

12. *B.J.* ii 12, 1 (224); *Ant.* xx 5, 3 (108).

13. *B.J.* ii 12, 1 (224–7); *Ant.* xx 5, 3 (105–11). In the *B.J.* passage some manuscripts read, 'more than myriads', *ὑπὲρ τοὺς μυρίους*. Niese, on good testimony, gives the figure 30,000; the same figure in Euseb. *Chron.*, ed. Schoene II, pp. 152–3, and *HE* ii 19, 1, proves that Eusebius is here following *B.J.*; see Schürer ZWTh (1898), p. 34.

neighbourhood of the place where the assault was committed were looted. Unfortunately, a new disaster very nearly resulted from this looting, in that a soldier tore up in the sight of the people a scroll of the Torah which he had found, accompanying his action with open insults. A mass deputation set off to Cumanus at Caesarea to demand revenge, and this time the procurator found it advisable to punish the culprit with death.[14]

Far more bitter and violent was a third incident under Cumanus which, although it did not cost him his life, lost him his office. Some Galilean Jews passing through Samaria on their way to a festival at Jerusalem were murdered in a Samaritan village. Since Cumanus, who had been bribed by the Samaritans, made no move to punish the guilty, the Jews took revenge into their own hands. An armed band led by two Zealots, Eleazar and Alexander, invaded Samaria and massacred old men, women and children, and laid the villages waste. But Cumanus with part of his troops then fell on the Zealots, and many were slain and others taken prisoner and carried off. Meanwhile, Samaritan envoys appeared before Ummidius Quadratus, the governor of Syria, and charged the Jews with robbery. Simultaneously, however, a Jewish delegation to Quadratus accused the Samaritans, and Cumanus, who had accepted a bribe from them. On hearing this, Quadratus himself went to Samaria and carried out a strict investigation. All the rebels captured by Cumanus were crucified; five Jews convicted of having taken part in the fighting were beheaded; and the ringleaders, Jewish and Samaritan, were sent to Rome, together with Cumanus, to answer for their conduct. Thanks to the intercession of the younger Agrippa who happened to be in Rome at the time, the Jews obtained their rights. Claudius decided that the Samaritan leaders should be executed as guilty, and that Cumanus should be removed from office and sent into exile.[15]

4. At the request of the High Priest Jonathan, one of the Jewish

14. *B.J.* ii 12, 2 (228–31); *Ant.* xx 5, 4 (113–17).

15. *B.J.* ii 12, 3–7 (232–46); *Ant.* xx 6, 1–3 (118–36). There is a divergence in essential points between Josephus's account and that of Tacitus, *Ann.* xii 54. According to Tacitus, Cumanus was only procurator of Galilee, while Felix was administrator of Samaria and apparently of Judaea also—'Felix . . . iam pridem Iudaeae impositus . . . aemulo ad deterrima Ventidio Cumano, cui pars provinciae habebatur, ita divisae, ut huic Galilaeorum natio, Felici Samaritae parerent'. Tacitus also reports that Felix and Cumanus shared the blame for the sanguinary excesses which took place, but that Quadratus charged Cumanus only, and even appointed Felix to sit in judgment over him at his trial.

It is impossible to resolve the contradiction between the reports of Tacitus and Josephus. According to Tacitus, the province was divided, with Felix as governor of Samaria (and apparently Judaea), and Cumanus concurrently in charge of Galilee. According to Josephus's exposition, Cumanus and Felix were appointed successively to rule over an undivided Palestine, the first in A.D. 48, the second

nobles whom Quadratus had sent to Rome,[16] the Emperor Claudius handed over the administration of Palestine to one of his favourites, Felix (A.D. *c.*52–60?),[17] the brother of the influential Pallas. Felix's term of office manifestly constitutes the turning-point in the drama which started in A.D. 44 and reached its bloody climax in A.D. 70. Whereas the period of the first two procurators was comparatively peaceful, and under Cumanus more serious uprisings occurred only sporadically set off by individual malcontents, under Felix rebellion became permanent.

Like his brother Pallas, Felix was a freedman of the imperial family,[18] and probably of Antonia, the mother of Claudius, whence his full name Antonius Felix.[19] The conferring of a procuratorship with military

---

after his recall in A.D. 52/53. Josephus states that the High Priest Jonathan, who was in Rome at the time of Cumanus's deposition from office, requested the Emperor Claudius to appoint Felix (see below). The detailed narrative of Josephus is clearly to be preferred to the vague remarks of Tacitus. Cf. R. Hanslik, RE s.v. 'Ventidius Cumanus' and E. M. Smallwood, 'Some Comments on Tacitus, Annals xii 54', Latomus 18 (1959), pp. 560–7.

16. *B.J.* ii 12, 5 (240); cf. *Ant.* xx 7, 1 (137); 8, 5 (162).

17. *B.J.* ii 12, 8 (247); *Ant.* xx 7, 1 (137); Suet. *Div. Claud.* 28. It seems probable that Felix's appointment fell in A.D. 52 because immediately after mentioning it, Josephus reports that Claudius, after ruling for twelve years, i.e. after the 24th January, A.D. 53, presented Agrippa II with Batanaea and Trachonitis, *Ant.* xx 7, 1 (138). Admittedly, A.D. 53 is also a possibility, and some writers actually adopt it. But it is an argument in favour of A.D. 52 that Tacitus, *Ann.* xii 54, reports the deposition of Cumanus among the events of that year; presupposing, of course, that Felix had already administered part of Palestine earlier, at the same time as Cumanus, see above, note 15. Although this assumption can hardly be right, the dating of the deposition of Cumanus in A.D. 52 may be accepted.

On Felix see P. v. Rohden, RE s.v. 'Antonius' (54); A. Stein, PIR[2] A 828.

18. Tac. *Hist.* v 9; Suet. *Div. Claud.* 28.

19. The *gentilicium* of Felix is given by Tacitus (*Hist.* v 9) as Antonius, but by Josephus, *Ant.* xx 7, 1 (137) as Claudius. His brother, Pallas, was a freedman of Antonia, the Emperor Claudius's mother, *Ant.* xviii 6, 6 (182). (See Tacitus, *Annales* xi 29, xii 54, and H. Furneaux on these passages.) Felix may have borne the name Claudius. Fragments of an epitaph, discovered between Dora and Athlit in Israel, mention a Tiberius Claudius (? Felix), an ἐπίτροπος, as the employer of a certain Titus Mucius Clemens. M. Avi-Yonah, IEJ 16 (1966), p. 259 and pl. 28, restores the inscription as follows:

[ΤΙ]ΤΩΙ ΜΟΥΚΙΩΙ ΜΑΡΚ[ΟΥ ΥΙΩΙ
[ΚΛ]ΗΜΕΝΤΙ ΕΠΑΡΧΩΙ ΣΠ[ΕΙΡΗΣ ΤΟΥ
ΒΑΣΙΛΕΩΣ ΜΕΓΑΛΟΥ ΑΓΡΙΠ[ΠΑ. ΕΠΙ
ΤΙΒΕΡΙΟΥ ΑΛΕΞΑΝΔΡΟΥ ΕΠΑΡ[ΧΟΥ ΑΙΓΥΠΤΟΥ
ΕΠΑΡΧΩΙ ΣΠΕΙΡΗΣ ΠΡΩΤΗ[Σ ΛΕΠΙ
ΔΙΑΝΗΣ ΙΠΠΙΚΗΣ. Β[ΕΝΕΘΙΚΙΑΡΙΩΙ
ΤΙΒΕΡΙΟΥ ΚΛΑΥΔΙΟ[Υ ΦΗΛΙΚΟΣ?
ΕΠΙΤΡΟΠΟΥ ΣΕ[ΒΑΣΤΟΥ ΙΟΥΔΑΙΑΣ?
*ΣΙΜΩΝΙΔΗΣ ΚΑΙ Τ (*or *Ξ)*
ΥΙΟΙ ΤΩ(Ν) ΕΑΥΤΩΝ
ΧΑ[ΙΡΕ]

command on a freedman was unprecedented, and can only be accounted for by the influence exercised by freedmen at the court of Claudius.[20] As procurator of Palestine, Felix was true to his origin. 'Practising every kind of cruelty and lust, he wielded royal power with the instincts of a slave.' Thus Tacitus's estimate of the man.[21]

Felix was married three times, and all his wives, two of whom are known to us, belonged to royal families.[22] One was a grand-daughter of the triumvir M. Antonius and Cleopatra, and through her Felix was related to the Emperor Claudius.[23] Another was the Jewish princess Drusilla, a daughter of Agrippa I and sister of Agrippa II, and the way in which Felix married her confirms the opinion expressed by Tacitus. When Felix assumed office, Drusilla was about 14 years old.[24]

The dead man is thus described as a b[eneficiarius] of Tiberius Claudiu[s Felix?], the im[perial?] procurator—but unfortunately the word 'Judaea' is not visible on the epitaph. Even the completion of *ΣΕ* as *σεβάστου* is not definitely established. The Tiberius Claudius in question may have been an *ἐπίτροπος* but not an imperial one. If that were the case, we cannot be sure that the *cognomen* of Tiberius Claudius was 'Felix'. See the quite different restoration and interpretation in AE 1967 525.

P. v Rohden originally thought that Felix bore the name 'Claudius', *De Palestina et Arabia provinciis Romanis questiones selectae* (1885), p. 35, but later changes his view. RE s.v. 'Antoninus' (54).

20. In Suet. *Div. Claud.* 28, the unusual nature of this appointment is singled out: 'Felicem, quem cohortibus et alis provinciaeque Iudaeae praeposuit'. See O. Hirschfeld, SAB 1889, p. 423; cf. F. Millar, Historia 13 (1964), pp. 181–2.

In the later years of Claudius's reign (A.D. 49–54), not only freedmen, but also his wife Agrippina exercised an unwholesome influence. Palestinian coins minted in the 13th and 14th year of Claudius afford evidence of her powerful position since the name 'Iulia Agrippina' appears on them alongside that of the emperor (see above, § 17, p. 380, note 123). It is probable that a town, or fort, east of the river Jordan was named after her, viz. אגריפינא, Agrippina, between Mount Sartaba and Haurân (see the Cambridge manuscript of Mishnah Rosh-Hashanah II, p. 4, ed. H. Lowe; a Hamburg manuscript and the *editio princeps* have *Agropina*; the Jerusalem Talmud and Codex de Rossi 138 read *Gripina*, the printed text, *Gropina*). The locality is named only in this place in the Mishnah. The Greek form would have been *'Αγριππῖνας* (cf. *Τιβεριάς*=טבריא). Cf. M. Avi-Yonah, *The Holy Land* (1966), p. 139.

21. *Hist.* v 9 'per omnem saevitiam ac libidinem ius regium servili ingenio exercuit'.

22. Suet. *Div. Claud.* 28, calls him 'trium reginarum maritum'.

23. Tac. *Hist.* v 9, 'Drusilla Cleopatrae et Antonii nepte in matrimonium accepta, ut eiusdem Antonii Felix progener, Claudius nepos esset'. The name 'Drusilla' is apparently due to a confusion with the other wife of Felix. Antonius had twins by Cleopatra, Alexander and Cleopatra Selene, and a son, Ptolemy Philadelphus (Dio xlix 32, 4). It is not known whose daughter the wife of Felix was. Cleopatra Selene married King Juba of Mauretania and died before 5 B.C., PIR² C 1148.

24. As is evident from *Ant.* xix 9, 1 (354), according to which she, the youngest of Agrippa I's daughters, was 6 years old when her father died.

Soon after, she was married by her brother Agrippa to Azizus, king of Emesa, after her first betrothed, a son of King Antiochus of Commagene, had declined to marry her because he did not wish to submit to circumcision.[25] Felix saw the beautiful queen soon after her wedding, desired her, and with the help of a magician from Cyprus called Simon, prevailed on her to marry him. In defiance of the law, which strictly forbade the marriage of a Jewess with a pagan, Drusilla became the wife of the Roman procurator.[26]

In public affairs Felix behaved no better than in his private life. As brother of the influential Pallas, 'he believed that he could commit all kinds of enormities with impunity'.[27] It is understandable that under a government such as his, hostility against Rome increased enormously. The various stages of its development under, and because of, Felix are easy to trace.[28]

First of all, in consequence of his misgovernment, the Zealots, who hated the Romans fanatically, gained more and more support among the citizens. How far Josephus was justified in calling the Zealots simply 'bandits' may be left undecided.[29] In any case, as the sympathy they evoked from the ordinary people shows, they were not ordinary bandits; and they confined their robberies to their political opponents.

25. *Ant.* xx 7, 1 (139).

26. *Ant.* xx 7, 2 (141–3). Cf. Acts 24:24. Since Azizus died in the first year of Nero, *Ant.* xx 8, 4 (158), this must have taken place in the time of Claudius in A.D. 53 or 54. Drusilla bore Felix a son called Agrippa, who 'together with his wife' (certainly not Drusilla, but her daughter-in-law, the wife of Agrippa) perished in the eruption of Vesuvius, *Ant.* xx 7, 2 (144).

27. Tacitus, *Annales* xii 54, 'cuncta malefacta sibi impune ratus tanta potentia subnixo'.

28. Especially in the account given in *B.J.* ii 13, 2–6 (252–65), which is even more lucid than *Ant.* xx 8, 5–6 (160–72).

29. Josephus is the only source of information on this period of Jewish history. It is necessary to remember that he is not an impartial witness as far as the yearning for Jewish independence from Rome is concerned. His own conduct during the war provides clear evidence of this. He represents all Jewish political groups hostile to Roman rule as 'bandits' or 'robbers'. But expressions which he occasionally uses, such as for instance, *ληστρικὸς θόρυβος*, cf. *B.J.* ii 12, 2 (228–31), show that it is not clandestine 'robbery' of which he speaks, but a form of civil war. When he speaks of *γόητες καὶ ληστρικοί*, 'impostors and brigands', *B.J.* ii 13, 6 (264), or says *ληστηρίων γὰρ ἡ χώρα πάλιν ἀνεπλήσθη καὶ γοήτων ἀνθρώπων*, *Ant.* xx 8, 5 (160), he equates the 'robber' (*ληστής*, Heb. פריץ) and 'seducer' (*γόης*, מסית). And this shows that he regarded people who 'seduced'—or inveigled—others to revolt as gangsters.

'Josephus consistently uses the word *ληστής* to describe the Zealots who had made armed resistance against Rome their aim in life', K. H. Rengstorf, ThWNT IV, pp. 262–7, on p. 263. See however B. S. Jackson, *Theft in Early Jewish Law* (1972), pp. 36–7. Compare also M. Hengel, *Die Zeloten* (1961), pp. 25–47; S. G. F. Brandon, *Jesus and the Zealots* (1967); also see above, pp. 381–2.

Felix, who was not very particular concerning his methods, contrived to get hold of Eleazar, the party leader, by treachery, and sent him to Rome with his companions, whom he had arrested also. 'But it is impossible to calculate the number of bandits whom he crucified, and of the citizens whom he tracked down and punished as their accomplices.'[30]

Such perverse severity and cruelty only provoked further lawlessness.[31] The 'bandits' of whom the country had been purged by Felix were replaced by the *sicarii*, an even more fanatical patriotic faction advocating the assassination of political opponents. Armed with short daggers (*sicae*), from which they received their name,[32] they mingled with the crowds, especially during the festival seasons, and unseen, struck down their opponents (τοὺς διαφόρους, i.e. collaborators of the Romans), afterwards affecting grief and thereby evading detection. Political murder became so frequent that soon nobody in Jerusalem felt safe. Among those who fell victim to the daggers of the *sicarii* was the High Priest Jonathan who, as a man of moderate views, was hated by the *sicarii* no less than by the procurator Felix. For he had often urged Felix to administer his office more worthily so that he, Jonathan, would not be blamed by the people for having recommended the emperor to appoint him as governor. Felix, wishing to be rid of his troublesome critic, found the easiest way to be assassination; to which end the *sicarii*, normally Felix's deadly enemies, willingly allowed themselves to be used.[33]

Political fanatics were joined by religious ones 'with cleaner hands but wickeder intentions'.[34] Claiming to have been sent by God, they incited the people to frenzied enthusiasm and led them in crowds into

30. *B.J.* ii 13, 2 (253); *Ant.* xx 8, 5 (160).

31. Tac. *Ann.* xii 54.

32. *Ant.* xx 8, 10 (186).

33. In *B.J.* ii 13, 3 (254–7), Josephus does not implicate Felix in the murder of Jonathan, but he does so in *Ant.* xx 8, 5 (161–3). The *sicarii* are also mentioned during the war, when they occupied the fortress Masada; cf. *B.J.* ii 17, 8 (433); iv 7, 5 (404), 9, 5 (516); vii 8, 1–9, 2 (252–406). The author of Acts knew them as a political party: Acts 21:38 mentions 4000 *sicarii* as adherents of 'the Egyptian' for whom Paul of Tarsus was mistaken. According to *B.J.* ii 13, 5 (261–3), 'the Egyptian' brought his followers from the desert, assembled them on the Mount of Olives, and prepared to seize Jerusalem by force.

In Latin *sicarius* is the usual designation for 'assassin'. The law against assassins issued under Sulla is called 'Lex Cornelia de sicariis'.

In bGittin 56a, the expression אבא סיקרא ריש בריוני ('ringleader of the *sicarii*, headman of the baryonê') indicates the leader of a political resistance party. In other talmudic passages the word occurs in a general sense, meaning 'outlaw', or 'assassin', See S. Krauss, *Griechische und lateinische Lehnwörter im Talmud* II (1899), p. 392; M. Hengel, *Die Zeloten* (1961), pp. 55–7.

34. *B.J.* ii 13, 4 (258).

the desert,[35] there to show them 'omens of freedom (σημεῖα ἐλευθερίας), a freedom which consisted in casting off the Roman yoke and establishing the Kingdom of God (or to use the language of Josephus, in reform and insurrection). Since religious fanaticism is always the most powerful and most persistent, Josephus is certainly right when he remarks that these visionaries and deceivers contributed no less than the 'bandits' to the downfall of the city. Felix also recognized the dangerous nature of the newly-formed sodalities and everywhere confronted them with the sword.[36]

The most notorious case of this kind was that of 'the Egyptian', a demagogue also mentioned in Acts 21:38. A Jew from Egypt proclaiming himself a prophet, he assembled in the desert a large number of supporters (4,000, according to Acts; 30,000, according to Josephus's account in *B.J.* ii 13, 5 (261); no figure is given in the Antiquities, but Josephus says there that 400 of the Egyptian's followers were killed and 200 captured, *Ant.* xx 8, 6 (171). He intended to lead them to the Mount of Olives, promising that at his command the walls of Jerusalem would collapse and allow them to enter the city. They would then overpower the Roman garrison and assume control. Felix did not give the prophet enough time to stage the miracle, but attacked with his troops, slaughtered and scattered his followers or took them prisoner. But the Egyptian himself escaped the massacre and disappeared.[37]

Abortive though it turned out to be, this incident led to a stiffening of the attitude of the anti-Roman forces. Religious and political fanatics (γόητες καὶ ληστρικοί) made common cause and 'incited many to revolt, exhorting them to assert their independence, and threatening to kill any who submitted willingly to Roman domination, and to suppress all those who would voluntarily accept servitude. Deploying in gangs throughout the country, they looted the houses of the nobles and killed their owners and set villages on fire, so that all Judaea felt the effect of their frenzy'.[38]

The abuse of governmental authority by Felix thus ended in alienating a great part of the nation; from this time on, the preaching of resistance against Rome continued incessantly and the agitation to take up arms never stopped until that objective was reached.

Side by side with this wild ferment among the ordinary people went

35. Retreat into the desert as a prelude to military action is characteristic of Jewish resistance groups from Maccabean times onwards.

36. *B.J.* ii 13, 4 (259–60); *Ant.* xx 8, 6 (167–8).

37. *B.J.* ii 13, 5 (261–3); *Ant.* xx 8, 6 (169–72). Undoubtedly the people believed in a miraculous deliverance and hoped for a return, to which Acts 21:8 also refers. See above, note 33 and Hengel, *op. cit.*, pp. 236–8; cf. also G. Vermes, *Jesus the Jew* (1973), p. 98.

38. *B.J.* ii 13, 6 (264–5); *Ant.* xx 8, 6 (168).

internal conflict amongst the priesthood. The chief priests were at odds with the rest;[39] and in the lawless conditions prevailing under Felix's government in Palestine, were even able to send their stewards to the threshing-floors to seize the tithes due to the other priests, many of whom died of starvation.[40]

The imprisonment of the Apostle Paul in Caesarea, an account of which is given in Acts 23–24, occurred during the last two years of Felix's governorship. Paul also had a personal encounter with the procurator and his wife Drusilla in which he did not fail to talk to them of what he thought they needed to hear—of righteousness, chastity and future judgment (Acts 24:25).

While Paul was held prisoner in Caesarea, a dispute arose there between the Jewish and the Syrian inhabitants over equality of citizenship (ἰσοπολιτεία). The Jews claimed precedence because Herod had founded the city. The Syrians, understandably, were reluctant to concede this priority to them. For some time there was street fighting between the two parties. In the end, Felix stepped in on an occasion when the Jews had won the upper hand, quelled them by force and handed over some of their houses to be plundered by the soldiers. When the rioting nevertheless continued, he sent notables from both sides to Rome for the emperor to decide the legal issue.[41] But before the matter could be settled, Felix was recalled by Nero, probably in A.D. 60, but possibly a year or two earlier.[42] [*Text continues on page* 467

39. S. G. F. Brandon, *Jesus and the Zealots* (1967), pp. 114, 118, 121, 125 f., 189, suggests that the latter were in alliance with both the Jewish adherents of Jesus and the Zealots.

40. *Ant.* xx 8, 8 (180–1); 9, 2 (206). Talmudic tradition complains of the violence of High Priestly cliques at this time. In bPes. 57a (a slightly different text also in bYom. 35b; tMen. 13:21, ed. Zuckermandel, p. 533, lines 33 ff.) we find the following song: 'Woe is me because of the house of Boethus; woe is me because of their staves! Woe is me because of the house of Ḥanin; woe is me because of their whisperings! Woe is me because of the house of Cantheras; woe is me because of their pens! Woe is me because of the house of Ishmael ben Ph(i)abi; woe is me because of their fists! For they are High Priests, and their sons are treasurers, and their sons-in-law are trustees, and their servants beat the people with staves!' (M. Freedman, *The Babylonian Talmud, Pesaḥim* (1938), p. 285). Cf. J. Jeremias, *Jerusalem in the Time of Jesus* (1969), pp. 195–6.

41. *B.J.* ii 13, 7 (266–70); *Ant.* xx 8, 7 (173–7). At the time, Caesarea may have had some 50,000 inhabitants, most of whom were Hellenized Syrians. The Jewish population—more than 20,000 according to *B.J.* ii 18, 1 (457)—was in the minority.

42. The exact dates of Felix's recall and the arrival of Festus are disputed. A.D. 60 may be suggested to be the most probable date. A. von Harnack, *Geschichte der altchristlichen Literatur* II/1 (1897), pp. 233–9, prefers an earlier date at the very beginning of Nero's reign, some time between A.D. 54 and 56. The grounds for this hypothesis are: (1) In the Chronicle of Eusebius according to the Armenian text, the recall of Felix is said to have taken place in the last year of Claudius,

i.e. A.D. 54 (Euseb. *Chron.*, ed. Schoene II, p. 152); in the Chronicle of Jerome, it is placed in the second year of Nero (Euseb. *Chron.*, ed. Schoene II, p. 155). (2) When after his recall Felix was accused in Rome by the Jews, Pallas secured his acquittal, *Ant.* xx 8, 9 (182). Pallas therefore still had great influence; but he fell into disfavour already at the beginning of Nero's reign, A.D. 55 (Tac. *Ann.* xiii 14). These statements have less force if the following facts are considered: (1) The statements in the Chronicle of Eusebius concerning the history of Judaea in this period are derived entirely from Josephus and so have no independent value. Where Eusebius finds no definite chronological data in Josephus, he uses his own judgment. He places the recall of Felix in the second year of Nero (for Jerome, not the Armenian, has the genuine text of Eusebius here; see ZWTh 1898, p. 35), probably because Josephus had previously, *Ant.* xx 8, 4 (158), mentioned the first year of Nero. (2) The dismissal from office of Pallas had already occurred by 13 February A.D. 55 (viz. before the birthday of Britannicus, Tac. *Ann.* xiii 15, 1; see ZWTh 1898, p. 39; on the evidence of Tacitus the year is quite definite), only a few months, therefore, after Nero's accession on 13 October A.D. 54. It is impossible that everything reported by Josephus on the administration of Felix during the reign of Nero could have happened in this short period, *B.J.* ii 12, 8 (247–70); *Ant.* xx 8, 5–8 (160–81). The above conclusion on the history of Pallas is consequently wrong. The contrary must rather be inferred from the history of Felix, namely that Pallas in spite of his dismissal remained influential—a conclusion which agrees completely with Tacitus's statement (cf. ZWTh, 1898, p. 40). A further argument against an early date for the recall of Felix arises from the revolt of 'the Egyptian' which, according to Josephus, *B.J.* ii 13, 5 (261–3); *Ant.* xx 8, 6 (169–72), occurred under Nero, and not at the beginning of his reign. But this revolt already belonged to the past, to the time when Paul was imprisoned under Felix (Acts 21:38). Paul then spent two years in prison, and it was only afterwards that Felix was recalled.

It is more possible to accept a date before A.D. 60 for Felix's dismissal though one cannot be quite certain about the year. It occurred in the summer, anyway, since Paul, who embarked for Rome not long after Felix's departure, arrived in Crete about the time of the Day of Atonement (i.e. in September/October; see Acts 27:9). But this cannot have been a later summer than that of A.D. 60. As Felix's second successor, Albinus, came to Palestine at the latest in the summer of A.D. 62, see Jos. *B.J.* vi 5, 3 (300–9), only one year, assuming that Felix did not leave till the summer of A.D. 61, would be left for Festus's procuratorship, which in view of the numerous incidents reported from his time, *Ant.* xx 8, 9–11 (182–96), seems too short. The argument in favour of A.D. 61, drawn from *Ant.* xx 8, 11 (193–5), is not convincing. Because Poppaea, in an incident which occurred some time after Festus had taken up office, is described as the wife of Nero, *Ant.* xx 8, 11 (195), which she became only in A.D. 62, Tac. *Ann.* xiv 60; it is argued that Festus's appointment cannot have taken place before A.D. 61. But nothing prevents us from placing that occurrence a year or so after Festus had taken up office. Moreover, Nero's marriage with Poppaea occurred around the time of Festus's death, perhaps even somewhat later. Since the incident referred to in *Ant.* xx 8, 11 (193–5) happened under Festus, Josephus has proleptically described Nero's concubine as his wife.

Some uncertainty remains concerning the year of the imprisonment of Paul in Caesarea. A.D. 57 or even 56 is not impossible. Since Paul was Felix's prisoner for two years, the latter's recall would fall at the earliest in A.D. 58 or 59. For the reasons stated, the date of A.D. 60 is preferable. Note that it was in A.D. 63/4 that Josephus went to Rome to assist priests who had been sent there by Felix, *Vita* 3 (13–14). Cf., for a different view, Ch. Saumagne, 'Saint Paul et Félix, procurateur de Judée', *Mélanges Piganiol* III (1966), pp. 1373–86.

5. As successor to Felix, Nero sent Porcius Festus (?A.D. 60–62)[43] to Palestine, a man of honest intentions but quite unable to undo the harm caused by his predecessor.

Soon after Festus's assumption of office, the dispute between the Jewish and Syrian townsmen in Caesarea was decided by an imperial rescript to the Syrians' advantage. The Jewish envoys in Rome were unable to press their complaint against Felix because Pallas used his influence on his brother's behalf. The two Syrian envoys, on the other hand, were able to win over by means of bribery a certain Beryllus who was in charge of Nero's Greek correspondence,[44] and thereby procure an imperial rescript which not only deprived the Jews of the equality with the Syrians with which they were dissatisfied, but declared the 'Hellenes' masters of the city. The bitterness caused by this decision among the Jewish inhabitants of Caesarea found an outlet a few years later, in A.D. 66, in seditious actions which Josephus regards as the beginning of the great war.[45]

Paul, whom Felix had left as a prisoner in Caesarea (Acts 24:27), was interrogated repeatedly by Festus, and in the end was sent, as a Roman citizen and at his own request, to be judged before the emperor in Rome.[46]

Disturbances caused by the *sicarii* were as bad under Festus as they were under Felix. Once again an impostor (this at any rate is what Josephus calls him) led the people into the desert, promising his followers redemption and deliverance from all evils. Festus proceeded

43. *B.J.* ii 14, 1 (271); *Ant.* xx 8, 9 (182). On Festus, see the extremely detailed treatment in RE s.v. 'Porcius' (39).

44. Instead of the name 'Beryllus' given in all manuscripts in *Ant.* xx 8, 9 (183) from Hudson and Haverkamp onward, some printed editions read 'Burrus'. Niese restored the traditional *Βήρυλλος*, while Naber resorted to *Βοῦρρος* again. This conjecture, which even induced some authors to engage in risky chronological speculations, is particularly regrettable since the characterization 'Nero's tutor who had been appointed secretary of Greek correspondence' does not fit Burrus, the well-known *praefectus praetorio*, who, by the way, was known as such to Josephus; cf. *Ant.* xx 8, 2 (152).

45. *B.J.* ii 14, 4 (284); *Ant.* xx 8, 9 (183–4). The two statements given by Josephus are inconsistent with one another. According to *Ant.* xx 8, 9 (182), the Jewish representatives from Caesarea did not travel to Rome to lodge their complaint against Felix until after Festus's accession to office. According to *B.J.* ii 13, 7 (270), both parties were despatched to Rome by Felix himself. This appears to have been the case, since even *Ant.* xx 8, 9 (183) reports that the Syrian representatives were also in Rome. From *B.J.* ii 14, 4 (284) it would appear that the emperor's decision was not given before A.D. 66. But this is impossible; Pallas, who died in A.D. 62 (Tac. *Ann.* xiv 65), played an important part in the proceedings.

46. Cf. e.g. P. Winter, *Trial*, pp. 83–5; A. N. Sherwin-White, *Roman Society and Roman Law*, pp. 48–70; P. Garnsey, JRS 56 (1966), pp. 182–5.

against him with the utmost severity, but it was too late to pacify the country permanently.[47]

The conflict which arose between the priests and King Agrippa II, in which Festus took Agrippa's side, will be discussed in detail in the section dealing with the history of that king.

Festus died in office after scarcely two years as procurator. He was succeeded by two men who, as true followers of Felix, did everything in their power to inflame the situation and bring on the final conflagration.

In the interval between the death of Festus and the arrival of his successor (A.D. 62), total anarchy reigned in Jerusalem. The High Priest Ananus profited from this to secure the death sentence for his enemies, whom he ordered to be stoned. He was a son of the elder Ananus or Annas known from the Gospel history of Jesus' passion. His despotism, however, did not last long, for King Agrippa deposed him even before the new procurator arrived, after he had been in office for barely three months.[48] Among those executed by Ananus was James, the brother of Jesus.[49]

6. Of the new procurator, Albinus (A.D. 62–64),[50] Josephus reports that he left no wickedness unexplored. His guiding principle, however, seems to have been to obtain money from any source. He plundered both public monies and private funds; the whole population suffered from his exactions.[51] But he also discovered that it was to his advantage to take bribes from both political parties in the country, from the pro-Roman faction and from their opponents. His venality knew no limits: he accepted presents from the collaborating High Priest Ananias, who although no longer in office was yet a man of considerable influence, and from his enemies, the *sicarii*, and then allowed them both to do as they liked. It is true that he gave the appearance of curbing the

47. *B.J.* ii 14, 1 (271); *Ant.* xx 10, 10 (188).

48. *Ant.* xx 9, 1 (199, 203). P. Winter, *op. cit.*, pp. 18 f.

49. Euseb. *HE* ii 23, 21–4 = Josephus, *Ant.* xx 9, 1 (200). Compare Excursus II to § 17 above, pp. 428–41.

Further, S. G. F. Brandon, *Jesus and the Zealots*, p. 121, and his 'The Death of James the Just: A New Interpretation', *Studies in Mysticism and Religion presented to Gershom Scholem* (1967), pp. 57–69.

50. The date of Albinus's succession to office may be gauged from *B.J.* vi 5, 3 (300–9). Albinus was already procurator four years before the outbreak of the war, and over 7 years and 5 months before the destruction of Jerusalem, when, at the Feast of Tabernacles, a certain prophet of doom, Jesus son of Ananias, made his appearance. These two dates point to the time of Sukkoth in A.D. 62. Albinus must therefore have assumed office at the latest during the summer of A.D. 62.

Our Albinus is probably identical with Lucceius Albinus, procurator of Mauretania under Nero, Galba and Otho, and put to death in A.D. 69 as a result of the rivalry between Otho and Vitellius by Vitellius's party (Tac. *Hist.* ii 58–59). See Pflaum, *Carrières* no. 33; PIR² L 354

51. *B.J.* ii 14, 1 (272–3). Cf. Brandon *Jesus and the Zealots*, p. 127.

sicarii, but anyone taken prisoner could, if he commanded sufficient money, buy his freedom. 'The only persons left in gaol were those who failed to pay the price.'[52] The *sicarii* soon found another method of setting free those of their party who were captured. They needed only to seize some of their opponents. Albinus, at the latter's request (by whom he was also bribed) would then exchange *sicarii* in return for the release of the pro-Romans. Once, the *sicarii* held the scribe of Eleazar, captain of the Temple guard and a son of the High Priest Ananias,[53] and in return for his liberation secured the release of ten of their own comrades.[54] In such conditions the anti-Roman party gained more and more power, or as Josephus puts it, 'the audacity of the revolutionaries was stimulated'.[55] And as their rivals also had a free hand to do as they liked, utter anarchy soon prevailed in Jerusalem. It was a free for all. Men of the 'middle-of-the-road',[56] of moderate views, were at the mercy of both the procurator and the insurrectionists. Ananias, the High Priest, behaved most outrageously. He quite openly ordered his servants to take the priests' tithes from the threshing-floors and those who dared to object were flogged.[57] Two worthy relatives of King Agrippa, Costobar and Saul, also tried their hand at banditry[58] and the man whose duty it was to maintain law and order, Albinus himself, vied with them in this game.[59] There was therefore nothing particularly remarkable in the fact that on one occasion a High Priest, Jesus son of Damnai, engaged in a pitched street-battle with his successor, Jesus son of Gamaliel, because he did not wish to relinquish his holy office.[60]

To please the city's inhabitants (and make his successor's task more difficult), when Albinus was recalled he left all the prisons empty,

52. *B.J.* ii 14, 1 (273); cf. *Ant.* xx 9, 2 (205).

53. This Eleazar, although still a supporter of the pro-Roman party when his secretary was waylaid by *sicarii*, later gave the signal to revolt by refusing to accept gifts or sacrifices on behalf of the Emperor and the Roman people, *B.J.* ii 17, 2 (409–10). Cf. Winter, *op. cit.*, p. 145; Brandon, *op. cit.*, p. 130.

Instead of *'Ανάνου* in *Ant.* xx 9, 3 (208), we should read *'Ανανίου* with Niese (according to Codex Ambrosianus and the Vetus Latina) and Feldman (Naber retains the incorrect *'Ανάνου*). Cf. J. Derenbourg, *Essai*, p. 248, n. 1, and E. M. Smallwood, 'High-Priests and Politics in Roman Palestine', JThSt n.s. 13 (1962), pp. 14–34, on pp. 27–8.

54. *Ant.* xx 9, 3 (208–9). Brandon, *op. cit.*, p. 126.

55. *B.J.* ii 14, 1 (274).

56. *B.J.* ii 14, 1 (275) *οἱ μέτριοι*.

57. *Ant.* xx 9, 2 (206–7). On the violence and repression exercised by the High Priests, see above, p. 465 and n. 40.

58. *Ant.* xx 9, 4 (214).

59. *B.J.* ii 14, 1 (272–5).

60. *Ant.* xx 9, 4 (213).

having executed the major criminals and released the rest. 'The prisons were thus empty of inmates, but the country full of robbers'.[61]

7. The last of the procurators, Gessius Florus (A.D. 64–66)[62] was also the worst. He came from Clazomenae and acquired the procuratorship of Judaea through the influence of his wife Cleopatra, who was friendly with the Empress Poppaea. Josephus is at a loss for words to describe the baseness which characterized his administration. Compared with him, Albinus was a 'most righteous' fellow (δικαιότατος). So measureless was his tyranny that the Jews regarded Albinus as benevolent by comparison. Whereas Albinus had committed his infamous deeds in secret, Florus was brazen enough to parade them openly.[63] The robbery of individuals seemed to him much too petty; he plundered whole cities and ruined whole communities. As long as bandits were willing to share their spoil with him, they could carry on without hindrance.[64]

Such malevolence was beyond endurance. So inflammable was the situation that it now needed but one spark. And the explosion followed with elemental force.

61. *Ant.* xx 9, 5 (215).

62. *B.J.* ii 14, 2 (277); *Ant.* xx 11, 1 (252–3). When the Jews openly took up arms against Rome in May A.D. 66, *B.J.* ii 14, 4 (284), Florus had started the second year of his procuratorship, *Ant.* xx 11, 1 (257). He must therefore have been installed in A.D. 64. The name Gessius Florus, and the adversities the Jews had to suffer under his rule and that of his predecessors, is attested by Tac. *Hist.* v 10 'duravit tamen patientia Iudaeis usque ad Gessium Florum procuratorem'. Cf. PIR² G 170.

63. Cf. Tac. *loc. cit.* (n. 62).

64. *B.J.* ii 14, 2 (277–9); *Ant.* xx 11, 1 (252–7).

EXCURSUS: AGRIPPA II A.D. 50–(?)92/3

Bibliography

Derenbourg, J., *Histoire de la Palestine*, pp. 252–4.

Saulcy, F. de, 'Étude chronologique de la vie et des monnaies des rois juifs Agrippa I et Agrippa II', Mém. Soc. Franç. de Num. et d'Arch. 3 (1869), pp. 26–56.

Brann, M., 'Biographie Agrippa's II', MGWJ 19 (1870), pp. 433–44, 529–48; 20 (1871), pp. 13–28.

Baerwald, H., *Josephus in Galiläa, sein Verhältniss zu den Parteien, insbesondere zu Justus von Tiberias und Agrippa II* (1877).

Rosenberg, A., RE s.v. 'Iulius' (54).

Abel, F.-M., *Histoire de la Palestine* I (1952), pp. 475–7.

Winter, P., *On the Trial of Jesus* (1961), pp. 75 ff., 127 ff.

Frankfort, T., 'Le royaume d'Agrippa II et son annexion par Domitien', *Mélanges Grenier* (1962), pp. 659–72.

Seyrig, M., 'Les ères d'Agrippa II', RN 6 (1964), pp. 55–65.

Avi-Yonah, M., 'The Epitaph of Mucius Clemens', IEJ 16 (1966), pp. 258–64.

See also the bibliographies above in §§ 16–18.

Agrippa II, whose full name as given on coins and inscriptions was Marcus Iulius Agrippa,[1] son of Agrippa I, seems like almost all the members of the Herodian family to have been educated in Rome. He was there, in any case, when his father died in A.D. 44 and Claudius wished to appoint him as successor to the throne.[2] As has been seen, at the instigation of the emperor's counsellors, who pleaded Agrippa's immaturity, this did not happen. The young prince remained for a time in Rome, where he made use of his connexions at court to be of service to his compatriots, as in the dispute over the High Priest's vestments,[3] and in the conflict during the time of Cumanus.[4] It was mainly due to him that Cumanus did not escape the punishment he

1. On the coins of Agrippa cf. F. W. Madden, *History of Jewish Coinage*, pp. 113–33; *Coins of the Jews* (1881), pp. 139–69; *BMC Palestine*, pp. xcviii–c, 239–47; A. Reifenberg, *Ancient Jewish Coins* (²1947), pp. 25–7, 49–54; Y. Meshorer, *Jewish Coins of the Second Temple Period* (1967), pp. 81–7, 141–53; *idem*, 'A New Type of Coins of Agrippa II', IEJ 21 (1971), pp. 164–5. The basic modern study of the eras of Agrippa II, attested mainly by the coins, is H. Seyrig, 'Les ères d'Agrippa II', RN 6 (1964), pp. 55–65. The name Marcus occurs on a coin from the time of Nero: *Βασιλέος* (*sic*) *Μάρκου Ἀγρίππου* (Madden, *Coins*, p. 146). In the light of this, an inscription at Helbun, not far from Abila of Lysanias, should probably be completed in the following manner: *Ἐπὶ Βασιλέος μεγάλου Μάρκο[υ Ἰουλίου Ἀγρίππα φιλο]καίσαρος καὶ φιλορωμαίων* (*sic*), OGIS 420. The name Iulius appears on an inscription at El Hît, north of Hauran; *Ἐπὶ βασιλέω[ς . . . . Ἰου]λίου Ἀγρίππα*, OGIS 421. The connexion of the inscription with Agrippa II is not absolutely certain but very probable. In any case, even without this evidence the appellation Iulius may be assumed *a priori* for Agrippa II, since the whole family bore the name; see above, p. 452.

2. *Ant.* xix 9, 2 (360–3).

3. *Ant.* xx 1, 2 (10–14); xv 11, 4 (403–9). Cf. above, p. 456.

4. *Ant.* xx 6, 3 (134–6). Cf. above, p. 459.

deserved. But this incident occurred already in A.D. 52,[5] by which time Claudius, in compensation for the loss of his father's territories, had bestowed on him another, though smaller, kingdom. For, some time after the death of his uncle, Herod of Chalcis (see Appendix I), in perhaps A.D. 50, he was given the latter's kingdom in the Lebanon and the same charge of the Temple and right to appoint the High Priests that his uncle had enjoyed.[6] He made frequent use of this right, deposing and nominating High Priests, until the outbreak of the war in A.D. 66. He probably stayed in Rome at first, and did not actually assume the government of his kingdom until after A.D. 52.

He can barely have returned to Palestine, and perhaps not at all, when in A.D. 53 (the 13th year of Claudius) he was granted, in return for the surrender of the small kingdom of Chalcis, a larger realm, namely, the tetrarchy of Philip (Batanaea, Trachonitis and Gaulanitis), the tetrarchy of Lysanias (Abila), as well as the territory of Varus.[7] This territory was enlarged still further after the death of Claudius by Nero, who added to it important parts of Galilee and Peraea, namely

5. About this time, probably in A.D. 53, a text partially preserved in Egyptian papyri, the *Acta Isidori*, represents Agrippa as being accused in Rome by an Alexandrian Greek delegation led by Isidorus. See H. A. Musurillo, *The Acts of the Pagan Martyrs: Acta Alexandrinorum* (1954), no. IV; see the commentary on pp. 117–40; the Agrippa concerned may however be Agrippa I, and the date A.D. 41; see CPJ, no. 156, and p. 398 above.

6. *Ant.* xx 5, 2 (104); *B.J.* ii 12, 1 (223); cf. *Ant.* xx 9, 7 (222) Ἐπεπίστευτο γὰρ ὑπὸ Κλαυδίου Καίσαρος τὴν ἐπιμέλειαν τοῦ ἱεροῦ. There is no mention of the transference of the right to appoint High Priests, but only of its actual exercise (cf. below, § 23, iv). That the grant of the kingdom was not made before A.D. 50 may be concluded from *B.J.* ii 14, 4 (284), according to which Agrippa had reached the 17th year of his reign when war broke out in the month of Artemisius (Iyyar) of A.D. 66. So if he is regarded as a Jewish king and his reign reckoned, in accordance with mR.Sh. 1:1, from 1 Nisan to 1 Nisan, his seventeenth year began on the 1st Nisan A.D. 66, and his first, on the 1st Nisan A.D. 50 at the earliest, but probably somewhat later.

7. *Ant.* xx 7, 1 (138); *B.J.* ii 12, 8 (247). To the tetrarchy of Lysanias doubtless belonged Helbun (not far from Abila Lysanias), where the inscription mentioned above (note 1) was found. Josephus explains ἐπαρχία Οὐάρου in *Vita*, 11 (48 ff.). For the Varus mentioned here (=Noarus, *B.J.* ii 18, 6 (481–6)), whom Josephus describes as ἔκγονος Σοέμου τοῦ περὶ τὸν Λίβανον τετραρχοῦντος, is most probably identical with our Varus. Again, his father Sohaemus was none other than the Soaemus who at the end of A.D. 38 obtained from Caligula τὴν τῶν Ἰτυραίων τῶν Ἀράβων . . . ἀρχήν (Dio lix 12, 2), which territory he governed until his death in A.D. 49, when it was incorporated into the province of Syria (Tac. *Ann.* xii 23). It may therefore be assumed that part of the territory in the Lebanon had been left to his son Varus for a time, and that this is the ἐπαρχία Οὐάρου which Claudius bestowed on Agrippa. Since Agrippa received the new territory in the 13th year of Claudius (24 January 53 to the same date in 54) after ruling over Chalcis for four years (δυναστεύσας ταύτης ἔτη τέσσαρα), and since his 4th year according to the reckoning above (note 5) began on the 1st Nisan A.D. 53, the gift must have been bestowed towards the end of A.D. 53.

the cities of Tiberias and Tarichea with their surrounding districts, and the city of Julias with fourteen neighbouring villages.[8]

8. *Ant.* xx 8, 4 (159); *B.J.* ii 13, 2 (252). In the latter passage, Abila is mentioned as being in Peraea; cf. vol. II, § 23, i. By Julias, A. Schlatter, *Zur Topogr. und Gesch. Palästinas*, p. 50, understands not Julias-Bethsaida, but Julias-Livias, in the vicinity of which there was also an Abel or Abila (see vol. II, § 23, i). These possessions must therefore have been enclaves in southern Peraea widely separated from the rest of Agrippa's territory, cf. A. H. M. Jones, *Cities of the Eastern Roman Provinces*, p. 275, and Frankfort, *op. cit.*, p. 662. A fragment of an inscription bearing Agrippa's name, which was found in southern Peraea, allegedly east of Philadelphia, appears to support this supposition (C. Clermont-Ganneau, CRAI 1898, p. 811; also his *Archaeological Researches in Palestine* I (1899), pp. 499–501). However, the locality of the find is doubtful (Wadi el Kittar? east of Philadelphia), and so is the connexion of the inscription with King Agrippa II (definitely legible is only *φιλο . . . . ιου Αγριπ . . . Κοκκηιου Ακ*; the completion *φιλο[ρωμαιου]* is not certain, and the completion *[Ιουλ]ιου* unlikely according to the remains available, since before *ιου* there is not *Λ* but *N* or *H*) If one of the two kings of this name is meant at all, Agrippa I is the more likely. Thus this evidence does not amount to further proof that the possessions of Agrippa II extended so far to the south. When exactly Nero's gift was made, cannot be determined with certainty. On the later coins of Agrippa, his regnal years are reckoned according to an era beginning in A.D. 61. It is possible that the basis of this era is that this was the year in which Agrippa's territories were increased by Nero. The separation of the respective regions of Galilee and Peraea would then have taken place immediately after the departure of Felix and assumption of office by Festus. This could be the meaning of a passing reference according to which Tiberias remained under Roman rule *μέχρι Φήλικος προεσταμένου τῆς Ἰουδαίας*, *Vita* 9 (37). Yet this *μέχρι* does not of itself mean 'until the end of Felix's term of office'; and this lends uncertainty to the assumption concerning an era of Agrippa beginning in A.D. 56. Nero's enlargement of Agrippa's territory might be adduced as the basis of this also (so Graetz, MGWJ (1877), pp. 344–9, for whom the rebuilding of Caesarea Philippi = Neronias is the basis of the era starting in A.D. 61; this view may be supported by the hypothesis of Meshorer, *op. cit.*, pp. 85–7, that certain coins marked *ΕΠΙ ΒΑΣΙΛΕ(ΩΣ) ΑΓΡΙΠΠ(ΟΥ) ΝΕΡΩΝΙ(ΑΔΟΣ?) Ε* refer to the refoundation in the fifth year of Agrippa's era). The era of A.D. 61 can be calculated from certain coins on which the 26th year of Agrippa is made to synchronize with the 12th consulship of Domitian (Meshorer, *op. cit.*, nos. 141–3) and another on which the 25th year of Agrippa is likewise synchronized with the 12th consulship of Domitian (Meshorer, no. 140). Since this consulship occurs in A.D. 86, the 26th year of Agrippa also began in that year, and consequently the era according to which he reckons, in A.D. 61. For a new type with this era see Y. Meshorer, 'A New Type of Coins of Agrippa II', IEJ 21 (1971), pp. 164–5. An era beginning five years earlier is indicated by two coins and an inscription. Both coins bear the date *ἔτους αί τοῦ καὶ ϛ* (the figure represents the number 6); see Meshorer, nos. 99 and 100. The 11th regnal year of Agrippa according to one era is therefore identical with the 6th according to the other. Both of these eras are applied on an inscription found at Sanamen in Hauran: *ἔτους λζ' τοῦ καὶ λβ' βασιλέως Ἀγρίππα*, OGIS 426 = IGR III 1127, and one from Soueida (years 16 and 21), Syria 5 (1924), p. 324 = SEG VII 970. In each case, one era begins five years before the other. H. Seyrig, *op. cit.* (n. 1), argues that the era of 56 is the basis of the great majority of the year numbers on Agrippa's coinage. Apart from a few coins with the head of Nero, and attributed by Meshorer (above) to A.D. 61 as foundation coins of Neronias, the known coins of Agrippa will thus stretch from A.D. 69/70 to 90/91,

Of Agrippa's private life there is little favourable to report. His sister Berenice,[9] widowed by the death of Herod of Chalcis in A.D. 48 (see below, Appendix I), lived from then on in her brother's house and soon had that weak man so much in her power that—the mother of two children—she was credited with the worst reputation. When the scandal became public, Berenice took steps to quash the evil gossip by inducing King Polemon of Cilicia to marry her and to submit to circumcision for that purpose. The marriage probably did not take place until after A.D. 64.[10] Berenice did not persevere long with Polemon but returned to her brother and seems to have resumed the old relationship with him. At least, this was later spoken about quite openly in Rome.[11]

In matters of foreign policy, Agrippa renounced even the small measure of independence which his father had sought to secure and subordinated himself unconditionally to Rome. He provided auxiliary troops for the Parthian campaign (A.D. 54),[12] and when the new procurator, Festus, came to Palestine in about A.D. 60, he and his sister Berenice hastened with great pomp (μετὰ πολλῆς φαντασίας) to welcome him.[13] He named his capital, Caesarea Philippi, Neronias in honour of the emperor, and the city of Berytus, which his father had adorned with magnificent specimens of pagan art, owed further gifts to his gracious favour.[14] His coins, almost without exception, bear the

9. On Berenice, see RE s.v. 'Berenike' (15); PIR[2] I 651 (Iulia Berenice); E. Miraux, *La reine Bérénice* (1951).

10. Polemon was king of Pontus from A.D. 38 to 64. In A.D. 41, he was awarded in addition part of Cilicia, which he retained when in A.D. 63 Pontus became a Roman province. He ruled in Cilicia until at least the time of Galba (see above, p. 450). As Josephus describes him on the occasion of his marriage merely as *Κιλικίας βασιλεύς*, *Ant.* xx 7, 3 (145), it probably did not take place until after A.D. 64. Support for this is found in the fact that Berenice had already been a widow for a long time after A.D. 48, when Herod of Chalcis died (πολὺν χρόνον ἐπιχηρεύσασα). She was at any rate back in Judaea from A.D. 66; but the period A.D. 64–66 leaves enough time for the marriage, which was of short duration. According to the context in Josephus, it seems that the wedding took place before the death of Claudius (A.D. 54). But as is now apparent, this implication is deceptive. Berenice's age causes least difficulties for she was still able to charm Titus in A.D. 70.

11. *Ant.* xx 7, 3 (145). Cf. Juvenal, *Sat.* vi, 156–60:

> . . . deinde adamans notissimus et Berenices
> in digito factus pretiosior; hunc dedit olim
> barbarus incestae, dedit hunc Agrippa sorori,
> observant ubi festa mero pede sabbata reges,
> et vetus indulget senibus clementia porcis.

12. Tac. *Ann.* xiii 7.

13. Acts 25:13, 23

14. *Ant.* xx 9, 4 (211). The city is named Neronias also on the coins (see n. 7 above). That the capital was not Tiberias—and therefore certainly Neronias—is clear from Josephus, *Vita* 9 (37–9).

names and images of the reigning emperors: Nero, Vespasian, Titus and Domitian. Like his father, he too styled himself *βασιλεὺς μέγας φιλόκαισαρ εὐσεβὴς καὶ φιλορώμαιος*.[15]

That he was altogether more attached to the Roman rather than to the Jewish side is evident from an incident characteristic in yet another connexion of his indolence and weakness. When he visited Jerusalem, he used to stay in the former palace of the Hasmonaeans.[16] This building, which was already tall, he made considerably higher by the addition of a tower so that he could survey the city and the Temple from there, and during his idle hours observe the sacred proceedings. To the priests, this indolent onlooker was offensive, and they blocked his view by building a wall. Agrippa then turned for assistance to his friend, the procurator Festus, who was ready to help. But a Jewish deputation went expressly to Rome and through the mediation of the empress Poppaea arranged that the wall should stay. So from then on Agrippa had to dispense with his pleasant pastime.[17]

In spite of his unconditional submission to Rome, Agrippa nevertheless tried to keep on good terms with Judaism. His brothers-in-law, Azizus of Emesa and Polemon of Cilicia, were required on their marriage to his sisters to submit to circumcision.[18] Rabbinical tradition tells of questions concerning the law which Agrippa's minister, or the king himself, addressed to the famous Rabbi Eliezer (ben Hyrcanus).[19] Even Berenice, who was as bigoted as she was dissolute, appears once as a Nazirite in Jerusalem.[20] Although, according to the Acts of the Apostles, Agrippa and Berenice were curious to see and hear Paul (Acts 25:22 ff.), to the Apostle's fervent testimony, the king would only reply, 'You think it will not take much to make a Christian of me!' (Acts 26:28); from which it is clear that he was admittedly free from fanaticism, but also from any real involvement in religious questions.[21]

15. So OGIS 419=IGR III 1244 (see above, n. 1); cf. OGIS 420=IGR III 1089, 1090, corr. in CRAI 1928, p. 213=SEG VII 217. *βασιλεὺς μέγας* is also found in OGIS 422=IGR III 1194 and OGIS 425=IGR III 1144.

16. According to *Ant.* xx 8, 11 (189 f.) and *B.J.* ii 16, 3 (344), this palace was situated on the so-called Xystus, a public square, from which a bridge led direct to the Temple, *B.J.* vi 6, 2 (325).

17. *Ant.* xx 8, 11 (190–5).

18. *Ant.* xx 7, 1 (139); 3 (145).

19. See Tanḥ., *Lekh* 20; bSuk. 27a; bPes. 107b. Cf. J. Derenbourg, *op. cit.*, pp. 252–4; Graetz, MGWJ (1881), pp. 483–93. Tradition cites sometimes Agrippa's steward, sometimes the king himself, as the questioner.

20. *B.J.* ii 15, 1 (313–14).

21. The words of Agrippa (Acts 26:28) are not meant to be taken ironically: 'The king confesses that with the few words he had spoken Paul had made him feel inclined to become a Christian.' (F. Overbeck, *Kurzgefasstes exegetisches Handbuch zum N.T.* I/4 (1870), pp. 446 f. Cf. also E. Haenchen, *Die Apostelgeschichte* (1956), p. 620, n. 1; E.T. (1971), p. 689, n. 2.) But the fact that he does

Whether motivated by personal conviction or by considerations of mere political expediency, Agrippa certainly promoted the cause of Judaism in various connexions. To support the Temple when its foundations began to sink, and raise it by 20 cubits, he had timber of immense size and beauty imported from the Lebanon at much expense. But owing to the outbreak of the great insurrection, the wood was never put to the use for which it was intended, and later served for the manufacture of engines of war.[22] At their request, he allowed the Levites who sang the psalms in the Temple to wear the linen garments which until then had been a privilege of the priests—a departure from the law of which Josephus expressly disapproves.[23] When in the time of Albinus the building of the Herodian Temple was completed, Agrippa had the city paved with white marble so that the crowds of building workers should not be unemployed.[24] 'And thus at least as costume-maker, woodcutter, paver and an active inspector of the Temple, he deserved well of Jerusalem in its last years.'[25]

When the revolution broke out in the spring of A.D. 66, Agrippa was in Alexandria, where he had gone to pay his respects to the Prefect of Egypt, Tiberius Iulius Alexander, while his sister Berenice remained in Jerusalem because of a Nazirite vow.[26] Agrippa immediately hastened back, and both brother and sister did all in their power to avert the threatening storm. But in vain. Open hostilities began in Jerusalem between the parties for and against the war, in which the king's troops participated on the side of the peace party. When the latter were defeated, and the palaces of Agrippa and Berenice, among others, fell victim to popular fury, the choice of party was decided for him.[27] He stood by the Romans unhesitatingly throughout the war. When Cestius Gallus undertook his unfortunate expedition against Jerusalem, King Agrippa was in his train also, with a considerable number of auxiliary troops.[28] In the further course of the revolt, which proved favourable to the Jews, he lost a large part of his territory. The cities of Tiberias, Tarichea and Gamala joined the revolution. But the king

---

nothing further about it, shows his indifference. Agrippa's saying may also be rendered: 'Soon you will persuade me to play the Christian.' Here ποιεῖν (to act) is to be understood as a theatrical *terminus technicus* (cf. Haenchen, *ibid.*).

22. *B.J.* v 1, 5 (36); *Ant.* xv 11, 3 (391).

23. *Ant.* xx 9, 6 (216–18). See J. Jeremias, *Jerusalem in the Time of Jesus* (1969), pp. 212–13.

24. *Ant.* xx 9, 7 (219–22).

25. Th. Keim, *Bibellex.* III, p. 59.

26. *B.J.* ii 15, 1 (309–14).

27. *B.J.* ii 17, 6 (426).

28. *B.J.* ii 18, 9 (500–3); 19, 3 (523–5).

remained unswervingly loyal to the Roman cause.[29] After the capture of Jotapata in the summer of A.D. 67, he entertained the commander-in-chief Vespasian most splendidly in his capital, Caesarea Philippi,[30] and having in the meanwhile been slightly wounded at the siege of Gamala,[31] was soon afterwards able to repossess his kingdom. For towards the end of A.D. 67, the whole of northern Palestine submitted once more to the Romans.

After the death of Nero (9 June A.D. 68), Titus went to Rome, accompanied by Agrippa, to pay homage to the new emperor, Galba. On the way, they received the news of Galba's murder (15 January A.D. 69). While Titus hastened back to his father, Agrippa continued his journey to Rome, where he stayed for the time being.[32] But after Vespasian was elected emperor by the Egyptian and Syrian legions in July A.D. 69, Berenice—who throughout had strongly supported the Flavian party—hurried to recall her brother to Palestine to pay homage.[33] From this time on, Agrippa was to be found in the company of Titus, to whom Vespasian had entrusted the continued prosecution of the war.[34] And when Titus sponsored magnificent games at great expense in Caesarea Philippi to celebrate the conquest of Jerusalem[35], King Agrippa was no doubt also present, rejoicing as a Roman in the defeat of his people.

After the war ended, Agrippa, as Vespasian's faithful ally, was not only confirmed in the possession of his kingdom but presented with considerable territorial increments, though no details are known of

29. Full details of Agrippa's conduct during the war are given in Keim, *op. cit.*, pp. 60–3. Agrippa was not in Palestine during the interval between the defeat of Cestius Gallus and the advance of Vespasian. He delegated the administration of his kingdom to a certain Noarus or Varus, and when he began to indulge in gross high-handedness, to a certain Aequus Modius (*B.J.* ii 18, 6 (481–3); *Vita* 11 (48–61) and 36 (180); cf. 24 (114). Of the three cities (Tiberias, Tarichea, Gamala), Gamala was of special importance as a strong fortress. It was at first held faithfully for the king by Philip, an officer of Agrippa, *Vita* 11 (46 ff.). But when Philip was recalled by Agrippa, the city went over to the rebels, *Vita* 35–7 (177–85); *B.J.* ii 20, 4 (568) and 6 (574). Agrippa then ordered Aequus Modius to recapture Gamala, *Vita* 24 (114). But a seven months' siege failed to take it, *B.J.* iv 1, 2 (10). Another of Agrippa's officers, Sulla, fought against Josephus, *Vita* 71–3 (398–406). Agrippa remained in Berytus until the spring of A.D. 67, *Vita* 36 (181); 65 (357), then awaited with his troops the arrival of Vespasian in Antioch, *B.J.* iii 2, 4 (29), advanced with Vespasian to Tyre, *Vita* 74 (407) and Ptolemais, *Vita* 65 (342–3) and 74 (410), and seems generally to have kept in close contact with Vespasian, *B.J.* iii 4, 2 (68); 9, 7–8 (443–61); 10, 10 (540–1); iv 1, 3 (14–15).

30. *B.J.* iii 9, 7 (444).

31. *B.J.* iv 1, 3 (14).

32. *B.J.* iv 9, 2 (498–500); Tac. *Hist.* ii 1–2.

33. Tac. *Hist.* ii 81.

34. Tac. *Hist.* v 1.

35. *B.J.* vii 2, 1 (23–4).

their extent.[36] Josephus notes in passing that Arcea (Arca in northern Lebanon, north-east of Tripolis) belonged to the kingdom of Agrippa.[37] From this it may be inferred that his new possessions stretched far to the north. Josephus's failure to mention these northern possessions when describing Agrippa's territory in *B.J.* iii 3, 5 (56–7), might be explained by the hypothesis that at the time of writing these increases in his former territory had not yet taken place; in fact, Josephus does not mention them because in that particular passage he is not concerned to describe the whole of Agrippa's kingdom, but only areas more or less inhabited by Jews. It is perhaps possible that certain of his southern

36. Photius, *Bibliotheca* 33, on Justus of Tiberias, says about Agrippa: *παρέλαβε μὲν τὴν ἀρχὴν ἐπὶ Κλαυδίου, ηὐξήθη δὲ ἐπὶ Νέρωνος καὶ ἔτι μᾶλλον ὑπὸ Οὐεσπασιανοῦ, τελευτᾷ δὲ ἔτει τρίτῳ Τραϊανοῦ.*

37. *B.J.* vii 5, 1 (96–9). Josephus tells here how Titus, on the march from Berytus to Antioch, came upon the so-called Sabbatical river which flows *μέσος Ἀρκαίας τῆς Ἀγρίππα βασιλείας καὶ Ῥαφαναίας*. Thus a city to the north of Berytus is intended, this being undoubtedly the Arcea which, according to the ancient Itineraries, lay between Tripolis and Antaradus, 16–18 Roman miles north of Tripolis, and 32 Roman miles south of Antaradus (18 *mil.pass.*—*Itinerarium Antonini*, ed. Cuntz, p. 21; 16 *mil.pass.*—*Itinerarium Burdigalense, ibid*, p. 94; *Itinera Hierosolymitana*, ed. Geyer (1898), p. 18; CCL clxxv, p. 12; they agree on the figure 32 for the distance from Antaradus). The name is preserved to the present day in a village in northern Lebanon in the place indicated in the Itineraries. In ancient times the city was very well known. The Arkites are named in the genealogical table of the nations in Genesis (Gen. 10:17). Josephus, *Ant.* 1 6, 2 (138) calls it, *Ἄρκην τὴν ἐν τῷ Λιβάνῳ* (to be distinguished from the Arce mentioned in *Ant.* v 1, 22 (85), which lay much further south; in *Ant.* viii 2, 3 (37) Niese reads *Ἀκή*, but for this, *Ant.* ix 14, 2 (285) has *Ἄρκη*). Pliny, *NH* v 18/74, and Ptolemy v 15, 21, simply mention the name. Stephanus Byzant. remarks: *Ἄρκη, πόλις Φοινίκης, ἡ νῦν Ἄρκαι καλουμένη*. Jerome interprets Gen. 10:17: 'Aracaeus, qui Arcas condidit, oppidum contra Tripolim in radicibus Libani situm' (*Quaest. Hebr. in Genesin, opp.* ed. Vallarsi III, 321 = PL xxiii, col. 954; CCL lxxii, p. 13). In the period of the empire, Arca was especially known as the birthplace of Severus Alexander (SHA *V. Sev. Alex.* 1, 5, 13; Aurel, Victor, *Caes*, 24). It was now also called Caesarea (SHA *V. Sev. Alex.* 13: 'apud Arcam Caesaream'; Aurel, Victor, *Caes.* 24; 'cui duplex, Caesarea et Arca, nomen est'). On coins this name occurs as early as the time of Marcus Aurelius (*ΚΑΙΣΑΡΕΩΝ ΤΩΝ ΕΝ ΤΩ ΛΙΒΑΝΩ* or *ΚΑΙΣΑΡΕΙΑΣ ΛΙΒΑΝΟΥ*). From the time of Elagabal, if not earlier, it appears on coins as a Roman colony: *Col. Caesaria Lib(ani)*. An inscription found by E. Renan in the neighbourhood of Botrys refers to a boundary dispute between the Caesareans and Gigartenians (CIL III 183 = ILS 5974 = Renan, *Mission de Phénicie*, p. 149: *Fines positi inter Caesarenses ad Libanum et Gigartenos de vico Sidonior(um) iussu . . .*), from which it should not be concluded that their frontiers adjoined continuously (see Mommsen's remarks in CIL and Renan's, *loc. cit.*; the position of Gigarta may be determined from Pliny's specification, *NH* v 17/78: 'Botrys, Gigarta, Trieris, Calamos, Tripolis'). The plural form, *Ἄρκαι*, used by Stephanus Byz. is confirmed by the Itineraries, Jerome, Socrates (*HE* vii 36) and Hierocles (*Synecdemus*, ed. Parthey, p. 43). Cf. RE s.v. 'Arka' (3); Jones, *Cities of the Eastern Roman Provinces*, esp. pp. 281–2. On the coins, see *BMC Phoenicia*, pp. lxxi–iii and 108–10.

possessions were taken from Agrippa before his death. At the time, anyway, when Josephus wrote his Antiquities (A.D. 93/94) the Jewish colony of Bathyra in Batanaea no longer belonged to Agrippa.[38] It is more probable, however (see below), that Agrippa had died before this.

In 75 A.D. Agrippa and Berenice arrived in Rome and there Berenice continued the love affair with Titus which had started in Palestine.[39] The Jewish queen lived with Titus on the Palatine, while her brother was favoured with the rank of praetor. It was generally expected that there would soon be a formal marriage, a union to which Titus had allegedly committed himself. But dissatisfaction over this in Rome was so great that Titus found himself obliged to send Berenice away.[40] After the death of Vespasian (23 June A.D. 79), she was once more in Rome. But Titus had come to the conclusion that such liaisons were not compatible with the dignity of an emperor, and he ignored her.[41] Thus disappointed, she doubtless returned to Palestine.

Almost nothing more is known of the later life of Berenice and

38. *Ant.* xvii 2, 2 (28). In *B.J.* iii 3, 5 (56), Batanea is reckoned as still part of the territory of Agrippa. On an inscription found by Ewing at Sur in Trachonitis appears: *Ἡρῴδ(ῃ) Αὔμου στρατοπεδαρχήσαντι ἱππέων κολωνειτῶν καὶ στρατιωτῶν καὶ στρατηγήσας* (*sic*) *βασιλεῖ μεγάλῳ Ἀγρίππᾳ κυρίῳ* (OGIS 425 = IGR III 1144; the inscription dates from the year 20, viz. of Agrippa). The *ἱππεῖς κολωνεῖται* were presumably a cavalry division, formed from the descendants of the colonists settled in Trachonitis and Batanea by Herod the Great (see above, pp. 338, 419). They therefore also served under Agrippa II.

39. Even Titus's return to Palestine on the news of Galba's death was ascribed by cynics to his longing for Berenice (Tac. *Hist.* ii 2).

40. Dio lxvi 15, 3–4; Suet. *Div. Tit.* 7: 'insignem reginae Berenices amorem cui etiam nuptias pollicitus ferebatur'. Berenice even publicly assumed the role of Titus's wife (*πάντα ἤδη ὡς γυνὴ αὐτοῦ οὖσα ἐπόιει*, Dio *loc. cit.*). Any approaches made to her evoked Titus's jealous suspicion (*Epit. de Caes.* 10: 'Caecinam consularem adhibitum coenae, vixdum triclinio egressum, ob suspicionem stupratae Berenices uxoris suae, iugulari iussit.'

41. Dio lxvi 18, 1; *Epit. de Caes.* 10: 'ut subiit pondus regium, Berenicen nuptias suas sperantem regredi domum . . . praecepit'; Suet. *Div. Tit.* 7: 'Berenicen statim ab urbe dimisit, invitus invitam'. The *Epitome* and Suetonius speak only of a dismissal of Berenice after Titus's accession to the throne (for *statim* in Suetonius can be understood only in this sense). But Dio distinguishes clearly between two occurrences: the compulsory dismissal before his accession to the throne, and the disregard of Berenice after his accession. On her travels between Palestine and Rome, Berenice seems also to have formed certain connections in Athens, which the council and people commemorated in the following inscription (OGIS 428 = IG II/III² 3449); on the name Iulia, see above, p. 452:

Ἡ βουλὴ ἡ ἐξ Ἀρείου πάγου καὶ
ἡ βουλὴ τῶν χʹ καὶ ὁ δῆμος Ἰου-
λίαν Βερενείκην βασίλισσαν
μεγάλην, Ἰουλίου Ἀγρίππα βασι-
λέως θυγατέρα καὶ μεγάλων
βασιλέων εὐεργετῶν τῆς πό-
λεως ἔκγονον . . . . . .

Agrippa. We are told only that Agrippa corresponded with Josephus about his history of the Jewish war, praised it for its reliability, and bought a copy of the work.[42] Numerous coins of Agrippa confirm the continuance of his reign at least into that of Domitian. The many inaccuracies on these coins in respect to the imperial title have caused much trouble to numismatists. But it is precisely these inaccuracies that are instructive.[43]

In a chronological notice preserved by the so-called Chronographer of A.D. 354, Agrippa's reign, as it seems, lasted until A.D. 85 or 86. Although little weight can be attached to this remark because of the unreliable transmission of the text, it is none the less possible that it stems from sound tradition. It would then be necessary to regard

42. *Vita* 65 (362–7); *c.Ap.* i 9 (51–2).

43. For the literature on the coins, see above, p. 471. The facts of the case are as follows. Besides coins of the time of Nero (see above, p. 473, n. 8) we have coins of Agrippa, (1) from the years 14, 15, 18, 26, 27, 29 of his reign with the inscription *Αὐτοκρά(τορι) Οὐεσπασι(ανῷ) Καίσαρι Σεβαστῷ*, (2) from the years 14, 18, 19, 20, 21, 26, 29 of Agrippa with the inscription *Αὐτοκρ(άτωρ) Τίτος Καῖσαρ Σεβασ(τός)*, (3) from the years 14, 15, 18, 19, 21, 24, 25, 26, 27, 29, 35, of Agrippa with the name of Domitian: to the year 23 inclusive only *Δομιτιανὸς Καῖσαρ*, from the year 24, though not consistently, with the addition *Γερμανικός*. From the years 34 and 35 we have coins based on the era of A.D. 56, in the latter year with the inscription *Αὐτοκρά(τορα) Δομιτια(νὸν) Καίσαρα Γερμανι(κόν)*. See Seyrig, *op. cit.*, and Meshorer, *loc. cit.* The agreement in the year numbers on the coins of all three Flavians puts it beyond doubt that on all these coins the same era is employed, and that Agrippa in his 14th year simultaneously stamped coins bearing the names of Vespasian, Titus and Domitian, and so on. But the era used can only be that of A.D. 61, which is employed on the bilingual coins of Agrippa from his 25th and 26th regnal years (=Domitian's 12th consulate, i.e. A.D. 86; cf. above, n. 7). From these data emerge the following results. (1) The coins from the years 26, 27 and 29 were minted after the deaths of Vespasian and Titus; nevertheless, the term 'divus' is missing from the title of both emperors, perhaps on religious grounds. (2) The coins of the years 14, 15 and 18 were minted during Vespasian's lifetime; nevertheless, Titus is already called *Σεβαστός*. Incorrect though this is, it is indicative of the opinion held in the East in regard to Titus's standing. He was regarded as nothing less than co-regent. (3) The title of Domitian is correct in so far as he is called on the coins of the years 14–19 only *Καῖσαρ*, and on the coins from the year 24 (=A.D. 84) bears the title *Γερμανικός*, which he in fact received in A.D. 84. On the other hand, it was a serious mistake to omit the title *Σεβαστός*, and in some instances also the title *Αὐτοκράτωρ*, on the coins of the years 23–35, which all belong within the period of Domitian's reign, i.e. A.D. 83/4–89/90 and 89/90–90/91. The coins therefore show 'that in Galilee they were not altogether informed concerning the kingdom of this world' (Mommsen). Only the bilingual coins of the year 26 have the correct Latin title: *Imp*(*erator*) *Caes*(*ar*) *divi Vesp. f*(*ilius*) *Domitian*(*us*) *Au*(*gustus*) *Ger*(*manicus*). The attributions of the coins of the years 34 and 35 to the era of A.D. 56 is a hypothesis based on two considerations: (1) the existence of two concurrent eras is clearly attested (n. 7); (2) there are other reasons (see n. 47 below) for concluding that Agrippa had ceased to rule a few years before the death of Domitian (A.D. 96). Cf., however, the survey by B. Kanael in Jahrb. f. Num. u. Geldgesch. 17 (1967), pp. 177–9.

A.D. 85 or 86, not as the year of Agrippa's death,[44] but merely as marking the end of his reign over Jewish territory: the year, that is to say, in which he was deprived of the Jewish colonies which, according to *Ant.* xvii 2, 2 (28), were no longer part of his realm when Josephus wrote his antiquities.[45] It is, however, more likely that Josephus is referring by implication to the death of Agrippa and the passage of his whole kingdom to direct Roman rule (see below).

According to the testimony of Photius,[46] Agrippa died in the third year of Trajan (A.D. 100). The validity of this evidence has been much discussed, but both from Josephus and local inscriptions it seems necessary to conclude that it is unreliable and that Agrippa died about A.D. 92/3.[47] It would appear that he left no

[*Text continues on page* 483

44. So C. Erbes, who bases his investigation concerning the year of Agrippa's death on this passage, ZWTh 39 (1896), pp. 415–32; but cf. e.g. RE s.v. 'Iulius' (54), col. 150.

45. On the Chronographer of A.D. 354, see RE III, 2477 ff.; H. Stern, *Le calendrier de 354* (1956). In this collective chronographic work, at the end of the *liber generationis* is the following computation (*Chronica minora saec.* IV, V, VI, VII, ed. Mommsen, vol. I = *Monum. Germ., Auct. antiquiss.*, IX, 1 (1892), p. 140; the related editions of the *liber generationis* do not have this section): *Ex quo ergo mundus constitutus est usque ad Cyrum regem Persarum anni sunt $\overline{IIII}$DCCCCXVI. deinde Iudei reversi sunt in Iudeam de Babilonia et servierunt annos CCXXX. deinde cum Alexander Magnus Macedo devicit Darium et venit in Iudeam et devicit Perses et deposuit regnum eorum, et sub Macedonibus fuerunt Iudei ann. CCLXX. inde reversi sunt a Macedonibus et sub suis regibus fuerunt usque ad Agrippam, qui novissimus fuit rex Iudaeorum ann. CCCXLV. iterum ab Agrippa usque ad L. Septimum Severum urbis consulem . . . anni sunt $\overline{V}$ DCCCLXX. iterum a Severo usque ad Emilsanum* (*sic*) *et Aquilinum conss. anni sunt LVII. ab Emiliano usque ad Dioclecianum IX et Maximianum VIII. cons. anni sunt LV.* On the various errors in the received text of this section, see Mommsen, *loc. cit.* At the place indicated by dots something has obviously been omitted. Since the years previously mentioned (4916+230+270+345) amount to 5761, whereas the final total is given as 5870, the number 109 must have been omitted, covering the time from Agrippa until the consulship of Septimius Severus, which fell in A.D. 194. Accordingly, Agrippa's reign must have ended in A.D. 85. This coincides remarkably with the date of the bilingual coins from the 12th consulship of Domitian (A.D. 86), which bear on the reverse side, *ἐπὶ βασ(ιλέως) Αγρί(ππα) ἔτ(ους) κζ'* or *κε'*. The coins bear the letters S.C. and were therefore minted *senatus consulto*. This seems to point to some alteration in Agrippa's circumstances at that time. If the Jewish territory was taken from him then, as is perhaps to be inferred from the Chronographer, he must still have retained the region around Trachonitis for the inscription mentioned above (n. 7) of the year 37=32 of his reign (*ἔτους λζ' τοῦ καὶ λβ' βασιλέως Ἀγρίππα*, therefore A.D. 92), was found in Sanamen on the northwestern border of Trachonitis.

46. *Bibliotheca, cod.* 33; see above, n. 35.

47. For discussion of this problem see M. Brann, MGWJ (1871), pp. 26–8; Graetz, MGWJ (1877), pp. 337–52; N. Brüll, Jahrbücher für jüd. Gesch. und Literatur 7 (1885), pp. 51–3; A. Schlatter, *Der Chronograph aus dem zehnten Jahre Antonins*, TU XII 1 (1894), pp. 40 ff.; C. Erbes, *loc. cit.*; RE s.v. 'Iulius' (54),

cols. 149–50; A. H. M. Jones, *The Herods of Judaea* ([2]1967), p. 259; *idem, Cities of the Eastern Roman Provinces* (1941; [2]1971), p. 271; T. Frankfort, 'La date de l'autobiographie de Flavius Josèphe et des oeuvres de Justus de Tiberiade', Revue Belge de philologie et d'histoire 39 (1961), pp. 52–8; 'Le royaume d'Agrippa II et son annexion par Domitien', *Hommages Grenier* (1962), pp. 659–72; Seyrig, *op. cit.* (in n. 1 above); PIR[2] I 132.

A number of different items of evidence have to be taken into consideration. Most are unfortunately open to some doubt:

(1) The statement of Justus of Tiberias, as reported by Photius, *Bib.* 33, that Agrippa died in the third year of Trajan. The epigraphic evidence (see (7) below) makes it certain that Agrippa had ceased to rule at least in Auranitis and Batanaea by the end of the reign of Domitian (A.D. 96), and a reference in the *Antiquities* (see (3) below) that Batanaea had passed to Roman control by A.D. 93/4. Note also that the sentence in Photius *loc. cit.*, τελευτᾷ δὲ ἐν τρίτῳ Τραιάνου οὗ καὶ ἡ ἱστορία κατέληξεν (which refers, if to a work of Justus, to his χρονικόν, not to the work on the Jewish war which Josephus attacks in his *Vita*), falls between that part of the entry relating to Agrippa II and that relating to Justus himself. Furthermore, in Jerome's *de viris illustribus* the entry on Justus (xiv) is followed by that on Clement, which contains the words 'obiit tertio Traiani anno' (PL xxiii, cols. 631–4). These uncertainties serve to weaken further the claim of this passing reference in a late source to refute the implications both of Josephus, (2)–(4) below, and contemporary documents, (5)–(7).

(2) Josephus, *Vita* 65 (367) πορρῷ γὰρ ἦν ἐκεῖνος (Agrippa) τοιαύτης κακοηθείας. The reference is to Agrippa's approval by letter of Josephus's account of the war, but the tense seems none the less to imply that Agrippa was by now dead. Moreover in 65 (359–60) he states clearly that Vespasian, Titus and Agrippa οὐκέτ' εἰσι μεθ' ἡμῶν. If Photius's evidence is rejected, it becomes unnecessary to suppose a second edition of the *Autobiography* and *Antiquities* (so most recently M. Gelzer, 'Die Vita des Josephos', Hermes 80 (1952), pp. 67–90, and A. Pelletier, *Flavius Josèphe, Autobiographie* (1959), pp. xiii–xiv. The natural implication of *Vita* 76 (430) (and cf. Euseb. *HE* vii 10, 8) is that the *Autobiography* was completed near in time to the *Antiquities* (A.D. 93/4) and formed a pendant to it. Note also that *Vita* 76 (429) refers favourably to Domitian, but mentions no later Emperor. Cf. p. 54 above.

(3) Josephus, *Ant.* xvii 2, 2 (28) Ἀγρίππας μέντοι γε ὁ μέγας καὶ ὁ παῖς αὐτοῦ καὶ ὁμώνυμος καὶ πάνυ ἐξετρύχωσιν αὐτούς (the Babylonian Jewish colony at Bathyra in Batanaea), οὐ μέντοι τὰ τῆς ἐλευθερίας κινεῖν ἠθέλησαν. παρ' ὧν Ῥωμαῖοι δεξάμενοι τὴν ἀρχὴν. . . . As mentioned above, the passage is compatible with merely the loss of some territory by Agrippa, but reads more naturally as if his reign had ended altogether by the time (A.D. 93/4) at which the *Antiquities* was completed.

(4) The report of the rumoured incest between Agrippa and Berenice, *Ant.* xx 7, 3 (145), is more likely to have been written after Agrippa's death. This argument cannot of course be decisive.

(5) The coins giving the years 34 and 35 of Agrippa could relate either to the era of 56 or that of 61, so to either 89/90 and 90/91, or to 94/5 and 95/6 (see n. 43).

(6) The latest inscriptional evidence for Agrippa's reign is OGIS 426=IGR III 1127 (see n. 7) from Aere (Sanamein) in Batanaea which gives the years 37 and 32, i.e. 92/3.

(7) An inscription carved on the local basalt stone and now in the museum at Soueida in the Hauran (Auranitis), M. Dunand, *Mission archéologique au Djebel Druze: le musée de Soueida* (1934), p. 49, no. 75., is dated by the 16th year of Domitian, A.D. 96. It clearly implies that Agrippa's rule had ended, as does IGR III 1176 from Aeritae in Trachonitis, dated to the first year of Nerva,

children.[48] His kingdom was without doubt incorporated in the province of Syria.

A.D. 96/7. These inscriptions constitute the decisive evidence for rejecting the date apparently quoted by Photius from Justus of Tiberias.

(8) Compare now the inscription emanating from the Hauran or Djebel Druze and now in the Musée National in Beirut, published by H. Seyrig, Syria 42 (1965), pp. 31–4, *'Αρχιεὺς ὁ ἐπὶ 'Αγρίππου βασιλέος γενόμενος κεντυρίων δεκαοκτὼ ἔτους καὶ ἐπὶ Τραιανοῦ στρατηγὸν* (*sic*) *δέκα*. But for (7) above it would undoubtedly suggest that the man's service under Trajan had succeeded that under Agrippa directly.

48. It is not known whether he married. In the Talmud (bSukk. 27a) the story is told that Agrippa's steward (*epitropos*) addressed a question to R. Eliezer in view of which it was assumed that the questioner had two wives, one in Tiberias, the other in Sephoris. On the strength of this, writers, supposing that the steward asked the question in the name of the king, ascribe two wives to Agrippa (so Derenbourg, *op. cit.*, pp. 252–4; Brann, MGWJ (1871), pp. 13 f.), but this is purely speculative.

§ 20. The Great War with Rome A.D. 66–74(?)

Sources

Josephus, *B.J.* ii 14 (271)–vii end (455); *Vita* 4 (17)–74 (413).
Michel, O., Bauernfeind, O., *Flavius Josephus, De Bello Iudaico: Der jüdische Krieg* I–III (1960–69). [Text, German translation, notes and excursuses.]
Pelletier, A., *Flavius Josèphe, Autobiographie* (1959). [Text, French translation and notes.]
Tac., *Hist.* v 1–13.
Suet., *Div. Vesp.* 4–5, 7–8.
Suet., *Div. Tit.* 4–5.
Cassius Dio lxvi 4–7.
Sulpicius Severus, *Chron.* ii 30.

Bibliography

Mommsen, Th., *Römische Geschichte* V (1885), pp. 529–40. [E.T. *The History of Rome: The Provinces of the Roman Empire from Caesar to Diocletian* II (1886) pp. 206–18.]
Graetz, H., *Geschichte der Juden* III ([5]1905–6), pp. 426–558.
Weber, W., *Josephus und Vespasian* (1921).
Abel, F.-M., *Histoire de la Palestine* I (1952), pp. 483–505, II, pp. 1–43.
Plöger, O., 'Die makkabäischen Burgen', ZDMG 71 (1955), pp. 141–72.
Brandon, S. G. F., *The Fall of Jerusalem and the Christian Church* ([2]1957).
Brandon, S. G. F., *Jesus and the Zealots* (1967).
Farmer, W. R., *Maccabees, Zealots and Josephus* (1957).
Hengel, M., *Die Zeloten* (1961).
Vaux, R. de, *L'archéologie et les manuscrits de la Mer Morte* (1961), esp. pp. 30–3.
Richmond, I. A., 'The Roman Siegeworks of Masada, Israel', JRS 52 (1962), pp. 142–55.
Roth, C., 'The Constitution of the Jewish Republic of 66–70', JSS 9 (1964), pp. 295–319.
Yadin, Y., 'The Excavation of Masada—1963/64. Preliminary Report', IEJ 15 (1965), pp. 1–120.
Yadin, Y., *Masada: Herod's Fortress and the Zealots' Last Stand* (1966).
Prigent, P., *La fin de Jerusalem* (1969), pp. 11–67.
Kreissig, H., *Die sozialen Zusammenhänge des judäischen Krieges* (1970).
Neusner, J., *A Life of Yohanan ben Zakkai* ([2]1970), pp. 145–95.
Neusner, J., *Development of a Legend* (1970), pp. 228–39.
Neusner, J., 'Judaism in a Time of Crisis: Four Responses to the Destruction of the Second Temple', Judaism 21 (1972), pp. 313–27.

On the Jewish coinage minted during the War (see Appendix IV):

Reifenberg, A., *Ancient Jewish Coins* ([2]1947), pp. 28–33.
Kadman, L., *The Coins of the Jewish War of* 66–73 *C.E.* (1960).
Roth, C., 'The Historical Implications of the Jewish Coinage of the First Revolt', IEJ 12 (1962), pp. 36–46.
Yadin, Y., *Masada* (1966), pp. 108–9.

Muehsam, A., *Coin and Temple* (1966), pp. 45–52.
Meshorer, Y., *Jewish Coins of the Second Temple Period* (1967), pp. 88–91.

I. The Outbreak and Triumph of the Revolution A.D. 66

The outbreak of the long threatened revolt was provoked by an act of Florus which, although no worse than many others, was felt more keenly because it injured at the same time the religious sensitivities of the people. Whereas he had until then robbed the citizens, he now ventured to relieve the Temple treasury of seventeen talents. At this, the patience of the people came to an end. There was a great uproar and a couple of wits had the idea of ridiculing the procurator's greed by passing round baskets and collecting donations for the poor unfortunate Florus. Hearing of this, he quickly made up his mind to take bloody revenge for their mockery. He came to Jerusalem with a detachment of soldiers and, despite the entreaties of the chief priests and men of rank, turned over part of the city to be sacked by his troops. A great number of citizens, among them Roman knights of Jewish birth, were seized at random, scourged and crucified. Even the petitions of Queen Berenice, who happened to be in Jerusalem, were unable to check the fury of the procurator and his soldiers.[1]

This took place on 16 Artemisius (Iyyar, April/May) of A.D. 66.[2]

On the following day, Florus demanded that the citizens should give a ceremonious welcome to two cohorts on their way back from Caesarea, and thereby prove their submissiveness and repentance. Although the people were disinclined to do so, the chief priests nevertheless saw to it that, for fear of worse, they agreed to this humiliation. They went out in solemn procession to meet the two cohorts and presented friendly greetings. But the soldiers, apparently under instructions from Florus, offered none in return. At this, the people began to grumble and shout insults against Florus. The soldiers immediately seized their swords and drove the crowds back into the city, killing continuously. A fierce street battle then developed during which the people succeeded in gaining possession of the Temple mount and in cutting the connexion between it and the Antonia fortress. Florus could see that he was too weak to subdue the masses by force. He therefore withdrew to Caesarea, leaving only one cohort behind in Jerusalem and having made the city leaders responsible for the restoration of law and order.[3]

King Agrippa was at that time in Alexandria. When he heard of the

1. *B.J.* ii 14, 6–7 (293–308).
2. *B.J.* ii 15, 2 (315); cf. ii 14, 4 (284). *Ant.* xx 11, 1 (257) (in Nero's 12th year). Though Josephus uses the Macedonian names of the months he actually means the Jewish months; these correspond only approximately to the Julian calendar. For further details, see Appendix III.
3. *B.J.* ii 15, 3–6 (318–22).

disturbances he hurried back to Jerusalem, summoned the people to a meeting at the Xystus (an open square in front of the palace of the Hasmonaeans where he lived), and delivered a long and impressive speech to the crowd with the aim of persuading them to give up their hopeless, and therefore unreasonable and reprehensible resistance.[4] The people declared themselves ready to return to obedience to the emperor. They began to rebuild the corridors between the Antonia and the Temple which they had demolished, and to collect the tax arrears. But when Agrippa demanded that obedience should be shown to Florus also, the Jews' patience was exhausted. He was rejected with scorn and contempt and was obliged to return to his kingdom with his task unachieved.[5]

Meanwhile, the rebels had succeeded in occupying the fortress of Masada. In addition, at the instigation of Eleazar, the son of Ananias the High Priest, it was now decided to suspend the daily sacrifice for the emperor and to accept no more sacrifices whatever from Gentiles. The suspension of the sacrifice for the emperor was tantamount to an open declaration of revolt against the Romans. All the attempts of the leading men, chief priests and Pharisees to persuade the people to revoke this dangerous measure were fruitless. They adhered to their resolution.[6]

When the peace party—primarily the chief priests, the Pharisaic notables, and those related to the Herodian house—saw that nothing was to be achieved by amicable means, they decided to resort to force. First they approached King Agrippa for support. He sent a detachment of three thousand cavalry under the command of Darius and Philippus and with their aid the peace party gained control of the upper city, while the rebels retained possession of the Temple mount and the lower city. A bitter conflict now raged between the two factions. But the king's troops were too weak to withstand the infuriated mob and were obliged to evacuate the upper city. To take vengeance upon their opponents, the rebels set fire to the palaces of Ananias the High Priest and of Agrippa and Berenice.[7]

4. *B.J.* ii 16, 1–5 (345–404); cf. 15, 1 (309–14). The statistical details introduced by Josephus into this speech of Agrippa, were probably obtained from an official record; see L. Friedländer, *De fonte quo Josephus, B.J.* ii 16, 4 *usus sit* (1873); A. von Domaszewski, 'Die Dislokation des römischen Heeres im Jahre 66 n. Chr.', Rhein. Mus. 47 (1892), pp. 207–18.

5. *B.J.* ii 17, 1 (405–7).

6. *B.J.* ii 17, 2–4 (408–21). On the fortress of Masada, see below, p. 511. On the daily sacrifice offered for the emperor, see vol. II, § 24, iv; cf. C. Roth, 'The Debate on the Loyal Sacrifices A.D. 66', HThR 53 (1960), pp. 93–7.

7. *B.J.* ii 17, 4–6 (421–9). The troops sent by Agrippa were *ὑπὸ Δαρείῳ μὲν ἐπάρχῳ* [or *ἱππάρχῃ*], *στρατηγῷ δὲ τῷ Ἰακίμου Φιλίππῳ* , *B.J.* ii 17, 4 (421). Philip was thus the commander-in-chief. He was the grandson of the Babylonian Zamaris who during the time of Herod the Great had founded a Jewish colony in Batanaea,

A few days later—it was the month of Lous (Ab, July/August)—they succeeded in capturing the Antonia fortress also, and then began to lay siege to the upper palace (of Herod), where the troops of the peace party had taken refuge. Resistance was impossible here too, so when Agrippa's troops were guaranteed safe conduct, they gladly accepted. The Roman cohorts escaped to the three fortified towers of the palace (named Hippicus, Phasael and Mariamme). The rest of the palace was set ablaze on the 6th Gorpiaeus (Elul, August/September) by the rebels.[8] On the following day, the High Priest Ananias, who had been in concealment, was seized in his hiding-place and murdered.[9] The one weak support now remaining to the peace party was the Roman cohort besieged in the three towers of Herod's palace. In the end, it too had to yield. In return for surrendering their arms, the soldiers were guaranteed a free withdrawal. But the rebels, who were now masters of the entire city, crowned their victory with murder. Scarcely had the Roman soldiers withdrawn and laid down their arms, when they were treacherously set upon and cut down to the last man.[10]

While the triumph of the revolution was thus being decided in Jerusalem, bloody battles were taking place in many other cities inhabited by both Jews and Gentiles. Where the Jews were in the majority, they massacred their Gentile fellow-citizens, and where the latter had the upper hand they struck down the Jews. The effects of the revolt in the homeland extended as far as Alexandria.[11]

Finally, after long delay and preparation, Cestius Gallus, the governor of Syria, made a move to put down the disturbance in Judaea. With the 12th legion, two thousand picked men from other legions, six cohorts and four *alae* of cavalry, as well as a sizeable number of auxiliaries obligatorily supplied by friendly kings (among them Agrippa), he started out from Alexandria, marched by way of Ptolemais, Caesarea, Antipatris and Lydda—where he arrived at the feast of Tabernacles in the month of Tishri (September/October)—and finally, by way of Beth-Horon, arrived at Gibeon, fifty stadia from Jerusalem, where he

---

Ant. xvii 2, 3 (29). On him, see also *B.J.* ii 20, 1 (556); iv 1, 10 (81). *Vita* 11 (46–61); 35 (177–8); 36 (179–84); 74 (407–9). On an inscription from Deir esh-Shair, Waddington read *Δομήδης [Δ]αρήιος ἔπαρχος βασιλέως μεγάλου Ἀγρίππα. . . .* Le Bas & Waddington, *Inscr.* III, no. 2135. The man would then be identical with our Darius; but OGIS 422 reads *Δ(ι)ομήδης [Χ]άρη(τ)ος.*

8. *B.J.* ii 17, 7–8 (430–40); cf. v 4, 4 (172–83). The leader of Agrippa's troops, Philip, was later called to account because of his behaviour, Josephus, *Vita* 74 (408–9).

9. *B.J.* ii 17, 9 (441).

10. *B.J.* ii 17, 10 (449–56). Cf. Meg. Taan. § 14: 'On the 17th Elul the Romans withdrew from Judah and Jerusalem' (ed. Lichtenstein, HUCA 8–9 (1931–2) pp. 304–5, 320; Derenbourg, *op. cit.*, pp. 443, 445).

11. *B.J.* ii 18, 1–8 (457–98).

pitched camp.[12] An attack made by the Jews from Jerusalem brought the Roman army into great danger but was eventually repulsed.[13] Cestius moved closer to the city and encamped on Mount Scopus, seven stadia from Jerusalem. Four days later, on the 30th Hyperberetaeus (Tishri), he occupied the northerly suburb of Bezetha without encountering resistance, and set it on fire.[14] But when a subsequent assault on the Temple mount failed, he abandoned further attempts and withdrew.[15] Josephus cannot explain this withdrawal. Probably, Cestius realised that his forces were inadequate for an assault on the strongly fortified and boldly defended city. He was to learn the extent of Jewish resolution and determination in battle during the course of his retreat. In a gorge near Beth-Horon through which his route led, he suddenly found himself surrounded on all sides by Jews, and was attacked with such force that his retirement developed into a rout. It was only by leaving behind a great quantity of his equipment, in particular valuable war material which later proved useful to the Jews, that he was able to escape to Antioch with the nucleus of his army. With great jubilation the returning victors entered Jerusalem on 8 Dius (Marḥeshvan, October/November).[16]

12. *B.J.* ii 18, 9–10 (499–509); 19, 1 (513–16). *Γαβαώ* is the Gibeon mentioned frequently in the OT (=El-Jib, north-west of Jerusalem). Cf. Abel, *Géog. Pal.* II, pp. 335–6.

13. *B.J.* ii 19, 2 (517–22).

14. *B.J.* ii 19, 4 (527–30). The *Σκοπός* is mentioned again in *B.J.* ii 19, 7 (542), v 2, 3 (67), 3, 2 (106–8); *Ant.* xi 8, 5 (329) *εἰς τόπον τινὰ Σαφὶν* (so the best MSS.) *λεγόμενον· τὸ δὲ ὄνομα τοῦτο μεταφερόμενον εἰς τὴν Ἑλληνικὴν γλῶτταν Σκοπὸν* (so Niese) *σημαίνει.* צפין is an Aramaizing expression for צופים, as the place is called in the Mishnah, mPes. 3:8. From here, there was a fine view of the city, *Ant.* xi 8, 5 (329); *B.J.* v 2, 3 (67–8). The suburb *Βεζεθά* is referred to again in *B.J.* ii 15, 5 (328); v 4, 2 (151); 5, 8 (246). (Niese would add to this list, *B.J.* ii 19, 4 (530), but the text there is uncertain). It is the most northerly suburb enclosed by the so-called wall of Agrippa, *B.J.* v 4, 2 (151). The interpretation 'New City', given by Josephus, *B.J.* ii 19, 4 (530); v 4, 2 (151), is linguistically not without difficulty; one would rather have expected 'Place of olives' (ב ית זיתא). Cf. C. K. Barrett, *The Gospel according to St. John* (1955), pp. 209–11; J. Jeremias, *The Rediscovery of Bethesda* (1966), pp. 11–12.

15. *B.J.* ii 19, 5–7 (533–45).

16. *B.J.* ii 19, 7–9 (540–55). It is remarkable that Josephus places this event still within Nero's 12th year, *B.J.* ii 19, 9 (555). Since, until the end of the first century A.D., the regnal years of an emperor were calculated from his day of accession (according to Mommsen) and Nero came to the throne on the 13th October A.D. 54, his twelfth year extended only until the 13th October A.D. 66. But 8 Marḥeshvan falls, with rare exceptions, *after* the 13th October. For this reason, Niese, Hermes 28 (1893), pp. 208 ff., assumed that Josephus calculated Roman regnal years in the Jewish fashion, always beginning the year with Xanthicus (Nisan), i.e., in the Spring (that Niese in fact presupposes not the Jewish, but the Tyrian calendar, is irrelevant). According to Niese (*l.c.*, p. 212), Nero's first year was to be counted from the Spring of A.D. 55 (*sic*), as has been observed in, for example, the chronological schema of Porphyry and Eusebius

In face of the exhilaration which now seized Jerusalem the spokesmen for peace were obliged to remain silent. After such decisive blows a change of attitude was unthinkable. Even those opposed to the war were swept along by the force of the circumstances. The inveterate pro-Romans left the city. All the rest were won over to the side of the rebels, partly by force, partly by persuasion (τοὺς μὲν βίᾳ . . . τοὺς δὲ πειθοῖ).[17] They now began to organize the revolution methodically and to prepare for the expected Roman attack. It is characteristic that, in contrast to the later period of the war, the men in whose hands power lay at this stage belonged entirely to the upper classes. It was the chief priests and eminent Pharisees who led the country's defence organization. A popular assembly held in the Temple elected the provincial commanders. Two men, Joseph ben Gorion and the High Priest Ananus, were entrusted with the defence of the capital. Jesus ben Sapphias and Eleazar ben Ananias, both of High Priestly lineage, were sent to Idumaea. Almost every one of the eleven toparchies into which Judaea was divided received its own commander. Galilee was given Josephus son of Matthias, the future historian.[18]

Without doubt, the most difficult and demanding task of all fell to Josephus. For the first Roman attack was to be expected in Galilee. The appointment of Josephus to this vital command reflected his prominent position within the aristocratic society of Judaea. It is this fact which explains why a man who besides his innate intelligence could boast only of a religious education, should suddenly be required to form an army from the untrained Galilean population and with it withstand the attack of legions experienced in war led by seasoned generals. According to his own account, he set about his insoluble task with enthusiasm. For the government of Galilee he appointed on the pattern of the Jerusalem Sanhedrin a council of seventy men to deal with serious legal matters and capital cases; for less important disputes

---

(see above, p. 126: the full calendar year following the accession is counted as the first). These assumptions are, however, extremely improbable since it is more than doubtful that Josephus is to be credited with his own highly artificial method of calculation; he would surely, simply have used the customary one of that time. The most probable explanation seems to be that he made a slip here; he says in *B.J.* ii 14, 4 (284) that the war began in the twelfth year of Nero and thinks that that same year is still current. The date is in fact very close to the limit of the twelfth year.

17. *B.J.* ii 20, 1 (556), 3 (562).

18. *B.J.* ii 20, 3–4 (563–8); *Vita* 7 (28–9). In the latter passage Josephus has the temerity to claim that the purpose of his mission was the pacification of Galilee. As is clear from what has been said, the conduct of the war was in the hands of the commune of Jerusalem (τὸ κοινὸν τῶν Ἱεροσολυμιτῶν, *Vita* 12 (65), 13 (72), 38 (190), 49 (254), 52 (267), 60 (309), 65 (341), 70 (393) and, as its representative, the Sanhedrin: τὸ συνέδριον τῶν Ἱεροσολυμιτῶν . . . *Vita* 12 (62).

a council of seven was appointed in every town.[19] He intended to demonstrate his zeal for the Torah by destroying the palace of Tiberias ornamented with unlawful animal figures. But the revolutionaries had already anticipated him.[20] He endeavoured to meet military needs by, above all, fortifying cities. All the more significant towns of Galilee —Jotapata, Tarichea, Tiberias, Sepphoris, Gischala, Mt. Tabor, even Gamala in Gaulanitis, and many smaller places—were made more or less defensible.[21] But it is with a special pride that he boasts of his efforts to organize the army. He claims to have called up no less than 100,000 men and to have trained them on the Roman model.[22]

While Josephus was thus preparing for war against the Romans, bitter and armed opposition rose against him in his own province. Its moving spirit was John of Gischala, a daring, reckless partisan filled with burning hatred for the Romans and determined to fight them to the last. But while he had sworn death and destruction to the tyrants, he was himself a tyrant in his own circle. To be subordinate was intolerable to him. And least of all could he obey Josephus, whose cautious conduct of the war seemed to him no better than friendship with Rome. He accordingly bent all his efforts towards removing the man he hated and to persuading the people of Galilee to be disloyal to him.[23] His mistrust of Josephus was in fact not unjustified. Josephus knew the Romans too well to believe in a real and final success of the rebellion. From the outset, his heart was not wholly in the cause he represented and at times he somewhat uncautiously permitted this to be seen. On one occasion, some youths from the village of Dabaritta having taken valuable spoil from an official of King Agrippa, Josephus ordered the booty to be handed over to him with the intention—if we may believe him—of returning it to the king when a favourable opportunity presented itself. When the people realized this plan, their mistrust, already stimulated by John of Gischala, rose to the point of

19. *B.J.* ii 20, 5 (570); *Vita* 14 (79). Whether Josephus created the council (cf. *B.J.*) or recognised an existing organisation (cf. *Vita*) remains unsure, but the latter alternative is more likely.

20. *Vita* 12 (65).

21. *B.J.* ii 20, 6 (573–4), *Vita* 37 (188). Of the seven places named, Sepphoris never sided with the revolt but while it was without Roman protection adopted a vacillating position. Thus it attended to the building of its walls, and then when Roman troops were available allowed them to enter. Three of the six remaining cities or strongholds—Tarichea, Tiberias and Gamala—belonged to the territory of Agrippa, and after internal conflicts partly went over to the side of the revolt. A special position was adopted by Gischala, where John the son of Levi, the later hero of the revolt, seized control. He was dissatisfied with Josephus's tepid attitude and did not, therefore, hand over to him the fortification of the city but took it in hand himself.

22. *B.J.* ii 20, 6–8 (572–84).

23. *B.J.* ii 21, 1–2 (585–94); *Vita* 13 (71–6).

open insurrection. In Tarichaea, where Josephus was staying, there was a serious riot. The traitor's life was threatened. It was only by the most excruciating self-humiliation and low cunning that Josephus was able to avert the danger.[24] Some time later in Tiberias he evaded by flight the murderers sent against him by John of Gischala.[25] In the end, John contrived to obtain from Jerusalem the dismissal of Josephus. Four dignitaries were sent for this purpose to Galilee, and were provided with a detachment of 2500 men so that, if necessary, they could enforce the resolution. But Josephus succeeded in having the decree rescinded and the four emissaries recalled. When they would not comply, he had them arrested and sent home to Jerusalem. The inhabitants of Tiberias who continued to rebel were put down by force, and peace was temporarily restored.[26] When the city defected once more a few days later, this time in favour of Agrippa and the Romans, it was again subdued by a ruse.[27]

Meanwhile, Jerusalem had not remained inactive. There too preparations were made to receive the Romans. The wall was strengthened, war materials of every kind were made ready, and the young people trained in the use of their weapons.[28]

Thus the spring of A.D. 67 arrived, and with it the time of the expected Roman onslaught when the young republic would suffer its baptism of fire.

2. The War in Galilee A.D. 67

Nero received in Achaea the news of the defeat of Cestius.[29] Since the continuation of the war could not be left to the defeated general—he seems in any case to have died soon afterwards[30]—the difficult task of subduing the Jewish revolt was transferred to the experienced Vespasian, who made provision for the campaign while it was still winter. Whereas he himself travelled to Antioch and marshalled his

24. *B.J.* ii 21, 3–5 (595–613); *Vita* 26–30 (126–48).
25. *B.J.* ii 21, 6 (614–19); *Vita* 16–18 (84–96).
26. *B.J.* ii 21, 7 (620–30); *Vita* 38–64 (189–335), esp. 38–40 (189–203), 60–64 (309–35).
27. *B.J.* ii 21, 8–10 (632–46); *Vita* 32–34 (155–73). According to *Vita* 66–68 (381–9), the πρῶτοι τῆς βουλῆς of Tiberias sent once again to Agrippa for a garrison. Because of its mixed population, Tiberias was partly pro- and partly anti-Roman, cf. *Vita* 9 (33–42), which is why it sometimes appears as an ally of King Agrippa, and sometimes of John of Gischala. But it is difficult to say anything certain about its attitude in detail because Josephus's account is deliberately distorted.
28. *B.J.* ii 22, 1 (648–9).
29. *B.J.* ii 20, 1 (558); iii 1, 1 (1–3).
30. 'Fato aut taedio occidit', Tac. *Hist.* v 10. In the winter of A.D. 66–7, Cestius Gallus was still in the province. See *Vita* 8 (31), 43 (214), 65 (347), 67 (373–4), 71 (394 ff.).

army there, he sent his son Titus to Alexandria to bring him the 15th legion.[31] As soon as the season allowed, he set off from Antioch and marched to Ptolemais where he meant to await Titus. But before Titus arrived, emissaries from the Galilean town of Sepphoris appeared before Vespasian asking for a Roman garrison.[32] Vespasian hastened to meet their request. A detachment of 6000 men under the leadership of Placidus was sent to the town as a garrison. Thus, without striking a blow the Romans were in possession of one of the most important and heavily fortified places in Galilee.[33] Soon afterwards, Titus came with his legion. The army now at Vespasian's disposal consisted of three complete legions (5th, 10th and 15th), twenty-three auxiliary cohorts, six *alae* of cavalry, and finally the auxiliaries provided by King Agrippa, King Antiochus of Commagene, King Soaemus of Emesa and King Malchus II of Nabataea: in all, some 60,000 men.[34]

When everything was organized, Vespasian set out from Ptolemais and pitched camp on the border of Galilee. Josephus had already taken up a position near the village of Garis, 20 stadia from Sepphoris, *Vita* 71 (395), to await the Roman attack there. The military proficiency of this army proved itself immediately doubtful. As Vespasian's approach became known, the courage of most of the Jewish troops failed even before the Romans became visible; they scattered in all directions. The lowlands of Galilee were abandoned without a sword having been raised and Josephus found himself compelled to flee with the rest to Tiberias.[35] Vespasian had now only to conquer the fortresses.

Josephus at once reported to Jerusalem and requested that, if the war was to continue at all, they should send him an army 'of equal quality to the Romans', a plea which came too late.[36] The main part

31. *B.J.* iii 1, 2–3 (4–8). According to the traditional text of *B.J.* iii 1, 3 (8), Titus had to bring two legions from Alexandria, τὸ πέμπτον καὶ τὸ δέκατον. But it is said of the return of Titus to Vespasian, *B.J.* iii 4, 2 (65) κἀκεῖ (i.e., at Ptolemais) καταλαβὼν τὸν πατέρα δυσὶ τοῖς ἅμα αὐτῷ τάγμασιν, ἦν δὲ τὰ ἐπισημότατα τὸ πέμπτον καὶ τὸ δέκατον, ζεύγνυσι τὸ ἀχθὲν ὑπ' αὐτοῦ πεντεκαιδέκατον. This can only mean that Titus combined the 15th legion, which he had brought from Alexandria, with the 5th and the 10th which were with Vespasian. This also agrees with the fact that, according to Suet. *Div. Tit.* 4, Titus was commander of a legion (*legioni praepositus*), i.e. the 15th. Thus *B.J.* iii 1, 3 (8) should probably be corrected to τὸ πεντεκαιδέκατον. Niese and Thackeray adopt the reading, τὸ πέμπτον καὶ δέκατον.

32. *B.J.* iii 2, 4 (30–4). Sepphoris had already acquired a Roman garrison before Vespasian arrived, *Vita* 71 (394); *B.J.* iii 2, 4 (30–1). Whether this had in the meantime withdrawn, or was only now relieved and strengthened, is not wholly clear. See vol. II, § 23, i.

33. *B.J.* iii 4, 1 (59), *Vita* 74 (411). On Placidus, who was in Galilee prior to Vespasian's arrival, see *Vita* 43 (215).

34. *B.J.* iii 4, 2 (64–9).

35. *B.J.* iii 6, 2–3 (115–31).

36. *B.J.* iii 7, 2 (138–40).

of his army had taken refuge in the strong fortress of Jotapata.[37] He too arrived there on 21 (?) Artemisius (Iyyar, April/May), to conduct the defence in person.[38] By the evening of the next day, Vespasian reached the city with his army, and then began the famous siege, described by Josephus at length, of the not unimportant mountain stronghold. The first assaults brought no result. It was necessary to resort to a regular siege. For a long time a stubborn struggle made the outcome doubtful. Military skill and experience achieved for the one side what the courage of despair, and the astuteness of its commander-in-chief, did for the other. For though a general Josephus may not have been in the proper sense of the term, he was certainly a master of minor tricks and stratagems. He relates with immense gratification how he deceived the Roman generals over a water shortage in the city by having clothes dripping with water hung on the battlements; how he ensured food supplies by dressing his people in skins and sending them out to creep past the Roman sentries at night; how he broke the force of the battering ram by lowering sacks filled with chaff; how he poured boiling oil on the soldiers, or tipped boiled fenugreek onto the assault ramps, thus making the attackers lose their foothold. But the city's fate was not to be averted, either by such tricks or by the boldness of the sorties, in one of which Vespasian himself was wounded. After the besieged had given of their utmost, a deserter betrayed the fact that fatigue was so great that even the sentries were no longer able to stay awake till morning. The Romans made use of this. In absolute silence, Titus one morning scaled the wall with a small detachment, struck down the sleeping sentries and penetrated the city. The legions followed, and the surprised garrison only noticed the Roman entry when they were no longer able to repulse them. Whoever fell into Roman hands, armed or unarmed, men or women, were struck down or enslaved, and the city and its fortifications were razed to the ground. It was on 1 Panemus (Tammuz, June/July) in A.D. 67 that this most important Galilean fortress fell into Roman hands.[39]

37. Jotapata is referred to in the Mishnah (Arak. 9:6) as יודפת. It is described there as an ancient city, surrounded by walls since the time of Joshua. Its location was re-discovered in 1847 by E. G. Schultz at Jefat, due north of Sepphoris. See ZDMG 3 (1849), pp. 49 ff., 59 ff. Cf. Abel, *Géog. Pal.* II, p. 366.

38. *B.J.* iii 7, 3 (142). Since according to *B.J.* iii 7, 33 (316) and 8, 9 (406), the siege lasted 47 days, and according to *B.J.* iii 7, 36 (339), ended on 1 Panemus, the date 21 Artemisius cannot be correct. Niese, Hermes 28 (1893), pp. 202 ff., works out the 47 days by reckoning from 17 Artemisius, as Vespasian's siege-works began four days before Josephus's arrival, *B.J.* iii 7, 3 (142), and by giving 31 days to Artemisius and Daisius. But *B.J.* iii 7, 3 (142) is not concerned with siege-works, but with the building of a road before the siege started.

39. *B.J.* iii 7, 4–36 (145–339).

Josephus had found shelter with forty comrades in a cavern. When he was discovered, he wished to surrender to the Romans, but was prevented from doing so by his companions. They left him only the choice of dying with them, either by their hand or his own. By some kind of ruse—he claims to have proposed that they should kill each other in an order established by lot, and by the luck of the draw to have been the last man remaining—he contrived to escape and carried out his decision to surrender to the Romans.[40] Brought before Vespasian, he assumed the role of a prophet and foretold the general's future elevation to the throne. The result of this, at least was that, although fettered, he was treated more considerately.[41]

On 4 Panemus, Vespasian broke camp and left Jotapata, marching first by way of Ptolemais to Caesarea, where he allowed his troops to rest.[42] While they were recovering from the exertions of the siege, the general travelled to Caesarea Philippi, to his ally King Agrippa, and there took part in festivities for twenty days. After this, he ordered Titus to fetch the legions from Caesarea Maritima and advanced on Tiberias, which, when faced with the Roman army, voluntarily opened its gates and for Agrippa's sake was treated leniently.[43] From there he went on to Tarichea.[44] By a bold stroke on

40. *B.J.* iii 8, 1–8 (340–92).

41. *B.J.* iii 8, 9 (408); Dio lxvi 1; Suet. *Div. Vesp.* 5. According to Zonaras, *Annal.* xi 16, Appian, in the 22nd book of his *Roman History*, also mentioned the Jewish oracle referring to Vespasian (=Appian, ed. Viereck, Roos, F 17). The matter is discussed in detail by W. Weber, *Josephus und Vespasian* (1921), pp. 44 ff., where other references are also given. It is noteworthy that rabbinic tradition ascribes the same prophecy to R. Yoḥanan b. Zakkai. Cf. Weber, *op. cit.*, p. 43, n. 5; J. Neusner, *A Life of Yohanan ben Zakkai Ca. 1–80 C.E.* ([2]1970), pp. 157–66; *Development of a Legend* (1970), pp. 115–19, 163. For similar oracles given by pagan priests to Vespasian and Titus, see Tac. *Hist.* ii 4; ii 78; Suet. *Div. Vesp.* 5; *Div. Tit.* 5.

42. *B.J.* iii 9, 1 (409).

43. *B.J.* iii 9, 7–8 (443–61).

44. *Ταριχέαι* or *Ταριχέα* (both spellings occur) obtained its name from the curing of fish carried out there, Strabo xvi 2, 45 (764). It is first mentioned during the time of Cassius who, during his first administration of Syria in 52–51 B.C., took the city by force, *Ant.* xiv 7, 3 (120); *B.J.* i 8, 9 (180), and returned there during his second administration (in 43 B.C. he wrote to Cicero 'ex castris Taricheis', Cicero, *ad Fam.* xii, 11). According to Jos. *Vita* 32 (157), it lay thirty stadia from Tiberias; it was situated on the Lake of Gennesaret at the foot of a hill, *B.J.* iii 10, 1 (462); Pliny (*NH* v 15/11) places it at the southern end of the lake ('a meridie Tarichea'). The town must therefore have stood on the site, or in the neighbourhood of, Kerak (Beth Yeraḥ). Cf. Robinson, *Biblical Researches in Palestine* II, p. 387; Guérin, *Galilée* I, pp. 275–80. On the other hand, some writers have deduced from Josephus that Tarichea lay north of Tiberias, in the proximity of Mejdel (Migdal Nunayya). Cf. H. Graetz, MGWJ (1880), pp. 484–7, and more recently W. F. Albright, AASOR II/III (1923), pp. 29–46, followed by M. Avi-Yonah, *Atlas of the Period of the Second Temple, the Mishnah and the Talmud*

the part of Titus, this too fell into the hands of the Romans at the beginning of Gorpiaeus (Elul, August/September).[45]

In Galilee, only Gischala and Mount Tabor (Itabyrion) now remained in the hands of the rebels; and in Gaulanitis, the important and strongly fortified Gamala.[46] It was to this last place that Vespasian next turned his attention. The siege soon appeared to be successful. The Romans managed to storm the walls and force their way into the city. But here they met with such bitter resistance that they were forced to withdraw with very heavy losses. The set-back was so severely felt that it needed all Vespasian's authority to restore the morale of the soldiers. Finally, on 23 Hyperberetaeus (Tishri, September/October), the Romans again broke into the city, and on this occasion were able to occupy it completely.[47] During the siege of Gamala, Mount Tabor was also taken by a detachment sent there.[48]

Vespasian left the capture of Gischala to Titus with a detachment of

---

(1966), map 85. But the course of Vespasian's march described by Josephus does not prove that Tarichea was situated north of Tiberias. Vespasian evidently went from Scythopolis, therefore from the south, to Tiberias, *B.J.* iii 9, 7 (446). But there is no ground for supposing that he continued his march towards the north. Rather, after occupying Tiberias, he pitched his camp at Ammathus 'between Tiberias and Tarichea', as appears from a comparison of *B.J.* iv 1, 3 (11) with iii 10, 1 (462). But since the warm springs of Ammathus (cf. the rabbinic **חמתא**, vol. II, § 23 i) are clearly south of Tiberias, Vespasian after the occupation of Tiberias must have turned again towards the south. Those who place Tarichea to the north of Tiberias must do the same to Ammathus. They must then, if they wish to be consistent, deny the identity of the Ammathus mentioned by Josephus and the modern Hammam, a fact that cannot be reasonably questioned. Cf. vol. II, § 23, i. See, however, Abel, *Géog. Pal.* II, pp. 476–7, emphasising the absence of mountains in the neighbourhood of Kerak, a fact irreconcilable with *B.J.* iii 10, 1 (464) *ὑπώρειος*.

45. *B.J.* iii 10, 1–5 (462–502). Suet. *Div. Tit.* 4, ascribes to Titus the conquest of Tarichea and Gamala, the latter place wrongly. After Tarichea was taken by surprise, some of the inhabitants escaped in boats on the lake. Vespasian sent after them on rafts and they all met their death, either by the sword or in the water. This is presumably the 'victoria navalis' celebrated on coins and in the triumphal procession of ships, *B.J.* vii 5, 5 (147) *πολλαὶ δὲ καὶ νῆες εἵποντο. . . .* Cf. Eckhel, *Doctr. Num.* vi, p. 330; *BMC Roman Empire* ii (1930), nos. 597, 599, 616–17 (but see p. xlvii).

46. *B.J.* iv 1, 1 (2). Gamala is mentioned in the Mishnah (Arak. 9:6) among the cities walled since Joshua's time. Historically, its existence can be proved from the time of Alexander Jannaeus, *B.J.* i 4, 8 (105); *Ant.* xiii 15, 3 (394). Josephus describes it as a city in lower Gaulanitis, *πόλις Ταριχεῶν ἄντικρυς ὑπὲρ τὴν λίμνην κειμένη*, *B.J.* iv 1, 1 (2). He states that it stood on a hill that fell away sharply on both sides and in front and was only level at the rear; on the southerly slope, the houses were built close together, one over the other. It is probably to be located near the village of Jamli, in the immediate neighbourhood of Tell el-ehdēb, by the Nahr er-ruḳād. See Abel, *Géog. Pal.* II, p. 325.

47. *B.J.* iv 1, 2–10 (9–83), esp. 10 (83).

48. *B.J.* iv 1, 8 (54–61; esp. 61).

1000 cavalry. He himself led the 5th and 15th legions into winter quarters at Caesarea; the 10th he placed at Scythopolis.[49] Titus made light work of Gischala. On the second day of his presence before the walls of the city, the citizens voluntarily opened the gates, John with his band of Zealots having secretly left the city the night before and fled to Jerusalem.[50]

Thus towards the end of A.D. 67 the whole of northern Palestine was once again subject to the Romans.

3. From the Subjugation of Galilee to the Siege of Jerusalem A.D. 68–69

The fiasco of the first year of the war was disastrous for the leaders of the rebellion. The fanatical nationalists ascribed—not without justification—the unfortunate course of events to a lack of drive in the conduct of the war. They therefore turned all their efforts to obtaining control of the situation and displacing their former leaders. As these would not voluntarily vacate their posts, a fearful and bloody civil war broke out in Jerusalem in the winter of A.D. 67–68.

The head of the fanatical nationalists or Zealots, to use their own name, was John of Gischala. After escaping from Titus, he went to Jerusalem with his troop, in about the beginning of November 67, and tried to rally the people to his side and to stimulate them to carry on the war with greater force and daring. He had no trouble in winning over the young men. And since all sorts of militant elements from the country were in any case pouring into the city, the Zealot party soon had the upper hand.[51] Their first move was to get rid of those suspected of pro-Roman sympathies. A number of the most prominent, among them Antipas, a member of the Herodian house, were locked up and murdered in prison.[52] Another High Priest was then chosen by lot, for the previous ones all belonged to the aristocratic party. This Phannias (or Phanni, Phanasus, Pinḥas) from Aphthia had not the least under-

49. *B.J.* iv 2, 1 (84–7).

50. *B.J.* iv 2, 2–5 (92–120). Gischala (Heb.: גוש חלב) is also named in the Mishnah (Arak 9:6) among the cities walled since Joshua's time. Its name means, 'Fat Soil'. It did in fact produce first-class oil, *Vita* 13 (74–5); *B.J.* ii 21, 1 (591–2); tMen. 9:5; bMen. 85b. According to Jerome, it was the home of the parents of the Apostle Paul, *de viris illustr.* 5 (PL xxiii, 615). In the Jewish tradition of the Middle Ages, it was famed for its graves of rabbis and its ancient synagogue. Identical with el-Jish in Northern Galilee, it is situated about 6 miles north-west of Safed. Some ruins of the ancient synagogue still remain. See Abel, *Géog. Pal.* II, p. 338.

51. *B.J.* iv 3, 1–3 (121–37).

52. *B.J.* iv 3, 4–5 (135–46; esp. 140).

standing of the High Priestly office, but he was a man of the people, and that was the main thing.[53]

The authorities, in the persons of Gorion son of Joseph,[54] the famous Pharisee Simeon ben Gamaliel,[55] the two High Priests Ananus son of Ananus and Jesus son of Gamaliel, tried for their part to rid themselves of the Zealots by force. They exhorted the people to put an end to their wild behaviour.[56] A speech delivered by Ananus to this effect did in fact encourage some of them to fight the Zealots.[57] These were in the minority, and were obliged to withdraw into the inner forecourt of the Temple where, since there was no wish to storm the sacred gates, they were carefully guarded.[58]

To obtain support, the Zealots secretly sent messengers to the warlike Idumaeans and urged them to join them in an alliance on the pretext that the ruling party in Jerusalem was surreptitiously in league with the Romans. The Idumaeans appeared before the walls of the city, but as word had been received of their association with the Zealots they were not admitted.[59] During the night following their arrival there was a fearful storm; the wind howled and the rain poured in torrents. Screened by this, the Zealots managed to open the gates to their allies.[60] Hardly had the Idumaeans set foot in the city when they too began to rob and murder, faithfully supported by the Zealots. The establishment was too weak to offer resistance. The triumph of a reign of terror in Jerusalem was declared. Zealot fury, and that of the Idumaeans in league with them, was directed mainly against the prominent, respected, and well-to-do. All the leaders of the rebellion were disposed of as alleged friends of Rome. Conspicuous among those who fell victim to their blood lust were the High Priests Ananus and Jesus.[61] Once, to give an appearance of legality to their savage operations, they even staged the farce of a formal trial. But when the court summoned for the purpose acquitted the accused, Zacharias ben Baruch, he was killed

53. *B.J.* iv 3, 6–8 (147–57; esp. 155–6). Cf. Derenbourg, *op. cit.*, p. 269; J. Jeremias, *Jerusalem in the Time of Jesus* (1969), pp. 192–3. On the variations of the High Priest's name, see vol. II, § 23, iv.

54. *B.J.* iv 3, 9 (159). But he is probably identical with the Joseph ben Gorion, mentioned above (p. 489).

55. See also *Vita* 38–39 (190–8), 44 (216–27), 60 (309 ff.); W. Bacher, *Die Agada der Tannaiten* I (^{2}1903), pp. 12, 74, 86, 234; II (1890), pp. 322, 385; Derenbourg, *op. cit.* pp. 270–2, 474 ff.; A. Guttmann, *Rabbinic Judaism in the Making* (1970), pp. 182–4.

56. *B.J.* iv 3, 9 (159–61).

57. *B.J.* iv 3, 10 (163–92).

58. *B.J.* iv 3, 12 (196–207).

59. *B.J.* iv 4, 1–4 (224–82).

60. *B.J.* iv 4, 5–7 (283–300).

61. *B.J.* iv 5, 1–3 (305–33).

by a couple of Zealots with the sarcastic cry: 'You have our vote too'.[62]

When the Idumaeans had had enough of murder and, moreover, realized that the allegedly imminent treachery would only slanderously implicate law-abiding citizens, they wished to have nothing more to do with the Zealots and left them.[63] But the Zealots continued their reign of terror with even less restraint. Gorion fell under their lash also. The party of the well to do, and the authorities generally, were by now so intimidated that there was no longer any thought of resistance. John of Gischala was all-powerful in the city.[64]

It may have been at this time, if not earlier, that the Christian community fled from Jerusalem. They left the city 'as a result of divine guidance' and travelled to the Gentile, and therefore undisturbed, city of Pella in Peraea.[65]

Vespasian's generals were of the opinion that these conditions should be exploited and the capital attacked immediately. They believed that with the fighting going on in the city, it could be taken with ease. Not so Vespasian. He considered it wiser to allow full vent to the internal struggle, which would thus lead to exhaustion.[66] To give the capital time to destroy itself, he directed his next operations against Peraea. He set off from Caesarea even before the good season had arrived, occupied Gadara, which had requested a garrison as protection against the anti-Roman elements in the city, on 4 Dystrus (Adar, March), and then returned to Caesarea.[67] A detachment of 3000 infantry and 500 cavalry which he left behind under the leadership of Placidus completed the subjugation of the whole of Peraea as far as Machaerus.[68] With the arrival of better weather,[69] Vespasian once again set off from Caesarea, this time with the greater part of his army, occupied Antipatris, captured Lydda and Jamnia, posted the 5th legion outside Emmaus, made successful forays throughout Idumaea, then turned back northwards by way of Emmaus and marched through Samaria to Neapolis (Shechem) via Corea, where he arrived on 2 Daisius (Sivan,

62. *B.J.* iv 5, 4 (334–43). This Zacharias has also been identified (erroneously) with the man named in Mt. 23:35; Lk. 9:51.

63. *B.J.* iv 5, 5 (345–52); 6, 1 (353).

64. *B.J.* iv 6, 1 (355–65).

65. Euseb. *HE* iii 5, 2–3. Epiphanius, *Haer.* 29, 7; *De mensuris*, 15. The emigration took place κατά τινα χρησμὸν τοῖς αὐτόθι δοκίμοις δι' ἀποκαλύψεως ἐκδοθέντα κ. τ. λ. (Euseb. *HE* iii 5, 3). On Pella, see vol. II, § 23. Cf. S. G. F. Brandon, *The Fall of Jerusalem and the Christian Church* ([2]1957), ch. ix.

66. *B.J.* iv 6, 2–3 (366–7).

67. *B.J.* iv 7, 3–4 (413–19). On Gadara, see vol. II, § 23, i. Because of the description μητρόπολις, *B.J.* iv 7, 3 (413), only the well-known Gadara can be meant, though the context seems to favour a more southern location.

68. *B.J.* iv 7, 4–6 (419–39).

69. *B.J.* iv 8, 1 (443) ὑπὸ τὴν ἀρχὴν τοῦ ἔαρος.

May/June), and then to Jericho.[70] At Jericho and Adida he stationed Roman garrisons, while Gerasa (?) was taken and destroyed by a detachment under the command of Lucius Annius.[71]

The country was now sufficiently subjugated for the siege of the capital to begin. Vespasian therefore turned back to Caesarea and had just started preparations when news arrived of Nero's death (9 June A.D. 68). With this, the situation suddenly changed. The future of the whole empire was uncertain. He accordingly suspended his military projects and decided to await further developments. When news came in the winter of A.D. 68/9 of Galba's elevation to the throne, he sent his son Titus to Rome to pay homage to the new emperor and await his commands. But Titus had reached no further than Corinth when he heard of Galba's assassination (15 January A.D. 69), at which he returned to his father in Caesarea. Vespasian continued for the time being to play a waiting game.[72]

Soon, however, circumstances compelled him once again to take action. A certain Simon Bar-Giora, 'son of the proselyte',[73] a man of the same cast of mind as John of Gischala, inspired by the same fierce desire for freedom and just as intolerant of authority, had profited from the cease-fire to assemble a band of followers with whom he roamed the southern districts of Palestine, robbing and looting. Wherever he went, devastation marked his path. Among other exploits he made a surprise attack on Hebron and made off with a valuable haul of plunder.[74]

Vespasian therefore found it necessary to occupy Judaea even more completely than before. On 5 Daisius (Sivan, May/June) A.D. 69, after letting a full year pass without operations, he set off once again from Caesarea, subjugated the districts of Gophna and Acrabata and the

70. *B.J.* iv 8, 1 (449). On Corea, see above, p. 238. The other towns are known. The 5th legion probably stayed in the fortified camp at Emmaus until A.D. 70, cf. *B.J.* v 1, 6 (42); 2, 3 (68). The inscriptions of soldiers of this legion discovered at Emmaus thus apparently derive from this period (CIL III 6647; 14155 $^{11-12}$). On all three, the man in question is termed 'mil(es) leg(ionis) V Mac(edonicae)'. For further evidence see RE XII, col. 1575, and cf. L.-M. Vincent, F.-M. Abel, *Emmaüs* (1932), pp. 319–25.

71. *B.J.* iv 9, 1 (486). On Adida, see above, p. 186. It seems dubious whether 'Gerasa' can be the famous Hellenistic city of the Decapolis, since this was certainly on the Roman side; see C. H. Kraeling, *Gerasa* (1938), pp. 45–6. L. Annius is possibly L. Annius Bassus, PIR² A 637.

72. *B.J.* iv 9, 2 (497–9). For further details on the journey of Titus, see Tac. *Hist* ii 1–4.

73. Josephus constantly writes *υἱὸς Γιώρα*. The form *Βαργιορᾶς*, Bargiora, appears in Dio lxvi 7, 1, and Tac. *Hist.* v 12. (Tacitus erroneously ascribes this surname to John). גיורא is the Aramaic form of גר 'proselyte'. See vol. III, § 31, v.

74. *B.J.* iv 9, 3–8 (503–29). Cf. O. Michel, 'Studien zu Josephus', NTSt 14 (1967/8), pp. 402–8.

towns of Bethel and Ephraim, and approached the vicinity of Jerusalem, while his tribune Cerealis conquered and destroyed the city of Hebron, which had offered resistance. With the exception of Jerusalem and the fortresses of Herodium, Masada and Machaerus, all Palestine was now subject to Rome.[75]

Even before Simon saw himself prevented from continuing his raids through Idumaea by this campaign of Vespasian, the gates of the capital had already opened to him. Here, until the spring of A.D. 69, John of Gischala had played the all-powerful tyrant. Josephus has fearful tales to relate of the anarchic state of affairs prevailing in Jerusalem under his regime.[76] The people, who had for a long time cursed his rule, saw in the arrival of Simon Bar-Giora a favourable opportunity to get rid of their tyrant. On the suggestion of the High Priest Matthias, Simon was invited to enter the city. He readily accepted the invitation and marched into Jerusalem in the month of Xanthicus (Nisan, March/April), A.D. 69. But whereas the people had hoped to be freed by him from the tyranny of John, they now found themselves with two tyrants, who although they fought each other, nevertheless regarded moneyed citizens as their common enemy.[77]

Vespasian had scarcely returned to Caesarea when news arrived that Vitellius had been raised to the throne as emperor. It then occurred to the legions in Egypt, Palestine, and Syria, that they could provide the empire with an emperor just as well as their comrades in the West, and that Vespasian was more worthy of the throne than the gormandising Vitellius. On 1 July A.D. 69, Vespasian was proclaimed emperor in Egypt. A few days later the Palestinian and Syrian legions followed suit. Before the middle of July, Vespasian was recognized as emperor throughout the entire east.[78]

He now had other things to do than prosecute the war against the rebellious Jews. After receiving embassies at Berytus from many Syrian and other cities, he travelled to Antioch and from there sent Mucianus overland to Rome with an army.[79] He himself went to Alexandria. During his stay there he received word that his cause in

75. *B.J.* iv 9, 9 (550–5). On Gophna and Acrabata, see vol. II, § 23, i. On Bethel and Ephraim, see above pp. 175 and 182.

76. *B.J.* iv 9, 10 (556–65).

77. *B.J.* iv 9, 11–12 (573–7); v 13, 1 (527–33).

78. *B.J.* iv 10, 2–6 (592–620); Tac. *Hist.* ii 79–81; Suet. *Div. Vesp.* 6. Tacitus and Suetonius assert that the Egyptian legions were the first to proclaim Vespasian emperor; according to Josephus, those of Vespasian led the way. Further, according to Tacitus, the proclamation took place 'quintum Nonas Iulias'; according to Suetonius, 'Idus Iul.' After his proclamation as emperor Vespasian gave Josephus his freedom in thankful remembrance of his prophecy, *B.J.* iv 10, 7 (623–9).

79. *B.J.* iv 10, 6 (621); 11, 1 (630–2); Tac. *Hist.* ii 81–3.

Rome had triumphed and that Vitellius had been murdered (20 December A.D. 69). But he stayed on in Alexandria until the beginning of the summer of A.D. 70,[80] whilst his son Titus, to whom he had entrusted the continuance of the Jewish war, led an army to Palestine.[81]

In Jerusalem during this time the internal disruption had grown even worse. Instead of the two parties of John and Simon, there were now three; a new party under Eleazar, Simon's son, had split off from John's party. Simon dominated the upper city and a large part of the lower city; John, the Temple mount; and Eleazar, the inner forecourt of the Temple. All three were locked in ceaseless fighting and had turned the city into a continuous battlefield. In addition, they were rash enough to destroy by fire the enormous stores of grain in the city in order to prevent each other from obtaining it, not realizing that they were thereby robbing themselves of the means of defence.[82] Meanwhile, Titus made preparations for the siege.

4. The Siege and Capture of Jerusalem A.D. 70[83]

The army at Titus's disposal consisted of four legions. Apart from his father's three legions, the 5th, 10th, and 15th, he also had the 12th, which had already been in Syria under Cestius and had started the war so unfortunately. In addition, he had the numerous contingents of the allied kings.[84] The commanders of the legions were Sextus Vettulenus Cerealis for the 5th legion, A. Larcius Lepidus Sulpicianus for the 10th, M. Tittius Frugi for the 15th; the commander of the 12th is not named. At Titus's side as supreme adviser was Tiberius Iulius

80. According to Josephus, *B.J.* iv 11, 5 (658), Vespasian wished to set off for Rome λήξαντος τοῦ χειμῶνος. Tacitus, however, states that he waited in Alexandria for the summer winds and the prospect of a safe voyage (*Hist.* iv 81 'statos aestivis flatibus dies et certa maris opperiebatur'. On his route, see esp. Jos. *B.J.* vii 2, 1 (21–3). But he did not reach Rome until in the second half of A.D. 70. See W. Weber, *Jos. u. Vesp.*, pp. 250 ff.

81. *B.J.* iv 11, 5 (658–63). On Titus's march from Alexandria to Caesarea, see Chambalu, Philologus 51 (1892), pp. 729 ff. On the constitutional position of Titus during the war, see RE VI, cols. 2700–13.

82. *B.J.* v 1, 1–5 (2–35); Tac. *Hist.* v 12. On the destruction of the grain stores, see also the rabbinic tradition (bGit. 56a; Eccl.R. 7:11) in Derenbourg, *op. cit.*, p. 281. On provisioning during the siege see A. Büchler, 'Zur Verproviantirung Jerusalems im Jahre 69/70 n. Chr.', *Gedenkbuch zur Erinnerung an David Kaufmann* (1900), pp. 16–43.

83. The short report of Dio, lxvi 4–6, on the siege of Jerusalem gives a few details absent from Josephus. They are however insignificant, and we cannot be certain where they should be inserted into Josephus's account. Cf. also W. Weber, *Jos. u. Vesp.*, pp. 185 ff.

84. *B.J.* v 1, 6 (41–2); Tac. *Hist.* v 1.

Alexander, the former procurator of Judaea.[85] While a part of the army received orders to meet him outside Jerusalem, Titus himself set off with the main force from Caesarea[86] and reached the walls of the Holy City a few days before Passover of A.D. 70.[87]

Titus had hurried on ahead of the legions with 600 cavalry to reconnoitre, and in doing so had advanced so far that he had run into serious danger from an attack by the Jews. It was only thanks to his own bravery that he escaped.[88] Generally speaking, the Romans had painful experiences of their opponents' fanatical courage from the moment of their arrival. While the 10th legion which had marched from Jericho was still occupied with fortifying its camp on the Mount of the Olives, it was attacked with such ferocity that it almost suffered total defeat. It was only through the personal intervention of Titus that the legion was brought to stand its ground and repulse the attack.[89]

But the fighting between the parties in the city had still not abated. With the Romans standing before the gates, another massacre took place during the Passover festival. Eleazar's party had opened the gates of the Temple forecourt to the festival visitors. John of Gischala exploited this to smuggle in his men with concealed weapons and they fell on Eleazar and his men without warning. Taken unawares, they were too weak to resist and were forced to yield the forecourt to John's

85. *B.J.* vi 4, 3 (237). On the officers mentioned, see L. Renier, 'Mémoire sur les officiers qui assistèrent au conseil de guerre tenu par Titus . . .', Mém. Inst. de France 26, 1 (1867), pp. 269–321. On the individuals (1) Sex. Vettulenus Cerialis, see below, p. 515; (2) (A.) Larcius Lepidus (Sulpicianus), PIR² L 94; (3) 'Titus' Frugi is properly Tittius Frugi, PIR¹ T 208; (4) Tiberius Iulius Alexander (see above, pp. 456–8) is described by Josephus *τῶν στρατευμάτων ἄρχων*, *B.J.* vi 1, 6 (46), *πάντων τῶν στρατευμάτων ἐπάρχων*, *B.J.* vi 4, 3 (237). On the basis of this Mommsen restored the Aradus Inscription (CIG III, p. 1178, n. 4536 f. = Hermes 19 (1884), p. 644 = OGIS 586 = IGR III 1015 *[Τιβερίο]υ Ἰουλίου Ἀλ[ε]ξ[άνδρου ἐπ]άρχου [τ]οῦ Ἰουδαι[κοῦ στρατοῦ]*. Tiberius Iulius Alexander was thus 'Chief of the General Staff'. The position of this official of equestrian rank in an army commanded by a senatorial general was similar to that of the *praefectus praetorio* in an army commanded by the emperor himself. Cf. CIL III 6809. Indeed, a papyrus, P. Hibeh 215, does in fact describe him as *γενομένου καὶ ἐπάρχου πραι[τωρίου]*. This may refer to his role in Titus's army or to an actual tenure of the Praetorian Prefecture in Rome; for the latter view E. G. Turner, JRS 44 (1954), pp. 54–64; cf. PIR² I 139. See now IGLS 4011.

86. *B.J.* v 1, 6 (40).

87. As appears from v 3, 1 (98–9); cf. v 13, 7 (567). It was once supposed that the elder Pliny was also in Titus's army as *ἀντεπίτροπος* of Tiberius Iulius Alexander, following Mommsen's restoration of the Aradus Inscription (CIG III, p. 1178, n. 4536 f.), see n. 85 above. But the identification is untenable. See most recently R. Syme, 'Pliny the Procurator', HSCPh 63 (1965), pp. 201–36.

88. *B.J.* v 2, 1–2 (47–66).

89. *B.J.* v 2, 4–6 (71–97).

supporters. From then on, there were again only two parties in Jerusalem, those of John and of Simon.[90]

To understand the siege which now followed, it is necessary to possess a general idea of the layout of the city.[91] Jerusalem lay on two hills, a higher western one, and a smaller one to the east, divided by a deep ravine running from north to south, the so-called Tyropoeon. On the larger western hill stood the upper city, on the smaller eastern hill, the lower city. The latter was also called the 'Acra' because it was here that the fortress of Jerusalem built by Antiochus Epiphanes had formerly stood.[92] North of the Acra lay the site of the Temple, the extent of which had been considerably enlarged by Herod the Great. Adjoining the Temple area on its northern side was the Antonia fortress. The Temple site was surrounded on all four sides by a strong wall and thus constituted a small fort in its own right. The upper and lower cities were enclosed by a common wall which joined the western wall of the Temple area, then ran westward, swept around the upper and lower cities in a great southern curve, and finally came to an end at the south-eastern corner of the Temple site. Furthermore, the upper city must have been separated from the lower city by a wall running from north to south along the Tyropoeon. For Titus, when already in possession of the lower city, still had to direct his battering-rams against the wall of the upper city. On the west, south and east, the outer wall stood on high precipices; only to the north was the ground reasonably level. Here, there was a second wall forming a northerly curve and enclosing the older suburb; and then, in a still wider northerly sweep, a third wall begun by Agrippa I and only completed during the revolt when necessity demanded it. This third wall enclosed the so-called New City or suburb of Bezetha.[93]

As the city's layout itself demanded, Titus directed his offensive against the northern side, hence against the outermost third, or from the standpoint of the attackers, first wall. It was only then, as the battering-rams began their work at some three points, that the internal fighting ended and both parties, those of John of Gischala and Simon Bar-Giora, joined forces. In one of their attacks they fought with such success that it was due only to the intervention of Titus (who himself shot down twelve of the enemy) that the machines were saved.[94] After fifteen days' work, one of the powerful battering rams knocked a hole

90. *B.J.* v 3, 1 (99–105); Tac. *Hist.* v 12.
91. Cf. the description in *B.J.* v 4 (136–83).
92. For the site of the Acra see above, pp. 154–5.
93. On Bezetha, cf. above, p. 488.
94. *B.J.* v 6, 2–5 (258–90); Suet. *Div. Tit.* 5 'duodecim propugnatores totidem sagittarum confecit ictibus'.

in the wall, the Romans broke in, and on 7 Artemisius (Iyyar, April/May) obtained control of the first wall.[95]

The assault on the second wall began. Five days after the capture of the first, this too gave way before the onslaught of the Roman battering-ram. With a picked band, Titus moved in but was repulsed by the Jews. Four days later, however, he took it again, and this time retained control of it permanently.[96]

He now threw up two ramparts against the upper city and two against the Antonia; each of the four legions had one rampart to build. Simon Bar-Giora conducted the defence of the upper city, John of Gischala that of the Antonia.[97] While the works were in progress, Josephus was ordered to call on the city to surrender.[98] This had no result, but food had already begun to run short and many of the poorer inhabitants went out to look for something to eat. Whoever fell into the hands of the Romans was crucified in full view of the city so as to strike terror into the besieged, or was driven back into the city with mutilated limbs.[99]

On 29 Artemisius (Iyyar, April/May), the four ramparts were completed. Simon and John had been biding their time until they were finished in order to direct all their energy to demolishing these products of exhausting and laborious toil. John of Gischala dealt with those set against the Antonia by digging under them a tunnel supported by posts, to which he then set fire. As a result, the ramparts fell in and were destroyed in the blaze. Two days later, Simon Bar-Giora fired and destroyed the ramparts against the upper city also.[100]

Before attempting to construct new ramparts, Titus resorted to another device. He ringed the whole city with a continuous stone wall (τεῖχος) so as to cut off supplies and starve it out. The task was completed with amazing speed within three days. Numerous armed guards prevented anyone from emerging.[101] As a result, starvation in the city reached fearful proportions: Josephus's imagination was fertile, but even if only half of what he says is true, it was still horrible enough.[102]

95. *B.J.* v 7, 2 (299–302).
96. *B.J.* v 7, 3–4 (303–30); 8, 1–2 (331–47).
97. *B.J.* v 9, 2 (358); cf. 11, 4 (467–72).
98. *B.J.* v 9, 3–4 (362–419).
99. *B.J.* v 10, 2–5 (424–45); 11, 1–2 (446–59).
100. *B.J.* v 11, 4–6 (466–85).
101. *B.J.* v 12, 1–32 (499–511); cf. Lk. 19:43.
102. *B.J.* v 12, 3 (512–18); 13, 7 (567–72); vi 3, 3–4 (193–213). Cf. *Aboth de R. Nathan A*, 6 (ed. Schechter, p. 32); cf. bGit. 56 ab. One famous story is that of Maria of Beth-Ezob who, driven by hunger, devoured her own child. See *B.J* vi 3, 4 (201–13); Euseb. *HE* iii 6; Jerome, *ad Joel* 1:9 ff. (CCL lxxvi, p. 170). But the eating of one's own children is a customary part of the portrayal of the horrors of war: thus as a threat: Lev. 26:29, Dt. 28:29, Jer. 19:9, Ezek. 5:10; or as history, 2 Kg. 6:28–9, Lam. 2:20, 4:10; Bar. 2:3.

But only a Josephus can, in such circumstances, reproach John of Gischala for applying the sacred oil and wine to profane purposes.[103]

In the meantime, Titus also built new ramparts, this time four against the Antonia. Owing to the complete devastation of the surrounding district, the timber for these had to be brought from a distance of 90 stadia (4½ hours journey).[104] After twenty-one days of labour they were completed. An attack on them made by John of Gischala on 1 Panemus (Tammuz, June/July) misfired because it was not carried out with the same vigour as before, whereas the Romans had redoubled their vigilance.[105] Scarcely had the Jews withdrawn when the battering rams began to beat against the wall, at first without much success. Nevertheless, it was so badly shattered by the blows that it soon afterwards subsided of its own accord at the spot where the rams had been at work. Even so, the storming operation was still difficult because John of Gischala had already erected a second wall behind it. On 3 Panemus, after a rousing speech by Titus, a Syrian soldier named Sabinus tried with eleven comrades to scale the wall, but fell with three of them in battle.[106] Two days later (5 Panemus) some twenty to thirty others combined to renew the attempt. They scaled the wall secretly by night and struck down the first sentries; Titus pressed on quickly after them and drove the Jews back to the Temple zone. The Romans were indeed driven back from there, but they captured the Antonia, which was at once razed to the ground.[107]

In spite of war and famine, the daily morning and evening sacrifice had continued to be offered regularly. But on 17 Panemus it finally had to be suspended, though even then not so much due to the famine as the lack of men.[108] Since a further call for surrender by Josephus brought no result, and a night assault on the Temple area by a picked military detachment proved a failure,[109] Titus now made preparations for a full-scale attack. The Temple formed a fairly regular square surrounded by stout walls along the inside of which ran colonnades. Within this great area, the inner forecourt, which was likewise surrounded on all sides by strong walls, formed a second line of defence offering safety to the besieged even after the loss of the outer court. Titus had first to secure control of the outer walls. Once again four

103. *B.J.* v 13, 6 (562–6). Cf. mMid. 2:6, referring to the 'Chamber of the House of Oil' situated in the south-west corner of the Court of the Women where the wine and oil were stored.

104. *B.J.* v 12, 4 (522–4).

105. *B.J.* vi 1, 1–3 (3–25).

106. *B.J.* vi 1, 3–6 (26–67).

107. *B.J.* vi 1, 7–8 (68–92); 2, 1 (93).

108. *B.J.* vi 2, 1 (94). Cf. mTaan 4:6, 'On 17 Tammuz the daily offering (**תמיד**) ceased'. This is listed among the five disasters which took place on that day.

109. *B.J.* vi 2, 1–6 (94–148).

ramparts were erected, the building materials for which had to be brought from a distance of 100 stadia (5 hours journey),[110] On 27 Panemus, while this work was going on, a number of Romans met their death. Deceived by the Jews' retreat from the top of the western colonnade, they climbed it. But it had been crammed with combustible materials, and once the Romans were up, the Jews set fire to the colonnade. The blaze spread with such rapidity that the soldiers were unable to escape and perished in the flames.[111]

When on 8 Lous (Ab, July/August) the ramparts were finished, the rams were produced and the siege operation began. But they could do nothing against the gigantic walls. To achieve his aim, Titus therefore fired the gates and thus opened a way into the outer Temple court.[112] On the following day (9 Ab), when the gates were completely burnt down, he held a council of war at which it was decided to spare the Temple.[113] But a day later (10 Ab), the Jews mounted two attacks in quick succession from the inner forecourt. In repelling the second of these, one of the soldiers previously busy extinguishing the blaze in the colonnades, threw a brand into a chamber of the Temple proper.[114] When Titus was informed of this, he hurried to the scene, the generals and legions after him. He gave orders to extinguish the blaze. But in the wild battle which now developed, his commands were ignored and the flames took an ever-increasing hold. He still hoped to save at least the inner Temple, and repeated the orders to extinguish the fire. But in their fury, the soldiers no longer paid attention to his commands. Instead of putting it out, they threw in new firebrands and the whole magnificent edifice fell prey to the flames with no hope of its being saved. Titus was just able to inspect the interior before it was overwhelmed.[115]

110. *B.J.* vi 2, 7 (149–51).

111. *B.J.* vi 3, 1–2 (177–92).

112. *B.J.* vi 4, 1–2 (220–35). The use of fire is also mentioned by Dio lxvi 6, 1, but he ascribes it to the Jews, who employed it to hinder the Romans from advancing. This seems very improbable.

113. *B.J.* vi, 4, 3 (237–43).

114. *B.J.* vi 4, 4–5 (244–53).

115. *B.J.* vi 4, 6–7 (254–66). According to the foregoing, the date of the Temple fire is 10 Lous = Ab, as Josephus also expressly states, *B.J.* vi 4, 5 (250). Rabbinic tradition, however, places the destruction of the Temple on 9 Ab (mTaan. 4:6), and in fact on the eve of that day (bTaan. 29a), i.e. by our reckoning, on 8 Ab. It thus regards as the day of the destruction the day on which Titus fired the gates of the Temple. Rabbinic tradition records (bTaan. 29a) that it was precisely at the 'going out' of the Sabbath that the Temple was destroyed. Dio represents Jerusalem as destroyed *ἐν αὐτῇ τῇ τοῦ Κρόνου ἡμέρᾳ* . . . (lxvi 7,2).

Josephus's narrative, quoted above, presents Titus as striving to preserve the Temple proper, *B.J.* vi 4, 3 (241–3). An alternative view is that of Sulpicius Severus, *Chron.* ii 30, 6–7; 'Fertur Titus adhibito consilio prius deliberasse, an

While the Romans butchered all who fell into their hands, children and the aged, priests and people, and deliberately fanned the terrible conflagration so that nothing would be spared, John of Gischala with his Zealot band managed to escape into the upper city. The Temple had not yet burnt out before the legions had set up their standards in the outer court and hailed their general as Imperator.[116]

The destruction of the Temple did not, however, mean that the conquest was completed. The upper city, the final sanctuary of the besieged, still remained to be taken. Titus once again called on Simon and John to capitulate. But the besieged demanded a free withdrawal, which could not be granted them.[117] At Titus's command, those parts of the city occupied by the Romans—Ophlas, the Archives, the council chamber, the lower city as far as Siloam—were now set ablaze, while in the upper city the tyrants engaged in murder and plunder.[118]

---

templum tanti operis everteret. Etenim nonnullis videbatur, aedem sacratam ultra omnia mortalia illustrem non oportere deleri, quae servata modestiae Romanum testimonium, diruta perennem crudelitatis notam praeberet. At contra alii et Titus ipse evertendum in primis templum censebant, quo plenius Iudaeorum et Christianorum religio tolleretur: quippe has religiones, licet contrarias sibi, isdem tamen ab auctoribus profectas; Christianos ex Iudaeis extitisse: radice sublata stirpem facile perituram.' With a somewhat different motivation, Orosius, vii 9, 5–6, also ascribes the destruction to Titus. This view, which would suggest that Josephus may have deliberately altered the account to clear Titus of the 'nota crudelitatis', is upheld by W. Weber, *Josephus und Vespasian* (1921), pp. 72 ff., following J. Bernays, *Ueber die Chronik des Sulpicius Severus* (1861), pp. 48–61 = *Ges. Abhandlungen* II, pp. 159–81, etc. Cf. Mommsen, *Röm. Gesch.* V(1885), 538 ff. = ET II, pp. 217 ff., and H. Montefiore, 'Sulpicius Severus and Titus' Council of War', Historia 11 (1962), pp. 156–70. In support of the latter view it may be urged that the account in Josephus was written to 'whitewash' Titus, whereas his conduct elsewhere (e.g., in the slaughter of thousands of Jews in the 'games') does not suggest that he would be any less brutal here. Valeton has drawn attention to the fact that the false impression in Josephus is conveyed by his failure to mention (a) that in the War Council it was expressly resolved to occupy the Temple, and thus, if need be, to take it by force, if not also to destroy it; and (b) that the Temple was occupied by the Jews, and consequently had to be stormed. Both follow from Dio lxvi 6, 1–3, and indirectly also from Josephus himself, *B.J.* vi 4, 5 (249); 5, 1 (271–80). But whatever may have been the case, a definite directive on the part of Vespasian (which Valeton claimed) cannot be discovered. If there had been one, the Council of War would have been superfluous; see I. M. J. Valeton Verslagen en Mededeelingen der K. Akad. van Wetenschappen, Afd. Letterkunde, 4. reeks, deel 3 (1899), pp. 87–116.

116. *B.J.* vi 5, 1–2 (271–87). For the hailing of Titus as Imperator, see *B.J.* vi 6, 1 (316); Suet. *Div. Tit.* 5; Dio lxvi 7, 2; Oros. vii 9, 6. On the significance of the proceedings, see esp. Suet., *loc. cit.* (Titus was suspected of wishing to defect from Vespasian and make himself the independent ruler of the East). Further details RE VI, col. 2490.

117. *B.J.* vi 6, 2–3 (323–53).

118. *B.J.* vi 6, 3 (353–5); 7, 2–3 (363–73).

Since there was no prospect of a voluntary surrender, it was once again necessary to erect ramparts. They were thrown up at the north-western corner of the upper city near Herod's palace, and at the north-eastern corner, close to the so-called Xystus. Their construction began on 20 Lous (Ab, July/August) and finished on 7 Gorpiaeus (Elul, August/September). The battering-rams soon breached the wall and the soldiers forced their way in with little difficulty; the besieged in their desperate condition were no longer able to offer serious resistance.[119] Some of them tried to fight their way through the surrounding walls at Siloam. But they were repulsed and fled into underground galleries. Meanwhile the entire upper city was occupied by the Romans. The military standards were set up and the hymn of victory sung. The soldiers ranged through the city, murdering, burning and looting. After a siege of five months during which laboriously, step by step, they had gained one position after another, on 8 Gorpiaeus the whole city was at last in the hands of the victors.[120]

Those of the inhabitants who had not yet fallen victim to famine or sword, were executed or sent to the mines, or reserved for gladiatorial combat. The handsomest and strongest of the men were selected for the triumph. Among the refugees compelled by hunger to emerge from the underground galleries was John of Gischala. As he begged for mercy, his life was spared, but he was sentenced to life-long imprisonment. Simon Bar-Giora, who was not arrested until some time later, was kept as a victim for the triumph.[121] The city was levelled to the ground. Only the three towers of Herod's palace—Hippicus, Phasael and Mariamme—and one part of the wall were left standing, the first as memorials to the city's former strength, the other as protection for the garrison remaining behind. The hard-won victory was celebrated by Titus with a panegyric addressed to the army, rewards for outstanding acts of valour in battle, a sacrifice of thanks-giving and a festive banquet.[122]

5. The Sequel to the War A.D. 71–74(?)

While the 10th legion remained behind in Jerusalem as a garrison, Titus marched with the rest of the army to Caesarea Maritima, where

119. *B.J.* vi 8, 1–5 (274–407).

120. *B.J.* vi 8, 5 (407); 10, 1 (435). For preliminary reports of recent archaeological evidence of the destruction of Jerusalem see B. Mazar, BA 33 (1970), pp. 47–60; N. Avigad, IEJ 20 (1970), pp. 6–8.

121. *B.J.* vi 9, 2 (415–19), 4 (427–34); vii 2, 1–2 (21–36).

122. *B.J.* vii 1, 1–3 (1–17). The so-called Tower of David in Jerusalem incorporates the remains of one of these three towers (Phasael).

the booty was deposited and the prisoners placed in custody.[123] From there, Titus went to Caesarea Philippi, where some of the prisoners were made to take part in fights with wild animals and gladiatorial games.[124] At Caesarea Maritima, where he returned once more, he celebrated the birthday of his brother Domitian (24 October), again with spectacular games. Similarly, at Berytus he celebrated his father Vespasian's birthday (17 November). After a rather protracted stay in Berytus,[125] Titus marched to Antioch, celebrating in the cities through which he passed with shows in which the Jewish prisoners were forced to kill each other in gladiatorial combats. A brief halt in Antioch was followed by a further march to Zeugma on the Euphrates; from there, he returned to Antioch, and from there travelled to Egypt. At Alexandria he discharged the legions. Seven hundred prisoners distinguished for their handsome appearance, together with the ring-leaders Simon and John, were reserved for the triumph.[126] Titus then sailed for Rome,[127] where he was received by his father and the people with jubilation and celebrated (in A.D. 71) a joint triumph with his father and brother despite the fact that the Senate had granted each of them a triumph of his own.[128] In the course of it, Simon Bar-Giora,

123. *B.J.* vii 2–3 (5, 17, 20). At the time of Cassius Dio (the beginning of the third century A.D.), the 10th legion was still based in Judaea, Dio lv 23, 4. Eusebius is the first to mention it as the garrison of Aela on the Red Sea (*Onomast.* ed. Klostermann, p. 6). Inscriptions referring to it have been found at Jerusalem, e.g., CIL III 6638; 6659=12090; 14155[3, 23]; AE 1904, 202; 1939, 157; cf. 1926, 136; 1928, 36; 1964, 189. Cf. ILS 9059 referring to the discharge in A.D. 93 of veterans 'qui militaverunt Hierosolymnis (*sic*) in leg. X Fretense'. Cf. RE XII, cols. 1673–5 and B. Lifshitz, 'Sur la date du transfert de la legio VI Ferrata en Palestine', Latomus 19 (1960), pp. 109–11. See also IEJ 14 (1964), pp. 244, 250–2 (*vexillationes* at Caesarea); D. Barag, 'The Countermarks of the *Legio Decima Fretensis*', in *The Patterns of Monetary Development in Phoenicia and Palestine in Antiquity*, ed. A. Kindler (1967), pp. 117–25; *idem*, 'Brick Stamp-Impressions of the Legio X Fretensis', Bonn. Jahrb. 167 (1967), pp. 244–67 (=Eretz Israel 8 (1967), pp. 168–82, in Hebrew).

124. *B.J.* vii 2, 1 (23–4).

125. *B.J.* vii 3, 1 (39).

126. *B.J.* vii 5, 1–3 (96–118).

127. Chambalu placed Titus's arrival in Rome in 'about the middle of June 71', Philologus 44 (1885), 507–17. See RE VI, col. 2706.

128. *B.J.* vii 5, 3–7 (119–58); Dio lxvi 7, 2. The triumphal arch of Titus, which still stands, was not erected 'divo Tito' until after his death. The Jewish War is not commemorated in the inscription on the Arch of Titus (CIL VI 945=ILS 265). On the other hand, another Arch which stood in the Circus Maximus and was destroyed in the 14th or perhaps the 15th century, bore the following pompous and, as far as the earlier history of Jerusalem is concerned, untrue inscription (dated A.D. 81 and preserved in Codex Einsiedlensis): 'Senatus populusque Romanus imp. Tito Caesari divi Vespasiani f. Vespasian[o] Augusto . . . quod praeceptis patri(s) consiliisq(ue) gentem Iudaeorum domuit et urbem Hierusolymam omnibus ante se ducibus regibus gentibus aut frustra petitam aut omnino intem[p]tatam delevit', CIL VI 944=ILS 264. Coins of Vespasian, Titus and

the enemy leader, was by ancient custom carried from the procession to prison, and there executed.[129] Among the prizes of war carried in the triumphal march were the two precious golden objects from the Temple at Jerusalem—the Table of Shewbread and the Seven-branched Candlestick.[130] Vespasian deposited these in the Temple of the Goddess of Peace (*Εἰρήνη*, Pax) which he had rebuilt,[131] but which was later burnt down under Commodus.[132] It is not known what happened to them afterwards. They were probably taken to Africa by Geiseric when the Vandals sacked Rome in A.D. 455, and from there transferred to Constantinople by Belisarius when he destroyed the Vandal empire in A.D. 534.[133]

Domitian have also been found bearing the words: Ἰουδαίας ἑαλωκυίας, *devicta Iudea, Iudaea capta. BMC Roman Empire* II (1930), p. 473; *BMC Palestine*, pp. 276–9; Reifenberg, *Ancient Jewish Coins* ([2]1947), pp. 59–60; Meshorer, *Jewish Coins of the Second Temple Period*, pp. 107–9.

129. *B.J.* vii 5, 6 (153–5); Dio lxvi 7, 2. Simon was taken 'to the place adjoining the Forum', *B.J.* vii 5, 6 (154), εἰς τὸν ἐπὶ τῆς ἀγορᾶς ἐσύρετο τόπον . . . Havercamp rightly comments here: '*scil.* carcerem, quem Livius dicit Foro imminere'. The *carcer Mamertinus* was situated by the Forum. It was here, in its lower part, the *Tullianum*, that for example Jugurtha and the Catilinarian conspirators were strangled. Cf. RE s.v. 'Tullianum', and Platner and Ashby, *Topographical Dictionary of Ancient Rome* (1929), s.v. 'carcer'.

130. *B.J.* vii 5, 5 (148). Both are represented on the Arch of Titus in Rome. Cf. W. Eltester, 'Der Siebenarmige Leuchter und der Titusbogen', *Festschrift J. Jeremias* (1960), pp. 62–76; L. Yarden, *The Tree of Light* (1971), pp. 5–7.

131. *B.J.* vii 5, 7 (158–62). The temple of *Pax* was not dedicated until A.D. 75 (Dio lxvi 15, 1). Vespasian kept a Book of the Law taken from Jerusalem and the purple curtains from the Temple in his palace, *B.J.* vii 5, 7 (162).

132. Herodian i 14, 2.

133. On the later fate of these items of spoil, see F. Gregorovius, *Geschichte der Stadt Rom im Mittelalter* I ([4]1886), pp. 204–7; also Yarden, *op. cit.*, pp. 7–8. Among the treasures accumulated by Alaric in Carcassone were 'precious objects belonging to King Solomon', namely articles adorned with gems brought from Jerusalem by the Romans (πρασία γὰρ λίθος αὐτῶν τὰ πολλὰ ἐκαλλώπιζεν, ἅπερ ἐξ Ἱεροσολύμων Ῥωμαῖοι τὸ παλαιὸν εἷλον. . ., Procop. *de bello Gothico* i 12, 42. But other things, and among them, as it seems, the Temple vessels, must have remained in Rome, for in the sack of Rome in A.D. 455, Geiseric took among other things: κειμήλια ὁλόχρυσα καὶ διάλιθα ἐκκλησιαστικά, καὶ σκεύη Ἑβραϊκά, ἅπερ ὁ Οὐεσπασιανοῦ Τίτος μετὰ τὴν ἅλωσιν Ἱεροσολύμων εἰς Ῥώμην ἤγαγεν . . ., Theophanes, *Chronographia*, ed. de Boer, I (1883), p. 109; cf. Georgius Cedrenus, ed. Bekker, I, p. 606; Anastasius *Biblioth.*, in de Boer's edition of Theophanes, II, 109. It was these items that Belisarius brought to Constantinople in A.D. 534 from Carthage (Procopius, *de bello Vandalico* ii 9, 5 ἐν οἷς καὶ τὰ Ἰουδαίων κειμήλια ἦν, ἅπερ Οὐεσπασιανοῦ Τίτος μετὰ τὴν τῶν Ἱεροσολύμων ἅλωσιν ἐς Ῥώμην ξὺν ἑτέροις τισὶν ἤνεγκε. So also, Theophanes, *Chronographia* (ed. de Boer), I, 199, and Anastasius, *Biblioth.* (*ibidem*) II, 138. Procopius goes on to say that when a certain Jew saw these objects, he drew the attention of one of the emperor's trusted men to the fact that their unlawful possession had been the downfall of Rome and Carthage. Justinian therefore sent them at once to Jerusalem (ἐς τῶν Χριστιανῶν τὰ ἐν Ἱεροσολύμοις ἱερά . . .).

The capture of the capital certainly entitled Titus to the celebration of a triumph. But Palestine was still not completely subdued, for the fortresses of Herodium, Machaerus and Masada remained in rebel hands. Their reduction was assigned to Lucilius Bassus, the governor of Palestine at that time. In the case of Herodium he seems to have succeeded without difficulty.[134] The siege of Machaerus lasted longer.[135] Nevertheless, it too surrendered before any attack was necessary, against a guarantee of free withdrawal. The decision to capitulate seems to have been brought to a head by the capture of a young man named Eleazar who had distinguished himself in the defence. Bassus threatened to crucify him in full view of the city, and the Jews surrendered the city to prevent this.[136] Meanwhile Lucilius Bassus died, and it fell to his successor, Flavius Silva, to capture Masada.[137] The Sicarii, under the leadership of Eleazar son of Yair and descendant of Judas the Galilean,[138] had established themselves in this fortress at the very beginning of the war, and since then controlled it. The siege was extremely difficult, since the rock on which the city was built was so high and precipitous on every side that it was almost impossible to bring up siege instruments. Only on one side, and even then only after difficult and elaborate preparations, could a battering-ram be set up. When it had breached the wall, the defenders had already erected another barricade behind it of wood and earth which, owing to its elasticity, could not be destroyed by the ram. But the Romans managed to overcome this obstacle also by the use of fire. When Eleazar saw that there was no longer any hope of resisting the assault, he addressed the garrison, asking them first to kill their own families,

134. *B.J.* vii 6, 1 (163).

135. Machaerus (Gr.: *Μαχαιροῦς*—so Josephus, Strabo xvi 2, 40 (763), and Steph. Byz. s.v.) reflects the Semitic מכוור or מכבר (cf. mTam. 3:8; see J. Levy, *Neuhebr. Wörterbuch* III, pp. 111 f.; M. Jastrow, *Dictionary* II, p. 781b). According to *B.J.* vii 6, 2 (171), Machaerus was originally fortified by Alexander Jannaeus. Gabinius demolished the fortress, *Ant.* xiv 5, 4 (89); *B.J.* i 8, 5 (167–8). It was re-fortified by Herod the Great, *B.J.* vii 6, 2 (172). On its importance, see Pliny, *NH* v 16/72 'Machaerus, secunda quondam arx Iudaeae ab Hierosolymis'. It was situated on the southern border of Peraea, *B.J.* iii 3, 3 (46–7), next to Nabataean territory, *Ant.* xviii 5, 1 (112). It is doubtless present-day Khirbet el-Mukawer. See above, p. 344, n. 20.

136. *B.J.* vii 6, 1–4 (163–209).

137. On Masada (מצדה) 'mountain stronghold', in Strabo xvi 2, 44 (764), corrupted to *Μοασάδα*, see in particular the monograph of Y. Yadin, *Masada: Herod's Fortress and the Zealots' Last Stand* (1966), together with the preliminary reports in *IEJ* 15 (1965), pp. 1–120. The Roman siege-works of A.D. 73 are still to be seen. Cf. I. A. Richmond, 'The Roman Siegeworks of Masada, Israel', JRS 52 (1962), pp. 142–55. The excavation of the site, conducted between 1963 and 1965, by a group of archaeologists under the leadership of Y. Yadin, has strikingly confirmed much earlier information, known only from Josephus.

138. *B.J.* ii 17, 9 (447), vii 8, 1 (252–3).

and then one another. This was done. When the Romans entered, they discovered with horror that no work remained for them to do. Thus the last bulwark of the revolt was conquered, in April of probably A.D. 74.[139]

After the fall of Masada, further Jewish disturbances occurred in Alexandria and Cyrene; those in Alexandria led to the closure of the temple of Onias at Leontopolis.[140] But these last spasms of the great revolt in the homeland are, by comparison, barely worth mentioning. Palestine's fate was sealed with the conquest of Masada. Vespasian held the land as his private possession and leased it out to his own advantage.[141] He allotted landed property in Emmaus near Jerusalem to some eight hundred veterans.[142] The former Temple tax of two

139. *B.J.* vii 8, 1–7 (252–388); 9, 1–2 (389–406). See also Yadin, *op. cit.*, pp. 193–201. On the Ben Yair ostracon, cf. p. 201. Note V. Nikiprowetsky, 'La mort d'Eléazar fils de Jaïre et les courants apologétiques dans le *de Bello Judaico* de Flavius Josèphe', *Hommages Dupont-Sommer* (1971), pp. 481–90. According to *B.J.* vii 9, 1 (401), the mass suicide of the garrison of Masada took place on 15 Xanthicus (Nisan, March/April), i.e. on the feast of Passover. The year is not mentioned. But since just prior to this, vii 7, 1 (219), there is a reference to the fourth year of Vespasian, it has always been thought that the conquest of Masada must have occurred in the spring of A.D. 73. But two new inscriptions giving the career of Flavius Silva show that he can not have gone as *legatus* to Judaea before A.D. 73. See p. 515 below.

140. *B.J.* vii 10–11 (409–42), *Vita* 76 (424). See vol. III, § 31, iv.

141. *B.J.* vii 6, 6 (216–17) *κελεύων πᾶσαν γῆν ἀποδόσθαι τῶν Ἰουδαίων· οὐ γὰρ κατῴκισεν ἐκεῖ πόλιν ἰδίαν αὐτῷ τὴν χώραν φυλάττων*. . . . The nature of Vespasian's treatment of the land, and its legal background, remains obscure. See A. D. Momigliano, *Richerche sull'organizzazione della Giudea sotto il dominio romano* (1934), pp. 85–9; S. Applebaum, 'The Agrarian Question and the Revolt of Bar Kokhba', Eretz Israel 8 (1967), pp. 283–7 (Hebrew). Some land in the immediate vicinity of Jerusalem was assigned to the 10th legion, cf. *Vita* 76 (422).

142. *B.J.* vii 6, 6 (217) *ὀκτακοσίοις δὲ μόνοις ἀπὸ τῆς στρατιᾶς διαφειμένοις χωρίον ἔδωκεν εἰς κατοίκησιν, ὃ καλεῖται μὲν Ἀμμαοῦς, ἀπέχει δὲ τῶν Ἱεροσολύμων σταδίους τριάκοντα*. . . . Since the reading *τριάκοντα* is supported by 6 MSS. in Niese's edition, with only one reading *ἑξήκοντα*, the question naturally arises whether this latter is not an assimilation to Lk. 24:3. Accordingly, our Emmaus cannot be identical with the Emmaus attested elsewhere, about 160–70 stadia from Jerusalem and known since the time of Julius Africanus (early 3rd century A.D.) as Nicopolis (cf. vol. II, § 23, ii, and the literature noted there). Admittedly, Sozomenus maintains that the latter had already received the name Nicopolis *μετὰ τὴν ἅλωσιν Ἱεροσολύμων καὶ τὴν κατὰ τῶν Ἰουδαίων νίκην*, *Hist. eccles.* V 21, 5; and the coins from Emmaus-Nicopolis are supposed to have an era dating from A.D. 70 (see Belley, in MAIBL, 30 (1764), pp. 294–306; Eckhel, *Doctr. Num.* III, p. 454; Mionnet, *Description de médailles ant.* V, pp. 550 ff., Suppl. VIII, 376. de Saulcy, *Num. de la Terre Sainte*, pp. 172–5, 406, pl. VI, 3–5; *BMC Palestine*, pp. lxxix–lxxxi. But in spite of the figure given by Josephus for the distance from Jerusalem, a number of writers (e.g. Marquardt, *Röm. Staatsverwaltung* I ([2]1881), p. 428; Gelzer, *Julius Africanus* I, pp. 5–7) identified the military colony of Vespasian with Emmaus-Nicopolis, thus following Sozomen (who in any case may well have merely inferred the identity from the name 'Nicopolis'). Another view

drachmas was from then on extracted from all Jews for the temple of Jupiter Capitolinus.[143] The people of Palestine were impoverished and fearfully reduced by the seven-year war. A Jewish authority (in the earlier sense) no longer existed. The only centre left to the people was the Torah. They now rallied around it with anxious and scrupulous fidelity, in the unwavering hope that it might once again, in a political community and indeed in the world itself, acquire practical validity and use.

---

is represented by Eusebius and other chroniclers, who state quite definitely that Nicopolis was not founded until the time of Julius Africanus, and only then received its name. Cf. Euseb. *Chron. ad ann Abr.* 2237, ed. Schoene, II, 178 ff. = *Chron. paschale*, ed. Dindorf I, p. 499, where it is put in the time of Elagabal; or, Syncellus, ed. Dindorf I, p. 676, in the time of Severus Alexander; cf. generally also, Jerome, *De viris illustr.* 63 (PL xxiii, 673–5), and an anonymous notice probably stemming from the *Church History* of Philip of Side, *c.* A.D. 430 (ed. de Boer, TU V, 2 (1888), p. 169, 174 f.). The *locus classicus* in Eusebius, *Chron.*, ed. Schoene II, pp. 178 ff., according to the Armenian text reads: 'In Palaestina antiqua Emaus restaurata est Nicopolisque vocata cura (praefectura) et interpellatione Iulii Africani chronographi ad regem'; according to Jerome, *Chron.* ed. Helm, p. 214, 'In Palaestina Nicopolis quae prius Emmaus vocabatur urbs condita est, legationis industriam pro ea suscipiente Iulio Africano scriptore temporum', following the *Chronicon paschale: Παλαιστίνης Νικόπολις ἡ πρότερον Ἐμμαοῦς ἐκτίσθη πόλις, πρεσβεύοντος ὑπὲρ αὐτῆς καὶ προϊσταμένου Ἰουλίου Ἀφρικανοῦ τοῦ τὰ χρονικὰ συγγραψαμένου*. . . . In support of this, writers before Elagabal use only the name Emmaus (so Pliny, *NH* v 14/70; Ptolemy v 16, 7; etc.). Similarly, Josephus, who frequently mentions Emmaus, never once comments that it is also called Nicopolis, although he does often make observations of that sort. None the less, the coins seem to show that the name 'Nicopolis' was in use in the period A.D. 70–221; *BMC Palestine, loc. cit.*, though cf. Vincent & Abel, *Emmaüs*, pp. 321–3. Against the identity of Emmaus-Nicopolis with Vespasian's military colony, however, the following facts seem decisive: (1) Josephus refers to the military colony as though it were a place otherwise unknown (*χωρίον ὃ καλεῖται Ἀμμαοῦς*. , . .), whereas the other Emmaus was very well known, and is often mentioned by Josephus at earlier points in *B.J.*; (2) Josephus does not say that Vespasian's military colony was named Nicopolis; (3) for Emmaus-Nicopolis, every characteristic of a colony is absent. Thus, our Emmaus is most probably identical with that mentioned in the NT (Lk. 24:13), even though the distances in both cases—30 and 60 stadia—are only roughly correct. It is quite likely that the military colony is to be identified with Kulonieh (Colonia) near Jerusalem. See Abel, *Géog. Pal.* II, pp. 314–16. Both Talmuds (ySukk. 54b, bSukk. 45a) associate Colonia (קלוניא) with Moẓa, a place situated in the neighbourhood of Jerusalem and mentioned in mSukk.4:5, but no great weight need be attached to this view.

143. *B.J.* vii 6, 6 (218); Dio lxvi 7, 2. For the evidence on the Jewish tax see M. S. Ginsburg, 'Fiscus Iudaicus', JQR 21 (1930/1), pp. 281 ff.; CPJ I, pp. 80–8; II, pp. 119–36, 204–8 (the most important treatment); cf. I. A. F. Bruce, 'Nerva and the Fiscus Iudaicus', PEQ 96 (1964), pp. 34–45.

§ 21 From the Destruction of Jerusalem to the Downfall of Bar Kokhba

I. Conditions in Palestine from Vespasian to Hadrian

Whereas Judaea prior to the war had been ruled by governors of equestrian rank (procurators), it was now allotted governors of senatorial standing. The earlier subordination to the governors of Syria (manifest in certain circumstances at least) was thereby abolished. The official name of the province was now as before, 'Judaea'.[1] Since it had as a garrison only one legion, the *legio* X *Fretensis* (see above, p. 509), and apart from this only auxiliaries (see above, p. 367), the legion's commander was at the same time governor of the province. These governors were at first of praetorian rank. It was only at a later period—at some point in the 120's when the *legio VI Ferrata* also was stationed in Judaea, and the legate was not simultaneously governor—that the province was administered by men of consular rank.[2]

Of the series of governors only isolated names are known.[3] The

1. The name 'Judaea' is widely attested, e.g., in the diploma of A.D. 86, CIL XVI 33; an inscription of Pompeius Falco (cf. below, p. 517); an inscription of Iulius Severus (CIL III 2830=ILS 1056); cf. also CIL III 5776=ILS 1369, VIII 7079= ILS 5549; and on coins (e.g. a coin attesting and celebrating Hadrian's presence in Judaea, 'adventui Aug. Iudaeae', *BMC Roman Empire*, nos. 493–4). Compare now the Egyptian diploma of A.D. 105 mentioning two cohorts transferred 'in Iudaeam', H.-G. Pflaum, Syria 44 (1967), pp. 339–62. The designation 'Syria Palaestina', found already in Herodotus, later becomes the rule. An early attestation of the official use of this term is given by a diploma of A.D. 139 found in Palestine, CIL XVI 87 (see above, p. 367). But even so, the old name 'Judaea' did not entirely disappear. The geographer Ptolemy (v 16, 1) uses both terms.

2. See P. von Rohden, *De Palaestina et Arabia provinciis Romanis*, pp. 30 ff.; and for the change in the status of the province, now known to have taken place before the war of A.D. 132–5, see S. Safrai, 'The Status of Provincia Judaea after the Destruction of the Second Temple' Zion 27 (1962) pp. 216–22 (in Hebrew); H.-G. Pflaum, 'Remarques sur le changement de statut administratif de la province de Judée', IEJ 19 (1969), pp. 225–33. For the later period, see S. Krauss, 'Les gouverneurs romains en Palestine de 135 à 640', REJ 80 (1925), pp. 113–30; cf. M. Avi-Yonah, *Geschichte der Juden im Zeitalter des Talmud* (1962), pp. 41–3. In an inscription found in Jerusalem, and coming from the time of Severus and Caracalla, there is mention of one M. Iunius Maximus 'leg(atus) Augg. (i.e. duorum Augustorum) leg(ionis) X Fr(etensis)' (CIL III 6641). If this man were concurrently governor as well as commander of the legion, the designation 'pro praetore' should not be missing.

3. Compare the now out-dated lists in E. Kuhn, *Die städtische u. bürgerliche Verfassung des röm. Reiches* (1864–1865) II, pp. 184 ff.; Marquardt, *Röm. Stadtsverwaltung* I ([2]1884), pp. 419 ff.; P. von Rohden, *De Palaestina et Arabia . . .*, pp. 36–42; RE XII, cols. 1675–6. But note the recent lists in Pflaum, *op. cit.* and W. Eck, *Senatoren von Vespasian bis Hadrian* (1970), p. 243.

earlier ones in office during the war of A.D. 70–74 have already been briefly mentioned, namely:

1. Sex. Vettulenus Cerialis,[4] who commanded the 5th legion at the siege of Jerusalem (cf. above, pp. 501–2). He remained after Titus's departure as commander of the garrison troops, i.e. of the 10th legion and the detachments associated with it, and handed them over to Lucilius Bassus.

2. Lucilius Bassus, who captured the fortresses of Herodium and Machaerus.[5] He died as governor.[6] He is to be identified with a Sex. Lucilius Bassus who appears several times during the same period.[7] The procurator who served under him, L. Laberius (not Λιβέριος) Maximus,[8] is also mentioned in the Acts of the Arval priesthood (CIL VI 2059=ILS 5049), and in the diploma of A.D. 83. (CIL XVI 29=ILS 1996). According to the latter he was then prefect of Egypt.[9]

3. L. Flavius Silva, between A.D. 73/4 and 81; the conqueror of Masada.[10] He became consul in A.D. 81. The *Acta Arvalium* give his full name, L. Flavius Silva Nonius Bassus (CIL VI 2059). Two new inscriptions show clearly that he cannot have become *legatus* of Judaea before A.D. 73, and consequently that the fall of Masada must belong in spring A.D. 74, at the earliest.[11]

4. Cn. Pompeius Longinus, A.D. 86. On a diploma of Domitian from A.D. 86, the veterans of two *alae* and four cohorts are mentioned 'qui . . . sunt in Iudaea sub Cn. Pompeio Longino' (CIL XVI 33). Henzen thought it necessary to conclude from certain statements in the diploma that military operations had taken place in Judaea at that time. The inference, however, is not imperative.[12] This Cn. Pompeius

4. *B.J.* vii 6, 1 (163–4). See PIR[1] V 351, but note R. Syme, Athenaeum 35 (1957), pp. 312–3.

5. *B.J.* vii 6, 1–6 (163–218).

6. *B.J.* vii 8, 1 (252).

7. See PIR[2] L 379.

8. *B.J.* vii 6, 6 (216).

9. See PIR[2] L 8.

10. *B.J.* vii 8, 9 (252–406).

11. See Eck, *op. cit.* (in n. 3 above), pp. 93–111. Before being *legatus*, he was given praetorian rank by Vespasian and Titus in their censorship, which began in spring 73. Earlier evidence in PIR[2] F 368.

12. Cf. W. Henzen, Jahrbuch d. Vereins von Alterthumsfreunden im Rheinlande 13 (1848), pp. 34–7. Henzen's grounds were: (a) The *coh. I Augusta Lusitanorum* mentioned in the diploma was shortly before this stationed in Pannonia. It must therefore have been sent there just then to reinforce the garrison of Judaea. (b) According to the diploma the veterans were indeed granted *civitas*, but not their discharge (*honesta missio*); they were therefore still needed. The latter argument is not convincing, and the *coh. I Augusta Lusitanorum* mentioned in the diploma is a different one from the *coh. I Lusitanorum* traceable in Pannonia in A.D. 85.

Longinus should be identified with the *cons. suff.* of the same name from A.D. 90, and with the Cn. Aemilius Pinarius Cicatricula Pompeius Longinus, who was governor of Moesia Superior in A.D. 93, and of Pannonia in A.D. 98.[13]

5. Sex. Hermetidius Campanus, A.D. 93. The wooden diptych from Egypt,[14] which contains an edict of Domitian granting favours to veterans, also mentions soldiers 'qui militaverunt Hierosolymnis in leg. X Fretense (see above, p. 509) honesta missione stipendis emeritis per Sex. Hermetidium Campanum, legatum Aug. pro praetore', and the date, A.D. 93. He was possibly consul in A.D. 97.[15]

6. Atticus, ? A.D. 99/100–?102/3. In two fragments of Hegesippus cited by Eusebius, it is reported that Simeon son of Cleopas, a cousin of Jesus of Nazareth and alleged to have been the second bishop of the Jerusalem church, died as a martyr 'under the Emperor Trajan and the governor Atticus' (*HE* iii 32, 3 *ἐπὶ Τραϊανοῦ Καίσαρος καὶ ὑπατικοῦ Ἀττικοῦ* . . .; *ibid.*, iii 32, 6 *ἐπὶ Ἀττικοῦ τοῦ ὑπατικοῦ* . . .). In Eusebius's *Chronicle*, this event is placed in Trajan's tenth year (A.D. 107),[16] in the *Chronicon paschale*,[17] during the consulate of Candidus and Quadratus (A.D. 105). Neither statement has any independent value, least of all that in the *Chronicon paschale*, which is based solely on Eusebius. These dates seem to be excluded by documentary evidence for other *legati* of Judaea in this period (see below). It has been suggested, in view of Simeon's possible age, that the martyrdom is more likely to have taken place in the first, rather than the second half of Trajan's reign. The period A.D. 99–103 is therefore a reasonable possibility. Atticus may be identical with Ti. Claudius Atticus Herodes, the father of the famous orator, Herodes Atticus.[18]

7. C. Iulius Quadratus Bassus, *c.* A.D. 102/3–104/5, whose career is known from a long inscription found at his native Pergamum (AE 1933, 268; 1934, 176), is to be identified with the suffect consul of A.D. 105. His governorship of Judaea, attested on the inscription, will have fallen immediately before his consulship.[19]

8. Q. Roscius Coelius Pompeius Falco, *c.* A.D. 105–7. The *cursus*

13. Cf. E. Ritterling, Archäol.-epigr. Mittheilungen aus Oesterreich-Ungarn 20 (1897), p. 13; and on the governorship of A.D. 93, see E. Bormann, JOAI 1 (1898), pp. 171, 174; see RE s.v. 'Pompeius' (90); R. Syme, *Tacitus* (1958), p. 647.

14. ILS 9059=Cavenaille, *Corpus Papyrorum Latinarum*, no. 104=CIL XVI, App. no. 12.

15. See PIR² H 143; cf. R. Syme, *Tacitus* (1958), p. 641.

16. *Chron.*, ed. Schoene II, pp. 162–3.

17. Ed. Dindorf I, p. 471.

18. See E. M. Smallwood, 'Atticus, Legate of Judaea under Trajan', JRS 52 (1962), pp. 131–3.

19. See Smallwood, *op. cit.*, and PIR² I 508.

honorum of this man, a correspondent of the younger Pliny, is known from inscriptions.[20] He has the title 'leg(atus) Aug(usti) pr(o) pr(aetore) provinc(iae) [Iudaeae e]t leg(ionis) X Fret(ensis)'; in ILS 1036 (Hierapolis Castabala), 'leg. Aug. leg. X Fret. et leg. pr. pr. provinciae Iudaeae consularis' (a mistake of the stone-cutter for 'cos.'—he was suffect consul in A.D. 108). From Pliny, *Ep.* vii 22, the governorship of Judaea should probably be dated to A.D. 107, for in the letter written at or about that time, Pliny recommends a friend to Falco for the post of a tribune. But this, according to the other details of his *cursus honorum*, can only have taken place during the period of his governorship of Judaea. The letters addressed by Pliny to Falco are *Ep.* i 23; iv 27; vii 22; ix 15.[21]

9. A recently published inscription from Side in Pamphylia reveals a senator whose fragmentary name *may* have been C. Avidius Ceionius Commodus, and who governed Judaea under Trajan at some time subsequent to A.D. 102. He has the title *πρεσβευτὴν* [*ἀντιστράτη*]*γον λε*[*γε*]*ῶνος ί καὶ ἐπαρχ*[*είας Ἰουδαίας . . .*]. See Pflaum, *op. cit.* in n. 2. above.

10. ?Tiberianus, *c.* A.D. 114. Joannes Malalas (ed. Dindorf, p. 273) gives the text of a communication which Tiberianus, governor of 'Palaestina Prima', addressed to Trajan during the latter's stay in Antioch in A.D. 114 (*ἐν τῷ διατρίβειν τὸν αὐτὸν Τραϊανὸν βασιλέα ἐν Ἀντιοχείᾳ τῆς Συρίας βουλευόμενον τὰ περὶ τοῦ πολέμου ἐμήνυσεν αὐτὸν Τιβεριανός, ἡγεμὼν τοῦ πρώτου Παλαιστινῶν ἔθνους, ταῦτα*). Tiberianus brings to the emperor's notice the fact that the Christians are foolishly competing with each other to achieve martyrdom, and asks for appropriate instructions. At this, Trajan orders him and all other magistrates in the entire empire to suspend the persecutions. The same story in somewhat different form is also reported by John of Antioch (in Müller, FHG iv, pp. 580–1, F 111). The latter's account is reproduced word for word in the Suda, *s.v. Τραϊανός*). Both reports, which agree in essentials, are highly suspicious due to their contents. Further, the partition of Palestine into 'Palestina Prima' and 'Secunda' did not take place before the middle of the fourth century. The reports of John of Antioch and Malalas support one another so strongly here and in many other places that one, in any case, has borrowed from the other. Malalas wrote in the late sixth, and John of Antioch in the first half of the seventh century; his version is in fact patently a summary of that

20. ILS 1035–6.

21. See R. Syme, *Tacitus* (1958), pp. 243, 245; *idem*, Historia 9 (1960), p. 344; A. N. Sherwin-White, *The Letters of Pliny* (1966), pp. 115, 138–40, 306, 429, 497, 499–500; cf. Smallwood, *op. cit.*, pp. 131–2.

of Malalas.[22] Neither version can be accepted as positive evidence for the existence of a governor of Judaea called Tiberianus.

11. Lusius Quietus, *c.* A.D. 117. This distinguished general was appointed governor of Judaea after suppressing the Jewish rebellion in Mesopotamia (Euseb. *HE* iv 2, 5 *Ἰουδαίας ἡγεμὼν ὑπὸ τοῦ αὐτοκράτορος ἀνεδείχθη* . . .; *Chron.* ed. Schoene II, p. 164, in the 18th year of Trajan (2131 Abr.); Greek in Syncellus, ed. Dindorf I, p. 657 *ἡγεμὼν τῆς Ἰουδαίας διὰ τοῦτο καθίσταται*). Dio merely says that he was governor of Palestine after his consulship (A.D. 115), Dio lxviii 32, 15 *ὑπατεῦσαι τῆς τε Παλαιστίνης ἄρξαι* (Boissevain III, p. 206). That Trajan sent to Palestine a legate of consular, and not merely of praetorian rank, was justified by the special circumstances of the time. Lusius Quietus was deposed by Hadrian (HA, *vita Hadr.*, 5, 8 'Lusium Quietum . . . exarmavit'), and soon afterwards executed (*ibid.*, 7, 12; Dio, lxix 2, 15).[23]

12. Q. Tineius Rufus, A.D. 132.[24] At the time of Bar Kokhba's rebellion a 'Rufus' was governor of Judaea, Euseb. *HE* iv 6, *Ροῦφος ἐπάρχων τῆς Ἰουδαίας*. In the Chronicle of Eusebius, he is called Tinnius Rufus (ed. Schoene II, 166–7). Greek in Syncellus, ed. Dindorf I, p. 660, *ἡγεῖτο δὲ τῆς Ἰουδαίας Τίννιος Ῥοῦφος*. Latin in Jerome, 'tenente provinciam Tinnio Rufo', *Chronik*, ed. R. Helm, p. 200. The correct form is Q. Tineius Rufus, as is shown by the *Fasti Ostienses* for A.D. 127 (*Ins. Italiae* XIII, i, p. 205). This document reveals the important fact that Rufus held the suffect consulship in that year. In consequence, the change in the status of Judaea to that of a consular province (with two legions) must already have occurred, at what date is not clear. But there are indications that the status of the equestrian *procurator* of the province had risen by A.D. 123; see Pflaum, IEJ 19 (1969), pp. 232–3. One Q. Tineius Rufus, who was consul under Commodus, is attested by a number of inscriptions. He may have been the son or grandson of our Rufus.[25]

13. C. Quinctius Certus Publicius Marcellus, formerly governor of Syria, was also sent to Judaea to put down the revolt (IGR III 174 *ἡνίκα*

22. John Malalas, *Chronicle* (*Χρονογραφία*), ed. L. Dindorf (CSHB, 1831); Migne, PG xcviii, 9–790. Critical text: (Bks. 9–12), A. Schenk Graf von Stauffenberg, *Die röm. Kaisergeschichte bei Malalas* (1931). See W. Weber, 'Studien zur Chronik des Malalas', in *Festgabe für A. Deissmann* (1927), pp. 20–66. Cf. B. Altaner, *Patrologie* ([7]1966), p. 234 [E.T. (1960) pp. 282–3]. Books 1–17 in their present form reach only to A.D. 563 (though originally to 574). On John of Antioch see K. Krumbacher, *Geschichte der byzantinischen Literatur* ([2]1897), pp. 334–7.

23. See PIR[2] L 439; cf. E. M. Smallwood, 'Palestine c. A.D. 115–118', Historia 11 (1962), pp. 500–10.

24. See PIR[1] T 168; R. Syme, JRS 52 (1962), p. 90.

25. CIL VI 1978; PIR[1] T 169.

Πουβλίκιους Μάρκελλος διὰ τὴν κίνησιν τὴν Ἰουδαϊκὴν μεταβεβήκε[ι] ἀπὸ Συρίας: cf. IGR III 175). This reinforcement of Judaea's fighting strength is also mentioned by Eusebius (*HE* iv 6, 1 *στρατιωτικῆς αὐτῷ συμμαχίας ὑπὸ βασιλέως πεμφθείσης*. Cf. *Chron., ad ann. Abr.* 2148).[26]

14. (Cn. Minicius Faustinus) Sex. Iulius Severus, A.D. 135. The suppression of the Jewish revolt was achieved by Iulius Severus, who was sent to Judaea from Britain where he had been governor (Dio lxix 13, 2). His *cursus honorum* is given in an inscription (CIL III 2830=ILS 1056), where the higher offices are listed in the following order: [l]eg(ato) pr(o) pr(aetore) imp(eratoris) Traiani Hadria[n]i Aug(usti) p[r]ovinciae Dacia[e], cos., leg. pr. p[r]. provinciae Moesia[e] inferioris, leg. pr. pr. provinciae Brittaniae, leg. pr. pr. [pr]ovinciae Iudeae, [l]eg. pr. pr. [provi]nciae Suriae.' This confirms Dio's statement that he came to Judaea from Britain.[27] On the other hand, his assertion, or rather that of his epitomizer, Xiphilinus, that after the end of the Jewish revolt Severus became governor of Bithynia (Dio lxix 14, 4), rests on a confusion with another Severus. The name of our Iulius Severus, who was consul in A.D. 127, was Sextus Iulius Severus; that of the governor of Bithynia was C. Iulius Severus (see PIR² I 573).

Another name probably belonging to the list of governors of Judaea is that of Cl(audius) Pater(nus) Clement(ianus) who, according to an inscription (CIL III 5776=ILS 1369) was 'proc(urator) Aug(usti) provincia(e) Iud(aeae) v(ices) a(gens) legati', (i.e. procurator and representative of the (dead or recalled) governor. But his date is not certain. For it may not be inferred, as Rohden would have it, that because the province is named 'Judaea' and not 'Syria Palaestina', the inscription is certainly pre-Hadrianic.[28] Just as little information emerges from rabbinical legends concerning a Roman *ἡγεμών* said to have put trick questions to Yoḥanan b. Zakkai towards the end of the first century A.D., for the poor condition of the text makes it impossible even to establish his name.[29] He seems to be identical with 'Hegemon Agnitus' (אגניטוס הגמון) who according to *Sifre Dt.* § 351 (ed. Finkelstein, p. 408), is supposed to have addressed a similar question to Gamaliel II at the beginning of the second century A.D.[30]

26. See RE s.v. 'Publicius' (36).

27. For details of his career see RE s.v. 'Minicius' (11) and PIR² I 576.

28. RE s.v. 'Claudius' (262); PIR² C 953; Pflaum, *Carrières*, no. 150 bis.

29. In ySanh. 19b (top), he is called אגנטוס (Agnitus, ? Ignatius); ySanh. 19c (bottom), 'Antoninus'; *ib.*, 19d (top) 'Antigonus'. In other places still further forms are to be found; cf. J. Neusner, *A Life of Yohanan ben Zakkai* (²1970), p. 218, n. 3.

30. On the whole matter, see J. Derenbourg, *op. cit.*, pp. 316 ff.; W. Bacher, *Agada d. Tannaiten* I (²1903), pp. 36 ff.; J. Neusner, *A Life of Yohanan ben Zakkai ca.* 1–80 *C.E.* (²1970), pp. 218–23; *Development of a Legend* (1970), pp. 139–41.

The residence of the governor was, as in the time of the procurators, not in Jerusalem but Caesarea, the important port built by Herod the Great.[31] It was transformed into a Roman colony by Vespasian and bore the official name 'col(onia) prima Fl(avia Aug(usta) Caesarensis', or Caesarea.[32] Jerusalem had been so completely razed to the ground 'that those who visited it could not believe it had ever been inhabited.[33] It was primarily only a Roman camp, the headquarters of the major part of the 10th legion and its baggage and camp-followers.[34]

Only scattered items of information are available concerning other changes in the organization of the Palestinian communities. It cannot be determined with any certainty from Josephus's vague statements to what extent Vespasian held the land as his private possession (see above, p. 512). It seems to have been a matter not only of the actual area of Jerusalem but of all Judaea—in its narrower and proper sense—(*πᾶσαν γῆν τῶν Ἰουδαίων*). The only new settlement which Vespasian founded here was the military colony of Emmaus (see above, p. 512). In Samaria the rapidly flourishing town of Flavia Neapolis was founded at that time, a fact attested not only by its name and a mention by Pliny, but also by the city's era, which begins in A.D. 72/3.[35] Its site was now on that of a place formerly called Mabortha or Mamortha in the immediate vicinity of Shechem, for which reason it quickly came to be identified with Shechem.[36] In the later imperial period it was

31. After Flavius Silva had conquered Masada, he returned to Caesarea, *B.J.* vii 10, 1 (407). Tacitus also terms Caesarea 'Iudaeae caput', *Hist.* ii 78.

32. For details, see vol. II, § 23, i.

33. *B.J.* vii 1, 1 (3) τὸν δ' ἄλλον ἅπαντα τῆς πόλεως περίβολον οὕτως ἐξωμάλισαν οἱ κατασκάπτοντες ὡς μηδὲ πώποτ' οἰκηθῆναι πίστιν ἂν ἔτι παρασχεῖν τοῖς προσελθοῦσι.

34. In A.D. 116, a detachment of the 3rd legion (vexillatio leg. III Cyr.) was also stationed in Jerusalem (ILS 4393).

35. The full name is found in Justin, 1 *Apol.* 1 1 ἀπὸ Φλαουΐας Νέας πόλεως τῆς Συρίας Παλαιστίνης (ed. G. Krüger ([4]1915), p. 1); cf. Euseb. *HE* iv 12. And also on coins. Cf. Eckhel, *Doctr. Num.* III, 433–8; de Saulcy, *Num. de la Terre Sainte*, 244–74, pl. xii–xiv; *BMC Palestine*, pp. xxvi–vii.

36. *B.J.* iv 8, 1 (449) παρὰ τὴν Νεάπολιν καλουμένην, Μαβαρθὰ δὲ ὑπὸ τῶν ἐπιχωρίον. Pliny, *NH* v 14/69: 'Neapolis quod antea Mamortha dicebatur'. Euseb. *Onomast.*, ed. Klostermann, GCS 11, 1 (1904), p. 150: Συχὲμ· ἡ καὶ Σίκιμα ἢ καὶ Σαλήμ. πόλις Ἰακὼβ νῦν ἔρημος· δείκνυται δὲ ὁ τόπος ἐν προαστείοις Νέας Πόλεως. *Ibid.*, p. 120 s.v. Λουζά ἑτέρα. Παρακειμένη Συχὲμ ἀπὸ θ' σημείου Νέας Πόλεως (the text of Jerome *ibid.*, is in fact more correct: 'in tertio lapide Νέας πόλεως). The Bordeaux Pilgrim writes: 'Civitas Neapoli. Ibi est mons Agazaren (i.e. Gerizim) . . .inde ad pedem montis ipsius locus est, cui nomen est Sechim'. (*Itinera Hierosolymitana*, ed. P. Geyer, CSEL xxxix (1889), pp. 19–20=CCL clxxv, p. 13. Also, on the mosaic map of Madaba, Νεάπολις and Συχεμ ἡ καὶ Σικαι Σαλημ are shown as two different places, as also on the so-called 'map of Jerome' (A. Schulten, 'Die Mosaikkarte von Madaba und ihr Verhältnis zu den ältesten Karten u. Beschreibungen des heiligen Landes', AAG, phil-hist. Kl. N.F., 4, 2 (1900), esp. pp. 8–11, 83–87. Cf. also M. Avi-Yonah, *The Madaba Mosaic Map* (1954), Pl. 6.

one of the most important towns of Palestine.[37] Its citizens were predominantly Gentile, if not wholly so, as the cults attested by the coins prove. Mt. Gerizim is depicted on not a few of them (from Hadrian onwards) and on its summit a temple dedicated, according to Damascius, to *Ζεὺς ὕψιστος*.[38] In the second century, and later also, the games of Neapolis were among the most celebrated in Palestine.[39] The founding of Capitolias in the Decapolis took place in the time of Nerva or Trajan; its era begins in A.D. 97 or 98.[40] Hadrian founded Aelia on the site of Jerusalem; more will be heard of it below, in the history of the war. The founding of other new Palestinian cities belongs to a period later than that treated here, e.g. that of Diocaesarea = Sepphoris (known under the new name since Antoninus Pius; see vol. II, § 23, 1), Diospolis = Lydda, Eleutheropolis (both under Septimus Severus),[41] Nicopolis = Emmaus (under Elagabal).

The destruction of Jerusalem resulted in a violent upheaval in the inner life of the Jewish people. The disappearance of the Sanhedrin and the suspension of the sacrificial cult were two great factors which profoundly affected Jewish life. It must first, of course, be established that the sacrificial service really did cease.[42] Not only the Letter to the Hebrews, the date of which is not certain, but also Clement of Rome and the author of the *Letter to Diognetus*, who certainly wrote after the destruction of Jerusalem, speak as though in their time the sacrificial cult was still practised.[43] Indeed, even Josephus expresses himself similarly. He uses the present tense not only when describing

37. According to HA, *Vita Sept. Sev.* 9, 5, the *ius civitatis* was withdrawn by Septimius Severus, although he later restored it (*ib.*, 14, 6, 'Palaestinis poenam remisit, quam ob causam Nigri meruerant'. Under Philip the Arabian, it became a Roman colony, see *BMC Palestine*, pp. xxvii–viii. Ammianus Marcellinus describes it as one of the largest cities of Palestine, xiv 8, 11.

38. Serapis, Apollo, Diana and other deities appear on the numerous extant coins ranging in date from Domitian to the middle of the third century A.D. On the temple at Mt. Gerizim see Damascius in Photius, *Bibliotheca*, cod. 242., ed. Bekker, p. 345b, *ἐν ᾧ Διὸς ὑψίστου ἁγιώτατον ἱερόν*. For the archaeological evidence see R. J. Bull, G. E. Wright, 'Newly Discovered Temples on Mt. Gerizim in Jordan', HThR 58 (1965), pp. 234–7; R. J. Bull, 'The Excavation of Tell er-Ras on Mt. Gerizim', BA 31, 2 (1968), pp. 58–72.

39. Cf. the inscription from the time of Marcus Aurelius, in L. Moretti, *Iscrizioni agonistiche greche* (1953), no. 72.

40. The era of Capitolias can be determined from its coins. See A. Strobel, art. 'Capitolias', in LThK II, col. 927, and the literature given there, especially F.-M. Abel, *Géog. Pal.* II, p. 295. It appears to have been located between Gadara and Adraha (Der'a), and presumably corresponds to Bet-Rās in 'Ajlun.

41. On Lydda (= Diospolis), see Abel, *Géog. Pal.* II, p. 370. On Eleutheropolis, RE V, cols. 2353 ff.; Abel, *Géog. Pal.* II, p. 272.

42. Compare A. Guttmann, 'The End of the Jewish Sacrificial Cult', HUCA 38 (1967), pp. 137–48.

43. 1 *Clem.* 41:2–3; *Diogn.* 3.

the biblical sacrificial cult,[44] but also when apparently speaking of customs and institutions of his own day.[45] He employs it even when referring to sacrifice for the Roman people and the Roman emperor, although this was a later custom and not prescribed by the Bible.[46] There is also a rabbinic text which some interpret as alluding to sacrificial worship after A.D. 70.[47] In itself, this could well have been possible. In an interesting passage in the Mishnah, R. Joshua testifies:[48] 'I have heard that one may offer sacrifice even though no Temple is there; that one may eat the Most Holy Things even though no curtains (around the outer court) are there; that one may eat less holy things and the second tithe even though there is no wall; for the first consecration (of the Temple) sanctified for the future as well as for its own time'. Accordingly, it would not have been a positive contradiction of the views of certain rabbis if, after the destruction of the Temple, sacrifice had continued to be offered. But in fact this did not occur. In an enumeration of Israel's black days it is stated simply that 17 Tammuz saw the end of the daily sacrifice;[49] there is nowhere any mention of its being subsequently restored. In the description of the Passover festival in the Mishnah, an account of the dishes to be laid on the table closes with the comment, 'In the Temple they used to bring before him the body of the Passover victim'.[50] It was in other words no longer offered, since the Temple was destroyed. In the legal rulings for the determination of the New Moon it is said: 'While the Temple existed, the Sabbath was permitted to be profaned because of any one of the New Moons, to determine aright the time of the offerings.'[51] The unanimous testimony of these passages from the Mishnah is confirmed by others even more direct from the Babylonian Talmud, which take for granted that the whole sacrificial cult had ended by the time of R. Yoḥanan b. Zakkai, R. Gamaliel II, and R. Ishmael, i.e. the first decade after the destruc-

44. *Ant.* iii 9–10 (224–57).

45. *C. Ap.* ii 23 (193–8).

46. *C. Ap.* ii 6 (77) 'facimus autem pro eis continua sacrificia et non solum cotidianis diebus ex impensa communi omnium Iudaeorum talia celebramus verum . . . solis imperatoribus hunc honorem praecipuum pariter exhibemus . . .'

47. Cf. mPes. 7:2, where the question is discussed whether the Passover (lamb) may be roasted on a grill: 'Rabban Gamaliel once said to his slave Tabi, 'Go and roast the Passover-offering for us on the grill'.' The validity of the argument hinges on the identification of the Gamaliel who had a slave named Tabi. See also mBer. 2:7; Suk. 2:1. If he was Gamaliel II (floruit *c.* A.D. 90–110), a survival of the Passover sacrifice is alluded to, but not so if Rabban Gamaliel I is meant, for he lived before the destruction of the Temple. On the whole, the latter alternative is more likely. See also n. 55 below.

48. mEduy. 8:6.

49. mTaan. 4:6.

50. mPes. 10:3.

51. mR.Sh. 1:4.

tion of the Temple.[52] Finally, there is Justin's evidence. He says to his opponent, Tryphon: 'God permits the Passover Lamb to be sacrificed nowhere except in the place where His name is called on, knowing that after Christ's passion the days will come when the place of Jerusalem shall be given over to your enemies, and all the offerings shall cease. . . .'[53] Elsewhere, Tryphon himself, replying to Justin's question whether it was still possible to observe all the Mosaic commandments, answers: 'No. For we know that, as you have said, it is not possible anywhere (except in Jerusalem) to sacrifice the Passover Lamb, or to offer the goats ordered for the fast, or, in a word, to present all the other offerings.'[54] Thus, when Christian writers and Josephus, long after the destruction of the Temple, speak in the present tense of the offerings of sacrifice, they are merely describing what was lawful, not what was actually practised. Precisely the same happens in the Mishnah, from the first page to the last, in that all legally valid statutes are presented as current usage, even when as a result of prevailing circumstances their performance was impossible.[55]

Two facts of the greatest consequence are therefore established: the dissolution of the Sanhedrin and the suspension of sacrificial worship.[56] The Sanhedrin embodied the last vestige of Jewish political independence, and with it the last remains of the power of the Sadducean nobility. The latter's influence had already been reduced since the time of Alexandra by the growing power of Pharisaism. Nevertheless, as long as the Sanhedrin existed, it still had a role to play. For the competence of this aristocratic senate of Judaea was, during the time of the procurators, quite far-reaching; and at its head were the Saduccean High Priests. Now, with the downfall of Jerusalem, this Jewish administrative authority was abolished: there no longer existed any city of Jerusalem. And with it, Sadducean power vanished from history. Another consequence was the suspension of the sacrificial cult and the gradual withdrawal of the priesthood from public life. It was, however, a long time before the situation was accepted as definitive.

52. bR.Sh. 31b, bPes. 72b, bZeb. 60b.

53. Justin, *Dial. c. Tryph.*, 40, *εἰδὼς ὅτι ἐλεύσονται ἡμέραι μετὰ τὸ παθεῖν τὸν Χριστόν, ὅτε καὶ ὁ τόπος τῆς Ἰερουσαλὴμ τοῖς ἐχθροῖς ὑμῶν παραδοθήσεται καὶ παύσονται ἅπασαι ἁπλῶς προσφοραὶ γινόμεναι.*

54. *Ibid.*, 46, *οὐ· γνωρίζομεν γὰρ ὅτι, ὡς ἔφης, οὔτε πρόβατον τοῦ πάσχα ἀλλαχόσε θύειν δυνατὸν οὔτε τοὺς τῇ νηστείᾳ κελευσθέντας προσφέρεσθαι χιμάρους οὔτε τὰς ἄλλας ἁπλῶς ἁπάσας προσφοράς.*

55. In the paragraph on Gamaliel and his slave Tabi (cf. n. 47 above), Gamaliel I is probably meant, and Tabi, the servant of his grandson, has slipped in by mistake. But it is also possible that as a young man Tabi served the grandfather, and when old, the grandson, or that the name Tabi was passed down in the slave's family just as that of Gamaliel in the master's.

56. Cf. mSot. 9:11.

It seemed probable that the priests would soon be able to resume their duties. Needless to say, all the taxes were paid to them as before. Only those directly intended for the support of the Temple and public sacrifice were declared by the rabbis to be suspended. Dues appointed for the personal maintenance of the priests remained a legal duty.[57] But in spite of all this, now that priesthood was unable to carry out its functions, it lost its significance as well. It became a relic of bygone days which, as time passed, fell more and more into dissolution and decay.

The Pharisees and the rabbis entered into the heritage of the Sadducees and the priests. They were excellently prepared for this role, for they had been pressing for leadership during the last two centuries. Now, at one stroke, they acquired sole supremacy, as the factors which had stood in their way sank into insignificance.

After the catastrophe, Jamnia (Yavneh) became a special centre of scholarly activity. During the first decade after the destruction of the Temple, Yoḥanan ben Zakkai worked there, and at the end of the first century and beginning of the second, Gamaliel II, around whom gathered a whole circle of scholars. The most famous of his contemporaries were Joshua ben Ḥananiah, and Eliezer ben Hyrcanus from Lydda. Younger contemporaries and pupils of these men were R. Ishmael, R. Akiba and R. Tarphon.

Work on the Torah was resumed by them and their numerous colleagues and students with greater zeal than ever. It was as though, after the political collapse, the whole of the nation's energy was concentrated on its true and supreme task. Everything pertaining to the Torah, criminal law, civil law and the various religious statutes, was examined with most painstaking thoroughness and impressed on the students by their teachers. It was of no consequence whatever whether circumstances permitted these statutes to be performed, or not. All the subtleties of Temple worship, the entire ritual of the sacrificial cult, were discussed with as much industry and seriousness as the laws of purity, of the Sabbath, and of other religious duties the practice of which was in fact possible. Nothing gives a more vivid

57. mShek. 8:8, '(The laws concerning) the Shekel dues and First-fruits apply only to such time as the Temple stands; but (the laws concerning) the Tithe of Corn and the Tithe of Cattle and Firstlings apply to such time as the Temple stands and to such time as it does not stand.' These three imposts are named here only by way of example, as being the most important. For instance, the laws relating to the Terumah (mBik. 2:3) also remained in force, as well as the contribution of the three pieces of a slaughtered animal, namely, the right foreleg, the cheeks and the stomach (mḤul. 10:1; cf. also vol. II, § 24, ii). The tax of the right foreleg is attested by the emperor Julian as a custom of his own time, in Cyril of Alexandria, *adv. Iulian*, 306A καὶ τὸν δεξιὸν ὦμον διδόασιν ἀπαρχὰς τοῖς ἱερεῦσιν (PG lxxvi, col. 964).

idea of the people's faith in its future than the conscientiousness with which even the rules concerning Temple and sacrificial worship were treated by the guardians of the Law. Whether the time of desolation was long or short, the day of renewal must surely dawn. Hence, the written codification of Jewish law in the second century A.D. into a *corpus iuris* (the Mishnah) included a topography of the Temple (Middoth) and a description of the daily duties of the priests (Tamid). Posterity, to whom would be granted the privilege of the restoration of the cult, must know how it had been conducted in the time of their fathers.

These scholars who in such fashion cultivated Israel's greatest good, now constituted, more exclusively and unrestrictedly than ever before, the nation's supreme authority. The priests, who had otherwise been the most important mediators in performing their religious duties, were doomed to inactivity. The zeal of the pious was subjected to the guidance of the rabbis. No external compulsion was needed. Whatever was laid down by the distinguished teachers was accepted as valid by the devout without further ado. In fact, they were not only recognized as legislators in spiritual and worldly affairs; they were appealed to as judges in disputes, even in questions relating to property. There is nothing unusual during this period in, for example, R. Akiba, simply by virtue of his spiritual authority, sentencing a man to pay 400 zuz in damages because he had uncovered a woman's head in the street.[58]

The highest esteem towards the end of the first and the beginning of the second century A.D. was enjoyed by the academy of Jamnia (Yavneh), a college of scholars with scarcely any proper authorization from the Roman administration, but in fact occupying the role of the old Sanhedrin of Jerusalem as the supreme law-court of Israel. The decrees enacted by R. Yoḥanan ben Zakkai in Jamnia after the destruction of the Temple to adapt certain legal ordinances to the changed conditions of the times, were looked upon as binding.[59] R. Gamaliel II and his academy supervised the correct operation of the calendar; even the older R. Joshua accepted his decisions, though he regarded them as incorrect.[60] Generally speaking, legal decisions made in Yavneh were held as normative.[61] Indeed, Yavneh's full

58. mB.K. 8:6. On the whole question, see J. Juster, *Les Juifs dans l'Empire romain* II (1914), esp. pp. 19–23, 95–106, 108–9, 149–52, etc.

59. mSuk. 3:12, mR.Sh. 4:1, 3, 4; mMen. 10:5. Cf. J. Neusner, *A Life of Yohanan b. Zakkai* (²1970), pp. 196–215. On the establishment of the Yavneh academy, see pp. 164–9. Cf. also *Pharisees* II (1971), p. 4 and *passim*.

60. mR.Sh. 2: 8–9. According to mEduy. 7:7, on one occasion, during Rabban Gamaliel's absence, a year was declared a leap-year on condition that he should approve the decision on his return. Cf. H. Mantel, *Studies in the History of the Sanhedrin* (1961), p. 21.

61. mKel. 5:4, mPar. 7:6. Cf. also mBekh. 4:5, 6:8.

succession to the rights of Jerusalem was considered the rule; a lack of it was diagnosed as an exception.[62] The Sanhedrin seems to have been imitated even in regard to the size of its membership. There is mention at least once of the '72 elders' who appointed R. Eleazar ben Azariah president.[63] In matters of civil law the tribunal of Yavneh may, in accordance with circumstances of general legislation, have been positively authorized by the Romans. For as far as can be discovered, Roman legislation in general accorded to Jewish communities in the Diaspora the power to administer justice in civil disputes provided the contending parties themselves brought the matter before the community's law-court.[64] But in criminal cases, this seems to have been a usurped power rather than a jurisdiction granted by the emperor. Origen describes this state of affairs very clearly and authentically. In his defence of the story of Susanna and Daniel he seeks to show that even in the Babylonian exile the Jews may very well have had their own jurisdiction. As proof he refers to conditions in Palestine in his own day, known to him from his own observation. The power of the Jewish ethnarch (Origen's own term) was so great as to be similar to that of a king (ὡς μηδὲν διαφέρειν βασιλεύοντος τοῦ ἔθνους). 'Secret legal processes also took place according to the Law, and some are sentenced to death, with no general authorization for it, but not without the knowledge of the emperor.'[65] This was the situation in the first half of the third century. In the decades following the destruction of Jerusalem, matters would not yet have gone so far. Nevertheless, movement in that direction had begun. To this Jewish central authority in Palestine, the president of which later bore the title of Patriarch (*Nasi*), flowed contributions from the Diaspora too, so far as these continued to be exacted after the destruction of the Temple. This is certainly attested

62. mSanh. 11:4; mR.Sh. 4:2.

63. mZeb. 1:3, mYad. 3:5, 4:2. Cf. vol. II, § 25, iv.

64. Jos. *Ant.* xiv 10, 17 (235). *Codex Theodosianus* II 1, 10 'ex consensu partium in civili dumtaxat negotio'. According to mEduy. 7: 7, Rabban Gamaliel II once travelled to the governor of Syria 'to obtain authority' (לטול רשות). This may have had to do with the bestowal, extension or exercise of juridical powers. Cf. J. Juster, *op. cit.* II, pp. 95–101, 110 ff.; H. Mantel, *op. cit.*, pp. 21–2. On the theory that Yoḥanan b. Zakkai's move to Yavneh resulted from a Roman war measure directing loyalist Jews to the coastal region, and that the 'academy' was originally an unofficial body of scholars, see G. Alon, *Studies in Jewish History* I ([2]1967), pp. 219–52 (in Hebrew). Cf. a critical evaluation of the thesis by J. Neusner, *A Life of Yohanan ben Zakkai* ([2]1970), pp. 243–5.

65. Origen, *Epist. ad Africanum*, 14. Cf. Th. Mommsen, *Röm. Strafrecht* (1899), p. 120. Mommsen saw in this 'the most remarkable proof of the toleration under the imperial rule, of institutions running counter to the Roman ordinances themselves'. On the power of the ethnarch in this period see M. Avi-Yonah, *Geschichte der Juden im Zeitalter des Talmud* (1962), pp. 52–63.

for at least the later imperial period. On this point, also, the rabbis replaced the priests. For until then the taxes were paid into the priestly central treasury in Jerusalem. Now, it was a rabbinical body that collected them by means of its 'apostoli' and supervised their proper use.[66]

Zeal for the Torah during this later time, among the great majority of the devout anyway, found its mainspring in a belief in the nation's glorious future. This was so already before the great disaster; and it continued to be so, to an even greater degree, after it. If people now strove more keenly than ever towards a meticulous observance of God's commandments, their strongest impulse was simply the desire that they might thereby become worthy of the future glory in which they believed so confidently. The Apocalypse of Baruch and IV Ezra, which originated at this time, provide a vivid and authentic explanation of the religious mood prevailing in the first decades after the destruction of the Holy City.[67] The immediate sequel to the terrible blow was, indeed, profound shock. How could God permit such a misfortune to strike his people? But this great riddle was really no more than a particular example of the universal riddle: how, in general, is the wretchedness of the just and the good fortune of the unjust to be explained? Israel's piety had long since found a way through the obscurity of these questions. Now, too, it soon discovered the solution. It is a chastisement inflicted by God on the people because of their sin. It has its appointed time. If the people allow themselves to be instructed by it, the promised day of salvation will soon dawn. Such is the basic idea of both apocalypses. Their purpose was to comfort the people in their distress, to revive their courage and zeal with a prospect of sure and imminent redemption. Their confident faith was thus only strengthened and established by the heavy blows of the time. From their mourning for the ruin of the sanctuary, the messianic hope drew new nourishment, new strength. This was also important and fateful in regard to the political situation. For the messianic hope was a remarkable mixture of political and religious ideals. The former were never renounced; and the dangerous element consisted precisely in their association with religious motives. The political freedom of the nation which they longed for was viewed as the goal of God's ways. The more firmly this was believed, the more easily was a cool consideration of the humanly possible brushed aside, the bolder grew the resolve

66. Cf. Juster, *op. cit.*, I, p. 405; Mantel, *op. cit.*, pp. 190–5; on the title שליח, see *ibid.*, p. 191, n. 112.

67. Cf. P. Volz, *Die Eschatologie der jüdischen Gemeinde* (1934), pp. 35–48, etc.; W. Bousset, *Die Religion des Judentums im späthellenistischen Zeitalter* ([4]1966), pp. 35 ff.; M. Simon, *Verus Israel* ([2]1964), pp. 25–7. Cf. vol. III, § 32, v.

to attempt the impossible. It was this outlook which had led to a revolt already in Nero's time. It now contained the seeds of further catastrophes.

Under the Flavian emperors (up to A.D. 96), there seem to have been no serious conflicts, though there would have been sufficient occasion for them. For the command to send the former Temple tax to Rome for Jupiter Capitolinus was an insult to Jewish religious sentiment which must have been exasperated afresh every year when the tax was levied. Under Domitian this tax was exacted with great severity in line with this emperor's general behaviour as the determined opponent of the Jews. Conversion to Judaism was punished with heavy penalties.[68]

Eusebius, on the authority of Hegesippus, speaks of a real persecution of the Jews after the destruction of the Temple, still during the reign of Vespasian. According to Hegesippus, Vespasian, Domitian and Trajan hunted down all Jews of Davidic descent and executed them in order to extirpate the royal line on which the Jews had set their hopes.[69] Under Vespasian, this order led to a great persecution of the Jews.[70] There is no way of checking the historical truth of this story. Since a Messiah of the house of David was beyond doubt expected, men claiming Davidic descent may really have been viewed as a political danger. But this 'persecution' of certain Palestinian Church leaders (reputed to have been blood relations of the Christ) may well represent an apologetical legend intended to emphasize the Davidic-Messianic status of Jesus. If at all historical, the repression cannot have been of any great extent or significance, for no other writer seems to know anything about it. It is equally uncertain whether political disturbances occurred under Domitian. Certain indications in the diploma of A.D. 86 led to a belief that such disturbances must have taken place. But these conclusions do not amount to certainty (see above p. 515). By contrast, the revolts which broke out under Trajan and Hadrian, first outside Judaea and then in the country itself, were of terrible violence and extent.[71]

68. On the exaction of taxes: Suet. *Dom.* 12; the prosecutions for conversion, Dio lxvii 14, 2; see in general E. M. Smallwood, 'Domitian's Attitude towards the Jews and Judaism', Classical Philology 51 (1956), pp. 1–13.

69. Euseb. *HE* iii 12 (Vespasian); *ibid.*, iii 19–20 (Domitian); *ibid.*, iii 32, 3–4 (Trajan); all derived from Hegesippus.

70. Euseb. *HE* iii 12 *Οὐεσπασιανὸν μετὰ τὴν τῶν Ἱεροσολύμων ἅλωσιν πάντας τοὺς ἀπὸ γένους Δαβὶδ . . . . . ἀναζητεῖσθαι προστάξαι, μέγιστόν τε Ἰουδαίοις αὖθις ἐκ ταύτης διωγμὸν ἐπαρτηθῆναι τῆς αἰτίας*.. Cf. Mantel, *op. cit.*, pp. 46–7, 164, 169. See also J. Liver, *The House of David* (1959) (Hebrew) and Vermes, *Jesus the Jew* (1973), p. 157.

71. For a discussion of the social history of Judaea in this period, see A. Büchler, *The Economic Conditions of Judaea after the Destruction of the Second Temple* (1912).

II. The Wars under Trajan A.D. 115–117

Sources

Appian, *Bell. Civ.* II 90/380; *Historia Romana* Fr. 19 (ed. Viereck, Roos, pp. 534–5).
Dio lxviii 32, 1–3.
Eusebius, *H.E.* IV 2; *Chron.* ed. Schoene II, pp. 164–5.
Orosius vii 12, 6–7.
Papyri: Tcherikover, V., and Fuks, A., *Corpus Papyrorum Judaicarum* II (1960), nos. 435–50.
Świderek, A., *ΙΟΥΔΑΙΚΟΣ ΛΟΓΟΣ*, Journ. Jur. Pap. 16/17 (1971), pp. 45–60.
Inscriptions (Cyrene): Applebaum, S., *Greeks and Jews in Ancient Cyrene* (1969), pp. 308–10 (in Hebrew).

Bibliography

Derenbourg, J., *Essai sur l'histoire et la géographie de la Palestine* (1867), pp. 402–12.
Mommsen, Th., *Römische Geschichte* V (1885), pp. 542–4 (E.T. (1886) II, pp. 221–3).
Graetz, H., *Geschichte der Juden* IV ([5]1908), pp. 113–21.
Büchler, A., *The Economic Conditions of Judaea after the Destruction of the Second Temple* (1912).
Abel, F.-M., *Histoire de la Palestine* II (1952), pp. 60–3.
Fuks, A., 'Aspects of the Jewish Revolt in A.D. 115–117', JRS 51 (1961), pp. 98–104.
Smallwood, E. M., 'Palestine *c.* A.D. 115–118', Historia 11 (1962), pp. 500–10.
Alon, G., *History of the Jews in Palestine in the Period of the Mishnah and the Talmud* I ([4]1967), pp. 202–89 (in Hebrew).
Applebaum, S., *Greeks and Jews in Ancient Cyrene* (1969) (in Hebrew).

In the last years of his life (A.D. 113–117), Trajan was continually taken up with extensive campaigns in the far east of the Empire.[71a] It was while he was occupied with the conquest of Mesopotamia in A.D. 115 that the Jews in Egypt and Cyrene, taking advantage of his absence, began 'to rise against their non-Jewish fellow-countrymen, as if possessed by a wild spirit of mutiny'.[72] By the following year (A.D. 116)

71a. On Trajan's wars in the East, see especially Mommsen, *History of Rome* V, pp. 387 ff., CAH XI, pp. 236 ff., 889 ff.; F. A. Lepper, *Trajan's Parthian War* (1948).

72. Euseb. *HE* iv 2, 2 ἔν τε γὰρ Ἀλεξανδρείᾳ καὶ τῇ λοιπῇ Αἰγύπτῳ καὶ προσέτι κατὰ Κυρήνην ὥσπερ ὑπὸ πνεύματος δεινοῦ τινος καὶ στασιώδους ἀναρριπισθέντες ὥρμηντο πρὸς τοὺς συνοίκους Ἕλληνας στασιάζειν. The earliest literary evidence on the war in Egypt is unfortunately very brief: it is provided by two passages of Appian. (1) *BC* ii 90/380. This reports that Caesar dedicated a shrine at Alexandria as a memorial to Pompey, and then continues: ὅπερ ἐπ' ἐμοῦ κατὰ Ῥωμαίων αὐτοκράτορα Τραϊανόν, ἐξολλύντα τὸ ἐν Αἰγύπτῳ Ἰουδαίων γένος, ὑπὸ τῶν Ἰουδαίων ἐς τὰς τοῦ πολέμου χρείας κατηρείφθη. (2) Fr. 19 of Appian tells how, at the time of the war, he had to flee from Egypt to escape the Jews and crossed into the Province of Arabia.

the revolt reached such proportions that it took on the character of a formal war.[73] The Roman Prefect of Egypt, M. Rutilius Lupus, appears to have been no match for the Jews, who defeated the 'Hellenes' in an engagement and forced them to flee to Alexandria. But in the capital the Greeks obtained the upper hand, and Jews living there were seized and put to death.[74]

A number of papyri now provide isolated but vivid glimpses of the course of the war. For instance, CPJ 435 is almost certainly an edict of the Prefect M. Rutilius Lupus dating to October 13, A.D. 115, and refers to a battle (μάχη) between the Romans and the Jews; 438, dating to the second half of A.D. 116, refers to a Jewish victory in the Hermoupolite district and to the arrival of 'another legion of Rutilius'

73. According to Eusebius, *Chron.*, ed. Schoene II, pp. 164–5, the revolt seems to have begun in the 17th year of Trajan, *ann. Abrah. 2130*. (So also Jerome.) This would be A.D. 114. In *HE* iv 2, 1, he says ἤδη γοῦν τοῦ αὐτοκράτορος εἰς ἐνιαυτὸν ὀκτωκαιδέκατον ἐλαύνοντος αὖθις Ἰουδαίων κίνησις ἐπαναστᾶσα. He thus places the start of the revolt towards the end of the 17th year of Trajan or near the beginning of the 18th. If this rests on accurate information, we would be led to the end of A.D. 114 or beginning of 115; for the 18th year of Trajan corresponds essentially to A.D. 115, whether the year is counted from the date of his accession (27 January), or from the Tribunician New Year (10 December), as was the official custom from the time of Trajan. In the following year, i.e. the 19th of Trajan= A.D. 116, while Lupus was governor of Egypt, the revolt assumed greater proportions: αὐξήσαντές τε εἰς μέγα τὴν στάσιν τῷ ἐπιόντι ἐνιαυτῷ πόλεμον οὐ σμικρὸν συνῆψαν, ἡγουμένου τηνικαῦτα Λούπου τῆς ἁπάσης Αἰγύπτου, *HE* iv 2, 2. To check the later literary evidence we may use contemporary documentary sources relating to the Prefects of Egypt and the events of their governorships; see A. Stein, *Die Präfekten von Ägypten in der römischen Kaiserzeit* (1950), pp. 55–63; corrections in O. W. Reinmuth, 'A Working List of the Prefects of Egypt 30 B.C. to A.D. 299', Bull. Am. Soc. Pap. 4 (1967), pp. 76–128, on pp. 92–3. For the disproof of the notion that Q. Marcius Turbo was Prefect in A.D. 117, see R. Syme, 'The Wrong Marcius Turbo', JRS 52 (1962), pp. 87–96.

(1) M. Rutilius Lupus was certainly governor of Egypt prior to the summer of A.D. 115 (SB 4383, dated to 28 January 113). That he was still in office in January A.D. 117 is shown by a rescript of his dated L κʹ θεοῦ Τραιανοῦ Τῦβι δεκάτῃ=5 January A.D. 117, BGU 114, col. 1,5. He must be taken as the author of the edict probably dating to October 13 A.D. 115 (see above) which refers to a battle between Romans and Jews.

(2) It is known that Q. Rammius Martialis was Prefect in the first Egyptian regnal year of Hadrian, so A. Fuks, JRS 52 (1962), p. 101; he is attested between 11–28 August A.D. 117, P.Oxy. 1023. He is certainly the addressee of the petition for leave from the *strategos* Apollonios (CPJ 443) which dates to November 28 A.D. 117, and indicates that by that time fighting had ceased.

On the chronology of the revolt, see the excellent article by A. Fuks, 'The Jewish Revolt in A.D. 115–117', JRS 52 (1962), pp. 98–104, along with the literature cited there.

74. Euseb. *HE* iv 2, 3; *Chron.* ed. Schoene II, pp. 164 ff. (*ad ann. Abrah.* 2130, following Jerome; or 2131, following the Armenian). Oros. vii, 12: 'In Alexandria autem commisso proelio victi et adtriti sunt'. See A. Fuks, *op. cit.*, p. 99.

at Memphis; 443 is an application to the Prefect (Rammius Martialis) from the *strategos* of Apollinopolis-Heptakomias, dated November 28, A.D. 117, and asking for leave on the grounds that 'because of the attack of the impious Jews, practically everything I possess in the villages of the Hermoupolite nome and in the metropolis needs my attention'. 445 and 448 (and two papyri published by Świderek, *op. cit.*, above) are concerned with the confiscation of Jewish property after the revolt, and 447 and 449 with property damaged during it. Most striking of all, 450, dating to A.D. 199/200, reveals that an annual festival was still celebrated in Oxyrhynchus to commemorate the victory over the Jews.

Even more furious was the rage of the Jews in Cyrene. Dio paints a gruesome picture of atrocities perpetrated there against their non-Jewish fellow-citizens: they are said to have eaten their flesh, painted themselves with their blood, sawed them through from end to end, or fed them to the wild animals. The toll of those massacred apparently reached 220,000.[75] But however certain we may be of the unbridled fantasy of this account, it nevertheless discloses the scope and importance of the rebellion. The ringleader of Cyrenaican Jewry—whom they hailed as their king—is named Lucuas by Eusebius, Andreas by Dio.[76]

Here too there is now considerable documentary, and also archaeological, evidence to confirm the accounts of the literary sources. For instance, a number of temples in the city of Cyrene—including those of Apollo, Zeus, Demeter, Artemis, and Isis—were destroyed or damaged; milestones refer to roads near the city destroyed 'tumultu Iudaico'; an inscription mentions the sending by Trajan of 3,000 veterans to settle in Cyrenaica, evidently to assist repopulation.[77]

Trajan sent one of his best generals, Marcius Turbo, to put down the revolt,[78] and by means of protracted and stubborn fighting (*πολλαῖς*

75. Dio lxviii 32, 1–3. Cf. Oros. vii 12, 6–7. 'Incredibili deinde motu sub uno tempore Iudaei, quasi rabie efferati, per diversas terrarum partes exarserunt. nam et per totam Libyam adversas incolas atrocissima bella gesserunt: quae adeo tunc interfectis cultoribus desolata est, ut nisi postea Hadrianus imperator collectas illuc aliunde colonias deduxisset, vacua penitus terra, abraso habitatore, mansisset. Aegyptum vero totam et Cyrenen et Thebaidam cruentis seditionibus turbaverunt'.

76. Euseb. *HE* iv 2, 4; Dio lxviii 32. Cf. P. M. Fraser, 'Hadrian and Cyrene', JRS 40 (1950), pp. 77–90, esp. 83–4.

77. For surveys of the extensive evidence for destruction and restoration, see P. M. Fraser, JRS 40 (1950), pp. 77–90; S. Applebaum, 'The Jewish Revolt in Cyrene in 115–117, and the subsequent Recolonisation', JJS 2 (1951), pp. 177–86; A. Fuks, *op. cit.*, pp. 98–9; and now the general work by S. Applebaum, *Greeks and Jews in Cyrene* (1969) (in Hebrew).

78. Euseb. *HE* iv 2, 3–4, *ἐφ' οὓς ὁ αὐτοκράτωρ ἔπεμψεν Μάρκιον Τούρβωνα σὺν δυνάμει πεζῇ τε καὶ ναυτικῇ, ἔτι δὲ καὶ ἱππικῇ. ὁ δὲ πολλαῖς μάχαις οὐκ ὀλίγῳ τε χρόνῳ τὸν πρὸς αὐτοὺς διαπονήσας πόλεμον, πολλὰς μυριάδας Ἰουδαίων, οὐ μόνον τῶν ἀπὸ Κυρήνης, ἀλλὰ καὶ*

μάχαις οὐκ ὀλίγῳ τε χρόνῳ) Turbo brought the war to an end, putting to death many thousands of Jews, not only from Cyrene but also from Egypt, who had attached themselves to their 'king', Lucuas.[79]

The revolt had also spread to the island of Cyprus. Under the leadership of a certain Artemion, the Jews here followed the example of their Cyrenaican co-religionists and murdered some 240,000 non-Jewish islanders.[80] Even the capital, Salamis, was devastated by them.[81] No information is extant regarding the suppression of the revolt, but from then on, no Jew was allowed to set foot on the island; if any were driven onto its coasts by bad weather, they were put to death.[82]

Finally, when Trajan had advanced as far as Ctesiphon, the capital of the Parthian empire, the Jews in his rear in Mesopotamia also became restive. Such a disturbance on the empire's frontier was most serious. Trajan commanded the Moorish prince Lucius Quietus, who was at the same time a Roman general, to sweep the insurrectionists out of the province (*ἐκκαθᾶραι τῆς ἐπαρχίας αὐτούς*). Quietus followed his directions with barbaric ferocity, and thousands of Jews lost their lives. Peace was thus restored and Quietus was rewarded with the governorship of Palestine.[83]

The Jewish rebellion seems not to have ended completely until the beginning of the reign of Hadrian (A.D. 117). Eusebius in any case refers to disturbances in Alexandria which the emperor was obliged to

---

τῶν ἀπ' Αἰγύπτου συναιρομένων Λουκουᾳ τῷ βασιλεῖ αὐτῶν ἀναιρεῖ. Cf. HA, *vit. Hadr.* 5, 8, 'Marçio Turbone Iudaeis congressis ad deprimendum tumultum Mauretaniae destinato'. For a solution of the complicated problems relating to the career and identity of this man, see R. Syme, 'The Wrong Marcius Turbo', JRS 52 (1962), pp. 87–96.

79. Euseb. *HE* iv 2, 4. According to Euseb. *Chron.*, ed. Schoene II, pp. 164 ff., and Oros. vii 12, 6–7, the rising spread even beyond Thebes.

80. Dio lxviii 32. See also ILS 9491.

81. Euseb. *Chron.*, ed. Schoene II, p. 164 (the 19th year of Trajan, *ann. Abrah.* 2132) following the Armenian: 'Salaminam Cipri insulae urbem Iudaei adorti sunt et Graecos, quos ibi nacti sunt, trucidarunt, urbemque a fundamentis subverterunt.' Greek in Syncellus, ed. Dindorf I, p. 657: *τοὺς ἐν Σαλαμῖνι τῆς Κύπρου Ἕλληνας Ἰουδαῖοι ἀνελόντες τὴν πόλιν κατέσκαψαν*. Orosius vii 12, 8 'Sane Salaminam, urbem Cypri, interfectis omnibus accolis deleverunt.'

82. Dio lxviii 32. Cf. also A. Fuks, *loc. cit.*, p. 99.

83. Euseb., *HE* iv 2, 5; *Chron.*, ed. Schoene II, pp. 164–5 (in the 18th year of Trajan, *ann. Abrah.* 2131); Oros. vii 12, 7; Dio lxviii 32, 4–5 (here also for personal details concerning Quietus). On his activity in Mesopotamia and Palestine, see E. Groag, RE s.v. 'Lusius Quietus'; cf. PIR² L 439. It appears from CIL III 13587=ILS 4393, dated to about A.D. 116–117, that part of the force at his disposal was a detachment of the *legio III Cyrenaica*.

quell.[84] Hadrian's biographer, Spartianus, reports that Palestine also showed signs of rebellion.[85] But order seems to have been completely restored within the first year of the reign. This, or the following year, provides the probable dramatic setting for the scene from the 'Acts of the Pagan Martyrs', called the Acta Pauli et Antonini,[86] representing a hearing before an emperor, most probably Hadrian, of accusations and counter-accusations by Jewish and Greek ambassadors from Alexandria in connexion with their mutual conflicts there.

Palestine does not seem to have been involved to any great extent in the revolt, but there is scattered evidence to suggest that real upheavals took place there and had to be repressed.[87] Rabbinical tradition is aware of a 'War of Quietus' (פולמוס של קיטוס),[88] though this may simply refer to the war of Quietus in Mesopotamia. In the vulgar text of Meg. Taan. §29, 12 Adar is described as the 'Day of Trajan' (יום טורינוס),[89] intended to commemorate the following event.[90] Two brothers, Julianus and Pappus, were seized by Trajan in Laodicaea, whereupon he mockingly said to them: 'If you belong to the people of Hananiah, Mishael and Azariah, may your God come and deliver you from my hand as he saved them from the hand of Nebuchadnezzar.' The two brothers replied that neither he nor they were worthy of such a miracle, but God would require their blood from him if he killed them. And Trajan had not yet left that place before a command came from Rome in consequence of which he was executed. This fable (which merits no attention because Trajan is depicted as a subordinate official) was once advanced as principal evidence of Trajan's Judaean War! Clearly, there is no question here either of war, or of Judaea (but expressly of Laodicea).[91] The only point in favour of this view is the

84. Euseb. *Chron.* II, pp. 164–5 (in Hadrian's first year=*ann. Abrah.* 2133) using the Armenian version: 'Adrianus Iudaeos subegit ter (tertio) contra Romanos rebellantes'; according to Jerome: 'Hadrianus Iudaeos capit secundo contra Romanos rebellantes; following Syncellus: *Ἀδριανὸς Ἰουδαιοὺς κατὰ Ἀλεξανδρέων στασιάζοντας ἐκόλασεν.*

85. HA, *vita Hadr.* 5, 2: 'Lybia [Lycia] denique ac Palaestina rebelles animos efferebant'.

86. H. A. Musurillo, *Acts of the Pagan Martyrs* (*Acta Alexandrinorum*) (1954), no. ix.

87. See E. M. Smallwood, 'Palestine *c.* A.D. 115–118', Historia 11 (1962), pp. 500–10.

88. mSot. 9:14; S. Olam, ed. Neubauer, p. 66.

89. Ed. Lichenstein, HUCA 8–9 (1931–2), pp. 321 and 272–3; J. Derenbourg, pp. 443, 446. The form טוריינוס is given also by A. Neubauer, *Mediaeval Jewish Chronicles* II (1895), p. 19 and yTaan. 18b. But the MSS. of Meg. Taan. and yMeg 70c, yTaan. 66a read טירין.

90. Lichenstein, p. 346; J. Derenbourg, pp. 406 f.; A. Neubauer, *op. cit.*, p. 19.

91. The tale possibly goes back to a hazy recollection of the fact that Lusius Quietus, the oppressor of the Jews, was recalled by Hadrian and later executed (HA, *vita Hadr.* 5, 8; 7, 2).

statement by Spartianus quoted earlier, according to which Palestine, at the outset of Hadrian's rule, *rebelles animos efferebat*. But it can hardly have come to a real war. Otherwise our sources would say something about it.[92]

III. The Great Revolt under Hadrian A.D. 132–135

Literary sources:

Appian, *Syriaca* 50/252.
Justin, 1 *Apol*. 31, 6.
Fronto, *Epistulae* ed. Naber, p. 218; ed. Van den Hout, p. 206.
Dio lxix 12–14.
Eusebius, *HE* iv 5, 2; 6. (On Ariston of Pella, see pp. 37–9 above.)
Eusebius, *Chron*. ed. Schoene II, pp. 166–9.

Documents and archaeological finds

Benoit, P., Milik, J. T., de Vaux, R., *Discoveries in the Judaean Desert II: Les grottes de Murabba'at* (1961), esp. nos. 22–46.
Avigad, N. & al., 'The Expedition to the Judean Desert, 1960', IEJ 11 (1961), pp. 3–72, esp. pp. 21–30, 36–62.
Avigad, N. & al., 'The Expedition to the Judean Desert, 1961', IEJ 12 (1962), pp. 167–262, esp. 190–214, 227–62.
Lifshitz, B., 'Papyrus grecs du désert de Juda', Aegyptus 42 (1962), pp. 240–56.
Yadin, Y., *Finds from the Bar-Kokhba Period in the Cave of Letters* (1963).
Meshorer, Y., *Jewish Coins of the Second Temple Period* (1967), pp. 92–101, 159–69.
Yadin, Y., *Bar Kokhba* (1971).
Kanael, B., 'Notes on Dates Used During the Bar Kokhba Revolt', IEJ 21 (1971), pp. 39–46.

Bibliography

Derenbourg, J., *Essai sur l'histoire et la géographie de la Palestine* (1867), pp. 412–38.
Graetz, H., *Geschichte der Juden* IV (^{5}1908), pp. 125–67.
Weber, W., *Untersuchungen zur Geschichte des Kaisers Hadrianus* (1907), pp. 240–5, 275–6.
Abel, F.-M., *Histoire de la Palestine* II (1952), pp. 83–102.
Yeivin, S., *Milḥemet Bar Kokhba* (*The War of Bar Kokhba*) (^{2}1952).

---

92. The chronology of the last Jewish wars is given in *Seder 'Olam* (ed. Neubauer, p. 66) as follows: 'From the war of Asverus (Varus? cf. p. 332 above) to the war of Vespasian: 80 years whilst the Temple existed. From the war of Vespasian to the war of Quietus: fifty-two years. And from the war of Quietus to the war of Ben Koziba: 16 years. And the war of Ben Koziba: three and a half years. מפולימוס של אסוירוס עד פולמוס של אספסינוס פ׳ שנים. אלו בפני הבית. מפולימוס של אספסינוס עד פולימוס של קיטוס חמשים ושתים שנה. ומפולימוס של קיטוס עד מלחמת בן כוזיבא י״ו שנה. ומלחמת בן כוזיבא שלש שנים ומחצה.

Smallwood, E. M., 'The Legislation of Hadrian and Antoninus Pius against Circumcision', Latomus 18 (1959), pp. 334–47.
Smallwood, E. M., 'Addendum', *ibid.* 20 (1961), pp. 93–6.
Abramsky, S., *Bar Kokhba n^e^si' Yisra'el* (*Bar Kokhba Prince of Israel*) (1961).
Alon, G., *Tol^e^dot ha-Y^e^hudim b^e^-'Ereẓ Yisra'el bi-t^e^ḳufat ha-Mishnah v^e^ha-Talmud* (*History of the Jews in Palestine in the Period of Mishnah and the Talmud*) I (⁴1967), pp. 290–354, II (²1961), pp. 1–47.
Applebaum, S., 'The Agrarian Question and the Revolt of Bar Kokhba', Eretz Israel 8 (1967), pp. 283–7 (in Hebrew).
Mantel, H., 'The Causes of the Bar Kokba Revolt', JQR 58 (1967–8), pp. 224–42, 274–96. 'Postscript', *ibid.* 59 (1968–9), pp. 341–2.
Prigent, P., *La fin de Jérusalem* (1969), pp. 92–146.

A late Jewish legend relates that in the days of R. Joshua ben Ḥananiah (i.e. during Hadrian's time), the Gentile government directed that the Temple should be rebuilt. The Samaritans, however, raised objections. As a result, the emperor, while not actually withdrawing the permit, decreed that the new building should not be erected on the precise site of the old Temple, which was equivalent to an actual prohibition. At this, the Jews gathered in crowds in the valley of Beth-Rimmon. To pacify them, R. Joshua told them the fable of the lion and the stork: as the stork was happy to have extracted its head uninjured from the jaws of the lion, so they should be happy to be able to live in peace under Gentile rule.[93] The historical value of the legend is nil, and yet it forms the main basis of the view put forward by some scholars that Hadrian consented to the rebuilding of the Jewish Temple and that his withdrawal of this permission was the true cause of the great Jewish revolt.[94] To support this theory, appeal is also made to Christian accounts. But they too are little suited for the part. Chrysostom, Cedrenus and Nicephorus Callistus say merely that the Jews in Hadrian's time revolted and tried to rebuild the Temple, and that Hadrian thwarted this enterprise; the *Chronicon paschale* speaks of the destruction by Hadrian of a Temple that had actually been rebuilt.[95] There is thus no question of a permit originally given by Hadrian and subsequently withdrawn; the attempted reconstruction of the Temple was itself an act of rebellion. The one apparent confirmation of this hypothesis appears in a passage from the *Letter of Barnabas*, the interpretation of which is however debatable. Barnabas wishes to show that Jewish observance of the Law does not conform to God's will. Their Sabbath is not the true one. 'And they have worshipped God in a temple almost like the heathen.' To prove the heathen character of the Jewish Temple, Barnabas quotes the prophecy of Isaiah (Is.

93. Gen. R. 64:8. For an English translation, see the Soncino *Midrash Rabbah, in loc.*

94. E.g. Graetz, *op. cit.*, pp. 125 ff., Derenbourg, *Histoire*, pp. 412 ff.

95. See n. 146 below.

49:17) 'See, those who have destroyed this temple will themselves rebuild it'; and he then continues: *γίνεται· διὰ τὸ γὰρ πολεμεῖν αὐτοὺς καθῃρέθη ὑπὸ τῶν ἐχθρῶν· νῦν καὶ αὐτοὶ [καὶ] οἱ τῶν ἐχθρῶν ὑπηρέται ἀνοικοδομήσουσιν αὐτόν* (16:4). It is only if the bracketed *καί* is retained, that this passage expresses the expectation that Jews and pagans together will rebuild the Temple. If the *καί* is omitted, the meaning is that the pagans themselves will build the Temple, for pagan purposes. But on external grounds as well, the latter reading is to be preferred. Barnabas thus seems to be alluding to Hadrian's intended pagan edifice.[96] The alleged permission given by Hadrian to rebuild the Jewish Temple must therefore be disregarded as a cause of the revolt. Such a consent, especially one accompanied by active encouragement, is also inherently unlikely. For whereas Hadrian did indeed promote the Graeco-Roman cults with enthusiasm, he despised alien religions.[97]

Only two reports on the causes of the great revolt should be considered with any seriousness. The Historia Augusta says,[98] 'moverunt ea tempestate et Iudaei bellum, quod vetabantur mutilare genitalia'.

96. A careful discussion of the passage is to be found in H. Windisch, HNT, Ergänzungsband, *Die apostolischen Väter* III: *Der Barnabasbrief* (1920), pp. 387, 388–90. Windisch (as also J. B. Lightfoot, *The Apostolic Fathers* (1907), p. 261) accepts the omission of the *καί*, and refers the verse to the building of the temple of Jupiter. The words *οἱ τῶν ἐχθρῶν ὑπηρέται* best suit the construction of a pagan temple. Cf. also A. von Harnack, *Gesch. d. altchristl. Literatur bis Euseb.* II, 1 (1897), pp. 423–7. The wording of the passage implies that the rebuilding of the actual temple is involved. According to Barnabas, this temple was no better than a heathen one; the proof is that it has now been rebuilt by the pagans. In support of this, note the *αὐτόν* at the end.

97. HA, *vita Hadr.* 22, 10, 'sacra Romana diligentissime curavit, peregrina contempsit'. According to A. Schlatter, *Die Tage Trajan's und Hadrian's*, p. 67 n., this remark has absolutely nothing to do with the matter. He himself construed the causes of the revolt as follows (*op. cit.*, pp. 59–67): The letter of Barnabas tells us that Hadrian authorised the construction of the Jewish temple. We also know that it was under construction and that it was so nearly finished that the Day of Atonement could again be celebrated. Everything seemed to be going as well as possible. Then suddenly conflict broke out because the Jews refused to offer the sacrifice for the emperor. The latter is attested by the story of a certain Bar Ḳamẓa (b. Git. 55b–56a and Lam. R. to Lam. 4:2). This man felt insulted by the rabbis because of the treatment he had experienced at a banquet, and maligned the Jews to the emperor by saying that a sacrificial victim donated by him would not be accepted. The emperor thereupon sent a fat calf. But the trouble makers secretly injured the animal, thus rendering it unsuitable for sacrifice. When, as a result, the Jews did in fact reject it, the emperor despatched Nero, and shortly after, Vespasian, and the Temple was destroyed. Despite the anecdotal character of the story, Schlatter treats it as historical and places it in Hadrian's time. He makes of *a* sacrifice sent by the emperor, *the* sacrifice for the emperor, and so obtains the interpretation set out above. In doing so, he clashes with the real sources, Dio and the Historia Augusta.

98. HA, *vita Hadr.* 14, 2.

Dio, on the other hand, observes,[99] 'When Hadrian founded a city of his own at Jerusalem on the site of the ruined one, calling it Aelia Capitolina, and erected on the site of the Temple another (temple) to Zeus, a great and protracted war resulted. For the Jews regarded it as an abomination for foreigners to settle in their city and for alien sanctuaries to be built in it.' As the Historia Augusta names only the one cause, and Dio only the other, it seems debatable whether the two can be combined without further ado. Gregorovius rejected the statement in the Historia Augusta and gave credence exclusively to that of Dio. In fact, a ban placed on circumcision for no special reason seems to accord little with Hadrian's mild disposition, however comprehensible its use as a method of exterminating the Jews after the suppression of the revolt.[100] But in spite of this, the Historia Augusta's reference may be accepted.

To evaluate it correctly, it must be remembered that circumcision was not peculiar to the Jews.[101] Herodotus lists as nations among whom it was customary from time immemorial, the Colchians, the Egyptians and the Ethiopians; from the Egyptians it passed also to the Phoenicians and the 'Syrians in Palestine' (i.e. the Jews). From the Phoenicians he excludes 'those in contact with Hellas'.[102] Other writers also mention the fact that the Egyptians' practised circum-

99. Dio lxix 12, 1–2. But H. Windisch, *Barnabasbrief*, p. 389, stresses that this passage cannot rightly mean that the completed Aelia and temple of Jupiter were the cause of the revolt.

100. F. Gregorovius, *Der Kaiser Hadrian*, pp. 188 ff. Both Dio and the Historia Augusta partially depend on Hadrian's autobiography (cf. Dio lxix 11, 2, ὥς Ἀδριανὸς γράφει. HA, *vita Hadr.* 1, 1, 'in libris vitae suae Hadrianus ipse commemoret'; 7, 2, 'ut ipse in vita sua dicit', cf. also 3, 3; 3, 5). In Dio, moreover, the account of the Jewish War follows almost immediately on a quotation from the autobiography and may very well have been drawn from it; for Dio's sources on Hadrian see F. Millar, *A Study of Cassius Dio* (1964), pp. 60–72. In the case of the Historia Augusta, on the other hand, circumstances are not so favourable. Even if it cannot be proved that the actual comment on the Jewish war does not stem from a good source, examination of the *Scriptores historiae Augustae* has shown that as presently extant they are a later work in which the underlying original source has been considerably retouched and combined with dubious material. Cf. e.g. E. Hohl, 'Über die Glaubwürdigkeit der Historia Augusta', SBA, Klasse für Gesellschaftswissenschaften, 1953, Nr. 2; and R. Syme, *Ammianus and the Historia Augusta* (1967).

101. For a valuable discussion of this whole question, see E. M. Smallwood, 'The Legislation of Hadrian and Antoninus Pius against Circumcision', Latomus 18 (1959), pp. 334–47, and 'The Legislation of Hadrian and Antoninus Pius against Circumcision: Addendum', Latomus, 20 (1961), pp. 93–6. H. Mantel's attempt at refuting this thesis (JQR 58 (1967–8), pp. 231–6) is unconvincing.

102. Herodotus ii 104, 2–4. Josephus twice quotes this passage, *Ant.* viii 10, 3 (262); *c. Ap.* i 22 (169–71), remarking on both occasions that by the term 'the Syrians in Palestine' only the Jews can be meant.

cision.[103] As a generalization, this statement is probably incorrect, for Jer. 9:24–5, according to the correct interpretation of the passage, indicates that the Egyptians were uncircumcised. Circumcision seems therefore to have been practised only in the narrower circles of the more highly placed. In Roman times, at any rate, only the priests in Egypt were regularly circumcised.[104] On the other hand, circumcision was general among the Arabs,[105] whereas the Ituraeans and the Idumaeans (i.e. the Jews' nearest neighbours to the north and south) did not accept circumcision until their forced conversion to Judaism by the Hasmonaean princes John Hyrcanus and Aristobulus I.[106]

Accordingly, if the Jews were not the only people in the Roman empire to practise circumcision, it is unlikely that the ban applied to them alone. In point of fact, it is plain from the factors which led to the prohibition that it was a general one. Hadrian first of all intensified the ban on castration already decreed by Domitian; it was to be punished 'in accordance with the *lex Cornelia*', i.e. as murder.[107] But circumcision was placed on a par with castration, as may be seen from

103. Also, Herodotus ii 36, 3, *Αἰγύπτιοι δὲ περιτάμνονται*. Agatharchides: *Geographi graeci minores*, ed. C. Müller I, p. 154, 'the Troglodytes *καθάπερ Αἰγυπτίους πάντας*'. Diodorus i 28, 'The Egyptians, and after them the Colchians and the Jews'; iii 32, 4, 'the Troglodytes as the Egyptians'. Diodorus in this section is reproducing Agatharchides almost verbatim. Strabo xvii 2, 5 (824). Philo, *de spec. leg.* i 1 (2). Celsus, in Origen, *Contra Celsum* v 41, 'the Egyptians and the Colchians practised circumcision before the Jews did'; cf. i 22; v 48. Further references in E. M. Smallwood, Latomus 18 (1959), pp. 334 ff.

104. Artapanus, in Euseb. *Praep. Evang.* ix 27, 10=FGrH 726 F3 (Artapanus wrote before Alexander Polyhistor and probably in the second century B.C.). Jos. *c. Ap.* ii 13 (141), *ἐκεῖνοι* (the Egyptian priests) *ἅπαντες καὶ περιτέμνονται καὶ χοιρείων ἀπέχονται βρωμάτων*. Horapollon, ed. Leemans, I 14, p. 23. Origen, *Com. in ep. ad Rom.* ii 13 (ed. Lommatzsch VI, 138 ff., PG xiv, cols. 910–11) 'Apud Aegyptios . . . nullus aut geometriae studebat aut astronomiae . . . nullus certe astrologiae et geneseos . . . secreta rimabatur, nisi circumcisione suscepta. sacerdos apud eos, aruspex aut quorumlibet sacrorum minister, vel, ut illi appellant, propheta omnis, circumcisus est. Litteras quoque sacerdotales veterum Aegyptiorum, quas hieroglyphicas appellant, nemo discebat nisi circumcisus.' *Id.*, *in Jerem. hom.* v 14 (GCS Origenes III, pp. 43–4). Jerome, *Comm. ad Gal.* 5: 1 (PL xxvi, col. 394). Epiphanius, *Haer.* 30, 33. The story of Apion also shows that circumcision was not general in Egypt. Cf. Jos. *c. Ap.* ii 13 (171–2); note however, W. Otto, *Priester u. Tempel im hellenistischen Ägypten* I (1905), pp. 214–15.

105. Gen. 17:23–7 (circumcision of Ishmael at the age of thirteen). Jos. *Ant.* i 12, 2 (214) *Ἄραβες δὲ μετὰ ἔτος τρισκαιδέκατον. . . .*). *Barn.* 9: 6, *περιτέτμηται . . . καὶ πᾶς Σύρος καὶ Ἄραψ καὶ πάντες οἱ ἱερεῖς τῶν εἰδώλων* (only partially correct). Origen, *Com. in Gen.* iii 10 (ed. Lommatzsch VIII, 33) quoted by Eusebius, *Praep. Evang.* vi 11, 69 (GCS Eusebius VIII, pp. 357–8) *τῶν δὲ ἐν Ἰσμαηλίταις τοῖς κατὰ τὴν Ἀραβίαν, τοιόνδε ὡς πάντας περιτέμνεσθαι τρισκαιδεκαετεῖς· τοῦτο γὰρ ἱστόρηται περὶ αὐτῶν*. Cf. preceding note.

106. Jos. *Ant.* xiii 9, 1 (257–8); 11, 3 (318–19).

107. *Digest* xlviii 8, 4, 2 (from Ulpian), 'Divus Hadrianus rescripsit: constitutum quidem est, ne spadones fierent, eos autem, qui hoc crimine arguerentur, Corneliae legis poena teneri'. By this is meant the *Lex Cornelia de*

a later decree of Antoninus Pius permitting Jews to practise circumcision once again.[108] Hadrian thus forbade circumcision in general as a barbaric custom. He did not simply apply the ban to the Jews on religious grounds. Hence under Antoninus Pius, the general ban remained in force, but circumcision was permitted to the Jews as a special case for the sake of their religion.[109] There is direct evidence for the universality of the ban in regard to the Arabs, Samaritans and Egyptians. (1) In Nabataean Arabia, circumcision prevalent until then was abolished by the Romans.[110] (2) Among the Samaritans in the time of Origen it was forbidden on pain of death.[111] In Egypt, priests in the second half of the second century A.D. required, in each individual case, a special official permit to perform circumcision. Permission to circumcise a boy was only granted once his priestly descent and absence of

---

sicariis et veneficis. Domitian and Nerva had already banned castration (Dio lxvii 2, 3; Suet. *Dom.* vii 1), but there does not seem to be any indication that prior to Hadrian circumcision was assimilated to it. Further, his rescript goes on to impose the death penalty on both the circumcised and the circumciser. On the whole matter, see E. M. Smallwood, 'The Legislation of Hadrian and Antoninus Pius against Circumcision', Latomus 18 (1959), pp. 334 ff.

108. Modestinus, *Digest* xlviii 8, 11, 'Circumcidere Iudaeis filios suos tantum rescripto divi Pii permittitur: in non eiusdem religionis qui hoc fecerit, castrantis poena irrogatur'. Cf. J. Juster, *Les Juifs dans l'Empire romain* I, pp. 263–71; E. M. Smallwood, *art. cit.*, p. 334. Note that this rescript exempts Jewish families from the ban, but apparently does not extend exemption to adult converts. This implies the universality of the ban hitherto, as affecting all races, not merely the Jews.

109. Modestinus, *Digest* xlviii 8, 11 (as in previous note). See also Paulus, *Sent.* V 22, 3–4, listing the penalties for Gentiles submitting to circumcision: 'Cives Romani, qui se Iudaico ritu vel servos suos circumcidi patiuntur, bonis ademptis in insulam perpetuo relegantur; medici capite puniuntur. Iudaei si alienae nationis comparatos servos circumciderint, aut deportantur aut capite puniuntur'. According to Smallwood, *art. cit.*, p. 345, this concerns the period after the issue of Antoninus's rescript.

110. In the Syriac dialogue on Fate, ascribed to Bardesanes, the fact that when kings have conquered foreign lands they have often, without hindrance from the stars, annulled existing laws and introduced their own, is illustrated principally by the Roman annulment, shortly after the conquest of Arabia, of local laws, and in particular that relating to circumcision. Cf. W. Cureton, *Spicilegium Syriacum* (1855), pp. 29–30; H. J. W. Drijvers, *The Book of the Laws of Countries* (1965), pp. 56–7. In the somewhat abridged version (in Greek) in Euseb. *Praep. Evang.* vi 10, 41, the prohibition of circumcision is not mentioned. The same author speaks immediately afterwards of the circumcision of Jews as an existing custom.

111. Origen, *c. Cels.* ii 13, notes that Christians alone would be persecuted for their faith, and then continues: *ἀλλὰ φήσει τις, ὅτι καὶ Σαμαρεῖς διὰ τὴν ἑαυτῶν θεοσέβειαν διώκονται. πρὸς ὃν τοιαῦτα ἐροῦμεν· οἱ σικάριοι διὰ τὴν περιτομήν, ὡς ἀκρωτηριάζοντες παρὰ τοὺς καθεστῶτας νόμους καὶ τὰ Ἰουδαίοις συγκεχωρημένα μόνοις, ἀναιροῦνται*. So it is not on account of their religion that they will be punished as 'murderers' (in accordance with the Lex Cornelia), but because of circumcision, permitted only to Jews.

physical defect had been proved, i.e., his fitness to assume priestly office.[112] In general, therefore, it was forbidden.

The ban on circumcision promulgated by Hadrian was in consequence not directed specifically at Judaism; but obviously the Jews felt that it dealt them a mortal blow. To this was now added the other vexation, namely that Hadrian intended to build a new pagan city on the ruins of Jerusalem. Here again, the motive was not enmity towards Judaism: splendid architecture and the founding of cities characterized Hadrian's life work as a whole. But the proposal must have given the Jews profound offence. While Jerusalem lay in ruins they could look for its restoration. The establishment of a pagan city, the erection of a pagan temple on the holy place, put an end to these hopes. It was an outrage similar to that once perpetrated by Antiochus Epiphanes, and the reaction to it was, as before, a general uprising of the people. Thus neither cause is in itself unlikely. A combination of the two is therefore quite conceivable, if Hadrian's two directives were not too widely separated from one another in time.

Various statements appear in the sources in regard to the date at which the construction of Aelia Capitolina started. Epiphanius claims that Hadrian, on a visit to Jerusalem, commanded that the city (not the Temple) should be rebuilt, and entrusted the task to Aquila, forty-seven years after its destruction.[113] This would point to A.D. 117, immediately after Hadrian's accession. He was in any case in the east at that time; but Epiphanius is apparently thinking of one of his later long journeys from Rome, and his information consequently loses all its value. The *Chronicon paschale* places the founding of Aelia in the year A.D. 119, but only because it dates the great Jewish rebellion to the same year, the foundation of Aelia taking place just after the revolt was suppressed.[114] With the date given for the Jewish rebellion,

112. This interesting point is shown by several papyri e.g., BGU I, 82, and 347=L. Mitteis, U. Wilcken, *Grundzüge u. Chrestomathie* I, no. 76. One of these contains two contemporary documents from A.D. 171, the other, a similar document from A.D. 185. A similar text, edited by R. Reitzenstein, *Zwei religionsgeschichtliche Fragen* (1901), pp. 1–46, includes two documents from the time of Antoninus Pius (=Mitteis, Wilcken, *op. cit.*, no. 77). The legal process according to all four texts is the same. A priest wishing to submit his son to circumcision has first to present a petition to the officer in charge of his home district, who then certifies the boy's priestly origin on the basis of the roll of inhabitants. Armed with this certificate, father and son go to Memphis, to the Roman Chief Priest of all Egypt. This man how has the boy examined by his priestly officials (to see if he is free from physical defect—εἰ σημεῖόν τι ἔχοι ὁ παῖς. . .). Only when he is certified to be 'free' (ἄσημος) and thus eligible for the priesthood, does the Chief Priest issue the written authorization for the circumcision. It may be mentioned as a parallel that the Prefect of Egypt was able also in exceptional cases to permit castration, Justin, 1 *Apol.* 29.

113. *De mensuris et ponderibus*, 14.

114. *Chron. pasch.*, ed. Dindorf, I, p. 474.

which is demonstrably false, collapses that for the foundation of Aelia.[115] Eusebius, too, views the work on the new city as subsequent to the revolt.[116] This is right inasmuch as the plan was not carried out until then. But according to Dio, building was unquestionably started prior to the uprising, though not very long before. For he says that the Jews, who were scandalized over it, nevertheless remained calm while Hadrian stayed in Egypt and Syria, but that they flared up as soon as he had left those regions.[117] It may therefore be assumed that the foundation of Aelia occurred during Hadrian's sojourn in Syria in A.D. 130.[118]

Hadrian went to Syria at that time from Greece: it was his last great journey to the east. From there he travelled to Egypt, and then back again to Syria.[119] Coins, papyri and inscriptions attest that he was in Syria in A.D. 129/30, in Egypt by August 130, and in Syria again in 131.[120] Everywhere he went, he furthered works of civilization. Buildings were erected, ornamental and utilitarian, and games were

115. Cf. CAH XI, pp. 313–14.

116. *HE* iv 6, 4.

117. Dio lxix 12, 2.

118. Compare L. Kadman, *The Coins of Aelia Capitolina:* Corpus Nummorum Palaestinensium I (1956), pp. 17–18; note also the observation of Y. Meshorer, *op. cit.*, pp. 92–3, that a coin of Aelia was found with a hoard from the Judaean Desert which included denarii of Bar Kokhba. The probable inference is that it was minted before the war and buried with them during it.

119. Dio lxix 11–12. Cf. W. Weber, *Untersuchungen zur Geschichte des Kaisers Hadrianus* (1907), pp. 231–40; W. F. Stinespring, 'Hadrian in Palestine 129/30 A.D.', JAOS 59 (1939), pp. 360–5.

120. Eckhel demonstrated in *Doctr. Num.* VI, pp. 489–91 that Hadrian was in Egypt in A.D. 130. Cf. W. Weber, *Untersuchungen*, pp. 198–263, 265 ff. In favour of such a view are the following points:

(1) An inscription at Palmyra in the temple of Zeus (Ba'alsamin), dated to Nisan 442 *aer. Sel.* (=130–131), indicates that Hadrian had stayed there before (IGR III 1054). The inscription is bilingual, in Aramaic and Greek.

(2) The coins of Gaza from Hadrian's time have an era dating from A.D. 130, the occasion of which was almost certainly his presence in the city and the benevolence shown by him then (*BMC Palestine*, p. 146, n. 14).

(3) Coins were minted in Alexandria to celebrate Hadrian's presence. Most are dated to the 15th year, but one is to the 14th (*BMC Alexandria*, p. 101, n. 867). Since according to the reckoning commonly used in Egypt, the 15th year of Hadrian began on 29 August A.D. 130, his arrival in Alexandria is to be dated to August 130.

(4) The inscription on the statue of Memnon at Thebes, indicates that Hadrian was there precisely in the month of Athyr, in the 15th year of his reign: *κοιράνω[ι] Ἀδριάνῳ πέμπτῳ δεκότῳ δ' ἐνιαύτῳ, (φῶτ)α δ' ἔχεσχε(ν) Ἄθυρ εἴκοσι καὶ πέσυρα. εἰκόστῳ πέμπτῳ δ' ἄματι μῆνος Ἄθυρ* (Nov. 21, A.D. 130). Cf. A. and E. Bernand, *Les inscriptions grecques et latines du Colosse de Memnon* (1960), no. 31.

(5) The inscription on the triumphal arch at Gerasa, in the Decapolis, dated to A.D. 130, i.e. 192 of the city's own era, commencing in autumn 63 B.C. Cf. C. H. Kraeling, *Gerasa* (1938), pp. 401–2 (n. 58).

celebrated: to all the provinces he became a 'restitutor'.[121] Signs of his presence appear in the cities of Palestine also. Caesarea and Tiberias had an *Ἁδριάνειον*, Gaza a *πανήγυρις Ἁδριανή*, Petra named itself *Ἁδριανὴ Πέτρα* in appreciation of the emperor's benefactions.[122] His presence in Judaea is commemorated by coins bearing the superscription 'adventui Aug(usti) Iudaeae'.[123]

The founding of Aelia was without doubt associated with these endeavours. Further, Pliny calls Jerusalem 'longe clarissima urbium orientis, non Iudaeae modo'.[124] This famous city now lay in ruins, or was no more than a Roman camp. What greater temptation than to raise it again in new magnificence? But needless to say, it would be a pagan magnificence. A temple to Jupiter Capitolinus should stand in place of the former Temple to the God of the Jews. This was the fatal proposal. The Jews were already extremely angry on account of the ban on circumcision promulgated perhaps not long before, if we accept the evidence of the Historia Augusta.[125] Now came this new outrage bringing matters to a head. The people remained quiet while the emperor stayed in Egypt and, for the second time, Syria. But once he was no longer in the neighbourhood—in A.D. 131/2 therefore—the revolt broke out:[126] an uprising that in scope, dynamic power and

121. On many city inscriptions Hadrian is styled *σωτήρ, οἰκιστής, εὐεργέτης, κτίστης*. He is also described on his coins as 'restitutor' of Achaia, Africa, Arabia, Asia, Bithynia, Gallia, Hispania, Italia, Lybia, Macedonia, Nicomedia, orbis terrarum, Phrygia, Sicilia. Cf. Eckhel, *Doctr. Num.* VI, pp. 486–500; Cohen, *Médailles impériales* II ([2]1882), pp. 209–14; *BMC Roman Empire* III, pp. 628–9.

122. A *Ἁδριάνειον* in Caesarea is mentioned in an inscription from the Christian period, RB 4 (1895), pp. 75 ff.; PEFQS (1896), p. 87. The coins of Petra have *Ἁδριανὴ Πέτρα* (*BMC Arabia*, p. 35, no. 8).

123. Eckhel, *Doctr. Num.* VI, pp. 495 ff. Madden, *Coins of the Jews* (1881), p. 231. Cohen, *Médailles*,[2] II, pp. 110 ff.; *BMC Roman Empire* III, nos. 493–4. Analogous coins exist for practically all the other provinces. Cf. Eckhel, *Doctr. Num.* VI, pp. 486–501; Cohen, *op. cit.* II, pp. 107–12; *BMC Roman Empire* III, p. 607, listing—in addition to Judaea—Africa, Alexandria, Arabia, Asia, Bithynia, Britannia, Cilicia, Gallia, Hispania, Italia, Macedonia, Mauretania, Moesia, Noricum, Parthia, Phrygia, Sicilia, and Thracia.

124. *NH* v 14, 70.

125. Cf. E. M. Smallwood, Latomus 18 (1959), p. 336.

126. It is clear from Dio lxix 12, 1–2, that the foundation of Aelia occurred during Hadrian's first stay in Syria (129/30), but the outbreak of the revolt after his second visit (131), thus in A.D. 131/2. In point of fact, Eusebius's *Chronicle* dates it to the 16th year of Hadrian, or *ann. Abrah.* 2148 = A.D. 132, *Chron.*, ed. Schoene II, pp. 166 ff. Note that the new date, A.D. 131, proposed for the beginning of the war by J. T. Milik in DJD II, p. 125, is rejected in favour of A.D. 132 by M. R. Lehmann, 'Studies in the Murabba'at and Naḥal Ḥever Documents', RQ 4 (1963/4), pp. 53–81, on p. 56. The discussion concerns a contract taken up in the Second Year of the Liberation, for five harvests, up to but not including, the next Sabbatical year (A.D. 138/9). The first year will

destructive consequences was at least as violent as that of the time of Vespasian. It is only due to the relative poverty of the sources that it has seemed less important.

With the various discoveries in the Judaean desert (Murabba'at, 1951; Naḥal Ḥever and Naḥal Ẓe'elim, 1960–1) of literary and archaeological material, first-hand Hebrew, Aramaic and Greek information relative to the second Jewish war has increased beyond all expectation. In addition to contracts, the documents include correspondence between the leader of the revolt, district governors and local chiefs. Apart from the Murabba'at texts, all the other sources are as yet unpublished and known only from preliminary studies.[127]

Until the recent finds, there was some uncertainty concerning the name of the leader of the rebellion. Christian sources designate him as Kokheba or Bar Kokheba. The latter form is known also in rabbinic writings, but there he is usually referred to as Ben (or Bar) Koziba.[128] The spelling displayed in the new documents is כוסבה, כוסבא or כסבה, pronounced no doubt as Kosiba, as its Greek transliteration (**Χωσιβα**) indicates.[129] From this it would follow that both Christian and rabbinic forms represent puns. The former—Bar Kokhba, Son of the Star—was coined by R. Akiba and alluded to the leader's messianic dignity;[130] the latter—Bar Koziba, Son of the Lie=Liar—was probably invented by his opponents, and those of Akiba, and was regularly used by later

therefore be A.D. 132/3. The most recent dated text was written 'on 21 Tishri in the fourth year of the Liberation of Israel', i.e. October 134 or 135 (Mur. 30, 8, see DJD II, p. 145). Cf. Lehmann, *ibid.* For the view that the period A.D. 132–134/5 corresponds to the duration of Bar Kokhba's 'kingdom' founded at the end of several years of hostilities, see H. Mantel, *op. cit.*, JQR 58 (1967/8), pp. 237–42.

127. See the bibliography at the head of this section.

128. He is called *Χοχεβᾶς* and 'Chochebas' in Eusebius's *Chronicle* and Jerome *ad. ann. Abr.* 2149 (ed. Schoene II, pp. 168 ff.; the Greek form in Syncellus, ed. Dindorf I, p. 660). Similarly, in Oros. vii 13. *Βαρχωχέβας* in Justin, 1 *Apol.* 31, 6, and Eusebius, *HE* iv 8, 4. In the rabbinical sources on the other hand, he is always either Bar Koziba' or Ben Koziba'. In the passage from the *Seder 'Olam*, only the Munich MS. reads בר ככבא.

129. See IEJ 11 (1961), pp. 41–50. For the Greek *Σιμων Χωσιβα*, cf. *ibid.*, p. 44.

130. yTaan. 68d. 'R. Simeon ben Yoḥai said, R. Akiba my teacher used to explain the passage, "A star shall go forth from Jacob" (Num. 24:17) thus. "Koziba (read, Kokhba) goes forth from Jacob." Again, when R. Akiba saw Bar Koziba (Kokhba), he cried out, "This is King Messiah". Thereupon R. Yoḥanan b. Torta said to him: "Akiba, grass will grow out of your cheek-bones and the Son of David will still not have come".' The correct explanation of Kokhba=ἀστήρ also appears in Eusebius, *HE* iv 6, 2 and Syncellus, ed. Dindorf I, p. 660. According to Eusebius, *loc. cit.*, even Bar Kokhba himself had claimed to be an ἐξ οὐρανοῦ φωστὴρ. On the messianic application of Num. 24:17 in the Qumran texts, see CDC 7:19; 4Q Testimonia 9–13 (esp. 12); 1QM 11:6–7. Cf. G. Vermes, *Scripture and Tradition*, pp. 165–6; ALUOS 6 (1969), pp. 92, 94–5. See also *Jesus the Jew*, pp. 133–4.

writers only too aware of his failure and its disastrous consequences.[131]

Coins minted by the revolutionaries,[132] as well as the new texts, attest that his first name was Simon and his official title 'Prince (נשיא or נסיא) of Israel'.[133] A few coins bear the image of a star above the figure of a temple.[134] Others dating to the first and second year mention, together with Simon or singly, Eleazar the Priest (אלעזר הכהן), possibly a joint head of the rebellion. Since in the rabbinic sources R. Eleazar of Modiim is described as the uncle of Bar Koziba,[135] it has been suggested that he was identical with the 'Priest Eleazar' named on the coins.[136] The priestly descent of Eleazar of Modiim is admittedly never asserted, but neither is it denied. In consequence, he remains the least unlikely of several weak candidates for the office of Bar Kokhba's deputy.[137]

The association of Simon ben Kosiba with 'the Star' rising from Jacob (Num. 24:17) indicates that he was regarded as the Messiah. As has been noted, R. Akiba definitely announced him as such.[138] And though not all his colleagues agreed with him, the people did. As in Vespasian's time, so now, also, it was believed that the days had come when the ancient prophecies would be fulfilled and Israel would cast off the Gentile yoke.[139] Christian legends declare that Bar Kokhba

131. E.g. Lam. R. 2:2, 'Do not read Kokhab (Star) but Kozeb (Liar)'. See also the preceding note.

132. They are referred to in rabbinic writings as מעות כוזביות, Coins of Koziba. See tM.Sh. 1:6; bB.K. 97b.

133. A. Reifenberg, *op. cit.*, nos. 190, 192–3, 199, in addition to the many coins inscribed 'Simon'. See also Y. Meshorer, *op. cit.*, nos. 167, 169–72, 181–2, 186–7, 192–3, 195, 199, 201, 204, 206, 209B, 210–12, 215. For literary evidence, see DJD II, pp. 124–33; IEJ 11 (1961), p. 41; 12 (1962), pp. 249–50, 255.

134. Cf. Reifenberg, *op. cit.*, pp. 36–7 and nos. 167–8; Meshorer, *op. cit.*, nos. 165, 178–81, 199–201.

135. See bGit. 57a; Lam.R. 2:5. Cf. W. Bacher, *Tannaiten* I, pp. 187–211.

136. Cf. Reifenberg, *op. cit.*, nos. 169–70, 189, 189a, 196, 203; Meshorer, *op. cit.*, nos. 166, 173–4, 197, 213.

137. See G. Alon, *op. cit.* II, p. 37. According to this author, R. Eleazar ben Azariah, suggested for the role by Reifenberg, *op. cit.*, p. 34 (cf. also Abel, *op. cit.* II, p. 87), was dead by that time.

138. See n. 131 above; Bacher. *Tannaiten*, I, p. 284.

139. Sundry references in the Murabba'at and Naḥal Ḥever documents reveal a strong emphasis laid by the leadership of the revolt on the observance of traditional religion. For instance, Eleazar bar Ḥitta was to travel before the sabbath (IEJ 11 (1961), p. 44; Yadin, *Bar Kokhba*, p. 128); Bar Kosiba's envoys were to rest on the sabbath (DJD II, p. 162); order was issued to provide palm branches, citrons, myrtles and willows required for the celebration of the feast of Tabernacles (IEJ 11 (1961), p. 48; Yadin, *op. cit.*, pp. 128–9); taxes were to be paid with tithed corn (DJD II, pp. 125 ff.). The otherwise unknown Batniah bar Mesah is mentioned with the title *Rabbenu* (our Master = the Aramaic *Rabban*), a designation reserved in rabbinic terminology for teachers of outstanding authority (IEJ 11 (1961), p. 46). For reference to the sabbatical year, see Mur. 24 (DJD II, pp. 125, 129, 131).

deluded the people with fraudulent miracles.[140] It was precisely because of the Messianic nature of the movement that Christians were unable to participate in it without denying their Messiah. They are said by Justin and Eusebius to have been severely persecuted for this reason by Bar Kokhba.[141]

The revolt extended speedily to the whole land; wherever strongholds, forts, caves and underground galleries offered a hiding-place, there collected the fighters for Palestine's indigenous customs and freedom. They avoided open conflict, but ravaged the country from their places of concealment and fought all who did not join their cause.[142] Jerusalem, too, was certainly occupied by them. The doubt on this point which many have expressed derives from the absence of any reference in the more reliable accounts (Dio, and Eusebius's *Ecclesiastical History*) of a battle for Jerusalem. It is inherently probable, however, that the initially successful rebels would have taken Jerusalem, which was at that time not a heavily fortified city but only a Roman camp. This probability is confirmed by evidence of two kinds. First, the coins.[143] Those which can be dated to this period with the greatest confidence bear on one side Simon's name (שמע[ו]ן) and on the other the inscription: 'For the freedom of Jerusalem' (לחרות ירושלם). Thus, the liberation of Jerusalem was extolled by Simon on coins. But there are others from the same time which, besides the date 'Year I of the Liberation of Israel', or 'Year II of the Freedom of Israel', bear only the name of the city of Jerusalem. These, therefore, were minted by the city in its own name, from which it is clear that it was held by the rebels during the first and second year. To the evidence of the coins is to be added that of a contemporary, Appian, who, as will be mentioned later, attests the re-conquest of Jerusalem by the Romans.[144] Whether in these troubled

140. Jerome, *ad Rufin.* iii 31 (PL xxiii, col. 480). Jerome tells his opponent Rufinus that he spits fire 'ut ille Barchochabas, auctor seditionis Iudaicae, stipulam in ore succensam anhelitu ventilabat, ut flammas evomere putaretur'.

141. Justin, 1 *Apol.* 31, 6 *καὶ γὰρ ἐν τῷ νῦν γεγενημένῳ Ἰουδαϊκῷ πολέμῳ Βαρχωχέβας, ὁ τῆς Ἰουδαίων ἀποστάσεως ἀρχηγέτης, Χριστιανοὺς μόνους εἰς τιμωρίας δεινάς, εἰ μὴ ἀρνοῖντο Ἰησοῦν τὸν Χριστὸν καὶ βλασφημοῖεν, ἐκέλευεν ἀπάγεσθαι.* Eusebius, *Chron.* (ed. Schoene II, pp. 168 ff.) *ad ann. Abrah.* 2149 (in the Armenian version) 'Qui dux rebellionis Iudaeorum erat Chochebas, multos e Christianis diversis suppliciis affecit, quia nolebant procedere cum illo ad pugnam contra Romanos'. Cf. also Oros. vii 13, 4.

142. Dio lxix 12, 3. Cf. Jerome, *Chron. ad ann. Abr.* 2148 (Euseb. *Chron.*, ed Schoene II, p. 167; Jerome, *Chron.*, ed. Helm, p. 200), 'Iudaei in arma versi Palestinam depopulati sunt'. The Armenian version of Eusebius has: 'Iudaei rebellarunt et Palestinensium terram invaserunt'.

143. See Meshorer, *op. cit.*, pp. 95–6.

144. See below, n. 161. Note, however, that only one of the contemporary documents discovered in Judaea mentions Jerusalem with the formula לחרות ירושלם; see Mur. 25, 1 (DJD II, p. 135).

years, the rebuilding of the Jewish Temple was also begun straight away remains to be decided. Later Christian sources speak of it, and the intention to do so must certainly have existed.[145]

The data offered by the Bar Kokhba documents are too scanty, and at present, owing to our limited information, too vague to allow a proper history of the war to be written. They provide, however, valuable insight into the system of administration adopted by the rebels, the discipline imposed on his forces by Bar Kosiba and to some degree the extent of the territory under his control.

The beginning of the uprising was taken as the start of a new era and all the legal documents are dated according to the year of 'the Liberation of Israel'. See for 'first year' Mur. 22 (DJD II, p. 118); for 'second year' Mur. 24B (*ibid.*, p. 124); for 'third year' Mur. 25 (*ibid.*, p. 135) and for 'fourth year' Mur. 30 (*ibid.*, p. 145).

The various districts are described as being under military government. Several of them are named in the letters. Jonathan bar Ba'ayan and Masabala bar Simon commanded the region of En-gedi (IEJ 11 (1961), pp. 43–7), Judah bar Manasse that of Kiryath Arabaya (*ibid.*, pp. 48–9); Joshua ben Galgula was in charge of the area in which was situated the otherwise unknown Beth Mashku (Mur. 42, DJD II, p. 155).

Localities in the districts were administered by פרנסין, or community leaders (Mur. 42, DJD II, p. 156; IEJ 12 (1962), pp. 249–50). Their duties included, in addition to normal communal activity, acting as liaison officers with the district commander (Mur. 42, DJD II, p. 156), and in particular the leasing out of land belonging to the head of state (Mur. 24, DJD II, pp. 122–32; IEJ 12 (1962), pp. 249–55) and the collection of the yearly rent, a tenth of which was apparently to be paid directly into the state treasury (Mur. 24, *ibid.*).

Central government was strong and authoritarian. The commanders of En-gedi were to assist the leader's envoy, Elisha, in every way (IEJ 11 (1961), p. 43). The governor of a district was threatened with imprisonment for disobeying directives (Mur. 43, DJD II, 160). Lack of enthusiasm in the war effort provoked immediate rebuke ('You sit and eat and drink from the property of the House of Israel, and care nothing for your brothers', IEJ 11 (1961), p. 47). The inhabitants of Tekoa were threatened with severe punishment for repairing their houses (*ibid.*, p. 42) and refusing to fight (*ibid.*, p. 48). Orders were issued for the disarming and arrest of a certain Joshua bar Tadmoraya (*ibid.*, p. 42).

Little new is learnt about the conduct of hostilities. The Romans

145. Cf. Chrysostom, *Orat. adv. Iudaeos*, v 10; Georgius Cedrenus, ed. Bekker, I, p. 437; Nicephorus Callistus, *Eccl. hist.* iii 24 (PG clxv); *Chronicon paschale*, ed. Dindorf I, p. 474. Cf. p. 535 above.

are rarely mentioned (IEJ 11 (1961), p. 46); in Mur. 42 (DJD II, p. 157) a visit by local leaders to the district commander was rendered impossible because of the proximity of the Gentiles (הגיים קרבים אלנו). The regular title given to the rebels in Greek documents is that of ἀδελφός (brother) (IEJ 11 (1961), pp. 44, 59–61). All the identifiable places held by Bar Kokhba which appear in the texts lie in the Judaean desert: Herodium,[146] Tekoa, En-gedi, etc.[147] The Galileans whose ill-treatment by Joshua ben Galgula was strongly condemned by Bar Kosiba (Mur. 43, DJD II, pp. 159–60) were probably refugees from the northern province under Roman occupation rather than either rival Galilean troops or Judeo-Christians.

Neither the new sources, nor the classical and rabbinic texts report much about the actual course of the war. At the time of its outbreak, Tineius Rufus was governor of Judaea.[148] As he and his troops were no match for the rebels, the uprising not only swept victoriously through Palestine, but spread beyond its frontiers as well. Indeed, unruly elements of another kind allied themselves to the Jewish revolt so that ultimately 'the whole world, as it were, was in turmoil'.[149] An enormous effort was necessary to control the disturbance. Large numbers of troops were brought in from other provinces as reinforcements; 'the best generals' were assigned to Palestine.[150] Even the governor of Syria, Publicius Marcellus, hastened to the aid of his

[*Text continues on page* 549

146. Against the view that Herodium was Bar Kokhba's headquarters (cf. J. T. Milik, DJD II, pp. 123 ff.), see Y. Yadin, IEJ 11 (1961), p. 51. But cf. E.-M. Laperrousaz, 'L'Hérodium, quartier géneral de Bar Kokhba?', Syria 41 (1964), pp. 347–58.

147. The identification of מצד חסדין (Fortress of the Pious) in Mur. 45 with Qumran, advanced by Milik, (DJD II, pp. 163–4), is based on the problematic derivation of 'Essene' from *Ḥasid*. See G. Vermes, RQ 2 (1960), pp. 429–30; 3 (1962), pp. 501–2.

148. See above, p. 518.

149. Dio lxix 13, 2, *πάσης ὡς εἰπεῖν κινουμένης ἐπὶ τούτῳ τῆς οἰκουμένης*.

150. Reinforcements: Euseb. *HE* iv 6, 1; *Chron. ad ann. Abrah.* 2148. Generals: Dio lxix 13, 2, *τοὺς κρατίστους τῶν στρατηγῶν ὁ Ἀδριανὸς ἐπ' αὐτοὺς ἔπεμψεν*. The inscriptions establish that the following troops took part in the war (cf. RE XII, cols. 1291–2):

(1) The *legio III Cyrenaica*, which had been stationed in Egypt from the time of Augustus to that of Hadrian, and from the latter's time was to form the garrison of the newly established province of Arabia (see G. W. Bowersock, 'The Annexation and Initial Garrison of Arabia', Zeit. Pap. u. Epig. 5 (1970), pp. 37–47); a *vexillatio leg. III Cyr.* was already in Jerusalem in A.D. 116 (CIL III 13587 = ILS 4393)). A tribune of this legion was presented 'donis militaribus a divo Hadriano ob Iudaicam expeditionem' (CIL XIV 3610 = ILS 1071); one of its centurions likewise 'ab imp. Hadriano corona aurea torquibus armillis phaleris ob bellum Iudeicum (*sic*)' (CIL X 3733 = ILS 2083).

(2) The *leg. III Gallica*, which had probably belonged to the garrison of Syria since Augustus. One of its *emeriti* was 'ex voluntate imp. Hadriani Aug. torquibus

et armillis aureis suffragio legionis honorat(us)', doubtless as a result of the Jewish war (CIL XII 2230=ILS 2313). Cf. also CIL VI 1523=ILS 1092.

(3) Needless to say, the *leg. X Fretensis* as garrison of Judaea (see above, p. 509) also participated in the war.

(4) The *leg. VI Ferrata* will also have been involved, for it had previously belonged to the garrison of Syria, and from Hadrian's time formed the garrison of Judaea with the *leg. X Fretensis*. Add now N. Tzori, 'An Inscription of the Legio VI Ferrata from the Northern Jordan Valley', IEJ 21 (1971), pp. 53–4. The transfer of VI Ferrata probably took place before the war, see B. Lifschitz, 'Sur la date du transfert de la legio VI Ferrata en Palestine', Latomus 19 (1960), pp. 109–11.

(5) Concerning auxiliary cohorts, a considerable number of which doubtless took part, the *coh. IV Lingonum* is mentioned in the inscriptions. Its commander was presented 'vexillo mi[l. d]onato a divo Hadriano in expeditione Iudaic[a]' (CIL VI 1523=ILS 1092). From a diploma of A.D. 139 three *alae* and twelve cohorts are known to have been at that moment stationed in Syria Palaestina (CIL XVI 87). Some of them, though not all, will have taken part in the war (e.g., the *coh. I Damasc.* was still in Egypt in A.D. 135).

(6) A legionary detachment involved in the Jewish war is mentioned in CIL VI 3505, 'Sex. Attius Senecio praef. alae [I] Fl. Gaetulorum, trib. leg. X Geminae missus a divo Hadriano in expeditione Iudaica ad vexilla[tiones deducendas in . . .' Note also CIL VIII 6706=ILS 1065 which describes Q. Lollius Urbicus (PIR² L 327) as 'legato imp. Hadriani in expedition. Iudaica . . . leg.. leg. X Geminae' (reverse chronological order, possibly but not certainly indicating that he was in Judaea as *legatus* of the legion).

An inscription at Bittir (Beth-ther) refers to detachments of the *leg. V Macedonica* and the *leg. XI Claudia*; Clermont-Ganneau, CRAI 1894, pp. 13 f.; the attribution of the inscription to this war is made more probable by a foundation-coin of Aelia Capitolina with the legend 'LE. V'. See J. Meyshan, 'The Legion which reconquered Jerusalem in the War of Bar Kochba (A.D. 132–5)', PEQ 90 (1958), pp. 19–26.

The Gerasa inscription of 128–138, C. H. Kraeling, *Gerasa* (1938), p. 390, n. 30, shows the emperor's *equites singulares* wintering there possibly during the war, but more probably in A.D. 129/30.

An inscription from Campania, CIL X 3733=ILS 2083, mentions a man decorated by Hadrian, 'corona aurea torquibus armillis phaleris ob bellum Iudaicum'. He was successively centurion of *III Cyrenaica* and *VII Claudia* and *primus pilus* of *II Traiana*. It was probably in the latter post that he took part in the war, for an inscription from Caesarea shows a *vexillatio* of *II Traiana* there, A. Negev, IEJ 14 (1964), pp. 245–8.

The presence of part of the praetorian cohorts with the emperor at the war may be reflected in CIL XI 5646=ILS 2081, referring to military honours awarded by Hadrian to a *trecenarius* of that cohort.

If the disappearance of the *legio XXII Deiotariana* was due to its total destruction in the Jewish war, it might be the subject of Fronto's remark (p. 218 Naber; p. 206 Van den Hout), 'Hadriano imperium optinente quantum militum a Iudaeis . . . caesum?' This legion disappears from the Roman army-list sometime between A.D. 119, when it is attested in Egypt (BGU I. 140) and *c.* A.D. 145, when it is missing from an inscription from Rome listing the legions in geographical order (CIL VI 3492=ILS 2288). But the fact that it ceases to be mentioned in Egypt in the late 120s weakens the theory (RE XII, col. 1795).

(7) The Syrian fleet (*classis Syriaca*) may also have taken part, for its commander was presented 'donis militaribus a divo Hadriano ob bellum Iudaicum'

harassed colleague.[151] But it seems that Rufus remained in control for some time yet, for Eusebius names no other Roman commander, and speaks as though the rebellion was suppressed by him.[152] In rabbinical sources, too, 'Turranius Rufus' (טורנס רופוס) is presented as the arch-enemy of the Jews at that time.[153] From Cassius Dio, however, whose statements are corroborated by an inscription, it appears that Iulius Severus, one of Hadrian's most outstanding generals, was in supreme command during the later period, and that it was he who effected the suppression of the revolt. He was recalled from Britain to direct the campaign and took a considerable time in crushing the rebellion. Nothing could be accomplished by open battle. He had to hunt out the rebels one by one, and where they remained hidden in caves, wear them down by cutting off their supplies. The burial niches in the 'Cave of Letters' and the 'Cave of Horror' in Naḥal Ḥever provide a gruesome archaeological illustration.[154] It was only after long and costly individual battles that it was finally possible to 'annihilate, exterminate and eradicate' them from the land (*κατατρῖψαι καὶ ἐκτρυχῶσαι καὶ ἐκκόψαι*).[155]

It is not entirely sure where Hadrian stayed during the war. He was probably at the scene of action during the critical years. When the revolt broke out, he had left Syria. The bad news then seems to have led him to return to Judaea, for his presence there is not only

---

either in this post or his previous one, *praefectus alae I Augustae geminae colonorum* (CIL VIII 8934 = ILS 1400; see PIR² G 1344). On the Syrian fleet in general, see RE III, cols. 2642 ff.; C. G. Starr, *The Roman Imperial Navy* (²1960), pp. 114–15. A fragmentary inscription, CIL VI 1565, also mentions the activity of the fleet in a 'bellum Iudaicum'. In this case also, the Hadrianic war should be understood (so Th. Mommsen, *Ephem. Epigr.* III, 331).

151. IGR III 174–5. See p. 518 above. The two inscriptions, which are all but identical in text, mention that Severus was commander of the *leg. IV Scythica* and governed Syria as praetorian *legatus* after Publicius Marcellus had left Syria on account of the Jewish war. Publicius Marcellus thus brought to Judaea a section of the Syrian garrison consisting of three or four legions, while Severus took over the administration of Syria, retaining meanwhile command of his legion. The *leg. IV Scythica* therefore remained behind in Syria with its commander.

152. *HE* iv. 6, 1 *πολέμου τε νόμῳ τὰς χώρας αὐτῶν ἐξανδραποδιζόμενος.*

153. bTaan 29a. Cf. J. Derenbourg, *op. cit.*, p. 422; J. Levy, *NhWb* II, p. 149; M. Jastrow, *Dictionary* I, p. 527 s.v. טורנוס; W. Bacher, *Die Agada der Tannaiten* I, 287–93. Although the name Turranius does appear in PIR¹ III, 344; and cf. *Ἀπόλαυστος Τυράνιος Ῥοῦφος* in Phrygia, Mittheil d. deutsch. archäol. Inst. Athens, 25 (1900), p. 407, the form Tineius is now assured (cf. p. 518 above). The rabbinic טורנוס may reflect the title 'Tyrannus'.

154. Cf. Y. Yadin, 'Expedition D', IEJ 11 (1961), pp. 37–8; Y. Aharoni, 'Expedition B—The Cave of Horror', IEJ 12 (1962), pp. 186–99; Yadin, *Bar Kokhba*, pp. 60–65.

155. Dio lxix 13, 3. The summoning of Iulius Severus to Judaea from Britain is also attested by CIL III 2830 = ILS 1056, see PIR² I 576 and p. 519 above.

presumed in rabbinic tradition[156] but is also suggested by inscriptions[157] and by a letter from Hadrian to his architect Apollodorus enquiring about siege-engines to be used against tribes holding out in mountainous areas.[158] There is no reference to his being in Rome again until 5 May, A.D. 134.[159] He will have returned immediately success was assured, without waiting for the complete cessation of operations.

Both Dio and Eusebius are silent concerning the fate of Jerusalem, but it is unlikely to have been a centre of battle as in the war under Vespasian. Its fortifications were inadequate. Even if the rebels had managed to drive out the Roman garrison, recapture would have presented little difficulty to a sufficiently strong Roman force. That violence did occur there is nevertheless plain from the evidence of a contemporary, Appian.[160] When Appian speaks of 'destruction' (*κατασκάπτειν*), this is surely correct, in so far as a violent conquest is inconceivable without it. But, of course, after Titus's thoroughness, its object was but a limited one. On the other hand, once they were in control of the city again, the Romans will not have taken destruction any further than was necessary for founding the new city of Aelia. Eusebius also assumes that the city was besieged.[161] Certain Church fathers (e.g. Chrysostom, Jerome and others) maintain that Hadrian completely destroyed the vestiges of the old city left standing after the devastation by Titus. By this they merely mean that Hadrian completely demolished the old Jewish city and erected a new pagan one in its place.[162] It is stated in the Mishnah that on 9 Ab a plough was

156. bGit. 57a. Cf. J. Derenbourg, *op. cit.*, pp. 433–4.

157. Cf. CIL VIII 6706=ILS 1065, which describes Q. Lollius Urbicus as 'legatus imp. in expeditione Iudaica . . .', thus suggesting that Lollius was a personal adjutant to the emperor; also, possibly, CIL VI 974, probably A.D. 134 or 135, Hadrian '[lab]oribus max[imis rempublicam ab ho]ste liberaverit . . .'.

158. Cf. Ernest Lacoste, 'Les poliorcétiques d' Apollodore', REG 3 (1890), pp. 234–81, revised by R. Schneider, Gött. Abh. hist.-phil. Kl. N.F. 10 (1908), pp. 1 ff. Cf. F. Millar, *Cassius Dio* (1964), pp. 65–6.

159. CIG 5906=IG XIV 1054=IGR I 149=Moretti, IGUR I 235. Cf. W. Weber, *Untersuchungen*, p. 276.

160. *Syr.* 50/252 *τὴν μεγίστην πόλιν Ἱεροσόλυμα —, ἣν δὴ καὶ Πτολεμαῖος ὁ πρῶτος Αἰγύπτου βασιλεύς, καὶ Οὐεσπασιανὸς αὖθις οἰκισθεῖσαν κατέσκαψε, καὶ Ἀδριανὸς αὖθις ἐπ' ἐμοῦ.*

161. Euseb. *Demonstr. evang.* vi 18, 10 notes that the prophecy of Zech. 14:2 *ἐξελεύσεται τὸ ἥμισυ τῆς πόλεως ἐν αἰχμαλωσίᾳ* was fulfilled in Vespasian's time; the other half of the city, i.e. of the inhabitants, was then besieged in the time of Hadrian and expelled, *τὸ λεῖπον τῆς πόλεως μέρος ἥμισυ πολιορκηθὲν αὖθις ἐξελαύνεται, ὡς ἐξ ἐκείνου καὶ εἰς δεῦρο πάμπαν ἄβατον αὐτοῖς γενέσθαι τὸν τόπον.* Thus Eusebius does not speak of a destruction of the city, but only of an expulsion of its Jewish inhabitants after a preceding siege. He mentions the siege also in *HE* iv 5, 2.

162. Chrysostom, *adv. Judaeos* v 11; Cedrenus ed. Bekker I, p. 437; Nicephorus Callistus, *Eccl. hist.* iii 24; Jerome, *Comm. in Ies.* I 1:6 (CCL lxxiii, p. 10), 'post

driven over Jerusalem. As the context shows, the time alluded to is that of Hadrian. The Babylonian Talmud and Jerome ascribe the deed to Rufus; but these two authorities speak of ploughing up the Temple area, not the city.[163] At most, the brief comment in the Mishnah is worth noting. But the rite would have signified, not the destruction, but the new foundation; it would consequently have taken place prior to the outbreak of the revolt.[164]

The last refuge of Bar Kokhba and his supporters was the strong mountain fort of Bether, not very far from Jerusalem according to Eusebius,[165] and in all probability on the site of present-day Bettir, 10 km south-west of Jerusalem.[166] An inscription found in Bettir, in which reference is made to detachments (*vexillationes*) of the *legio V Macedonica et XI Claudia*, may well date to this period and be regarded as a confirmation that this was the scene of the last great battle between Romans and Jews.[167] After long and stubborn resistance, this

---

Titum et Vespasianum et ultimam eversionem Ierusalem sub Aelio Hadriano usque ad praesens tempus nullum remedium est'. Cf. in *Ezech.* vii 24 (CCL lxxv, p. 326), 'post quinquaginta annos, sub Hadriano civitas aeterno igne consummata est'.

163. mTaan. 4:6 lists five disasters on 9 Ab. 'On 9 Ab it was decreed against our fathers that they should not enter into the Land (of Israel), and the Temple was destroyed the first and the second time, Beth-Tor(=Bethar, Bittir) was conquered and the City was ploughed up' (נחרשה העיר). Further, bTaan. 20a relates that it was 'Turnus Rufus' who ordered the Temple site (ההיכל) to be ploughed up. The whole passage is reproduced almost word for word by Jerome, who expressly acknowledges the Jewish tradition ('cogimur igitur ad Hebraeos recurrere'), *in Zachariam* 8: 19 (CCL lxxvi A, p. 820), 'In hoc mense et a Nabuchodonosor et multa post saecula a Tito et Vespasiano templum Ierosolymis incensum est atque destructum; capta urbs Bether, ad quam multa millia confugerant Iudaeorum; aratum templum in ignominiam gentis oppressae a T. Annio (*leg.* Tinnio) Rufo'.

164. That a plough was driven over Jerusalem as a sign of devastation is not improbable, because the establishment of a new city was in fact envisaged, but it may well have been done as an act of inauguration. The rite was the same in both cases. See Servius *ad Virgil. Aeneid.* iv 212 'cum conderetur nova civitas, aratrum adhibitum, ut eodem ritu quo condita subvertatur'. The passage from Varro, cited by Servius, *Virgil. Aeneid.* v 755, provides a precise description of the rite.

165. Euseb. *HE* iv 6, 13. Cf. yTaan. 68d–69a; mTann. 4:6. The name of the locality is variously spelt, ביתתר or ביתר in Hebrew, *Βίθθηρ*, *Βέθθηρ* or *Βήθθηρ* in Euseb. *HE*, and Bethar in Rufinus.

166. Cf. Abel, *Géog. Pal.* II, p. 271. For a survey see E. Zuckermann, 'Chirbet el-jehud (bettîr)', ZDPV 29 (1906), pp. 51–72. The unexcavated site reveals traces of a Roman wall of circumvallation, see A. Schulten in ZDPV 56 (1933), pp. 180–4, and remains of what might have been a mint of Bar Kokhba have been found, see B. Kirschner, 'A Mint of Bar-Kokhba?', Bull. J. Pal. Explor. Soc .13 (1946), pp. 153–60 (Hebrew; English summary, p. xi). Cf. Yadin, *Bar Kokhba*, pp. 192–3.

167. See p. 548 above.

bulwark too was taken in the 18th year of Hadrian = A.D. 134/135[168] on the 9 Ab, according to rabbinical tradition.[169] In the conquest of the town, Bar Kokhba, 'the author of their madness', paid 'the just penalty'.[170] Nothing is known of the siege and capture. Rabbinic legends give various accounts of the struggle, but these are products of the imagination. The only story deserving mention relates that before the capture, R. Eleazar, the uncle of Bar Kokhba, was put to death by his nephew because he falsely suspected him of having come to an understanding with the Romans.[171]

With the fall of Bether, the three and a half years of war (A.D. 132–135) were at an end.[172] During it, many rabbis had died a martyr's death. Ten such martyrs, among them R. Akiba, are particularly honoured in rabbinic tradition.[173]

168. Euseb. *HE* iv 6, 3.

169. mTaan. 4:6, and Jerome, *in Zachariam* 8:19 (CCL lxxviA, p. 820). If this tradition is to be believed, Ab of A.D. 135 is probably meant, for the war is likely to have lasted until that year.

170. Euseb. *HE* iv 6, 3.

171. The legends relating to the fall of Bether are to be found mainly in yTaan. 68d–69a, and Lam. R. 2:2. On the death of Eleazar, see J. Derenbourg, *op. cit.*, pp. 433–4; W. Bacher, *Tannaiten* I, pp. 187–8. In describing the frightful bloodbath caused by the Romans, rabbinical legend employs the same hyperbole as used by the writer of the Book of Revelation, viz., that the blood came up to the horses' nostrils (Rev. 14:20, 'up to their bridles, *ἄχρι τῶν χαλινῶν τῶν ἵππων. . .*). Cf. also 1 Enoch 100:3, 'A horse will wade up to its chest in the blood of the sinners. . .'

172. That the war of Bar-Kokhba lasted 3½ years is attested by *Seder Olam* (see above, p. 534). Jerome also gives it as the view of some *Hebraei* that the last septennium of Daniel 9:27 is to be divided between the time of Vespasian and that of Hadrian, *Com. in Daniel.* 9:27 (CCL lxxvA, p. 888), 'tres autem anni et sex menses sub Hadriano reputentur: quando Hierusalem omnino subversa est et Iudaeorum gens catervatim caesa'. In the Palestinian Talmud (yTaan. 68d) the 3½ years are given as the duration of the siege of Bether; in Lam. R. 3½ years for the siege of Jerusalem by Vespasian and 3½ years for that of Bether by Hadrian, see J. Derenbourg, *op. cit.*, p. 431. Although these sources are not of great weight, it is in fact correct that the war lasted about three and a half years (the late sources confuse the duration of the war with that of the siege of Bether). For the beginning of the war in A.D. 132, see p. 542 above. For the evidence that it ended in 135 see p. 553 below.

173. According to bBer. 61b R. Akiba was martyred by having the flesh ripped from his body with iron combs. But he continued to utter the words of the *Shema'*, and just as he was prolonging the word אחד (one), as prescribed, he breathed his last. Thereupon a Bath Kol (voice from heaven) proclaimed, 'Blessed are you, R. Akiba, that your soul departed with אחד'. There are numerous references elsewhere in the older Midrashic literature and in the Talmuds to the martyrdom of other rabbis, but the list of ten martyrs is first found in the post-Talmudic midrash *Elleh Ezkerah*. Cf. Zunz, p. 150; Strack, pp. 226–7. Cf. M. Beer, 'An Ancient saying regarding Martyrdom in Hadrian's Time', Zion 28 (1963), pp. 228–32 (in Hebrew).

The victory brought Hadrian his second acclamation as *Imperator*.[174] Iulius Severus was granted the *ornamenta triumphalia*, and officers and men were given the usual rewards.[175] It was a victory gained at a heavy cost however. So great were the casualties that Hadrian, in his letter to the Senate, omitted the usual opening formula that he and the army were well.[176] Even more serious than the direct loss of men was the spoliation of the fruitful and prosperous province. 'The whole of Judaea was practically a desert.' Fifty forts were destroyed and 985 villages, 580,000 Jews (?) fell in battle and those who succumbed to illness or starvation were uncounted.[177] Innumerable multitudes were sold as slaves. So many were offered for sale at the annual market at the Terebinth at Hebron that a Jewish slave fetched no more than a horse. Those who could not be disposed of were taken to Gaza and sold there, or were sent to Egypt, many of them dying on the way from hunger or shipwreck.[178]

In Jerusalem the plan conceived already before the war was put into effect; the city was turned into a Roman colony with the name Aelia Capitolina.[179] To ensure the permanence of its purely pagan character, Jews still residing there were driven out and Gentile colonists settled in their place.[180] From then on no Jew was permitted to enter the city area; any Jew seen there was punished with death.[181] The official name of the newly-founded city appears on the coins as 'Col(onia) Ael(ia) Cap(itolina)', though writers as a rule call it simply 'Aelia'.[182] Its

174. In Hadrian's titulature, the title *Imp*(*erator*) II is still missing from two diplomas dated from 2 April and 15 September A.D. 134 (CIL XVI 78–9). It is also absent in other inscriptions from A.D. 134 (CIL VI 973; IX 4359). But it appears in A.D. 135, see RE I, cols. 514–15 .

175. On Sex. Iulius Severus, see p. 519 above.

176. Dio lxix 14, 3. Cf. Fronto, *Epistulae*, ed. Naber, pp. 217–18; Van den Hout, p. 206, 'Quid? avo vestro Hadriano imperium optinente quantum militum a Iudaeis, quantum ab Britannis caesum?'.

177. Dio lxix 14, 3.

178. Jerome, *in Zachariam* 11:5 (CCL lxxviA, p. 851); *in Hieremiam* 6:18 (CCL lxxiv, p. 307). *Chronicon paschale*, ed. Dindorf I, p. 474. On the Terebinth at Hebron, see Jos. *B.J.* iv 9, 7 (533).

179. See Abel, *Histoire* II, pp. 97–102; CAH XI, pp. 313–14; A. H. M. Jones, 'The Urbanisation of Palestine', JRS 21 (1931), pp. 77–85, esp. 82 ff.

180. Dio lxix 12, 2; Euseb. *HE* iv 6, 4; *Demonstr. evang.* vi 18, 10; Malalas, ed. Dindorf, p. 279. Cf. M. Avi-Yonah, *Geschichte*, pp. 50–1, 79–81.

181. Justin, 1 *Apol.* 47, 6 *ὅτι δὲ φυλάσσεται ὑφ' ὑμῶν ὅπως μηδεὶς ἐν αὐτῇ γένηται, καὶ θάνατος κατὰ τοῦ καταλαμβανομένου Ἰουδαίου εἰσιόντος ὥρισται, ἀκριβῶς ἐπίστασθε*. *Dial c. Tryph.* 16; Ariston of Pella, in Euseb. *HE* iv 6, 3. Tertullian, *adv. Iudaeos* 13. Cf. pp. 37–9 above.

182. The name 'Aelia Capitolina' is given in full in Dio lxix 12, 1; Ulpian, *Dig.* L 15, 1, 6 and the Peutinger Table ('Helya Capitolina'); Ptolemy v 16, 8 and viii 20, 18 reads *Αἰλία Καπιτωλιάς*. On milestones it is found abbreviated as *Κολ. Αἰλία Καπιτωλ.* (CIL III 6649). It was called 'Aelia' after Hadrian's family name, and 'Capitolina' after Jupiter Capitolinus. For the coins, see L. Kadman, *The Coins of Aelia Capitolina* (1956).

constitution was that of a Roman colony, although it did not have the *ius Italicum*.[183] Needless to say, it was not lacking in the usual splendid buildings: the *Chronicon paschale* lists τὰ δύο δημόσια καὶ τὸ θέατρον καὶ τὸ τρικάμαρον καὶ τὸ τετράνυμφον καὶ τὸ δωδεκάπυλον τὸ πρὶν ὀνομαζόμενον ἀναβαθμοὶ καὶ τὴν κόδραν.[184] The image of a pig is said to have been carved on the southern gate of the city, facing towards Bethlehem.[185] The main cult of the city was that of Jupiter Capitolinus, to whom a temple was erected on the site of the former Temple of the Jews.[186] It appears to have contained the statue of Hadrian, of which Christian writers speak.[187] Besides Jupiter, the following deities of the city are represented on coins: Bacchus, Serapis,

183. Ulpian, *Dig.* L 15, 1, 6: 'In Palaestina duae fuerunt coloniae, Caesarensis et Aelia Capitolina, sed neutra ius Italicum habet'. Cf. Paulus, *Dig.* L 15, 8, 7; CIL III 116 = 6639. The coins of the colony extend as far as Valerian (A.D. 253–260). According to the *Chronicon paschale*, ed. Dindorf I, p. 474, the city was divided into seven districts: καὶ ἐμέρισεν τὴν πόλιν εἰς ἑπτὰ ἄμφοδα καὶ ἔστησεν ἀνθρώπους ἰδίους ἀμφοδάρχας καὶ ἑκάστῳ ἀμφοδάρχῃ ἀπένειμεν ἄμφοδον.

184. *Chron. paschale*, ed. Dindorf I, p. 474. The Bordeaux Pilgrim mentions a tombstone of the Patriarchs in Hebron 'per quadrum ex lapidibus mirae pulchritudinis' (*Itinera Hierosolym.*, ed. P. Geyer, CSEL xxix (1889), p. 25 = CCL clxxv, p. 20), and in Jerusalem, by the Pool of Siloam, a 'quadriporticum' (*ibid.*, p. 22; CCL clxxv, p. 16).

185. Jerome, *Chron. ad ann. Abr.* 2152 (Eusebius, *Chron.*, ed. Schoene II, p. 169; Jerome, *Chron.*, ed. Helm, p. 201). 'Aelia ab Aelio Hadriano condita, et in fronte eius portae qua Bethleem egredimur sus scalptus in marmore significans Romanae potestati subiacere Iudaeos'. The image of a pig, or rather of a boar, is also found on a coin discovered in Jerusalem, belonging to the *leg. X Fretensis*, see Kadman, *op. cit.*, pp. 57–8. Likewise on stamps of the *leg. X Fret.* found in Jerusalem, see D. Barag, Bonn. Jahrb. 167 (1967), pp. 245–6.

186. Dio lxix 12, 1. Jupiter is represented relatively rarely on the coins from Aelia, see Kadman, *op. cit.*, pp. 42–3. Note the questionable testimony of Hippolytus, in a fragment of commentary on Matth. 24:15 f. preserved in Syriac: 'Vespasian placed no idolatrous image in the Temple, but rather that legion which Traianus Quintus, a Roman commander posted there, erected an idol named *Core*'. GCS Hippolytus Werke I. 2 ed. Achelis (1897), pp. 244–5. Cf. Harnack, TU VI, 3, pp. 141–2, 147. The temple erected by Hadrian was certainly devoted to Jupiter, but a pagan cult was surely not established on the site of the Sanctuary in the period between Vespasian and Hadrian. There is therefore some confusion in this statement which may have arisen subsequently to the original text of Hippolytus.

187. Jerome, *in Esaiam* i 2, 9 (CCL lxxiii, p. 33) 'ubi quondam erat templum et religio Dei, ibi Hadriani statua et Iovis idolum collocatum est'; *Com. in Matt.* 24:15 (CCL lxxvii, p. 226), 'potest autem simpliciter aut de Antechristo accipi aut de imagine Caesaris, quam Pilatus posuit in templo, aut de Hadriani equestri statua quae in ipso sancto sanctorum loco usque in praesentem diem stetit'. This would seem to imply that the statue of Hadrian stood in the temple of Jupiter. Cf. also Chrysostom, *Orat. adv. Iudaeos*, v 11; Cedrenus, ed. Bekker I, p. 438; Nicephorus Callistus, *Eccl. hist.* iii 24. The Bordeaux Pilgrim speaks of two statues of Hadrian (*Itinera Hierosolym.*, ed. P. Geyer, CSEL xxix, p. 22 = CCL clxxv, p. 16).

Astarte and the Dioscuri. A shrine to Aphrodite (Astarte) stood on the traditional site of Jesus' tomb;[188] or according to another version, a shrine to Jupiter stood on the grave; and a sanctuary to Venus on the place of the crucifixion.[189]

The total paganisation of Jerusalem was the fulfilment of a scheme long before attempted by Antiochus Epiphanes. In another respect, too, the measures adopted by Hadrian resembled his. The ban on circumcision, promulgated before the war and not specifically directed against the Jews (see above, p. 538), was now unquestionably maintained. Not until the time of Antoninus Pius were Jews permitted to circumcise their children again (see above, p. 539). Jewish tradition, which likewise commemorates this ban, maintains that it was also forbidden to celebrate the Sabbath and to study the Torah.[190] Whether or not this statement is reliable, the prohibition of circumcision was, to the Jewish mind, tantamount to a ban on Judaism itself. As long as it was maintained, there could be no question of pacification. In point of fact, another attempted rebellion under Antoninus Pius needed to be put down by force.[191] Here the Roman administration were faced with the choice of either tolerating the religious rites or totally destroying the people. Presumably, it was the recognition of these alternatives that persuaded the emperor Antoninus to permit circumcision again and exercise tolerance.

Under Hadrian's successor, therefore, essentially the same state of affairs prevailed as had existed since Vespasian. It in no way corresponded to the political ideals of the Jews. But as regarded their religion they could be satisfied with it. It was, in effect, precisely the annihilation of Israel's political existence which led to the triumph of rabbinic Judaism.

Development now continued along the lines marked out earlier by the great upheaval resulting from the destruction of Jerusalem. Without a political home and unified only by the ideal of the Torah, the Jews from then on held all the more tenaciously to this common

188. Euseb. *Vita Constant.* iii 26; cf. A. H. M. Jones, JRS 21 (1931), p. 82.

189. Jerome, *Epist.* 58 *ad Paulinum*, 3 (CSEL liv, pp. 531–2): 'Ab Hadriani temporibus usque ad imperium Constantini per annos circiter centum octoginta in loco resurrectious simulacrum Iovis, in crucis rupe statua Veneris a gentibus posita colebatur'. Jerome's divergence from Eusebius obviously has its basis in the legend of the discovery of the Cross. Cf. RE VII 2, cols. 2830 ff.

190. See, e.g., Mekh. on Exod. 20:6 (ed. Lauterbach II, p. 247). Cf. E. M. Smallwood, 'The Legislation of Hadrian and Antoninus Pius against Circumcision', Latomus 18 (1959), pp. 334–47. See also J. Derenbourg, *op. cit.*, p. 430; G. Alon, *op. cit.* II, pp. 56–8. Cf. S. Klein, 'The Hadrianic Persecution and the Rabbinic Law of Sale', JQR 23 (1932–3), pp. 211–31.

191. HA, *vita Ant. Pii* 5, 4, 'Iudaeos rebellantes contudit per praesides ac legatos'.

treasure and cherished it. In the process, the division between them and the rest of the world became more pronounced. Whereas in the heyday of Hellenistic Judaism the boundaries between the Jewish and Graeco-Roman philosophy of life had threatened to vanish, Jews and Gentiles now joined forces to ensure that the gulf between them remained deep. Proselytism slowed down, and pagans ceased to flock to the God of the Jews, partly because the Roman state, without revoking the toleration of Jewish religion guaranteed since the time of Caesar, none the less erected legal barriers to its propagation.

The Jews thus tended to become more and more strangers in the Gentile world, despite the many surviving bonds linking them to it.[192] The re-establishment of a Jewish state was, and remained, an object of religious expectation. But the contrast between the ideal and reality was at first, and continued for centuries to be, so sharp and severe that Jews were not even permitted to enter the capital of their hoped-for kingdom as visitors. Even by the fourth century, they were only allowed access to the city once a year by Constantine, on the anniversary of the destruction of Jerusalem (9 Ab), to make their lamentations on the site of the Temple.[193] Jerome depicts in graphic terms how the Jews used to come there on that day in pitiful proces-

192. For a fuller understanding of the evolution of Judaism, many other factors must also be taken into account. Note for the development of the political position of the Ethnarchy and its holders' contacts with the outside world, M. Avi-Yonah, *Geschichte der Juden im Zeitalter des Talmud* (1962); for the presence of Greek influence in rabbinic writings, S. Lieberman, *Greek in Jewish Palestine* (1942; [2]1965); *Hellenism in Jewish Palestine* (1950); for Greek inscriptions on tombs, including those of leading rabbis, B. Lifshitz, 'L'hellénisation des Juifs de Palestine: à propos des inscriptions de Besara (Beth-Shearim)', RB 72 (1965), pp. 520–38; *Beth She'arim* II: *The Greek Inscriptions* (1967) (in Hebrew with English summary); cf. also J. N. Sevenster, *Do you know Greek?* (1968); J. Brand, 'Concerning Greek Culture in Palestine during the Talmudic Period', Tarbiz 38 (1968–9), pp. 13–17 (in Hebrew); for the architecture and decoration of synagogues of the third century A.D. onwards, E. L. Sukenik, *Ancient Synagogues in Palestine and Greece* (1934); E. R. Goodenough, *Jewish Symbols in the Greco-Roman Period* I: *The Archaeological Evidence from Palestine* (1953); for the more liberal rabbinic attitude to representational art in this period, C. H. Kraeling, *The Excavations at Dura-Europos, Final Report* VIII.1: *The Synagogue* (1956), pp. 340–6; E. E. Urbach, 'The Rabbinical Laws of Idolatry in the Second and Third Centuries in the Light of Archaeological and Historical Facts', IEJ 9 (1959), pp. 149–65, 229–45; J. Guttmann, 'The Second Commandment and the Image of God', HUCA 32 (1961), pp. 161–74; E. R. Goodenough, 'The Rabbis and Jewish Art in the Greco-Roman Period', *ibid.*, pp. 269–79; cf. G. Vermes, CHB I (1970), pp. 217–18; for the survival of Jewish proselytism, M. Simon, *Verus Israel* ([2]1964), pp. 334–51, 482–8; B. Blumenkranz, *Juifs et chrétiens dans le monde occidental* (1960), pp. 159–62; cf. also S. Zeitlin, 'Proselytes and Proselytism during the Second Commonwealth and The Early Tannaitic Period', *H. A. Wolfson Jubilee Volume* II (1965), pp. 871–81.

sions, how they lamented and bought permission from the Roman guards to remain longer at their place of wailing.

'Usque ad praesentem diem, perfidi coloni post interfectionem servorum, et ad extremum Filii Dei, excepto planctu prohibentur ingredi Hierusalem, et ut ruinam suae eis flere liceat civitatis pretio redimunt, ut qui quondam emerant sanguinem Christi emant lacrimas suas et non fletus quidem eis gratuitus sit. Videas in die, quo capta est a Romanis et diruta Hierusalem, venire populum lugubrem, confluere decrepitas mulierculas et senes pannis annisque obsitos, in corporibus et in habitu suo iram Domini demonstrantes. Congregatur turba miserorum; et patibulo Domini coruscante et radiante ἀναστάσει eius, de Oliveti monte quoque crucis fulgente vexillo, plangere ruinas templi sui populum miserum, et tamen non esse miserabilem: adhuc fletus in genis et livida brachia et sparsi crines, et miles mercedem postulat, ut illis flere plus liceat; et dubitat aliquis, quum haec videat, de die tribulationis et angustiae, de die calamitatis et miseriae, de die tenebrarum et caliginis, de die nebulae et turbinis, de die tubae et clangoris? Habent enim et in luctu tubas, et iuxta prophetiam vox sollennitatis versa est in planctum. Ululant super cineres sanctuarii, et super altare destructum et super civitates quondam minitas et super excelsos angulos templi, de quibus quondam Iacobum fratrem Domini praecipitaverunt.'[194]

Yet the tears of mourning concealed hope, and hope refused to die.

193. See M. Avi-Yonah, *Geschichte* . . ., pp. 165–6.

194. Jerome, *in Sophon.* 1:15–6 (CCL lxxviA, pp. 673–4). Cf. also Origen, *in Iosuam* 17:1 (GCS Origenes VII, pp. 401–2). The Bordeaux Pilgrim (*Itinera Hierosol.*, ed. P. Geyer, CSEL xxxix, p. 22 = CCL clxxv, p. 16).

Appendices

APPENDIX I

History of Chalcis, Ituraea and Abilene

Bibliography

Münter, F. C., *De Rebus Ituraeorum* (1824).

Renan, E., 'Mémoire sur la dynastie des Lysanias d'Abilène', Mém. Acad. Ins. et Belles-Lett. 26. 2 (1870), pp. 49–84.

Beer, G., s.v. 'Ituraea', RE IX, cols. 2377–80.

Kahrstedt, U., *Syrische Territorien in hellenistischer Zeit* (1926), pp. 88 ff., 106, 116.

Dussaud, R., *Topographie historique de la Syrie antique et médiévale* (1927), pp. 285–90, 396–412.

Jones, A. H. M., 'The Urbanisation of the Ituraean Principality', JRS 21 (1931), pp. 265–75.

Buchheim, H., *Die Orientpolitik des Triumvirn M. Antonius* (1960).

Coins and Inscriptions

BMC Syria, pp. lxxiv, 279–81.

Lévy, I., 'Tétrarques et grands-prêtres ituréens', *Hommages à J. Bidez et à F. Cumont* (1949), pp. 183–4.

Seyrig, H., 'Sur les ères de quelques villes de Syrie: Chalcis du Liban', Syria 27 (1950), pp. 46–9 = *Antiquités Syriennes* IV (1958), pp. 108–11.

Mouterde, R., 'Antiquités de l'Hermon et de la Beqâ'', MUSJ 29 (1951/2), pp. 19–89.

Inscriptions grecques et latines de la Syrie VI: Baalbek et Beqa', ed. J.-P. Rey-Coquais (1967); esp. IGLS 2851, the inscription of Zenodorus, son of Lysanias.

Seyrig, H., 'L'inscription du Tétrarque Lysanias à Baalbek', *Archäologie und Altes Testament: Festschrift für Kurt Galling* (1970), pp. 251–4.

The Old Testament mentions among the sons of Ishmael a Jetur (יטור, Gen. 25:15, 1 Chr. 31:5, 19). It is without doubt the same tribe as that encountered in later history under the name of *Ἰτουραῖοι* or *Ἰτυραῖοι*.[1] The earliest reference to it in Greek sources is in the writings of the Jewish Hellenist, Eupolemus (mid-second century B.C.), who lists the Ituraeans among the tribes fought by David.[2] Furthermore,

1. In inscriptions, the form *Ἰατουραῖος* is also found. E.g. in two inscriptions from Atil in the Hauran, MDPV 5 (1899), pp. 83–4, no. 42 *Ἀλεξάνδρου Μαξίμου βουλευτοῦ Ἰατουραίου . . .*; no. 43 *Ἀ]λεξάνδρου Ῥαού[δου βου]λευτοῦ Ἰατουρα[ίου.]*. Cf. C. Clermont-Ganneau, *Rec. d'arch. or.* IV, pp. 118–19.

2. Jacoby, FGrH 723 F 2 (3) *στρατεῦσαι δ' αὐτὸν καὶ ἐπὶ Ἰδουμαίους καὶ Ἀμμανίτας καὶ Μωαβίτας καὶ Ἰτουραίους καὶ Ναβαταίους καὶ Ναβδαίους.*

we know from Josephus, and his authorities, Strabo and Timagenes, that the Jewish king, Aristobulus I (104–103 B.C.), attacked the Ituraeans and took from them a part of their territory (*Ant.* xiii 11, 3 (318–19)). From then on, they are mentioned frequently. Sometimes they are described as Syrians, sometimes as Arabs.[3] As they are traced back to Ishmael in Gen. 25:15, they were probably by origin a tribe of nomads which settled within the region of Aramaic culture and absorbed Aramaic elements. Thus the proper names of Ituraean soldiers, as found in Latin inscriptions, are often Aramaic.[4] At the time of the Roman conquest they were still rough brigands, though greatly esteemed as accomplished archers.[5] Caesar used Ituraean bowmen in the African war[6]; the triumvir, Marcus Antonius, employed them as his bodyguard, and terrorized the Senate with them, much to the dismay of Cicero.[7] Poets and historians commemorate the Ituraean bowmen down to the later period of the empire.[8]

They will not always have lived in the same areas. According to 1 Chr. 5:19, they were once neighbours of Reuben, Gad and Half-Manasseh. But in the period during which more is known about them, there is no trace of their presence except in the mountains of Lebanon. Owing to Lk. 3:1, some Christian authors endeavour to place it as close as possible to Trachonitis. Indeed, Eusebius even identified Trachonitis and Ituraea.[9] But all the historical evidence points clearly to Lebanon. Thus first and foremost Strabo, who repeatedly describes the Ituraeans as mountain dwellers, and to be precise, as living on

3. Appian, *BC* v 7/31 *τὴν Ἰτουραίαν καὶ ὅσα ἄλλα γένη Σύρων*. Vibius Sequester, ed. Gelsomino (1967), *Gentes* 335 'Ityraei, Syri, usu sagittae periti'. Pliny, *NH* v 23/81 lists them among the peoples of Syria. Dio lix 12, 2, *τὴν τῶν Ἰτουραίων τῶν Ἀράβων*. Strabo xvi 2, 18 (755) connects them with 'Arabians'; cf. *ib.* 2, 19 (756).

4. E.g., Bargathes, Baramna, Beliabus, Bricbelus (CIL III 4371); Monimus son of Jerombal (ILS 2562). Caeus son of Manelus, and his brother 'Iamlicus' (CIL XIII 7040). Most of these names are also attested elsewhere in Syria. *Βαράθης*, JA 16 (1900), p. 274; BCH 21 (1897), p. 70 (near Emesa); ברעתה, RB 6 (1897), pp. 595, 597; AJA 12 (1898), pp. 88, 89, 108; a bilingual inscription from England has 'Barates Palmyrenus natione, ברעתא', Clermont-Ganneau, *Rec. arch. or.* III, pp. 171 ff. = RIB I 1065. *Βεελίαβος* (בעליהב), JA 8 (1896), p. 328 (Anti-Lebanon); Rev. Arch. 30 (1897), p. 285 (near Damascus); MDPV 1898, pp. 81–6 (Damascus region and Anti-Lebanon); IGLS 2695 (near Emesa); *Βηλίαβος*, Clermont-Ganneau, *Rec.* I, p. 22; *Μόνιμος*, Waddington, *Ins.* 2117–8, 2128 etc. Jerombal is the equivalent of the biblical ירבעל. *Ἄννηλος*, Waddington, *Ins.* 2320, 2437 etc.; *Ἰάμλιχος*, e.g. IGLS 2339.

5. Strabo, *loc. cit.* Cicero, *Phil.* ii 44/112.

6. *Bell. African.* 20 'sagittariisque ex omnibus navibus Ityraeis Syris et cuiusque generis ductis in castra compluribus frequentabat suas copias'.

7. *Phil.* ii 8/19; ii 44/112; xiii 8/18.

8. Virgil, *Georg.* ii 448. Lucan., *Pharsal.* vii 230; vii 514. E.g. the diploma of A.D. 110 (CIL XVI 57), 'cohors I Augusta Ituraeorum sagittaria'.

9. Euseb. *Onomast.*, ed. Klostermann, pp. 110, 166.

the mountain which extends to the Plain of Massyas or Marsyas, and has Chalcis as its capital.[10] This is the plain between Lebanon and Anti-Lebanon;[11] it begins in the north near Laodicea in the Lebanon, and stretches south as far as Chalcis.[12] As the Ituraeans are quite often named together with the Arabs,[13] they are probably to be looked for in the mountain-range bordering the Plain of Massyas on the east, i.e. in Anti-Lebanon. They also appear in all later accounts as inhabitants of the Lebanon. Dio (xlix 32, 15) designates the elder Lysanias simply as 'king of the Ituraeans'. But he was the son and successor of Ptolemy Mennaeus, whose kingdom embraced the Lebanon and the Plain of Marsyas, with the capital city, Chalcis (see below, p. 564). In the well-known inscription from the time of Quirinius, a *praefectus* serving under him, Q. Aemilius Secundus, says 'missu Quirini adversus Ituraeos in Libano monte castellum eorum cepi'.[14] At the time of the war under Vespasian, Josephus, *Vita* 11 (52) mentions a Οὔαρος βασιλικοῦ γένους, ἔγγονος Σοαίμου τοῦ περὶ τὸν Λίβανον τετραρχοῦντος. This Soaemus is probably the man described by Dio and Tacitus as ruler of the Ituraeans.[15] There is no indication at all that the Ituraeans settled anywhere else but in the Lebanon. Wetzstein's opinion that they inhabited the eastern slopes of the Hauran[16] is as incorrect as the older view that the Plain of Jedur south of Damascus obtained its name from them. Even on philological grounds this is impossible.[17]

In the last decades before the arrival of Pompey, the Ituraeans

10. Strabo, xvi 2, 10 (753); xvi 2, 18 (755); xvi 2, 20 (756).
11. Polyb. v 45, 8–9.
12. Cf. Strabo, *loc. cit.*, in n. 3 above.
13. Strabo xvi 2, 18 (755). Cf. also n. 3 above.
14. CIL III 6687=ILS 2683.
15. Dio lix 12, 2; Tacitus, *Annal.* xii 23.
16. J. G. Wetzstein, *Reisebericht über Hauran und die Trachonen* (1860), pp. 90–2.
17. Wetzstein's opinion finds support only in one of the three passages from Strabo noted earlier, xvi 2, 20 (756), where the Trachones appear in connexion with Damascus and the 'inaccessible mountains in the territory of the Arabs and the Ituraeans'. Perhaps the order here points to the Hauran. At any rate this region must have been included. But if the passage which follows this is compared with Josephus, *Ant.* xv 10, 1–3 (344–64), a different viewpoint emerges. Strabo asserts that in these mountain ranges there were large caves used as hiding-places by bandits. But by this time the companies led by Zenodorus had been destroyed by the Romans. The state of affairs described by Josephus (*l.c.*) is the same. The latter, however, relates that the domain of Zenodorus was the district of Panias, *Ant.* xv 10, 3 (363), but that he made common cause with the robbers infesting Trachonitis and Auranitis, xv 10, 1 (343–4). The territory of Zenodorus thus seems to have been part of the previously more extensive Ituraean kingdom. When therefore Strabo says that this cave-riddled range lay 'in the territories of the Arabs and the Ituraeans' (πρὸς τὰ Ἀράβων μέρη καὶ τῶν Ἰτουραίων . . .), he apparently means by the term μέρη Ἰτουραίων the country of Zenodorus. From his words then, it cannot be argued that the Ituraeans as a whole dwelt in the Hauran.

belonged to an important political entity ruled by Ptolemy the son of Mennaeus (*Πτολεμαῖος ὁ Μενναίου*), for according to the first passage from Strabo, referred to earlier, xvi 2, 10 (753), his kingdom included the mountain country of the Ituraeans and the Plain of 'Massyas', with the capital, Chalcis.[18] The Plain of Massyas runs northwards to Laodicea in the Lebanon.[19] But Ptolemy, like Alexander Jannaeus, seems to have made conquests in all directions. His territory (for Strabo's reference, xvi 2, 18 (755), to the inhabitants of Lebanon applies to him) stretched westward as far as the sea. He possessed Botrys and Theuprosopon (*Θεοῦ πρόσωπον*); Byblus and Berytus were threatened by him. To the east, the Damascenes were made to suffer at his hands.[20] To the south, the district of Panias was his, as may be inferred from the story of Zenodorus, Josephus, *Ant.* xv 10, 1–3 (344–64); cf. also, p. 565 below). Indeed, at the time of the Jewish king, Aristobulus I, the kingdom of the Ituraeans seems to have included Galilee as well.[21] In any event, the Ituraeans at that time shared a common frontier with the Jews, and formed part of a state constituted very similarly to theirs.

Ptolemy Mennaeus reigned from *c.* 85 to *c.* 40 B.C. About 85 B.C., the Damascenes were impelled by their fear of him to call on Aretas, the king of the Nabataean Arabs, *Ant.* xiii 15, 2 (392); *B.J.* i 4, 8 (103). About 70 B.C., Aristobulus, the son of Queen Alexandra, led an expeditionary force to Damascus, supposedly to protect it from Ptolemy, *Ant.* xiii 16, 3 (418); *B.J.* i 5, 5 (115). When Pompey arrived, Ptolemy purchased impunity from him by the payment of 1,000 talents, *Ant.* xiv 3, 2 (38–9). Nevertheless, Pompey destroyed the fortresses in Lebanon, Strabo, xvi 2, 18 (755), and no doubt also reduced Ptolemy's territory in much the same way as he did that of the Jews.[22] In 49 B.C., Ptolemy took into his care the sons and daughters of the Jewish king, Aristobulus II who had been deposed and recently murdered by the supporters of Pompey, *Ant.* xiv 7, 4 (124–6); *B.J.* i, 9, 2 (185–6). In 42 B.C., when Cassius had left Syria, Ptolemy supported Antigonus the son of Aristobulus in his efforts to gain control in Judaea, *Ant.* xiv

18. Josephus also names Chalcis in the Lebanon as Ptolemy's capital, *Ant.* xiv 7, 4 (126); *B.J.* i 9, 2 (185). It lay, according to Pompey's line of march, *Ant.* xiv 3, 2 (39–40), south of Heliopolis. It is to be distinguished from another Chalcis further north in Syria called by Pliny 'Chalcidem cognominatam ad Belum' (*NH* v 23/81).

19. Strabo xvi 2, 18 (755). Laodicea in the Lebanon (not to be confused with Laodicea on the sea) lay 18 *mil. pass.* south of Emesa, according to the *Itinerar. Antonini* 198, 1 (*Itineraria Romana* I, ed. Cuntz (1929), p. 27).

20. Jos. *Ant.* xiii 16, 3 (418) *ὃς βαρὺς ἦν τῇ πόλει γείτων.*

21. Cf. A. Alt, *Kleine Schriften* II, p. 407; A. H. M. Jones, 'The Urbanisation of the Ituraean Principality', JRS 21 (1931), pp. 265–75, esp. p. 266.

22. See Appian, *Mith.* 106/499; Eutrop. vi 14, 1; Orosius vi 6, 1.

12, 1 (297 ff.). Ptolemy died in 40 B.C. during the Parthian incursion, *Ant.* xiv 13, 3 (330); *B.J.* i, 13, 1 (248). As he is nowhere designated 'king', the coins with the legend restored as *Πτολεμαίου τετράρχου καὶ ἀρχιερέως* (all examples are defective) are attributed to him.[23]

Ptolemy was succeeded by his son Lysanias, *Ant.* xiv 13, 3 (330); *B.J.* i 13, 1 (249), whose kingdom will thus have extended as far as that left to his father by Pompey. Dio calls him 'king of the Ituraeans', xlix 32, 5. His reign falls in the time of Antonius, who also imposed heavy tribute on the Ituraeans, Appian, *BC* v 7/31. At Cleopatra's instigation, Antonius executed Lysanias in 34 B.C. (on the date, see above, pp. 287–9) for alleged conspiracy with the Parthians, after he had presented her in 36 B.C. with a large part of his territory, Jos. *Ant.* xv 4, 1 (92); *B.J.* i 22, 3 (440); Dio xlix 32, 5.[24] Because Dio and Porphyry call him 'king', it has been doubted whether the coins bearing the inscription *Λυσανίου τετράρχου καὶ ἀρχιερέως* belong to him, for there were one or more later princes of this name.[25] This is unnecessary for later writers often apply the title *βασιλεύς* to tetrarchs as well.

The subsequent history of the area cannot be pursued further but it is certain that the one considerable kingdom of Ptolemy and Lysanias was gradually carved into smaller territories. Four different regions can be distinguished quite definitely, all of them arising from the former kingdom of Chalcis.

1. Around 23 B.C. (for the chronology, see p. 291 above), Josephus mentions one Zenodorus who had leased from Cleopatra the territory formerly belonging to Lysanias, *Ant.* xv 10, 1 (344) *ἐμεμίσθωτο τὸν οἶκον τὸν Λυσανίου*; *B.J.* i 20, 4 (398–9) *ὁ τὸν Λυσανίου μεμισθωμένος οἶκον.* When Zenodorus became involved in banditry in Trachonitis, the region was removed from his sphere of influence and granted to Herod, *Ant.* xv 10, 1–2 (342–53); *B.J.* i 20, 4 (398–9).[26] Three years later, in 20 B.C., Zenodorus died, whereupon Augustus conferred his land on Herod, namely, Ulatha and Panias, *Ant.* xv 10, 3 (359–60) *τὴν τούτου*

23. Cf. *BMC Syria*, pp. 279–80. H. Seyrig, *Ant. Syr.* IV, p. 115, suggests that he began issuing coins with his name and titles from the moment of his confirmation by Pompey in 63 B.C.

24. See Porphyry's comment in Euseb. *Chron.* ed. Schoene, I, col. 170; cf. Jacoby, FGrH 260 F 2 (17). *Τὸ δ' ἑκκαιδέκατον* (that is, the sixteenth year of Cleopatra) *ὠνομάσθη τὸ καὶ πρῶτον, ἐπειδὴ τελευτήσαντος Λυσιμάχου τῆς ἐν Συρίᾳ Χαλκίδος βασιλέως, Μάρκος Ἀντώνιος ὁ αὐτοκράτωρ τήν τε Χαλκίδα καὶ τοὺς περὶ αὐτην τόπους παρέδωκε τῇ Κλεοπάτρᾳ.* It is generally accepted that *Λυσανίου* is to be read here in place of *Λυσιμάχου.*

25. For the coins see *BMC Syria*, p. 280. H. Buchheim, *op. cit.*, p. 19, accepts that Antonius granted Lysanias the title of king. But there is no reason not to attribute the coins, and hence the title 'tetrarch', to this Lysanias; see Seyrig, 'L'inscription du tétrarque', p. 252.

26. Cf. Strabo xvi 2, 20 (756) *καταλυθέντων νυνὶ τῶν περὶ Ζηνόδωρον λῃστῶν.*

μοῖραν οὐκ ὀλίγην οὖσαν . . . Οὐλάθαν καὶ Πανιάδα καὶ τὴν πέριξ χώραν: cf. *B.J.* i 20, 4 (400), Dio liv 9, 3, *Ζηνοδώρου τινὸς τετραρχίαν.*[27] There is a difficulty here in so far as Zenodorus is first alluded to merely as lessee of the *οἶκος Λυσανίου*, whereas afterwards mention is made of his own land, called by Dio a 'tetrarchy'. One might be inclined to regard these two as different territories. But against this it may be argued that in his first reference to him Josephus would have designated him by his own land if it had been distinct from the territory which he leased. The two must therefore be accepted as identical. It is in any case probable that the region of Ulatha and Panias belonged previously to the territory of Lysanias, i.e. to the kingdom of Ituraea, since the latter extended to the borders of the Jewish kingdom (see above, p. 564). It appears that after the death of Lysanias, Zenodorus leased a part of his land from Cleopatra, and that when she died this 'leased' territory, subject to tribute, remained his with the title of tetrarch.[28]

A fragmentary inscription on a monument belonging to the dynasty of Lysanias at Heliopolis mentions a certain 'Zenodorus, son of the tetrarch Lysanias'.[29] This is generally taken to mean our Zenodorus, who is held in consequence to be the son of the Lysanias executed by Antonius. Although this is uncertain because Lysanias is described as 'tetrarch', the inscription nevertheless proves that there was a genealogical connexion between the two families, in which the names may have been often repeated. It may be accepted as certain that the coins bearing the legend *Ζηνοδώρου τετράρχου καὶ ἀρχιερέως* belong to our Zenodorus.[30] They apparently have the year numbers *ΠΣ, ΒΠΣ, ΖΠ(Σ)*, i.e. 280, 282, 287 of the Seleucid era, or 32, 30 and 25 B.C., which would fit our hypothesis. Of these figures, *ΒΠΣ*, i.e. 31/30 B.C., has recently been confirmed, and thus suggests the restoration of the third figure to the equivalent of 25 B.C.[31] However, it has recently been argued that the inscription from Baalbek/Heliopolis cannot refer to this Zenodorus because it does not give him the title tetrarch, but must refer to a son of Lysanias of Abilene (below).[32]

After the death of Herod the Great, a part of the former tetrarchy

27. Ulatha=חולתא (cf. Neubauer, *La géographie du Talmud* (1868), pp. 24, 27 f.) designates the region of Lake Merom or Semechonitis, known also as Lake Ḥuleh. Cf. Abel, *Géog. Pal.* II, pp. 143 ff.; A. Alt, *Kleine Schriften* II, p. 391.

28. On Zenodorus, see also PIR[1] Z 8.

29. Cf. CIG 4523, Le Bas & Waddington, *Inscr. gr. et lat.* III, no. 1880. See E. Renan, *Mission de Phénicie*, pp. 317–19; IGR III 1085; IGLS 2851 . . . *θυγάτηρ, Ζηνοδώρῳ Λυσ[ανίου τ]ετράρχου καὶ Λυσ[ανίᾳ. . . καὶ τ]οῖς υἱοῖς [καὶ] (Λυ)σαν[ία . . . . καὶ τ]οῖς υἱοῖς μν[ήμ]ης χάριν [εὐσεβῶς] ἀνέθηκεν.*

30. See *BMC Syria*, p. 281.

31. Seyrig, *Ant. Syr.* IV, pp. 113–14.

32. So H. Seyrig, 'L'inscription du tétrarque Lysanias à Baalbek', *Festschrift Galling* (1970), pp. 251–4.

of Zenodorus passed to Herod's son, Philip, *Ant.* xvii 11, 4 (319); *B.J.* ii 6, 3 (95).[33] The evangelist Luke probably has this part in mind when he says (3:1) that Philip ruled over Ituraea also (τῆς Ἰτουραίας). Philip's tetrarchy later passed to Agrippa I and Agrippa II.

2. Another tetrarchy split off from the former Ituraean kingdom in the east, in the neighbourhood of Abila in the Lebanon, between Chalcis and Damascus. This Abila lay, according to the *Itinerarium Antonini*[34] and the Peutinger Table, eighteen Roman miles from Damascus, on the road linking it to Heliopolis, and thus on the site of the present village of Suk on the Barada, where the remains of an ancient town are to be found. The location is confirmed by the discovery of a milestone two Roman miles from Suk bearing the inscription *mil. pass. II.*[35] Nearby, an inscription on the cliff face records that the emperors Marcus Aurelius and L. Verus 'viam fluminis vi abruptam interciso monte restituerunt . . . inpendiis Abilenorum'.[36] In the same neighbourhood, too, is the legendary tomb of Abel (*Nebi Abel*), suggested by the place-name, Abel. The identity of Abila with Suk is therefore beyond doubt.[37] Less certain is the identification proposed by several numismatists of a town called 'Leucas', from which numerous coins have been recovered, with our Abila. Support for this theory is found in a coin bearing, besides the words [Λευκ]αδίων Κλαυ[διέων], the name of the river Χρυσορόας. In ancient times, the Barada was certainly called Chrysorrhoas, and apart from Damascus, no other city lay on it but Abila.[38] But the name Chrysoroas occurs elsewhere also (see e.g. an inscription from Gerasa, vol. II, § 23, i); furthermore, the name of the town on the coin in question has to be restored.[39]

Before the time of Caligula, Abila was the capital of a tetrarchy often mentioned by Josephus. On Caligula's accession (A.D. 37), Agrippa I was awarded not only the tetrarchy of Philip, but also 'the tetrarchy of Lysanias', *Ant.* xviii 6, 10 (237) τὴν Λυσανίου τετραρχίαν. By this is meant the tetrarchy of Abila. For when Claudius came to the throne in A.D. 41, he confirmed and increased the domain of Agrippa by transferring to him the entire kingdom of his grandfather Herod as an hereditary possession, together with Ἄβιλαν τὴν Λυσανίου καὶ

33. In Jos. *B.J.* ii 6, 3 (95), for Ἰάμνειαν read Πανειάδα. Cf. *Ant.* xv 10, 3 (360); xvii 8, 1 (189).

34. *Itineraria Romana*, ed. Cuntz (1929), p. 27.

35. Clermont-Ganneau, *Receuil d'archéol. orient.* II, pp. 35–43.

36. CIL III 199=ILS 5864.

37. Cf. art. 'Abilene' in IDB I, p. 9; IGLS VI, p. 29. Cf. R. Mouterde, MUSJ 29 (1951/2), pp. 77–89.

38. Cf. *BMC Syria* pp. lxxviii–ix. A. H. M. Jones, 'Urbanisation', p. 267, n. 11, rejects the identification of Abila with the Leucas on the Chrysorhoas of the coins and argues in favour of Abila = Balaneae.

39. See *BMC Syria*, pp. lxxvii–ix, 296–7.

ὁπόσα ἐν τῷ Λιβάνῳ ὄρει, *Ant.* xix 5, 1 (275); cf. *B.J.* ii 11, 5 (215) βασιλείαν τὴν Λυσανίου καλουμένην.[40] After the death of Agrippa I in A.D. 44, his territory was administered by Roman procurators. But in A.D. 53 (i.e. in the 13th year of Claudius), Agrippa II was awarded the former tetrarchy of Philip, together with Abila of the tetrarchy of Lysanias, *Ant.* xx 7, 1 (138) σὺν Ἀβίλᾳ [Niese: Ἀβέλλᾳ]· Λυσανία δὲ αὕτη ἐγεγόνει τετραρχία. Cf. *B.J.* ii 12, 8 (247) τήν τε Λυσανίου βασιλείαν . . .).

From these passages it appears that prior to A.D. 37, the tetrarchy of Abila belonged to a certain Lysanias.[41] And because Josephus alludes earlier only to the Lysanias who was a contemporary of Antonius and Cleopatra, it has been assumed that there was no other since then, and that the Abilene tetrarchy got its name from that older Lysanias. This is impossible. Under Lysanias I, Ituraea possessed the same frontiers as under his father, Ptolemy. Its capital was Chalcis.[42] It is true that the region of Abila belonged to it, for the kingdom of Ptolemy bordered the territory of Damascus. But it certainly formed only a small part of that considerable kingdom, which embraced practically the whole of Lebanon. So it is impossible that the region of Abila would have been described as 'the tetrarchy of Lysanias'. It should rather be assumed that the Abilene region was in the meantime divided from the kingdom of Chalcis and ruled by a later Lysanias as tetrarch.

The existence of a later Lysanias is also attested by the following inscription found at Abila:[43]

> Ὑπὲρ (τ)ῆ(ς) τῶν κυρίων Σε[βαστῶν]
> σωτηρίας καὶ τοῦ σύμ[παντος]
> αὐτῶν οἴκου, Νυμφαῖος Ἀέ[τοῦ]
> Λυσανίου τετράρχου ἀπελε[ύθερος]
> τὴν ὁδὸν κτίσας κ. τ. λ.

As the correctness of the restoration Σε[βαστῶν] is not in question, the inscription cannot be placed earlier than the time of Tiberius. For previously there had never been several 'Augusti'. The first contemporary Σεβαστοί are Tiberius and his mother Livia, who took the title *Augusta* after the death of Augustus in accordance with the

40. In regard to Abila, this is not a new gift, but confirmation of the award made by Caligula.

41. The designation βασιλεία in *B.J.* ii 11, 5 (215) and 12, 8 (247) is clearly inexact.

42. See PIR² L 467.

43. CIG 4521=OGIS 606=IGR III 1086; second copy, also from Abila, RB 9 (1912), pp. 533 ff.; cf. Rhein. Mus. 68 (1913), pp. 634 and E. Gabba, *Iscrizioni greche e latine per lo studio della Bibbia* (1958), no. 47.

instruction expressed in his will.[44] But at the time of Tiberius (at least fifty years after the death of Lysanias I), it is hardly likely that one of Lysanias's freedmen would have built a road and erected a temple, as the inscription records. Nymphaeus is unquestionably the freedman of a later tetrarch Lysanias. The Heliopolis inscription given above[45] also makes it probable that there were several dynasts by the name of Lysanias. Thus, when Luke (3:1) suggests that in the fifteenth year of Tiberius a certain Lysanias was tetrarch of Abilene, he would seem to be right.[46]

The tetrarchy of Lysanias probably remained in the possession of Agrippa II until his death. But the name of Lysanias clung to the place for a long time. In Ptolemy v 14, 18, Abila is still called *Ἄβιλα ἐπικαλουμένη Λυσανίου*, presumably because Lysanias not only possessed the city at one time, but founded it (cf. Caesarea Philippi).

3. The territories of Zenodorus and Lysanias lay on the periphery of the former Ituraean kingdom. During the governorship of Quirinius, one of his *praefecti*, Q. Aemilius Secundus, undertook a military expedition against the Ituraeans, as he himself reports in an inscription ('missu Quirini adversus Ituraeos in Libano monte castellum cepi').[47] This may have been the occasion when the Ituraean kingdom was dismembered. Under Claudius, in any case, a kingdom of Chalcis and a kingdom of Ituraea existed side by side. In A.D. 38, Caligula bestowed power over the Ituraeans on a certain Soaemus (Dio lix 12, 2, *Σοαίμῳ τὴν τῶν Ἰτυραίων τῶν Ἀράβων . . . ἐχαρίσατο . . .*).[48] This Soaemus died in A.D. 49, after which his territory was incorporated with the province of Syria (Tac. *Ann.* xii 23, 'Ituraeique et Iudaei defunctis regibus Sohaemo atque Agrippa provinciae Suriae additi'). But at the same time a Herod reigned in Chalcis (see below), so the old kingdom of Ptolemy and Lysanias was partitioned into at least four regions. Presumably, the kingdom of Soaemus included the more northerly parts (roughly from the boundary of the territory of Heliopolis to that of Laodicea ad Libanum.[49] Its capital was probably Arca, Caesarea ad Libanum.[50]

44. Tac. *Annal.* i 8, 'Livia in familiam Iuliam nomenque Augustum adsumebatur'. Tiberius and Livia (Julia) are called *Σεβαστοί* on some inscriptions, see PIR² L 301.

45. See above, n. 29.

46. Cf. E. Meyer, *Ursprung u. Anfänge des Christentums* I (1921), pp. 47–9.

47. See n. 14 above.

48. The name 'Soaemus' also appears in the dynasty of Emesa. An Ituraean 'Soaemus' during the time of Herod the Great: *Ant.* xv 6, 5 (185); 7, 1–4 (204–29).

49. See IGLS VI, pp. 36–7.

50. A. H. M. Jones, 'Urbanisation', p. 267. Cf. Pliny, *NH* v 16/74; Jos. *B.J.* vii 5, 1 (97). See H. Seyrig, 'Une monnaie de Césarée du Liban', *Ant. Syr.* VI (1966), pp. 11–16.

When, on Soaemus's death, his territory was confiscated, it would seem that his son Varus, or Noarus, as he is called in *B.J.* ii 18, 6 (481)[5], was endowed with a small territory, which he held only till A.D. 53. This was the year in which Claudius bestowed upon Agrippa II, in addition to the tetrarchies of Philip and Lysanias, *τὴν Οὐάρου γενομένην τετραρχίαν*, *B.J.* ii 12, 8 (247); on the date, see *Ant.* xx 7, 1 (137–40). According to Josephus, *Vita* 11 (52), this Varus was probably a son of the Soaemus who died in A.D. 49 (*Οὐᾶρος βασιλικοῦ γένους, ἔγγονος Σοαίμου τοῦ περὶ τὸν Λίβανον τετραρχοῦντος*).[52]

After the amalgamation of Ituraean territory with the province of Syria, regular Roman auxiliary forces were raised there. From the final decades of the first century, and occasionally even earlier, Ituraean *alae* and *cohortes* made their appearance in widely separated provinces of the Roman empire.[53]

51. For the name 'Noarus', see CIG n. 4595, 8652; Waddington, *op. cit.* n. 2114 = IGR III 1137 (*Νοαίρου*), 2412 (*Νοέρου*).

52. The identity of this Soaemus is not fully established because there is another Soaemus from Emesa, a contemporary of Nero and Vespasian (Jos. *Ant.* xx 8, 4 (158); *B.J.* ii 18, 6 (481), etc.; Tac. *Hist.* ii 81; v 1). However it is unlikely that Josephus describes him as 'tetrarch in the Lebanon district', especially since he ruled also over the distant Sophene, situated beyond the Euphrates, north of Edessa. Cf. Jones, 'Urbanisation', p. 267 and n. 2.

53. Compare RE I, col. 1250 (s.v. 'ala') and IV, cols. 305–7 (s.v. 'cohors'), now out of date.

(1) The *ala I Augusta Ituraeorum* was in Pannonia in A.D. 98 (CIL XVI 42), and in Dacia in A.D. 110 (CIL XVI 57, 163); back again in Pannonia perhaps in A.D. 139 (CIL XVI 175; cf. AE 1960 19), certainly between A.D. 150 (CIL XVI 99) and 167 (CIL XVI 123); cf. CIL XVI 179–80 (A.D. 148). Compare CIL III 1382, 3446, 3677, 4367–8, 4371 = ILS 2511. In the 140s the unit was seconded temporarily for operations in Mauretania, see CIL XVI 99, AE 1955 31, and J. Baradez, Libyca 2 (1954), pp. 113–16. In Rome there is a dedication to Jupiter Heliopolitanus by a *vexillatio alae Ituraeorum* (CIL VI 421 = ILS 2546).

(2) The *cohors I Augusta Ituraeorum sagittaria* was based in Pannonia in A.D. 80 (CIL XVI 26), A.D. 98 (CIL XVI 42), and A.D. 102 (CIL XVI 47). In A.D. 110 (CIL XVI 57) it was in Dacia, where it still was in A.D. 144 (CIL XVI 90) and 158 (CIL XVI 158).

(3) The *cohors I Ituraeorum* was at Mainz in Germania Superior for some period in the first century A.D. (CIL XIII 7040–2, cf. AE 1901 86, and 1929 131). It is found in Syria in A.D. 88 (CIL XVI 35, AE 1939 126) and in Dacia in A.D. 110 (CIL XVI 57).

(4) The *cohors Ituraeorum civium Romanorum* is found in Mauretania Tingitana between A.D. 109 and *c.* A.D. 160 (CIL XVI 161, 165, 169–70, 173, 181–2, AE 1960 103).

(5) The *cohors II Ituraeorum* was already at Syene, on the southern border of Upper Egypt, in A.D. 39 (CIL III 14147^1 = ILS 8899); the *coh. Itur.* referred to here is almost certainly this one. It appears among the auxiliary units of Upper Egypt in a diploma of A.D. 83 (CIL XVI 29), and was still at Syene in A.D. 99 (CIL III 14147^2 = ILS 8907). It is mentioned on an Egyptian diploma of A.D. 105, Syria 44 (1967), pp. 339–62, and on a diploma from Karanis of A.D. 157/61 (CIL

4. The history of Chalcis, the centre of the former Ituraean kingdom, is unknown from the death of Cleopatra until the accession of Claudius (A.D. 41). On that occasion, the emperor presented it to a grandson of Herod the Great, similarly called Herod.[54] He was a brother of Agrippa I, and thus a son of Aristobulus, the son of Herod the Great.[55]

Herod of Chalcis had the title *βασιλεύς* and praetorian rank.[56] He married twice. His first wife was Mariamme, a granddaughter of Herod the Great. By her he had a son, Aristobulus,[57] who married Salome, the daughter of Herodias, the widow of Philip the Tetrarch, and was made king of Lesser Armenia by Nero.[58] Herod's second wife was Berenice, the daughter of his brother Agrippa, who gave her to him in marriage after the death of her first husband, Marcus Iulius

---

XVI 184). A papyrus of A.D. 177 (SB 7362=S. Daris, *Documenti per la storia dell'esercito romano in Egitto* (1964), no. 97) is the *epikrisis* of a veteran of this unit. Cf. BGU 2024 (A.D. 204). Greek inscriptions from the reign of Hadrian and Antoninus Pius, found in temples at Talmis (IGR I 1348=SB 8521), Pselchis (IGR I 1303; CIL III 14147[7]) and Hiera Sycaminis (IGR I 1370=SB 8537), all of them places on the borders of Upper Egypt and Ethiopia, show soldiers of this unit worshipping there. In the Late Empire it was based in Lower Egypt (*Notitia dignitatum, Or.* 28, 44, ed. Seeck, p. 60). See J. Lesquier, *L'armée romaine d'Égypte* (1918), p. 90.

(6) The *cohors III Ituraeorum* was also based in Upper Egypt in A.D. 83 (CIL XVI 29). It was in Egypt in A.D. 103 (P. Oxy. 1022=Wilcken, *Chrestomathie* no. 453=Cavenaille, *Corp. Pap. Lat.* no. 111=Daris, *Documenti* no. 4—enrolment of recruits), and also appears on the diploma of A.D. 105, Syria 44 (1967), pp. 339–62. At some stage it provided a guard for the quarries at Ptolemais Hermiu (CIL III 12069). See also CIL VIII 2394–5, 17094; IX 1619=ILS 5502; IGR III 1339–40; AE 1952 249. P. Mich. III, no. 164=Cavenaille, *Corp. Pap. Lat.* no. 143=Daris, *Documenti*, no. 27 shows the unit in Egypt in A.D. 230. See Lesquier, *op. cit.*, p. 91.

(7) A *cohors V Ituraeorum* is very dubiously restored on the Egyptian diploma of A.D. 157/61 (AE 1952 236, cf. CIL XVI 184).

(8) A *cohors VII Ituraeorum* is mentioned in an inscription on the statue of Memnon at Thebes, CIL III 59=A. and E. Bernand, *Les inscriptions grecques et latines du colosse de Memnon* (1960), no. 26. But it is likely that VII was mistakenly inscribed for III. This unit is also very dubiously restored on the diploma of A.D. 157/61 (AE 1952 236=CIL XVI 184).

(9) An *ἔπαρχος σπείρης Ἰτουραίων* (the number unspecified) occurs in an inscription from Phrygia (OGIS 540).

(10) Reference to the dispatch of Ituraean troops to Moesia may perhaps be found in the fragmentary inscription in Le Bas and Waddington, *Inscr. gr. et lat.* III, n. 2120=IGR III 1130 (at el-Hit, north of the Hauran): [*Μνῆμα Πρ*]*ηξιλάου τοῦ εἰς Μοισία*[*ν πεμφθέντος καὶ ἄρξαντος σπείρης Ἰ*]*τουραίων καὶ στρατη*[*γήσαντος* . . .]

54. *Ant.* xix 5, 1 (274–5); *B.J.* ii 11, 5 (215). See PIR² H 156.

55. *Ant.* xviii 5, 4 (137 f.); *B.J.* I, 28, 1 (552).

56. He is always described as king by Josephus. Dio lx 8, 3, states that Claudius gave him praetorian rank (*στρατηγικὸν ἀξίωμα*).

57. *Ant.* xviii 5, 4 (134); xx 5, 2 (103 f.); *B.J.* ii 11, 6 (221–2).

58. *Ant.* xviii 5, 4 (137); xx 8, 4 (158); *B.J.* ii 13, 2 (252).

Alexander, a son of Alexander the alabarch of Alexandria.[59] He had two sons by her, Berenicianus and Hyrcanus.[60]

Herod of Chalcis was present at the assembly of dynasts summoned to Tiberias by Agrippa I but dispersed by the *legatus* of Syria, Marsus.[61] After the death of Agrippa I in A.D. 44, Herod requested the emperor to grant him the superintendence of the Temple and the Temple treasury, together with the right to appoint the High Priests. His plea was granted; and he exercised his authority by means of frequent depositions and new nominations.[62]

On his coins he named himself *Φιλοκλαύδιος*, a natural act of homage to the emperor to whom he owed all his splendour.[63] Whether an Athenian memorial inscription for a *Ἡρῴδης Εὐσεβὴς καὶ Φιλόκαισαρ* refers to him, appears questionable.[64]

He died in the eighth year of Claudius, A.D. 48, after reigning for about seven years. His kingdom was bestowed on his nephew, Agrippa II, although probably not until somewhat later.[65]

Agrippa retained possession of Chalcis only till A.D. 53, when he was presented with a larger kingdom in return for surrendering this territory.[66] The history of Chalcis then recedes once more into obscurity.

59. *Ant.* xix 5, 1 (276–7). There is some doubt whether Berenice married Marcus or was only promised in marriage to him. Josephus writes (after mention of Alexander the alabarch), *καὶ αὐτοῦ υἱὸς Βερενίκην τὴν Ἀγρίππου γαμεῖ θυγατέρα. καὶ ταύτην μὲν (τελευτᾷ γὰρ Μᾶρκος ὁ τοῦ Ἀλεξάνδρου υἱός) παρθένον λαβὼν ἀδελφῷ τῷ αὐτοῦ Ἀγρίππας Ἡρώδῃ δίδωσιν Χαλκίδος αὐτῷ τὴν βασιλείαν εἶναι αἰτησάμενος παρὰ Κλαυδίου.* If this is continued as the brackets suggest, Berenice was only affianced to Marcus, which is the interpretation adopted in the Latin translations of the editions of J. Hudson, S. Havercamp and F. Oberthür. The opposite view was advanced by R. Ibbetson, in a footnote to Hudson's edition (vol. II, p. 865), emphasizing the preceding *γαμεῖ* and including *παρθένον λαβών* in the parenthesis as well. He was followed by Dindorf, Bekker, Niese, and Feldman; see also U. Wilcken in RE III, col. 287, s.v. 'Berenike', and PIR² I 651. But in the second view, the phrase *παρθένον λαβών* is quite pointless, whereas in the first it makes good sense; further, Berenice was 16 years old when her father died in A.D. 44, *Ant.* xix 9, 1 (354), and thus aged about 13 on her marriage with Herod of Chalcis, which took place at about the same time as his appointment to the throne, i.e. A.D. 41. An earlier marriage is consequently improbable.

60. *Ant.* xx 5, 2 (104); *B.J.* ii 11, 6 (221).

61. *Ant.* xix 8, 1 (338–42); cf. above, p. 448.

62. *Ant.* xx 1, 3 (15–16); 5, 2 (103).

63. For his coins, see A. Reifenberg, *Ancient Jewish Coins* (²1947), pp. 23–4.

64. OGIS 427 (from Athens): [*Ὁ δ*]*ῆμος* [*Βασι*]*λέα Ἡρῴδην Εὐσεβῆ καὶ Φιλοκαίσαρα* [*ἀ*]*ρετῆς ἕνεκα καὶ εὐεργεσίας*. Another inscription at Athens (OGIS 414) similarly honours one *βασιλέα Ἡρῴδην Φιλορωμαῖον*. The difference in titulature points to different men; it is probable that 414 refers to Herod the Great, and 427 to Herod of Chalcis. On the other hand, the fact that he names himself *Φιλοκλαύδιος* on his coins presents difficulties.

65. *Ant.* xx 5, 2 (104); *B.J.* ii 11, 6 (221); 12, 1 (223).

66. *Ant.* xx 7, 1 (138); *B.J.* ii 12, 8 (247).

In the time of Vespasian there is a mention of a king Aristobulus of Chalcidice, who may be identical with the son of Herod of Chalcis and king of Lesser Armenia.[67] But even if this is conceded, it is very much open to question whether by 'Chalcidice' is meant Chalcis ad Libanum or the territory of Chalcis ad Belum. According to the coins, the city of Chalcis had an era commencing in A.D. 92, possibly the year of its incorporation in the province of Syria.[68]

67. *B.J.* vii 7, 1 (226) *τῆς μὲν Χαλκιδικῆς λεγομένης Ἀριστόβουλος*. On Aristobulus see PIR² A 1052. A coin from the time of Nero, bearing the inscription *Βασιλέως Ἀριστοβούλου ET H* (year 8) *Νέρωνι Κλαυδίῳ Καίσαρι Σεβαστῷ Γερμανικῷ* is given by F. Cumont, RN 4me sér. 4 (1900), pp. 484 ff. = Reifenberg, *op. cit.*, no. 72. It was found in Nicopolis in Armenia Minor, but minted in Syria, as the stylistic affinities testify. A coin from Vespasian's time, with the words *Βασιλέως Ἀριστοβουλου ET IZ* (year 17), *Τιτῷ Οὐεσπασιανῷ Αὐτοκράτορι Σεβαστῷ* is given by de Saulcy (*Mél. de numism.* 3 (1882), pp. 339–49, and J. Babelon, RN 3me sér., 1 (1883), p. 145, pl. IV, n. 9). See Reifenberg, *op. cit.* no. 73, who suggests (p. 15) that this was his son, also called Aristobulus. For a coin of Aristobulus and his wife Salome, with the legend *Βασιλέως Ἀριστοβούλου, Βασίλισσης Σαλώμης* and busts of both, see Reifenberg, *op. cit.*, no. 71.

68. Note, however, that A. H. M. Jones, 'Urbanisation', JRS 21 (1931), p. 267, following *BMC Syria*, pp. liv–v, and B. V. Head, *Hist. Num.*,² p. 785, asserts that the coins inscribed *ΦΛ ΧΑΛΚΙΔΕΩΝ* and having an era commencing in A.D. 92, are to be attributed to Chalcis ad Belum.

APPENDIX II

HISTORY OF THE NABATAEAN KINGS

Bibliography

Clermont-Ganneau, C., *Recueil d'archéologie orientale* I–VIII (1888–1924).
Dussaud, R., Macler, F., *Voyage archéologique au Safa et dans le Djebel ed-Drûz* (1901).
Dussaud, R., Macler, F., *Rapport sur une mission scientifique dans les régions désertiques de la Syrie moyenne* (1903).
Brünnow, R. E., and Domaszewski, A. von, *Die Provincia Arabia* I–III (1904–9).
Dalman, G., *Petra und seine Felsheiligtümer* (1908).
Jaussen & Savignac, *Mission archéologique en Arabie* I–II (1909–14).
Dalman, G., *Neue Petra-Forschungen und der heilige Felsen von Jerusalem* (1912).
Bachmann, W., Watzinger, C., Wiegand, Th., *Petra* (1921).
Kennedy, A. B. W., *Petra, Its History and Monuments* (1925).
Kammerer, A., *Pétra et la Nabatène* I–II (1929–30).
Cantineau, J., *Le Nabatéen* I–II (1930–2).
Grohmann, A., 'Nabataioi', RE XVI, cols. 1453–68.
Glueck, N., *Explorations in Eastern Palestine* I–IV (1934–51).
Horsfield, G. and A., 'Sela-Petra, the Rock of Edom and Nabatene', QDAP 7 (1938), pp. 1–42; 8 (1939), pp. 87–115; 9 (1942), pp. 105–205.
Dussaud, R., *La pénetration des Arabes en Syrie avant l'Islam* (1955), pp. 21–61.
Starcky, J., 'The Nabataeans: a Historical Sketch', BA 18 (1955), pp. 84–106.
Starcky, J., 'Pétra et la Nabatène', DB Supp. VII (1960), cols. 886–1017 (the most complete modern survey).
Wright, G. R. H., 'The Khazne at Petra: a Review', ADAJ 6–7 (1962), pp. 24–54.
Parr, P. J., 'The Date of the Qasr Bint Far'un at Petra', Jaarbericht ex Oriente Lux 19 (1965/6), pp. 550–7.
Wright, G. R. H., 'Structure et date de l'arc monumental de Pétra', RB 73 (1966), pp. 404–19.
Glueck, N., *Deities and Dolphins: the Story of the Nabataeans* (1966).
Negev, A., 'Oboda, Mampsis and Provincia Arabia', IEJ 17 (1967), pp. 46–55.
Negev, A., 'Mampsis, a Town of the Eastern Negev', Raggi 7 (1967), pp. 67–87.
Starcky, J., 'Le temple Nabatéen de Khirbet Tannur', RB 75 (1968), pp. 206–35.
Parr, P. J., Wright, G. R. H., Starcky, J., Bennet, C. M., 'Decouvertes récentes au sanctuaire du Qasr à Pétra', Syria 45 (1968), pp. 1–66.
Negev, A., 'The Chronology of the Middle Nabataean Period', PEQ 101 (1969), pp. 5–14.
Bowersock, G. W., 'The Annexation and Original Garrison of Arabia', Zeitschr. Pap. u. Epig. 5 (1970), pp. 37–47.
Bowersock, G. W., 'A Report on Arabia Provincia', JRS 61 (1971), pp. 219–42.
Negev, A., 'The Necropolis of Mampsis (Kurnub)', IEJ 21 (1971), pp. 110–29.

Coins, Inscriptions and Papyri

CIS II, nos. 157–3233.
Lidzbarski, M., *Handbuch der nordsemitischen Epigraphik* I–II (1898).
Cooke, G. A., *A Textbook of North Semitic Inscriptions* (1903).
Littmann, E., *Princeton University Archaeological Expedition to Syria*, 1904–5, *and* 1909, *IV A: Nabataean Inscriptions* (1914).
Dussaud, R., 'Numismatique des rois de Nabatène', JA 10 (1904), pp. 189–238.
BMC Arabia (1922), pp. xi–xxii, 1–13.
Starcky, J., 'Un contrat nabatéen sur papyrus', RB 61 (1954), pp. 161–81.
Milik, J. T., Seyrig M., 'Trésor monétaire de Murabba'at', RN sér. 6 (1958), pp. 11–26.
Milik, J. T., 'Nouvelles inscriptions nabatéennes', Syria 35 (1958), pp. 227–51.
Negev, A., 'Nabataean Inscriptions from Avdat (Oboda)', IEJ 11 (1961), pp. 127–38; 13 (1963), pp. 113–24.
Yadin, Y., IEJ 12 (1962), pp. 228–48 (The archive of Babata).
Yadin, Y., 'The Nabataean Kingdom, Provincia Arabia, Petra and En-Geddi in the Documents from Naḥal Ḥever', Jaarbericht Ex Oriente Lux 17 (1963), pp. 227–41.
Starcky, J., 'Nouvelles stèles funéraires à Pétra', ADAJ 10 (1965), pp. 43–9; cf. RB 72 (1965), pp. 93–7.
Starcky, J., Strugnell, J., 'Pétra: deux nouvelles inscriptions nabatéennes', RB 75 (1966), pp. 236–47.
Winnet, F. W., Reed, W. L., *Ancient Records from North Arabia* (1970).
Starcky, J., 'Une inscription nabatéenne de l'an 18 d'Arétas IV', *Mélanges Dupont-Sommer* (1971), pp. 151–9.
Negev, A., 'New Dated Nabataean Graffiti from the Sinai', IEJ 17 (1967), pp. 250–5.
Negev, A., 'A Nabatean Epitaph from Trans-Jordan', IEJ 21 (1971), pp. 50–2.
Yadin, Y., *Bar Kokhba* (1971), pp. 222–53 (the archive of Babata).
Negev, A., 'Notes on some Trajanic Drachms from the Mampsis Hoard', Jahrb. f. Numism. u. Geldgesch. 21 (1971), pp. 115–20 and plates 9–12.

Besides the Syrian empire in the north and that of Egypt in the south, Palestine had during the Graeco-Roman period a third powerful neighbour: the Nabataean kingdom in the south and east. Its history can be assessed with some degree of coherence now that the scattered written reports, particularly those of Josephus, have been amplified by copious material in the form of coins, inscriptions and, most recently, papyri.

So little is known of the Nabataean people (*Ναβαταῖοι*, נבטו) that not even their ethnic origin is certain. The language of coins and inscription, without exception Aramaic, indicates that they were Arameans. On the other hand, they are repeatedly spoken of as Arabs by ancient writers, not only by those remote from them in time, but also by Josephus, to whom the distinction between Syrians and Arabs must have been quite familiar. In addition, the names on the inscriptions are Arabic throughout. It has therefore been concluded that they were Arabs who, because Arabic had not yet developed into a written language, made use of Aramaic, the civilized language of the time, for literary purposes.[1]

Almost nothing is known of the history of the Nabataeans prior to the Hellenistic period. Their identity with the נביות, mentioned in Gen. 25:13, 28:9, 36:3; 1 Chr. 1:29; Isa. 60:7 as an Arab tribe, is very improbable.[2] Nor do the cuneiform inscriptions yield much information. It is only from the beginning of the Hellenistic period that a fairly coherent picture of them emerges. They were at that time settled where the Edomites previously lived, between the Dead Sea and the Gulf of Aqaba, in the region of Petra, probably not identical with the old Sela of the Edomites.[3] After Antigonus had driven Ptolemy Lagus from Coele-Syria in 312 B.C., he sent his general Athenaeus against the Nabataeans with 4000 infantry and 600 cavalry. Athenaeus attacked their fortress of Petra by surprise, and went off with a great deal of booty. But due to his own carelessness, his army was soon afterwards almost annihilated by the Nabataeans in a night assault; only fifty horsemen, and most of these wounded, are said to have survived. Antigonus then sent his son Demetrius against the Nabataeans with a fresh army. But he, too, achieved no decisive victory. After a fruitless siege of Petra, he withdrew, contenting himself with the placing of hostages and a pledge of friendship on the part of the Nabataeans. Diodorus, who reports all this,[4] also provides a description of the Nabataeans. They were at that time uncivilized pastoral nomads with no agriculture but only cattle-raising and trade, and were evidently still without a king. But civilization must have gradually reached them, and some sort of political order under monarchical rule have taken shape. Their power extended further towards the south and the north, and Petra, which in the time of Antigonus had been their stoutest sanctuary, remained their capital.[5]

The first known Nabataean dynast is Aretas (I), with whom Jason the High Priest sought refuge in vain in 168 B.C. (2 Mac. 5:8).[6] As Aretas is designated *τύραννος*, the Nabataean princes do not seem to

1. See, e.g. Th. Nöldeke, ZDMG 17 (1863), pp. 703 ff., 25 (1871), pp. 122 ff. J. Cantineau, *Le Nabatéen* (1930–32); J. Starcky, 'Pétra et la Nabatène', cols. 924–6.

2. Cf. Starcky, 'Pétra', col. 903.

3. So Starcky, 'Pétra', cols. 886–96.

4. Diodorus xix 94–100; cf. ii 48, 5 and Plut. *Demetr.* 7.

5. On Petra as the capital of the Nabataeans, see esp. Strabo xvi 4,21 (779); Pliny, *NH* vi 28/144. Jos. *Ant.* xiv 1, 4 (16), 5, 1 (80–1), 13, 9 (362); xvii 3, 2 (54); xvii 3, 2 (54), 5, 3 (120); *B.J.* i, 6, 2 (125–6), 8, 1 (159), 13, 3 (267), 29, 3 (574). Plut. *Pomp.* 41. *Periplus maris erythraei*, 19. On its name *Raḳmu*=*Reḳem*, see J. Starcky, 'Nouvelle épitaphe nabatéenne donnant le nom sémitique de Pétra', RB 72 (1965), pp. 95–7.

6. 2 Mac. 5:8 reports that Jason was imprisoned by Aretas, the Prince of the Arabians and that he subsequently fled from city to city. Cf. Abel, *Les livres des Maccabées, in loc.*

have taken the title of 'king' at that time.[7] After the outbreak of the Maccabean revolt, the Nabataeans adopted a friendly attitude towards the leaders of the Jewish national party (Judas, 164 B.C.; Jonathan, 160 B.C. See 1 Mac. 5:25, 9:35). Their power now reached as far as the region east of the Jordan.

The kingdom of the Nabataeans did not, however, rise to greater eminence until approximately the end of the second century B.C., when the collapse of the Ptolemaic and Seleucid empires facilitated the foundation of a powerful and independent state on their borders. In Justin's epitome of Pompeius Trogus, it is said of the period around 110–100 B.C. that the kingdoms of Syria and Egypt themselves had at that time become so weak 'ut adsiduis proeliis consumpti in contemptum finitimorum venerint praedaeque Arabum genti, inbelli antea, fuerint; quorum rex Erotimus fiducia septingentorum filiorum, quos ex paelicibus susceperat, divisis exercitibus nunc Aegyptum, nunc Syriam infestabat magnumque nomen Arabum viribus finitimorum exsanguibus fecerat'.[8] This Erotimus is thus to be regarded as the founder of the royal Nabataean dynasty.[9] He is perhaps identical with Aretas II (Ἀρέτας ὁ Ἀράβων βασιλεύς) referred to at the time of the siege of Gaza by Alexander Jannaeus about 100 B.C. He had promised to assist the people of Gaza but the city fell into the hands of Alexander Jannaeus before he could give support, Jos. *Ant.* xiii 13, 3 (360–4).

Some years later, about 93 B.C., Alexander Jannaeus attacked King Obodas I (Ὀβέδαν τὸν Ἀράβων βασιλέα), but suffered a crushing defeat at his hands east of Jordan, *Ant.* xiii 13, 5 (375); *B.J.* i 4, 4 (90). This Obedas I is possibly to be identified with the Obodat appearing on certain coins and inscriptions.[10]

A few years later, in 87 B.C., Antiochus XII advanced from Coele-Syria against an unnamed king of the Arabs. Again the Arabs were victorious. Antiochus himself fell in battle at Cana, Jos. *Ant.* xiii 15, 1 (391); *B.J.* i 4, 7 (101–2). There is some difficulty concerning the identification of this king, but most likely this is still Obodas I, referred

7. It is possible, however, that this ruler is identical with the 'Aretas, king of Arabia' mentioned in a Nabataean inscription from Elusa. See A.E. Cowley, PEFA 3 (1914–1915), pp. 145–7. For palaeographic discussion see F. M. Cross in JBL 74 (1955), p. 160, n. 25.

8. Justin xxxix 5, 5–6.

9. The two 'Arabians' mentioned *c.* 146–145 B.C., Zabdiel, 1 Mac. 11:17; Jos. *Ant.* xiii 4, 8 (118) perhaps identical with Diocles in Diodorus xxxii 27, 9d/10.1; and Imalkue, 1 Mac. 11:39; cf. Malchus in Jos. *Ant.* xiii 5, 1 (131) and Jamblichus in Diodorus xii 33, 4a.1, are probably minor dynasts, not Nabataean princes; see A. v. Gutschmidt in Euting, *Nabat. Inschr. aus Arabien* (1885), p. 81.

10. For inscriptional evidence see G. Dalman, *Neue Petra-Forschungen*, pp. 90 f., no. 90; cf. also CIS 354; J. Starcky, 'Pétra', col. 906: 'Year 1 of Obodat, king of Nabatu, son of Ḥaretat, King of Nabatu'.

to earlier by Josephus.[11] Alternatively, according to an inscription found in Petra (CIS II, 349) a king Rabbel (on whose statue the inscription appears), was followed in office by another called Aretas. It would seem that this cannot be the Rabbel whose reign closed the history of the Nabataean kingdom in A.D. 106. It has therefore been suggested that the unnamed king who defended himself against Antiochus XII in 87 B.C., and who was in any case followed by Aretas III, should be identified as this Rabbel, who would then be known as Rabbel I and assigned a period of approximately 90–85 B.C. This poses a certain problem in that it requires kings to be placed between Aretas II (*c.* 100 B.C.) and Aretas III (*c.* 85 B.C.), Obodas I and Rabbel I, concerning neither of whom much information is extant. It is therefore more likely that this Rabbel (I) belongs earlier, before Obodas I; the statue will have been restored under Aretas III.[12]

The last king in the period prior to the Roman domination is Aretas III, who is reported by Josephus as having gained possession of Coele-Syria and Damascus in about 85 B.C., following the death of Antiochus XII. Thereafter he defeated Alexander Jannaeus at Adida, *Ant.* xiii 15, 2 (392); *B.J.* i, 4, 8 (103). The coins bearing the inscription *Βασιλέως Ἀρέτου Φιλέλληνος* must be assigned to Aretas III. They cannot belong to an earlier Aretas because they were struck in Damascus

11. So Starcky, 'Pétra', col. 906.

12. Note the passage from the *Arabica* of Uranius, Jacoby, FGrH 675 F25 preserved in Steph. Byz., s.v. *Μωθώ· κώμη Ἀραβίας, ἐν ᾗ ἔθανεν Ἀντίγονος ὁ Μακεδὼν ὑπὸ Ῥαβίλου τοῦ βασιλέως τῶν Ἀραβίων, ὡς Οὐράνιος ἐν ε*. For *Ἀντίγονος* it has been common to read *Ἀντίοχος* and to interpret this as meaning Antiochus XII (cf. Josephus, *Ant.* xiii 15, 1 (391); *B.J.* i 4, 7 (101–2). In this case the 'Rabilus' mentioned would possibly be the otherwise unnamed king. Clermont-Ganneau then suggested that this 'Rabilus' might well be identified with the 'Rabbel' mentioned in CIS II 349 (Brünnow und Domaszewski, *Die Provincia Arabia* I, pp. 312 ff. The inscription was found by P. Germer-Durand at Petra, in 1897). The inscription is dated to the eighteenth year of 'Aretas'. G. Dalman thought the Aretas in question was Aretas III (*c.* 87–62 B.C.). In this case its date would be *c.* 70 B.C. (Dalman, *Neue Petra-Forschungen* I, p. 100). Cf. also J. Starcky, *op. cit.*, cols. 903–5. As to the question whether two kings or only one are to be 'inserted' here between Aretas III (87–62 B.C.) and Aretas II (110–96 B.C. approx.), opinion is divided. Partly it depends on how line 2 in CIS 349 is restored. The inscription runs:
1. [This is the im]age which Rabbel, King of the Nabataeans
2. [br 'bd]t [son of Oboda]t, king of the Nabataeans erected . . .
But, of course, the lacuna can be filled in with [Areta]s [Ḥarita]t, instead of ['Oboda]t.

In this case Rabbel (I) could be a son of Aretas I. Furthermore, if the king who defended himself against Antiochus XII was in fact Obodas I, the passage of Uranius quoted above does not have to be emended, but will refer to the event of 312 B.C. and give the name of the ethnarch then in power, Rabbel. See Starcky 'Pétra', cols. 903–4, 905–6. See E. T. Newell, *Late Seleucid Mints in Ake-Ptolemais and Damascus*: Num. Notes and Monographs 84 (1939), pp. 92–4.

between 84 and 72 B.C.;[13] but neither should they be ascribed to Aretas IV, since the latter named himself 'Friend of his people'.[14] The coins, all with Greek inscriptions, are thus evidence of the penetration of Hellenism in the Nabataean realm at that time. It was also during the reign of this same Aretas that the first encounter with the Romans took place. It is known from Jewish history that, in the struggle between Hyrcanus and Aristobulus, Aretas III sided with the former, supported him with troops and besieged Aristobulus in Jerusalem, but then withdrew on the command of the Roman general Scaurus and whilst retreating was defeated by Aristobulus, *Ant.* xiv 1, 4 (14)–2, 3 (33); *B.J.*, i 6, 2–3 (123–30). Pompey thereupon determined to march against Aretas himself. But on the way to Petra, he was obliged because of the hostile attitude of Aristobulus to turn towards Judaea, *Ant.* xiv 3, 3–4 (46–53). After the conquest of Jerusalem, Pompey handed over the province of Syria to Scaurus, *Ant.* xiv 4, 5 (79) who led an expedition against Petra in 62 B.C. All he obtained from Aretas, however, was the payment of a sum of money, *Ant.* xiv 5, 1 (81–2); *B.J.* i 8, 1 (159). This was the limit of the subjugation of Aretas of which Pompey boasted,[15] and which is even proclaimed on coins.[16] The city of Damascus was occupied by Pompey's legates when the Romans first entered Syria, *Ant.* xiv 2, 3 (29); *B.J.* i 6, 2 (127), and from then on remained under Roman control.[17] The reign of Aretas III extended from about 85 B.C. to 62 B.C.

13. Damascus, however, did not remain in the possession of the Nabataeans. In 72/1 B.C., Tigranes, the Armenian king, invaded Coele-Syria, with the result that Aretas's troops withdrew from Damascus; for his coinage of 72/1 to 69 B.C. in Damascus see Newell, *op. cit.*, pp. 95–100. There is no indication that Aretas and his men were there when the Romans occupied the place in about 66 B.C. Further, in about 70 B.C. Damascus seems to have been under the control of the Jewish queen, Alexandra, Jos. *Ant.* xiii 16, 3 (416–8); *B.J.* i 5, 3 (115–16).

14. For the coins of Aretas III see *BMC Arabia*, pp. xi–xii, 1–2 and Newell, *op. cit.* (previous note). The title Φιλέλλην cannot be regarded as a translation of the title *rḥm ʿmh* used by Aretas IV.

15. Diodorus xl 4. Cf. also Dio xxxvii 15, 1–2; Plut. *Pomp.* 41; Appian, *Mith.* 106/497; Oros. vi 6, 1.

16. *BMC Roman Republic* I, pp. 483–4. On the coin, Aretas is shown kneeling, with the inscription, 'Rex Aretas, M. Scaurus aed. cur. ex. S.C.' Cf. p. 244 above.

17. It has been held, on the basis of 2 Cor. 11:32, that Damascus remained subject to the Nabataean king from the beginning of the Roman period until A.D. 106. The argument against this is as follows:
(1) According to Pliny, *NH* v 18/74 and Ptolemy, V 15, 22, it belonged to the Decapolis, i.e. to those cities which had received their freedom through Pompey and were merely under the supervision of the Roman governor of Syria. It cannot therefore, have been returned to the Nabataean king by Pompey. On the status of Damascus in the period compare H. Bietenhard, 'Die Dekapolis von Pompeius bis Traian', ZDPV 79 (1963), pp. 24–58.
(2) After the territory of the Nabataeans had been converted into a Roman

Aretas III may have been followed in 62 B.C. by an Obodas II (*c.* 62 B.C. to *c.* 57 B.C.), to whom it is possible, though not obligatory, to assign a series of didrachms on the Phoenician standard, with the years 1 to 3 and 5 to 6 of an Obodas of Nabataea.[18] It is this Obodas who is probably mentioned in an inscription from Petra, in a tomb-complex near Bab es-Siq.[19] At any rate, Malichus I will have acceded by 56 B.C., for there is a coin of his with the year 28, and his successor was on the throne by 28 B.C.[20] In 56 B.C., Gabinius launched a campaign against the Nabataeans. Josephus does not name their king, *Ant.* xiv 6, 4 (103–4), *B.J.* i 8, 7 (178), but it will have been Malichus.

In 47 B.C., Malichus provided Caesar with cavalry for the Alexandrian War (*Bell. Alex.* 1). When the Parthians conquered Palestine in 40 B.C., Herod wished to take refuge with Malichus but was not accepted by him, *Ant.* xiv 14, 1–2 (370–5); *B.J.* i, 14, 1–2 (274–8). Because of his support for the Parthians, Ventidius in 39 B.C. exacted a sizeable tribute from him, Dio xlviii 41, 5. Antonius presented a part of his territory to Cleopatra, Dio xlix 32, 15; Plut. *Ant.* 36; Jos. *B.J.* i 18, 4 (360). In 32 B.C., Malichus sent Antonius auxiliary troops for the war of Actium, Plut. *Ant.* 61. Because he paid no tribute for the territory handed over to Cleopatra, he was invaded by Herod at the command of Antonius. The war began in the Arabs' favour, but ended with their total defeat in 32–1 B.C. *Ant.* xv 5, 1 (108–20); 5, 4–5 (147–60); *B.J.* i 19, 1–6 (364–85). The last heard of Malichus is that he promised to support the aged Hyrcanus in the revolt planned against Herod in 30 B.C., *Ant.* xv 6, 2–3 (167–75). He may be the person referred to in a Nabataean inscription from Boẓra mentioning 'the eleventh year of Maliku the King'.[21]

Obodas III (or II), *c.* 28 B.C., was king at the time of the campaign led by Aelius Gallus against the southern Arabs in 26–25 B.C. in which a thousand Nabataean auxiliaries also took part. He entrusted the

---

province in A.D. 106, Damascus belonged not to the province of Arabia, but to Syria, Justin, *Dial. c. Tryph.*, 78.

(3) In the frontier dispute between the Sidonians and the Damascenes under Tiberius, Jos. *Ant.* xviii 6, 3 (153–4), the jurisdiction is that of the Roman governor, not that of the Nabataean king.

(4) The coins of Damascus with the images of Augustus, Tiberius and Nero do not favour the assumption that it was part of the Nabataean kingdom.

18. See Starcky, 'Pétra', cols. 910 and 911, who assigns these coins to the Obodas of 29/8–9/8 B.C.

19. G. Dalman, *Neue Petra-Forschungen*, pp. 99 ff. (no. 90). Dalman after detailed discussion of this inscription, dates it to 62 B.C., identifying 'Obodat' with Obodas II. For further discussion, see G. and A. Horsfield, 'Sela-Petra, the Rock, of Edom and Nabatene', QDAP 7 (1938), pp. 41–2 and 8 (1939), pp. 87–115.

20. See Starcky, 'Petra', col. 909.

21. CIS II 174; E. Renan, JA 7th ser. 2 (1873), pp. 366–82 = CIS II 158.

business of government entirely to his ἐπίτροπος, Syllaeus,[22] who advised Aelius Gallus badly as to the route he should take, Strabo xvi 4, 23–4 (780–2). Obodas is still mentioned as king towards the end of Herod's reign, when Syllaeus went to Jerusalem to ask for the hand in marriage of Salome, Herod's sister, *Ant.* xvi 7, 6 (220–8); *B.J.* i 24, 6 (487), and when Herod undertook an expedition against the Arabs, *Ant.* xvi 9, 1–2 (279, 282–5). Obodas died at about that time (9/8 B.C.) allegedly from poison administered by Syllaeus, *Ant.* xvi 9, 4 (294–9). A few coins can be attributed to his reign.[23] It is also very probable that there is a connexion between Obodas III and the inscription on a statue of the god Obodat (*'lh' 'bdt*) erected by the children of Ḥoneinu to the prosperity of King Aretas, the friend of his people (i.e. Aretas IV) in the 29th year of his reign.[24] It is interesting as providing definite evidence of the apotheosis of dead kings among the Nabataeans, and confirms the observation of Uranius (in Steph. Byz., s.v. Ὄβοδα = Jacoby FGrH 675 F 24, ὅπου Ὀβόδης ὁ βασιλεύς, ὃν θεοποιοῦσι, τέθαπται).

Aretas IV, whose original name was Aeneas, succeeded Obodas in about 9 B.C. and ruled till A.D. 40, *Ant.* xvi 9, 4 (294). Augustus was at first displeased on account of his arbitrary accession to the throne, but later recognized him as king, *Ant.* xvi 10, 9 (353–5). Aretas laid repeated complaints against Syllaeus before Augustus, *Ant.* xvii 3, 2 (54 ff.); *B.J.* i 29, 3 (574–7), with the result that Syllaeus was executed at Rome, Strabo xvi 4, 24 (782). When after Herod's death in 4 B.C. Varus, the legate of Syria, was forced to undertake an expedition against the Jews, Aretas provided auxiliaries for his army, *Ant.* xvii 10, 9 (287); *B.J.* ii 5, 1 (68). Of the later period of the long reign of Aretas IV, only a few events are known. The tetrarch Herod Antipas married one of his daughters, but divorced her in order to marry Herodias. The resulting hostility between the two rulers was exacerbated by border disputes. These ended in war, in the course of which Herod's army was defeated by Aretas. Because of his high-handedness, Aretas, on the command of the emperor Tiberius, was to have been chastised by the governor, Vitellius. But while he was on his way to Petra, Vitellius received in Jerusalem the news of Tiberius's death and turned back leaving his task undone, *Ant.* xviii 5, 1 and 3 (109–15, 120–5). These events thus occurred at the end of the reign of Tiberius, A.D. 36–7. The flight of Paul from Damascus took place

22. See RE s.v. 'Syllaios' (IVA, cols. 1041–4). Note the bilingual (Greek and Nabataean) inscription of Syllaeus, called ἀδελφὸς βασιλ[έως], a dedication for Obodas to Dusares at Miletus, CRAI 1907, pp. 389–91; G. Kaweran, A. Rehm, *Das Delphinion in Milet* (1914), p. 387, no. 165. There is a similar, unpublished, one from Delos, see Starcky, 'Pétra', col. 913.

23. *BMC Arabia*, pp. xiv–xvii, 4.

24. CIS II, 354 (Brünnow und Domaszewski, no. 290, vol. I, p. 283). Cf. also Starcky, BA 18 (1955), p. 99, fig. 6.

not long after this, when the city seems to have been governed by an ἐθνάρχης of King Aretas (cf. 2 Cor. 11:32). This could indicate that it belonged once more to the territory of the Nabataean king, a possibility supported by the apparent lack of Damascene coins from the reigns of Caligula and Claudius bearing the image of the Roman emperor. Caligula, who enjoyed making such gifts, may have conferred the city on Aretas.[25] On the other hand, it may be argued that there is inadequate positive evidence for the transference of the city to Aretas. Furthermore, the term ἐθνάρχης, normally denotes an independent minor dynast, not a subordinate of a king; it has therefore been suggested that this ethnarch was head of the Nabataean colony at Damascus.[26] But the story implies the actual exercise of power by the ethnarch.

Of no other Nabataean king is there such a rich fund of inscriptional and numismatic material to hand as of Aretas IV.[27] It is probably he who is mentioned in an inscription from Sidon,[28] and in two inscriptions from Puteoli.[29] He is also not infrequently represented on coins.[30] An Aretas is also commonly referred to in inscriptions and on coins as *ḥrtt mlk nbtw rḥm ʿmh*—'Aretas King of the Nabataeans, friend of his people'. The title *'Raḥem 'ammeh'*, which may be Hellenized as 'Philodemos', is an expression of national feeling and contains an implicit rejection of such titles as *Φιλορώμαιος* or *Φιλόκαισαρ*. It corresponds to the Greek *Φιλόπατρις*, a title borne, for example, by King Archelaus of Cappadocia.[31] This Greek title may also be a protest against the servility of other kings.[32] It is therefore unlikely that *'Raḥem-'ammeh'* is to be interpreted, 'who loves his great-grandfather', as Clermont-Ganneau suggested, even if *'am* really does mean 'great-

25. So Gutschmidt, in Euting, *Nabat. Inschr.*, p. 85. The coins of Damascus with the image of Tiberius run to the year 345 of the Seleucid era = A.D. 33/34. (Mionnet, *Description des méd.*, V, p. 286; de Saulcy, *Numism. de la Terre Sainte* p. 36); those of Nero begin with the year 374 of the Seleucid era = A.D. 62/63 (Mionnet, *op. cit.* V, p. 286; de Saulcy, *op. cit.*, p. 36; cf. *BMC Syria*, p. 283, (no example with Tiberius). In the interim, Damascus may have belonged to the Nabataean kingdom.

26. So Starcky, 'Pétra', col. 915.

27. Cf. CIS II 182, 196, 197, 198, 199, 201, 204, 206, 207, 209, 212, 213, 354, etc.; J. T. Milik, 'Nouvelles inscriptions nabatéennes', Syria 35 (1958), pp. 227–51 esp. 249 ff.; A. Negev, IEJ 11 (1961), pp. 218–30. Note especially, J. Starcky, J. Strugnell, 'Pétra: deux nouvelles inscriptions nabatéennes', RB 73 (1966), pp. 236–47, on the inscription of a statue of Aretas IV from the *temenos* of the Qasr Bint Farun, which provides a conclusive dating of this major temple to the Augustan period.

28. CIS II, 160.

29. CIS II, 157, 158.

30. *BMC Arabia*, pp. xvii–xix, 5–10; cf. now the hoard from Murabbaʿat, Milik, RN, sér. 6, 1 (1958), pp. 11–26.

31. See above, p. 322.

32. So Gutschmidt, *Kleine Schriften* IV, p. 116.

grandfather, *proavus*'.[33] Also, in the title of King Rabbel to be mentioned below—'who has given life and freedom to his people'—*'am* certainly means people. This Aretas may therefore confidently be identified with Aretas IV, for the inscriptions from el-Hegra mention the 48th year of his reign; in fact, some express the actual figure in words.[34] The coins similarly extend to the 48th year.[35] But only one Aretas, Aretas IV, can have reigned for so long. In consequence, the Aretas mentioned in the closing years of Herod the Great must be identical with the opponent of Herod Antipas. Inscriptions help to reconstruct more or less satisfactorily the composition of Aretas's family.[36]

Malichus II (Maliku), the son of Aretas and his first wife, succeeded his father in A.D. 40 and ruled until A.D. 70. He provided Vespasian with auxiliaries for the Jewish War in A.D. 67, *B.J.* iii 4, 2 (68), and is mentioned as 'King of the Nabataeans' in the *Periplus maris Erythraei* 19, ed. Frisk (1927), *Λευκὴ κώμη, δι' ἧς ἐστὶν εἰς Πέτραν πρὸς Μαλίχαν, βασιλέα Ναβαταίων* ⟨*ἀνάβασις*⟩ (cf. also A. Dihle, *Umschrittene Daten* (1965), pp. 9–35). An inscription at Salkhat in the Hauran is dated from 'the seventeenth year of Maliku King of the Nabataeans, son of Aretas IV'.[37] Epigraphic evidence extends as far as the 24th, possibly the 25th regnal year of Maliku.[38] There are also coins dated to the years 3–11, 15–17, 20, 22–3,[39] and now three fragments of a papyrus in Nabataean, dated by the 20th–29th years of Malichus.[40] According to CIS II 161, Rabbel II came to the throne in A.D. 70; Malichus II therefore ruled from A.D. 40–70. During his reign, Damascus, if ever under Nabataean control, seems to have been once more separated from that kingdom.

Malichus II was succeeded by his son, Rabbel, in A.D. 70.[41]

33. CIS II 214, 215. Cf. C. Clermont-Ganneau, *Recueil d'arch. orient.* II, pp. 372–6; J. T. Milik, Syria 35 (1958), p. 228.

34. E.g. CIS II, 209, line 9, the 'fortieth year'; CIS II, 212, line 9, the 'forty-fourth year. . .'.

35. *BMC Arabia*, p. xviii.

36. He had two, possibly even three, wives: Shakilat, Ḥalidu (and Hagiru?). Shakilat bore him six children: Maliku, Obodat, Rabbel, Phasael, Sa'udat and Hagiru. There are two more sons and a daughter. See G. Dalman, *Neue Petra-Forschungen*, pp. 106–7; C. Clermont-Ganneau, *Recueil* II, pp. 376–8. For a new inscription from Avdat (Oboda), mentioning Aretas's children 'Obodat and Phasael, see A. Negev, IEJ 11 (1961), pp. 127–8. On Aretas in general, see J. Starcky, 'Pétra', cols. 913–16; PIR² A 1033.

37. CIS II 182=Lidzbarski, *Handbuch*, p. 450, Taf. XXX, 1.

38. Year 24. Jaussen & Savignac, *Mission en Arabie*, no. 38; year 23, E. Littman, *Nabatean Inscriptions*, no. 23 (to be read instead of the '33' there suggested).

39. *BMC Arabia*, p. xix, 11. See now J. T. Milik, H. Seyrig, 'Trésor monétaire de Murabba'at', RN sér. 6, 1 (1958), pp. 11–26.

40. J. Starcky, 'Un contrat nabatéen sur papyrus', RB 61 (1954), pp. 161–81.

41. On the question whether there could have been another Nabataean king between Aretas IV and Malichus II, viz. the 'Abias, *ὁ Ἀράβων βασιλεύς*, mentioned

Rabbel II Soter (A.D. 70/1–106), is known through fairly numerous coins, inscriptions and papyri from his reign. The year of his accession to the throne can be determined quite precisely from the Dmeir inscription, which is dated to the month of Iyyar 'in the year 405 according to the Roman reckoning, that is, the 24th year of King Rabbel'.[42] The expression 'according to the Roman reckoning' designates the Seleucid era. Therefore the date is May A.D. 94, and the first year of Rabbel II, A.D. 70/1. Two inscriptions from el-Hegr allude to the second and fourth years of Rabbel,[43] an inscription from Salkhat in the Hauran refers to the twenty-fifth;[44] and two others from the Hauran give the twenty-third and twenty-sixth.[45] Papyrus documents from the Cave of Letters date to the twenty-third (A.D. 92), and twenty-eighth year (A.D. 97).[46] Since Rabbel II is mentioned on some of the coins with his mother, Shakilat (*škylt 'mh*),[47] he was probably still a minor at the time of accession. A 'Queen Shakilat' is also referred to on coins of Malichus II as the latter's 'sister' (*škylt 'ḥth mlkt nbṭw*); and an 'Oneisu, brother of Shakilat, Queen of the Nabataeans' (*'nysw 'ḥ sḳylt mlkt nbṭw*) appears on an inscription in Petra.[48] If the same Shakilat is meant throughout, it would follow that she was the sister-consort of Malichus II, that Rabbel was their son, and that Oneisu was not her brother in the real sense of the word but her *ἐπίτροπος*, as Clermont Ganneau perspicaciously remarked[49] on the basis of Strabo xvi 4, 21 (779) *ἔχει δ' ὁ βασιλεὺς ἐπίτροπον τῶν ἑταίρων τινὰ καλούμενον ἀδελφόν*. It may further be noted that Rabbel reigned later jointly with his wife, Gamilat (who also seems to have been his sister).[50]

In several inscriptions, Rabbel bears the title *dy 'ḥyy wšyzh 'mh*, i.e. 'who has given his people life and freedom', which appears to be a

---

by Josephus, *Ant.* xx 4, 1 (77 ff.), see J. Starcky, BA 18 (1955), p. 100. He thinks that the term 'Arabs' is used vaguely by Josephus in this passage. The Abias who unsuccessfully attacked Adiabene on the invitation of the subjects of Izates, was not a Nabataean king. Cf. also Dalman, *op. cit.*, pp. 100–6.

42. CIS II, 161.

43. CIS II, 224, 225. See further A. Negev, IEJ 13 (1963), pp. 113–17.

44. CIS II, 183.

45. Clermont-Ganneau, *Recueil* IV, pp. 170, 174.

46. IEJ 12 (1962), pp. 239–41; Jaarbericht 17 (1963), pp. 229–32.

47. Note the 11 *denarii* from Murabba'at with the effigies of the young king and his mother from years 1–4, RN sér. 6, 1 (1958), pp. 13, 20.

48. CIS II, 351. Cf. CIS II, 354.

49. Clermont-Ganneau, *Recueil* II, p. 380.

50. See RN sér. 6, 1 (1958), pp. 14, 20–2. A complication is caused here by one of the Nabataean documents from the Cave of Letters dated to the year 28 = A.D. 97. It is additionally dated as 'in the lifetime of Obodat, the son of Rabbel, the king . . . and of Gamilat and Hagira, his sisters, queens of the Nabataeans, children of Manichu (Malichus II) . . . the son of Ḥaretat (Aretas IV)? See Y. Yadin, IEJ 12 (1962), pp. 239–40; Jaarbericht 17 (1963), pp. 230–1; *Bar Kokhba* (1971), p. 235.

rendering of the Hellenistic Σωτήρ.[51] Mention of Rabbel in the inscription at Dmeir east of Damascus, on the road to Palmyra, confirms the spread of Nabataean influence into that region.

The latest inscription of Rabbel comes from his thirty-sixth year,[52] and therefore dates to immediately before the Roman conquest. This effectively excludes the theory that there was a later king Malichus III, which was postulated by Dussaud and Macler.[53] The suggestion of a Malichus III is rendered even more improbable by the document of A.D. 97 mentioning Rabbel's son Obodas.[54]

In A.D. 106, 'Arabia belonging to Petra' was made a Roman province by Cornelius Palma, governor of Syria, on the orders of Trajan.[55] In extent, it seems to have corresponded more or less to that of the former Nabataean kingdom.[56] The task seems to have been accomplished without a struggle, although no detailed information exists. Dio (lxviii 14, 5) reports that Cornelius Palma had to 'subdue' the territory in the vicinity of Petra, but archaeological evidence reveals no trace of destruction at this date.[57] There is also an inscription referring to the 'year of the War of the Nabataeans', but it is not clear that it alludes to the events of this year.[58] The event is also proclaimed by Trajan on coins bearing the inscription, 'Arab. adqu(isit.)'.[59] In any case, Petra in the south and Bostra in the north (in the Hauran district), both of which reckoned according to the provincial era of A.D. 106,[60] were the province's most important cities,[61] although

51. E.g., CIS II 184, 183; cf. J. T. Milik, 'Nouvelles inscriptions nabatéennes', Syria, 35 (1958), pp. 227–31, and A. Negev, IEJ 13 (1963), p. 115.

52. Jaussen & Savignac, *Mission*, no. 321.

53. Dussaud et Macler, *Voyage archéologique*, pp. 169–73. Cf. J. T. Milik, Syria 35 (1958), pp. 231–5, and J. Pirenne, *Le royaume sud-arabe de Qatabân et sa datation* (1961), pp. 185–93.

54. See n. 50 above.

55. Dio lxviii 14, 5, *κατὰ δὲ τὸν αὐτὸν τοῦτον χρόνον καὶ Πάλμας τῆς Συρίας ἄρχων τὴν Ἀραβίαν τὴν πρὸς τῇ Πέτρᾳ ἐχειρώσατο καὶ Ῥωμαίων ὑπήκοον ἐποιήσατο.* On A. Cornelius Palma Frontonianus, see PIR[2] C 1412.

56. Cf. Brünnow and Domaszewski, *Die Provincia Arabia* III, pp. 250 etc.

57. See A. Negev in IEJ 17 (1967), pp. 46–55, and PEQ 101 (1969), pp. 5–14.

58. See Bowersock, 'The Annexation . . .', p. 38.

59. See *BMC Roman Empire* III, pp. 608–9.

60. All doubts as to the precise year of the provincial era have been settled by Document 6 from the Cave of Letters, an Aramaic deed of gift which is dated, 'In the consulship of Lucius Catilius Severus for the second time and Marcus Aurelius Antoninus, in the third year of Imperator Caesar Traianus Hadrianus Augustus, and according to the era of this province, on the 24 Tammuz, year 15', i.e. July 13, A.D. 120. See Y. Yadin in IEJ 12 (1962), pp. 241–4; Jaarbericht 17 (1963), pp. 232–3; *Bar Kokhba*, p. 236. Cf. Bowersock, 'The Annexation . . .', p. 39.

61. *Chron. paschale* (ed. Dindorf I, 472): *Πετραῖοι καὶ Βοστρηνοὶ ἐντεῦθεν τοὺς ἑαυτῶν χρόνους ἀριθμοῦσι.* The *Chron. pasch.* has this note against the year A.D. 105. Cf. Brünnow and Domaszewski, *Die Provincia Arabia* III, p. 250.

Petra, it seems, was pre-eminent and ranked at first as the metropolis.[62] The further history of the province cannot be pursued here. But it should be mentioned that a few years after its establishment, Trajan built a great road, the via Traiana, running 'from the Syrian frontier to the Red Sea'.[63] Bostra was now called Nova Traiana Bostra, while Petra, after Hadrian's visit in A.D. 131, took the title *'Αδριανὴ Πέτρα*.[64] From the fourth century A.D. Arabia was divided into two provinces, *Arabia* with its capital at Bostra, and *Palaestina tertia* (or *Palaestina salutaris*) with Petra as chief city.[65]

62. For Petra as the metropolis see the Greek document in IEJ 12 (1962), p. 260, and Jaarbericht 17 (1963), pp. 234–5, issued in A.D. 124 *ἐν Πέτρᾳ μητροπόλει τῆς 'Αραβίας*. Cf. also Jaarbericht, pp. 237–8, the judgement seat of the governor at Petra, and *Bar Kokhba*, p. 240. But cf. Bowersock, 'A Report', pp. 231–2.

63. An inscription found on various milestones of A.D. 111 and 114, states that Trajan 'redacta in formam provinciae Arabia viam novam a finibus Syriae usque ad mare rubrum aperuit et stravit per C. Claudium Severum leg. Aug. pr. pr.' References in PIR² C 1023. Cf. Brünnow and Domaszewski, *Die Provincia Arabia* II, pp. 83–6; III, p. 287.

64. This title is now attested for June or July A.D. 131, on Document 24 (in Greek) from the Cave of Letters, Jaarbericht 17 (1963), p. 241.

65. Brünnow and Domaszewski, *op. cit.*, III, p. 277.

APPENDIX III

Principal Features of the Jewish Calendar

The Jewish and, according to Josephus, corresponding Macedonian months compare with the Julian calendar as follows:

1.	ניסן	Nisan	*Ξανθικός*	Mar./Apr.
2.	איר	Iyyar	*'Αρτεμίσιος*	Apr./May
3.	סיון	Sivan	*Δαίσιος*	May/June
4.	תמוז	Tammuz	*Πάνεμος*	June/July
5.	אב	Ab	*Λῷος*	July/Aug.
6.	אלול	Elul	*Γορπιαῖος*	Aug./Sept.
7.	תשרי	Tishri	*Ὑπερβερεταῖος*	Sept./Oct.
8.	מרחשון	Marḥeshvan	*Δῖος*	Oct./Nov.
9.	כסלו	Kislev	*'Απελλαῖος*	Nov./Dec.
10.	טבת	Ṭebeth	*Αὐδυναῖος*	Dec./Jan.
11.	שבט	Shebaṭ	*Περίτιος*	Jan./Feb.
12.	אדר	Adar	*Δύστρος*	Feb./Mar.

The Jewish names are of Assyro-Babylonian origin; their Akkadian equivalents are: ni-sa-an-nu, a-a-ru, sí-ma-nu, du-ú-zu, a–bu, ú–lu–lu, taš-ri-tú, a-ar-aḫ-sam-na, ki-si-li-mu, ṭe-bi-tum, ša-ba-ṭu, ad-da-ru; see B. Landsberger, *Materialen zum Sumerischen Lexicon* V (1957), pp. 25–6. Cf. in general, S. Langdon, *Babylonian Menologies and Semitic Calendars* (1935).

Within the sphere of Judaism, the earliest document listing all the months in succession is *Megillath Ta'anith*. It was compiled in the first or early second century A.D. since it is already quoted in the Mishnah (see p. 114 f. above). Of later authorities, it is necessary only to mention the little-known Christian, Josephus, who in his *Hypomnesticum* (PG cvi, col. 33) has *Νησάν*, *Εἴαρ*, *Σιουάν*, *Θαμούζ*, *"Αβ*, *'Ελούλ*, *'Οσρί* [read *Θισρί*], *Μαρσαβᾶν*, *Χασελεῦ*, *Τηβήθ*, *Σαβάθ*, *'Αδάρ*. For the individual names of the Jewish months, the earliest Hebrew evidence appears in the following passages:

1. *Nisan:* Neh. 2:1; Est. 3:7; mPes. 4:9; mShek. 3:1; mR.Sh. 1:1, 3, 4; mTaan. 1:2, 7; 4:5; mNed. 8:5; mBekh. 9:5. Greek *Νισάν* in Ezra 5:6; Ad. Est. 1:1; Jos. *Ant.* i 3, 3 (81), ii 14, 6 (311), iii 8, 4 (201), 10, 5 (248), xi 4, 8 (109).
2. *Iyyar:* mR.Sh. 1:3, *'Ιάρ* in Jos. *Ant.* viii 3, 1 (61).
3. *Sivan:* Est. 8:9; mShek. 3:1; mBekh. 9:5; *Σιουάν* in Bar. 1:8.

4. *Tammuz:* mTaan. 4:5–6.

5. *Ab:* mPes. 4:5; mShek. 3:1; mR.Sh. 1:3; mTaan. 2:10, 4:5–7; mMeg. 1:3; mBekh. 9:5. In Jos. *Ant.* iv 4, 7 (84), the reading Ἀββά (better Ἀβά) is merely a conjecture introduced by E. Bernard, but one that is fully justified. For the Σαβά adopted in accordance with the manuscripts by Niese cannot possibly have been written by Josephus.

6. *Elul:* Neh. 6:15; mShek. 3:1; mR.Sh. 1:1, 3; mTaan. 4:5; mBakh. 9:5, 6. Ἐλούλ in 1 Mac. 14:27.

7. *Tishri:* mShek. 3:1; mR.Sh. 1:1, 3–4; mBekh. 9:5–6. In Jos. *Ant.* viii 4, 1 (100), where editions since Hudson have Θισρί, Niese reads Ἀθύρει. But Hudson's reading, which is supported in particular by that of the Latin Josephus, is undoubtedly the correct one.

8. *Marḥeshvan:* mTaan. 1:3–4. Μαρσουάνης in Jos. *Ant.* 1:3, 3 (80).

9. *Kislev:* Zech. 7:1; Neh. 1:1; mR.Sh. 1:3; mTaan. 1:5. Χασελεῦ in 1 Mac. 1:54; 4:52; 2 Mac. 1:9, 18; 10:5; Jos. *Ant.* xii 5, 4 (248), 7, 6 (319).

10. *Tebeth:* Est. 2:16; mTaan. 4:5. Τεβέθος in Jos. *Ant.* xi 5, 4 (148).

11. *Shebaṭ:* Zech. 1:7; mR.Sh. 1:1. Σαβάτ in 1 Mac. 16:14.

12. *Adar:* is frequent in the Book of Esther; mShek. 1:1; 3:1; mR.Sh. 1:3; mMeg. 1:4; 3:4; mNed. 8:5; mEduy. 7:7; mBekh. 9:5. Ἀδάρ in 1 Mac. 7:43, 49; 2 Mac. 15:36. Jos. *Ant.* iv 8, 49 (327), xi 6, 2 (202), xii 10, 5 (412). *Adar ha-rishon* and *Adar ha-sheni* in mMeg. 1:4; mNed. 8:5.

The Jewish months have continued always to be what the 'months' of all civilised nations were by origin; namely, genuine lunar months. As the astronomical duration of a month is 29 days 12 hours 44′ 3″, months of 29 days must alternate fairly regularly with months of 30 days. But twelve lunar months amount to only 354 days 8 hours 48′ 38″, whereas the solar year comprises 365 days 5 hours 48′ 48″. The difference between a lunar year of twelve months and a solar year amounts, therefore, to 10 days 21 hours. To compensate for this difference, at least once in every third year, and sometimes in the second, one month must be intercalated. It was observed in very early times that a sufficiently accurate compensation was attained by intercalating a month three times in every eight years (during which period the difference amounts to 87 days). The quadrennial Greek games already depended on a recognition of this 8-year cycle ('octaeteris'), the 4-year cycle being arrived at simply by halving it.[1] But as early as the fifth century B.C., the astronomer Meton of Athens had drawn up a still more exact system of compensation in the form of a 19-year cycle in which a month was to be intercalated seven times.[2] This considerably

1. On the age of the 'octaeteris' cf. L. Ideler, *Handbuch der Chronologie* I, pp. 304 f.; II, p. 605; A. Boeckh, 'Zur Geschichte der Mondcyclen der Hellenen', Jahrb. f. class. Philol. 1. supp. (1855–6), pp. 9 ff.; A. Schmidt, *Handbuch der griechischen Chronologie* (1888), pp. 61–95. On the precursors of the 'octaeteris' see F. K. Ginzel, *Handbuch der math. u. techn. Chronologie* II (1911), pp. 370–3. Cf. RE s.v. 'Octaeteris'.

2. According to Diodorus xii 36, 2–3, Meton published his system in 433/32 B.C. Cf. also Theophrast. *de signis tempestatum* 1/4; Aelian. *Var. hist.* x 7; Ideler, *op. cit.* I, pp. 309 ff; cf. RE s.v. 'Meton' (2). Boeckh believed that the Metonic

excelled the 8-year cycle in accuracy because in nineteen years there remained only a difference of a little over two hours, whereas in eight years it was one of one and a half days. Of later astronomers who provided even more accurate computations, Hipparchus of Nicaea (*c.* 180–120 B.C.) deserves especial mention.[3] The fact that after every nineteen years the courses of the sun and moon coincide again almost exactly, was also well known to the Babylonians. In fact, cuneiform inscriptions have been thought to show that they regularly employed a nineteen-year intercalary cycle as far back as the time of Nabonassar, long before Meton therefore.[4] Even if this is not yet proved, the use of a nineteen-year intercalary period in the Persian and Seleucid eras may nevertheless be accepted as verified, though it is still not absolutely certain whether priority belongs to the Greeks or (as is probable) the Babylonians.[5] That the nineteen-year cycle was in use in the kingdom

---

cycle was introduced at Athens but not until some time later (according to Usener in 312 B.C., according to Unger between 346 and 325 B.C., see Philologus 39 (1880), pp. 475 ff. But it is now a matter of dispute as to whether it was ever in practical use in calculating intercalations. Cf. in general on the calendar of the Athenians, Mommsen, *Chronologie. Untersuchungen über den Kalenderwesen der Griechen, insonderheit der Athener* (1883); A. Schmidt, *Handbuch der griechischen Chronologie* (1888); W. S. Ferguson, *The Athenian Calendar* (1908); W. Kendrick Pritchett, O. Neugebauer, *The Calendars of Athens* (1947); B. D. Meritt, *The Athenian Year* (1961); W. Kendrick Pritchett, *Ancient Athenian Calendars on Stone* (1963); *idem, The Choiseul Marble* (1970).

3. Cf. L. Ideler, *op. cit.* I, pp. 352 ff.; F. K. Ginzel, *op. cit.* II (1911), pp. 390 f.; T. L. Heath, *A History of Greek Astronomy* (1932), pp. 142 ff.; G. Sarton, *A History of Science* II (1959), pp. 296–302.

4. Cf. E. Mahler, 'Der Schaltcyclus der Babylonier', ZA 9 (1894), pp. 42–61; *id.*, 'Zur Chronologie der Babylonier', AAB 62 (1895), pp. 641–4; *id.*, 'Der Saros-Kanon der Babylonier und der 19 jährige Schaltcyclus derselben', ZA 11 (1896), pp. 41–6; *id.*, 'Der Schaltcyklus der Babylonier', ZDMG 52 (1898), pp. 227–46; M. D. Sidersky, *Étude sur la chronologie assyro-babylonienne* (1916), pp. 25–40; R. A. Parker, W. H. Dubberstein, *Babylonian Chronology 626 B.C.–A.D. 75* (1956), p. 1. For a different view see F. X. Kugler, *Sternkunde und Sterndienst in Babel* II (1912), pp. 362–71, 422–30.

5. H. Martin, 'Mémoire ou se trouve restitué pour la première fois le calendrier lunisolaire chaldéo-macedonien dans lequel sont datées trois observations planetaires citées par Ptolémée', Rev. arch. 10 (1853), pp. 193–213, 257–67, 321–49, showed from three astronomical observations recorded in Ptolem. ix 7, and xi 7 for the years 67, 75 and 82 of the Seleucid era = 245, 237 and 229 B.C., that the calendar used by the Babylonians at that time was based upon the 19-year cycle, and indeed, as Martin assumed, in the improved form devised by Callippus (4th century B.C.) in which it was brought by the Macedonians to Babylonia. Forty years after Martin, and without having known of his predecessor, E. Meyer, 'Die chaldäische Aera des Almagest und der babylonische Kalender', ZA 9 (1894), pp. 325–9, again showed, from the same passages in Ptolemy, that the 19-year cycle had been used in Babylonia in the third century B.C. Cf. also J. Epping and J. N. Strassmaier, 'Der Saros-Canon der Babylonier', ZA 8 (1893), pp. 149–78; J. Oppert, 'Die Schaltmonate bei den Babyloniern',

of the Arsacids in the first century B.C. and A.D., has been shown by Th. Reinach from coins on which the years 287, 317 and 390 of the Seleucid era appear as intercalary years.[6]

How far had Jews of the inter-Testamental era advanced in these matters? They had some general knowledge of them, of course. But, unless we are altogether deceived, at the time of Jesus they still had no fixed calendar, but on the basis of purely empirical observation, began each new month with the appearance of the new moon, and similarly on the basis of observation, intercalated one month in the spring of the third or second year in accordance with the rule that in all circumstances Passover must fall after the vernal equinox.[7]

(1) The author of the astronomical portions of the *Book of Enoch* is aware that the year has six months of 30 days and six months of 29 days;[8] and Galen (second century A.D.) says that 'those in Palestine'

ZDMG 51 (1897), pp. 138–65 (who accepts that the 19-year cycle came from Greece to Babylonia in the 4th century B.C.); F. K. Ginzel, *Specieller Kanon der Sonnen- und Mondfinsternisse für das Ländergebiet der klassischen Alterthums-wissenschaften* (1899), pp. 235–43 (this section was revised by C. F. Lehmann); F. X. Kugler, *Die babylonische Mondrechnung* (1900), pp. 69 f., 210 f.; F. H. Weissbach, 'Ueber einige neuere Arbeiten zur babylonisch-persischen Chronologie', ZDMG 55 (1901), pp. 195–220 (against Mahler); F. K. Ginzel, 'Die astronomischen Kenntnisse der Babylonier' in *Beiträge zur alter Geschichte*, ed. C. F. Lehmann, I (1901), pp. 1–25, 189–211 (shows on pp. 201 f., following Kugler, that already some time before Hipparchus, the Babylonians determined the period of the moon's revolution as exactly as he did; namely, at 29 days 12 hrs. 44′ 3⅓″).

For later work see F. X. Kugler, *Sternkunde und Sterndienst in Babel* I–II (1907–24); R. A. Parker, W. H. Dubberstein, *Babylonian Chronology 625 B.C.–A.D. 75* (1956), taking 382 as the starting-point of the 19-year cycle. O. Neugebauer, 'The Metonic Cycle in Babylonian Astronomy', *Studies and Essays . . . in Honor of G. Sarton* (1946), pp. 435–48, argued that the use of the 19-year cycle in Babylonia can be traced back to 480 B.C. Parker and Dubberstein, *op. cit.*, p. 1, note considerable regularity in intercalation back to 747 B.C.

6. Th. Reinach, 'Le calendrier des Grecs de Babylonie et les origines du calendrier juif', REJ 18 (1889), pp. 90–4. Reinach here assumed as a matter of course that the 19-year intercalary cycle originated in Greece.

7. Wieseler championed the view that the Jews already had a fixed calendar at the time of Christ, *Chronologische Synopse*, pp. 437 ff. (E.T., pp. 401–33); *Beiträge zur richtigen Würdigung der Evangelien*, pp. 290 ff.). The correct view is given e.g. in Ideler, *op. cit.* I, pp. 512 ff.; Ginzel, *op. cit.* II (1911), pp. 67 ff.; G. Ogg, *Chronology of the Public Ministry of Jesus* (1940), pp. 262 ff.; E. J. Bickerman, *Chronology of the Ancient World* (1968), pp. 24–6.

8. *1 Enoch* 78:15–16, trans. R. H. Charles, 'And three months she makes of thirty days, and at her time she makes three months of twenty-nine days each, in which she accomplishes her waning in the first period of time, and in the first portal for one hundred and seventy-seven days. And in the time of her going out she appears for three months (of) thirty days each and for three months she appears (of) twenty-nine each.' On the Astronomic Book of Enoch (1 En. 72–82) in the light of the Qumran material, see J. T. Milik, HThR 64 (1971), pp. 338–43.

divide the time of every two months amounting to 59 days into two unequal halves, reckoning 30 days to the one month, and 29 days to the other.[9] It would, however, be a mistake to conclude that, except in some particular Jewish circles, the duration of the month was fixed in advance. This cannot yet have been the case even in the time of the Mishnah (*c.* A.D. 200). For the entire legislation of the Mishnah rests on the presupposition that, without any previous reckoning, each new month began when the new moon became visible. As soon as the new moon's appearance was confirmed by trustworthy witnesses before the competent court in Jerusalem (later in Jamnia), it was 'sanctified', and messengers were sent out in all directions to announce the opening of the new month (thus at least in the six months in which this announcement was of importance because of a festival: in Nisan because of Passover; in Ab because of the Fast; in Elul because of the New Year; in Tishri because of the arrangement of its festival days, namely, the Day of Atonement and Tabernacles; in Kislev because of the Feast of the Dedication of the Temple; in Adar because of Purim; and while the Temple stood, in Iyyar because of the Little Passover).[10] As it was obviously known with a fair degree of accuracy when the new moon was to be expected, every effort will have been made to fix it on the correct day. But the duration of each individual month was not fixed. This is confirmed by the following two passages in the Mishnah: (1) mErub. 3:7; 'If before the New Year a man feared that [the month Elul] might be intercalated . . .';[11] (2) mArak. 2:2, 'In a year there are never less than four 'full' months [of thirty days], nor do more than eight months require to be considered.' The first passage discloses that it was by no means determined in advance whether a month was to have 29 or 30 days. And the second passage shows how uncertain the calendar was under this empirical system: even in the age of the Mishnah (second century A.D.) it was considered possible that there might be years in which there were only four months of thirty days, and again others in which there were eight such months (i.e. that the

9. Galen, *Opp.* ed. Kuhn, XVII, p. 23 *τοὺς δύο μῆνας ἡμερῶν γινομένους θ' καὶ ν' τέμνουσιν εἰς ἄνισα μέρη, τὸν μὲν ἕτερον αὐτῶν λθ' ἡμερῶν ἐργαζόμενοι, τὸν δ' ἕτερον θ' καὶ κ'.*

10. Cf. mR.Sh. 1:3 ff.; 2:1–9; 3:1; 4:4. Also see especially B. Zuckermann, *Materialien zur Entwickelung der altjüdischen Zeitrechnung im Talmud* (1882), pp. 1–39. According to mSanh. 1:2 (cf. mR.Sh. 2:9, 3:1) a tribunal of three was sufficient for the declaration of a new moon and an intercalary year, which does not, however, mean that it was as a rule carried out in this way. On intercalation in general see J. B. Segal, 'Intercalation and the Hebrew Calendar', VT 7 (1957), pp. 250–307; E. J. Wiesenberg, 'Calendar', Enc. Jud. V, cols. 43–50.

11. It is clear from mSheb. 10:2 that the later rule according to which Elul must always have 29 days, did not exist at that time.

lunar year might extend from 352 to 356 days, whereas in fact it lasts from 354 to 355 days).[12]

(2) The system of intercalation was still not fixed in the second century A.D. It is true that Julius Africanus says that the Jews, like the Greeks, intercalated three months every eight years;[13] and there is no reason to doubt this statement respecting his own time (the first half of the third century A.D.) even though it is inexact in regard to the Greeks, the majority of whom had long since adopted the more accurate nineteen-year cycle.[14] It is also generally valid for the time of Jesus, because even with the purely empirical method, the three intercalations during the course of eight years is a result that emerges of itself. Nevertheless, knowledge of this eight-year cycle in the astronomical section of the *Book of Enoch* and the *Book of Jubilees* is still extremely vague; and it was not yet adapted to a fixed intercalary system. In the *Book of Enoch*, the erroneous view is expressed that in eight years, the moon is only about eighty days behind the sun, the lunar year being put at 354 days and the solar year at 364 days (*Enoch* 74:16; see in general chs. 72–82). The same inexact statements appear also in ch. 6 of the *Book of Jubilees* (Charles, *Apocr. and Pseudep.* II, pp. 21–3).[15] A calendar constructed on these suppositions would very

12. In the context of the passage cited (mArak. 2:2), possible minimum and maximum limits are given with regard to the most varied things. The above-mentioned oscillation in the length of the year was therefore actually observed, and in the time of the Mishnah was still regarded as possible. As a matter of fact, the statement appeared so remarkable to the authorities of the Babylonian Talmud that attempts were made to give it a new interpretation, see bArak. 8b–9a; Zuckermann, *Materialien*, pp. 64 f.

13. Julius Africanus, in Euseb. *Demonstr. evang.* viii 2, 54 = Syncellus, ed. Dindorf I, p. 611 = M. J. Routh, *Reliquiae Sacrae* II, p. 302, Ἕλληνες καὶ Ἰουδαῖοι τρεῖς μῆνας ἐμβολίμους ἔτεσιν ὀκτὼ παρεμβάλλουσιν, cf. Jerome, *in Daniel.* III, 9:24 (CCL lxxvA, p. 868).

14. By the Ἕλληνες Julius Africanus probably means the Syro-Macedonians. See G. F. Unger, SAM (1893) II, p. 467.

15. On the calendar of the *Book of Jubilees* cf. R. H. Charles, *The Book of Jubilees* (1902) pp. lxvii f., 54–7. Since the Qumran sect used the same calendar reckoning as *Jubilees*, the question has recently received much attention; A. Jaubert, 'Le calendrier des Jubilés et la secte de Qumrân. Ses origines bibliques', VT 3 (1953), pp. 250 ff.; J. Morgenstern, 'The calendar of the Book of Jubilees, its origin and its character', VT 5 (1935), pp. 37 ff.; A. Jaubert, 'Le calendrier des Jubilés et les jours liturgiques de la semaine', VT 7 (1957), pp. 35 ff.; E. R. Leach, 'A Possible Method of Intercalation for the Calendar of the Book of Jubilees', VT 7 (1957), pp. 392 ff.; J. M. Baumgarten, 'The Beginning of the day in the Calendar of Jubilees', JBL 77 (1958), pp. 355 ff.; J. van Goudoever, *Biblical Calendars* ([2]1961), pp. 62 ff.; J. T. Milik, *Ten Years of Discovery in the Wilderness of Judaea* (1959), pp. 107–13; H. Cazelles, 'Sur les origines du calendrier des Jubilés', Biblica 43 (1962), pp. 202–12; J. Finegan, *Handbook of Biblical Chronology* (1964), pp. 49 ff.; J. Meysing, 'L'énigme de la chronologie biblique et qumrânienne dans une nouvelle lumière', RQ 6 (1967–9), pp. 229–51.

soon have given rise to utter confusion.[16] It was fortunate then that it was dispensed with, and that intercalation was carried out as the need arose, on the basis of an empirical observation made on each occasion without any advance calculation. The following two passages demonstrate that this was still the case in the time of the Mishnah: (1) mMeg. 1:4, 'If the Megillah (the Scroll of Esther) has been read in the First Adar, and the year is intercalated, it must be read again in the Second Adar'; (2) mEduy. 7:7, '[R. Joshua and R. Papias] testified that the year may be declared a leap-year at any time during Adar; for previously this could be done only until Purim. They testified that the year may be declared a leap-year conditionally. Once when Rabban Gamaliel had gone on a journey to obtain authority from the governor of Syria, and he was long absent, the year was declared a leap-year on condition that Rabban Gamaliel approved. And when he returned, he said, "I approve"; and so it was a leap-year.' The two passages are so clear that they require no further commentary. It could be decided even at the end of the year, in the month of Adar; after the feast of Purim had been celebrated, whether a month should be intercalated or not. There was absolutely no calculation in advance.[17]

The rule according to which it was decided whether to intercalate or not was very simple: the feast of Passover, to be celebrated at full moon in the month of Nisan (14 Nisan), must always fall after the vernal equinox (μετὰ ἰσημερίαν ἐαρινήν) when the sun stood in the sign of *Aries*. Anatolius, in a fragment of great importance for the history of the Jewish calendar preserved in Eusebius, *HE* vii 32, 16–19, characterizes this as the unanimous view of all the Jewish authorities, and above all of Aristobulus, the famous Jewish philosopher of the time of Ptolemy Philometor (not Philadelphus, as Anatolius erroneously says). The statements of Philo and Josephus also accord with it.[18] If, therefore, it was noticed towards the end of the year that Passover would fall before the vernal equinox, the intercalation of a month before Nisan was decreed.[19] The intercalated month was given the same

16. The statements in the later *Slavonic Book of Enoch* (in English, R. H. Charles, *The Book of the Secrets of Enoch*) 14:1; 15:4; 16 and 18 are more correct. For an attempted reconciliation of the solar and lunar calendars in 4 Q *Mishmaroth*, cf. Milik, *op. cit.*, p. 41.

17. Everything said in tSanh. 2, bSanh. 11a–12a, and elsewhere, concerning the reasons for, and procedure of, intercalation, serves to confirm this. It is assumed throughout that the decision to make an intercalation, or not, is to be taken every time during the course of the year and in accordance with the principles stated. See n. 19 below.

18. Philo, *de spec. leg.* II 19; *Quaest. et solut. in Exodum* 1. 1 (Eng. trans. of Armenian in Loeb ed., Supp. II). Cf. also *Vita Mosis* II, 41 (221–4). Jos. *Ant.* iii 10, 5 (248) ἐν κριῷ τοῦ ἡλίου καθεστῶτος.

19. On other reasons for intercalation see especially tSanh. 2, bSanh. 11a–12a; B. Zuckermann, *Materialien zur Entwickelung der altjüdischen Zeitrechnung im*

name as the last month of the year, Adar. A distinction was then made between אדר הראשון and אדר השני (first and second Adar).

Primitive as this calendar is, its great advantage was that it avoided the serious and permanent inaccuracies that necessarily appear in the course of the years in a calendar based on inexact calculation. Nevertheless, it is remarkable that the purely empirical procedure survived so long when the Greeks and the Babylonians (the Egyptians with their solar year are not involved here) had for centuries possessed a fixed calendar based on accurate computation. Only the association of the calendar with the religious cult, and the stubborn opposition of the cult to all scientific reforms, make such a state of affairs comprehensible. But in the end, scientific understanding made its impact here too, and did so from Babylon. The Babylonians, Mar Samuel in Nehardea and Rabbi Adda bar Ahaba in Sura, both from the third century A.D., are named as rabbis who made a particularly important contribution to the calendar system. The latter was accurately acquainted with the nineteen-year cycle in the improved form given it by Hipparchus. The introduction into Palestine of a calendar based on it is to be ascribed to the patriarch Hillel in the first half of the fourth century A.D.[20]

On the different year beginnings (spring and autumn) see pp. 126 ff. above.

The literature on the Jewish calendar, particularly in its later development, is very comprehensive. On a controversy in the tenth century between Ben Meir in Palestine and Saadia in Babylonia see S. Poznański, JQR 10 (1898), pp. 152–61; A. Epstein, REJ 42 (1901), pp. 173–210. A systematic exposition was presented as early as the twelfth century by Maimonides in the section on the 'sanctification of the new moon' in his great work, *Yad Ha-Ḥazaḳah* or *Mishneh Torah*. See *The Code of Maimonides, Book Three, Treatise Eight, Sanctification of the*

Talmud (1882), pp. 39–45. The most noteworthy statements are the following: 'A year may be intercalated on three grounds: on account of the premature state of the corn-crops; or that of the fruit trees; or on account of the lateness of the *Teḳufah* (vernal equinox). Any two of these can justify intercalation, but not one alone' (bSanh. 11b). 'The year may not be intercalated on the ground that the kids or the lambs or the doves are too young. But we consider each of these circumstances as an auxiliary reason for intercalation' (bSanh. 11a). An excerpt from a letter by Rabban Gamaliel to the communities in Babylonia and Media reads: 'We beg to inform you that the doves are still too tender and the lambs still too young and that the crops are not yet ripe. It seems advisable to me and to my colleagues to add thirty days to this year' (bSanh. 11b).

20. See Ideler, *op. cit.* I, pp. 573 ff., also Ginzel's account of later discussion of this matter (*op. cit.* II, pp. 70 ff.). Since Julius Africanus says that in eight years the Jews intercalated three months (see n. 13 above), they cannot yet have had (in the beginning of the third century A.D.) a calendar based on the 19–year cycle. On the Patriarch's privilege concerning the fixing of the calendar, cf. H. Mantel, *Studies in the History of the Sanhedrin* (1961), pp. 179–87.

New Moon, astron. com. by O. Neugebauer (1956). Cf. Ideler, *op. cit.* I (1825), pp. 477–583; Wieseler, *Chronologische Synopse* (1843), pp. 437–84, E.T., 1864, pp. 401–33; *id.*, *Beiträge zur richtigen Würdigung der Evangelien und der evangelischen Geschichte* (1869), pp. 290–321; B. Zuckermann, *Materialien zur Entwickelung der altjüdischen Zeitrechnung im Talmud* (1882); L. Loeb, *Tables du calendrier juif depuis l'ère chrétienne jusqu'au XXXe siècle, avec la concordance des dates juives et des dates chrétiennes et une méthode nouvelle pour calculer ces tables* (1886); E. Mahler, *Chronologische Vergleichungs-Tabellen, nebst einer Anleitung zu den Grundzügen der Chronologie, 2. Die Zeit- und Festrechnung der Juden* (1889); B. M. Lersch, *Einleitung in die Chronologie* I (1899), pp. 193–205; S. B. Burnaby, *Elements of the Jewish and Muhammedan Calendars* (1901); J. Bach, *Zeit- u. Festrechnung der Juden* (1908); F. K. Ginzel, *op. cit.* II (1911), pp. 1–119; E. Mahler, *Handbuch der jüdischen Chronologie* (1916); J. van Goedoever, *Biblical Calendars* ([2]1961); J. Finegan, *Handbook of Biblical Chronology* (1964), pp. 40–4. Cf. also R. de Vaux, *Ancient Israel* (1961), pp. 178–93; JE s.v. 'Calendar' III, pp. 498–505; Enc. Jud. V, cols. 43–50.

The Jewish year having sometimes twelve, and sometimes thirteen months, they correspond of course only approximately to the twelve months of the Julian calendar. The Macedonian names were adopted in Syria from the beginning of Seleucid dominion. They were employed in three different ways: (1) to designate real lunar months; for it seems that a lunar year based on the eight-year cycle existed in Syria too, until well into Christian times;[21] (2) to designate the twelve months of a solar year identical, generally speaking, with the Julian, the individual months of which do not, nevertheless, correspond exactly with those of the Julian calendar because the beginnings are fixed differently, and indeed vary from one large city to another. For example, in Tyre the year began on 18 November, in Gaza and Ascalon, on 29 August (Bickermann, *Chronology*, p. 50); (3) the Julian months were later simply called by the Macedonian names (Ideler, *op. cit.* I,

21. The details are of no concern in this connexion and cannot in any case be traced with certainty. From the statement of Julius Africanus cited in n. 13 above, it appears that in his time the lunar year based on the 8-year cycle was still prevalent among the Ἕλληνες in Syria. On the other hand, the basic source of the *Apostolic Constitutions*, which probably originated in Syria in the third century A.D., already reckons according to the Julian calendar, except that it begins the year in the spring (*Const. Apost.* v 17, 3: the vernal equinox falls on the 22nd of the twelfth month, i.e. Dystrus; v 13, 1: the birth of the Lord on the 25th of the ninth month). See F. X. Funk, *Didascalia et Constitutiones Apostolorum* (1905), pp. 289, 269. The great cities along the Philistine-Phoenician coast (Gaza, Ashkelon, Tyre, and Sidon) seem, as a result of their proximity to Egypt, to have been the first to accept a solar year related to the Julian, in that the Alexandrian calendar was variously modified there.

pp. 429 ff.). In addition to the Macedonian names, the native Syrian names (many of which were identical with the Jewish) were also used; and it may safely be assumed that their employment was always in conformity with that of the Macedonian names. Thus, for example, the Syrian date on Palmyrene inscriptions corresponds exactly to the Macedonian (24 Tebeth = 24 Audynaeus, 21 Adar = 21 Dystrus), see de Vogüé, *Inscriptions* n. 123a, 111, 124 = Le Bas and Waddington, *Inscriptions grecques et latines* III, 2, n. 2571b, 2627; OGIS 629 [22]. This is also the case in the later Syriac calendar, where both Syriac and Macedonian names simply designate the months of the Julian calendar.[23]

In these circumstances it is not self-evident what Josephus has in mind when, as he frequently does, especially in his *Bellum*, he makes use of the Macedonian names of the months. In general, he places them exactly parallel to the Jewish names, in the same way as on the Palmyrene inscriptions (Nisan = Xanthicus, Iyyar = Artemisius, Ab = Lous, Tishri = Hyperberetaeus, Marḥeshvan = Dius, etc.; for evidence of this see p. 588 above, and on the Palmyrene inscriptions, see the evidence in Le Bas and Waddington n. 2571b). But does he mean simply the Jewish months when he uses the Macedonian names? In many instances, undoubtedly. (1) The Jewish Passover was celebrated on 14 Xanthicus, *Ant.* iii 10, 5 (248); *B.J.* v 3, 1 (98); 13, 7 (567). (2) In the time of Antiochus Epiphanes, the Temple was desecrated and reconsecrated on 25 Apellaeus, *Ant.* xii 5, 4 (248); 7, 6 (319), cf. 1 Mac. 1:59; 4:52. (3) During the siege by Titus, the daily morning and evening sacrifice was discontinued on 17 Panemus, *B.J.* vi 2, 1 (94); according to mTaan. 4:6, this took place on 17 Tammuz. (4) The destruction of the Temple by Nebuchadnezzar took place on 10 Lous, *B.J.* vi 4, 5 (250); according to Jer. 52:12, on 10 Ab. (5) The festival of the yearly offering of wood for the altar of burnt offering (on this see vol. II, § 24) fell, according to *B.J.* ii 17, 6 (425) *τῆς τῶν ξυλοφορίων ἑορτῆς οὔσης*, cf. ii 17, 7 (430) *τῇ δ' ἑξῆς, πεντεκαιδεκάτη δ' ἦν Λώου μηνός*, on 14 Lous; according to rabbinical sources, on 15 Ab (Meg. Taan. § 11, ed. Lichtenstein, HUCA 8–9 (1931–2), p. 319; mTaan. 4:5, 8). In spite of the difference of a day, the two dates are to be regarded as equivalent, Josephus having included the preceding evening in the festival. In view of these facts, scholars ancient and modern have assumed that when he uses the Macedonian names of the months, Josephus always means the

22. Nöldeke, ZDMG 39 (1885), p. 339, doubted that this was the case in the Palmyrene inscriptions. Cf. however J.-B. Chabot, *Choix d'inscriptions de Palmyre* (1922), p. 13, and the Palmyrene and Greek inscriptions in *Excavations at Dura-Europos, Seventh and Eight Seasons* (1939), pp. 307–9.

23. See now L. Bernhard, *Die Chronologie der Syrer*, OAW Ph.-hist. Kl. S-B. 264, 3 (1969), pp. 64–7.

corresponding Jewish months.[24] But O. A. Hoffmann, following the example of Scaliger, Baronius and Usher, raised objections against this view.[25] He emphasized above all that Josephus was hardly in a position (and if he had been, would certainly not have bothered) to convert to the Jewish calendar dates transmitted to him in another calendar. He simply followed the calendar used by his sources. Hoffmann believed, however, that the source for the numerous dates in the *Bellum* must have been the official documents kept in the Roman camp itself. It may therefore be assumed that they were given according to the Julian calendar, the months of which Josephus designated only by their Macedonian names. The basis of this theory is not unreasonable. A writer such as Josephus does not put himself to the trouble of converting dates, but gives them as they are transmitted. One should therefore not take for granted that he uses the same calendar for all his dates. Many are doubtless given according to the Jewish, others according to the Roman calendar.[26] But whether the main body of the dates in *B.J.* goes back to Roman military documents, seems more than doubtful. It is not correct, as Hoffmann maintains, that Josephus provides definite dates almost exclusively for Roman enterprises, but not for Jewish internal affairs. A consideration of the passages referred to in the present study (§ 20) shows that many of them relate to Jewish internal events, whilst on the other hand, more accurate statements concerning the Romans increase from the time when, as a prisoner of war and later as a freedman, Josephus was himself in the Roman camp. He thus had a personal knowledge of these matters. Indeed in vindicat-

24. So Ideler, *op. cit.*, I, pp. 400–2; Wieseler, *Chronol. Synopse*, p. 448 [E.T., p. 408]; Unger, 'Die Tagdata des Josephos', SAM (1893) II, pp. 453–492; Ginzel, *Chronologie* II, pp. 68 f.

25. O. A. Hoffmann, *De imperatoris Titi temporibus recte definiendis* (1883), pp. 4–17.

26. Josephus obviously uses the Roman calendar for, e.g., the regnal periods of the emperors Galba, Otho and Vitellius. The dates concerned are: Nero died on 9 June A.D. 68, Galba on 15 January A.D. 69, Otho on 16 April A.D. 69, Vitellius on 20 December A.D. 69. But according to Josephus, Galba reigned 7 months 7 days, *B.J.* iv 9, 2 (499), Otho 3 months 2 days, *B.J.* iv 9, 9 (548), Vitellius 8 months 5 days, *B.J.* iv 11, 4 (652). If the day of the accession and the day of death are included in the reckoning, it agrees exactly with the above dates of the Julian calendar, which therefore Josephus follows here. The day of Vitellius's death appears to be given according to the calendar of Tyre. Whereas in the Julian calendar it falls on 20 December, Josephus dates it to 3 Apellaeus, *B.J.* iv 11, 4 (654). But this in the Tyrian calendar corresponds to 20 December in the Julian. So possibly Josephus is following a Phoenician source here. Cf. Ideler I, p. 436; O. A. Hoffmann, *op. cit.*, p. 6; Niese, Hermes 28 (1893), p. 203. The correctness of this view was contested by Unger, who in *op. cit.*, pp. 456–65 attempted to show that Vitellius's death fell not on 20, but on 21 December, and that there is a corruption of the numeral in Josephus B.J. iv 11, 4 (654) (pp. 491 f.).

ing the credibility of his exposition he appeals exclusively to the records which he himself made during the occurrences, and not to Roman official documents, *c. Ap.* i 9 (49) *τὰ κατὰ τὸ στρατόπεδον τὸ Ῥωμαίων ὁρῶν ἐπιμελῶς ἀνέγραφον*. He therefore obviously did not use them. But the argument that he made his records according to the Jewish calendar derives its support, partly from the inherent probability of such a thing, and from the fact that some of the dates are undoubtedly given according to the Jewish calendar; thus *B.J.* vi 2, 1 (94) (see p. 505 above) and *B.J.* vi 4, 1–5 (220–53) (see p. 506 above). The frequent formula, *Πανέμου νουμηνίᾳ*, *B.J.* iii 7, 36 (339); v 13, 7 (567); vi 1, 3 (23), cannot, of course, be urged as proof that the months of Josephus actually began with the new moon. For in later usage, *νουμηνία* usually signifies the first day of the month, even when, according to the calendar concerned, the months did not begin with the new moon, as e.g. in the Roman calendar. Cf. Dio lx 5, 3 *τῇ τοῦ Αὐγούστου νουμηνίᾳ*, Plut., *Galba* 22 *ἡ νουμηνία τοῦ πρώτου μηνός, ἣν καλάνδας Ἰανουαρίας καλοῦσι*. Cf. Stephanus, *Thes.*, s.v. Analogous to the view of O. A. Hoffmann were those of Schlatter and Niese. Schlatter[27] was of the opinion that, with few exceptions, the dates in *B.J.* are given according to the Roman (Julian) calendar; and saw in this confirmation of the belief that, in the main, the *Bellum* is really a work of Antonius Julianus (see p. 34 above). Niese[28] also recognized that particular dates are given according to the Julian calendar but believed that he had 'sufficiently shown that the calendar used by Josephus was the same as the Tyrian' (*op. cit.*, p. 204). It would not matter that this was also in use in Jerusalem and Judaea; the old lunar months were retained only for the determination of the feasts, just as the Jews still preserve this calendar side by side with the civil one (*op. cit.*, p. 207). This view of Niese—that in civil life the Jews used the Tyrian calendar, i.e. a reckoning according to the solar year, whilst retaining a reckoning according to lunar months for religious festivals—is in such sharp contradiction to all that is known of the history of the Jewish calendar that it must simply be described as impossible. There was, of course, a distinction between the civil and the sacred year; but it consisted merely in the commencement of the one in the autumn and the other in the spring; the months were the same (see pp. 18 ff. above). Apart from the isolated note regarding the death of Vitellius, which seems indeed to be given according to the Tyrian calendar (see n. 26), Niese adduced only one noteworthy ground for the view that Josephus in his statements in the *Bellum* reckoned according to the solar year: namely, the remarks concerning the duration of the siege of Jotapata. But from the account

27. A. Schlatter, *Zur Topographie und Geschichte Palästinas* (1893), pp. 360–7.

28. B. Niese, 'Ueber den von Josephus im *bellum Judaicum* benützten Kalendar', Hermes 28 (1893), pp. 197–208.

given on p. 493, this does not hold water either. Nor are Schlatter's calculations in the least conclusive vis-à-vis the other arguments.[29] If it is certain that Josephus reckons in several instances according to the Jewish calendar, this must also be regarded as holding good for those in which the contrary cannot be proved; and that means most of them. It is highly probable, therefore, that the majority of the dates in the *Bellum* are given according to the Jewish calendar.

Niese's contention that the Jews used the Tyrian calendar is resumed by E. Schwartz in section ix of his important article 'Christliche u. jüdische Ostertafeln'.[30] (1) He finds the argument confirmed by the fact that Josephus equates the Hebrew, or more correctly Aramaic, names of the months with the Macedonian. (2) He maintains that the dates given for certain events in the *Megillath Taanith* agree with those given for them in the *Bellum*, provided it is assumed that the latter are according to the Tyrian calendar. (3) He maintains further that as regards the dates of Passover which Josephus gives for the period A.D. 66–70, there is no indication whatsoever that he borrowed them from a calendar other than the one by which he dates the events of the Jewish war, and that some of them are irreconcilable with the assumption that his reckoning was according to lunar months. But in the judgement of Ginzel, *op. cit.* II (1911), pp. 69 f., Schwartz's conclusion that the great mass of the Jewish people used the Tyrian calendar is 'too sweeping'. Particular cities may for certain purposes have found themselves obliged to resort to a calendar based on the solar year, but there is ample evidence that such a calendar was not used by the Jews generally in the first century A.D.

There is general agreement among authorities on the Dead Sea Scrolls that the Qumran community deprecated the use of the luni-solar calendar described above, and adopted a calendar very similar to, and probably identical with, the one figuring in the *Book of Jubilees*, and

29. Schlatter (*op. cit.*, pp. 360–1) attempts to point out three occasions on which Josephus assumes months of 31 days. (1) According to *B.J.* ii 19, 4 (528), Cestius Gallus began the assault on Jerusalem on 30 Hyperberetaeus; according to ii 19, 9 (555), he was decisively defeated when retreating on 8 Daisius. In between, appear the following dates (535) πέντε . . . ἡμέραις . . . τῇ δ' ἐπιούσῃ, (542) τῇ δ' ἐπιούσῃ, (545) τῇ τρίτῃ. Schlatter counts ten days between the two events, which result emerges only if Hyperberetaeus has 31 days. But as regards τῇ τρίτῃ, the preceding τῇ ἐπιούσῃ is probably included in it, in which case there are only nine days, and Hyperberetaeus needs only 30 days. (2) Schlatter derives his second proof from the dates of the siege of Jotapata (see *op. cit.*, p. 361). (3) The assault on the final wall of Jerusalem began, according to *B.J.* vi 8, 1 (374), on 20 Lous, and the ramparts were ready on 7 Gorpiaeus, after eighteen days' labour, *B.J.* vi 8, 4 (392). If Schlatter requires 31 days here for Lous, this rests only on a mistaken calculation; for 20 Lous to 30 Lous amounts to 11 days (the first and last days being included), and 11 plus 7 makes 18.

30. In AGGW, N.F. 8 (1905), pp. 138 ff.

known also to the compilers of the *Book of Enoch* and the *Testaments of the XII Patriarchs.*

Mlle A. Jaubert has subjected to a thorough analysis the principles underlying the calendar of the *Book of Jubilees,* and pointed out its connexion with the solar calendar used in the priestly traditions of the Bible and with the antique pentecontad calendar of the Western Semites.[31] Her reconstruction of it is based for the most part upon statements in the book itself, particularly in *Jub.* 6:23–38. The year consisted of 364 days, i.e. 52 weeks exactly. In consequence, it always began on the same day of the week, Wednesday. The year had four seasons of equal length, each therefore of 13 weeks=91 days. They also began on a Wednesday.[32] Each season contained three months, each of 30 days' duration to which was added an intercalary day. These details permit the following tabulation:

Months	Sun.	Mon.	Tue.	Days Wed.	Thu.	Fri.	Sat.
I. IV. VII. X.				1	2	3	4
	5	6	7	8	9	10	11
	12	13	14	15	16	17	18
	19	20	21	22	23	24	25
	26	27	28	29	30		
II. V. VIII. XI.						1	2
	3	4	5	6	7	8	9
	10	11	12	13	14	15	16
	17	18	19	20	21	22	23
	24	25	26	27	28	29	30
III. VI. IX. XII.							
	1	2	3	4	5	6	7
	8	9	10	11	12	13	14
	15	16	17	18	19	20	21
	22	23	24	25	26	27	28
	29	30	31				

A noteworthy feature of this calendar is that a festival determined by its date fell every year on the same day of the week; e.g. Passover,

31. See *La date de la Cène* (1957), pp. 30–59. The pentecontad calendar divides the year into seven periods of seven weeks (7×7=49 days) followed by a fiftieth or pentecontad festival day. It has left traces in Mesopotamia and in the Bible, as well as in later Jewish and Christian texts. Cf. J. and H. Lewy, 'The Origin of the Week in the Oldest West Asiatic Calendar', HUCA 17 (1942–3), pp. 1–152; J. Morgenstern, 'The Calendar of the Book of Jubilees', VT 5 (1955), pp. 37–61; *Some Significant Antecedents of Christianity* (1966), pp. 20–31.

32. The opening festal day of each season is designated as 'the day of Remembrance' (Jub. 6:23); the four seasons figure in the Dead Sea Scrolls as 'season of harvest', 'season of summer fruits', 'season of sowing' and 'season of grass' (1QSer. 10:7).

which had to be celebrated on the 15th day of the first month (Exod. 12:6), was always kept on a Wednesday; the Day of Atonement, the 10th day of the seventh month, on a Friday; and the Feast of Tabernacles, the 15th day in the same month, on a Wednesday.[33]

33. In regard to the Qumran calendar see, in addition to the works listed in n. 15 above, J. Oberman, 'Calendric Elements in the Dead Sea Scrolls', JBL 75 (1956), pp. 285–97; A. Jaubert, *La date de la Cène* (1957), pp. 13–30, 142–9; J. T. Milik, 'Le travail d'édition des manuscrits du Désert de Juda', VT Suppl. IV (1957), pp. 24–6; S. Talmon, 'The Calendar Reckoning of the Sect from the Judaean Desert', Scrip. Hier. IV (1958), pp. 162–99; G. R. Driver, *The Judaean Scrolls* (1965), pp. 316–30.

APPENDIX IV

Hebrew Coins

Bibliography

Eckhel, J., *Doctrina numorum veterum* I, 3 (1794).
Saulcy, F. de, *Recherches sur la numismatique judaïque* (1854).
Madden, F. W., *History of the Jewish Coinage* (1864).
Madden, F. W., *Coins of the Jews* (1881).
Reinach, Th., *Les monnaies juives* (1887).
Hill, G. F., *A Catalogue of the Greek Coins in the British Museum . . . Palestine* (1914).
Sukenik, E. L., 'The oldest Coin of Judaea', JPOS 14 (1934), pp. 178–84. Cf. *ibid.* 15 (1935), pp. 341–3.
Reifenberg, A., *Ancient Jewish Coins* (1940, [2]1947).
Mildenberg, L., 'Numismatische Evidenz zur Chronologie der Bar-Kochba Erhebung', Schweizer Numism. Rundsch. 34 (1948/9), pp. 19–27.
Mildenberg, L., 'The Eleazar Coins of the Bar Kochba Rebellion', Hist. Jud. 11 (1949), pp. 77–108.
Kanael, B., 'The Beginning of Maccabean Coinage', IEJ 1 (1950/1), pp. 170–5.
Kanael, B., 'The Greek Letters and Monograms on the Coins of Jehohanan the High Priest', IEJ 2 (1952), pp. 190–4.
Kanael, B., 'The Historical Background of the Coins "Year Four . . . of the Redemption of Zion" ', BASOR 129 (1953), 18–20.
Kindler, A., 'The Jaffa Hoard of Alexander Jannaeus', IEJ 4 (1954), pp. 170–85.
Kindler, A., 'The Coinage of the Hasmonaean Dynasty', in *The Dating and Meaning of the Ancient Jewish Coins and Symbols* (1958), pp. 10–28.
Kadman, L., 'The Hebrew Coin Script', IEJ 4 (1954), pp. 150–69.
Kadman, L., 'A Coin Find at Masada', IEJ 7 (1957), pp. 61–5.
Kadman, L., *The Coins of the Jewish War of 66–73 C.E.* (1960).
Roth, C., 'The Historical Implications of the Jewish Coinage of the First Revolt', IEJ 12 (1962), pp. 33–46.
Kanael, B., 'Ancient Jewish Coins and their Historical Importance', BA 26 (1963), pp. 38–62.
Mayer, L. A., *A Bibliography of Jewish Numismatics* (1966).
Kanael, B., 'Altjüdische Münzen', Jahrb. f. Numism. u. Geldgesch. 17 (1967), pp. 159–298 [a complete survey of numismatic literature, referred to as Kanael].
Meshorer, Y., *Jewish Coins of the Second Temple Period* (1967) [a comprehensive study of Palestinian coinage with 32 plates, referred to as Meshorer].
Naveh, J., 'Dated Coin of Alexander Janneus', IEJ 18 (1968), pp. 20–5.
Kindler, A., 'The dated Coins of Alexander Janneus', IEJ 18 (1968), pp. 188–91.
Meyshan, J., *Essays in Jewish Numismatics* (1968).
Ben-David, A., 'When did the Maccabees begin to strike their first Coins?', PEQ 124 (1972), pp. 93–103.

Numismatic research and archaeological discoveries in recent times have proved erroneous the attribution by earlier scholars of the Shekel, 'Freedom' and 'Redemption' coins to the Maccabee brothers

(Judas, Jonathan and Simon). Since excellent and up to date bibliographies and surveys (Mayer, Kanael, Meshorer) are now available, it will suffice here to sketch very briefly the history of Jewish coins with Hebrew or Hebrew and Greek inscriptions.

These coins belong to four distinct periods: (1) the end of the Persian domination (fourth century B.C.); (2) the Hasmonaean period from John Hyrcanus I or Alexander Jannaeus to Antigonus; (3) the first revolt against Rome; (4) the Bar Kokhba rebellion. The legends are mostly in the palaeo-Hebraic script though occasionally the square Aramaic characters are also used.

(1) *The Persian Domination*

Five types of coins are known to have been struck in the decades immediately preceding the rise of Alexander the Great. They are all marked *Y^ehud* (יהד), the Aramaic name of the province of Judaea, but one of them bears also the name of Y^eḥezḳiyo (יחזקיו) sometimes considered identical with the High Priest Ezechias mentioned by Josephus, *c. Ap.* i 22 (187–9). See, in general, Kanael, pp. 164–5; Meshorer, pp. 35–40, 116–7, and now L. Y. Rahmani, 'Silver Coins of the Fourth Century B.C. from Tel Gamma', IEJ 21 (1971), pp. 158–60, showing that Y^eḥezḳiyo *ha-peḥah* was a Persian governor.

(2) *The Hasmonaean Period*

Since the attribution of the 'Freedom of Zion' coins to Simon or any other Maccabee brother has been universally abandoned, the only major issue still unresolved is whether Jewish coinage starts with John Hyrcanus I (134–104 B.C.) around 110 B.C. (so Kanael, p. 167; cf. *idem*, IEJ 1 (1951), pp. 170–5), or with Alexander Jannaeus (103–76 B.C.). In the latter theory (see Meshorer, pp. 41–55) all the Y^ehoḥanan and Y^ehudah coins are ascribed to (John) Hyrcanus II and (Judas) Aristobulus II. Cf. above, pp. 210, n. 24, 217, n. 7.

(i) John Hyrcanus I (?) (134–104 B.C.)

Legend:

Y^eḥoḥanan the High Priest and the congregation of the Jews	יהוחנן הכהן הגדל וחבר היהודים

(ii) Judas Aristobulus I (?) (104–3 B.C.)

Legend:

Y^ehudah, High Priest and the congregation of the Jews	יהודה כהן גדול וחבר היהודים

These coins are rare (see Kanael, p. 167).

(iii) Alexander Jannaeus (103–76 B.C.)

A large number of coins minted during the reign of Y^e^honathan surnamed Alexander have survived, and represent three different styles. Their most likely sequence is High Priest, King, High Priest (so Kanael, pp. 169–71). Some of the royal coins were re-struck with the words High Priest. The change is usually explained as the outcome of Alexander's conflict with the Pharisees (see pp. 221 ff. above). Cf. in general, Kanael, pp. 167–71; Meshorer, pp. 56–9. On the other hand, it has been argued that some of Jannaeus's coins with Aramaic and Greek royal inscriptions bear datings to the twentieth and twenty-fifth years of his reign, 83 and 78 B.C. See Naveh and Kindler, IEJ 18 (1968), pp. 20–5, 188–91. This would imply that two years before his death he still called himself, or called himself again, 'King Alexander'.

Legends:

(1) Y^e^honathan the High Priest and the congregation of the Jews — יהונתן הכהן הגדל וחבר היהודים

(2) Y^e^honathan the King — יהונתן המלך
King Alexander — *ΒΑΣΙΛΕΩΣ ΑΛΕΞΑΝΔΡΟΥ*

(3) Yonathan the High Priest and the congregation of the Jews — ינתן הכהן הגדל וחבר היהודים

(4) King Alexander מלכא אלכסנדרוס/*ΒΑΣΙΛΕΩΣ ΑΛΕΞΑΝΔΡΟΥ*

See Meshorer, pp. 118–21; IEJ, *loc. cit.*

(iv) John Hyrcanus II ([76–67], 63–40 B.C.)

Most Y^e^hoḥanan coins (see Kanael, pp. 171–2) if not all of them (so Meshorer, pp. 41–52) belong to Hyrcanus II. Some display the Greek letter *A*, thus alluding to Antipater (Kanael, IEJ 2 (1952), pp. 190–4), or Alexandra (cf. p. 229 above). The substitution of the phrase 'the head of the congregation of the Jews' for 'and the congregation of the Jews' may echo Hyrcanus's re-appointment by Caesar in 47 B.C. as High Priest. Cf. Jos. *Ant.* xiv 8, 3 (137); *B. J.* i 9, 5 (194).

Legends:

(1) Y^e^hoḥanan the High Priest and the congregation of the Jews — יהוחנן הכהן הגדל וחבר היהודים

(2) Y^e^hoḥanan the High Priest, the head of the congregation of the Jews — יהוחנן הכהן הגדול ראש חבר היהודים

See Meshorer, pp. 121–3.

(v) Judas Aristobulus II (?) (67–4 B.C.)

The rare coins attributed by Kanael to Aristobulus I are ascribed by Meshorer (pp. 53–5) to Aristobulus II. For the legend see (ii) above.

(vi) Mattathias Antigonus (40–37 B.C.)

Antigonus was the last Jewish head of state to use, in the Greek legend of his coins, the royal title. His large bronze coins have all been discovered in Judaea proper, and it is likely that their circulation was restricted to that province (see Meshorer, p. 63). The Jewish name of Antigonus is known only from numismatic sources.

Legends:

(1)	Mattithyah the High Priest and the congregation of the Jews	מתתיה הכהן הגדל וחבר היהודים
	King Antigonus	*ΒΑΣΙΛΕΩΣ ΑΝΤΙΓΟΝΟΥ*
(2)	Mattithyah the High Priest	מתתיה הכהן הגדל
	King Antigonus	*ΒΑΣΙΛΕΩΣ ΑΝΤΙΓΟΝΟΥ*
(3)	Mattithyah the Priest	מתתיה הכהן
	King Antigonus	*ΒΑΣΙΛΕΩΣ ΑΝΤΙΓΟΝΟΥ*
(4)	Mattithyah the Priest	מתתיה הכהן
(5)	Mattithyah	מתתיה

See Kanael, pp. 172–3; Meshorer, pp. 60–3, 124–6

(3) *The First Revolt against Rome*

After an interruption of a century, during which Herod and his successors issued coins with Greek legends, Hebrew inscriptions reappeared between A.D. 66 and 70 on bronze coins as well as on silver shekels, half shekels and quarter shekels. They are dated year 1 to year 5 of the new era of the 'Freedom of Zion' which started on 1 Nisan A.D. 66. The recent excavations at Masada have yielded sixty-seven silver shekels and half-shekels as well as hundreds of bronze 'Freedom' and 'Redemption' coins. See Y. Yadin, IEJ 15 (1965), pp. 1–120, esp. pp. 64 ff., 73 ff.; *Masada* (1966), pp. 97–8, 108–9, 168–71.

Legends:

(1)	Shekel of Israel/Jerusalem is holy	שקל ישראל/ירושלם קדשה
(2)	Shekel of Israel/Jerusalem the holy	שקל ישראל/ירושלם הקדושה
(3)	Freedom of Zion	חרות ציון
(4)	Of the Redemption of Zion	לגאלת ציון

See L. Kadman, *The Coins of the Jewish War of 66–73 C.E.*, Corpus Nummorum Palestinensium III (1960); Kanael, pp. 182–4; Meshorer, pp. 88–91, 154–8.

(4) *The Bar Kokhba Rebellion*

The revolutionary government of Simeon ben Kosiba (A.D. 132–5) issued silver and bronze coins dated from year 1 to year 3. The style of the inscriptions varied annually. The exact meaning of the 'Jerusalem' and 'Freedom of Jerusalem' legends continues to be debated. They may express the aim of the uprising, viz. the eventual capture of the capital (so Mildenberg, Hist. Jud. 11 (1949), pp. 77–108, esp. p. 91); or possibly 'Jerusalem' of years 1 and 2 reflects the occupation of the city by Bar Kokhba, whilst 'For the freedom of Jerusalem' of year 3 proclaims his programme of reconquest (so Meshorer, pp. 95–6, following G. Alon); or, more likely, both phrases imply that Jerusalem was in rebel hands, the latter being an elliptic form for (Year 3) 'of the freedom of Jerusalem' (so Kanael, p. 185; *idem*, Bar Ilan 1 (1963), pp. 149–55 [Hebr.], xxxiii f. [Engl.]). On Eleazar the Priest, see p. 544 above.

Legends:

Year 1

(1) Year One of the Redemption of Israel	שנת אחת לגאלת ישראל
(2) Jerusalem	ירושלם
(3) Simeon Prince of Israel	שמעון נשיא ישראל
(4) Sime(on)	שמע(ון)
(5) Eleazar the Priest	אלעזר הכהן

Year 2

(1) Y(ear) 2 of the Free(dom) of Israel	ש ב לחר(ות) ישראל
(2) Jerusalem	ירושלם
(3) Sime(on), Simeon	שמע(ון) שמעון

Undated coins attributed to Year 3

(1) Of (or For) the Freedom of Jerusalem	לחרות ירושלם
(2) Sime(on), Simeon	שמע(ון) שמעון
(3) Jerusalem	ירושלם

See Kanael, pp. 184–7; Meshorer, pp. 92–7, 159–69.

For Herodian and Roman Palestinian coins, see Kanael, pp. 173–82; Meshorer, pp. 64–87, 102–9, 127–53, 170–8. For coins found at Qumran, cf. R. de Vaux, *L'archéologie . . .*, pp. 26–30, 35–6, 52–4.

APPENDIX V

Parallel Years of the Olympic, Seleucid and Christian Eras[1]

The Olympic Calendar begins in 776 B.C. The games were held at the height of summer.[2] The Seleucid Era begins in 312/11 B.C. and is reckoned from October 1, 312 B.C., but in Babylonia from April 311 B.C.[3] In the following table the respective years of the Olympic and Seleucid (Macedonian) calendars are equated with the years of the Christian calendar in which they begin. Accordingly:

Ol. 151, 1 = summer 176 to summer 175 B.C.
Sel. 137 = autumn 176 to autumn 175 B.C.

Ol.	*Sel.*	*B.C.*	*Ol.*	*Sel.*	*B.C.*
1, 1		776	154, 2	150	163
6, 4		753	3	151	162
117, 1	1	312	4	152	161
. . .	. . .	. . .	155, 1	153	160
151, 1	137	176	2	154	159
2	138	175	3	155	158
3	139	174	4	156	157
4	140	173	156, 1	157	156
152, 1	141	172	2	158	155
2	142	171	3	159	154
3	143	170	4	160	153
4	144	169	157, 1	161	152
153, 1	145	168	2	162	151
2	146	167	3	163	150
3	147	166	4	164	149
4	148	165	158, 1	165	148
154, 1	149	164	2	166	147

1. See H. Clinton, *Fasti Hellenici*, III, pp. 472 ff. Cf. E. J. Bickerman, *Chronology of the Ancient World* (1968), pp. 146–53; A. E. Samuel, *Greek and Roman Chronology. Calendars and Years in Classical Antiquity* [*Handbuch der Altertumswissenschaft* I, 7] (1972).

2. Ideler, *Handbuch der Chronologie*, I, p. 377; Bickerman, *op. cit.*, pp. 75 f.

3. Ideler, *op. cit.*, I, pp. 450–3; Bickerman, *op. cit.*, pp. 71 f.; R. A. Parker–W. H. Dubberstein, *Babylonian Chronology 626 B.C.–A.D. 75* (1956).

Ol.	Sel.	B.C.	Ol.	Sel.	B.C.
158, 3	167	146	169, 2	210	103
4	168	145	3	211	102
159, 1	169	144	4	212	101
2	170	143	170, 1	213	100
3	171	142	2	214	99
4	172	141	3	215	98
160, 1	173	140	4	216	97
2	174	139	171, 1	217	96
3	175	138	2	218	95
4	176	137	3	219	94
161, 1	177	136	4	220	93
2	178	135	172, 1	221	92
3	179	134	2	222	91
4	180	133	3	223	90
162, 1	181	132	4	224	89
2	182	131	173, 1	225	88
3	183	130	2	226	87
4	184	129	3	227	86
163, 1	185	128	4	228	85
2	186	127	174, 1	229	84
3	187	126	2	230	83
4	188	125	3	231	82
164, 1	189	124	4	232	81
2	190	123	175, 1	233	80
3	191	122	2	234	79
4	192	121	3	235	78
165, 1	193	120	4	236	77
2	194	119	176, 1	237	76
3	195	118	2	238	75
4	196	117	3	239	74
166, 1	197	116	4	240	73
2	198	115	177, 1	241	72
3	199	114	2	242	71
4	200	113	3	243	70
167, 1	201	112	4	244	69
2	202	111	178, 1	245	68
3	203	110	2	246	67
4	204	109	3	247	66
168, 1	205	108	4	248	65
2	206	107	179, 1	249	64
3	207	106	2	250	63
4	208	105	3	251	62
169, 1	209	104	4	252	61

Ol.	*Sel.*	*B.C.*	*Ol.*	*Sel.*	*B.C.*
180, 1	253	60	190, 4	296	17
2	254	59	191, 1	297	16
3	255	58	2	298	15
4	256	57	3	299	14
181, 1	257	56	4	300	13
2	258	55	192, 1	301	12
3	259	54	2	302	11
4	260	53	3	303	10
182, 1	261	52	4	304	9
2	262	51	193, 1	305	8
3	263	50	2	306	7
4	264	49	3	307	6
183, 1	265	48	4	308	5
2	266	47	194, 1	309	4
3	267	46	2	310	3
4	268	45	3	311	2
184, 1	269	44	4	312	1
2	270	43	195, 1	313	1
3	271	42	2	314	*A.D.* 2
4	272	41	3	315	3
185, 1	273	40	4	316	4
2	274	39	196, 1	317	5
3	275	38	2	318	6
4	276	37	3	319	7
186, 1	277	36	4	320	8
2	278	35	197, 1	321	9
3	279	34	2	322	10
4	280	33	3	323	11
187, 1	281	32	4	324	12
2	282	31	198, 1	325	13
3	283	30	2	326	14
4	284	29	3	327	15
188, 1	285	28	4	328	16
2	286	27	199, 1	329	17
3	287	26	2	330	18
4	288	25	3	331	19
189, 1	289	24	4	332	20
2	290	23	200, 1	333	21
3	291	22	2	334	22
4	292	21	3	335	23
190, 1	293	20	4	336	24
2	294	19	201, 1	337	25
3	295	18	2	338	26

Ol.	Sel.	A.D.	Ol.	Sel.	A.D.
201, 3	339	27	212, 2	382	70
4	340	28	3	383	71
202, 1	341	29	4	384	72
2	342	30	213, 1	385	73
3	343	31	2	386	74
4	344	32	3	387	75
203, 1	345	33	4	388	76
2	346	34	214, 1	389	77
3	347	35	2	390	78
4	348	36	3	391	79
204, 1	349	37	4	392	80
2	350	38	215, 1	393	81
3	351	39	2	394	82
4	352	40	3	395	83
205, 1	353	41	4	396	84
2	354	42	216, 1	397	85
3	355	43	2	398	86
4	356	44	3	399	87
206, 1	357	45	4	400	88
2	358	46	217, 1	401	89
3	359	47	2	402	90
4	360	48	3	403	91
207, 1	361	49	4	404	92
2	362	50	218, 1	405	93
3	363	51	2	406	94
4	364	52	3	407	95
208, 1	365	53	4	408	96
2	366	54	219, 1	409	97
3	367	55	2	410	98
4	368	56	3	411	99
209, 1	369	57	4	412	100
2	370	58	220, 1	413	101
3	371	59	2	414	102
4	372	60	3	415	103
210, 1	373	61	4	416	104
2	374	62	221, 1	417	105
3	375	63	2	418	106
4	376	64	3	419	107
211, 1	377	65	4	420	108
2	378	66	222, 1	421	109
3	379	67	2	422	110
4	380	68	3	423	111
212, 1	381	69	4	424	112

Ol.	Sel.	A.D.	Ol.	Sel.	A.D.
223, 1	425	113	226, 1	437	125
2	426	114	2	438	126
3	427	115	3	439	127
4	428	116	4	440	128
224, 1	429	117	227, 1	441	129
2	430	118	2	442	130
3	431	119	3	443	131
4	432	120	4	444	132
225, 1	433	121	228, 1	445	133
2	434	122	2	446	134
3	435	123	3	447	135
4	436	124	4	448	136

APPENDIX VI

THE SELEUCIDS

Seleucus I Nicator
d. 281 B.C.

Antiochus I Soter
d. 261 B.C.

Antiochus II Theos
d. 246 B.C.

Seleucus II Callinicus
d. 226/5 B.C.

Seleucus III Ceraunus (Soter)
d. 223 B.C.

Antiochus III, the Great
d. 187 B.C.

Seleucus IV Philopator
d. 175 B.C.

Antiochus IV Epiphanes
d. 164 B.C.

Alexander Bala
(pret. son of
Antiochus IV)
d. 145 B.C.

Demetrius I Soter
d. 150 B.C.

Antiochus V Eupator
d. 162 B.C.

Antiochus VI
Epiphanes Diony
d. 142 B.C.

Demetrius II Nicator
d. 126/5 B.C.

Antiochus VII Euergetes (Sidetes)
d. 129 B.C.

Seleucus V
d. 126/5 B.C.

Antiochus VIII Epiphanes Philometor
(Grypus)
d. 96 B.C.

Antiochus IX Philopat
(Cyzicenus)
d. 95 B.C.

Seleucus VI
Epiphanes
Nicator
d. 95 B.C.

Antiochus XI
Epiphanes
Philadelphus
d. 93 B.C.

Philip I
Epiphanes
Philadelphus
d. 84 B.C.

Demetrius III
Philopator
Soter
(Eucaerus)
d. 88 B.C.

Antiochus XII
Dionysus
d. 84 B.C.

Antiochus X Euseb
Philipator
d. 83 B.C.

Philip II
d. 66/5 B.C.

Antiochus XIII Philadelph
(Asiaticus)
deposed 64 B.C.

APPENDIX VII

THE HASMONAEAN FAMILY

Mattathias
d. 166/5 B.C.

on (Maccabaeus)
d. 134 B.C.

Judas (Maccabaeus)
d. 161 B.C.

Jonathan
d. 142 B.C.

n Hyrcanus I
l. 104 B.C.

ristobulus I
d. 103 B.C.

Alexander Jannaeus —— Alexandra
d. 76 B.C. d. 67 B.C.

Hyrcanus II
d. 30 B.C.

Aristobulus II
d. 49 B.C.

Alexandra —— Alexander
d.? 28 B.C. d. 49 B.C.

Antigonus
d. 37 B.C.

Aristobulus III
d. 35 B.C.

Mariamme
d. 29 B.C.

Daughter who married Antipater III, son of Herod the Great.

APPENDIX VIII

The Herodian Family*

- Antipater I
  - Antipater II, d. 43 B.C. (Cyprus I)
    - Phasael I. d. 40 B.C
      - Phasael II (Salampsio)
        - Cyprus II (Agrippa I)
    - Herod the Great d. 4 B.C.
      - (Doris of Jerusalem [Idumaean])
        - Antipater III d. 4 B.C. (daughter of the Hasmonean Antigonus)
      - (Mariamme [Hasmonaean]), d. 29 B.C.
        - Alexander (d. 75 B.C. Glaphyra
        - Aristobulus IV d. 7 B.C. (Berenice I)
          - Herod of Chalcis (Berenice II)
          - Agrippa I d. A.D. 44 (Cyprus II)
            - M. Iulius Agrippa II d. before A.D. 93 (or A.D. 100)
            - Berenice II (1. Herod of Chalcis 2. Polemon of Cilicia)
            - Drusilla (1. Azizus of Emesa 2. Antonius Felix the Procurator)
              - Agrippa d. A.D. 79
          - Herodias (1. Herod Philip 2. Herod Antipas)
        - Salampsio (Phasael II)
        - Cyprus III (Antipater IV)
      - (Mariamme II)
        - Herod Philip (Herodias)
          - Salome II (Philip)
      - (Malthace [Samaritan])
        - Herod Archelaus (1. Mariamme IV 2. Glaphyra)
        - Herod Antipas (1. daughter of Aretas IV of Nabataea 2. Herodias)
      - (Cleopatra of Jerusalem)
        - Philip d. A.D. 34 (Salome II)
    - Joseph II d. 38 B.C.
    - Pheroras d. 5 B.C.
    - Salome I d. c. A.D. 10 (1. Joseph, d. 35/4 B.C. 2. Costobar, d. 28 B.C. 3. Alexas)
      - (by Costobar)
        - Antipater IV Antipater IV
        - Berenice I (Aristobulus IV)
  - Joseph I, d. 35/4 B.C. (Salome)

* Following A. Schalit, *König Herodes, der Mann und sein Werk* (1969).

Sources:

1. *Ant.* xiv 7, 3 (121); *B.J.* i 8, 9 (181) (parents, brothers and sisters of Herod the Great).
2. *Ant.* xvii 1, 3 (19–22); *B.J.* i 28, 4 (562, 3) (wives and children of Herod the Great).
3. *Ant.* xviii 5, 4 (130–42); *B.J.* ii 11, 6 (220–2) (Mariamme's children).